DATE DUE

MAY - 5 2008		
APR 0 6 2009		
5/4/09		

SOCIAL PSYCHOLOGY

SOCIAL
PSYCHOLOGY

The Science and the Art
of Living Together

WAYLAND F. VAUGHAN

Professor in Boston University. Fellow, Society
for the Psychological Study of Social Issues
of the American Psychological Association

The Odyssey Press   New York

301.15

V465

Dedicated to
My Five Children

ELEANOR COLTON
WAYLAND FARRIES, JR. (deceased)
MARILYN FRANCES
WAYLAND EDWARD
EMILY-LOUISE

who have taught me more social psychology
than I ever could have learned from books

PREFACE

THIS BOOK has grown out of my experience in teaching social psychology at Boston University over a period of some twenty years. Beginning in a modest way as a two-hour, one-semester affair, the course has now matured into a three-hour, two-semester program. The expansion was made inevitable by the increasing demand for enlightenment in this sphere of psychology. The large student enrollment and occasional senior-class votes honoring the course as "the most valuable" attest to a lively interest in the material covered.

The writing of SOCIAL PSYCHOLOGY began some years ago when a colleague, J. Rea Butler, persuaded me to team up with him in the project. Shortly after he had talked me into it, Butler was side-tracked by becoming a Dean, and I was left "holding the bag." The momentum I had gathered under his inspiration made the continuance of the task inescapable. Perseveration and perseverance did the rest.

No person can possibly do justice to everything that might legitimately be included under the general heading of "social psychology." Therefore, I have selected topics which seem to be of primary concern to the student who is seeking a satisfactory personal orientation amidst the social chaos of our time. The central theme is based on the conviction that human beings can achieve happiness in their social relations by discovering just how we've gone about it to make one another so miserable. Surely we can profit by our mistakes.

The depression of the nineteen-thirties, the Second World War, and the postwar problems have stimulated me to search for psychological principles by which we may be guided in planning a brighter future. I am optimist enough to believe that we can use our collective intelligence to better advantage than we have used it in the past. The objective of this book is a very practical one: to show how we can apply to our everyday problems what we already know about human-beings-living-together, for better or worse, in modern society.

There are many evidences of a growing interest in human relations. One shining example is the establishment of the Department of Social Relations at Harvard College. A significant purpose of this new program, at the graduate level, is to equip specialists in clinical psychology with a clear appreciation of the cultural influences which help to shape the patterns of our interpersonal relationships. I believe that, in the years ahead, psychology will concern itself more and more with the problem of learning to live together with a minimum of friction and a maximum of satisfaction. This text is admirably suited to such a course in human relations. Moreover, its content and method are such that it may be used successfully even with students who have not had the traditional training in elementary psychology.

Every effort should be made to encourage the student of social psychology to develop his critical judgment. The preparation of a term thesis is ideal for the acquisition of skill in independent research. The footnotes in the text suggest numerous books and articles which will serve as a "starter." The recently published *Readings in Social Psychology,* edited by Newcomb and Hartley under the sponsorship of the Society for the Psychological Study of Social Issues, is recommended for supplementary study; the *Journal of Social Issues,* sponsored by the same organization, is also recommended.

I have received valuable aid from many persons, among them: Walter Muelder, Henry Weinberg, Robert Meikle, Donald Miller, Marjorie Conklin, Cory Snow, Doris Maslach, Evelyn Orne, Gloria Regali, Dorothy Sacks, Joanne Sim, Alice Angyal, Blanche Kimoto, Arthur Littlefield, Roselle Johnson, Cecilia Krawiec, Elinor Trowbridge, Allen Hunting, Fredric Coulon, Naomi Goldstein, and J. Garton Needham.

Special thanks go to Elsie Wyzanski for extensive research, gathering data, and checking references; and to Armine Barseghian, Barbara Phillips, and Elizabeth White, all of whom typed *ad infinitum.*

I am grateful to Philip L. Harriman of Bucknell for many helpful criticisms.

Babson Park, Florida   WAYLAND F. VAUGHAN
January, 1948

CONTENTS

PART I. THE PROVINCE OF SOCIAL PSYCHOLOGY

Contents

Contents

SOCIAL PSYCHOLOGY

Part I

THE PROVINCE OF SOCIAL PSYCHOLOGY

SOCIAL PSYCHOLOGY is defined in Chapter 1 as the study of "The Individual in Social Situations." The social psychologist is always concerned with the behavior of individuals, even when he is investigating the actions of groups. Our frame of reference is human relations. A social situation exists when two or more people interact, whether it be face-to-face or symbolically. Our behavior is determined under some circumstances by the fact that we are members of an established organization; when we conform to the regulations of such a group, we are engaged in institutional behavior. We shall *describe* social behavior—and *evaluate* it. We shall be concerned chiefly with the ways in which group membership modifies individual behavior, as exemplified in such phenomena as conventional codes, the presence of spectators, the pressure of group opinion, the effects of competition. It is important to relate the individual to the total social situation in order to understand his reactions. The radical, for example, cannot be explained merely by attributing some maladjustment to him. One of the most fundamental human satisfactions is the pleasure of belonging to a group. There is no "group mind" over and above the minds of the individuals composing the group. We shall approach social psychology with the idea of learning some facts that can be applied to the problem of living together most successfully.

Chapter 2 discusses "Social Psychology in Relation to Other Social Sciences." There is an increasing realization that our social problems are too complicated to be solved by any *one* social science. The need for collaboration is urgent. Social psychologists will find it helpful to combine their efforts with those of experts in sociology, criminology, anthropology, economics, political science, and history, and to attack problems which are of common interest to these several disciplines. The inter-relatedness of the various fields just cited is elucidated by a few significant samples.

Chapter 1

THE INDIVIDUAL IN SOCIAL SITUATIONS

IN WATCHING HUMAN BEINGS, you have probably noticed that a person's behavior is influenced by the presence of other individuals, and that it makes a great deal of difference who these other people are. The child who does clever stunts for the entertainment of his immediate family may appear nonplused and stupid when teased into performing his antics for the amusement of visitors. The youngster who is ordinarily a model of good behavior within the privacy of the family circle may "cut up" before guests until his parents are much embarrassed. The individual who is at ease in conversing with one other person may become tongue-tied, tense, and nervous in the midst of a larger company. The inexperienced speaker may rehearse his oration with faultless eloquence in the homey precincts of his own cellar and then turn mute the moment he meets his audience face to face. These observations are cited to emphasize the fact that an individual may act one way when he is alone and quite another way in the presence of other people. This fact is a basic datum of social psychology.

I. DEFINITION

Taking human relations as our primary concern, we shall conceive social psychology to be *the study of the human being in social situations.* We shall recognize, of course, that ants, and bees, and apes enjoy a social life that may be explored to advantage by the social psychologist. Man is not the only social animal. It will be wise, however, for us to limit ourselves to *human* relations because we shall be interested chiefly in problems which directly touch us as human beings living in a modern civilized society. Our task may be defined in terms of three main objectives: to describe patterns of interaction which develop whenever two or more persons come into psychological contact; to evaluate our social behavior; to search for ways of improving our social adjustments.

A. Typical Problems

Social psychologists are concerned with various situations in which human beings react to one another. We may consider, by way of illustrations, what happens when one person is frustrated by others, what psychological adjustments must be made by the serviceman returning to civilian life, what it means in terms of international maladjustment when we misjudge foreigners or foreigners misunderstand us.

1. frustration and aggression

Extensive research on frustration and aggression has been conducted at the Yale Institute of Human Relations. How do people get frustrated? What do they do when they are frustrated? We find that aggressive behavior is the usual reaction to frustration. Applying this formula to strikes, suicides, race prejudice, sibling jealousy, lynching, satire, crime, reading detective stories, wife-beating, and war, we learn that "aggression is always a consequence of frustration . . . the existence of frustration always leads to some form of aggression." [1] We learn further that the aggression is mainly directed at the frustrator, but it may be displaced (indirectly expressed) upon the world in general, as the frustrated person looks around for a scapegoat: farmers vote out officeholders in time of drought; subjects rate a series of jokes zero after they have been deprived of their sleep; people register dislike for foreigners when they discover that filling out a questionnaire on race attitudes is going to prevent them from attending a special feature at the local movie-house. This research on the patterns of frustration and aggression is cited because it illustrates how the formulation of a problem depends upon the concepts around which an investigation is organized. It is important to learn how people react when they are thwarted. Such an insight helps us to understand, for example, why vengeful peace settlements issue sooner or later in the outbreak of new wars and thus perpetuate a vicious circle from which mankind is still struggling to escape. It becomes clear that aggression cannot be outlawed effectively by non-aggression pacts. The key to amicable relations is rather to be found in the insurance of satisfaction for the vital needs of peoples everywhere.

2. soldier to civilian

The conversion of the civilian into a soldier, and the soldier back again into a civilian are two processes of profound interest to the stu-

[1] J. J. Dollard *et al.: Frustration and Aggression*, p. 1. 1939.

dent of social psychology. The psychological training by means of which the peace-loving citizen is educated to be a fighter with a good morale, will be discussed in Chapter 11. At this point let us restrict ourselves to a consideration of some of the psychological adjustments required when the serviceman and his family, and the folks in his community face the task of getting reacquainted.[2]

The serviceman who returns to his father and mother needs a psychological "climate" in the home which may be aptly described as mature sympathy. Such an atmosphere will be one of understanding without any taint of mawkish sentimentality. The soldier who has been disfigured is worried lest his family instinctively recoil upon seeing his disability and in his anxiety he craves the assurance of love and moral support, expressed in actions rather than words. Forced joviality, unrealistic Pollyannaism, constant babying will prove irritating. Parents can do much unintentional harm if they lack psychological insight. Thus Mother may urge her son to recount his exploits, only to be told, "I don't remember," which is the truth, although she suspects he is deliberately concealing horrors; if the son does tell about his experiences, Father, who was in the last World War, may try to match every story with a better tale of his own; parents may forget that their boy has grown up, and still try to govern him in the style of "Mother and Dad know best." To the homesick veteran who has been dreaming of his home-coming for months, the reality may prove disappointing. He has dissociated from his thinking the prewar habit Mother had of asking him where he was going and what time he'd be back. Meddlesomeness of this sort is exasperating to one who has been away from his parents, out on his own, for so long.

The returning veteran is glad to be home, at the same time he is annoyed by so many little intrusions. This ambivalence is characteristic of the many contradictions that beset the soldier-turning-civilian: he is pleased to be through with military discipline, confused by his liberty; he wants social activities, is uneasy in company; he yearns for the security of a routine existence, rebels with restlessness when he tries in vain to settle down. A stranger to his family, conflicted with all these incompatible trends in his personality, the veteran feels lost in a sense of his own isolation. Through his grumbling and his griping he attempts, in an uncertain way, to convey to his family his inner confusion. Having found security in the army by identifying himself with

[2] The following discussion is based upon G. K. Pratt's excellent book, *Soldier to Civilian*. Whittlesey House, copyright, 1944, by the McGraw-Hill Book Company, Inc.

his buddies in uniform, the veteran finds it difficult to get the feel of belonging to his family again.   The readjustment takes time, requires patience of all concerned.

The serviceman returning to his wife and children faces similar psychological problems.   Perhaps he had welcomed the bachelor freedom of military life after chafing under the restrictions of marital routine; in any case, he must now be redomesticated.   Extensive travel and meeting many kinds of people may have broadened him to such a degree that he is bored with the provincialism of his wife, who still lives in the little world of their own home town.   Sometimes "the little woman" has enjoyed being the head of the family in her husband's absence, is reluctant to relinquish her prerogatives; or maybe a son has taken his father's place as "the man of the house" and as the main object of mother's affection and, if so, the youngster may jealously resent his replacement by "the old man."   A wife who has gone to work may have found a satisfying experience that prejudices her against going back to household drudgery; if her husband happens to be the kind of man who needs the role of provider to bolster up his ego, a difficult situation is in the making.   He may not like the friends she has made while he was away.   The old crowd he looked forward to rejoining may have evaporated, leaving him high and dry.   If in all this frustration, when nothing turns out as he had expected, he seems gruff and uninterested in his wife, his boredom is not to be interpreted as loss of love. He is projecting his own annoyance when he peevishly asks, "What's the matter with everybody?"   War has made him less romantic, more realistic, more vulgar in his language and his humor.   Husband and wife, in each other's absence, have idealized each other; disillusionment is bound to follow during the process of readjustment.

Then there are all the psychological problems involved in restoration to the community, such as finding a job despite the ignominy of a discharge, perhaps a label of P.N. (psychoneurosis), or a code number designation for it which makes a prospective employer a bit wary, and the attempt to feel friendly toward old acquaintances who may have remained safe at home, often for good reasons, which do not seem excuse enough, however, in the irrational eyes of men who have risked their lives in battle.   Society will show appreciation for the veteran's services, traditionally, too little, too late, and then in an unintelligent way by bonuses that may easily encourage an unhealthy dependency. What he really needs is a new kind of bonus which will "pay the debt of disability in the currency of opportunity."   The community should aim, above all, to help the veteran to help himself.

3. UNDERSTANDING FOREIGNERS

Erroneous conceptions concerning the psychologies of foreign peoples—notions based upon complacent ignorance, patriotic bigotry, and general hostility toward the outlandish ways of strangers—have vitiated human relations in the international sphere, interfering with efforts toward cooperation and laying the psychological groundwork for war. How much do you, as an American citizen, really know about the pet attitudes and emotional slants which may be peculiar to the British or the Russians or the Chinese or the Germans or the Japanese? Our schools have done practically nothing to enlighten us, beyond courses in history or geography which tell us little about present-day national character. Indeed, the paucity of knowledge in these matters is appalling evidence of our indifference to the need for a clearer understanding.

For example, how well informed are we about the Russians, the people who may be a potential enemy unless we learn to get along with them and they with us? Public opinion polls reveal that only one American in ten is even reasonably well informed about the Soviet Union. Evidence from the polls indicates that the clearest single determinant of confidence in Russia's postwar cooperation is the amount of information one has about the Soviets.[3] In the light of the great need for American-Soviet teamwork, it is sad to note the large number of American citizens who prefer to damn the Russians as Bolsheviks or Communists and to let it go at that. When Boston University, in 1945, sponsored some meetings to acquaint school teachers with Russia, there was strong protest in the Hearst press and letters poured in to the Governor urging him to fire the Commissioner of Education who presided at the Conference. William S. White's *Report on the Russians* (1944) is typical of our American refusal to understand the Russians; instead of understanding, we get a capitalistic condemnation of the residents of the Soviet Union for their backwardness in the installation of modern plumbing. And the Russians, in their turn, exhibit a lamentable ignorance of American mores. At the time of the San Francisco Conference in 1945 a high-ranking Russian officer, asked to caption a photograph in which he appeared with several others, remarked of a junior officer in the picture, "You don't want his name; he's not important." This was true, commented an American witness, but the Russian officer lacked insight into the fact that Americans, with their

---

[3] See W. B. Walsh: "What the American People Think of Russia." *Public Opinion Quarterly*, 1944, 8, 513-522.

dislike of brass hats and their sympathy for the little guy, would get peeved at Eisenhower himself if he were to make such a disparaging remark about his jeep driver. Russian military heroes showed their annoyance at American bystanders who congregated to get a look at them; they failed to appreciate that in the United States everybody loves to see a celebrity. One editor explained that part of the difficulty with the Russians lies in the fact that they have been so busy completing a revolution and winning a war that they have paid no attention to the mores of other nations. Yes, indeed, but can we say any more for ourselves!

Americans don't even understand adequately their traditional allies, the British, nor they us, with a resulting dislike and suspicion which might well be brought out in the open and threshed out for our mutual benefit.[4] The English reserve is mistaken by Americans for high-hat snobbishness. An Englishman may snub conversational advances in a train with a cold indifference which seems appallingly rude, but which often conceals pure terror. Americans may offend the British by poohpoohing their royal family without inquiring what the symbolism of King and Queen means to a British subject. The English are apt to misinterpret the free and easy way of Americans, their quick assumption of intimate address, their incessant kidding, their cajoling flattery which is intended merely to give the British girl a pleasant evening. Americans are upset when the English insist on cooling their toast and when they persist in eating with fork in left hand, knife in right. American soldiers in England were warned against likely "boners" by a movie called "Welcome to Britain," in which the typical American visitor is portrayed as saying boastfully, "I know all about this country. I've been here three weeks." Britishers are cursed with a similar, though not such a cocky, misunderstanding of American ways. Fear was expressed in British homes, for example, that children evacuated to America would return to England talking like Damon Runyon characters. The misapprehension proved unfounded. However, one mother was distressed when she asked her daughter if she preferred pie or tart, and her youngster replied, "I don't care," which to the English implies a discourteous suggestion that both are unappealing.

How much less do we Americans and the Germans know about each other, or the Americans and the Japanese? To the German brought up on the Nazi ideology, "democracy" and "liberty" are not values to be cherished but evils to be abhorred. Our "Four Freedoms" touched no responsive chords in a people who espoused their own *Three* Freedoms:

[4] We shall return to this point in Chapter 21.

freedom from Anglo-Saxon imperialism, freedom from Bolshevism, and freedom from Jews. Americans, at a loss to understand how Germans can be as cruel as their atrocities attest, try to explain everything by assuming that sadism runs in the German blood. This explanation is too easy to be of much aid. The real key to German character is to be found in German culture: the tradition of Prussian militarism, the exploitation of the people by the Junker class, the education for submissiveness to leadership, the role of the husband and father as the almighty ruler in the home. Germans "get that way" because they are brought up according to a certain system of values.

It is difficult to ascertain which is sense and which nonsense in our notions about foreigners like the Germans. We must ever remind ourselves that the study of individual differences has established the principle that individuals within a nation will differ more from one another than will peoples of different nationalities. With this principle in mind, we can still study what may be called national character. What traits characterized the people of pre-Republican and Nazi Germany? Clarence Leuba has uncovered certain qualities which Americans are likely to attribute to the Germans, such as the following:

Might makes right.
Higher standing accorded the military.
Greater respect for laws.
Greater emphasis on the importance of men as contrasted with women.
Women considered important chiefly in so far as they make men comfortable.
Stricter discipline imposed on children.
Greater obedience demanded from children.
More respect for adults inculcated in children.
Leader worship.
Greater willingness to sacrifice personal desires for the alleged "good of the state."
Greater fondness for group excursions and other group activities, especially group singing and beer drinking.
Emphasis on the value of sports for body-building rather than as recreation.[5]

The above characteristics, if accurately ascribed to modern Germans, are certainly not to be considered as native qualities, ineradicable and

[5] In G. Murphy (Editor): *Human Nature and Enduring Peace*, pp. 82-109. 1945.

unmodifiable. Such conclusions are only too congenial as an escape from the responsibility of learning more about these strangers. Extensive reconditioning, based on a far more intimate body of information than psychologists have accumulated to date, will provide the surest method by which we can modify German character in desirable directions. That such character changes are possible has been amply demonstrated by many German Americans—and Nisei, too—who have benefited by the influence of American culture, and even have come to appreciate their adopted country more than do some of the native born.

We know less about the Japanese than we do about the Germans. According to hearsay, Americans believe the Japanese are characterized by their cleanliness, frugality and self-discipline, imperturbability, face-saving pride, sensitiveness to ridicule, and so on. It is not surprising that many contradictions appear when the reputed qualities are listed. For example, the Japanese are reported to be imitative, to be ingenious, to be devoted to family, to be indifferent to home ties.[6] How ignorant we have been concerning the Japanese character is revealed in an open letter sent to the press in 1944 by a Presbyterian minister in Brooklyn, the Reverend John Paul Jones:

I turn to the *Encyclopædia Britannica*. . . . My edition bears copyright as late as 1939. . . . I was somewhat surprised at what I read in the encyclopædia. The article was by no means uncritical. After all it was written by "foreigners." But these are some of the sentences which appear. I quote them at random. "The Japanese are essentially a kindly hearted, laughter loving people. . . ." "From many points of view there is no more beautiful type of character than that of the Japanese woman." . . . Then, after recording weaknesses and excesses, there is this further sentence: "But no nation is free from failings, and when due account is taken of those of the Japanese there still remains a people of remarkable energy and intelligence, of marvelous achievement, and of great attractiveness." I am almost reluctant to quote one further sentence, for just now its acceptance may seem too much to expect. But in fairness I include it. "Contact with a ruder outside world may perchance since have blunted a little the fine edge of the national courtesy. . . ."[7]

What a rude awakening Pearl Harbor brought to dormant Americans who doped themselves with such happy nonsense!

[6] *Ibid.,* pp. 110-131.
[7] Quoted in an editorial in the *Christian Century*, February 16, 1944.

These three topics—frustration and aggression, the transformation of soldier to civilian, and international misunderstanding—have been reviewed briefly to show the student the kinds of problems with which the social psychologist is very much concerned. These problems have been selected because they are timely and because they demonstrate how much research is required of the psychologists before any of us can deal with the issues at all adequately.

In fact, the Second World War has brought home vividly to us the importance of studying the social psychology of the peoples with whom we Americans must deal, foe and friend alike. One phase of the program of familiarizing the armed forces with the manners and morals of the various peoples was a series of guides issued by the Office of War Information (OWI). Another phase was the intensive training in Foreign Area Studies given to men in the service, to prepare them for Military Government abroad. A report of the Foreign Area Studies program at Yale, by its Director, A. W. Griswold, tells the story of this development in international understanding.

The Second World War confronted us with an immediate need for still a different and more specialized type of training and personnel. Our troops were fighting the war in literally every quarter of the globe, in strange lands and among peoples of whom we had the scantiest and generally most inaccurate knowledge. This was true not only of the more distant nations of the Orient but also of many of our more familiar European neighbors. If the number of Americans with even a bowing acquaintance with Japan, Russia, and India was small, the number of those with a truly informed and intimate knowledge of Germany, Italy, and the Mediterranean was hardly greater. The supply of each was speedily exhausted as the armed forces and the government recruited their war staffs. The barrel was scraped in the early months of the war. The demand for Americans who could speak the languages and understand the ways of the nations with and against which we were fighting kept increasing out of all proportion to the supply. . . .

The military government official . . . cannot function successfully without as keen and sympathetic an understanding of the environment in which he is working as the Tammany district leader has of the sidewalks of New York. Both British and American officers returning from North Africa have testified to this. Not a textbook knowledge of the procedures of government, but an ability to speak to foreign peoples in their own languages and according to their own ways of behavior and thought, has been found to be the primary essential in military government. . . .

In its curriculum, Foreign Area Studies is a blend of old and new elements. There is nothing new in studying a foreign language or the history, culture, and economy of a foreign nation. Courses of this type have long formed a basic part of the typical university curriculum. What is new about Foreign Area Studies is the way in which the courses are combined and presented. Ordinarily the subjects of instruction in a university curriculum are arranged according to theoretical fields or special disciplines, rather than according to particular national cultures or civilizations. Thus a normal undergraduate program of study might include history, mathematics, literature, economics, philosophy, and a foreign language. Though a student might devote the major portion of his time to one of these special disciplines, he would study them all as fragments, related abstractly to his major field but never concretely to a given human society.

Foreign Area Studies places its primary emphasis on the human society, in which the diverse elements of history, economics, sociology, philosophy, language, literature, and art are observed and studied as in real life. From the teacher's point of view, this means a departure from the conventional departmental organization of teaching, which gathers the teachers of the various disciplines into separate and distinct groups, and substitutes for it groups of teachers organized according to particular national cultures: Japan, the Pacific Islands, Italy and the Mediterranean, Russia, Germany and Western Europe, Latin America, China, and the like. As the various facets of each of these civilizations are presented—the cultural, the economic, the political—the specialist makes his contribution. The sum of these contributions is an interpretation of human life in a representative community rather than the exposition of one or the other theoretical methods of arranging human affairs. This may well cast the shadow before the coming event of a change in our university curricula. In their efforts to establish themselves as exact sciences during the past half century, the social sciences have become so overspecialized as to make a maze of human society instead of an orderly pattern. . . .

Can the reader remember any course he took in college or any book he has read since then which presented an accurate, vivid, and fully rounded picture of a foreign country? History offered one perspective, literature another, economics (if it looked abroad at all) a third. The separate disciplines rarely merged in any particular national society or culture, and when they did they formed a hodgepodge of information rather than a composite interpretation.

It is no easy task for Americans who have never visited a foreign country to come by the familiar understanding of its inhabitants required by the military government officer. Nor has this type of understanding been conveyed to us in the writings of foreign correspondents, for the most part absorbed in political developments and insensitive to folkways and history. . . . Many an academic prejudice went by the board as educational and fictional movies, museum exhibits, travel books, maps, photographs, and even immigrants complete with native food and dress were pressed into service. . . . The American officer will not set foot on *terra incognita* when he arrives at his post abroad. He will not view the inhabitants with the amused condescension and bewilderment characteristic of the innocents abroad. When in Rome he will truly be prepared to do as the Romans do.[8]

B. INDIVIDUAL BEHAVIOR

Sometimes the exploration of human relations means observing what a group as a whole is doing; sometimes it means concentrating on particular individuals to determine just how they are influencing the group pattern and just how they as individuals are affected, in turn, by the group. Ultimately the description of any group activity resolves itself into a delineation of what individuals are doing and the explanation of what is happening will be found only by discovering why individuals interact the way they do in the situation under scrutiny.

C. SOCIAL SITUATION

When we say that the social psychologist is interested in observing the behavior of the individual in a social situation, it must be understood that an interaction may occur with or without the physical presence of the parties involved. In the former case, there is a direct interaction; in the latter, a symbolic interaction.

1. DIRECT INTERACTION

When several people respond to each other as social stimuli, a direct interaction takes place. It may be two persons howdy-doing on the street and exchanging comments on the weather; it may be a husband and wife greeting each other after a prolonged separation; it may be the members of the British Parliament responding to a speech by the Prime Minister. In each case, the persons reacting to each other constitute a face-to-face group. The meeting of such a group may be momentary and casual, as it is when motorists signal each other at an intersection, or it may involve a more stable relationship, as it does in the case of a fraternity, where mutual interests are sustained and promoted by organized cooperation. The direct interaction is a person-to-person contact between individuals in the flesh. It is a social situation with the actors there in person.

2. SYMBOLIC INTERACTION

A social situation just as truly exists when the influence of one person upon another person is mediated through symbolism, as is fre-

---

[8] A. W. Griswold: *Education for War and Reconstruction.* Pamphlet issued by the Alumni Board of Yale University, June, 1943.

quently the case. An interaction may be engineered through the medium of imagination, as when one person thinks of another person, recalling some incident, some remark, some facial expression.

When a son in a distant place writes a letter home on Mother's Day, expressing his appreciation for all that "Mom" has done for him in days gone by, and wishing her happiness in days to come, he is functioning in a symbolic situation that is as essentially social in nature as if he were actually to return to the old family home—and his mother, responding to his symbolic evidence of filial affection, will be thrilled to be remembered on "her" day.

We are, to a large extent, products of the past, since tradition plays such a dominant role in our lives. We are influenced by the customs established by remote ancestors and handed down from generation to generation through the ages. It is the task of the social psychologist to trace the effects of our heritage upon our behavior, to find out why we persist in doing things the way people always have done things since time immemorial. Here again we encounter a social situation where the actual participants may be noticeably absent only in the physical sense. Our ancestors may mold us even more extensively than our contemporaries, as we try to live up to family tradition or pride in our national heroes. Because we are given to reverence for the past, George Washington may be more influential than a next-door neighbor in conditioning our ideals of character. We live in a world that extends far beyond the range of the immediate present, the here and the now. The social situation must be thought of in these larger terms.

D. Institutional Behavior

Our conduct as members of the community is organized and regulated by certain rules or standards. Members of a group who agree that certain regulations should be respected function as an institution. The behavior of such group members we shall designate as institutional behavior, the subject of our Part V.

A typical institution is the *family.* A man and a woman, who must be old enough to be responsible for what they are doing, go through a ceremony called a *wedding,* maybe a formal occasion in a church, maybe an informal appearance before a justice of the peace. They pledge allegiance to each other and symbolize their mutual promise by the *ring.* Then they go away for awhile on a *honeymoon,* if they can afford a trip, and on their return they live together in the same house and they are expected to stay together. The husband goes to work to earn a living, and his wife, if the arrangement is the traditional one, tends the home. When children come, the parents are supposed to care for them: clothing them, feeding them, and rearing them to become good citizens; and children are supposed, in return, to honor their father and mother. The fulfilling of these obligations, in accordance with these specified patterns, constitutes family life.

An institution, like the family or the church or the state, is not an abstract entity, but it is individuals thinking and acting in certain ways because they are parents or children, church members, or American citizens.

Institutional rules are usually respected by members of the organized group to which they apply. Most people are conformists. This generalization is represented statistically by the fact that behavior patterns in institutional situations tend to be distributed along a characteristic curve resembling a J in reverse, consequently called a J-curve, as proposed by F. H. Allport, who was the first to note this means of plotting degrees of social conformity.[9] Pedestrian behavior in response to a traffic light was observed and tabulated according to four degrees of respect for the law (legal *institution*):

1. Waiting on the intersection curb while the light showed **RED**.
2. Waiting just off the intersection curb.
3. Proceeding to the middle of the intersection and waiting.
4. Walking across the street in disregard of the light.

Plotting the behavior of the pedestrians (*when a traffic officer was present*) resulted in the following J-curve: 89.8 per cent of the persons conforming to the highest degree, 7.9 per cent waiting off the curb, 2.0 per cent in the middle, 0.3 per cent proceeding across regardless.

Note that in the J-curve most instances fall upon the step at the extreme left; that as we proceed by successive steps toward the right, there is a diminishing number of instances, and that this decline in the number of instances becomes less and less abrupt. The same type of curve is obtained in plotting other forms of institutional behavior: communicants crossing themselves in a Catholic Church, employees arriving at work, automobile drivers reacting to the change of color in a traffic light. Institutional regulations ordinarily produce uniform behavior, since individuals usually "do what they're told."

[9] See F. H. Allport: "The J-curve Hypothesis of Conforming Behavior." *Journal of Social Psychology*, 1934, 5, 141-183.

The normal curve for psychological traits in non-institutional situations shows a few people at one extreme, a few at the other, and most people in the middle region.

It is very important to understand how our institutions came into being, how they function, and particularly to appreciate how they affect our lives for good or ill. Our present sufferings—depressions, wars—are mainly the result of the kinds of institutions we have developed, ways of doing things that satisfy some needs while frustrating others: economic institutions, evolved as the means for producing and distributing the goods of life, may degenerate into instruments of greed, with depressions as a consequence; war, established as a device for settling in-group vs. out-group differences, may become a weapon for exploitation and may eventuate in hardship and destruction for everybody, winner and loser alike Our hope for a brighter future will depend on changing our institutions by modifying habitual patterns in individuals.[10]

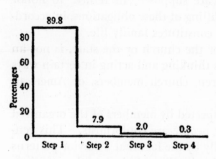

J-Curve of 996 Pedestrians at Traffic Light with a Traffic Officer Present.*

Instead of excusing our follies by arguing, as so many do, that wars are inevitable, it would be healthier for us to look into our plight, to ascertain the causes and consequences of our habitual actions, to allocate the blame where it belongs. Pursuing this scientific approach to an understanding of international conflict, we will discover that *human nature* is not the explanation for our troubles. The answer will be found, rather, on the institutional level: war has been developed by human beings as the *customary* way of settling differences among individuals who belong to special interest groups called nations.

Those persons who are seriously concerned with eliminating war from the functions of our institutions must see that superficial changes in personnel or in the form of society will not be sufficient; but that thoroughgoing revisions must be made in the structure of our civilization. These revisions involve changes, it seems to me, that would extend into the basic structure of every contemporary institution, and into the fundamental values and attitudes of every person. The establishment of a permanently peaceful world is no easy matter.

* See S. H. Britt: "Pedestrian Conformity to a Traffic Regulation." *Journal of Abnormal and Social Psychology*, 1940, 35, 114-119.
[10] This thesis is further presented in Chapter 13, "Custom."

This paper rests upon two beliefs: (a) Most of our social institutions have arisen and developed around some need or want of society; but since this development has been a growth largely of accident, happenstance, and minor opportunism, these institutions may not serve their functions well and may even be perverted. (b) As a consequence of our present stage of development, however, it is possible for us as members of society to change, voluntarily, many of the forms of our society so that our institutional habits will efficiently and pleasantly serve our needs. . . .

The psychological basis for war and peace lies in the fundamental emotional organization of mankind. We have some institutions, such as the family, which are based on love, considerate kindness, and cooperation. The aim and justification of these institutions is the development of happy human beings. Other institutions demand dominance and mastery over people, or the reciprocal feelings and the frustration of being dominated. The motivation and rewards in these institutions must be changed.

Our capitalistic society predominantly emphasizes the emotional attitudes of dominance and mastery. Only persons who are exceedingly dominant are able to succeed. The emphasis upon dominance as the basic and primary emotional attitude is so strong that it colors and distorts into its pattern even situations which are basically love relations.

The solution goes to the roots of society. No superficial adjustments will suffice. The solution consists not in denying that men and women are naturally aggressive under certain circumstances, for we actually need and enjoy vigorous aggressive behavior; nor in denying that we are bound to face many frustrations in our lives. The proposal offered by some pacifists that peace will come when man stamps out his aggressions, and that dominant, aggressive behavior is evil, demands an improbable change in human nature.

The root of the matter is that we cannot get rid of love or of anger; but we can arrange our society so that our love is expressed with regard to people, and our dominance and anger directed against "things"! There are "things" enough to dominate, such as the forces of inanimate earth, sea, and air, and the conditions of ignorance, disease, and hardship. No changes in the superstructure of our institutions will do. It is futile to tinker with the techniques of the international political organizations, or with the national political organizations, or even with many features of the economic and social institutions. We must see that our current institutions are wrong in so far as they encourage success through the dominance of man by man. Our goal must be a society where exploitation of human beings is impossible.[11]

It all comes down to a problem in values: do we want peace or do we want other things—war, military glory, imperialism, exploitation —more? We can have peace if we seek intelligently to modify human

[11] R. H. Gundlach: "The Psychological Bases for Permanent Peace." *Journal of Social Psychology,* S.P.S.S.I. *Bulletin,* 1942, 16, 297-334.

behavior patterns in the direction of less competition and more cooperation, in the home, in the business world, and in international relations.

E. VALUES AND EVALUATION

Psychologists may deal with values as data, investigating the standards with reference to which people are judged praiseworthy or censurable. Thus social psychologists may describe the norms which differentiate the adjusted person from the maladjusted person. There are criteria, socially defined, which determine our judgments of other individuals, as to whether they are "the right kind" or "the wrong kind." Certain kinds of acts or habits brand a person as an outlaw, as being immoral, delinquent, degenerate, or criminal: paupers, tramps, hoboes, pimps, prostitutes, gigolos, homosexuals, confidence men, pickpockets, gangsters, drunkards, dope fiends, lunatics—all are regarded as maladjusted persons, judged by the standards in our culture. Other kinds of persons are considered well-adjusted and, accordingly, are admired and respected: children who obey their parents, boys who play manly games, girls who preserve their virginity, men who show community spirit by joining service organizations, women who get married and have children, oldtimers who work till the end and die in the harness. The norms which determine our admiration and condemnation are socially defined; therefore, they fall within the jurisdiction of the social psychologist.

Some psychologists, with whom the author disagrees, question whether social science should concern itself at all with the weighing of values: the problem of how we *should* behave. They insist that social science should follow the practice of natural science by limiting itself to a description of how we *do* behave. Thus, in line with this view, the social scientist may legitimately study what people value, but he may not pronounce judgment on what people should value. It is not up to the scientist, therefore, to instruct us regarding our obligations. According to this view, Dr. Carle Zimmerman, Harvard sociologist, is out of order when he tells the public that "every family should have at least four children to keep the population up to its present level and to maintain the welfare of the country." [12]

We may assume that social psychology is a science in so far as it is concerned with the existent norms, merely describing their operation, examining impartially the ends that are set by our wishes without any decision as to whether they are beneficial or harmful. There is no

[12] Boston *Herald*, September 28, 1941.

compelling reason, though, why we must limit ourselves as social psychologists to the scientific approach. Must we conceive of psychology as only a *science?* Perhaps we would gain some worth-while knowledge if we branched out to include inquiries into the *art* of living together. Such a course, viewing psychology as a science and an art, may be justified if we are honest enough, and conscientious enough, to recognize when we are merely delineating facts and when we are evaluating them. If we are going to expand psychology to include the weighing of facts, we must be careful to realize that the resultant values cannot be demonstrated scientifically. Evidence, for example, can be cited to convince the reader that Americans in 1938 spent one dollar in every twelve for alcoholic beverages, but no amount of evidence could persuade these drinking consumers that they would have been better off *(values)* had they spent this money on education or on foreign missions, if they are not inclined to see the situation in that light.

Psychologists do weigh patterns of living, whether or not they are conscious of going beyond *science* in doing so. Numerous cases could be cited as evidence for this assertion. Let us just note one example, that of Lehman and Witty, who conclude from their studies of the effects of play upon personality, that too much social participation in play is just as unwholesome as too little.

Witty says:

> These data suggest that certain sociologists and educators should revise or abandon their pleas for indiscriminate sociability. One frequently hears that the non-social child is a misfit, that wholesome growth is consummated only through numerous and varied social contacts. It seems, from the data presented in this study, that one should not encourage indiscriminate sociability if one desires the most wholesome development of the growing child It appears to be the kind of social contacts made, not the number, which should be of great concern to the person charged with the guidance of children.[13]

Evidence of this nature lends support to Huxley's contention that "the emancipation of natural science from considerations of value is a fiction . . . values and all that they connote of motive, emotion, qualitative hierarchy, and the rest constitute some of the most important data with which the social scientist must deal." [14] Theoretically, psycholo-

[13] P. A. Witty: *A Study of Deviates in Versatility and Sociability of Play Interests,* p. 50. 1931.

[14] J. S. Huxley: "Science, Natural and Social." *Scientific Monthly,* January, 1940.

gists who regard themselves as strictly scientists would not pass judgment on the behavior patterns passing under their observation. In actual practice, however, they do become involved in discriminating between values: "science" may not be concerned with values, but "scientists" frequently are. Dealing as he often does with human relations, it is not uncommon for a psychologist to register his preference in favor of a certain mode of conduct by characterizing it as a sane, rational, or mature adjustment to the particular life-situation under consideration. Being human, the psychologist like other people is inclined to refer to behavior in terms that express or imply evaluation.

Assuming that social psychology may be both a science and an art, we are going to subject the facts we survey to critical evaluation. Educators say that pupils should be trained to think. This dictum will guide us. Surely social psychology offers an ideal field of study for stimulating thoughtful investigation, since many problems arise for which no satisfactory solutions have been found. We shall examine the patterns of conduct prevalent in our culture and then we shall evaluate them—conventions, customs, fashions, superstitions, prejudices, and propagandas—to determine which practices can pass muster as intelligent modes of behavior, which ones bring us satisfaction. From time to time we may suggest that certain lines of conduct appear maladjustive, possibly even stupid, and we may mention procedures for ridding ourselves of insidious habits like superstitions and prejudices, in the hope that reeducation may enable us to conform more closely to standards of *sanity*. Studying social psychology with a critical eye will prove much more exciting than would a bare review of the facts. We need the facts, let us remember, as a basis for intelligent evaluation. We are not likely to profit from an overhauling of our social habits unless we know pretty well what we are doing.

II. THE INDIVIDUAL IN THE GROUP

One essential datum of social psychology, as we have noted, is the fact that an individual acts differently in a group from the way he would act were he alone. A person must adapt himself to the unique canons of each group with which he becomes associated. Mental conflict is frequently engendered by the inconsistency involved in adjusting to the divergent standards imposed by different groups. By means of various forms of pressure, especially the censure of public opinion, the individual is educated in conformity. He cannot be "himself." He must recognize the demands of his fellows and adjust himself to their expectations if he wants to "belong." The influence exerted by the group upon its members is an important factor in modifying individual conduct.

Conformity to Group Standards: African Aborigines after Feasting.
(Black Star Photo.)

A. Conventional Codes in Sports

Conventional rules regulate athletic contests, each game being subject to its own peculiar etiquette. In baseball the players are expected to protest the umpire's decisions as a matter of course. The player who fails to dispute a crucial ruling is not carrying out his assignments conscientiously. Base coaches make faces and derogatory remarks in their efforts to "razz" the pitcher. Chatter and catcalls are resorted to in vociferous vehement vituperation. Raillery is expertly used as a technique for "goat-getting." [15]

At the ball park spectators occasionally throw pop bottles at the players and umpires, shout for the removal of players who muff flies, and yell, "Kill the umpire," or "empire," as the illiterates out in the

---

[15] See S. Frank: "Rough Riders of the Dugouts." *The Saturday Evening Post,* May 17, 1941.

center-field bleachers call him. Baseball is a virile game; players and fans are expected to let off steam in a manly fashion.

Tennis, in contrast with baseball, is a "sissy" game, according to the popular conception. Scoring by "love" seems to sustain this charge. Dirty uniforms, such as are worn on the ball field, are out of place. The players must dress and act like gentlemen; likewise, the spectators. The tennis player must never, under any provocation, protest the decisions of the umpire or the linesman. If he believes that his opponent has been the victim of an unfair ruling, he is called upon by the unwritten code of the game to throw away the next point by hitting the ball out intentionally. Spectators at a tennis match do not rise in unison from their seats at the end of a set, as they do in the seventh inning at a ball game, nor do they shout for the murder of the umpire. Members of a tennis audience do not appropriate errant balls that are hit by mistake into the bleachers, the way fans do with foul balls at a baseball game or with pucks drifting over the sideboards at a hockey rink.

Cricket, like tennis, is a game for gentlemen. The contestants must be garbed in white flannels. They are dressed not merely to play a certain game but to conduct themselves in keeping with a certain code. Players must not "ride" opponents or attempt to "rattle" the bowler. Resorting to such unfair practices in order to win "is not cricket." Loudly voiced opinions are ruled out. Umpire's decisions must be accepted at face value. To dispute a decision of the umpire in cricket is as unthinkable as to stand up in church and contradict the preacher.

Players must adapt themselves to the etiquette peculiar to the particular game in which they are competing, since the rules of propriety differ so much from game to game. If a tennis player hired Nick Altrock to run up and down the sidelines performing antics to distract his opponent, he would soon be disqualified as a "rowdy" of the worst sort. It would never do. The individual must always conform to the demands of the specific situation.

B. Experimental Evidence on Effects of Various Social Situations

Some experimenting has been done to measure the influence of a group upon an individual. The general technique for such experimentation involves "a comparison between measured achievements of the individual person when under influences from other persons physically present, with the measured achievements (in identical functions) of the same individual when working alone." [16] It is very difficult to control the conditions involved because the interrelationships of persons are subject to so many complicating factors. An individual may be working alone, but at the same time he may be competing with others in his own mind: while he may be physically alone he nevertheless is not functioning mentally as an isolated individual. Then again, he may be acting much like the expert golfer who plays against par rather than against his opponent. What the individual is doing can only be determined by reference to introspective revelations as to what is going on in his mind. Such data are liable to considerable error; and, further, different persons react to instructions so differently that it is impossible to keep the conditions exactly uniform with reference to the various individuals being studied.

When it comes to situations where individuals are working in the presence of others, the experimenter must arrange conditions so that he can tell whether the subjects are working together non-competitively, competing as rivals, or reacting to others as spectators. In the last case, we see how complicated the experimental situation may be when we recall the way athletes differ in the presence of a cheering crowd, an indifferent audience, or a booing crowd; when we stop to realize what a difference it sometimes makes as to whether the spectators are males or females. A woman-shy man facing a Woman's Club audience would be considerably ill at ease; so would an effeminate man when face to face with rough-and-ready factory strikers. It is obvious that the possibilities in any social situation are vast. Quantitative experimentation is, therefore, especially difficult. A good start, however, has been made in delimiting certain problems and in developing techniques for their investigation.

1. SPECTATORS

The influence of spectators on an individual's performance was tested by Travis. The task was to hold a flexible pointer on a target mounted on a revolving disk turning once per second, the contacts being electrically registered. The subject was tested in the presence of the experimenter alone, and in the presence of four to eight student spectators. Eighteen of the twenty-two students made better scores before the group than before the experimenter only.[17]

[16] J. F. Dashiell: "Experimental Studies of the Influence of Social Situations on the Behavior of Individual Human Adults," Chapter 23 in *Handbook of Social Psychology*, C. Murchison, Editor. 1935.

[17] See L. E. Travis: "The Effect of a Small Audience upon Eye-Hand Coordination." *Journal of Abnormal and Social Psychology*, 1925, 20, 142-146.

2. SOCIAL ENCOURAGEMENT AND DISCOURAGEMENT

Experiments have been conducted to determine the comparative effects of social encouragement and discouragement on the individual's work. It has been traditionally assumed that encouragement is facilitating, blame inhibiting. In support of this assumption, writers have cited Laird's experiment in which he reported that fraternity initiates suffered a loss of speed and coordination in motor tests when they were "razzed" during their performances.[18] More recent experimentation on the effects of praise and blame upon learning indicate that the situation is not as simple as it has been customarily represented. Praise was found to be more effective with grade-school boys, in an experiment conducted by Schmidt, whereas with girls at this level it made no difference which incentive was applied, praise or blame. Analysis of the complete results did indicate that the relative effectiveness of the two modes of treatment was dependent upon the test situation and specifically on the kind of person the tester was, as he was the one who was administering the "reward" or the "punishment."[19] Obviously, people differ in their sensitivity to encouragement and discouragement, and it makes a lot of difference *who* is providing the incentive, even with standardized procedures.

3. PRESENCE OF THE TESTER

Significant for psychological testing is the fact that the presence of the tester in the testing situation exerts a definite influence on the results obtained. Ichheiser subjected youths to a block-assembling problem, some of them going through the test in an isolated room, some of them under the experimenter's observation. A majority of the performers were retarded by the presence of the experimenter.[20] Ekdahl found a similar retardation, in measuring reactions based on word associations.[21] In an experiment reported by Bingham, subjects were tested for steadiness, skill in adding, and typing ability, with the examiner present and with the examiner absent, the results proving

[18] See D. A. Laird: "How the College Student Responds to Different Incentives to Work." *Pedagogical Seminary,* 1923, 30, 366-370.

[19] H. O. Schmidt: "The Effects of Praise and Blame as Incentives to Learning." *Psychological Monographs,* No. 240. 1941.

[20] See G. Ichheiser: "Ueber die Veränderung der Leistungsbereitschaft durch das Bewusstsein einen Zuschauer zu haben." *Psychotechnische Zeitschrift,* 1930, 5, 52-53.

[21] See A. G. Ekdahl: "Effect of Attitude on Free Word Association-Time." *Genetic Psychology Monograph,* 1929. 5. 253-338.

to be less precise when the examiner was present.[22]   There is a general tendency for the individual to work faster but more inaccurately in the presence of others.[23]

4. GROUP OPINION

Group discussion tends to bring extremists into conformity with majority opinion.   Bekterev instructed an audience to judge a time interval.   Only nine out of fifty-eight estimated the interval correctly; there were more who overestimated than underestimated it.   After a discussion the judgments came nearer the true interval: more were correct and there were fewer gross overestimates and underestimates.[24]

A similar trend in a group which was estimating stick lengths, was reported by Vaughan.   Though there was no discussion, the subjects were influenced in revising their estimates by the figures for the group, which were recorded on the blackboard for the subjects to study previous to the final trial.[25]   Wheeler and Jordan demonstrated that majority opinion affects individual opinion regarding social, political, and economic problems.   They found a sixty per cent shift of opinion toward the majority attitude after that attitude had been made known to the subjects.[26]

Allport discovered that when individuals rated the pleasantness or unpleasantness of odors, in the presence of a group, extreme judgments in either direction were avoided.   The pleasant ratings were less pleasant, the unpleasant ones less unpleasant, in the group situation.   This leveling influence of the group was attributed to "a basic human tendency to temper one's opinions and conduct by deference to the opinions and conduct of others." [27]

5. CO-WORKERS

The effect of co-workers upon the individual worker was also measured by Allport.   The rivalry motive was minimized by instructing

[22] See W. E. Bingham: "A Study of the Effect of the Presence of the Examiner upon Test Scores in Individual Testing." *Journal of Applied Psychology*, 1944, 28, 471-476.

[23] See J. F. Dashiell: "An Experimental Analysis of Some Group Effects." *Journal of Abnormal and Social Psychology*, 1930, 25, 190-199.

[24] See W. Bekterev and M. de Lange: "Die Ergebnisse des Experiments auf dem Gebiete der kollectiven Reflexologie." *Zeitschrift für angewandte Psychologie*, 1924, 24, 305-344.

[25] See W. F. Vaughan: "An Experimental Class Demonstration of Suggestibility." *Journal of Abnormal and Social Psychology*, 1935, 30, 92-94.

[26] See D. Wheeler and H. Jordan: "Change of Individual Opinion to Accord with Group Opinion." *Journal of Abnormal and Social Psychology*, 1929. 24. 203-206.

[27] F. H. Allport: *Social Psychology*, p. 278.   1924.

the subjects that their work was non-competitive, that their results were not going to be compared afterwards, and that they were not to make any comparisons themselves. He found that the presence of co-workers favored speed, that individual differences in susceptibility appeared, that the slower subjects were more affected than the fast, that individual variability was increased in the group in most of the tests. The general effect obtained was a social facilitation of performance.[28]

a. *Competition.* The influence of competition on individual performance was tested by Whittemore, who discovered that every one of twelve subjects turned out more work when competing than when not competing, that the slower workers seemed more speeded up by the rivalry situation, and that all twelve did poorer jobs in quality when adopting the competing attitude. The subjects were asked to give introspective reports, as a means of checking on their attitudes under the different experimental conditons.[29]

There are various forms of competition that must be differentiated: (1) competition in which the competing individual is a member of a group competing against another group, as in a football game, (2) competition of one individual with another, as in boxing, and (3) competition against one's own record, as in running a time trial. Each brand of competition is characterized by its own unique psychology.

Much more needs to be learned about the psychological effects of competition, for rivalry is one of the major incentives in our society, as Margaret Mead has shown in her portrayal of American culture (*And Keep Your Powder Dry,* 1942). There are many questions to be answered. Does competition in the schoolroom promote socialization, or does it foster unwholesome jealousies? Does Phi Beta Kappa really further the ends of scholarship? Should athletic coaches inculcate the will to win? Would people strive for social recognition just as hard as for financial rewards? Might it not be wiser for us to place more stress all along the line on cooperation? These questions do not even rise in the mind of the average American because he has been trained to believe that competition is the very essence of human nature, that the spur to outdo the other fellow is responsible for our national achievements, that cooperation is an impractical ideal. Such convictions are soon exploded when one joins the anthropologist in a

[28] See F. H. Allport: "The Influence of the Group upon Association and Thought." *Journal of Experimental Psychology,* 1920, 3, 159-182.
[29] See I. C. Whittemore: "The Influence of Competition on Performance: an Experimental Study." *Journal of Abnormal and Social Psychology,* 1924, 19, 236-253.

comparison of our system with that of other societies where competition is practically unknown, and cooperation is the supreme rule of life.

b. *Cooperation.* Unfortunately, students of human behavior have paid too little attention to the psychology of getting along with others on a friendly basis. What counsel we do receive is predominantly concerned with the most effective ways of exploiting friendship, in the manner of Dale Carnegie. Psychologists know more about the competitive patterns of human behavior than they do about the cooperative ones. The paucity of experimental evidence on cooperation is well exemplified in the meagerness of the chapter devoted to the topic in Murphy, Murphy, and Newcomb's *Experimental Social Psychology.*[30] I believe it is significant that the authors devote 132 pages to "Aggression and Competition" and only 43 pages to "Cooperation, Friendship, and Group Activity." The lengthier discussion of aggression is symbolic of our whole culture, where the desire to get ahead for oneself is given special weight in preparing the child for the struggle of existence. "Stand up for your own rights," "Don't let people run over you," "Hit back if anybody hits you," are lessons taught early in training the child to hold his own in the fight for dominance and success, in a culture that calls for a certain amount of aggressive behavior if a person is going to "get anywhere"—and be a credit to his parents, who will bask vicariously in the reflected glory.[31] The complete picture of *homo sapiens,* however, should include the story of man's socialization, beginning with the immature egocentric infant and culminating in the mature adult who has learned to discipline his own desires in deference to his fellows.

This evolution from a self-centered to a cooperative being may be simply illustrated by the progressive development of play patterns in the growing child. Two-year-olds in the nursery school are given to *solitary* play, each child preoccupied with himself despite the group around him. There is no group cohesiveness, no sense of community, no cooperation. Children, aged two to four, engage in *parallel* play. Each child still plays pretty much by himself but he is influenced by the presence of other children, enjoying himself more because they are there, exchanging ideas occasionally, staying with a given activity longer than he would, were he alone. Friendship scarcely exists, for one playmate will do about as well as another. Nevertheless, the per-

---

[30] Chapter 8, "Characteristic Social Behavior of Children in Our Culture: Cooperation, Friendship, and Group Activity."

[31] See M. Mead: *And Keep Your Powder Dry.* 1942.

sonal contacts furnish experiences which are necessary to the child's social development. The three-year-old child, though still largely self-absorbed, may become increasingly aware of others if the proper opportunities are provided. For example, he may learn to take turns at the swing or slide and he may, with encouragement, share the available toys. Four-year-olds are just old enough to become aware of themselves as a group. Thus, in nursery school, a four-year-old will ask, "Is that what the children do here?"—evidence of growing identification of himself with other children. "Whereas a two-year-old is seldom successful in eliciting a desired response from other children, a four-year-old often succeeds, and shows such a wide repertory of social responses as reaction to the distress of others, making requests for assistance from other children, making suggestions for dramatic play, and utilizing a variety of technics of acceptance, refusal, evasion, or transformation of the situation." [32] Expressions of sympathy, at this stage, are rudimentary, such as asking, "Does it hurt?" Children of three to five enjoy looking at things together, or hearing a story together. From four to eight, children play in *shifting groups,* "a form of play in which group activity goes on but the form of organization is so loose that any individual child may abandon the group for his own activities without disturbing the project. Highly popular projects at this age are keeping store, or playing show or playing school." [33] If they elect to play store, one child may appoint himself delivery boy long before there is anything on hand to deliver, and another child may wander off to ride his wagon for a while in the middle of "business hours." Eight to ten is the *gang age,* characterized by separation of the sexes in play, interest in clubs, and enthusiasm for team games in which the team, and not the individual, wins or loses. Through the gang the pre-adolescent becomes imbued with the "we-feeling," learning cooperation through common interests and common activities pursued by the group. During adolescence the individual learns how "to take it," perfects his self-control, gains an insight into the needs and wishes of others, acquires a fair skill in adjusting himself to his companions. "At this stage there should be at least occasional demonstrations of submerging immediate personal gratification in favor of team or school welfare, of taking blame, or suffering or sacrificing for some other person or persons." [34] The individualist, at last, is becoming a social being.

[32] M. E. Breckenridge and E. L. Vincent: *Child Development,* p. 445. W. B. Saunders Company, 1943.
[33] *Ibid.,* p. 446.
[34] *Ibid.,* p. 456.

Perhaps, through the social chaos of our era, we shall find that we have been betting on the wrong horse in encouraging competition rather than cooperation. Inadvertently, we are discovering that co-operating is even more satisfying than winning while somebody else is losing. Such, at least, has been the experience of many persons who have shared in the growth of consumer cooperatives in which members have organized initially for economic benefits, only to discover later the psychological returns to be shared in working together.

C. Radicalism: Personality and Social Conditions

It is easy for the psychologist to get so interested in analyzing the personality of an individual as to lose sight of the situation within which the individual is acting. Representatives of the *Gestalt* school have helped to correct this fault by calling attention to the importance of including all the relevant factors involved in the determination of a behavior pattern, which means a comprehensive study of the-individual-in-the-situation. This suggestion has been largely ignored by psychoanalysts when they have essayed to explain how radicals "get that way." The limitations of the psychoanalytic account become apparent as we consider the psychological basis of radicalism with due regard for the social conditions contributing to its psychogenesis.

Psychoanalysts see the radical as a maladjusted person who is pro-jecting his own failure on the environment. They attribute his atypical conduct to unsolved emotional conflicts hanging over from an unhappy childhood. They "explain" the radical by asserting that he is suffering from an unsuccessful rebellion against his father, a revolt that is displaced to resistance against the employer as a father-surrogate (substitute). The radical projects the blame for his personal shortcomings in order to depersonalize his problems and imper-sonalize his motives. The psychoanalyst suspects him of chicanery in this self-justification, for to the analyst "nothing is ever what it seems."

The worker unwittingly becomes a labor agitator, according to the psychoanalytic interpretation, to compensate for his family maladjust-ments. Industrial unrest is thus attributed to emotional deficiencies in the individual. It is assumed that nothing could be "wrong" with the environment, that the "normal" person learns to accept the *status quo*. This acceptance, indeed, is taken to be the criterion of nor-mality. Anybody who is not satisfied with the way things are run is announcing his own emotional immaturity every time he complains.

Placing the blame for industrial unrest upon the worker, without reference to the conditions under which he labors, is a travesty on the truth because the person who sponsors such a view is remiss in failing to see the picture as a whole. An observer who is well versed in the field of industrial relations, who can see things from the standpoint of the worker as well as from the vantage of the employer, may wonder how any psychologist has the "nerve" to propose such fantastic explanations for radicalism. The psychoanalytic account is misleading because it oversimplifies a very complex situation. There are undoubtedly some radicals who are emotionally retarded, but what of it? That is only part of the story. There are others who are mature enough to recognize abuses that need correction, and they are courageous enough to say so. It is possible that the person who "explains away" the radical by calling him neurotic, is the one who is "maladjusted," since he refuses to "face reality" by blinding himself to the evils involved in our economic system.

People who have been conditioned to adopt the employer's way of seeing things, as most of us have been trained to do, will be inclined to discount the radical's talk about exploitation and to agree with the psychoanalysts that there must be some unhealthy complex somewhere in the individual's unconscious to account for such unpleasant grumbling. Accordingly, the popular reaction to such "agitation" is to wonder what ails the "agitator." Whether this reaction is justified or not will depend ultimately on the decision as to whether the system should be adapted to man, or man to the system. And by "man" we mean both employers and employees.

The psychogenesis of radicalism has been discussed—and some questions raised—in order to point out the necessity for including both personality factors and situational factors in accounting for behavior. The recognition of this truth has been facilitated by the extensive work of social psychologists and anthropologists, who have been set by the very nature of their interests to see the social conditions under the influence of which people act. As we come to see the individual against the background of his cultural milieu, we get a more complete picture of the factors determining behavior.

D. The Sense of Belonging to a Group

Belonging to a group means a great deal to an individual in the way of social satisfaction.[35] This fact is vividly illustrated in the tragedy of the foster child who discovers, after years of believing that he is the true child of his supposed parents, that he is "merely" a foster child.

[35] This topic is the theme of Chapter 11, "Social Consciousness: Morale."

The result is frequently devastating beyond all expectation. There are cases where the child who was a good student at school loses his high rank, stops taking any work seriously and turns into a vagabond. Such reactions have been observed where the foster parents continue to give the child every proof of their undiminishing love and loyalty, and nothing has changed in the "objective" relations of the household. In such cases the deplorable effect seems to be excessively out of proportion. For nothing else than the child's feeling of belongingness to his foster parents has been changed.[36]

The group to which an individual belongs, as Lewin would express it in his topological terminology, is the "ground" on which he stands, providing him social status and emotional security. According to the topologists, a person and his psychological environment must be treated dynamically as one "field." The disillusioned foster child becomes disoriented when the stability of his ground is undermined. The reactions of such a child cannot be understood by a study of the objective conditions. We must discover what *meaning* the situation carries for the person who is surprised to learn that he has been an adopted child. The meaning of the experience must be interpreted in terms of how much "the structure of the life-space" of the individual is changed by the insecurity resulting from the disruption of his accustomed attachments.

Lewin finds in this foster child situation a parable that helps us to understand the precarious psychological position of the modern Jew.

The breakdown of the foster child has its parallel in the fact that the most severe breakdowns resulting from Nazi anti-Semitism have occurred among half or quarter-Jews who had believed themselves to be good Catholics or Protestants. These unhappy people experienced a collapse of their social ground when the right of belongingness to the group of which they had felt as a part all their years was suddenly denied them. Only to a lesser degree, the foundations upon which the Jews have been living all over the world were shaken when Germany, a country considered one of the most enlightened and best educated, resorted to violent Jewish persecution. This was a blow to the favored ideology of many Jews that anti-Semitism should be regarded as a "prejudice" which "well educated people do not have" and which one can hope to overcome with "enlightenment." It made obvious the fact that this problem cannot be treated on an individual, private basis; it has to be recognized as a social problem of groups.[37]

[36] K. Lewin: "Bringing Up the Child." The *Menorah Journal,* Winter, 1940. Copyright, 1940, The Menorah Association, Inc.
[37] *Ibid.*

Chief sufferers from the lack of a sense of belonging are the "marginal" individuals, Jews who do not belong to their own group, who do not fit among the Gentiles, people on the fence, neither here nor there. A girl, who describes herself as typical of the Jewish people, confesses that she is unappreciative of her Jewish heritage, owing, in part, to the fact that her education has been exclusively Christian. She isn't wholeheartedly American either because she still feels conscious that she is Jewish. "So what am I?" she asks, in trying to determine her status. "According to Jews, I'm American. According to Americans, I'm Jewish." Double loyalty of this sort does not necessarily lead to ambiguity. It is not the fact of belonging to many groups that is the cause of the difficulty, Lewin maintains, but the *uncertainty* of belongingness. Many Jews, to their misfortune, are uncertain about what it means to belong to the Jewish group, and they cannot decide whether they should identify themselves with their own people or try to break away.

It is becoming apparent that all psychotherapy is a social process, based upon satisfactions to be derived from interpersonal relations, whether through psychoanalysis, play therapy, psychodrama, cottage life in an institution, or Alcoholics Anonymous. The personal element plays the essential role in effecting a cure, as Adolph Meyer has long insisted. Group therapy has proved particularly valuable in the reeducation of children who, feeling rejected by family, gang, or school, respond by manifesting hostility toward a world that seems unkind. Aggressive children and quiet children are mixed together because they are good for one another, each tempering the unwholesome tendencies in the other, all profiting from the group dynamics set up by the various interpersonal reactions. The children are allowed to express themselves freely in the "permissive environment" established by the therapist who makes it a point to tolerate the outbreak of destructive impulses, even to the degree of allowing the members to throw clay at the walls, pull the furniture apart, or fight with each other. Gradually the more aggressive child learns to control his violent proclivities in deference to group discipline because he wants to be accepted by the others—he *wants to belong.* "The child's desire to be accepted, or at least not to be excluded, is an incentive for modifying egoic trends. The desire to be accepted by the group we designate *social hunger,* which in our opinion is one of the strongest drives in human beings . . . all psychotherapy takes place in relation to other people." [38]

[38] S. R. Slavson: *An Introduction to Group Therapy,* pp. 15, 16. 1943.

The group approach to the treatment of behavior problems and mental disorders is just beginning to be appreciated. It has great possibilities because it appeals to the desire to belong to somebody, the need to feel that there is another person who cares about one's happiness. The forlorn English *évacuée* who had been separated from her parents too long, expressed the thought aptly when she lamented, "I'm nobody's nothing."

This need-for-belonging deserves more attention from the psychologists. Eric Fromm sees this desire for relatedness-to-others as a basic motive in contemporary social behavior. The dread of physical isolation, the fear of moral aloneness, the need to feel one with others, are all ways of describing this fundamental drive. Persons who believe Hitler's leadership was built upon a cunning that enabled him to foist his domination on the German people are fooling themselves, for "millions in Germany were as eager to surrender their freedom as their fathers were to fight for it." [39] Many individuals are afraid of freedom because it means a threat to their personal security. The whole philosophy of individualism has neglected this fact, that human beings want to merge themselves with their fellows in order to enjoy a feeling of communion. Emphasis on individual power and individual achievement in our "extroverted" Western culture has not allowed sufficient opportunity for expression of the "basic human need for belonging," in the opinion of Angyal, who urges Americans to pay more heed to this fundamental "trend toward homonomy." [40]

III. THE GROUP-MIND FALLACY

We must recognize that the social psychologist is fundamentally concerned with individuals even when he is observing their behavior in group situations. He is not concerned with a group mind, however plausible such a concept may appear on the surface. The psychologist who is conscientious about his terminology, using words that represent realities, terms that have referents, will not speak of "the Boston Mind," as Van Wyck Brooks does in depicting New England, nor will the scientist write about cities, as Brooks does, as if they were persons: "One could foresee a New England turned in upon itself, while Boston, sulking in its tent, refused to play with Denver and San Francisco. . . ." [41] Nor will he set out with W. J. Cash to describe *The Mind of the South* (1941). Personifications of this sort may be ex-

[39] E. Fromm: *Escape from Freedom*, p. 5. 1941.

[40] A. Angyal: *Foundations for a Science of Personality*, Chapter 6, "The Trend toward Homonomy." 1941.

[41] V. W. Brooks: "Dr. Holmes's Boston." *Harper's Magazine*, July, 1940.

cused by literary or poetic license, but they are not to be tolerated for a moment by anybody who is interested in using words to describe reality.

Some people speak of the "mass mind" as if there were a mind of a group over and above the minds of the individuals composing the group. This concept of a "group mind" appears in three forms. First, the *Crowd Mind.* Le Bon in his book *The Crowd* advanced the theory that people in a crowd act the way they do because the personal consciousness of each individual disappears and is replaced by a crowd consciousness. The people are then supposed to be "swept away" or to be "seized" by this crowd mind that "gets hold of them." Thus we can account for their bizarre actions, which otherwise would remain inexplicable. Such a resort to mythology is unscientific and unnecessary. Consciousness, as far as we know, is dependent upon a nervous system. The crowd has no nervous system. Furthermore, the activity of the mob is actually the activities of the individuals who make up the mob. The behavior may be best understood on a scientific basis if we start from the viewpoint that we are studying *the individual in the crowd situation.* Proceeding with such a formulation of the problem we find that mob actions can be adequately accounted for in terms of the psychology of the individual, with reference, of course, to the situation in which he is functioning. We know that the anonymity of the person lost in the crowd dulls his sense of responsibility and we know that one person is affected by other persons with whom he is associated, especially so where there is a large number of people. "Human nature in the raw" is released under such conditions—the human nature of each individual person.

Second, the *Collective or Class Mind.* A mind is fallaciously attributed to the group because there is a sameness of thought and action involved, as in an army, a political party, or a trade union. The *esprit de corps,* however, is really an attitude in each individual. "Public opinion" is the way separate individuals think. As Cooley has said, the nation thinks only as the individuals who compose it think. The individual, however, would not think as he does were he not a member of the nation. All thinking is a social process but social as a cooperation of individuals and not as a process in a super-individual mind. So a university exists really in the attitudes which individual teachers, students, and administrative officers have toward one another and toward the traditions of the school. The mind is in the members.

Third, the *Group or Social Mind.* Permanent organization is supposed to generate a group mind. Again, we may note that the group activity consists in the behavior of its personnel. The continuity of the group does not require the same personnel, but some personnel there must be. The apotheosis of this idea of a group mind was reached in Hegel's philosophy of the state, the influence of which is found in the concept of the totalitarian state, which was followed so conscientiously by the Nazis. According to this philosophy, individuals exist only for the state. The individual has no value *per se.* Hegel felt that humanity in social groups should be regarded as the expression of a spiritual principle, a *Volksgeist* or *Folk-Soul,* which is an emanation of a World-Spirit in a particular form. This Hegelian concept was exploited by chauvinists to rationalize the expansive nationalistic ambitions of Prussia. Critics of this totalitarian view are of the opinion that society exists for the good of the individual—it is his happiness that counts. Hence the measure of the value of group life would lie in the opportunity it offers the individual to realize himself through the give and take of social contacts.

Many people who regard the idea of a group mind as absurd, act, nevertheless, as if they accepted the idea as sound. A few illustrations of how the idea is applied in practice will suffice to indicate how we succumb unconsciously to the illogic involved in this concept.

A news item from Germany in 1935 told us that a kiss from one of his pretty Aryan salesgirls cost a Jewish merchant a month in jail. Another salesgirl chanced upon the embrace, and tattled. The court ruled that the Jew had "insulted not only a German maiden but also the entire German people," although the girl said she had offered no resistance.[42]

One of the arguments in favor of prohibition was that federal control made it possible to prevent "wet states" from shipping liquor into "dry states"; but, there were teetotalers in the former states and thirsty citizens in the latter. The states themselves did not do the drinking.

There are definite motives for indulging in the group-mind fallacy, as F. H. Allport points out so well in his treatise, *Institutional Behavior* (1933). Institutional idolatry leads us to neglect the happiness of individuals in our impetus to satisfy the needs of society. When we regard our country as high-minded and peace-loving, we do not feel the need to prove these qualities in ourselves. Thus we evade the test of ourselves as individuals by means of lip service to our collective symbols. A pertinent example of this process is "Middletown's tendency to regard civil liberty as an absolute, something all Americans

[42] Boston *Herald,* October 28, 1935.

practice, while the intervention and very existence of a Civil Liberties Union is an impertinent denial of American institutions." [43]   Men and women, as Allport contends, do not acquire good motives through being grouped together as an institution.   Our flag stands for what you and I aim to be, not for a great nation already embodying these noble qualities.   It is wiser to judge institutions by the people than to judge the people by their institutions.

Society does not solve the problems of mankind through its institutions.   Instead, specific men and women try to solve their own problems through the behavior which they call their institutions.   The government is not a wise agency, but a method by means of which individuals attain what they want.   The acts of the government are the acts of individuals and, consequently, there is always a chance for mistakes.

Citizens do not struggle for the nation, but through the nation, as a method of organization, for something which they, as individuals, want.   Nationalistic loyalty may conceal self-interest.   Nations have grown up in support of the interests of certain groups of people. Walter Lippmann has stated the case in a nutshell: "If these essentially private disputes could be handled, without patriotic fervor and without confusing an oil prospector with the nation as a whole, with governments acting as friends of the court and not as advocates for a client, the balance of power between governments would be easier to maintain."

One of the best sections in *Institutional Behavior* is on "the Psychology of Nationalism; the Nationalistic Fallacy as a Cause of War." Individuals want peace, says Allport, but society is organized upon a basis of competing national groups.   The system of settling international disputes by fighting will be abolished as soon as we change the behavior of individuals.   People must realize that the Nation for which they do battle is merely a symbol, obscuring the fact that they are really fighting on their own behalf in defense of values which they personally deem precious.

IV. THE PRACTICAL VALUE OF SOCIAL PSYCHOLOGY

This book on social psychology has been designed with the idea of presenting information, gathered by psychologists, that may guide us toward an intelligent solution of our social problems.[44]   World War II

---

[43] R. S. Lynd and H. M. Lynd: *Middletown in Transition*, p. 432.   Harcourt, Brace and Company, 1937.
[44] Consult the Preface.

awakened leaders in the *social* sciences to a sense of their *social* responsibilities.[45] The time has come, Lynd tells us, for social science to attack practical problems.[46]

In 1936, leading social scientists, among others, convened at Harvard's tercentenary celebration to engage in symposia on the progress of science. These meetings left an impression on some people that social science was not making any considerable contribution to our welfare. This reaction was expressed by Link, a man well known in the field of applied psychology:

> In September, 1936, a great tragedy occurred at Harvard University, a tragedy far more profound than the World War. . . . The net conclusion, both stated and implied, was: that the physical sciences had made tremendous contributions to man's physical progress—the automobile, the X ray, insulin, and thousands of other things; but that the social studies, such as economics, history, anthropology, sociology, had contributed little or nothing to man's understanding of himself. While physics, chemistry, and biology had given man a miraculous control over his physical environment, they had added practically nothing to his control of his personal and social behavior.[47]

The Society for the Psychological Study of Social Issues (S.P.S.S.I.), founded in 1936, is giving organized expression to the growing interest in a psychology that is applicable to everyday affairs. A committee of the S.P.S.S.I. collaborated on *Industrial Conflict: a Psychological Interpretation,* which was published in 1939. Another S.P.S.S.I. project was consummated in the Second Yearbook (1942), on *Civilian Morale.* The Third Yearbook (1945), *Human Nature and Enduring Peace,* edited by Gardner Murphy, is the best treatise to date on the psychological approach to the abolition of war. These projects represent an increasing conviction among psychologists that they should be contributing some insight to the settling of social issues. If we do not concern ourselves with the issues of our time, we may be charged with "failure to pay our way in the civilization that is sustaining us." [48] The time has come for us to surrender the happy seclusion of our ivory towers, to mix in the affairs of the everyday world, to use what expert

[45] The need for a sense of responsibility among scientists will be discussed at length in Chapter 6, "The Socialization of Intelligence."
[46] See R. S. Lynd: *Knowledge for What?,* Chapter I, "Social Science in Crisis." 1939.
[47] H. C. Link: "Man in Chains." *Saturday Evening Post,* May 7, 1938.
[48] G. W. Allport: "The Psychologist's Frame of Reference." *Psychological Bulletin,* 1940, 37, 1-28.

knowledge we may have to help solve the critical problems that threaten to undermine our happiness.

Psychologists share with other scientists a responsibility for informing the public concerning the views that experts hold upon matters of social concern. When the United States entered the First World War, psychologists volunteered their services through their professional societies. They made some valuable contributions, notably, the development and application of group intelligence testing. After the war, psychologists as an organized group subsided into their old indifference to practical issues, and during the depression the journals and association meetings revealed little interest in the fact that our social institutions were "rattling about our ears." This situation led some observers to comment that the world at large knew very little about the findings of scientific psychologists, that the latter seemed to be equally unconcerned about what was going on outside the academic walls. This unwholesome state of affairs prompted the Western Psychological Association, in 1939, to give some thought to ways in which psychologists could contribute to the understanding of social issues. Subsequently, Gundlach conducted an investigation to discover how far apart expert opinion and uninformed opinion would be on certain problems of vital concern, using a questionnaire which was administered to college students at the University of California and to members of the American Psychological Association who were attending meetings of the Association at Leland Stanford University. A.P.A. members were found to differ perceptibly from the university undergraduates: more A.P.A. members registered faith in the capacity of the individual citizen to participate in our democratic government, more recognized the doctrine of racial superiority as a fallacy, more labeled as untrue the belief that women are less capable than men, more rejected the idea that war is due to a fighting instinct. The questions touched on some fundamental notions concerning democracy: race, sex, class discrimination, educational handicaps, social reconstruction. Experts were found to hold views differing considerably from those held by a "psychologically naïve college population." Moreover, the psychologists indicated a willingness to extend themselves in correcting fallacious views affecting public policy. They recognized "that as scientists and as citizens they have an obligation to their fellow man." [49]

Many psychologists contributed their professional services to the

[49] See R. H. Gundlach: "The Psychologist's Understanding of Social Issues." *Psychological Bulletin*, 1940, 37, 613-620.

prosecution of the Second World War, in the selection of personnel, in the planning of training programs, in the designing of instruments to fit particular sensory and motor capacities, in the measurement of public opinion and morale, in the waging of psychological warfare. The Office of Psychological Personnel, for a time under the direction of S. H. Britt, helped in assigning psychologists to posts where their special aptitudes and experience could be utilized to best advantage. The Emergency Committee and the National Council of Women Psychologists were also organized to extend the practical service of psychology to the war effort. The War Service Committee of the S.P.S.S.I. did its bit to help the cause. Its report in 1943 reviewed many researches of practical value to the war program and then arrived at the following conclusion:

It seems inevitable that the focusing of research upon everyday problems, with the end in view of making the results immediately applicable to the enhancement of social values, will engender good habits for the future. Social psychology will become less esoteric in its outlook, and more closely geared to application. The limit of this revolutionary trend cannot now be foreseen. But for a whole generation, at least, the mere fact that the majority of social psychologists have directly or indirectly worked for the government cannot fail to have a significant effect upon their outlook and upon their teaching. . . .

The present survey has frequently strayed from the narrow confines of social psychology academically defined. But narrow definitions of social psychology, futile enough in peacetime, are obviously out of place in time of war. If the revolutionary changes that are taking place succeed in destroying the artificial boundaries that have been erected between various branches of psychology or between psychology and other sciences, there will probably be few mourners.[50]

There is manifest a growing desire to develop psychology as a profession which will be devoted in concrete ways to the advancement of social welfare. Evidence of this development is the increasing cooperation among the various professional groups within the American Psychological Association. The sense of social responsibility demonstrated by psychologists during World War II has been so impressive as to make it seem likely that this time, in contrast to the 1920's, there will be a carry-over of concern for the practical problems of everyday peacetime living.

[50] G. W. Allport and H. R. Veltfort: "Social Psychology and the Civilian War Effort." *Journal of Social Psychology, S.P.S.S.I. Bulletin*, 1943, 18, 165-233.

Psychology can help us solve our personal and our social problems, not only in wartime but in peacetime as well. We shall assume that society can be improved only by educating individuals to appreciate the social conditions affecting their behavior and to realize how far such conditions can be modified for the better by the development of keener insights and the assertion of independent judgment. Unconsciously we absorb and perpetuate traditional modes of conduct as if they were inevitable—"human nature being what it is," as we say in defending our inertia. As mature persons we should take stock of ourselves by making an inventory of the social influences underlying our reactions and then we should evaluate those influences in terms of their adjustment value under modern conditions. People continue blindly in their old, confirmed ways unless they come to turn aside the blinders of habit long enough to become conscious of their narrow, rutted lives. Every phase of our social life should be weighed by critical intelligence and, if found wanting, should be discarded in favor of some adaptation more satisfying in its consequences. We shall only touch on some of the more important phases of this reevaluation. Our keynote will be a search for intelligent modes of living. It will be our hope that social science can contribute more effectively to the more intelligent direction of human affairs.

Chapter 2

SOCIAL PSYCHOLOGY IN RELATION TO OTHER SOCIAL SCIENCES

THE SOCIAL PSYCHOLOGIST can borrow to advantage from all the "departments" of knowledge which are interested primarily in the nature of man as a social creature. Students of social psychology should aim to get a broad training in sociology, criminology, anthropology, economics, political science, and history; for all the "social sciences," or better, the "social studies," contribute to our understanding of man-in-society. In seeking to achieve an over-all view of man, we come early to the conviction that knowledge should not be rigidly compartmentalized, even though a college catalogue does list various departments. The interdependence of the several fields of study was recognized at Harvard by the establishment of a roving professorship. Some means must be provided to integrate the different courses in the curriculum, and to impress upon the student the fact that the several avenues of learning converge into the essential unity of knowledge. We shall carry out this suggestion by concentrating here on one phase of that *community* of learning: the relating of social psychology to other social sciences.

I. SOCIOLOGY

The province of social psychology cannot be sharply defined. Its problems are the common concern of several social studies.

Sociology and social psychology, for example, are intimately interrelated. Sociology deals with the agencies which care for the sick, the poor, the delinquent, the unemployed; handling these unfortunate persons with tact and wisdom requires a thorough mastery of psychological principles. Fundamentally, the sociologist concentrates on groups rather than persons, interesting himself in the structure of human society, the characteristics and interrelations of human groups, and the cultural institutions that grow out of human associations.

41

Sociologists measure shifts in urban and rural populations to determine how many people are moving from city to country, how many in
the reverse direction.   The determination of the trend is the distinctive task of the sociologist; the search for the motives actuating change
of residence is the function of the psychologist.   Similarly, sociologists
gather statistics on births and they report the lowest number of births
in the families of architects, physicians, surgeons, dentists, artists,
teachers, engineers, designers, draftsmen, and inventors; the highest
number, in the lowest-income brackets or among those who have no
income at all.[1]   The assignment of the psychologist is to explain *why*
"the rich get richer while the poor get children," as the old saying
goes. Voluntary childlessness among city dwellers is usually motivated
by the hope of improving their competitive position in the economic
and social scale of urban living.[2]   One cannot divorce the sociological
research on differential birth rates from the psychological research of
Terman who finds, by exploring the intelligence quotients of various
occupational groups, that gifted children are usually the offspring of
parents in the professional or higher occupational groups.[3]   Cooperative research is particularly desirable among sociologists and social
psychologists because they are concerned so much of the time with
common problems.   Indeed, one writer remarks: "The facts of psychology and sociology are inevitably coexistent . . . , they are the
same phenomena seen in different frames of reference." [4]

The overlapping interests of sociology and social psychology are
evidenced in the fact that a number of books on the subject of social
psychology have been written by sociologists, notably: Ross, Ellwood,
Bogardus, and Kimball Young.   One textbook, under the title of
Social Psychology, has been written by LaPiere, a sociologist, in collaboration with Farnsworth, a psychologist.   This sort of cooperation symbolizes the spirit of teamwork that is growing among workers
in these two fields.

The distinctive subject matter of sociology may be apprehended
by consulting a typical textbook in the field.   Taking Bogardus'
Sociology as a sample, we find that it is organized around the concept
of groups: family, occupational, play, educational, religious, racial and

[1] See F. Lorimer and F. Osborn: *Dynamics of Population,* p. 72.   1934.
[2] See J. Popenoe: "Childlessness: Voluntary or Involuntary." *Journal of Heredity,* 1943, 34, 83-87.
[3] See L. M. Terman: *Genetic Studies of Genius,* Vol. I, *Mental and Physical Traits
of a Thousand Gifted Children.*   1925.
[4] K. F. Walker: "Sociology and Psychology in the Prediction of Behavior." *Psychological Review,* 1940, 48, 443-449.

community. Among the topics treated are such psychological ones as instinctive reactions, habitual reactions, gregariousness, suggestion, attitudes and values, the socialization of leisure, control by custom, control by public opinion, group leadership. One approach mentioned is the ecological. The naïve person would never guess how much psychology is involved in ecology. A few quotations will prove enlightening on this point:

> Human ecology may be explained as the study of the nature and effect of the spatial relationships of people. These spatial relationships vary from sparse to dense. . . .
>
> The location and development of human groups have been conditioned by natural factors such as hills and mountains. . . . Certain areas, whether natural or artificial, have developed distinctive characteristics which in turn have separated people widely or brought them together. . . .
>
> Spatial relationships help to determine a person's attitudes, values, and his status. Sparseness permits the growth of independent attitudes, self-reliance, and hinders cooperative activities. . . .[5]

These sample citations illustrate how much psychology may enter into a discussion that is primarily sociological in its design.

The relation between psychology and sociology has been described by a sociologist in these words: "I am inclined to think of these overlapping subjects, not as separate fields of knowledge, but as representing differences in approach and emphasis, even though in practice we have accepted a somewhat limited and conveniently stabilized content for each. The dividing lines, like those separating courses by departments in the college catalogue, are arbitrary and administratively useful rather than in line with reality." [6] This statement reflects an important trend in modern education, that of emphasizing the connections and common aims of various fields of study instead of insisting upon the distinctive peculiarities of each special department. This broader view of the unity underlying the several branches of learning is supplanting the excessive specialization and departmentalization which were so characteristic of the scientists a generation ago when each specialist jealously guarded his private precinct of academic learning from encroachment by any and all trespassers.

The sociologists have much to offer the social psychologist. Of spe-

---

[5] From E. S. Bogardus: *Sociology*, p. 17. By permission of The Macmillan Company, publishers. 1935.

[6] Statement made by Albert Morris, Professor of Sociology, College of Liberal Arts, Boston University, in answer to a question raised by the author.

cial interest to us in formulating our program for social psychology is the point of view sponsored by Lester F. Ward, who was one of the pioneers in American sociology (1841-1913). Ward advocated the thesis that man would some day be able to control his destiny by applying scientific knowledge to the management of his social relations as well as to the manipulation of the physical world.[7]   In his enthusiasm for the vision of a man-made world he was following in the footsteps of Auguste Comte, the French sociologist and positivist, who has been called the founder of scientific sociology.[8]   Ward, like Comte, refused to accept Herbert Spencer's dictum that evolution just goes in in its own sweet way no matter what human beings may try to do to influence its course, the doctrine of *laissez faire* that was to be expounded in later years by Yale's famous William Graham Sumner, who wrote in his essay "The Absurd Effort to Make the World Over":

If this poor old world is as bad as they say, one more reflection may check the zeal of the headlong reformer.   It is at any rate a tough old world.   It has taken its trend and curvature and all its twists and tangles from a long course of formation.   All its wry and crooked gnarls and knobs are therefore stiff and stubborn.   If we puny men by our arts can do anything at all to straighten them, it will only be by modifying the tendencies of some of the forces at work, so that, after a sufficient time, their action may be changed a little and slowly the lines of movement be modified.   This effort, however, can at least be only slight, and it will take a long time.   In the meantime spontaneous forces will be at work, compared to which our efforts are like those of man trying to deflect a river. . . .   The great stream of time and earthly things will sweep on just the same in spite of us. . . .   The men will be carried along with it and be made by it.   The utmost they can do by their cleverness will be to note and record their course as they are carried along, which is what we do now, and is that which leads us to the vain fancy that we can make or guide the movement.   That is why we sit down with a slate and pencil to plan out a new social world. . . .[9]

(Sumner should have lived to read *Mein Kampf.*)

Ward had no sympathy for this attitude of helpless resignation because he believed so firmly in the creative potentialities of human intelligence.   Instead of a do-nothing outlook, he adopted a utilitarian view of science combined with a faith in social meliorism and a teleological conception of social progress.   These basic postulates in

[7] Francis Bacon was influential in educating the people of his time regarding the utopia that science could establish, once men devoted themselves to that goal.

[8] See F. B. Karpr: *American Social Psychology*, p. 218.   1932.

[9] W. G. Sumner: *War and Other Essays*, pp. 208-210.   Yale University Press, 1911.

Ward's system are of special concern to us, since our treatment of social psychology will be guided by the same faith that man can use his knowledge to improve the social conditions under which he lives. For this reason it is appropriate that we examine Ward's ideas with some care.

Ward's *Dynamic Sociology* was inspired by the conviction that sociology might discover laws of social life that could be utilized to advantage in promoting human welfare. Ward lamented the sterility of the social science then prevailing—and he would mourn over some of it today, too. "There are," he said, "dead sciences as well as dead languages. The real object of science is to benefit man. . . ." [10] Sociology, he felt, had become a polite amusement, and had sacrificed its chance to become a practical scientific discipline.

Ward was optimistic enough to feel that it was entirely possible for man to improve his lot by getting knowledge and applying it intelligently. Social forces must be understood before they can be controlled. Prerequisite to any constructive effort will be the faith that we can do something about the defects in our present society, that we can bring our world into line with our aspirations. In this hope Ward anticipated John Dewey's confidence in human intelligence as an instrument for social amelioration.

II. CRIMINOLOGY [11]

The study of crime is the specialty of the criminologist. He must be well versed in psychology if he is to discover why some people become criminals while others develop into respectable citizens. Our penal practices are grossly inefficient if we measure the results of our system of punishment in terms of rehabilitation rather than revenge. Our Houses of Correction do not correct and our Reform Schools do not reform, as the Gluecks have demonstrated in their studies of 1,000 bad boys whose careers they have followed since the boys were first referred to the Judge Baker Guidance Center by the Boston Juvenile Court during the years 1917 to 1922. The Gluecks reported their findings first, in 1934, in *One Thousand Juvenile Delinquents;* and later, in 1940, in *Juvenile Delinquents Grown Up.* The boys, whose average age was 13½ years, were subjected to various modes of treatment: probation, fines, correctional schools, reformatories, jails, institutions for the feeble-minded. Only one-tenth of the boys went straight. Within a five-year period four out of five were arrested—an average of

[10] L. F. Ward: *Dynamic Sociology*, Preface to the first edition, p. vii. 1883.
[11] There will be further discussion of crime in Chapter 6.

more than three times apiece.   Nearly half of them served time.   After 15 years, six out of ten were still getting arrested, three out of ten had become hardened criminals.   The evidence suggests that our handling of the lawbreakers is ineffective because our penal system is not built on sound psychology.

Some criminologists have attempted to delineate a special type of personality that predisposes an individual to a criminal career.   Lombroso advanced the theory that the criminal can be detected by certain "stigmata of degeneration," such as woolly hair, oblique eyes, receding forehead, large ears.   These organic idiosyncrasies were supposed to reveal an atavistic nature.[12]   This theory was exploded by Goring and Pearson, who compared English prisoners with students and army men, measuring their physical characteristics with great care.   They reported in *The English Convict* (1913) that the stigmata of degeneration appeared to be just as prevalent among students at Oxford as among the inmates of London's penal institutions.   Hooton has revived interest in Lombroso's theory by virtue of his anthropometric studies, the results of which have led him to state that "the primary cause of crime is biological inferiority." [13]   Though no single feature distinguishes the criminal, the list of inadequacies adds up to "a deteriorated organism," according to Hooton.   Hooton's conclusions, however, are invalidated, it is claimed, by the fact that he failed to exercise proper precautions in equating his criminal and non-criminal groups with respect to all essential characteristics except the two under comparison, namely, criminality and physical characteristics.   On this account, says Klineberg, we should not take his view too seriously.[14]

While some criminologists are centering their attention on the criminal's personal traits, others are concentrating on the social conditions that breed crime.   They find in a large city, for example, that there are definite delinquency areas where the density of the population and the economic level show significant correlations with the kinds of crime and the amount of crime; that rates of truancy, delinquency, and adult crime vary inversely in proportion to the distance away from the center of the city; that areas high in juvenile delinquency are also high in adult crime.   Records over the years reveal the fact that there is an annual quota of crimes for a given district, a certain number of robberies, a certain number of homicides, and so on.   The number will remain fairly constant from year to year, indicating that any commu

---

[12] See C. Lombroso: *Crime, Its Causes and Remedies.*   1911.
[13] E. A. Hooton: *Crime and the Man*, p. 130.   1939.
[14] See O. Klineberg: *Social Psychology*, p. 529.   1940.

nity tends to suffer the crimes it deserves in full measure, a principle designated by Ferri as "the law of criminal saturation." This observation implies that the responsibility for crime rests squarely on the community as a whole. Every citizen is contributing his bit in so far as he tolerates poverty, unemployment, undernourishment, overcrowded living quarters, inadequate recreational facilities, or any other social conditions that are favorable to the genesis of the criminal.

The explanation for crime will undoubtedly be found in a combined analysis of personality and environment. Social psychologists join the criminologists in a search for better methods of preventing crime and of reeducating the criminal who has come into conflict with the forces of legal control. Here again we see that the individual and his situation must both be taken into account.

III. ANTHROPOLOGY

Anthropology, the study of man and his civilization, concerns itself with the growth of language, the significance of inventions, the discovery of tools, the development of myths. Anthropology embraces *ethnography*, the study of races, and *ethnology*, the science of culture.[15]

The anthropologist is interested in the "Arts of Life," which include weapons of warfare, carpenter's tools, hunting and fishing and agriculture, caves and huts and tents and houses, dress and tattooing, cookery, navigation, commerce, music, dancing, painting. Tylor's *Anthropology* (1920) is devoted largely to this topic, as the author traces each art historically from its origins among primitive men. It is obvious that much of this material is of interest to the social psychologist, and the same might be said of Goldenweiser's *Anthropology: an Introduction to Primitive Culture* (1937), the theme of which is the psychic unity of man regardless of his geographic location or the stage of his social or cultural evolution. Sections in Goldenweiser that will appeal especially to psychologists deal with the mental characteristics of the various races, the nature of human invention, the psychology of cultural diffusion, the symbolism of primitive art.

The anthropologists, we have noted, take an interest in the study of tools, especially directing their research to the effects that various in-

[15] Our exposition of anthropology is restricted to cultural anthropology as distinguished from physical anthropology.

A group of anthropologists at Harvard University are expanding the scope of anthropology by defining it as "the science of human relations." This extension of the province of anthropology is sure to prove confusing, since it is an attempt to appropriate the functions of social psychology. *Principles of Anthropology*, by E. D. Chapple and C. S. Coon, 1942, exemplifies this very broad concept of anthropology.

ventions have had upon man's estate.   The import of these studies for the psychologist is suggested in this discussion of "Wheels":

I have always been interested in the relationship of the wheel to the advance of civilization and the rise of man from the state of savagery.   There has been a good deal of exploration as to where the wheel was discovered and how it first was used.   It is suggested that it came from putting logs under heavy objects to roll them about, and then gradually went on to more refined uses, from transporting of objects and men to more creative or manufacturing uses, such as in the potter's wheel, the spinning wheel, and the mill wheel.   Our own early American life and our spread across this continent owed much to the wheel, and it now plays a predominant role in our economic structure.

We know that the Eskimos have been able to build up a fairly satisfactory culture without the use of the wheel; what they do, though, is of a very simple character, and their snowy environment has not been conducive to the use of wheels.   But upon nearly every civilization of the world wheels have had a profound influence.   Few of us pause to realize the power of wheels in our daily life, whirling about us everywhere in the civilization which they have played such a large part in creating.   Literally, "Wheels That Make the World Go Round," and "Wheels within Wheels."   Not just the obvious wheels we all see rolling under us on trains, automobiles, or bicycles.   There are the tiny wheels tucked away in watches to tyrannize over us in the matter of time.   There are the wheels in typewriters and presses, in engines and machines and other devices about us everywhere.   Steamships, airplanes, the tractor, and the armored tank alike are impotent without them.   Wheels have done much in building up and bringing together man's world; misused, they can the more rapidly destroy it.

Perhaps the most significant effect of the development of the wheel was that it gave mobility to man and increased his range of activities.   This mobility has been vastly increased by the steam and now the gas engine in conjunction with wheels, tracks, roads, or water.   Wheels mean movement. Movement means danger, unless that movement is controlled.   Wheels have made possible a military attack which is unprecedented and which, as we have recently watched it develop on this earth, may bring revolutionary changes in all human affairs.[16]

The historical-ethnological approach to anthropology was promoted by Boas, who maintained that a culture can be understood only in relation to its historical orientation, its geographical setting, its physical environs, and its interrelations with surrounding cultures.   The historical treatment of culture as developed by ethnologists is sometimes classified as *cultural anthropology.*

[16] R. L. Wilbur: "Wheels." *School and Society,* October 12, 1940.

Anthropologists have enlightened us with respect to the distinction between "common human characteristics," which are popularly called "human nature," and "culturally imposed artifacts," which are the habits acquired under a certain system of conditioning peculiar to a given society. This problem of ascertaining just what constitutes *human nature* is the core of many investigations of culture. It was this problem that prompted Margaret Mead's study of Samoa, where she went to discover whether Samoans undergo the stress so characteristic of American adolescents, thus to determine by the comparative method whether the strain undergone by our adolescents is attributable to adolescence *per se* or to the cultural taboos enforced in American society. She reached the conclusion that our neurotic conflicts are produced by our frustrating mores, thus substantiating the claim of the behaviorists that our troubles are traceable to our habits rather than to native impulses. Further research of a comparative nature was conducted by Mead among the inhabitants of New Guinea. Her studies of *Cooperation and Competition among Primitive Peoples* (1937) have already been mentioned, as supporting the thesis that training determines whether people are going to work together harmoniously or whether they are going to cut each other's throats, figuratively or literally speaking. Ruth Benedict has engaged in similar investigations and come to similar conclusions in her survey of the customs prevalent among three primitive peoples, namely, the Pueblos of New Mexico, the Dobuans of Melanesia, and the Indians of the Northwest Coast of America; and Bronislaw Malinowski has conducted investigations of the same general nature among the inhabitants of the Trobriand Islands. The anthropologists as a rule subscribe to the thesis that the environment is of primary importance in the determination of behavior patterns, that habit rather than instinct will supply the key to man's social activities. According to this view, people settle their differences by resort to war, practice monogamy, or strive to amass wealth, because of their upbringing and not because of any hereditary needs that impel them to act in these ways. The anthropologists have gathered valuable information on the significance of habit formation, information that is very useful to social psychologists.

Psychologists who are well acquainted with the anthropological point of view are not likely to commit the fallacy of "community-centrism," the error of thinking that one's own cultural patterns are the universal rule. We may avoid this mistake by recognizing that, as we are going to confine our attention very largely to American culture, our remarks should not be interpreted as general principles that will hold for people everywhere. Perhaps we may find justification for limiting our discussion in the thought that social psychology may prove more enlightening if it is conceived in terms of a particular culture. At least the narrowing of our focus will enable us to use words for which referents may be easily found. We shall try to avoid overgeneralizing on the basis of vague abstractions supposed to account for human conduct anywhere, any time, anyhow. By limiting our scope in this manner, we may increase our accuracy.

Psychology and ethnology have been nicely integrated by Klineberg, who has shown that certain "dependable motives," such as the parental drive, aggressiveness, acquisitiveness, self-assertiveness, and sex, are expressed in forms that are culturally conditioned. A real service has been performed by thus calling attention to the many contributions made by ethnology to social psychology. This anthropological emphasis is stimulating psychologists to adopt a broader view of human behavior, more comprehensive in scope because it is derived from a comparison of differing cultural backgrounds.

IV. ECONOMICS

Economics is another social science that bears an intimate relationship with social psychology.[17] Economic laws are principles of human behavior. Economic forces are not powers external to human beings but, rather, the dynamic reaction patterns that constitute human action. Thus the economist's Law of Supply and Demand may be viewed by the psychologist as the stimulation and satisfaction of human wants. Capitalism is predicated upon competitive reactions, which are habits cultivated in the interest of individual enterprise. Foreign trade depends upon many psychological factors: fluctuating consumer demands abroad, prohibitive tariffs based on fear, reciprocal agreements worked out by mutual accommodation, inventions eliminating the need for importing materials, and nationalistic ambitions. "Buy American" is a popular slogan with both economic and psychological connotations. Economics deals with the principles underlying our system of producing and distributing goods. Those principles cannot be fully understood without reference to the psychological media through which men influence each other. Inflation, too, can be understood better when it is interpreted in terms of the psychology of expectation.

[17] A discussion of economic planning will be included in Chapter 6.

Inflation, a sustained and general upward movement of prices, is not an automatic effect of economic factors, such as excess purchasing power. It takes men and their decisions and actions to put the mechanism of inflation into operation. Psychologists may therefore contribute to the study of inflation and the fight against inflation.

Whether a rise in price of a commodity will be followed by increase or decrease of demand for it depends on what consumers expect of subsequent developments. Laboratory experiments concerning the origin and strength of expectations seem to show: a) Reiterations of statistical data, or categorical statements and pronouncements (e.g., that shoe prices will remain stable or will go up), create relatively weak expectations. b) Presentation of comprehensive context with a clear and consistent structure, from which the subjects gain an understanding of why prices may advance or remain stable, influences the attitudes and expectations to a much greater extent.[18]

Bookkeeping is more than a matter of the sheer economics of accounting. Psychological factors are also involved. Failure to appreciate the psychology of accounting was responsible for much of the condemnation directed against the Roosevelt administration. A New York investment banker, speaking at the Summer Institute for Social Progress at Wellesley College, defended the New Deal spending as "necessary, even at the cost of an unbalanced budget," but criticized the administration's system of bookkeeping. He explained his position in these words: "I do not believe that the excess expenditures would have appeared so alarming had the government prepared a balance sheet indicating value received as a result of spending. There should have been a better accounting system, one in which capital expenditures and current expenses might quickly be distinguished." *Words* make the difference.

Economic thinkers base their theories on their ideas of what people want most of all in life. There is plenty of evidence to demonstrate that fantastic doctrines evolve when economists adopt some view of human motivation which happens to serve as a convenient premise for a pretty theory. Adam Smith and his disciples, for example, concocted a picture of *Economic Man,* which they used to rationalize the capitalistic system of free competition and private enterprise. For ages, this view of man—an egocentric being dominated by the profit

---

[18] G. Katona: "Psychological Studies of Inflation and Inflationary Expectations." Report that was to have been delivered at the 1942 meeting of the American Psychological Association—canceled on account of the War.

See G. Katona: *War without Inflation: the Psychological Approach to Problems of War Economy.* 1942.

motive as his supreme inspiration—prevailed as the authoritative explanation of man and society.   Rare were the sceptics who ventured to question the astonishing myth that a free-for-all society would issue happily in blessings for everybody.   The collapse of this notion of Economic Man is one phase of the present revolutionary cataclysm which is shaking the world to its foundations, while man gropes for some new insight into human needs which will enable him to understand society better and to control it more effectively in the interest of communal well-being.

Homo economicus was a fictional character invented by economists who lacked any adequate comprehension of man's psychological make-up.

Every organized society is built upon a concept of the nature of man and of his function and place in society.   Whatever its truth as a picture of human nature, this concept always gives a true picture of the nature of the society which recognizes and identifies itself with it.   It symbolizes the fundamental tenets and beliefs of society by showing the sphere of human activity which it regards as socially decisive and supreme.   The concept of man as an "economic animal" is the true symbol of the societies of bourgeois capitalism and of Marxist socialism, which see in the free exercise of Man's economic activity the means toward the realization of their aims.   Economic satisfactions alone appear socially important and relevant.   Economic positions, economic privileges, and economic rights are those for which man works.   For these he wages war, and for these he is prepared to die.   All others seem mere hypocrisy, snobbism, or romantic nonsense.[19]

The acceptance of this handy abstraction facilitated the development of a "science" of economics.   "Laws" were established in conformity with which society supposedly behaved.   It was a beautiful logical construct that the classical economists evolved—but grossly untrue and fantastic, for history did not bear out the theory: economic freedom did not prove a trustworthy sesame to security and abundance for all, as predicted, and man, we have since discovered, does not labor just for money.[20]

V. POLITICAL SCIENCE

Political Science describes and evaluates the governmental machinery which has been designed to express the will of the citizens.   "Poli-

---

[19] Peter F. Drucker: *The End of Economic Man,* p. 45.   The John Day Company, 1939.

[20] The motives actuating work will be discussed at length in Chapter 18.

tics as a science," says Rice, "is concerned among other things with the nature, content, and distribution of attitudes among individuals, and with the manner in which they have practical effect in the machinery of government." [21] Votes may be used as one means of measuring those attitudes.

The political scientist is interested, too, in the techniques of creating and controlling public opinion, as practiced in political campaigns, particularly. The wooing of public support—and its maintenance— has become a very important function of the party in power. When the federal government expanded its responsibilities to include the care of the aged and the unemployed, regimentation of wages, hours, drugs, and stock speculation, officials had to quell the protests of those citizens who objected to the strong being penalized so that the weak could be pampered with handouts. Publicity bureaus were busy persuading the public that its money was being expended (invested) wisely in priming pumps and in conserving natural resources. Some encouraging word had to be passed along to pacify anxious citizens who were worrying about the mounting public debt. The political scientist and the social psychologist are both interested in observing the way of the officeholder with the voter. There is a lot of psychology involved in legislating a higher income tax and then making the taxpayer like it.

Political action would be far more intelligent if our citizens, and particularly our leaders, were guided more by the counsel of social scientists. When we need a faucet repaired, we call the plumber; when we need a tooth cavity filled, we see the dentist; but, when we are afflicted with a social-economic-political ill, we fall back on the "uninformed dogmas of the man on the street," content to allow "the body politic to be butchered by ignorant, corrupt politicians." Why? We offer incentives to inventors of material things—prizes, patent royalties, prestige; to the social inventor we extend our patronizing ridicule.[22] If we applied to our political problems the intelligence that we devote to making our business prosper, our social ills would soon be alleviated or cured. The price we pay for our indifference to incompetent and even psychopathic leadership is social disaster, as we have witnessed in the careers of the neurotic Kaiser Wilhelm, the megalomaniac Mussolini, and the paranoiac Hitler.

The art of vote-getting is a topic of common concern to the political

---

[21] S. A. Rice: *Quantitative Methods in Politics*, p. 53. 1928.
[22] See H. E. Barnes: "The Responsibility of Education to Society." *Scientific Monthly*, September, 1940.

scientist and the social psychologist. The seasoned politician knows that emotional appeals get the votes. As a candidate of a minority party, in an election held in Allentown, Pennsylvania, in 1935, Hartmann (a psychologist) prepared two different campaign pamphlets, one a statement designed to excite emotional reactions, the other a statement phrased to encourage dispassionate deliberation, with the idea of comparing the relative effectiveness of emotion and reason in political campaigning. In the rational pamphlet he outlined some suggestions for changes of a social and economic nature. The other pamphlet was a sentimental letter to voters designed to wring the hearts of parents.

RATIONAL

You've heard of intelligence tests, haven't you? Well, we have a little examination right here which we are sure you will enjoy taking, even if you didn't care much for school when you were a youngster. The beauty of this test is that you can score it yourself without any teacher to tell you whether you passed or failed.

This is how it works. First read each one of the seven statements printed below. If you approve of the idea as it stands, underline the word AGREE; if you disapprove of the idea, underline the word DISAGREE. Simple, isn't it? All right, then. Get your pencil ready. All set? Go!

1. We would have much cheaper electric light and power if this industry were owned and operated by the various governmental units for the benefit of all the people. AGREE—DISAGREE.

2. No gifted boy or girl should be denied the advantages of higher education just because his parents lack the money to send him to college. AGREE —DISAGREE.

3. The federal government should provide to all classes of people opportunity for complete insurance at cost against accident, sickness, premature death and old age. AGREE—DISAGREE.

4. All banks and insurance companies should be run on a non-profit basis like the schools. AGREE—DISAGREE.

5. Higher income taxes on persons with incomes of more than $10,000 a year should be levied immediately. AGREE—DISAGREE.

6. The only way most people will be able to live in modern sanitary homes is for the government to build them on a non-profit basis. AGREE— DISAGREE.

7. Many more industries and parts of industries should be owned and managed cooperatively by the producers (all the workers) themselves. AGREE—DISAGREE.

Have you answered them all? Fine. Now go back and count the number of sentences with which you AGREED. Then count the number with which you DISAGREED. If the number of agreements is larger than the number of disagreements, you are at heart a Socialist—whether you know it or not!

Now that you have tested yourself and found out how much of a Socialist you really are, why don't you try voting for the things you actually want? The Republicans and Democrats don't propose to give these things to you, because a mere look at their records will show that they are opposed to them. Do you get the point?

> *HELP BUILD THE AGE OF PLENTY*
> *VOTE SOCIALIST*

SENTIMENTAL

Dear Mother and Father:

We youngsters are not in the habit of giving much thought to serious things. You have often told us so and we admit it.

But while we like to play football and have a good time dancing and cause you a lot of amusement as well as worry with our "puppy loves," we sometimes think long and hard. You ought to know what many of us young folks are saying to ourselves.

Our future as American citizens in 1940 looks dark. We want jobs—and good jobs, too—so that we can help in the useful work of the world. But we know that many of our brightest high-school and college graduates find it absolutely impossible to get any kind of employment. We also know that this condition is not temporary, but that it will last as long as we stick to harmful ways of running business, industry, and government.

We want to continue our education, but we haven't the heart to ask you to make that sacrifice. With Dad working only part time on little pay and Mother trying to make last year's coat and dress look in season, we feel we ought to pitch in and help keep the family's neck above water. But we can't. The world as it is now run has no use for us.

Many of our teachers know what is wrong, although we can see that most of them are afraid to say what they really think. Luckily, the textbooks and school magazines keep us in touch with new ideas, and we have learned how to read between the lines of the ordinary newspaper. Please don't be frightened if we tell you that we have decided!

We young people are becoming Socialists. We have to be. We can't be honest with ourselves and be anything else. The Socialist party is the only party which is against all wars—and we have learned from our history courses what awful wars have taken place under Republicans and Democrats. We refuse to be slaughtered (like Uncles Bob and Charles were in 1918) just to make profits for ammunition manufacturers.

The Socialist party seeks to create a world in which there will be no poverty. In our science classes we learn how power machinery and other modern inventions make it possible for all of us to have enough of all the goods and services we need. Yet look at our town with its unpainted shacks, suffering parents, half-starved children! We might have everything, but we continue to live on next to nothing.

It is all so unnecessary. You have had to lead a poor workingman's life, because you and most of the workers and farmers of this country have regularly voted for either the Republican or Democratic parties, between which there is no real difference. These old machines are not for us.

The Youth of 1935 want to build a Better America, in which there will be no poverty, no fear of unemployment, no threat of war. We ask you to follow the lead of the Socialist party this year because that is the most direct way for you to help hasten the day when Peace and Plenty and lasting Prosperity will be the lot of all men. Good parents such as you desire these things for us. But we can never have them as long as you are controlled by your old voting habits.

We are profoundly earnest about this. Our generation cannot enjoy the beauty and justice of the New America if you block our highest desires. There was a time when you too were young like us. We beg you in the name of those early memories and springtime hopes to support the Socialist ticket in the coming elections!

Your Sons and Daughters[23]

In certain wards 5,000 copies of the rational pamphlet were handed personally to voters. In other wards the same number of emotional pamphlets were given out. The remaining wards received neither pamphlet. When the votes were counted, the Party ballots were compared with a previous year's returns. By far the greatest increase was in the wards where the emotional appeal was used. The emotional appeal, according to Hartmann, was twice as effective as the rational one. Through a check-up two weeks later, it was discovered that three times as many people recalled the emotional leaflet as remembered the factual one.

Political science and social psychology are both interested in finding out how different forms of government affect the personalities of the citizens. It is easy for an American to say that democracy produces the healthiest kind of personality but is there any specific, concrete evidence to support this contention? There is evidence but it is hardly conclusive. We may cite, as a sample, an experiment in self-government conducted at the New Haven Children's Center. The leaders of the Center were treating some problem children who had been upset by too much discipline. Children of this type, they found, are diffi-

[23] G. W. Hartmann: "A Field Experiment on the Comparative Effectiveness of Emotional and Rational Political Leaflets in Determining Election Results." *Journal of Abnormal and Social Psychology*, 1936, 31, 99-114.

cult to handle because they are hostile toward anybody who represents authority; on this account, leaders stir resentment whenever they try to dominate the child, a situation that is especially unhappy because it prevents the establishment of an intimate rapport between the Staff Members and their protégés. The leaders agreed that the children needed a period of relative freedom during which they could rid themselves of their hostilities. The problem of providing this freedom without encouraging anarchy was solved by inaugurating a modified form of self-government. The group of twenty-four children, ranging in age from four to twelve years, were called together and enlightened as to the need for self-discipline in governing themselves. It was explained to them that they would have to work out a practical basis for their morals: if they wanted their own property to remain unmolested, they would be wise to refrain from stealing the belongings of the others. It was pointed out that the enjoyment of freedom entailed the shouldering of responsibilities for themselves. With these instructions to prepare the way, the children were given the opportunity to regulate themselves. One result of this program was better child-adult relationships based upon mutual understanding.[24]

If the schools are preparing youngsters for citizenship, as they claim they are doing, there should be more of this sort of democracy in the classroom, less of the dictatorial regime so characteristic of the traditional schoolroom. This idea of giving the pupils a chance to learn about government in school is being tried out with notable success in many of our up-to-date schools. There are possibilities in this recent educational development that merit the attention of political scientists and social psychologists.

VI. HISTORY

History is concerned with human behavior. The historian reviews the shifting patterns of human relations, with special attention to their temporal sequence. The traditional subject matter of history has been war, peace, and more war, and historians have all too often confined themselves to describing and explaining how people become involved in these ever-recurring conflicts. We have come to feel that no account of events can be complete without considering "the personalities behind the news." History, as Carlyle said, is collective biography. No student of the Reformation, for example, can compre-

---

[24] See O. H. Mowrer: "Authoritarianism vs. Self-Government in the Management of Children's Aggressive (Anti-Social) Reactions as a Preparation for Citizenship in a Democracy." *Journal of Social Psychology,* 1939, 10, 121-126.

hend the meaning of that period without some insight into the mental conflicts of Martin Luther. The psychological approach to history has been very enlightening.

History is more than a mere chronicle of events related in a meaningless sequence; life, we might say, is more than "just one darned thing after another." The *raison d'être* of history is interpretative; it should enable us, through an appreciation of man's past, to understand how he has arrived at his present estate and to anticipate what the future may hold in store for him. Psychology will, of course, play a significant role in such a program, as James Harvey Robinson demonstrated so ably in his psychological approach to history. In his *Mind in the Making* (1921) he proposed that the study of history should enable us, by creative thought, to reevaluate the authority of tradition and thus to lay aside the vicious habit of using our intellects to defend by subtle rationalizations the old ways of doing things. He pointed out that our debts to the past are handicapping us. Operating unconsciously, our established habits impede intelligent consideration of our problems. This hold on us of the hoary past is particularly paralyzing in our social relations, as vestiges of our animal and barbaric heritage prevent us from attaining the level of civilization we could achieve if we were able to emancipate our intelligence from these inhibitive controls. Among such controls we find our mystical and animistic tendencies, our notions of the sacred, our tribal taboos. We sanctify the habits we happen to acquire and then refuse to reconsider our customary ways of acting. By viewing the evolution of the human mind and getting an historical perspective on ourselves, we gain a new insight into the inertia that keeps us from capitalizing on our creative powers. The great mass of mankind and their leaders and teachers unfortunately "continue to operate on the basis of presuppositions and prejudices which owe their respectability and currency to their great age and uncritical character. . . . A great part of our beliefs about man's nature and the rightness or wrongness of his acts, dates from a time when far less was known of the universe and far different were the conditions and problems of life from those of today. . . . We should have a dynamic education to fit a dynamic world. The world should not be presented to students as happily standardized but as urgently demanding readjustment." [25] An intelligent attitude toward the past, the kind of attitude that historical studies should encourage, will help us steer a course between uncritical cre-

[25] From *The Humanizing of Knowledge*, by J. H. Robinson, copyright 1924, 1926 by Doubleday and Company, Inc. Pp. 41, 42, 69.

dulity and cynical contempt. The wise student will sift the human heritage to ascertain what is worth preserving.

One of the chief lessons to be gleaned from history, according to Robinson, is an appreciation of the fact that all things change, even our most precious institutions. Historians learned from biologists the "advantage of finding out how things had come about in order to comprehend the more fully how they are." [26] History introduces us to "the living past" and reminds us of our humble beginnings.

Robinson's outlook on life, gained by years of historical research, may be summarized by quoting a few passages from *The Human Comedy:*

Knowledge certainly comes in rapidly enough, but Wisdom tarries . . . a great many of our disappointments and woes are gratuitous and unnecessary, the result of tragic stupidity and want of insight. . . . The older longing to be "good," with the hope of making all things right, is giving way to the suspicion that intelligence is what we most need. . . . (p. 1.)

Our present problems cannot be understood by just looking them in the face. We have to ask how they arose—in trenchant slang, "How did we get that way?" (pp. 2-3.)

All advancement in intelligence and insight depends upon our ability to call in question and reconsider what we have hitherto taken for granted. . . . (p. 5.)

Rarely do we come later to doubt in any comprehensive fashion what we are taught in childhood. . . . (p. 47.)

History . . . should not be regarded primarily as an accumulation of information about the past, but as a means for cultivating intellectual freedom and sagacity. This precious historical-mindedness, so essential to estimating man's plight, has hitherto been rare even among historians. . . . (pp. 67-68.)

History I am now inclined to describe as an effort to recall those reminiscences of the past which cast most light on the present. It is an extension of our personal memories. Memory alone renders us sane and able to make judicious terms with things. History properly conceived should vastly augment our insight by widening our memories. It should contribute to precisely the same end as personal recollection, namely, that of orienting us in a world we never made, where we are strangers and afraid. . . . (p. 379.)

We cannot attack our political, religious, economic, educational and social standards directly, although we may well suspect they must *perforce* be anachronisms. They may all, however, issue into a clearer light when we think how everything that now goes on came about. So history might be the great illuminator. As yet it is highly imperfect; but some day it may well become the most potent instrument for human regeneration. (pp. 388-389.)

[26] J. H. Robinson: *The Human Comedy,* p. 8. Harper & Brothers, 1937.

The two main obstacles to a proper socialization of modern applied science, according to Robinson, are the profit-making objective of our economic system and nationalistic patriotism.   Defenders of our modern scheme of things, who believe they stand to gain by its continuance, are vehement in opposing reform.   Yet if history proves anything, it is that excessive suppression of progressive tendencies is as ill-advised on the part of the vested interests as it is detrimental to society at large.   Conservatism of this sort merely postpones change, making it both violent and expensive when it comes.

Intelligent persons learn from past mistakes and revise their conduct accordingly.   History can point the way to a wise solution of our social problems.   History is a prelude to a science of society, enabling us to predict the future in terms of the past.

VII. SUMMARY

A survey of the relation of social psychology to the other social studies offers abundant evidence of the need for cooperation among the workers in the several fields.   Coordination of the research projects carried on in the various social sciences is being fostered by the Social Science Research Council, which "exists for the one comprehensive purpose of advancing the study of man in his relations to man."   The comprehensiveness of its program is revealed in the fact that the directors of the Council are elected by seven different national scientific societies:

American Anthropological Association
American Economic Association
American Historical Association
American Political Science Association
American Psychological Association
American Sociological Society
American Statistical Association

The variety of projects for which the Council lends its financial assistance each year shows the wide scope of its interests.   Teamwork among social scientists is effectively promoted by such a program.

In addition to the urgency for cooperation among the social scientists, there is need for a reorientation of the basic aims inspiring research in the social studies.   The emphasis in social psychology, as in social science generally, has been too much on the *science,* not enough on the *social.*   Social science differs from natural science, though some

persons seem to be unaware of the distinction. "The obvious difference between a *social* science and a *natural* science," says Childs, "is
the fact that one is social and the other is not." [27] Childs goes on to
point out that a *social* science deals with criteria of social welfare,
standards of evaluation, by reference to which it interprets its observations. The need for more attention to the *social* aspect of social science is well illustrated in the field of public relations. It is unfortunate, comments Childs, that "much of the prevailing interest in public
relations is often based upon no broader idealism than the desire to
find out how to promote some profitable cause irrespective of its social usefulness." [28]

The *social* psychologist, as a *social* scientist, will study events and
their implications. He will not content himself with the cataloguing
of unrelated facts. This search for the social significance of scientific
discoveries is especially important today, for men live, not by inco-
herent fragments of fact, but by values.

[27] Reprinted by permission from *An Introduction to Public Opinion* by H. L.
Childs, published by John Wiley & Sons, Inc. P. 22. 1940.
[28] *Ibid.*, p. 23.

Part II

OBSERVATION AND EVALUATION

PSYCHOLOGY is both a science and an art.

In Chapter 3, "Investigating Social Behavior," we shall study how methods of measurement are applied to the recording of social attitudes and reactions, how field studies are used to explore the ways in which human beings act in real-life situations. In this chapter we are dealing with psychology in its role as a science.

The psychologist may observe how people behave, and then he may proceed to weigh patterns of behavior in terms of the satisfaction or dissatisfaction they produce. It is natural that fact-gathering should issue in interpretation and evaluation. This role of the psychologist as a student of "the problem of protracted human happiness," is examined in Chapter 4, "Values and the Art of Living." Since psychology is usually considered to be a science—and is seldom recognized as an art—it will be wise to justify our thesis that psychology is both a science and an art. The psychologist can find out how people live and how much satisfaction they gain from their particular modes of life, and then on the basis of such knowledge suggest some practical means for increasing the chances of happiness. The subject of values—both descriptive and normative—is coming more and more to occupy the serious attention of those psychologists who are interested in promoting better personal adjustments. Examination of the sources of values reveals their cultural determination. By discovering just what we want to get out of life we can plan society to facilitate the fulfillment of our more important needs. Democracy seems especially favorable to the satisfaction of *personal* needs.

The task of evaluation is illustrated in Chapters 5 and 6.

Chapter 5, "The Unemployment of Intelligence," analyzes in a negative, critical manner some of the reasons why we have failed so miserably in our collective pursuit of happiness: we do not choose our goals wisely; we lack social-mindedness in our daily contacts whether it be as business men, lawyers, or doctors; we are so egocentric that we fail to see how we hurt ourselves in the long run by trying to outwit the other fellow for our own immediate gain; our sense of values is immature; we set up barriers to defeat intelligence by prohibiting non-conformists from expressing their disturbing ideas or we interfere with the acquisition of knowledge by censoring the news; we dupe each other with propaganda, we let our emotions misguide us, and we excuse our immoralities by transmuting them into collective blessings.

Chapter 6, "The Socialization of Intelligence," deals with the significance of the fact that the social sciences lag far behind the physical sciences. We know more about running machines than we do about governing human relations. Our social backwardness is evidenced in our emotional resistance to the obvious necessity for social planning. Scientists are not yet aware of their social responsibilities. We still await the day when our scientific knowledge will be utilized to benefit mankind. Science must be socialized to insure the constructive application of all that we learn about the physical and the human world.

Chapter 3

INVESTIGATING SOCIAL BEHAVIOR

STUDENTS with a background in elementary psychology have a fairly good idea as to what is meant by *scientific* psychology. The application of the scientific method involves (1) the formulation of an hypothesis, and (2) the testing of this hypothesis by means of experiment under controlled conditions for verification or revision. The investigator, impartial and objective, guards himself against the inclination to prove what he himself prefers to believe. These tenets provide the frame of reference for psychology-as-a-science.

The experimental approach is not limited to laboratory investigations, though persons with a naïve conception of science are prone to think of the scientist as strictly a laboratory technician. Social psychologists would sacrifice their touch with reality if they were to restrict themselves to "brass instrument" research. Accurate knowledge of human behavior in society can be gained only by including the approach of the field worker: observing individual persons in their everyday contacts, in the home, in the school, in the market place. In such a world of intercourse, it is impossible to control conditions as a scientist would like to do in order to be sure of discovering the significant factors in a situation. It is difficult to establish valid principles when we are dealing with the personal variables involved in human relations. Unfortunately, crowds, strikes, elections, wars, and similar mass phenomena cannot be duplicated in the laboratory. The social psychologist is limited, too, by the fact that precise measurements in many cases are difficult to obtain. Despite these obstacles, there are encouraging features in the situation: statistical controls are available to make possible significant measurements of many kinds of social phenomena in real-life situations; descriptive methods of investigation may be used to good advantage if care is taken to be accurate. Qualitative (non-quantitative) reports may give us just as true an account of reality as that attained through the experimental methods of the laboratory.

Our discussion of scientific research in psychology will not be comprehensive. We shall limit ourselves to a few notable kinds of *measurement* and to a few outstanding illustrations of *field studies*. These examples will be discussed with the idea of furnishing the student with a glimpse of what can be done by the social psychologist who is interested in applying the scientific method to the investigation of human behavior in society.

I. MEASUREMENT

There are distinct advantages in measuring the phenomena under observation, for a quantitative record of results is a step in the direction of the two goals of scientific progress, prediction and control. The prediction of group tendencies, of course, lies more within the realm of probable accuracy than does the prediction of an individual's actions, since statistical methods can be utilized to full advantage in studying groups. This means that the data of social psychology, in so far as they are obtained from the study of groups, are peculiarly suited to mathematical treatment. Advantages accruing to this quantitative recording of social facts are that it reduces individual bias to a minimum, makes evident any margin of error, and permits verification by other investigators.

Statistical data give us the material for interpreting trends, and enable us to predict the future by following the direction of a development over a period of time. The accuracy of prediction will depend upon exact measurement and sane interpretations, both equally essential to sound prognostication. Analyses of census reports over a period of years will enable the social scientist to envisage the pattern of things to come: whether in the years ahead there will be more people or fewer people; whether there will be a preponderance of older folks and a scarcity of children, with all the ramifying effects of these shifting proportions in terms of needed playgrounds and golf courses, the demand for school teachers, the relative consumption of milk and whiskey. The census analyst, looking back to earlier reports to catch the "drift" of change, observes that as recently as 1870 America was almost entirely a young man's country, persons over 45 making up only 15.5 per cent of the population; in 1940 they constituted 24.4 per cent. Medical advance is prolonging life, and war still takes its toll of young people. The trend over the years indicates that we are heading toward a larger proportion of older people. This shift in age distribution carries many implications for the social psychologist: problems of unemployment aggravated by the tendency of business concerns to avoid the hiring of persons over 45; the growth of adult education and recreation programs; increasing production of articles in demand by elderly people and decreasing manufacture of goods for children; an increment in the mental and physical diseases of senility; and different parent-child relationships since parents are older and children fewer. Definite figures, secured by scientific measurement, give us something concrete on which to base our "prophecies," thus enabling us to go beyond mere conjecture to well-grounded prediction.

To show the value of the quantitative method in operation, we may look into the exploration of attitudes, as an experimental procedure, and then see how it is applied to market analysis or consumer research, and to public opinion polls.

A. EXPERIMENTAL STUDY OF ATTITUDES

An attitude is a mental-physical (psychophysical) set which determines how an individual will feel and how he will act in a given situation. It is a state of readiness inclining the individual toward a certain pattern of behavior, conditioned by past experience, often operating in a dynamic fashion outside the person's awareness. Thus we say, speaking in proverbs, "The wish is father to the thought." The truth of this observation was confirmed by Cantril, who sent out a questionnaire in the spring of 1937 to twelve selected groups: bankers, newspaper editors, lawyers, magazine editors, life-insurance executives, public-relations counsels, Communists, historians, economists, sociologists, social psychologists, and laymen. Members of these several groups were asked to predict whether there would be another depression in the United States between 1943 and 1950, whether the Roosevelt Supreme Court Bill would pass, which faction would win the Spanish Civil War, what would be the future for the C.I.O. At the end of the questionnaire was a short test on attitudes on which the subjects were requested to record their own views regarding the issues involved in their predictions. Analysis of the results showed a tendency for some persons to forecast the outcome they personally favored: wishing affected the judgments of life-insurance executives, bankers, lawyers, and Communists; personal desires did not exert any significant influence upon the judgments of historians, economists, sociologists, and social psychologists. Social scientists apparently learn to appraise issues objectively, keeping their own feelings out of their evaluations in the interest of objectivity. It is significant, too, that the persons who felt least certain about their predictions coming true were the social psychologists and sociologists.

Methods of measuring attitudes fall into two general categories: the questionnaire and the rating scale.

The questionnaire technique consists of questions calling for answers which the subject writes down as he reads the queries, or the questions may be asked orally by the interviewer who then records the replies which the subject voices. Two types of questions are most commonly used: (1) The open or free answer question, such as, "What do you think about a national sales tax?" (2) The categorical or dichotomous question which calls for a "yes" or "no" answer, such as, "Are you in favor of a national sales tax?"

By counting ballots or by tabulating answers to questions, the investigator can ascertain how prevalent an attitude may be in a sample population. We shall deal with this sort of opinion census in more detail in our discussion of public opinion polls. At this point it may be sufficient for our purpose to cite a census of students' attitudes at Syracuse University, conducted by Katz and Allport. In this census, which was very comprehensive, 4,248 students answered hundreds of questions about college life. Among the items was the following questionnaire concerning the reasons for coming to college (multiple choice or "cafeteria" type of question):

Place a check mark (√) on the short line to the left of *three* of the following statements which you consider the three most important of your reasons for coming to college:

———In order to prepare for a certain vocation

———Because of the social attractions or athletic opportunities of college life

———Because my parents wished it

———Because a person with a college degree can obtain a better position and earn more money

———Because a person with a college education has more prestige and a higher social standing

———Because of my interest in specific studies and my desire to pursue them further

———Because so many of my friends and relatives had gone to college that it seemed the thing to do

———In order to show people I have as good a mind as anyone

———For general self-improvement in culture and ideals

———For some other reason not mentioned [1]

[1] D. Katz and F. H. Allport: *Students' Attitudes.* 1931.

Other items dealt with attitudes toward fraternities, snobbishness, coeducation, moral standards, religious beliefs, the University. The data were analyzed to determine possible implications for academic and administrative policies.

For uncovering the "why" of opinions, an "omnibus" questionnaire is especially useful. This may be a list of two hundred or three hundred questions requiring a whole afternoon or evening to answer.

"Filter" questions are employed to sort out the views of informed and uninformed persons and to record their respective replies separately. A sample filter inquiry would be, "Do you happen to know what is meant by a reciprocal trade agreement?" If the respondent answers in the affirmative, he is then requested to explain the term. If he does so satisfactorily, his views are then explored. Those who confess ignorance or reveal it by an attempted bluff, are listed separately as having no adequate comprehension of the issue.

Even on the most intimate subjects—questions of religion and sex —the majority of people show little reluctance to speak their minds, provided they are interrogated skillfully. Some individuals express views which are intended to make a good impression on the interviewer. This "prestige" factor can be detected by employing a secret ballot. If results of face-to-face interviews and of secret ballots differ substantially, there is good reason to suspect the respondent is "putting his best foot forward."

The second technique of attitude measurement—the rating scale— gives the subject an opportunity to register how much he is in favor of or opposed to each proposition submitted to him for his reaction. One variation of this procedure is to arrange the responses in order from most to least, such as,

strongly approve
approve
undecided
disapprove
strongly disapprove

the subject to check the one that expresses his view. These steps are assumed to represent equal-appearing intervals, and, accordingly, they may be assigned numerical values ranging from 1 to 5, to indicate exactly the amount of favor or disfavor, with 3 as the point of neutrality. Allport calls such a scale an *a priori scale* because the author of the test arbitrarily assigns numerical values to denote the intervals. Sometimes it is considered advantageous to prepare a series of statements ranging from favorable to unfavorable, then allow the subject to place them in rank order according to his preference—this is the *order-of-merit method.*   Or the subject may just check one item in the scale.   The Syracuse University Reaction Study mentioned above employed this sort of scale arrangement on some of its items, with steps carefully graded to bring out the range and incidence of opinion on a specific issue.   For example:

Check the *one* statement which most nearly expresses your point of view on cribbing:

——A student who would crib would lie and cheat under any similar circumstances.

——Cribbing shows a serious defect in character, but it is not as bad as lying and cheating.

——Cribbing is not playing fair to one's fellow students or to the faculty, but it is not otherwise immoral.

——As an ideal, honesty in examinations deserves my support; but students are human and cannot be expected at present to attain this ideal.

——Cribbing is not desirable, but it is generally recognized to be the only way in which a student can gain his rights when others cheat, or when a wrong emphasis is put upon grades.

——Cribbing is merely playing the game with the professor.   He proctors the examination and is on the alert and suspicious for cheating.   Successful cribbing is beating him at his own game.

——Every student should take what he can get in this world.   If he can get his degree by cribbing that is the thing to do.[2]

In another case expert judges sort out hundreds of statements and the results are tabulated and analyzed until certain ones are sifted out as representing the degrees of preference ranging by equal steps from favor to disfavor.   This particular technique, perfected by Thurstone, is known as the *psychophysical scale* (the *method of equal-appearing intervals*).   Rating preferences by comparing propositions in pairs, each statement being evaluated with reference to every other, two at a time, is the *method of paired comparisons,* a technique that is too laborious for general use.

A simple device which serves as a rating scale is a thermometer, graded from 0 to 100, which represents clearly the degree of enthusiasm for or against a proposition or a candidate.   Descriptive phrases may be placed alongside the appropriate numbers to denote how strongly the respondent feels one way or another about the issue presented.

[2] Katz and Allport, *op. cit.,* p. 215.

Questionnaire and rating scale can be employed to discover how one attitude is related to other attitudes. With such evidence available, one can predict approximately how a person will look at a certain situation if it is known how he feels about other issues. Data on attitudes, furthermore, can be correlated with various factors in an individual's personality or his environment in order to reveal the influences responsible for his views. Murphy and Likert investigated the attitudes of students at several universities concerning issues related to internationalism, imperialism, race relations, and the economic order. A wide battery of tests was used, supplemented by laboratory studies. It was found that a person's views on internationalism, for example, provide an index for determining how he will feel about imperialism, race relations, and economic questions. A retest five years later showed a marked drift toward radical views; the data were analyzed to ascertain the reasons for this trend.[3]

What makes a person a radical? The psychologists can get the answer by first measuring a person's attitudes to find out how radical they are and then correlating these findings with the individual's upbringing, education, and other influences in his life which might possibly have affected his views. Following this procedure, Goodwin Watson discovered that prolonged schooling—not unemployment—is the principal source of America's economic radicals. It is commonly assumed that "the experience of being unable to find jobs leads men and women to rebel against the unjust economic order." The facts, he reported, show that unemployment is negligible in the genesis of radicalism. This observation was so striking in the analysis of his results that Watson was led to conclude that the real problem is to learn why the unemployed are so little radicalized by their experience of being out of work. Thousands of America's employed and unemployed were examined in the course of this investigation.[4] It was found that persons without jobs for two years were just as unaffected in their attitudes toward radicalism as those who had been jobless for three months or less. One of the main factors leading to economic radicalism appeared to be schooling, particularly going to high school and college. "Those who carried on into graduate study include ten times as large a proportion of radicals as those who have barely finished the eighth grade." The most radical group was the

---

[3] See G. Murphy and R. Likert: *Public Opinion and the Individual: a Psychological Study of Student Attitudes on Public Questions, with a Retest Five Years Later.* 1938.

[4] See G. Watson: "Morale during Unemployment," Chapter 16, in *Civilian Morale,* G. Watson, Editor. Houghton Mifflin Company, 1942.

professional and sub-professional people; the most conservative group was the factory workers. These findings are in line with the conclusion drawn by numerous investigators that the more radical students on the whole rate higher on intelligence tests than the conservative students.

The United States Department of Agriculture enlisted Likert's skill in a program of testing designed to gather facts as a basis for remedial policies in behalf of farmers. Instead of relying, as hitherto, upon information culled from whirlwind campaigns and stump speeches trained interviewers are sent out to study the farmers' ideas, feelings attitudes, and hopes. Meetings are organized by county representatives of the Department, at which farmers are encouraged to express their opinions freely, and other means are utilized to impress upon the farmers that the Department of Agriculture is their Department. The method developed by Likert and his staff goes far beyond mere "sampling" of opinion to a conversational exchange of ideas between farmer and interviewer. The interviewer, in each case, is a person who knows the particular area and the farmers' immediate problems in that district; by way of preparation he has spent whatever time was necessary to get the feel of the local situation. This program has revealed valuable information concerning the interrelation of various attitudes and the relation of the attitude-syndrome to the personality and the socio-economic situation of the individual farmer.[5]

The measurement of attitudes is subject to a number of limitations all of which should be taken into account in evaluating the studies made in this field. Attitudes may be covert or overt. We all know in this connection, that there are apt to be inconsistencies between inward thoughts and outward actions, discrepancies which may invalidate the observations of the investigator who is necessarily an outsider when he attempts to measure another person's attitudes. The investigator must accept the subject's say-so, with the reservation that his words and actions might not agree. There is always the risk that rationalization and deception on the part of the subject may distort the true picture, especially if morals or values are involved. Thus it is difficult to get a person to answer truthfully questions concerning sex, even though the protection of anonymity be granted, since feelings of guilt or lack of personal insight may prompt the individual to say the thing that is "expected" rather than the thing he really believes. Even prolonged questioning—the so-called depth interview—may fail

[5] See H. E. Skott: "Attitude Research in the Department of Agriculture." *Public Opinion Quarterly*, 1943, 7, 280-292.

to get at the subject's real feelings, since further probing may merely give the interviewee an opportunity to engage in some fancy rationalizing. It must be remembered, too, that the questionnaire presents a situation in verbal terms to evoke a verbal response on an imaginal basis. The subject may think he would act in a certain way, should the situation arise, but when the occasion actually presents itself, he may do the opposite of what he had predicted for himself, as in the case, say, of a pacifist face to face with an actual international crisis.

Public and private attitudes may not coincide. Schanck conducted a study of this problem in a rural community by obtaining from Baptists and Methodists a statement of their attitudes as *church members* (public) and also a statement of their *private feelings* concerning the proper form of baptism. As church members, the Methodists were unanimously in favor of *sprinkling only* and the Baptists were unanimously in favor of *immersion only;* in their private feelings, 71 per cent of the Methodists and 59 per cent of the Baptists regarded either form of baptism as acceptable. Further investigation of public and private attitudes toward various institutional practices revealed a similar situation: as members of a group, people frequently hold attitudes that are opposite to their private feelings; the institutional attitudes tend to be more uniform for all members of a given group than do their private attitudes.[6]

In spite of precautions taken to avoid ambiguities, words are liable to convey different meanings to different persons. Results may be misleading if terms are subject to several interpretations. Thus, a subject gave a low rating to the slogan "America First" on one occasion because he conceived of it as a "jingoistic phrase," but, on another occasion, he rated the same phrase high because he thought of it as meaning, "America should take the lead in attempting to settle foreign affairs." Ambiguity of this sort is a dangerous source of error.

Consumer research and public-opinion polls are practical applications of the techniques which have been evolved for investigating attitudes.

B. MARKET ANALYSIS AND CONSUMER RESEARCH

Successful merchandising depends very much upon a foreknowledge of what the consumer wants. It is worth while, therefore, to study the attitudes of the buying public. One index of buyers' preferences

[6] See R. L. Schanck: "A Study of a Community and Its Groups and Institutions Conceived of as Behaviors of Individuals." *Psychological Monographs*, No. 195. 1932.

is the obvious one of sales volume. Thus the musical selections fo the Lucky Strike Hit Parade are ranked from 1 to 10 in their orde of popularity, the ranking being based on estimates from the sales o sheet music and records, the number of nickels inserted into juk boxes for certain recordings, requests to orchestra leaders, and simila data. The planning of this radio program is a familiar example o an opinion survey.

It is one thing to discover what people want, after they have spen their money for various articles, but it is quite another thing to fin out ahead of time what they will be likely to buy. Anticipation i more difficult, of course, and also more advantageous. Busines leaders are recognizing the need for such foresight. A departmen store hired a psychologist to help find out what people actually hope to get for Christmas presents. The information gained in this surve was used in guiding customers in their choice of gifts. The store wa particularly interested in such a survey as a step toward reducin the backwash of gift-returning and gift-exchanging that inevitabl follows when guesswork on the part of the buyer results in dissatis faction on the part of the recipient. Useless gift-giving usually mean trouble for the store in the end. Guiding the Christmas shopper in telligently promotes customer satisfaction both on the giving and o the receiving end.

Large-scale sampling of consumer demand is conducted by th Psychological Corporation under its division of *Marketing and Socia Research;* this program includes surveys of selling, advertising, an public opinion. Interviewers are sent out to question housewive concerning slogans, advertising appeals via newspaper, magazine, bil board, or radio, and preferences for individual brands. These dat are correlated with week by week analyses of actual retail sales, as check on the effectiveness of various advertising media. Trends i buying behavior and public opinion are reported every three month in the form of "Psychological Brand Barometers." These consume surveys are based on 10,000 interviews conducted in cooperation wit psychologists throughout the country. By means of such researc it has become possible to predict with a considerable degree of ac curacy how many people are going to buy a given article and wha brand they will purchase.

Market research is conducted by radio chains to measure the exac size of their audiences; this information can be passed along to ad vertisers as an inducement to buy time on the air. Telephone sur veys, personal interviews, mail analyses, and the automatic recorde are all used to determine the audiences for various individual radio programs.

Telephone surveys are widely employed. They are less expensive than personal interviewing, take less time, and allow for easy checking since the investigators can remain in one place and compare notes. Most homes with telephones have radios, but the limitation on the technique of telephoning for information is that many homes with radios have no telephones. The coincidental telephone technique involves calling up a home and asking which station or program the radio is tuned to at the time. This method eliminates the memory hazard, but it fails to give a representative picture of the programs listened to for the whole day or even of a whole program heard all the way through. The *unaided recall* telephone survey is conducted by asking the listener to report the periods the radio was in operation and the programs heard during a certain period. Several calls a day are necessary to reduce the memory loss during the period between exposure and report. Unaided recall alone is, of course, unreliable. Errors in unaided recall have been demonstrated by installing an automatic recorder, unknown to the listener, the device being connected with the radio so as to record the exact times and stations to which the radio is tuned. In one experiment where these recorders were operating it was found, on calling the listeners the next day to question them about their previous day's listening experience, that "the subjects could recall correctly or account for about 31 per cent of the program time they had heard. However, when they were supplied with a list of all programs available to them the previous day they correctly identified 59 per cent of their listening experience, almost doubling the 'pure recall' report—but still leaving 41 per cent unaccounted for!" [7] This memory discrepancy has been demonstrated, too, by telephoning homes and questioning the respondents on program reception at the time, and then calling the same homes again the next morning; roughly, only one-third of the previous evening's listening was reported correctly.

A second type of technique is the *personal interview*. A trained staff of interviewers call directly on selected listeners. The sample can be carefully controlled, and detailed information, such as specific reactions to different phases of a single program, can be obtained. One drawback to this method is the expense involved. Interviewers may use *unaided recall* by simply asking "What radio programs did

[7] F. N. Stanton: "Checking the Checkers." *Advertising and Selling*, December 19, 1935.

you listen to today?" or they may employ the technique of *aided recall* based on recognition. In this latter method two printed lists are submitted, one a listing of broadcast periods by fifteen-minute intervals, the other a complete list of the programs of each station in the area under consideration, with identification by talent, broadcast time and (for commercial programs) sponsor and product. The person interviewed checks the periods during which he listened on Schedule No. 1 and then checks the programs to which he listened on Schedule No. 2. The first (recall) results are then checked against the second (recognition) findings.

Mail analyses proceed by means of the *mail questionnaire* and the study of audience mail. Sending questionnaires by mail enables the investigator to cover a wide territory simultaneously, but the value of the method is limited by the fact that a 20 per cent return is about all that can be expected even under favorable conditions. *Audience mail* is an inaccurate index because some programs make a bid for mail, and some people are more inclined than others to write in. The responsive portion of the audience, therefore, may not be at all representative of the audience as a whole.

Surveys of radio audiences should be supplemented by careful analysis of radio-listening habits. The advertiser who pays for time on the radio makes the investment upon the assumption that the radio is turned on at a certain time, as revealed in a survey, and that people are paying attention to the program, especially to the commercial "plugs." This latter is a big assumption that can only be proved by finding the answer to the question, "What does the listener do while the radio is in use?" Stanton sought an answer by sending out a mail questionnaire reading:

The radio is turned on while I—write—dance—dress—bathe—sew—eat—study—lie in bed—clean the house—read—play—iron—work—rest—talk—ride—cook—boat—and listen (that is, doing nothing else).

Space was provided for the listing of additional activities, and listeners were asked to check only those things they did regularly. Most of the men spent their time listening, eating, resting, and reading, while the women mostly were listening, sewing, resting, ironing, eating, cleaning, reading, and cooking. A complete analysis of radio-listening habits would include finding out who listens, where and when he listens, to what he listens, why he listens, what he does while he is listening, and how he is influenced by listening. These are all problems of interest to the psychologist, and to the advertiser who is in search of the best medium for enlisting the patronage of consumers.

Surveys of the public's wants are of interest to the people engaged in advertising and in selling, as we have noted, and they are also of concern to the manufacturer who must plan his production wisely if advertising and selling are to be carried on effectively. The General Motors Customer Research Staff has done some excellent work in determining "the proving ground of public opinion." Detailed questionnaires are prepared dealing with the appearance, dependability, economy, pick-up, smoothness, comfort, ease of control, first cost, safety, and speed of automobiles; the motorist is invited to express his preferences for various features which he would deem important in selecting a new car. Drawings make the experiment

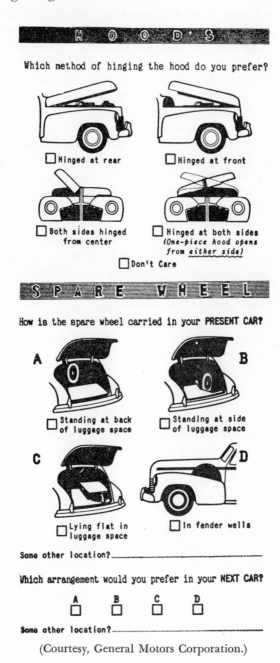

HOODS

Which method of hinging the hood do you prefer?

☐ Hinged at rear

☐ Hinged at front

☐ Both sides hinged from center

☐ Hinged at both sides (*One-piece hood opens from either side*)

☐ Don't Care

SPARE WHEEL

How is the spare wheel carried in your PRESENT CAR?

A ☐ Standing at back of luggage space

B ☐ Standing at side of luggage space

C ☐ Lying flat in luggage space

D ☐ In fender wells

Some other location?_____

Which arrangement would you prefer in your NEXT CAR?

A ☐   B ☐   C ☐   D ☐

Some other location?_____

(Courtesy, General Motors Corporation.)

concrete, graphic, interesting; "trifles" are considered in detail because little things like the hood opening or the spare wheel mounting may influence the buyer in choosing a particular make of automobile. Issued in booklet form, these questions enlist cooperation because they provide the motorist with information that is helpful to him in spending his money wisely; the answers supply the manufacturer with a first-hand knowledge of the public's preferences with respect to such things as headlight mountings, colors and shades, streamlining, upholstery, split windshields, running boards, automatic chokes, rear doors hinged at front or rear edge, hydramatic drive. The aim of General Motors in sounding out public opinion is to harmonize "manufacturer's products and policies on the one hand and consumer's tastes and desires on the other hand," with benefit to both in terms of more desirable cars, more good will, more sales, more profits. Closer *rapport* between producer and consumer becomes a necessity when a business institution grows to the size of the General Motors Corporation. One reason this accord is needed is that large stocks must be built up in advance; unforeseen changes in taste, under such conditions, would prove disastrous.

"The proving ground of public opinion," as used in a customer research, is a variety of the public opinion poll. Indeed, the polling of political sentiment was an outgrowth of market research, as we shall now observe.

C. Public Opinion Polls

1. history

The evolution of polling technique began with newspaper polls which were designed more for increasing the newspaper's circulation than for gauging the actual state of public opinion. Then came the "Golden Age" of the *Literary Digest*. Starting in 1916, the *Literary Digest* conducted nine nation-wide polls on Prohibition, the New Deal, presidential candidates. Millions of ballots were sent out, returns were widely publicized. More accurate polling came with the introduction of sampling techniques developed by experts in marketing research who had been exploring public reactions to advertising, marketing, and corporate relations. Gallup began experiments with nation-wide polls on social and political issues in 1934, organized the American Institute of Public Opinion in 1935; Cherington and Roper inaugurated the *Fortune* polls in 1935; the Crossley poll was launched during the presidential campaign of 1936. Methods are being steadily refined by applying the mathematical laws of chance to sampling, by increasing care in the phrasing of questions, by taking more pains in the training of interviewers.

Gallup's concern with polling developed as a hobby, a search for some means of gauging reader interest in newspapers and magazines. Rich tells the story in the *Saturday Evening Post*:

Convinced that editors not only didn't know their readers' preferences but didn't know how to determine them, he spent six years and discarded fifty trial methods before he found one that satisfied him. This method, now known as "the Gallup Method," he made the subject of his thesis for a doctor's degree, written in 1928. The degree was only a by-product of this remarkable document. The chief products were the picture magazine *Look*, the first advertisement in the form of a comic strip, and the American Institute of Public Opinion. It was, in short, the springboard from which Gallup jumped from local to national recognition.

The method is dazzlingly simple. The way to learn what interests people is to learn what they read, and the way to learn what they read is to hand them a newspaper or magazine and ask them to go over it with you. Says Maulsby, "No one but Gallup would bother to do a thing like that."

Since his research was being financed by the Cowles brothers, publishers of the Des Moines *Register & Tribune,* he handed people this paper. The survey established two facts: That interest in comics and pictures was tremendous, and that most adults, too, read the comics. The *Register & Tribune* had planned to economize on these features. It now bought more of them. It also experimented with the roto section, arranging the pictures to tell a story. Circulation soared. Presently the roto section began to run away with the rest of the paper. A national magazine of nothing but pictures was indicated. They named it *Look*.

Gallup was so excited by the success of his discovery that he conducted other surveys and published them in trade magazines. One of them caught the attention of Mr. Hearst. As a test, Hearst offered the advertising agencies a page of his syndicated comic section. Young & Rubicam, of New York, snapped it up for a breakfast food. It was the first full-page commercial comic, and it pulled in enough purchasers to make Raymond Rubicam grab his hat and set out on Gallup's trail. He found him teaching journalism at Northwestern University. Gallup asked assurance that his findings would be accepted, favorable or not, and that he wouldn't be used for sales promotion. He joined the firm in June, 1932.

He was short on advertising technique, but his surveys made him long on what people who read the ads thought about them. Here are some of his findings:

If you're selling with printed matter, break it into short paragraphs; lighten it with conversation; sprinkle it with italics. If you're selling with pictures, make them pictures of people, not products; and if they aren't photographs, the drawings should be photographic in detail.[8]

Elmo Roper, director of the *Fortune* poll, was likewise a market-researcher before entering the field of political polling. Experience in making accurate surveys of public taste for private industry gave him a good background for his work in conducting the *Fortune* Survey.

So much for the history of polling—an evolution of much interest to social psychologists.

2. TECHNIQUES

The *Literary Digest* relied upon sheer numbers in its polls, sending out some 10,000,000 ballots in 1936 to people whose names were culled from lists of automobile owners and telephone subscribers, about one in four ballots being returned. Victory for Landon and defeat for Roosevelt were predicted on the basis of the returns, despite warnings from Gallup that the *Digest's* old-fashioned methods would point to the wrong man. The subsequent election of Roosevelt was a source of grievous embarrassment to the *Literary Digest,* and was a factor in its subsequent collapse.

The failure of the *Literary Digest* poll in 1936 was a dramatic demonstration of the necessity for employing sound statistical methods in trying to gauge public opinion. The experts had discovered a fact that had escaped the notice of the *Literary Digest* pollers—a fact of tremendous significance for social psychology—that political sentiment varies strikingly with different income levels. Telephone subscribers and automobile owners were largely in favor of Landon, but people too poor to qualify as members of the "tel-auto" public were largely voting for Roosevelt. The lower-income group was not counted in on the *Literary Digest* balloting, but their votes were just as good as anybody else's in the regular election. The mistaken prophecy of Landon's election was based on an error in sampling. You cannot leave any section or class out of your calculations if you want to get the correct answer. The pollsters take great pains to get a fair, representative cross section of the population by means of "stratified" or "controlled" sampling; their aim is to sound public opinion on a wide scale by a small sample so carefully chosen as to reflect very accurately the opinion of the total electorate. Both time

---

[8] W. Rich: "The Human Yardstick." *Saturday Evening Post,* January 21, 1939.

and expense are saved in this way, rendering it possible to conduct frequent polls in short order, to keep the gauge up to date, and to make timely reports of shifting sentiment.

"Building the miniature electorate" is done by planning a cross section with due respect for statistical principles. The character of the cross section and the size of the cross section must be carefully determined in preparing a poll.

The person who plans the character of the cross section for a pre-election poll must use census figures in combination with information about how many people can and do vote. Voting participation differs according to the type of election, geographic areas, sex, and income levels. Women do not vote to the same extent as men, people in the lower-income levels do not vote in such a high proportion as those in the middle and upper groups. The miniature electorate is built with six statistical keys or "controls" in mind, to make sure the sample mirrors the voting population as a whole. The cross section must contain the proper numbers of:

(1) voters from each state
(2) men and women
(3) farm voters and voters in towns of 2,500 population or less; 2,500 to 10,000; 10,000 to 100,000; 100,000 to 500,000; and 500,000 or over
(4) voters of all age groups
(5) members of the following income groups: wealthy, above average, average, poor plus, poor, relief, home relief
(6) Democrats, Republicans, and members of all other political parties

Quotas for each of these categories must be constantly checked and rechecked against actual election returns to see that each group is weighted in proportion to its voting strength, for elections are the laboratories in which the polls are tested. Economic class appears at present to be the most important factor in determining the political alignment of voters.

Accurate results can be secured with a small sample, provided it is carefully selected. According to the laws of chance, a sample is considered adequate in size when an increase in the number of cases fails to produce significant differences in results. The *Fortune* staff feel that 5,000 is plenty; the American Institute of Public Opinion figure is anywhere from 3,000 to 60,000, depending on the closeness of the contest and the degree of accuracy desired. A survey which predicts an election within 5 per cent is generally regarded as amazingly ac-

curate.   Yet this degree of accuracy can be attained with as few as from
600 to 900 ballots.

Controlled sampling is usually preferred to random sampling.   The
latter would be involved if every fortieth person in a selected group of
cities, towns, and farming communities, were asked to express his
views.   It is obvious that a random technique of this sort would lead
to some inaccuracy if the data were interpreted as representing the
views of the population as a whole.

Selection of certain specific diagnostic areas is called "pin-point"
sampling.   Thus a "barometer county" may be chosen, a county which
has proved a reliable reflector of the consensus of opinion in the nation as a whole.   Accurate poll results have been obtained by interviewing every fourth, fifth, or tenth person in such a county.   Prior to
1940, there were five counties in the United States which could lay
claim to being reliable barometers: Erie County, Ohio; Bay County,
Michigan; Allen County, Indiana; Summit County, Utah; and Sheri-
dan County, Wyoming.

The modern polls are conducted by means of personal interviews.
The mail method is recognized as deficient, since it is difficult to reach
the poorer classes through mailing lists and even more difficult to get
them to respond, and since some groups of voters will answer through
the mail while others refuse to cooperate.   The personal canvass is
more accurate in that it circumvents these sources of error.   Interviewers are carefully trained before they are dispatched on their assignments to areas strategically located throughout the country.   Home
interviews are preferred because they are apt to be more leisurely than
street interviews and because the home visit gives the fieldworker an
opportunity to gain information helpful in checking on the accuracy
with which the individual has been allocated to a given economic
class.   The work of the interviewers is supervised and checked to make
sure the canvass is being conducted in a competent fashion.

Bias must be scrupulously avoided in the choosing of issues and the
wording of questions.   These matters are settled by a group of editorial and research executives, who confer at length in the planning
of every ballot.   Issues are chosen only after careful evaluation of
their real importance, apart from any personal interests or hobbies that
the opinion surveyor may be inclined to feature as matters that should
be of concern to everybody else.   It is easy to confuse one's private
world with the public world if personal enthusiasm is allowed to run
away with one's judgment.   Political trends and social tendencies
must be charted and contemporary events comprehensively surveyed

to provide the basis for an objective selection of vital questions. Certain broad guiding principles must be borne in mind in planning polls on national issues:

(1) The issues must deal with all possible aspects of the contemporary scene, and cover political, economic, social, and moral issues of common concern.

(2) The issues must be of direct interest to the mass of the public, and involve questions on which large sections of the people may be expected to have formed an opinion. People, for example, are not conversant with details of government finance or the nuances of diplomatic negotiations.

(3) The issues selected must be of current, topical interest. In many cases, it is difficult to elicit attitudes related to events which are rooted in the distant past, or events so far in the future that public attitudes have not had the chance to form.

(4) The issues must try to impinge closely on the everyday life experiences of ordinary people and must avoid being too remote and hypothetical. They need not be "profound," but may deal with manners as well as with politics.[9]

Issues are thus singled out with four definite criteria in mind: inclusiveness, widespread public interest, timeliness, and concreteness.

Questions must be carefully worded to avert a bias that might influence the respondent to answer one way or the other, in favor of or in opposition to the statement as presented to him. The interviewer would be angling for a negative reply if he asked the question and appended, "You wouldn't approve of that, would you?" Such a procedure would obviously invalidate the questionnaire. There are phrases that operate less obviously to sway the respondent, subtle nuances which are just as devastating to scientific opinion-measurement, though superficially they may look fair enough. Consider this one:

Do you approve of Mr. Blank's stand for good faith in international affairs and will you support his demand for the reestablishment of peace through the World Security Council?

This question is loaded because the question suggests the answer and it calls for a decision between two views, only one of which is given. The wording is equivalent to an ultimatum: Vote for Blank's view or proclaim yourself against good faith in international affairs and against the World Security Council. Link reports that the wording of a question definitely influences the answers; then he adds, "The critical question is not whether a question is leading but whether it is fair. In other words, it must not be misleading." [10]

If a poll is to be valid, the wording of the question must be free of any possible ambiguities. Anybody who has had experience with the formulation of objective tests—true or false—is aware of the fact that one little word can have many meanings for many different people, thus invalidating the particular test item as a measure of the students' knowledge. Ambiguity was involved in the question: "When the war is over do you think our government will be less democratic, more democratic, or the same as now?" What is meant by *democratic?* If 26 per cent of a sample think that our government will be less democratic, what can that mean specifically unless the tester ascertains what the respondents have in mind when they see the word *democratic?* [11]

Questions should be brief, the vocabulary simple, the words unemotional, all important alternatives provided, and if the choices are numerous they should be listed on a card for the respondent to read. As a check against biased wording, the "split-ballot" technique is used: the question is worded one way on ballot form A and another way on form B, then A is put to one-half the voters of a cross section, B to the other half, with the same types of voters in both groups, and the results are tabulated and compared, to determine whether approximately the same results are obtained with the two different ballot forms. Care must be taken to use terms that are readily understood. One contribution made by the polls has been the mapping of areas of ignorance. The masses have demonstrated that they do not know the difference between municipal, state, and Federal judges, or the meaning of "security regulation." "Phrasing a public-opinion ballot has been called 'a nightmare in semantics.' But gradually, through the process of continuous questioning, the Institute is building up a neutral vocabulary—a public-opinion glossary—within the comprehension of the mass of people." [12]

3. SIGNIFICANCE

The polls have already proved their value in the measurement of public taste and in the prediction of elections. Experience has demonstrated how accurately a certain number of interviews, held ac-

[10] H. C. Link: "The Eighth Nation-Wide Social Experimental Survey." *Journal of Applied Psychology,* 1943, 27, 1-11.
[11] See H. C. Link: "The Perils of Peace: a Study of Public Opinion and Morale." The Psychological Corporation. 1941.
[12] Gallup and Rae: *op. cit.,* p. 106.

cording to a definite plan of distribution, will represent the people as a whole: this is the question of reliability, involving the problem of getting a sample that will give consistent results of a known degree better than chance. We now know exactly how many persons have to be polled from various categories to get a certain degree of reliability. Experience has also shown that the polls can be valid. The question of validity involves the problem of ascertaining whether the people mean what they say: will they act as their verbal responses have indicated? Election polls, of course, are validated by election results. Market surveys are validated by purchasing behavior. Some years ago the question was asked in connection with a brand barometer: "What brand or make of automobile tire did you buy last?" A follow-up research, inspecting the tires on the cars of the respondents, revealed such a discrepancy between reported brand and actual brand that the question was abandoned. Check-ups have proved that there is a high degree of validity for answers to questions in regard to the purchase of common household articles. This fact was discovered by having interviewers make pantry inventories to see what brands of coffee, flour, tea, soaps, and cereals the respondents had actually purchased. Another check on barometer answers was obtained by having grocers make records of the brands sold to the particular customers who were being interviewed. The basic criterion for validity is behavior: it is in the respondent's doing that the investigator is ultimately interested.

Now that the techniques of polling have been perfected, the question naturally arises: how can they be used by the social psychologist to solve some of the problems of vital import in our society? The data can be analyzed by the social psychologist to find out how attitudes are influenced by economic class, age, sex, political affiliation, and geographic section. The Rockefeller Foundation has contributed funds to the Princeton School of Public and International Affairs to support public-opinion research. Investigators are tracing the fluctuations of public opinion on various questions and seeking to discover geographical as well as general patterns of opinion.

The polls are performing a useful service of a political nature, in that they facilitate the operation of our democratic form of government. They can go behind the election returns to find out what the public intends when it elects a candidate to office. Does his election mean a *carte blanche* blessing on all his prospective policies? By means of the polls the public mandate can be defined more exactly.

Another important function of the polls is that of checking the actual as opposed to the claimed strength of pressure groups. When a candidate asserts the public is for him, when lobbyists announce that their plan is endorsed by majority support, when political machines corrupt elections, when purists tell us the people do not wish to consider birth control or measures for reducing the toll of venereal disease—the pollsters go to the public for an authoritative answer that leaves no doubt as to how the public feels about the issue involved. Between elections the polls trace the trend of public sentiment, recording the rise and fall of popularity for persons and measures, enabling the officeholder to sense the public will. Trends are interpreted through the correlation of events occurring contemporaneously, and thus the investigators can ascertain what factors may be responsible for shifts in sentiment. Periodic canvasses of American attitudes toward all-out aid to Britain, toward convoys, toward intervention and non-intervention, toward the draft, kept the public and its leaders well informed regarding majority and minority opinion on these crucial issues of World War II, at regularly recurring intervals. Such data were important in determining policies. The records were of tremendous value for the study of the psychological factors that determined the direction of public opinion.

The polls have shown that the masses are surprisingly competent in passing judgment on matters of public policy, if they are given the facts upon which to base a decision. The aristocrats and the crowd psychologists have been telling us for a long time—the aristocrats since the days of Plato and Aristotle—that the average run of people are not bright enough to reach wise conclusions when faced with questions governing their welfare, that they need to be protected against their own stupidity by a few rare intellects who will volunteer to serve as custodians of their best interests. This myth, so dear to those members of the intelligentsia who bask in their own self-conscious superiority, has been exploded by the pollsters, who have gathered plenty of evidence to support the conclusion that the masses are blessed with a fair share of common sense.[13] Students of public-opinion polls are much impressed with the wisdom of the masses. Childs offers this judgment:

One of the principal contributions of nationwide polls . . . has been the light they have thrown on the matter of the competence of the masses, the wisdom of the electorate, to pass upon questions of public policy. The results of these surveys tend, I believe, to reestablish faith in the underlying

[13] See the editorial, "American Man-in-the-Street." *Fortune,* December, 1942. Condensed in the *Reader's Digest,* February, 1943.

tenets of democracy, the theory that, by and large, over reasonably long periods of time, public opinion is as safe a guide to follow as the opinions of smaller and select groups. Of course these experiments cannot establish, in the absence of objective absolute standards, the wisdom of the masses. They do suggest, however, that the masses are by no means as destitute of common sense as is sometimes commonly supposed.[14]

Gallup is likewise convinced that "we can place great faith in the collective judgment or intelligence of the people," as indicated by "results of sampling referenda on hundreds of issues." [15] His confidence in democracy is strong:

In scanning the record, it is not difficult to find individual cases of ignorance, stupidity, and apathy. The polls have discovered some people who do not know the difference between the Supreme Court and the local police court. . . . It is important to realize that ignorance, stupidity, and apathy are the exception, not the rule. The serious observer of public opinion on scores of issues cannot fail to come away with a feeling of intense admiration for the honesty and common sense with which an enormous number of ordinary people in all walks of life and at all levels of the economic scale have continued to meet their responsibilities as citizens. He will be profoundly impressed with the grasp of broad principles which voters of all types possess, and with their capacity to adjust themselves to the ever-changing movement of events. . . .

The conduct of government does not merely involve specialized knowledge. It deals primarily with human needs and human values. . . .

As a democratic nation, we have chosen to take the road of majority rule. Our leaders are chosen by the mass of the people, and the main lines of governmental and social policy are continuously referred back to the people for their approval. There is a wealth of available evidence proving that the common people can see through the shams of political life and can hold fast to what they value. Conclusive evidence supports the late Theodore Roosevelt who wrote: "The majority of the plain people of the United States will, day in and day out, make fewer mistakes in governing themselves than any smaller group will make in governing them." [16]

4. CRITICISMS

It has been asserted by some critics that the polls, by reducing the variety of points of view to a "yes"-or-"no" kind of response, tend to

[14] Reprinted by permission from *An Introduction to Public Opinion* by H. L. Childs, published by John Wiley & Sons, Inc. P. 26. 1940. Examples to support this thesis are offered by Childs on pp. 27-30. See also, H. Cantril *et al.: Gauging Public Opinion*, p. 230. 1944.
[15] G. Gallup: *Public Opinion in a Democracy*, p. 14. 1939.
[16] Gallup and Rae: *op. cit.*, pp. 286, 288, 289.

oversimplify the picture of public opinion. This all-or-none, black-or-white dichotomizing discourages discriminating analysis of issues, it is charged, forcing the respondent to align himself for or against, when he would rather qualify his support of either side. The pollsters are aware of this danger. They are guarding against it by breaking down the for-and-against responses into more than two mutually exclusive categories and they are investigating the "no-opinion" neutral type of vote to see why it occurs, what sorts of people are inclined to be non-committal, on what kinds of issues.

Another indictment of the polls is the charge that they operate as a band-wagon vote. The pollsters announce the winner before the election even takes place, encouraging the voters to share the elation of victory by casting their votes for the candidate who is obviously going to be elected. It is also charged that the polls destroy interest in the election itself. Neither of these charges is substantiated by the evidence, according to Gallup.[17] It is possible, however, for a politician to exploit the poll that picks him to win, employing it as a propaganda device to promote his own campaign, quoting its results as authoritative proof of his inevitable election, warning the voters against "throwing their votes away" by voting for the loser.

A third charge is that the polls will destroy representative government by reducing officeholders to rubber stamps. Thus Senator Bilbo was heard addressing the Senate after this fashion: "Mr. President, my amendment is an attempt to meet the demand of the American people as it has been evidenced by various polls taken by Mr. Gallup. . . ." The answer to this indictment is that "representatives will be better able to represent if they have an accurate measure of the wishes, aspirations, and needs of different groups within the general public, rather than the kind of distorted picture sent them by telegram enthusiasts and overzealous pressure groups who claim to speak for all the people, but actually speak only for themselves";[18] that legislation is unenforceable unless it is endorsed by the public will; that the function of the political expert is to devise the ways and means by which the values of the electorate can be embodied in common practice. This last point is expressed by Gallup and Rae in these significant words:

But all the experts can do . . . is to tell *how* we can act.

The objectives, the ends, the basic values of policy must still be decided. The economist can suggest what action is to be taken if a certain goal is to be

[17] *Ibid.*, Chapter 20, "Is There a Band-Wagon Vote?"
[18] *Ibid.*, p. 266.

reached. He, speaking purely as an economist, cannot say what final goal *should* be reached. The lawyer can administer and interpret the country's laws. He cannot say what those laws should be. The social worker can suggest ways of aiding the aged. He cannot say that aiding aged persons is desirable. The expert's function is invaluable, but its value lies in judging the means—not the ends—of public policy. . . . For the ultimate values of politics and economics, the judgments on which public policy is based, do not come from special knowledge or from intelligence alone. *They are compounded from the day-to-day experience of the men and women who together make up the society we live in.*[19]

Such are the main objections to the practice of polling public opinion—and the answers to the objections. Regardless of possible abuses, the polls will probably be continued and be steadily improved because they provide a much needed instrument for bridging the gap between the people and those who are responsible for making decisions in their name.

A poll to check on polls was initiated at the University of Denver in September, 1941, by the National Opinion Research Center. This organization, the first noncommercial group to measure public opinion in the United States, takes its own polls on all sorts of public questions, analyzes the results of other polls, and studies how polling methods may be improved. The Center conducts polls, at cost, for legislators and Congressmen who may want to know what their constituents think about specific issues, for Government departments, and for educators. The investigators are concentrating on the scientific wording of questions and on methods for measuring how strongly people feel on a given question.

Proponents of democracy will cherish any instrument for giving the public the opportunity, at frequent intervals, to register its will. Serving as such an instrument, the polls have proved their merit.

II. FIELD STUDIES

Measurement is only one of the methods used in the investigation of social behavior. There are other ways of getting at vital facts concerning man's conduct in the community, techniques that must be used to counteract the limitations inherent in the measurement situation. A poll of public opinion will tell us how the people are going to vote, but it will not tell us just why the electors have decided to vote for one candidate rather than another. The need for going be-

[19] *Ibid.*, pp. 264, 266.

yond mere quantification was well exemplified in a survey conducted
to find out why the people of Erie County, Ohio, intended to vote in
1940 for one presidential candidate in preference to others. A representative cross section was interviewed in person once every month beginning in the May previous to the election of 1940, and people who
changed their minds during the May-November interval were carefully questioned about their reasons for shifting allegiance. This
procedure of interviewing the same persons several times is known as
a "panel study." Taking the panel as representative of the county
voters as a whole, the investigators found that 55 per cent of the voters
preserved their voting intentions unchanged throughout the five
months, while 45 per cent changed their minds at least once.

As a group, those who did not change their minds evidenced more interest
in the elections than those who did—indicating that the most eager followers
of campaign news and debate are people looking for arguments to bolster
opinions formed during pre-campaign years. But, with full allowance for
the indifferent, the size of the percentage who did form opinions during the
campaign indicates that Americans as a whole are far more open-minded, less
set in partisan prejudices, than many critics think.[20]

Strongest determinants of voters' intentions were the income, age, religious, and residence groups to which they belonged.

Those who were in poor to middling economic circumstances, those who
were young, those who were Catholic, those who lived in the city—all of these
tended to vote Democratic. . . . The people of Erie County who were prosperous, who were old, who were Protestant or who lived in the country, inclined toward Republicanism.[21]

Voting did not follow class factionalism, largely because the great
middle class included supporters of both the candidates and a large
percentage who were undecided or indifferent. Of particular interest
to the investigators were the group of people who "won't vote" and
the group who intended to vote but didn't know for which candidate.
The former consisted mostly of women in the lower income level, who
were not interested in the elections, who skipped the political news
in the papers, who listened to serial dramas over the radio in preference to campaign oratory. The second group, the "Don't Knows,"

[20] *Life*, November 11, 1940.
[21] *Ibid.*

who included 9 per cent of the panel, intended to vote, but in October they were still undecided, torn and teetering, as they were, between conflicting campaign arguments.

This investigation into the formation of political opinion is a natural outgrowth of polling. Figures come to mean a great deal more when we discover the reasons determining each individual's own personal choice; statistics plus a detailed analysis of the genesis of opinion in particular individual samples, each unique, each a study in itself, gives us an ideal combination. This type of research belongs in the category of *field studies,* involving, as it does, an intimate association with people on the spot. The technique goes beyond ordinary polling, for individuals are interviewed not once and casually, but repeatedly and thoroughly, and the questionnaire is supplemented by a "clinical" search into the background factors responsible for the person's choice.

The *field-study method* gives the observer an opportunity to watch human beings functioning in real-life situations. The explorer in the field is privileged to note how man behaves in his "natural habitat," just as the naturalist heads for the jungle to discover how animals act under "un-laboratory" conditions. The investigator engaged in field work may employ tests and measurements as an incidental phase of his research, but his chief reliance is likely to be on a non-quantitative survey of people meeting their problems in everyday life unaffected by the consciousness of being under observation, as subjects are who submit to scientific experiment. Intimate glimpses of life at firsthand are gained best by means of "functional penetration," a fancy term for describing the fact that the observers become, as far as possible, accepted members of the community they are exploring, do their questioning indirectly, subtly, whenever it happens to be feasible. This technique is also referred to as "participant observation." Anthropologists have been using this technique successfully for years in their studies of primitive communities, notably Malinowski among the Trobriand Islanders and Margaret Mead among the natives of Samoa and New Guinea. The investigators just move right in, become identified with the life of the community, and report on what they see from the inside. The value of this method for the social psychologist is obvious.

The Lynds have shown the social scientists how a field study should be done in their classic studies of Muncie, Indiana, reported in *Middletown* (1929) and *Middletown in Transition* (1937). In his foreword to the former volume, Wissler remarks:

Experience with social phenomena is bringing us nearer and nearer to a realization that we must deal directly with life itself, that the realities of social science are what people do. Seemingly in full realization of this, the authors of this book have patiently observed an American community and sketched out for us, in the large, the whole round of its activities. . . . To study ourselves as through the eye of an outsider is the basic difficulty in social science, and may be insurmountable, but the authors of this volume have made a serious attempt, by approaching an American community as an anthropologist does a primitive tribe. It is in this that the contribution lies, an experiment not only in method, but in a new field, the social anthropology of contemporary life.[22]

The Lynds approached the life of the people in Muncie as a unit composed of interwoven trends of behavior. Instead of employing the usual piecemeal attack traditionally associated with scientific study, they sought to get an integrated perspective of the multifarious "gross-total thing" called "Middletown," everything interrelated in its complete cultural pattern. This large order guided them in the pursuit of details and the final report gives us a remarkable bird's-eye survey of "Middletown" as a typical small American city. In planning the study, the investigators organized their approach according to the following six main-trunk activities:

Getting a living
Making a home
Training the young
Using leisure in various forms of play, art, and so on
Engaging in religious practices
Engaging in community activities[23]

In order to learn how past experience conditions present behavior, the Lynds traced the genesis of conduct-patterns from 1890 through to 1925. Some of this historical evidence was gleaned from records, some from "folk talk." Apology for the latter source of data is offered on the ground that "the rattle of conversation that goes on around a luncheon table, on street corners, or while waiting for a basketball game to commence, affords indispensable insights into the moods and habits of thought of the city, even though it is not defensible as scientifically valid evidence." [24]

---

[22] R. S. Lynd and H. M. Lynd: *Middletown*, pp. v-vi. Harcourt, Brace and Company, 1929.
[23] *Ibid.*, p. 4.
[24] *Ibid.*, p. 8.

A "Note on Method" in the Appendix of *Middletown* explains the general procedure adopted in this field study.

The first intimation that Middletown had that it was being studied was the unheralded opening of an office in a local office building by a group of people who had come to "study the growth of the city." The writers of the report and . . . the staff secretary . . . lived in Middletown from January, 1924, to June, 1925, . . . Miss Davis for a year and Dr. Williams for five months. . . .

The various techniques employed included the following:

1. *Participation in the local life.* Members of the staff lived in apartments or in rooms in private households. In every way possible they shared the life of the city, making friends and assuming local ties and obligations, as would any other residents of Middletown. In this way a large measure of spontaneity was obtained. . . . Week in and week out they attended churches, school assemblies and classes, court sessions, political rallies, labor meetings, civic club luncheons, missionary meetings, lectures, annual dinners, card parties. . . .

In reporting meetings attended, as in individual interviews or casual conversations, the method followed was to take such inconspicuous notes as were possible in the course of the meeting, service, or interview and then immediately afterward to write them up in detail according to the standardized form adopted. In cases where it was impossible to take notes at the time, the record was made immediately afterward from memory.

2. *Examination of documentary material.* Census data, city and county records . . . daily papers . . . the minutes of various organizations . . . diaries . . . "boom books" . . . were used. . . .

3. *Compilation of statistics.* Such data included figures on wages, steadiness of employment, industrial accidents . . . club memberships . . . attendance at motion picture theaters. . . .

4. *Interviews.* These varied all the way from the most casual conversations with streetcar conductors, janitors, barbers, or chance associates at luncheon or club meetings to carefully planned interviews with individuals especially qualified to give information on particular phases of the city's life. Among the latter, for instance, were detailed interviews with the six leading Protestant ministers and the secretaries of the Y.M.C.A. and the Y.W.C.A., lasting about four hours each and covering with a long schedule intimate phases of the life of their organizations and of their personal problems as religious workers in Middletown. Such questioning, coming at the close of many months of close contact with these persons, elicited what is believed to have been almost complete frankness of response.

As the study progressed it seemed desirable to test in individual families certain hypotheses as to trends observed in the behavior of the community. Accordingly, schedules were drawn up on the basis of these observed charac-

teristics, and a group of forty families clearly belonging to the business class
were interviewed. . . .

5. *Questionnaires.* As extensions of the interviews, questionnaires were
used at some points in the study. A questionnaire on club membership and
activities was sent to the more than 400 clubs in the city. A questionnaire,
dealing with the life of the high school population, was given to all sopho-
more, junior, and senior English classes . . . of the high school. . . . A
"true-false" questionnaire, given to all junior and senior social science classes
. . . dealt largely with points of view on certain public questions.[25]

The survey was carefully planned, expertly carried out, and reported
in a masterful literary style, with the data all coordinated into meaningful patterns by the authors, who interpret their observations
against the background of their experience in social science. The
reader of *Middletown* will learn how human beings live together in
a community.

Middletown in Transition (1937) is a review of the changes in practice and faith produced by the experience of weathering a major depression. This second study is of special interest to the psychologist
because the people of "Middletown" were "on" to the fact that they
were under scrutiny; indeed, many of the citizens had read the first
report and others had "gotten wind" of the publicity to which they
had been exposed. Despite the handicap of being forced to work
without the protection of anonymity, against some animadversion
from citizens who resented their role as "guinea pigs," *Middletown in
Transition* is generally regarded as being more revealing than the earlier *Middletown.*

Special attention has been given to the problems of youth in a number of field studies. One survey which inquired into the situation of
young people during the depression period of the 1930's was *Youth
Tell Their Story* (1938), a project sponsored by the American Youth
Commission of the American Council on Education. Thirty-five
trained interviewers consulted 13,528 typical youths sampled from all
walks of life. They found the respondents cooperative and eager to
air their problems, for "We don't usually get asked," one of them said.
It was revealed that Maryland youngsters left school, on the average,
at the end of the ninth grade, most of the respondents (aged 16 to 24)
felt their education had helped them enjoy life, but about one-third
expressed the opinion that their schooling had not helped them much
in earning a living. Three out of ten were jobless, some had been looking seven years for their first full-time job, median pay for those with

[25] *Ibid.,* pp. 505-509.

jobs was $12.96 a week.   Their biggest worry, as voiced by one young-
ster, was "how to get married on $15 a week."   Four out of five, in-
cluding almost half of those who were married, were living with their
parents.   Despite all the obstacles, they were still marrying early,
median age for boys being 21, for girls, 19.   They learned about sex
mostly "in the gutter."   For recreation they liked the movies, dancing, music, reading, "cokes" and sodas at the corner drugstore.   They
did a lot of loafing but they would rather be doing something.   They

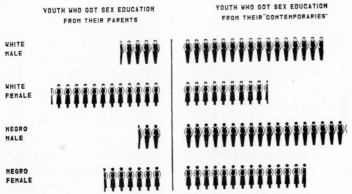

THE JOBS YOUTH WANT AND THE JOBS THEY GET

| | WHAT THEY WANT | WHAT THEY GET |

PROFESSIONAL OR TECHNICAL

MANAGERIAL

OFFICE OR SALES

SKILLED

SEMI-SKILLED

UNSKILLED

DOMESTIC OR PERSONAL

RELIEF PROJECT

THE CHIEF SOURCE OF SEX EDUCATION—
HOME OR STREET ?

| | YOUTH WHO GOT SEX EDUCATION FROM THEIR PARENTS | YOUTH WHO GOT SEX EDUCATION FROM THEIR "CONTEMPORARIES" |

WHITE MALE

WHITE FEMALE

NEGRO MALE

NEGRO FEMALE

From Bell's *Youth Tell Their Story*.   (Courtesy, American
Council on Education.)

felt they were "up blind alleys," getting nowhere. "In so far as love of one's work is a part of one's enthusiasm for living," the survey concludes, ". . . about all that can be said for this younger generation is that they are a rather sorry and depressed lot."

Social psychologists must get the facts by means of the various methods at their disposal, since a scientist cannot afford to rely on guesswork, casual notice, or armchair speculation. Measurement of attitudes, market analysis and consumer research, and public opinion polls, all give us fairly accurate data to go by in formulating our ideas and policies on social questions. Gathering tabulative and non-tabulative records, using informal interviews and questionnaires, correlating by statistical techniques and interpreting the data in the light of scientifically accepted knowledge, the social scientist is conducting community surveys, thus availing himself of another instrument for gaining knowledge about human behavior.

All of these procedures, quantitative and non-quantitative, are being improved by practice and reexamination. With the perfection of the instruments and with more adequate training in their use, social psychologists are rapidly obtaining results that are most enlightening.

Chapter 4

VALUES AND THE ART OF LIVING

In the preceding chapter we observed how the social psychologist, operating as a scientist, gathers his data about human beings acting and interacting within the social milieu. We saw how effectively the scientific method can be utilized as an instrument for promoting accurate observation. The aim of psychology, however, is broader than mere scientific exploration. Our interest as students of human behavior is sure to transcend the bare record of what people are doing —we want to know, too, whether they achieve temporary or lasting satisfaction through their particular ways of life. Even the scientist who rigorously limits himself to the description of phenomena in his research, is called upon constantly in the course of his daily life to make value judgments profoundly affecting his personal welfare. Indeed, the exigencies of living compel all of us to supplement observation with evaluation. In the light of this need, we may assume that, beyond the confines of science, the larger task of psychology becomes the job of integrating facts and values into a workable system of conduct. In thinking about this task and in viewing our situation in perspective, we come to realize the necessity for a proper sense of values to guide us in selecting the *important* fields in which to do research, to provide a frame of reference for us in interpreting our findings, and to aid us in applying our results to the best advantage.

In the midst of our concern for values we must respect the canons and practices prescribed by science, for good intentions are futile unless they are directed by scientific understanding. Scientific training is, indeed, primary. With a sound grasp of the facts at our command we are prepared to plan our lives intelligently. Training in psychology as a science may thus be regarded as a necessary preparation for the examination of human behavior and for the study of the art of living.

I. SCIENCE AND THE ART OF LIVING

The social psychologist may profitably concern himself with both psychological values (what people want) and ethical values (what people should want if they are going to succeed in the quest for happiness). His interest in the science of human relations prompts him to study the way people live; his interest in the art of living leads him to interpret his observations with reference to patterns of life that might be better suited to human needs. The analysis of behavior in terms of acts and consequences tends naturally toward the evaluation of conduct as happy or unhappy, moral or immoral, wise or unwise, rational or irrational.

Values have long been associated exclusively with the realm of ethics, whose main concern is determining what is the Good. Much of this search for goodness has been carried out in the abstract by appealing to authoritarian premises and logical deductions. Too little heed has been paid to the psychological bases for moral conduct. How can we learn what is good unless we find out something about the people for whom certain principles of conduct are supposed to be good? Psychology and ethics are not separate disciplines. Perhaps a combination of the two fields will give us a workable applied social psychology.

Significant for both psychology and ethics is the fact that man can "delay behavior by thought," deliberating so that he may "know before he does." Schoen explores the import of this fact:

This ability of man to look before he leaps, and thereby learn by looking rather than by leaping, assumes two forms. Human selective activity can be either activity that consists of discriminated means for the accomplishment of unconsidered ends, or of discriminated ends that necessarily also imply considered means. In other words, the thought problem before the person may be only that of determining the most expedient way of accomplishing a goal that appears desirable, or it may consist of an examination of the desirability of the goal itself. And it is these two forms of human selective activity that lead to an identification of morality with human intelligence. . . . To be moral is to know what you are doing, and to be responsible for what you are doing, because you know where you are going, why you are going there, and how you are to get there.[1]

The psychologist cannot deal adequately with the concept of *intelligence-in-action* unless he considers the individual's capacity to dis-

[1] M. Schoen: "A Scientific Basis for Moral Action." *Scientific Monthly*, March, 1939.

riminate between ends. This ability to weigh values makes *reflective living* possible. To comprehend man in his social relations, we must nclude the view of him as a moral creature conscious to some extent of what he wants to get out of life and conscious, too, of what he should want for his own good and the welfare of others. The human being may commit errors in selecting his ends, but there can be no mistaking the fact that his judgments of value are of profound importance for all persons concerned. Social relations and values will fall naturally together under our survey of social psychology since we are going to interest ourselves in determining what patterns of living we may wisely adopt as intelligent members of society.

Social science has given a distorted view of reality in so far as it has left out of account the matter of values. Doob has called attention to the significance of this omission by pointing out that "no conscientious and thoughtful scientist who applies his science to the people and events that surround him can avoid the problem of value and the role of science in social affairs." [2] Those who hold that human affairs are not amenable to the scientific method are confusing the methods of natural science with scientific method in general. "Social science differs inevitably from natural science in many important respects, notably in its lesser capacity for isolating problems, and more generally in its lesser degree of isolation from other aspects of human activity and its consequent greater entanglement with problems of value," says J. S. Huxley, who predicts that social science will evolve its own technique and its own methodology, just as natural science has done.[3]

Some psychologists, conforming to their own circumscribed view of scientific orthodoxy, have tended to dehumanize psychology by adopting the mechanistic explanation of animal behavior as the prototype of human behavior. These scientists have scrupulously avoided any reference to spiritual values, with the result that they frequently have less than they might have to offer by way of enlightenment in the understanding of human relations. The cult of pure science has its priests who "make such a fetish of objectivity that they shun all significant social problems. . . . It is not wholly objective to deny that a scientist has personal and social values to which he is loyal." [4] It is a pseudo-objectivity that misleads a scientist to restrict his pro-

[2] L. W. Doob, in a review of P. W. Bridgman's *The Intelligent Individual and Society*. *Psychological Bulletin,* January, 1939.

[3] J. S. Huxley: "Science, Natural and Social." *Scientific Monthly,* January, 1940.

[4] H. Cantril and D. Katz: "Objectivity in the Social Sciences," Chapter 1 in *Industrial Conflict: a Psychological Interpretation* (pp. 9, 4), G. W. Hartmann and T. Newcomb, Editors. The Dryden Press, 1939.

gram of research to simple colorless problems that can be neatly geared
to laboratory exploration.   Real objectivity comes from the employ
ment of sound methods, not from the observer's success in detaching
himself from real life.

Dehumanized science ignores the fact that appraisals are bound up
with our knowledge of the world we live in.   Scientific analysis of bare
unappreciated facts gives us an artificial view of man's place in the
universe.   It is not surprising that a science grounded on a naïve ad
herence to the dogma of man-as-a-machine should have so little to
offer in helping us to solve our social problems.   A broader concept
of the science of man is coming into its own.   It is important for the
student of social science, particularly, to realize that an adequate view
of the human being—inclusive of values—is basic to an accurate com
prehension of the role the individual plays in modern society.

With these comments clearly in mind, it will be understood why we
conceive of social psychology in a two-fold way: first as a science
second as an art.   The term *art* as we shall employ it in this context
is well exemplified in the concept of medical practice as the art of heal
ing.   The physician is an artist in the sense that he resorts to the "em
ployment of given means to accomplish a given end, the combination
of things to effect a definite purpose, in the hands of especial skill."
The physician spends years studying facts, preparing himself for his
profession.   He masters the science of medicine as embodied in physi
ology, histology, anatomy, endocrinology, pharmacology, and other like
disciplines.   The accumulation of knowledge, however, does not make
a *good* doctor.   The skillful physician must know a great deal and
he must also know how to make use of his fund of information.   Be
yond science is the art of applying science, whether it be in the prac
tice of medicine or in the social adjustments of everyday life.   Psy
chology as a science gives us the facts about human nature; psychology
as an art is the study of how to use this information to obtain what
we value.   Learning facts is easy compared to learning how to make
use of them.   Psychologists may grasp all the theories without being
clever in handling people.   Very likely it was this possibility Gordon
Allport had in mind when he suggested that an apprenticeship as
a headwaiter in a restaurant should be required of all graduate stu
dents in psychology.

"Art," then, may be defined as a skill or technique facilitating

[6] J. P. Warbasse: *The Doctor and the Public*. Paul B. Hoeber, Inc.   (Medical
Book Dept. of Harper & Bros.), 1935. See the section discussing this concept, pp
399-401.

he superior performance of some task. Thus we may speak of "the
rt of public speaking," or we may refer to the methodology of cookery
s "the culinary art." Now, the art of living depends upon the effec-
ive coordination of numerous skills under the integrating influence of
life-plan. The sort of person who excels in this comprehensive art
s the individual who aims at goals that are satisfying, adjusts his am-
itions to his capacities, works some and loafs some, sets his ideals
igh enough to maintain his zest for the struggle but not so high as to
roduce frustration, adapts his standards of living to his income,
etains his individuality while cooperating in the give-and-take of
ocial contacts, insists on his rights when he feels it is necessary to
aaintain his self-respect, and yields to others when he deems it dis-
reet to do so; in short, he is the picture of mental health because he
.nows the game of life and he is skillful in applying that knowledge.
uch a person gets the most out of life. The "how" of this enviable
ccomplishment is an art, not a science. There is no mathematical
ormula to determine how ambitious a man should be, how much he
hould love his wife and children, how much religious faith he ought
o have to protect his morale against unanticipated misfortunes.
Building up one's self-confidence to just the right amount so that the
pitfalls of overconfidence and underconfidence are avoided, cannot be
educed to a statistical equation. The attainment of this ideal bal-
nce involves evaluation based on insight, a procedure that is not susceptible to precise measurement. The artistry of living wisely is more
than a science; science is used as an instrument for achieving well-
chosen ends.

Most students who enroll for instruction in psychology are more
likely to be interested in the art than in the science of psychology and
they are more than likely to be disappointed, for they will usually
encounter in the course little that will help them in dealing effectively
with other people. The undergraduate, if he takes his work seriously,
will learn the facts and the principles about human behavior; the
professor will leave it up to him to discover for himself how to apply
what he has learned from text, laboratory experiment, and lectures.
Academic learning, however, is not enough as a preparation for effective living. It must be supplemented by "knocking around" in the
world, dealing with people, observing which techniques work and
which ones fail. Counselors can tell us to take an interest in the
other fellow's problems, to make the other person feel important, to
avoid the dictatorial manner in seeking to get our own ideas across—
all sound advice—but for the most part we have to pick up what we

can by firsthand experience in living with people. A person canno
become an orator by taking a course in public speaking; a theologica
student cannot master the art of preaching by electing a semester'
course in homiletics. The successful speaker knows the tricks of th
trade and by practice he learns how to use them: speaking with
serious emphasis at the right times, letting his audience relax with a
touch of humor at the appropriate moments, closing before he exhaust
their patience. Such finesse is an art rarely mastered. Comparable to
this art of public address, on a larger scale, is the art of living, requir
ing a keen perception for the worth-while, the discipline of desire
friendliness, and other attributes, all integrated into a working har
mony.

Art as skill in achieving a desired end, may be illustrated by a de
scription of how Abraham Flexner succeeded in raising money for a
medical school. Flexner set out one morning to interview Mr. George
Eastman, the Kodak executive, with the idea of securing a large gift to
finance a medical school at the University of Rochester. When Flex
ner arrived at the Eastman home, he found his host listening to organ
music, his favorite hobby. From eight-thirty to ten Flexner and East
man sat in silence, listening to the music. Notice that Flexner did no
force his request at an inopportune moment when the mention of busi
ness matters would have been in "poor taste," at a time when financia
considerations would have suffered from the competition of musica
preoccupation. When the concert was over and the two men had
repaired to Eastman's study, Flexner let Eastman speak first concern
ing the reason for the visit. Then in response to this invitation for
enlightenment, Flexner told his prospect all about medical education
in this country, mentioning the great school at Johns Hopkins, citing
Rockefeller's gifts, picturing what could be done at Rochester. At
noon luncheon was ordered for two—an indication of progress—and
they talked of other things. At four Eastman left for his office, after
inviting his guest for dinner, on which occasion they were to be joined
by President Rhees, head of the University of Rochester. *After* din
ner—a good time to approach any normal person with a request—the
talk turned to the medical school project. Eastman asked what it
would cost, learned it would take $10,000,000, offered $2,500,000.
Flexner had spent the good part of a day preparing the way for such
an offer but he was not ready yet to "close in for the kill." Instead, he
suggested that Eastman should do better, backing the school as his own
personal protégé, not sharing the venture with others. Despite this
urging, Eastman was adamant. "That's the best I can do now," was

is dictum. Flexner did not press the issue. "There's no hurry," e assured him. "Wait until you sell more Kodaks." On that note lexner left for New York. Several days later Eastman wired him to ome to Rochester and he offered to raise the amount to $3,500,000. lexner still did not jump at the gift; instead he protested that East-1an should go the whole way on his own, insisting he was sure the lonor would go higher. Again Flexner left for New York and again 1e was invited by wire to return. Again Flexner hastened to Roch-ster. Eastman rose behind his desk, smiled, pointed his finger at 'lexner, and said, "I shall make you one more offer and then I never vant to see your face again." Flexner expressed his regret and asked or the offer. It was $5,000,000. Flexner accepted, informed the lonor that he knew he would give more later on, and Eastman denied t. Flexner was right, though, and Eastman contributed generously o the project for years, left still more in his will. Confided Eastman o a friend concerning Flexner:

He himself is the worst highwayman that ever flitted into and out of Roch-ester. He put up a job on me and cleaned me out of a thundering lot of my 1ard-earned savings. I have just heard that he is coming up here June 2nd to speak at the graduating exercises of the allied hospitals. I have been 1sked to sit on the stage with him, but instead of that I shall probably flee the town for fear he will hypnotize me again.

Flexner took the measure of his man. He knew when to speak and when to keep quiet. His timing was perfection itself. He jested, he kidded, he used subtle persuasion, in just the right proportions. The real secret of his success was his technique of allowing Eastman to con-vince himself that the investment was a grand opportunity to put his savings to good use, with Flexner lending a little encouragement to provide extra momentum when the psychological moment called for a push. Flexner's skill was an artistic exhibition of consummate psy-chology in practice.[6]

Timing, as we have just noted, is an important factor in the art of selling. It is just as essential to skillful social adjustments. The wise parent knows there is a time to be gentle with a child, and a time to be firm; a time to let him play and a time to make him work; a time to be patient with him, and a time to put the foot down. This matter of timing is a cardinal principle of wisdom in all our social relationships.

[6] See A. Flexner: "Adventures in Money-Raising." *Harper's Magazine,* August, 1940.

There are occasions when we should be sympathetic for the unfor tunate, but there are also occasions when we should insist upon thei helping themselves out of their troubles. There are situations wher we should be tolerant of others' mistakes, and there are situation where it is equally obligatory to condemn with uncompromising se verity. The fine art of living is to know *how much is due when,* tha is, how kind, how generous, how forgiving, how serious one shoul be in any particular situation that calls for just the right amount o the correct (apt) behavior pattern.

The art of achieving happiness has been too long neglected by th psychologists. This feeling was expressed by Dodge as he looked bacl over his distinguished career in psychology:

> I am desirous of participating in the solution of one more problem ir applied psychology. That is the problem of protracted human happiness Whether or not it fits in with one's philosophy of life, the fact is incontestabl that happiness is an important if not the most important aim of human en deavor. Notwithstanding this fact, it has received no commensurate scien tific attention. The theory of the happy life remains at about the level wher Greek philosophers left it. There has been an immense amount of ameli orative activity and human welfare work, but it is practically all a treatmen of symptoms without fundamental analysis. We are trying to correct a num ber of the supposed major conditions of unhappiness. Personnel studies tr to avoid putting round pegs in square holes. Studies of family life, like tha of Hamilton's, try to develop adaptive behavior in the smallest social group Medicine and hygiene try to cure and prevent ailments of body and mind But these symptomatic and ameliorative activities touch only small section of human unhappiness.
>
> Scientific information as to the fundamental positive conditions of pro tracted happiness are conspicuous for their absence. We do not even know the laws by which pleasant situations become unpleasant and unpleasant sit uations become bearable or even pleasant. The positive conditions of hap piness are left largely to accident, such as the satisfaction of instinctive wants with its tragic disillusionments and negative adaptations, the economic pres sure to provide a market for manufactured products, the exigencies of the labor market, the desire to amass wealth, or the abolition of private wealth. There are numerous wise protests that protracted happiness is achieved by none of these things; but positive scientific data on the real conditions are as inconspicuous as scientific interest in the problem. If there were a real so licitude for intelligent adaptation, our science would be busy with very dif ferent tasks.[7]

[7] R. Dodge, in *History of Psychology in Autobiography*, Volume I, pp. 119-120. Clark University Press, Worcester, Mass. 1930.

The time has come for psychologists to investigate the conditions that are basic to human satisfaction and euphoria.

II. THE GROWING INTEREST IN THE SOCIAL PSYCHOLOGY OF VALUES

Despite protests from some psychologists who insist that social psychology is a science and, therefore, has nothing to do with values, there appears to be an increasing concern with valuation as a fundamental concept for interpreting the social implications of individual behavior. Defining a value in psychological terms as "anything that any individual desires for any reason whatever," [8] Freeman built his *Social Psychology*, published in 1936, around this concept as his basic frame of reference. His position is expounded in Part II, "Individual and Cultural Determination of Values," where he says, among other things:

Beyond the mere association of affective tone with value lies the fact that, aside from a restricted category of objects like food, the selection of objects and situations for the attachment of pleasantness is never constant or innate, but always socially determined, and conditioned largely by the stereotypes of local usage. In one society personal decorum is a value; in another it is possession by spirits and mystical excitement. Within each society its special values, whatever they may happen to be, become crystallized and eventually assume the character of immutable properties of the natural order, which the individual may ignore only at the peril of losing social status and the opportunity of enjoying the approbation of his fellows. Aside from the absence of any tendency to disobey articulated prohibitions, even the mere *temptation* toward violation occurs but rarely, because the individual is unfamiliar with, and hence does not suspect the existence of, the alternatives of behavior provided by other cultures. On grounds such as these individuals come to regard their God, their form of economics, morality, and patriotism as the only conceivable values.[9]

This frame of reference gives Freeman an opportunity to evaluate the assets and liabilities of our social setup, particularly in the industrial sphere, and to point out where our institutions are found wanting. As an approach to social psychology, value proves to be, in Freeman's resourceful scheme of thought, most stimulating and enlightening. Since the publication of Freeman's original text, social psychologists have come out into the open in their avowal of the role

[8] E. Freeman: *Social Psychology*, p. 123. Henry Holt and Company, 1936.
[9] *Ibid.*, pp. 124-125.

that value must occupy in any satisfactory treatment of social be
havior.

As a matter of fact, it is difficult to avoid evaluative language in th
exposition of social psychology. It is so difficult that some writers us
evaluative terms, accompanying them with protests against peopl
who allow values to intrude within the realm of social science. Kline
berg, for example, states on page 341 of his *Social Psychology* tha
". . . value judgments are not usually regarded as within the prov
ince of a social psychologist. . . ." And then on page 549 of the sam
book he apologetically injects in his "Conclusion," as a sort of after
thought, these significant comments:

It may seem premature to speak of an Applied Social Psychology, or to
attempt to relate our findings to the problems of human welfare. The goal
of civilization are not adequately defined, nor are satisfactory technique
available for a constructive program of social engineering. At the same time
the social psychologist has a contribution to make. If there is one genera
conclusion which may be said to emerge from this survey of the availabl
knowledge in the field, it is that most of the characteristics as well as the
institutions of modern society are to be explained in terms of social rathe
than biological factors. This has far-reaching practical implications. With
out denying the significance of man's biological nature or the importance o
the physical organism in determining individual differences in personality, i
remains true that improvements are to be sought more profitably in an ameli
oration of the social environment than in the creation of a superior genetic
stock.

More precisely, the following statements may with some safety be made
Criminality and mental abnormality may best be attacked by social better
ment, and not by sterilization; wars and conflicts are not inherent in human
nature, but in the structure of our social and economic system; racial hos
tilities are not due to the innate characteristics of biologically distinct groups
but to historical and economic forces; the functioning intelligence and
achievement of a people may be raised by making the best education available
to the largest number, rather than by selective breeding. The list might be
continued, but the additions would merely be variations on this same theme.
Man is primarily a social animal, and his hope for the future lies in the im
provement of his society.[10]

These are very important ideas, too important to be appended as an
afterthought, too important to be covered on one page, the last page
at that. This exposition of the evaluative point of view belongs at
the beginning as a statement of basic principles; its theme should be

[10] O. Klineberg: *Social Psychology*, p. 549. Henry Holt and Company, 1940.

terwoven with the descriptive account of man's social conduct, giv-
ng the facts meaning and direction.

Britt did just that in his *Social Psychology of Modern Life* (1941).
The last chapter, in summary, dealt with the question, "Knowledge
or What?" Britt suggested that the student ask himself whether a
society is logical and rational which permits 42 per cent of its families
to subsist on an income of less than $1,000 a year, which tolerates peri-
odic unemployment, which defends the *status quo* in its courts on the
grounds that "the law is the law and must be preserved," which
preaches equality and practices discrimination. Britt proposed that
the student adopt an attitude of healthy skepticism. What, he asked,
are you going to do to make our society more rational?

First of all, if you are content with the *status quo,* you will do nothing
about it. If you believe that the ways of your grandfather are good enough
for you and that, "It's a pretty good old world after all," then for you there
is no problem of a logical society.

An attempt has been made in this book, however, to engender a certain
degree of *healthy skepticism.* The word "skepticism" is used to denote an
intellectual curiosity about the society in which we live. . . . Skepticism
should *not* be confused with cynicism—they are not at all synonymous. The
word "healthy" in healthy skepticism may be explained by an analogy. If
you are occasionally skeptical about your own good health, a careful physical examination may reveal certain changes in your living which will be
desirable. Likewise, an objective examination of society may suggest certain
desirable social changes. This book is in no sense intended to suggest that
society as a whole is illogical or abnormal. In fact, we have examined many
phases of both normal and abnormal behavior and of both rational and irrational behavior.

A famous teacher once said that if he could not upset the views of a student
who came into his class and make him think for himself, then it was a waste
of the student's time to come. The same thing may be said for this book on
social psychology. Unless you have been forced to think about some old
problems and have worried a little bit about them, your time has been
wasted. No attempt has here been made at indoctrination in favor of any
one "philosophy of life." Instead, stress has been laid upon a scientific examination of your own attitudes and behavior in relation to your fellows.

One difficulty with any analysis is that the one who makes it may be accused of attacking society. Again, an analogy may be useful. Suppose that
this were a book on the physiology of teeth. Critics might say: "This man
is attacking teeth for he does not show up their beautiful characteristics. He
does not say much about the good that teeth do, and he offers us no substitute." That would be analogous to a belief that the present book is an

attack on society, because we have not always "pointed with pride" but hav
realistically examined our social behavior.

The question of what we can or will do about our society always depenc
upon our aims and ideals. . . .

This book began with a plea for objectivity, that is, for an impartial scrt
tiny of all the facts concerning any problem.   Objectivity, however, shoul
not make you colorless, neutral, or completely lukewarm.   The demand :
simply that you make up your mind about a problem, not in terms of in
pulses and prejudices, but through an objective analysis of all sides of th
question.   After such an analysis, you are entitled to carry your thought
into action.   In a democracy you have a right, like other citizens, to "d
something about it."   Democracy today needs social scientists both inside an
outside the universities.[11]

The topic of *value* was featured at the 1939 and 1940 meetings o
the American Psychological Association, where, on each occasion, th
Chairman's address before the Society for the Psychological Study o
Social Issues gave considerable attention to the subject.   At the 193
meeting Hartmann, speaking on "Value as the Unifying Concept o
the Social Sciences," said, in part:

It is no more possible to build a system of human and social relations upot
any foundation other than an extensive knowledge of man's values than i
is to erect a numberless arithmetic or a non-symbolic algebra. *Values ar*
both the basic data and the explanatory tools of all the social sciences. Be
cause they refer to realities with which every social science, including psy
chology, sooner or later must grapple, they are the necessary intellectual cor
structs that workers in these fields must use.   Just as inevitably the notio:
of value is that which unites all the cultural sciences in a common enterprise

I believe the judgments of many leaders in these areas support my inter
pretation.   Charles Beard has personally told me that the events of histor
are meaningless without the ascription of certain values to the participant
and that the historian himself cannot write, much less criticize, without som
principle of selection to guide his hand.   Much of anthropology is a recorc
of the ways in which values are ordered by different ethnic groups.   *Mid*
dletown is essentially a study of the preferences, attitudes, and beliefs of :
representative American community, none of which have any meaning sav
in terms of some system of values. . . .   In his most recent and equally im
portant volume called *Knowledge for What?* Lynd pleads in the unashamec
spirit of the reformer that social research accept the alleviation of tension
and frustrations as its inescapable task.   It is not necessary to multiply illus

[11] S. H. Britt: *Social Psychology of Modern Life*, pp. 490-491.   Rinehart and Com
pany, 1941.

trations from many sources all indicating that the value-problem is the basis of every effort to explain institutional behavior. . . .

Thus the real subject matter of all the social sciences is clearly identified as the cataloging of human needs and the construction and testing of devices for their satisfaction. This was undoubtedly the insight that McDougall had when he wrote his *Social Psychology*. . . .

If the study of a culture cannot be pursued without an examination of the premier values that the culture embodies, then I think it follows that physical science and technology are affected by, if not saturated with, the special values of the persons who transmit and develop them. That the natural sciences came into being at all must mean that they represented experiences of worth to those who cherished them. . . . If life *as such* and scientific and intellectual activity are themselves values (and they must be such to everyone in this audience or you would not be among those present), then we as psychologists are not only *justified* in studying the value-experiences of individuals and groups—we are *compelled* to do so; and in addition we are forced to make maturer and more critical value-judgments about the human and social values our research reveals. The ceaseless reconstruction, refinement, and improvement of our notions of what constitutes worthy behavior is the chief business of the student of social issues. . . .

We have adhered too long to the superstitious separation of values from so-called "facts." . . . The barrenness of so much psychologizing may be a consequence of this self-denying ordinance which restricts scientific reporting to a *minimum* of arguable features rather than seeking to convey the true *essentials* of an observable situation. To create a world without values may seem like a curious ideal, but that is precisely the exhortation conveyed by the scientific *ethos* of the last century. Such a view must be repudiated, because so long as it persists it fosters an artificially and narrowly restricted glimpse of reality while posing as the full substance of truth.[12]

In 1940, Chairman Tolman's address on "Psychological Man" closed with these words, especially impressive because spoken by a psychologist who has devoted years of study to animal behavior:

This would be my Utopia, and the sermon I would try to preach, though Utopias and sermons are, I realize, inexcusable in such a company as this. But our fellow human beings today all over the world are giving up their lives in the name of new loyalties. And, if we psychologists here in America don't preach our own sermons, we shall be caught by theirs. If we don't

---

[12] G. W. Hartmann: "Value as the Unifying Concept of the Social Sciences." *Journal of Social Psychology, S.P.S.S.I. Bulletin*, 1939, 10, 563-575. Hartmann has written a textbook with value as a frame of reference. See *Educational Psychology*, especially Chapter 13, "The Improvement of Social Behavior and Social Relations." 1941.

say our say, not merely as to how to detect and measure and tabulate social change, but as to what good social changes would be, then we shall deserve no better fate than the one which otherwise undoubtedly lies in store for us. America will have to be not only a surviving America, but also a New America. For, if it be not a New America, it will not survive.[13]

This address, like Hartmann's the year before, constituted a new note in American psychology, a call to social psychologists to concentrate their research upon *evaluation*.

Thorndike has transferred his interest from the synaptic S-R bond to problems of value. His research in this field began with the assumption that you can tell what people value by studying how they spend their time and their money. "What we spend our money for" and "What we spend our working time for," combined, will give "some idea of the gratifications for which all our days are spent." Investigation showed that "time not spent at work or in sleep" was spent "largely for entertainment (including the pleasures of the senses and of the love life), companionship, affection, and approval." Adults in the United States spend the sixteen hours of the waking day about as follows:

25 per cent for subsistence and perpetuation
 2 "   "   to avoid or to reduce sensory pain
 7 "   "   for security
 8 "   "   for the welfare of others
30 "   "   for entertainment
10 "   "   for companionship and affection
10 "   "   for approval
 4 "   "   for intellectual activity
 2 "   "   for dominance over others
 2 "   "   for other wants

These figures are "impartial conjectures based on facts."

Man does not put first those wants the satisfaction of which ensures survival, the production of offspring and their survival, and attend to others only after these have been satiated. His craving for social intercourse and the approval of self and others is for greater amounts and different sorts than are needed for survival; his craving for sex pleasures is out of all proportion to what is needed for the production of offspring; his craving for entertain-

[13] E. C. Tolman: "Psychological Man." *Journal of Social Psychology, S.P.S.S.I. Bulletin,* 1941, 13, 205-218.

ment may even operate against the nourishment of the young and the protection of the community.[14]

Thorndike is correct in assuming that we may learn much about a person's values by discovering what he spends his money for.   Most of us have to work for our money; it represents effort.   A Gloucester sea captain was sued by a beautician for breach of promise and the jury awarded the lady damages of $6,250.   Said the news account:

> The young fisherman was stunned by the verdict.   "I haven't got that much money," he told reporters, "and I don't know how I'll ever be able to get it. Six thousand dollars runs into a lot of mackerel." [15]

People who cannot pay their doctor's or their grocer's bills seem to find enough cash on hand to take care of their tobacco and liquor needs.   It doesn't require any wizard to detect that self-indulgence for such persons takes precedence over a sense of financial obligation. When a woman wills $5,000 to her cat so that "Lilly can live in luxury on an allowance of $50 a month," she is revealing how lightly she values her fellow human beings.

Thorndike estimates that we spend "about one ninth of our money to ward off hunger, about one tenth to keep warm (or cool) and dry, that only a few eccentrics pay money for exercise (our payments for games and sports being for entertainment rather than exercise), that we spend much time but little money for rest, that the mental features of sex life cost us about five times as much as the physical, that the reproduction of the species comes chiefly as a by-product. . . .   We pay more to get companionship than to get affection. . . .   For entertainment . . . we spend more than for mental activity and the welfare of others combined. . . .   *Homo* (of U.S.A. 1939) seems much more sociable than *sapiens*.   He seems to be mainly a hedonist, but most of the pleasure he seeks is not of the senses." [16]

Pursuing the problem of valuation on a larger scale, Thorndike set himself the task of finding out what specifications characterize a city as a good place for good people to live in.   From 117 cities 120 "items

[14] From E. L. Thorndike, *Human Nature and the Social Order*.   By permission of The Macmillan Company, publishers.   Pp. 134-135.   1940.   See also, E. L. Thorndike: "How We Spend Our Time and What We Spend It For."   *Scientific Monthly*, May, 1937.

[15] Boston *Herald*, May 14, 1936.

[16] E. L. Thorndike: *Human Nature and the Social Order*, pp. 132-133.   See also E. L. Thorndike: "What Do We Spend Our Money For?" *Scientific Monthly*, May, 1937.

of fact," all measurable, were collected, and from these data a composite score of General Goodness (G) was derived, based on the 23 items selected by competent judges as the essential traits determining goodness. These constituents of the G Score involved such matters as the rate of infant mortality; amount of money spent for schools and teachers' salaries, for libraries, for recreation and for public parks; percentage of persons between sixteen and twenty attending school; infrequency of poverty; average wage of workers in factories; frequency of home ownership; number of homes with electricity, gas, telephones, automobiles, and radios; circulation of the better magazines.[17]

Cities, he postulated, are made better when able and *good people* settle as residents—people who are intelligent, who read books, who don't commit murder. For each city Thorndike computed a score, P, representing the personal qualities of its population. P is the weighted average of these 11 items:

Per capita number of graduates from public high schools in 1934; Percentage which public expenditures for the maintenance of libraries was of the total public expenditures; Percentage of illiteracy (reversed); Percentage of illiteracy among those aged 15-24 (reversed); Per capita circulation of public libraries; Per capita number of physicians, nurses, and teachers minus male domestic servants; Per capita number of telephones; Number of male dentists divided by number of male lawyers; Per capita number of deaths from syphilis (reversed); Per capita number of deaths from homicide (reversed); Per capita number of homes owned.[18]

G and P tend to go together, high P accompanying high G; low P, low G. Good people tend to live in good cities.[19]

In his colossal volume, *Human Nature and the Social Order,* Thorndike explains why he has become so concerned with the subject of values. Psychology, he says, has given more attention to the operation of the sense organs than to the functioning of purposes. Yet it is important for us to study how purposes work. If we are observing

[17] See E. L. Thorndike: "Individual Differences in American Cities: Their Nature and Causation." *American Journal of Sociology,* 1937, 43, 191-224; *Your City.* 1939; *Human Nature and the Social Order,* p. 279. 1940; *144 Smaller Cities.* 1940; "American Cities and States: Variation and Correlation in Institutions, Activities, and the Personal Qualities of the Residents." *Annals of the New York Academy of Science,* 39, No. 4. 1939.

[18] E. L. Thorndike: "Individual Differences in American Cities." *American Journal of Sociology,* 1937, 43, 191-224. University of Chicago Press.

[19] Thorndike has also evaluated the press in 28 cities. See "The Press in American Cities." *Scientific Monthly,* January, 1941.

the stars, we are not likely to get involved in problems of value; but if we are studying human relations, we inevitably run into the factor of value. Values are tied up with consequences. This being so, psychologists interested in studying values must inquire into what happens to human wants. In the past, values have been so widely established by *authority* that people have neglected to weigh acts in terms of natural consequences. The way to improve the world, according to Thorndike, is to use our abilities to gratify our good wants. In this enterprise we find that ethics and psychology are intimately related.[20] The procedure to follow in attaining the fulfillment of our desires is to study first the needs of human beings and then to "fashion the social machinery which will make for human happiness."[21] In preparing our plans in this direction, it is incumbent upon us to discover for ourselves what sorts of organizations have produced what sorts of consequences. Happiness, the chief aim of "the art of living," is principally a psychological problem. It is up to psychologists, therefore, to concern themselves with these problems of value.[22]

In a civilized culture, it is reasonable to assume, human rights would be deemed more important than property rights, should the occasion arise for these rights to come into conflict. To determine the relative weighting of these rights or values, Alfred Winslow Jones investigated the *attitude toward corporate property* as exhibited by the citizens of Akron, Ohio, using the field-study approach—a community survey with one specific problem in view. The title of his book gives us in a nutshell the nature of his project: *Life, Liberty, and Property: a Story of Conflicting Rights*.[23] The investigation was conducted in Akron during the late months of 1938 and the early months of 1939. Some 1,700 citizens were subjected to an interview that lasted from a half-hour in some cases to over an hour in others. The procedure of the interview was prepared and tested out in advance. It was rigidly adhered to in every case. Instead of dumbfounding the respondent with queries about "corporate property," Jones adopted the roundabout procedure of telling some anecdotes and asking the individual for his reactions. These stories "are not fictitious episodes, but the simple account of events that have taken place during the past few years—events affecting corporate property on the one hand, and the personal fate of a considerable number of individuals on the

[20] See E. L. Thorndike: *Human Nature and the Social Order*, p. 355.
[21] *Ibid.*, p. 524.
[22] See *ibid.*, Chapter 13, "Conflicts of Wants, Conscience, and Judgments about Values," and Chapter 14, "Valuation."
[23] Published in 1941.

other." [24]   The stories told of unemployed miners in the hard coal districts of Pennsylvania taking coal from the idle mines, of the Goodrich Company's threat to move part of its production away from Akron, of a farmer whose neighbors came to his rescue when a bank was foreclosing on his farm, of a stay-in strike in a power company, of the use of tear gas by police in dislodging sitdown strikers, and of other similar problem situations.   The story about the Goodrich Company's moving part of its plant hit pretty close to home with many of the Akron citizens for whom this possibility constituted a very real source of anxiety; this particular anecdote was related as follows:

The B. F. Goodrich Company in early 1938 asked the workers in its plant in Akron, Ohio, to accept a wage cut and a longer working week.   The company maintained that if the workers refused, some departments would have to be moved away from Akron, involving the removal of some four or five thousand jobs.   They held that only in this way could they compete with the other rubber companies which already had a smaller proportion of their operation in Akron, where a strong union exists and maintains high wages. Assume that the Goodrich Company can stay in business and continue to pay the old wages.   They will not make much money, if any, and they will not be able to pay much dividends, if any, but they will at least not be driven into bankruptcy.   Assume also that if they move out of Akron they will be able to hire workers cheaper, make more money and pay more dividends, at least at first.

The workers at a meeting held by the union refused to accept the wage cut.

Question: The company has the next move.   What would you think of its action if the company should move these jobs away from Akron?

Answers: 0. I would disapprove.
1. I would disapprove, but with qualifications.
2. I cannot decide.
3. I would approve, but with qualifications.
4. I would approve.[25]

The respondent was given an opportunity to speak his mind on the issue and then his answer was scored according to the scale of 0 to 4 delineated above.   The response to each of the eight anecdotes was scored in like manner and then the sum of the scores gave a total score representing with fair accuracy the individual's *attitude toward*

---

[24] A. W. Jones: *Life, Liberty, and Property*, p. 21.   J. B. Lippincott Company, 1941.

[25] *Ibid.*, pp. 359-360.

corporate property.   Quantification made it easy to compare persons and groups in this respect.

INTERVIEW SCORES

	Number	Mean
a. Control group	303	12.3
b. Business leaders	18	29.1
c. Technicians (chemists)	24	19.5
d. Farmers	22	19.5
e. Employee Association members (rubber workers)	37	17.6
f. Female office workers	97	15.9
g. Teachers	40	15.7
h. Non-C.I.O. (rubber workers)	69	12.6
i. Small merchants	52	12.1
j. Ministers	26	12.0
k. W.P.A. white collar workers	72	11.0
l. A.F. of L. members	59	8.0
m. W.P.A. manual workers	110	7.8
n. C.I.O. members (rubber workers)	193	6.2 [26]

A score of 32 signifies a very high regard for property rights; a score of 0, no respect. Attitude toward corporate property, according to Jones, depends in part upon a *subliminal set toward authority* and in part upon *socio-economic position.* The highest regard for corporate property was found among the industrial executives and business leaders, the lowest among members of the C.I.O.

The leaders of industry in Akron have prospered under the auspices of the corporate form of organization. They advanced themselves to managerial positions of power and prestige and have acquired wealth in the form of corporate securities. It would have been a handicap to them, to say the least, if they had turned aside to show sympathy for the other side in any of the conflict situations in which they found themselves. This applies, of course, to the struggle they have had with each other as well as to the conflicts—as in our stories—in which the general rights of corporate property were involved. The leaders of economic life in Akron are in the main line of American business with its tradition of self-reliance and ruthless, competitive acquisitiveness.[27]

At the other extreme are the workers who have rejected the old authorities and the persons of all classes who have embraced radical, extreme

[26] *Ibid.,* p. 378.
[27] *Ibid.,* p. 318.

left-wing, Marxist, socialist, communist or other similar doctrines. Contrasting the business leaders (29.1) and the C.I.O. rubber workers (6.2), we note that the C.I.O. rubber workers are not so near to a complete disregard of corporate property rights as the business leaders are to a complete disregard of personal rights, and comparing both groups with the random sample (12.3), it is obvious that the business leaders are much farther from the average feelings of Akronites than are the C.I.O. rubber workers.

Jones studied the attitude toward corporate property against the background of Akron's history and its contemporary community life, in order "to make clear and plausible why certain attitudes and opinions should develop, and to give the reader the feeling that they have not developed in a vacuum." Thus he combines, to good effect, opinion study with a community survey. Present attitudes of Akronites can only be understood in terms of the long and bitter history of industrial conflict that has characterized its major industry, rubber. For a long time unions could make no headway against *company executives* and against *public opinion;* collective bargaining just was not recognized. By the time of the middle 1930's, with help from above in the form of the New Deal's National Industrial Recovery Act (1933) which guaranteed to labor the right of collective bargaining, unions found they could count on public support from the great middle class. Akron had become union-conscious. Executives were forced to yield to the union demands, though still seeking to retain control by wielding the threat of decentralizing plant operations if wages were to be raised or hours shortened. The first full-fledged sitdown strike occurred in Akron's Firestone plant in January, 1936. It is significant that labor desisted from using this weapon, after the first flurry of sitdowns, because workers sensed public disapproval. Thus we see how public opinion affects industrial relations, including both employers and employees. The story of Akron's conflict is a story of labor's slow progress against stubborn resistance from the business leaders. The variations in the attitude toward corporate property become comprehensible when they are viewed in the light of this longtime struggle.

III. THE CULTURAL DETERMINATION OF VALUES

A person's attitudes and values are developed, in part, by means of identification with his parents. Parental ideals are appropriated consciously and unconsciously as the guiding norms of conduct. Precept and example insure transmission of the family tradition, the family honor, the family style of life.

Personal values are influenced very much, also, by the kind of work the individual does to earn his livelihood. The stockbroker is apt to absorb a sense of values characteristic of stockbrokers in general, the farmer has his own way of looking at things, the small-business man learns by his experience what to expect of life:

The Manufacturers' Association and the Bar Association present such a nicely articulated set of values that the behavior of these groups in any given crisis can be closely anticipated. While a Presbyterian in Ohio and another in New Jersey may be as unlike each other as are Tarzan and Little Bo Peep, manufacturers from the same quarters are more than likely to be as kindred in spirit as two sardines from the same can. Should a young man find his way into the private utilities and see some promise of a career in this field he begins to take on the spiritual coloring of the machine he serves, and in a few years his reactions to social problems involving taxes or state interference in business, or to a sermon, are typical of his associates.

Insurance and investment companies with their nicely calculated risks determine attitudes and active commitments on such vital questions as the race problem, labor disputes, and war. . . .

So true is this job-genesis of our values that a preacher, a teacher, or a candidate for public office finds himself addressing, not Americans or men and women with common aspirations, but lawyers, political bosses, union members, organized farmers, real estate magnates, bankers, and stockholders of this or that ilk.[28]

Individual psychology and comparative psychology have both amassed evidence to show that our desires are determined largely by the cultural standards to which we are attuned from the earliest stages of the conditioning process.[29] A man's hopes, his ambitions, his aspirations, depend upon the time in which he lives, the place wherein he dwells. In America the race is to the swift, and first prize goes to the man who can hurry, make more, sell more, own more, do more; among the Dakota Indians the most important person is the woman who can do the best beadwork; among the Plains Indians the thing that used to count was prowess in war. What we ourselves consider abnormal may be the norm of another culture. Among the Indians of Northwest America the Chief boasts of his remarkable merit and no one steps forward to denounce him as a braggart when he sings without embarrassment:

[28] A. H. MacLean: "Back of the Moral Crisis." *Christian Century*, January 22, 1941. Obviously, there is a danger of oversimplifying into stereotypes here.
[29] See O. Klineberg: *Race Differences*, Chapter 14, "The 'Fundamental Drives.'" 1935.

I am the great chief who vanquishes
I am the great chief who vanquishes. . . .
I sneer at the chiefs below the true, real chief.
I am the great chief who makes people ashamed.[30]

The Chief can get away with his sneering arrogance among his own people; here in America we would diagnose his case as one of grandiose delusions and assign him to the psychopathic ward to continue his proud paeans of self-praise. We would also provide psychiatric care for the Buddhist who has mastered the art of self-absorption in attaining Nirvana—an enviable accomplishment in India, just another case of schizophrenia in America.[31] In speaking of the Buddhist practice, Klineberg comments: "It may require years of careful training to reach a state which we would regard as the greatest of all misfortunes." [32]

The cultural determination of values is further evidenced in the fact that it is customary for people to eat certain foods, to live in certain kinds of dwellings, to follow definite rules concerning competition and cooperation, to settle disputes by resort to procedures generally recognized as binding on the parties in conflict. Each of these group patterns adopted by individual members of the group is a so-called "institution." An institution, then, is a pattern of behavior practiced by an individual in common with other individuals who share the same general norms and values for regulating the communal life. Thus political habits, religious habits, family habits constitute what we usually refer to as the institutions of government, church, and family. These habits are all customs because they are patterns of conduct sanctified by practices of long standing; they are institutions because they are a functional part of our organized group life. The sum total of the customs, conventions, and institutions which determine our behavior as members of an enduring group, such as the tribe or nation, is designated as the "culture." Thus our culture sets our values for us, determines whether we shall seek gain in terms of cattle, bananas, money, or military power; whether we shall have one wife, two wives, or many wives; whether we shall dwell in a penthouse, igloo, hovel of sod, or hut of thatch. Wherever our habitat, whatever our condition, if we live in an organized community, we are subject to cer-

---

[30] See R. F. Benedict: *Patterns of Culture,* pp. 192-193. 1934.

[31] See F. Alexander: "Buddhistic Training as an Artificial Catatonia." *Psychoanalytic Review,* 1931, 18, 129-145.

[32] O. Klineberg: *Race Differences,* p. 293. 1935.

tain privileges and obligations. Our duties and our functions are defined for us by the culture in which we are reared.

Cultural values can be appreciated by studying what sort of person the group sets up as its ideal. In America, for example, we exalt the go-getter who works hard, who is smart enough to make more money than his competitors, who is a winner. The Pueblos of New Mexico have a very different idea of what constitutes the ideal man: he is a person of dignity and affability who has never tried to get ahead, never shown any urge to win notice, never manifested any personal ambition. The man who habitually wins in contests of skill is debarred from further competition. The ideal man is a nice, polite man who never gets into any trouble and who never pushes himself into the limelight. The Dobu Islanders (Southwestern Pacific) favor a still different ideal. Among the Dobuans treachery is regarded as the supreme virtue. The good man, the successful man, is the one who can cheat the best. If he can trick another by sharp dealing—"wabu-wabu," as they call it—he is a hero. The person who excels at getting away with something is highly respected. "The Dobuans prefer to be infernally nasty or not nasty at all." [33] Dr. Fortune of Columbia, who studied these Islanders, found one Dobuan who was a social misfit: a man whose liking for work and for helping others was just too strong for him, who could not repress his smiling good will, with the result that he became the laughing stock of the Island.

The economic system operating among any given people is simply a customary arrangement that has evolved into an institution accorded increasing sanction with the passing of time. In our American culture, one of the main ideas is to accumulate money in the bank and to amass property in the form of real estate, stocks, or bonds. The more you can get—and hold on to—the more prestige you win. The profit motive is widely regarded as inherent in human nature, as basic to our common welfare. The Indians of Northwest America feel differently about this "basic" principle. These tribes do not use wealth to get an equivalent value in economic goods but as a counter in the game of social climbing. The idea is to shame rivals by giving them more property than they can give in return (the rival is supposed to double the original gift) or by destroying more property than anyone else at feasts staged for the purpose of burning blankets, canoes, and other possessions. A man may lose all he owns in the contest but in doing so he gains unparalleled prestige—which is the main thing. The

[33] A remark of Dr. Fortune quoted by R. F. Benedict: *op. cit.*, p. 171.

winner can indulge in uncensored self-glorification. Undisguised ego-tism of this sort would never do in our culture.

Anthropological studies which compare the folkways of various peo-ples show that our patterns of behavior are developed as habits pecul-iar to our particular culture. It is easy for a person growing up in our economic order to believe that capitalism is the only sound system, human nature being what it is; that socialism assumes a cooperation that is foreign to human nature; that war is Nature's way of weeding out the unfit so that only the fittest may survive. The individual who is naïve enough to think that his own way of doing things is the only way that is suited to man in general needs to take a look around at other peoples and other cultures where different practices prevail. Such a survey would convince the observer that customs are relative; that behavior patterns are local, variable, man-made; that the cultural determinants of behavior must be taken into account in explaining man's social life. Knowledge of other people's customs may render us less dogmatic in the pronouncement of our personal judgments, less inclined to identify our personal reactions with the Universal Will, more prone to consider the social influences that govern conduct. Comparative anthropology can do much to open our minds to the ne-cessity of adopting an objective approach to the observation and in-terpretation of human behavior.

The recognition that our values and our conduct patterns are cul-turally determined provides us with a sound psychological basis for an optimistic philosophy of social reconstruction. Armed with this in-sight, we can no longer excuse our follies by laying the blame on *hu-man nature*. Our institutions are of our own making. For better, for worse, they are our own handiwork. If culture is the basic source of our social behavior patterns, if institutions are fundamentally hab-its ingrained by experience rather than grooves set by biological des-tiny, if values are what we make them, then there is some hope that by our own efforts we may better ourselves by changing things until we discover, by experiment, the best ways of gaining our common and our individual goals.

IV. ORGANIZING SOCIETY TO MEET HUMAN NEEDS: DEMOCRACY

We can create the kind of society we want for the satisfaction of our needs if we plan our institutional arrangements to accord with what we already know about human values. Such a program would be "sci-entific management" on a huge scale, for as Odum defines the phrase, we should be practicing management as "an art or science or technique of organizing and directing human effort, applied to control the forces and to utilize the materials of nature for the benefit of mankind." [34] We are not suggesting the Nazi type of regimentation. Organizing society in terms of dominance by a super-race and submission by everybody else is not in keeping with the ideal that has largely inspired our civilization: *respect for persons.*

We can all subscribe to the desirability of some fundamental principles though our tastes may differ regarding the details. Employment is better than relief, plentiful goods better than artificial restriction, mutual accommodation better than pogroms and war, conciliation better than strikes, just as health is better than sickness in any rational scale of values. Almost any person in his right mind would chuckle if he heard a fellow human being moan: "It just kills me to spend so much money on doctor's bills, but I suppose health is a necessary evil." If we are in doubt as to what people want, we can ask them—that's simple and direct enough. That is exactly what the American Youth Commission did in Maryland and they found three things youth wanted most: education, jobs, fun. Facilities for the realization of all of these desires must be encouraged in a society whose members are conscious of their responsibilities. Schools and recreation centers cost money; the money must be forthcoming, somehow; it is up to our economists to find a way for ministering to these basic wants. The Maryland study revealed a tragic lack of leisure-time facilities for the large number of youth who "just hang around" in poolrooms, bars, drugstores, and on street corners. "For no less than millions of young people in America," the investigators concluded, "this situation calls for an awakening, on the part of communities, to the social . . . values of satisfying recreation, and a determination to develop leisure-time programs that will not only absorb energies that often lead to delinquent behavior, but which will add something valuable to the spiritual stature of those who participate in them." [35]

In planning to meet human needs, it is obvious that we must have accurate information as to what people really want. Tests have been developed to discover the nature of human desires through the measurement of attitudes, market research, public opinion polls, and the like. Jones demonstrated in Akron how values can be ascertained.

---

[34] H. W. Odum: *American Social Problems*, p. 72. 1939.
[35] H. M. Bell: *Youth Tell Their Story*, p. 255. American Council on Education, Washington, D.C. 1938.

In addition to all of the techniques we have mentioned for investigating wishes and hopes, there is available a very useful means of getting information on values in the personality test developed by Allport and Vernon, *A Study of Values: a Scale for Measuring the Dominant Interests in Personality* (Houghton Mifflin Company), first issued in 1931. Based on Spranger's *Types of Men* (1928), "this study aims to measure the relative prominence of six basic interests or motives in personality: the theoretical, economic, aesthetic, social, political, and religious." [36] Allport and Vernon claim that their test unearths evidence of much importance for social psychology. Typical test items are:

Do you believe that contemporary charitable policies should be curtailed because they tend to undermine individual initiative?

In your opinion, has general progress been advanced more by: (a) the freeing of slaves, with the enhancement of the value placed on individual life; (b) the discovery of the steam engine, with the subsequent industrialization and economic rivalry of European and American countries?

Do you think that a good government should aim chiefly at:
a. more aid for the poor, sick, and old;
b. the development of manufacturing and trade;
c. introducing more ethical principles into its policies and diplomacy;
d. establishing a position of prestige and respect among nations?

These are significant questions and the answers are of special interest to the social psychologist who is attempting to evaluate our society in terms of the opportunities it provides for fulfilling human aspiration.

The time is auspicious for a study of human needs. Murphy calls attention to the importance of such an undertaking:

In view of the general recognition of the infinite diversity of tensions and miseries traceable to the placing of man in an environment which does not satisfy him, there is surely little sense in continuing to speak as if man could adapt himself equally well to any environment. Here the concept of cultural relativism has done immense damage, indeed as great damage, I believe, as the concept of unchanging human nature. Both notions are blatantly at variance with the findings of the cultural sciences. If man is to be molded to society, society must also be molded to man. In short, one of the greatest research needs in social psychology is to discover what social arrangements, what human values, are really sound. And no one can begin to do research on such a problem unless he knows the human organism, its needs, its capacity to create and to adapt, the limits of its adaptation, and the individual dif-

[36] Quoted from the *Manual of Directions*, p. 3. 1931.

ferences in each creative or adaptive function, with their implications for the total social pattern.[37]

The merit of a culture depends on how the needs of men are met, curbed, controlled, or frustrated. The soundness of our social order cannot be weighed in the abstract; it must be measured in terms of personal happiness—the happiness of the individual human beings who are affected by our institutions.

People in modern cities, it is charged, do not know how to live. They exist in crowded tenements or apartment houses, with little fresh air and less sunlight, descending underground for a ride, popping up into an office building, working their daily stretch in dark, stuffy rooms, descending for another ride in subterranean vehicles, popping up in due time into a tiny suite called "home." Our cities have grown without any orderly social effort and in view of this fact Lewis Mumford has concluded that "a seventeenth century Dutch peasant, in his little village, knew more about the art of living in communities than a nineteenth century municipal councilor in London or Berlin. Statesmen who did not hesitate to weld together a diversity of regional interests into national states, or who wove together an empire that girdled the planet, failed to produce even a rough draft of a decent neighborhood." [38] Robert Lynd is equally strong in his indictment of our city life:

The dweller in a large American city tends to be a highly developed roving predatory animal. His culture resembles a frontier boomtown, with everywhere the clatter of new buildings going up and disregard for the niceties of living in pursuit of the main chance. He is free—free to swim or drown, free to bet all his life on "the big money," free to turn on the gas as a lost and beaten atom in the anonymity of his furnished hall-bedroom. . . . We have not as yet addressed ourselves to the task of building urban *communities,* in the social sense. . . . At point after point our culture plays down extensive, acute and subtle feeling. . . . And democracy, interpreted largely as the right to be free to take or leave the world about one and to acquire private property, has afforded little basis for deep common sentiment. . . . We must somehow manage to rewrite our institutions in terms of organized community of purpose.[39]

[37] G. Murphy: "The Research Task of Social Psychology." *Journal of Social Psychology, S.P.S.S.I. Bulletin,* 1939, 10, 107-120.
[38] L. Mumford: *The Culture of Cities,* pp. 7-8. Harcourt, Brace and Company, 1938.
[39] R. S. Lynd: *Knowledge for What?,* pp. 79, 80-81, 84, 85, 87. Princeton University Press, 1939.

Lynd also feels that we cheat ourselves by concentrating so much upon the achievement of financial success, for in such a quest so many fail, and even those who succeed discover that the narrowing of their interests has robbed them of numerous important satisfactions. We have not yet found out what institutions and what elements in our culture satisfy healthy human cravings and what do not. Lynd suggests that the social scientists "review our democratic assumptions in the light of what we now know about individual differences in intelligence and other personality traits and the degree to which such things are innate or culturally conditioned," analyze American culture to learn how democracy is working and how it might work, and then "chart the ways of remolding institutional behavior radically in the light of these findings." [40]

In contemplating schemes for social reconstruction, it is easy to embrace alluring panaceas that promise to end all our problems, but experience is bound to convince us that life is too complicated to allow for handy final solutions. Humanitarian employers have been often disillusioned in their attempts to improve the lot of their employees. The employer who wants to do the right thing by his workers builds them houses, provides recreational programs, inaugurates profit sharing, pensions, insurance, employee representation, and then finds, to his grief, that his employees are still unhappy. They feel the rent for their houses is too high; they want to choose their own form of recreation; they are annoyed because there are no profits to be shared when a depression comes along; they object to pensions and insurance because these provisions tie them to the plant and encourage discrimination against the older workers, and they resent being docked for their contributions; they discover that employee representation doesn't mean much because an aggressive representative is apt to get penalized and because a timid representative does not win any gains for the employees. When the various schemes have all collapsed and good will has failed to materialize, the kindly employer discovers his employees are more interested in *how* management does things for them than in *what* is done. Two things the worker cannot stand: regimentation and paternalism. If he suspects either, humanitarian efforts are wasted from the start.[41] The wise employer finds out ahead of time what his employees want and works out his plans accordingly.

[40] *Ibid.*, p. 216.

[41] See H. M. Somers: "Methods of Harmonizing Capital and Labor: Industrial Relations Programs," Chapter 17 in *Industrial Conflict: a Psychological Interpretation,* G. W. Hartmann and T. Newcomb, Editors. The Dryden Press, 1939.

The same care should be taken in planning our educational program. The schools should be reconstructed only after a careful survey of youth's needs. A beginning in this direction has been made by a committee of ten distinguished American educators appointed by the American Youth Commission to chart a new curriculum for high schools in the United States. The committee's investigation revealed the fact that modern high schools were busy preparing youth for white-collar careers, nonexistent for most of them. Thus the schools were succeeding only in making youth "grossly unprepared" for life. The committee proposed that high schools teach youth how to read, be good citizens, wives, husbands, keep their health, solve their personal and family problems. Above all, young people need to be taught how to work. "The ability to work steadily for eight hours is not a natural possession; it has to be acquired." Suggestions for a curriculum more adapted to youth's needs included the following proposals:

Let every pupil be taught to work with his hands, in school shop or home-making laboratory.
Let schools sponsor community work projects, such as cleanup campaigns.
Let schools and private employers collaborate in cooperative education, whereby pupils work part time for wages.
Let schools stimulate young people to invent jobs.[42]

Educational policy must be framed in terms of definite values based on a knowledge of human needs.

Americans believe that democracy is essential to the realization of human values. This conviction is based on the recognition that the democratic guarantees of religious freedom, free speech, freedom of the press, the right to assemble peaceably, the right to petition the government, the right to life, liberty, and property, are all aimed to assure the conditions most favorable to the fullest development of the individual. Under such a system a person has a say in the running of the government, an opportunity for education, access to information, a right to express his opinion—all guaranteed, with minor reservations such as the stipulation that he should not abuse his privileges by inciting sedition. Freedom of religion, freedom of citizenship, freedom of education—these are values we cherish. If we prize them enough, we will see to it that our economic life is brought into harmony with our belief in human freedom, for nothing is so inimical to religious, political, or educational freedom as economic chaos—as Europe has

---

[42] B. G. Graham *et al.: What the High Schools Ought to Teach.* American Council on Education, Washington, D.C. 1940.

so disastrously demonstrated. "We need to create for ourselves a new American wisdom—a wisdom about how we shall produce and distribute and enjoy the products of our ingenuity in such ways as will advance rather than obstruct the decent development of our life." [43] We must create an economic democracy if democracy as a political order is to survive.

"Democracy," asserts historian James Harvey Robinson, "may get its setbacks, may vanish temporarily, but rest assured no society will be permanently satisfactory unless it guarantees man some voice in the control of his actions and aspirations." [44]   Psychologists may step forward to second Robinson's judgment.   Psychiatrist Strecker, for example, expresses his opinion: "Among the extant political ideologies and practices, democracy comes closest to a fulfillment of mental hygiene ideals of mature and independent thinking." [45]   The Society for the Psychological Study of Social Issues states its position as follows:

We believe that the widest possible dispersion of verifiable factual information and of mature attitudes that rest upon this base will strengthen rather than weaken democracy as a social system.   There are many undesirable conditions in our American institutions; and the "way of life" to which this nation is verbally committed is something still to be achieved rather than considered as fully attained.   Nonetheless, the great virtue of democracy as contrasted to any form of dictatorship lies in its ability to assimilate criticism and to change accordingly.   A democratic society is not to be cherished solely because it harmonizes with our history and tradition, but because it is the only method of organizing human relations that permanently meets the major needs of all participants.   In this spirit we study the American people, their thinking, their emotions, their wise or foolish conduct, their desires and aspirations.   We shall seek to educate them to a higher level of self-knowledge for the sake of the emerging culture in which man may live more happily and freely than ever before.

While democracy is probably the best system for promoting human happiness, authorities agree that there are numerous respects in which we could reform our ways to gain more satisfaction for ourselves. There are still too many occasions for frustration, as minority groups in our midst could amply testify.   If we value our way of life, we will be ready to recognize the need of improving it so that the democracy

---

[43] H. A. Overstreet in a symposium on the topic, "How Can Philosophy and Religion Meet Today's Needs?"   *Bulletin of America's Town Meeting of the Air,* March 18, 1940.

[44] J. H. Robinson: *The Human Comedy,* p. 235.   Harper & Brothers, 1937.

[45] E. A. Strecker: *Beyond the Clinical Frontiers,* p. 180.   1940.

we treasure will deserve to be the "wave of the future." The surest way to guarantee its survival is to demonstrate its merit through the evidence of our own happy experience. Max Schoen has given expression to his faith in democracy:

It is a vicious social habit to classify high and low, noble and ignoble, thereby fixing the social worth of a human being by his occupation.

Because one is a physician, minister, engineer or teacher, he is held to be more deserving of honor and respect than is the barber, the plumber, street cleaner, or ditch digger. A plumber may be several times better than some physician is a physician, or a minister a minister, or professor a professor. By this false standard, one man is penalized for doing a good job and another is rewarded for being a failure.

This is the reason for the rush to higher vocations, with the result that many a promising butcher, instead of cutting steaks skilfully, often wields a surgeon's knife fatally. Many a promising hair-cutter makes a botch of cutting into the minds of youth in the classroom.

If some barbers would do as poor a job cutting hair as is done by some teachers and preachers, they would not last a month in their trade. Yet the barber is accepted socially as being, in the main, a utility or tool, thereby becoming a social slave, while the minister and teacher are respected as persons no matter how poorly one may preach and the other teach. . . .

Social stability depends on the recognition and the practice that it is the person who matters, and not the label. Before a person is a Jew or a Christian, he is a human being.

This is the principle on which the structure of American democracy was erected in theory, and it is this principle carried out in practice which is our guarantee that, while its natural foundations may be shaken, its walls will never crumble.[46]

We have yet to achieve a real democracy. Much remains to be done to attain such a goal.[47]

[46] Report at a meeting of the American Association for the Advancement of Science, June, 1941.
[47] The means of establishing industrial democracy will be treated in our Chapter 18, "Industry."

Chapter 5

THE UNEMPLOYMENT
OF INTELLIGENCE

INTELLIGENCE is usually conceived as the capacity to achieve a given end. The value of the end to be achieved is not taken into consideration. The merit of the goal should be examined, however, since the devotion of a keen mind to a stupid cause is a waste of talent, both for the individual and for society. Whether the end is worth while may be as important as the amount of ability needed for its attainment.

I. INTELLIGENCE AND VALUES

The intelligent person, we may assume, should care about things that are most worth while—at least, in so far as he is intelligent, he should. A wise discrimination should be manifest in his judgment of relative values. Measuring ourselves with this criterion in mind, we may find ourselves often sadly deficient. Our shortcomings we excuse by blaming our fellowmen. Certainly the fear of being different is partly responsible for the tendency in each one of us to approximate the lowest common denominator of intelligence in our conduct.

The measurement of intelligence is an important task which the psychologists have performed very well. The effective application of what intelligence we have is even more important. It makes a lot of difference to us as social beings what we think about, what sorts of persons we revere, what we care enough about to work for. The more we consider this thesis, the more convinced we become that intelligent living depends upon the devotion of our energies to ends that are worth while. In the preceding chapter, we studied how the art of living hinges upon a person's sense of values. Our attention will now be centered on the social significance implied in the goals that enlist our devotion. It will become apparent, in the course of our discussion of the relation between intelligence and values, that much of our social unhappiness is due to the fact that we dissipate our strength in accomplishing purposes that do not really matter, with the result that we have little energy left over to attack the problems that are most vital to our welfare. The consequent waste of intelligence is appalling. The thought of what society could be like if we all used our minds more fully and for better purposes should encourage us to give these problems our most careful consideration.

An investigation of college students, conducted by Tuttle, revealed no significant relationship between intelligence quotients—or college grades—and social concern. This finding is interpreted to mean that a high degree of intelligence is no guarantee of a high degree of social-mindedness and that the acquisition of information may proceed without any concomitant growth in social attitudes. Tuttle became interested in following up this line of research when he attempted unsuccessfully to formulate a program of character-building based upon data collected from 275 college executives. He had asked them to describe situations and procedures which they had found effective in cultivating "social-mindedness." The replies were characterized by a lack of unanimity. Failing to get the light he wanted from this source, Tuttle made a study of 400 freshmen in four selected colleges to determine the correlation between all measurable campus agencies and gains in social attitudes. He computed the degree of social concern at the beginning of the freshman year and the degree attained by the end of the year. The larger gains in social-mindedness were noted among those who read progressive magazines, those who worked to help pay their way through college, those who participated in off-campus service projects, and those who enrolled with certain staff members. Tuttle concludes from his evidence that more attention to the cultivation of social concern is needed in the college curriculum, that special agencies should perhaps be developed to see to it that this aspect of education is adequately taken care of.[1] Much might be done to develop a skill for discriminating between values. Here is an important opportunity we have neglected too long.

The direction of intelligence to useful ends should be one of our foremost considerations, as Jastrow points out in the *Betrayal of Intelligence,* when he says:

Everyone above the moronic level has, in John Erskine's phrase, "the moral obligation to be intelligent"—as intelligent as one's endowment permits. Brains cannot be exchanged; but good, bad or indifferent, they can be tuned in on the wave-lengths of sapience. . . .

There are nearly as many good minds gone wrong as there are poor minds.

[1] See H. S. Tuttle: "Cultivating Social Motives." *Journal of Higher Education,* 1937, 8, 321-328.

. . . Sapience must have a conscience. The sad side of social history is the fact that superior brains have so often been directed to exploitation—exploitation of the dull by the sharp, of the foolish by the wise, of the ignorant by the learned. . . . The need of the hour is the better employment of mind.[2]

The failure of much of our education to provide the citizen, dull or bright, with an intelligent sense of values is a serious defect in our society, as we shall observe when we turn to the evidence. This neglect reduces our chance for happiness in a myriad of ways.

II. EGOISM AND THE LACK OF SOCIAL-MINDEDNESS

There has been a long controversy among students of human nature as to whether man is essentially a selfish creature occupied exclusively with the preservation of his own well-being or is just as essentially a social creature with an inherent inclination to interest himself in the welfare of his fellows.

A. Is Man Social by Nature?

Was Aristotle correct when he insisted that man is social by nature? Does the human being just naturally seek to promote the common welfare? Or is man an egoist?

Thomas Hobbes stands out as one of the most enthusiastic sponsors of the egoistic theory of behavior. "That atheist Hobbes," as he was contemptuously called by some of his contemporaries, wrote *The Leviathan* (1651) to expound his view. Man, he says in that book, is always looking out for himself. Then why does the individual submit to limitations on his self-seeking as a member of society? There is nothing in man's native tendencies to account for such an acceptance of restrictions. The natural state of mankind is *bellum omnium contra omnes,* a state in which everybody is fighting everybody else. A society based on continual warfare among its individual members could not survive. It would be in the same economic "fix" as the community in which each family is reputed to have supported itself by taking in another family's washing. Endless war would defeat its own end. Consequently, each individual agrees to respect the other man's wants in return for a like guarantee from him. Since man is an egoist and regards his fellows as like unto himself, he knows that such promises mean nothing until some power is set up to enforce the

---

[2] J. Jastrow: *The Betrayal of Intelligence*, pp. 15, 18, 20. Greenberg: Publisher, 1938. See J. Erskine: "The Moral Obligation to be Intelligent," in *American Character and Other Essays.* 1927.

contracts to which the several parties have agreed.   Thus the state is set up and "rights" are established.

According to Hobbes' theory human association is based primarily on mutual fear.   There is no recognition of positive mutual attraction.   Hobbes fails to allow for congeniality.   Human beings may enjoy one another's company, just for the sake of being together.   A lonely wife whose husband was away during the war, reported that "sitting home and reading when there is a man opposite you reading, too, is completely different from sitting by yourself.   It's the same with resting, listening to the radio, knitting, and all the other things included in doing nothing with someone."   Most of us feel that love is as fundamental as fear.   Hobbes has exaggerated the picture to give his thesis a more striking effect.   The result is a caricature rather than an accurate description of human nature.

Felix Alexandre LeDantec has written a more modern version of Hobbes' theory in his *L'Egoïsme, Base de Toute Société* (1911).   Self-interest, he insists, is the basic fact in human nature and hence in society.   People would not join together were it not considered advisable to do so for defense against a common enemy.   The ego, unfortunately, is deformed by the influences of the life in common.   Under the conditions imposed by communal living a man cannot be himself.   Beverley Nichols has expressed this same thought, in explaining why he avoids marriage:

I can go when and where I want. . . .   The other day I went to Paris on my way to Salzburg.   Within twenty-four hours I was speeding in somebody else's car to Biarritz.   And in the end we arrived at Juan-les-Pins.   My companion was another bachelor, and nobody but a bachelor could have been so irresponsible.

If I choose, I can get on board a steamer tomorrow and sail to Hawaii and start a trade in illicit drugs.   I can grow a beard and screech anarchy in Hyde Park.   I can stay in bed and eat macaroons.   I can fill the house with monkeys.   I can keep goldfish in the bath.   I can wear sandals.

In other words, I can "be myself," as the Americans say.   No married man can ever "be himself" unless he is so overbearing that his wife is a mere obedient shadow.

You are going to tell me that "if everybody thought as I did the world would cease altogether, and humanity would perish from the face of the earth."

To which I can only reply, "Why not?"

If man is inherently selfish and individualistic, then certainly the demands of married life deform his ego in lamentable ways; if, however, man is by nature inclined to seek a mate and to reproduce his kind, then he is not deformed in being socialized by the rigors of family life —he is merely "coming into his own." If man is social by nature, society provides the medium through which he achieves self-realization. LeDantec, though, feels otherwise, and, proceeding from his premise that man is an out and out egoist, he is consistent in his conclusion that social life "cramps his style."

Most people are so deformed by moral codes that they are afraid to "be themselves." They stick in the conventional ruts because they lack the courage to defy the ethical demands imposed upon them. "Good people" are cowards, according to LeDantec. Mr. Dooley once confessed: "When I give a tip, 'tis not because I want to, but because I am afraid of what the waiter will think. It takes a strong man to be mean." Not many of us are strong enough. We succumb to the dictates of law and religion which, LeDantec says, represent unattainable transcendental ideals. These ideals become absolute. They are beyond examination or reevaluation. It is the absoluteness of such demands upon the individual that deforms the ego so irresistibly.

As egoism is the basis of society, so hypocrisy is its keystone, LeDantec maintains. Civilization has only veneered the cave man underneath. Socialization, therefore, is a poor sham. Being polite means being a liar: agreeing, for example, that the bride looked "simply lovely" when actually she was a "sight." If the society columns told the truth, an account of some wedding might read like this:

Billy H—— and Miss Alice L—— were married at noon Monday, at the home of the bride's parents, Mr. and Mrs. P. D. L——, Rev. M. L. G—— officiating.

The groom is a popular young bum who hasn't done a lick of work since he got shipped home in the middle of his junior year at college. He manages to dress well and keeps a supply of spending money because his dad is a soft-hearted old fool who takes his bad checks instead of letting him go to jail where he belongs.

The bride is a skinny, fast little idiot who has been kissed by every boy in town since she was twelve years old. She paints like a Sioux Indian, smokes cigarettes in secret and drinks mean corn liquor when she is out joy-riding in her dad's car at night. She doesn't know how to sew, cook, or keep house.

The house was newly plastered for the wedding and the exterior newly painted, thus appropriately carrying out the decorative scheme for the groom who was newly plastered and the bride who was newly painted.

The bride wore some kind of a white thing that left most of her legs sticking out at one end and her bony upper structure sticking out at the other. The young couple will make their home at the bride's parents, which means they will sponge upon the old man until he dies and then she will take in washing.

Postscript—This may be the last issue of the *Tribune* but my life ambition has been fulfilled. Now that it is done, death where is thy sting? [3]

What it would mean to speak the truth regardless of the costs is shown by the contrast between two letters written to a counselor. They speak for themselves:

I am a girl liked by many and popular in my own home town, but I have an ugly and selfish disposition. No person knows it but myself, as I conceal it in every possible way so far as others are concerned. Yet I do not readily sympathize with or share the joy of my friends and relatives, and when I say pleasant things to them my friends think I am sincere, but down in my heart I know I am not. This is a very unpleasant sort of character to have, and I would greatly appreciate any help you can give me to change it.

———————

I try under all circumstances to tell the truth, and by doing so I find myself in a bad plight. I have not hesitated, when asked for my opinion of others, to say exactly what I thought. As a consequence many whose friendship I desire to retain now shun me and I am gradually getting into a state of isolation. Would you advise me to stop telling the truth?

"Good breeding," said Mark Twain, "consists in concealing how much we think of ourselves and how little we think of the other person." Social intercourse seems to demand some hypocrisy. If people were entirely free with their honest opinions, social life would degenerate into internecine chaos.

The question as to whether social behavior is invariably hypocritical is one that cannot be answered by evidence or argument. Your conviction on the matter will be determined largely by your temperament. Some people are inclined to believe the worst of their fellows while others are disposed to look on the brighter side. The cynic is apt to feel that socialization is all sham.

"Do you know," complains a woman-hater, "that women never go into politics from lofty, patriotic motives, but go into politics to get their names into the newspapers? There are few sadder sights than to see women hobbling on high-heeled shoes up to the legislative bodies, dressed so as to show their bosoms and their bunions, while they clamor for the passage of laws the

[3] From the Fountain Inn (S.C.) *Tribune*, January, 1930. Robert Quillen, Editor and Publisher.

purport and effect of which they have not the mental capacity even faintly to comprehend?"

The "nothing but" interpretation of human motives is a very common fallacy in psychologizing: certain actions, so the theory goes, are prompted by *nothing but* ambition, greed, or some other selfish desire. Human nature is too complicated to fit such an oversimplified description. How can anyone assert dogmatically that women go into politics just to get their names in the papers? Selfishness there is in our human nature but that does not tell the whole story. Man must become socialized, no matter how individualistic he may be to start with, in order to exist happily with his fellows. There are generous impulses in all of us, along with the meaner motives, and they must be recognized in the complete picture of the human being. It would be erroneous to say that man is *nothing but* kind, and just as untrue to maintain that man is *nothing but* selfish. Certain it is that original nature needs to be modified through socialization.

There are occasions when human beings resort to delusions of altruism to conceal from themselves their own egoistic purposes. Self-interest is often an important incentive even in the motivation of our social activities. A frank recognition of our own selfish desires would probably be conducive to better mental health and a saner society. Being honest with ourselves does not mean that we should see only our baser natures but rather that we should get a more adequate picture of ourselves, envisaging how far we have already gone toward becoming socially conscious and how much further we can go for our own good as social beings. Man will become adequately socialized when he comes to realize that the most intelligent egoism involves the recognition of social needs—for selfishness can be enlightened.

B. Short-sighted Egocentrism

The intelligent person will presumably realize that his own happiness is inevitably interwoven with the happiness of his fellows. The stupid person is apt to be concerned only with his own welfare, ignorant of the fact that an individual cannot live by himself, for himself, to himself satisfactorily in a society founded on the principle of living together and struggling together for survival. Egocentrism is foolish because it involves a denial of the real community of our interests; it is short-sighted because it is costly to the individual himself in the long run. Our egocentric habits function as a serious detriment to our welfare, as Ogburn asserts:

Perhaps the psychological factor underlying the largest number of social problems is selfishness. . . . A highly developed accumulation of material culture such as we have in modern society provides a wonderful opportunity for an apparently ruthless exploitation of selfish interests.[4]

A small boy exemplified a spirit that is all too prevalent. His mother had instructed him that gambling is wrong. A few days later she overheard him saying that he had been playing marbles. Gently she suggested that she hoped he had not been playing for keeps. "Oh, don't worry, Mother," he explained, "I aways win."

We are lacking in social-mindedness when we do not pause to consider the social consequences of our deeds.[5] Some people become so absorbed in the task of earning a living that they do not see beyond their incomes to the bearing their work may have upon the lives of others. A man's occupation influences his own set of values, as we have noted; how he makes his money also affects other persons, often in ways so subtle as to escape his notice. Important social values centered in the well-being of other people may have been sacrificed by an individual in the process of "getting ahead." This failure to appreciate the social implications of the job is responsible for some of the ills we blame on "the inevitability of the natural course of events." It is time for us to discover for ourselves that we build our own unhappiness in so far as we fail to apply intelligence to beneficial objectives. Let us see how the lack of social-mindedness operates at times to our disadvantage in business, in law, and in medicine.

1. BUSINESS

One of our major industries is the motion picture industry. Pictures are produced with an eye to box-office receipts, not with an eye to the effects they may have on their audiences. Emotions are aroused, but there is no particular concern for the kinds of emotions. Pictures suitable only for adults are shown to children, with damaging effects, frequently, upon their personalities, as investigators found in the studies made of *Motion Pictures and Youth* (1933), a project sponsored by the Payne Fund. Some of the pictures, of course, are not even suitable for adults. But with regard to children, especially, Mortimer Adler interprets the predominance of common, and even of

---

[4] W. F. Ogburn: *Social Change*, pp. 334-335. 1922.
[5] Social-mindedness is a phase of social consciousness. This relation will be explored further in Chapter 11, "Social Consciousness: Morale."

expert, opinion as agreeing that motion pictures have a somewhat undesirable influence.[6]

The movies are first, last, and all the time a business, according to
Howard S. Cullman, manager of a large New York film theater, who
discussed the question as to whether movies are an art before a group
at New York University. Any aesthetic values they may contain, he
explained, are unimportant and usually accidental. The screen aims
to please the masses. Her sister Muses are the comic strip, the pulp
magazines, the radio and all other forms of entertainment based on
"democratic" rather than aesthetic principles. Cullman stated that
he and his fellow exhibitors keep two essential factors in mind in selecting their pictures: first, that, to the average American, thinking is
the direct antithesis of entertainment; and, second, that successful mass
entertainment depends on emotional excitation of some kind, usually
of the primary passions of love, fear, hate, and pity.[7] This statement
is a frank admission by one man in the business, that the motion picture industry does not recognize its educational and social responsibilities.

"Business is business" seems to be the code, too, which inspired the
brewers to initiate a campaign in 1937 for stepping up sales. Aroused
by an impending decline in profits, they banded together, pooled
their collective resources, and hired public relations experts to promote their products. In the days before Prohibition, according to
the propaganda distributed in behalf of the brewers, the average family had spent much of its time, especially on Sundays, at home drinking beer. Even when the folks made a holiday trip to some resort,
the "principal pleasure for the elders consisted in sitting quietly on
some beach or in some beer garden and there taking ease and drinking beer at leisure." But in the years since then automobiles, golf,
radios, and movies have changed all this. Instead of sitting down
quietly and tending to the business of drinking beer, we are informed
by the brewers' propagandists, the American people, under peacetime
conditions, gad about the highways, spending money for gasoline
that should be devoted to beer, or rushing to the movies, or listening to the radio, or playing golf. And, of course, a man cannot
drink his way around the links; hence, that is a lot of time diverted
from the main thing, getting enough beer. "All of these things are
contrary to the spirit of beer. Constant action, travel, movement, are
out of harmony with a beverage which is conducive to relaxation,

---

[6] See M. J. Adler: *Art and Prudence.* 1937.

[7] Summarized in an editorial in the Boston *Herald,* January 24, 1936.

quiet, and even tempo." Here is a real problem. What is the answer? After much thought, the solution was arrived at. "If the automobile and gasoline are competitors to beer, why not make the automobile trip a time when beer is to be consumed? It would require
but a little urgence on the part of the brewing industry to get the
major manufacturers of cars to include refrigeration among the facilities offered in the most modern models. . . . A traveling ice-box
. . . snuggled under the back seat or placed in the rear compartment
. . . could provide for bottled beer. . . . The time might come when
the movie patron could enjoy his favorite screen star while sipping a
glass of beer at his seat." A collapsible seat arm would make this
achievement possible. As for the radio fan, it would be easy for him
to take care of his quota of beer while relaxing beside his set, thus
providing a picture which might be regarded as "just perfect from the
brewing standpoint. . . . In a word, the leisure moments of our average Americans should be inextricably intertwined with beer." [8] If
we are all intertwined with beer, what is going to become of the manufacturers of soft drinks? How can we find enough room for our
quota of spaghetti, fruit juices, and yeast cakes?

This preoccupation with money-making regardless of whether the
results are beneficial or detrimental to the welfare of the people who
are affected by it, is all too characteristic of business ethics in practice,
not only in the movie industry and the brewing industry but in other
lines as well. There is a tendency, too, for private enterprise, in many
cases, to go along as if it were indeed "private," unaware of the need
for working together with other enterprises directly or indirectly related to its own endeavors. In line with this observation, some authorities feel that businessmen would better their own lot considerably if they would open their minds to a recognition of the fact that
individualism must give way to cooperation.[9] Management in some
instances has discovered economic salvation in combining efforts with
union representatives to cut costs. Threatened with a wage cut, the
employees in a steel mill proposed, instead of a strike, a Union Shop
Betterment Committee to work with the management in improving
production methods. Suggestions from the Union members resulted
in substantial savings, and the business was rescued from collapse.[10]

---

[8] See F. Eastman: "Missionary for the Brewers." *Christian Century*, February 19,
1936.
[9] See Chapter 18 of this present volume, "Industry."
[10] See H. J. Ruttenberg: "The Fruits of Industrial Peace." *Harvard Business Review*, Spring, 1940. Condensed in the *Reader's Digest*, May, 1940.

Employers and employees must eventually come to appreciate the fact that they share a common fate, standing to win or lose together.

It is among the business leaders of the nation, however, that the real need exists for social-mindedness. In a notable address to the American Management Council, William Hard warned the businessmen of America that they will have to lead the way in a cooperation that will ensure prosperity for all economic groups—or else the government will be forced to intervene more and more in the public interest. Charging that businessmen had failed to assume the responsibility of intelligent leadership, he asserted that farmers, labor leaders, and organized consumers were getting the better of the businessmen, by going to Washington to secure "relief" through "regulation." Representatives of these various groups were turning to the government for remedy because businessmen, standing their ground on the excuse of defending "individualism," refused to work with them in an effort to solve their common problems. Businessmen, according to Hard, no longer operate as *individuals* themselves, but through corporations and trade associations; then they have the "nerve" to tell other groups that they should not organize to get what they want. Mr. Hard did not mince words:

> You men who manage American business—and you alone—can save our private economic system, and you don't.
>
> You are the very center of it. It is in the form of a square. The four sides are Investment, Agriculture, Labor, the Consumers. You are the central link through which they are united. I mean, you could be. You could be the vitalizing element in our Economic Union.
>
> Why not work toward such a union? Economic society today is a lot of individuals gathered together into a living whole. When its parts start quarreling among themselves, government has to step in and restore order. The only way to prevent the governmental intervention is to be first in preventing the quarrels.
>
> That is why I am imagining an Economic Congress. . . . Think this over: "I get ahead through *me*" is dead. The motto for your walls is "I get ahead through *us*." [11]

2. THE LEGAL PROFESSION

The legal profession, on the whole, is behind the times in the recognition of its social obligations. Law, for many, becomes simply a means of livelihood. The money-making motive blinds the lawyer, in

[11] W. Hard: "We Get Together—or Else." An address to the American Management Council, condensed in the *Reader's Digest*, June, 1940.

many instances, to his social responsibilities. The rise of the university law school, from the 1870's, paralleled the rise of the great corporations and the tremendous expansion of American industry. The bar entered on a new phase of development and the law schools went with it. For the first time in our history it was taken for granted that the bar was the servant of commerce, industry, and finance. It became possible for lawyers to amass substantial fortunes. As the bar came to see the law as a means of making money, law students inevitably came to see it in the same light. If the aim of most lawyers is financial success, and if the best way of achieving it is guile, students are not likely to be much interested in a course of study resting on the notion that the law is a learned profession, and that a university is a place for the pursuit of truth and the cultivation of the intellectual virtues. So says President Hutchins of the University of Chicago, former Dean of the Yale Law School. He is not referring, he explains, merely to shysters and ambulance chasers, but to the more respected members of the bar as well.

Hutchins reiterated this warning in an address on legal education, before the American Bar Association, in which he urged the lawyers to "do something pretty promptly" if they wished to "command sufficient respect to impose on the country their conception of justice." He went on to say:

If they (the lawyers) continue to accept what is done as the standard of what to do; if they continue to seek large fees under the impression that they are the common good; if legal ethics mean little more than a protective tariff in favor of the bar; if we are regarded as the spokesmen of special privilege; if our chief claim to public admiration is our agility in making the worse cause appear the better, then we are lost; then we cannot hope to make the community accept our moral leadership.[12]

Training in the social psychology of law has been strongly advocated by Britt. His counsel in this matter is especially worth heeding since he speaks as a lawyer and as a psychologist, and as one who has given a course for law students on the "Social Psychology of Law." Britt explains the value of such training:

Law students get a one-sided view of the law, simply as a profession to be practiced—with little or no realization of the sociological effects of the law and courts in operation, or of the psychological assumptions underlying various legal theories. . . .

[12] Boston *Herald,* September 30, 1937.

A thorough background in the social sciences is excellent training for the work of the law school . . . in government, economics, history, the natural sciences, psychology, sociology, and anthropology. . . .

Room (in the law school curriculum) must be made for a study of the cultural aspects of law. This includes the place of law and custom in society, the nature of sanctions, the basis of authority, the character of primitive law, the application of the social codes to individual conduct. . . .

Rather than a mere emphasis on what the established "rules" of the law are, attention is given to the study of law as a social institution. This means the study of how legal doctrines and institutions actually work, especially in our own society. . . .

A selection is made of only those particular phases and materials of sociology and psychology which are also of a legal nature or have a bearing on the law. A few examples:

> Domestic relations of the family
> Divorce
> Social control
> Social change and legal change
> Testimonial qualifications of witnesses
> The psychology of testimony
> The judging process
> Punishment
> Mental and emotional disturbances
> Guilt

The attempt is made . . . to give an initial understanding of the legal system . . . and of the problems and responsibilities of the law practitioner—always pointing out the sociological and psychological implications. . . .[13]

A seven-year law course has been instituted at Harvard in an effort to train lawyers who will know their law and also the social implications of their profession. Dean Landis explains the purpose of this new program:

The increased complexity of our social and economic order has expanded private law and enlarged greatly the field of public law. Modern industrial society calls for government to exert a greater influence in the ordering of affairs. These changes demand the mastering of new techniques and new disciplines by any student who chooses to pursue the law as a calling rather than as a trade. . . .

A lawyer isn't hampered by education. Lawyers, whatever their political demands are, will be able to represent the interests of their clients better if they understand what's going on about them.[14]

[13] S. H. Britt: "The Social Psychology of Law." *Illinois Law Review*, 1940, 34, 802-811.
[14] Boston *Sunday Herald*, September 15, 1940.

Instead of the usual pattern of four years of college and three years of law school, Harvard's seven-year plan calls for three years of study in ordinary college courses, two years at straight law, and two years of law combined with specialized study of government and economics. The plan has two major features: (1) of the 16 courses studied in the first three years, nine are prescribed, ensuring the student a broad knowledge of history, social sciences, English literature, a foreign language, and a natural science; (2) a specialized study of government and economics is reserved until two years of law have been mastered. The intensive study of the social sciences is saved until the end of the seven-year course, so the student will have the background and the maturity to appreciate the relationships between his specialty, the law, and the social factors which are affected by our legal institutions.

Some investigators in the field of social science have called attention to the role of the lawyer in our society, and the picture is not a flattering one. Harold J. Laski finds that the most influential type of American lawyer is the corporation lawyer, the legal strategist of high finance, who spends a good part of his time in protecting the wealthy from the "deleterious" consequences of social legislation.[15] In that service he, too, becomes rich. His reward is a reflection of his success in preserving his clients; and his success in this capacity is incompatible with the public good. The evidence for this assertion is bountiful in the history of the public utilities, the investment banks, and the oil industry. The Securities Act was intended to protect the public from the labyrinthine ingenuities of the Wall Street lawyer. The Federal Trade Commission is largely concerned with this same objective. The corporation lawyer, despite these bothersome measures to restrain him, still finds time to invent, for the rich, ways and means of avoiding the income tax. A famous man of wealth once said to his legal advisor: "What I like about you is that other lawyers tell me what I can't do, while you tell me how to do what I want to do." This sort of lawyer is not so crude as to break the law. Rather he devotes his skill to finding ways around the law of which, to the public detriment, his clients can take advantage. Under his guidance the law is bent to the service of those who control the financial power of society. Ultimately, if he excels in his labors, he is promoted to the bench, where he merely acts for his clients from the bench instead of advising them in the chambers. It is not that he is avowedly dishonest. It is simply that he has become unconsciously imbued with what Justice Holmes called

---

[15] See B. R. Twiss: *Lawyers and the Constitution: How Laissez Faire Came to the Supreme Court.* 1942.

"inarticulate major premises" in favor of property. The commercialization of the legal profession has rendered it dependent upon the business empire. With its loss of independence has gone also any profound social consciousness it may once have professed.[16]

The conservatism of the lawyer is due in part to the fact that he is involved in protecting persons with property.[17] Associating as he does with persons of means, it is natural for the barrister to operate in collusion with the financial interests who are his clients. Calvert Magruder of the Harvard Law School faculty has called attention to this role of the lawyer:

Much of the best brains of the legal profession has been spent on financial manipulations of the corporate device—all the familiar paraphernalia of pyramided holding companies, subsidiaries, security affiliates, mergers, non-voting stock, investment trusts—too often at the behest of financial adventurers who with a comparatively small investment thereby have obtained control of vast pools of money contributed by the public and control of basic industries. Whatever else you may say, lawyers certainly have not been (beneficent) leaders here; they have been hired agents of the supposed financial geniuses who have reached out for power, with scant attention to the social implications of their policies.[18]

The late Chief Justice Harlan F. Stone, also noted this lack of social conscience in the legal profession. He said:

When we know the significant facts in the professional life of the lawyers of the present generation and appraise them in the light of the altered world in which we live, we shall better understand how it is that a bar which has done so much to develop and refine the technique of business organization, to provide skillfully devised methods for financing industry, which has guided a world-wide commercial expansion, has done relatively so little to remedy the evils of the investment market; so little to adapt the fiduciary principle of Nineteenth-century equity to Twentieth-century business practices; so little to improve the functioning of the administrative mechanisms which modern government sets up to prevent abuses; so little to make law more readily available as an instrument of justice to the common man. . . . There is little to suggest that the bar has yet recognized that it must bear some burden

[16] See H. J. Laski: "The Decline of the Professions." *Harper's Magazine*, November, 1935.

[17] See J. M. Williams: *Principles of Social Psychology*, Chapter 16, "The Conflict of Interests in the Legal Profession." 1922. The conservative habits of the lawyer will be discussed in the chapter on "Custom" (Chapter 13).

[18] Quoted by F. Lundberg in an article entitled "The Legal Profession: a Social Phenomenon." *Harper's Magazine*, December, 1938.

of responsibility for these evils. But when we know and face the facts we shall have to acknowledge that such departures from the fiduciary principle do not usually occur without the active assistance of some member of our profession, and that their increasing occurrence would have been impossible but for the complaisance of a bar too absorbed in the workaday care of private interests to take account of these events of profound import or to sound the warning that the profession looks askance upon these, as things that "are not done." [19]

Working as he does with the basic rules that govern society, the lawyer is in a peculiarly favorable position to promote the enforcement of the rules—or to circumvent them. Knowledge of the rules, says Lundberg, "has a different effect upon different members of the profession. Some few become impressed by their social responsibility; others—probably the majority—are enabled to see how the facts can be bent to their own uses. They discover loopholes in the law, but instead of bringing them to the attention of the legislature, they go to someone in a position to profit by their discoveries." [20]

The conservative attitude of the legal profession is exemplified in the furor that broke loose when President Wilson nominated Louis D. Brandeis to the Supreme Court in 1916. Every living former president of the American Bar Association signed a statement declaring him unfit for judicial office. A former President of the United States, William Howard Taft, headed the protest registered by the legal profession. Why all the resistance? "It was the record which Mr. Brandeis had made as a crusader for public rights in a famous list of legal contests that made his elevation anathema to the conservatives of the pre-war era. He had fought the traction interests in Boston, the utilities in that same city, the New York, New Haven and Hartford Railroad, the Equitable Life Assurance Society. He had upheld the constitutionality of the Oregon minimum wage law for women, and he had fought the attempt of the railroads to secure increased rates from the Interstate Commerce Commission." [21] This "monster" who opposed the concentration of power in business monopolies or in governmental agencies, because he saw in such concentration a threat to personal and economic liberty, turned out, despite all the criticisms

---

[19] Quoted, *ibid.* For a description of some of the methods the lawyers use in lining their own pockets, see Thurman Arnold's accounts in his book, *The Folklore of Capitalism*, especially Chapter 10, "The Ritual of Corporate Reorganization." 1937.

[20] Lundberg: *loc. cit.*

[21] Editorial in the *Christian Century*, February 22, 1939.

of his supposed incompetence, to be one of the most able and respected Justices of the Supreme Court.

The legal profession does not devote itself to the promotion of justice, Lundberg charges. Aside from the fact that a large percentage of the people cannot get justice through the courts because they cannot pay for legal services—"only through the application in the courts does the law have life and force" [22]—Lundberg indicts the lawyers for failing to fulfill their proper role as champions of justice:

> The causes of injustice are many, and some will say that the legal profession is not to blame for them. But the legal profession in theory is supposed to acquaint society with the causes of injustice in order that they may be removed. The legal profession has not been given its position by society, nor do its spokesmen say it has, simply to serve private clients who are able to pay. It has higher duty, the duty to combat the general causes of injustice. This duty it has pretty carefully shirked. Outstanding individuals, like Louis D. Brandeis before he ascended the bench, seriously accepted this duty and this responsibility. But that such individuals have contravened the desires of the bar as a whole has been shown by the consistent organized opposition offered to them by the most eminent lawyers. The nomination of Mr. Brandeis to the Supreme Court, it may be recalled, met with denunciation from the leaders of the profession; and the late Robert M. LaFollette, who as a public prosecutor in Wisconsin was active in bringing to light the misdeeds of the railroads, was similarly denounced by his brethren at the bar.[23]

The lawyer succeeds in evading his responsibility in securing justice by resorting to a mystical metaphysics which obscures the issues under consideration, by taking refuge in concepts which are not susceptible to empirical verification. "Legal concepts (for example, *corporations* or *property rights*)," says Felix S. Cohen, "are supernatural entities which do not have a verifiable existence except for the eyes of faith. *Rules of law,* which refer to these legal concepts, are not descriptions of empirical social facts (such as the customs of men or the customs of judges) nor yet statements of moral ideals, but rather theorems in an independent system. It follows that a *legal argument* can never be refuted by a moral principle nor yet by an empirical fact. Jurisprudence, then, as an autonomous system of legal concepts, rules, and arguments, must be independent both of ethics and of such pos-

---

[22] See R. H. Smith: *Justice and the Poor.* Published by the Carnegie Foundation. 1919.

[23] From F. Lundberg: "The Priesthood of the Law." *Harper's Magazine,* April, 1939.

itive sciences as economics or psychology. In effect, it is a special branch of the science of transcendental nonsense." [24] We look to the lawyers for light to clarify our problems, and we get darkness.

SICKNESS COSTS FALL UNEVENLY

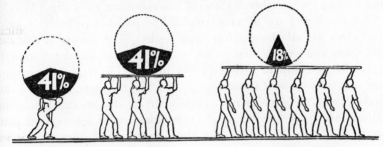

10% of families
BEAR 41%
OF COSTS

32%
BEAR 41%

58%
BEAR ONLY 18%

INCOME AND PHYSICIANS' CALLS

PHYSICIANS' CALLS

INCOME

UNDER $2000

$2000-$5000

$5000-$10,000

$10,000 & OVER

Each symbol represents one call per year per person

From Public Affairs Pamphlet No. 10, Revised. 1940. (Courtesy, Public Affairs Committee, Inc., New York.)

3. THE MEDICAL PROFESSION

We have pointed out, largely by quoting the commentaries of lawyers on their own profession, that the average lawyer is not adequately trained to appreciate the social responsibilities that go with his calling; the same deficiency in social consciousness is prevalent among the members of the medical profession. Doctors, on the whole, may be well grounded in medicine but many of them are still backward in seeing the need for developing more efficient means of distributing medical care. People cannot postpone their illnesses while the doctors rest contented with a fee-for-service system which has demon-

[24] F. S. Cohen: "Transcendental Nonsense and the Functional Approach." *Columbia Law Review,* June, 1935.

strated its inadequacy. The figures speak for themselves, some 28
volumes of them compiled by the Committee on the Costs of Medical
Care. These findings, along with other facts, have been condensed in
a Public Affairs pamphlet entitled "Doctors, Dollars, and Disease." [25]
Sickness costs fall unevenly. People need care; doctors need patients.
They cannot get together because of the economic difficulty. Would
it work out better for all concerned if the patients collectively paid
the doctors flat salaries to keep them well? "The answer is that we
don't know and won't unless we are willing to try at least a few experiments with new ways of paying doctors' bills." The facts indicate that
some new arrangement should be given a try, for more than half the
avoidable deaths of mothers at childbirth are due to deficiencies of
medical care; only one dollar of every thirty spent for medical care
goes to public health services for the prevention of disease. Under
our present setup "the practice of medicine cannot keep pace with
the science of medicine." Proponents of group practice feel that it
can be superior to private practice in providing expert care—specialists and expensive equipment—at a price patients can afford to pay.

The sociology of medical practice should be a fundamental phase
of the medical school course. Sigerist, world authority on the history
of medicine, has given his attention to developing such a course at
Johns Hopkins on "Medicine and Its Relations to Society." "To Dr.
Sigerist . . . medicine is not only a science whose triumphs are technical improvements, but a service whose success is measured by the
ability of a small group of men to make mankind's life more livable.
Even in his first enthusiasm over the United States, Dr. Sigerist felt
medical care was unevenly distributed, that physicians had not yet
found their proper place in a complex new society. . . . A No. 1
Medical Historian, he is convinced that history spirals toward socialization. . . ." [26] He asserts that state control of medicine is not
a radical departure. In support of this contention, he points out that
more than 60 per cent of all hospital beds are owned and operated by
the Government, that the duties of the Public Health Service have expanded to include care for cases of tuberculosis, blindness, and the
like. Persons who say that salaried doctors would lose their incentive
are insulting the profession, Sigerist charges. Doctors on salary, he
predicts, would be more competent because they would have time and
money for frequent periods of postgraduate training; the relationship

---

[25] Prepared by William Trufant Foster.
[26] *Time*, January 30, 1939. See H. E. Sigerist: *Medicine and Human Welfare.*
1941.

between physician and patient would be more human, once the money question was removed; socialization need not lower standards of medical care.

Another authority on the history of medicine, J. P. Warbasse, sees the need for training in "Medical Sociology" as a means of helping the doctor to attain a broader view of his profession, to achieve better harmony with his colleagues, to treat his patients more effectively, to get more satisfaction out of his practice. Ways and means are considered for promoting the mutual interests of the doctor and the patient, and it is suggested that things might be arranged so that it would be to the advantage of the doctor to prevent sickness, to cure the patient sooner, to operate less frequently. Public health is not just a medical question; it involves issues both social and economic. The successful doctor must learn to cooperate with the sanitarian, the nurse, the chemist, the engineer, the statistician, the social executive. Health insurance is coming, Warbasse predicts, because socialization is the answer to a real need, just as public education came into being in response to popular demand. The medical profession cannot stop it, but they can guide it if they wake up in time. It is important to note that socialization of medicine does not necessitate political control. This is a significant point because the opponents of socialization resort to this charge as a means of discrediting the idea with the public.[27]

The American Foundation wrote to representative medical men all over the country asking them to express their opinions about the present organization of medical care. The 5,000 letters received from 2,000 doctors are summarized in a report entitled *Medicine: Expert Testimony out of Court* (1937). According to this survey, leading physicians are almost unanimous in the conviction that modern medical service is not available to the great majority of our population. This report caused a sensation in medical circles. It was followed a few months later by a statement, signed by 430 internationally known

[27] Based on J. P. Warbasse: *The Doctor and the Public*. Paul B. Hoeber, Inc. (Medical Book Dept. of Harper & Bros.), 1935. Warbasse cites six different plans that are already in operation, some of them with state control, and some without state control:

1. Socialized medicine under the State, such as workingmen's compensation.
2. Guild socialism: Government owns hospitals, doctors organize staffs.
3. Medical syndicalism: group practice, as at the Mayo Clinic.
4. Groups of patients organize themselves, as in the mining industry or the railroads.
5. Consumers' cooperative, in which the patients exercise control.
6. Group cooperation: a combination of (3) and (5), by which doctors and consumers organize independently and then negotiate a contract.

American physicians, renouncing the American Medical Association's policy of stubborn opposition to any form of socialization. The 430 doctors came forward with "certain principles and proposals" such as: "The health of the people is a direct concern of the government. A national health policy directed toward all groups of the population should be formulated." They even went so far as to demand "adequate medical care for the medically indigent, the cost to be met from public funds." The New York *Times,* commending the stand of these insurrectionists, declared: "If this is socialized medicine, let us have more of it." [28]

Apparently some members of the medical profession are getting aroused over the fact that people are not receiving the care necessary for maintaining good health. The public still remains shockingly indifferent to the values at stake:

Early in the spring of 1938 the U.S. Technical Committee on Medical Care issued a quietly worded government report on "the state of the nation's health." The committee indicated that, with adequate medical care, more than 200,000 deaths a year could be prevented; that medical science, fully applied, could every year save the lives of:

  7,000 women who die in childbirth;
70,000 children who die in the first year of life;
20,000 people who die of pneumonia;
35,000 who die of tuberculosis;
40,000 who die of the after-effects of syphilis;
12,000 who die of diabetes;
24,000 who die of cancer.

That works out to nearly 600 persons a day, all of whom can be saved if we can put our present knowledge to work.

The human mind is peculiar. If 600 men, women, and children were stranded on an island in a Mississippi flood, and if we knew they would be drowned unless we saved them by midnight, the whole nation would be aroused. We would call the Army, the Navy, and the Red Cross. Headlines would scream and radio announcers would shout bulletins. Thousands of volunteers would stand ready to lay down their lives in the rescue attempt.

But because these 600 persons who die unnecessarily every day are on separate islands—little islands of neglect—we don't pay much attention. [29]

If the public were fully aware of the facts, they would probably demand some immediate reform that would ensure better care. The

[28] *Literary Digest,* November 20, 1937.
[29] Beverly Smith: "Diagnosing the Doctors." *American Magazine,* June, 1938.

public is "getting wise."   It is significant, in this connection, that the California Medical Association felt it best to suppress the findings of the California Medical Economic Survey.[30]   The truth will break out, though, in time, and remedial action is likely.   It is encouraging to realize that scores of doctors in good standing are beginning to say openly that the profession must not oppose "valid experimentation in meeting social needs."

The medical profession has been resisting experimentation, through its organized medical societies.   The history of this resistance is an interesting study in social psychology, showing how human beings incline to conservatism by virtue of the mere fact that they are organized. We shall now examine this history to learn something about the techniques available for discouraging innovation.

Rapidly growing are cooperative clinics, established and owned by laymen who pay, in addition to initial stock investments, a small annual sum for medical care.   One of the most successful of these cooperatives is the Community Hospital in Elk City, Oklahoma, a clinic which serves 15,000 farmers throughout the southwestern part of the State.   This institution was started on the initiative of Michael Shadid, a doctor in that section who came, in 1928, to realize that the farmers had no hospital they could afford to use, that they were forced to pay exorbitant prices for medical care, that they were often cheated by unscrupulous doctors.   Shadid proposed to the farmers that they build their own hospital:

Two thousand of you can pay $25 a year for your families, and with the $50,000 you will have collectively, you can hire eight or more good doctors and specialists who will provide you with free examinations. . . .   You can have expensive equipment, preventive medical treatment.[31]

The Oklahoma Farmers' Union backed the plan and in August, 1931, the Community Health Association, Inc. formally opened a trim, two-story brick hospital.   Then things began to happen, as the forces of resistance got going.   Shadid had been a member of the Beckman County Medical Society for more than twenty years.   The Society suddenly expelled him.   Then the State Board of Medical Examiners tried to revoke his license as a penalty for "steering" patients into his

[30] See A. D. Carlson: "The Doctors Face Revolt." *Harper's Magazine*, September, 1938.
  [31] See M. Shadid: *A Doctor for the People*. 1939. See also, J. D. Ratcliff: "Co-op Hospital." *Collier's*, July 31, 1943.

office. When this measure failed, the Board placed obstacles in the path of young doctors from other states who wanted Oklahoma licenses to work in the Elk City hospital. As a final, desperate measure, the State Medical Association tried to get a bill passed in the Oklahoma Legislature against medical cooperatives, but the Farmers' Union was too strong and the bill was defeated. The Association staggered under these various blows, delivered and attempted, but it finally weathered the storm.[32]

The same story has been repeated in other cases where group medicine has been established, notably in the instance of the Group Health Association in Washington, D.C. Even before this plan began to operate in Washington, the *Journal of the American Medical Association* featured a long, bitter article attacking it as illegal. The hospitals of the district were closed to the physicians who joined the staff of the Group Health Association. A patient ready for an operation had to be sent home because his surgeon was on the Group Health staff. The staff pediatrician was expelled from the District of Columbia Medical Society because he had not secured the Society's approval of his contract. In the words of Dr. Hugh Cabot, organized medicine is defending the system of private practice "to the last ditch, with the reactionary tactics of a short-sighted labor union."[33] The Department of Justice charged the American Medical Association and its affiliate, the District of Columbia Medical Society, with violation of the anti-trust laws in attempting to prevent the functioning of the Group Health Association, Inc. by expulsion or threatened expulsion of doctors employed by the Association. Conviction of the American Medical Association and the District of Columbia Medical Society for violating the Sherman Anti-trust Act was upheld by the Supreme Court in January, 1943. In explaining his prosecution of the case, on behalf of the Department of Justice, Thurman Arnold stated that the action was taken not with the idea of planning a solution to the question of providing medical care for all persons of moderate or low incomes, "but with the idea of keeping the situation free from restraint" so that groups formed voluntarily would not be prevented from carrying out their experiments.[34] This statement deals with the crux of the issue: shall we experiment with new plans for distributing medical care, or shall we stick with our antiquated methods, no matter what the cost in terms of unnecessary illness and death? Intimidation

[32] *Time,* May 1, 1939.
[33] Boston *Herald,* March 6, 1940.
[34] Boston *Herald,* August 1, 1938.

by means of boycotts against physicians participating in group medical service, browbeatings by older doctors, threats of forcing resignations, do not represent an open-minded attitude toward intelligent experimentation in this field.[35]

The American Medical Association, through its spokesman, Dr. Morris Fishbein, has registered vehement opposition to socialized medicine, charging that group plans involve the corruption of medical practice by bureaucrats and politicians, that such plans call for compulsory subscriptions from everybody, that patients will no longer be able to choose their physicians, that contract practice is sure to be damaging to the public health. Most of these arguments are patently spurious, for we have cited the fact in the footnote on p. 147 that there are various plans, proposed or in operation, which involve none of these alleged difficulties.[36]

The Physicians' Committee for the Improvement of Medical Care, Inc., a nationwide group of 33 doctors within the American Medical Association, advocate "free experimentation with plans aimed at raising the nation's health standards, especially those including group practice and budgeted pre-payment of costs." This Committee published a statement bluntly taking issue with the A.M.A.'s contention that "compulsory sickness insurance, state medicine and similar technics" lead to communism or totalitarianism: "Methods of finance are quite as valid fields of inquiry as methods of therapy or prophylactic procedures. The real road to totalitarianism lies in the arbitrary limitation of the attempts of the people to improve their condition by peaceful methods consistent with the philosophy of democratic government." [37]

An editorial note in the spring issue of the *Yale Law Journal* for 1938, deals with the legal remedies open to a doctor who suffers expulsion from a medical society for engaging in group practice, and then offers this observation:

Regardless of the ultimate outcome of the various experiments to spread and reduce the costs of medical care, the public obviously has a vital interest in assuring a fair trial to organizations like the Group Health Association.

But as long as medical societies can brandish the bludgeons of expulsion, free experimentation, long extolled by the medical profession itself as the very lifeblood of scientific progress, will be throttled.

[35] Boston *Herald,* February 11, 1940.
[36] The reactionary policies of the American Medical Association are delineated in J. Rorty: *American Medicine Mobilizes.* 1939.
[37] Boston *Herald,* February 27, 1940.

In the last analysis, the solution lies not in the decree of judges but in overcoming the stubborn intolerance of organized medicine.[38]

The problems of private and public health will not be solved by name-calling, a propaganda device hardly consistent with the intelligent policies one would expect of the American Medical Association. Conservatism dies hard—even in the kindly care of a doctor who wrote, at Christmas time:

The spirit of Christmas symbolizes some thought for others. State medicine in the long run would nullify that "good will toward men" which is exhibited by the watcher at the bedside a million times daily throughout this land of ours.[39]

That is a dire prediction hardly justified by the evidence; it is based more on prejudice than on straight thinking. There are objections to group plans of medical practice but there is no call for highly emotionalized arguments on a problem that is important enough to merit careful consideration and hardheaded thinking.[40]

III. POPULAR VALUES

Social living can be intelligent only if conduct is guided by a wise discrimination between the important and the unimportant. "The public should take some pains," Thorndike warns us, "to learn what sorts of persons and abilities are its real benefactors." [41] Why, we may ask, is this matter of evaluation so significant? What "sorts of persons and abilities" are ordinarily glorified? Does the level of popular values make any difference to us?

It is sometimes difficult to appreciate the full significance of current events when we are immersed in the immediacy of adjusting ourselves to what's going on at the time. The perspective of the newspaper and the perspective of history may differ radically in setting the interpretation given to events that affect us. September 3, 1929, was an historical day, but none of the newspapers headlined the fact that it marked the climax of the Coolidge-Hoover prosperity and the begin-

---

[38] See Editorial Notes, *Yale Law Journal,* Vol. 47, No. 7, May, 1938, pp. 1193-1201.

[39] Boston *Herald,* December 27, 1938. By Dr. Irving S. Cutter. Reprinted by permission of Chicago Tribune-New York News Syndicate, Inc.

[40] Reactions to the Truman proposals for national health insurance indicate that the American Medical Association is becoming more tolerant toward the basic principles involved in socialized medicine.

[41] From E. L. Thorndike, *Human Nature and the Social Order.* By permission of The Macmillan Company, publishers. P. 75. 1940.

ning of the decline into the great depression.[42]   The newspapers may
be excused for failing to detect the significance of the Dow-Jones average for that particular day.   Few were the prophets who could read
the signs of the times.   How hard it is to see the import of events
when we confront them close to; how easy it is to get a better perspective with the passage of time!

Newspapers, unfortunately, aggravate our human proclivity for
glorifying the insignificant by concentrating their ballyhoo on events
and personalities which do not amount to much when evaluated from
a long-range perspective.   The report of the Hall-Mills murder case
in a single newspaper required twice as many words as Will Durant
needed to tell *The Story of Philosophy*.   Pulitzer set the style for
news reporting when he asserted that the newspaper's function is not
to instruct but to startle.   He did not designate "social importance or
economic or historical magnitude as a factor in the news." [43]

If news space reveals the popular judgment, then Rudolph Valentino was a more important man than Charles W. Eliot, J. Pierpont
Morgan more important than Stephen Vincent Benét.

People experience little appreciation for their real benefactors.   Napoleon Bonaparte and Edward Jenner were contemporaries.   Bonaparte's name is known by almost everybody, Jenner's by very few.
James Simpson, an Edinburgh doctor, once wrote: "During the long
European wars connected with and following the French Revolution,
it has been calculated that five or six millions of human lives were
lost.   In Europe, vaccination against smallpox has already preserved
from death a greater number of human beings than were sacrificed
during the course of these wars.   The lancet of Jenner has saved far
more human lives than the sword of Napoleon destroyed.   On these
devastating European wars, England lavished millions of money, and
freely bestowed honors, peerages, and heavy annual pensions upon the
soldiers who were most successful in fighting her battles and destroying their fellow men.   She grudgingly rewarded Jenner with thirty
thousand pounds for saving thirty thousand of her subjects annually."
Over eighty years have passed since that contrast was drawn by Simpson, yet the regard in which these two men are held has not changed
materially.   We are savages in our tastes, admiring ruthless destructive
power and remaining indifferent to constructive humanitarianism.
Perhaps if personal worth were judged on the basis of benefits to hu-

---

[42] See F. L. Allen: "One Day in History." *Harper's Magazine*, November, 1937.
[43] S. Bent: "The Art of Ballyhoo." *Harper's Magazine*, September, 1927; *Ballyhoo.* 1927.

man welfare, Napoleon's greatest claim to distinction would come from the fact that he was an ardent supporter of Jenner.[44]

Check yourself:

What did Pasteur do for mankind?   Lister?   Semmelweiss?   Hideyo Noguchi?

Who discovered the use of anaesthetics?

Who discovered insulin as a control for diabetes?

Who discovered liver as a cure for pernicious anaemia?

Who discovered penicillin?   Streptomycin?

How are you doing?   Maybe you can show to better advantage on the following?   Just identify them:

> John L. Sullivan
> Jim Thorpe
> Alonzo Stagg
> Byron Nelson
> Joe Di Maggio
> Clarence De Mar
> Red Grange
> Joe Louis
> Frankie Brimsek
> Alice Marble

Probably you know more of the athletes than you know about the great doctors.   If that is the case, you are quite normal in your range of information.   A list of 150 allegedly famous persons was submitted to a random group of 200 Chicagoans.   The only two known to all were John Barrymore and Joan Crawford.   Texas Guinan, a night-club hostess, was better known than Mahatma Gandhi, Mae West than Stalin, Aimee McPherson than Einstein.   Several thought the Mayo brothers were a circus team.   Such is fame!

The author asks his class, "Who discovered insulin?"   Hardly anybody knows.   He poses the same question to them again a month later.   They still won't know.   They don't know and, furthermore, they "don't give a hoot."

Topping our list of heroes are athletes and movie stars.   Society

[44] Digested from a radio talk by Howard W. Haggard, Professor of Applied Physiology at Yale University, author of *Devils, Drugs, and Doctors.*

encourages certain types of achievement by the bestowal of its hero-worship. Therefore, it gets the heroes it deserves.

No man in history, perhaps, ever inspired such adoration from women as did Rudolph Valentino. In 1928 his English admirers formed the Valentino Association, which now has branches in many places, ranging from Stockholm to Calcutta. . . . With the women of other countries they raised a large sum of money toward the erection of a memorial to Valentino in a Hollywood public park. This takes the form of a fountain, surmounted by a bronze figure signifying "Aspiration." Valentino's memory is kept alive in many ways: by correspondence among the members of the association; by selling postcards, photographs, biographies of the star, and copies of his book of poems, called "Day Dreams." Some have personal souvenirs of him, which they keep in a sort of shrine, constantly surrounded by fresh flowers. They arrange for revivals of his films everywhere, and travel incredible distances to see them, even bringing wreaths to leave in the cinema vestibule.[45]

Reichenbach, who publicized Valentino, would be proud of the fruits of his labors.[46] He took advantage of the fact that the public is uncritical in its praise.

In 1844 Haydon, the painter, was exhibiting his *Banishment of Aristides* in the same building where Tom Thumb was showing. The midget's receipts for the first week were $3,000; the painter's, $35. Haydon committed suicide a few days later, leaving this entry in his diary: "They rush by thousands to see Tom Thumb. They push, they fight, they scream, they faint. They see my bills but do not read them. It is an insanity of which I could not have believed England could be guilty." [47]

Carlton Parker once raised the question as to why Florence produced so many artists. The answer lies in an incident he relates. He tells us that back around 1300 Giotto painted a picture. The day it was hung in St. Mark's the town closed down for a holiday. The people with flowers and garlands and songs escorted the picture from the artist's studio to the church. Parker suggests that we shall never be able to produce such artists as Florence turned out until we have developed a company such as followed Giotto's picture. Education must train consumers of culture. Unless our system can somehow train more effectively for consumption of culture, the producers of culture

[45] *Literary Digest,* February 7, 1931. See also, *Life,* June 20, 1938.
[46] See H. Reichenbach and D. Freedman: *Phantom Fame: the Anatomy of Bally-hoo,* pp. 203-208. 1931.
[47] The *Reader's Digest,* January, 1935. Condensed from the book, *It's a Small World,* by W. Bodin and B. Hershey. Coward-McCann, Inc., 1934.

will, many of them, find themselves "all dressed up but nowhere to go." [48]

We are uncivilized in our conception of value. We are indifferent to important things, such as the care of women at childbirth. What we do for mothers at such a time is a fair measure of our civilization. Our mortality record for mothers at childbirth in the United States is disgraceful. "Why Do They Die?" asks a writer in the *Literary Digest:*

> Most of them could have been saved. Most of them died because we did not care enough to save them.
>
> As a nation we care enough to stamp out smallpox, diphtheria, tuberculosis, typhoid fever, and a host of other diseases. After the mothers die, we care enough about their orphaned children . . . to support institutions for them.
>
> But we let mothers and babies go right on dying. You have seen the figures before, because they have been almost the same figures for twenty years. . . .
>
> Some die because mothers have no care whatever when their babies arrive. . . .
>
> Among social and medical welfare groups, the answer is always the same: "We can cut the maternal death toll when enough people demand it. . . ."
>
> Any effective program for cutting the maternal death-rate must . . . include attendance at childbirth.
>
> But that would cost money. If we were embarking on a serious campaign to save the mothers, it would take more than $3,800,000. We spend almost that much annually to conserve wild life. We have spent more than four times that much to prevent cholera in hogs.[49]

The persisting high rate of mortality for mothers in the United States is not due to the economic condition of this country; it is merely an index of our indifference. The care of mothers should be a paramount concern. "The men who have worked on this problem, whose praise is unsung and whose names are unknown to most people, rank higher in the advance of our civilization and are greater men by every standard than any of the kings and statesmen whose names are taught to school children and whose works are measured by the ephemeral boundaries which they won for the countries where they fought and intrigued." [50] When Mothers' Day comes, it is suggested that, instead

---

[48] T. M. Carter: "Education for Production and Education for Consumption of the Elements of Culture." *School and Society*, December 7, 1935.

[49] *Literary Digest*, January 15, 1938.

[50] From a radio talk by Howard W. Haggard, in honor of Mothers' Day.

of sending Mother flowers, you send a check to a maternity hospital in honor of your mother. That would be a constructive gift.

The use of leisure time is as good a measure as there is of a person's sense of values. What we do when we are free from our tasks is a fair criterion by which to judge our culture. Technological advances are increasing the amount of leisure. Is this spare time being devoted to worth-while creative pursuits or is it being devoted to listening to music rendered by others, watching games played by others, and just plain frittering away of time. "A civilization that creates a leisure which it cannot rationally use may well be in greater danger of destruction than one that has no leisure at all. . . . The great problem before us today is to create a civilization that does not degenerate under leisure." [51]

Philosophers and moralists have contended for ages that human beings missed the blessings of culture because they had to labor too hard for a living. Give them more time to themselves, the theory went, and they will use it in the pursuit of wisdom, science, and beauty. Will they? Thorndike and a number of other psychologists computed how people occupy themselves during their spare time, by analyzing the studies made by Janet Fowler Nelson of 500 New York Y.W.C.A. girls in 1931 and 1932. They found the craving for entertainment to be the dominant note in the repertoire of leisure-time activities. "I prophesy," states Thorndike, "that historical and anthropological research will increasingly reveal that the great majority of people have spent their free time for entertainment up to or beyond thirty hours a week, if a supply was available. The desire for approval may counteract it widely, as in waves of Puritanism or patriotism. . . . The human nervous system is very adaptable and can learn to operate with satisfaction in a humdrum world. But its lines of least resistance go toward cheerful sociability, free play, sensory stimulation, and emotional excitement." [52] Most people would not hesitate if they were forced to choose between the opera and a burlesque show, between a lecture on Plato and a poker game, between a trip through an art museum and a ringside seat at a wrestling bout. Our devotion to culture is not characterized by any sweeping enthusiasm. More energy is burned up in dancing than in the cultivation of the mind.

Certainly our colleges should be centers of culture. But are they?

[51] G. W. Alger: "Leisure—For What?" The *Atlantic Monthly*, April, 1925.
[52] E. L. Thorndike: "How We Spend Our Time and What We Spend It For." *Scientific Monthly*, May, 1937.

What do they care most about? [53] Academic progress or athletic prowess? The answer is easy, if it is the undergraduate we have in mind, for he would rather see a winning football team than an illustrious chemistry department. If it is the typical graduate we have in mind, the answer is still easier, for football is his one indissoluble tie with Alma Mater. A revolution in the academic curriculum occasions no excitement among the alumni, but a shift in a coaching staff produces a general alarm. When Blank College was changing its football coaches, an alumnus who had carried the ball down the field in his palmier days wrote the authorities that "if you don't give us a say in picking the coach, we won't contribute to the endowment fund." Subsidizing and proselyting of athletes are fostered more by organized alumni than by coaches. The alumni of one institution seek to outbid the alumni of a rival institution in securing star athletes. Who ever heard of the alumni organizing to outbid a rival for an outstanding professor?

In 1929 Bertrand Russell was invited to give a lecture at the University of Wisconsin. The largest and most convenient auditorium on the campus, where important lectures were given, was the gymnasium (quite appropriately). It so happened that the basketball coach needed the gymnasium on that particular night for practice, since, as he himself said, "I must either practice or get licked, and my job is to turn out basketball teams." The coach's statement was paraphrased by E. L. Meyer of the *Capitol Times* as follows:

> If the five men on my squad, sir,
> Learn the tip-off and the passes,
> It is better far, by God, sir,
> Than to aid one thousand asses.
> For my basket quint will hustle,
> Bring renown to Alma Mater,
> While the thousand who hear Russell
> Soak up nonsense like a blotter.
> Can this fellow toss a ball, sir?
> Can he pivot, can he dribble?
> No? Good day, then. That is all, sir!
> Bertrand Russell? Ish kabibble! [54]

The prevailing conception of the relative importance of coaches and professors was revealed at one university where, during the last de-

---

[53] See J. L. Graham: "Social Change and Higher Education." *Journal of Social Psychology*, S.P.S.S.I. *Bulletin*, 1944, 19, 339-350.

[54] From a letter to the Editor, *The Nation*, November 27, 1929.

pression, the athletic coaches had been paid in full without taking the cuts applied to professorial salaries. A high school in Oregon faced the problem of faculty curtailment during the depression and solved it by firing the principal and making the football coach both principal and coach. One college was up against a tough problem in securing a coach for its football team in 1941. The newspaper account ran as follows:

COACHES SPURN BLANK POST
Pay Too Small
Even High School Mentors Refuse Job

Blank University's avowed intention of paying its coaches the same scale as professors is causing the trustees not a few headaches.

While we are on this subject of professorial salaries, we might quote a comment from one professor:

It is stated that 250,000 teachers in the United States were paid less than $750 each last year (1937). Laborers building motor cars are better paid than people charged with building the mentality of citizens of the United States. It is not money we lack, but perspective in social values.[55]

An item in *Time* is very revealing on this point.

AMERICAN IGNORANCE

In the way they scrimp and save to send their children to school and college, and spend money on school buildings and equipment, Americans in general act as though they believe education is a cure for every social ill. But in the way they fail to bestow pay, respect, and freedom on their teachers, Americans seem not to understand the first thing about education. Last week the National Opinion Research Center (University of Denver) supplied further evidence of this national ignorance.

In a nationwide survey, Denver polltakers asked a scientific sampling of citizens: "Is there any kind of change you would like to see made in our public schools?" More than half (57 per cent) of the pollees were satisfied with schools as they are. Of the 43 per cent who suggested changes, most spoke of such things as curricula, administration, equipment. Only 10 per cent of the discontented minority wanted better paid and better qualified teachers. Approximately 96 out of every 100 Americans seem unaware of the

[55] E. V. Cowdry: "Science and Social Values." *Scientific Monthly*, November, 1938

unchallenged fact that a log with Mark Hopkins at one end of it is still a
far better school than the most expensive modern classroom presided over by
a mediocre teacher.[56]

We are equally myopic in our attitude toward Old Age Pensions: in
some states, the citizens care so little about the provision of security
for the aged that horse racing and dog racing are relied upon for the
funds necessary to attain this humanitarian goal.

Many of our universities have failed to put first things first. For
one thing, Flexner observes, they have worshiped size, growing by
all sorts of irrational accretions, such as schools of cookery and schools
of physical education, expanding in the belief that by getting bigger
and bigger they were getting better and better.[57]   The aim seems to be
to develop into a "whale of a university."   The same lack of discriminating judgment has been expressed in the practice of doing things
on a costly and pretentious scale, especially in the erection of impressive stadia and magnificent dormitories.   Some of the colleges have so
much money tied up in buildings that they have to cut the professors'
salaries to pay the bills, or must even get rid of some of the faculty.
"To what degree do sumptuous dormitories and dining halls, palatial
classroom and laboratory buildings, the appointment of ordinary
people to extraordinary professorships, *rarissima* in the library, really
contribute to the prestige that matters?" asks a baffled professor.   The
universities could educate their students by demonstrating a more intelligent appreciation of what is really important.   Our schools have
not succeeded as they should in training young people to attain a mature sense of values.   Dean Malcolm MacLean of the University of
Minnesota's General College wanted to know what his charges needed
to prepare themselves for life, so he sent out a questionnaire to
1,600 Minnesota alumni concerning his "University of Tomorrow."
Shocked but undaunted by the replies, the Dean commented:

It is appalling to discover that there are few, if any, observable differences,
in other respects than earning power alone, between the graduates and non-
graduates and between those who in college were known as "good" students
and those who were known as "poor" students.   They are culturally much
alike: they listen to the same radio programs, read the same magazines, go to
the same movies, feel much the same about their jobs and families, and almost

[56] *Time,* July 3, 1944.
[57] See A. Flexner: *Universities: American, English, German.*   1930.

uniformly find democratic participation in social and civic affairs dull as dishwater and comparatively unimportant.[58]

Four years in college should make a difference, James Harvey Robinson thinks, but it is disillusioning to anyone who expects that they will to see how immature is the perspective of the typical college graduate.[59] The faith that the typical American has in the power of education to convert a pagan into a civilized person is seldom justified. Perhaps we need to start earlier in building a more discerning sense of values, as Frances Morehouse of Hunter College suggested in her contribution to *The Future of the Social Studies,* when she proposed that American youngsters should get a new set of heroes: to conventional United States heroes such as Washington, Jefferson, and Lincoln, *add* Buffalo Bill, Harriet Beecher Stowe, the Wright Brothers, Elias Howe, Booker T. Washington, G. W. Carver, Cyrus W. Field, Jane Addams, Dan Beard, and Richard Byrd.[60]

Possibly some of the names just mentioned are strange to you. Let us assume, for the sake of the theme we are considering, that what you care about is revealed by what sorts of things or people you know. You have undoubtedly studied American history. You should, therefore, be informed concerning the important events and personages of our past. Check your knowledge of American history by answering the following questions:

1. Who invented linotype?
2. Who discovered how to vulcanize rubber?
3. Who invented short-exposure X-ray photography?
4. Who invented the electric lamp?
5. Who delivered the lecture, "Acres of Diamonds"?
6. Who was Maria Mitchell?
7. Who invented the sound film?
8. Who wrote *Uncle Tom's Cabin?*
9. Who was Joseph Pulitzer?
10. Who was Horace Mann?
11. Who was Gilbert Stuart?
12. Who was Luther Burbank?
13. Who was John Audubon?

[58] Quoted in "What the Colleges Are Doing," January, 1940. Published by Ginn and Company.

[59] See J. H. Robinson: *The Human Comedy,* Chapter 12, "Ever Learning." 1937.

[60] See *The Future of the Social Studies,* James A. Michener, Editor. 1940.

14. Who was Eugene Debs?
15. Who was Thomas Mott Osborne?
16. Who was Joseph Story?
17. Who was Emma Lazarus?
18. Who founded Hull House?
19. Who was Dorothea Dix?
20. Who was Edward Bok?
21. Who was Stephen Foster?
22. Who was Clara Barton?
23. Who invented the rotary press?
24. Who was Henry Ward Beecher?
25. Who was John Burroughs?
26. Who founded the playground movement?
27. Who was Alice Freeman Palmer?
28. Who was Walter Reed?
29. What New Englander discovered ether as an anesthetic?
30. Who was Matthew Fontaine Maury?
31. Who was Booker T. Washington?
32. Who invented the spring bed?
33. Who was Augustus St. Gaudens?
34. Who was Simon Newcomb?
35. Who was Hiram Maxim?
36. Who was Joseph Henry?
37. Who was Asa Gray?
38. Who was Susan B. Anthony?
39. Who was Orville Wright?
40. Who was Adoniram Judson?
41. Who founded life insurance in America?
42. Who wrote *Little Women?*
43. Who was Noah Webster?
44. Who was Charles P. Steinmetz?
45. Who wrote *A Message to Garcia?*
46. Who invented the roller bearing?
47. Who invented condensed milk?
48. Who founded the American Federation of Labor?
49. Who discovered how to make paper from pulp?
50. Who invented baseball?

(The correct answers will be found at the end of this chapter.)

For your own enlightenment, run through the Name Indexes of some American History textbooks and see how many of these benefactors are mentioned. Notice the names included in the texts. Are they the names of men and women who have contributed constructively to human progress? Are we teaching children to revere the right people?

A number of the names included in the test you have just taken are enshrined in the Hall of Fame. Do you know which ones? We venture to guess that you do not know many of the persons upon whom this honor has been conferred. It seems a bit ironical to call it a Hall of Fame when there is so little fame involved. Perhaps it should be renamed the Hall of Those Who Should Be Famous.

We have analyzed some popular values to determine whether people as a general rule do succeed in distinguishing between the important and the unimportant. The answer is so much in the negative as to challenge our serious reflection, for here we have a fundamental problem in social psychology, the problem of training people, including ourselves, to appreciate the significant things in life, to cease the pursuit of the trivial.

IV. HINDRANCES TO INTELLIGENT ACTION

There are many reasons why we do not employ our minds to our best advantage. Two of them we have already noted: our shortsighted egocentrism and our immature sense of values. There are other reasons which we should also include in our account of social behavior if we want to get a reasonably complete picture of why our intelligence is so widely unapplied or misapplied, notably: *censorship* which prevents us from knowing the truth, *regimentation* which discourages us from working out our own ideas, *propaganda* which distorts reality by means of deliberate misrepresentation, *emotionalism* which aims to get us so excited we cannot think straight, and our *collective immorality* which excuses our uncivilized behavior by disguising it as noble loyalty to group ends. We shall review these points in the order mentioned.

A. Censorship

It is especially important in a democracy that the people be accurately and thoroughly informed about goings-on in their own country and in the world at large. They must have ready access to the truth if they are to exercise their suffrage intelligently. Suppression, misrepresentation, coloring the news, omitting embarrassing incidents, concealing significant happenings in obscure sections of the paper—

all of these devices frustrate the employment of intelligence. Wise decisions on public issues cannot be reached in the absence of sound information.

How was the average American citizen to form an intelligent opinion about American policies with regard to World War II, say in 1940, when he did not know what was going on in Europe and had no way of finding out? News reports via the press or radio were being censored at the source, with the result that we learned only what the authorities abroad wanted to tell us. Consequently, news consisted of claims and counterclaims: the British shot down forty Nazi planes with the loss of only five of their own planes, according to the British version of an air battle; the Nazis destroyed sixty-five British planes and lost only one of their own, according to the report from Berlin. How could the bewildered citizen find his way through this maze of conflicting reports to formulate an attitude based on reality? Nazi prisoners brought to America during the war were surprised—and chagrined—to discover New York and Chicago still existed, for they had been told that these great American cities had been wiped out by German bombs. What a disillusionment it must have been to learn the facts after being sheltered so long in a world of unreality! Let us not forget our own plight, however, for as long as avenues of communication are blocked, we, too, shall live in a world of fiction.

Packer's "War-Blinded." (Courtesy, New York *Mirror* and Fred Packer.)

If the ordinary American citizen were to believe all he reads in the newspapers, he would be as much at home in the realm of delusion as any seasoned paranoiac. The individual would be a lost soul if he could honestly say, "All I know is what I saw in the newspaper." According to the news reports, just to take a sample, the Finns won all the battles in their war with the Soviet Union, but Russia won the war. Beneath "Tall Stories and Tall Headlines" ran stories of incredible Finnish feats and colossal Russian setbacks.

Less than a month after the conflict started, Irving Pflaum, foreign news editor of the Chicago *Times,* tried to deflate the bubble of Finnish successes: "These stories more often than not bear a dateline some hundreds of miles from the crash of bombs and daring encounters. Copenhagen is offender No. 1, with Oslo, Stockholm, Paris, and London all guilty in fostering rumors as well as fact. Sooner than most readers have been encouraged to believe, the Russians are going to spoil the pretty pictures being concocted in certain journalistic centers." But Copenhagen and Stockholm and other capitals were not the prime offenders. Helsinki was. Not until after two months of camouflage from the Finnish front (or rear) did the one tangible truth about the war emerge: it was an invisible war.

To the New York *Herald Tribune* on February 3, Walter Kerr cabled: "Old-time newspaper correspondents say the war in Finland is the first in many years without war correspondents. It probably is. . . . Even if the American correspondents were skilled with skis, which they are not, or spoke the Finnish language, which they cannot, the Army would not allow them to visit the front lines unless it were a relatively quiet day. That is why no correspondent, so far as I know, has ever seen the troops in action. . . ."

Thus the rival censorships blanketed the battlefields. But to superficial readers of the American press it wasn't immediately plain that news of the Finnish war was largely manufactured in Helsinki for foreign consumption—and domestic morale. . . . Late in February Leland Stowe cabled a saga which the New York *Post* headlined: "100 Finns Stood Off 300,000." Surfeited with tales of military miracles, newspaper readers probably weren't startled by the typographical error when the St. Louis *Globe Democrat* reported on February 9:

250,000 REDS ROUTED
By Thomas F. Hawkins
Associated Press Staff Writer. . . .

If the war was a circulation manager's holiday, it was a newspaperman's nightmare. What sources could be trusted, even granting the noblest intentions? [61]

Wherever revolution and social unrest exist, interference with the Fourth Estate is employed to suppress counter-revolution and to foster the regimentation necessary to a successful dictatorship. It is no coincidence that several of Europe's dictators were former newspaper men; they were well aware of the central importance of journalism in securing their ends. Lenin in 1917, Mussolini in 1922, and Hitler in 1933 shackled the press by imposing a strict censorship and seeing to it

---

[61] "Russia, Finland, and the U.S.A." *Propaganda Analysis,* April 30, 1940. Institute for Propaganda Analysis. Reproduced by permission of Alfred McClung Lee, Executive Director.

that news was corrupted at its source. With the best intentions in the world, the representatives of United States press bureaus and newspapers cannot escape the flood of biased news transmitted by foreign agencies under governmental domination.

Most of the foreign news America gets comes through three press associations: the Associated Press, the United Press, and the International News Service. The accuracy of the news transmitted is diminished by foreign government agents who tap correspondents' telephones, steam open their letters, read their private telegrams, and inspect their office wastebaskets.[62] Correspondents who are found guilty of speaking the truth that hurts are forced into hasty retreat, as David Darrah, Dorothy Thompson, and others can testify.[63]

The value of the press as an agency of enlightenment depends upon the free and speedy flow of news from all parts of the world. After World War I, particularly, the control of communication came to be considered a prerogative of the nationalistic state and was deemed indispensable to its existence. There was more and more tampering with the stream of news. The chief source of corruption, according to Riegel, was nationalism: "As long as nationalism remains the dominant factor in political life, the interchange of information will remain subject to the whims of nationalistic expediency . . . national barriers will prevent the existence of an informed world public." [64]

Freedom of the press in America is in danger of being circumscribed, not by dictator's decrees but by concentrated financial control which is increasing with the consolidation of independent newspapers into chains. The fact that newspaper income depends to such a large extent upon advertising is prejudicial to impartial reporting of the news.[65]

A man who lives on an unbalanced diet of news is not only injuring himself but he is a source of danger to everyone with whom he comes in contact. Intelligence cannot operate effectively when it is proceeding upon the basis of false information.

B. REGIMENTATION

Regimentation, formal and informal, decreases the exercise of intelligence by inhibiting independent thinking. The individual who does

---

[62] See W. P. Carney: "Fighting the Censor." *Scribner's Magazine*, June, 1937.

[63] David Darrah was expelled from Italy at Mussolini's order on June 13, 1935. Dorothy Thompson was given twenty-four hours to get out of Germany in 1935, because of her book, *I Saw Hitler!* published in 1932.

[64] O. W. Riegel: *Mobilizing for Chaos*, pp. 210, 211. 1934.

[65] See S. Bent: *Ballyhoo*. 1927.

not conform in his opinions to the beliefs sanctioned by those in authority, whether the persons in power are dominant by reason of political, economic, or social preeminence, may get into serious trouble if he insists on expressing his ideas and trying to influence others to adopt his way of thinking.

There is a fundamental problem of social organization involved, one of great import to the social psychologist: the reconciliation of individual freedom and centralized control. Bertrand Russell has treated this question exhaustively in his book, *Freedom versus Organization, 1814-1914.*[66] Planning requires the focalization of control and the limitation of individual initiative. Some kinds of planning are desirable, even necessary; liberty likewise is a desideratum. The task of achieving both to the highest possible degree is a major problem of our time. The solution, of course, in a democracy, must be some sort of compromise, satisfying in some ways and annoying in some ways, to all concerned.

Some cynic has described the democratic fallacy as the conviction that multiplying wrong conclusions a sufficient number of times results in the correct answer. In a democracy, it is charged, we count noses, not brains. It is fair to assume that the individual citizen can learn to arrive at sound conclusions, only by being allowed the opportunity to use his intelligence in making choices on his own. Even then, of course, his decisions may sometimes be wrong; whether or not his decision is right will depend on his intelligence, his educational background, and his capacity for straight thinking. It is exactly this possibility of error that gives other persons the feeling that they should do his thinking for him. A democracy, however, is not really democratic unless the citizens think for themselves.

Independent thinking is considered dangerous because it may be fallacious and, more essentially, because it may undermine authority. The man who hints that the Constitution may be defective is supposedly promoting anarchy and is suspected of concealing a bomb. The man of foreign birth who finds fault with our economic system is damned as an unappreciative alien who ought to go back to where he came from if he doesn't like it here. Thus criticism is mistaken for conspiracy against all that we hold dear. The 100 per cent American accepts "what is" with a stolidity that ensures stability and security, and he resents anybody who entertains an opinion differing from his own. If such a conservative devotes his intelligence to an uncritical maintenance of the *status quo,* his ability is being wasted. An open

[66] Published in 1934.

mind is as important as native ability for the creation of a social order that will satisfy the longings of human nature to the fullest degree. If the radical rushes headlong to the promotion of ill-conceived ends, he may likewise be a social liability instead of an asset. Epimetheans must get out of their ruts, Prometheans must be sure they are headed on the right roads. Freedom of thought, in any case, is necessary to render intelligence effective.

Years are spent in teaching youth to think. "Since character is the result of choice," states President Hutchins, "it is difficult to see how you can develop it unless you train the mind to make intelligent choices." [67] This view is seconded by Joseph Jastrow, who speaks his mind: "The fundamental purpose of all schooling is to teach young minds to think straight and avoid shooting wildly at illusory targets, and not less to think responsibly with a right perspective of values." [68] Fine in theory, but how does it work out in practice? Suppose we do train young people in the exercise of critical judgment. To what end? When they graduate from the cloistered seclusion of the college classroom into the unacademic realities of everyday citizenship, they discover that unusual ideas may be regarded as evidence of an unbalanced mind. Anything different from the ordinary run is suspect. When a minister in Republican "Middletown" explained in a sermon why he intended to vote for Roosevelt in 1936, the rumor circulated that he was "mentally unbalanced," that while he was a "brilliant man, he has done a number of unaccountable things," and that he "intends consulting a doctor in the East about his condition." Such a mild variation from the local "norm" was sufficient to provoke the wrath and malediction of his fellows. The penalty for being different is ostracism, with all that may mean in scorn and contempt.

No social problem today requires more serious consideration than the ethics of war. Surely this issue calls for the clearest insight. When a crisis comes, however, critical judgment is strictly forbidden. In other words, thinking is taboo at just the time when it is most needed. It seems to be the general feeling that pacifistic convictions should be suppressed during wartime. War is not a problem to be discussed but a program to be prosecuted.

In this matter of war, the nonconformist is apt to be regarded as a nuisance. In 1935 the Nobel peace prize was awarded to Carl von Ossietzky, a German pacifist who was active in opposing militaristic

[67] R. M. Hutchins: "The Confusion in Higher Education." *Harper's Magazine* October, 1936; *The Higher Learning in America.* 1936.
[68] J. Jastrow: *The Betrayal of Intelligence*, p. 102. Greenberg: Publisher, 1938.

sentiment in Germany in the years following World War I and who suffered terribly for his convictions. He had already been in prison for his views before the Nazis came into control of the government. He was among the first to be sentenced by the Nazi authorities to a concentration camp, where his health was ruined before his release. Upon the award of the Nobel prize to von Ossietzky, German official-dom announced that the honor of the nation had been affronted by the granting of so high a distinction to a man just released from jail— a man "guilty of treachery."

The case of Douglas Clyde Macintosh, a Yale professor, illustrates the taboo against *thinking* about the issues of war. Macintosh was not a pacifist—he merely insisted upon his right to use his judgment re-garding the justice of any particular war in determining whether he would or would not support its prosecution. The question arose in connection with his application, as a Canadian, for United States citizenship in 1929. His application was turned down because he re-fused to promise to bear arms in case of war. In explanation of his stand he made this statement:

On this matter of bearing arms, there are just three stands you can take. One is out-and-out pacifism. One is the stand I have taken, that I will bear arms if I believe it is for the welfare of mankind. The third is that you will bear arms in any war, the position Judge Burrows holds is necessary for citizenship. I believe the first two are the only ones possible for a Christian.

Christian ethics, as I view them, make it a man's duty to act for the welfare of all mankind, including his own nation. A man's first duty is toward his family, but not against the welfare of all mankind.

Another great war would be such an irreparable calamity for the world that I cannot pledge myself in advance to support it. I am not a pacifist. If the welfare of the world were threatened, I would fight for it.[69]

Dr. Macintosh had served with Canadian troops as a chaplain in World War I, and later with the American Army. The Supreme Court voted in 1931 to deny him citizenship.

The issue was clear in this case. Dr. Macintosh believed that pa-triotism should be subservient to religious convictions. He was will-ing to fight but he demanded the right to think it over first. He re-garded loyalty to conscience as the supreme object and was firm in his conviction that ethical scruples must be operative in all situations, no matter what the cause at stake.

There are certain principles that should be kept in mind in disciplin-

[69] See the *Literary Digest* for June 6, 1931 and June 20, 1931.

ing such nonconformists. The late Chief Justice Stone stated some of them. After examining conscientious objectors in World War I, Justice Stone wrote:

> However rigorous the State may be in repressing the commission of acts *injurious to the community,* it may well stay its hand before it compels the commission of acts *which violate the conscience.* . . . All our history gives confirmation of the view that liberty of conscience has a social and moral value which makes it worthy of preservation.

Justice Stone combined his legal views and his personal views in an essay on the Common Law, in which he said:

> There comes a point in the organization of a complex society where individualism must yield to traffic rules and where the right to do as one wills with one's own must bow to zoning ordinances or even to price-fixing regulations. Just where the line is to be drawn between individual liberty and government action for the larger good is the perpetual question of constitutional law. It is necessarily a question of *degree* which may *vary* with the *time* and with the *place.*[70]

Unless people are allowed to think and to express their thoughts, without fear of prosecution and persecution, social conduct runs the risk of being stupid. A certain amount of freedom is indispensable to intelligent action. "The only method which I have observed to be effective in the production of rationality," states Bridgman, "is deliberate criticism on the part of members of the community and consequent self-conscious modification of their actions." [71]

C. PROPAGANDA

Propaganda is another serious threat to intelligent behavior.[72] As an agency for social control propaganda cannot always be distinguished clearly from censorship, for the two forms of regulation are often combined in one person or office. Hence a newsman reported during World War II that getting information was like telephoning the hospital for news concerning a sick friend—a quest ending in futility: "Newsmen in Germany had nothing to write about except official propaganda. . . . Goebbels wrote the script and there was no

---

[70] Both quotations are cited by W. Hard in an article entitled "Our New Chief Justice—Old-Line American." *Reader's Digest,* August, 1941.

[71] P. W. Bridgman: *The Intelligent Individual and Society,* p. 221. 1938.

[72] A thorough discussion of "Propaganda" will follow in Chapter 10.

ad-libbing. . . . The correspondents reported what they heard. And what they heard was Dr. Goebbels." [73]

"Propaganda," states Doob, "is a systematic attempt by an interested individual (or individuals) to control the attitudes of groups of individuals through the use of suggestion and, consequently, to control their actions." [74] Propaganda may be intentional or unintentional, revealed or concealed, according to Doob, who feels that no absolute distinction can be drawn between propaganda and education. Most readers of the New York *Times,* he suggests, would not think of the *Times* as a vehicle of propaganda but they would regard the *Daily Worker* as such. Propaganda, some wit has remarked, is the other side of the picture presented so convincingly it makes you mad.

The techniques of propaganda were perfected during World War I. The creation and maintenance of morale was an important factor in the achievement of victory. Truth was one of the first casualties in the conflict. Faked stories and pictures were circulated widely by both sides. One famous hoax was the tale about the Baby of Courbeck Loo:

Captain Wilson of the London *Daily Mail* was in Brussels when the war broke out. A telegram came from the home office instructing him to get stories of war atrocities. There were none at the time. He wired to that effect. Word came to get stories about refugees. The Captain tells how he proceeded. "There was a little town outside of Brussels where one went to get dinner. I heard the Huns had been there. I supposed there must have been a baby there. So I wrote a heart-rending story about the baby of Courbeck Loo being rescued from the Huns in the light of the burning homestead. The next day they telegraphed to me to send the baby along, as they had about five thousand letters offering to adopt it. The day after that, baby clothes began to pour into the office. Even Queen Alexandria wired her sympathy and sent some clothes. Well, I couldn't wire back to them that there wasn't a baby. So I finally arranged with the doctor that took care of the refugees that the blessed baby died of some very contagious disease, so it couldn't even have a public funeral."

One of the immediate reasons for the entry of the United States into World War I was the sinking of the *Lusitania.* The impression was fostered that the ship was sailing innocently with no war supplies in

[73] H. Lavine and J. Wechsler: *War Propaganda and the United States,* pp. 169-170. Yale University Press.

[74] L. W. Doob: *Propaganda: Its Psychology and Technique,* pp. 75-76. Henry Holt & Co., 1935.

its cargo. In 1915 the Senate attempted to expel Robert LaFollette on the charge that he had falsely declared that the *Lusitania* carried ammunition. When Dudley Field Malone, Collector at the Port of New York, proposed to testify in the Senator's behalf, that the *Lusitania's* consignments to the British government on her last voyage included 4,200 cases of Springfield cartridges, the prosecution was dropped. But the administration refused to permit the publication of the facts.

Brigadier General Charteris, Chief of Intelligence[75] of the British army, was responsible for concocting the tale of the German corpse factory, as a means of winning the sympathy of China for the Allied cause. Two pictures came to his office—one of dead horses being taken by train to the rear where the cadavers were to be used by the Germans for producing fertilizer, the other of dead German soldiers being transported to the rear for burial. The Chief of Intelligence simply transposed the captions so that it appeared the Germans were making a dreadful use of their own dead.

One striking photograph of a shipwreck, showing forlorn passengers struggling in a heavy sea, appeared simultaneously, during World War I, in both the British and German press as an official Government photograph. In the British version, it was another case of a German submarine atrocity; in the German, another example of the heartless cruelty of the British navy. The London *Daily Herald* dug up for its readers the original of the picture, which had appeared widely in the British and Continental press back in 1909, an old photograph representing an ordinary peacetime shipwreck. One is reminded of the notorious instruction sent by William Randolph Hearst to his Cuban correspondent in 1898: "You furnish the pictures, and I'll furnish the war."

In the prosecution of a war, truth is often sacrificed in the service of hatred. Lies are fabricated freely as a part of the game. When facts are withheld, when falsehoods pass for the truth, when prejudice is enkindled by deliberate provocation, straight thinking is rendered difficult and intelligence disabled. Unfortunately, the intelligentsia seem to be just as susceptible to hysterical propaganda as *hoi polloi*.

Since 1919, propagandists have been operating very successfully in politics. The Coolidge legend is a noteworthy illustration. Coolidge was nominated for the Vice-Presidency in 1920 because of a popular belief that he had handled the Boston police strike of 1919 with masterly tact and vigor. Actually, in the weeks before the strike he

---

[75] What a sardonic title!!

vas extremely vacillating in dealing with the situation. On the day f the strike, the Mayor of Boston was unable to locate Governor Coolidge. The Mayor himself brought order out of chaos. Governor Coolidge then reappeared and coined a neat phrase in a telegram to he President of the American Federation of Labor: "There is no right o strike against the public safety by any body, any where, any time." 'rom that moment on, the propaganda of the Coolidge machine and f the Republican Party built him up as the strong, silent man of lestiny.[76]

D. EMOTIONALISM

Words may be used to facilitate the exchange of ideas, thus to stimulate thought; words may also be used to arouse strong emotions, thus o inhibit thought. Exciting language serves frequently as a convenent instrument for obscuring the issue under consideration. Problem-solving is promoted by a conscientious adherence to objective erminology, and it is discouraged by a resort to words which touch off motionally toned prejudices. A comparison of newspaper accounts lealing with the same news story as presented in the New York *Times* nd in the Chicago *Tribune* will reveal how the same situation may e described in emotional or non-emotional terms:

New York *Times*	Chicago *Tribune*
Progressive	Radical
Senate investigation	Government witch-hunting
Regulation	Regimentation
Maritime leader	Communist CIO leader
Labor organizer	Labor agitator
Home relief	The dole
Crop control	Farm dictatorship
Nonstrikers	Loyal workers
Investigator	Inquisitor
CIO chieftain	CIO dictator
Foreign	Alien
Picketing	Mass picketing[77]

The *Tribune* language is not chosen with the main objective of clari-ying thought, but rather with the idea of arousing affective reactions o the situation at stake.

[76] See E. L. Clarke: *The Art of Straight Thinking*, p. 320. 1929.
[77] S. S. Sargent: "Emotional Stereotypes in the Chicago *Tribune*." *Sociometry*, 939, 2, 69-75.

If everybody would learn to use the right words, words that repre
sent accurately the world of reality, our misunderstandings and ou
muddled thinking would be greatly reduced and many of our ill
would be miraculously cured.   This thesis constitutes the major them
of semantics as developed by Korzybski in his *Science and Sanity* (1933
and as popularized by Stuart Chase in his *Tyranny of Words* (1938)
Chase once compiled a glossary to guide Government examiners; i
it he specified "good" words to use and "bad" words to avoid in attack
ing monopolies.

> *Savings* is a "good" word, tenderly regarded in the folkways. . . .   If sav
> ings are not invested, they become hoardings, or idle money. . . .   *Invest
> ment* is a "good" word. . . .   *Hoarding* is a "bad" word. . . .   Alway
> remember that one context pleases the layman and the other distresse
> him. . . .
>   *Spending* is a "bad" word.   Avoid it like a copperhead.   Talk about *Gou
> ernment running expenses* and *Government plant.*   Talk about putting th
> Government budget on a *business basis,* rather than about *triple budgets o
> capital budgets.*   If spending must be discussed, always remember that ever
> dollar spent by the Government is usually a dollar of *sales* on the books o
> some business man.   Keep *spending* firmly associated with *sales, wages, pu
> chasing power*—all good words.
>   *Economy* is a beautiful word.   Visions of thrifty Uncle Abner, rolling ball
> of waste string.   *Economy,* however, means *loss* to somebody else—loss o
> *sales* or *wages.*   Keep *economy* and *loss* firmly associated.[78]

Children used to shout "Sticks and stones may break my bones, bu
names will never hurt me," but that immunity does not apply to name
calling in a discussion of economic or social problems.   It makes
tremendous difference whether you call disbursements *spending* o
plant expansion because one touches off emotional reactions, the othe
does not.

A wise lawyer will recognize the value of mastering an effective vc
cabulary, for the winning of a case may depend more upon rhetori
than upon legal erudition.   The skillful lawyer, practiced in the a
of tergiversation,

> surrounds some spoilsman with an aura of sanctity. . . .
>   Lacking any great issues in his two-penny case, the advocate of commo
> practice seeks to create them out of resounding words, referring to sacre
> rights, the blood of the forefathers, the Bill of Rights, the inalienable pe

[78] Quoted in *Time,* June 19, 1939.

quisites of free men, the holiness of the Constitution, and the freedom of the press, when the issue may simply be: Shall the defendant be permitted to pay children five dollars for a sixty-hour week? . . . or Shall collective-bargaining rights be denied newspapermen on the plea that freedom of the press is endangered? To listen to the arguments in such cases, knowing in what causes the rhetoric was originally invoked, is like listening to the Ninth Symphony rendered on a penny whistle.[79]

Clear thinking may be impeded by religious ardor and patriotic fervor, two of the strongest of all our sentiments. Religious excitement reached the heights of hysterical nonsense in the sawdust trail, the anxious seat, the holy-rolling, and the holy-jumping of the old-fashioned religious revival. A thing of the past in most communities, kinesthetic religion is still prevalent among some colored people of the South who express their spiritual glow in seizures, swoons, sways, and trances. Father Divine knows the art of provoking religious ecstasy by means of a gibberish all his own. Listen:

Because God made Himself flesh, it was observable; it was concentratable; in other words, could be concentrated upon. By individuals concentrating on something, the reaction of such concentrating thoughts caused the reproduction of that which was invisible incarnated in that on which that individual, or those individuals concentrated, to be transmitted to those who have concentrated on such you see. So that is the mystery, according to my version.[80]

Ministers of the gospel who are better educated than Father Divine would not feel it necessary to speak so obscurely, but many a successful preacher achieves a similar obliteration of cerebration by means of dramatic, oratorical appeals that incite the emotions. When an evangelist gets wound up on the subject of rum or women, and paints word pictures of degenerate drunkards and lewd sirens, it is difficult for anybody in the congregation to keep a clear head. When oratory is a thing of beauty, it is apt to be a deadly menace to critical judgment, and we should certainly ask ourselves whether fundamental problems of conduct should be settled in a poetic mood.

If patriotic excitement becomes intemperate, it is likely to be conducive to irrationality. One case in point is that of the eminent German psychologist, E. R. Jaensch, who reported an experiment in which

[79] F. Lundberg: "The Priesthood of the Law." *Harper's Magazine*, April, 1939.
[80] J. Alexander: "All Father's Chillun Got Heavens." *Saturday Evening Post*, November 18, 1939.

he discovered that, since the Nordic chicken is inwardly integrated, it is better behaved and more efficient in feeding than the Mediterranean chicken, thus paralleling the typological superiority of the German citizen. Under Nazi encouragement Erich Jaensch, like the Nordic chicken, had become coordinated.

We may find it enlightening to examine a few more samples to demonstrate how far the prostitution of science and learning may proceed under the domination of a narrow, passionate patriotism. At a meeting of the German Academy of Science, a Nazi mathematician announced: "Mathematics may be variously interpreted. There are English mathematics, Jewish mathematics, German mathematics. German mathematics is the best." This supercilious claim for the superiority of German mathematics was matched by a similar claim for the preferential status of German physics: "Nobel Laureate Lenard dedicates the first volume of his work *Deutsche Physik* with a sweeping denial of the existence of any but Aryan physics, or the physics of the Nordic species of man. Further, he insists that science, like every other product, is racial and conditioned by blood. Monsieur Verdun remarks that the German likes to put Prussian boots on his feet . . . and also on his head."

Nazi patriotism reached the pinnacle of tomfoolery in the employment of sport as an instrument of politics. A paragraph from the *Frankfurterer Zeitung* tells us of a tennis-match victory that was declared forfeited because the winners were not one-hundred-per-cent Nazi. The account reads:

> The governing body of the Reichsbund district in Leipzig decided upon an important step which has been carried out with full cooperation of the district meet supervisor, Herr Stolze. The victory won by members of the Blue-White tennis club in Dresden at the last Meden games was declared void following an unsatisfactory discussion of national problems which took place after the games between Herr Stolze and the victorious players. Lack of appreciation or silent refusal of Nazi ideology becoming evident during the interview prompted the authorities to take this action. Nobody in the Third Reich can be declared winner in any sport competition who does not also demonstrate that he is well-grounded in Nazi theory and willing to do his utmost not only in the field of sport but also in the field of national socialistic endeavor.

The theory of Nazi physical superiority was endangered by the startling performances of a Negro runner representing the United States in the 1936 Olympic Games staged in Germany. The speed of Jesse

(Courtesy, the Baltimore *Sun* and the Artist Yardley.)

Owens on the running track apparently provided an exception to the rule of Nordic superiority, an exception which was explained away by Nazi theorists by resort to the unique hypothesis that Negroes are able to run faster because they are not really human beings, but animals.

We shall consider the social consequences of our religious and patriotic passions in subsequent chapters: religion, in Chapter 20 on "The Church"; patriotism, in Chapter 21 on "The Nation."

E. Collective Immorality

Man in his collective capacity, that is, as a member of a group, can without any compunctions do things which he would not countenance in himself were he acting in an individual capacity. This observation has been very well phrased in the title of a book by Reinhold Niebuhr, *Moral Man and Immoral Society* (1932). Most men feel that honesty is a categorical imperative when they are acting as individuals, even in business matters. In the realm of sport, a player or coach whose idea was victory at any cost, would be unhesitatingly condemned. But victory at any cost is the recognized practice in war.

If I lie in a lawsuit involving the fate of my neighbor's cow, I can go to jail. But if I lie to a million readers in a matter involving war and peace, I can lie my head off, and, if I choose the right series of lies, be entirely irresponsible.[81]

The life of a secret agent abounds in intrigue. One of them confessed: "For more than a quarter of a century I lied and stole and deceived and bribed and killed men suddenly and ruthlessly—all in doing my appointed everyday job. Not once did my conscience reproach me. Rather did I feel that I have deserved well of the country I served. . . . The one wholehearted allegiance of my life was the Army, and the Government behind it which symbolized my native land." [82]

It was Lincoln Steffens who popularized the thesis that the individual person in public office is not deliberately corrupt—the fault lies in the rules of the game, rules which require a certain type of behavior from the office-holder in the fulfillment of his role. Similarly, critics have been prone to blame wars upon munitions manufacturers and in-

---

[81] From W. Lippmann, *Liberty and the News*. By permission of The Macmillan Company, publishers. Pp. 39-40. 1920.

[82] H. W. Lanier: "The Secret Life of a Secret Agent." *Harper's Magazine*, August, 1936.

ernational bankers, forgetting that these people are engaged in activities which are sanctioned by our culture.

Our traditional codes permit a system of doing business which makes some people rich regardless of what their commercial activities may do to upset international relations. In our ignorance and nonchalance we have taken no steps to outlaw conduct of this sort, even though it is seriously antisocial in its effects. Men can still operate within our cultural bounds to make money at the expense of our collective well-being. A striking example of this was the unhappy case of Sterling Products, Inc. This concern, an American pharmaceutical house, was faced with the necessity of making deals with a German corporation (*I. G. Farbenindustrie*) in order to protect its monopoly privileges with respect to patented drugs. Through these agreements (cartels), Sterling officials were gradually compelled to sacrifice vital American interests for the sake of their own personal gain. Commitments which played into Nazi hands were made without any apparent concern for our national welfare. The transactions were legal, fair enough according to the existing rules, loopholes included. Indeed, there are instances of other firms which have prospered in a similar manner, to the public detriment.

It is hard to find norms by which to judge such conduct. The standards of personal morality will hardly do. The officials of Sterling were like hundreds of their kind. They did not, with evil and wanton intent, set out to cripple their country for a war just ahead. They did not formally decree that thousands of men must die, and tens of thousands suffer, for the want of adequate medicines. Like men of affairs, they minded their own business; ignored moral inhibitions, social considerations, national loyalty; refused to be diverted from their resolute purpose. They willed their specific acts, not the larger consequences of what they did. . . . The officials did not indulge a feeling that medicine is more than merchandise; they did not compromise money-making just because they were dealing in ethical drugs. 'If they are sick enough they'll pay the price" is the epitome of salesmanship pure and undefiled. Sterling was impelled throughout by a cardinal business virtue—an intense, steadfast, uncompromising devotion to the pursuit of gain. . . .

If an old story is not to be repeated, we must think, not in terms of personal guilt, but in terms of institutional reform. To secure the common health is one of the great offices of state. A monopoly in anything is odious and a monopoly in medicines intolerable. . . .

The story of Sterling reveals a cleavage that runs through our culture. . . . The American concern does not plan, or even intend, to betray the nation.

It simply neglects to take into account the larger implications of its own acts.[83]

Sterling officials, regarding their venture as a game, did not feel obligated to guard their country—and ours—against the Nazi threat. It was not their job, they could argue, to shape our foreign policy. There was nothing in the rule book commanding a corporation to subordinate its business interests to patriotic loyalty. The individuals who bartered away American rights in order to gain their own personal advantage were not violating any canons of our traditional morality. They did not *will* the evil that issued from their complacent practice of the philosophy that "business is business." The remedy for this kind of evil, as Steffens would suggest, is to bring our ethics up to date, to modernize our rules to fit modern conditions, to make it clear to all concerned that we will no longer give our institutional sanction to a mode of conduct that values individual profit more than it cares for our common welfare.

Answers to questions on pages 161-162.

1. Ottomar Mergenthaler. 2. Charles Goodyear. 3. Michael Pupin. 4. Thomas Edison. 5. Russell Conwell. 6. An astronomer. 7. Thomas Edison. 8. Harriet Beecher Stowe. 9. A newspaper publisher. 10. Leader in public education. 11. A painter. 12. A naturalist. 13. An ornithologist. 14. A socialist leader. 15. A penologist. 16. A jurist. 17. A poetess. 18. Jane Addams. 19. A leader in the care of the insane. 20. Publisher of the *Ladies Home Journal.* 21. Composer of folk songs. 22. Leader in the Red Cross movement. 23. Robert Hoe. 24. A preacher. 25. A naturalist. 26. Joseph Lee. 27. A president of Wellesley College. 28. A doctor, investigator of yellow fever. 29. William Morton. 30. An hydrographer. 31. A Negro educator. 32. James Liddy. 33. A sculptor. 34. An astronomer. 35. Inventor of numerous mechanical devices. 36. A physicist. 37. A botanist. 38. A leader in the movement for woman suffrage. 39. An inventor of the airplane. 40. A missionary to Burma. 41. Judge Willard Phillips. 42. Louisa Alcott. 43. A lexicographer; Webster's Dictionary. 44. An electrical engineer and inventor. 45. Elbert Hubbard. 46. John Hyatt. 47. Gail Borden. 48. Samuel Gompers. 49. B. C. Tilghmann. 50. Abner Doubleday.

[83] W. Hamilton: "The Strange Case of Sterling Products." *Harper's Magazine,* January, 1943.

Chapter 6

THE SOCIALIZATION
OF INTELLIGENCE

MANY OF OUR MISFORTUNES, as we have just noted in the previous chapter, can be attributed to the fact that we fail to use our capacities for ends that will ensure us lasting satisfaction. If we are correct in assuming that the unhappiness we bring upon ourselves is of our own making, then the remedy lies in our own hands. As we learn more about human relations by devoting ourselves more assiduously to the development of the social sciences, we will eventually be in a position to apply our intelligence, our education, our enlightened sense of values, to better advantage. It is exactly this sphere of social relations that scientists have been neglecting too long. We need to know more about the techniques of living together successfully; we need to apply more effectively what we already know. Leaders in all the sciences must be induced to participate in a unified program for organizing society to meet human needs.

I. MODERNIZING SOCIAL SCIENCE

Observers of our contemporary society have pointed out that the social sciences have not kept pace with the development of the physical sciences. The physical sciences, they say, have been making remarkable progress but the social sciences lag. This fact has been dramatically illustrated in the confusion over methods of controlling the use of the atomic bomb. Human beings are at a loss as to what to do with the newly discovered atomic power.

The lag of social science will be illustrated by our outmoded attitudes toward the treatment of the criminal and by our backwardness in economic planning. To counteract the negative emphasis which permeated the preceding chapter on "The Unemployment of Intelligence," we shall supplement our discussion of *lag* in matters of crime and planning by showing what can be done in a constructive way when we take advantage of modern scientific knowledge and apply it intelligently to improve human relations. Thus we shall demonstrate that intelligence *can* be employed. This positive emphasis, after all, must characterize any fruitful approach to the solution of our social problems.

A. THERAPY FOR CRIMINALS

Our concept of the criminal is still very naïve. We think of the criminal as a person who has spent some time in prison. We do not stop to think that there may be persons who belong in prison, just as truly as the people already there, for committing acts we have not yet learned to regard as "antisocial" or "criminal." As long ago as 1907 Ross asserted that modern interdependence was giving rise to new sins, the motivation for which was to be found not in personal ill will but in the ruthless pursuit of gain. The modern sinner—who may be accorded a position of unsullied respectability in your own home town —"picks pockets with a railway rebate, murders with an adulterant . . . burglarizes with a 'rake-off' instead of a jimmy, cheats with the company prospectus instead of a deck of cards," [1] maims through neglect to fence dangerous machinery in a mill, robs as a tax dodger, tells lies and distorts news, promotes crooked reasoning, loans trust funds to friends without adequate collateral, sponsors fake testimonials, pyramids holding companies on watered capital, adjusts insurance claims by bluffing the injured party out of his lawful indemnity. These are not black sins but just grayish, so subtle as to be hardly recognized as iniquities, for, as Ross says, the time-honored insignia of turpitude are missing. Fagin and Simon Legree have been replaced, in part, by respectable sinners, men who are loving in their family relations, faithful to friends, generous to the needy. The villain today is a quasi-criminal, what Ross calls a "criminaloid." The key to the criminaloid is not evil impulse but moral insensibility. The criminaloid operates in an impersonal fashion: he would not rob a specific individual but holds up people in general. He may sin by syndicate. There is nothing like distance to disinfect dividends. Thus the retired professor who invests in stock accepts the welcome dividends without inquiring to discover that the company may be oppressing Tennessee miners in order to create profits. The corporation, as Ross puts it, transmits the greed of investments but not their conscience.

The designation of certain persons as "criminals" will accord with

[1] E. A. Ross: *Sin and Society*, p. 7. Houghton Mifflin Company.

the social norms prevailing at the time. People are continually devising new ways of sinning they can get away with. Sensibility
changes, too. Society no longer tolerates the predatory practices
which built up the fortunes of John D. Rockefeller, Andrew Carnegie,
and the other "robber barons." [2] Ross was making allowance for such
an evolution in our norms when he suggested an annual supplement
to the Decalogue.

Despite some advances in our concept of *crime,* we still do not appreciate, most of us, the dangers of "white-collar criminality." Citing as
white-collar criminals the "robber barons" of the Nineteenth Century
and the Kreugers, Staviskys, Insulls, Whitneys, Coster-Musicas of the
Twentieth, Sutherland calls attention to a great welter of less spectacular white-collar rascality, such as misrepresentation in financial statements of corporations, manipulation in the stock exchange, bribery of
public officials indirectly in order to secure favorable legislation, misrepresentation in advertising and salesmanship, misapplication of
funds, short weights and measures and misgrading of commodities,
food and drug-law violation, fee-splitting by doctors, tax frauds, mis-
appropriation of funds through receiverships and bankruptcies—what
Al Capone would have called "the legitimate rackets." This sort of
top-drawer malfeasance does not reach the courts nearly so often as the
crimes of violence such as murders, assaults, robberies, and sex offenses which flourish among the lower-class criminals. Such being the
case, white-collar criminals receive scant attention from criminologists.
Indeed, statistics of upper-class criminality are bound to be incomplete
because the culprits are usually regarded as respectable and influential
citizens in the community, and are seldom apprehended, prosecuted,
or convicted. Consequently, there are no substantial criminal records
upon which to estimate the cost to society of crimes of greed as compared with crimes of violence. Some students of the problem hazard
the guess that the social cost of white-collar criminality is far more serious than the damages done by violence.[3] Here is a field in which we
should long ago have been collecting data to guide us in the formulation and administration of our legal codes.

The attitude of the public toward criminals is extremely unreliable,
inconsistent, and unscientific. Chance circumstances, passing sympathies, and incidental moods play an unwarranted role in producing
condemnation or leniency. Our present-day feeling about criminals is

---

[2] See M. Josephson: *The Robber Barons.* 1934.
[3] Paper on "White-collar Criminality," presidential address delivered by E. H.
Sutherland at the 1939 meeting of the American Sociological Society.

tied up with our attitude toward the law. Criminals, obviously, do not feel any great respect for the law; but neither do many respectable citizens, like the ones who persistently flouted the Prohibition Amendment without losing caste or prestige. Persons who have been arrested "merely" for speeding or overtime parking or heading the wrong way down a one-way street, or persons who have argued in public with brutal, officious policemen, may fail thereafter to accord the "proper" respect for officers of the law. The popular contempt for the law as represented by the police is evidenced in detective plays where the sadistic detective gives a third-degree manhandling to a frail little woman suspect, and the audience cheers when the guilty party eludes the fumbling search of the police. Disrespect for the law affects our attitude toward the criminal.

One of the chief contributory causes of crime is the morbid state of public opinion about crime. When a murder has been committed, maudlin sentimentalists protest against the assassin's doom, disparage the law which decrees it, pursue the officials charged with its administration, rail against the penalty prescribed for the deed, compose letters and editorials which reverse the real order and paint the convicted murderer as a hero or his executioner as a villain. These sentimentalists give aid and comfort to the criminal population. The comparative immunity from punishment now enjoyed by many criminals in the United States is traceable to respectable people who are given to exalting clemency for the guilty at the expense of protection for the unoffending.

It is not difficult to find instances of misdirected sympathy. An Associated Press dispatch described what happened when the jury returned a verdict of murder against Gerald Chapman, the man who had been writing lovely poetry while he languished in prison:

Hartford, a New England bulwark of law and order, was decidedly "for" the vivid Chapman, and made no bones about it. Crowds in motion picture houses had for the past week hissed pictures of Walter E. Shean, Springfield, Mass., advertising man, who first accused Chapman of murder. These same crowds, when Chapman's striking visage was flashed on the screen, applauded. So, when Hartford heard of Chapman's fate, it mourned as though in anticipatory requiem. Men in the streets cursed volubly and long. Women openly wept.[4]

When a boy stole a car and drove it at a high speed through the streets of Boston's North End, "thousands lined the streets to see him

[4] Boston *Herald*, April 7, 1925.

pass. That the sympathy of the majority was with the youthful des-
perado and not with the police was evidenced by the cheers that
greeted him each time he appeared." [5] In the case of one speedster
who toured the loop, only to be killed by a policeman, the reporter
wrote this harrowing story:

With tears streaming down her wrinkled cheeks, a 55-year-old mother lived
in retrospect the last hours with her 15-year-old son, Harry, at their modest
little home, on Kennard street, Cambridge, last night, before a police officer
had sent a bullet crashing through the boy's skull accidentally.

"He was the only one left of three," Mrs. Catherine Haskett, mother of
Harry, and a native of Cheshire, Eng., sobbed. "And he was the one I loved
most. He was a good boy. But he was in bad company."

Harry Haskett was killed by a policeman's bullet as he sped over the loop
on the now famous Charlestown speedway. His two companions, James
Slattery, 15, of Donovan court, Charlestown, and George Taylor, 16, are
under arrest.

Mrs. Haskett, surrounded by a group of friends and neighbors who tried to
console her, wept unrestrained.

"Harry was a good boy," she cried, "but I told him he would get into
trouble associating with bad company." [6]

The moment a man is arrested and put on trial for a crime, some
people take the attitude that a game is on. They see the poor, lone,
unbefriended defendant on one side, with the uniformed, powerful
hosts of the law on the other. Sympathizers begin to root for the defendant, who seems to be playing a losing game. Because of reports
of the bravery and heroism of the defendant, and of the way he stands
up under the strain, which appear repeatedly in some of the newspapers, the defendant comes to be regarded as a martyr to the cause
of liberty. Newspaper readers are familiar with accounts such as this
one:

ILLICIT LOVERS DIE ON GALLOWS

Sheriff Charles Pecot went to Mrs. Lebouef's cell at noon and told her to
come with him.

She was sitting on the edge of her cot, dressed in a plain pink linen slip-
dress and white silk stockings.

"Sheriff, you know I am innocent, why do they want to hang me?" she
asked.

---

[5] Account in a Boston newspaper.
[6] The Boston *Herald Traveler*, September 19, 1933.

"I know, Miss Ada, but we have done all we can. Come on," said Pecot
Arthur Martel, the jailer, reached down to put on her patent leather black
pumps. When his hands fumbled she reached down and fastened the straps.

She hesitated a moment and looked at Father J. J. Rousseau, pastor of the
Church of the Assumption, seated in front of her. "Oh, well, I suppose I
must change this life for a better one," she said.

She walked from the cell with her left arm around the neck of Jailer Martel. She had only seven feet to walk from her cell to the two steel double
doors extending out from her cell tier, making the death trap.

Her eyes were blinded by a white handkerchief and she did not see the
rope, hanging from a steel eye in the roof to the corner of an adjoining cell.
As she stood there, with the jailers trussing her hands behind her back, and
her legs at the knees with clothes line, she exclaimed:

"My mother! My mother! Oh, my God. Isn't this a terrible thing?
Don't let me hang there too long. Don't let me suffer. God forgive everybody. Isn't this a terrible thing? This is awful. This is murder itself."

The black cowl was placed over her head. The rope was adjusted with the
knot at the right ear.

"That rope is too tight around my neck," she protested. Then as her knees
gave way and she struggled with the jailer, the trap was sprung.

The body swung for eleven minutes, and at 12:16 the physician officially
pronounced her dead. The body was cut down, the prayer beads with the
cross were twisted from her fingers and she was carried to a cell cot by four
men.

Meanwhile, Dr. Dreher was held a few feet away in a cell behind a solid
steel door. He could see nothing but could hear all.[7]

Stories of this nature give the average person the creeps, thereby evoking sympathy for the abused criminal.

The same tender feeling for the criminal may be developed by a
college course in criminology—or psychology. The student who has
discovered that behavior is the resultant of hereditary and cultural influences may no longer retain the moralistic attitude that it is our duty
to "teach the criminal a lesson" by subjecting him to punishment.
The student who has learned to understand the psychology behind
the criminal's action, tends to be more lenient in his feeling for the
man who has come to a bad end, perhaps through little fault of his
own. To determine how college courses affect students in this regard,
Telford administered the Thurstone Scale of Attitude toward Treatment of Criminals to members of four college classes, at the beginning
and at the end of the semester. Changes, all in the direction of increased leniency, were found among the students in all four classes:

[7] Boston *Herald,* February 2, 1929.

least in general psychology, more in educational psychology, still more in introduction to sociology, most of all in criminology. The degree of change correlated positively with the amount of attention paid to the topic of treating criminals or to allied topics.[8]

What does the student of criminology learn that causes him to become more lenient in his attitude toward the criminal? He learns that crime results from the impact of certain environmental influences upon the personality of the malefactor, that unwholesome habits are acquired under unfortunate conditions of life, that the criminal is a "sick" person in the same sense that an individual is said to be ill when he is suffering from a mental disorder. The criminologist does not see the criminal as one who has exercised his free will to choose the path of law-violation just for the sake of being antisocial. Rather he interprets the misconduct in the light of the individual's past—his family background, economic circumstances, physical deficiencies, mental aberrations, his motives, and the like. The criminal is a human being; as such he is a proper subject for investigation by physiologists, psychologists, psychiatrists, and sociologists. These scientists, working together, look first for the causes that will account for the antisocial conduct, and then they explore the possible techniques available for reforming or rehabilitating the *individual,* or possibly decide upon the basis of what they learn about his personality that he should be permanently segregated for the protection of society. There is no notion of punishing the evildoer in a spirit of retaliatory moral discipline. The treatment is scientifically designed to modify the personality in the desirable direction. Thus the old idea of fixing blame is supplanted by a search for the understanding of causal relationships.

A scientific attitude toward criminality does not imply the sentimental conclusion that the criminal should be excused from punishment, for an adequate comprehension of psychological principles will certainly suggest that something must be done to reform the offender or to protect society from his malefactions. The mature person, well grounded in scientific criminology, will not demand expiation for sin or "an eye for an eye" retribution; he will be interested, instead, in studying the personality of the criminal and in planning what can be done to convert him into a law-abiding citizen. The underlying principle in an objective view of crime is to fit the punishment, not to the crime, but to the criminal. Warden Lawes, on the basis of long experience at Sing Sing, describes the newer attitude very well. Instead

[8] C. W. Telford: "An Experimental Study of Some Factors Influencing the Social Attitudes of College Students." *Journal of Social Psychology,* 1934, 5, 421-428.

of giving the criminal thirty days for this, or five years for that, Lawes proposes:

> Why not say to the boy or man charged with crime, "You have done wrong. Let us find out about you. We are concerned not only with your particular act, but also with your personality. Perhaps we can ascertain the exact nature of your delinquency. Are your home influences bad? . . . Would teaching you a trade help? Is there something wrong with your physique? Or, is your mentality so warped as to necessitate your permanent segregation?" [9]

Penologists and psychiatrists agree that our criminal jurisprudence is archaic, unscientific. They advocate *individualization* in the treatment of the offender. To attain this end they favor radical changes in legislative enactments, legal procedure, and penal practice, including these modifications of our present trial procedure:

1. The disposition of all misdemeanants and felons should be based on study of the individual offender by properly qualified and impartial experts cooperating with the courts.
2. Such experts should be appointed by the courts with provision for remuneration from public funds.
3. No maximum term should be set for any sentence.
4. Prisoners should be discharged or released upon parole only after complete and competent psychiatric examination indicates that there is a prospect for successful rehabilitation.
5. The incurably inadequate, incompetent, and antisocial offenders should be interned permanently, without regard to the particular offense committed.

These proposals for a more scientific procedure in the treatment of criminals were approved by the delegates to the Ninth International Prison Congress in 1925 and by the American Psychiatric Association in 1927. I mention the dates in this connection to impress upon the reader the fact that scientific authorities in the field of criminology have felt for a long time that our system of jurisprudence is antiquated. Progress in introducing these revolutionary procedures is slow because public opinion regarding these matters is still guided more by sentimental whim than by scientific understanding. It appears reasonable to anyone who has studied criminology and penology to assume that justice is more likely to be done if we have one group of experts to determine the matter of guilt and another group

[9] L. E. Lawes: *20,000 Years in Sing Sing*, p. 365. 1932.

of experts to decide how the convicted person should be treated for his own good and the good of society. The achievement of a scientific jurisprudence would mean the abolition of the jury trial which is a hangover of the archaic idea of "trial by combat." [10] It would also mean the abolition of the practice which allocates to the judge the responsibility for imposing sentence. Presumably, in most cases, the judge is a man trained in the law but not necessarily trained in psychology, psychiatry, and sociology. S. Sheldon Glueck of the Harvard Law School believes that the time may come fairly soon for abrogating the sentencing power of jurists and for delegating this power to a board of experts empowered to impose a sentence based entirely on the circumstances surrounding each individual defendant—and later to release on parole when exhaustive scientific study indicates that the public interest would be served by doing so.

The objection may be raised, of course, that psychologists and psychiatrists do not know enough to justify delegating to them so much responsibility in handling the criminal. It is true that psychologists and psychiatrists do not know as much as they ought to know—but it is equally true that they are likely to know far more about the art of modifying human habits than a judge trained principally, and usually exclusively, in the fine points of the law. And professional experts in psychology or psychiatry are not likely to be any more subject than judges to the influences of prejudice or corruption.

As social scientists we should concern ourselves not primarily with the offense but with the offender, and we should aim, not to punish, but to understand and to readjust the individual offender to normal life in the community.

What can be accomplished when criminals are treated scientifically has been demonstrated by the Federal Bureau of Prisons and by the Judge Baker Guidance Center.

The Bureau of Prisons, created by Congress in 1930, operates under the Department of Justice for the purpose of managing and regulating all Federal penal and correctional institutions (except those maintained by the Army and Navy). The Bureau "is responsible for the safekeeping, care, protection, instruction, and discipline of all persons charged with or convicted of offenses against the United States." In the selection of personnel, the importance of professionalizing the penal service is recognized and, consequently, "with a few exceptions, all officers and employees of the Bureau are appointed in accordance

[10] See T. Arnold: *The Symbols of Government,* Chapter 8, "Trial by Combat." 1935.

with the rules and regulations of the United States Civil Service Commission." This is a very significant requirement in the prison system since it takes the administration of penology out of the hands of political appointees who may know little about criminology and places it in the hands of persons who must prove themselves by examination. The same objective of expert care has been furthered by the inauguration of a "comprehensive plan of in-service training for custodial officers," according to which "all promotions and salary raises will be made upon the basis of the completion of training requirements as well as the maintenance of satisfactory service records."

The fundamental policy which governs all activities of the Bureau is stated thus: "Our prisons and reformatories should not be conducted in the interests of the prisoner solely, but with the thought in mind of *protecting our communities.*" The true protection of society, it is explained, "can only be achieved through a program of individual treatment involving custody, discipline, and rehabilitation. Prisons do not protect our communities if men leave prison more antisocial and more desperate than when they went in. The task of the modern prison includes an effort to prepare prisoners for normal social life." Individual treatment is sought by studying offenders, classifying them, and committing or transferring each one to an institution especially prepared to care for a particular type of criminal: narcotic addicts are assigned to Leavenworth Annex, insane prisoners to the United States Hospital for Defective Delinquents, intractable persons with serious records of violent crime to Alcatraz, and so on. Classification of prisoners is "based upon a careful consideration of all factors, including age, previous criminal record, personality characteristics, and social background." Transfers are planned so as "to place the most hopeful offenders in those institutions which offer the best rehabilitative opportunities."

The thoroughness of this penal program, which aims to do the best thing for each inmate, may be gleaned from a Bureau report:

INDIVIDUAL TREATMENT WITHIN EACH INSTITUTION

Individual treatment within each institution begins with an initial quarantine period of thirty days which is devoted to the investigation, interviewing, and examination of each new prisoner by the following members of the staff or their assistants:

Record Clerk
Deputy Warden or Assistant Superintendent
Senior Warden's Assistant

Chief Medical Officer
Psychiatrist
Psychologist
Supervisor of Education
Chaplain
Director of Recreation
Parole Officer

Each of these staff members studies the new inmate for the purpose of discovering what problems he presents in his field in order that he may make the recommendations for remedial and corrective measures to be undertaken during the period of incarceration. At the end of the quarantine period every case is brought before the institution's Classification Committee consisting of the Warden or Superintendent and the above members of his staff.

This Committee reviews all of the information available secured during the quarantine period, considers the recommendations of the various specialists and outlines a definite program embracing the following elements:

Custody and discipline
Transfer to another institution when indicated
Social service
Medical and surgical treatment when indicated
Psychiatric and psychological treatment when indicated
Education
Employment
Religious training
Recreation

Periodic reclassifications are made with the idea of reducing supervision gradually in case the prisoner's conduct and previous record offer convincing evidence that society will not be jeopardized by the extension of his freedom.

Every effort is made to administer discipline in a constructive manner by inculcating acceptable attitudes and desirable habits. The medical and psychiatric services are consulted freely in dealing with disciplinary problems. Brutal punishments are not permitted; there must be no beating or other form of corporal punishment; no handcuffs, no shackles, no other form of physical restraint may be used for punishment purposes. "Throughout the system every energy is bent to avoid the traditional brutality of prisons without sacrificing fairness and firmness."

In the educational program, instruction is highly individualized. "Learning as a means of better social adjustment rather than learning for its own sake is the goal." Industrial training is provided, where it is indicated, as a means of preparing men for their return to society.

Religion is utilized as an instrument for reformation. Constructive recreation is offered to train the inmates for successful release. In some institutions prisoners are allowed to participate in the management; thus, they are taught, by experience, to respect rules and regulations.

Regional jails have been established by the Bureau to demonstrate the fundamentals of decent jail management.[11]

The Bureau of Prisons stands for progressive, scientific penal treatment. It is understandable, therefore, why the public attitude toward the criminal is deplored in so many reports by the Director of the Bureau:

While many people give lip-service to the idea that our prisons must be primarily rehabilitative, I am afraid that the basic attitude of people in general still is one of vengeance. They think men go to prison not only as punishment but also for punishment. If this obvious method of controlling crime had proved successful, our prisons would not now be growing in size and number, and crime would be steadily decreasing.[12]

I sometimes wonder that we get as good results as we do considering the situation in many of our prisons. After all, the American people get the kind of prisons they want and deserve. By and large most American prisons are antiquated structures, shockingly overcrowded, operated under the spoils system, and starved for funds.[13]

Treatment of the offender, I think you will admit, reflects the philosophy and culture of those who conceive and administer criminal justice.[14]

Public sentiment, it is pointed out, constitutes a very important factor in dealing with crime. The public is being educated to share the point of view of the psychiatrist who is trying to *understand* the prisoner so that he can reeducate him successfully. Many taxpayers still remain blind to the fact that money would be saved in the long run by devoting more funds to prevention and to adequate programs for rehabilitation.

[11] This outline of the Bureau's program, and the quotations cited, are from "A Brief Account of the Penal and Correctional Activities of the Bureau of Prisons, U.S. Department of Justice." 1936.

[12] J. V. Bennett: "Prisons and Law Enforcement." Address before the Pacific Northwest Conference on Banking, Pullman, Washington, April 5, 1940.

[13] *Ibid.*

[14] J. V. Bennett: " 'There is a Tide'—a Religious and Social Approach to the Criminal Offender through Parole." Address before the National Conference of Catholic Charities, Denver, Colorado, August 8, 1939.

We have not yet begun to tap the possibilities of readjusting the anti-social, the psychopathic and the handicapped. But we cannot do very much until we are willing to spend some money to study physical and mental illnesses of the prisoner. Our prisons provide an opportunity for research unparalleled elsewhere in our social system and yet by and large little or nothing is being done. You can see this when you realize that at least 100,000 of 175,000 prisoners come under no rehabilitative or reformative force whatsoever during the entire period of the incarceration. Not much can be done on a budget of about one dollar per man per day for all housing, guarding, feeding, clothing, and maintenance costs. It is only within the past few years and in a comparatively few institutions that any effort whatsoever has been made to study the mental and social problems of the prisoner.

However, in the Federal service we are making some effort not only to find out what accounts for the type of individual who gets into prison, but also we are using the psychiatrist and the medical officer to an increasing extent to help us solve the workaday problems of prison administration. The U.S. Public Health Service, which is responsible for furnishing and supervising medical and psychiatric care in the Federal correctional institutions, has made notable contributions to the improvement of our rehabilitative program.[15]

Prison psychiatry in this modernized penal program is regarded as a special branch of mental hygiene. Its job is to find out what can be done to "cure" the constitutional psychopathic inferior, the incipient paranoid, the happy-go-lucky alcoholic addict, the drug addict, the intelligent individual who is totally incapable of governing his own passions and controlling his wants. Progress is being made through studying how to prevent and how to cure the psychopathic personalities developed by our culture "rather than cavalierly trying to bury our mistakes behind prison walls." Not all criminals, of course, are insane or psychopathic. Some fifteen or twenty per cent of the Federal prisoners possess definite mental defects clearly recognizable by the trained psychiatrist.

The Bureau of Prisons is seeking through the United States Public Health Service to provide psychiatric diagnostic service in the Federal District Courts. A panel of psychiatrists certified by the American Board of Psychiatry and Neurology is selected for each city listed in this limited program. This service, the Bureau feels, should be broadened: "in larger jurisdictions there should . . . be a full-time psychiatric officer attached to the probation department so that pre-trial and pre-sentence investigations of offenders may be made and appropriate

---

[15] J. V. Bennett: "Psychiatry in the Federal Correctional System." Address before the American Psychiatric Association, Cincinnati, Ohio, May 20, 1940.

psychotherapy and other forms of treatment may be made available to probationers and to offenders under the jurisdiction of the court." [16]

The constructive penal policies of the Bureau of Prisons are exhibited at their best in the matter of parole. The philosophy underlying the parole system is interest in readjusting the offender to society so that he may become an asset instead of a liability. The idea is sound, authorities agree; what is most needed is improvement of its administration. In too many instances the parole system is closely allied to politics. Adequate funds must be made available to provide for competent, well-paid, politically independent supervisors; at present "we spend ten times as much to keep men in prison as to supervise them on parole." [17] The right kind of parole permits the release of a prisoner only under conditions which are most favorable for his reestablishment in the community. "Now we can achieve the right kind of parole if we focus public opinion upon the need for taking it out of politics and provide the necessary funds for its intelligent administration." [18] The period of imprisonment must be utilized to prepare the offender for his release into the community. Parole can be successful only when it is administered as an integral part of a coordinated program for treating the offender. "You can't have a poor, antiquated, cruel system of prison management and at the same time a good parole procedure. It should also be plain that it is of equal importance to have the right kind of community cooperation." [19] This means planning ahead: securing employment, preparing the family group for the return of the offender, providing a suitable home and environment for the homeless and friendless man. The prisons, strange to say, are expected to teach men how to use their liberty by depriving them of their freedom. This problem is a difficult one. Parole is one answer, and it has proved to be a good one by successfully reducing crime.[20]

Probation should not be considered merely as leniency, letting the offender off scot-free, but rather as a realistic system of making the offender abide by the law at the same time he continues to work, support his family, and

[16] *Ibid.*

[17] J. V. Bennett: "Parole: One Way or Round Trip." Address before the International Association of Chiefs of Police, San Francisco, California, October 9, 1939.

[18] *Ibid.*

[19] Bennett: " 'There is a Tide'—a Religious and Social Approach to the Criminal Offender Through Parole." *Loc. cit.*

[20] See S. Bates: "Probation Today and Tomorrow." Address before the New York Probation Officers Association Conference, New York City, October 18, 1937.

go about his normal duties.[21]   Among both the accidental or "temporary" criminals and the improvable type of prisoner are many for whom only access to community resources can possibly provide the essentials of rehabilitation.   For these the prison will never have enough personnel, enough facilities, or enough money to complete the rehabilitative process.   For these only a fraction of what we call rehabilitation can possibly be accomplished within prison walls; the real job of rehabilitation must be performed in the community itself under normal conditions where access to all the many opportunities and facilities and personal elements essential to the process can be had for each individual.[22]

The modern psychiatric approach, then, aims to select the persons who are reclaimable and to apply sound therapy to assure their redemption.   It represents an humanitarian endeavor, intelligently directed.

The Judge Baker Guidance Center in Boston, directed by Healy and Bronner, is another illustration of the modern scientific approach to the study of delinquency.   The Center concerns itself first and foremost with the development of character by guiding personal growth in the right channels.

The quality of family relationships in the early years of life; the way frustrations and real or fancied wrongs are met; the types of compensations for handicaps and inferiorities; the goals for which physical and mental assets are utilized—these are some of the main factors basic in the structuring of personality. . . . [We] must guide both parents and children, learning ever better to recognize and treat emotional ills.[23]

This is the philosophy which has grown out of years of experience in dealing with young delinquents and other problem children referred to the Center by families, by juvenile courts, by schools, and by other social agencies.   Healy established the first child-guidance clinic in Chicago, in 1909; he was the leader in the founding of the Judge Baker Guidance Center in Boston, in 1917.   The Boston clinic became a model which inspired the spread of the child-guidance movement in many parts of the world.   This movement has made important contributions to crime prevention by checking early delinquency through helping young people to solve their behavior, personality, and educational or vocational problems.

[21] Bennett: "Prisons and Law Enforcement."   *Loc. cit.*
[22] J. V. Bennett: "Breaking the Delinquency-Crime Chain on the Adult Level." Address before the National Conference of Social Work, Atlantic City, New Jersey, June 3, 1941.
[23] Judge Baker Guidance Center: *Annual Report, 1941.*

The service of the Judge Baker Guidance Center was almost entirely diagnostic back in 1917—causes and recommendations for handling cases were reported to juvenile courts and a few other social agencies, all of whom assumed responsibility for treatment. "After a few years, gradually more and more psychiatric treatment was undertaken, involving both parents and children, until at present it is our chief task." [24]   This shift in policy is graphically portrayed in the pictogram on this page.[25]

In the old days, theorists were inclined to attribute crime to a single cause: to birth, to degeneracy, to physical defects or diseases, to mental

Growth of the Judge Baker Guidance Center
Changes in Sources of Referral

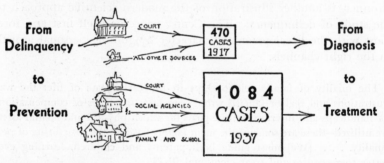

defect, to bad habits, to poor recreation, to economic pressure—each interpreter boosting one of these factors as his pet explanation for the evolution of the criminal.   The modern student of delinquents looks for a plurality of interrelated causes.   On page 197 the Judge Baker Guidance Center presents this point of view.[26]   Each case is studied as an individual problem, and treatment is selected according to individual needs—some children are placed in foster homes, some are given remedial training to overcome school disabilities.   Family contacts are sought in an effort to educate parents in handling their children effectively.   Psychologists and social workers are trained at the Center and considerable research is conducted to determine the exact nature of different forms of delinquency, the causes and the cures.

Under the sponsorship of the Yale Institute of Human Relations, Healy and Bronner made an extensive investigation into the genesis

[24] Judge Baker Guidance Center: "Twenty Years of Growth—1917-1937."
[25] *Ibid.*
[26] *Ibid.*

How Problems of Youth Are Met
Through Present Day Child Guidance Procedure
Many Interrelated Causes—Scientifically Evaluated

By Study of

1. The Entire Physical Organism

Sensory and organic conditions and the physical self as a whole with its weaknesses and assets are studied as related to the mental, emotional and social life of the growing individual.

2. The Mental Equipment

Besides general intelligence, capacities for dealing with ideas and with actual materials is estimated by many psychological tests in order to determine talents and handicapping disabilities in educational, vocational and social adjustments. Judgment is made of personality.

3. The Total Social Milieu

Physical features of the home are not nearly so important as the attitudes, behavior and feelings of members of the family towards each other. Neighborhood conditions are not so important as the effects of school and other social contacts upon the children. Parents gradually tell their stories of the deeper issues involved.

4. The Emotional Factors

The sources of unhappiness, of feelings of frustration and deprivation and inferiority as well as goals represented by the behavior of the child are elicited through his own story. It is a story of desires and fears and hates and loves in terms of human relationships.

5. Interplay of above as Causes

In staff conference a picture is built up of all that bears upon the particular problem that the child presents. Each of the contributed facts is interpreted in the light of the outlined sketch of all the causes. The needs are discernible as those of the family as well as those of the child.

6. Subsequent Treatment

The multiple causes always found signify multiple needs, ranging perhaps from endocrine treatment, betterment of recreations, or special tutoring, to resolving mental conflicts and continuance of psychiatric interviews with parents and children to aid them in living more adequately and happily.

of criminals, using a control technique of comparing the delinquent with a non-delinquent child in the same family, following the psychiatric approach throughout. Searching for the meaning of delinquent behavior, the investigators developed a new orientation based on the assumption—later a conviction—that delinquency is the result of the frustration of basic human needs, that crime is resorted to because it fulfills a purpose in the individual's life, that the family should be taken as the unit of treatment rather than the individual by himself. Thwarted in "the wish for various sorts of affectional response, . . . desires for recognition, security, and adequacy, . . . urges . . . for accomplishment satisfying to oneself, for new experiences and adventures, for outlets for physical and mental energies, for ownership of possessions, . . . self-assertion, . . . independence, and self-direction," the individual turns to crime as a substitutive activity to gain satisfaction.[27] He is disposed toward antisocial outlets, partly because of external circumstances—evil companions, opportunities to pick up easy money—and partly because of ideas he has been entertaining in his mind over a period of time. The determinants of crime can be traced to emotional maladjustments within the family circle, specifically to "the less tangible facts, namely, those related to emotional attitudes and to values held."

In Boston, New Haven, and Detroit, 133 families were studied, families which had produced 194 delinquent children out of 461 who were old enough to be delinquent. Sample careers were followed through. In each case a critical study was made of the assets and liabilities of the family life.

For the entire 153 delinquents with whom we began to work . . . there was real disharmony between the parents in 54 per cent and distinct harmony in only 30 per cent. This, of course, means that in a large share of the families there was between the parents open exhibition of disrespect, discontent, and friction, with disagreement (in 41 per cent) about discipline of the children, especially of the delinquent. Sexual incompatibility was freely spoken of in 63 per cent of 75 families where parents discussed their sexual adjustments. . . . There was definite conflict between parents and children resulting from the clash between old and new world standards in one quarter of the families.

Personality characteristics were examined carefully, in the delinquents and in their comparable non-delinquent siblings, to determine

[27] W. Healy and A. F. Bronner: *New Light on Delinquency and Its Treatment.* Yale University Press, 1936. All of the quotations hereafter in this section on the work of Healy and Bronner are from this book.

whether any traits could be found that would distinguish the criminal from the law-abiding children in the same family. The outstanding trait of the delinquents was discovered to be great restlessness or over-activity manifested in uninhibited physical impulses, extreme aggressiveness, and an excessive fondness for excitement. Some evidence was gathered which indicated that "emotional thwartings and dissatisfactions, themselves dating back to very early years, may be the inciting cause of hyperactivity. In reviewing the family relationships of the overrestless cases we discovered that the vast majority had highly disturbing emotional situations in the family life."

In studying the social adjustments of their subjects, Healy and Bronner learned that among the delinquents family relationships were reasonably satisfactory in only 20 per cent of the cases. "Love for the father was expressed or evidenced in only about one fifth of the cases. In very numerous instances the child was either thoroughly indifferent to him or resented him." Strong affection for the mother was detected in somewhat less than half the cases. The thwarting of such normal emotional needs of childhood affords a clue to a deeper understanding of fundamental sources of antisocial conduct. It is significant, too, that 40 per cent of the delinquents expressed a marked dislike of school and 13 per cent said they hated some one or more of their teachers. Findings of dissatisfaction in home and school were combined and "the startling fact emerged that in no less than 75 per cent there was evidence of marked dislike either of school or of father or of mother."

Major emotional disturbances were noted in 131 out of the 143 delinquents accepted for treatment:

Feelings of being rejected, unloved, or insecure in affectional relationships —53 cases.

Deep feelings of being thwarted in self-expression and other self-satisfactions—45 cases.

Marked feeling of inadequacy or inferiority in some situations or activities—62 cases.

Emotional disturbance about family disharmonies, discipline, etc.—43 cases.

Great persisting sibling jealousy or rivalry—43 cases.

Deep-set internal emotional conflicts—19 cases.

Delinquency in many cases seemed to function as a compensatory satisfaction for profound feelings of not being understood and of being isolated in the family circle.

The investigators studied the non-delinquent siblings to find out

why they had not taken to crime. They found these law-abiding
youths less active, less gregarious, less subject to emotional disturbances. Granting that different children in the same family are not exposed to the same objective and subjective conditions, it was observed
that non-delinquents, when they were unhappy, reacted to their discontent by seeking education, associating with the right kind of companions, or gaining substitute satisfactions in athletic or other social
activities. The evidence points unmistakably to this significant conclusion:

Many children living under conditions which seem to offer sufficient reason
for the development of delinquent tendencies do not become delinquent.
This is an outstanding fact not to be lost sight of when family situations are
stressed, as they properly should be, as partial causes of delinquency. The
point is that if some children are able to withstand a given inimical asocial
environment, particularly as represented by the family life and its neighborhood setting, the environment considered by itself cannot logically be regarded as the only factor in the production of delinquency.

For various reasons the non-delinquents demanded less from the environment, were able more readily to obtain satisfactions through interests within the law.

Eight pairs of non-identical twins were included in the study, one of
each pair appearing as the control, one as the delinquent. "Assem-
bling the records of these twins we find a one-to-one correlation between affective discomforts and the onset or continuance of delinquency. Every one of the delinquents proved to have these inner
stresses and every one of the controls proved to be free from them."
In one case, quite typical, the parents were thoroughly incompatible,
engaged in much open quarreling and counter-accusations in front of
the children. "There was violent disagreement about discipline; the
mother charged her high-tempered husband with whipping too severely and he maintained that although she was rather well-educated
she was really dull, incompetent, and too lenient." The father acknowledged that he disliked the delinquent, that he liked the control;
he attributed his aversion for the delinquent to the fact that the child
showed a "stubborn lack of response" even in his early infancy; later
the father repulsed the boy when he tried to climb on his knee. The
delinquent deeply sensed the deprivation of his father's love, commented frankly on his being hatefully rejected, expressed his own antagonism for his father, stated that he felt greatly discriminated against
and that he experienced exceeding jealousy for his siblings. Such evi-

dence suggests that we should "pay more attention to the emotional implications of human relationships. Herein will lie the guiding principle of a new orientation." The figures speak for themselves: "*ninety-one per cent of the delinquents* gave clear evidence of being or having been very unhappy and discontented in their life circumstances or extremely disturbed because of emotion-provoking situations or experiences . . . but *only 13 per cent of the controls*." Many children were found who had never suffered from serious, persisting emotional maladjustments; the 14 controls who had experienced some considerable degree of emotional discomfort, had found counterbalancing satisfactions.

Why did the delinquents react to frustration by turning to crime? Various motives were uncovered by the investigators, such as *escape* or *flight* from an unpleasant situation, attempt to achieve substitutive *compensatory satisfactions,* effort to *bolster up the ego, revenge, antagonism to authority, urge for emancipation, wish for punishment* (response to a conscious or unconscious sense of guilt). Delinquency serves a purpose, "offering itself as a vehicle for reactive urges because ideas of delinquency have already been a part of the thought content of the individual." A person is more apt to accept the idea of crime if it happens to accord with his special needs, if he is frustrated, restless, looking for a chance to do something about it.

Usually the juvenile delinquent is the sole recipient of treatment, though it is generally recognized that he is not the only person who is to blame. Such a procedure is unfair and illogical, especially if the treatment consists merely of incarceration, for under such circumstances the fundamental sources of trouble still remain untouched. Healy and Bronner were keenly interested to find out what could be accomplished by treating the delinquent's whole family, inasmuch as the evidence was convincing that the source of crime lay in the emotional maladjustments within the family circle. It would seem sensible, such being the case, to reconstruct unfortunate behavior tendencies by modifying the unhappy family relationships. This was done as one aspect of a comprehensive treatment which included medical and dental care, attention to school problems, recreational plans, country vacations, placing in foster homes, and psychiatric interviews. Psychiatric counsel was employed to help the youth gain an insight into the real source of his unsocial behavior, outlets were sought for emotional tensions, tensions were reduced by consultations with parents and siblings. "In 123 cases reconstruction of the parental attitude was clearly necessary for the solution of the delinquent's problem." The staff found it very difficult to reeducate the parents, owing to resentment against interference, unwillingness to relinquish long-established patterns of bad living, and like reasons. Modification of the parents, nevertheless, was accomplished in some cases and the results were very encouraging. "These families that responded so well showed by far the greatest proportion of successes" as far as rehabilitation was concerned.

This very significant investigation confirmed the thesis which has been the directing principle in the child-counseling program of the Judge Baker Guidance Center and of other such clinics: "Delinquency is a symptom, a symptom of some personal or social maladjustment, and its rational treatment should be analogous to therapy in medical science." Carrying out this analogy, Healy and Bronner ask whether a physician who has diagnosed the symptom, fever, as due to tuberculosis, would be equally successful by treating all patients alike, irrespective of their living conditions or their personal peculiarities. Irrational as such a procedure would appear in the medical field, it is just as absurd in the treatment of delinquency.

The Bureau of Prisons and the Judge Baker Guidance Center, along with other progressive agencies, are demonstrating the constructive possibilities inherent in a scientific approach to the problems of crime and delinquency. Unfortunately, such rational procedures are the exception rather than the rule. Healy and Bronner—and the Director of the Federal Bureau of Prisons would second their assertion—lament the obsolete practices which prevail in our handling of criminals, in these words, applicable not only to young but also to old delinquents:

What we do see very plainly is that at present there is very little general conception of the possibilities of getting away from largely worthless and noncurative methods of dealing with cases of serious delinquency. It might almost be said that we are still in the dark ages, or at least in the prescientific era, of treatment of juvenile delinquents.

Enlightenment is needed if the public is to view the problem of crime intelligently.

B. Economic Planning

The ability to plan ahead is certainly one of the most significant requisites for intelligent living. We have failed miserably to capitalize on our opportunities in this connection, particularly in the economic sphere.

New Russia's Primer states the case with discomfiting clarity:

The Americans are proud of their machines, of their factories. . . . But how do these factories work? According to some general plan, do you suppose? No, they work without a general plan.

What happens when they work without a plan?

Mr. Fox acquires money—one million dollars. But money must not remain idle. Mr. Fox looks through the newspapers, he consults friends, he employs agents. From morning to night the agents comb the city, look about, and make inquiries. What is to be done with the money of Mr. Fox?

At last a business is found. Hats. That is what one should make. Hats sell; men get rich.

There is nothing to hesitate about. Mr. Fox builds a hat factory.

The same idea occurs at the same time to Mr. Box, and Mr. Crox, and Mr. Nox. And they all begin to build hat factories simultaneously.

Within half a year there are several new hat factories in the country. Shops are filled to the ceiling with hatboxes. Storerooms are bursting with them. Everywhere there are posters, signs, advertisements: Hats, Hats, Hats. A great many more hats are made than are needed—twice as many, three times as many. And the factories continue to work at full speed.

And here something happens that neither Mr. Fox, nor Mr. Box, nor Mr. Nox, nor Mr. Crox anticipated. The public stops buying hats. Mr. Nox lowers his price twenty cents; Mr. Crox, forty cents; Mr. Fox sells hats at a loss in order to get rid of them. But business grows worse and worse.

In all of the papers advertisements appear:

> You may have only one head, but that does not mean at all that you should wear only one hat. Every American should have three hats. Buy the hats of Mr. Fox.

Mr. Box offers to sell hats on a three-year installment plan.

Mr. Nox announces a sale.

But this does not help. Mr. Fox lowers the wages of his workers one dollar a week. Mr. Crox lowers the wages two dollars a week. Again business grows worse and worse.

All at once—Stop. Mr. Fox closes his factory. Two thousand workers are discharged and permitted to go wherever they please. The following day the factory of Mr. Nox stops. In a week practically all the hat factories are standing idle. Thousands of workers are without work. New machines grow rusty. Buildings are sold for wreckage.

A year or two pass. The hats bought from Nox, Fox, Box, and Crox wear out. The public once more begins to buy hats. Hat stores become empty. From the top shelves dusty cartons are taken down. There are not enough hats. Prices on hats go up.

And now, not Mr. Fox, but a certain Mr. Doodle thinks of a profitable business—the building of a hat factory. The same idea also enters the heads of other wise and businesslike people—Mr. Boodle, Mr. Foodle, and Mr. Noodle. And the old story begins all over again.

The experience with hats is repeated with shoes, with sugar, with pig iron, with coal, with kerosene. Factories are blown up like soap bubbles and burst. One would think that people had lost their minds.[28]

Such social maladjustments were responsible for the initiation of the long-term plans in Russia and the more modest planning programs of the New Deal. In plotting the economic future, surveys of needs should be made and production adjusted accordingly. Thus we would be using foresight instead of proceeding in the helter-skelter fashion to which we are accustomed. In our traditional planless, individualistic, each-man-for-himself scheme of things, a farmer may hear there is money in raising turkeys. Without any ado he takes a plunge. The price of grain goes up, his expenses are doubled. When Thanksgiving time approaches, it is discovered that a myriad other farmers have been raising turkeys, too, so the price drops and heavy losses are suffered. The critical observer may suggest that the farmer should not undertake such an enterprise without a better knowledge of the market conditions, and that it is proper, under a competitive system, for the loser to accept the penalty as part of the game. But it must be pointed out in the farmer's defense that no single individual is in a position to predict the national need for turkeys or to call the turns on the fluctuating prices of grain. Whether it is fair or not, the system is wasteful to a shameful degree. Large-scale planning would diminish the risks substantially; at the same time, however, it would involve centralization of authority and, to some extent, the suppression of individual enterprise, both of which are contrary to the American tradition.

The need for planning is widely accepted in wartime. Efficient production of armaments depends upon the establishment of priorities, putting first things first, utilizing every resource to the best advantage. Schedules of production are set up as objectives to be achieved and careful records are maintained to measure periodically the approximation to these goals, progress being evaluated in terms of indexes of production. Comparison of various phases of output may reveal an unevenness in acceleration. In his second report on progress, during World War II, Chairman Nelson, of the War Production Board, made this significant observation:

The big job ahead of us right now (August, 1942) is to bring our program into balance and make sure that we use our materials and facilities as wisely

[28] M. Ilin: *New Russia's Primer*, pp. 6-9. Houghton Mifflin Company, 1931. Translated by G. Counts and N. P. Lodge.

s possible. This is one of the principal tasks on which the War Production Board is engaged. We must make sure that we produce promptly those most important fighting weapons the services must have; but in addition, we must speed up the slow items and slow down some of the fast ones so that the unbalance which now marks part of the program is brought into adjustment.[29]

On the basis of our consideration of values in Chapter 4, it is appropriate to suggest that there are priorities that should be respected in peacetime, too, when planning may be really just as important as it is in time of war.

The basic problem involved in planning is a very serious one: How can we use our intelligence to the best advantage in plotting the path ahead without sacrificing the freedom of individual initiative we hold so dear? Plowing under crops, dumping coffee in rivers, and like measures designed to maintain high prices, do not seem to be in keeping with a rational economic order where human needs should be the primary consideration.

We must evolve better means for distributing the goods which may now be produced in greater abundance as a result of our increasing technological efficiency. A sane economic order would be designed to meet human needs on the broadest possible scale.

Our system of distribution depends upon money as the medium of exchange. The function of money is to make it possible for all the people to obtain food, shelter, clothes, education, recreation—all the things and privileges which are valued as the means for sustaining life in a satisfying manner. Money, theoretically, should facilitate the relations between producer and consumer. But, practically, money has one important drawback—it is susceptible to hoarding: some people accumulate more than they can possibly spend while others cannot acquire enough to satisfy their elemental needs.

The hoarding can be done by individuals or by corporations or by both. In the case of the individual, the idle money does not usually go under a mattress, but into banks or insurance companies, which often can make no productive use of the funds entrusted to them. Mr. Manuel cited the case of a manufacturer who has $85,000 in his checking account in Mr. Manuel's bank. It has lain there for years, "leached out of our economy." In the case of the corporation, the idle money may accumulate in depreciation or depletion reserves, or in surplus account. In all cases, the effect is to interrupt the circuit of dollars.

And there we are, impaled again on the paradox of plenty. Too much

[29] Boston *Herald*, August 23, 1942.

money—or better, not enough circulation of the available supply. No conspirators plotted this impasse. No fell clan of economic royalists is responsible. No New Deal dictated the accounting principles upon which depreciation rests. It just happened. It has happened all over the civilized world. It cannot be corrected by putting Mr. Stettinius or Mr. Roosevelt or the American Institute of Accountants in the doghouse. The war, by speeding up investment in munitions, may screen the effect for a time, but presently it will be back in the center of the stage. It is impossible to operate a matured economy with financial methods appropriate to a rapidly expanding one.

If this dilemma were not so serious it would be funny. We have, as a nation, so much money that millions of us are close to the starvation line. It is serious to the point of tragedy. And the paradox will never be resolved by calling names, impugning motives, or summoning the shades of Adam Smith or Karl Marx. It will be resolved when enough Americans of intelligence and good will sit down together to examine the facts, patiently and exhaustively.[30]

Hoarding occurs in our culture partly because the accumulation of money brings the possessor prestige and power. In so far as we admire and respect people for the wealth they hoard, we are paying homage to the very persons who prevent us from satisfying our wants.

One reason we do not secure a broader distribution of income is that the "haves" want to "hang on to what they've got." The individual or group which organizes any society, whatever its intentions or pretensions, arrogates an inordinate portion of social privilege to itself. In our culture the dominant type of power is economic. Granted that differentials in economic rewards are morally justified and socially useful, it is impossible to justify the *degree* of inequality which develops in a complex society as a more elaborate civilization brings with it an increased centralization of power. Most justifications for these inequalities are specious. Even though superior services merit higher rewards, it may be taken as axiomatic that the rewards will sometimes be higher than the services warrant. The rewards are not rationally or impartially determined, the apportionment being made by those who are in control. When special ability is not allied with power, as in the case of the modern professional man, the compensation is absurdly low as compared with the income of the economic overlords who rule our industrial society. "The greatest mental abilities," says Thorndike, who has made an exhaustive study

[30] S. Chase: "Capital Not Wanted." *Harper's Magazine*, February, 1940.

of comparative incomes, "are as a rule the poorest paid so far as money is concerned." [31]

Another obstacle to the attainment of a better order of things is the fact that political opinions are inevitably rooted in economic interests. Comparatively few citizens can view a problem of social policy without regard to their own personal financial loss or gain. Evidence for such a thesis is plentiful. Public-opinion surveys have shown that the most significant opinion "chasm" in the United States today is determined by income groupings, according to Claude Robinson, Associate Director of the American Institute of Public Opinion. Polls demonstrated that the controversy over the New Deal was mostly a struggle between those who "have and own" and those who do not: at the bottom of the income scale, low-economic and relief groups were die-hard New Dealers, supporting every Roosevelt measure; at the other end of the scale the well-to-do were equally die-hard against the spending, taxing, and labor policies of the New Deal. Several investigators, reporting on the use of correlational techniques in exploring voting behavior, state that "a considerable proportion of the voters who shifted from one party to another during the depression did so in direct response to the way in which government policies affected their well-being." [32]

We have the brains to solve our economic problems, once we develop the desire to work out our salvation:

We've been smart enough to make tractors and mechanical corn-pickers and dial telephones; are we smart enough to find work for the folks they've thrown out of work? . . .

Personally, I think we can, and that what we need most is a redirection of our genius as a people. Heretofore, we've concentrated on methods of efficient production. Henceforth, we must concentrate on efficient and businesslike methods of increasing domestic consumption no matter how much violence it may do to some of our preconceived notions. We know how to produce almost anything—but we haven't learned how to distribute such things to the jobless who ask only the chance to work for them. This nightmare of under-consumption is the black plague of the 20th century; we've got to make up our minds to wipe it out—with a vengeance. Only one thing can stop us and that's a mental sit-down strike—a kind of smug,

[31] E. L. Thorndike: *Human Nature and the Social Order*, p. 92. The Macmillan Company, 1940.

[32] H. F. Hosnell and N. Pearson: "The Study of Voting Behavior by Correlational Techniques." *American Sociological Review*, 1939, 4, 809-815.

19th century faith that things will work themselves out if only we don't do anything about it.[33]

Our best brains, unfortunately, are too apt to be preoccupied with the business of exploiting the situation for the individual's personal benefit.

If we are going to use our intelligence to advantage, we must plan ahead. This entails economic planning, as we have observed—the search for the means of balancing production and consumption, scarcity and abundance. But *planning* connotes more than the preparation, in advance, of economic policies. It involves, in addition, comprehensive "blueprinting" to take care of flood control, soil and timber preservation, diversification of crops, social security, public welfare, public health, public education.

What we most need engineers for today is not the primary constructions. We need engineers who can deal with the consequences of engineering. We need economic and sociological engineers, who know as much about human nature as they do about the modulus of elasticity. We need them for recreational plans and civic plans, in all kinds of communities, from the borough to the great metropolis.

The task awaiting this generation is to make a world in which human beings are not necessarily unhappy.[34]

Coordinated effort is a necessity in our modern complex society. Some problems call for national planning, as is the case with railroads; some for regional planning, as in flood control; some for local control, as in the matter of barber shops. Part of our planning program should be determining what we are interested in planning, so we can get our bearings to begin with.

There is a widespread prejudice against "blueprint planners" which is bound to complicate the picture. "It won't work," shout the unbelieving populace, "it's visionary." The Russians were planners, the obstructionists used to argue, and therefore Roosevelt was a "Communist" because he was a "planner." Freedom, pleads Lippmann, is preferable to planning, and therefore, planning is bad. Freedom for what? when? where? Planning for what? when? where? Let's cling to our referents when we consider the issue. If we do not try to control our future by planning for it, we shall never discover better ways of organizing our lives more effectively.

[33] M. Perkins: "Let's Wipe It Out!" *Consumers' Guide,* April 1, 1940.
[34] R. Helton: "Born in 1921." *Harper's Magazine,* August, 1940.

This is the rub: how to put planning into operation without curbing *"unduly"* our precious liberties—that is a task which is sure to puzzle the wisest of men. It is a fine art to arrive at just the right balance between "compliant and encroaching behavior. . . . Self-restriction and encroachment upon the freedom of others are the two basic aspects of all forms of living together. . . ." [35] Sociality demands that we learn how to compromise between the desire to mind our own business, to fend individually for ourselves, and the necessity of working together with other members of our group.

II. THE SOCIALIZATION OF SCIENCE

We have not really discovered what could be accomplished by applying science to the developing of saner social relations. The attainment of this important end requires not only a knowledge of science, but also of social relations. For this very reason the social psychologist should be peculiarly concerned with the impact of science on society.

Scientists, as we shall now show by their own testimony, are becoming increasingly aware of the need for examining the social implications of scientific progress. Let the scientists speak for themselves.

Max Schoen, a psychologist, states our problem in an article entitled "Can We Be Socially Intelligent?" Please note that this article, like many others we shall cite, appeared in the *Scientific Monthly,* a journal which provides a medium through which scientists can express their views. Schoen says:

So intelligence . . . consists of a conscientious effort to get at the facts in the case. But a knowledge of the facts will not in itself result in control, for such knowledge may be used only to carry out a destructive purpose, and consequently, the more knowledge there is the more mischief-producing it may be in its application. We have a capital example of this fact in the socially destructive results that have followed in the wake of the progress of research in the physical sciences. The fault here does not lie in the knowledge, but in its application. The more knowledge that the schemer and plotter possesses in the field of his activities, the more destructive he becomes. Consequently, a second factor in intelligence is an examination of the ends or purposes to be achieved by the knowledge of a situation. This is the factor of self-examination, or knowledge of oneself: the distinction between the worthy and the unworthy, the fit and unfit, the human and the inhuman, and constitutes the ethical or moral phase of intelligence, as the other is the material phase. And the two are inseparable, for where there

[35] K. Goldstein: *Human Nature,* pp. 207, 214. 1940.

is no knowledge of the human situation, or motive, and action in keeping with this knowledge, the human being is victimized by himself by being enslaved to himself. There can be no real control of a situation, and therefore no intelligence, apart from self-control.

We fail to be intelligent in social affairs in two ways: first, by misusing the fruits of the physical sciences and thereby bringing numerous social evils down upon ourselves, and second, by our failure to apply to social ills even as much scientific knowledge about social life as we possess.[36]

Generally speaking, the education of the scientist fails to train him in an awareness of his social responsibilities. His consequent indifference to the social implications of his role in society is lamented by Lancelot Hogben, English scientist, as one important factor in the *Retreat from Reason*.[37] There are others who are worried, too, about this serious omission in the preparation of the scientist. For instance, the Maurice Falk Foundation in Pittsburgh, an organization devoted to the financing of projects related to economic welfare, is sponsoring a professorship designed "to bring the engineering undergraduate to a point of development where, upon graduation, he will possess a social intelligence and outlook and a sense of social responsibility to parallel his technical proficiency." [38]

The type of training sponsored by the Falk Foundation answers an important educational need stressed by Freeman in his *Social Psychology*, where he cites the social blindness so prevalent among engineers. Freeman is particularly critical of efficiency engineers who devise ways of pushing the worker to the limit of his producing capacity, treating him as a mere unit in the cost of production, with no apparent concern for him as a human being. Hours of work, under such a setup, are determined exclusively by a regard for profit. Any socially minded person recognizes that industry has social functions, that there must be some purpose beyond the generation of profits. Freeman searched through the proceedings of societies of engineers for papers that might show some consciousness of the wider implications of the engineering profession. A typical paper was "Scientific Management and Its Effect upon Manufacturing." The effect upon society was not mentioned. These papers, as evidence of the social awareness of a whole profession, Freeman comments, are a depressing spectacle.[39]

[36] M. Schoen: "Can We Be Socially Intelligent?" *Scientific Monthly*, December, 1937.

[37] See L. T. Hogben: *Retreat from Reason*, especially pp. 2-3. 1937.

[38] The Falk Foundation Report for 1937 and 1938, pp. 22-23.

[39] E. Freeman: *Social Psychology*, p. 205. 1936.

Evidently, the situation has been improving. At a meeting of the Society for the Promotion of Engineering Education at the Massachusetts Institute of Technology in 1937, Dean Edwin S. Burdell stressed the fact that engineers must take a social view. Engineers, he said, must be educated to meet their social responsibilities so that they can control the complex machinery they have created. In the past so much emphasis has been put upon training men to take their places in industrial and commercial processes that there has been no time to enable these men to gain an understanding of the profound changes they were creating in the pattern of human society. To put it in another way, there has been no training, much less education, in the technique of living in a machine age. Today, more and more, experienced engineers are beginning to realize that members of their profession have a personal responsibility to think of their products and their contributions to society, not merely in their technical aspects but also in the light of their social effects and how these effects can be controlled and guided. If the engineer can be educated as well as trained—that is to say, if he can develop judgment, if he can acquire wisdom as well as techniques—he will be that much more able to command intelligently a situation which now threatens confusion, chaos, and defeat.[40] The program in Industrial Relations at the Massachusetts Institute of Technology is specifically designed to acquaint the engineer with his role as a human being working in relation to other human beings. It is a step in the right direction.

There is a growing conviction that a higher education should aim to acquaint all students with the social implications of science. Such is the aim of a course in Social Technology offered at Colby College for the first time in 1939 by Dr. William T. Bovie, who is widely known as the inventor of the electric scalpel which made bloodless surgery possible. The purpose of this course, as described in the announcement, is twofold: to give students going into chemistry or physics an idea of the sociological implications of their work; and to give students entering the fields of economics, social service, or government a background knowledge of present-day scientific techniques and the problems in human welfare which scientific discoveries may solve or the new problems which they may bring about.

The need for enlightening scientists can be appreciated by studying the social effects of recent inventions. Such a study will reveal at once that an invention means something more than a mere mechanical innovation. To the banker it brings insecurity to his securities; to

[40] Boston *Herald*, May 30, 1937.

the wage-earner it may mean the loss of his job.   All of us are affected either directly or indirectly.   Consider five inventions which were little known, or at least were unimportant, in 1900, but which are now dominant factors in our civilization: the automobile, the moving picture, the airplane, radio, and rayon.   They have revolutionized our modes of living.   Think of the changes that will be brought about in the next few years by the mechanical cotton-picker, prefabricated houses, air-conditioning equipment, plastics, the photo-electric cell, artificial cotton and woolen-like fibres made from cellulose, television, the automobile trailer, gasoline produced from coal, steep-flight airplanes, jet propulsion, tray agriculture, and nuclear fission (splitting the atom).   These developments may have great potential effects upon our economic and social order, introducing improvements in our ways of living and yet, at the same time, involving dislocations of a serious nature in our system.   The inventors of the mechanical cotton-picker, John D. and Mack D. Rust, are aware of the influence their labor-saving device may have, particularly in displacing the workers and thus bringing unemployment and starvation to some million men, and, consequently, they have taken measures to mitigate the ill effects that might ensue.   Instead of selling their machines outright, the Rusts lease them to planters who must meet their specifications with respect to labor, hours, wages, and other conditions.   Nine-tenths of the profits of the machine will go to start a series of cooperative farms, cooperative stores, and educational projects for both white and colored workers.   The Rust brothers see their invention in its social context.

The American Association for the Advancement of Science (A.A.A.S.) has been very much concerned, of late, over the role of science in modern society.   At the 1938 meeting, Sir Richard Gregory, retiring editor of *Nature* and chairman of the Division for the Social and International Relations of the British Association for the Advancement of Science, attacked the view that "the sole function of science is the discovery and study of natural facts and principles without regard to the social implications of the knowledge gained" and spoke of the scientist's duty "to assist in the establishment of a rational and harmonious social order."   Expanding on this theme in a *Scientific Monthly* article, he reported:

In every department of human life—at any rate, in Great Britain—there has been a stupendous awakening to a sense of social responsibility, a very real development in man's mentality and the growth of society.   In effect it now demands that the latest results of all branches of scientific research, but more especially of those affecting hygiene, both physical and mental, should be applied to the conditions of life of the population as a whole. This is not philanthropy or religion as such in the narrow sense, but arises from a broadening in the conception of the relations and obligations of man to man.[41]

At the 1937 meetings of the A.A.A.S. the presidential address by E. G. Conklin, Princeton biologist, dealt with the subject of "Science and Ethics." During the course of his remarks Conklin said:

I know full well that there are many scientific specialists who maintain that science has no concern with ethics, its sole function being to seek the truth concerning nature irrespective of how this truth may affect the weal or woe of mankind. They may recognize that the use of science for evil threatens peace and progress, but they feel no responsibility to help avert disaster. The world may be out of joint, but they were never born to set it right; let the shoemaker stick to his last and the scientist to his laboratory.

During the dark days of the World War, I once spoke to a distinguished scientist of some major event in the course of the war and he looked up from his work and said sharply, "What war?" Concentration upon our various specialties is essential, but it should not cause us to lose our sense of orientation in the world. It is pleasant and at times necessary to avoid "the tumult and the shouting," but there is no excuse for the scientist who dwells permanently apart from the affairs of men. . . .

The greatest problems that confront the human race are how to promote social cooperation; how to increase loyalty to truth; how to promote justice and brotherhood; how to expand ethics until it shall embrace all mankind. [But these problems are problems] for science as well as for government, education, and religion.[42]

At the 1939 meeting of this same Association, this general topic was the keynote of the presidential address by Wesley C. Mitchell, internationally known economist of Columbia University. He called upon scientists of America to become members of

an organization that would bring into focus all the intelligence available in the community and increase knowledge of human behavior, as the most urgent item in the unfinished business of science.

If we had a keener insight into individual psychology, we might not be able to alter fundamental drives, but we might be able to direct them into beneficent channels.

[41] Sir Richard Gregory: "Religion in Science." *Scientific Monthly*, February, 1939.
[42] Published in *Science*, December 31, 1937.

If we can come to a clearer understanding of how we behave, perhaps—and perhaps is all we can say—we can learn how to condition men so that their energies will go less into making one another miserable. . . .

In addition to the responsibilities they share with all other citizens, scientific men have the special duty of trying to increase the kind of knowledge required to deal intelligently with public problems.[43]

The idea of organizing scientists for an investigation of their role in society was embodied in a Committee on Science and its Social Relations instituted by the International Council of Scientific Unions, in May, 1937. The work of this Committee was very seriously interrupted by the war. The inquiry as originally planned was to be conducted through nationally representative scientific organizations in the various countries: in America, the National Academy of Sciences; in Britain, the Royal Society of London; and so on. Individuals were to be canvassed, too, to get their opinions on the following points:

(1) The part played by scientific thought in the outlook of various social groups.

(2) The forms in which scientific workers and their work are involved in the various struggles and conflicts of human society.

(3) The forms in which the consciousness of a social responsibility of science and of scientific workers is taking shape.[44]

In commenting on this program, an authority remarks: "These are matters of extreme importance in the large vistas of the world. If they seem less important than fast-marching current affairs, it is largely a matter of perspective. The fear is that the forces of violence will throttle the opportunity of such deliberate assaying of the science that has made civilization." [45]

Our primary need, as members of modern society, is the definition of our ideals. Social relations are facilitated when the rights and responsibilities of the citizen are clearly defined. F. Cyril James, Principal and Vice-Chancellor of McGill University, expresses his convictions on "Science and Society" in these terms:

Men cannot live together in a society unless there is a dominant philosophy or ethos that they share in common. The ideals towards which society is

[43] Boston *Herald,* December 28, 1939.

[44] Report on "World Inquiry into Social Effects of Modern Science." *Scientific Monthly,* November, 1938.

[45] *Ibid.*

directing its efforts, and the standards by which the conduct of its members will be judged, must be comprehended (however dimly) by each member of the group. . . .

The adaptation of means to ends; the charting for society of a course that is most appropriate in the light of the existing fund of human knowledge, is the primary function of the social sciences. . . .

If we are willing to face the major problem of deciding upon our ideals, the forces that science has placed at our disposal are already sufficient to make the attainment of those ideals a practical possibility.[46]

This point of view is ably corroborated by Howard E. Jensen, Duke University sociologist, in a discussion of "Science and Human Values." Jensen says:

The ultimate problems of our civilization are social and moral, and science, while it has placed new and powerful instruments in the hands of men, has done nothing to clarify the moral and social purposes which these instruments are to serve.

Even the social scientists have of recent years made common cause with the natural scientists in washing their hands of all concern with human values. The economist, the political scientist, the sociologist, we are told, must study a social situation as the astronomer studies a nebula or the biologist an organism, to describe what exists, and to predict, if he can, what must exist tomorrow, but that is all. He may study suicide, divorce, crime, poverty, unemployment, strikes, lynchings, war, but whether these things are good or bad he does not know. Any interest in their ethical implications, or any concern about human welfare, is scientifically taboo. He is a social technician solely. He can teach us efficiency in attaining our ends, but not wisdom in choosing them. He tries to learn, for example, how depressions are caused and how they may be prevented, but whether we should have bigger and better depressions or smaller and fewer, is a question of social ethics or social welfare, and he does not know.

We might for the present accept this defense of the scientist, that science is concerned with what is, not with what ought to be, and that for knowledge of human values we must turn not to him, but to the philosopher, if the scientist were in fact such a humble person as this answer implies. . . . But the scientist is rarely so self-effacing . . . he thrusts aside the work of the philosophers as worthless, and proceeds to formulate a view of human life and destiny in harmony with his own professional bias.

This shattering of confidence in spiritual values is the most damaging blow that science could strike mankind. It has centered attention upon the tangible and the ponderable, exalted material possessions as the measure of

---

[46] F. C. James: "Science and Society." *Scientific Monthly*, July, 1941.

human worth, and substituted comfort, excitement, and entertainment for truth, goodness, and beauty, as the supreme values of life. This concern of modern man with material things has left a void in his soul, and, shut up between the darkness of the birth from which he came and the darkness of the grave to which he goes, he can only fill the void with an increasing volume of material possessions and an increasing intensity of sensuous satisfactions. It has made of life a system of tensions, a continuous succession of strains which is never followed by relaxation.

A science which assumes that its basic concepts of materialism and mechanism and quantity exhaust the possibilities of dependable knowledge has ceased to be science, and degenerated into a dogma which has betrayed civilization. For if we can discover no dependable knowledge of the good life which the intelligence must recognize as valid and the will as obligatory, our civilization cannot survive the forces which science has let loose within it. . . .

It is high time for all who call themselves scientists, whether physical or social, to make common cause with philosophy and the humanities in the defense of human values, and in the competence of scholarship and research to find a rational basis for them in human experience which all men must accept. For let there be no mistake about it, in the midst of the passionate social conflicts that rage about us, if scholarship and research are unable or unwilling to determine the ends of economics and politics by reason, economics and politics will determine the ends of scholarship and research by force.

The knowledge most desperately needed is knowledge concerning the principles of social organization and the ends of social action. No social science is adequate to this task that is descriptive only, that confines itself to exploring what is and predicting what will be. For human nature and human society are vastly richer and more complex in their potentialities than in their accomplishments. An adequate social science will of course begin with a careful collection of facts about how men carry on their common life together as families and communities, as economic classes and political parties and religious sects, as nations and races, but it will not stop there. It will pass on from this concrete knowledge of social actualities to the consideration of social possibilities.

It is a grim task, but beyond it there lies a great hope, the hope that by means of a social science that has become intelligent enough to extend its scope from social facts to social values, from a consideration of what is to what might be and ought to be, we may formulate a rationally valid conception of the general social welfare, and develop a social organization adequate to mediate between the conflicting interests of human groups.[47]

[47] H. E. Jensen: "Science and Human Values." *Scientific Monthly*, September, 1941.

The opportunity for scientists to lead the way to a new social order, better designed to promote human welfare, is especially favorable in a democracy. The essential basis for a happier future, under any system of government, is the achievement of a rational control of social relations. It is the sad truth that "the organization of society has been left to the chance operation of individual self-interest and the uncertain pressure of mass opinion, in the expectation that a beneficence not of men's devising would somehow shape the course of events to a desired but undefined good end." [48]

If scientists will take their social functions seriously, if they will provide us with the facts and then help us in clarifying our ideals, if scientists will organize themselves to devise the most effective means for achieving our goals, then we may face the future with confidence. In the words of A. J. Carlson, famous physiologist at the University of Chicago: "We *will* nurse the hope that the hairy ape who somehow lost his tail, grew a brain worth having, built speech and song out of a hiss and a roar, and stepped out of the cave to explore and master the universe, may some day conquer his own irrational and myopic behavior towards his kin." [49]

[48] C. Becker: *Progress and Power*, p. 196. 1936.
[49] A. J. Carlson, in the *Sigma Xi Quarterly*, Vol. 28, No. 4, 1940.

Part III

THE STIMULATION AND CONTROL
OF SOCIAL BEHAVIOR

INFLUENCING PEOPLE to buy a product, to accept an idea, to support a cause, is often effected by resort to the subtle arts of suggestion. The techniques employed in providing just the right stimulus to secure the desired response and the nature of the personal *rapport* involved, are explained in Chapter 7, "Suggestion," with some additional observations on the circumvention of resistance, the exploitation of the public by advertisers, and the role of imitation in our social behavior.

Handling human beings in a leader-follower relationship, on a large scale, depends to some extent on a knowledge of the principles of "crowd psychology": stimulation of emotional excitement, direction of attention to a common objective, curtailing of critical judgment, oratorical appeals to hatred, and the like. Social movements, such as Nazism, demonstrate what can be accomplished by leaders who are well versed in the art of controlling the public's responses. The working principles are described in Chapter 8, "The Creation and Manipulation of Crowds."

Chapter 9, "Popular Credulity, Rumor Mongering, and Public Acclaim," cites various examples of public gullibility: the persistent clinging to traditional myths, the ready acceptance and facile transmission of rumors, the "unpredictable" shifts in public fancy.

The remainder of Part III is concerned with the general topic of propaganda and morale. Chapter 10, "Propaganda," deals with the techniques of propaganda, their practice in psychological warfare, the agencies for conducting propaganda (in war or peace), and the development of propaganda as a political tool in the United States, Russia, and Germany.

Propaganda is usually employed to promote the morale of the in-group and to demoralize the out-group. Chapter 11, "Social Consciousness: Morale," explains how people come to identify themselves with the group, how individual and group morale can be fostered, how morale is developed to secure athletic and military victories.

Part III, we thus observe, shows how suggestion functions in the determination of social behavior, whether it is used by the advertiser, the crowd leader, the rumor monger, the propagandist, or the Office of War Information. The clever person, whatever the situation, can manipulate people to his own advantage if he knows "how to sway human emotions" in the appropriate manner.

Chapter 7

SUGGESTION

CONTROLLING THE BEHAVIOR of other people, a very important phase of social psychology, depends to a large extent upon the skillful use of suggestion.

I. DEFINITION

Suggestion is the provision of a stimulus that will evoke the desired response, with personal influence brought to bear upon an individual to induce in him an uncritical acceptance of a belief that will issue in action. Personal pressure is employed rather than rational persuasion.

Numerous experiments have been performed to demonstrate how an individual may be led to accept a belief or to modify his judgments under the influence of one or more persons. In certain situations the individual will tend to defer to expert opinion or to majority opinion, as the case may be. The author planned an experiment to demonstrate how individual judgments may be influenced by majority opinion. Ten sticks of various lengths ranging from fifteen inches to fifty inches were presented in haphazard order to a class in experimental psychology. The students were instructed to record their visual estimates for each stick held before them by the instructor. The fact that the experiment was designed to test suggestibility was concealed from the subjects, who were presumably just testing out their visual perception. After all ten sticks had been exposed, the instructor presented sticks three inches long, six inches, twelve inches, twenty-four inches, thirty-six inches and forty-eight inches, in each case informing the subjects of the exact length of the stick. The class was instructed "to register the way each stick looks and keep it in mind as a standard of comparison," with the idea of revising estimates when the original sticks were again exposed. After this second exposure, the estimates for all the subjects were recorded on the blackboard. The class was requested to compare estimates as a preliminary to a third exposure of the original sticks. The estimates for this last step became standards as some individuals modified their estimates to conform to the majority opinion.[1]

Moore performed an experiment to ascertain the relative influences of expert and majority opinion. Students recorded, at the start, their judgments on topics such as:

Which of the two following errors in grammar do you find more offensive? "Everybody loves their mother"; "She sort of avoided him."

Another series called for judgments with respect to offensive character traits; a third involved musical preferences. The test was made twice and the chance percentage of change from day to day computed. Some months later, the two tests were repeated, with this modification: the judgments in the second application were influenced by providing the subjects with the vote of the majority on each pair of items. Students who had previously differed from the majority opinion were quick to alter their judgments to conform to the prevailing reaction. The shift was most noticeable in matters pertaining to speech and morals, less in degree with respect to musical preferences. When choices of experts were cited, the subjects were influenced to shift their opinions in the direction of expert opinion, but the changes were not so marked as in the case of majority opinion.[2] This finding accords with a common observation in social psychology that man feels more secure when he "goes with the crowd," even though it means disregarding the experts to do so. This "band-wagon" appeal is a very potent one.

II. THE TECHNIQUES OF SUGGESTION

There are certain principles which should be followed in attempting to influence other people by means of suggestion. These principles have been validated in actual practice.

A. THE APPEAL TO WANTS, EMOTIONAL DRIVES, AND EXISTENT BELIEFS

The suggester must direct his appeals to wants or desires that are generally recognized as basic human wishes, just as Tom Sawyer did

[1] See W. F. Vaughan: "An Experimental Class Demonstration of Suggestibility." *Journal of Abnormal and Social Psychology*, 1935, 30, 92-94.
[2] See H. T. Moore: "Comparative Influence of Majority and Expert Opinion." *American Journal of Psychology*, 1921, 32, 16-20.

when he succeeded in getting his fence whitewashed by exciting the vanity of his chum. Macy's store in New York invented a clever slogan to fit the depression pocket-book—"It's smart to be thrifty." In this case two desires are kindled, thus rendering the appeal doubly efficacious.

Influencing people through the art of salesmanship is effected by appealing skillfully to common human desires and predispositions. We may illustrate this art in practice by studying the procedure used by the Willmark Service System in training retailers how to sell more goods. *Incognito* investigators, making a preliminary survey, bought things from 1,000 different clerks, to determine how good these clerks were at "suggestive selling," that is, in influencing customers to spend more than they had intended to. More than 300 of them restricted themselves to such clichés as "And what else?" and "Will that be all?" Nearly 150 did make specific suggestions, but they were pretty feeble: "Got plenty of handkerchiefs?" "Any coffee, sugar, salt, or butter today?" "You wouldn't be interested in any lace collars, would you?" or "Would you be interested in a flashlight?" Some let slip such things as "Here's a cheaper hat that looks twice as good as your old one," and "Do you use an astringent? You're inclined to be oily around the nose, you know." Willmark is convinced that suggestive selling, done right, can work wonders. "We have a new-model shoe that will look perfect on a small foot like yours" was a line recommended for a shoe store. A Midwest drug chain found that only 3.8 per cent of their luncheon customers were responding to "Would you care for any dessert?" They switched to "Will you have apple pie à-la-mode? It's special today," and 22.5 per cent bought. A word picture of a specific food, they discovered, is much more likely to arouse appetite than the vague, colorless term "dessert." [3]

"Tested Selling Sentences," invented and patented by Elmer Wheeler, are designed to touch the customer in his most vulnerable spots, by applying suggestion in an expert manner. An unschooled soda jerker will ask if you will have an egg in your malted milk. When he has been trained by Wheeler, he is more skillful in the wording of his suggestion: holding up an egg in each hand, he asks whether you'd like one egg or two. Automatically you answer, "One," and the cash register rings up an extra dime. "Don't ask *if*," counsels Wheeler, "ask *which*. Don't ever give a customer the choice between something and nothing; don't ask questions easily answered in the negative;

[3] "Foolproofing America." *Reader's Digest*, February, 1937.

frame your questions so as to lead to the answer you want." Wheeler searches carefully for the key words that will be most effective in producing the purchase the salesman is after:

In 1927 Wheeler was on the advertising staff of the Baltimore *American*. A store owner complained that, while his merchandise was good and newspaper ads pulled crowds into his store, people didn't buy enough when they got there. Wheeler went behind the counters, listened, watched, and soon realized that the clerks' words and actions were haphazard, mechanical; that a counter could be a bottle-neck where even the best sales campaign got stuck. He experimented with shirts. He taught the clerks to say, "These buttons are anchored on," meanwhile letting the customer tug at the buttons. This, and the vivid word "anchor" moved mountains of shirts.

Here was born one of those ideas which, like most original ideas, are so simple that no one else has thought of them. For ten years it has been Elmer Wheeler's profession to find out for his clients what words, spoken across the counter, will sell merchandise. It is shrewd psychology applied to a neglected link in the chain of business. Wheeler and his staff, when they set to work, do not immediately fill the clerks' mouths with polished, ready-made slogans. For a long time they listen, test, keep score, eliminate. Often the selling sentence finally chosen comes from one of the clerks, who was saying it without quite knowing why.

Engaged by the Barbasol Company, Wheeler set up his "field word laboratory" in a retail store and found that clerks were using 146 different sentences to interest men shoppers in Barbasol. By trial and error he eliminated all but one sentence, and had the clerks say, "How would you like to save six minutes shaving?" Sales of Barbasol doubled. Later this sentence was further simplified, and at a store where the clerks said, "How would you like to cut your shaving time *in half?*" sales of Barbasol tripled. . . . People who ordered Coca Cola at a Brooklyn department store soda fountain were being asked by the attendants whether they wanted a large one or a small one. Few ordered large ones. When Elmer Wheeler had finished his tests, the clerks merely said, "Large one?" and a large one it was two out of five times. . . .

A shoe store asked him to help dispose of a surplus of children's moccasins. Mothers, and the children who came with them, were indifferent to sales talk about the moccasins' stitching, wired beads, or blunt toes, but when Wheeler taught the clerks to drop a pair in front of the child and say "The kind the *real* Indians wear, Sonny," every fourth boy made his mother buy him a pair.[4]

In explaining his principles to salesmen, Wheeler likes to use two unusually apt examples to drive home his ideas. One is the observation that a sign reading "Beware of the Dog" is not so effective as one

[4] *Literary Digest*, January 22, 1938.

warning "Beware of the Hungry Dog." The other illustration is the story of the blind man who was getting no coins in his cup in response to his appeal "Help the Blind," while another blind beggar working the same street was cleaning up with a sign reading "It is May—and I am Blind."

Suggestion may work because it satisfies certain wants of the customer, as we have noted, or it may succeed because it arouses powerful emotional drives. The emotional excitement may facilitate suggestion by inhibiting critical judgment, in which case any proposal within reason or even beyond reason may be accepted. An example of this principle is found in White Owl's campaign to sell their cigars by showing in their advertisement a pretty girl being kissed by a handsome man who presumably has just finished smoking his favorite cigar —guess which brand?—or perhaps he has set aside his smoke for the moment in deference to the call to romance. *Life* showed some closeups in the filming studio, with this explanation:

THIS GIRL'S KISSES MAKE MEN BUY CIGARS

To advertising men throughout the U.S. blonde Sheila Kerry is known as "The Girl of a Million Kisses." From coast to coast her image, langorously embracing a dark young man, persuades sensitive smokers that they may smoke White Owl cigars and still win a mate. Accompanying catch lines: "Keep Fit for Breath-taking Moments," "Kiss and Tell," "Every Woman Wants to Be Kissed." Miss Kerry is a notable figure in the business world not only because she has sold millions of cigars, but because she has brought The Kiss back to advertising. . . . Notice Miss Kerry's wedding ring, an essential to all kiss advertising.[5]

Selling cigars by picturing kisses is an irrational procedure but it works just the same. The man who sees the advertisement knows that the photograph represents a clinch that has been carefully posed under the direction of studio cameramen, he knows that smoking is not the best means of enhancing one's sex appeal, he doesn't know that the man in the ad smokes White Owls or any other brand of cigar, yet unconsciously he is lured into the inference that a cigar is the gate to romance. The picture provokes memories or daydreams that shut out all else from the mental focus. With critical thought rendered out of commission by emotional preoccupation, the suggestion is put over with eminent success.

German leaders used the appeal to fear as a means of developing

[5] *Life,* December 26, 1938.

a high degree of morale for war. Regularly Hitler hammered home the theme of "we're—all—alone—against—the—world," warning the people that they'd better work and fight harder than ever before because "there'll be no mercy for us next time." This technique for building German morale was very effective because it appealed to the strong emotional drive of fear, and because it fitted into the patterns of belief already prevalent among the people. Suggestion is more apt to be successful when it reinforces beliefs already firmly held. The Germans felt the world was against them—Hitler simply made the feeling "more nearly unanimous." That is exactly the procedure to be followed by any leader who wants to use suggestion effectively. The speaker who tells the audience to do something they are all set to do beforehand just pulls the trigger of a gun that's already loaded. People are attracted to the man who gives voice to beliefs which they approve. By appealing to the dominant convictions of the group such a leader demonstrates that his judgments are sound. So the propagandist must direct his campaign to fit the traditional creeds of his audience, for otherwise he will get no welcome, hence no acceptance for his appeals.

B. Association through Contiguity

Suggestion often depends for its effectiveness on the "irrational relationships that mere contiguity can establish." This is readily understood because suggestion is effected through the mechanism of the conditioned response. By the principle of partial identity lovely music comes to share its loveliness with the cigarettes which make the music possible. Thus one company increased its cigarette sales by 47 per cent in two months after going on the air with dance music. Air-conditioned gasoline must be superior since an air-conditioned home is more comfortable. Germ-processed motor oil must be better for the car because germs in the human system undermine the health of the individual. Streamline refrigerators must preserve food more adequately because streamline trains run faster; both belong to our streamline age.

C. Recommendation by Persons of Prestige

Suggestion may be effected by personal influence alone, without resort to rational considerations. The point, in such a case, will be carried by the sheer weight of personal authority. A typical case is the socialite who recommends the dietetic benefits to be derived from the consumption of Blank's Soft-Bun Bread. This bread has been endorsed by Mrs. ——, who knows her bread by virtue of the following qualifications: 1. She is the wife of the Dean of the —— School of Law; 2. She is the mother of two sturdy sons and a charming daughter; 3. She winters in Brookline; 4. She summers on Buzzard's Bay; 5. She is at home abroad, where she travels extensively; 6. She is a collector of American antiques; 7. She is on the Board of the Boston Children's Friend Society; 8. She is on the Board of the Wednesday Morning Musicales; and 9. She is a good squash racquets player. Most of these qualifications are irrelevant, but what matter? The mind is not always logical in its demands for authority. The point is carried by non-logical considerations.

D. THE RELATIVE EFFECTIVENESS OF VISUAL AND AUDITORY APPEALS

Allport and Cantril conducted an investigation at Harvard to determine the relative effectiveness of visual impressions and auditory impressions for the transmission of suggestion.[6] These experiments to settle the Eye versus the Ear controversy were watched with considerable anxiety by persons concerned with the sponsorship of newspaper and magazine advertising and by others equally devoted to the promotion of radio advertising. On the whole, the verdict was in favor of the Ear, much to the delight of the radio chains. The fundamental reason for this superiority of the auditory medium is that the human voice is personal and consequently carries more weight in putting a suggestion across. People, it was found, are less critical of things heard than of things read. The listener to the radio is especially receptive, being less critical, less analytic, and more passive. The Columbia Broadcasting System issued a circular, "The Truth about the Harvard Findings," in which it quoted Cantril as saying:

Since advertising is so largely dependent on suggestion, rather than on pure logic and analysis, a medium which enhances the power of suggestion should be particularly valuable for the advertiser.

The fact that it is much easier to listen to the radio than it is to read, may account, in part, for the fact that we are becoming a nation of inveterate listeners. We have already arrived at the point where many people resort to oral book reviews to save themselves the effort entailed in getting a copy of the book and reading it. News,

---

[6] The full story of the experiments is reported in Cantril and Allport's *The Psychology of Radio* (1935).

music, tabloid versions of plays and stories, instruction in spelling or Spanish, may all be had by turning a dial and placing the ears in a receptive attitude. A member of the information-service staff of the Social Security Board reports that it is almost impossible to get people to read pamphlets explaining the various provisions of the Social Security Act and that, when it is necessary to reach the public, the staff finds it advisable to send out speakers or to arrange for them to talk over the radio.

A survey, reported by Lazarsfeld in his book *Radio and the Printed Page*,[7] discovered that it is the people on the lower cultural levels who do most of the listening to the radio, while those on the higher cultural levels prefer reading. In seeking an answer to the question as to who listens to what, the investigators analyzed the audiences of those radio programs which compete with the printed word in conveying ideas, information, interpretations of news, and political opinions, and they found that the lower the level of education, the fewer are the people who listen to such programs. Radio is the medium preferred by those strata of the population who are more suggestible, who read little or nothing, who are "easy marks" for the advertiser on the air. People who are most interested in the news prefer the newspaper to the radio; they report that the radio news fare is too sketchy. Habitual non-readers whose curiosity is aroused by radio news programs may develop into newspaper readers. The radio even leads some people to book-reading. Radio is definitely not replacing the printed word, because reading is a more efficient process than listening for those who happen to be skilled readers. Interviewers frequently heard the statement: "You can concentrate on reading more than on listening. Listening is easier, but you get more out of reading." The reader can choose his own material, set his own pace, reread difficult passages, mull over the ideas as he goes along. "Serious reading requires more effort than listening, but intellectually it is more satisfactory."

III. *RAPPORT:* A PERSONAL RELATIONSHIP

Suggestion involves a relationship between the person doing the suggesting and the person to whom the appeal is made. Of course, one or more persons may be concerned on each side of this reciprocal relationship. We shall consider first the factors determining sugges-

---

[7] See P. F. Lazarsfeld: *Radio and the Printed Page: an Introduction to the Study of Radio and Its Role in the Communication of Ideas.* 1940.

tibility and then the factors determining the effectiveness of the suggester.

A. Suggestibility of the "Receiver"

When we analyze the susceptibility of the person on the receiving end, we are dealing with suggestibility or gullibility. Some people, we say, are more suggestible than others. What factors influence the nature and the degree of suggestibility? Is a person who is susceptible to suggestion in one field likely to be susceptible in other fields as well —that is, is suggestibility a specific or a general trait?

1. factors determining the acceptance of a suggestion

Among the factors influencing suggestibility we shall mention ignorance, age, sex, emotional excitement, and the desire to believe.

a. *Ignorance.* Ignorance certainly is one important condition of suggestibility. In the slang of our day we hear it said that so-and-so is "so dumb he'll swallow anything." A child is easily led to believe that there is a Santa Claus. He may be convinced of Santa's reality when his father picks up the telephone and presumably engages Kris Kringle in conversation. In such a case, ignorance, like distance in the old proverb, lends enchantment. By the same token, the pupil tends to believe what his teacher tells him, the patient accepts the doctor's diagnosis, especially if it is couched in esoteric language he cannot understand, and the neophyte in any group, such as a fraternal order, follows the lead of some associate who has been on the inside for a long time.

b. *Age.* Age is another factor in determining suggestibility. Younger boys and girls were found by Messerschmidt to be more suggestible than the older ones, in an age range of from six to sixteen years. One test used by him was originally devised by Binet. It called for the presentation of twelve lines, exposed one at a time. Each line exhibited was longer than the preceding one except for the sixth, eighth, tenth, and twelfth lines, each of which was the same length as the line immediately preceding. Many subjects were led by the progressive increase in the series to estimate the four "trap" lines as longer than they really were. Another phase of the experiment was the use of leading questions suggesting the presence of an object not actually in the picture exposed. From the eleven tests of suggestibility which he employed Messerschmidt concluded that the greatest susceptibility to indirect suggestion occurs in the seven-year-old group.

From this age on to sixteen, the highest age level tested in the experiment, there was a progressive decrease in suggestibility.[8]

c. *Sex.* Women are more suggestible than men, and girls are more suggestible than boys, according to a number of investigators. Between the sexes, however, the differences are relatively small in comparison with those existing among members of the same sex. It is likely that the higher suggestibility of the female is a product of our cultural system, which still places a premium on the "ladylike" woman who refrains from contradicting the male. Possibly the emancipation of women from masculine dominance, reinforced by the enlightenment provided by higher education, will reduce, in time, the small difference between the sexes in this matter of suggestibility.

d. *Emotional Excitement.* A person in an emotional state is more suggestible than when he is calm and unexcited. This observation is illustrated in the case of a man who heard that his son had been drowned. Brokenhearted, he went to the morgue where, he had been informed, the body of a boy had been brought in for identification. The man identified the body as that of his son and, shaken with grief, proceeded home. When he arrived at his house, lo and behold there was his son sitting at the kitchen table eating his supper. The coincidence of the rumor and the finding of a body set the stage for the erroneous identification. The average person visiting a morgue would be in a perturbed state of mind. It is understandable how the sight of a corpse would add to the emotional disturbance. A leading question from the man in charge would suffice to evoke a mistaken perception in the "bereaved" parent.

Fright over the Orson Welles radio version of "The Invasion from Mars," which occasioned such a panic in 1938, is attributed by Cantril to "susceptibility-to-suggestion-when-facing-a-dangerous-situation." [9] Insecurity, lack of self-confidence, fatalism, and religiosity prepared the emotional setting conducive to the acceptance of the idea that Martians were attacking the United States. Analysis of this incident convinced Cantril that the most important insurance against susceptibility to panic is *critical ability:* "a person's readiness to reevaluate interpretations he first receives, to look for new standards of judgment and juxtapose them against others." [10] This critical procedure

---

[8] See R. Messerschmidt: "The Suggestibility of Boys and Girls between the Ages of Six and Sixteen Years." *Journal of Genetic Psychology*, 1933, 43, 422-437.

[9] See H. Cantril *et al.: The Invasion from Mars*, p. 130. Princeton University Press, 1940.

[10] *Ibid.*, p. 196.

is not likely to be employed when an emergency arises which provokes an intense emotional response. Emotional excitement thus facilitates suggestibility.

Inspired by Cantril's analysis of the public reaction to the Welles broadcast, Coffin planned an ingenious experiment to test the influence of critical judgment upon suggestion. Problems chosen from a college textbook on mathematics were mimeographed (to disguise the nature of the investigation) under the title, "Richardson Number Facility Test." The subjects were told it was a test of mathematical aptitude. Suggestions were introduced in the form of "hints" penciled in the spaces provided for working out the problems.

It was "explained" to the subjects that the test had been found to require more time for completion than had been anticipated, so the authors had reduced the labor necessary by giving hints as to the answers or by indicating the first steps in procedure. The hints were inserted in pencil in order to suggest their addition as an afterthought and to render plausible the statement as to their origin and purpose. Later questioning of the subjects revealed that they accepted without suspicion this explanation of the hints. Most of the hints suggested incorrect procedures. However, to establish confidence in the suggestions, two of the problems in the first two groups . . . were given "correct" hints.

Introspective reports were used to supplement the scoring, in order to learn how the stimulus was experienced, that is, to find out which characteristics of the situation aroused false standards of judgment. In summarizing his findings, Coffin says: "It is found that . . . the reactions to the suggestion-situation are comparable with the analysis of radio listeners' reactions to the broadcast of the *War of the Worlds,* as presented by Cantril. Individuals who made successful external or internal checks tended to be non-suggestible, while persons who made ineffective external or internal checks, or no check whatsoever, tended to be suggestible." [11]

e. *The Desire to Believe.* The most important factor in suggestibility probably is the desire to believe. There is in some people a strong urge to accept authority, possibly because it gives them a feeling of security to believe that there are those who know. A sick person wants to believe in the expertness of his physician because it is reassuring to have such a faith. If he is at all in doubt, he consults a special-

[11] T. E. Coffin: "Some Conditions of Suggestion and Suggestibility: a Study of Certain Attitudinal and Situational Factors Influencing the Process of Suggestion." *Psychological Monographs,* No. 241. 1941.

ist. Sophisticated people may suspect that "a specialist is just an ordinary doctor a long way from home."

Anybody who finds lawn-mowing tedious is prepared to welcome a salesman announcing a labor-saving grass seed that he claims will never grow higher than three inches. The Boston Better Business Bureau reports that canvassers soliciting orders for this marvelous non-growing grass seed just get the orders, ship the seed, and let the owner plant his own lawn. In rural communities the sales force employs a more elaborate plan of attack, setting up a landscaping company which assures skeptical inquirers that this unbelievable boon to the caretaker has actually been discovered. The schemesters tell their customers that they cannot proceed with the planting until they have a sufficiently large number of orders to warrant their going ahead. When the time is ripe, they tear up all the lawns and replant them with this "seed" which consists largely of sawdust. The grass, just as they claim, does not grow higher than three inches—in fact, it does not grow at all. By the time the culprits have skipped town, scores of lawns in the community have been left "looking like the battlefields of France."

A person who would fall for such a proposition is dominated by "wishful thinking," that is, he tends to believe what he wants to believe. Lund investigated the relation of belief to desire by submitting to his subjects a list of thirty propositions concerning various issues, such as:

Is Christianity losing its influence in this country? . . .
Does a black cat crossing your path cause bad luck?

Students were instructed to mark these propositions on a scale ranging from absolute belief through neutral to absolute disbelief. After this task was completed, the subjects marked the same issues on a similar scale to indicate how much they desired each proposition to be true. The results revealed a strong inclination to believe what was desired.[12]

Observing that groups of subjects in experiments on suggestion will accept some suggestions and reject others, Coffin sought an explanation for the differences in reaction. He was not satisfied to classify persons into suggestible and non-suggestible categories—he wanted a more concrete answer to his problem. Investigation showed

[12] See F. H. Lund: "The Psychology of Belief." *Journal of Abnormal and Social Psychology*, 1925-1926, 20, 63-81; 174-196.

him that suggestion is a function of attitudes and the situations in which they are operating. Exploring the relation between a person's attitudes and his reactions to propaganda rumors bearing on the war as it stood in January, 1940, the time of his research, he found a rather close relation between attitude and acceptance of propaganda: the stronger the pro-Ally attitude, the more likely the acceptance of pro-Ally propaganda. Coffin particularly cites the importance of *pre-existing attitudes* in determining whether a person will accept or reject suggestions. "Subjects accept, in general, those suggestions which 'fit' with their existing attitudes, even when alternative suggestions are available, offered simultaneously, and in a similar manner." [13] The determining tendency operates as a very significant factor in suggestion.

The will to believe, an important determining tendency, is connected, at times, with the nature of the person's temperament. The optimistic person, for example, is apt to believe the salesman who is kind enough to want to let him in on something good, say some stock in oil wells or gold mines. Such a gullible individual is perhaps better known as a "sucker." Very intelligent people are betrayed by their eagerness for easy money into accepting the wildest tales about treasure ships and other "sure things." Their faith is akin to that of the man who, in marrying for the fifth time, demonstrated the triumph of hope over experience.

2. SPECIFICITY OF SUGGESTIBILITY

Suggestibility is often referred to as if it were a general personality trait. It is not a general trait but rather it is specific to particular situations. No one is gullible in all circumstances. Each one of us is vulnerable only under certain conditions. A plumber whose wife had joined a thought-control cult was much impressed by the good she was deriving from attending their services. Finally he decided to give it a try himself. He accompanied his wife to a testimony meeting where various people recited how they had been cured of hay fever, poor vision, cancer. The evidence appeared convincing to him. He returned to another meeting the next week. Among those testifying was a lady who had been upset when the cold weather froze the water pipes in her home. When the water failed to respond to the turning of the faucet, she sat down nearby, opened her book of readings, perused it awhile, and meditated on the fact that all is love, all is good. After she had attained a composed mind, she arose and

[13] Coffin: *op. cit.*

tried the faucet again. The water poured forth. This bit of testimony was too much for the plumber. He scratched his head and departed, never to return.

B. Prestige of the Suggester

The term *rapport* which we have been using to designate the personal relationship inherent in suggestion, was first employed to explain hypnotic suggestion. Hypnosis can be induced only in cases where the subject is amenable to the suggestion that he is going into a "sleep," where the hypnotizer has the prestige to carry his suggestions. This means that there must be a reciprocal relationship of dominance and submission. It also means that some subjects can be hypnotized, others cannot, depending in some cases on the personality of the subject, in other cases on the personality of the suggester, in some cases on both factors.

Though hypnotic suggestion is a special kind of suggestion, the condition of *rapport* is just as necessary in normal suggestion: there must be a subject who is susceptible and a suggester who is respected as one having authority. We have examined some of the influences determining suggestibility. Now we shall analyze the nature of prestige, legitimate and illegitimate, and the factors responsible for the power some persons have for influencing others effectively by means of suggestion.

1. THE POWER OF PRESTIGE

Anything that makes a person prepossessing, any quality that contributes to dominance, any value that is impressive, lends prestige to the suggester. The influence of prestige can be demonstrated and even measured by asking subjects to compare statements as to convincingness, first without names attached, then with names attached. The statements are scaled by the method of paired comparisons, and the first scale is subtracted from the second; that is, the "weight" of the statement without the name is compared with the "weight" of the statement with the name. Thus a scale of prestige-values of the names is obtained with respect to the influence they carry for the particular subjects involved.[14] This technique for measuring prestige is based on the observation that a literary passage is likely to be given a higher rating if the author is known to have achieved top standing in this field. Thus, a Shakespeare passage attributed to Edgar Guest

[14] See W. A. Lurie: "Measurement of Prestige and Prestige-Suggestibility." *Journal of Social Psychology*, 1938, 9, 219-225.

is regarded as poor; the same passage accredited to Browning is considered excellent. A political idea attributed to Marx is labeled false; the same idea attributed to Coolidge is marked true.[15]

Sherif reports an experiment in which the subjects rated various authors. Then passages from Stevenson, ascribed to the different authors, were rated. The Stevenson passages which were attributed to authors rated high in the first step of the experiment were graded as superior in the second procedure, the ones attributed to authors rated low, were graded as inferior. The *name* of the author, concludes Sherif, serves as a "reference point" influencing the judgment of the merit of a passage ascribed to that *name*.[16] The situation is analogous to that of the person with a reputation for being "good," who, on that account alone, can do no wrong. The stereotype seals the estimate which the person will rate, deserved or not deserved.

It has been shown by experiment that prestige effect is influenced by whether or not the subject likes the person who is being featured as a prestige source. Saadi and Farnsworth established this thesis by having students check the names of people liked and disliked; then the students were divided into three groups, all receiving the same statements, the statements being accredited for each group to different persons as the sources. Group A thus received an opinion credited to a person they liked; group B estimated the same opinion as attributed to a disliked person; group C reviewed the same proposition with no name attached. The results demonstrated a significant difference in favor of accepting statements when they are ascribed to persons liked.[17]

The prestige of a famous name is of great value in the endorsement of any enterprise. The Buchmanites used effectively the weight of illustrious names in promoting their program of MRA (moral rearmament). "Testimonials" included names of prominent people who presumably had joined Buchman's Oxford Group Movement, when the truth of the matter was, they simply signed their names as subscribing to certain self-evident propositions. One Congressional leader who had signed a statement for the meeting of the Group in Washington, explained later: "Sure, I'm for MRA, whatever that is. It's just like being against Sin." Commenting on this promotional technique,

[15] See H. Cantril: "Experimental Studies of Prestige Suggestion." *Psychological Bulletin*, 1937, 34, 528.
[16] See M. Sherif: "An Experimental Study of Stereotypes." *Journal of Abnormal and Social Psychology*, 1935, 29, 371-375.
[17] See M. Saadi and P. R. Farnsworth: "Degrees of Acceptance of Dogmatic Statements and Preferences for Their Supposed Makers." *Journal of Abnormal and Social Psychology*, 1934, 29, 143-150.

an observer noted: "Yet the Oxford Group uses these names freely; the not-too-alert listener gets the impression that most of the great of the earth have actually joined." [18]   The association of a project with famous persons is one of the most effective ways to "build up" the prestige of an organization.   Prestige has *A-Number-One* promotional value.

2. KINDS OF PRESTIGE

The exploitation of famous names in order to lend "class" or merit to an enterprise suggests that prestige may be employed to advantage in illegitimate as well as legitimate ways.

a. *Legitimate Prestige.*   Legitimate prestige is involved when the suggester is exerting his influence in a field where he is an expert, or at least in a field where he is recognized as an expert.   Emily Post is exercising prestige in a legitimate fashion when she tells us how to put the best foot forward, Ely Culbertson when he instructs us to play second hand low, as was Ignace Paderewski when he recommended the Steinway piano.   Emily Post knows her etiquette, Culbertson his bridge, and Paderewski knew his pianos.

b. *Illegitimate Prestige.*   Prestige is illegitimate when an expert in one field poses as an authority in other matters.   Red Grange endorsing spinach, Conchita Montenegro recommending the Frigidaire, Irene Bordoni backing Miller Tires, and Shirley Temple praising the Dodge ("My goodness! . . . what a grand car!") are cases in point.   A noted philanthropist, director in many important business and welfare organizations, testified that he was enthusiastic about the Lucky Strike cigarette because "It's Toasted."   He said that the ultra-violet-ray toasting of the Lucky Strike was a splendid example of an industry's obedience to the basic principle of philanthropy: action for the good of others.   In this instance, he declared, the tobacco company had made a most beneficial contribution, one that would be heartily hailed by the consumer.

A writer in *Advertising and Selling,* however, is not so naïve:

In stressing "It's Toasted," George Washington Hill, President of the American Tobacco Company, is on solid ground.   We say this in spite of the fact that the Lucky Strike process of heat-drying tobacco is, we are told practically identical with that of all other makers of popularly priced cigarettes.

[18] M. A. Rose: "Buchman and Moral Re-Armament."   *Christian Herald,* October 1939.

One brand of cigarettes is recommended with the claim that a blindfolded smoker would "know the difference."

Louis Goodman, at Reed College, put this matter to scientific test.
He found that our senses, minus vision, are totally unable to recognize
the heart leaves of the tobacco plant.   There was one chance in nine of
picking the favorite.   Twenty students, all seasoned smokers, all confident they could select their favorite brands, served as subjects in the experiment.   Their choices turned out to be very inconsistent.   In a
series of presentations, Lucky Strikes were liked, disliked, and considered indifferent by the same smoker.   Five blindfolded subjects
were presented Old Golds, among others.   The recognition of Old
Golds occurred as follows among the five men:

Presented	11	times		Correct	0
"	9	"		"	0
"	7	"		"	1
"	10	"		"	1
"	7	"		"	0

In 44 presentations, Old Gold was but twice correctly named.   Rather
it was called:

Camel	13	times
Lucky Strike	10	"
Fatima	7	"
Chesterfield	5	"
Stroller	4	"
Three Castles	1	"
Tareyton	1	"
One Eleven	1	"

The statistics of chance would allow 7 identifications out of 44, but
there were only two.   In other words, false confidence increased the
errors.   One man, a Fatima smoker paying the few cents for that
"whale of a difference," could not tell them from Strollers at half
the price.[19]

The author applied to several tobacco companies for permission to
use, in this section, quotations from their advertisements.   Permission
was refused.

There has been something treacherous in the connotation of the
word "prestige" from its beginning, for it is derived from the Latin

---

[19] S. Chase: "Blindfolded You Know the Difference." *The New Republic*, August 8, 1928.

word *praestigium,* meaning "sleight of hand." A study of moder
advertising—witness the samples just cited—would indicate that pre
tige in some cases is still quite often underhanded in nature. Th
possibility of deception through the authority of prestige is certainl
present when we are led by the mention of "big names" in the medica
profession to believe that yeast must be good for any ailment if it i
of value in the treatment of staphylococcic infections. Even thoug
we feel well, the advertisers tell us, we might feel better.

Illegitimate prestige of this sort was demonstrated experimentally b
an investigation in which Hoover, Lindbergh, Einstein, Pershing, Mo
gan, and Theodore Roosevelt were rated for their command of fifteen
different fields of knowledge. All of them were regarded by the sul
jects as authorities in most of the fields listed. Roosevelt, for example
was rated as an authority on government, military affairs, economic
education, and the law. Uncritical individuals thus tend to attribut
superior knowledge on all subjects to a person who happens to be a
authority in one particular field. This tendency to rate a person hig
in all traits because he is rated high in one respect, is known as th
"halo effect." The halo effect accounts for much of the illegitimat
prestige influencing our human relations.

3. FACTORS INFLUENCING PRESTIGE

We have observed how prestige, legitimate and illegitimate, fun
tions. Now let us analyze, sketchily, what factors lend a person pre
tige in our particular culture.

a. *Athletic Prowess.* First, there is athletic prowess. In 1932 th
nonpartisan fact-finding committee for Hoover released a statemer
listing the names of five college football coaches who had endorse
President Hoover's campaign for reelection: Amos Alonzo Stagg (
Chicago, Dr. Marvin Stevens of Yale, Andy Kerr of Colgate, "Tuss
McLaughry of Brown, and "Pop" Warner of Stanford.

Red Cagle, famous Army halfback, endorsed both Hoover and th
Royal portable typewriter. In the Royal advertisement he was quote
as saying: "It is the greatest aid I ever knew in keeping up my grades.
Some one reading this statement was curious enough to look up Cagle
grades, found them uniformly low. It is still true, of course, that h
might have fared worse without his Royal.

b. *Science.* A second factor in prestige is science. The word of th
scientist is the last word today. Hugh Manity, N.D., F.S.D., M.T.D
is the originator of Egoatrics, the new science of Bio-dynamics, accord
ing to his own say-so. One of his lectures discusses "How to Acquir

a Dynamic Magnetic Personality Egoatrically." This is "a new method
of self-treatment through the ductless glands for fatigue, poor memory, debility, nervousness, timidity, underweight and overweight . . .
an exotic, subtle principle of self-improvement within reach of every
earnest seeker."

Foreign doctors, with hyphenated names and strings of degrees appended, advocate for middle-aged persons "less feasting and more
yeasting," without any mention of the need for proper exercise and a
sensible diet. Bearded scientists in long white aprons, in the midst of
beakers and test tubes, testify to the potency of chewing gum and shaving creams. Vitamins A, B, C, and D, with some more added on, are
recommended in certain foods, toothpastes, and hair tonics. Scientific endorsement is all that is required to convince the gullible public.

The *scientist* is one of the most useful iconographic symbols in the
advertising art—a prominent type among the images which people the
advertiser's world.

He is grave, efficient, deliberate, unlikely to be swayed by carnal passions.
He is shown at his work-desk looking through a microscope or inspecting a
test tube or some curious mechanism. All about him is a medley of retorts,
bunsen burners, and carboys of magical ingredients—in fact, all the attributes
of the scientific passion. He may be shown alone, or with disciples of only
slightly less probity. . . . This modern savior, the embodiment of the
shibboleth of Science, is the court of appeal of the advertiser. Proof, in advertising, only too often consists of the significant words: "Modern Science
tells us." The Scientist is one of the few characters in the advertising
pantheon who never smiles. He is felt to be even above humor. In this
modern day He is the Man Who Knows. He is the magician who makes the
ideal world created by advertising possible.[20]

Much of the research for which the Scientist stands as a convenient
symbol, takes place in the office of the advertising agency where some
clever person discovers a new "fact" or "principle" by means of the
armchair method. A genius in this line is William Cole Esty, President of Esty and Co., New York advertising agency, who thought up
the slogans that carried Camel cigarettes right out in front of the field,
in a campaign characterized by *Fortune* as "$57,000,000 Worth of
Whizz and Whoozle." [21]

Science probably carries more prestige today than any other single

[20] P. Parker: "The Iconography of Advertising Art." *Harper's Magazine,* June,
1938.
[21] See *Fortune,* August, 1938.

source of authority.   Even religion has been endorsed by the scientists.   Dr. Harry Emerson Fosdick writes:

The men of faith might claim for their positions ancient tradition, practical usefulness, and spiritual desirability, but one query could prick all such bubbles: Is it scientific?   Science has so cowed religion that many throw up their hands at the mere whisper of it.   When a prominent scientist comes out strongly for religion, all the churches thank Heaven and take courage, as though it were the highest possible compliment to God to have Eddington believe in Him." [22]

c. *Academic Degrees.*   Academic degrees carry prestige, since it is assumed that the trappings of Master and Doctor invariably represent superior learning.   Some students become degree hunters, continuing in school for years and years to collect sundry academic honors.   Just to be able to say "I am a college graduate" is still a mark of some distinction, often an open sesame to a job.   Teachers must get advanced degrees to be promoted.   Some colleges strive to build up a faculty limited to men with Ph.D.'s because it looks so impressive in the school catalogue.

d. *Social Position.*   Social position is one of the most important factors in the creation of prestige.   Junior Leaguers have endorsed so many commercial articles that the national organization has considered it necessary to take some action to control the practice.   Members of the Social Register whose names appear in the Blue Book and whose families "go way back" exert a marked influence because they are notables.   Their names mean something.   A chief of the Chudasama tribe in India, who ordered his shoes from London, by chance received a pair that squeaked.   His barefooted subjects were very much impressed by the chief's loud footwear, thereafter demanded shoes with a squeak, the squeakier the better.

e. *Wealth.*   Wealth is another condition conferring prestige.   We assume that money and good taste go together, that whatever the rich do with their time and money must be worthy of imitation and respect. Sometimes people who are well off set a worthy example, sometimes they do not.   Imitators need to use some discrimination.

f. *Success.*   The last factor in prestige which we shall mention is success.   Nothing, we say, succeeds like success.   Sometimes this is legitimate, as it is when a successful novelist explains how to write novels; more often it is illegitimate, as it is in the case of a big investment

[22] H. E. Fosdick: *As I See Religion*, p. 130-131.   1932.

counsel who gives instruction pertaining to matters of health. Some wit has remarked that you know a man is successful when the newspapers start quoting him on subjects he knows nothing about. Whether it be a musician taking an advance peep at a new car or a movie actress displayed in graphic, eating spaghetti, the principle is the same: a person who can forge his way to the top of his profession must be qualified to pass judgment on all matters, inside or outside his field.

IV. CONTRA-SUGGESTION: NEGATIVISM

The converse of suggestion is contra-suggestion. The contra-suggestible person does just the opposite of what he is asked to do. If he sees a sign saying "Keep off the grass," he immediately feels a compulsive urge to get *on* the grass. Scientists call such an individual negativistic; ordinary people call him "just plain cussed."

Young children pass through a negativistic stage from about two to four years of age, when they are beginning to assert their individualities and "I won't" is the characteristic response to parental commands. Children sometimes have more won't than will power, as someone has well expressed it. It is a wise parent who circumvents negativism by avoiding the use of direct commands. The parent who orders, "Tie your shoe!" may arouse nothing more than defiance. How much wiser he would be to call the child's attention to the situation in a matter-of-fact way by simply saying, "Johnnie, your shoe is untied." In the latter approach the assumption is made that Johnnie has brains enough to see that something should be done and Johnnie appreciates the compliment enough to do something about the untied shoe.

Instead of urging a child repeatedly to "Hurry! Hurry! Come on and get dressed quick!" the mother would secure the desirable speed more readily by purchasing a sandglass and placing it on a table in the child's room, with the simple challenge: "Have a race with this sandglass and see how few times it will have to be turned over before you are dressed." A mother in Cleveland who discovered a remedy for the wandering shirttail, was also using her wits to gain her purpose. Her little boy was careless about letting his shirttail hang out, so she cured him by sewing bits of lace and embroidery on the tails. According to last reports, he now keeps the tails out of sight.

A mother was puzzled because her three-year-old daughter cried every time she told her that she could not do or have what she wanted. The mother began to substitute "Yes" for "No." If the daughter wanted candy just before mealtime, Mother would say: "Why, certainly, you may. We are going to eat lunch in a few minutes, and when you have finished, you may have a piece of candy." If the child wanted to go and play just before nap time, Mother said: "Yes, you may go and play in just a little while, but first let's go find a book and read a story. Then we'll take a nap and then it will be time to play." The little girl never seems to see the "No" side of her mother's answers, and consequently, she has ceased to cry on such occasions.[23]

The art of influencing children has been investigated in the laboratory elementary school at the University of Michigan. Using 40 matched pairs of children, ages $2\frac{1}{2}$ to $8\frac{1}{2}$ years, as subjects, Johnson tested the relative effectiveness of 26 different varieties of persuasion, including such techniques as cajolery, flattery, commands, threats, and scolding. Simple instructions were found to be most persuasive. When a teacher pointed to some glass toys and said, "Put them away in the red box," 34 of the 37 children did so. But when she said, "We have to be very careful of these glass animals. We wrap them up in tissue paper. We put them away in a red box. . . . It would be too bad to break them. . . . You put them away," only 7 children responded correctly. A positive request proved to be more effective than a negative one. The children, for example, were almost twice as careful when a teacher said, "Keep the clay on the board," as when she said, "Try not to get it all over everything." [24]

Children who play too strenuously around the house, upsetting furniture and scratching floors, are usually ordered to stop at once by an angry parent who shouts, "Be careful of my floor." They do not stop. Why should they, if they don't feel like respecting papa's or mama's floors! Quiet and order could be restored more readily by a personal reference to "our floors which we all want to take care of, don't we?"

Negativism is not limited to children, by any means. Adults can be just as "cussed" in resisting suggestions. A good example of this is seen in the story of the opening session of the Peace Conference back in 1918, when Clemenceau, in a derby, and Lord Balfour, in a silk topper, walked out together. Balfour apologized. "I was told," he said, "that it was obligatory to wear one." "So," Clemenceau answered, "was I." Such a reaction as Clemenceau's is typical of negativistic behavior.

Since so many people are contra-suggestible in a number of situations, it is necessary to learn the art of slantwise suggestion as a technique for handling such persons. The father who condemns the

[23] See "Child Problems," a regular feature of *Parents' Magazine*.
[24] See M. W. Johnson: *Verbal Influences on Children's Behavior*. 1939.

young man his daughter is going with is not nearly so clever as the father who damns the upstart with faint praise. The individual who wants to use flattery should be subtle in his compliments, for "soft soap" is apt to be identified as such unless it is well disguised. The girl who wants to impress her suitor with her maternal craving can do so more effectively by proclaiming her thrill over a friend's baby, in the young man's presence, than by the blunt assertion, "I do love children so much."

The minister was employing slantwise suggestion, who put this notice in a June issue of the church calendar:

During the absence of his family, the pastor is devoting the dinner hour to fellowship with the families of the church.

Just as subtle was the theater owner who discovered an effective means of getting the women to remove their hats. Just before the performance, this notice appeared on the screen:

The management wishes to spare elderly ladies any inconvenience. They are therefore invited to retain their hats.

All hats, it is rumored, came off.

The cigarette "moocher" is an expert in the technique of slantwise suggestion.

Question: Now, as I understand it, Mr. Gooch, you are what is called a cigarette moocher?

Answer: Yeah. I don't never buy any.

Q. How do you operate, Mr. Gooch? Do you just ask people for cigarettes?

A. Naw, that's just bumming. I mooch 'em. I use psychology. Suppose I see a guy take out a package. I say, "Boy, that reminds me. I'm fresh out of cigarettes." The other guy nearly always says, "Won't you have one of mine?" [25]

The master of slantwise suggestion gets his own way but makes other people think they are having things their way. Lincoln used this method very successfully in handling his recalcitrant cabinet. Sir James M. Barrie's play, *What Every Woman Knows,* depicts the ways in which a woman made her husband's career for him without his ever

[25] D. Welch: "Moocher," *Saturday Evening Post* ("Post Scripts"), March 28, 1936.

suspecting, until the end, the working of "the power behind the throne."

White, in *The Psychology of Dealing with People*,[26] gives some concrete advice relative to slantwise suggestion. Assume acceptance, he advises. If a woman wants her husband to use his razor on his beard, she may say, "You'll have time, dear, to shave before dinner." That is much better than to command him to shave, for one should avoid the impression, at least, of dictating.

The preacher must learn how to circumvent negativism because, as soon as he starts his sermon, some members of his congregation will be on the defensive. The teacher, likewise, is handicapped by the fact that some of her pupils may regard school as something to be endured and resisted as far as possible. The wise teacher does not impose her assignments upon the child but "eggs him on" by discovering his interests, then appealing to them, and tying them up with other lines of activity that may seem to the child to be unrelated. Thus a child who can draw can be inveigled, through the study and reproduction of maps, into a liking, even though mild at first, for geography and history.

One of the cleverest devices for handling negativism is to suggest just the opposite of what you want done. The man with a contrary wife will suggest going to the mountains for the summer when he really wants to go to the seashore. A tobacco-advertising calendar has a picture attached to the cardboard, with these instructions printed below the picture:

DO NOT LOOK UNDER THE PICTURE

Your curiosity is aroused and you peek under it to find a hint as to where you should purchase your cigarettes to obtain the best quality at the most reasonable prices. A variation of this technique is a real-estate advertisement arranged as follows:

DO NOT LOOK

at this ad unless
you care about
obtaining a new house
at a price reduced to
suit your pocketbook.

Contra-suggestible people fall for such bait very readily.

[26] Published in 1936.

Fond parents, of course, will want to rear their children in such ways that negativism will not be nourished into an habitual attitude. There are two techniques for avoiding such an eventuality. One is to give the child attention when he is being agreeable, so that he will not learn to resort to stubbornness in order to win notice; the other is to avoid the dictatorial manner that is sure to arouse opposition, by resorting, instead, to the use of slantwise suggestion.

V. EXPLOITATION OF SUGGESTION BY ADVERTISERS

Utilizing the various kinds of prestige and employing the latest promotional techniques discovered by psychology, some advertisers have succeeded in exploiting the credulous buying public whose sales resistance is no match for the canny experts. Capital is sometimes expended on fooling the consumer rather than on improving the commodity.

Advertisers, encouraged by our obvious gullibility, tell us without "cracking a smile" of tooth pastes that will cure acid mouth, when all the time it is a well-known fact among medical authorities that our saliva is normally acid and that it should stay that way.[27] Acid stomach is another bugbear the advertisers use for all it's worth.[28]

Irrational conclusions can be promoted by suggestion in as much as there is an inhibition of critical judgment involved in the process. "You wouldn't eat a green orange, why drink unripe ginger ale?" It would be equally logical to ask, since you would not eat a ripe egg, why drink ripe ginger ale? The magazine *Ballyhoo* satirized the nonsense of the advertisers. The fact that their fun-poking helped the sales of the products whose advertisements they ridiculed offers clinching evidence of the consumers' disregard for the canons of reason. Advertisers, according to Chase, lay down "a smoke screen of psychological appeals to shame, fear, sex, mother love, success, and greed. . . . If all consumers should wake up literate tomorrow morning, the commercial fabric would be torn to pieces. It has been patiently reared on the assumption that we are natural-born damn fools." [29] Playing upon our irrationality, the advertisers calmly inform us that "exclusive people buy inexpensive tooth paste." The advertisement then goes on to tell us about the things we could buy with the money saved in the purchase of this cheaper article. We are not informed, how-

[27] See J. W. Ephraim: "The Truth about Dentifrices." *American Mercury*, September, 1934.
[28] L. J. Henderson: "Alkali Ads." *Harvard Business Review*, Autumn, 1937. Condensed in the *Reader's Digest*, February, 1938.
[29] S. Chase: *A New Deal*, pp. 232, 235. 1932.

ever, of the wonderful things we could get for ourselves with the money saved by not brushing our teeth at all.

Advertisers use suggestion to intensify and multiply our wants.[30] Luxuries are converted into necessities as we desert the coal shovel for the oil burner and protect the family's health with a nice, new, gleaming white refrigerator. The automobile used to be considered a "rich man's toy." Now we cannot do without one. We must keep up with our neighbors and a little ahead of them, if possible—and a little ahead of the installment collectors, too. Spending money is satisfying when an impression of affluence can be created to stir the admiration of persons not so well off. Thus we engage in "conspicuous waste." Meanwhile the advertising agencies prosper while the consumer wonders how in the world he is going to meet his bills. The acquisition of new needs is illustrated by the Baltimore woman who demanded a separation on the ground that her husband refused to buy her an electric refrigerator, which she declared to be "a necessity of life."

The naïveté of the average consumer is taken for granted by the advertiser. Why, when you stop to think about it, should anybody believe the praise of a product delivered by a man hired to promote its sale? The eulogist is naturally not going to be half-hearted in his panegyric. His vacuum cleaner is the best on the market, for scientific experiments have demonstrated such and such. Experiments conducted by whom? And for what purpose? No doubt most advertising is honest, but consumers must be ever on their guard lest suggestions penetrate which are inconsistent with the world of reality. *Caveat emptor* is still the common practice. The consumer must save his own skin or perish before the cleverly designed maneuvers of those who are out to get his dollar. "You have got to look right down into their pocketbooks," Madame Rubenstein reputedly instructs her salesgirls, "and get that last nickel." [31] Against this sort of artful pressure, a healthy skepticism is a first line of defense.

The fraudulent and misleading claims of some advertisers have given rise to several organizations which aim to give the consumer the truth. Consumers' Research has exposed many products which do not live up to their reputations. A soap powder was not recommended because it contained substances other than soap which should not be

---

[30] Multiplying our wants can be regarded as raising the standard of living. Advertisers have performed a useful function in stimulating the large consumption which makes mass production and lower prices possible.

[31] *Life,* July 21, 1941.

used on colored cottons, wool, or silk without special precautions. These precautions were nowhere noted in the advertising or the directions on the container. The advertising manager protested against the adverse judgment of Consumers' Research, though he admitted the correctness of the findings; he insisted that since so many millions of women used the soap with little or no complaint, there was no reason for his bothering to change the formula for it. A manufacturer of fire extinguishers whose product was not recommended sent a picture of his sales force and asked if it was likely that such a fine looking group of people could give their time to the sale of an inefficient article. These examples may be multiplied many times, as they are in *100,000,000 Guinea Pigs*[32] and other books exposing the frauds that are perpetrated on the consumer. Consumers' Union has gone further than Consumers' Research in its examination of goods, by furnishing not only an estimate of the quality of the product, but also information on the working conditions at the plant where the article is made. The assumption behind this plan is that people with a social conscience will boycott goods turned out under sweatshop conditions or other circumstances unfair to the worker.

Consumers' Research and Consumers' Union, well known by now, are only two developments within the widening program of *consumer education* carried out by home-economics courses in high schools and colleges, sponsored elsewhere by women's clubs, parent-teacher associations, consumer cooperatives, the Department of Agriculture and the Department of Labor in Washington, and other organizations interested in training the consumer to demand full value for his dollar. As a result of this expanding program, the consumer is learning to be wary of fraudulent advertising and fraudulent merchandise.

VI. SUGGESTION AND IMITATION

Imitation is usually the response to suggestion, made unintentionally, with the imitator set or predisposed to copy the behavior of the suggester, as in the case of a pupil who absorbs the mannerisms of his favorite teacher. Not all suggestion calls forth imitation. Imitation is involved only when there is a similarity between the stimulus and the response. If the teacher suggests that a mischievous student mend his ways, and the pupil does so, the response is not an imitative one. If the instructor sits erect in his chair, urges the class to do likewise, and they all straighten up, the response is imitative. In this case the suggestion is made deliberately. Ordinarily, however, the

[32] By A. Kallet and F. J. Schlink. 1933.

person who is copied is not aware that he is the model for those who admire his opinions or his way of doing things. Frequently, the imitator too is unaware of the fact that he is "following suit." It is the unconscious nature of the process, both on the side of the suggester and of the imitator, that explains why we do not fully realize how

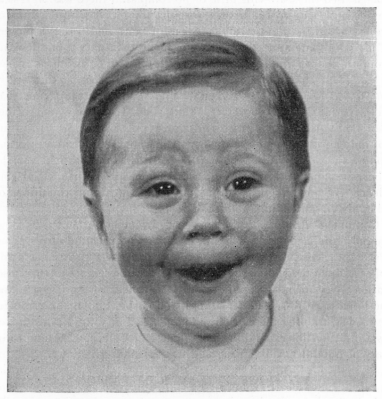

Can You Resist the Impulse to Imitate This Smile?   (Courtesy, Edgar L. Obma, photographer.)

certain patterns of behavior like fashions and customs are diffused until they become the prevailing modes of conduct.

A. Learning to Imitate

Most of our imitation is the result of *learning-to-imitate-others,* learning to follow a good example because it "pays" to do so, learning to avoid a bad example because experience has demonstrated that failure to do so results in dissatisfaction. The motivational factor in imitation is an important one, as Miller and Dollard point out in their treatise on *Social Learning and Imitation* (1941). Imitative behavior, they assert, can only occur when four conditions are present:

1. *Drive:* wanting something—such as candy.
2. *Cue:* noticing something—the candy is hidden under a particular kind of object.
3. *Response:* doing something—the person must be able to make the appropriate response.
4. *Reward:* getting something—satisfaction reinforces the correct response.

The child who follows in the footsteps of his elders is praised. This secondary reward, parental favor, encourages him to imitate when further situations afford him the opportunity. Doing the same as others do is regularly rewarded and in this way can be utilized in maintaining social conformity and discipline. Being different results in anxiety; conforming results in relief. Thus the child acquires a motive impelling him to copy, to conform. He will generalize to other similar persons and situations, too: he will imitate persons resembling previous good models and he will non-imitate those who are similar to previous bad models. The leader's prestige for one type of response will carry over to other situations (illegitimate prestige).

B. KINDS OF IMITATION

Imitation may be unconscious or deliberate, as we have noted. Miller and Dollard prefer to designate these two forms of imitation, *matched-dependent* and *copying*. In the matched-dependent situation, the matcher need not know his behavior is the same as that of the model. A familiar form of this pattern is exhibited when younger people match behavior with, and are dependent upon, older people. In a typical case the leader will afford the imitator an easy relevant cue which the latter makes use of without being aware of the fact that he is imitating. For example, Jim, the older brother, ran to the door when he heard his father's footsteps; his younger brother, Bobby, happened to be running behind Jim; both got candy from father. The next time Bobby saw Jim run to the door, Bobby ran, too—not in response to the cue of father but to the cue of Jim-running. In the *copying* sort of imitation, the copier knows when his behavior is the *same,* when it is *different,* sees the distinction, recognizes that the *same* mode of adjustment is a better one, worth following, copies it more or less exactly. This pattern of behavior proving by experience to be economical, the copier takes a short cut to success by adopting a solution which the model has already demonstrated to be successful.

Imitation is selective.   We do not copy another person unless he has prestige and unless we are interested in what he is doing.   The young lawyer does not adopt the platform antics of the religious evangelist but rather the suave fluency of the successful barrister, whom he seeks to emulate.   Thorndike found that one ape would not learn how to extricate himself from a puzzle box by watching another ape solve the problem.[33]   One reason probably was that the observer was not definitely interested in what was going on, did not feel any vital concern in the situation.   Only where interest is aroused does imitation occur. There must be an appeal based upon effective prestige.

C. Social Significance of Imitation

Since we all pattern ourselves after the likeness of our heroes, hero-worship offers one approach for ascertaining the shifting interests that characterize the process of growing up.   During the various stages of development circus performers, railroad conductors, traffic cops, and ball players excite, in their turn, the admiration of the boy who is coming of age, while cooks, seamstresses, dancers, and aviatrix are stirring the homage of the maturing girl.

Discrimination is often lacking in the process of imitation.   The emulator is apt to copy the nonessential aspects of the hero's character.   Thus the anemic undergraduate may ape the football captain's walk instead of taking measures to acquire a sturdy physique.   The younger brother will discard his garters to keep pace with the collegiate practices of his older brother just home from the university. The child who sees his professorial father underlining important passages in a textbook will seize a pencil and mark up *Black Sambo* with an abandon that makes it evident he has missed the point.   The advantages of intelligent emulation are lost because observation fails to select the significant item that renders the model worthy of adoration.

Imitation commonly occurs when the imitator is unaware of the fact that he is matching somebody else.   The person who follows his model demonstrates by that very act that he considers the exemplar his superior.   The open admission of inferiority in such a situation would not come easily with most people.   It is, therefore, less damaging to one's self-respect to imitate without knowing it.

Imitation involves certain social consequences which it would be well for us to keep in mind as we survey its role in human society—

[33] See E. L. Thorndike: *Animal Intelligence*, pp. 219-222.   1911.

notably its relation to originality and standardization, and its function in promoting progress and stagnation. We shall consider each of these effects briefly.

Originality may be sacrificed for the advantages of being one of a crowd. There is a feeling of security that comes with conformity to the group pattern. Being different lays one open to ridicule and censure. Falling in line saves the effort involved in creative activity.

THE SNOB

(Courtesy, Francis Dahl and the Boston *Herald*.)

Imitation is the easier way because it requires no initiative and because it secures the blessings accorded to those who "belong" by virtue of their compliance with the mores. Thus imitation promotes standardization.

Originality is indirectly stimulated by imitation. The upper classes seek to be distinguished from the lower classes by living in exclusive neighborhoods and by membership in the social register. In these matters they are fairly immune to the threats of imitators. It is more difficult, however, to dress in a distinctively upper-crust manner because technological improvements have made it possible for manufacturers to produce cheaper articles which cannot be readily recognized as substitutes for the "real thing." Rayon has blurred the lines between the classes. A well-dressed girl may be a debutante or a stenographer —it is hard to tell them apart by superficial signs. Exclusive modes of dress are sure to give rise to imitation, with the result that they are no longer exclusive. White shoes for men used to be the mark of "blue bloods" who went yachting in their leisure time. Now every member of *hoi polloi* can boast of at least one pair which he sports the year around. The aristocrats are smart enough to wear them only in the summer. Spats and colored underwear, which used to be worn only by dandies, are no longer the subject of lower-class ridicule, since the practice of wearing them has seeped down to the masses.

Under such circumstances the upper classes are forced to use their originality in order to maintain lines of distinction. Socialites are forced to devise new means of confounding their pretentious imitators. Thus innovation is encouraged as the classes endeavor to set themselves apart from the masses in a race that never lacks for competition.

It is important to recognize that it is human to want to be like others, and that it is just as human to want to be different. In spite of the standardizing influences of imitation, individuality is still maintained as idiosyncrasies are cultivated in the pursuit of distinctive charm. Though we identify ourselves with others, we still remain ourselves, like the small colored boy who was greeted by the old lady:

"So your name is George Washington," she mused.
"Yassum," replied the boy.
"I'll bet you try hard to be like him, don't you?"
"Lak who?"
"Why, like George Washington, of course."
"Ah kaint help bein' lak Jawdge Washington, 'cause dat's who Ah is."

Individuality is never completely sacrificed for conformity.

Imitation affects social progress in that it spreads the new and preserves the old.

Imitation plays a significant role in learning. Young children learn much from the examples set by their elders, a fact that should impress parents with a profound sense of responsibility. Plato was familiar with the import of parental example and in his *Republic* stipulated that all people over ten years of age should be removed from the city so that the young could grow up without being contaminated by their elders. Children are roving exhibits of parental deficiencies, especially when they dramatize family life in their play. A small boy and a little girl agreed to make believe they were married. As soon as their status had been established by mutual recognition, the boy imparted a push to his mate, accompanied by an assertion of masculine prerogative, "Get out of the way. Papa wants to do tricks!" Such a demonstration of domestic relations affords considerable insight into the patterns of adjustment practiced within the privacy of a neighbor's home.

A three-year-old child stuck a pipe in one corner of his mouth and seated himself in a Morris chair to read the newspaper. The fact that the paper was upside down did not detract seriously from the picture he presented of his father similarly lost with his "nose in the paper." As the boy gets older, he may get sick smoking corn silk in order to convince himself of his manhood. He wants to be grown up "the worst way."

Two boys, emulating the Wild West heroes of books they had been reading, shot up the town of Ellsworth, Maine, after stealing two guns and two bicycles to aid them in their rampage. William Edward Hickman, Los Angeles kidnaper and slayer, got his start by reading crime stories in the Public Library of Kansas City where he was employed during after-school hours. Tony Dziedzic, thirteen years old, read in the newspapers of the exploits of Hickman and decided to do something similar. He wrote a ransom letter to his former employer, the neighborhood butcher, demanding $10,000 and threatening to kidnap the butcher's daughter. Tony, however, made two mistakes. He forgot to say where the money was to be delivered and he signed his own name. Placed on six-months' probation, Tony marvelled at the intelligence of the police who were able to track him down.[34]

The movies also teach their lessons to immature and impressionable minds, not always convincing the young persons that "crime does not pay." Betrayed by his gang, which he had led in more than fifty robberies near Gloucester, Massachusetts, Smoky Joe told the police he got his ideas from the movies. Members of the gang admitted that they robbed homes, stores, and boats under the guidance of their movie-struck leader, who said, "It took me weeks to teach my gang up-to-date methods used by 'big shots.'" Smoky Joe, at the time, was eight years old.

Children's urge to do just what mama and daddy do is revolutionizing the toy industry. A third of all the toys manufactured in the United States are of the vehicle type because children love playthings that go. A large proportion of the vehicle toys are miniature reproductions of modern machinery or transportation devices. Concrete mixers, street sprinklers, steam shovels, iceboxes, and electric stoves

[34] Boston *Herald*, January 14, 1928.

which actually cook are put forth in tiny models for youngsters who prefer replicas of the prosaic things of modern life to the wooly left-overs from the playthings of other generations. Dolls constitute merely one-sixth of the toy-maker's product. Moreover, little mothers like their babies of the modern type. Bisque blondes with that doll-baby stare have been driven off the toy counter by snappy models with well-rouged cheeks and lips and hair of dramatic shade—preferably black.

Learning one's way around socially depends to a large extent upon imitating persons who are recognized as authorities in matters of eti-quette. So the guests may watch the hostess to see what fork she is going to use to eat the salad. How embarrassing it would be if the hostess happened to be at a loss in the situation and waited herself for somebody else to take the lead!

Imitation helps to preserve the old ways of doing things, but it often functions to preserve the old long after the days of its usefulness have passed. Some procedures are thus endowed with so much momentum that they endure to handicap generations whose needs they do not meet. As a result survivals are produced, a survival being a custom that was adjustive at an earlier time but is now maladjustive because of changed conditions.[35]

D. Uniformity of Action

People often do the same things in the same way: eating, working, re-producing, worshiping, all are much alike the world over. This sort of similarity has been attributed to imitation by some superficial observ-ers who chose the most convenient explanation at hand instead of probing further to uncover the variety of factors that might be respon-sible for the particular uniformity. Such was the case with Walter Bagehot who leaned heavily on imitation in his *Physics and Politics* (1884); later with Gabriel Tarde, in his *Les lois de l'imitation* (1890). [36] Both of these observers suspected that man was guided more by im-pulse than by reason, despite the optimistic assertions of Descartes and other rationalists who had allowed a personal stake in philosophy to influence their accounts of human motivation. Reason had been con-sidered the mark which distinguished man from the animals, the one evidence of God's special interest in creating man in his own image. Bagehot and Tarde refused to be prejudiced by such a consideration

---

[35] Survivals will be discussed at length in Chapter 13, "Custom."

[36] Tarde's book was published in English as *The Laws of Imitation*, translated by E. C. Parsons, in 1903.

in their efforts to reach the roots of social behavior. Impulse seemed to them more fundamental than reason in explaining the evolution of fashions, conventions, customs, and other phases of our social life. Imitation, they believed, was the real explanation for the similarities and uniformities of conduct characteristic of men in society.

The term *imitation* was used loosely by these two writers to account for the fact that people resembled one another in their social behavior, whether or not there had been any personal contacts among the individuals concerned. Apparently Bagehot and Tarde did not realize that similarities in custom may exist because human nature is much the same the world over and because the physical environment, to which man must adapt himself, is much the same everywhere. If they had defined the term more carefully, by recognizing that imitation is involved only when the response is similar to the stimulus, many of their errors could have been avoided. Similarity of response is not an adequate criterion in itself, either, since the uniformity in behavior may be due to the fact that the individuals are reacting to a common stimulus. Two citizens rushing from opposite ends of a village to a fire in the center of the town are obviously not aping each other, even though they both happen to run with their chests heaving; the running is provoked by a common interest in a common stimulus and the shortness of breath may be attributed to their respective waistlines. It is unlikely that anyone would lay their resemblance in obesity to imitation. The abundance of fattening foods in that particular region might be a more plausible explanation. If both men, however, were dashing from the same end of town, they might be imitating each other, though not necessarily. If one of them started for the fire and the other rushed in pursuit without any knowledge of the conflagration, running simply because he saw somebody else running, imitation would be involved. Conditioned by past experience to realize that a running citizen is probably headed for some exciting event, the second person would be inclined to follow the lead of the first. The mere fact that one man was pursuing the other would not be *prima facie* evidence of imitation, however, for it might be a case of a person chasing a man who had tried to rob him. These various possibilities are mentioned to demonstrate how easily similarity in behavior patterns may be mistaken for imitation.

Two girls in the same family being afflicted with the same speech defect, the question immediately arose as to whether or not the younger one was copying the older one. Their audiograms revealed a similar defect in hearing. Suspecting a family difficulty, the investigators gave audiometer tests to the mother and father. The mother's hearing was normal at all frequencies. The father's audiogram revealed a high-frequency deafness almost exactly like that of his two daughters, except that his was farther up in the range of frequencies and, therefore, had not affected his understanding of spoken words. On the basis of the evidence, it seemed likely that the younger daughter's speech difficulty was attributable to a common hereditary defect shared with her older sister, rather than to imitation.

Obviously, uniformity may be due, in some cases, to imitation. Much of the time, however, uniform behavior is likely to be a resultant of other factors. An enumeration of some of these other conditions will suggest how complex is the problem of explaining why people act alike, when they do:

1. Practically identical innate structures, plus common stimuli, result in common behavior. The way men and monkeys use their hands is a case in point.

2. Uniformity of action is economical and time-saving. Most men wear raiment called "suits" cut very much alike, largely because of the economy and time-saving of mass production.

3. If you act differently from others, embarrassment may result, or even the disapproval of others. If you do not conform to the folkways, customs, and mores of your group, you may be scorned or perhaps become a complete outsider. This is motivation enough for uniformity.

4. Conversely, uniformity is rewarded by the approval or even friendship of others. You are a "jolly good fellow" or at least "O.K." if you conform.

5. The group may have the same mores and habit patterns. In other words, through a long period in the culture of a particular group, the same ways of thinking and acting may have evolved so that every member of the group takes these "ways" for granted.

6. There may be a common language and other symbols of thought and action. If individuals in a particular group speak and think by use of the same sorts of symbols, this in itself promotes uniformity.

7. The actions of others may call attention to certain things and conditions (for example, food or danger). You may see someone on a street corner with his neck tilted back and his eyes pointed up. You then tilt your neck back and your eyes up, not with any desire to imitate him but simply because of your attention to outward stimuli.

8. In groups, there is often stimulation by enthusiasts or specialists in certain lines. In religious ceremonies, fraternal rituals, activities of audiences, some one individual may stimulate the group to behave or think a certain way. In fact, we hear a great deal today about "rabble-rousers."

9. Conditioning is an important factor. That is, your early background and experiences may result in your behaving very much like the other members of your group.

10. Uniformity in certain manners and activities may result in self-elevation. That is to say, going with the group may mean not only approval of others, but a boosting of your own self-esteem.[37]

Thus people dress alike because they wish to practice economy, because they don't want to be embarrassed by social disapproval, because they are eager to boost their own self-esteem.

[37] See J. Peterson: "Imitation and Mental Adjustment." *Journal of Abnormal and Social Psychology*, 1922, 17, 1-15.

Chapter 8

THE CREATION AND MANIPULATION
OF CROWDS

CROWD PSYCHOLOGY has become increasingly important, owing in part
to the introduction of universal suffrage and to the concentration of
people in cities. Popular suffrage has made it necessary for the politician to develop the techniques for inciting and swaying the masses.
Urbanization has encouraged the growth of crowd behavior by herd-
ing the masses into densely populated areas, thus providing the physical conditions conducive to mob action. The loudspeaker has furnished the leader with an effective instrument for manipulating the
multitudes by means of verbal symbols. Mass movements which for
centuries had been brought about only in time of riot or revolution
are deliberately cultivated today by persons who, in their search for
power, make their appeals to the electorate for support.

Observers of our modern political scene have been deeply disturbed
by the increasing prevalence of crowd psychology, especially in countries where the crowd has become the tool of leaders expert in manipulating the masses in the interest of their own personal programs.
There is a serious menace to civilization in the exploitation of herd
behavior. Civilized living depends upon the wisdom of the individual
as manifested in thoughtful conduct. Crowd behavior is impulsive,
unthinking, highly emotionalized, and primitive. If we are interested
in using our intelligence to the best advantage, we must resist the pressure of crowd influences by exercising independent judgment and by
refusing to be carried away by a surge of emotion that is blinding in
its very intensity. Some immunity to collective madness may be
gained by studying the manner in which crowd psychology operates
and by acquainting ourselves with some of its disastrous consequences.

I. THE CREATION OF A CROWD

A crowd is something more than a mere gathering of people; it is
a gathering of people who have gotten into a certain state of mind.

A. Theories

Usually there is a situation involving conflict, such as a strike of employees against employers, a student riot in defiance of academic authorities, or an athletic contest where some violation of a rule has stirred up animosities. Everybody gets to thinking emotionally about the same thing. The emotional excitement is intensified by circular reinforcement, that is, each person who is angry himself grows more angry as he sees others about him in the same frame of mind. The pace is set by those individuals who are highly excitable. As the members of the crowd give way to their passions, ordinary inhibitions are lost. Individuals no longer feel responsible for what they do since they realize that the group gives them an anonymity which makes detection impossible. Persons who are ordinarily respectable are thus provided with an opportunity to give vent to elemental impulses long held in check. The release of tension is thrilling. There is a sense of abandon. Almost anything goes. There is a "kick" in going barbarian, in casting aside the cloak of civilization. Such is the state of mind that characterizes a crowd.

1. LE BON'S THEORY

Gustave Le Bon postulated a "Psychological Law of the Mental Unity of a Crowd" to explain how an assemblage of people becomes converted into a crowd. According to his theory there are three steps in the process: first, the sentiments and ideas of all the persons take one and the same direction; second, their conscious personalities vanish; third, a collective mind is formed.

Whoever be the individuals that compose it, however like or unlike be their mode of life, their occupations, their character, or their intelligence, the fact that they have been transformed into a crowd puts them in possession of a sort of collective mind which makes them feel, think, and act in a manner quite different from that in which each individual of them would feel, think, or act were he in a state of isolation. . . .

It is more especially with respect to those unconscious elements which constitute the genius of a race that all the individuals belonging to it resemble each other, while it is principally in respect to the conscious elements of their character—the fruit of education, and yet more of exceptional hereditary conditions—that they differ from each other.

It is precisely these general qualities of character, governed by forces of which we are unconscious, and possessed by the majority of the normal individuals of a race in much the same degree—it is precisely these qualities, I say, that in crowds become common property. In the collective mind the intellectual aptitudes of the individuals, and in consequence their individuality, are weakened. The heterogeneous is swamped by the homogeneous, and the unconscious qualities obtain the upper hand.

This very fact that crowds possess in common ordinary qualities explains why they can never accomplish acts demanding a high degree of intelligence. The decisions affecting matters of general interest come to by an assembly of men of distinction, but specialists in different walks of life, are not sensibly superior to the decisions that would be adopted by a gathering of imbeciles. The truth is, they can only bring to bear in common on the work in hand those mediocre qualities which are the birthright of every average individual. In crowds it is stupidity and not mother-wit that is accumulated.[1]

Three conditions operate to produce a crowd, according to Le Bon. First there is the large number of people, which gives the individual member a sense of power, and encourages him "to yield to instincts which, had he been alone, he would perforce have kept under restraint." Second is a contagion of a hypnotic order. "In a crowd every sentiment and act is contagious, and contagious to such a degree that an individual readily sacrifices his personal interest to the collective interest. This is an aptitude very contrary to his nature, and of which a man is scarcely capable, except when he makes part of a crowd." Third is a heightened suggestibility, likewise hypnotic in its nature, which is responsible for the contagion just described.

Le Bon's observations of crowd behavior are keen, but his theories are far-fetched in the light of our present knowledge. The concept of the collective mind is untenable, a flagrant example of the group-mind fallacy.[2] Contagion and suggestibility are both important factors in accounting for the phenomena of crowd action but neither should be imputed to events of a hypnotic order. Le Bon is guilty of overstatement in asserting that a crowd of imbeciles will arrive at as intelligent conclusions as a crowd of eminent persons. All of us, as human beings, share many characteristics in common, but imbecility is not one of them, even though we grant that crowd behavior is often stupid. The crowd situation brings out "human nature in the raw" by releasing our primitive passions. There is no need to resort to the concept of a collective mind to account for our barbarous conduct under such circumstances.

[1] All of the quotations in this section on Le Bon are from his book *The Crowd*. 1917. Originally published in French in 1895. The quotations are reprinted here by permission of The Macmillan Company, publishers.

[2] We discussed this fallacy in Chapter 1.

Le Bon performed a real service in stressing the psychological significance of number, contagion, and suggestibility as factors in the creation of crowds. By translating his theories into more modern terminology, even altering them considerably in the interest of a more scientific exposition, we are afforded a good insight into the conditions which favor the patterns of behavior characteristic of crowds. We shall return to this task of modernizing Le Bon after we have outlined Martin's theory of crowd behavior.

2. MARTIN'S THEORY

Everett Dean Martin, in his *Behavior of Crowds,* agrees with Le Bon that a gathering may be converted into a crowd if the members of the group can be led to concentrate upon some one thing in unison. He also agrees that the conscious personality ceases to function. Martin, however, does not believe that a collective mind comes into play at this point. Instead, he suggests that the lapse of conscious personality turns the dominance of action over to primitive impulses which operate unconsciously in the Freudian manner. Passions ordinarily taboo escape the censor, which is dulled by the anonymity enjoyed in the confusion of the mass; the censor is thrown off guard too by the fact that unanimity of action places the stamp of social approval upon behavior which would be highly condemnable under other circumstances.

In the crowd the primitive ego achieves its wish by actually gaining the assent and support of a section of society. The immediate social environment is all pulled in the same direction as the unconscious desire. . . . The crowd is always formed for the unconscious purpose of relaxing the social control by mechanisms which mutually justify such antisocial conduct on the part of members of the crowd.[3]

The real motives, being antisocial in their nature, remain unrecognized. Sometimes they are disguised by a cloak of righteousness, by a noble purpose that will justify a resort to wicked means for its realization. Excuses of this kind are none the less effective because they are manufactured by rationalization; for the members of a crowd, in the frenzy of their zeal, lose the capacity to distinguish between fiction and reality.

[3] Except for the section on revolution, all the quotations in this discussion of Martin's theory will be taken from his book, *The Behavior of Crowds.* Harper & Brothers, 1920.

As a crowd . . . we find ourselves moving in a fictitious system of ideas uncritically accepted as real—not as in dreams realizing our hidden wishes, merely in imagination, but also impelled to act them out in much the way that the psychoneurotic is impelled to act out the fixed ideas which are really the symbols of his suppressed wish. In other words, a crowd is a device for indulging ourselves in a kind of temporary insanity by all going crazy together.

Crowd behavior, Martin asserts, is psychopathic. It is a mass attempt to evade reality. Every crowd has its peculiar "illusions," ideals, dreams, akin to the delusions of the paranoiac.

When one's beliefs or principles become ends in themselves, when by themselves they seem to constitute an order of being which is more interesting than fact, when the believer saves his faith only by denying or ignoring the things which contradict him, when he strives not to verify his ideas but to "vindicate" them, the ideas so held are pathological.

The reason why the pathology of crowd-ideas "is not more evident is the fact that they are simultaneously entertained by so great a number of people."

Delusions of grandeur are common among the leaders and followers in a revolutionary uprising. Revolutionists are hopeless romanticists, allowing their emotions to obscure their intellects, denying the significance of reality and substituting for the truth what they wish to believe, and finding compensation for inner boredom by resort to imaginary and exotic heroics and adventure. Professing love for humanity, they ordinarily exhibit an intensity of hatred which is probably nowhere else in civilized society manifest to such a degree.

Revolutionary mobs, like all crowd movements, are the victims of fixed ideas and of the delusion of infallibility. . . .

Those who participate in such activities are filled with frenzied zeal, sometimes with a kind of ecstasy. They believe themselves to be men of destiny, moving in an historical pageant. . . . People imagine that a revolution is a moral crusade, with all the right on one side. They picture it as a victorious stage in the long process of the triumph of liberty, justice, and humanity over the forces of darkness. . . .

Revolutionary ideas are . . . justifications for the seizure of power and wealth by violent means. . . .

Mankind as a whole—the criminal class excepted—is too decent to plunder and destroy and kill unless people can justify such action by fictions and plausibilities which enable them to go wild with mutual moral approval. . . .

Propaganda furnishes that needed distortion of ideas and facts which permits people to do wrong with good conscience.[4]

When ideas and institutions are in a state of transition, there is a special need for constructive thinking.

Unfortunately it is precisely at such times . . . that the unadjusted are likely to lose their heads completely, resort to mob action, and demand the adoption of policies which are designed to resolve their own inner psychic conflicts rather than to solve any social problem.

Social problems are solved only when people of varying types are enabled to live peaceably in the same community. They are not solved when one faction massacres all its critics and rivals. A social revolution occurs when people abandon the attempt to solve their problems and resort to infantile temper tantrums. . . .

Revolutionists are apt to claim that they are leading the revolt of "the people" against the established authorities because they want to see justice done to all.

There is a commonly accepted fiction that a revolution is an uprising of the whole people against established injustice. There never was an uprising of a whole people—or even of a substantial majority of the people. All revolutions have been perpetrated by rather small desperate minorities. These revolutionary minorities often profess to be "the people," or to act in the people's interests. Invariably they have set up their own crowd dictatorship over the people. What the people get out of revolution is new tyranny for old.

The professed aims of revolution, therefore, are a snare and a delusion. Beneath the profession of humanitarianism is the lust for power. A study of history has convinced Martin that revolutions have accomplished less for liberty than is commonly supposed. Evidence for this conclusion may be seen in a critical evaluation of such revolutionary movements as the French Revolution, or the seizure of power by the Communists in Russia, or the Fascists in Italy, or the Nazis in Germany. Nothing is so disastrous to liberty as a successful revolution. "Such liberties as we have . . . we owe not to revolution but to the gradual development of culture." A free people must be a thinking people who prize wisdom. The ideal of justice for all cannot be

---

[4] All of the quotations in this exposition of Martin's theory of revolution are taken from his book, *Farewell to Revolution*. Harper & Brothers, 1935.

achieved by a resort to physical violence. That is fundamentally why a revolution is merely a drama of delusion.

Martin stresses the fact that the crowd situation constitutes a psychological "field" within which the individual can give free rein to his more primitive impulses. A member of a crowd, for example, may vent his sadism without any moral compunctions. In its milder forms we may observe the cruel "boohs" of the sports fans when a player fails to measure up to their expectations, even though he may be giving his best to the team. When the great Babe Ruth, idol of the baseball fans for so many years, was closing his career as a big-league player—and he did not retire quite soon enough—he made an error that provoked the uninhibited wrath of the crowd. Their intolerant attitude toward his decline was reported in the sport columns as follows:

The crowd, nevertheless, gave the great man the raspberry in the fifth inning when he let Lary's comparatively easy fly drop by him for a double The Bambino looked on this try like a one-legged man galloping through a cabbage patch.

In its more severe forms we may note the orgies of sadism found in lynching-bees where the victim may be tarred and feathered and tortured in various ways before he is "strung up" to a limb of a convenient tree.

Man has become civilized enough to find it necessary to invent justifications for his barbarism under such circumstances. The motive of a lynching-bee is euphemistically described as "a defense of the purity of American womanhood." By means of this fiction the crowd can give unbridled expression to its fury with the full sanction of whatever conscience may be functioning at the time. Racial hatred is effectively concealed by the noble aims professed by those who participate in the mob vengeance. Primitive passion is stirred to its depths by the ecstasy of the crowd; rationalization gives the "bee" its blessing and dulls any qualms of conscience that might spoil the "party."

Another primitive delight shared by the members of a crowd is found in the destruction of property. The lack of personal responsibility makes it possible for the crowd to smash things with a thrilling abandon, whether the occasion be one of malicious sabotage during a labor strike or the playful demolition of a hotel by visiting college football rooters. Hotels which accommodate conventions devoted to convivial hilarity can count on considerable damage to their premises, for on occasions of this sort grown-up men cast aside momentarily their respect for the property rights of others—a reverence that is carefully imbued in us in our capitalistic culture—and enjoy themselves like boys who get a "kick" out of a Halloween sortie into the backyard of a cranky neighbor.

In 1935 a Negro, charged with a serious sex crime, was incarcerated in the courthouse at Shelbyville, Tennessee. The courthouse was stormed by a formidable mob of local citizens bent on lynching the man in custody. Their murderous intentions were frustrated by the prompt action of the Governor, who dispatched a strong force of militia to the scene. The Negro was spirited out of the building, disguised in a uniform and a gas mask, and was taken to Nashville. Enraged by the escape of its quarry, the mob attempted to dynamite the building and was successful in completely destroying it by fire. A more stupid exhibition of blind passion it would be difficult to imagine. The incendiarists were citizens of the county and town. The courthouse was their house, paid for by themselves. They were destroying their own property as a protest against the escape of their intended victim. It was an expensive way to relieve their insensate rage.

The impulse of the mob to take the law into its own hands is a denial of one of the basic factors in the promotion of social order: the willingness to settle conflicts in a civilized manner by submitting them to properly constituted authorities for deliberate review and judgment. The lynching mob in Shelbyville was not only destroying its own courthouse—it was also attacking its own social order, which is a much more serious offense. Modern man cannot enjoy the privileges of civilized living and at the same time practice the law of the jungle. It has taken ages to instill into the human being an appreciation of how important it is to live in a socialized manner, respecting the rights of others as commonly recognized in a particular culture and delegating the authority for arbitrating conflicts to persons duly constituted to exercise such functions in a peaceable manner. Nations—that is, individuals acting in behalf of their particular nations—have yet to grasp the social significance of what it might mean in terms of good citizenship if people would forsake the doctrine that a nation can do what it pleases and that there is no one who can rightfully interpose a valid objection.[5] In our national capacities we act in the

[5] This matter will be discussed under the heading of "National Sovereignty" in Chapter 21.

irresponsible manner characteristic of the mob bent on self-aggrandizement and destruction, oblivious to the fact that we may be destroying ourselves by the unleashing of our passions.   In panics, riots, lynching bees, and wars, we all go crazy together, as Martin suggests; we give our emotions free rein and so supplant the intelligent regulation of behavior.

B. Conditions Conducive to Crowd Behavior

We have mentioned, in our digest of Le Bon and Martin, a number of phenomena which facilitate the formation of a crowd.   By way of review, we shall select some of the more important of these observations for further elucidation.

1. physical contact

In a large gathering under the influence of a dynamic leader, the individual, aroused by emotional oratory, notices that many others are likewise moved, as evidenced by shouts, by restless milling about, or by facial expressions and gestures.   The contact of elbows, the united rise to the feet, and the surge of cheer on cheer all furnish physical stimuli conducive to a sense of invincible power.   Indulging in social projection, the individual gets an impression of universality; that is, he feels that everybody else is experiencing the same emotions as he is feeling.   Thus the influence of mere number is exaggerated to an even greater degree of importance.

Physical conditions are very significant in the promotion of crowd psychology.   An interesting example in support of this assertion was the Democratic convention held in New York in 1924.   The convention was held in Madison Square Garden.   There was a still larger gathering outside in Madison Square listening in to the addresses relayed through a loud speaker.   Inside, according to reports, the crowd rose to a fury in their cheers and demonstrations of approval and disapproval.   Outside, the crowd listened amid a silence as of the grave.   The difference in the reactions of the two assemblages, inside and outside, was largely due to the fact that the people outside were not in the physical presence of the speaker.   Lacking the inspiration of his personality as manifested in his facial expressions and forensic gestures, the people outside were not stirred individually and therefore their emotions were not functioning to intensify the excitement in the others by mutual reinforcement.   The gathering inside became a crowd; the gathering outside remained a group of individuals.

The radio, with its unseen speaker addressing an unseen audience, has introduced a unique situation into the political psychology of our day. More and more, politicians are resorting to the air lanes in order to reach the voters through campaign oratory or fireside chats. The radio has made it possible to obtain a vast audience without the need of traveling from town to town in an effort to win supporters. Though the radio has extended the range of listeners, it has deprived the speaker of the opportunity to bring the graces of his personal presence to bear upon his audience. Thus he lacks one of the important facilities for creating a crowd. An individual who, in the privacy of his home, listens to a demagogue over the radio, is apt to be somewhat on his guard against spurious arguments, and he is less given to an emotional response. Furthermore, the radio listener can shut off the speaker by a mere turn of the dial, a device that is definitely missing when the voter is physically exposed to the speaker. The increasing use of the radio is making it more difficult for the politician to exploit the resources inherent in crowd psychology. Franklin Roosevelt was unusually successful in overcoming this difficulty. Whereas most politicians speak over the radio in the same way that they address a crowd in a hall, Roosevelt had the knack of talking to the unseen audience in a manner that suggested personal intimacy.

2. EMOTIONAL EXCITEMENT

Festivals, parades, and rallies are helpful in the fostering of crowd psychology, not only because of the large number of people involved but also because of the ease with which emotions may be kindled in such situations. The conditions are favorable for the spread of fear or hatred, as the case may be, by a process of circular reinforcement. Responses are intensified under such circumstances by social facilitation (mutual stimulation). The European dictators found that unity was strengthened by patriotic demonstrations. Typical in such spectacles were gigantic throngs of people, massed ranks of uniformed troops, bands playing patriotic and martial airs, voices declaiming from a hundred mechanical mouths, ecstatic marchers carrying flickering torches, flags and emblems everywhere.

Emotional excitement accentuates suggestibility. Thinking is inhibited by intense emotion. A person cannot think straight when he is all stirred up "inside." He gives way readily to an impulse be-

cause conflicting tendencies are blotted out in the excitement of th
moment. Consequently he is prepared to accept a suggestion that fit
his mood and that allows him a release of tension. He is set for im
mediate action. The trigger is ready. All it needs is the proper pull

3. UNITED ACTION

Marching is particularly conducive to a crowd state of mind, a
Duranty noted in Russia:

> The Bolsheviki must be right psychologically. A crowd in movement i
> a dynamic force, thrilling and terrific. A crowd standing, in whatever num
> bers, has potential power, but it is static—a reservoir, not a mighty river flow
> ing. In the Bolshevist system of marching crowds there are . . . sound psy
> chological factors. First, when you march, when you advance in solid ranks
> stepping disciplined to music, you cannot fail to feel that you are a part o:
> something moving; that you yourself are an instrument of progress, howeve
> humble; that you and the millions like you that form your nation are going
> somewhere, moving forward, all together.[6]

Group activity builds a feeling of group solidarity. Thus the people
are encouraged to "get on the band wagon," a device used by the prop
agandist to facilitate the acceptance of his program *en masse*. The
impression that "everybody's doing it" helps to stir the emotions with
the thrill of belonging to a vast movement that is "going places."
Each individual derives a sense of importance from the realization
that he is counting for something in his loyalty and devotion to a great
cause.

4. CONCENTRATION OF ATTENTION ON A COMMON STIMULUS

The individual in a crowd is suggestible because he has a "one-track
mind," as a result of the fact that all the members of the group have
been induced by the leader to think of one thing, some symbol like the
flag or some abstraction such as "justice." Thinking of one thing pro
motes suggestibility because it limits the field of attention and thus inhibits distracting stimuli. "This one thing I do" seems to describe the
set of a person who belongs to a crowd.

A good slogan may serve as an instrument for stirring united loyalty.
Politics, according to Beard, is largely a question of finding slogans
that will capture the crowd, or discovering candidates that will awaken
enthusiasm. "Tippecanoe and Tyler, Too" and "Fifty-four Forty or
Fight" proved very effective back in the 1840's; "Millions for Freedom,

---

[6] Walter Duranty, in the New York *Times Magazine*, February 3, 1935.

Not One Cent for Slavery," "Free Homes for Free Men," in 1860; "The Full Dinner Pail," in 1896; "The Square Deal," in 1904; "Back to Normalcy," in 1920; "Keep Cool with Coolidge," in 1924; and "The New Deal" for "the Forgotten Man," in 1932. Wilson was a master sloganeer: "Too Proud to Fight," "Making the World Safe for Democracy," "Watchful Waiting," "Disentangling Alliances," "Open Covenants, Openly Arrived At" were products of his knack for the apt phrase. Skill in this line may depend upon certain tricks that are sure to appeal to the crowd. One technique is alliteration, typified in the Democratic Party cry of "Rum, Romanism, and Rebellion" that sent Blaine down to defeat in 1884. Another device is the nursery jingle. Famous examples of this are:

"Van, Van is a Used Up Man." (1840)
"Blaine, Blaine, Blaine of Maine." (1884)
"Grover, Grover, Four Years More of Grover,
    In he comes, out they go, then we'll be in clover." (1888)

Note the similarity of these rhythmic slogans to the metric lines characteristic of the football cheer. Rhythm is a fundamental technique in stirring people to the pitch of crowd excitement. A slogan in the style of a childish jingle, therefore, may knit supporters together in feverish devotion to their common cause. As the group recites its ditty in rhythmic unison, embarrassed not one whit by their childishness, members are bound together, ready to do battle for the party.

5. INHIBITION OF CRITICAL JUDGMENT

Critical judgment is inhibited by the mere presence of a group, even more so, of course, by the overstimulating influence of a crowd. F. H. Allport found that students could not work as effectively in a group as they could alone, when they were assigned the task of preparing arguments to disprove didactic passages of a uniform character chosen from the writings of two ancient philosophers. The quantity of the arguments was better in the group but the quality was poorer.[7] The inhibition of thought is one factor in heightening suggestibility.

Both Le Bon and Martin emphasize the fact that the motivation of behavior in the crowd situation is largely unconscious. Primitive emotions prevent the exercise of critical judgment. Intelligence fails to function. The result is stupid behavior. How stupid we can be in crowds we shall now proceed to illustrate.

[7] See F. H. Allport: *Social Psychology*, p. 272 ff. 1924.

Dr. Karl Muck was the leader of the Boston Symphony Orchestra at the outbreak of World War I. He was a German. In fact, the Orchestra had been German trained and German led from its inception. When the Orchestra entered upon the season of 1917-1918 the feeling engendered by the War was growing in intensity. Major Henry L. Higginson, founder and sustainer of the Orchestra, was loyal to America and to Dr. Muck during this trying period when the conductor was becoming more and more of a storm center. It needed but a stray match to ignite the gunpowder that lay scattered all about. The match was dropped in Providence, Rhode Island. An overzealous and afterwards discredited spy-hunting editor of the Providence *Journal* dropped the match by declaring that Muck and his men should play the "Star Spangled Banner" at the Orchestra's concert in Providence that evening. Various patriotic societies backed him up, and the matter was laid before Major Higginson and C. A. Ellis, the manager of the Orchestra. They decided that since there was no time for rehearsal the anthem had better not be played. Dr. Muck was not consulted and knew nothing of the affair until the next morning. Yet all over the country there spread like wildfire the false report that a German conductor had refused to play our national anthem. Agitation against Muck mounted, and scandalous charges were made against him. In March, 1918, he was interned at Atlanta by the Federal Government as an enemy alien, on grounds that were never made public. In fact no reason has ever been shown why he should have been punished as an enemy alien.[8]

The extent to which the crowd situation dulls the critical judgment may be appreciated if one examines, privately, speeches that have been effectively delivered under the conditions of crowd excitement. In many cases, an oration is found to be largely "blah-blah," with a few meaningful remarks interspersed which serve to create an illusion of significance. When a person is alone he may be critical enough to recognize the inanities that elude him when he is a member of a responsive audience. A biographer of Aimee Semple McPherson Hutton says: "Let Mrs. McPherson's deliverances be divorced from Mrs. McPherson's personality, and they fall to the depths of the banal."[9] In support of this assertion, he cites some typical excerpts from her most famous sermons:

[8] M. A. De Wolfe Howe and J. N. Burk: *The Boston Symphony Orchestra, 1881-1931*, Chapter VIII, "Interlude, 1914-1918." 1931.

[9] S. Comstock: "Aimee Semple McPherson." *Harper's Magazine*, December, 1927.

How wonderful are the forces of nature! How mighty!

You and I are gardens, like trees of the planting of the Lord.

Little butterfly flitting hither and yon—little humming birds that come humming around to get what honey you can—where are you when the storm comes?

A mother with trembling hands was stroking back the dampened yellow curls from a marble-white brow.

A tear trickled down the weather-beaten face and hung like a sparkling jewel in the rough-looking beard.

In an objective mood one is led to wonder how such "blarney" even "gets by." It does "go over big," however, when the proper conditions are present to induce an enthusiastic reaction to its touching, poetic nothingness. It "gets 'em" when the circumstances are favorable, no matter how meaningless the remarks may appear upon careful analysis.

The irrational nature of crowd behavior was attributed by Le Bon and by Martin to motivational sources outside the realm of the conscious personality. Individuals, of course, are guilty of stupidities even when removed from the baneful influence of an excited mob, but it must be observed that the crowd situation encourages any nonsensical proclivities which may come naturally to the individual. The intensified emotional excitement is not conducive to deliberate judgment; under such circumstances intelligent decisions are not likely to result. Impulse prevails before cogitation can get under way. The lack of inhibitions precludes the exercise of critical judgment. The crowd must act to relieve its emotional tension, come what may.

The absence of critical judgment explains, according to Le Bon, why the impossible does not exist for the crowd. "Let us leave reason, then, to the philosophers, and not insist too strongly on its intervention in the governing of men. It is not by reason, but most often in spite of it, that are created those sentiments that are the mainsprings of all civilization—sentiments such as honor, self-sacrifice, religious faith, patriotism, and the love of glory." [10]

II. LEADERSHIP

Leadership cannot be considered apart from followership, for both aspects of the relationship are involved whenever one person assumes the dominant role over another. In the past it has been customary in analyzing the psychology of leadership merely to list a number of per-

[10] Le Bon: *op. cit.,* pp. 131-132.

sonal traits, such as "masculinity" and "aggressiveness," without any reference to the psychological needs of the people to whom the leader must appeal for support.   Sociometric studies in this field have been enlightening because they have stressed the desirability of defining the term leadership "situationally" as a function of the inter-personal relations which constitute the give-and-take of living in a community. One of the reasons that a certain kind of person can be dominant in a given situation is that there are present other people who find it satisfying to submit to his authority.   Thus *Der Führer* was able to become a dictator because he arrived on the scene when many Germans felt the need for somebody to tell them what to do.   The psychologist who seeks to understand Hitler's leadership must study *Der Führer's* personality *and* the personalities of the individual Germans who were induced to pledge their loyalty to the man who embodied the Nazi cause.

There are a few basic specifications for a leader that will apply to most leadership situations where crowd psychology is involved: he must be a man of action, invariably and eminently successful, respectful of religious convictions, skilled in speechcraft, expert in the art of salesmanship.   If psychologists are correct in asserting that leaders are not born but made, then the understanding and practice of some of the requisite skills will prepare a person to qualify as a leader when the proper occasion arises.[11]

A. Action

Since leadership often depends upon the ability to create and manipulate crowds, a leader must, first of all, be a man of action.   The crowd wants to do something without hesitating too long about it. A man who pauses to deliberate may arouse the suspicion that he is not sure of himself.   Such a person cannot win the respect of the crowd which wants a man it can follow without question.   Delay of action being subject to interpretation as a sign of weakness, the leader must act and act at once, relying on the guidance of impulse rather than reason.   Careful planning for the long-range future is, under the conditions, impossible.   The highly intelligent person who is aware of a multiplicity of conflicting issues and who consequently feels the need for time to think things through is apt to be disqualified for leadership by the very fact that he insists on suspending his judgment until all the evidence is in.   The extroverted individual stands a much better chance of being a leader than the introverted person be-

[11] See the quotation on leadership in connection with military morale on pp. 453-4.

cause the extrovert sees only one course to follow, while the introvert is paralyzed by the need to sift all the evidence before he can plot a line of action which will satisfy his discriminating standards. Theodore Roosevelt waving his "big stick" and rushing into action enjoyed a much greater hold on the popular imagination than did Woodrow Wilson with his scholarly procrastination. Leaders are not usually profound thinkers; it is often our misfortune that we are inclined to follow the man who does not know where he is going but who, at least, is going somewhere or other.

B. SUCCESS

The leader must show by success that he is worthy of a following. He must have the prestige that goes with a winner. Once he suffers failure, no matter how good the excuses may be, he has lost his authority to command respect and obedience. Today's hero may be insulted tomorrow should he be overtaken by failure. Nothing succeeds like success in the rise to power. "Coolidge luck" is a great blessing to a leader because it gives the people the feeling that the gods are with their chief and so no harm can befall him or them. Misfortune undermines that confidence in divine destiny and provokes an uneasy suspicion that worse disaster may soon follow. Bad luck, even though trivial, is a sign that a man is only human like the rest of us. The wise leader will not encourage tests of his strength if he thinks there is any likelihood of defeat.

C. RESPECT FOR RELIGION

A true leader will always respect the religious sentiments of his followers, for, as Machiavelli once advised, "the sagacious politician will respect religion even if he has no belief in it himself . . . because through inculcating it even by craft much valor has been aroused for the defense of the country." Certainly a leader will give evidence of religious faith, sincere or not, if he wants to retain the confidence of his supporters, that is, if they themselves are believers. Consequently, the wise politician has himself photographed on the church steps. Somehow people feel that a man who attends "worship," particularly if he has a large family to go with him, has his heart in the right place and can, therefore, be trusted with the responsibilities of a high place.

D. SPEECHCRAFT

One of the most important assets for a leader is the ability to speak effectively. Johnson O'Connor has found that an extensive vocabulary correlates highly with executive ability.[12]   This observation is not surprising when we stop to realize that speech is the medium through which the leader can bring the force and charm of his personality to bear upon his subordinates.   A man must have more than a wide vocabulary, however, to become a good speaker—he must also master the basic techniques involved in a good delivery.   He will find that training in public speaking will at the same time be training for leadership.   Learning how to face and master an audience will develop self-assurance which is a great asset to an executive; in the process of learning how to dominate his audience he will also be acquiring skills useful for handling people successfully.   The speaker should talk on a subject that is of vital interest to himself; catch the attention of the audience by starting right in—with a concrete illustration and then proceeding to general remarks; avoid a platitudinous preface, such as "I come to you tonight to speak on a subject that should be of interest to every one of us . . ."; relax the throat so that the voice will be pleasantly resonant; appear natural; leave at home any paraphernalia that tend to bulge the pockets; arouse curiosity and then satisfy it; pause before and after important ideas by way of emphasis.   Such devices are all helpful in winning the favor of an audience.   A leader should be adept in the practice of these precepts concerning the art of public speaking.

The public speaker is, for the time being, at least, a leader.   As a public speaker he assumes the leadership of the thinking of the group to whom he speaks.   Man likes his leaders to be men of strength, of self-confidence . . . and of superior knowledge.   We do not think of a leader as being a man who cannot look people in the eyes, who twists and squirms, whose voice is weak, whose speech is halting, who cannot express himself because of either lack of a good vocabulary or lack of ideas.   It is therefore essential that the young public speaker give his first attention to looking in a straightforward manner into the eyes of the people with whom he is conversing, that he speak in a clear ringing voice after the manner of one enthusiastic about his proposition and confident of its worth, that he stand as though at ease and at the same time determined and full of energy, and that he lack neither ideas nor the words with which to express them accurately and fluently.   This it is necessary for the speaker to do in order to get the favorable attitude of the audience toward him.   This favorable attitude is practically necessary in order that the audience may have confidence in him as a leader, and this confidence is necessary to a speaker's success.   *But doing this is not public speaking;* it is

[12] See J. O'Connor: *Vocabulary Builder,* Foreword, "Vocabulary and Success." 1937.

simply creating a favorable attitude toward the speaker in order that his speaking may be effective. Good posture, diction, enunciation, gesture, etc., hold about the same position in the public speaker's work as scenery does for the actor. They are simply mechanical aids to his work; his real work is mental and consists of adapting his superior knowledge of a subject to an audience in view of his knowledge of human nature. Gesture and correct pronunciation are no more the end of the public speaker than operating a typewriter is the end of a novelist.[13]

Expertness in speechcraft is an asset to a leader, but it is far more important that he know the psychological devices that make it possible to create and manipulate crowds with the proper finesse. A good speaker must know his crowd psychology if he intends to master the art of persuasion. Once an audience has been converted into a crowd, there are five techniques for influencing them which are of special value: affirmation, repetition, the use of emotionalized words, the evocation of imagery, and the appeal to hatred. Some of these techniques are useful, too, in creating a crowd.

1. AFFIRMATION

First, the speaker should affirm his view, that is, simply state that it is so, and not attempt to prove his assertion by offering evidence or by reasoning with his hearers. If the speaker tries to prove his statement, he demonstrates that there may be some legitimate doubts as to its validity. Such an interpretation is damaging to the conviction he wants to convey to his listeners. When Calvin Coolidge was a member of the Massachusetts legislature, a certain member who was noted for his long-winded speeches addressed the house for an hour in support of a measure, during which he used a succession of affirmations always beginning with "It is—." When Mr. Coolidge rose to speak on the question, he said, "Mr. Speaker, it isn't," and sat down. That's the idea: be concise, and to the point, just say it's so, and that's that.

2. REPETITION

Drive the point further home by saying it's so and then saying it again. Repetition may carry conviction by virtue of accumulated power and of suggestibility brought on by fatigue. Mr. Dooley used to say, "I'll belave anythin' at all if ye tell it to me aften enough." An old colored preacher was once asked to explain the unusual effectiveness of his sermons. "Firstly," he replied, "I tells 'em what I'm gwine

[13] H. H. Higgins: *Influencing Behavior through Speech*, pp. 28-29. Expression Company, Boston, 1930.

to tell 'em; secondly I tells 'em; and thirdly, I tells 'em what I done tole 'em."

3. EMOTIONALIZED WORDS

Persuasion is facilitated by resorting to emotionalized words like speakeasy, booze, saloon, brewery, Bolshevik, Fascist, economic royalist, Tory, or Communist.[14]

James M. Curley, famous Boston politician and widely recognized

Why Politicians Get That Way.   (Courtesy, the *Saturday Evening Post.*)

as a silver-tongued orator, was asked what he considered the ten most beautiful words in the English language. Without hesitation he replied: "Mother, home, love, charity, health, happiness, friendship, kindness, success, and loyalty." This selection is interesting because it includes so many of the key words employed by public speakers to touch the hearts of their listeners. "Mother" is especially potent in this respect. Any time a man is honored by a testimonial banquet, he can almost be counted upon to say:

> In closing, I would like to pay tribute to my mother as the one who is alone responsible for whatever success I may have had and whatever success may be in store for me in the future.[15]

If a critical person should suggest that the closing remarks were absurd, he would probably be accused of cynicism. There can be no doubt that it is very decent of a man to say he owes everything to his

---

[14] Refer to section on Emotionalism in Chapter 5.
[15] Adapted from a speech delivered by a man who was being honored for his services as a District Attorney.

mother. Certainly no man could go far without some effort of his own. And what about dear old Dad? Where does he come in?

4. EVOCATION OF IMAGERY

Another device employed by the public speaker in manipulating his audience is the use of "word pictures" to stir their imagination. Poetic metaphors involving symbols like "the flag unfurled on the ramparts" or "the hearth with the family gathered 'round" stimulate imagery that has been loaded with emotion by years of conditioning. When the Sacco-Vanzetti League sent out an appeal in behalf of "the victims of archaic laws and cruel prejudice," they referred to the condemned men as "The Good Shoemaker" and "The Poor Fish Peddler." How much more effective than to have asked us to help Mr. Sacco and Mr. Vanzetti! Men are moved by symbols more often than by logic.

Word pictures are good, but the concrete evidence is much better for arousing the imagination. Mark Anthony's great oration on Caesar, appealing to the populace to avenge his murder, was rendered far more effective by the fact that he had Caesar's corpse right in front of him to point to. There was something the mob could see, something far more stimulating than mere rhetoric. Napoleon once explained how he based his power on the popular imagination: "It was by becoming a Catholic that I terminated the Vendean war, by becoming a Mussulman that I obtained a footing in Egypt, by becoming an Ultramontane that I won over the Italian priests, and had I to govern a nation of Jews I would rebuild Solomon's temple." [16]

William Hale Thompson, former Mayor of Chicago, was an expert in the art of getting elected. He had the tabloid touch in everything he did. He gave the people pictures they could understand. The Irish and the Germans had stirred up considerable agitation about alleged pro-British school histories. "Thompson simplified the issue with a stroke of genius: he denounced William McAndrew, superintendent of the Chicago schools, as 'King George's stool pigeon.' That is as plain as the picture on the front cover of a tabloid; like the picture, it may be faked, but few of the customers are going to be curious enough to inquire into that." [17] He called his Irish Catholic opponent a tool of the King of England and promised that if the royal nose were ever unveiled in Chicago, he would "hand King George one on the snoot." It would be difficult to discover a campaign platform com-

---

[16] Le Bon: *op. cit.*, pp. 77-78.
[17] E. Davis: "Portrait of an Elected Person." *Harper's Magazine*, July, 1927.

parable to Thompson's in irrelevance and bad taste; but it worked, for "Chicago's citizens just couldn't resist the temptation to reward the man who dared from stump to stump to take the King of England by the scruff of the neck and dangle his heels." [18]   Thompson depicted the water situation, in which high rates were involved, by declaring that you could go into the flats of the poor and see five children taking their bath in the same tub of water because their parents could afford no more.   The water situation was complex and obscure; but there was nothing complex or obscure about Big Bill's picture of the five children bathing in the same tub.

Aimee Semple McPherson Hutton relied heavily upon symbols to convey the message of the Four-Square Gospel.   A typical service at Angelus Temple was described as follows:

> The atmosphere bubbles over with love, joy, enthusiasm; the Temple is full of flowers, music, golden trumpets, red robes, angels, incense, nonsense, and sex appeal.   The service may be described as supernatural whoopee.   It is balanced by the stronger medicine concocted and dispensed at the Gospel Lighthouse, Sister's third creation.   The Lighthouses have been so successful that Sister now has them scattered throughout the United States.   Here she introduced a Military Note—the Old Reliable!—with thrills and bold adventure.   The Lighthouse was also built to a sure-fire theme song: "Throw out the Life Line!"   The ladies of the chorus are clad in dapper uniforms so much like those of American Bluejackets that the Navy went to court in a vain effort to prevent Mrs. McPherson from belittling the dignity of Our Boys.   The typical Lighthouse service leads up to a Rescue.   The grand finale shows a dozen nightgowned virgins clinging to the Rock of Ages, while the wind howls, the thunder roars, the lightning flashes and the waves beat about them.   Sister—magnificent in an Admiral-General's uniform—directs the girlish sailors as they throw out the lifeline, while a corps of male Coast Guard workers for the Lord sweeps a prop sea with searchlights.   The virgins are Saved; the curtain descends as the band crashes, the audience stands and cheers, and the American Flag waves triumphantly over all.[19]

A cause or truth should be dramatized if it is going to reach the understanding and arouse the devotion of the common man.   Humanity's moving convictions come not through reason but through the avenues of emotion.   People are stirred by the individual who symbolizes a cause by giving his life to its realization.   Such a person exerts more influence by his example than he could ever attain through the pale abstractions of reason.   So Garrison with a halter around his

[18] The Cleveland *Plain Dealer.*
[19] M. Mayo: "Aimee Rises from the Sea." *The New Republic,* December 25, 1929.

neck and John Brown on a scaffold demonstrated the evil of slavery; Mahatma Gandhi with his loin cloth and spinning wheel dramatizes his oneness with the conditions and aspirations of India's toiling peasant millions and symbolizes the conflict he is waging with the materialistic West; Kagawa living in the slums of Japan and devoting himself unselfishly to the spread of cooperatives dramatized the economic and social plight of the Japanese masses; and Christ becomes a living reality for millions as we relive each Christmas his humble birth in the stable at Bethlehem. Dramatic symbols appeal to the imagination and stir the emotions. The man who wants to be a leader must learn the art of moving crowds by giving them something they can see as a symbol of the cause for which they are uniting their efforts. This art is a basic technique in the achievement of leadership.

5. APPEAL TO HATRED

.The most effectual emotion for the leader to arouse is hate, for, as Martin says in his *Behavior of Crowds,* the crowd is a creature of hate. Hatred and fear are closely allied. By pointing out some menacing dangers—it does not make much difference what they are, as long as the people get scared—a leader can readily exhort the populace to follow him in the defense of their homes and the extermination of the dread foe.

Evangelist Billy Sunday could get himself all worked up over the communists, socialists, and other "ists":

Our country is filled with a socialistic, I.W.W., communistic, radical, lawless, anti-American, anti-church, anti-God, anti-marriage gang, and they are laying the eggs of rebellion and unrest in labor and capital and home; and we have some of them in the universities. I can take you through the universities and pick out a lot of black-hearted communistic fellows who are teaching that to our boys and sending them out to undermine America. If this radical element could have their way, my friends, the laws of nature would be repealed, or they would reverse them: oil and water would mix; the turtle dove would marry the turkey buzzard; the sun would rise in the West and set in the East; chickens would crow and roosters would squeal; cats would bark and dogs would mew; the least would be the greatest; a part would be greater than the whole; yesterday would be day after tomorrow if that crowd were in control.

Hatred for an enemy may be all the more bitter if the fighters are not quite sure who it is they are fighting. Vague references to a foe may, therefore, be particularly effective.

Dangers dire and deadly are covertly crouched on all sides desirous of devouring our country. Insidious evils, steadily creeping in, are subtly establishing themselves in strategic positions in preparation for the day of America's doom.[20]

The writer seems to be more interested in alliteration than in striving for an exact description of who these monsters are. The vagueness and the alliteration are both very effective. Alliteration was used to good effect, likewise, in a campaign against publishers of indecent magazines, who were attacked as persons who "gratify lust for putrid pelf, those peddlers, those panderers, exploiting sensuality and sexuality."

Many speakers prey upon our hatreds. A good example of this technique of emotional exploitation is the speech delivered by Governor Hanley of Indiana at the National Convention of the Prohibition Party in 1916. Note the appeal to hatred, the use of repetition, the emotionalized word pictures.

I bear no malice toward those engaged in the liquor business, but I hate the traffic.

I hate its every phase.

I hate it for its intolerance.

I hate it for its arrogance.

I hate it for its hypocrisy, for its cant, and craft and false pretense.

I hate it for its commercialism; for its greed and avarice; for its sordid love of gain at any price.

I hate it for its domination of politics; for its corrupting influence in civic affairs; for its incessant effort to debauch the suffrage of the country, for the cowards it makes of public men.

I hate it for its utter disregard of law, for its ruthless trampling of the solemn compacts of State constitutions.

I hate it for the load it straps to labor's back; for the palsied hands it gives to toil; for its wounds to genius; for the tragedies of its might-have-beens.

I hate it for the human wrecks it has caused.

I hate it for the almshouses it peoples; for the prisons it fills; for the insanity it begets; for its countless graves in potters' fields; I hate it for the mental ruin it imposes on its victims; for its spiritual blight; for its moral degradation.

I hate it for the crimes it commits; for the homes it destroys; for the hearts it breaks.

I hate it for the malice it plants in the hearts of men; for its poison; for its bitterness: for the dead-sea fruit with which it starves their souls.

[20] W. J. Simmons: *America's Menace or the Enemy Within.* 1926.

I hate it for the grief it causes womanhood—the scalding tears, the hopes deferred, the strangled aspirations, its burden of want and care.

I hate it for its heartless cruelty to the aged, the infirm, and the helpless; for the shadow it throws upon the lives of children; for its monstrous injustice to blameless little ones. . . .

There is a speech! It gives one a lift just to read it, makes one feel that one should be up and doing for the cause.

E. Salesmanship

Observers of political psychology often comment on the illogical behavior of the voter. Munro, in his *Personality in Politics,* points out how an unsophisticated person might be fooled if he thinks voting is going to accord with the rules of logic:

People vote their resentment rather than their appreciation. It is not good political strategy to do something that pleases a majority of the voters but bitterly offends a minority. The novice in politics would reason, of course, that by such action a mayor must necessarily gain more votes than he loses, but it does not work out that way. The approving majority forgets all about the matter long before the next election arrives; the vindictive minority does not forget.[21]

Munro's statement is not always true, either. People are apt to vote for the candidates who appear first on the ballot and since the names are arranged alphabetically, it is obvious that Adams often stands a better chance of getting elected than Zukor.

In January, 1932, the Seattle *Times* decided to poke fun at the mayoral campaign as a protest against the roster of inferior candidates. They prepared a burlesque of the ballyhoo methods being employed, a harlequinade on electioneering. As a roaring joke they telephoned Victor Aloysius Meyers, trombone-playing jazz-band leader, to invite him to run for mayor as their candidate. Meyers consented, and the *Times* spread his name all over the first page of their last edition that night. For thirty days the *Times* entertained its readers with its sardonic jest. Nine other candidates cringed as they saw their extravagant campaign promises parodied in a series of daily articles appearing under the by-line of Vic Meyers, but actually written by Reporter Doug Welch. Almost a promise a day was made by Meyers: hostesses on streetcars; flower boxes on hydrants; cracked ice on mid-

---

[21] W. B. Munro: *Personality in Politics,* p. 26. 1924. By permission of The Macmillan Company, publishers.

night streetcars. The *Times* jokesters found their candidate tractable, eager to lend himself to any and all farcical plans to build up the jest. To a business-club luncheon went Meyers, dressed as Mahatma Gandhi. In a street parade he rode on an old-time beer truck. Meyers, of course, was not elected mayor. But—let the *Times* laugh last—Meyers ran for Lieutenant Governor of Washington in the next election and was swept into office on the Democratic slate. The *Times* felt by that time that the joke had gone far enough, if not too far. According to reports gallery crowds came to the Senate to get a good laugh at the presiding officer but were much surprised to find that the bandmaster was a good showman and a good politician to boot.[22]

H. L. Mencken considered politics as the subtle art of "boob bumping." [23]   A sound knowledge of mob psychology, he said, is the chief asset of the politician. What, in such a case, should he know? Does a politician get farther by slapping backs and haw-hawing, in the manner of Jim Watson of Indiana, or by maintaining an aloof and superior reserve, in the manner of Henry Cabot Lodge? Does it profit him more to be thought shrewd or to be thought honest? These are practical questions. The answers to them, Mencken says, are essentially matters of scientific salesmanship. The politician is a salesman. He must know how to make *Homo boobiens* do what he doesn't want to do—in fact, what it is plainly to his interest to avoid doing. A candidate for office must get at the voter by appealing to his weaknesses. Is he vain? Then he can be fetched by flattery. Is he timorous? Then he can be nailed by searching out his fears. The task of the politician is to convince the mob, first, that it is confronted by some grave danger, some dreadful menace to its peace and security, and secondly, that he can save the situation. The horrors that politicians talk of are mainly imaginary. They gabble darkly of famine, oppression, slavery. The remedies they hawk belong mostly to the realm of quackery. Only once in a blue moon, indeed, are the ills of mankind curable by purely political means. When they are disposed of, it is usually by an economic process, and when it is not by an economic process, it is by an undiluted act of God.

But the plain people always believe otherwise. They trust to the vote, the palladium of their liberties. They believe the way to get more money for less work is to turn A out and B in. When the scheme fails, they turn to C. When C is caught *in flagrante* they go back to A or B. This, in brief, is the process of politics in a democracy. It is the aim of every politician to be to-

---

[22] The *Literary Digest*, December 24, 1932.

[23] Childs, Gallup, and others have more respect for the political intelligence of the average citizen than Mencken ever had. See pp. 86-87.

day's savior. If the mob is not already scared, he must scare it by the devices of his ancient and wily art. And once it is scared, he must convince it that he can succor and secure it.

For this art some men have a great natural talent. There was, for example, the late Colonel Roosevelt. He radiated bugaboos as a New Thoughter radiates optimism. At least once a month until the advance of age overcame him, he started a new one—and then set the mob to howling for him by pursuing and scotching it. Most of these bugaboos, I believe, were without substance, and few of those that were real were actually scotched. Nevertheless, Roosevelt knew how to make the hunt seem genuine, and even perilous, and so he had the mob with him so long as he kept his health. . . .

The underlying principles . . . are few and simple. . . . The most successful politician, taking one year with another, is the one who sticks most faithfully to a few well-tried tricks. What worked last year will work again today, and yet again tomorrow. The worst disasters of politics are due to ventures outside the narrow circle. The ambitious politician, made imprudent by success, decides to be original. At the next ensuing plebiscite he is retired to the icehouse.

Only too often, I believe, that originality takes the form of overestimating the intelligence of the rabble. Soon or late almost every politician above the city boss level decides to make a bold appeal to the enlightenment of his lieges. It is fatal. The beaches of politics, in fact, are strewn with the corpses of such logicians. They pass out under great suspicion. They have addled the public mind, and so caused public pain. Any idea, to the mob, is radical.

The professionals lower down never make such mistakes, and in consequence their season lasts far longer. The average city boss survives 20 mayors, a dozen Governors, and six or eight Presidents. Why? Simply because he sticks to the tried and true stuff. His appeal is never to the imaginary intelligence of his customers; it is to their immemorial weaknesses. He plays upon their cupidity, their vanity, their ignorance—above all, upon their fears. He knows that uneasiness is their dominant mood—that the struggle for existence, even at best, falls just short of being too much for them. He makes life easier for them—or makes them believe that he has made it easier. He is safe so long as they cling to that pathetic delusion.[24]

An illustration of this technique is furnished by a news item used as a filler in a local small-town newspaper, to the following effect:

KANSAS CITY—Former U. S. Senator James A. Reed is of the opinion that he is needed in Washington again to curb Bolshevik trends and is reported as being in the race to regain his Senate seat.

It's all a part of the great game of politics.

[24] H. L. Mencken, in a syndicated column, 1925. By permission of the Chicago *Tribune* and H. L. Mencken.

The great problem in a democracy is to secure a government run by men who are best fitted for administrative work.   Such an end is difficult to attain in a system where so much depends upon the art of getting elected, where advantage accrues to the man who is expert in manipulating crowds and exploiting them for his own preferment. Internships in government service may, in time, provide us with leaders who have proved their worth by long experience in public office. Perhaps the inauguration of brain trusts in Washington during the depression of the 1930's was a tardy recognition that the political problems of our day can be handled adequately only by men who are more than just professional politicians.   The need is being felt for men who are versed in the intricacies of economic and political science, for individuals who can approach social problems with the disinterested attitude of the scientist in so far as that is humanly possible.   It is obvious that politicians who are only amateurs in economics and political science cannot solve complicated problems requiring expert knowledge of the facts and principles involved.

The exploitation of crowd psychology is not a phenomenon peculiar to democracies.   A study of the Nazis' rise to power will show us how Hitler took full advantage of his opportunities to create crowd support for himself and his party.

III. NAZISM AS A SOCIAL MOVEMENT

It is easy for an ambitious person to assume the reins of leadership if there are potential followers who are eagerly waiting for a savior to rescue them from an intolerable existence.   Hitler arrived on the German scene at the psychological moment.   The time was ripe; the people were ready for a *Führer.*

Numerous developments had come to a focus to prepare the way for a redeemer.   Nationalism was achieved late in Germany.   The country was still functioning as separately organized states long after England and France had become nations.   The United States had been a homogeneous political federation for almost a century before the Germans awoke to a sense of their national identity.   Cantril suggests that the Kaiser's effort to overrun Europe in 1914 was a case of "overcompensating for a feeling of national inferiority." [25]   By 1918 the German people had fused themselves into a self-conscious nation, just in time to go down together in humiliating defeat.   "German nationalism," says Shotwell, "was wounded at the height of its pride." [26]

---

[25] H. Cantril: *The Psychology of Social Movements,* p. 212.   1941.   Our discussion of Hitler's leadership is based largely on Cantril's Chapters 8-9, "The Nazi Party."
[26] J. T. Shotwell: *What Germany Forgot,* p. 66.   1940.

The Versailles Treaty came as a final insult to the hard-won German nationalism. The people were waiting for a leader to rekindle their patriotism, a man who would enable them to recover their self-respect by organizing the nation into a first-rate world power.

Economic hardship in the post-war period was so severe that the German people were all set to follow anybody who could promise salvation. The middle class had been liquidated in the inflationary collapse of the mark. By 1932 one-half the German population was living on a starvation level. All classes of society were plagued with a sense of insecurity. Hitler held out a hope for each of them, proposing remedies to allay their anxieties. To the Junkers, the landed aristocracy, he pledged protection against industrialists, peasants, republican governments; they liked Hitler's nationalist emphasis and his militarist program. To the industrialists the Nazi Party represented a bulwark against communistic counter-revolution. To the middle class the Nationalist Socialist program promised a restoration of status, economic stability, sponsorship for their rights to employment and social insurance, a political ideology to justify their needs. Said the official party platform: "We demand the creation of a sound middle class." To the proletariat whose standards of living had been steadily declining and whose hopes for government aid had been persistently frustrated, Hitler extended the hand of friendship, guaranteeing them trade unions and state succor in their fight for workers' rights. To the peasants the *Führer* pledged himself to lift the burden of debts, to abolish "interest slavery," to confiscate the large estates. To the youth of Germany, Hitler assured a bright future with jobs and education for everybody.

It mattered little that Hitler told the rich one thing, the poor another, promising anybody whatever might be expedient as a means of evoking hope and loyalty. The Nazi program was psychologically clever in singling out definite evils to oppose, at the same time remaining vague as to any positive proposals. Hitler capitalized on the free-floating allegiance of the citizens who craved protection against impending dangers. Under the circumstances the sentiment was readily created that God had sent the *Führer* to be "the savior of Germany." The *savior* got off to a good start by blaming the Jews for all the ills the people had suffered. Thus he incited the persecution of the Jews, which offered an outlet for pent-up aggression. Hitler denied the German war guilt; he boasted and strutted and vaunted the superiority of the German race; he nourished the national self-consciousness which had long been starved.

Hitler was the answer to many needs. His greatest service was the fact that he had an explanation to offer for all the troubles the German people had endured. He understood the meaning of their hardships; he knew what the remedy would be. Folks were no longer baffled when their faith in themselves had been restored by the sureness and directness of their new leader. Through oversimplification he turned confusion into conviction, stirring and canalizing their fear and hatred. The Nazi philosophy gave the people an interpretation of events that brought a much needed "order into their confused psychological worlds." The German people enjoyed being assured that they were not personally responsible for their ills. The "escapist" solution for the crisis, by diverting attention to the guilty parties outside Nazi circles, carried a deep appeal.

Hitler was eminently successful in achieving his leadership because he was a master of the art of manipulating people by the exploitation of their hopes and fears—especially their fears, as White has brought out through his analysis of Hitler's speeches. In White's study of Hitler's utterances, each paragraph was classified in terms of its dominant meaning or "theme." Contrary to the prevalent American notion that Hitler's propaganda glorified war, his speeches were found to be overwhelmingly preponderant in anti-war themes.

Whether or not he himself consciously wants war as such, he at least recognizes that most of his hearers do not. To justify specific aggressive acts, he consistently resorts to the creation of a "paranoid" world-picture, which represents other nations or groups as wanting to destroy Germany, and which invokes the motive of fear as a reason for fighting against the foreign warmakers. To put it quantitatively, more than 80 per cent of the paragraphs are elaborations of four basic themes: "they are evil"; "we are good"; "they are weak"; and "we are strong." Since this combination involves ideas of both grandeur and persecution, it is perhaps more aptly characterized by the word "paranoid" than by any other single word.

Within these four basic themes, subthemes were differentiated. For instance, the pronoun "they" has a varying content (the Jews, the Marxists, the bourgeoisie, the English, etc.), and various sorts of evilness are attributed to them (e.g., they kill, they rob, they enslave, they lie, they are cowards, they poison our blood, they are different from Us). By totalling up the relative frequency with which these various subthemes occur, with reference to a particular group, it is possible to characterize quantitatively several of the official Nazi stereotypes.[27]

[27] R. K. White: "A Quantitative Analysis of Hitler's Speeches." Program planned for the 1942 meetings of the American Psychological Association.

The *Führer* was keen enough, early in his political career, to realize the importance of speechcraft. He tells us in *Mein Kampf* that the speaker can be much more influential than the writer because the orator can adjust himself to his audience, he can vary his arguments to suit the occasion, he can repeat strategic points until even the dullest understand, he can anticipate and answer objections, he can arouse enthusiasm undampened by the calm scrutiny ordinarily accorded the printed word.[28] Furthermore, Hitler attended to every detail, as evidenced by his arranging meetings of his cohorts for the evenings when he knew they would succumb most easily to his pointed suggestions. Under optimum conditions provided by history and by personal manipulation, the *Führer* spoke, and the Germans listened, inspired with frenzied dreams of *Lebensraum* in a Nazi-dominated world.

IV. CONCLUSION

It is to be hoped that education in the techniques by means of which crowds are manipulated may provide some immunity against the wiles of scheming politicians, be they presidents or dictators, ward bosses or "ministers of public enlightenment." The best protection against mob rule is a clear realization of the values that are sacrificed in succumbing to the surge of crowd excitement. The individual who wants to live intelligently must guard himself conscientiously against the temptation to indulge in the passions of the pack and the herd.

[28] See A. Hitler: *Mein Kampf,* pp. 705-716. Edition by J. Chamberlain, S. B. Fay *et al.* Reynal and Hitchcock, 1939.

Chapter 9

POPULAR CREDULITY, RUMOR-MONGER-ING, AND PUBLIC ACCLAIM

NUMEROUS WRITERS on crowd psychology have called attention to the irrational beliefs and the unpredictable whims that result from "mass suggestibility." It is true, as we have noted, that people are highly suggestible under crowd conditions, doing many foolish things of which they will be individually ashamed when the prevailing emotional excitement subsides. These follies, however, cannot always be attributed legitimately to crowd psychology since many of our naïve conceptions and our passing crazes are derived from person-to-person contacts where there is no congregated mass of people and where there is no leader. In the casual contacts of everyday life individuals accept uncritically what they are told, pass the word along to other credulous persons who, in turn, disseminate what they hear. Thus we all do our bit toward circulating among contemporaries and preserving for posterity rumors, untruths, fallacies. In the same uncritical way individuals acquire some of their enthusiasms and aversions. Sometimes, of course, clever persons exploit the popular gullibility by manipulating the factors responsible for beliefs, prejudices, and tastes, as "pluggers" do who are employed by music publishers to get their songs played over the radio, knowing that the more a song is rendered over the air, the more popular it will become. Public acclaim may thus be subtly manufactured, though often it operates in reverse, as it does when the fickle public fools the manipulator by transferring its enthusiasm elsewhere for no apparent reason. Some of these variations in taste might be "explained," as the psychoanalysts would claim, in terms of the psychopathological workings of the "unconscious mind," some of them more simply by reference to the functioning of suggestion and imitation. It is chiefly through suggestion-and-imitating that ideas and behavior patterns are spread among the masses of the people. Fear is contagious in a stock-market panic, a movie starlet becomes a star, popular sentiment grows in favor of a political party, because of the tendency in each of us to do as others are doing. Imitating those who set the lead, is largely responsible, too, for the spread of fads like the mania for chain letters, for the dissemination of rumor, and for the sudden rise to popularity of songs, plays, and books that happen to catch the public fancy.

We have grouped credulity, rumor, and acclaim together because they all involve the same person-to-person influences which play upon suggestibility to generate beliefs and values. In so far as we accept uncritically hearsay evidence and diffuse it by word-of-mouth publicity among our friends, we serve as tools for the aggravation of credulity and the perpetuation of irrationality.[1]

We shall begin our discussion by showing how gullible we are in absorbing fiction which we mistake for fact; popular fallacies and hoaxes to support this thesis are plentiful. Then we shall proceed to show how this credulity of ours operates in the field of rumor, with special reference to its exploitation in the prosecution of war. Finally, we shall examine how people, following the herd, are manipulated by persons whose business it is to secure popular support for their particular commodities. In this connection, some of the difficulties confronting the promoter will be reviewed.

I. POPULAR CREDULITY: COMMON FALLACIES AND HOAXES

Many of our beliefs have no better basis than hearsay evidence. It is commonly held, for example, that it is dangerous to leave food in a can after the can has been opened. Yet the United States Department of Agriculture has issued the following bulletin:

It is just as safe to keep canned food in the can it comes in—if the can is kept cool and covered—as it is to empty the food into another container. Thousands of housewives are firm in the faith that canned goods ought to be emptied as soon as the can is opened, or at least before the remainder of the food goes into the refrigerator—one of the persistent food fallacies. The

---

[1] Anthropologists have employed the term *diffusion* to connote the process by which "culture traits," practices characteristic of a given society, pass from one group to another. Patterns of behavior are said to "diffuse" or spread from a common source. We find, for example, that people smoke tobacco in widely separated regions of the world. How is this fact to be explained? Anthropologists used to attribute such a similarity to independent "inventions" on the part of different peoples, each group having discovered tobacco for itself; now anthropologists are coming to favor diffusion rather than invention as the explanation for such phenomena.

question keeps coming to the bureau of home economics in letters from home makers.

A few acid foods may dissolve a little iron from the can, but this is not harmful, not dangerous to health. Cans and foods are sterilized in the proc essing. But the dish into which the food might be emptied is far from sterile. In other words, the can is less likely to have on it bacteria that cause food to spoil.

Whether in the original can or in another container, the principal precau tions for keeping food are—keep it cool and keep it covered.

The following list of 100 common misconceptions may impress the reader with the prevalence of fallacies which are given a ready cre dence. How many of these statements would you ordinarily regard as true? Try it as a test on an unsuspecting friend. The number of statements considered true is an index of his credulity.

POPULAR FALLACIES

Instructions:

The following is a list of 100 statements to be labeled T (True) or F (False). The decision is to be based on the accuracy of the statement with reference to its factuality or its actual occurrence either now or in times past.

1. The precocious child is apt to have a puny body.
2. The Bible relates that three wise men visited the infant Christ.
3. Women mature earlier in hot climates.
4. Playing wind instruments induces consumption of the lungs.
5. It is harmful to your watch to turn the hands backward.
6. "As Maine goes, so goes the nation."
7. Water can be found by a dowser by the use of a divining rod.
8. The needle of a compass points to the North Pole.
9. Lightning conductors do more harm than good because they attract electricity.
10. Quicksand sucks.
11. Lightning never strikes twice in the same place.
12. Tropical parents are the most prolific.
13. Most automobile accidents are due to excessive speed.
14. An electric fan cools the air of a room in which it is operating.
15. Cleopatra was an Egyptian.
16. Byron had a clubfoot.
17. On learning that the French poor could not get bread, Marie An toinette said: "Then why do they not eat cake?"
18. Aesop wrote Aesop's Fables.
19. Opposites are more likely to be happily mated in marriage.
20. Pheidippides ran the marathon distance to Athens with the tidings of the glorious victory of the Greeks over the Persians.

21. Watts' observation of a steaming teakettle led to his invention of the steam engine.
22. Wellington said: "The Battle of Waterloo was won on the playing fields of Eton."
23. Singeing the hair is beneficial, aiding it to grow more abundantly.
24. William Tell shot an apple off his son's head with a bow and arrow.
25. Horatius defended the Sublician bridge over the Tiber with the aid of two friends.
26. The narcotic addict is the most dangerous and desperate of criminals.
27. It is more dangerous to prick oneself with a pin than with a needle.
28. The Old Testament says that a whale swallowed Jonah.
29. According to Darwin, man is descended from monkeys.
30. The Bible says that Adam and Eve ate an apple.
31. Brilliant scholars do not succeed in business.
32. Child prodigies peter out.
33. The principle of evolution was discovered by Darwin.
34. Columbus discovered North America.
35. The fall of an apple suggested to Newton his theory of gravitation.
36. A red rag will madden a bull.
37. Marconi invented wireless telegraphy.
38. Nero played a fiddle while Rome was burning.
39. George Washington cut down a cherry tree and when confronted by his father said: "I cannot tell a lie."
40. Man is the only animal that laughs.
41. The beaver uses its broad flat tail as a trowel.
42. There is a law of compensation in nature—e.g. beautiful women are dumb; blind persons have an extraordinary sense of touch.
43. A snake, cut or hack it as you please, will never die till sunset.
44. An ostrich, when pursued, hides its head in sand and thinks that as it cannot see its pursuers, therefore they cannot see it.
45. Crocodiles shed tears.
46. Tortoise shell is obtained from tortoises.
47. The earth is nearest the sun in June and farthest away in December.
48. Shooting stars are stars.
49. The sun sets earliest on December 22 each year, that being the shortest day.
50. Robert Fulton invented the first American steamboat.
51. A frosty winter is more healthful than a mild one.
52. Red cheeks are a sign of health.
53. Night air is unwholesome.
54. Adding certain powders to the bath will reduce body weight.
55. Stuff a cold and starve a fever.
56. Dead teeth do not ache.
57. It is more dangerous for an adult than for a child to have whooping cough.
58. Moths eat clothes.

59. Fish is a brain food.
60. Chop suey originated in China.
61. Cocoa is made from cocoanuts.
62. Wine kept in glass bottles becomes stronger with age.
63. Drinking hot tea cools you.
64. The human heart is on the left side of the body.
65. A drowning person always rises three times before finally sinking.
66. Exercising the body rests the mind.
67. Alcoholic liquors keep out the cold.
68. Blood is purified during its passage through the heart.
69. Some people are double-jointed.
70. Eating green apples will cause stomach-ache.
71. The ninth wave in the surf is always the largest.
72. The Hudson seal is a seal from Hudson Bay.
73. A declining birth rate means depopulation.
74. Rain before seven means clear before eleven.
75. A halo around the moon is a sign of approaching rain.
76. There is soda in soda water.
77. Camel's hair brushes are made from the hair of camels.
78. The only way to avoid scurvy is to eat fresh vegetables.
79. Cork legs are made of cork.
80. A laughing jackass is a mammal.
81. India ink comes from India.
82. Explosions produced by firing big guns, or by other means, bring down heavy rain.
83. George Washington was the first President of the United States.
84. The number of man's senses is five.
85. The criminal can be readily distinguished by certain definite physical stigmata, such as a big jaw or protruding ears.
86. Alcohol is a stimulant.
87. Women are inferior to men in intelligence.
88. Lindbergh was the first man to make a non-stop flight across the Atlantic.
89. All men are created equal in capacity for achievement.
90. Women possess a power of intuition absent in men.
91. The slow learner retains what he gets better than the fast learner.
92. A person is apt to get indigestion if he consumes fruit and milk because milk curdles in the stomach when fruit is present.
93. Shaving makes the hair grow faster.
94. One hour's sleep before midnight is worth two after midnight.
95. The Caesarian operation in obstetrics derives its name from the manner in which Julius Caesar was born.
96. Tan shoes are noticeably cooler for summer wear than black.
97. If a man had faith enough he could heal a broken limb.
98. Women are by nature purer than men.

99. Long, slender hands indicate an artistic nature.
100. Ministers' sons usually turn out poorly.

There are various sources for the items included in this list. The author leaned mostly upon the excellent compilation in A. S. E. Ackermann's *Popular Fallacies* (third edition, 1924), which not only cites the misconception but also cites the evidence that the belief is erroneous. Many of these fallacies are widely accepted. Probably you found yourself a bit credulous on some of these matters.

We do not have to be gullible, though, if we are willing to make the necessary effort to curb our inclination toward accepting statements as facts without even examining the evidence.[2] The most important step to take as a means of minimizing erroneous beliefs is to develop the habit of asking questions, of other people, of yourself. You may find that some people resent your probing attitude, for it is usually more pleasant all around if the members of a group can agree substantially upon their convictions. When you start resisting the social pressures impinging upon you, you may become aware for the first time of how powerful is the urge to conform to standardized opinions.

The advice was given to ask questions. What kind of questions? You may begin your training by raising a basic question: Is the evidence sufficient to justify a conviction or is it so inadequate as to demand a suspension of judgment? Raising questions of this sort is the way scientific experiments get started. Scientific training should imbue a healthy skepticism of this kind. This is especially true of psychology because the psychologist is very much concerned with the ways in which beliefs grow; it is a favorite sport among psychologists to explode popular beliefs that do not accord with reality. For example, consider No. 91 in the list of Popular Fallacies just cited: "The slow learner retains what he gets better than the fast learner." This fallacy is popular because it protects the ego of the slow learner. Experiments have shown that fast learners retain better but such evidence is ignored because it doesn't seem fair for things to work out that way. So, in spite of the evidence, or perhaps because of ignorance, people continue to believe what they prefer to believe.

Making an inventory of our beliefs and finding out where we got them, checking them and double-checking them with what is known by reliable authorities, will convert living into an exciting intellectual adventure, a kind of life which is never discovered by people who are contented with their present store of "knowledge." It is so easy to

[2] We shall return to this topic in Chapter 16, when we deal with "Prejudice: Dogmatism and Ignorance."

be intellectually lazy and uncurious, to allow wishes to speed us on to prejudgments that settle the issues once for all and thus bestow upon us a certain satisfying peace of mind.   The person who desires to wake up and live must cultivate assiduously the *wish to know the truth* by practicing the art of asking questions.   We suggested above that it is wise to consult reliable authorities.   Who are reliable authorities?   Why do I trust them?   Do they deserve such confidence? Why?   Are any of them grinding axes?   For what purpose?   Is the supposed expert intellectually honest or does he reveal his prejudice by being dogmatic and by overgeneralizing?   Do I find myself eager to accept a person's say-so?   Why?   For example, take the erroneous idea current among many Americans about the system of pay in Russia.   More than half of all Americans believe, according to a survey made by Elmo Roper for the New York *Herald Tribune,* that everybody in Soviet Russia gets the same income regardless of the work he does or the job he holds.   Peter F. Drucker tells us that business executives in Russia are being very highly paid; as compared to what the workers get, the managers receive much more relatively than managers get in the United States.   This observation on the part of Drucker will prove disturbing to many Americans because it unsettles their whole picture of Russia, so disturbing, in fact, that they will be inclined to reject the evidence.   The person who is scientific-minded will ask himself: Who is this Drucker?   What is the nature of his evidence?   Did he go to Russia to see for himself what was going on? Where did I get my previous opinion about the Soviet economy?   Was it on equally good authority?   Where can I find more evidence to confirm Drucker or to disprove his testimony? [3]

On any important issue the curious individual will want to examine his beliefs against the background of his culture.   We pointed out in Chapter 4 that values are culturally determined.   Values, of course, are simply beliefs which involve a judgment of merit.   Such being the case, we are safe in assuming that our beliefs, too, are influenced very much by the particular milieu in which we have been conditioned. It is suggested that the reader put himself through this cross-examination, asking himself these searching questions.   What do I believe because of:

My nationality
My color
My religious training

[3] P. F. Drucker: "Stalin Pays 'Em What They're Worth." *Saturday Evening Post,* July 21, 1945.

My age
My occupation
My sex
My status as a married man or a bachelor
The fact that I am a parent or not a parent
The fact that my parents were happy or unhappy
My income level
My educational level
My physical condition
The section of the country I live in, the city or suburb in which I dwell, the part of town in which I own or rent a house
The time of day, the day of the week, the season of the year

It is not being proposed that all of these questions are relevant in every case. The reader will have to learn by experience what questions need to be raised in any given situation to stimulate and to guide him in his search for beliefs that will stand the test of truth.[4]

Stefansson is the sort of person who applies his scientific training to make sure his observations and his conclusions fit reality. Reading his books is an experience that should help to immunize the student against credulousness, for Stefansson obviously derives considerable enjoyment from exploding some of our traditional beliefs that "ain't so." He ate nothing but meat for a year in an experiment to prove that accepted ideas on scientific dieting were notions without any sound basis in facts. He wrote *The Friendly Arctic* (1921) and *The Standardization of Error* (1927) to convince the public that knowledge based on hearsay instead of first-hand evidence is dangerously liable to error. In the former book he called attention to some of the fallacious ideas about life in the Arctic:

The popular picture of the Arctic as a land covered with the ice of everlasting winter, an intensely cold, lifeless waste of eternal silence, is erroneous. That Arctic does not exist, though it may be a pity to destroy the illusion.

One land in the North, Greenland, *is* covered with glaciers, and from it all the rest of the North has been pictured by analogy. Greenland is a mass of high mountains. . . .

"But surely the Arctic is covered with deep snow," many people say. The snowfall in the Canadian Arctic and on the north coast of Alaska is in many

[4] The student of psychology should supplement his training in psychology by taking courses in logic and philosophy in order to become well informed concerning the criteria by means of which we can distinguish correctly between truth and error.

places less than a quarter of what it is in Montreal or Leningrad. It is les
than in Chicago. The annual snowfall of Ellesmere Island, the most north
erly island yet discovered, is less than that of California. Most of what littl
snow falls in the far North is swept by the wind into gullies or the lee of th
hills, so that about 80 per cent of Arctic land is comparatively free from snov
all year.

Closely allied to the idea that all land in the North is covered with eterna
ice and snow is the one that the climate is an everlasting winter of intens
cold. Canada has for years maintained a weather observatory at Hersche
Island, about 200 miles beyond the Arctic Circle, and the lowest temperatur
recorded has been 54 degrees below zero. This is not cold when compare
with some permanently inhabited countries. As you go south from the Arctic
you find more intensely cold winters, for you get away from the moderatinj
effect of the comparatively warm water that underlies the ice of the polar se
and that forms a great radiator which prevents the temperature from drof
ping exceedingly low. . . .

The north of Iceland is within the Arctic Circle; yet, thanks to the Gul
Stream, Iceland is temperate. At sea level the temperature in some winter
never falls to zero Fahrenheit, and 15 below is more often experience
around New York City than in Reykjavik. The mean temperature o
January in Reykjavik averages 30 degrees above zero, or about that of Mila
in Italy.

A corollary to the myth of everlasting cold in the North is belief in th
absence of summer heat. . . . I spent one summer 75 miles north of th
Arctic Circle, and for six weeks the temperature rose to 90 degrees nearl
every day. Nor did it fall low at night, for in that region the sun does not se
and there is no respite through the cooling darkness. All my party agree
we had never suffered as much from cold as we suffered from heat tha
summer.[5]

Stefansson goes on to point out that the North is not lifeless and it i
not silent. And he could go on, as could other first-hand observer:
to indicate that many of our beliefs about other matters are just a
contaminated with erroneous assumptions and prejudices, for whicl
hearsay is largely responsible.

One of the reasons for "the standardization of error" is the menta
satisfaction derived from believing that we understand something,
satisfaction which is not diminished one whit by the fact that we hav
oversimplified the situation in order to arrive at that happy state o
comprehension. We do not realize, of course, that we have distorte
reality in the process of trying to grasp its meaning. We have learne

[5] V. Stefansson: "The North That Never Was." Condensed from *The Friend*
Arctic (The Macmillan Company, 1921), in the *Reader's Digest*, February, 1942.

by experience that it is simpler to have a rule to follow, even though the rule be misleading, than to have no rule at all. "Facts," according to Stefansson, "have usually the unfortunate defect of being complicated . . . it is therefore often necessary and sometimes desirable to ignore them." [6] It is a common assumption, for example, that the farther north you go, the colder it gets, no matter what the time of year. There are numerous exceptions to this generalization. Teachers of geography, however, find that it is practical to acquaint their pupils with this general formula, without any mention of exceptions or qualifications. "We would certainly have to lengthen out our school courses if we went into such hair-splitting, and our millions of potential workers would be kept out of the mills and factories even longer than they are now. Besides, the complexities of facts are bewildering and confusing to the average mind, and never give the feeling of enlightenment you have when you grasp a simple principle which throws a flood of logical light on a previously haphazard world." [7]

One of the impressive characteristics about our credulity is the fact that once we have accepted a hoax, we are inclined to continue our confidence in it. The perpetrator may confess his trick but to no avail—nobody pays any attention, nobody believes it could have been a joke. A good example of this thesis is the famous bathtub hoax started by H. L. Mencken in 1917. "My motive," he explains, "was simply to have some harmless fun in war days. It never occurred to me that it would be taken seriously." The story was originally published in the New York *Evening Mail,* December 28, 1917, under the title, "A Neglected Anniversary." It reviewed the history of the bathtub, essentially as follows:

The first American bathtub was displayed December 10, 1842, by Adam Thompson of Cincinnati, inspired on a European trip by the example of Lord John Russell who, ten years earlier, had introduced the convenience in England. Thompson's tub was constructed of mahogany and lined with sheet lead; he inaugurated it with a stag party at which the entertainment consisted of trying it out.

Although Thompson, a wealthy cotton and grain dealer, looked upon himself as a public benefactor, he was surprised and chagrined to find that others thought otherwise. Physicians denounced the bathtub as a menace to public health. In Boston a city ordinance prohibited its use except on medi-

[6] V. Stefansson: *The Standardization of Error,* pp. 52-53. 1927. By permission of the Macmillan Company, publishers.
[7] *Ibid.,* p. 57.

cal advice. Virginia imposed a thirty-dollar tax on each installation of a bathtub. Hartford, Connecticut, Wilmington, Delaware, and Providence, Rhode Island, all charged extra rates for water used in bathtubs. The Philadelphia city council considered an ordinance forbidding its use from November to May, but the measure was defeated by two votes.

Despite this opposition, it was impossible to legislate the bathtub out of existence. President Fillmore had one put into the White House in the fifties and took the first presidential bath.

Mencken became alarmed by the widespread acceptance of his hoax, confessed his little "joke" in a syndicated article, "Melancholy Reflections," which appeared May 23, 1926, in thirty widely separated big city newspapers.

Pretty soon I began to encounter my preposterous "facts" in the writing of other men. They began to be used by chiropractors and other quacks as evidence of the stupidity of medical men. They began to be cited by medical men as proof of the progress of public hygiene. They got into learned journals. They were alluded to on the floor of Congress. They crossed the ocean, and were discussed solemnly in England and on the continent. Finally, I began to find them in standard works of reference.

In his sixth volume of *Prejudices* Mencken revealed that his story had appeared in the Boston *Herald* with a four-column head and a two-column cartoon labeled satirically, "The American Public Will Swallow Anything." And then three weeks later, but promoted to page one, the same *Herald* reprinted the ten-year-old fake—soberly, as a piece of news. The *Herald's faux pas* elicited a second Mencken confession which was given wide publicity on July 25, 1926. Innumerable attempts have been made to check the spread of the hoax since then but it refuses to be downed and is well on its way to immortality. Among the prominent persons who helped in its dissemination as historical truth were Hans Zinsser, Alexander Woollcott; and Carroll Dulaney in Mencken's own newspaper, the Baltimore *Evening Sun*.

II. RUMOR-MONGERING

Credulity is manifest in the acceptance and circulation of rumor. Crowd behavior—inspired by fear, hatred, demoralization, panic—may be brought about by gossipers who spread their own fabrication or by tongue-waggers who give word-of-mouth publicity to the stories

---

[8] This account is digested from C. D. MacDougall: *Hoaxes*, pp. 302-309. 194 By permission of The Macmillan Company, publishers.

hey have picked up and passed along as the unhappy dupes of enemy propagandists.

The spread of reports based solely on hearsay evidence will be discussed now with reference to gossip, the chain-letter craze, panics, the Lindbergh kidnaping case, and psychological warfare.

A. Gossip

Gossip is ordinarily associated with malicious remarks concerning the personal transgressions of friends and neighbors. This sort of story-telling is sometimes labeled *idle* gossip. Chance observations give rise to the wildest inferences. If a married man joins the church choir, it's because he wants to be near the pretty soprano who wouldn't be there herself if she were tending to her children as every mother should be. Such slanderous scandalmongering is probably due, in some cases at least, to envy rising from the repression of polygamous impulses still surging within. Certainly the malicious satisfaction derived from the invention and circulation of idle tales is evidence of a desire to believe the worst about others because we ourselves are not quite sure of our own uprightness.

Whispering campaigns are now organized on a nation-wide basis. One firm tells prospective clients that its "trained sentiment spreaders" can, on a few hours' notice, do any job that requires altering of opinion by word-of-mouth campaigning under clever disguises anywhere in the country. It has served some of America's greatest corporations in labor disputes by breaking strikes through whispering campaigns. It works in general by having its operatives appear as salesmen of such products as small kitchen utensils, hosiery, or polish. Its customary line of approach is through the women of a community where a strike is in progress. The "salesman" will present himself at a house. After a feeble attempt to sell his product, he will sigh and shake his head at the wife, mother, or sister of the striking worker. "I don't blame you for not buying," he will say. "It's not your fault you have no money. It's the union leaders. Look at me. I'm a union man. Used to make good money in my trade. But I listened to corrupt union leaders and went on strike. Now look at me. Nope, unions and strikes hit us poor people pretty hard." Sighing, he will move to the next door to spread his message further.

One firm . . . is prepared to furnish men in units of two to spread word of mouth propaganda by conversation in subways, theatres, railroad trains, baseball games and all other places of public assembly. . . .

In a recent strike of piano workers in a Midwestern plant, operatives of an organization engaged for the purpose circulated rumors that the plant would be moved to another city unless the workers surrendered. . . .

. . . One great corporation has set up a special counter-espionage department to combat malicious rumors which have already cost it many thousands of dollars worth of business. To mention its name or the names of other firms and products which have been victims of whispering campaigns would further the purposes of the rumor mongers.

The article manufactured by this corporation is used daily by millions of buyers. The campaign against it opened simultaneously in a score of cities along the Atlantic seaboard. . . .

The rumors spread were (1) that several employees in one of the many plants where the product is manufactured suffered from leprosy, and (2) that executives of the firm had contributed large sums of money to the Nazi movement. . . .

Someone—all efforts to trace the source have proved futile—started a whisper in a Middle Western city that in every thousandth package of the firm's product a stamped number would be found inside the package. The firm was paying $100 in cash to everyone who mailed in the package with the number, the whisper said. From mouth to mouth, in offices and over lunch and dinner tables, the rumor was spread by innocents who had heard it from others.

Within a week the company was getting 500 letters a week enclosing numbered packages and demanding $100.

As every package of the product bears a number inside, it was within the realm of possibilities that every customer would demand his $100 and grow indignant when it was not forthcoming.

Despite the frantic denials of the company and the polite explanatory letters, customers believed they were being cheated of a legitimately won prize.

Firms are reluctant to talk about being victimized because of the fear of further spreading of the whisper. Mathematics of rumor-mongering are startling. If one man told ten friends a derogatory story about a certain product and each one told it to ten friends, at the rate of five minutes to talking, in twenty-five minutes 100,000 people would know it.

An agency engaged in an effort to trace down and stamp out a malicious whisper affecting the business of a famous firm worked two months but was unable to find a single person who did not say: "Somebody else told it to me."

"The field is already fertile for the rumor campaign to start," the head of the agency said, "because there are so many sensitive minorities who already have the will to believe that others are persecuting them. Racial minorities particularly, with a sensitive complex, are ready to believe.

"There are firms that play on this situation. They spread stories that competitors are discriminating against the particular minority in employing workers, by contributing to anti-organizations or in other ways.

"Our experience in attempting to combat these campaigns is that the person who is unable to tell from whom he heard the malicious story will say he 'heard it on the radio.' That answer is becoming more and more prevalent.

"We had one instance in which a firm hired cab drivers. We don't know, but we suppose that the firm had its salesmen or other employees say casually to the cab drivers, 'Did you know that the people who manufacture —— were caught with lepers working in their plant?' And who can better spread a story than a cab driver, who passes idle conversation with passengers all day and all night?

"We are having to meet this sort of thing every day. By far the most prevalent now (1934) are racial and religious whispers. Unscrupulous firms are taking advantage of controversies and prejudices.

"Naturally a lot of these things start spontaneously and not designedly. But important corporations are in a jittery state. Their psychological instability now can be turned into panic by further whispering campaigns.

"The power of the whispering campaign lies in the fact that those who hear the rumor believe it comes from an unbiased source. Printed matter which boosts a product or firm is discounted by the readers, who realize those who paid for it have a selfish motive, but gossip is not protected by any such safeguard."

A recent rumor campaign (1934) seriously threatened the commercial stability of an island vacation resort owned by a foreign country but which regularly draws a vast American tourist trade. Merchants of the island gathered a fund and advertised in newspapers here and elsewhere, denying the whisper that the American dollar was worth sixty cents and less in the resort.

In the order of their prevalence (1934), the whispers now frightening business are:

1. That poisonous, rancid or deleterious ingredients are used in a product.
2. That the financial condition of a firm is shaky.
3. That employees of a plant have leprosy.
4. That a firm is secretly owned by foreign interests.
5. That executives of a firm are contributing heavily to the Nazis.
6. That a firm is failing to comply with NRA codes and rules of fair competition. . . .

The whispering campaign has always been a stock weapon in political campaigns and in wars. The last classic example in politics was that of the cruel and vicious rumors flung against Alfred E. Smith because he is a Catholic. Untold thousands of votes were lost to him because there swept from lip to lip through the areas where illiterate laborers and dirt farmers live, the word that "Al Smith will bring the Pope to Washington and make him ruler of America if we vote for him." . . .

In politics and warfare the endless record of effective whispering campaigns attests the fierce power of unprincipled tongues. The whisperers said Harding had Negro blood, that Grover Cleveland's private life was immoral, that the name Roosevelt is not a real Dutch name but a corruption of the Jewish Rosenfeld.

And the use of whispered untruths, few of which ever find their way into print, has been frequent in business.

But until now there have never, apparently, been organizations directed by masters of psychology, hiring themselves out to whisper whatever words employers put into their mouths.[9]

The term *rumor* suggests that the story in circulation gets distorted in the telling.   This falsification, resulting from deliberate or unintentional fabrication, prompted by envy and sadism and the desire to appear excitingly informative, is the basic reason why hearsay evidence is barred from courtroom testimony.   Bartlett tested the amount of distortion experimentally by having a person read a short folk-story twice, and then after a filled interval of from fifteen to twenty minutes, reproduce it from memory in writing.   A second subject read the account as written by the first subject, later reproduced it for a third subject, and so on in a series of from ten to twenty persons. Changes in the story were classified as: omissions; rationalizations— such as rearranging details into meaningful wholes; transformations of unfamiliar names; and transpositions in the order of events and in the order of words.[10]

Read the following passage to the individual next to you in a group; have him repeat what he has heard to his neighbor; and so on around the group.   The last person will write down what he hears.

The average man has a vocabulary of 7,500 words.   He can repeat seven numbers he hears but if asked to repeat eight, he leaves out one of them.   He leaves school at the eighth grade.   On a standardized intelligence test he makes about the same score as a boy of fourteen.   He marries at an early age, and has from three to five children.

Sample final account of the above:

There are a great many words in the American vocabulary.   We don't like the American family.

There is no malice involved in the spreading of this tale about the average man.   Where emotional sets operate to influence the story

---

[9] Lionel Houser: "Guaranteed Whispers For Sale."   New York *World-Telegram* October 18, 1934.

[10] F. C. Bartlett: *Remembering*, Chapter 5, "Experiments on Remembering: (b) The Method of Repeated Reproduction."   1932.

telling, as they do in everyday, over-the-phone, over-the-fence, neighborly gossip, fabrication will be exaggerated.

Emotional excitement may stir the imagination to conjure up all sorts of stories based on the flimsiest foundations. Often there are no facts to substantiate the suspicions involved in the concoction of rumors. The play, *Tobacco Road,* was alleged by the rumor-mongers to be salacious and many persons who attended the drama, according to the producer, went away disappointed, to spread the news that "it's not very exciting." Despite their criticisms, the word got around that the play was unfit for decent people to see. The producer, Sam H. Grisman, was considerably upset by the unfortunate publicity:

Why the stories that have got around about this play! We'd arrive in Kansas City to find that there was a ban because people believed that a baby was born on the stage, or rather that that was depicted. We'd have to get an injunction against the censor and we'd always get one because none of the stories were true.

Governor Talmadge of Georgia said it was a foul libel on the fair state that he had the honor of leading, because Georgians did not eat snakes. There's nothing in the play that says they do.

Some patriotic congressman from Georgia got up in Congress and waved his arms and said, "Our people don't act thataway and it sho'nuf ought to be stopped." When someone asked him if he'd ever seen it, he said he hadn't.[11]

irascible inhabitants and officials sought to ban it in Chicago, Newark, Washington, Albany, and other cities on the ground of indecency. Censors, however, were forced to agree that the play was not salacious but was a serious study of life among Georgia's "po' white trash."

B. THE CHAIN LETTER CRAZE

The chain letter craze, motivated by the desire for easy money, was facilitated in its spread by the propagation of rumors to the effect that So-and-So made $550 the previous week. Advisers confided, "You'd better get in on it early, so your name will come to the top and you can cash in on it." The story was passed along that money was being made by lots of people and the amounts were exaggerated in each telling. The hope that it was all true precluded any check on the accuracy of the information. Rumors circulated, devotees imparted their enthusiasm to their friends, postmen were burdened with more mail, a few people "cleaned up," more people parted with

[11] Boston *Herald*, April 11, 1936.

their money without any return, economists exploded the theory behind the scheme, interest waned, and the speculators turned their attention to Bank Night at the movies and to Bingo over at the church. It was the old story of the Tulip Mania and the South Sea Bubble—the craze for quick money, bred of hard times.

C. PANICS

In the fall of 1938 a widespread panic was unexpectedly precipitated by Orson Welles' radio broadcast of "The War of the Worlds," depicting an imaginary invasion from Mars. Many listeners who tuned in late were disposed to accept the fictitious bulletins as news; others who tuned in at the start to hear a play by the Mercury Theatre thought the regular dramatic program had been interrupted for the purpose of inserting some special news bulletins, a practice to which listeners had become accustomed during the war crisis in October, 1938. A large number of the late "tuner-inners" had picked up the program after excited friends had telephoned to warn them of the fearful invasion. Fright was communicated as one terrified person passed along the rumor to another in this way. A larger proportion of people who listened to the broadcast in a public place were scared than of persons who were secure in the privacy of their own homes "Those who listened in public places saw more people who were frightened and their own behavior seemed to be more violent. . . [They] were more confused and more terror-stricken because they were away from home, worried about their families, surrounded by so many other people who were frightened." [12] Even sophisticated people were "taken in" by the dramatic portrayal of parachuting Martians. Preexisting mental sets made the account so understandable that persons ordinarily critical did not bother to check the broadcast Subsequent investigation of panicky listeners led to the conclusion that "the general characteristic of personality that made people vulnerable to the broadcast was what we might call susceptibility-to-suggestion-when-facing-a-dangerous-situation." [13] Feelings of insecurity over chaotic world conditions predisposed listeners to misinterpret the play as a real event; they had never experienced an interplanetary war, so customary standards of judgment were lacking for supplying a reliable check on the "truth" and for enabling the individual to orient himself. Still another factor in the situation was the lis-

[12] H. Cantril *et al.: The Invasion from Mars,* p. 146. Princeton University Press 1940.

[13] *Ibid.,* p. 130.

tener's failure to realize that his first snap interpretation might be wrong. "Perhaps," says Cantril, "the clearest index of critical ability is a person's readiness to reevaluate interpretations he first receives, to look for new standards of judgment and to juxtapose them against others. One of the outstanding indices of suggestibility is the complete absence of the awareness that things might be otherwise than they are made out to be." [14]

Financial panics may be precipitated by the diffusion of rumors of impending insolvency. The psychology of a business depression is summed up in a French story which shows how gloom travels by word of mouth.

While waiting to be served in a Paris restaurant, a regular habitué picked up a newspaper he saw protruding from behind a picture. When the waiter came, the customer said: "Henri, I shall take a cheaper wine from now on. I see by this paper times are going to be very hard, so I must commence to economize." The waiter reported the matter to the proprietor, who said: "If that is the case, I also must economize." So he phoned the automobile company, saying, "Times are getting very hard; my customers are cutting down on their orders, so I shall have to cancel that order for a new car." The manager of the automobile company phoned the artist: "Times are getting pretty hard; customers are canceling orders for automobiles, so I shall have to cancel that order for my wife's portrait." The artist phoned his wife: "You will have to do without that fur coat; times are very hard, people are canceling their orders."

Next day, the same customer went as usual to his restaurant, picked up the paper, and found the news the same as he had read the day before. Looking at the date, he found the paper two years old. To the waiter he said: "Henri, that was a mistake about the hard times; I had an old newspaper. Bring me my usual wine again." Again the waiter reported the matter to the proprietor, who promptly ordered the new car. The automobile manager got his wife's portrait, and the artist's wife got her fur coat.

Every person who spreads the sad news about the gloomy prospects of his own business and the tragic outlook of other people's business makes his contribution to the maintenance of depression, economic and psychological. Traveling men who report how business is falling off for themselves and how they have heard it is the same all along the line, distribute more melancholy than sales. They are a source of discouragement to every listener who has the time to heed their tale of woe.

Rumor plays a prominent role in the rise and fall of the stock

[14] *Ibid.*, p. 196.

market.   Optimistic rumors were given a cordial reception and quick repetition during the summer of 1929, even by business men of experience and otherwise sound judgment.   Hardheaded business men listened to discussions about the "new era" in business and began to wonder if the old economic laws of their youth were applicable to modern conditions.   The same confusion of thought seemed to exist among leading economists.   Small wonder, therefore, that the public believed practically everything it heard.   In less than sixty days this situation was entirely reversed.   Excessive declines took place as people lost confidence in their securities.   Fear soon resulted in widespread liquidation.

A run on a bank in Millbury, Massachusetts, in the summer of 1929 was precipitated by the verification of a report that a small shortage existed in the accounts.   The Bank Commissioner announced that he could not determine without further investigation whether the shortage was due to larceny or mismanagement.   He declared, however, that all employees of the bank were bonded and that the bank would lose nothing through the $6,000 shortage.   The treasurer, meanwhile, was asked to resign by the state banking department.   He refused to do so.   Instead of resigning, he simply failed to go to the bank as usual.   He was seen on the streets of the town by the chief of police.

The clerk in charge of the books had been missing for several weeks.   She left her desk one noon, told her associates that she was going out for a sandwich and coffee, and was not seen thereafter.

Unfounded stories concerning the bank's affairs had been circulated for several days.   It was known that a large concern had made a sizable withdrawal.   The appearance of the treasurer on the streets during banking hours, the disappearance of the clerk, and the sizable withdrawal started some gossip, though it was stated on good authority that the three incidents were not connected.   The coincidence added fuel to the public gossip, with the result that a small line appeared at the paying teller's window.   There were fifteen or twenty in it and each had his passbook and sought withdrawals.

Millbury is a small, compact town where news and rumor travel fast and within an hour the line had swelled into hundreds.   Bank officials appealed to the police when the press of the mob inside the bank became so great that it was impossible to do business.   The chief strove valiantly to clear the main foyer of the bank and to prevail upon the people to form a line and be orderly.   He finally had to summon the state police for help.

In the meantime the throng outside and inside the bank had been growing larger.   Inside the bank, they became ill and hysterical in the press of the crowd.   The line outside grew longer.   On this first day of the run $150,000 was withdrawn.

A 90-day moratorium was finally declared to prevent the run from being disastrous.[15]

All of the public excitement, whipped up by rumor, was completely irrational, since the state banking authorities had issued an assurance that the bank was in a sound condition. The assurance was unavailing, however, in the face of the mounting public hysteria. Nerves were jittery in those days and it did not take much in the way of a rumor to provoke unfounded conclusions.

D. The Lindbergh Kidnaping Case

The genesis and dissemination of rumor were nicely illustrated in the search for the Lindbergh baby and its kidnaper, back in 1932.[16] As soon as the crime was announced, people here, there, and everywhere began to help out by telling how they had noticed somebody with a baby somewhere, acting "peculiar and kind of nervous." The newspapers reported tips like the following:

> The furor that swept the country as news of the crime spread over it brought in an avalanche of clues and "tips," most of which proved worthless. It seemed that every constable between Mexico and Canada spent the day searching automobiles at bridgeheads and ferries, and the number of women and babies who came under suspicion was staggering.
>
> These meager clues were augmented by tales of suspicious looking cars mysteriously parked on lonely roads, of strangers inquiring the way to the Lindbergh home, and endless theories offered by neighboring farmers.
>
> Trenton, N.J.—A Pennsylvania Railroad brakeman noticed two men and a woman, the latter with a crying baby in her arms, acting oddly in the Clinton St. station. The child was whimpering. He thought from the sound it had a cold. One of the men asked when a New York train was due. Both men seemed nervous.
>
> New York Police Headquarters sent a message to look for all Hudson sedans with license numbers 4U—99—. Police near Manlius, N.Y., chased in vain a Hudson licensed 4U—99— which carried two men in front and one in the rear holding something in a blanket.
>
> Wheeling, West Virginia—Joseph Schlantz, contractor, reported that a car bearing a New Jersey license went by him very fast, forcing him into a ditch. It was a coupe, carrying three persons. . . . Two were slumped into the seat, holding something, and he could not say whether one was a woman.

[15] Boston *Herald,* July 18, 1930.
[16] This account of the Lindbergh rumors is based on a study made for the author by Elsie Wyzanski.

Providence, R.I.—Police chased a car that had been reported to carry four men and a baby but they were only hockey players—and there was no baby.

Babies resembling the stolen infant were seen in Buffalo, Philadelphia, Portchester, Washington, and Nashua, N.H.

Paris—Hamburg authorities have been asked to verify the identity of an eighteen-month old child aboard the liner *President Roosevelt*.

Gibraltar—A report that the kidnaped Lindbergh boy was aboard the liner *Roma* stirred excitement here. A search revealed nothing to substantiate the rumor.

Bergen, Norway—Twenty-eight babies of various ages were aboard the liner *Bergensfjord* when she arrived here today, but none of them was the kidnaped Lindbergh boy.

Hamburg—A girl baby on the S.S. *City of Baltimore* proved not to be the child.

Havana—Baby reported in Cuba. . . .

Bogota, Colombia—A report from Manizales states that a "reliable authority" there knows the kidnaped Lindbergh child is being held on an island near the coast city of Buenaventura, Colombia. . . .

Mexico City—Telegrams from Oklahoma received here report that Governor Murray is of the opinion that the Lindbergh baby may be in Mexico. . . .

Madrid—The Spanish police today received orders to search for the Lindbergh baby. The Madrid press prints rumors that the child was brought into Spain at Vigo.

Johannesburg, South Africa—A John M. Long was arrested here in connection with the Lindbergh case. . . .

It is a well-known fact among students of psychology that testimony is notoriously inaccurate even when it is given immediately after the event under observation. Experiments have also demonstrated that an extended lapse of time between the observation and the report tends to aggravate the errors. Experiences during the intervening period interfere with the recall of earlier events owing to retroactive inhibition. Prior to the announcement of the Lindbergh kidnaping many people had been noticing many sorts of things only in a casual manner because there had been no particular reason to give special attention to them. As soon as people became aware of the tragedy sympathy for the distraught parents prompted an effort to ransack their memories for any possible clues. Events that were practically ignored at the time of their occurrence and later only dimly recalled suddenly took on a new meaning that transfused them with a vividness hitherto nonexistent. Hope and expectation filled in the gaps by secondary elaboration until a clear and coherent reminiscence resulted which accorded very little with the facts involved. Phantasies supplemented realities to such an extent that imaginary events could not be distinguished from actual ones. Several persons, eager for publicity or money, carried fancy so far that the law had to step in to curb their fertile imaginations. Almost every one wanted to help in some way. Feeling ran high. Under such circumstances it was inevitable that emotional excitement would distort both observation and recall.

It is obvious that rumors, in many cases, do not rise from a single origin. They seem to spring simultaneously from many diverse sources. This fact would indicate that rumor is more than a mere transmission of a report in a chain-like fashion—it is a social phenomenon in which each individual is influenced by many other persons, all of whom are likewise centering their attention upon the same situation. There is a common interest that inspires a large number of people to keep the story in circulation until the zest for gossiping about it has spent itself. By that time the tale has gone around and around and come out everywhere.

E. WARTIME STORIES

War and rumor are bedfellows. "Inside dope" is constantly being passed along. Stories of the wildest sort are invented by highly imaginative citizens or are promulgated from enemy headquarters for purposes of demoralization. The manufacture and dissemination of rumors is an important phase of psychological warfare.

Why is it that wartime is so productive of rumors? The answer is twofold, says Gordon Allport.[17] First, war demands secrecy on many vital topics. When the public cannot get complete information on all matters, it begins to imagine things. Imagination issues in the fabrication of rumors. Secondly, people in wartime are deeply emotional and they find it difficult to bottle up their feelings. They want to talk; especially they want to give vent to their hopes, fears, and hatreds. Rumor-mongering provides a satisfactory outlet for this purpose. With facts lacking and emotions running high, the field is wide open for the initiation and transmission of unfounded reports. Some

---

[17] See "The ABC's of Wartime Rumor." *Worksheets in Morale,* Department of Psychology, Harvard University, 1942-1943.

of them are invented out of whole cloth, some of them are subtle distortions of fact.

There are three common types of wartime rumors, continues Allport. The first is the *pipe-dream* rumor. This kind is characterized by wishful thinking. It springs from desire and hope.

A tells B he wishes the Norwegians would plant a bomb on the *Scharnhorst.* B tells C that maybe the Norwegians will blow up the *Scharnhorst.* C says he heard from reliable sources that the *Scharnhorst* has been blown up. D says the whole German navy in Norwegian waters has been secretly sunk.

Such rumors foster a groundless optimism. In aiding us to escape the harsh realities of war, they breed complacency and overconfidence, thus softening us up for enemy attack.

The second type of rumor is the *wedge-driving* variety, designed to promote distrust of leaders, of the army and navy, of our government. Stories are circulated to encourage race hatred and class conflicts, to incite suspicion and resentment toward our allies, to destroy confidence in our news sources.

The third kind of rumor is the *fear* rumor. Like a child who wakes up from a nightmare in a dark bedroom and imagines all sorts of hobgoblins, people in the excitement of war spread stories of impending disasters which may not be in the offing at all. Stark panic may result, as unwarranted anxiety and despondency are provoked. Persons who convey such forebodings are "low morale carriers" who help to nourish a spirit of defeatism.[18]

Rumors, of course, may turn out to fit the facts. Stories of troop movements and factory production may be in accord with actual conditions—they are still properly labeled as rumors if they are based principally on hearsay evidence and circulated by person-to-person communication. Modern warfare, with its well-organized espionage and its planted fifth columns, cannot be prosecuted effectively if people are careless in their conversational references to matters that need to be kept confidential. Early in World War II campaigns were conducted to educate people to maintain a discreet silence, lest a casual remark conveying some bit of information might be overheard by a listener in the employ of the enemy. Posters carried the appeal to people to stop talking so much. "Zip Your Lip."

A few samples of the rumors which emanated from Axis sources will reveal how stories were engineered to demoralize the Allied Nations. Most of these illustrations were garnered by the Rumor Clinic sponsored by the Massachusetts Committee on Public Safety and were published Sundays during World War II in the Boston *Herald*. Here are some typical ones:

Negroes are forming secret clubs to decide how best to take over our government when the war is ended; these clubs even consider methods of torture to apply to white people; such clubs are called Eleanor Roosevelt clubs.

There is a pneumonia epidemic in —— training camp. Hundreds of the boys are sick and there are already forty-two bodies in the morgue.

[18] Boston *Herald*, March 13, 1942.

You're lucky not to be down at —— camp in Georgia.   It's full of influenza. The food stinks.   The officers kick you around.

Food prices are soaring in the United States while ships with food cargo bound for England anchor off our coasts and dump innumerable crates overboard to boost prices here.

The scrap metal collected from millions of housewives is of no value. The whole drive was a hoax put over on an innocent public.

Anonymous postcards sent to soldiers at Fort Dix, read: "Your wife was seen parked in a country lane in an automobile.—A Friend."

All Italian aliens are to be moved back 20 miles from the Massachusetts coast.

A local Italian mother, not a citizen, who lost a son at Pearl Harbor, and has another in the Navy, has been put in a concentration camp.

British pilots in training in this country remain here a year or more, but American pilots are trained much more rapidly and sent overseas.

State Street is betting war will be over this fall.

Lloyds of London is betting on peace by fall.

Florida has been bombed.

Commanders of ships of the Navy always order all food, left on board on return to the home port, dumped overboard because otherwise the ship's food allowance will be cut the next time.

A woman has received a letter from a soldier in camp who had found her name and address on a slip of paper inside a Red Cross sweater.   He thanked her for the sweater but said he had paid $2.50 for it.

A woman bought a sweater in Jordan Marsh Company's store and found a slip pinned in the sleeve reading: "I hope this keeps you warm and comfortable, buddy."   That indignant woman took the sweater and her story to the local Red Cross and was told they had a surplus of sweaters and sold them to get their money back for the yarn they had supplied.

The Red Cross is charging the Army and Navy $25 a pint for the blood which is collected free from volunteer donors, and pocketing the money as profit.

The blood is not properly preserved and large quantities of it have spoiled.

No test is made for venereal diseases, and blood contaminated with such disease has been given to soldiers and sailors, thus transmitting the disease to them.

Because Negro donors are accepted, white soldiers and sailors who receive donations of Red Cross blood will have Negro children.

A number of people around Boston have died from poisoning and ground glass which were traced to canned crab meat packed in Japan.

England is letting its colonial and dominion soldiers (or soldiers of allied nations) fight the war while carefully protecting its own troops.

New cruisers have been returned to the Boston Navy Yard because they were not fitted with anti-aircraft guns. They were completely forgotten.

Pipe lines carry petroleum products to Canada, thus enabling Canadians to have plenty of fuel oil and gasoline, while Americans have to ration these essentials.

The British are poor fighters because they stop fighting in the middle of the afternoon to have tea and crumpets.

When in Maine last week, I was told by a friend (who said she had learned it from an eye witness) that a tanker came into Portland recently full of gasoline, and because all storage facilities were full, the gasoline was pumped into Portland harbor. This does not seem logical to me, but she was firmly convinced and I believe the rumor has become quite widespread.

We are sending so much lend-lease aid to England and Russia that United States forces are badly in need of war materials.

The British are intercepting American aid to China because the Tory class in England does not wish China to emerge from this struggle as a first-class power in the Orient.

Observers noted that the same rumors tended to appear almost simultaneously in various parts of the country, the story in each case being adapted to the particular region. A Californian who recorded rumors on the Pacific coast wrote to the Massachusetts Rumor Clinic as follows:

Some of the rumors which you publish are almost exactly like those current here with slight changes to fit the locale. That is, if your rumor has the bodies of Nazi sailors washed up on a beach, ours will naturally have Japanese sailors; if your rumor has an enemy submarine captured near Gloucester, ours will have it sunk in Monterey Bay; and so on. We even had Japanese parachutists here in rumor before the recent wave of parachutist rumors in the East. Our sugar rationing rumors are almost identical with yours.[19]

Many of the rumors which were so innocently circulated by Americans were engineered by Goebbels from Berlin. Nazi agents in this

[19] Boston *Herald*, August 9, 1942.

country functioned as "Trouble Seekers," looking for trouble-spots, or what the Nazis called *Stoerungskerne:* signs of friction, such as labor trouble, racial discrimination, political skulduggery, and the like. These sore spots were reported to the home office of the Ministry of Propaganda in Berlin. Then short-wave broadcasts instructed the "Trouble Makers" how to proceed to implant disruptive and demoralizing tales in the minds of gullible Americans who unknowingly did the rest by disseminating the unhappy stories. Gabby gossipers thus served as dupes to further the strategy of "Divide and Conquer."

One alert American spotted a gross pleasantry perpetrated by Herr Goebbels. On January 13, 1942, this amateur rumor detective wrote a clever note to the Editor of the Boston *Herald:*

You published a dispatch from Washington dated January 7 to the effect that "an official report by an Allied government telling of dissension, hunger, and disease among German troops on the Russian front and of a plot by German army officers to overthrow Adolf Hitler and his accomplices was handed today to the War Department, which did not authenticate or comment on the document." Follows a very sinister and, for us, satisfying story of dire happenings in the Reich. But the last sentence seems to give the game away: "All preparations for an army revolt are said to be in the hands of Admiral Canaris, head of the German intelligence service."

Admiral Canaris! Canaris is strangely like canard, a French word meaning, literally, a duck, and figuratively, a newspaper hoax. This gross pleasantry smacks distinctly of Goebbels and it is a well-known trick of German propaganda to ridicule and discredit in advance adverse rumors especially when they are founded on facts.

We can be pretty sure that Hitler's goose is cooked, but that is no reason to swallow gullibly Goebbels' ducks.

The Committee for National Morale was organized to detect and expose the Axis rumor-propaganda. Working on one such project, Ruch and Young set out to learn how many people were hearing the totalitarian propaganda directly, how many indirectly, what sorts of people, and how many were falling for the rumors to which they were exposed. One of their most significant discoveries was that people in the big cities were the most effective rumor-mongers.

The average New Yorker is more gullible than the rank and file of Bostonians, but both are bigger suckers for Herr Goebbels' propaganda brain storms than the residents of Dover, New Jersey. Why? Because the bigger the city, the better the stamping ground for the professional rumor monger. In the smaller communities, people know one another and make allowances for the source of unconfirmed tales. But in the larger cities, the resident has many acquaintances but fewer friends, and is more vulnerable to enemy stories.

The research was conducted by means of a standard public-opinion sampling technique. Interviewers, with a background training in psychology and the social sciences, made contacts with a cross section of the general public in their homes and in public places. Each person was shown a series of cards on which items from recent Axis broadcasts were printed. As each card was presented, the person was asked this question:

Have you heard or seen this statement anywhere within the past few weeks? I don't care whether you believe it or not, just tell me whether you have heard or seen it.

The object of this question was to measure the *degree of circulation*. To facilitate this end, the question was so phrased as to obviate any sense of guilt in replying affirmatively. The following items were used in this survey—items A, B, C, and E were obtained from Jack Gerber of the Short-Wave Listening Post of the Columbia Broadcasting System; item D was "home-grown" in the Committee's headquarters in New York City and had not been used by the Axis at the time of the study:

Card A—"More than 300 draftees recently deserted from Fort Dix in New Jersey."
Card B—"Hawaii was so effectively attacked by Japanese forces that American authorities now consider that its further defense is not possible, and are withdrawing forces to use in the defense of the West Coast, which is in serious danger."
Card C—"During the night of December 6, a formation of American bombers appeared over Formosa from the Philippines, and were driven off by Japanese reconnaissance planes before they could launch their attack."
Card D—"Labor union pickets will be excluded from air-raid shelters, according to a recently issued order from Washington."
Card E—"Young men with religious convictions against war who choose non-military service instead, are being blacklisted so that they cannot get their jobs back after their service is over."

After all of the cards were presented and the answers to the questions recorded, they were shown again in the same order, this time with the query: "Now read the statement carefully once more, and tell me whether you think it is true. I don't care whether you have heard it before or not, just tell me whether you think it is true." The aim of this phase of the investigation was to measure the *acceptance* of the propaganda. In the last stage of the interview an attempt was made to discover the *source* of the rumor. The interviewer handed the person only those cards containing the items which had been heard, and asked: "Do you happen to remember who told you this, or where you heard or read it?"

Four hundred interviews were conducted in Greater Boston and the same number in Greater New York. The average figures for the five rumors considered *in toto,* based on the 800 cases in the two cities covered, were 6.8 per cent for circulation (had heard) and 6.6 per cent for acceptance (believed). These figures might lead one to assume that the Nazis were not making any important headway, and that was just the conclusion the Nazis aimed to foster, for their technique in the war of nerves was to keep the rumors flowing continuously, each item a shell in a barrage, all designed to summate gradually into a final impression of inevitable defeat. With this fact in mind, it is interesting to learn that 22.8 per cent of the population of the two cities had heard *one or more* of the rumors—and that 23.4 per cent believed *one or more.* The average Acceptance Index for New Yorkers was 9.4 per cent; for Bostonians, 3.8 per cent. Women proved less susceptible than men, the average Acceptance Index being 6.2 per cent for all women, 7.0 for all men. The Index of Circulation, however, showed a slight superiority for the women, 7.1 per cent, as against 6.4 per cent for the men.[20]

The Committee for National Morale was only one of the agencies engaged in the task of frustrating the Axis tongue-wagging plots. The Special Defense Unit of the Department of Justice kept a sharp eye on the pro-Axis press in the United States, reading and translating all foreign-language newspapers, cataloguing and filing editorials and news articles which could be converted into rumors. Field workers of the Soil Conservation Service of the Department of Agriculture played an important role in discovering and quashing rumors in the rural areas of the United States. Two simple rules promulgated by Ruch for combating rumors effectively were these:

Do not accept unconfirmed stories told by comparative strangers. Ask them politely where they got the information.

Ask yourself, "Whose axe am I grinding if I believe this story—and spread it around?"

[20] Boston *Herald,* March 22, 1942.

Perhaps the best defense against rumors was to give people the facts. The Rumor Clinic in Massachusetts employed this technique to good effect by publishing statements from various authorities with reference to the falsity of particular rumors submitted to them for comment. Too much censorship, by keeping people in the dark, facilitated the genesis of anxiety and panic—frames of mind which rendered individuals vulnerable to rumor campaigns.

The Allied Nations did not neglect this potent weapon of rumor

(Courtesy, Joe Stern and the Boston *Herald*.)

in the war of nerves. Stories of an invasion of the Continent and the opening of a second front continually worried the Nazis, and dire penalties were threatened from Berlin for citizens in the occupied countries who dared to spread such disquieting tales.

The deliberate invention and organized dissemination of rumors was developed during World War II as an important technique in psychological warfare. In the emotional excitement of wartime, it was discovered repeatedly, people proved an easy prey to this subtle weapon of demoralization.

III. PUBLIC ACCLAIM

Suggestion and imitation, operating through word-of-mouth publicity, play an important role in the popularizing of people, books, plays, songs. *Gone With the Wind,* for example, became a best seller because critics praised it, because individuals read it, liked it, and told others it was worth reading, because the publishers publicized it well through advertising and other means, and because it became the fashion of the day—a person had to read it to be in the swim, to enter into conversations intelligently when somebody at a party happened to mention Scarlett O'Hara or Rhett Butler, or to maintain the reputation for being well-read. Some readers discovered the novel, reported their "find," *suggested* it to friends, others *imitated* by following suit, passed the word along, and the "rumor" got around that it was a good book—and it was.

A. Errors in Predicting the Public Taste

Publishers and producers would give a good deal to be able to pick "winners" when they look over books, plays, and songs. Experts and critics "pull some awful boners" in judging what the public will take to. Ambitious authors, with reputations yet to make, console themselves, when the rejection slips come their way, by recalling some of the hits which have met with outstanding success despite the disparagement of critics and the condemnation of publishers.

1. books

Why do some books catch the public fancy, while other books, seemingly just as meritorious, go unnoticed? Many good books do not become best sellers. Publishers wish they knew how to select the good ones that are destined to "click." If they only knew how to evaluate a manuscript accurately in terms of its possible sales, their business would be considerably less hazardous. One publisher, in desperation, formulated a questionnaire to guide the editorial staff. "Points on the Art of Book Selection or the Elements Involved in Editorial Judgment" consisted of a series of questions. If all the firm's editors answered "Yes" to the questions, the book was to be considered worth publishing. The publisher himself evaluated one book as follows:

1. Is it a good book? *Not particularly.*
2. How important or how interesting is its purpose? *Reasonably important.*

3. How well does the book achieve its purpose? *Reasonably well.*

4. Will it sell? *I have no idea.*

5. Did I personally enjoy it? *Not particularly.*

6. Is it news, by virtue of message, novelty, author or special situation? *No.*

7. Is it likely to receive enthusiastic reviews? *No.*

8. Will the bookstores feature it? *Not unless it sells.*

9. Does it say something not said by any other book in its particular field? *No.*

10. Does it meet some basic human need? *No.*

11. Is the manuscript so extraordinary, so novel, or so unique in style, content, or appeal as to command special attention? *No.*

The book was published, in spite of the publisher's personal judgment, and more than 200,000 copies were sold.[21] Other books have proved surprises, too:

> *The Education of a Princess,* by Grand Duchess Marie, was turned down by practically every leading publisher in the nation. Yet it turned out to be the national non-fiction best seller in 1931. The publisher said: "We figured, when we took it, that it was good for a sale of 4,000 or 5,000 copies, but I guess we reckoned without the drawing power of royalty in the flesh autographing copies of its book in the stores." A few weeks after publication, one shop sold more than 1,000 copies in a single afternoon. Upon hearing this, one of the publishers who had turned it down, remarked: "That book should have been called *The Education of a Publisher.*"

> Reviewers praise many a flop and condemn a best seller. Critical acclaim hasn't much to do with a book's zooming into the ranks of best-sellerdom. *The Winning of Barbara Worth,* panned by every highbrow critic, reached a sale of 1,500,000 copies.

> Nearly every tremendous money-maker of the past fifty years has been rejected by leading publishers before it was launched on its career. *David Harum* was hawked in the streets, and turned down by virtually every publisher before finally someone was found who had faith in it. The sales amounted to 1,200,000 copies.

> The publisher who first held a contract to produce Will Durant's essays on the great philosophers in book form practically begged another publisher to take it off his hands—and succeeded—only to see *The Story of Philosophy* turn overnight into one of the most astonishing successes of our time.

[21] J. A. Goodman and A. Rice: "Big Books; the Story of Best Sellers." *The Saturday Evening Post,* November 17, 1934.

Timing is the all-important factor in the success of the topical-interest best seller. Had *This Side of Paradise* been published five years earlier, the public would not have been ready for it and would not have believed it; had it come out five years later, they might have yawned at it. Published today, it might not have a sale of 10,000 copies—it actually went to 600,000. The great *All Quiet on the Western Front* might conceivably have never come into the limelight if published just after the war, when people wouldn't believe anything but evil of the enemy.[22]

Katherine Brush's most famous story, "Night Club," was rejected by five editors who had been asking for some of her work, but who did not take kindly to that particular bit. The story was eventually published in *Harper's Magazine* and instantly it became a sensation. It has since been reprinted in several different anthologies and in the *Golden Book;* it has been translated into several languages; Famous Players Lasky made a talking motion picture of it; and at New York University, Columbia University, and many other institutions of like standing, it has been used as a model in teaching the technique of the short story to aspiring writers.

Ring Lardner wrote a yarn about a baseball rookie which contained such gems of moronic wit as this:

He called me a dumb ox, and I said, "Oh, is that so?" And he didn't have no comeback.

The manuscript was rejected with such speed that Lardner maintained that it was physically impossible for it to have traveled from Chicago to Philadelphia and back. But two of his friends finally persuaded George Horace Lorimer of the *Saturday Evening Post* to give it a personal reading. Although Lorimer liked it, his sub-editors argued that no baseball player could be quite so dumb as Lardner's Jack Keefe. Lardner produced several letters he had received from heroes of the diamond, and his case was won. The *Post* published the story, the first of a series. "You Know Me, Al" became a national by-word, and Lardner an established author.

Charles M. Sheldon wrote a series of stories concerning what Jesus would do if he were alive in our modern day, which he read to the congregation of his church in Topeka, Kansas. Simultaneously a religious weekly was printing *In His Steps* as a serial. When it was finished, the college students who had listened to the reading asked if it could be put out in book form. Three book publishers re-

[22] *Ibid.*

fused it on the ground that it was "too religious." "Nobody is interested in religion," they said. Finally, a weekly magazine plucked up courage enough to put out an inexpensive edition. So anxious was the magazine to save every possible penny that only one copy of the book was sent to the copyright office in Washington, instead of the two copies which the law requires. Hence, the copyright was never completed, and the book was anyone's property. Sixteen publishers issued it in America, and sixty in Great Britain and on the Continent. The book was published in 1896. Some 8,000,000 copies have been sold; it tops the list of best sellers published since 1880.

2. PLAYS

Channing Pollock worked out a similar idea in writing his play, *The Fool,* which depicted what would happen to a man who tried to live like Christ. He took it to thirty-one managers who refused the piece with unanimity and enthusiasm. At last, two men were found who were willing to take a chance. For several weeks after its opening, business was pretty bad. And then came the flood. For nearly fifty weeks *The Fool* led every other attraction in New York City in gross receipts. The movie rights sold for $150,000. The next season five companies took the piece on the road and played it for three years. *The Fool* was translated and performed in every civilized nation. It has netted some $1,000,000.

In 1922 John Golden decided to produce *Seventh Heaven.* His friends all tried to dissuade him from the venture. The play, as the cast pointed out, is about a dirty sewer rat who pops up and down through a manhole in a Paris alley and the characters are drunkards, thieves, and prostitutes. The cast, disgusted, resigned. Golden was determined to go through with the production despite all protests. At length the curtain rose upon *Seventh Heaven.* It ran in New York two years, was played by stock company theaters, and was produced in the movies.

Indelible memories of his war experience as an infantry officer impelled an obscure London clerk in an insurance office to write a play, *Journey's End.* It was his spare-time hobby. He made something beautiful, just for the joy of the making. London managers, however, turned it down because, they asserted, the author knew the dugout but he didn't know the drama. Finally Maurice Browne, an Englishman who founded the Little Theatre in Chicago and who had been active in America for many years, decided to open his season at the Savoy with this play. Its triumph was immediate and overwhelming. The play made a fortune for Browne and for the author, R. C. Sherriff. It was hailed as "the greatest war play ever written."

The manuscript of *Abie's Irish Rose* was hawked about among New York producers by its author, Anne Nichols. No one would sponsor it. Miss Nichols eventually became her own producer. Critics almost universally condemned the play. Seats could be obtained at cut-rate prices for the first thirty-five weeks. After that the play moved with irresistible momentum. It is estimated that 11,000,-000 persons, in all parts of the world, have seen this comedy. It enjoyed an uninterrupted run on the New York stage of 2,327 performances, covering a span of five years, and exceeding the previous theatrical record by more than eleven performances. New York was not alone in its acceptance of the offering. In Washington it was patronized more enthusiastically than any other play, before or since. Other cities, too, yielded in the same unconditional fashion to what the pundits had termed "cheap hokum." The author became many times a millionaire.

Hellzapoppin did all right on Broadway despite the critics; so did *The New Hellzapoppin,* with Olsen and Johnson still in the role of producers and head comedians. Said the *Time* reviewer:

> When *Hellzapoppin* opened last season the critics muttered a curt No, but the public howled an emphatic Yes, has been howling Yes, Yes, a Thousand Times Yes ever since. When the new *Hellzapoppin* opened last week, the critics acknowledged themselves licked. They knew they might just as well reason with an earthquake or talk back to a cannon. . . .
>
> Stripped of its unsurpassable insanity, the new *Hellzapoppin,* like the old, is the worst kind of ham vaudeville. But, as a tourist once grumbled, "Take away the mountains and the lakes, and what is there to Switzerland?" [23]

The screen version of *Little Women* was made with considerable hesitancy because the producers were very dubious as to whether it would appeal to audiences of the present time. There was talk of modernizing it, with Constance Bennett tentatively cast as Jo. Fortunately, wiser heads saw the folly of such a course. The picture was made in its historical context, with Katherine Hepburn as Jo, and its reception was so enthusiastic as to dwarf all predictions. The commentary of Elinor Hughes summarized the situation:

> Beautifully directed, admirably cast, it was staged so perfectly that inhabitants of Concord might well feel that they were right at home while the pic-

[23] *Time,* December 25, 1939.

ture was unreeling. There was no hysterical excitement, no gun-play, no last-minute rescue, no hard-boiled characters talking out of the sides of their mouths, no shady ladies and no mysterious strangers or evil influences. In short, a film that violated all the accepted canons of screen tradition has been a tremendous money-maker and there will probably be plenty of headaches as a result.[24]

3. SONGS

Experts whose profession it is to judge the merits of new songs have the same difficult time trying to guess what the public will like. Snap judgments or any other kinds of intuitive evaluations are apt to prove erroneous. Billy Hill's *Last Round-Up* was stowed away in a publisher's safe for two years to make room for more promising material. It was "discovered" in the process of housecleaning when a staff member tried it out, and decided maybe it wasn't so bad after all. Out of the rubbish into the "big-time"!

There's a Long, Long Trail was headed for the limbo of forgotten melodies until it finally won favorable attention.

No song of World War I was more popular than *There's a Long, Long Trail;* no other has remained so poignantly associated with the marching troops of 1917. Yet few realize that the music was composed a year before war broke out, and that the composer, Alonzo Elliott, a Yale senior, had Napoleon's retreat from Moscow in mind when he first picked out the tune on his piano. It made a hit when he sang it at a fraternity banquet; but American music publishers weren't interested.

In 1914, Elliott went to Cambridge University, and while shopping for a piano for his room, he tested each instrument with the *Long, Long Trail*. The tune so enchanted the dealer that he advised a music publisher to buy the song.

From the day when homesick Canadian soldiers rolled out the tune from a ship coming down the Thames its popularity was assured. It sold 4,000,000 copies.[25]

4. SPEECHES

Lincoln's Gettysburg Address was not hailed with enthusiasm by the hearers or by the editors who commented on the occasion which has since come to be regarded as so historic. Newspapermen were practically unanimous in their condemnation. The *Patriot and Union* of nearby Harrisburg took Lincoln to task for his dedicatory remarks: "The President acted without sense and without constraint in a pan-

---

[24] Boston *Herald,* December 25, 1933.
[25] *Reader's Digest,* November, 1939.

orama that was gotten up more for the benefit of his party than for the honor of the dead. . . . We pass over the silly remarks of the President; for the credit of the nation we are willing that the veil of oblivion shall be dropped over them and that they shall no more be repeated or thought of." And the Chicago *Times* fumed: "The cheek of every American must tingle with shame as he reads the silly flat, and dish-watery utterances of the man who has to be pointed out to intelligent foreigners as the President of the United States." Wrote the correspondent of the London *Times:* "Anything more dull and commonplace it would not be easy to produce." [26]

B. SAMPLING

Since it is so difficult to predict what the public will like, it is advisable, wherever possible, to apply sampling techniques such as those developed in consumer research and market analysis.[27] In the realm of the theater, for example, the sound-level meter for registering the volume of applause has been employed to good advantage by the Marx brothers to improve their shows. Before opening in New York they made a tour of the "tank" towns to try out their jokes. Puns and clown skits that registered low on the sound-level meter which they had secreted backstage were replaced with new gags. By the time the Marx brothers reached New York, any producer could tell them their show would be a success by glancing at their sound chart.

It has long been a custom for producers to try out their shows in New Haven because they know that collegiate audiences are critical and relatively uninhibited in the expression of their feelings about the performances. It would save time and money, of course, to be able to evaluate a play or movie or book ahead of time but such a feat would require a more intimate knowledge of human nature *en masse* than any student of social psychology can claim at present.

Better still, where the problem of taste calls for a study on a wider scale, is a poll of public likes and dislikes, like the one Gallup conducted in 1941 to uncover the habits and attitudes of U.S. movie-goers. This poll was sponsored by R.K.O. as a means of obtaining more accurate "tabs" on the American movie audience. Gallup set up a special organization to conduct the study: the Audience Research Institute.

[20] From *Abraham Lincoln: The War Years* by Carl Sandburg, as condensed in *Reader's Digest,* July, 1936. Reprinted by permission of Harcourt, Brace and Company, Inc.

[27] Refer to pp. 73-78.

The Institute proceeded to explode a number of Hollywood illusions. It was learned that 54,275,000 go to the movies each week, not 80,000,000 as the Hays office had claimed; admissions in 1940 added up to $700,000,000 cash, not a billion-dollar-a-year box-office gross, as claimed by the movie Czar. On Sundays 11,500,000 movie fans throng the theaters while 34,000,000 radio fans listen to Jack Benny on the air; on Mondays 5,428,000 go to the movies, while 26,000,000 stay home to hear the Lux Radio Theater program. Of movie-goers under 30 (85 per cent of all movie audiences), 54 per cent are male; of those over 30, 53.5 per cent are female. This proportion varies, of course, for different shows: *Rebecca* attracted a 71 per cent female audience, *Arizona*, 75 per cent male. Men go alone to the movies more often than women. When mixed couples attend the cinema, the woman selects the picture more often than the man. Women don't go for comedians. . . . Propaganda features fizzle. Ace cinemaddicts are 19-year-olds. The typical movie-goer is 27 years old, earns $28 a week. Laggard are folks over 30, who grow out of the habit of going to the movies, as they marry, have babies, and spend more time at home. Since 65% of the U.S. bolts the evening meal before 6:30, 90% before 7:30, fans have plenty of time to sit through double features. Only 4% of the cinemaudience stays away because of double features. People are overwhelmingly in favor of the double bill in towns showing a twin program, just as overwhelmingly against the twin bill in single-feature towns. Fans go to see the stars, and a majority of them think the stars are not overpaid. The fourteen leading favorites with men and boys are all males; the fourteen favorites with women are evenly split between male and female stars. Women, however, generally go to pictures to see women. Most cinemaddicts are inclined to bestow their greatest affection upon stars of their own age and sex. . . . Advance publicity is very important to a picture's box-office success. From now on competition from radio and other entertainment media and an increasingly more critical public are likely to make flops flop harder, give Hollywood all it can do to stay out of the red. No picture can expect to achieve a big box-office success without drawing customers from all age levels and groups. But there is no sure-fire formula for producing that kind of picture. . . . At present Hollywood is missing the velvet by failing to make pictures for people over 30 years of age in the average and above-average income groups.[28]

Gallup has taken some of the guesswork out of movie production by finding out ahead of time, through Audience Research, Inc. (ARI), what the people think of a particular theme and the stars who might be enlisted to play the leading roles. Armed with a brief summary of a movie story, ARI interviewers in some 100 cities and towns ask people: Would you like this movie? How much? Why? Poll results are translated into an *index of audience interest.* The average

[28] *Time,* July 21, 1941.

"A" picture rates 100, will gross $1,000,000; a rating of 125 will mean around $2,000,000. The index on *White Cargo,* for example, was 121; on *For Me and My Gal,* 129; and these pictures grossed several million apiece. ARI predicted success for *Random Harvest,* and failure for *The Devil and Daniel Webster.* The forecasts were accurate within a few per cent.

A good example of how the tests help Hollywood is the case of RKO's Cary Grant picture *Mr. Lucky.* The main character was to be a colorful immigrant Greek gambler who helps some society ladies promote a charity ball and then makes off with the proceeds. The consumer poll showed that the story had two drawbacks. People did not like having the gambler represented as a Greek and they didn't like the idea of a hero's robbing a charity ball.

So the studio changed the hero to a Greek-American, and the robbing was done by the hero's rivals in his own gambling outfit. The hero tried to thwart their attempt and was wounded, thus redeeming himself in the eyes of the audience. With these changes, ARI's tests indicated that *Mr. Lucky* would gross three times as much as the average "A" picture. Its record thus far has more than borne out this prediction.[29]

Polling has thus minimized the risks in movie production. Perhaps we can now revise the famous witticism, "The public always knows what it wants just after it has seen it."

C. Fickleness of the Public Fancy

It is one problem to predict what the public will like; it is another to foretell how long the popularity will last. Public fancy is very fickle. Edgar Bergen and his impudent dummy, Charlie McCarthy, toured the United States and Europe in vaudeville with only moderate success until Bergen broke into radio via a night club, to become the radio sensation of 1937. Charlie McCarthy was momentarily the People's Choice, but, like Trotzky, he may be acclaimed today and forgotten tomorrow. When Napoleon was being cheered as he rode through the streets of Paris, a friend asked him why the applause did not seem to elicit any enthusiasm on his part. Napoleon replied that the crowds would cheer just as loudly the next day if he were being led to the guillotine. It is ever so. Why, some one asked, did the crowds cheer Dempsey when he fought Tunney for the championship of the world?

[29] Quoted from W. A. Lydgate: "Hollywood Listens to the Audience." Condensation in the *Reader's Digest,* April, 1944, of an article entitled "Audience Pre-testing Heads Off Flops, Forecasts Hits, for Movie Producers" which appeared in *Sales Management,* March 15, 1944.

Tunney was a marine overseas in World War I. He fought for his country. Dempsey went to a shipyard and stayed awhile. The movies showed him in new overalls and patent leather shoes. He was called a slacker, and whether justly or not, public opinion was decidedly against him. But a few years later when he entered the ring against the fighting marine, the big majority was roaring for Dempsey to win. Possibly the public reaction was due to rumors that Tunney read Shakespeare.

Popularity depends on so many subtle factors: the timeliness of an achievement, the mood at a given moment, sponsorship by persons of prestige, the spread of rumors, and the appearance of rivals for public acclaim. Anything that becomes the rage is apt to be short-lived in its monopoly of attention. Shifting interests call for new persons, new programs to applaud. Suggestion and imitation build up new things to get excited about, the public fancy is centered upon some object until the next interest comes along that happens to carry appeal. Whether, in each case, we can say that "such popularity must be deserved" is a moot question of values that we may leave for other investigations to determine.

Chapter 10

PROPAGANDA

THE PERSON who engages in propaganda presents an emotional stimulus to other individuals for the purpose of influencing them to adopt a certain belief or to follow a certain line of action. Suggestion is the fundamental process, though persuasion may be employed to clinch the case. The propagandist is essentially a promoter interested in stirring up enthusiasm for some program that is dear to him. He may paint a poster urging young Americans to enlist and to take up arms against the foe, or to buy War Bonds to beat the Nazis; or he may be a Nazi cartoonist seeking to discredit the Atlantic Charter; or he may be a Japanese flier dropping leaflets ("surrender tickets") among American Marines in the Solomons, depicting a female nude on one side, offering an invitation to surrender on the other; or a Japanese radio broadcaster aiming to undermine Chinese morale:

America is China's ally. Americans say they love and admire the Chinese. But can you go to America, can you become citizens? No. Americans don't want you. They just want you to do their fighting. Their Exclusion Act names you and says you are unfit for American citizenship. If Generalissimo Chiang really has influence in America, why has he not had this stigma erased from American law? There will be no such discrimination against you in the Greater East Asia Co-Prosperity Sphere.[1]

Many persons erroneously think that propaganda is synonymous with deception based upon lies. This is a mistaken notion. Some propaganda is founded upon prevarication, as, for example, the fake radio news flash presumably from Boston, actually from Berlin, to the effect that Boston customers of the black market in meat were very well "pleased" with the "quality" of their purchases, and that it was a government trick to say black market meat contained disease germs. The most effective propaganda, however, is based upon truth, pre-

[1] *Time,* June 14, 1943.

sented forcefully and consistently. It is best to stick to the truth because such a policy obviates worrying about one's lies being exposed, and because, in the long run, a reputation for being reliable encourages credence. An appeal is no less propaganda for being honest: thus Hitler was resorting to truthful propaganda when he goaded the Nazi fighters by predicting in vivid terms the suffering they would

(Courtesy, James Montgomery Flagg.)

(Courtesy, Belmont Radio Corp.)

German Jibe at Atlantic Charter.

Surrender Ticket.

have to face if they lost the war; so was Eisenhower when he told the Italians in Sicily they would get more to eat if they laid down their arms; and so, too, was the *March of Time* newsreel, back in 1941, in warning America of Japan's militaristic designs on the Dutch East Indies and on American possessions in the Pacific.   In each of these cases, the propagandist was telling the truth but telling it with an end in view: to precipitate action by arousing emotion.   Propaganda is sometimes true, sometimes untrue; it is always an appeal to emotion, made for some deliberate purpose.

For our purposes, the subject of propaganda may be conveniently treated in terms of the techniques used for influencing others "with reference to predetermined ends" and in terms of the agencies carrying on propaganda in modern society.   We shall consider these two phases separately, though in actual practice they belong together. Our concluding section will be a brief review of political propaganda in the United States, Russia, and Nazi Germany, respectively.[2]

I. TECHNIQUES OF PROPAGANDA

The expert propagandist must be well versed in the psychology of suggestion in order to succeed in manipulating others for the purposes he has in mind, whether he is engaged in peacetime propaganda or in wartime propaganda.[3]

A. GENERAL PRINCIPLES

Authorities agree that the wise propagandist will inform himself thoroughly concerning the human attitudes to which appeals are going to be directed, for it is only through the enlistment of social values that the desired action can be evoked.   Thus the Nazi short-wave propaganda was clever in appealing to the American sense of fair play by urging Americans to stop the Allied air forces from bombing helpless civilians in German cities.   That this well-designed appeal hit the right (soft) spot was evidenced in subsequent speeches and letters-to-editors condemning such unnecessary brutality.   Japanese propaganda also appealed to our ideal of fair play by citing examples of racial discrimination and by charging us with "white imperialism." American counter-propaganda, conversely, had to be formulated to fit the Japanese character.   Menefee suggested Americans improve their treatment of Nisei in the United States and then publicize this fact;

---

[2] The role of propaganda in fostering morale is discussed in Chapter 11, "Social Consciousness: Morale."

[3] Refer to the early section in Chapter 7, "Suggestion."

he warned that pro-democratic appeals would be futile because these would have no meaning for the Japanese, that attempts to scare the Japs by hinting about the great hardships in store for them would only be interpreted as a challenge; rather, the American propagandist should exploit the Japanese fear of ridicule and their superstitiousness, and combat their "win or die" idea by persuading them that defeat would not mean destruction for the nation.

The propagandist, according to Doob, must be acquainted with the various kinds of propaganda—*revealed, concealed,* and *delayed revealed*—and plan his approach with reference to the particular kind of perception he is going to evoke. In the *delayed revealed* type of appeal, for example, the propagandist does not reveal his aim immediately. He postpones the revelation until he has aroused auxiliary and related attitudes first; in other words, he prepares the ground thoroughly before planting the seed. "Some of the more sophisticated advertisements use this latter type of propaganda: a lengthy introduction serves to arouse related attitudes and then, in the last paragraph, the advertiser finally reveals his purpose by indicating inconspicuously the particular product he desires to have purchased." [4] This principle of preparing the way before delivering the suggestion is endorsed by Rogerson, who cites the technique of the commercial advertising expert who "has long recognized the necessity for a general goodwill background against which he can press the advertisement of a particular branded product." [5] One can see the truth of this principle demonstrated in the failure of Nazi propaganda in the United States during Hitler's campaign to conquer the world. The Germans sent out plenty of literature, but little was gained by their machinations since Americans were in no mood to "fall" for such claims as the one that the people of Holland were happy at last to find employment under the beneficent Nazi occupation. One cannot put an idea across in an unfriendly atmosphere. Winning friends comes first as a prelude to influencing people.

Seven devices of the propagandist were described by the Institute of Propaganda Analysis. They were first delineated by the bulletin entitled "How to Detect Propaganda" which appeared in *Propaganda Analysis,* November, 1937. The purpose of each device is to lead the respondent into accepting or rejecting a proposition without examining the evidence. The seven devices may be designated as follows:

[4] L. W. Doob: *Propaganda: Its Psychology and Technique,* p. 105. Henry Holt & Co., 1935.
[5] S. Rogerson: *Propaganda in the Next War,* p. 160. 1938.

1. *Name-Calling*

Calling names is a familiar device for discrediting the other fellow: "im ported radical," "Communist Jew," "international banker."

2. *Glittering Generality*

An indefinite, vague, high-sounding abstraction may evoke emotional support for a proposition by inhibiting critical discrimination. For example:

"If our opponents get control of our government, it will mean the end of *civilization.*"

3. *Transfer*

A rally for a political candidate may feature the "Star Spangled Banner" and a salute to the American flag—then the candidate is brought to the focus of attention, carrying with him the loyalty that was originally stirred by our national anthem and our flag.

4. *Testimonial*

This device consists of quoting well-known people as endorsing a cause. The prestige invoked may be legitimate or illegitimate. Our advertisements abound in this sort of appeal based on a quotation from Mrs. Astor bilt upon almost any topic.

5. *Plain Folks*

The politician mixes with the people, talking with farmers, hobnobbing with truck drivers, kissing babies, and generally giving the impression that he is a regular fellow.

6. *Card Stacking*

"The selection and use of facts or falsehoods, illustrations or distractions, and logical or illogical statements in order to give the best or the worst possible case for an idea, program, person, or product." Certain implications can be encouraged by stating that the office-holder possesses the virtue of being loyal to his friends. Unwarranted conclusions can be fostered by means of emphasis, by omitting relevant details, by arranging statements in a certain order so as to provoke inferences based upon mere juxtaposition of ideas.

7. *Band Wagon*

Everybody's doing it—why not you? Cast your vote for the winner.

This appeal is especially effective when it produces the "impression of universality" which we mentioned in our discussion of crowd psychology.[6]

---

[6] For the full discussion see A. M. and E. B. Lee: *The Fine Art of Propaganda,* New York, Harcourt, Brace and Co. and the Institute for Propaganda Analysis, 1939.

So much for the general principles involved in the preparation and dissemination of propaganda. Now for a study of how the art is practiced in promoting war.

B. Tricks of Wartime Propaganda

The art of propaganda really came into its own during World War I; it was perfected during World War II.[7] There were various techniques employed during the earlier conflict: suppressing bad news, until it could be offset with good news; disguising reverses by calling them euphemistically "strategic retreats"; evoking bitter hatred for the barbaric Hun and the Beast of Berlin (the Kaiser); inspiring moral zeal "to make the world safe for democracy." These tricks of the trade were exposed by numerous writers who had seen the art in practice from the inside.

As we look back now we realize that these pioneers were mere amateurs in molding public opinion. Instead of returning to that earlier period, therefore, it will be more worth while for us to concentrate our attention on World War II, limiting our discussion to some of the salient phases of propaganda featured in this world-wide conflict of armed forces and contradictory ideologies.

1. Attributing barbarism to the enemy

The British painted a dark picture of Nazi decadence and depravity, citing in one *White Paper* the gruesome details of life in Nazi concentration camps. This charge was immediately parried by radio broadcasts from captured British soldiers who told the world, under Goebbels' sponsorship, that German prison camps were actually better than first-class hotels back home. P. G. Wodehouse did his bit in recommending these camps for a happy stay.

The German Library of Information distributed its periodical bulletin, *Facts in Review,* informing Americans of the eminent progress being made by Germans in the fields of literature, art, and science, with the implication that more progress had been made under Hitler's benevolent encouragement than people had witnessed during any similar period in the past history of mankind. One of the outstanding achievements of "the present German government," we were told, was "the Nazi program of securing farms against the depredations of mortgages and economic depressions," a dramatic demonstration of the humanitarian ideals that were motivating the German leaders,

---

[7] There was a brief discussion of propaganda in World War I, you remember, in Chapter 5, "The Unemployment of Intelligence."

while by way of contrast we were reminded that the inhuman British navy was at that very moment starving the poor people of Europe by means of a cold-blooded blockade.   Research in the German Library of Information succeeded in uncovering statements by various British authors that living conditions were not entirely wholesome in some parts of the British Empire; indeed, health conditions among the London masses turned out to be appalling, for "every seventh child in London is infested with vermin . . . and only every sixth child is properly nourished . . . in the heart of London alone there are twenty-five thousand underfed children . . . nearly half of the five-year olds have bad teeth . . . nearly every third child of that age has defective eyesight . . . and besides, one per cent of Britain's population possesses fifty per cent of her wealth"—all of which should convince any fair-minded person that the British were not fit even to rule the waves.   Playing on the same theme, Lord Haw Haw, an expatriated Englishman who served the Nazis well as a broadcaster, sought to drive a wedge between the British common people and their rulers by informing the English laboring class that their callous leaders had inveigled them into a stupid imperialistic war which they could not win.   To make his point more vivid, Lord Haw Haw one night had the "British Minister for Muddling Through" arrive at the gates of Heaven.   "Get away," cried Saint Peter. "Go and live for a year in a London slum.   That will be your Purgatory and Hell itself couldn't be any worse."   Light on slum conditions was offered by the German Library of Information in the form of citations from a book entitled *The Slum Problem* (1928), written by an Englishman named Townroe while he was in charge of the Housing Problem for the Ministry of Health.   In this book the Nazis discovered conditions which were very shocking to their German sensibilities, such as three families asleep in a single room upstairs in a house in a prosperous township in Lancashire, where, according to the Nazi version, "the air was foul, with so many human beings herded together like pigs, except that each litter of pigs would have had a sty for itself." [8]

In the propaganda war it is easy to prove that the enemy is uncivilized—the evidence can be witnessed in the inexcusable atrocities he commits.   Almost everybody recognizes that there are certain things that decent people do not resort to even in the heat of battle. The enemy cannot be forgiven for bombing non-military objectives, for killing civilians indiscriminately, for crippling helpless women and innocent children, for destroying churches, libraries, hospitals,

[8] *Facts in Review,* October 2, 1940.

nuseums, and other priceless heritages of mankind. It was the enemy
who started this inhuman destruction and the only effective way to
top it is to pay him back in kind. Such reprisals become inevitable,
ach side charging the other with the responsibility of initiating the
unfair tactics. One characteristic bit of propaganda from Danzig
harged the British with having supplied mustard gas to the Poles.
This charge-of-atrocity device is employed to confirm the claim that
he enemy needs civilizing.

2. UNDERMINING CONFIDENCE IN THE ENEMY'S LEADERSHIP

The Nazis harped on the theme that the British upper classes
brought on this war, that the British workers were, consequently, dupes
o offer themselves as cannon-fodder just to preserve the privileges of
he effete English aristocracy. Lord Haw Haw in broadcasting to the
English people liked to refer to Anthony Eden as the man who is
"known for his good tailor and poor speeches"; in his references to
Churchill he labeled the Prime Minister as the "First Lord of the
Sea Bottom." The British propaganda agency was contemptuously
branded "The British Ministry of Mis-Information." Meanwhile,
Churchill and Hitler were engaging in *Name-Calling,* in which pastime they both excelled.

The British, on their part, kept circulating the prediction that at
any moment the rank and file of the German people would start a
revolution to force the abdication of the Nazi Party leadership. This
prediction was engineered, in part from Berlin, to promote wishful
thinking. The British, in turn, may have kept the rumor alive for
the purpose of reminding Nazi listeners that revolution might be a
good idea.

3. PINNING THE GUILT UPON THE ENEMY

If we were to accept the say-so of each nation, we would be forced to
conclude that every government has always worked steadfastly and consistently for peace. Germany told the world that she was fighting
against encirclement; that she had been forced to fight as a last resort for
self-preservation. *White Books* and *Blue Books* were written by both
sides to explain how the enemy was solely responsible for plunging the
world into conflict.[9] According to the Nazis the British had stirred
up Polish attacks on harmless German citizens. The *German White*

---

[9] *German White Book: Documents concerning the Last Phase of the German-
Polish Crisis.* Published by the German Library of Information, New York. 1939.
See "White Book and Blue Book: Who Started the War?" *Facts in Review,* July
8, 1940.

Book said so.[10] The Nazis explained that they invaded Norway to "protect" Norway against threatened invasion by the British, and they published "The Stratforce Plan" as evidence of collusion between the British and the Norwegians. *The German White Book, No. 4,* published by the German Library of Information for American readers, was entitled "Britain's Designs on Norway" and the announcement promised "Startling Revelations on British Intrigue in Norway." [11]

One of the most effective documents influencing American opinion on the question of who started all the trouble was Neville Henderson's *Failure of a Mission,* excerpts from which appeared in *Life* (March 25-April 8, 1940). According to Henderson the war was made in Berlin. Incidentally, Henderson's inside story of Hitler's psychopathic personality—a sort of clinical case-study—must have influenced many readers to believe that Hitler's leadership was definitely psychotic.

4. PROCLAIMING NOBLE WAR AIMS

"War aims or peace aims—which are used interchangeably—cannot be separated from the propaganda which helps to win wars. A clear understanding of aims builds and maintains morale. Without it, soldiers and citizens are assailed by doubts. They ask, 'What are we fighting for?' They say, 'It's a phoney war.' Morale declines; fighting spirit droops." [12]

The Nazis told the world confidentially that all they wanted was *Lebensraum*. This term was explained by *Facts in Review:*

"Lebensraum" simply means "living space"—or perhaps "breathing space." A man occupies only a few cubic feet of space, but to live he must have around him a space from which he can draw the elements necessary to life. An individual is an organism. So is a nation. Both must have breathing space or they suffocate.

When translated or interpreted into its equivalent English terms, the German word "Lebensraum" loses its sinister appearance. It simply becomes a normal and fundamental aspiration.[13]

The Nazis also insisted that the German people were entitled to their share of the earth's resources, that they could not see just why God

---

[10] *Polish Acts of Atrocity against the German Minority in Poland.* Published by the German Library of Information, New York. 1940.

[11] *Facts in Review*, August 26, 1940.

[12] "War Aims in War Propaganda." *Propaganda Analysis*, March 27, 1941. Reproduced by permission of Alfred McClung Lee, Executive Director.

[13] August 16, 1939.

had chosen the British to monopolize the largest part of the earth's surface. The have-nots were due for their inning, Hitler warned, as he promised his followers to get the material goods necessary for maintaining a standard of living befitting the superior German race. Hitler professed that his aims included no "territorial ambitions" in Europe or elsewhere. All he had in mind was economic cooperation under German domination. The Germans, he explained, merely wanted living space and something to live on, for a change. This claim to a share in the good things of life was sufficiently justified by the facts in the case to constitute a very effective propaganda weapon for the Nazi cause. The alleged injustice even touched the British conscience so keenly that Englishmen were led to confess they had made a botch of the situation following the last war, and to promise to do better next time.

"The British had a war aim: crush Hitler. It was immediate, peremptory, and it was constantly reiterated by Winston Churchill." [14] The British propagandists, in response to public demand, felt that Britain should define its aims more elaborately and more exaltedly. Consequently they claimed that it was a war between democracy and dictatorship, with Britain acting as the last line of defense for the civilized world. This definition of the war aim provoked some confusion when later on Russia complicated the picture by joining hands with the British in an effort to stop Hitler: the line-up of democracy vs. dictatorship seemed no longer valid. The British fought on, despite the confusion in verbalizing their aims, in the hope that Hitler could be stopped first and a philosophical justification could be developed subsequently, when there would be more time for thought. Still some people were wondering just what the future would bring and so in response to this demand for clarification, numerous books were published to explain what the British were fighting for, notably Angell's *For What Do We Fight?* (1939), and Nicolson's *Why Britain Is at War* (1939). To bolster up the morale of the home folks, British leaders paused in their prosecution of the war to promise that the fruits of victory would be distributed equitably to all classes in English society. Some of the more excitable Britons even pictured a classless society in which Dukes and Lords would no longer ride to the hounds, shouting "Tally-ho" while the working classes were shouting for bread. In short, the British leaders pledged themselves to usher in an economic democracy after the war, thus to justify the assertion that the war was being waged on behalf of democracy against the threat of dictators.

[14] "War Aims in War Propaganda." *Loc. cit.*

The Beveridge plan was announced to give weight to this promise of security for all classes of English society.

C. War Propaganda and the United States

Both the Nazis and the British had to face the problem of influencing American public opinion, the Nazis to stop the Yanks from intervening, the British to induce the Yanks to come to the rescue. The aims and programs were necessarily different in the two cases.

1. THE NAZI PROGRAM

From the start the Nazis realized that they could never enlist American aid in their search for *Lebensraum;* the best they could hope to accomplish would be to keep the United States from meddling in European affairs. This sentiment was prominent in the broadcasts of Kaltenbach, a former Iowan, who was the chief Nazi radio spokesman when appeals were addressed to the United States. His communications to "Dear Harry" ran something like this:

Man, what a picture it is to see Hermann Goering's war birds soaring overhead! Boy, are they fast! Now, don't let the British drag America into this thing, Harry. Don't pull Britain's chestnuts out of the fire again.[15]

Until they were "exported" by President Roosevelt in the summer of 1941, the propaganda experts at the German Library of Information in New York were doing a fair job keeping down American sympathy for the British cause by stating the German case in as favorable a light as the facts would allow. And sometimes they did even better than the facts would allow, with pictures of bombed hospital wards, demolished churches, German doctors ministering to wounded Poles, German scientists advancing knowledge for the sake of all humanity, German women tenderly caring for kindergarten children, German soldiers home on furlough expressing their love for home and family, German poets and dramatists carrying on their noble work in spite of war's unhappy distractions. Frequent references were made to British misrule in India, to the atrocious conditions in England's industrial centers, to British misrepresentation of war casualties, to the English perfidy in general, to the hopelessness of the Allied cause. *Facts in Review* was distributed regularly to many American readers. The publication was cleverly conceived and cleverly executed. It was an uphill task, however, to enlist American sympathy.

[15] A. A. Michie: "War as Fought by Radio." *American Legion Magazine,* June 1940

2. THE BRITISH PROGRAM

The aim of the British was to win the United States as an ally. America was looked upon as "The Greatest Neutral." [16] It was easy to persuade Americans to participate in relief either in the form of Bundles for Britain or of knitting for the soldiers at the front. In this way, Americans were led to identify themselves with the Allies.

Thus were America's humanitarian impulses mobilized. . . . In the swift parade of events there was little attempt to conform to even the outward forms of neutrality. . . . As a method of stirring devotion, the relief pleas were invaluable. . . . The relief movement was, in short, a roll-call of affluent and high-placed men and women. Their professions of support were an early and major victory for the Allied Armies in America.[17]

One of the devices for enlisting American aid was the issuing of pessimistic bulletins stressing the critical need for American aid—at once. Rogerson, the English authority who wrote *Propaganda in the Next War,* had warned the British propagandists in 1938 that the security of the United States would have to be drastically threatened before Americans could be induced to join hands in common cause with the British. The British Ministry of Information, evidently heeding Rogerson's warning, circulated reports repeatedly concerning the increasing Nazi menace in South America.

The British had learned from their campaign of 1914-1917 how to overcome American neutrality. One thing that they remembered was the value of sending over prominent lecturers to reach the American public by enlisting the support of prominent Americans, particularly the intellectuals associated with the universities, men who could be counted on to volunteer their services in promoting pro-British sentiment.[18] One similarity between 1914 and 1939 was this fact—that the best propagandists for England and France were not British or Frenchmen; they were native Americans with attachments of various natures for the older lands.

King George VI and Queen Elizabeth, on a royal visit to Canada, stopped over in the United States. The king intimated on a number of occasions that Europe was looking to America for hope and guidance. His speeches referred pointedly to the fact that Britain and

---

[16] See H. Lavine and J. Wechsler: *War Propaganda and the United States,* Chapter 2, "The Greatest Neutral." Yale University Press, 1940.

[17] *Ibid.,* p. 112.

[18] See *ibid.,* Chapter 6, "Expeditionary Force."

America were sister democracies whose interests were substantially identical.

Also fitting into this pattern is Britain's exhibit at the New York World Fair. Center of the exhibit is the Magna Charta, Britain's famous charter of liberties, from which America's liberties are in part derived. Nearby is George Washington's family tree, emphasizing that the "Father of Our Country" was of British stock.[19]

Much of the British propaganda was carried on informally by means of personal contacts. Friendships were readily formed because of pro-Ally sentiment among Americans. These preexistent kindly attitudes were helpful to the British propagandists, for the British, though less so than the Germans, were faced with the task of surmounting isolationist, anti-war, anti-propaganda attitudes which were well developed in the United States.

3. AMERICAN RESISTANCE TO PROPAGANDA

The First World War was followed by a widespread reaction against the horrors of militarism and against the machinations of the propagandists. Many books were published exposing the futility of war. Among these were Remarque's *All Quiet on the Western Front* (1930), Stallings' *The First World War* (1933), and Trumbo's *Johnnie Got His Gun* (1939). Pacifism gained in popularity as people had time to look back and evaluate the consequences of our participation in the war to make the world safe for democracy. University undergraduates became particularly resistant to the pleas of the militarists. Some of them founded the Veterans of Future Wars, an organization for satirizing the folly of modern war. When World War II broke out, it has been estimated that undergraduates were predominantly isolationist and university faculty members predominantly interventionist.

Idealistic proclamations were viewed [by young people generally] with uneasy and continuing suspicion. It was possible for commentators to say that "the Allies are the lesser of two evils." But a "lesser evil" is not a fighting faith. Men are mobilized to die "for" ideals; negative slogans are not enough. Like the rest of America, undergraduates and others of the "draft age" saw distinctions between Germany and Britain; but the distinctions were not sufficiently clear-cut. So, at least, it appeared on American campuses, as

[19] "Britain Woos America." *Propaganda Analysis*, June 10, 1939. Reproduced by permission of Alfred McClung Lee, Executive Director.

in other sectors of American life, during the first months of the second World War.[20]

There was a conviction that we had wasted our time and our money back in 1917 fighting a war to end war, and that it would be unwise to make the same mistake again. We were fed up with the idea that we were obliged to fight other peoples' wars for them. This feeling was a very serious obstacle in the way of British propaganda and it explains in part why Americans took such a long time before committing themselves to active support of the British cause.

Americans had been subjected for some time to peace propaganda against war propaganda. Conspicuous in the anti-war propaganda were the spectacular advertisements of World Peaceways, to which magazines gave free space. The "Hello, Sucker" drawing, which was the most famous of these peace advertisements, appeared in 1935. This was only one phase of a vast effort to propagandize the American public in favor of peace. The resultant pacifistic sentiment was another obstacle to be overcome by the British Ministry of Information.

Another formidable obstacle in the path of British propaganda lay in the fact that the American people had been "put wise" to the tricks of the propagandists and did not intend to be "taken in" again. The propagandists of World War I had gone out of their way to tell us how clever they had been in deceiving us. Some of the most effective exposures of war propaganda were engineered by the editors of *Look* magazine. In January, 1938, they began publication of a series of articles revealing the techniques by means of which the war propagandists exploited the public in the promotion of World War I. These articles were later grouped together and published as *A Contribution to the Cause of Peace,* an exposé that was read by some forty million Americans.

The *Look* campaign was just one phase of an educational program designed to immunize Americans against propaganda appeals. In October, 1937, a group of Americans organized the Institute for Propaganda Analysis. They were motivated in this undertaking by the conviction that there was a special need for "propaganda analysis" in a democracy, for under our form of government the citizens must learn to "search things out for themselves." The Institute was founded "as a non-profit educational institution to analyze the propagandas of today and to formulate methods whereby American citizens can make

---

[20] Lavine and Wechsler: *op. cit.,* p. 152.

their own analyses of 'attempts to persuade them to do something that they might not do if they were given all of the facts.' " [21]   The editors stated in a prefatory note explaining the purposes of their program that "there are three possible ways to deal with propaganda.   You can suppress it, meet it with counter-propaganda, or analyze it and try to see how much truth there is in it.   We are going to analyze it."   The following are some of the articles published in *Propaganda Analysis:*

"How to Detect Propaganda."   November, 1937.
"How to Analyze Newspapers."   January, 1938.
"Newspaper Analysis."   February, 1938.
"The Movies and Propaganda."   March, 1938.
"Propaganda Techniques of German Fascism."   May, 1938.
"Propaganda on the Air."   June, 1938.
"Public Relations Counsel and Propaganda."   August, 1938.

Each of these bulletins included "Suggested Activities and Discussion Notes," and also "References." [22]

Interest in this campaign against propaganda was apparently at a high peak in 1937, for in that year the Institute for Propaganda Analysis was organized and in that same year the Seventh Year Book of the National Council for the Social Studies was devoted to *Education Against Propaganda*.   Included in this volume were such articles as "Teaching Resistance to Propaganda," and "Teaching Students in Social Studies Classes to Guard against Propaganda."

Educators tend to be overoptimistic in the confidence that they place in the effectiveness of such a program for inoculating people against propaganda.   There is undoubtedly some value in training the public to detect the tricks of the propagandists, but perhaps we should go no further than to adopt the "timid" and "not too pious" hope expressed by Doob when he stated reservedly that "the ability to label something propaganda and someone a propagandist and a simultaneous insight into the fundamental nature of the process of propaganda will combine to render many kinds of propaganda less effective." [23]

The debunking of old slogans had succeeded in "disarming" the United States by instilling a cynicism that left us "defenseless before an aggressor," Archibald MacLeish penitently confessed, speaking for

[21] *Propaganda Analysis,* Volume I, p. iv.
[22] The Institute for Propaganda Analysis suspended publication of its bulletins in 1941 "for the duration."
[23] Doob: *op. cit.,* p. 5.

himself, for Ernest Hemingway, and for other "debunkers." [24]   Jesse
Homer Newlon, addressing the 1940 summer session of Teachers
College, Columbia University, broke down and admitted that he was
guilty, along with other educators, of misleading the younger generation into believing that there is nothing worth fighting for.   This
devaluation of war, he confessed, had been a mistake, one that should
be corrected before it was too late:

> We have taught many fallacies.
> We have taught that war never settles anything.   Look at the Revolution-
> ary War and tell me that war never settled anything. . . .   Try to tell a na-
> tive of Norway that war never settles anything, or a native of Denmark or
> the Baltic countries.
> We have taught that the last war was caused by the munitions makers.   I
> think only simple people can find things that simple.
> Another fallacy is all this propaganda about propaganda. . . .   I believe
> in propaganda analysis, but there is such a thing as carrying it too far.   We've
> been bringing up a group of young people who don't believe in anything any
> more. . . .   Some day someone will cry "Wolf" when there is a wolf, and
> we'll say it's propaganda, and we'll be destroyed.
> We have been teaching a sentimental program of peace education.
> There'll be no peace in the world . . . until we solve world problems. . . .
> We must teach loyalty to American democracy directly and deliberately—
> loyalty to our institutions so that youth will . . . fight for them if necessary.[25]

Whether or not Americans generally were influenced by these ex-
posés of propaganda it may be categorically stated that many United
States citizens were wise enough to the ways of the propagandists
to maintain a skeptical attitude toward the pleas of the intervention-
ists.   Most of the appeals recalled the hectic days of World War I:
there was a "deadly parallel," in as much as the words and the slogans seemed definitely reminiscent of the earlier propaganda.   The
mention of fighting again for democracy brought back "deep and
angry recollections" of the disillusionment that followed our last attempt to straighten out Europe's complicated animosities.

The greatest obstacle to Allied propagandists in World War II was the
propaganda that preceded American entry into World War I.   Skeptics are
not crusaders, and disbelief was the chief inheritance of America from the
last war.   In the long and depressing postwar hangover, three propositions
had been deeply entrenched: first, that the war to end war and save democ-

[24] See *Time,* June 3, 1940.
[25] See *Time,* July 22, 1940.

racy had enthroned war and created totalitarianism; second, that the war to protect democracy had deep commercial roots; third, that the altruistic banners under which the war was fought had been devised by glib-tongued propagandists. For the first proposition the evidence was September 3 and Adolf Hitler; for the second, the widely publicized findings of the Nye committee; for the third, the postwar revelations and confessions of wartime propagandists. Justly or erroneously, the bulk of America was convinced that the last war was a futile enterprise sold under false pretenses.[26]

In view of these developments, it was not surprising that a Gallup poll of April, 1937, showed that 71 per cent of the American public believed that American entry into World War I had been a mistake. Obviously the average American did not mean to abandon peace for war again unless a serious emergency developed. Americans endorsed the lend-lease policy for aiding Britain, with some reluctance. Only by degrees did we come to see the wisdom of helping the Allies to stem the Nazi tide.

Raymond Swing noted a widespread skepticism here in America that prevented us during the early months of the conflict from following the war news in any intelligent fashion.

With the outbreak of the war, many Americans set themselves deliberately not to believe most of what they read or were told about it. The memories of the World War were already blurred, but there could be no forgetting the propaganda of that period. . . . Since the truth was in any case to be incomplete, and was also to be artfully distorted, the best attitude, these people thought, was one of aloof skepticism. Newspapers reminded their readers that their own foreign dispatches were not to be trusted; radio stations, before the reading of the news, repeated the reminders; and for the first part of the war, news was subjected to an initial welcome of incredulity. . . . Only after many months did the warnings against propaganda become less strident, and the preconceived suspicions die down. This was when the war of itself had taken shape and meaning. It had become too clear and too menacing to be dismissed as the product of suppressed truth or the diabolical twisting of fact.[27]

The pressure of events was needed to arouse America from its lethargy and its nonchalance which were in part products of the long campaign against propaganda. Strenuous measures were required to make us realize how serious was the threat to our security. Members of the Committee to Defend America by Aiding the Allies, headed by

[26] Lavine and Wechsler: *op. cit.*, p. 89.
[27] Foreword, by Raymond Swing, to E. McInnis: *The War: First Year.* Oxford University Press (Canadian branch), 1940.

the late William Allen White, did all they could to stir their fellow citizens, even to the extent of featuring a "Stop Hitler Now" advertisement in leading newspapers. England had been a long time waking up and America was taking even longer.

When Japan treacherously attacked American outposts in the Pacific on December 7, 1941, while official Japanese representatives were in Washington supposedly negotiating terms for the maintenance of peace, propaganda in behalf of American participation became superfluous, for Americans were inspired, a nation united, to make sure that no such menace should endanger us again. The Japanese could not have planned a situation more likely to promote American morale in favor of an all-out war on the Axis.

D. Psychological Warfare

The "Tricks of Wartime Propaganda" described earlier in this present chapter are phases of psychological warfare. Let us examine in more detail now the means by which war is waged psychologically.

It was the Nazis who perfected to the highest degree the psychological weapons of warfare. In characteristic German fashion, they went about their preparations with remarkable thoroughness. On April 1, 1937, Hitler signed a decree creating a permanent psychological department within the German army, thus organizing psychologists to play an important role in preparing the people for a total war: selecting and training officers and men, indexing and "typing" the "new German race," developing a morale offensive, designing political activities to engender an effective leadership-followership relation. Studies were made of soldiers' homesickness, the effect of war on civilian morale, the nation's religious and ethical attitude toward war, the problem of political faith, the manipulation of popular opinion through the press, radio, and film. Investigations were conducted to discover the strong points and weak points in foreign nations, the information gathered to be used as a basis for directing the Nazi foreign policy. Mass psychological training encouraged the people to take a masculine pride in competition, brawn, and the aggressive spirit. Contrary to the practice in the old German army whereby commissioned officers maintained a social distance between themselves and the common soldiers, Nazi officers were required to smoke and chat with their men, to attend mess frequently, to take an interest in barrack affairs, never to ridicule or reprimand a man before a whole company, to unearth good qualities, to extend felicitations on birthdays even to members of soldiers' families, never to "dress down" a whole company for individual mistakes. Objectors, religious or intellectual, were singled out as "germs of destruction" and turned over to the army psychologists for "treatment." Despite the Government hostility to religion, the army favored the presence of chaplains on the front and in the garrisons where they were regarded as morale-building agents. All means were employed to indoctrinate the German people with a positive attitude toward war. The Nazi system, dominated by the army, aimed to construct a personality integrated around racial pride, aggressiveness, and violence. The German psychologists did a superb job for the Fatherland.

The Nazis demonstrated their psychological acumen in preparing for war; they displayed the same keen insight in their prosecution of the war. During the early days of the conflict the Nazis kept everyone in suspense as to where they would strike next. They seemed to be threatening at all times. Periodic announcements informed the anxious world that "a secret weapon" had been discovered. The impression conveyed was that this new weapon would be devastating; henceforth there would be no use for the enemy even to try holding out any longer against the invincible Nazi machine.

The German propaganda experts developed a neat trick of timing their bulletins on the progress of the war in such a way as to achieve the maximum effect. In the early stages of the campaign, German bulletins would be brief; simply stating in a quiet, self-confident manner that the German offense was proceeding "according to schedule." The Nazis allowed the enemy to circulate all kinds of optimistic reports to the general effect that the Nazis were about to taste defeat. When these hopeful, wishful announcements from the enemy had built up a cumulative expectation of German failure, the Nazis would suddenly announce that "this phase of the war is over. The enemy have surrendered." Against the background of hope-for-Nazi-defeat such announcements were extremely demoralizing.

The Germans kept insisting on their ultimate victory. Short-wave broadcasts from Berlin described the increasing discontent among the British laboring class, the mounting toll of submarine destruction; then contrasted this "unhappiness" among the Allies with Germany's plentiful supply of food, her united home front, the "purposeful" reconstruction work being conducted in Poland and other occupied countries. The Nazi propagandists asserted that German dominion over the inferior races was predestined.

The concept of the *Blitzkrieg* was promulgated as a "strategy of terror." In physical terms, the *Blitzkrieg* meant a sudden attack initiated without the formality of declaring war, demoralizing the civilian population with explosive bombs and fire bombs and time bombs, as the Nazi *Luftwaffe* did over Warsaw, Rotterdam, and London. On the psychological side, the *Blitzkrieg* meant inspiring fear. Motion pictures of horrible air raids were shown to intimidate people who contemplated resisting Goering's irresistible air force. One of the most gruesome of these films was *The Baptism of Fire,* photographed by Nazi flyers while they devastated Poland. Based on the theory that "Might Makes Fright" this film was used to terrify audiences in neutral nations, to instill in them a fear of German strength. *Blitzkrieg im Westen* was another film designed to spread terror. To the world such photographs served notice of the might of German arms.

Fear-photography is a purely Nazi weapon. Ever since Hitler came to power, Europe has been slowly hypnotized by pictures of Nazi might: the fanaticism of mass gatherings, the virility of German males stripped to the waist, the unending columns of guns, tanks, and square-jawed soldiers. Each year the columns grew longer, the guns and tanks seemed more deadly, the goose-stepping soldiers looked more ominous. Since Poland, fear-photography has become a psychological prelude to invasion—standard procedure in the strategy of conquest.[28]

Another phase of the psychological warfare, as conducted by Germany, was a program of inconsistency designed to confuse the enemy. Threaten war in the interest of peace, thus leaving the enemy, potential or actual, bewildered. Sign a non-aggression pact with Russia and then attack Russia. The Nazi propagandists aimed to demoralize the enemy by destroying the cohesion, discipline, and collective morale of all his social groups. This strategy included the following tactics:

1. *Whispering Campaigns* to spread defeatist rumors and false news.
2. *Anti-Semitism Campaign* to get the Gentiles fighting among themselves over the Jewish question.
3. *Defeatist Propaganda* to undermine confidence.
4. *Ridicule of Authority*—poking fun at officials so as to destroy public respect for them.
5. *Violence* "displayed excessively, gratuitously, but not too frequently; the threat always remains a little shadowy and therefore all the more terrible."
6. *Rousing False Hopes* by circulating imaginary tales of Nazi defeats and then publishing the news of another major Nazi victory.

[28] See J. S. Bruner and G. Fowler: "The Strategy of Terror: Audience Response to *Blitzkrieg im Westen." Journal of Abnormal and Social Psychology,* 1941, 36, 561-574.

By means of these devices the Nazis were very successful in spreading panic abroad and disuniting their enemies so that they could take them on and beat them one at a time.   The fundamental strategy was to destroy the enemy from within by inducing him to suffer from mental confusion, contradictions of feeling, indecisiveness, and panic. Thus, propaganda for American consumption was aimed at encouraging debate and dissension so that war preparations would be held up by strikes and internal conflict.   Measures were adopted to counteract the effects of this insidious campaign, as the Office of Facts and Figures in Washington went into action to expose the artifices of the enemy to the American people.

IF YOU BELIEVE THESE THINGS, YOU'RE HITLER'S LITTLE SUCKER

The Office of Facts and Figures declared today that Hitler has adapted his propaganda strategy of "divide and conquer" to fit a United States at war and is trying to make this country believe that:

Democracy is dying.

Our armed forces are weak.

The "new order" is inevitable.

We are lost in the Pacific.

Our West Coast is in such grave danger there is no point in fighting on.

The British are decadent and "sold us a bill of goods."

The cost of the war will bankrupt the nation.

Civilian sacrifices will be more than we can bear.

Stalin is getting stronger and Bolshevism will sweep over Europe.

Our leaders are incompetent, our government incapable of waging war.

Aid to our Allies must stop.

Our real peril is the Japanese, and we must join Germany to stamp out the "yellow peril."

We must bring all our troops and weapons back to the United States and defend only our own shores.

The Chinese and the British will make a separate peace with Japan and Germany.

American democracy will be lost during the war.

The Office of Facts and Figures issued this list today, saying these were the propaganda objectives which "Hitler wants us to believe."   The list was contained in a pamphlet labelled "Divide and Conquer" which also embraced a discussion of propaganda technique used by Hitler in European nations both before and after they became involved in war.[29]

The radio has proved to be a convenient instrument for waging the "war of nerves."   In the strategy of war via the radio the speaker

[29] Boston *Herald*, March 29, 1942.

seeks to create a state of anxiety by engendering a mental conflict which cannot be resolved by unified action. The procedure begins with an effort on the part of the speaker to gain the listener's confidence and to reduce his resistance. Then the speaker attacks the institutions, traditional beliefs, and moral values revered by his audience, taking great care not to put anything in their place; thus the hearer is encouraged to become cynical and to doubt the validity of his own normal judgments. This skepticism is built up until a total loss of faith is presumably secured. The victim is then ready to be subjected to the strategy of terror, tales of imminent death and destruction. Lest this threat evoke a united defense, the speaker injects some "confusion" propaganda, suggesting that the corrupt society in which the person lives is not worth fighting for, that it would be better to lay down arms and to cooperate in the establishment of a New Order. In this process of weakening the enemy, there are four distinct phases which constitute the *Angstkrieg* (War of Nerves); first, a good-neighborly period; second, an aggressive stage consisting of a semi-factual approach, followed by a verbal bombardment, the vituperation being accurately timed to accompany an offensive on the military front; the third phase includes sinister threats, superlative lies, repeated warnings of the wrath to come, with frenzied injunctions to "get rid of your corrupt leaders and appeal for peace"; the fourth phase, prolongation of the state of confusion in order to keep the victims at the mercy of their new masters.

The United States was late in developing the machinery and the techniques of psychological warfare; we blissfully allowed the Germans a long head-start in psychological as well as in military preparedness. The American version of the psychological offensive—like the German—was predicated on the belief that warfare, to prove effective, must aim at changing the enemy's mind, must attempt to *"convert determination to resist into willingness to accept defeat."* The Roosevelt-Churchill demand for unconditional surrender, proclaimed at Casablanca and reiterated at Quebec, backed by the threat to "bomb, burn, and ruthlessly destroy" the people responsible for creating the war, was a decisive phase of the campaign to break down the Axis will to resist. This campaign had been planned with four steps in view:

1. Propaganda, based on truth, starting from a fact, should be properly timed to get the maximum effect. An auspicious time to soften up the enemy is when he is weary.
2. Doubt, insecurity, and frustration furnish a fertile soil for psychological

demolition. At the right moment, interpret the enemy's defeat for him by pointing out that his cause is hopeless—he was beaten because he lacked ammunition and he is never going to get enough—and thus turn disillusionment into despair.

3. Promise something better—food and comfort, a fair peace—show him a way out of his despair.

4. Get the enemy to fix the blame where it belongs—on his leaders.[30]

This psychological offensive was supplemented by its corollary, a psychological defensive. The best defense, we were told, is "sophistication"—learning all about what the enemy is up to in his propaganda warfare and discovering what he is trying to do to you, so you will not be duped.

The chief agency in formulating and carrying out the program of psychological warfare in the United States was OWI, or Office of War Information—the nearest thing we had to a Ministry of Propaganda. Before the OWI was set up, a vast number of New Deal information agencies had been experimenting with the control of public opinion. There developed a need for some coordinating agency when we entered the war and so the OFF, or Office of Facts and Figures, was created. The Office was given this prosaic, harmless title because it was feared that American citizens might not take kindly to propaganda emanating from the Government. The OFF's principal achievement was its publication of "A Report to the Nation," intended to give the American people a complete picture of the nation's war effort to date. It was a dull document, unhappily interpreted by critics as a white-wash of the Administration's leadership. *A Song Book for the United Nations* and a geography book followed in due course—both flops. It was becoming increasingly obvious that something more and better was needed. Consequently OFF was supplanted by OWI, established by executive order on June 13, 1942, with Elmer Davis, news analyst and radio commentator, as its head. OWI's functions were defined by the executive order, as follows:

1. To increase understanding of the war effort by means of information programs conducted through the use of the press, radio, and motion picture.

2. To coordinate the war-information activities of all the Federal agencies so as to assure an accurate and a consistent flow of war information to the public and to the world at large.

[30] Based on *Psychology for the Fighting Man*, Chapter 20, "Psychological Warfare." 1943. Prepared for the Fighting Man Himself by a Committee of the National Research Council with the collaboration of Science Service as a contribution to the war effort.

3. To obtain and study information concerning the war effort and to advise agencies about the most effective means of keeping the public informed.

4. To record, clear, and approve all proposed radio and motion-picture programs sponsored by the government.

5. To maintain liaison with the information agencies of the United Nations and to relate our information programs to theirs.

6. To fulfill other duties the President might authorize.

In his testimony before the House Appropriations Subcommittee, Davis carefully pointed out that OWI was not a propaganda or morale agency:

A good many people seem to think that we are specifically charged with the maintenance of national morale. We are not; and in my opinion there is no need of such an agency.

In taking this position, Davis cited a Congressional document to this effect:

There are no privations which the people will not willingly endure, no sacrifices which will not be unflinchingly faced, as long as they are truthfully informed as to the reasons for making such demands on them. . . .

Then he summarized his own attitude on the matter:

The people must be satisfied that the great sacrifices which all of us will be called on to make are being distributed as fairly and evenly as possible. Once they are sure of that, once they know what is going on, why they are being asked to make sacrifices, how much we have to do, or why we have to do it—once they understand all that (as it is the job of this office to make them understand), in my opinion nobody needs to worry about national morale.

Davis was denying any concern with morale-building because he did not want his Office to be regarded as a propaganda agency—he was going to confine himself just to information. OWI, in other words, was not out to *campaign,* but just to *explain.* Such a separation of its function as a disseminator of war information from its influence with respect to morale and propaganda was, of course, impossible to maintain in practice. Having been kept in the dark about the losses at Pearl Harbor, as represented in Government releases through the press, and then recanted a year later, many Americans found themselves considerably heartened by Davis' honest efforts to give the people the truth about the war. Davis took seriously his own dictum: "This is a people's war, and the people are entitled to know as much as possible about it." Davis' regular weekly series of war analyses, broadcast from Washington, exerted an important influence on the morale of the home front despite the many protestations that OWI was not at all concerned with the maintenance of morale.

OWI put its faith in the Strategy of Truth. In its messages to the peoples of the world concerning our leaders, our aims, and our growing armed might, OWI stuck to facts, shunned exaggeration. *The Unconquered People,* issued in July, 1942, told the story of Europe enslaved and China in chains, both eager to fight alongside us for human freedom. It was a good "plug" for the United Nations, a moving, dramatic story. In the August résumé of the war situation, there was the blunt statement: "We can lose this war." October's report was an objective comparison of our air strength with that of the Axis. Davis described our position in his usual realistic manner when he stated in a radio speech about this time, "We are ankle deep in this war." Later he was able to announce, "Our side is on the offensive, strategically"—news that was good news to American listeners who had been eagerly awaiting an initial victory for a long time. At daily conferences with representatives of the Army and Navy, Davis discussed the news and projected releases with military men, checking on the substance and *timing* of such releases, to make sure the psychological warfare fitted just exactly into the scheme of total war.

Among its many assignments, OWI prepared leaflets to be dropped by Allied planes over Axis territory, telling the enemy about their corrupt leaders and our kindly intentions. Sometimes these pamphlets were concealed in babies' diapers, sometimes attached to a needle and thread; sometimes the information was printed on badly needed folders of matches. OWI also published *Victory,* an ambitious picture magazine, distributed bi-monthly overseas only, "selling" America to other peoples. *Victory* sought to counteract the influence of a similar magazine gotten out for foreign consumption by the Nazis, called *Signal,* a publication that had been very successful in winning friends for Germany. The first issue of *Victory* contained air views of New York City and Boulder Dam, a fine shot of a tree-shaded, American residential street, a picture of an Indiana dirt road complete with rugged farmer, a three-page color spread of Marines training for combat, a double-truck photo of a bomb-battered, sinking Jap cruiser, three pages of pictures showing camouflaged Berlin buildings which had been bombed.

This brief survey of OWI at work on the home front and on the foreign front may give the reader some idea of the nature and scope of psychological warfare as waged on a modern scale. We shall refer to this warfare in connection with the "radio as a propaganda agency" later in this chapter and then again in connection with "morale in war" in the chapter that follows.

(Courtesy, the Chicago *Tribune*.)

II. AGENCIES OF PROPAGANDA

Some of the important agencies of propaganda are the press, the radio, the theater, the school, and the public relations counsel. We shall consider each of them in turn.

A. THE PRESS

Magazines and newspapers are ready vehicles for the transmission of propaganda. Propaganda of a subtle sort, distorting the truth by the encouragement of logical fallacies, is exemplified in the newspaper cartoon on page 353.   The cartoonist wields a mighty pen.

Even the "funnies" carry propaganda.   "Little Orphan Annie," the Chicago *Tribune's* syndicated comic strip, was used as a medium for airing political convictions.   James Clendenin, editor of the Huntington, West Virginia, *Herald Dispatch,* registered a protest against the strip, because Daddy Warbucks, guardian of Orphan Annie, was being made the mouthpiece of extreme reactionary doctrines.   Harold Gray, the creator, used the strip to attack the New Deal, and to denounce the organized labor movement.   Slugg, a capitalist-employer and rival of Warbucks, hires a set of "liberal" politicians to ruin his competitor. One of these hirelings resembles vaguely Senator Norris of Nebraska. Failing to gain his end through political manipulation, Slugg resorts to the labor movement to further his evil designs.   Three labor "agitators," wearing black slouch hats and long, fuzzy beards, gather outside Warbucks' factory, and are made to say: "Above all, we must keep them (the workers) organized."   "Yes, of course, otherwise we cannot collect our dues."   "Ah, my friends, do not forget the initiation fees, the fines and assessments."   Warbucks engages a squad of kindly, Adonis-like armed guards, and the union leaders cry disappointedly: "We cannot even bomb the plant.   There are too many guards. There should be a law against guards."   Finally, the workers, in a burst of grateful loyalty to Warbucks, beat up the union leaders and tar and feather them.   Through all of these episodes, Little Orphan Annie herself appears only fitfully, and her sole function is to create sympathy for Daddy, his anti-union policies and guards.

The "Little Orphan Annie" strip is published by 135 daily and 100 Sunday newspapers.   Until Mr. Clendenin made his protest, readers of the strip were being prejudiced against the reform legislation of the Roosevelt administration and were also being informed that those who now rule industry are good and kindly, and their rivals evil.   In an editorial on the first page of his paper, Mr. Clendenin declared that " 'Annie' has been made the vehicle for a studied, veiled and alarmingly vindictive propaganda," and announced that the strip would no longer be printed in his newspaper.   He immediately received a telegram from the Chicago *Tribune's* syndicate service reading: "Orphan Annie artist ordered stop editorializing and has already started new series.   Feel sure you will like it." [31]

---

[31] "Fascism in the Funnies."   Editorial in the *New Republic,* September 18, 1935.

The press as a propaganda agency functions largely in the interest of the moneyed, conservative class, as Irving Brant asserted in an address to the National Council for the Social Studies (1937). Brant, an editor of the St. Louis *Star-Times,* was speaking on "The Press and Political Leadership." Among other things he said:

The greatest shock ever experienced by the newspaper publishers of America was to wake up on the morning of November 4, 1936, and discover that they had no influence in a presidential election. . . . I invite you to look at the amazing phenomenon we have in the United States today—a political philosophy which we call the New Deal, completely triumphant in national policy as expressed in a presidential election, yet practically unrepresented in that upper stratum of the American press which dignifies itself by the title of the fourth estate. If journalism were quickly responsive to political trends, there would have sprung up long before this a mushroom growth of liberal newspapers, all of them devoted to the New Deal and appealing for the blessings of its followers. Why has there been no such development? For two reasons. First, the cost of establishing a daily newspaper. Men wealthy enough to buy or establish newspapers are not usually interested in an extension of liberalism. In the second place, the established conservative newspapers protect themselves against public disfavor in a very creditable way. They put out newspapers which satisfy the main necessities and desires of liberal readers, to an extent at least sufficient to discourage the entry of new competition. What are these necessities and desires? To know the news of the world, and to be entertained. A newspaper which presents the news fairly and comprehensively, and which has appealing comic strips, can weather an astounding amount of opposition to its editorial policies. . . .

However, the inescapable fact is that we have no press today representing the dominant political thought of the country, and there is no immediate prospect of such a press being established on a national scale. . . . It is impossible to point to one important constructive step taken in the United States in the last eight years which represents either the inventiveness, the initiative, or the supporting activity of the American press. . . .

From the day the newspapers were invited to put a curb on child labor in their own industry, from the day they were asked to limit the hours of their employes to forty per week and to pay reporters a minimum wage of twenty-five dollars, from the day they were told that the law guaranteed newspaper employes the right to organize for collective bargaining, from that day the metropolitan newspapers of the United States have been substantially regimented against the New Deal, the agent of regimentation being the American Newspaper Publishers Association.[32]

[32] I. Brant: "The Press and Political Leadership." *Social Education,* January, 1938.

B. THE RADIO

The radio provides an excellent vehicle for the dissemination of propaganda, as President Roosevelt demonstrated in his Fireside Chats. Mr. W. J. Cameron's talks on the Ford Sunday Evening Hour promulgated a definite economic philosophy with expert subtlety, with a good word now and then, cleverly inserted, for the Ford Motor Company, though no resort was made to direct advertising in his remarks. The promotion was there, well enough hidden to be in excellent taste.

Let us glance through the thirty-nine talks prepared and delivered by Cameron on the Ford Sunday Evening Hour from September, 1936, to June, 1937.[33] We shall ignore the excellent musical program which created, by conditioning, an attitude of appreciation for the beauty and efficiency of the V-Eight.

"There will be no sales talk, no commercial advertising in these programs." There was no sales talk, but there was talk that was good for sales. On May 23, 1937, Cameron took as his subject, "The Money Flow," in the course of which he explained where the money goes by stating that it just keeps on going. Specifically, checks for materials go to thousands of employees in various parts of the country; in fact, to 45 of the 48 states. In a time of unemployment and economic stress the above remarks might encourage listeners to think of a Ford when considering a new car. In the same talk it was asserted that those who know Mr. Ford "are sure that the principal satisfaction he gets out of business, and he gets plenty of it too, is the satisfaction of seeing his production ideas work out in the interest of the public and his men." The talk ended with an innuendo against the New Deal: "The country would seem to be making some progress in spite of the numerous and costly hindrances that have been put in its way."

Cameron gave the Roosevelt administration a good dig whenever an opening presented itself. Restriction of production by government order, with pay for creating scarcity, was condemned in no uncertain terms. " 'Tain't right!" is the way real Americans feel, even when they take the customary cut of the public money. Cameron's thesis—and Ford's—is that we need increased and more efficient production, lower prices, and higher wages. "Industrial improvement began where political hindrance partly ceased." A forward surge resulted when the government granted what was officially called a "breathing spell." How long will this improvement last? "Its answer depends on whether

[33] A reprint of these talks by W. J. Cameron may be obtained from the Ford Motor Company, Dearborn, Michigan. Cameron is no longer on the program.

men overfond of bizarre economic theories, men who never successfully managed a business themselves, are allowed to interfere with
industry again." The so-called intelligentsia, the brain trusters who
write books about themselves for themselves to read, are living on the
system they pretend to despise. They suffer from an ingrowing aberration which amounts to a group delusion.

A listener asked: "If all Ford profits had been given to the help,
how much additional would they have received?" Had the profits
all been divided amongst them, according to Cameron, there would
be no Ford employees, no Ford Motor, no Ford profits, since the profits
have been devoted to developing the business. Had all the dividends
paid out during these thirty-three years been added to wages and paid
exclusively to employees, it would have meant a wage increase for
each man of less than six cents a working hour. By stating the amount
in wage per hour it is made to appear that six cents a working hour
for thirty-three years does not amount to much. Not a very exciting
amount, he adds! The philosophy of "taking everything" is vicious,
whether it is practiced by labor, management, or the tax collector, for
in the end, nobody gets anything.[34]

Radio has been employed as a potent instrument for waging psychological warfare. The Nazis used this weapon to particularly good
effect in hastening the downfall of France. For example, German
propaganda units accompanied combat units to the front where they
used public address systems to talk directly to enemy soldiers. An
announcement would be made that a shell was coming over the Ma-
ginot Line and the French would be warned where it was going to land.
The Nazis explained that there was no desire on their part to harm
the Frenchmen who were really their friends. This kind of fraterniz-
ing helped to create the impression that it was a "phony war." Some
of the propaganda units were mobile, doing their broadcasting behind
the enemy lines.

It was such a German unit that broadcast to the French soldiers in June,
1940, the "news" that a French Armistice Commission was going to meet with
German authorities to sign an armistice. The broadcast had a devastating
effect on French morale. The French troops in the front line reasoned:
"Why hold the line and be shot today, when the war will be over tomorrow?"
Resistance crumbled.[35]

[34] For another study of Cameron as a propagandist, see "Propaganda on the Air."
Propaganda Analysis, June, 1938.
[35] *Psychology for the Fighting Man*, p. 442. 1943.

Nazi short-wave propaganda for American listeners stressed the cost of the war in the form of higher taxes, the secret designs of the British to incorporate the United States into the British Empire, the threat of Bolshevism if the Nazis failed to protect Western civilization against Stalin's Sovietized slaves, and "the conniving of the Jews who forced Roosevelt and America into the war." After Pearl Harbor, each broadcast was concluded with the sign-off—

Franklin Delano Roosevelt promised peace but he brought you war.

After the Russian offensive got under way in November, 1942, a new sign-off was introduced:

The world is divided into two camps: on the one side, Jewish Bolshevism and Jewed-up plutocracy, on the other the forces of a new and better order. Why is America still in the wrong camp?

Bait for listeners was provided in the announcement on each program of the names of several American airmen who had been captured. Dramatic descriptions of the sinking of American ships were broadcast by Nazi submarine crews who were just returning to base from successful convoy hunts in the Atlantic. Desecration of German cemeteries, cathedrals, universities, and hospitals, the brutal bombing of old people and children, were vividly depicted in an attempt to slow down the air drive by arousing sympathy. The Nazis did not pause in their programs to give the reason why so many of their churches were being bombed—that they were being used as ammunition depots. Among others, Robert H. Best and "Paul Revere," former American citizens, served faithfully as broadcasters for the Nazis on their regular programs to America.

International broadcasting can be a very effective means of building up good will. America had been tardy in availing itself of this instrument. While we sat idly by, Germany was using the radio to good advantage. Nazi broadcasts prepared the way for *Anschluss*, for the dismemberment of Czechoslovakia, for the disintegration of France, for the anti-British coup in Iraq, for hostility toward Uncle Sam in South America. Germany was sending our southern neighbors highly colored accounts of strikes in our steel industry and concluding them with such slogans as "The United States is truly repulsive to all honest people." Listeners in Ecuador and Peru, "enlightened" by Nazi propaganda, were convinced that England had invaded Norway.

Belgium, and Holland. After the United States had finally awakened to the seriousness of the Nazi influence, radio programs were developed to spread the good word in our behalf. The newscast proved to be our most effective program in international broadcasting. Our reputation for accuracy and objectivity in reporting news stood us in good stead as our strongest asset in this field. More funds and more radio time were at last devoted to wooing the South American countries away from pro-Nazi sentiments. Much still needs to be done in this respect to counterbalance some of the Hollywood movies purporting to describe life in South America. These movies may have done more to promote ill will between the Americas than did all of Goebbels' short-wave transmitters.

C. THE THEATER

The stage and screen are important agencies of propaganda. Many successful plays reach an extensive clientele through their screen versions. The vivid appeal to the visual sense, through which we get our most enduring impressions, gives the dramatist a remarkable opportunity to sway the minds of the people who come under his spell. We shall mention propaganda as exemplified by the stage and by the movies, particularly with reference to the theme of "social justice," also citing a few illustrations from other spheres of interest which demonstrate the power of the movie as an instrument for influencing attitudes.

Propaganda for social justice was a popular subject on the stage during the depression of the 1930's. Outstanding among the plays on this general topic was *Dead End,* an East River idyl, of which the *Time* reviewer said: "In teeming Manhattan no expert statistician is needed to point out that the city's wealth is unequally divided. Crisscrossed everywhere by hairlines of social distinction, with frowsy tenements rubbing their rumps against the flanks of patrician apartment houses, the island's very real estate proclaims the class war." [36] The drama showed how the criminal is produced by his sordid environment.

They Shall Not Die was a dramatic and simple telling of the story of the nine colored boys accused of rape in Scottsboro, Alabama. The author insisted that the play was a fiction but its fidelity to the actual case was obvious. Four Negroes were convicted of rape in a court that was undeniably prejudiced. There was an appeal to the members of the audience to join in a public protest against this

[36] *Time,* November 11, 1935.

travesty on justice.   Scenes of brutality were depicted as phases of "the struggle between classes."

Stevedore was produced by the Theater Union, an organization devoted to fostering the drama of radical propaganda.   The play dealt with a Louisiana race riot.   The events concerned were given a Marxian interpretation.   The reason for its effectiveness as melodrama and propaganda probably was "that it sticks with uncommon persistence to a single purpose, which is to inflame the passions of its audience and to sweep that audience forward on a wave of fighting hate."   The idea was to get the crowd going somewhere.   "A goodly percentage of those who saw *Stevedore* were probably ready to seize the nearest club and crack somebody over the head.   Most books and plays offered as proof that 'art is a weapon' remind me of wooden swords, but this particular work is really a bomb—homemade perhaps, but full of powder and quite capable of going off."   The main character was a huge Negro with firm ideas about the necessity of the class struggle and a talent for converting his more timorous fellows to the cause.   "Personally I should not be much surprised to hear any night," wrote reviewer Krutch, "that the infuriated audience had rushed out on to Fourteenth Street and lynched a white man just on general principles." [37]

Waiting for Lefty, produced in 1935, was an appeal for the revolution: "Workers of the World Unite!"   The play began on the platform at a strikers' meeting, and "plants" interrupting from the audience created the illusion that the meeting was actually taking place at the very moment of representation.   From the platform the characters delivered their speeches in convincing style.   Brief flashbacks revealed the trials and tribulations in the lives of the striking cab drivers.   Joe and Edna were averaging six to seven dollars a week. Joe had nothing but a coffee cake and coffee all day.   The two kids had just been put to bed "so they wouldn't know they missed a meal." Edna urged a strike:

I know this—your boss is making suckers outa you boys every minute.   Yes, and suckers out of all the wives and the poor innocent kids who'll grow up with crooked spines and sick bones.   Sure, I see it in the papers, how good orange juice is for kids.   But dammit our kids get colds one on top of the other.   They look like little ghosts.

Betty never saw a grapefruit.   I took her to the store last week and she

[37] The quotations are from J. W. Krutch's review in the *Nation*, May 2, 1934.

pointed to a stack of grapefruits. "What's that!" she said. My God, Joe—
the world is supposed to be for all of us.[38]

The drama of "social significance" was given impetus in the late
1920's by the Workers' Laboratory Theater, a communist-inspired
group in America who were aiming to use "the theater as a weapon"
for enlisting interest in the worker-labor cause. There was a lack of
effective plays during this early period, as the message "outweighed
the dramatic quality of the productions." It was a beginning, however. In tracing the further evolution of this type of drama, Bosworth states:

The first plays of the left-wing theater in America were notable for their
crudity. Good example, *Unemployment* (1931). They revolved around a
sharp, clear-cut separation of sheep and goats, capitalists and labor, bosses
and workers. Characters were "over-classified" into symbolic groups, good
and evil, depicting in quasi-religious fashion a moral-religious issue, much
like that seen in the medieval morality plays. In the words of G. K. Chester-
ton (*Current History*, 1934), these plays suffered from a "hero-villain complex."
Subsequently the left-wing theater realized the need of expressing motives
in terms of the culture, and its problems in terms of current situations. By
the middle of the '30's decade, humor began to seep into the left-wing stage,
and the social drama became more truly American, shifting its technique
from the style of the mysteries to the style of Gilbert and Sullivan. For example, *The Class of '29*.
All of this early activity in the social drama was pretty much confined to
the Workers' Theaters, which sprang up in great numbers. They did give
the theater new converts, new actors, a new audience.
As the Workers' Theaters became more effective, and developed better
dramas, their influence began to seep into the commercial theater. In 1932
the Theater Guild formed the Group Theater, from which came in 1935 the
first really important left-wing play, Odets' *Waiting for Lefty*. This was a
really successful play, because it was "good theater." If a play is to be a
weapon, it must be a good play; it cannot succeed in the theater on the
strength of its argument alone. . . .
As propaganda, such plays probably do no more than "reconvert the converted." The dramatic method is perhaps too "usual" to be effective. The
illusory nature of the theater defeats its purposes as propaganda. The theater "works on the emotions inside the theater only." . . . The intense

[38] C. Odets: *Waiting for Lefty*, published in *Three Plays*. Random House, Inc.,
1935.

economy of the dramatic form forbids discussion, digression. . . . Historical survey reveals few if any plays which have influenced social evolution.[39]

The movies are more influential in the realm of propaganda because they reach a much wider audience. When Upton Sinclair was running for the governorship of California on his utopian platform, the movie magnates were sure that his election would mean ruin to their industry. So the screen entered politics. Patrons of neighborhood movie houses were treated to pictures of an army of hoboes disembarking from box cars on Los Angeles sidings. These ugly bums were supposed to be swarming in from all corners of the United States, eager to enjoy the easy pickings of the Sinclair regime. Their appearance was repulsive enough to instill terror into any citizen of the Golden State who had a job, and a roof over his head. The scene was strangely moving, though the more discerning wondered why the vagrants were wearing make-up and some with good memories at once recognized excerpts from the Warner Brothers' previous film fiction, *Wild Boys of the Road*.[40]

Amkino, a Russian film organization, has released a number of excellent propaganda pictures. *The Five Year Plan* showed graphically how, under Communist leadership, Russia was getting industrialized, and how standards of living were being improved for the masses of the people. The camera, we were told in the publicity releases for the picture, cannot lie. The scenes, however, were carefully selected to carry the message in the most telling fashion. *The New Gulliver* was cast with one boy and 3,000 puppets. The boy dreamt that he was cast ashore on the coast of Lilliput. When he witnessed a stage manager hitting a midget with a stick, the sad truth dawned upon him: Lilliput was a capitalist nation. Allying himself with the Workers' Party, he speedily brought order out of chaos. *The Road to Life* depicted the reclamation of the wild boys of the road, who swarmed over Russia after being orphaned by World War I. *Broken Shoes* dealt with the effects of modern strike conditions on the children of the worker. It was regarded by critics as one of the best propaganda films yet produced.

American film producers have turned out some pictures with a message. *Oil for the Lamps of China* was a tribute to the unflagging idealism of the Standard Oil Company in carrying the benefits of Oc-

[39] Excerpts from a lecture on "Propaganda and the Theater" delivered by Raymond F. Bosworth in the Simmons College Faculty Lecture Series, February 27, 1940.

[40] R. S. Ames: "The Screen Enters Politics." *Harper's Magazine*, March, 1935.

cidental civilization to the benighted peoples of the Orient, although the company was nowhere mentioned by name.[41] *Black Fury* was concerned with the plight of the coal miners of Pennsylvania. Its thesis was that the cause of all strikes in this country is the existence of certain sinister and mysterious strike-breaking organizations which foment trouble between worker and employer for the sake of financial gain. The only salvation for the misguided workers is to stick by their own regular unions, even when these unions fail to secure what they are after, for "half a loaf is better than no loaf at all." [42]

Propaganda disseminated through newsreels is particularly effective because its purpose is often well concealed. The *Hearst Metrotone News* and the *March of Time* have both been accused of stealthily promoting fascism.[43] The Hearst reel at one time became so offensive in this connection as to provoke a boycott in several university communities. The Young People's Socialist League instituted a nationwide campaign against the reel.[44]

Many movies appeared during World War II which were propagandistic in nature, though sometimes such a purpose was well concealed; for example, in *Mrs. Miniver* the story was so dramatically developed that the incidental anti-Nazi appeals were subordinated— they were there, nevertheless, and hours later, the audience would sense the build-up of pro-British feeling which was perhaps the main idea behind the picture. Other stirring appeals to the American war-spirit included: *Journey for Margaret, Hitler's Children, In Which We Serve, Desert Victory, Wake Island, Casablanca, Reunion in Paris, Moscow Strikes Back,* and *Paris Calling,* just to mention a few of the outstanding pictures.

The effectiveness of movies as a vehicle of propaganda has been checked by a number of experimenters. Some pictures like *All Quiet on the Western Front* may modify children's attitudes considerably. Several such pictures may exert a cumulative effect upon attitudes, producing striking changes.[45]

D. The School

Colleges and schools function as another agency for propaganda. The colleges have discovered the vital importance of cultivating good

[41] W. Troy, in the *Nation,* July 10, 1935.

[42] W. Troy, in the *Nation,* April 24, 1935.

[43] For an indictment of the *March of Time* see C. Menefee: "The Movies Join Hearst." *The New Republic,* October 9, 1935.

[44] *The New Republic,* October 23, 1935.

[45] See especially R. C. Peterson and L. L. Thurstone: *Motion Pictures and the Social Attitudes of Children,* pp. 25-28. 1933.

public relations. The promotion of such relations may be one of the services rendered by the college news bureau. The bureau educates the alumnus in loyalty to Alma Mater, calls the attention of prospective students to the special merits of Blank College, advertises the research being carried on in its laboratories, and throws out hints about the good that would result from increased endowments. The oldest and most dignified seats of learning in America now hire press agents, just as railroads and political parties do, whose function it is to foster friendly relations with the newspapers, and through the newspapers, with the public. The agent is not always known as a publicity man; sometimes he is disguised as the "Secretary for Infor mation."

With its existence ensured by well-devised propaganda, the school is in a position to proceed with its proper business of teaching the younger generation. There is some significance in the fact that the word "doctrine" means that which is taught. Education, unfortunately, is largely a matter of indoctrination. We regard education "not as a means for stimulating in the children a desire to know the truth, but as a means for inoculating them with the stereotypes and superstitions of the dominant groups in control." [46] Taxpayers may feel that they have a right to decide what shall be taught in the public schools, since it is their money that is being spent. In Chicago, for example, civics teachers were ordered to stop an essay contest on the merits of the City Manager Plan.[47]

Children develop into conceited chauvinists if they learn in school—or elsewhere—that their own country is the only country that ever really amounted to anything. The dice are loaded against the attainment of an intelligent world view when young people are given an inflated sense of their own importance while they are still too immature to weigh the evidence. A pupil's mind may be warped, for example, by the nationalistic bias which is often reflected in the teaching of history.[48] Thus French children and German children were taught very different versions of what happened in the Franco-Prussian War and in World War I.

Some critics feel that the schools are not sufficiently interested in ex-

[46] P. Odegard: *The American Public Mind*, p. 100. Columbia University Press. 1930.

[47] R. Littell: "These Schools Teach Practical Politics!" *Reader's Digest*, July, 1937.

[48] One of the great needs for assuring peace after World War II is the writing of history textbooks free of nationalistic rationalizations, prejudices, and misrepresentations.

ploring the truth in economics but, instead, propagandize in behalf of capitalism, communism, or whatever the prevailing system happens to be. In this country, the student is apt to get the impression that capitalism is the only system or at least the only sound system. The college student may complete a course in economics without appreciating the fact that capitalism is a comparatively recent development in the perspective of man's long history. Textbooks are written mostly by persons immersed in the stereotypes of capitalism. Students, as a rule, are not encouraged to digest Marx' *Das Kapital* as a part of their program. Some colleges still use textbooks published many years ago, and thus overlook recent discoveries in economic theory and practice. How can a student understand capitalism without a comprehension of its relations to other types of economic organization?

The viewpoint of the employer is the principal one that the pupils get a chance to absorb. School boards and university trustees are likely to look with disfavor upon the representation of labor's views when economic questions are under consideration.[49] "It is exceptional to find an opportunity in the established schools for free and open discussion of the social and economic questions that are of vital interest to workingmen. . . . Yet in the same schools the chamber of commerce, the American Legion, and similar organizations can send representatives at any time to talk to the students on any subject." [50]

Radicalism is often taboo. Teachers in some places dare not mention the word "Communism," even for the purpose of denouncing it. A high-school principal in a small town was discharged partly because he had paid a call on a communist family one of whose members was in his classes. The Lynds found Middletown uneasy about "radicalism out at the college."

Even today students at the local college who get a reputation for being "radical" are reported not to have the backing of the institution in seeking positions.

The D.A.R., always on a hair-trigger of watchfulness for "disloyalty," is reported to feel that both the high school and the college have "some pretty pink teachers"; and it is reported as characteristic of its activity that sons and daughters in the classrooms of suspected teachers have been enlisted to check up on the latters' teachings.

[49] See H. K. Beale: "Forces That Control the Schools." *Harper's Magazine*, October, 1934.
[50] Quoted by Odegard: *op. cit.*, p. 89.

If conditions of national and local strain continue even moderately sharp, Middletown's forward-looking teachers will either "tone down" their teaching or conceivably be quietly removed.

This culture which appears to be bending education to its special purposes is a culture dominated by a drive not for "individual differences" but for "community solidarity." [51]

In some states the public utilities exert a very definite influence over what the pupils learn about the relative merits of utilities controlled by the municipal or federal government and those operated by private corporations. At one time over two hundred thousand students in the public and private schools of Ohio were using *Aladdins of Industry,* a textbook prepared by the utilities. Connecticut introduced in many of its lower schools a *Public Utilities Catechism* in which the children were enlightened by these statements:

It has been found in every case that the costs of the service are higher [under municipal ownership] than when the service is furnished by a private corporation. . . .
The cost of living in cities that operate their own utilities is much higher.

Aladdins of Industry declared that under the existing regulations public utility companies cannot make profits in the way other businesses do. The fundamental aim of this instruction, according to the chairman of the Joint Committee of National Utility Associations, was "to demonstrate that the entry of the government, whether national, state, or local, into this field is constitutionally unsafe, politically unwise, economically unsound, and competitively unfair." The literature "demonstrating these basic truths" was distributed free of charge.[52]
Through the elimination of unhappy references from prospective textbooks and provision for the adoption of books kindly disposed to private ownership of public utilities, the education of the young has been steered into certain channels. Such corruption of the true purpose of education

. . . is not propaganda merely because it is one-sided and partisan. It is propaganda also because it was put in the schools by non-educational and irresponsible, self-seeking agencies as part of a much larger program, and was put in surreptitiously. . . . Not only did the school authorities become

[51] The quotations are all taken from R. S. Lynd and H. M. Lynd: *Middletown in Transition.* Harcourt, Brace and Company, 1937.
[52] Quotations from Odegard: *op. cit.,* pp. 90-91.

means to private ends—the while the taxpayers assumed the opposite and paid for it—but the pupils also became means to private ends, namely, the nullification of all public ownership movements. Possibly there has never been in our history a more gigantic and insidious attack on our public schools.[53]

Teaching and research must function in an atmosphere of freedom if education is to succeed in the encouragement of learning. Asserts Laski:

The enemy of the university without . . . is orthodoxy. It may present itself as the servant of wealth, of a political or economic creed, of a religious faith. In so far as any university submits to the demands of these, it prostitutes its power to serve truth. For, by such submission, it limits, both for its teachers and its students, that power to let the mind range unimpeded over fundamental questions through which alone essential discoveries can be made. Academic freedom is the nurse of intellectual inventiveness.[54]

Laski proposes an international organization for the protection of academic freedom and suggests that "no university that is not prepared to admit to its teachers freedom from all censure or penalty in respect of their expression of opinion in any sphere of thought should be permitted to join." Such a proposal is impractical, for any teacher knows that there are certain limits he must respect within the precincts of the classroom if he wishes to continue his work. He cannot, without risk, advocate free love, sabotage, or atheism. Freedom, however desirable, can never be absolute.

Organizations such as the American Legion and the National Association of Manufacturers have at times taken a paternal interest in determining what is to be taught in our schools. They can bring pressure to bear which may be effective in rooting out "subversive" teaching, that is, teaching which is out of line with the views espoused by those persons who are doing the criticizing. Pressure groups may thus interfere seriously with academic freedom. In so far as such

[53] F. E. Lumley: *The Propaganda Menace*, p. 316. D. Appleton-Century Company, 1933. See also pp. 309-316.

[54] H. J. Laski: "Universities in These Times." *The New Republic*, January 23, 1935.

Lynd reports: "A professor of economics remarked before the annual meeting of the American Economic Association in 1937 that, despite the fact that what Marx wrote makes more sense and is more nearly correct at a number of points than many of the things economists actually teach, the latter go on teaching these other things because they cannot afford to commit hari-kari." Footnote in *Knowledge for What?*, p. 116. Princeton University Press, 1939.

groups succeed in dictating what doctrines the educators shall teach and what textbooks they shall use, the school is made to function as an agency for spreading the propaganda approved by the pressure organizations.

In 1935 the National Americanism Commission of the American Legion conducted a survey of American colleges and universities to discover the extent of "radicalism" in these institutions. They were alarmed to find students all over the land studying books and listening to instructors who were working under cover for the overthrow of our government by destroying faith in our democratic institutions. Commander Belgrano, according to his biographer, was spared such a disquieting experience by not going to college: "After graduating from high school our National Commander had been wise enough not to waste four precious years of his youth striving to accumulate a modern university education." [55] Another writer in the *American Legion Monthly* reported that a "noted chemical engineer" stated "that his company refused to employ any graduate of Alma Mater (because) they found it difficult to drive the anti-Americanism, anti-government notions out of the heads of the chaps who attend that school." [56] The Commission advocated that teachers be required to take loyalty oaths. Thus it was hoped disloyalty would be crushed before there was any opportunity for subjecting pupils to ideas of "radical internationalism." One Commander proposed that education stick to "those things which the mind of man has evolved through the ages and which have proven themselves by the acid test of time. . . . The American Legion has fought and will fight to prevent the school from becoming the dumping ground for every idea of social change which is proposed and to prevent the school from becoming the fertilizing field for ideas which in the reasonable exercise of the power to look ahead shall never become part of our way of life." [57] In practice that would mean teaching only what Legion members cared to endorse. Anybody entertaining views contrary to Legion theories would be subject to the charge of being "un-American" and, therefore, unfit for instructing the younger generation.

In the fall of 1940 the National Association of Manufacturers, gravely concerned over school teachings, announced that textbooks were going to be scrutinized and abstracts furnished for readers who

[55] P. B. Kyne: "That Boy Belgrano." *American Legion Monthly*, January, 1935.
[56] "Fred": "The Shifting Background, a Letter from an Old Classmate." *American Legion Monthly*, October, 1935.
[57] J. V. McCabe, in the New York *American*, November 19, 1935.

were urged to examine the ideas to "determine whether there is any basis, and if so, how much, for the growing apprehension about the contents of school textbooks." Explained *Propaganda Analysis:* "The alarm springs from a belief that the schools are conditioning pupils to accept a new social order based on national planning. In the opinion of H. W. Prentis, Jr., the past president of the N.A.M., such planning amounts to 'creeping collectivism.' " [58]

One object of investigation by various agencies and individuals was the series of twenty volumes written by Harold Rugg and collaborators under the general title of *Man and His Changing Society.* These books had been responsible for some bitter controversies long before it was decided to look into them critically. One critic summarized the "objectionable" views expressed by Rugg in terms of what this critic called "the Rugg indoctrination."

First, the child is taught the great principle of Change—everything is in a constant state of change and we must expect all institutions to be changed in the future, especially forms of government and social organization. Second, the student is shown by numerous examples of factual and fictitious evidence that our present situation in this country is very unsatisfactory and our system has worked badly. Third, the child is disillusioned of any preconceived ideas that America has a glorious history or that the founding fathers were men of good intent. Rather, it is shown that our form of society was designed to benefit only the minority ruling class. Fourth, the panacea of social reconstruction and collectivist planning is advanced as the inevitable coming change.[59]

Other critics had objected that the Rugg texts pictured the United States as a land of unequal opportunity, that they gave a class-conscious account of the framing of the American Constitution. Favorite among critics was a Rugg quotation: "The merchants, landowners, manufacturers, shippers and bankers were given what they wanted . . ."—omitting the rest of the sentence which qualifies the assertion just quoted: ". . . namely, a government which would stabilize the money and trade, keep order within the country and defend the nation against foreign enemies." Digging up these citations, reciting

[58] "Propaganda over the Schools." *Propaganda Analysis,* February 25, 1941. Reproduced by permission of Alfred McClung Lee, Executive Director.
[59] *Ibid.* The criticism is the one directed against Rugg by Alfred T. Falk, Director of the Bureau of Research and Education of the American Federation of Advertisers. Falk was objecting to Rugg's philosophy in general and in particular to Rugg's remarks about advertising in his *Introduction to the Problems of American Culture* (1931).

them out of their contexts, charging the author with spreading communism, constituted "Rugg-beating," to use the parlance of *Time*.[60] In Philadelphia, for example, Mrs. Ellwood J. Turner, a Daughter of Colonial Wars, denounced the Rugg books because they "tried to give the child an unbiased viewpoint instead of teaching him real Americanism." [61] In banishing the books from the schools of Wayne Township, N.J., Board Member Ronald Gall justified the action: "In my opinion, the books are un-American but not anti-American. . . ." [62]

The N.A.M. inquiry into school textbooks was regarded with alarm in some quarters. The American Committee for Democracy and Intellectual Freedom considered it to be a serious threat to academic freedom, so serious, in fact, that a special committee was appointed by this organization to examine the same textbooks as those under scrutiny of the N.A.M. and to check on the N.A.M. findings.

Fourteen members of the faculty of the Harvard Graduate School of Education, headed by Dean Francis T. Spaulding, sensed "danger" in this investigation and strongly urged that it be carried out "without bias." In its reply to the Harvard group N.A.M. asserted that it did not seek to suppress any textbook and defended the following principles:

It is appropriate, however, for any citizen to recommend that generally unaccepted political and economic philosophies should be *explained* rather than *advocated;* that both the merits and disadvantages of such philosophies should be duly emphasized; that the characteristics of our traditional institutions should receive at least an equal hearing; and that controversial issues should be presented with due regard for the age and intellectual maturity of the student.[63]

The Harvard group answered with this statement (January 17, 1941):

The Association's [N.A.M.] thoroughgoing endorsement of certain educational principles which seem to us of the greatest importance is not merely a matter of encouragement to us as a group, but will, we believe, help to reassure many other persons who have been acutely conscious of the dangers pointed out in our statement. We agree with the Association that if these principles can be safeguarded, the Association's program may be of great constructive value to education in this country.

[60] See *Time,* September 9, 1940; March 3, 1941; April 7, 1941.
[61] The Boston *Traveler,* February 20, 1940.
[62] *Time,* September 9, 1940.
[63] Quoted from the N.A.M.'s statement on its textbook-abstracting project.

If we can in any way cooperate with the Association in seeing that such principles are safeguarded, we shall be happy to do so. In any event we shall watch with active interest the further progress of the Association's program.

A college education may become propaganda in behalf of certain economic or social dogma if the college authorities, in their eagerness to attract endowment funds, interfere with the academic freedom of the faculty. The files of the *Bulletin of the American Association of University Professors* include a number of cases in which professors have been dismissed on account of their socio-economic views. In such instances college administrators have been anxious lest some "radical" faculty member offend some wealthy person who might otherwise be inclined to favor the institution with his monetary blessing. Firing a "dangerous" professor may prevent the alienation of a prospective benefactor. Thus a professor may be discouraged from teaching the truth as he sees it, if money takes precedence over academic freedom in the eyes of the administration.

Education fails to fulfill its true function in so far as it promotes the spread of propaganda rather than the search for truth. Rational living must be based on full, honest information. The school should foster a desire for facts as the foundation of sane conduct. "There rests upon every one," says Morgan, "an increasing obligation to be intelligent; to insist that the materials that form his thinking and his attitudes shall bear an honest label. . . . To build into the life of every citizen an appreciation of the precious obligation to be intelligent is the primary task of the school." [64]

E. The Public Relations Counsel

The agent of propaganda *par excellence* is the public relations counsel, a phenomenon of our modern age. Many events seem to happen innocently enough; look behind them and you will uncover the counsel. When the unemployed of New York sold apples, for example, it was just a bright idea of Joseph Sicker of the International Apple Association. Publicity frequently emanates from some scheme hatched in the ingenious mind of some counsel who has been commissioned to sell some idea to the public. People, on a large scale, no longer think their own thoughts; their ideas are packaged for them.

A glimpse of the work of the public relations counsel may be gleaned by a brief look into the achievements of three leading men in this field—Reichenbach, Lee, and Bernays.

[64] J. E. Morgan: "Propaganda: Its Relation to the Child Labor Issue." *Education,* September, 1925.

It is significant that Reichenbach got his start in a circus. He learned from the carnival business that it is charity to cheat the small-town folk a little because it sharpens the folks' wits for bigger deals. The prototype from which his later stunts were refined was a barrel enclosed in wire netting, with a sign posted: "Danger: Snakes." Inside the barrel was an advertisement for those to read who dared to peek, and most people did. It was an easy transition from picking the pockets of gaping yokels whose necks were craned for the high diver, to promoting a faker on the vaudeville stage in the person of Reynard. "I found it easy," confides Reichenbach, "to make a world-famous handcuff king out of a man who couldn't get out of his own shirt."

One of Reynard's stunts was to extricate himself from a strait-jacket in front of an audience. He went through a ritual of contortions to impress his observers with the difficulties involved in emancipating himself. Actually, he was twisting to hold the jacket together long enough to make his escape look real. Another trick was getting out of jail by pinning the key on the man appointed to guard him. Reynard failed to show up for a scheduled jail break because Reichenbach had locked him in the hotel room by mistake. "Everywhere," we are informed, "the people clamored to be fooled and it was gratifying to see how much they appreciated it when they were well fooled. Every time he worked a fake jail break or a bogus handcuff release, Reynard felt like a public benefactor. . . . In writing the story of my life I find it is more properly the story of ballyhoo, the evolution of the circus barker into the public relations counsel, and I can see how much of scientific publicity had its source in the crude ways of the carnival." [65] Ballyhoo is an art, and given proper publicity a mediocre chorus girl becomes a star, a cheap painting becomes a work of art, a tawdry story of illicit love becomes a sensational novel.

It was Reichenbach who was responsible for the popularity of the painting, "September Morn." A New York art company turned to him to help them unload copies of the picture with which they were overstocked. They had been unable to sell it at any price. The nudity was so innocuous it had been rejected for a brewer's calendar. Reichenbach had an enlargement of the painting placed in the window of an art shop on West 3rd Street. He hired ten boys and girls of various ages and sizes to stand in front of the window and to act as if

[65] Reprinted from H. Reichenbach and D. Freedman: *Phantom Fame*, by permission of Simon and Schuster, Inc. Copyright, 1931, by Lucinda Reichenbach and David Freedman. Pp. 95, 8.

they were enjoying a "dirty picture." Then he called up Anthony Comstock, the vice crusader, and denounced the immoral display. Comstock rushed right over and ordered the owners to remove the picture from the window. They refused. The battle went to the courts. Songwriters rhapsodized about the picture, vaudeville artists joked about it, ministers stormed against it, newspapers featured the whole story, with the result that in the next six months 4,000,000 copies of "September Morn" were sold at a dollar apiece. Subsequently the sale mounted to some 7,000,000 copies. Later on, Reichenbach used the same technique in converting Elinor Glyn's novel, *Three Weeks,* into a best seller.

In the days when motion pictures were used as "chasers" to clear the theater after the vaudeville was over, Reichenbach entered the field as a promoter. *Over the Hill to the Poorhouse* was playing to an empty house. He changed the title to *Over the Hill,* thus eliminating the poorhouse at one stroke. Then he hired twelve couples in evening dress, all handsome and pretty movie extras, to go out on the crowded streets in teams of three and argue as to whether they should go to *Sally* or to *Over the Hill.* They debated loudly as they argued themselves right into the theater, a curious crowd following them past the box office. Once inside, they slipped out again and "worked" another street. *Over the Hill* became a success.

Clara Kimball Young, Rudolph Valentino, and many others became luminaries because of Reichenbach's enthusiastic publicity. One chorus girl who had been fired returned to the same theater several weeks later as the leading lady, with the aid of well-planned publicity. Reichenbach's commentary on his professional achievements gives us some insight into the art of promoting: "The only insidious element in all this personal publicity of stars, is that eventually they begin to believe it themselves and gradually the stories concocted to fool the public, fool them too."

Ivy Lee, familiarly known as "Poison Ivy," made a name for himself as a public relations counsel during the time when Hughes was exposing corruption in some of the big insurance companies, Lincoln Steffens was muckraking big business in general, and Ida Tarbell was assailing Standard Oil in particular. Lee, who had been a newspaperman, popularized the idea that what the public thinks of a company is a very important factor in determining its success. His first big assignment was with the Pennsylvania Railroad when that organization decided to "take the public into its confidence."

Lee was best known for his success in converting Rockefeller in the public mind from "an ogre into a Santa Claus." The Rockefellers had gotten a bad name as a result of the Ludlow Massacre in Colorado in 1914. John D. Rockefeller, Jr., shocked by the chorus of denunciation, determined to present his case to the public. Lee proposed that the affairs of the corporation be put into shape meriting public approval and the result was "the Rockefeller plan" for bettering mining conditions. The newspapers were supplied continuously with complete information about the good deeds of Standard Oil. Every action of the Rockefellers, especially their contributions to science and education, was brought by Lee to the public's attention. It was due to Lee's resourceful promotion that "the figure of the striding, ruthless monopolist in high hat and long coat, gripping his walking stick and entering a courthouse has been replaced by pictures of a frail old man, playing golf with his neighbors, handing out dimes to children, distributing inspirational poems, and walking in peace among his flowers."

Edward L. Bernays conceives of his profession as "the conscious and intelligent manipulation of the organized habits and opinions of the masses," and he believes that the role of the counselor of public relations is a particularly important one in a democratic society. Through his expert control over "the mass mind" the counselor functions as "the invisible government." Small groups of persons can, and do, make the rest of us think what they please about how our houses should be designed, what furniture we should put into them, what foods we should eat, what shirts we should wear, and what charities we should support. The intelligent minority leads the way, with the counselor setting the pace.

Bernays acts as an adviser to his client. Some product may not be selling up to expectations. The client wants to know how the public can be made to feel a need that will bear fruit in larger sales. Unlike Reichenbach, who did not want to see the article he was to publicize for fear he would be disillusioned, Bernays insists on knowing what it is he is pushing and he will not commit himself to its promotion until he is convinced of its value. He will not feature a product he believes to be fraudulent or a cause he believes to be antisocial. Bernays says that the chief assets of the public relations counsel are honesty and candor. Maybe so, but—Bernays' crowning achievement, the handling of Light's Golden Jubilee, the fiftieth anniversary of Edison's discovery of the electric light, was put over in a very subtle fashion. Let Wayne W. Parrish and John T. Flynn tell the story.

Parrish:

While the appropriateness of a national celebration for such a valuable invention and utility as the electric light is not to be denied, the newspapers were not immediately made aware that Mr. Bernays was directing the jubilee from behind the scenes.

Ostensibly, Henry Ford was sponsor for the mammoth affair. That it was a success in bringing countless columns of free newspaper publicity for the electric utilities was shown by the one fact that President Hoover and many other public officials journeyed to Dearborn, Michigan, as the guests of Mr. Ford.[66]

Flynn:

October 21, 1929, marked the climax of a celebration ostensibly designed to commemorate Edison's invention of the incandescent lamp. Edison re-enacted his procedure before a large audience in Detroit. . . . Henry Ford reconstructed the village in which Edison was born. The original laboratory was reproduced. Ostensibly a great man was being honored by a famous industrialist. Really, Mr. Bernays managed and directed this series of dramatic episodes, taking advantage of an opportunity to exploit and publicize the uses of the electric light.[67]

In behalf of piano sales Bernays enlisted the help of architects in designing homes to feature a music room. It was assumed that when people bought homes including such a room they would have to purchase a piano to occupy the floor space provided. Ivory Soap was promoted by competitions in the schools where the children were encouraged to sculpture in Ivory Soap. A sculptor of national reputation found this particular brand of soap an excellent medium for his skill. The Proctor and Gamble Company offered a series of prizes. The contest was held under the auspices of the Art Center in New York City, a reputable organization in the art world. School superintendents and teachers got behind Ivory Soap. An exhibition of the best pieces was held annually in an important art gallery in New York. Distinguished artists acted as judges. It was a good clean contest all the way through, acquainting the children with soap as well as with art.

Another campaign was carried through for the luggage industry. In the twenties, women began wearing fewer clothes and bobbing their hair. It was the "scanties" era. This caused a slump in the luggage business. Interviews with society women and film stars were arranged

---

[66] W. W. Parrish, in the *Literary Digest,* June 2, 1934.
[67] Summarized from J. T. Flynn: "Edward L. Bernays." *The Atlantic Monthly,* May, 1932.

by Bernays and it was reported that these ladies deplored the careless traveling habits of American women.   No woman, these leaders asserted, should ever go away for a week end without a complete ensemble and spare dresses.   Though luggage was never mentioned in these press interviews, the idea was put across that any lady who wanted to keep "in style" would have to buy more luggage to carry her complete ensembles.   The sales charts of the manufacturers showed an improvement.

Bernays became the press agent for the "United Brewers' Industrial Foundation" in their campaign to give beer its proper place in the drinking habits of the nation.[68]   The Foundation planned to spend $1,000,000 annually to interpret the brewing industry to the public and to interpret the public interest to the brewers.   If the public and the brewers could only get together and understand each other, it was hoped the brewers would come into their own.   Bernays was paid handsomely for "generating the industry's odor of sanctity."

In his investigations, Mr. Bernays already has found out a lot of surprising things about beer.   Its caloric value is nearly as high as that of milk.   It "aids digestion by creating a feeling of well-being."   It "replaces lost body salts"; it "acts as a toxic to cholera and typhoid germs"; it "stimulates the flow of milk in pregnancy." . . .   He can also quote authorities on "proof" of the impossibility of getting drunk on 3.2 beer.[69]

The campaign, launched at a "beer luncheon" in New York on April 14, 1937, was prompted by several untoward developments that distressed the brewers.   For one thing, the consumption of hard liquor was increasing faster than the consumption of beer.   The brewers desired to reduce the total amount of intoxication by inducing people to drink less of the spirituous liquors and more of the malt beverages.   Their interest, so they said, was temperance.   Such being the case, the brewers attempted to league themselves with various organizations devoted to the cause of temperance.   Thus, churches were invited to join hands with them in educating the coming generation to appreciate the advantages of beer.   The Foundation hoped in this way to disarm the drys whose increasing power was giving them the jitters.   The brewing interests promised to remedy all the abuses of their industry —in order to forestall more regulatory control.   One of Bernays' prob-

[68] See the section on Shortsighted Egocentrism in Business in Chapter 5, "The Unemployment of Intelligence."

[69] J. R. Dill: "Unhappy Days for the Brewer." *Christian Century,* June 30, 1937.

lems, therefore, was to convince people that the brewers had the public welfare at heart and, because of their sense of public responsibility, could be relied upon to clean their own house without any help from outsiders.

The Foundation began its project by making a survey of editors, educators, clergymen, lawyers, business executives, club women, and farm and labor leaders, to ascertain their attitudes toward drinking in general and beer in particular. Unhappily, it was found that 59 per cent of those replying did not think that the consumption of more beer would solve our social problems. This setback was compensated for by replies received from Women's Page editors who offered suggestions for getting women to drink and serve more beer. To further this end it was discovered that beer is non-fattening.

Through a survey of the history of such temperance organizations as the Anti-Saloon League and the Women's Christian Temperance Union it was determined that the propaganda of the drys could be counteracted most effectively by appropriating their techniques in behalf of beer. The Foundation, therefore, announced, "We have prepared three booklets dealing with the health, the economic, and social aspects of beer. We will be very glad to send them to you. . . ."

In the hope of increasing profits and protecting the brewers from the attacks of the drys, the Foundation decided that a paid advertising campaign was not "in the best interests of the industry" and that some groundwork such as "public education and public acceptance of the product" should first be laid. Propaganda works best when it is not recognized as the gospel of a pressure group. The program contemplated the circularizing of the colleges and the picturing of beer cans in movies.

Folksy communications suggested that beer should be featured more in the home, both as a beverage and as an ingredient of chocolate cake, salad dressing, and cabbage slaw. The brochure, "Beer in the American Home," stressed the food value of beer. A few dietitians and medical authorities were quoted in support of beer. However, none of the authorities to the contrary were mentioned. Most of the appeal was through poetizing on the "amber liquid," the "sparkling fluid," the jolly elbow friend of ye old British literati around tavern ingle nooks. Recipes based on beer were sent out to the editors of Women's Pages to aid them in their daily columns.

The respectability of beer was presumably established by citing the fact that ale helped to build and maintain some of the old English churches. Said the Foundation:

Committee members for modern church fairs and other "socials" from quilting bees to strawberry festivals can look back to Merrie England for the granddaddy of all popular community gatherings—the "church-ales" of the fourteenth century.

Now times have changed, brought new customs, but the old church-ales are still held in many sections of England, a survival of a period when beer helped maintain active churches and the true community spirit.

No stone was left unturned, not even Plymouth Rock, for another circular asserted that the Pilgrims landed on Plymouth Rock because their beer gave out and they dared not brave the seas without this beverage.

The appeal to business men was that large taxes are paid by the brewing industry; to farmers that beer offers them a market for their products; to laborers that beer is the cheap drink they can afford. The fact that many persons had been given employment was an appeal to everybody.

So much for the careers of some of our prominent public relations counselors. Now let us turn our attention to some of the problems in public relations involved in business.

American business in general was put "on the spot" by the depression of the 1930's. During this critical era executives were coming more and more to recognize the vital importance of cultivating friendly relations with the general public, especially as insurance against radicals who were exploiting the crisis to advance wild proposals for upsetting the old order of things. Paul W. Garrett, Director of Public Relations for the General Motors Corporation, explained the necessity of winning public endorsement of American industry when he delivered an address, in 1938, on "Public Relations —Industry's No. 1 Job." [70] In this talk he made several very significant observations:

Industry's destiny rests and must necessarily rest not on the system's benefits to capital, not on its benefits to labor, but in the final analysis on its benefits to that most important group that is the common denominator of all—the consumer, the group that outnumbers and includes all others. . . .

We have been generally alert in building a profit motive system that has brought to the American consumer the highest standard of living in the history of mankind. We have been inexcusably stupid in our failure to give him an understanding of how it is that consumer dreams and desires become

[70] See, in connection with this discussion, the exposition of the role of Consumer Research in the public relations program of General Motors, on pp. 77-78.

realities under our system of large-scale enterprise. We have made no appreciable effort even to explain the A B C's—the simple premises and processes —of the American plan; to explain that the standard of living for all goes up, and can only be made to go up, as the true price of goods for all is brought down.

And until this elementary concept is got across, how can we expect people to understand that their advanced standard of living—far beyond anything else in the world—is inextricably linked to the characteristic American plan of mass production in industry by which managements are forever striving to drive costs lower and lower to make more and more goods for more and more people? Were this principle understood people would have infinitely greater faith in their own security. They would see that hope ahead lies not in surrendering this basic formula, but in making it work better, and making people understand it better. . . .

Public relations, therefore, is not something that can be applied to a particular phase of a business—nor is it an umbrella covering everything but touching nothing. It is rather a fundamental attitude of mind—a philosophy of management—which deliberately and with enlightened selfishness places the broad interest of the customer first in every decision affecting the operation of the business. . . .

But it is no longer sufficient that business produce goods or services of the kind customers want at a price that customers can pay. Although heaven knows that in itself is hard enough to do. In addition—and here we break into a new field of management responsibility—business must provide and dispense those goods and services in a manner to win general approval and under circumstances that will promote social as well as economic progress. The great lesson that business is learning is that people are interested in more than just the product and the price. They are interested in the way things are done, in what might be called the social products of industry . . . the doing is more important than the saying. But the doing alone is not enough . . . good relations outside grow from good relations inside. . . .

First: A company's public relations program, to get anywhere, must begin in the outer office and inside the plant. If the immediate family is not happy and informed, those whom it meets on the outside will not be. To outsiders those who work for a company are the company—outsiders judge the company by the folks in the company they know. But good relations with employees depend upon something more than high wages. The pay, of course, should be right always, but to almost every employee a sense that he is being treated fairly is just as important as that he is being paid well. Lack of attention to grievances, real or fancied inequalities in treatment, failure to explain the whys and wherefores of company policies—these are the things that underlie most troubles. . . . How the employment office hires, what the foreman does, how the paymaster pays, and how management conducts and articulates itself—these are the A B C prerequisites to building harmony within the family. . . .

It is not always easy to transmit the philosophy of the president to the foreman.   It is not always easy to transmit the philosophy of the foreman to the
top management.   But unless two-way channels of communication are cleared
from top to bottom and from bottom to top, the industrial machine weakens
and one day bogs down. . . .

Second: A company's public relations is strongly rooted in its plant community relations. . . .

Third: With good relations inside the plant, and good relations within the
plant community, you have the base for good relations with the public outside.   But you can never take those relations for granted.   Living right is
not enough.   People must know you live right. . . .

The art of public relations is in the art of multiplication—that is, the art
of multiplying endlessly the good impressions of a company. . . .[71]

"Business Finds Its Voice," a series of articles appearing in *Harper's
Magazine* in early 1938, analyzed the campaign organized and conducted by American business leaders to regain public confidence by
justifying "the American Way" to the American people.   In 1934
Samuel Crowther had criticized business for not stating its case to the
public:

Business is highly skilled in informing the public as to its products . . .
but when it comes to making plain the relation of business to the public, of
the public to business, the efforts are mostly feeble and in nowise match the
vigor and intelligence, to say nothing of the plausibility, of those who would
bring in some other economic system in which private enterprise would not
have a part.

In a similar vein, Bruce Barton, in a speech before the National Association of Manufacturers in 1935, warned his auditors:

If any manufacturer says, "I do not care what the common mass of people
think about my business, whether it be popular or unpopular with them,"
that man is a liability to *all* industry.   No major industry has any moral
right to allow itself to be unexplained, misunderstood, or publicly distrusted;
for by its unpopularity it poisons the pond in which we all must fish.

The easiest way to tell the public something is to say it in advertisements and this is what General Motors did in a succession of
spreads in four colors in the *Saturday Evening Post* and other magazines, featuring the theme, "Who Serves Progress—Serves America,"

---

[71] Excerpts from a speech delivered by Paul W. Garrett at the Twenty-First Annual Convention of the American Association of Advertising Agencies on April
22, 1938.

and offering arguments for the advantages we enjoy as a result of "the American system of free opportunity, free initiative, free competition." One result of this effort on the part of General Motors was a new enthusiasm for "public-relations advertising."

Another avenue of appeal to the public was utilized by the Du Pont Company in its radio program, "Cavalcade of America," which consisted largely of dramatized incidents from American history and "outstanding episodes from the humanitarian side of America's progress." Among such features were the story of the "Seeing Eye" (the organization which trains dogs to guide the blind), the history of anti-tuberculosis Christmas seals, and dramas called *Women in Public Service, Willingness to Share,* and *The Humanitarian Urge.*[72]

Motion pictures proved effective in carrying the message of the service rendered by American business corporations. Du Pont's *The Wonder World of Chemistry,* General Motors' *Progress on Parade, Who Serves Progress, More Jobs for More People, A Car is Born,* the American Iron and Steel Institute's *Steel,* and U.S. Steel Corporation's *The Human Side of Steel* were shown to employee audiences and to the general public, advancing the theme that the abundant life of the typical American has been made possible by virtue of the efficiency and beneficence of our large corporations. The National Association of Manufacturers began making films in 1936, with a "short" entitled *America: Yesterday, Today, and Tomorrow.* Five more films followed, described by the NAM in these terms:

1. *The Light of a Nation* gives the story of American institutions . . . and discusses the various "isms" which threaten the nation.

2. *Men and Machines* is a picturized answer to the argument that machines destroy jobs.

3. *Flood Tide* analyzes the present-day tax situation, warns against rising costs of government.

4. *The Constitution* points out what this remarkable document means to us and how it preserves our individual freedom and our freedom of enterprise.

5. *American Standards of Living* forcibly portrays what the American workingman enjoys as the fruit of labor under the American system.

These films were so successful that NAM continued its program of movie production. Of special interest was the picture, *Everybody's*

---

[72] See S. H. Walker and P. Sklar: "Business Finds Its Voice: Part I." *Harper's Magazine,* January, 1938.

For an account of the "Cavalcade" program, see p. 42 of *Time,* February 26, 1940.

Business, which afforded "dramatic proof that what's 'good for business' is also 'good for the individual.' " [73]

The NAM also sponsored a series of booklets entitled the "You and Industry Series," including brochures on *The American Way, The American Standard of Living,* and *Pattern of Progress.* In *The American Standard of Living* comparisons were made with other countries by reference to various yardsticks: the amount of material goods that each of us has, the yardstick of leisure, expenditures for recrea-

AMERICAN
WAGE EARNER

FRENCHMAN

ENGLISHMAN

ITALIAN

RELATIVE AMOUNT OF WORK REQUIRED TO PURCHASE A RADIO

From *The American Standard of Living,* published by the
National Association of Manufacturers.

tion, advances in public health, and advances in education.   The thesis of this brochure is summarized in the "Conclusion":

A single idea permeates this pamphlet—that by any means of comparison the American standard of living is the highest known to man. It has not been suggested that every individual in the United States enjoys all the benefits of this high standard of living, but we have shown that an increasingly large number of Americans do, that the average for the entire country is extraordinarily high.

It has not been possible in these few pages to analyze every commodity to show its improvement and its increased use. Nor has space permitted the discussion of future standards of living, except as they may be judged by our amazing past performance under the American system of individual enterprise and freedom of thought and action.[74]

Business leaders of the more progressive sort have come to see that public relations cannot be soundly built upon propaganda alone. This point of view has been expressed by three men whose opinions merit quotation:

[73] See S. H. Walker and P. Sklar: "Business Finds Its Voice; Part II. Motion Pictures and Combined Efforts." *Harper's Magazine,* February, 1938.

[74] *The American Standard of Living.*

President Batten of N. W. Ayer & Son

Too many manufacturers . . . neglect their corporate health and then scream for the public relations herb doctor. . . . Any public relations worthy of the name must start with the business itself. Unless the business is so organized and so administered that it can meet at every point the test of good citizenship and of usefulness to the community, no amount of public relations will avail.

Vice-president Kobak of Lord & Thomas

The sooner we stop thinking of public relations as a job of mass hypnotism which will make the public think the way we want it to think, the better for all of us.

President Brown of the Johns-Manville Corporation

We must not think in terms of propaganda. We must think of public relations as a fundamental program to improve the product to be sold and to educate our own people and the public in the true facts about business.[75]

The functions of a public relations counsel in business are well illustrated in the achievements of Lewis H. Brown, President of the Johns-Manville Corporation, who gained widespread recognition for his public relations work in 1938. There were two basic problems facing Mr. Brown. One was Tommy Manville, Jr., whose repeated marital ventures caused much unhappy publicity inasmuch as he was always labeled the "asbestos heir," though not connected in a business capacity with the company from which he inherited his millions. This has been one public relations problem that Johns-Manville has been unable to solve. Another problem lay in the fact that the corporation was a "Morgan Company," a fact that grieved the ten thousand workers who felt, when J. P. Morgan took over the reins, that they had been "sold down the river." *Time* continues the story of the company's progress under Brown's leadership:

Business's new concept of public relations as exemplified by Johns-Manville is an operating philosophy rather than a promotional stunt, actually changing business management instead of just lifting its face. Its basis is the discovery that good public relations begin at home, that Business can "sell itself" permanently to the U.S. public only by developing leaders whose comprehension of public relations is as mature as their knowledge of their particular trades. . . . Lewis Brown went to work for Johns-Manville in 1927. . . . [His] first objectives were . . . plain—to win the confidence of his em-

[75] The three statements cited above are quoted by S. H. Walker and P. Sklar: "Business Finds Its Voice: Part III." *Harper's Magazine*, March, 1938.

ployes and fellow officers, and to last out the depression. . . . [He] had not been president of Johns-Manville very long before he discovered that J-M was anything but popular in most of the 17 towns where it had factories and mines—Waukegan, Ill., for example, where J-M supported a large part of the population. So Johns-Manville came down off its traditional perch, started a pictorial newssheet for employes, issued a series of booklets such as "This is our policy on the closed shop," hired Cartoonist Don Herold to do a set of down-to-earth advertisements for local newspapers. J-M plants, says Lewis Brown, are now getting known as "good neighbors."

J-M sells products to railroads, utilities, automotive concerns, but its chief interest lies in building materials (it sells 28 per cent of a modern house). In 1934 Lewis Brown started the National Housing Guild, a plan to educate local lumber dealers in all the phases of house-building so that a prospective builder can get all his information and all his work at one spot. So far, 5,000 men have spent two weeks at their own expense at the J-M school. It has spread goodwill for J-M into hundreds of hamlets.

Somewhat to Mr. Brown's surprise, something he did a year ago was hailed in the press as the smartest public-relations stunt of the year. He issued an annual report to J-M workers as well as stockholders, couching it in one-syllable words with simple diagrams to show what happened to the J-M dollar. . . . He also put his report to stockholders into plain English instead of accounting jargon. . . .

Last June, Lewis Brown was the first major corporation head to appoint a director to represent the public. He chose Dr. Walter Albert Jessup, president of Carnegie Foundation for the Advancement of Teaching. . . .

Said Businessman Brown . . . as an example of business enlightenment: . . . "In the complex industrial society under which we now live, management no longer represents, as formerly, a single interest; increasingly it functions on the basis of a trusteeship, endeavoring to maintain a proper balance of equity between four basic interlocking groups: the shareholders . . . the jobholders . . . the customers . . . the public." . . .[76]

Very few of the big corporation's thousands of stockholders can attend its annual meetings. Company managements, aware of this gulf between them and their shareholders, are attempting to bridge the gap by the issuance of more personalized information. The officers of General Mills have gone a step further by undertaking the innovation of going directly to their stockholders and talking over with them the company's methods of doing business. The president and other executives of the company hold informal discussions with their stockholders in various parts of the country. At these meetings the board chairman and his associates explain the company's policies and pro-

[76] *Time*, April 3, 1939.

cedures, then answer questions concerning various phases of its operations including labor relations, pension plans, the marketing and advertising of products. As a result the stockholders learn a great deal about their property and the management gains valuable information concerning popular reactions to the company's products and advertising. Expressing approval of this policy a Boston *Herald* editorial makes this comment:

There is such a thing as a pride of ownership which extends beyond the receipt of dividend checks. America's millions of investors are also interested in having a share in enterprises which manufacture good products, provide honest services, maintain fair prices, and give their employes adequate wages and proper working conditions. General Mills' experiment is a constructive attempt to make this sort of ownership more vocal and to adjust policies to it.[77]

The popular idea that public relations consists of tricks for winning friends and influencing people is being replaced by a more adequate concept which involves the removal of the sources for ill will. The Bell Telephone Company was among the first to see the necessity of redefining economic freedom in terms of growing social responsibilities. The relations of a corporation with the public will ultimately depend upon sound company policies based upon a respect for human beings. Business sooner or later has to justify itself at the bar of public opinion. As our personal freedoms become increasingly circumscribed, our social responsibilities have expanded, and, as Childs points out, our greater social interdependence increases the demand for intelligent public-relations counseling. Childs even goes so far as to propose that a corporation should include within its organization a social science division whose function it would be to interpret to the employees and to the public the social implications of the work done by the company. Such a division would go beyond the technological aspects of business procedure to advise the management concerning the environment in which it is operating.[78]

III. POLITICAL PROPAGANDA

We shall review briefly the development of political propaganda in the United States, in Russia, and in Germany.

[77] Boston *Herald*, February 24, 1940.
[78] See H. L. Childs: *An Introduction to Public Opinion*, pp. 13-21. John Wiley & Sons, Inc., 1940.

A. The United States

Propaganda has been used very successfully by the Democratic Party under the direction of Charles Michelson, whose spectacular rise to fame began in 1928.   John J. Raskob had failed in running the Democratic campaign of that year.   He sought a remedy and found it in Michelson, who was at that time serving as Washington correspondent for the New York *World*.   A journalist by training, he had a wide knowledge of politics and a special gift for remembering the missteps in the careers of many public figures.   Under Hearst's wing he had become a master of innuendo and satire.

Michelson directed a spectacular attack on the Republicans in 1929, charging that Hoover was in conspiracy with big-business interests to fix the tariff.   He wrote speeches to be used by prominent Democrats. Eminent men in the party gave him *carte blanche* to issue any statement he chose and to use their names if he cared to do so.

It was an age of personalities.   Michelson attributed every mistake of the Administration to Hoover.   Every unpopular policy was blamed on Hoover.   It was Michelson's strategy first to render Hoover's actions unpopular and then the man himself.   By summating little animosities against the President he hoped to build up hostile sentiment. The Republicans called it a "Smear Hoover" campaign.   Michelson then cast aside his anonymity in a radio talk in which he explained, "We haven't smeared Hoover, the man was already smeared." [79]

Frank R. Kent published an exposé of Michelson's tactics in *Scribner's Magazine*.[80]   Instead of hurting Michelson, the article boosted interest in a column of his, "Dispelling the Fog," and the increased attention was a boost to the Democratic cause.

A book appeared describing Hoover as an exploiter and despoiler of Chinese coolies.   The publishers tried to interest the Democratic Party in its promotion, but Michelson would not touch it.   The Republicans, however, made the blunder of accusing Michelson of fostering the book.   Whereupon, of course, he issued denials.   The book then became a best seller.   Michelson did not allow the occasion to pass without asserting that the Chinese mines failed because of Hoover's lack of administrative ability.

Another weapon in Michelson's smearing campaign was his charge

[79] W. Irwin: *Propaganda and the News*, p. 290 ff. Michelson pinned "the Wall Street tag" on Willkie in the 1940 Presidential campaign. See "The Presidential Campaign." *Propaganda Analysis*, October 15, 1940.

[80] F. R. Kent: "Charley Michelson." *Scribner's Magazine*, September, 1930.

that the Commission for Relief in Belgium, which Hoover directed, was really a plot for feeding Germany during the World War.

Hoover made a mistake which helped the Michelson cause indirectly, when he resisted news reporters who tried to pry into his domestic quarters at the White House. The reporters got even with the President by slanting all their stories against the Administration. They never mentioned Hoover's name without adding a sneer.

While "Al" Smith was opposing Roosevelt's reelection on the ground that the Administration lacked respect for the Constitution, Michelson was busy going through all of Smith's former speeches. He unearthed one that ruined Smith's political prestige. It was a talk before a religious group in which Smith had said that in times of great public emergency it was necessary to put the Constitution on the shelf.

During the summer months of 1935, Roosevelt took several Sundays off for recreation. He was severely criticized for this by a number of ministers. The President was then photographed with his family in their home church and publicity was given to the fact that he attended the vestry meeting there in the afternoon. A week later Roosevelt sent a letter to all the clergymen in the country, asking how the Government could better serve the people.

The President took the carrying of air mail from the civilian airlines and turned it over to the Army. Ten Army fliers were killed and in May, 1934, Roosevelt had to give the concession back to the civilian fliers. To counteract the unhappy publicity occasioned by this incident, Michelson featured the income-tax charges against Mellon and other prominent capitalists.

This was a new method in politics—employing a press agent to create and warp the news. Political propaganda had been languishing in the hands of amateurs until the publicity bureau of the Democratic National Committee brought it up to the times and gave it a professional cast. Roosevelt's secretaries, Howe, McIntyre, and Early, were all newspapermen. The White House established a close relationship with the newsmen and Presidential interviews kept the Administration favorably in the headlines. The slanting of all the news emanating from Washington stimulated the rise of syndicated columns purporting to give the inside story of political events, such as Paul Mallon's "Nation's Politics."

There is a law that no money may be used for the compensation of any publicity expert unless it is specifically appropriated for that purpose. According to a report made to a Senate committee in June, 1937, the Federal Government paid more than $500,000 in the 1936 fiscal year to gentlemen whose services were suspiciously like those of press agents. At one time there were more publicity men in Washington than bona-fide newspaper correspondents, many of the publicity experts busying themselves educating the public with regard to the accomplishments of their several governmental departments. These men were not called press agents, but rather "assistants" to members of the Cabinet, "Chiefs of Press Information," or "Chiefs of Current Information."

B. RUSSIA

Our discussion of political propaganda in Russia will be limited to the period between World War I and World War II.

Political propaganda was developed early in Soviet Russia, since it was necessary to educate a vast population in the ideology of Communism. The Red regime was faced with the task of persuading an illiterate, backward, hungry people that a new order was being ushered in under which there would, in time, be an abundance exceeding that enjoyed by the most prosperous capitalistic countries. Fundamental to the whole program was the introduction of compulsory education for children, for a literate people can be reached far more effectively by propaganda. *New Russia's Primer,* a widely used textbook, is a model of what can be done to train children to new attitudes and new ways of thinking.

While the people were learning how to read, the libraries were being liberally supplied with the proper literature. Books contrary to the communistic ideology were removed from circulation. In 1930 forty-eight per cent of all the books taken from circulation were removed on ideological grounds. Manuscripts for new books are carefully examined and passed on at Moscow by a special institute. Only those approved are printed. The old system of printing books first and censoring them afterward involved too much waste. Library facilities have been increased and the demand for books has grown prodigiously.

In Russia, libraries and schools serve the primary purpose of recording and glorifying the achievements of Communism. Every course of instruction in the public schools is judged not on the basis of its value to the child, but for its value to the Communist state. The school is not the only place where formal education is carried on. There are classes in connection with every factory, and workers are required to attend a certain number of hours each week. Many of the old textbooks have been discarded because they contained "too much church and too much czar." One of the most important centers of education is the Red Army, where picked young men are trained and then sent back to their communities to spread the good word.

Museums offer effective object lessons in the superiority of Communism. Leningrad's Museum of the Revolution is located in some of the 1,057 rooms of the old Winter Palace which once housed the glory of the czars. Bullet holes in the windows and shell scars in the façade have been left unrepaired as memorials of the revolution. Guides are trained to impress visitors with the outrages of the old regime. One guide explained how she enjoyed showing the peasants through the exhibit. "I love to show them the vulgar luxury of these rooms, and picture the corruption and extravagance of their former rulers. I point out the room where Alexander II received his mistress, and the private staircase she used. They see the gorgeous ballrooms and banquet-halls and I tell them about the czar's twenty personal cooks, the czarina's million-ruble gown. You should see them drink it in! Then I take them to the miserable boxes where the 2,000 servants were quartered, and I explain how 7,000 men slaved for seven years just to build the walls of this palace."

Radio and press are, of course, under strict government supervision. Radios are placed largely in clubs in urban communities and in the leading huts in the villages. The programs are devoted extensively to political education and feature news items and educational topics. The Party publishes newspapers especially for workmen and peasants, such as the *Workman's and Peasant's Newspaper*. The ideology of the publications is Bolshevik, and the editors are, for the most part, members of the Party.

The newspaper, as any other educational and cultural agency, exists first of all for the purpose of making Bolsheviks and putting across the program outlined by the government and Party. The information that the newspaper gives is interpreted in the light of Communism and must serve as a foundation for [assuring] the masses of readers that the dominance of the Communist Party is for their welfare. The Soviet government is realizing the advantages of a monopoly of all news agencies. The entire machinery of publication, scientific, technical, and literary, is controlled by the State Publishing Corporation (*Gosizdat*). Since the publishing of any work is dependent on the *Gosizdat,* it is clear that "nonconformist" literature has a slight chance. This is the more important since *Gosizdat* controls not only the publication but also the printing machinery and paper supply. . . . A censorship board examines all manuscripts intended for periodicals, books, scenarios for films, and even drawings, music, and maps—in short, everything that is to be published in the Soviet Union or imported from abroad. This efficient censoring board has local branches which supervise various cultural and other activities in localities. . . . In order to safeguard Soviet citizens from influences coming from abroad an index of prohibited works is kept at the receiving bureau of the post office, to which new titles are added from time to time.[81]

Motion-picture performances are likewise carefully supervised. The Soviet motion picture must not permit itself to become merely a form of amusement, but must help the spectators to understand the ideas of the revolutionary struggle. Films depicting the progress achieved under the Five Year Program were shown not only in Russia but in the United States and other countries. Two of the best propaganda films were *The Little Red Devil* and *Potemkin*. The latter was such a good picture that it gained a wide showing in America and it was such effective propaganda that it had to be censored before it could be shown to American audiences. Few events outside of Russia are included in the "News of the Week" reel that precedes the feature picture in every Russian moving-picture theater. Three types of events in Russia are always depicted. Invariably the Red Army or the Red Navy makes some kind of display.[82] Always some prominent figure of the government is shown in oratorical action. Always, too, Russian boys and girls are shown engaged in athletic sports or parading and demonstrating as Communist pioneers.

C. GERMANY

State propaganda was thoroughly organized in Germany with a unifying singleness of purpose.[83] The National Ministry of Popular Enlightenment and Propaganda was established by the National Socialist government immediately after their accession to power. A militant opposition had to be converted to the ideology of the new one-party rule in which the will of the individual was to be subordinated to the authority of the totalitarian state. The individual was to think as the government dictated. Various devices were employed to secure this end.

Homogeneity of political thinking was symbolized by inaugurating the German salute. Germans were "encouraged" to greet each other

---

[81] B. W. Maxwell: "Political Propaganda in Soviet Russia," in *Propaganda and Dictatorship*, H. L. Childs (Editor). Princeton University Press, 1936.

[82] Compare some of our newsreels here in America.

[83] See F. M. Marx: "State Propaganda in Germany," in *Propaganda and Dictatorship*.

with raised arm in recognition of their national solidarity. *"Heil Hitler"* was substituted for the older greeting of *"Guten Tag."* Printed handbills were distributed in the mail with the following instruction:

It must be the duty of each fellow-citizen who professes his allegiance to our Leader, to demonstrate his loyalty by adorning his dwelling on election day with the symbol of the New Germany, the swastika flag. There must be no house which does not display the sign of National Socialist Germany.

Subsequently an order was issued that "the display of the national flags, especially of the swastika flag, by Jews must cease."

The importance of the leader as a center of emotional investment was recognized in the building up of Hitler as *Der Führer*. The respect engendered for the one and only Leader helped greatly in uniting the quarreling factions which had been debilitating Germany since the end of World War I. The focusing of responsibility on one man meant the substitution of action for parliamentary wrangling. Individual initiative gave way before the supreme authority of *Der Führer*. One of Hitler's promoters, Rudolf Hess, in an appeal to the nation just before the "purge" in 1934, announced:

We see with pride: One man remains always excluded from all criticism—the Leader. That is due to the fact that every one feels and knows: He was always right and will always be right.

Officials who had been called *Führer,* like Dr. Ley, Staff Chief of the Political Organization (*Führer der Deutschen Arbeitsfront*), assumed different titles—Dr. Ley was converted from a *Führer* into *Stabsleiter der P O* by his own decree.

The Third Reich was very careful about what the people read. Just as in Russia, books, periodicals, and newspapers were under strict government surveillance. No newspaper editor, for example, could be employed unless he proved acceptable to the Propaganda Ministry, for according to the Editor Act of December 19, 1933, "Sense of responsibility to state and people and personal integrity shall determine the fitness for the editorial profession." "Inspired" releases were sent out regularly by the government to the editors and they printed them if they knew what was good for them. A recalcitrant newspaper could be suspended for several weeks; such action virtually meant its demise. Some "independent" newspapers were extinguished because they constituted "unsound competition." Publishers were required to trace their "Aryan" descent back to 1800.

The Propaganda Ministry under the leadership of Goebbels mobilized the radio as "the voice of the nation." The goal was "one single public opinion." To achieve this end, weak receiving sets were produced on a large scale at low prices and powerful transmitters were installed. The low price made the sets available on such a wide scale that some 56,000,000 Germans listened to the words of *Der Führer* when he went on the air. The weakness of the sets restricted their range to German stations. The powerful transmitters made that result doubly sure by drowning out foreign broadcasts by means of "jamming."

This brief survey of political propaganda in America, Russia, and Germany reveals how difficult it is for the average citizen to learn the facts necessary for the formulation of an intelligent opinion. Truth is often sacrificed for the furtherance of special ends.

Chapter 11

SOCIAL CONSCIOUSNESS: MORALE

SOCIAL-MINDEDNESS was discussed at some length in Chapters 5 and 6 to exemplify the need of appreciating how one's conduct affects other people. This awareness of our relations with one another as members of various groups in the family, the school, the club, the church, is a very important aspect of our experience as social beings, one that is especially significant for the social psychologist. We are going to explore social consciousness further by discovering how it develops and by what measures it can be fostered to produce good morale.

I. THE SOCIAL SELF

William James said that the social self is the recognition that a man gets from his mates. "We are not only gregarious animals, liking to be in the sight of our fellows, but we have an innate propensity to get ourselves noticed, and noticed favorably, by our kind. . . . [A man] has as many different social selves as there are distinct groups of persons about whose opinion he cares." [1]   A person shows a different side of himself to each of these groups.   He is not the same person alone in Paris as he is with his family in Peoria.   As James put it, "We do not show ourselves to our children as to our club-companions, to our customers as to the laborers we employ, to our own masters and employers as to our intimate friends." [2]   An individual may thus be divided into several selves; or to state the matter in more modern terms, a person develops specific habits in order to adapt himself to specific situations.

According to James, "a man's *fame*, good or bad, and his *honor* or dishonor, are names for one of his social selves." [3]   Every individual has his code of honor, certain requirements which he must measure up

[1] W. James: *Principles of Psychology*, I, pp. 293, 294.   1890.
[2] *Ibid.*, p. 294.
[3] *Ibid.*, p. 294.

to if he is to succeed in meriting the approval of those persons about whose opinion he cares.   Such a code of honor is apt to be definite in its demands, constituting a categorical imperative, in the Kantian phrase, which is to say that the code must be obeyed if, in the light of conscience, peace of mind is to be preserved.   Thus the gambler must pay his gambling debts, though he pay no other.   Edgar Allan Poe felt the disgrace bitterly when his father refused to pay the gambling debts incurred at the University of Virginia.   Poe never recovered from his feeling of shame.

According to a popular saying, there is no honor among thieves. It is true that thieves steal tobacco and dope from one another in prison.   It is true also that thieves frequently betray one another. These instances, however, do not constitute the whole story, for it is just as true that there is honor among some thieves.   Professional thieves, for example, adhere to very definite codes.[4]   Regardless of how strong the ill feeling may be between two thieves, neither of them would want to see the other arrested, and each would exert much effort to prevent it.   One thief will warn another of danger and will avoid doing things which might put other thieves in danger.

A thief will not stop to watch a booster (shoplifter) in a store since such an act might arouse suspicion and cause the booster to get pinched.

Professional thieves give assistance to other professional thieves who are in trouble.   Personal feelings are not allowed to enter if a fellow gets into trouble. . . .   In such a situation, the thief will send money to another doing a bit and the money is regarded as a gift, not a loan.

All thieves are united against one common enemy, the law enforcement agencies.   Their social consciousness is thus developed to a high degree.

If one mob (group) finds a spot heated (dangerous), it will pass the word along to another mob.

One thief will not ask another to reveal his technique.   If the other wanted to tell, he would do so without being asked.

Thieves are tolerant.   Their code is: let everyone grift (steal) as he sees fit.

Codes of ethics are much more binding among thieves than among legitimate commercial firms.   If one mob offers 10 per cent for a putup touch (tip), another mob would not think of offering 15 per cent to outbid the first.

If a mob is falsely accused of a crime, they pay the costs, knowing that the guilty mob will reimburse them.

A thief must never squawk (inform).

If a mob finds another mob working a spot, they move on.

[4] A professional makes a regular business of stealing.   His activities are well planned and organized, from the selection of "spots" to the disposal of goods and the "fixing" of cases if he happens to get "pinched."

If a thief makes a meet (date), he must be there on time.

Money is divided in accordance with a prearranged understanding. The nut (expenses) comes off the top of every touch. No questions are asked, no itemized expense accounts required.

If one member of a mob gets pinched and the fix costs, say, $500, each member contributes his share.

Thieves must deal honestly with each other. A mob must work as a unit.

A member of a mob should not be held responsible for untoward events which he cannot control. There are no complaints. Each member trusts the other to carry his end.

A fixer will not take a stranger until he has been guaranteed by a reliable thief. Once a fixer has taken a thief on, he will go for him after that.

If a thief is sent to prison, his associates contribute to the support of his wife while he is serving his sentence.[5]

Social consciousness is particularly strong among thieves because they must stick closely together for the sake of security; otherwise, they would be deprived of their livelihood and freedom. Their unity is based on an intense consciousness of kind, a strong feeling of solidarity, for they could not function individually without codes to protect them collectively.

The code of the actor's profession is that "the show must go on." Actors feel deeply their responsibility toward their publics; they will not allow illness or indisposition to interfere with their appearances because they realize it is a serious matter to disappoint their "fans." This sense of obligation has been the theme of innumerable dramas. De Wolfe Hopper demonstrated that it is no idle boast of the profession. His death notice in September, 1935, included the following comment:

True to the traditions of a trouper he appeared yesterday for his weekly broadcast with the Kansas City Rhythm Symphony although obviously in distress. He had to be persuaded by friends to go to a hospital afterward.

"His heart was gone," said Dr. H. P. Boughan. "His was a sick body with a mind and spirit that would not admit it." [6]

The medical profession has its code of honor. During an epidemic of infectious disease, laymen may abandon their residences and depart for safer environs; not so the doctor, who must remain at his post even at the risk of his life. Doctors answer sick calls at great inconvenience

[5] Digested from *The Professional Thief*, annotated and interpreted by E. H. Sutherland. University of Chicago Press, 1937.

[6] Boston *Herald*, September 24, 1935.

and accept charity cases at great financial sacrifice. They cannot advertise for patients. They are not supposed to keep secret their research discoveries or to capitalize on them for financial gain. Years ago the Chamberlens learned how to use the forceps in delivery at childbirth and they concealed the technique in order to make money on it; they were punished with disgrace for their dishonorable conduct. Contrast the Chamberlens with Banting, who received a paltry reward for his co-discovery of the value of insulin in the treatment of diabetes; or with Steenbock, who turned over his royalties on vitamin D to the University of Wisconsin. A man who invents a mechanical device can patent it, maintain a monopoly on its profits, and make a fortune for himself by selling the rights and collecting the royalties. Such a course is forbidden by the medical profession for its members because they believe that important discoveries should be made available to doctors everywhere for the relief of human ills.[7]

The business man, too, has a code of sorts. In our capitalistic society it is considered fitting and proper for a business man to profit from somebody else's hard luck or to exploit for personal gain the fruits of his own ingenuity for all they are worth. If business men adopted the code of the medical profession by sharing private discoveries with their "competitors" for the benefit of all the people, such action would revolutionize our economic order. In ordinary times such generosity or unselfishness would be considered so radical as to be absurd. Nevertheless, during World War II, one big industrial company did take this radical step:

AN IMPORTANT DECISION
ON SYNTHETIC RUBBER FOR TIRES

For more than a year this company's Buna rubber patents have been royalty-free to everybody for the duration of the war. Last Thursday we offered, subject to the approval of our stockholders, to transfer *permanently* to the U.S. government (through the government's rubber reserve company) patent rights on Buna-S, the tire rubber which forms the basis of the government's synthetic rubber program. The government's rubber director and rubber reserve company have accepted this proposal. This is the first time, to our knowledge, that any company has offered to government the right to license important patents—royalty-free—forever—to everyone—even to its competitors.

[7] "It is unprofessional to receive remuneration for patents for surgical instruments or medicines." Section 5, "Principles of Medical Ethics" of the American Medical Association. 1937. (535 N. Dearborn St., Chicago, Ill.)

Under the Proposal

1. The government will have a free license for itself not only during the war, but for the entire life of the patents.

2. During the war the government will have the right to issue royalty-free licenses for the entire life of the patents to everyone who cooperates with the government in its war rubber program and reciprocates with similar licenses under its own patents.

3. There will be no payments to us or to others for the patent rights used.

4. The government will increase its expenditures on rubber research to a total of not less than $5,000,000.

Our Purposes

1. To give every possible incentive to cooperation in the war rubber program.

2. To remove concern about the post-war patent situation from the minds of all those who have a contribution to make to this program.

3. To encourage American research and ingenuity—among independent workers, small companies and large—to build up a new and great American industry.

4. To continue to do everything we can to assure tires for America's cars—*always*.

STANDARD OIL COMPANY
(NEW JERSEY)

Scientists are ideally motivated by the quest for truth rather than by a desire for pecuniary gain. A study of 137 American inventors chosen at random in 1927 from the *Patent Office Gazette* revealed that only 16.5 per cent of them claim that they have invented for economic gain.[8] Scientific research workers, according to their own say-so, are motivated by the desire to serve humanity, by curiosity, and by a desire for social recognition far more than by a desire for high financial remuneration.[9] The Curies exemplified this spirit in their attitude toward the opportunity to make money from their discovery of radium. A letter came one day from technicians in America who wanted to exploit radium there. Pierre Curie consulted his wife.

[8] L. J. Carr: "A Study of 137 Typical Inventors." *Publications of the American Sociological Society*, 1929, 23, 204-206.

[9] R. Stagner: "Motivation of Scientific Research." *Sigma Xi Quarterly*, 1934, 22, 112-113.

"We have two choices," Pierre told her. "We can describe the results o our research without reserve, including the processes of purification. . . ."

Marie made a mechanical gesture of approval and murmured:

"Yes, naturally."

"Or else," Pierre went on, "we can consider ourselves to be the proprietors the 'inventors' of radium, patent the technique of treating pitchblende, anc assure ourselves of rights over the manufacture of radium throughout the world."

Marie reflected a few seconds. Then she said:

"It is impossible. It would be contrary to the scientific spirit."

Pierre's serious face lighted. To settle his conscience, he dwelt upon it mentioning, with a little laugh, the only thing which it was cruel for him to give up:

"We could have a fine laboratory too."

Marie's gaze grew fixed. She steadily considered this idea of gain. Almos at once she rejected it.

"Physicists always publish their researches completely. If our discover has a commercial future, that is an accident by which we must not profit And radium is going to be of use in treating disease. . . . It is impossible to take advantage of that."

She made no attempt to convince her husband; she guessed that he had spoken of the patent only out of scruple. The words she pronounced with complete assurance expressed the feelings of both, their infallible conception of the scientist's role.

Pierre added, as if settling a question of no importance:

"I shall write tonight. . . ."

They had chosen forever between poverty and fortune.[10]

Dr. George Washington Carver, famous Negro scientist, teacher a Tuskeegee, was another illustration of the scientist's indifference to monetary inducements. Whenever he discovered something he im mediately gave the idea away. "Mankind," the Doctor commented "is being benefited, and that is the purpose for which my work is in tended." From the peanut he made nearly 300 useful products, in cluding cheese, candies, instant coffee, pickles, oils, shaving lotions dyes, lard, linoleum, flour, breakfast foods, soap, face powder, sham poo, printer's ink, and axle grease; from wood shavings he made syn thetic marble; from the lowly sweet potato he extracted 118 products including starch, library paste, vinegar, shoe polish, ink, dyes, and mo lasses. Dr. Carver did more than any other man to rehabilitate agri culture in the South. He turned down an invitation from Edison to

[10] From *Madame Curie*, by Eve Curie, copyright, 1937, by Doubleday and Com pany, Inc.

work for him in his laboratories because he felt he was needed in the South; he rejected another offer with a salary of $100,000. Money meant nothing to him. He told some wealthy peanut growers in Florida how to cure their diseased crops. They sent him a check for $100, promising the same amount monthly as a retainer. He sent back the check, telling them that "God didn't charge anything for growing the peanut," and that he "shouldn't charge anything for curing it." He continued to live on his meager salary at Tuskeegee, devoting himself to his labors with no thought of financial gain. Such is the spirit of the scientist who finds his primary joys in his work.

Every profession has its written and unwritten traditions which govern the conduct of its members. What James described as the social self is simply the system of habits that a person develops in order that he may maintain his self-respect and merit the approval of those "about whose opinions he cares."

The social self evolves as the growing person learns how to meet the standards of behavior which others come to expect of him. For this reason Cooley described the social self as the looking-glass self, a reflection of the attitudes of one's fellows as these are incorporated into one's own style of life.[11] Early in life the child learns that other people react to him. Even the infant discovers that he can manipulate other persons by crying. In later years, girls and even women may employ the same technique to good advantage; men, according to the dictates of our culture, cannot resort to this device without a loss of prestige. There are certain privileges that a man does enjoy, however, such as the right to seek openly the esteem of a girl who catches his fancy; whereas the girl who sees a man she wants to notice her must be more subtle in her appeals for attention. Indeed, persons of both sexes learn by experience that it is wise in our society to win affection and respect by indirect means. A student who is eager to make a certain fraternity, for example, is not supposed to solicit the friendship of the active brothers by calling on them in their rooms and making them presents of choice cigars. Rather, the aspirant must be more subtle about it: make the basketball team, wear the right clothes, smile when smiled at, and indicate in a general fashion the direction of his fraternal inclinations. So it is in most social situations—we establish ourselves socially in the eyes of others not by begging openly for their good opinion but by conducting ourselves in such a way as to win their esteem.

[11] See C. H. Cooley: *Human Nature and the Social Order*, pp. 184-185. Revised edition, 1922.

The process of social adjustment depends, to a large extent, upon learning how to anticipate the reactions of others to our actions. Thus we are able to govern our own behavior in the light of its social effects. This consideration for the feelings of others is the essence of tact. As the individual becomes socialized, he learns to be thoughtful of others, to inhibit cutting remarks, to avoid unintended slights. Being tactful requires a high degree of the social sense, the ability to put oneself in the place of others and to appreciate their emotional responses in a given situation. The development of tact is one important factor in the evolution of the social self.

II. IDENTIFICATION WITH THE GROUP

The ability to identify oneself with one's fellows is the basis of social consciousness. The group self or "we" is an extension of the "I" to include other persons. When my wife says that *we* mowed the

Vicarious Football.   (Wide World Photo.)

lawn, she is using the "editorial we," that is, she means I mowed it and she engaged in the task vicariously by "feeling for" me as she watched me work. Credit is often appropriated where credit is not due by this process of introjection (identification). So some Americans boast that "we won the war," even though they did not fight or buy War Bonds or serve as air-raid wardens; and college students take great pride in a winning team, when their only contribution to the cause is a cheer as some star crosses the goal line. One of the induce-

ments for joining any group is the chance to share in the glory resulting from the achievements of any of its illustrious members.

The "we-feeling" is developed primarily in family relationships, as
children identify themselves with their parents, as husband and wife
share the responsibilities of parenthood and the companionship of
married life, as family ties are nourished by the intimate associations
within the home. Psychotherapists are stressing the importance of
building the right kind of "we-feeling" in children as a basic step
toward successful social adjustments outside the home. This kind of
a healthy "we-psychology" depends upon happy and adequate parent-
child relationships tending to security and satisfaction; upon an understanding of one's own values and a sensitiveness to the values of
others. It is by human affection that we live in other lives more than
in our own. Robert Southwell expressed this thought long ago, when
he said: "Not where I breathe, but where I love, I live."

"The original and elementary subjective fact in society," according
to Giddings, "is the consciousness of kind." [12] This "consciousness of
kind" manifests itself in the agreeable sense of belonging, as we noted
in Chapter 1; it is manifested in the like-mindedness fostered by imitation and other psychological processes which promote conformity
and uniformity in behavior patterns (Chapters 7-9); it is made manifest in the social-mindedness of those persons who show concern for
the ways in which their conduct may affect their fellows (Chapters
5-6). Despite the shortcomings we have noted in the matter of social
responsibility, despite the inhumanity of prize fighting, the third degree, concentration camps, and war, we are justified, I believe, in asserting that human beings, in the long perspective, have been gradually gaining in social consciousness. Evidence for such a claim may
be found in the increase of human kindness and the decline in cruelty,
complementary aspects of the sympathy that evolves as man becomes
more aware of his kinship with his fellow man.

Human nature has changed, and is changing, for the better. Despite
gloomy reversals and temporary tragic eras, the slow surge is away from ignorance and cruelty, and toward decency and kindness.

If you sometimes doubt this, glance back at life in the *best* of the good old
days. Consider the golden age of Elizabeth—around 1600. The strong were
boastful, drunken, and murderous; the weak were voiceless and uncham-
pioned.

Care of the insane, the halt and the blind was unknown. Lunatics were

---

[12] F. H. Giddings: *The Principles of Sociology*, p. 17. See especially pp. 132-152.
Third edition, 1920.

chained in dungeons, or exposed in cages to public view. . . . A sadism incomprehensible to the modern mind disfigured the games of the day; unless sport was cruel, spectators were bored. . . . At local fairs men fought each other with heavy clubs, the combat ending when one was beaten to insensibility. . . .

The cruelties of yesterday were nowhere better exhibited than on the high seas. Herman Melville's *White Jacket* describes how in the United States Navy a man could be flogged till his bones gleamed white. Hands trussed above his head, the dreaded "cat" was laid on, each blow raising an indelible weal on the man's back; usually before the last lash the victim was unconscious. Publication of *White Jacket* in 1850 led our Navy to abolish flogging, but merchant sailors were shredded piecemeal by the "cat" as late as 1870.

More murderous yet was the practice of keelhauling, common among American whaling ships during the first half of the 19th century. To keelhaul a man, you tied him to a rope that had been passed under the ship's bottom. His shipmates pulled at the other end of the rope, dragging the victim overboard, under the keel and up the other side of the hull, while the barnacles lacerated him to ribbons. Sometimes, mercifully, he was drowned. . . .

Within the memory of living men the fight for the twelve-hour day began. Mill and factory owners, slow to acknowledge the human rights of the employed, stubbornly resisted the movement toward shorter hours and better pay. Only the growth of an informed, organized, humane public opinion has brought about the change. . . .

The outstanding human development in the past century, and especially the past 25 years, is the growth of a sense of obligation to our fellows. Community consciousness grows ever stronger, more effective. . . . War, crime, and disease still rack our state—but we are even more painfully racked by a desire to abolish these evils. . . .

Human beings are not the ornery, cross-grained, calloused creatures they used to be.[13]

The growth of sympathy is predicated upon our increasing ability to identify ourselves with other individual human beings. Jesus set up the ideal in this respect when he said: "Inasmuch as ye have done it unto one of the least of these, my brethren, ye have done it unto me." Our sense of common humanity, as far as it goes, is kindled extensively by membership in groups. Identification with a group produces a feeling of comradeship, a "we-experience," that constitutes our predominant form of social consciousness. We shall examine this sense of belonging, first in the satisfactions derived from joining a frater-

[13] R. W. Riis: "Human Nature Has Changed." *Liberty,* November 29, 1941. Condensed under the same title in the *Reader's Digest,* December, 1941.

nity, second in the contrast between in-groups and out-groups, third in the development and prolongation of class distinctions.

A. Fraternities

A fraternity offers a gateway to a never-never land where ordinary persons escape their own insignificance by joining in mystic rituals of mutual flattery. The plain bank teller of the workaday world becomes, on lodge night, a Sir Knight Errant of the Mystic Order of Granada.

It is characteristic of secret orders that the names they bear are high-spirited and resounding, on a plane above the routine affairs of daily living. The Shriners are not simply Shriners; they are members of the Ancient Arabic Order of Nobles of the Mystic Shrine. The Grottos are not simply Grottos; they are members of the Mystic Order of Veiled Prophets of the Enchanted Realm. There are many other "Mystic" orders. There are many "Illustrious" orders, many "Imperial" orders, many "Exalted" orders. Frequently there are orders which are several of these at once. On the heels of the Illustrious and Exalted Order of Crusaders may come the Imperial and Illustrious Order of the Mystic and Exalted Cross. These are good adjectives, and possibly by this time some five million Americans have identified themselves with at least one of them. Possibly five million more Americans have identified themselves with two other adjectives which prefix the names of at least fifty thriving orders. These two are "Royal" and "Ancient"; and the popularity of each is understandable in a nation which has neither royalty nor antiquity, but a vicarious enthusiasm for them both.

To live in a modern world and be an ancient; to live in a humdrum world and be a knight; to live in a gabby world and have a secret—all this is possible. It is the essence of fraternalism that it does its best to make it possible. An illustrious name is only a beginning. . . . On the dais sits a Monarch or a Master, a Supreme Seignior, an Illustrious Potentate, a Grand Illuminator, or a Maharajah. No secretary is a secretary in this world of dreams come true; he is a Thrice Illustrious Scribe. No treasurer is a treasurer; he is an August Keeper of the Strong Box. No citizen is a citizen; he is a knight, a monk, a priest, a dervish, or an ogre. . . .

From the street outside you climb a flight of well-worn stairs to the second landing. There is a door of varnished oak, behind which stands the Lord High Seneschal. It is just an average door; but beyond lies mystery, drama, opportunity to share great names and take a hand in deeds well done, the satisfaction of "belonging." [14]

[14] C. Merz: *The Great American Band Wagon*, Chapter 3, "Sweet Land of Secrecy." The John Day Company, 1928.

B. In-groups and Out-groups

Group consciousness is stimulated by cooperation within and opposition outside the group. The formation of a club, fraternity, or some other kind of association establishes an in-group for those who belong and an out-group for those who remain on the outside looking in. It is fun to be on the "inside." Indeed, there is no sense in joining a group unless it excludes somebody. As one cynic put it: "Many a party is given for the pleasure of not inviting someone."

The conflict between the town and gown is an instance of the opposition between the ins and the outs. Townies from Cambridge, for example, will go to the Harvard Stadium and invariably root for the visiting team. Violent clashes sometimes occur between college boys and residents of the same town. G. Stanley Hall mentions the strong feeling of antagonism existing where he spent his boyhood, between the villagers and the out-of-towners. When the out-of-towners came to the village, they were always "dressed up" and self-conscious of their status as outsiders. Not a few intermarriages between the villagers and the out-of-towners resulted unhappily. The line of cleavage appeared in nearly all town affairs, such as the election of officers in town and church.[15]

The psychological significance of identifying oneself with a group is illustrated by the story of a preacher who delivered a very dramatic sermon that moved the congregation to tears. Only one man in the audience kept his composure. He explained afterward to an inquisitive neighbor that he was not weeping because he did not belong to the parish.

The feeling of group solidarity is fostered by group activities. Schanck describes how the service in a Methodist Church begins with two chants sung without recourse to song books; then later the Apostles' Creed is read in unison. Both of these ceremonies, says Schanck, make the non-member conscious of the fact that he is an alien.[16]

The assumption that one's own group is superior to all others is the basis of ethnocentrism. Ethnocentrism refers to the social consciousness of a race or nation, especially to the feeling of superiority that is shared by all the members who belong. Other peoples do not amount to much in comparison. The ethnocentric attitude is important in

[15] G. S. Hall: *Life and Confessions of a Psychologist*, p. 58. 1923.
[16] See R. L. Schanck: "A Study of a Community and Its Groups and Institutions Conceived of as Behaviors of Individuals." *Psychological Monographs*, 1932, No. 195, p. 75.

nourishing a naïve sort of patriotism and in promoting international ill will, thus contributing to the causation of war. Indeed, war is sometimes resorted to by nationalistic leaders to consolidate the citizenry of the nation in defense against a common enemy. Propaganda asserting the special virtues of the nation and disparaging all others is useful in building up group consciousness on a national basis.

In-groups are formed within groups, as members combine into cliques. Schopenhauer tells how this happens:

Take the case of a large number of people who have formed themselves into a league for the purpose of carrying out some practical object; if there be two rascals among them, they will recognize each other as readily as if they wore a similar badge, and will at once conspire for some . . . treachery. In the same way, if . . . there is a large company of very intelligent and clever people, among whom there are only two blockheads, these two will be sure to be drawn together by a feeling of sympathy, and each of them will very soon secretly rejoice at having found at least one intelligent person in the whole company.[17]

Satisfaction is derived from being on the inside, and if one can be on the inside of the inside, so much the better for one's vanity and self-complacency.

C. Class Distinctions

Another phase of grouping as it affects social consciousness is the identification of oneself with a particular class in society; this gives rise to so-called class-consciousness.

By class is meant two or more orders of people who are believed to be, and are accordingly ranked by the members of the community, in socially superior and inferior positions. Members of a class tend to marry within their own order, but the values of the society permit marriage up and down. A class system also provides that children are born into the same status as their parents. A class society distributes rights and privileges, duties and obligations, unequally among its inferior and superior grades. A system of classes, unlike a system of castes, provides by its own values for movement up and down the social ladder. In common parlance, this is social climbing, or in technical terms, social mobility.[18]

[17] A. Schopenhauer: *Essays*, p. 143. Home Library Edition.
[18] All of the quotations in this section on Yankee City (Newburyport) are taken from W. L. Warner and P. S. Lunt: *The Social Life of a Modern Community.* Yale University Press, 1941. This is the first volume of the six-volume Yankee City Series.

Warner and Lunt found Yankee City dominated by a class order. One would expect this observation to hold true of a New England town "with a social organization which had developed over a long period of time under the domination of a single group with a coherent tradition." The social life of the community was governed by a system of superordination and subordination, with each and every person ranked somewhere in the hierarchy. Personal relationships were regulated by the class context, particularly among the women, who "were very conscious of class. . . ." The percentage distribution of the population among the six discernible classes is represented in this diagram:

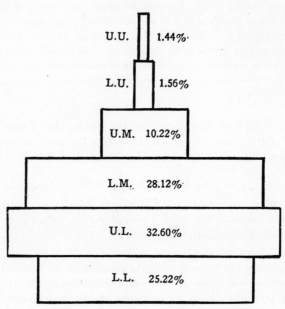

The Class Hierarchy of Yankee City

U.U. = Upper Upper; L.U. = Lower Upper;
U.M. = Upper Middle; L.M. = Lower Middle;
U.L. = Upper Lower; L.L. = Lower Lower.

Though smallest in number, the upper-upper and lower-upper classes exerted the predominant influence in politics.

Although the voters among the three lower classes far outnumber those in the three higher, they had a disproportionately small percentage of officers in the political hierarchy. In other words, the upper classes held a greater proportion of the higher offices than their numbers in the voting and general population would by mere chance allow them. Indeed, as the importance of the political offices increased, the proportion of upper-class officeholders increased. Class is therefore an important factor in Yankee City politics. . . .

The personnel of the school board was also examined for the class status of its several members. Because of the high importance of the educational structure in American society, the class position of the members of this board is of obvious importance. One member of the board was upper-upper, one lower-upper, five upper-middle, and one lower-middle. No members of the two low classes served on the school board. It is perhaps significant that the two unsuccessful candidates in the election in which these members took office were both of the lower-middle class.

This investigation of Yankee City is a pioneer venture in the application of anthropological techniques to the study of a modern civilized community. For this reason, the general line of procedure is worth noting. The research staff of thirty persons consisted of writers, analysts, and field workers, some individuals fulfilling several of these functions. The staff employed the interview, observation, questionnaire and schedule; they examined case histories, biographies, life histories, and autobiographies; they looked over genealogies and kinship charts; they delved into documentary material including directories, records, rules, membership lists; they analyzed newspaper and magazine clienteles; they made surveys of community activities, place of residence, source of income, family budgets, and so on. One important phase of the project was the analysis of memberships in various associations to determine their class structures.

As the associations increase in size, the opportunity increases for the members of the lower classes to move upward in the class hierarchy, inasmuch as in the large groups they are in contact with more individuals of the other classes. In like manner, the large association furnishes a device by which members from the upper brackets of the class system may subordinate and control those inferior to them. . . . The associations whose members were from six classes were few in number, and those of one class, still fewer. There is a tendency for those with six classes to be large associations, and those with one to be small.

The Yankee City investigators began their research with the assumption that class stratification would be determined by the economic level. This assumption had to be abandoned in the light of overwhelming evidence to the contrary: a person on a lower social level may make more money than a person on a higher social level. Indeed, the highest average income for each individual was in the lower-upper class. The most significant finding of the research turned out to be this: rank-status is determined by a complex of factors, *wealth* being only one factor in the total configuration. *Type of occupation* is important. It correlates closely with social position. Eighty-three per cent of the upper-upper class earn their living in professional or proprietary positions; none of them are "workers." *Family background* is significant. Upper-uppers are exclusively "Yankees."

No person is accepted by the upper-upper class as one of them unless he is a Yankee, and that in a special sense. His family origins must go back early in the city's history; the person must fit in the New England tradition and measure up, genealogically, to its important values.

"Family connections" are stressed particularly among the elite. Approved *geographical location of residence* is practically essential. "The right neighborhood" is a great social asset. It is a token of respect to remark that Jones "lives up on Hill Street"; it is conversely a symbol of low esteem to state that somebody is a "Riverbrooker." A spot map showed that not all "Hill Streeters" lived on Hill Street and not all on Hill Street were "Hill Streeters." "Hill Streeter" must be interpreted as a term of rank, not as an accurate designation of residence. This observation is significant in demonstrating that class is determined by a number of conditions, no one of which may be taken *per se* as an adequate criterion. *Clubs* influence class status. Some few associations, like the American Legion, embrace all classes. Higher classes belong to social clubs and charitable organizations; lower classes, to fraternal orders and their auxiliaries. Upper-middles are allowed in charitable associations; in fact, this class prefers this type of "club." Lower-middles are excluded from or refuse to join the charitable societies. *Cliques* (informal, intimate associations) play a role in the social ranking, as do *education* and *manners*.

There are other aspects of class behavior in Yankee City which deserve mention. The upper classes maintain a "social distance" by means of private schools—none of the upper-uppers were attending the local high school at the time of this research—by means of large grounds, nurses for the children, large houses, infrequent use of public conveyances. "Money is of importance only as it enables one to carry out the behavior which is felt to be inherently appropriate to the upper-class configuration. . . ." Let me summarize other findings in my own words:

In the upper-upper class, women predominate; in the lower-lower, men. Men in the upper-upper class leave town when they are old enough to go to work, for the sake of better opportunities. Many females among the upper-uppers remain single and stay at home because they are under pressure to marry within their own class—the eligible young men, as noted above, have departed in search of more promising employment. The uppers marry late, the lowers at an early age; the uppers have small families, the lowers large ones.

Uppers spend more time over their breakfast.

Uppers live in old houses, kept in good condition. Uppers own their houses or rent by the month. Lowers rent and pay by the week.

Lower-uppers go in for conspicuous display: expensive houses and cars and the like.

Uppers are more apt to attend the Episcopalian church; lowers, the Baptist.

Lowers spend a higher proportion of their smaller incomes for food and shelter.

Lowers are more liable to arrest. Uppers who commit the same crimes, go unmolested.

Uppers read the *Atlantic Monthly,* the Boston *Herald.* Lowers read *True Story,* the Boston *American,* or *Daily Record.* Middles read the Boston *Globe* or Boston *Post.*

Highest attendance at the movies is among the upper-lowers; lowest, among the upper-uppers.

People choose their doctors, dentists, undertakers from members of their own class: higher rank patients are cared for by higher rank doctors.

Rising in the class hierarchy is a slow process. Cliques allow social climbers to form intimate associations with people above them, thereby improving their chances for climbing. "Bettering oneself" is often accomplished by means of a "fine marriage." This step upward has to be achieved against pressure, since higher-ups are trained not to marry beneath themselves. These upward and downward pressures are exerted by the application of various effective sanctions: welcome or ostracism, as the case may be.

It is very significant, from the point of view of class psychology, that the exclusive uppermost class sends its children to private schools (in England, "public" schools) where ideals of distinction are absorbed. The boy who goes to Groton or Lawrenceville is bound to develop an awareness of his own social superiority; if he goes on to Harvard, he is not likely to identify himself with the "common people." Spartan cubicles and tin basins cannot disguise the fact that a "Grottie" is groomed to be an aristocrat.

The twenty-five cents weekly is the great equalizer at Groton. . . .
Despite this effort to build an economic proletariat and to submerge fifty-

cent Morgans, Groton remains "the" of American private schools. There
are several reasons for this. For one thing, waves of Adamses, Auchin-
closses, Biddles, Coolidges, Frothinghams, Gardiners, Lawrences, Morgans,
Motleys, Roosevelts and Whitneys have, over the years, formed a somewhat
well-knit clientele. Then, too, there have been outward marks of swank,
stiff collars for supper, patent leather shoes for evening study hall, and particularly the Groton accent—the very broad *a*, the lack of *r*, and the affectedly
clear enunciation of the last syllable of long words. . . .

Attributed to the Grottie alone is the ability to carry on a conversation
with a casual acquaintance and yet keep his eye focused two inches over the
other's head. . . .

Unmistakably, under the outward snobbery, there is something very inward about Groton. It is the simple fact that the whole school—graduates,
masters, boys, and all—considers itself one family. Grotonians feel about
other people that they may be very nice and that they may even someday be
friends of theirs, but unless it is a girl whom one of them will marry, another
person can never be a member of the family. As such, another person must
remain separated by that distance as if by blood. . . .

If, in all this, Doctor Peabody collected nice names, he did not mind.
And even the football coaching staff—Noble, Whitney, Wright, and Hallo-
well—read in any order, reaches the tone pitch of a State Street Boston law
firm. . . .[19]

Private school training like that provided at Groton instills a sense of
class.

Occupation—together with the property level and the family connections which often determine the choice of a line of work—influences
a person's status very definitely. Professional vocations such as the
law and the ministry carry more prestige than manual labor. A white-
collar job like that of a school teacher is considered more respectable
than a career in plumbing where the work gets a man dirty; a secre-
tarial job is more conducive to social acceptability than work as a
maid. Such distinctions are usually respected by all parties concerned.
A maid, for example, does not sit down and chat with the family in the
living room. Every occupation has its social status, a fact that must
be taken into account in contemplating the choice of a vocation, for
a man cannot be happy in a job, even if his abilities run in that direction, if he is ashamed of the way he is earning his livelihood. In this
connection it is of interest to note an experiment conducted by Counts
in which forty-five occupations were ranked by high-school seniors,
senior trade-school boys, freshmen in an agricultural college and by
school teachers; the rank orders assigned by these different groups

[19] C. Amory: "Goodbye, Mr. Peabs." *Saturday Evening Post*, September 14, 1940.

were found to be in remarkable agreement. These attitudes toward occupations must be taken into consideration by counselors engaged in vocational guidance. Counts suggests:

It has often been remarked by those interested in the problems of vocational guidance that an extraordinarily large proportion of the children in the high schools are looking toward the professions. This has been taken as evidence of defective knowledge on the part of the high-school pupil of the world in which he lives. The present investigation would suggest that high-school students know a great deal about this world. They look forward to the professional occupations because they are sensitive to the social judgment and because they recognize the prestige which is attached to these callings. The difficulty, perhaps, is that they know too much rather than too little about the world into which they are going.

The problem of guidance is greatly complicated by these differences in social status. If all occupations were of equal standing in the community, the counselor could be somewhat more arbitrary in advising individuals to enter or to avoid certain occupations. He could think chiefly in terms of the abilities of pupils and vigorously encourage each to enter the occupation for which he is best fitted. As it is, we must proceed very slowly in advising a pupil not to enter any occupation that attracts him. In our society, in spite of what is said about the dignity of labor, many occupations which are clearly necessary to the promotion of the common good are stamped as unworthy and are thus given an essentially negative standing. This situation must be faced frankly and honestly. We must either follow the policy of pointing out to our pupils the great differences in the social status of occupations or make some definite effort through the schools and other educational agencies so to alter the prevailing social attitudes that every occupation which is necessary to the life of society will be accorded positive social recognition.[20]

Among individuals who are engaged in occupations of the same general social status, mutual interests and mutual problems provide a basis for a feeling of comradeship. People of the same occupational status tend to stick together both in their work and in their social activities. Social adjustment is facilitated by a respect for such distinctions. Individuals who ignore the factor of status, who fail to "keep their places," are likely to be humiliated sooner or later by those persons who impose the sanctions of exclusiveness in order to maintain their social superiority. The conflict of occupational values in such a situation makes it clear that all concerned will get along better in the long run if "birds of a feather flock together."

[20] G. S. Counts: "The Social Status of Occupations." *School Review,* January, 1926.

Class consciousness is far more significant in our psychology than most of us realize. We shun talk about class privilege and make believe to ourselves that there really aren't any classes; that we're all just one happy family.

Current social science plays down the omnipresent fact of class antagonisms and conflicts in the living all about us. It studies industrial strikes and analyzes wage differentials and the operation of trade and industrial unions and the machinery for collective bargaining. But it is careful, in the main, to keep the word "class" out of its analysis and to avoid the issue of the possibility of the existence of fundamental cleavages which may not be remediable within our type of economy. Social science does this because the concepts of "class" and "class struggle" lead straight into highly inflammable issues. It is helped in so doing by the tradition that class divisions are un-American and that such differences as exist are transitory and will be eliminated by a rising standard of living and "the general movement of Progress." [21]

Classes there are in American society and they exert a considerable influence on our social behavior—facts that are borne out by the observations made in Yankee City. Similarly, Kornhauser's investigations of "class" feeling show that differences in attitude exist among occupational and income groups with respect to certain broad social-political questions. The greatest disagreement in attitude, he found, was between the highest and lowest income groups, and between major business executives and labor union officials, when the persons in these several groups were requested to register their reactions to such issues as the following:

The New Deal.
The Government should leave the business system alone as far as possible.
Wealthy businessmen have too much influence in running the affairs of the nation.
Strong labor unions.
Equalization of wealth.
Government ownership and operation of big industries. [22]

Analysis of the popularity of President Roosevelt as evidenced by a number of polls demonstrated that he was most popular with the lower

---

[21] R. S. Lynd: *Knowledge For What?*, p. 227. Princeton University Press, 1940.

[22] See A. W. Kornhauser: "Analysis of Class Structure of Contemporary American Society—Psychological Bases of Class Divisions," Chapter 11 in *Industrial Conflict: a Psychological Interpretation*, G. W. Hartmann and T. Newcomb (Editors). The Dryden Press, 1939.

income group, least popular with the upper income group, in between for popularity as far as the middle income group was concerned. This correlation of political attitude with income level was noted in Chapter 3 as one of the most significant developments in recent American political history.

It is easy to fall into the error of oversimplifying the situation when we notice such a connection between income and political views. Closer investigation of the matter will convince us that social opinions are not determined exclusively by economic factors. Attitudes are influenced by the personal traits, the schooling, the sex and age and race and religion of the individual, all of which play a part in generating the economic status—and the social attitudes, according to Kornhauser. This multiplicity of correlative factors helps to account, too, for another datum that must not be overlooked, namely, "the non-uniformity of opinion within homogeneous socio-economic groups." Evidence for such non-uniformity is not lacking. For example:

> The $3,000-$5,000 group tends to agree with lower classes on questions having to do with weaknesses in the present distribution of wealth and influence and with the need for reform. However, they swing toward the wealthy group in opposition to the lower classes when it comes to questions of strong labor sympathies and socialization of industry (threats to the present order from the under-privileged and radical). Variations of this sort from one type of issue to another constitute a further reason why the income groups cannot properly be thought of as clearly defined classes.[23]

One of the strange psychological facts about persons who are poor is that they are not as distressed over their condition as their economic plight would seem to warrant. A *Fortune* poll, for instance, showed that the poor were almost as much in favor of allowing the inheritance of an unlimited amount of money, as were the wealthy; and the poor were just about as firm as the prosperous in their faith that a young man has a good chance today to rise to the point of earning $5,000 a year.[24] Attitudes of this sort on the part of persons in poverty help us somewhat to understand how it is that they accept their lot without being particularly unhappy about it. When the Lynds asked residents of Middletown whether they thought the gap was widening between business people and workers as the depression (of the 1930's) continued, they found the question made businessmen uneasy. Busi-

[23] *Ibid.*
[24] *Fortune*, October, 1936.

ness people do not like to think of "classes"; they feel happier in ignoring the possibility of their existence.

Tradition aids them in thus disregarding such distinctions, for, according
to the "American way," even the workingman with a wife and four children
and eighteen dollars in his Saturday pay envelope is on his way to becoming,
if not a millionaire, at least independent and secure in his old age. Or, if he
isn't, it is because he is lacking in initiative or thrift or industry, and is therefore simply getting what he deserves—which is in itself a vindication of the
tradition.[25]

The workers themselves in Middletown appeared to be unconscious
of any class alignment even in the sixth year of a great depression.
The Lynds attributed this phenomenon to the fact that the working
people seemed to possess the capacity to adjust themselves to untoward
circumstances, getting along somehow with or without a job, existing,
come what might.

If the Lynds are correct in finding workingmen unconscious of class
distinctions, Marx's prediction of what the future would bring is definitely not applicable to the American scene to date. Marx believed
that manual workers would become increasingly discontented with
their lot; finally they would revolt and gain ascendancy by sheer force
of numbers; out of the class struggle there would come a classless society.[26] But there can be no class struggle in America until there are
classes which are clearly aware of their distinctive status and clearly
aware of the need for a struggle. Instead of a clearly defined *class*
struggle we now observe innumerable struggles—between rival industries, like oil versus coal; between chain stores and independent gro-
ceries; between the American Federation of Labor and the Congress
of Industrial Organizations. The term "class struggle," Chase maintains, is without tangible validity, though it does provide a useful psychological stimulus to labor organization, furnishing a feeling of solidarity and fighting morale.[27]

The laboring classes are being educated to see the wisdom of uniting
themselves for a common purpose. Labor unions have done much to
impress upon the workingman the necessity of organizing for the protection of his rights. Efforts are being made to organize labor for the
exertion of political influence in its own behalf. The Political Action

[25] R. S. Lynd and H. M. Lynd: *Middletown in Transition,* p. 444. Harcourt,
Brace and Company, 1937.
[26] See K. Marx and F. Engels: *The Communist Manifesto.* 1848.
[27] See S. Chase: *The Tyranny of Words,* pp. 269-273. 1938.

Committee (P.A.C.), established by the Congress of Industrial Organizations in 1943, is an outstanding instance of such an endeavor to develop a united labor front. Philip Murray, President of the C.I.O., defined the function of the P.A.C.: "To conduct a broad and intensive program of education for the purpose of mobilizing the five million members of the C.I.O. and enlisting the active support of all other trade unions . . . for effective labor action on the political front." [28] The immediate occasion for this move was the realization that too many persons were being elected to Congress who were reactionaries hostile to labor. The P.A.C. brought its pressure to bear in local and statewide elections in the fall of 1943 and conducted its own campaign in behalf of Roosevelt's reelection to the Presidency in 1944. This development is a sign of a dawning social consciousness among the members of labor. It is still too early to evaluate its long-range effectiveness.

The chief drawback to the development of a clear-cut economic alignment between the "haves" and the "have-nots" is still the fact that so many workers identify themselves with the middle class rather than the proletariat. This is especially true of white-collar workers such as clerks, salesmen, stenographers, teachers, beauticians, and keepers of roadside stands.

Service-trade folks do not consider themselves "masses." They are the despair of communist organizers. Even when they keep their overalls on, and shift from a robot job in a factory to running a garage, they inevitably take on a middle-class psychology. U. S. Route 1—or Route 101—is lined solidly with the new service trades. How many authentic proletarians can you find in its filling stations, tourist camps, Come-on-Inns and "flats fixed" emporiums? A man who leaves a factory bench and opens a filling station may earn less money than he used to, but he feels he has gone up in the social scale.

All this is enough to make Papa Marx heave in his grave. The whole communist philosophy is based on a proletariat which gets larger—and poorer—pitted against a small but powerful capitalist class, which gets richer and richer. The two great antagonists are supposed to work a squeeze play on the middle class, which is finally exterminated. But the facts show a declining proletariat getting richer rather than poorer as average wages increase, a capitalist class which lost its top hat in 1929, and a middle class which . . . is now the largest and most vital class in existence.[29]

[28] *Report, Sixth Constitutional Convention of the C.I.O.* 1943.
[29] S. Chase: "The Twilight of Communism." *Forbes Magazine*, August 15, 1941. Condensed under the title, "Twilight of Communism in the U.S.A.," in the *Reader's Digest*, September, 1941.

Among our many sorts and conditions of people in America, *Fortune* finds a prevailing sense of kinship.

Asked what class they belong to, one third of those questioned were vague or didn't know, replying with such terms as "American class," "good citizen class." Only 2.9 per cent think they belong to the upper class and only 14.9 per cent feel that they are lower class.

Conspicuously lacking is anything resembling the "underprivileged third" of the nation as a self-acknowledged group, nor does there appear any strong class consciousness such as a Marxist would wish for. Indeed only a quarter of the factory workers, and an even smaller proportion of farm and miscellaneous labor, call themselves the "working" or "laboring" class. And when those who thus described themselves were asked to be more specific, they would swing mainly into the middle grouping rather than identify themselves with a lower-class proletariat. At the other end of the scale, among the well-to-do, there are singularly few who tag themselves above plain "middle class." Seventy per cent of those who were actually poor, and 74.7 per cent of those who were actually prosperous, avowed that they belonged to the middle class. . . .

It is significant that in the face of powerful influences at work to make the labor movement more militant in dealing with employers, the average American thinks that employer and employee have common interests. To the question, *Do you think that the interests of employers and employees are, by their very nature, opposed, or are they basically the same?* the answers were:

	The same	Opposed	Don't know
Executives	80.2%	15.3%	4.5%
White-collar workers	69.8	23.1	7.1
Factory labor	41.3	37.3	21.4
Unemployed	45.1	29.2	25.7
Total	56.2	24.8	19.0

Thus by more than two to one, the U.S. public rejects the premise of class warfare.[30]

Gallup's studies of class stratification give us a good picture of the class lineup:

Despite the inequalities of life at different levels of the economic pyramid, there is little evidence that the people themselves are dividing into self-conscious blocs. If there are problems to solve, the dominant attitude is still

[30] "Fortune Survey: Heritage for the Next Generation." *Fortune*, February, 1940. Condensed in the *Reader's Digest*, May, 1940, under the title, "Self-Portrait of the American People."

that they will be solved not through the impact of hostile classes, but through unified national effort. The historian Charles A. Beard placed his finger on the central reason for this when he wrote of the "subjective consciousness" of the American people, a consciousness not solely of immediate economic surroundings such as unemployment and scanty diet, but also of common membership in a "middle class" which has a future as well as a past. The extent of this consciousness of belonging to the middle class—culturally and socially—was clearly indicated in an Institute survey conducted in 1939.

"To what social class in this country do you think you belong," voters were asked, "the middle class, the upper, or the lower?" It made little difference whether the voter was a Democrat or a Republican, whether he lived in a city or in the country, whether he worked in a factory or owned the factory himself. In all cases, nearly nine Americans in ten said they viewed themselves as members of the middle class:

Upper Class	6	per cent
Middle Class	88	" "
Lower Class	6	" " 31

The middle class boosts its ego, at times, by identifying itself with the upper class. This phenomenon evokes varying reactions among observers who take note of it. Leftist Kenneth Crawford, in his book *The Pressure Boys* (1939), decries this middle-class vanity because "no great progress can be made until the hard-pressed middle classes learn that their destiny is bound up with the welfare of fellow workers at the bottom, not the owners at the top." While Crawford expresses his regret over the stupidity of the middle class in this respect, Holcombe finds in the situation reason for joy, since a "strong and enlightened middle class" affords the best possible protection against the forces of revolution. Against Communist and Fascist claims that the peoples of modern states are divided into two main classes necessarily in conflict with one another, Holcombe sets up a strong case for the view that there are three important classes in the United States, that the middle class is the strongest of the three, and that its interests tend to harmonize with those of the people as a whole.[32]

As a general principle, Freeman asserts, a dominant minority (clique) will exploit an organization for its own benefit, though claiming to represent the interests of all the members.[33] This thesis is pertinent

---

[31] Reprinted from G. Gallup and S. F. Rae: *The Pulse of Democracy*, by permission of Simon and Schuster, Inc. Copyright, 1940, by George Gallup and Saul F. Rae. P. 169.

[32] See A. N. Holcombe: *The Middle Classes in American Politics.* 1940.

[33] E. Freeman: *Social Psychology*, pp. 378-397. 1936.

here, in that the upper class is able to exploit the middle class through making it appear that their interests are identical.

Marx counted on class consciousness on a world-wide scale: "Workers of the World, Unite!" It didn't "pan out" that way. *National loyalty* turned out to be more important as a social influence than class loyalty. National loyalty is especially apt to transcend class loyalty in time of war.

Mobility—moving from a lower status to a higher level or vice versa—is possible only in an open-class society. In some cultures status is fixed, as social position is settled once for all at birth. In India a caste system defines exactly the position into which an individual is born, and circumscribes the patterns of his behavior according to long-established traditions of social stratification. Caste distinctions are maintained in our country, too, in the South, where white and Negro groups are true castes, both intermarriage and mobility being barred. The caste division is rigorously and arbitrarily maintained by the whites through an elaborate system of observances from which they derive substantial economic and prestige gains. Social distance is established and stabilized by training the Negro to "know his place" in the system. Etiquette, reinforced by long-standing social usages (customs), requires respect for white superiority:

Segregation in hotels, churches, inns, theaters, street cars, parks, hospitals, schools, courts, police stations, jails, depots, residence sections, and cemeteries (Jim Crow laws).

A Negro shall never address a white person first.

Master-slave relations were upset by the Civil War and by the emancipation of the slaves. In the post-war period Negroes, in the first flush of their freedom, abandoned their servile patterns of conduct. As a result, the Ku Klux Klan was organized to put them back in their places. With the old intimacies between slave and master gone, segregation came to be more and more strictly enforced during the period of readjustment.

Within each caste, in the South, there are classes; not only are the inhabitants of a typical area divided into superordinate whites and subordinate Negroes, but each caste in turn is divisible into classes: the whites into upper, middle, and lower; the Negroes into middle and lower. The class position of the person within his own color-caste establishes an appropriate behavior norm which is accompanied by ideology and values peculiar to that position. Both caste and class are described as hierarchies in which the lowest group symbolizes all the negative values of the culture.   Persons may change position in the class hierarchy; never in the caste hierarchy.

Studies have been made to determine the influence of caste and class on the personalities of individual Negroes.   One research in this field was based on interviews with 197 Negro adolescents in New Orleans and Natchez, the aim being to discover the emotional significance of lower-caste status, the meaningfulness of social class, and the problems of child training and of education in relationship to social class. The investigators, Davis and Dollard, state that "a social class is to be thought of as the largest group of people whose members have intimate social access to one another. . . .   The individuals included have equal status in the sense that they may visit one another, have interfamily rituals such as meals or tea together, and may intermarry." [34]   Symptomatic of lower-class behavior in the Negro caste— more than three-fourths of all Negroes are lower-class—are the following: physical violence in settling family differences and in resisting white assaults, sexual precocity and promiscuity (girls exploiting men for their money), illegitimate births (with no loss of standing therefrom), repeated punishment of children and practically no rewards for them, mothers working outside the home and therefore giving their children very little supervision, retardation in school.[35] It is a prevalent belief among whites that Negroes are "contentedly servile."   Davis and Dollard report that this fiction is kept alive because white persons do not understand how Negroes feel about their lower-caste position.

In the first place, as soon as he begins to live in the South, a white person is taught the social dogma of *his* caste with regard to Negroes. On every hand he hears that Negroes are inherently childish and primitive.   He is taught that they lie and steal impulsively, "like children," that they are unable to control their sexual urges, and that they share none of the complex social and economic ambitions of white people.   Since Negroes are primitive and childlike, the story runs, they accept their restricted opportunities as matters of course (although children themselves do not do so), and consequently they feel no pain or deprivation in performing the heaviest, dirtiest work, or in undergoing the severest discriminations.   In many essential points, the

[34] A. Davis and J. Dollard: *Children of Bondage: the Personality Development of Negro Youth in the Urban South,* p. 13.   American Council on Education, 1940. See also, Chapter 11, "What Is Social Class?"

[35] Davis and Dollard account for this retardation not by reference to lower I.Q., but to emotional reactions against discrimination expressed in continuous punishment and no rewards.   See *Ibid.,* p. 280ff.

Southern dogma concerning Negroes is the same as that held by the slave-owning classes almost a century ago.

The second difficulty which white people meet in understanding the experience of Negroes as lower-caste people is the rigidity which the caste system has attained in the South. Negroes and whites, for example, seldom have face-to-face relationships, except in necessary economic transactions. In those immediate relations which they do have with whites, Negroes must always act deferentially. In life, this means that the colored individual seldom expresses to white people, by word or by action, the frustration or resentment which he may feel toward them. On the contrary, he must dramatize his subservience by using deferential forms of address, and by accepting without open aggression those punishments with which the whites subordinate him. To a white person who observes Negro behavior from his own caste position, therefore, Negroes may appear perfectly accommodated and "happy." . . .

Yet we know that Negroes in the Deep South are continually expressing to each other the sharpest antagonisms against whites and the deepest sense of frustration over their position in society. They verbalize these tabooed feelings only to their colored interviewers, and to Northern white men, that is, to members of those groups which will not punish them for such expressions. . . .

In both New Orleans and Natchez, a general form of subordination which Negroes meet from whites is that of being addressed by their first names. In November, 1938, a colored school teacher in New Orleans entered one of the leading stores on Canal Street to buy a suit. She is a brown-skinned woman, nineteen years old, of the upper-middle class. A white female clerk showed her one suit and left her. No other clerk returned to wait upon her. The colored woman then left the store and went to a small shop which catered to the middle-class whites. There she was waited upon and purchased a rather expensive suit. Finally she gave her name and address so that the suit might be delivered to her.

After writing down the information, the white saleswoman said, "Margaret, what time do you want this purchase delivered?" Neither woman had ever seen the other before that time.

The Negro woman later stated to the interviewer, who was her close friend, "I saw red. I was so mad. But I couldn't say a thing before all those white people. I made up my mind right then, though, that I'd never go there again to be insulted." . . .

When one gathers detailed accounts of these emotional reactions of Negroes to the impact of caste controls, it is not difficult to understand the basis of their frustrations and their consequent verbal aggression. Indeed, it becomes clear that only a vested societal interest in caste can account for the established dogma that most Negroes are completely "accommodated" to their caste status and that they are simple-natured, childlike beings with childish needs. It is necessary for the society to inculcate strong defensive teachings of this kind to prevent general human recognition of the basic deprivations and frustrations which life in a lower caste involves.   But it is certain that the sting of caste is deep and sharp for most Negroes. . . .[36]

In America, generally speaking, a person can rise from a lower class to a higher one, if he is persistent enough to overcome the obstacles placed in the way of his social ambitions and if he is clever enough to proceed in just the right manner.   Family background, educational affiliation, and financial eminence all enter into the situation, and few are the "climbers" who succeed in surmounting the barriers.

We have no official nobility in America but we do have "the four hundred" and the members of high society who belong to what is generally recognized as the social set in any given community.   Communities differ, indeed, in the prestige attached to their "upper crusts." The Boston Junior Leaguer would resent it if she were ranked on a par with one of her ilk from Chicago.   They both belong to exclusive circles, but some circles exclude more than others.

Listing in the Social Register is one recognition that a person belongs to the elite.   The field secretary in the Boston district, for the Social Register Association of New York, has described some of the criteria in reference to which names are judged for inclusion or exclusion.   If a girl whose name is already listed in the book marries a man who graduated from Harvard and who has become a member of some of the social clubs, there is little question of his admittance, although he may not be a member of one of the older families.

Club membership is of the utmost importance.   A man who has made the Somerset, Union, Tavern, or Tennis and Racquet, especially if he is a member of any two of them, is considered possessed of sufficient social standing to satisfy the requirements of the register, although some successful applicants never join a club.

The feminine short cut to the register is, and always has been, by way of marriage. . . .

A well-lined pocket book and a comely daughter are open sesames to social distinction.   A campaign must be carefully drawn up to storm the bulwarks of the elite.   The first line of attack in Boston would be by a foray into some charitable movements by several sizable donations.   Such largess would be followed, usually, by an invitation to dine at the home of the socially prominent sponsor.   A return dinner would give the social aspirant an opportunity to become host to a wider circle of important friends.   A box at the horse show, Country Club races and opera would help quite a bit, especially as the name of the intended applicant would find its way into the newspapers.

[36] *Ibid.,* pp. 237-240, 244-245.

A final assault on the fortress would be made by the comely daughter. She should become a student at an exclusive finishing school and, if talented, make every effort to join the Junior League or the Vincent Club. It might take a few years, but the process is about the surest way possible to attain the social goal.[37]

III. THE EXTENT OF SOCIAL CONSCIOUSNESS: LANGUAGE AS A DETERMINING FACTOR

The range of social consciousness is as wide as the scope of the individual's imagination. Many a person who never traveled much beyond the borders of his old home-town has enjoyed the adventures of the explorer and the globe-trotter vicariously by joining the National Geographic Society, reading the stories and absorbing the pictures of foreign lands. The success of the *National Geographic* magazine is due in no small measure to its clever psychology of making its subscribers members in a fellowship. They pay dues of $3 a year as members of the National Geographic Society, in response to the appeal:

Dear Sir:
    I have the honor of advising you that the Membership Committee extends you a cordial invitation to become a member of the National Geographic Society. . . .

"The main lure is the membership, which enables the janitor, plumber, and loneliest lighthouse keeper to share with kings and scientists the fun of sending an expedition to Peru or an explorer to the South Pole." [38]   This sort of armchair adventure carries a "sure-fire" appeal.

Imagination likewise extends the range of social consciousness backward and forward in time: to the symbols of our tradition, such as the town meeting, the cabin-in-the-clearing, the covered wagon, the lone prairie, the little red schoolhouse—and to the ideals we contemplate for our future realization, such as a more democratic society at home and leadership in a federation of nations abroad.

In terms of person-to-person interrelationships, the extent of social consciousness is dependent upon the means of communication that are available. Animals congregate for warmth and familiar smells, among other things; human beings associate with one another more for the

[37] Boston *Herald,* December 23, 1934.
[38] I. Ross: "Geography, Inc." *Scribner's Magazine,* June, 1938. Condensed in the *Reader's Digest,* July, 1938.

mental stimulation to be derived from an interchange of ideas, if it be no more than comments on the weather. Interest on the human level tends to vary proportionally with geographic distance: other things being equal, an individual is more interested in his own family than in his neighbors; more concerned about his neighbors than about his fellow-townsmen; more interested in people who live in his own town than in the residents of other towns; more interested in persons who live in his state than in those who reside elsewhere; more interested in members of his own nation than in members of other nations. The degree of interest is determined, in part at least, by knowledge. We do not care much about what is happening to people of other nations because we do not know much about them. Improved means of communication develop contacts and extend the range of interest. The telephone advertisements showing the traveling salesman calling up his wife every night to maintain the home ties illustrate how important communication is in the promotion of social consciousness. In a similar manner the growth of the railroads played a very significant role in the evolution of a sense of nationalism in the United States; and in like fashion the radio will eventually make the whole world much more akin. The printing press, the telegraph, the telephone, the automobile, the airplane, and the radio have contributed a great deal to the enlarging of our mental horizons. So did the Second World War, during which the folks at home "followed" their boys on distant battle fronts scattered over the world, with strange names of places which took on new meaning for us as we pictured our fathers, sons, and brothers fighting on foreign soil.

The Lynds concluded from their study of Middletown that the small city is losing its isolation under the cultural drenching of movies, radio, and other agencies of sophistication. In their newspapers Middletowners were reading, along with other Americans on a country-wide scale, Brisbane, Drew Pearson, Walter Lippmann, Paul Mallon, O. O. McIntyre's "New York Day by Day" and Walter Winchell's "On Broadway." Chain stores, too, serve to bind Main Street and Fifth Avenue.

Mail-order firms have found that a lag of six months in the cataloguing of women's fashions hurts their sales, for people in small towns all over the country keep abreast of the styles by watching what the movie queens are wearing. Through these various influences provincialism is decreasing and centers of belonging are shifting to conform to more distant centers of prestige.

Since language is the basic medium of communication between

human beings, it is of special concern to us in the study of social consciousness. There is a bond of sympathy tying those who speak the same tongue. The Dakota Indians, for example, are thus bound together.

> The social structure may be thought of as a series of circles within circles, each one complete, each like the other, varying only in the size of the circumference. The outermost circle is the tribe, the seven bands of the Teton Dakota. They are united by the same dialect of the Siouan language, by having the same heritage in the distant past, and by possessing the same ideals and way of life. Yet there are no records of the whole tribe's having come together at one place. Two or three or four of its component bands have met in the great camp circle, but never the whole tribe. Within this great circle the members know peace with each other, and outside it is the world of enemies.[39]

The fact that the Dakota tribe all used the same dialect is one important reason why the bands all shared the same heritage and the same ideals, for traditions and values are largely transmitted through speech or written records.

Sectionalism is promoted by the manner of speech peculiar to a definite region: the Southerner with his drawl and "you-alls," the New Englander with his extra r's as in "umbrellar" or "lawr" (law), the Westerner with his "laff" (laugh, in Boston, "loff"), and the Kentucky mountaineer with his English that is "Greek" to Americans who are strangers to those parts. A story of the Kentucky backwoods has to be accompanied by a glossary to aid the baffled reader:

Blinky—slightly sour, as milk turned in a thunderstorm; curdled.
Devyse—explain, make clear (to others).
Fere—sympathetic, kindly.
Gar—to compel, force, make.
Gramy—to vex.
Losel—good-for-nothing, ne'er-do-well.
Moldwarp—a slack-twisted, worthless man; a down-gone wastrel.
Treddan—think over, reflect upon, study out.[40]

Individuals who are inclined to be provincial tend to regard their own idioms and pronunciations as the correct ones, to experience a certain

---

[39] J. Mirsky: "The Dakota," Chapter XII in *Cooperation and Competition among Primitive Peoples,* M. Mead (Editor), p. 390. McGraw-Hill Book Company, 1937.
[40] M. Chapman: *The Happy Mountain.* The Viking Press, 1928.

amaraderie with those persons who share the same unique renditions
•f the mother tongue, to look down with a mild contempt or a super-
ilious scorn upon queer persons whose language differs from their
•wn norm.   It is difficult to feel any bond of comradeship with a per-
on who talks in a way you're not used to: somebody who, instead of
aying "Is that all?" says, "Is that the hull of it?"; instead of stating "It
nakes no difference," asserts, "It doesn't make any odds" (down Maine).
'The tongue spoken in Maine," notes a non-native, "is as different
rom the tongue spoken in New York as Dutch is from German.   Part
•f this difference is in the meaning of words, part in the pronunciation,
)art in the grammar.   But the difference is very great." [41]

People reveal their "class" or lack of it by the way they talk.   If
omeone says, "She ain't done nothin'," you could surmise the speaker
night be a "woiking goil"; but if someone asks, "Are you motoring to
he dawnce?" you would be fairly safe in classifying the speaker as a
nember of the aristocracy.

A person who is careful to speak grammatically may be laying him-
elf open to the charge of being thought unsportingly highbrow, es-
)ecially if he is associated with uneducated people who are accus
omed to their own special errors in speech.   An educated foreigner
vho tried to conceal his cultured background from his fellow workers
n an American factory says:

> I would repeatedly give myself away by some such form of address as
> 'Please," "May I?" or "Thank you."   They instinctively regarded such po-
> itenesses as the social affectation of an upper class.   Correct grammar was
> lso a high-hat pretense to them, and I soon caught myself saying "He don't"
>)r "I says." [42]

Slang plays an important role in promoting a sense of community
mong the members of a group who understand the esoteric terms
)eculiar to their particular social set.   Thus the zoot-suiters communi-
:ate with each other in a jargon that mystifies the outsider:

TOGGED TO THE BRICKS: FALL STYLE

No zoot-suiter who wants to be dicty this autumn can igg these solid threads
lished up for the hep cats.   The *London Drape* is sharp as a tack for truck-
ng on down to meet the barbecue in the early black when you are having
/ourself a ball.   The *Commando* is a lead sheet that's really ready.   Note the

[41] E. B. White: "One Man's Meat." *Harper's Magazine,* December, 1940.
[42] S. Pribichevich: "In an American Factory." *Harper's Magazine,* September,
938.

brand new cash flap, over the right mouse, to hold your beatup. Chicago cats who dug these drapes agreed they're solid murder. Yeah, Man! [43]

Sports fans share a slang all their own. Ball players never hit a ball—they "slug the apple" or "smack the horsehide." The late W. O. McGeehan wrote of "fistic dukes" and the "cauliflower industry," and of fighters with "educated portside mittens." What a contrast there is between the language of the editorial writer and this jargon of the sports writers!

Professional thieves use their own peculiar argot. The underworld is an exclusive society where strangers are not welcome. Indeed, a stranger is regarded as an invading alien and is referred to as a "weed in the garden." The argot serves as a means of identification. Thus a thief will ask a man, "Where were you nailed?" and the answer may be, "In the shed," meaning in a railroad station. Further questions will reveal what particular racket was being pursued in "the shed." The argot is not used, as so many suppose, to conceal meanings from the general public; thieves do not talk in this manner when people are around who might overhear the conversation, for the peculiar terminology would immediately attract embarrassing attention. Argot helps a thief identify another thief; further clues are obtained by asking what people the man knows. "Recognition as a professional thief by other professional thieves is the absolutely necessary, universal, and definitive characteristic of the professional thief." [44] There is a keen *esprit de corps*.

Mencken classifies the jargon of the underworld into the slang of three general classes: criminals, tramps, and prostitutes. [45] Typical of the first is prison argot:

slum	stew
punk	bread
skilley	gravy
sand, dirt	sugar
bombs	eggs
young horse	roast beef
beagles, pups	sausages
jamoca	coffee
big house	the prison itself

[43] *Time,* October 11, 1943.
[44] Sutherland: *op. cit.,* p. 211.
[45] H. L. Mencken: *The American Language; an Inquiry into the Development of English in the United States,* Chapter XI, "American Slang." Fourth edition. Alfred A. Knopf, Inc., 1936.

band-box	county workhouse
can	police station
to go stir-bug	to go crazy while in confinement
to do it all	imprisonment for life
to burn, fry, squat	electrocution

Tramps and hoboes speak a language of their own. ("Note: A hobo or bo is a migratory laborer; he may take some longish holidays, but soon or late he returns to work. A tramp never works if he can avoid it; he simply travels. Lower than either is the bum, who neither works nor travels save when impelled by the police.") [46] Subtle class distinctions!

Typical of the argot of tramps are the following slang terms:

bindle	bed roll
bindle-stiff	man who carries one
jungle, hang-out	place where tramps and hoboes foregather
panhandler	beggar
tank, jerkwater, filling station	small town
salve, axle-grease	butter
hot stuff	coffee[47]

All of these terms were originally esoteric; some of them have now passed over into common usage. In so far as they function as argot they contribute in an important way to fostering social consciousness among the members of a certain class.

In concluding our discussion of the place of language in the establishment of social consciousness, we may summarize by saying that everybody belongs to one or more groups and as a member of any one group he shares with his associates feelings of mutual interest which constitute the essence of social consciousness. The individual identifies himself with the group; this process is greatly facilitated by a common language that promotes a ready and sympathetic understanding.

IV. MORALE

The morale of a group is evidenced by its solidarity. The term "morale" was popularized during World War I, when patriotism in-

[46] *Ibid.*
[47] *Ibid.*

spired the boys at the front and the folks back home to cooperate in a common cause. Sustained efforts were made on both sides to promote morale by the wearing of uniforms, the singing of songs, entertainment programs, the suppression of news concerning defeats, the headlining of victories, the arousal by propaganda of hatred for the subhuman barbarians fighting on the other side. The unifying power of song was found to be of incalculable value for bolstering flagging spirits. Great songs have played their roles in other wars, too. During the Civil War the "boys in blue" marched to the Potomac and the James singing "John Brown"; the "boys in gray" had their "Dixie" and "Maryland, My Maryland." During World War I, "Tipperary," "The Long, Long Trail," "Pack Up Your Troubles in Your Old Kit Bag," "Keep the Home Fires Burning," and "Over There" helped the singing soldiers to renew their courage and their strength. The French sang of "Madelon," the little French girl who served wine at some obscure station "somewhere in France." "Madelon" was a symbol and an ideal. There was a swing to the melody that put life into tired legs. When the hungry, tired, dejected men picked up the strains of "Madelon" and every man joined in, backs straightened up again, and the weary marchers took a new lease on life. As the German troops tramped through Brussels they sang the songs of the Fatherland, not company by company, but mile by mile, all by prearrangement—so many paces between the lines and the verses—so that whole divisions at times were singing in unison. There is a thrill in martial music, a lift in the beat of the drums, that boosts morale, and when a group unites in song, every member is inspired with increased loyalty to the common cause.

A. Personal and Social

"Morale" may be conceived in three different senses:

I. (The individual-organic emphasis.) The term *morale* refers to a condition of physical and emotional well-being in the individual that makes it possible for him to work and live hopefully and effectively, feeling that he shares the basic purposes of the groups of which he is a member; and that makes it possible for him to perform his tasks with energy, enthusiasm, and self-discipline, sustained by a conviction that, in spite of obstacles and conflict, his personal and social ideals are worth pursuing.

II. (The group emphasis.) *Morale* refers to the condition of a group where there are clear and fixed group goals (purposes) that are felt to be important and integrated with individual goals; where there is confidence in the attainment of these goals, and subordinately, confidence in the means of attainment, in the leaders, associates, and finally in oneself; where group actions are integrated and cooperative; and where aggression and hostility are expressed against the forces frustrating the group rather than toward other individuals within the group.

III. (Emphasis on individual-within-the-group on any specific occasion.) Given a certain task to be accomplished by the group, *morale* pertains to all factors in the individual's life that bring about a hopeful and energetic participation on his part so that his efforts enhance the effectiveness of the group in accomplishing the task in hand.[48]

1. INDIVIDUAL

Group morale depends, of course, on the morale of the individuals who compose the group.

Morale is a matter of mental condition. Among athletes it is generally recognized that mental condition is just as essential for top-notch performance as physical condition. The individual whose morale is good is full of pep; he is confident of victory; he is "riding high," on the crest, keen for competition, fired with a zest for activity. Life is good because the best—or better—man will win. Such a person is on his toes, alert, mentally fit and physically fit, and therefore "raring to go."

A person is more apt to feel that life is good if he "feels good," that is, if he is physically sound, with his glands working efficiently. Physical health is important. A person with a "run-down feeling" cannot meet life on equal terms.

The feeling that life is good is dependent, too, upon a person's philosophy of life. If an individual is convinced that there is an intelligent plan behind the universe, that God is love, that virtue will get its reward, that this life is only preliminary to a better life to come, he will be predisposed to take his misfortunes in stride and to get a lot of fun out of this mundane struggle for happiness. On the other hand, if a person can see nothing but meaningless pain and sorrow in this vale of tears and is obsessed with the feeling "what's the use of trying, you can't come out on top?" it is likely that his morale will be poor. Sometimes it is hard to know which is cause and which, effect; the belief that life is empty may be due to a defective thyroid secretion, or it may be that the lack of a working philosophy has got the thyroid "down." Quite possibly the reaction is a reversible one. Since we might as well enjoy ourselves while we are here and get the most out of

---

[48] I. L. Child: "Morale: a Bibliographical Review." *Psychological Bulletin,* 1941. 38, 393-420.

living, for better or worse, it is highly important that a person attain a good morale.

There are certain signs of a healthy morale. A person with the right kind of spirit will do more than he has to in carrying out his assignments in cooperating with the group; he will endure disappointments cheerfully; he will not blame his comrades for any setbacks they collectively suffer; he will have faith in the loyalty of his co-workers; he will discipline himself to make sacrifices gladly for the cause; he will feel sure of ultimate victory.

There are various methods of investigating morale. One technique is the clinical interview, in which it is assumed that individual *morale* is analogous to the psychological *adjustment* of the individual to his general surroundings.

> Morale may be distinguished from *adjustment* primarily in that it involves the orientation of the individual to future goals and generalized ideals as well as to the situation immediately confronting him. A state of high morale might be said to be a condition of good adjustment which includes effective and confident striving for conditions that will make for good adjustment in the future.[49]

One example of this approach is the psychiatric study of the attitudes of tuberculous patients.[50] Rating procedures may be used to advantage by interviewers, the investigator asking questions and evaluating answers concerning the "happiness" of the respondent. This method has been employed in studying people who are receiving old-age assistance.[51] The subject may be asked to rate his own "customary and representative feelings" for different hours of the day, days of the week, and months of the year, apparently as an inquiry into his mood cycles, indirectly as an analysis of his morale.

The most widely used questionnaire in the field of morale is the scale constructed by Rundquist and Sletto. The items in this scale were predicated on the authors' concept of morale:

> The word connotes zeal, hope, confidence in oneself and in what the future will bring. It might be defined as confidence in one's ability to cope with the future. In addition, there are symptoms that are commonly assumed to

---

[49] Child: *op. cit.*, p. 395.

[50] See E. A. Strecker, F. J. Braceland, and B. Gordon: "Mental Attitudes of Tuberculous Patients." *Mental Hygiene*, 1938, 22, 429-453.

[51] See C. M. Morgan: "The Attitudes and Adjustments of Recipients of Old-Age Assistance in Upstate and Metropolitan New York." *Archives of Psychology*, 1937, 30, No. 214.

be present when morale is poor: distrust of people, the feeling that no one is friendly, and the belief that life is not worth living.[52]

The Rundquist-Sletto Scale has been used in studying the morale of the unemployed,[53] of slum dwellers,[54] of college graduates.[55] This last research, by Miller, is worth summarizing.

Miller sent a questionnaire, based on the Rundquist-Sletto Scale, to 1,381 former University of Minnesota students who had left the University from one to thirteen years before 1937. Returns were made by 951. For men and women separately, Miller selected the 100 who had the highest and the 100 who had the lowest morale score; then he examined the responses of these individuals on the various items to determine what variables were significantly associated with the difference in morale score. Some of the findings may be digested as follows:

1. High morale is associated with executives and managers.
2. High morale is associated with economic security.
3. Conformity—having a job approved by one's family, holding conservative political attitudes—tends to go with high morale.
4. Deep religious convictions are correlated positively with high morale.
5. Men with good morale are inclined to use realistic techniques in seeking social advancement and in solving their problems, as opposed to indulgence in wishful thinking by those whose morale is poor.
6. Individuals who rate their enjoyment of their leisure activities high, are apt to be characterized by a favorable morale.

2. GROUP

Group morale is developed by building a sense of teamwork in which each individual identifies himself wholeheartedly with his fellow members, with a spirit of all-for-one and one-for-all. Living in large population masses has unhappily resulted in attenuated sentiments of community in feeling. People sitting side by side watching

[52] E. A. Rundquist and R. F. Sletto: *Personality in the Depression*, p. 201. 1936.
[53] See F. S. Chapin and J. A. Jahn: "The Advantages of Work Relief Over Direct Relief in Maintaining Morale in St. Paul in 1939." *American Journal of Sociology*, 1940, 46, 14-22.
[54] See F. S. Chapin: "The Effects of Slum Clearance and Rehousing on Family and Community Relationships in Minneapolis." *American Journal of Sociology*, 1938, 43, 744-763.
[55] See D. C. Miller: "Morale of College-Trained Adults." *American Sociological Review*, 1940, 5, 880-889; "Personality Factors in the Morale of College-Trained Adults." *Sociometry*, 1940, 3, 367-382; "Economic Factors in the Morale of College-Trained Adults." *American Journal of Sociology*, 1941, 47, 139-156.

movies do not constitute "a community." With church, family, and local community ties weakened, we need a dramatization of our feeling of common purpose such as we achieve in times of war, seldom in times of peace.

The liabilities and assets of our civilian morale in the United States were ably evaluated by Gordon Allport in a timely study undertaken as America faced the threat of war in 1941. This was his frame of reference:

In everyday life, morale may be viewed as a zest for solving personal problems. In times of grave crisis when common enemies threaten common values, defense is a matter of dovetailing each person's efforts at problem-solving with the efforts of his neighbors. National morale is merely the morale of single persons supplementing the morale of other persons intent upon solving the same problems.

National morale, thus defined, may be said to be high when there are clear and fixed goals shared by a large majority of citizens; when there is confidence in the attainment of these goals, in leaders, in one's associates, and in oneself; when the actions of separate citizens are integrated and cooperative, and when hostility is expressed against the forces frustrating the national group rather than toward other individuals within the national group. We now ask what our chances are for attaining a high state of national morale in these terms.[56]

We shall summarize Allport's analysis.

Liabilities in American morale before Pearl Harbor:

1. *The cynicism of the deadly parallel.* Remembering the disillusionment over the last war, we do not intend to be lured again into a futile struggle.

2. *The ravages of the depression.* Privation has given rise to antidemocratic sentiments. Said a man on relief: "I suppose they'll be asking us now to make the world safe for unemployment."

3. *Our habit of destructive criticism.* We irreverently wisecrack about the President who has been our scapegoat.

4. *Americans take for granted their basic liberties.* We forget that we have had to fight for our freedom, that Rights call for corresponding Duties.

5. *We are preoccupied with making profits.* Imbued with the habit of "patriotism-plus-ten-per cent," we seem "almost incapable of practicing self-denial in the national interest."

[56] G. W. Allport: "Liabilities and Assets in Civilian Morale." *Annals of the American Academy of Political and Social Science,* July, 1941.

6. *Americans have lost confidence in the adaptability of democracy to swift action in emergencies.*

7. *There is a damaging amount of factionalism.* Fear of narrow partisanship and rumors of strife are deleterious to morale. Nazi dissolvent propaganda has been taking advantage of these internal dissensions.

Assets in American morale before Pearl Harbor:

1. *Our realistic problem-solving attitude toward difficulties.* Relatively free of censorship, we get the facts and face them. "War is hell—Hitler is worse."

2. *Democratic morale is potentially stronger than totalitarian morale.* "An integrated personality marshaling its energies is superior to a segmentalized personality behaving only under conditions of mental suggestion. The Nazi identifies himself with his leader, yields up his own responsibility, his own conscience, and a large portion of his intelligence. An almost trance-like state results which must be sustained by the trappings, the myths, and the hocus-pocus appropriate to hypnotism. In the exercise of democratic morale, all of one's sentiments, values, and knowledge can be employed. Among the Nazis, only blind followership is in order. Distortions of fact, forced enthusiasm, the specious logic of scapegoating—all conspire to tear the personality asunder. Deliberately suppressed are love of family, of personal freedom, of education, of butter instead of cannon, of the impulses of compassion and pity. In his memoirs a former Nazi wrote that the revolution was being fought by each individual German in the dark of night in the privacy of his own heart.

"Oddly enough, democratic morale is more total than totalitarian morale."

3. *A unity of national purpose is emerging,* as revealed by the progressive polling of public opinion, by the growth of societies dedicated to the preservation of our democratic way of life.

4. *The American habit of intense cooperation.* Sporadic though it may be, boosting is a national trait. "Americans do not want to dig in, but to put something over."

5. *Hatred of tyranny and persecution.* This is a tradition with us.

6. *"Group morale implies a division of labor, and a division of labor alleviates anxiety."* We have learned the value of teamwork, the necessity for sharing responsibilities. In a crisis we can subordinate our individualism to the group end.

7. *The American sense of humor.* This affords insight into ourselves, a powerful weapon against pompous enemies. "The pranks of the Norwegians, the Dutch, and the French, edged as they are with ridicule, cannot fail to deflate the artificial self-confidence engendered by the humorless Nazi training.

"Especially vulnerable to humor are the pomposities of the racial myth, the joylessness of *Kraft durch Freude,* the excessiveness of *Ordentlichkeit,* Nazi travesties on science, and the contradictions in Hitler's speeches." Americans are adepts in laughter.

8. *American inventiveness.*   Our morale is helped by our faith in American scientists, our confidence in our productive efficiency.

During World War II psychologists were eager to develop effective means for analyzing and measuring morale. Harding experimented with a scale designed to discover the attitudes that were especially vital for morale with respect to the task of national defense. The questionnaire, in his research, was administered to two criterion groups selected to represent high and low morale respectively:

High—44 distinguished social scientists and public servants engaged in furthering national morale
Low—settlement-house residents who were known to be "surly," with "a grudge against the world"
    —loafers on the Boston Common

Persons with high morale exhibited confidence in our capitalistic democracy, tolerance for minorities, realistic evaluation of the war situation, desire for active participation in world affairs, in contrast to the opposite attitudes characterizing those persons with low morale. Harding concluded: "No scale of attitudes on national and international problems can have a very long life in these troublous times, and it seemed better to construct a scale with a high degree of relevance for the issues of the moment than to try to build a scale of attitude for the ages." [57]

Another valuable approach to the development of group morale is provided in the sociometric techniques devised by Moreno.[58] The structure of small social groups is determined by asking each member of the group to express an attitude toward his individual fellow members. For example, students may be asked how they would feel about joining certain classmates in a discussion group, hospital inmates may be requested to state how they would like specific persons as house mates, soldiers may be instructed to name individuals they would prefer in their squads. The data for such records may be obtained by having the subject fill in a *Group Preference Record.*

[57] J. Harding: "A Scale for Measuring Civilian Morale." *Journal of Psychology,* 1941, 12, 101-110.
[58] See J. L. Moreno: *Who Shall Survive?* 1934. There is a journal called *Sociometry* which is devoted to these problems of group relations.

Name_____Group Number_____Date_____

On this sheet is a list of the names of all the members of the class. Will you please indicate how you feel about working with them in a class learning group? Those you choose may be assigned to your group later. The information you give will be treated confidentially and used for the improvement of class groups and for scientific study.

Instruction 1. Put a figure "1" to the *left* of the name of the person who is your first choice for membership in a class learning group of which you may be a member. Continue until you have made *five* choices in order from first choice to fifth choice. Put all answers to the left of the names.

Instruction 2. To the right of *each* name indicate how you feel about having this person a member of your class learning group. If you would like having the person in your group, encircle "L" for "like"; if you would dislike having the person in your group, encircle "D" for "dislike"; if you have no feeling one way or the other toward the person, encircle "I" for "indifferent."

1 First five choices	Names	2 Feeling toward each
————	Richard Roe	L D I
————	John Doe	L D I
————	Robert Smith	L D I
————	John Jones	L D I
————	Henry James	L D I
etc.	etc.	etc.[59]

A *Group Morale Blank* may be administered to determine how much the individual identifies himself with or fuses himself with a given group of which he is a member. The subject rates the extent to which he experienced "shared or mutual feelings of like" by marking an "x" on the line above the correct answer.

————	————	————	————	————
Experienced strong feelings of mutual dislike	Experienced mild feelings of mutual dislike	Participated without much feeling of like or dislike	Experienced mild feelings of mutual like	Experienced strong feelings of mutual like[60]

[59] L. D. Zeleny: "Sociometry of Morale." *American Sociological Review*, 1939, 4, 799-808.

[60] *Ibid.*

Graphic methods may be employed to plot the structures of relationships among the several members of the group. A morale quotient may be computed by ascertaining the ratio of "likes" received (times their average intensity) to the total possible "likes" which might be received.

Sociometric findings may be employed to facilitate morale by arranging groups in clubs, in public school classes, in institutional cottages, or in army squads so that members will be associating with fellow members who are congenial: interpersonal relations will thus be characterized by reciprocated positive attitudes. In this connection, it is of interest to note that the German Army reported improvement in morale as a result of "placing in the same regiment men who are congenial, who are interested in the same arts and crafts. The High Command feels that the results are astounding." [61]

National morale during war becomes a problem of paramount importance. After the United States entered World War II, polls dealt increasingly with problems of civilian morale. Research in this field was inspired by the conviction that knowledge of public opinion could indicate how unified the country was, what steps could be taken to improve morale, and where the danger spots lay. Surveys were periodically conducted to measure the public willingness to make sacrifices for defense and to check on the acceptance of war aims. As war costs mounted, surveys were conducted to learn which forms of taxation would meet with the least resistance among the taxpayers.

Time, in discussing popular dissatisfaction with the conduct of the war, cited "the consistent offense to millions of Americans of Washington speeches charging them with complacency and apathy, although the people have shown by every index that they were far ahead of the Administration in willingness to meet the price of war." [62] This sort of psychological fumbling on the part of the Government could have been averted if officials had given more heed to poll results. Polling showed, for instance, that very important for the fostering of an effective American morale were these considerations: "national policies that avoid frustrations; policies that do not give rise to false hopes; policies that make sacrifices worth while; above all, policies that demonstrate through actual works the ability of democracy to serve its people's needs." [63]

[61] M. M. Witherspoon: "Morale in the New World War." *Proceedings of the U.S. Naval Institute,* 1940, 66, 675-684.

[62] *Time,* October 12, 1942.

[63] "We Say Au Revoir." *Propaganda Analysis,* 1941, 4, No. 13. Reproduced by permission of Alfred McClung Lee, Executive Director.

B. MANIFESTATIONS

The fundamental factors in building up individual and group morale may be readily observed in athletic competition and in war. The principles involved are essentially the same for other lines of endeavor.

1. ATHLETICS

In sports such as boxing, tennis, and golf where the athlete may be striving as an individual for success, the element of confidence plays a very important role in the determination of the outcome. A man who assumes a "cocky" manner is a hard man to beat, particularly if he backs up his boastful attitude with skillful performance. Dizzy Dean, the baseball pitcher, was interviewed just before the St. Louis Cardinals faced the Detroit Tigers in the World Series. "I don't want to make them think I'm a windbag," he stated, "but I want to tell the truth. So just say the Cardinals will take them Tigers like a bulldog takes a pussy cat, and that if they get a good foul off me and Paul they can consider themselves lucky. That won't sound like braggin', will it? The way I sees it, braggin' is where you ain't got nothing to back it up." Walter Hagen, the famous golfer, has always been just as "cocky" as Dizzy Dean. Hagen would burst into the locker room just before a tournament and ask the other golfers which one of them was going to come in second. Hagen was not only expert in the execution of his strokes but also keen in his mental strategy, as illustrated by an incident that occurred when he was playing Leo Diegel in a championship match at Olympia Fields in 1925.

Hagen and Diegel, playing the third round, were all square at the end of thirty-six holes. The thirty-seventh and thirty-eighth were halved. It was at the thirty-ninth—or the third hole on the course—that Hagen staged his effective by-play. Both were well on with their seconds. Hagen rolled up to within four feet of the cup. Diegel was about a foot closer, but with a curving side-hill lie.

Putting first, Hagen sank his ball. At that moment he had an inspired thought. He picked up Diegel's ball and handed it to him. "I'll give you that one, Leo," he said. The crowd gasped. It was a difficult putt. If he missed, it was Hagen's match.

But Hagen was merely shrewd in his calculations. He figured that Diegel was more likely to make the putt than to miss it. In the circumstances, then, it would do no harm to concede it. And such an action was an open notification to Diegel that Hagen did not fear him.

It worked beautifully. Hagen hit a tremendous drive off the next tee, while Diegel looked up, topped his shot, and was through.[64]

A few great athletes are known as "money" players, that is, they "come through" when the crucial moment arrives; they are at their best when it counts the most. Players of this type keep their self-control and coordination when contestants with less "intestinal fortitude" fold up under the nerve-racking tension. The ability to do one's best under stress is just as important for achieving athletic prowess as is a strong physique or a mastery of the kinaesthetic skills involved in the game. Keeping one's head "under fire" is a matter of morale; self-confidence is the essence of such poise.

Confidence is the secret, likewise, of group morale. In football each player must be sure of himself and sure of his teammates. Each man on the team must feel that his mates can be counted upon to give their best in defeat or victory. A team that gets the jump and continues to function smoothly gathers momentum from its success and its morale is improved by the realization that things are clicking, while the opposition becomes demoralized by the prospect of defeat and attributes its failure to the bad "breaks" which fate seems to have decreed for the occasion. Whether defeat is going to be an asset or a liability depends upon the morale of the team. Some teams fight harder in the face of apparent defeat while other teams lose all their "scrap" under such discouraging circumstances. Rockne of Notre Dame used to say that no team could be great until it had been beaten. One observer points out that one defeat makes a good team mad; two defeats are too discouraging; many defeats, and the team is dangerous again because it doesn't care what happens.

The psychological odds favor the underdog in the pre-game betting, for the favorite has nothing to gain by victory and everything to lose by defeat, while the underdog has nothing to lose and everything to gain. The favored team is in serious danger of developing overconfidence, a menace that has harassed many a successful coach. It is becoming a tradition for coaches to predict a victory for the opposing team. In 1930, Cannell of Dartmouth suppressed overconfidence among his players by forecasting a Columbia win; the next day Dartmouth proceeded to rout the Lions by a score of 52-0. The coach may have succeeded in attaining his immediate objective in this case, but certainly his subsequent predictions would not be given respectful attention. The art of preventing overconfidence was perfected by Gil

[64] The *Literary Digest*, August 1, 1931.

Dobie, who came to be known as "Gloomy Gil" because of his pessimistic outlook at the start of every season. One year, at Cornell, he described his dismal prospects by reporting that his candidates looked like a bunch of Phi Beta Kappa men. Such an outlook might seem too hopeless to inspire any effort for overcoming the odds. The wise coach must build up just the right amount of confidence—not too little, not too much. Either extreme is an indication of an unhappy morale.

Mental condition is just as important as physical condition for winning games. A team that thinks it is suffering from a jinx is on the way to defeat from the start: it is suffering from low morale. Dartmouth had some great football teams in the ten years from 1924-1934 but none of them could beat Yale, partly because the boys from Hanover got to believing that the sons of Eli had the "Indian sign" on them. That "Yale Bowl jinx" beat the Dartmouth "Indians" year after year.

The average football spectator might not appreciate just why morale makes so much difference, but the coaches can see how poor morale affects every move of the players. P. D. Haughton, famous Harvard coach, was asked one time to explain the influence of morale:

Right mental condition wins a majority of the games between college football teams in the first class.

Let's get down to concrete facts, however, and show where mental condition is all important.

Tackling and blocking are vital assignments in any football game. . . . Now, what I want to make clear is that blocking and tackling are duties the performance of which depends almost wholly on the mental condition of the players. . . . If they have that keenness, that liking for body contact and the wish and will to go through with their assignments, then they will function. . . .

There are days, maybe after an extremely hard game on the preceding Saturday, or possibly against a foe which does not seem particularly worthy, when even your normally good blockers and tacklers do half-hearted work. And who ever saw half-hearted blocks or tackles win a big football game?

Any football team has its ups and downs, which are due primarily to its mental attitude. One week the players are bubbling over with enthusiasm for the approaching game; the next week they are not the least bit interested. It is this difference, mentally, which makes a team look sluggish one Saturday and appear as a perfect, well-drilled unit the next. It is this difference in mental attitude which causes the numerous upsetting results each Saturday afternoon. It is this factor that gives the underdog a chance. For this same reason, games between traditional rivals are even propositions, regardless of what has happened previously. One of the elements of good coaching is to work the team up to the proper pitch for each game. Most teams point to a few big games and try to take the other contests in stride. Rockne's genius lay in his ability to inspire his teams for big games Saturday after Saturday, so that the men were keyed up enough to win each game on a long schedule.

In the old days the coach relied on a fight talk to instill the will-to-win in his men, to get them to "go all out" for the glory of the school, to make "the old college try." The classic phrase "I'd die for dear old Rutgers" has become a bit of litany in American football lore. The old straight-from-the-shoulder fight talk does not go any more. Says Harry Kipke:

In the olden days, the Rutgers speech was delivered before the two big, hard games, but today every game is a hard game and our newest generation is too skeptical to make this possible on eight successive Saturdays. . . . They recognize hooey. . . .

Kipke adds that the young men of today may seem to be sophisticated and blasé and given to smug complacency, but when the ball is snapped, "the son of Man still goes forth to war" and when the smoke of battle clears, you will find that he has given all he has for the team.[65] The old "pep-talk" in which the coach asks the men if they want to break the hearts of numberless alumni, in which he recalls past humiliations at the hands of their arrogant opponents, is a thing of the past. The modern coach relies more on winning the loyalty of his men through his daily contacts, for he knows that if the players respect and honor him, they can be counted upon to do their best without any violent oratory.

One of the essentials in creating good morale is the maintenance of discipline. If there are training rules, they must be enforced on all the players in such a way that they will submit gladly to the rules for the sake of the team and the school. Players who violate the regulations and thereby demonstrate their lack of cooperation, are a serious menace to a good *esprit de corps*. The coach who lets his men get away with such infractions loses the respect of his players. It

[65] See H. G. Kipke and H. A. Fitzgerald: "Dying for Dear Old Rutgers." *Saturday Evening Post,* November 17, 1934.

is necessary for the right morale that each man feel that all his team-mates are just as interested as he is in subordinating personal desires to the larger good of the group.

The best foundation for athletic morale is the feeling, shared by the majority of the student body, that victory is very important to the welfare of the school. Rallies, cheering sections, torchlight parades, and band music are all designed to inspire a will-to-win, not only in the team, but also in all the loyal rooters whose happiness is staked on victory. F. Scott Fitzgerald was thinking of this spirit when he wrote to a Princeton undergraduate, expressing the hope that Princeton would beat Yale so his student friend could enjoy the winter at college. A whimsical educator who deplored the overemphasis on athletics in our colleges suggested the following course if defeats should come:

> *One defeat*—demote the whole first line.
> *Two defeats*—change the whole team.
> *Three defeats*—abolish the coach.
> *Four defeats*—abolish the college.

The average undergraduate of today, better oriented in his sense of values than the student of a generation ago, no longer feels that his happiness depends upon the success of the athletic teams representing his school. Oldsters sometimes decry this lack of school spirit. An alumnus of 1900 who now has a son in his own college puts the case:

The heart has gone out of college life; youngsters go to college now very much as they might go to a night school. They take their particular institution more or less for granted. In my time it was different. College life then revolved around two very deep-seated loyalties: the first one was to the undergraduate's particular class; the second was to his college as a whole, in which all classes joined. In our rushes or snowball fights we were willing to give our last ounce of strength and last drop of blood (and there was occasionally a little unnecessary blood-letting) for our class and our class-mates.

At the same time, we would go any lengths to back our college, and our football or even our baseball team represented in a tangible way the spirit and prowess of Alma Mater. We spent almost every afternoon down at the field watching the practice, and a defeat in a big game was a college disaster. My son does not see it that way. There was nothing smooth about us. The campus was our backyard and we dressed accordingly, but we were fiercely and unshakably loyal. You could count on us. All that is gone.[66]

[66] Quoted by Dean Christian Gauss, in the New York *Times Magazine*, April 3, 1932.

American youth have been tending more and more to adopt the traditional English attitude that sports are for recreation, that play should be taken in a playful mood, that the important thing is to have a good time; win or lose, it makes no difference. A will-to-win is lacking in such a philosophy. Big-time teams cannot be fostered in such an atmosphere. Why, the English students don't even train, that is, go to bed early, stop smoking, and refrain from alcoholic beverages, when they prepare for an approaching contest. The game is a lark, all for fun. American athletes have tended to take their sports seriously, training rigorously, with hearts set on victory as the goal, suffering defeat graciously if come it must; for we are taught that we must be good losers, whether it's the game of football or the game of life. Americans love competition; a game is a battle and may the better man or better team win! Our whole culture has been predicated on the beneficence of the struggle for existence, in the course of which the unfit are eliminated and only the fit survive. But our philosophy is changing. In the economic sphere we are restricting ruthless competition; in the social sphere we are feeding the unemployed; in the medical sphere we are giving aid to the infirm; and even in the field of sports we are beginning to appreciate that the aim is recreation, not the humiliation of one's opponent.

2. WAR

Wartime poses two problems in morale which are intimately interrelated: maintaining the cohesion of the home front, and instilling a confident aggressiveness in the fighting forces.

The first of these tasks, fostering civilian morale, is now recognized as a vital element in the prosecution of total warfare. Civilians are called upon to face danger, deprivation, and regimentation. Unlike the soldiers, they do not have ready outlets for releasing the tensions involved. The British, on the basis of observations made during bombing raids, discovered the value of enlisting every available person in organizations where duties were assigned which were clearly related to the achievement of war goals. It was found, too, that it was wise to keep a close watch of fluctuations in morale. Evidence for such a purpose was gathered regularly by the "War-Time Social Survey" conducted under the direction of the Ministry of Information. The Survey had accurately predicted that the bombing of England would "stiffen the public morale." The indiscriminate air attacks of the *Luftwaffe* did not shatter the nerves of the English people—instead they bred increased determination to "take it" and to "see it through."

"The humble workingman or artisan whose home has been blown to bits can scarcely fail to feel that his own stake in this conflict is a very real one indeed." [67]

Morale was measured and charted in the United States, too, by means of interviewing and other techniques. The information proved most valuable in the formulation of policy, and enabled those in authority to take action in a timely and effective manner. The data pertaining to "the state of mind of the nation" were collected by the Office of War Information, the Office of Strategic Services (War Department), the Section on Consumer Problems among Ethnic Minorities of the Civilian Supply Administration, the Bureau of Agricultural Economics of the Department of Agriculture, the War Savings Bond Section of the Treasury Department, and by other government agencies that were responsible for building up support for the war effort.

It is one of the fundamental tenets in our American credo to assume that morale can be established on a firmer, healthier basis in a democracy than in a totalitarian state.

The mark of a true democrat is that he sees no progress in any social action unless it is based upon sincere respect for the individual, and unless it results ultimately in the growth of human personality. From this fundamental creed of living (utterly opposed to the creed of all dictatorships) democratic morale draws both its power and its meaning.[68]

In our Chapter 4, "Values and the Art of Living," experimental evidence was cited to confirm this faith in the morale-building virtue of the democratic way of life. Lippitt has drawn certain pertinent conclusions regarding this matter from his study of leadership among groups of young people:

Whether the group's interpersonal unity is derived from mutual resistance to external pressures or from spontaneous inner sources of cohesion is a fact of considerable importance both in determining the extent to which the group will resist disrupting forces and persist in its efforts toward goal attainment and in determining what channelization the tension resulting from group frustration will take.

One of the best criteria for satisfactory or unsatisfactory democratic morale in a youth group is found in the manner in which the group functions in the

[67] E. Estorick: "Morale in Contemporary England." *American Journal of Sociology*, 1941, 47, 462-471. University of Chicago Press.
[68] G. W. Allport: "The Nature of Democratic Morale," Chapter 1 in *Civilian Morale*, G. Watson (Editor), p. 7. Houghton Mifflin Company, 1942.

absence of its adult leader.   The whisper, "teacher is out of the room," is an important symptom in our educational system.

Too much of our thinking about morale has been focused upon such factors as resistance to disintegration rather than upon such factors as productivity, enthusiasms for member responsibility, personal sacrifice for group goals. . . .

More "we-centered" constructive suggestions for the improvment of group practices and group policy arise from youth groups under demcratic adult guidance and having spontaneous cohesion than from groups in a freer (laissez-faire) or less free (authoritarian) climate.[69]

In his editorial preface to *Civilian Morale,* 1942 Yearbook of the Society for the Psychological Study of Social Issues, Goodwin Watson noted that all sorts of devices had been recommended for building up the right morale, from donning a toupee to getting a hair wave, drinking beer, or buying a new hat.   "Baseball, sermons, night clubs, red-white-and-blue posters, uniforms, vitamin pills, comfortable mattresses, martial music, V symbols, boys' clubs, morning calisthenics, newsreels of enemy atrocities, and hundreds of other activities have been defended as 'building morale.' "

Obviously, there are more important measures available for use in establishing a sound morale.

Some of the most constructive suggestions in the Yearbook were these: (1) There should be a positive goal, some definite concept of "a new and better order."   (2) Togetherness is important—a sense of purpose shared by fellow workers in a cause, the diminution of class barriers, the welcoming of minority groups, as embodied in the slogan "Together we stand or together we fall; we are United Nations." (3) Awareness of common danger generates community of feeling. (4) Confidence is improved if people are shown ways of helping and are encouraged to lend a hand.   (5) A sense of success is a boost in the right direction if it is based upon a faith in the trustworthiness of the news sources which are reporting the gains.

One of the best contributions to *Civilian Morale* was made by the editor, Goodwin Watson, who dealt with the problem of according recognition to labor for its vital role in the war production program.[70] The newspapers can help to build the right kind of morale within the ranks of American labor by representing fairly the case of labor, instead of slanting the news, as many of them did during World War II, in such a way as to encourage public hostility toward unions.   The

[69] *Ibid.,* R. Lippitt: "The Morale of Youth Groups," Chapter 7.
[70] Chapter 18, "Labor Unions and Morale."

press hurt national morale when it exaggerated the extent of wildcat strikes and failed to give credit where credit was due for meritorious performance. "We read that battleships are ready a year ahead of schedule, and the credit is given to a government official or to a corporation . . . rarely . . . is . . . tribute . . . paid . . . to the men in overalls." [71] Newspapers misrepresented the labor unions by exaggerated reports of the amount of racketeering in the unions, conveying the false impression that the few racketeer leaders were typical of the thousands of men and women holding influential posts in the labor movement. Lags in production were blamed on "conscienceless labor leaders" when the unions may not have been responsible at all; perhaps, indeed, working time was lost because the employer would not go ahead until he had taken plenty of time to negotiate a favorable contract with the government. Watson suggested that something should be done to prevent the press from acting as a propaganda agency to discredit labor, because the newspapers undermined our national morale by following such a policy:

What does it do to the morale of a group of American citizens, as patriotic as any, working hard to earn a wage which is meager enough at best, to find their organization consistently misrepresented and maligned? No very profound psychology is required to understand this problem. None of us likes to be misunderstood. If the union for us had been, as it has been for millions of workers, a means to greater self-respect, more democratic control over methods of work, and higher standards of living, then how would we react to allegations that we believed unfair and untrue? If the union leaders we knew happened to be conscientious, loyal men whom we fully trusted and were proud to have as spokesmen, how would we feel about the institutions that smear them? Would we not over-react and refuse to admit even the defects and limitations which another approach might have made us willing to recognize and to correct? . . .

The essence of the problem is to get the great instruments of communication out from the control of a single class, representing a small minority of Americans. There will be serious morale problems in our national life until the press and radio achieve at least that measure of impartiality and respect for truth which characterizes the scholars in our universities. . . .

The morale of labor is almost as vital for victory as is the morale of the fighting forces. At present there is little reason to fear for the morale of the workingmen of America. Four steps would help to preserve high morale: (1) insure a fair statement of labor's viewpoint, in the American press, radio, and movies; (2) encourage or require unions to extend democracy within their own ranks, purging organizations of dictators or racketeers; (3) provide

[71] *Ibid.*

such a control of profits and prices and wages, as will demand approximate equality of sacrifice from all groups in American life; and (4) dissuade the anti-labor extremists who are more interested in fighting labor than in winning the War for Democratic Survival.[72]

With the increasing centralization of government authority, it becomes more and more necessary to have leaders who inspire the confidence of the citizens.   Confusion is very demoralizing, as many citizens discovered when they were bombarded by conflicting announcements from various government officials concerning the rationing of gasoline and other consumer goods.   Rumors and counter-rumors were encouraged by the failure of Washington to come out with a definite statement of what people could expect.   The newspapers kept hinting that drastic sacrifices would be necessitated, warning the people that they seemed unaware of the seriousness of the situation. Under such uncertain conditions, people could not plan ahead.   The public began to get jittery.   When at long last officials made up their minds, about gasoline, for example, demoralization resulted in some parts of the country because other parts of the country were not being compelled to give up their gasoline, and some people were resentful because neighbors were getting more gas than they seemed to be entitled to.   Householders were urged to convert from oil to coal, only to discover after conversion, a serious shortage of coal.   The trouble, as a general rule, lay essentially in the "piece-mealness of much of the policy making and publicity." [73]   Such costly mistakes could have been avoided had more attention been paid to basic principles of morale-building.   Fortunately, some people could see the humor in the rationing program.   Tension was relieved somewhat by a story from Fort Custer, Michigan, about the following notice:

With the rationing of tires and sugar, and scarcity of many articles, civilians are having a tough time.   To bolster civilian morale, soldiers should write home more often.

During the Second World War, advertisers did a very effective job in boosting American morale.   With fewer or no products to feature, it looked like "curtains" for advertising for the duration.   Two things saved the situation: first, businessmen remembered that some firms had

[72] *Ibid.*
[73] B. S. Burks: "A Social Psychology Background for Civilian Morale." *Journal of Social Psychology, S.P.S.S.I. Bulletin,* 1942, 16, 150-153.

collapsed during the First World War because they stopped advertising; second, the advertisers got together and organized the Advertising Council to cooperate with the Government, by finding out what ideas the Government wanted to put across and then persuading advertisers to devote their space to Government's problems, thus giving the copywriters and artists something concrete and constructive to do in lieu of promoting their regular lines of products, which were more or less curtailed under wartime conditions. The advertisers fell to

(Courtesy, Francis Dahl and the Boston *Herald*.)

and did an excellent job, telling the story of the nation's war-production miracles, explaining the complexities of point rationing, selling billions of dollars' worth of war bonds, sending dance bands and radio entertainers to the various camps to keep up the spirits of the boys in uniform and also to war plants to pay tribute to the part the workers were playing in war production.

Advertising became a powerful home-front weapon. American Airlines featured a magnificent air map of the world; Consolidated Aircraft, a similar air-age globe, with the heading, "No spot on earth is more than 60 hours from your local airport"; Pan American ran a series of statements on the postwar world written by such world citizens as John Dewey and the Archbishop of Canterbury; the New Haven

Railroad's "The Kid in Upper 4" explained why the trains were crowded and urged people who could, to stay at home; Hood Rubber Company published a series on "How to Make Your Rubber Footwear Last Longer." One of the best ads was Texaco's Teuton, a fat repulsive person, with a text saying:

(Courtesy, The Texas Company.)

You've got a *real, personal* adversary to fight just as one of our marines who comes face to face with a Jap in the jungle. Your opponent is a "man-in-the-street" in Berlin . . . or Tokio. . . . It's you against him—your "morale" against his. "Morale" means driving under 35 miles per hour—and not grousing about it. It means cutting out pleasure driving—*with pleasure.* It means saving fuel oil, living in a colder home—with a *warmer* heart. . . . If that's "morale," we've got it—to spare.

Advertisers warned the public of the perils of black markets; pointed up the abiding faith of people in better years ahead. As *Time* put it: "For the duration, advertising has largely forgotten competition and is promoting one common product: the U. S." [74]

While we were busy developing a high morale in our own fighting forces and in our own civilian population, it was just as important to do everything we could to demoralize the enemy. For the accomplishment of this end, propaganda also furnished a very useful weapon. Reminding the Germans of what happened when the Yanks came over in 1917 provided a potent means of inducing the jitters among the Nazis in 1943.

London was clever in broadcasting the voice of Hitler more than that of any other man. Hour after hour and day after day for many months, the BBC has broadcast to Germany recordings of his war speeches so Germans will not forget his arrogant assertions and extravagant promises.

People in the occupied countries used humor very effectively to demoralize their captors. In Czechoslovakia, for example, a notice was posted on a cemetery wall, which read: "Hey, you Czechs, get out of here! Don't you know that this is the German Lebensraum?" Another quip was posted over a hen which had been hanged: "I'd rather commit suicide than lay eggs for Hitler."

The British "V" campaign was clever strategy for bolstering Allied morale and demoralizing the enemy. A Belgian refugee named Victor de Laveleye conceived the idea. On a short-wave broadcast from London he urged his countrymen to chalk the letter V (for *victoire*) in public places, as a symbol of confidence in their deliverance. A Colonel Britton "plugged" the V campaign on the short-wave programs of the British Broadcasting Corporation. He asked the people of the occupied countries to mark the letter everywhere, even on the backs of German officers—which some of them did. Listeners were informed how to tap it out in Morse Code, three dots and a dash. This rhythmic beat was recommended as a signal for calling waiters, knocking on doors, blowing auto horns, bugles, and train whistles. Soon the tat-tat-tat-too was heard all over Europe. Requests for Beethoven's Fifth Symphony multiplied because the opening motif, "fate-knocks-at-the-door," consists of three short bars and one long one.

The Colonel told Europeans to sit in cafés with their legs stretched out V-wise. He told them to wave to one another with the first two fingers of

[74] *Time,* March 22, 1943.

the hand spread V-wise. He told them to make the letter V with their knives and forks in restaurants, to set stopped clocks at five after eleven. The Moscow radio jammed German broadcasts with the Morse V. The R.A.F. flew over Europe in V-formation—and it was so noted in official communiqués. In Belgium the Flemish composer R.A.F. Verhulst became a

Blasphemy: This cartoon, by Bill Moran, appeared in a Japanese newspaper in Hawaii during World War II. To a Japanese it was blasphemous, because it showed the Emperor. Hirohito (*right*) asks Premier Tojo (*left*) and Admiral Yamamoto where the planes that bombed Tokyo came from. There could be no greater blasphemy than ignoring the Emperor's request.

national celebrity when posters advertising the performance of one of his operas featured his four initials. The Germans caught on and tore the posters down.

Like a fresh wind blowing in from the sea, the campaign spread over Europe. V, which stood for *victory* in English and *victoire* in French, became *vryheid* (freedom) in Dutch, *vitezstvi* (victory) in Czech, *vitestvo* (heroism) in Serbian, and in Norwegian *ve vil vinne,* which means just what it sounds like in pidgin English.

To Nazis all Europe's eternal tat-tat-tat-tooing was foolish and exasperating. First the Nazis tried to suppress or ignore it. Growled Norway's Quisling Propaganda Minister Gudbrand Lunde: "Don't think you will win the war by making silly noises in restaurants." In France 6,000 people were arrested for distributing paper V's. Then Germany's Propaganda Chief Paul Joseph Goebbels had what he thought was a bright idea, or perhaps it was given to him by a visiting friend, Italy's Popular Culture Minister Alessandro Pavolini, who was also on the receiving end of the campaign.

On the principle of if-you-can't-lick-'em-join-'em, the Nazi Propaganda Ministry announced that V stood for Nazi victory—*Viktoria*—thereby impairing the purity of the German vocabulary by importing a foreign word, for the native German word for victory is *Sieg*. Germans were urged to use the symbol. In rendering this decision Dr. Goebbels made a mistake: since the V-sign was no longer *verboten,* the Germans could not suppress it. . . .

Colonel Britton concluded:

"The Germans will not drown out the knocking of fate, however loud they beat. For when they tap out the V they are merely signaling their own impending doom. . . .

"I advise you to read from the Old Testament of the Bible, the Book of Daniel, Chapter 5, Verse 5, that is Chapter V, Verse V, and read to the end of the chapter. Good luck to you."

Colonel Britton's campaign was ingenious. It was more. It was the first antidote prescribed for the apathy of Europe. It was the first organized attempt to unite the spirit and forces of resistance. Symbols are strangely powerful in politics, and a symbol had been found for a future revolution against Fascism. If kept alive, V might come to stand, in Germany and all conquered countries, for a great underground movement against Nazism, for democracy's vast Column V.[75]

There are various technical problems peculiar to military morale that need the attention of psychological experts working in collaboration with military experts. Physical and mental conditioning are both necessary to convert the flabby peace-loving citizen into an effective fighter. To understand the task that faced the men in charge of conditioning the American inductee, we must look into the situation existing just prior to our entry into World War II.

The morale of the American Army was reported to be none too good in the period of mobilization previous to Pearl Harbor. The men in camp were demoralized during the national uncertainty by the uneasy feeling that the Army had no goal. They felt that the emergency was not serious. Other conditions contributing to a poor morale were:

> Little faith in the competency of the officers
> Training old-fashioned
> Idleness
> Lack of modern equipment

[75] *Time,* July 28, 1941.

Lower pay than that earned by civilians
Worry over their jobs back home
Nice girls avoid the army boys
Storekeepers overcharge them
Lack of recreational facilities.[76]

The 1941 "gripes" of the men in camps were well portrayed by cartoonist Thomas in the Detroit *News.*

Soldiers confessed they were bored and fed up, tired of sitting on their bunks of an evening, of hanging around street corners, of walking miles and miles for any sort of entertainment. The men confided

(Courtesy, Burt Thomas and the Detroit *News.*)

that they were satiated with army routine, that they yearned for a chance to chat with nice people, that they worried a lot about what would happen to them when they returned, if ever, to civilian life.[77] The peacetime soldier, of course, is by nature a grumbler. He is in the same unhappy situation as the boxer who is training for a fight which may never come off. It is very difficult to build up a sound morale in a peacetime army. When the enemy has been recognized, war declared, and the battle front fairly well defined, it is not hard to develop in either volunteers or conscripts that spirit of aggressive loyalty which is ordinarily called morale.

Entrance of the United States into the war in December, 1941, changed this whole frame of reference and it became less difficult to stir the nation, both civilians and fighting men, to a full awareness of the danger, and the need of making every effort to defeat our formidable enemies.

Wartime morale for the soldier must be built upon training to kill with zest and without compunction, to face peril without shrinking, to endure hardship without flinching. A will-to-win must be inculcated by tapping the love of American freedom, so the fighter will be able

[76] "What the Soldiers Complain About." *Life,* August 18, 1941.
[77] "Camp Morale—What Goes On?" *Liberty,* August 2, 1941.

o tolerate being deprived of his accustomed satisfactions, his physical omforts, and his normal social relationships. The morale-disrupting onditions of military life can be minimized by allowing leave, by upplying every comfort available, by providing for recreation, by enouraging relatives and friends to write letters. Too much leave is nadvisable—some authorities claim that relaxation between periods f fighting may be demoralizing.

There are definite symptoms of poor morale which officers must 10tice and then take steps to remedy: the lack of readiness of the men o volunteer for special duty, frequent violations of discipline, large 1umbers of men AWOL or in the guardhouse, a high incidence of 7enereal disease, susceptibility to rumors, fights over religious or racial lifferences, grouching and "beefing," chronic fatigue.[78] One of the nost important preventives of demoralization is a frank recognition hat it is natural for a soldier to be afraid. The experienced fighter earns that every man going into battle is scared, in fact, terrified, and 1e is not disturbed too much when he finds his hands trembling, his hroat dry, and he begins swallowing over and over because his "heart s in his mouth." These bad moments, experience shows, come in the oeriod of waiting; when combat begins, fear is forgotten. In order hat the fear preceding battle may not become overpowering, the sollier and his leader should be trained to make use of certain devices for allaying anxiety: do something, keep in sight of other men, have the roll called to reassure each man others are doing their part, keep the men informed of what is going on, remove panicky men from the presence of others, be mindful that one's chances of getting killed are very small. It is necessary, of course, to warn the soldier that shirking or desertion will lead to court-martial. Negative discipline of this sort is not enough, however, for it will not inspire a man to take the risks or to adopt the aggressive attitude that is essential to good fighting.

Obedience and respect must be demanded and merited by the commanding officers. Leaders must be men who are blessed with an understanding of human relations. Man-officer relations turn out to be "much more important to morale than beefsteak, warm socks, ball games, vaudeville shows, or what men believe about war."

What the men think of their leaders is, then, of the utmost importance to the Army and to the successful prosecution of the war.

[78] See *Psychology for the Fighting Man* Chapter 13, "Morale." National Research Council, 1943.

Roughly, in the order of their association with good leadership in the minds of the enlisted men, are the following points:

(1) Ability. Competence comes first. The good officer must know his stuff, for on this depends the men's confidence in his leadership.

(2) Next to ability is interest in the welfare of the soldier. The officer who can be trusted to help the soldier in time of need, or who would be accessible for personal advice, is a good officer.

(3) "Promptness in making decisions" is next.

(4) "Good teacher or instructor" follows. The leader who has the patience and the ability to make things clear to the men under him is valued for that reason.

(5) "Judgment," "common sense," and the ability to get things done follow next in order.

(6) The good leader does not "boss you around when there is no good reason for it." Soldiers dislike an officer who throws his rank around, who tests his own authority continually. They sense that he is not sure of himself.

(7) "The man who tells you when you have done a good job" rates well as a leader. Failure in commendation is a common complaint among men in the ranks. The best incentive to good work is the prospect that it will be noticed and remembered by the leader.

(8) Physical strength and good build come next.

(9) "Good education," "sense of humor," and "guts or courage" follow in that order.

(10) Impartiality is next. Leaders who do not "save the dirty jobs for the fellows they don't like" are valued. The good leader is fair to all his command.

(11) Next in importance is industry. Leaders who "do as little work as they can get away with" are not respected by the enlisted men.

(12) When an officer "gives orders in such a way that you know clearly what to do," that too is a mark of merit as a leader. Soldiers also like an officer with a "clear, strong voice." [79]

It is important, too, to instill a pride in group membership, which may be accomplished by means of uniforms, insignia, parades and reviews, colors, close-order drills, mass singing, and unit athletic teams. It is a good idea to plan the allocation of men so that men who have trained together will also fight together. Positive incentives can be utilized by conferring medals and decorations, awarding them promptly to get the maximum effect, and by fostering a firm belief in the cause that is being fought for. Confidence can be bred by training the soldier thoroughly in the skills of offense and defense and by keeping him

[79] *Ibid.*, pp. 373-374.

accurately informed of the risks he is undertaking. The spirit of the ideal soldier has been aptly expressed in this epitome of what it takes to make a great fighter:

I'll tell you what morale is. It is when a soldier thinks his army is the best in the world, his regiment the best in the army, his company the best in the regiment, his squad the best in the company, and that he himself is the best damn soldier-man in the outfit.[80]

[80] *Time*, August 18, 1941.

Part IV

INDIVIDUAL PATTERNS OF SOCIAL BEHAVIOR

IN PART IV we shall concentrate our attention upon the actions of the individual in his "informal" role, indicating how his thinking and his outward behavior are fashioned by the influences of the society in which he lives; in Part V our concern will be focused upon the patterns of "formal" behavior as they manifest themselves in particular organizations or institutions.

Chapter 12, the first chapter in Part IV, discusses "Convention," distinguishing it from custom, describes the exercise of social control through approval and disapproval, represents *conventionalization* as the recognition of a proper time-and-place for everything, and deals with the supervision of morals by the censor-reformer.

Chapter 13, "Custom," describes the adherence to traditional modes of conduct, modes established by long usage and revered for their time-honored sanctity. The "permanence" of customary habits is traceable to dread of the unfamiliar, veneration for the past, the strong affective tone involved, and resistance to innovations which upset the old ways of doing things. Cultural lag results when developments are accelerated in one phase of our culture while progress in some other phase is slower by comparison. Survivals are customs which have outlived their usefulness—we find them in ceremonials, politics, law, medicine, and economics, just to mention some outstanding examples. The intelligent person will seek to preserve only what is worth while in our heritage from the past. The wise conservative will encourage moderate change if he really wants to discourage revolution.

Chapter 14 treats the various aspects of "Fashion," with special emphasis upon changing patterns in clothes. The follower of fashion wears what "they're all wearing now"; the adherent of style wears what's becoming. Fashions change according to definite trends or cycles, engineered by interested persons who exploit prestige as a spur to "fashion racing." Sex differences appear in conforming to fashion. Rapid changes of an extreme sort are short-lived, come under the head of fads and crazes.

Chapter 15 deals with "Superstition." Fallacious beliefs of all kinds are popularly labeled "superstitions." This is unfortunate. We should limit the term to beliefs which assume the existence of super natural forces which can be influenced in one's behalf by resort to sorcery. Crooked thinking, emotionalized, wishful, compulsive, ma nipulates symbols to achieve magical results, in an endeavor to out maneuver the unknown factor "Chance." Certain superstitions are characteristic of particular localities: the Pennsylvania Dutch cling to their favorites, the Ozark Mountain folk to theirs. Pseudo-sciences like astrology and numerology, pose as sciences; their pretensions call for exposure. Religion is sometimes damned as mere superstition. This sort of wholesale indictment is due to confusion: *some* with *all*. Some religious beliefs may be superstitious, an observation which does not justify a wild generalization inclusive of all religious beliefs. Education can reduce superstitiousness but it is not likely to exterminate it very soon.

There are two chapters on prejudice. Chapter 16 analyzes "Prejudice" with reference to "Dogmatism and Ignorance," pointing out that prejudices exert a subtle influence upon our attitudes, all the more subtle when we maintain strong opinions on matters we know little about, being especially fond, under such circumstances, of our own convictions. Prejudice discourages learning by closing the mind to evidence, thus precluding investigation of the truth. Seeing both sides of an issue may result in paralyzing action but in everyday life we are often compelled to commit ourselves to some policy before we have time to gather all the relevant facts.

Chapter 17 treats of "The Genesis and Control of Prejudice." Prejudices are conditioned by personal experiences. The school, press, movies, and radio help to instill prejudices which will fit the individual for living comfortably in his culture. Prejudices are facilitated by the presence of individual differences—personal appearance, personality, cultural level, religion, race, and status. An effective diminution of prejudice must be based upon a desire for enlightenment. Tolerance can be promoted by education, through reading, classroom instruction, wide personal contacts, and propaganda for enlightenment. The individual who comes to understand the nature of his stereotyping is likely to become less prejudiced. Progress toward fairmindedness can be measured by tests designed for that purpose.

Chapter 12

CONVENTION

ONE IMPORTANT EVIDENCE that the individual is eager to be recognized as an accredited member of the society in which he moves is the
fact that he conscientiously conforms to certain standard usages, binding on all persons who feel constrained to practice the accepted amenities. These social norms are conventions. Their function is to facilitate social intercourse by defining the bounds of courtesy and decency,
so that good manners may be the rule rather than the exception.
What is seemly, what is decorous, what is of good report are made
manifest as the criteria of orthodoxy. Thus the writer of amateur
plays must be careful of his language lest he shock persons who are
duly sensitive to the proprieties:

Even as harmless an expression as "Holy Mackerel" might be criticized as
a sacrilegious reference to the parable of the loaves and fishes, and as mild
an exclamation as "My Stars and Garters" might be blue-penciled because
of its association with the leg.[1]

Conventions set the canons of good taste. Those who fail to conform
are ostracized as vulgar persons or heretics.

I. CONVENTION AND CUSTOM

Convention and custom both decree certain modes of accepted behavior. Convention is more concerned with the forms; custom, with
the essentials. It is customary to eat; it is conventional to set the
table with the silver arranged in a definite pattern and to use the appropriate knives, forks, and spoons for the various edibles served during the prearranged courses. The significant fact about eating is that
it provides sustenance for the body; the manner of food consumption,
from soup to nuts, is incidental. The formalities, even though incidental, must be rigidly observed by persons of quality, for table man-

[1] M. Denison, "Do You Know Aaron Slick?" *Harper's Magazine*, March, 1938.

ners are interpreted as a measure of breeding.   According to a seven
teenth-century authority on etiquette, the man of polish must no
scratch himself in company, or blow in his soup, or talk with his moutl
full, or pocket the fruit served for dessert.   Eating, apparently, is mor
than a process of stuffing the stomach; it is a ritual through which botl
body and soul may be momentarily satisfied.   Only a glutton woulc
think of mealtime in terms of carnal cravings.

It is customary for friends to greet each other upon meeting; th
manner of salutation is determined by the conventions.   Negro chief
in Africa snap the middle finger three times; Polynesians press noses
Eskimos rub noses; Sandwich Islanders kowtow by prostrating them
selves; Americans nod the head, shake hands, or kiss, depending on th
degree of intimacy.   The American gentleman tips his hat to a lady
in paying his homage.   The lady is not expected to uncover as a marl
of respect for the man to whom she is how-do-you-doing.   There is nc
particular sense to tipping the hat as a courtesy; a flip of the necktie
might do just at well if it were the recognized symbol of friendship
Some historians tell us that hat-tipping goes back to the days of chiv
alry when knights wore full armor in public and friends greeted eacl
other by raising the visor as a sign of mutual recognition.   Whatever
the origin, the practice is an established one in America and in othe
countries, supplemented at times by handshaking, bowing, curtsies
and, on special occasions, back-slapping.   Convention decrees what i
proper for whom, when and where.

It is the custom for people to be patriotic; the ways of expressing
love of country are prescribed by certain conventional forms.   These
forms are arbitrarily established by persons in authority, who may no
feel constrained by any laws of logic, in their formulation of the rules
This observation is borne out in the case of a woman who complainec
that her husband made her arise from bed and stand at attention while
the national anthem was being played over the radio at 10 P.M.   The
disgruntled wife was instructed by Mrs. Noble Newport Potts, Presi
dent of the National Patriotic Council, that there were no grounds for
the complaint, since American wives are supposed to roll out of bed
when the strains of the *Star Spangled Banner* are wafted into the bou
doir.   Mrs. Potts said that she spends her summers at Fortress Monroe
Virginia, where her cottage is within view of the flag that's raised a
6 A.M. every day.   "And as Old Glory is run up, I rise from my bed
and stand at attention.   There's nothing noble about it, it's just the
thing to do.   Why, if I heard the *Star Spangled Banner* being played
in the middle of the night, I would get up out of a sound sleep

here is no clarion call like the national anthem. It would rouse a patriotic woman no matter how soundly she slept." However, a different opinion about what's expected from patriotic citizens was offered by Colonel James A. Moss, President-General of the United States Flag Association, who stated that a person need not arise when the anthem is played while he or she is in bed, eating, telephoning, playing cards, or taking a bath.[2] Assuming that the Colonel speaks with more authority than Mrs. Potts and taking him at his word, it is difficult to see what rational basis there could be for ignoring the clarion call because the patriot happens to be busy trying to make his contract of four spades. Nevertheless, the Colonel says it's all right to keep your seat under the circumstances.

We have differentiated convention and custom with respect to form and essence. It is not a clear-cut distinction and in everyday parlance the two terms are often used interchangeably. There is another basis for distinguishing the two: custom, on the one hand, emphasizes the mores established by long usage, sanctified by generations of experience, endorsed by the oldest families. Convention, on the other hand, is a standard of behavior that is respected without reference to the sanctions of time, a norm that is adhered to now because it is what's being done in the present. Ross says that customs are borrowed from our ancestors, conventions from our contemporaries.[3] This statement is not strictly accurate because some conventions have endured from one generation to another. Ross would prefer to call such conventions "customs." Confusion may result from this usage since it ignores the first distinction we described, which is probably a better ground for differentiation than the difference in the time element. The matter of time is a criterion that must be kept in mind, however, and if it is combined with the form-essence criterion, we have a demarcation that may be helpful even though not definite enough to be wholly satisfactory.

II. APPROVAL AND DISAPPROVAL

One important reason why a person conforms to conventional usages is his desire for social approval. Every individual who wants to belong to a group must follow the rules that are recognized as binding upon all alike. Thus a college freshman who is eager to be accepted by upperclassmen must do what is expected of him, even though it means a rapid depletion of his funds and an appeal to home for more capital:

---

[2] The Boston *Herald*, October 13, 1938.
[3] See E. A. Ross: *Social Psychology*. 1908.

I joined the University store because everyone else was doing it. I als
bought a pressing ticket, a soccer ticket, a shoeshine ticket, subscriptions t
the *Princetonian,* the *Nassau Literary Magazine,* the *Tiger,* and a Ne
York paper, and I joined the Nassau Club which is a club just for freshme
So you see where all of my money went, but I guess I am in pretty good wit
the upperclassmen.[4]

Many a father who earned his own way through college is now earnin
his son's way through and helping him to get in the good graces c
people who "count."   Conformity is a prerequisite to social approva
whether it be in college or in the home community.

A stronger motive for following the dictates of convention is the fea
of social disapproval.   One form of this fear is the dread of gossi
Thus the individual who is tempted to violate the canons stops sho
when he asks, "What will people say?"   The prospect of becomin
the talk of the town will incite some apprehension even in those ind
pendent souls who are relatively insensitive to public opinion.   Pe
sons of more delicate sensibilities are careful not to offend good tast
lest the gossipers be given provocation for humiliating them.   Lik
Caesar's wife, they must be above suspicion.   It does not take much t
start tongues wagging, as a girl found out who was working on
W.P.A. sewing project.   She had been ill for several weeks.   Whe
she returned to work some of the older women on the project bega
"whispering."   The girl told her parents about the gossip, finally sai
she couldn't stand it any longer, left home and disappeared.   Misi
formed gossipers drove her to despair.

One man who was so disheartened by malicious gossip concernin
his illegitimate child that he could not bear it any longer had the chil
"done away with."   Just before he was electrocuted for his crime, h
wrote a letter moralizing on his sad end:

One little mistake on my part got me into a great mess of trouble.
have been ashamed of my illegitimate child that I did not want to take hom
and I had it boarded out at a stranger's house.   The shame came to m
through the gossip of my neighbors and disrespectful talk against the illegit
mate child, and in giving this child to place in a Jewish home in New Yor
till the gossip will die down.

This case is to teach us all not to make little mistakes and that when
little mistake has been made, we must try to do right by the innocent chil
in spite of gossip of neighbors, and the shame that comes with it.[5]

[4] A. Winsten: "A Story in Descending Discords." *Harper's Magazine,* Augus
1926.

[5] The Boston *Herald,* July 17, 1928.

Since people will talk, some wag has suggested the moral maxim: So live that you wouldn't be ashamed to sell the family parrot to the town gossip.

When Mrs. Grundy talks, conventional folks fall into line. Her ideas about morality are narrow and hidebound and she enforces them on others with a relentless will. It was Mrs. Grundy who condemned theater-going as sinful and who lumped in the same category: dancing, cosmetics, scanty clothing, tobacco; playing cards for money, playing cards on Sunday, or just playing cards; billiards, playing the fiddle, taking a nap, reading the Sunday paper. With the passing years the conventions concerning sin have become more liberal, but Mrs. Grundy gives way grudgingly, sure that the younger generation is "going to the dogs."

It is in the small town that the pressure of social disapproval becomes the dominant agency of social control. On Main Street all people are supposed to hold the same opinions. Heretics are hushed, or patronizingly told, "If you'll think these things over long enough you'll come around to agreeing with us." And agree they will, if they want to be known about town as boosters, not knockers. There is little tolerance for nonconformists.

A man who had lived for some time in New York City moved to a small town. In the new environment he discovered what fear can do to the human mind when people live at close quarters, as they must in a small community:

Why does one sit at parties [in Durham], and wish, for God's sake, that something awful would happen to crack the glassy smoothness of these happily ordered lives? . . . [the lives of] the grown-up married people, men and women, who foregather at one another's houses, and create all the taboos. . . . What price does one pay for assimilation into their world?

For their world has a price. As I see it, it is an adaptation, slow but irrevocable, to the small-town mind. Just as one adapts the household to an early dinner—maids in Durham fall into a faint if dinner is ordered later than six-thirty—so one must prune the reckless city-bred mind to an earlier un-metropolitan habit of thought. Axioms on Forty-fifth Street are blasphemies in Durham.

The newcomer to Durham found himself "making breaks" in his table talk. On one occasion he mentioned to a patrician dowager that a friend had just returned from Russia. The dowager immediately wanted to know what the friend thought about those dreadful murders.

"Which murders?" There are always so many murders in any social upheaval.

The lady gave me a look only to be described as dirty. Any murder was unpleasant, but the murders which harried her heart were those of the Royal Princesses, "those lovely girls." . . . This lady . . . rejected this revolution because of the extinction of a royal family. . . .

As the months go by, I have grown more wary. I say less at the wrong time, and I think more about fear and what it does to the human mind, that instrument potentially so daring and so precious. It is fear which makes Durham's nicer people so wary to avoid experience, so careful to stay with accustomed friends, to cheer for the happily ended book . . . to avoid the harsher plays when in New York.

On another occasion the mistake was made of mentioning a book which was concerned with moral decay.

"But think of all the people one knows who do decay."
"But, one doesn't have to have such people in one's home. Why should one have to read about them?"

Shakespearian drama in modern dress was severely condemned by Mrs Cobalt with the didactic comment: "Hamlet cannot be Hamlet in tweeds."

Mrs. Cobalt is an able intelligent woman, a reader of the *Atlantic Monthly*, a pillar of rectitude. She is courageous in behalf of her ideals, some specially chosen, others inherited from her sheltered youth. The ideals of other people are of little moment; her face assumes a granite-like frigidity when confronted with the unfamiliar and the unapproved. She distrusts immigrants, sophisticated novels, young people, and women who long for careers. Indomitably, she stands guard at the door of her own mind, lest any disturbing novelty enter in.

People in Durham would rather be dull forever than take a chance on the uncertainty of change.

Now beset as we are by repression, prohibition, shyness, dignity, it is difficult for people over thirty to have a good time at a party unless they are jazzed up with liquor.

At the Durham Country Club we hold each winter a set of dances . . . for the married set. Yet as the months go by, the committee in charge finds it hard to keep the dances going; pair by pair, couples drop out. Mrs. Henry Payne keeps her husband at home because he likes too well to dance with pretty Mrs. Duncan.   The men are bored by dancing with one another's wives. . . .

Upon a newcomer these connubial routs make a strange impression.   In the ballroom to the music of a jazz band, rhythmic but not riotous, one sees Durham's best, dancing about in one another's arms: the prominent, pudgy Mr. Henshaw with chattery Mrs. Dunn; the attractive lively Mrs. Henshaw with the dull Mr. Dunn.   The impeccably well-dressed Mrs. Evans parades by with her saturnine, indifferent spouse, who hates dancing.   Oh, dear God!

The next dance will present a fresh realignment.   The couples smile, reverse, banter; assume masks of hopeful gayety.   But the spectacle has neither the dignity of a ritual nor the abandon of a bacchanal.   Few of these men and women dance together because they want to dance with each other.   They are husbands and wives, breaking for one evening the routine of monogamy.   Where is that electric spark of sex—the man pursuing the woman, the woman eluding the man—which pervades all youthful parties, debutante balls, and college dances?   Yet how to introduce sex into a Durham ball, safely to enliven the evening without breaking up homes, is a problem for no committee, but for the gods.

Indeed, love and marriage are treated with evasions and reticences.

With innocent enthusiasm, we in Durham welcome early marriages.   The obvious unpreparedness of some youthful mates is obscured by veils of sentiment, chiffons, and wedding presents.   Indeed, financial suitability and perfectly darling girlhood, the world over, make a perfect match.   Yet a decade later, when these young people are in their early thirties, the best time of their lives, there are few to recognize the sad plight of a wife emotionally and intellectually mature mated to an eternally adolescent husband.   She married him, and she is a sinner if she does not love him, says society. . . . This same nicety of attitude is instanced in the general feeling of horror at the thought of a large family.   To bear six children is revolting, ostentatious, sloppy. . . .

The account of life in Durham closes with this trenchant observation:

Most people lose in the early thirties their passionate hunger for life.   It is so easy to cherish monotony for fear of something worse.[6]

III. CONVENTIONALIZATION

Certain acts are permissible only under certain circumstances.[7] Whether an act is to be accepted or censored depends upon the situa-

[6] Anonymous: "Fear in Small-Town Life."   *Harper's Magazine*, August, 1926.

[7] Conventional regulations for sports were described in Chapter 1, "The Individual in Social Situations," pp. 21-22.

tion. There is a time and a place for everything. "Conventializa tion creates a set of conditions under which a thing may be tolerated which would otherwise be disapproved and tabooed." [8] Special condi tions may excuse behavior ordinarily considered reprehensible. Cir cumstances alter cases.

Suppose a college professor is giving a course in summer school and one very hot morning he appears on the lecture platform in nothing but his underwear. He is not an exhibitionist; he merely wants to be comfortable during his labors. The effect would be shocking, no mat ter what his motive might be, no matter how well proportioned hi physique. Word would soon get to the president of the university and to the board of trustees that one of the professors had lost his mind The erring teacher would be "on the carpet" in no time, facing a de mand to account for his peculiar antics. He would lose his job regard less of any justifications he might offer and not even the Association of American University Professors would rise to protest against his un timely expulsion.

Suppose that the professor, instead of appearing in the classroom in only his underclothes, should turn out in his athletic underwear on the occasion of the university's annual Field Day. If he sits in the bleach ers to watch the baseball game, clad as we have specified, all the people around him would start talking and edge away from his vicinity. If he stands on the running track, or better still jaunts down the track, he will attract no particular censure, although a few people may won der just why the professor is resorting to such violent, and perhaps uncomely, exercise.

This general situation is not purely a theoretical one. A famous judge found himself in a similar predicament in an unwary moment. He was pressing his trousers in his office—in his early impecunious days—when he saw a client go by who owed him some money. In the excitement of the moment, he set out in pursuit of his prospect, absentmindedly forgetting his trousers were still on the ironing board. As he bounded down the sidewalk, he suddenly realized his legs were bare. Much embarrassed, he rushed back to cover, leaving his client to continue his way unmindful of his narrow escape. Now if the young lawyer had been thinking fast, he could have removed his shirt and garters, and, provided he had on athletic underwear, he could have run down the street without being taken into custody, since peo ple would have mistaken him for a marathon runner training for a holiday grind. It might not have done him much good, however, be-

[8] W. G. Sumner: *Folkways,* p. 68. Ginn and Company, 1906.

ause he could not have stopped on the sidewalk to talk with his
debtor. The underwear taboo would have prevented any sidewalk
interviews. Attired in running garb, he would have found it wise to
keep on running until he returned to the privacy of his office. These
are nice distinctions; the wise man observes them conscientiously.

There is a time and a place for everything. It is all right to make
a lot of noise on the Fourth of July. It is all right for people to destroy each other's property on Halloween, if it is done in the spirit of
fun and the damage is not excessive. In ancient times there were the
Saturnalia, carnival holidays which were celebrated with joy uncon-
fined, since at these special times ordinary social restrictions were re-
laxed and a period of license allowed a temporary release of inhibited
impulses.

Certain conventions have grown up around dancing. Some parents
may allow their children to dance in private homes but not in public
dance halls; others may draw the line on country clubs or night clubs
or debutante balls. Many persons would be shocked by the idea of a
girl dancing in front of a church congregation, even though she assured
the authorities that her dance was to symbolize the spirit of religion.
When a girl did actually render a rhythmic interpretation of a Biblical theme in a church at Waltham, Massachusetts, in September,
1934, a critic was prompted to editorialize in the following censorious
tone:

> After all allowances have been made, the fact remains that the church
> cheapens itself in the estimation of the general public, and probably out-
> rages the sensibilities of the great majority of church constituencies, by sub-
> stituting a series of interpretative dances for the usual order of Christian
> worship. The parish house is the place for such performances. A conse-
> crated auditorium is not.
> It is not that there is anything wrong with dancing itself. It is altogether
> a matter of judgment as to the time and place. On grounds both of expe-
> diency and of propriety, this variety of church service is of most dubious
> value to real religion.[9]

Times change, of course. A generation ago church people frowned
on the Bunny Hug, the Turkey Trot, the Subway Glide, and dancing
in general. Dancing in church, even in the parish house, would have
been considered irreverent and ungodly. At the present time dancing
in the parish house is permitted by many sects—but not on Sunday.

[9] The Boston *Herald*, September 23, 1934.

There is a time and a place even for rioting when Frenchmen are concerned.   There is no rioting after hours.

A riot in France is one of the most remarkable things in the world.   The frenzied combatants maintain perfect discipline. . . .   There was no fighting at all between about seven-thirty p.m. and nine when everyone took time out for dinner.   [During the riots of 1934] communists, royalists, fascists, socialists fought shoulder to shoulder under both red flag and tricolor against the police and Garde Mobile.   The fighting stopped on the stroke of twelve [midnight], because the Paris Metro [underground] stops running at 12:30 and no one wanted to walk all the way home.   Bloody, bandaged, fighters and police jostled their way into the trains together.   Promptly at seven thirty next morning, the fighting started again.[10]

In the summer of 1934 Park Commissioner Long of Boston was faced with the problem as to whether women should be allowed to wear shorts on the municipal golf links.   He ruled that women's shorts were all right for tennis but not for golf, admitted that it was a subtle distinction, defended himself by adding that "it is just a matter of practical taste.   Shorts go on the courts, but not on the links."   Legal authority for the ban was found in a law passed in 1880: "Women must be properly clothed from neck to knee" or be subject to fine.

By 1936 the problem of shorts and abbreviated bathing costumes had become a nation-wide issue.   Burgess Samuel A. Boyd of Forty Fort, Pennsylvania, expressed a common attitude when he inveighed against scanty costumes in public places, said he was not a bewhiskered grandpop, described himself as being in the prime of life and in full possession of his faculties, objected strenuously to pedestrians and residents who showed "too much anatomy and not enough common sense."   Shorts will go in Forty Fort, but not short shorts, for they constitute "indecent exposure." [11]

Sun suits—silk or cotton outfits consisting of a detached halter and matching shorts—were viewed with alarm when they first appeared on the streets of Rye, New York.   The authorities thumbed through the local law books and found a statute making appearance in lingerie in public subject to disciplinary action.   They promptly classified sun suits as lingerie and thus brought offenders within the scope of the law.   Thereafter shorts were allowed on the beaches of Rye and in the privacy of residents' backyards, but not on the streets.[12]

[10] J. Gunther: *Inside Europe*, pp. 154-155. Published by Harper & Brothers. Copyright, 1933, 1934, 1935, 1936, 1937, 1938, 1940 by John Gunther.
[11] New York *Times*, June 26, 1936.
[12] *Ibid.*

In some cases there was some question as to whether censorship of shorts should be based on moral or on aesthetic grounds. Dover, New Jersey, lined up against shorts and halters on the streets because of the immoral tendencies fostered by exposed backs and legs, with the local W.C.T.U. exerting its pressure to keep the body properly attired.

The Mores Change. (Photo at right, courtesy, Jantzen Knitting Mills.)

Yonkers opposed exposure for aesthetic reasons, being disturbed by the vulgarity of "too fleshy bodies." A lady suggested to the Yonkers Common Council that it appoint a committee to include a physician with a knowledge of reducing and a sociologist to cope constructively with the situation.

Meanwhile the Navy was also perplexed by the unconventional attire adopted unofficially by some of the members of the fleet. Finally Rear Admiral A. J. Rowcliff issued this opinion:

Neither nakedness nor underwear are authorized Navy outer uniforms at present. The sun's age and man's antiquity being what they are, sun-bathing has been practiced for some time in the past without a policy. However, the price of clothing, the progress of medical thermo and radio technique, and the existing inclination of mankind toward nakedness and idleness may require the establishment of a policy. Sun-bathing, by its very nature, seem to eliminate clothing, at least temporarily. . . . The use of trunks has been established as suitable for public swimming from ships of the Navy, for race boat crews, and other athletic exercises aboard ship. There appears no reason why they may not be used for sun-bathing, if desired.[13]

Many of these perplexing problems might never have arisen to plague the moralists if the doctors had not discovered the beneficent effects of the sun's rays upon the bare skin. A person can get his vita mins from cod liver oil without causing any profound social disturb ance, but basking in the ultra-violet rays of the sun necessitates the shedding of clothes. As soon as somebody's sensibilities are shocked the censors are provoked to take action. As the years go by, however there seems to be an increasing tolerance for bodily exposure. If the process of unclothing is a gradual one, with attire getting a little scantier each season, negative adaptation enters in so that the change attracts minimal notice. How far the process can continue in the di rection of nudity is difficult to determine.

There are conventional attitudes toward hat-wearing, which differ entiate between the two sexes, discriminating especially against the men, for in this matter, at least, women have the advantage over men Women are allowed variety, flexibility, in fact, a liberty that almost amounts to license, while their brothers are hemmed in by prohibi tions, by inhibitions, by relentless taboos. In styles, a woman may run in a single year the whole gamut of toques, turbans, and tams. Ex cept in church and theater she may practically decide for herself the question of taking her hat off or keeping it on; she may wear straw in January, and felt in July with perfect impunity—indeed, with a cer tain added prestige. But her brother is ridden by a hundred rules For fifty years, the stingy styles for men have kept him down to little beyond derbies, fedoras, and sailors, with an occasional silk top hat in which he is somehow made to feel that he looks like an ass. There are endless rules of etiquette which he must bear in mind. He must lift his hat to ladies, and to gentlemen when they are with ladies, and not to gentlemen when they are alone. He must keep it on in trolleys and off or on, according to the city, in elevators. He must guard it in restaurants with the tail of his eye, and ransom it in hotels. At an afternoon tea some other man gets it; in church there is nothing at all to do with it. He is allowed to wear felt in summer, to be sure

[13] *Time,* October 24, 1938.

but he is not supposed to put on straw before a special date or wear it after a special date fixed by no known statute. A New Yorker with the effrontery to wear a straw hat on September 16th, was attacked by several women who took his hat away from him and stamped on it till only the shreds remained. The brave fellow had the women arrested, charging them with assault and battery; the judge awarded him one dollar for damages. Man cannot count even on his fellow man for moral support. Still, Martin Lomasney, famous Boston political boss, wore a straw hat the year around at the Hendricks Club with no detraction from his prestige. He was *a man*, with plenty of nerve and plenty of protection. We must remember, too, that butchers wear straw hats during all seasons—within the precinct of the meat market. There is a place for straw hats, irrespective of time, and that place is the meat market. In other public places, the season must be respected.

When Charles Dawes was the United States ambassador to England, he committed a serious breach of decorum. There is a recognized rule that a person wearing civilian attire in attending the royal court must include knee breeches and hose of silk. Dawes sent a request to the proper court official for a special dispensation that would grant him the privilege of wearing long trousers. The dispensation was accorded him. The Boston *Transcript* was quick to censure Dawes without any mincing of words:

> In this case customs in the matter of costume were well known. They may not be customs that appeal in all particulars to Ambassador Dawes, but they are the customs sanctioned by long usage in England, and regarded there as worth continuing. Mr. Dawes saw fit to make himself an exception to this rule. He would not do as did the others, and as his predecessors have done. He put personal preference above a nice regard for the accepted amenities. He forgot what should be a distinguishing characteristic of the man who accepts hospitality. Looked upon in this light the incident cannot be said to redound to the credit of the Ambassador. There was a lesson in good manners that even an ambassador might take to heart.[14]

It is the essence of convention that such little things are of great importance, even though the cool analytic intelligence may wonder what difference it makes whether a diplomat intent upon adjusting international difficulties has on short pants or long pants while he is on his job. The decrees of convention are imperious. It is the part of good breeding to pay heed to these niceties of good taste, these fine points of gracious living. Such observances of courtesy are important only be-

[14] June 27, 1929.

cause the best people, people with polish, people who are cultivated, people who are chivalrous, believe that such trivialities are important. Deference to convention serves a useful function: it prevents individuality from interfering with sociality.   Thus the social machinery is oiled so that eccentricity cannot upset expectation, so that uncultured folk can be easily spotted when they attempt to be "social climbers." Good manners are a badge of recognition enabling ladies and gentlemen to distinguish themselves readily from men and women in general.

High-school students, eager to learn about manners, are demanding that instruction in the amenities be added to the school curriculum. Young people want to know whether a man should keep his hat on at a soda fountain, whether fish bones may be removed from the mouth with the fingers at table, whether a woman's name should be mentioned first or last in an introduction.   Students of the social graces consult their texts to solve the problems that puzzle them—and their parents.

When dancing, do not apologize for slight mistakes.   There is nothing more boresome.

When a boy and a girl meet, it is expected of the girl to speak first.

When a man is introduced to a woman, he takes his cue from her about whether or not to shake hands.

The formal introduction is worded in this order, "Mrs. Wood, may I present Mr. Graham?"   The man is always presented to the woman.

Practice in good manners is gained under supervision in dancing groups and in other social situations.   Educators are convinced that training in courtesy is one basic phase in preparing young people for good citizenship.[15]

How well versed are you in the rules and regulations prescribed by etiquette?   Test yourself on the following matters of decorum by indicating which of these statements are true and which, false:

1. The man should always precede the lady when approaching seats in a theater, when no usher is present.
2. It is proper for a gentleman to assist a strange lady in removing her coat at the theater.
3. The guest of honor at a party or dinner should sit opposite the hostess.
4. A gentleman should sit to the left of the lady at dinner.
5. At the dining table, you should keep quiet and attend to your eating.

[15] See E. M. Stern: "Manners Go to School."   *School and Society*, 1939, 50, 52-55.

6. Food should always be passed first to the ladies on each side of you when at a meal.
7. The mouth should always be wiped before drinking water.
8. At the conclusion of a formal dinner a guest should fold his napkin properly and place it at the left of his plate.
9. A wedding at high noon is always formal.
10. A young lady should be congratulated upon her engagement.
11. At a formal wedding, the bride should march up to the altar on the arm of the bridegroom.
12. A gentleman precedes a lady when ascending stairs.
13. A typewriter may be used to answer social letters.
14. It is necessary to excuse yourself from a group upon leaving the room temporarily.
15. It is necessary to wait for the hostess to begin before starting to eat.
16. It is correct form to "excuse your glove" and shake hands without removing it.
17. A gentleman may keep his hat on when in an elevator of a hotel or club if ladies are present, but should remove it when in the elevator of an office building or store.
18. It is proper for a lady to take the arm of a man when walking on the street during the day.
19. R.S.V.P. means that your presence is requested.
20. Smoking a pipe is always permissible in a restaurant.
21. If a person drops silver while eating at the table, he should immediately stoop to recover it.
22. When the proprietor of a restaurant waits on you, it is proper to tip him.
23. It is proper for a girl to applaud at a dance.
24. Sport clothes can be worn to informal evening parties.
25. A filet mignon is a white fish with a cream sauce.
26. It is always permissible to take a chicken leg in the fingers.
27. Lettuce, chicory, or endive may be cut with a knife when served as a salad.[16]

(The "correct" answers will be found at the end of the chapter.)

Respect for good manners may result in stupid behavior, as it does when the amenities serve to thwart effective manipulation of the material environment. Westbrook Pegler has called attention to the mal-

---

[16] Some of the items are borrowed from Hepner's "Sociability Test: Knowledge of the Upper Social Strata." See H. W. Hepner: *Finding Yourself in Your Work.* D. Appleton-Century Co., 1937. For further material, see the *Furbay-Schrammel Social Comprehension Test,* published by Bureau of Educational Measurements, Kansas State Teachers College, Emporia, Kansas.

adjustive table manners of the English and Americans, as contrasted
with the practical directness of the French:

The Frenchman, like the old Scotch golfer, endeavors to do what is to be
done without superfluous weapons or fancy gestures. He sits down, ties
his napkin behind his ears, picks up a knife and fork and goes to work with
admirable directness. He dunks his bread in the juice of the snail, he
chases fragments of steak and gravy with a piece of crust, he licks his fingers
and says "Ah!"

He is far too sensible ever to permit a desirable morsel to be carried back
to the kitchen out of respect for a rule devised by the English whose etiquette
decrees that a man at the table should never appear to be hungry. If it is too
small or too liquid for a fork he will not hesitate to use his knife for a
squeegee and wipe the knife on the bread. . . .

He does not require a special niblick to blast the peas out of the mashed
potatoes or a tweezer to overcome asparagus.

If a slice of mushroom reposes in a difficult downhill lie on the rim of the
plate he doesn't ignore it, as the American or Englishman would, but goes
after it and gets it even if he has to play three strokes off the tablecloth,
which some of us would consider out of bounds. . . .

The affectation of Americans at table is notorious, and they hamper them
selves by rules having no basis in common sense. They are afraid to dig
for the best fragments of chicken or lobster, they avoid the gravy as though
it were poison, and the last spoonful of soup always goes back to the kitchen
because somebody once made a law that tipping the plate is comparable to
teeing up on the fairway. . . .[17]

Now analyze each of the twenty-seven canons in our test on etiquette
in the same critical spirit that permeates Pegler's commentary on
French manners. Do the rules promote intelligent behavior, that is,
actions that secure the essential results with the least amount of effort?
How much does each rule contribute to the facilitation of social intercourse? Could the same ends be attained by more direct means?
These are all questions that bear on a critical understanding of the
social value of conventions.

IV. CENSORSHIP, REFORM, AND THE "REFORMER"

In Chapter 5 we considered some effects of the censorship which reg-
ulates the purveyance of world news. In our present context we shall
limit ourselves to "moralistic" censorship, the kind of "meddling" that
is concerned with the custody of our morals, sometimes labeled "re-

[17] W. Pegler: *'T Ain't Right*, pp. 115-116. 1936. Quoted by permission of Westbrook Pegler.

formism." Concentration on this one phase of social regulation is prompted by our present concern with convention: the establishment and enforcement of the rules of propriety and decency.

Before we examine moralistic censorship as exercised over the press, the radio, the theater, and the schools, it may aid our perspective if we pause to survey the agencies and the means for prescribing our morals, and to look for a moment into the definition of *decency*. Agencies include:

The Watch and Ward Society
Society for the Suppression of Vice
Legion of Decency
Methodist Board of Temperance, Prohibition and Morals
W.C.T.U. (Women's Christian Temperance Union)
D.A.R. (Daughters of the American Revolution)
Local School Boards
The Anti-Saloon League

Means of enforcement include the informal pressures exerted by gossip, satire, laughter, name-calling, and threats, and the formal pressures levied by legal prosecution and institutional punishment.

Moralistic censorship concerns itself chiefly with the eradication of obscenity, conceiving the obscene to be synonymous with the lewd, lascivious, vile, immodest, filthy, indecent, suggestive, and disgusting. Prosecutors of offenders in this realm of the salacious proceed on the false assumption that morality never changes, that obscenity, therefore, is inflexible and precisely definable. An historical approach to the problem of regulating sex mores shows impressively that the idea of what constitutes a "dirty" picture or a smutty remark may change from one generation to another.

Granting that perverted persons selling pornographic postcards to youngsters should be punished by the courts, it is fairly obvious why this sort of prosecution so often appeals to the prudish type of person who is eager to impose his own unchaste repressions upon other people who may resent the assumption that "sex is filthy and passion immoral." Sex taboos are apt to be prescribed by persons who are obsessed with the creed of man's constant degradation. It has been proposed that the air be cleared in favor of intelligent regulation by changing our terminology—the tyranny of words—substituting for "obscene," "unaesthetic"; for "lewd," "in poor taste"; and for "filthy," "ugly." In line with this suggestion, LaPiere has made this pertinent observation: "The justification for moralistic censorship has generally been that that which is censored would be bad for public morals. Some—e.g., the Legion of Decency—more realistically have placed censorship on the basis of taste." [18]

Books are banned if the official censors feel that they "corrupt the morals of youth" or "tend" in that direction. Fear of such prosecution is a source of real anxiety to publishers and booksellers who can never be sure somebody with an eye for the salacious may not unexpectedly uncover a suggestive passage, however obscure, which, torn out of its context, proves nasty enough to render the "guilty" parties liable to punishment. Legal action against a book, of course, provides a lot of free publicity, thus boosting sales, much to the chagrin of the vice suppressors. Books which gained fame via this route include:

> Elinor Glyn: *Three Weeks*
> Robert Keable: *Simon Called Peter*
> James Joyce: *Ulysses*
> Theodore Dreiser: *An American Tragedy*
> James Branch Cabell: *Jurgen*
> D. H. Lawrence: *Sons and Lovers*
> J. Gautier: *Mademoiselle de Maupin*
> Marie Stopes: *Married Love*
> Lillian E. Smith: *Strange Fruit*
> Kathleen Winsor: *Forever Amber*

Strangely enough, the Bible is unmolested despite its unveiled allusions to the "realities of life." Newspapers, too, are seldom suppressed, though the more lurid tabloids feature all manner of lewdness and immorality. In deference to censorial demands, books may be bowdlerized, that is, expurgated by the deletion of offensive words or by the translation of indelicate passages into acceptable euphemistic phraseology. Novels may be "cleansed" in this way, but not so books on sex enlightenment and birth control which cannot very well discuss the anatomy and physiology of the reproductive organs without "calling a spade a spade."

Radio programs must be very carefully censored for suggestive allusions because broadcasting systems do not care to offend their faithful listeners. Mae West was severely reprimanded for a radio drama in which she shocked the good taste of some of her audience. "Ad libbing" comedians are occasionally cut off the air. Writers of soap tragedies must respect the niceties of conventional decency because listeners tend to think of the strip characters as real persons.

[18] R. T. LaPiere: *Collective Behavior*, p. 233. 1938.

Let a hero propose an ignoble act, a heroine harbor an unworthy thought, dear old Aunt Emmie grow irascible with a visiting niece, or Uncle Eb speak harshly to the family horse, and the letters of censure begin to arrive.[19]

The *dramatis personae* in these episodic misadventure dramas must watch their p's and q's.　Lovely ladies can be put upon—but the "soap opera" or "strip show" must depict nothing sordid or degrading.

The *theater*, regarded in earlier times as a den of iniquity, is still subjected to close surveillance.　The content of films, for example, has been definitely affected by pressure from reform groups such as the Hays Office, the Legion of Decency, and the state and city review boards.　Typical of film censorship was the expurgation in 1941 of Greta Garbo's picture, *Two-Faced Woman*, which depicted a wife engaged in deceiving her husband.　Boston, renowned for its puritanical Watch and Ward, mystified the public by allowing the showing of the picture, *The Birth of a Baby*, produced by the American Committee on Maternal Welfare and widely endorsed by medical societies, whereas New York censors refused to issue a permit for its appearance; Boston, running nearer to form, banned the issue of *Life* magazine which printed a sequence of scenes from this same movie, and imposed a $500 fine on the newsdealer who was caught selling a copy to a customer.

One order from the Hays Office forbade the wearing of tight sweaters by shapely movie stars and starlets.　A sample list of *Don'ts* from the same source included "Words and Phrases to be Omitted from all Pictures":

> *Alley cat* (applied to a woman)
> *Broad* (applied to a woman)
> *God, Lord, Jesus, Christ* (unless used reverently)
> *"Fanny"*
> *Fairy* (in a vulgar sense)
> *Goose* (in a vulgar sense)
> *Hot* (applied to a woman)
> *Lousy*
> *Nuts* (except when meaning "crazy")
> *Razzberry* (the sound)
> *Tomcat* (applied to a man)
> *Buzzard* (too similar in sound to bastard)[20]

S. A. Rice, reviewing B. B. Hampton's *A History of the Movies* (1931), analyzes the philosophy behind such censorship in the following terms:

---

[19] M. Denison: "Soap Opera." *Harper's Magazine*, April, 1940.
[20] *Time*, June 16, 1941.

Attitudes toward the motion picture as a social institution are of two main types, which I shall call the moralistic and the realistic. The terms are not adequate, but they will serve to make a distinction which is important in appraising the present volume. Moralists tend to view the movies as a menace to social and individual standards, as distorters of social values, as baneful educational influence which inculcates false ideas and ideals in the young and dissipates the energies and serious purposes of adults. They recognize the potential power of the silver screen for good, and urge its utilization for social control in directions which these critics would approve. The realists, on the other hand, view the movies as a tremendously vital agency of escape from the harsh actualities which surround life for the masses of the population. In themselves they are neither to be praised nor blamed, since they accurately reflect the aspirations of the *genus homo* as does no other form of sublimation. If criticism there must be, it should be directed against man himself, for being what he is, or against his maker.[21]

The stage is scrutinized, too, by vigilant censors on the lookout for such plays as *The Children's Hour* and *The Captive.* Boston banned *Strange Interlude,* and so persons interested in seeing this O'Neill drama had to journey to suburban Quincy to satisfy their curiosity. Though the censors examine every line of the scripts of legitimate stage shows to eliminate "naughty" words and though they strictly forbid overexposure of the feminine form, burlesque theaters generally continue with their strip-teasing, fan or bubble dancing, their provocative gestures, and their vulgar *double-entendres.*

The *school,* like the theater, is under constant scrutiny. School teachers are haunted by the watchful eyes of school boards and anxious parents, for instructors of the young are deemed to be in a peculiarly favorable position to exert an influence for good—or evil. In some communities teachers who want to keep their jobs must avoid frivolity and remain in town on Sundays to sing in the choir and teach Sunday-school classes.

The hullabaloo over the appointment of Bertrand Russell to a professorship of philosophy at the College of the City of New York provides an illuminating instance of the popular feeling that educators should be persons of unquestionable character—which means they must conform in their theory and practice to the conventional standards of conduct, particularly in the sexual sphere. Russell's appointment was severely condemned by the Hearst papers, the Knights of Columbus, the Holy Name Society, the Sons of Xavier, and by many other organizations and individuals; just as vigorously championed by

[21] *American Journal of Sociology*, 1936, 41, 694-697. University of Chicago Press.

the American Civil Liberties Union, the American Committee for Democracy and Intellectual Freedom, the Parents' Association of City College, and numerous ministers and educators of liberal bent. The question of competence was not raised; the protests centered upon the immoral influence which would be exerted by the eminent professor. The dismissal of Russell through court action appeared to some to be a threat to academic freedom. In the excitement, the American Committee for Democracy and Intellectual Freedom issued a statement summarizing the crux of the controversy:

Shall a man's right to teach in an institution of higher learning, and particularly in a public institution, be determined solely by his competence, as established by the faculty and administration of the institution involved, or shall there be a further requirement of conformity with the religious and social views of the community? [22]

The executive board of this Committee affirmed:

(1) the irrelevance of a man's religious and social views in determining his right to teach at an institution of higher learning;
(2) the obligation of our colleges and universities to present conflicting points of view;
(3) the right and obligation of public institutions of higher learning to maintain the same standards of freedom of teaching and discussion as private institutions.

These affirmations illustrate how emotional excitement over rights and values may cause even the best educated people to become grossly unrealistic, for is it not fantastic to assume that a man's competence as a college teacher will be completely dissociated from his opinions about society and his private life outside the classroom—which is no longer private when the teacher writes books preaching the nonconformist doctrines he practices, as was the case with Russell? College teachers in small communities who transgress the mores even to a minor degree can testify that people—including faculty wives—do not divorce the academic and the private lives of a professor.

In the popular mind, censors are thought of as "reformers." This stereotype focuses within its constellation many of the attitudes that are resistant to reformation. Such resentment against "busybodies" must be overcome if reform is to succeed.

Let us grant, if we are to be impartial in our analysis of the "re-

[22] See New York *Times* editorial, April 20, 1940.

former," that there are defects in our society that need to be remedied —that somebody must make the effort necessary to change things for the better—that we need reformers. Such necessary reforms would be engineered more effectively if the reformer were not so inclined to rush blindly into the situation, never pausing to take account of the forces with which he must contend in order to put across his program. His headlong action suggests that the motive of personal satisfaction is the paramount factor in his zeal, the desire for improving society secondary.

Reforming, at best, is not a popular pastime. But what can a reformer accomplish in a society whose members eye him with suspicion and annoyance? Name-calling is provoked by clumsy attempts to influence people, and the reformer gets nowhere when his "victims" regard him as a joy-killer, crepehanger, self-appointed guardian of other people's morals, a pest who inflicts himself and his ideas on others, brother's keeper, unbearable nuisance. Ludwig Lewisohn voiced the popular resentment toward the vice crusader when he attacked "the fevered fanatics of the Anti-Saloon League and the Evangelical Churches."

No one seemed to understand the character of these poor creatures. They can no longer burn witches or whip Quakers. They have somehow lost their grip on the devil of old. So they have made the substance known as ethyl alcohol into an overshadowing myth—the evil thing in the world that must be fought and trodden under foot and exorcised by Christian men. Since they can not quite in this age say that I am an unbelieving dog, they say—with sternly pitying and averted faces—that I shall die a drunkard. It is, of course, because in their savage and yet festering souls they have not caught a glimpse of the meaning of humane culture—choice, self-direction, a beautiful use of things. These poor slaves of drink must either howl against it or reel in barrooms. One knows the type: thin-lipped, embittered by the poisons that unnatural repression breeds, with a curious flatness about the temples, with often, among the older men, a wiry, belligerent beard. You have seen them with their shallow-bosomed, ill-favored wives—stern advocates of virtue—walking on Sunday self-consciously to church. The wine they have never tasted, the white beauty they have never seen, the freedom of art they have never known—all their unconscious hungers have turned to gall and wormwood in their crippled souls.[23]

The figure of Anthony Comstock has come to symbolize this meddlesome sort of snooper. Unpopularity did not bother Comstock: in-

[23] From *Upstream* by Ludwig Lewisohn, published by Liveright Publishing Corporation. Pp. 221-222. 1922.

deed, he welcomed opposition as a spur to his own steadfastness. In the little leather diary which he kept during the year 1871, he recorded his indifference to public esteem:

As for me I am resolved that I will not in God's strength yield to other people's opinion but will if I feel and believe I am right stand firm. Jesus was never moved from the path of duty, however hard, by public opinion. Why should I be? [24]

This sense of duty is a dominant trait in the "reformer" personality.

What are the motives that may possibly actuate the reformer? In the opinion of some analysts the *parental* impulse may play a role. According to this view, the reformer is "endowed" with too much (overprotective) affectionate solicitude or he has failed to find adequate outlets. Evidence for this interpretation is found in the large number of spinsters among vice crusaders, childless women, women frustrated in love, women past the child-bearing age, old bachelors, men without children in their homes.

Pugnacity is another possible urge. The individual is aggressive as the result of some frustration. He finds in reforming a moral equivalent for physical combat. "The anger of the spinster who has remained unloved towards the woman of free love is not altogether impersonal or unbiased. Sex jealousy is at the basis, either consciously or unconsciously." [25] It is pointed out, too, that people who are anti-saloon are apt to be anti-other-things: anti-tobacco, anti-bridge, anti-dancing, anti-cosmetics.

Envy may be involved. A strict conscience and an ascetic disposition may deprive a person of fun that less inhibited people may enjoy. This idea is expressed in the famous jingle:

'Tis not the drink I object to, my brothers,
But I hate the pleasure it gives to others.

Envy may be sensed underneath this overemotional attack on the pleasures of our modern civilization by a pious soul:

Just because you dance, I don't say you will go to hell, but the sad thing about it is that you love these things better than the Bible and the prayer

---

[24] Quoted by H. Brown and M. Leech: *Anthony Comstock: Roundsman of the Lord,* p. 15. 1927.
[25] W. D. Tait: "The Menace of the Reformer." *Journal of Abnormal and Social Psychology,* 1927, 4, 343-353.

meeting. God pity your poor, shriveled-up, infinitesimal soul nature, if you can enjoy playing golf on Sunday or watch a half-naked girl whirl around on one toe on prayer meeting night.

Reform may function as a *defense mechanism*. A person may be alarmed at his own weakness when temptations present themselves. Sin being so attractive as to provoke self-distrust, the individual seeks to protect himself by the reassurance of social, moral, and legislative prohibitions. His attention is diverted, too, by projecting his own deficiencies on to others and then attacking those failings in other persons. Aggression against the self may be thus displaced through externalization.[26]

The Puritan hated the Flesh in himself and he hated even more fiercely that Flesh appearing as the vices of others. . . . It is useless to tell such a man to love his neighbor as himself; he hates so much of himself. His hate, reservoired within him, gets its drainage in raids on vice, in the persecutions and suppressions carried on by anti-vice societies and in campaigns of reform that call for the punishment of evil-doers.[27]

Morbid sexual curiosity may be satisfied by working as a reformer, exploring obscene literature, red-light districts, and dens of vice, delving into the haunts of sin without the risk of incurring social disapproval. By means of crusading the reformer is able "to have his cake and suppress it too."

The above account of the motivation behind the reformer ignores, of course, all the legitimate cases in which people are inspired to abolish real evils: Lincoln and slavery, Plimsoll and economic exploitation, Lincoln Steffens and corrupt politics. We have concentrated on the censurable motives of the reformer, as they look to the "victims" who set themselves to thwart the efforts of "kill-joys" seemingly bent upon interfering with their personal habits in a program of imposed amelioration. This hostile attitude toward the reformer is a serious obstacle to effective reform.

In his haste to mold recalcitrant human nature to his own conception of the model citizen, the reformer is likely to resort to the handiest means: legislation. Pass some laws and presto, people will lead nobler lives. Numerous Americans acquiesce daily in the passage of

[26] See K. A. Menninger: "Men, Women, and Hate." *Atlantic Monthly*, February, 1939; and *Man Against Himself*. 1938.
[27] H. O'Higgins and E. H. Reede: *The American Mind in Action*, p. 15. Harper & Brothers, 1920.

laws, ordinances, statutes that no intelligent man or woman believes can, or perhaps should, be enforced. The reformer, inspired by a deep and abiding responsibility for the shortcomings of others, is intolerant of individual differences, particularly of individuals who differ from him, and he finds it hard to reconcile himself to the idea that others may think differently and still be honest intellectually. Taking it for granted that he is right, he cannot compromise with "error." In his enthusiasm for the legislative approach to changing his fellow men, the reformer is inclined to underrate the practical difficulties which are involved in translating a good principle into good practice. Munro feels that most of our failures in reforming and administering government are due to lapses in the human equation:

Nothing is easier to make than an unworkable law; and nothing is harder than to execute it. The art of government is largely the art of adapting laws to the foibles of mankind. It is the art of managing large bodies of cantankerous, obstinate, fickle, apathetic, and emotional men and women. Frame the laws as skilfully as you may—and you have taken only the first step. Applying the laws, interpreting them, enforcing them, and developing a popular respect for them—these are also steps that count.[28]

Legislation is a superficial nostrum unless the way is prepared by a long process of enlightenment.

Education is a more satisfactory instrument for changing human beings in the "right" direction, but it doesn't appeal to the reformer as a methodology because he is too impatient to put up with the tedium and effort involved in bringing about, through education, a profound metamorphosis of values and habits. Educating a person to adopt new modes of life is a long-time job, as any woman can testify who has married a man to reform him. Reeducation—reform—takes time. The haste of the reformer tempts the observer to suspect that his interest in remodeling others is principally a disguise for indulging his own desire to dominate, a subtle means of assuring himself of his own self-importance.

When we view the slow progress of reform in the perspective of time, we are likely to conclude that the most important failing in the reformer is his tactlessness, bred of his zeal. Somebody once asked Dr. Cadman, a prominent minister, "Why are prohibitionists and other reformers so great a nuisance?" To which he replied:

[28] W. B. Munro: *Personality in Politics*, pp. 8-9. 1924. By permission of The Macmillan Company, publishers.

I am glad we are. I was talking once with Hugh Price Hughes. He was the son of a Jewish father and a Welsh mother, and when you get that combination, something will come of it. He said to me: "Cadman, until a man has made himself an insufferable public nuisance on any great question he cannot get other people to heed him." He was quite right. . . .

This observation of Cadman's, of course, is a dangerous half-truth, in that reformers sometimes aim to be unpopular as a symbol of their righteousness, but in so far as they succeed in arousing animosity against themselves as persons, they are ensuring the defeat of their precious cause, or at least, postponing victory. The public animadversion to tactless zealots is well phrased by Emerson in his essay on "Self-Reliance": "You will always find those who think they know your duty better than you know it." The expert reformer should attempt to forestall such active resistance if he wants to succeed in the promotion of his program.

It is obvious that some reformers should be reformed. Three suggestions are proposed for bringing about more expert reforming.

First, the reformer should study himself in order to prepare himself for his job of changing others. The idea here is similar to the strongly held belief of the psychoanalysts that practitioners should be allowed to treat others only after going through an analysis (didactic) themselves. The *raison d'être* is the same in both cases: the reformer or analyst should have enough insight into himself to prevent the projection of his own personal problems into his subjects or patients. It is easier to see faults in others than in oneself; it is more fun to cast the beam out of somebody else's eye than to remove the mote from one's own. If the reformer will first work on himself he will get some valuable practice in the art of character changing. Another advantage accrues to this order of procedure, a fact once noted by William Penn when he said: "Though good laws do well, good men do better."

Second, the reformer should study the human material he's going to work on, to get the measure of his man. It is easier to change a man's habits if you know just how to proceed in his particular case, with due respect for the ways in which he as an individual differs from others in his attitudes toward the person trying to influence him. This point is brought out vividly in a comment on Upton Sinclair, applicable, too, to reformers in general:

An idealistic reformer may protest against being compared with an army sergeant. But though their aims are on different levels, their means are much alike, since both are sculptors working in human material, with a visioned model in their minds. And if either is seduced by his eagerness into ignoring the limitations of his material, he is like a sculptor trying to shape granite with his thumb.

This is why one expects a serious reformer to have at least a working knowledge of men and women as they are before setting out to change them. Everybody knows that from his conception of God to his taking of a wife, a man is a knotted skein of prejudices. And a reformer's success will ultimately depend on his ability in drawing out those that best suit his purpose. Modern psychology has only rediscovered what story-tellers have always known, that every man is a hypocrite in the presence of his soul. He sweats to achieve goals which he hides from himself and occasionally succeeds in hiding from others. He has the appearance of a rational being, yet any politician knows the futility of trying to move him by reason. In fact, he is most open to suspicion when he is most convinced that he is acting on principle. And it is this chameleon creature the reformer is boldly engaging to remold. . . .

Any sensible person would think it impertinent to start repairing an engine until he understood what was wrong. And if he were a part of the engine, he would begin by discovering his own bias. The reformer, being a part of society, must begin by shedding the prejudices bred in him by his own time and place. For only when he has emptied his mind of what his contemporaries and neighbors take for axioms, will he be able to examine human nature realistically.[29]

Finally, there should be a transfer of emphasis in reform from the negative to the positive aspects of character formation. Too many don'ts, too much repression, characterize efforts at moral reform. It would be more helpful—and more constructive—to stress healthful expression. Thorough procedure should call for a probing that will go behind the symptoms to the underlying source of the trouble: if students whisper in the classroom, the professor may command, "Silence," or, if he is wiser, he can achieve the same end by making his lecture more interesting. A deacon once told Henry Ward Beecher that his minister was troubled by a parishioner who kept falling asleep during the sermon, and asked Beecher what he would recommend as a remedy. "I'd fix up a pin on the end of a pole," advised Beecher, "and give it to a deacon and have the deacon march down the aisle with the pole—and stick the pin into the minister." In other words, constructive reform will offer free concerts to keep men out of barrooms. Constructive reform will not aim to cure social ills by limiting itself to attacking a particular person but will go beyond personalities

---

[29] L. S. Morris: "Upton Sinclair; the Way of the Reformer." *New Republic,* March 7, 1928.

to social influences that make people what they are. Freemont Older learned his lesson in this respect. As a San Francisco newspaper editor he had a man named Ruef sentenced to San Quentin Prison for extortion. Older repented:

> I should not have directed my rage at one man, human like myself, but . . . I should have directed it against the forces that made him what he was. Those forces were not changed by putting Ruef in San Quentin.[30]

The sincere, intelligent reformer will make sure his policy is sound by asking himself two searching questions:

> Is it good for the community?
> Is it wise to take the measures necessary to enforce it?

"Americans," according to Lowell, "are far too much inclined to favor a law and oppose its enforcement." [31]

Answers to Test on Etiquette, pp. 472-3

1. True. 2. True. 3. False. 4. True. 5. False. 6. False. 7. True.
8. False. 9. True. 10. False. 11. False. 12. False. 13. False. 14. True.
15. True. 16. False. 17. False. 18. False. 19. False. 20. False. 21. False.
22. False. 23. False. 24. False. 25. False. 26. False. 27. True.

[30] Freemont Older in his autobiography, *My Own Story,* 1926.
[31] A. L. Lowell: *Public Opinion in War and Peace,* p. 167. 1923.

Chapter 13

CUSTOM

CUSTOMS are social habits which have proved useful in times past. They are inculcated in the younger generation by the older generation by precept and example. *Customs* are transmitted ways of doing; *traditions* are transmitted ways of thinking or believing. Customs are sanctioned by long usage and they concern the fundamentals of living, in contrast with conventions which are more ephemeral and more involved with the formalities conducive to gracious living. What we eat is a matter of custom; how we eat it, a matter of convention.

In our consideration of custom, we shall concern ourselves extensively with the psychological factors impeding social change. Patterns of behavior, once crystallized and fixated, tend to persist even though they are anachronistic, ill adapted to new conditions. People quite generally fail to bring their minds up to date, as Robinson reminded us in *The Mind in the Making* (1921). It is necessary in our collective living to preserve the past but we do not need to preserve all of it in wholesale fashion. Evaluation and discrimination must be used in discarding outmoded behavior patterns, in order to modify some which can serve our needs after alteration and to preserve others that fit our modern situation. It usually takes a crisis, a natural catastrophe, the depletion of available resources, a war, a depression, or some other emergency, to make us appreciate the urgency for changing our reaction patterns; out of tension and chaos new norms are evolved.

I. THE ORIGIN OF CUSTOM

Fear inspired by animistic beliefs influenced early man to follow the beaten path. Departures from the customary ways of doing things, he realized, were fraught with dangers. He preferred to take no chances. It was safer to adhere to the tried and true. Experimenting with anything new was too risky.

One of the strongest characteristics of primitive man is his fear of the Unknown. He is forever dreading that some act of his may bring down upon him the anger of the gods. He may not fear his fellow man, nor the beasts of the forest; but he lives in perpetual awe of those unseen powers which, from time to time, seem bent on his destruction. He sows his corn at the wrong season; he reaps no harvest, the offended gods have destroyed it all. He ventures up into a mountain, and is caught in a snowdrift. He trusts himself to a raft and is wrecked by a storm. He endeavors to propitiate these terrible powers with sacrifices and ceremonies; but they will not always be appeased. There are terrors above him and around him.

From this state of fear, custom is his first great deliverer. . . . What has been done once in safety, may possibly be done again. What has been done many times, is fairly sure to be safe. A new departure is full of dangers; not only to the man who takes it, but to those with whom he lives, for the gods are apt to be indiscriminate in their anger. Custom is the one sure guide to law; custom is that part of law which has been discovered. Hence the reverence of primitive society for custom; hence their terror of the innovator. Custom is the earliest known stage of law; it is not enacted, nor even declared: it establishes itself as the result of experience.[1]

Primitive man "played safe." He tried to do things the way he had done them before. Staying with the customary gave him a sense of security that inspired courage for meeting the innumerable uncertainties of life. This conservative attitude, of course, is still very active in modern man. It is responsible for much of the inertia that leaves unchanging man maladjusted in a world that undergoes incessant change. Though we seek to rationalize our laziness by convincing ourselves that what's old must be good for us or it wouldn't have survived, in our more lucid moments we recognize that this argument is only a resort to a half-truth justifying the path of least resistance. Honesty would compel us to admit that we stay in the rut because it requires too much effort and strain to get out of it. It is easier to follow custom and relax.

The role of fear in the evolution of custom is also manifested in the development of taboos. A thing was taboo if it was not to be touched. There were two kinds of objects that had to be avoided: *sacred* objects which were to be revered for their sanctity, and *impure* objects which were to be left alone because they might defile anyone coming into contact with their loathsome qualities. Awe should be felt toward sacred things, aversion toward the unclean.

The totem animal—the animal protecting the tribe—seems to have

[1] E. Jenks: *Law and Politics in the Middle Ages*, pp. 56-57. John Murray (London), 1898.

been the earliest object of taboo. No member of the tribe was allowed to kill the totem animal or to eat its flesh. The common observance of this regulation helped to bind together the members of the group in loyalty to the tribal organization. Persons knit by this mysterious tie usually bore the name of the totem and, believing that this bond meant they were of one blood, they prohibited marriage or cohabitation of members of the group with one another. Totemism, therefore, was a religion, and a form of social organization.

In the earliest stage only the totem animal was taboo; later certain men became taboo, privileged persons like the priest and the chieftain. Gradually class differences evolved as the upper class became taboo to the lower class. The property of the nobleman became taboo to every other person.

BY REMOTE CONTROL

EVER WONDER WHY **EMPEROR HIROHITO'S** CLOTHES LOOK AS THOUGH HE ORDERED 'EM BY MAIL? **THE IMPERIAL MEASUREMENTS ARE GUESSED AT** FROM 20 FEET AWAY —COMMONERS MUSTN'T COME CLOSER TO HIS SACRED PERSON.

(Courtesy, Edwin Cox and Publishers Syndicate.)

The taboo has not merely the force of a police law, similar to that whereby, in other localities, men of superior rank prohibit entrance to their parks; it is a religious law, whose transgression is eventually punished by death. It is particularly the chief and his property that are objects of taboo. Where the taboo regulations were strict, no one was allowed to venture close to the chief or even to speak his name. Thus, the taboo might become an intolerable constraint. In Hawaii, the chief was not allowed to raise his own food to his mouth, for he was taboo and his contact with the food rendered this also taboo. Hence the Hawaiian chief was obliged to have a servant feed him. The objects which he touched became taboo to all individuals. In short, he became the very opposite of a despotic ruler, namely, the slave of a despotic custom.[2]

[2] W. Wundt: *Elements of Folk Psychology*, p. 195. 1916. By permission of The Macmillan Company, publishers.

Taboos were extended in their scope to include relations by marriage, especially the mother-in-law and the father-in-law, who were to be avoided if possible.

Taboos were originally concerned with sacred objects. Later the emphasis shifted to fear of the unclean and the demoniacal. Primitive man felt as uneasy about touching a tabooed object as most of us would feel if we were asked to help an undertaker prepare a corpse for burial. If the savage touched an unclean object, he purified himself by washing in water, by removing the impurity by fire, or by transferring the demon to an animal. The belief in the demoniacal power of inanimate objects is known as fetishism. It was the basis of taboo and also an outgrowth of it. Another development was that of ancestor worship, the practice of revering tribal ancestors, from which evolved the hero cult, and later, the cult of the gods. These various modes of worship all go back to primitive totemism.

Modern man, hemmed in as he is by an ever increasing number of laws, is sometimes provoked to feel that he would welcome the freedom savages enjoyed when man lived close to nature. Little does this modern man realize how extensive and how binding were the taboos that restricted primitive man in his every move. Group life, indeed, was never too kind to freedom.

II. CUSTOMS AS STANDARDS OF CONDUCT

Customary modes of conduct represent patterns of behavior which are supposed to be followed religiously by all persons professing to belong to the group. Since these patterns prescribe uniform ways of doing things, they serve to standardize actions and thus they function as norms with reference to which persons can be subjected to the bar of communal judgment. Often customs are formally codified into laws. In America automobile drivers proceed on the right-hand side of the road; in England, on the left. These arrangements are determined by general agreement. Their effectiveness depends upon how universally they are respected within a given society. There is no higher moral law that makes it virtuous to stay on a particular side of the road. The prescription of one side rather than the other is merely for purposes of convenience and self-preservation; driving on the right is correct because we have made it so by ordinance and by mutual agreement. It is fairly easy to see that what we call "right" is just a matter of custom when we are considering traffic regulations; it is not so easy to see the same principle operative when we consider the "rightness" of monogamy or living up to one's promises. Comparative anthropologists, surveying the different customs of various cultures, generally favor the conclusion that whatever *is*, is right, that mores make morals.[3]

Most people are guided in their conduct by what Aristotle called customary virtue. They are governed by the prevailing practice— theirs not to reason why. When Porteus was giving intelligence tests to aboriginal Australians, he discovered that the natives were puzzled by his unwillingness to give them help. This was especially true of the members of the tribe into which he had been initiated, for they were accustomed to tribal cooperation. The refusal of Porteus to do his part in the test situation appeared to the tribesmen like a breach of loyalty, subject to moral condemnation. The idea that the tester's help would be vicarious cheating just did not occur to them because custom called for cooperation. The competitive nature of testing did not lie within their scheme of things and, consequently, no question of individual honor was involved.

It used to be considered immoral for American women to smoke. There were even those who felt that any woman who would smoke would do other things she wasn't supposed to do. Nowadays such an attitude would be considered queer, for numerous women smoke and few are the critics who offer any objections. The mores, according to Sumner, can make anything [seem] right; the goodness or badness of any act like smoking is evaluated in terms of its fitness relative to the time and place. Seeming right and being right are not necessarily identical, of course, as idealistic philosophers have insisted ever since Plato denied the relativism of the Sophists. When we state that mores make morals, we are speaking of people's attitudes, their subjective judgments of fitness, and we are not dealing with the objective rightness upon which the idealists put so much stress. Ordinarily, unsophisticated people, that is, persons unversed in the intricacies of philosophy, are apt to believe they are "good" when they are doing what is *customarily* the thing to do.

The conformity demanded by custom tends to reduce the range of individual differences, to standardize conduct according to certain norms. Though standardization may do violence to personal idiosyncrasies it still performs a valuable social function by fostering a sense of unity. Morale is improved by the realization that all persons respect the historic traditions which lend their sanction to certain customary modes of conduct recognized in the group as constituting the

[3] This thesis that mores make morals was defended by W. G. Sumner in his *Folkways*. 1906.

basic norms of behavior. Group solidarity is promoted by common practices; thus in the place of worship the Christian takes off his hat, the Jew keeps his hat on, and the Mohammedan takes off his shoes. If, in a Christian church, some men kept their hats on, others took their hats off, and still others removed their shoes, there would not be the same consciousness of oneness that now exists as a result of the fact that everybody is doing the same thing.

The role of custom in the promotion of group solidarity is illustrated in the Americanization of immigrants. Foreigners who settle in this country gradually abandon their old habits as they acquire the new mores of their adopted country. This transition to American ways is amusingly exemplified by the husky Italian laborer who asked the police department of Somerville, Massachusetts, for a permit to kill his wife, complaining that his wife was unappreciative of his labors, failed to cook his food properly, and was beginning to be attentive to another man. He applied for the permit to do away with her and it took the police lieutenant an hour to explain to the applicant that no such permit could be issued. At least, the newcomer was trying to adapt himself to American mores as he understood them, misled though he was.

Customs, like conventions, are enforced by group sanctions. The pressure of public opinion is a powerful influence in compelling the individual to conform to the prevailing folkways. Most people probably obey the mandates of the group without much resistance, since adherence to the mores saves the strain of thinking for oneself; for, as Cooley says, "All good citizens want the laws to be definite and vigorously enforced, in order to avoid the uncertainty, waste, and destruction of a lawless condition. In the same way right-minded people want definite moral standards, enforced by general opinion, in order to save the mental wear and tear of unguided feeling." [4] The unsettled condition engendered by mental conflict is a very unhappy one. Living becomes much simpler if we can rely upon axioms and canons that represent the accumulated wisdom of the ages. Thus experience has shown that it is folly for a young person to "sow his wild oats," because he will reap in bitterness. The individual who listens to the counsel of his elders spares himself the grief that may issue from dissolute living; the person who insists on experimenting with his own morals in the hope that he may be able to have the fun without paying the penalty and thus disprove the ancient precepts, is taking a big

[4] C. H. Cooley: *Human Nature and the Social Order,* p. 287. Revised Edition. 1922.

risk, learning the hard way.   After all, human beings have been seeking for happiness during countless ages, and surely lessons have been
learned that are bequeathed to us in the maxims endorsed by the
sages, both ancient and modern; our way is made easier if we choose to
let them guide us.   Most people enjoy the sense of security that comes
with a scrupulous obedience to the mores.   Of course, the mores in a
particular instance may be wrong, but the odds are overwhelmingly
in favor of the mores being right as a general rule, and it is the general rule that counts in the long run.   If you accept custom as your
standard of conduct, you will be fairly sure to be right; if you can feel
sure you are right, you will spare yourself the uneasiness of mental
conflict.

On the other hand, the intelligent person who wants to live thought-
fully will, of course, not be satisfied with any such blind adherence to
custom.   He will want to analyze situations as they arise and weigh
the dictates of custom in the light of his own judgment.   He will want
to distinguish between customs, studying particular customs to see
whether they promote happiness or interfere with the enjoyment of
life.   To the discriminating person every standard must prove itself a
value in terms of human experience.   Some generally accepted customs may prove wanting when thus examined.   A critical analysis of
the psychological bases of custom may reveal which of our customs we
should discard, which we should retain.   The criterion for judgment
in each case will be whether or not a specific custom actually is conducive to the long-range happiness of the human beings concerned.[5]
Some of our standards, we shall see, cannot pass muster when subjected to this vital test.

III. THE PERMANENCE OF CUSTOM

One important characteristic of a custom is the fact that it has endured for a long time.   It is hoary with age; it is sanctioned by long
usage.   The very permanence of custom is occasionally responsible for
its detrimental influence on human happiness, since an unchanging
mode of conduct is likely to prove maladjustive in a world of perpetual
change.   Fixed patterns of behavior may prevent a person from adapting himself to changing conditions.   Everything is subject to perpetual flux, as Heraclitus observed in ancient times—an observation that

---

[5] This criterion is not to be confused with the hedonistic exploitation of momentary pleasures by an individual for his own private satisfaction.   The happy
person must consider the effects of his conduct upon other people, since he lives together with other human beings in a *community*.

is even truer in our own day, since the process of change has been accelerated by numerous modern inventions. Precepts regarded as eternal verities may prove out of place in an evanescent, kaleidoscopic world where the ephemeral is the rule rather than the exception. Times change; behavior must be variable, too, if the individual is going to deal successfully with the vicissitudes of existence.

An analysis of human reactions will reveal some of the factors which underlie the permanence of custom. There are definite reasons why certain modes of conduct tend to persist in practically unalterable form.

A. Dread of the Unfamiliar

One reason why behavior patterns endure is the dread of the unfamiliar that seems so characteristic of the human being. The sudden abandonment of a custom produces a feeling of alienation. A person in this situation feels so uneasy that he is tempted to return at once to the old way of doing things, just as the convert backslides because the new life is too much of a strain on him. The average person is inclined to feel that his present mode of life is good enough even though it is not perfect. It requires no argument to convince people that it is wise to let well enough alone. It is an old rule of forensics that the burden of proof is on the reformer, not on the conservative. "We know what we have," we say sententiously, "the future is uncertain." There is always a risk in social experimentation. Changes are unwelcome because they disturb the orderliness and definiteness upon which our collective activities depend for their smooth operation. Innovations mean confusion—and, consequently, distress. We wish to progress but hope we can do so without making any changes in the customary ways of doing things. Thus we trust in playing safe to ensure our security.

The fear of change was prevalent among the natives of Tennessee when they learned that the Tennessee Valley program was going to involve shifts of one kind or another. A TVA appraiser found Isabel Brantley living on Cedar Creek. He offered her twelve hundred dollars for her log cabin and eroded acres. To which she replied, "I was born in this house and so was my pappy before me, and here I've lived and here I'll die, even if I have to bolt the door and let the flood come —but there hain't a-goin' to be no flood!" Finally she consented to have her house moved to a site below the dam, but she insisted on one concession: "You got to find me a place with a spring or a well. I don't want none of this new-fangled pipe water runnin' into my house."

B. REVERENCE FOR THE PAST

The permanence of custom is due also to the fact that people tend to revere the past. Custom has an *a priori* influence in that it is accepted without question. Thus a person may be a Methodist and a Republican because his parents were Methodists and Republicans, and for no better reason. Occasionally a son follows in his father's footsteps with meticulous respect for every detail of the paternal footprint, as in the case of George F. Baker, Jr., who went every day, when he was in New York, to his desk in the big gray-stone First National Bank at No. 2 Wall Street, where he had succeeded his father as chairman.

He and his father carried on the curious traditions of the bank, where every officer has an old-fashioned roll-top desk, strictly observes no-smoking rules during banking hours, and leaves his hat on the top of his desk at all times when in the building, to show he is somewhere about.[6]

Forgetting what is unpleasant to remember fosters a glorification of the past. "The good old days" were not as bright as memory paints them. This "old-oaken-bucket delusion," brought on by a process of selective forgetting, is an important factor in prolonging the established patterns of life.[7]

Children are taught from their earliest days that they must accord respect to their parents, grandparents, and others possessing certain rights by virtue of seniority. "Don't contradict your elders" is one of the first taboos enforced upon the child who insists upon developing a mind of his own; "children should be seen but not heard" is likewise designed to inculcate a proper attitude of veneration toward one's elders. We are trained to be deferent to the aged as a part of our education in the ways of etiquette. Since old people as a rule are conservative and since they must not be contradicted, the whole arrangement results in keeping things the way they always have been, sometimes for the better, sometimes for the worse.

The customary patterns tend to persist, too, because so many positions of responsibility are occupied by old-timers. Bank presidents, judges, and business executives are often past their prime when they

[6] The Boston *Herald*, May 28, 1937.
[7] See W. F. Ogburn: *Social Change*, pp. 186-189. 1922.

ascend to power. It is supposed to be best this way since the pattern of seniority is predicated on the assumption that as we grow older we also grow wiser, though no scientist has demonstrated that individuals past forty-five are any wiser than adults under forty-five who are blessed with the same degree of intelligence. Indeed, it should be said that often comparative intelligence does not enter into the situation except in a minor role; for rank, in many cases, is determined by age rather than ability. How many people really learn much from experience? Are you getting wiser as you get older, or do you find yourself repeating your mistakes and multiplying your errors with the passage of time? One reason we progress slowly is that we are afraid to entrust ourselves to young persons of high intelligence for fear they may be "too smart for their own good." Many people feel that we should progress slowly because it is dangerous to move ahead, particularly to move ahead fast. It is hard enough to decide whether we are moving ahead, so it's better "to make haste slowly," to proceed with caution. With old people at the helm, who will cling stubbornly to tradition, who will take no chances, we can relax, confident that nothing untoward can happen to disturb the even tenor of our ways.

Comparing the age of leaders during periods of reform and periods of quiet in modern history, Gowin discovered that the average age of the dozen leading men in ten historical periods of reform varied from 32 to 46 years; that the average age of leaders in more conservative periods varied from 54 to 66 years. The champions of change have been 15 to 20 years younger than the defenders of the *status quo*.[8]

Young men, said Roger Babson in 1941, are America's hope.

Most of the pessimism now floating about comes from the older businessmen who cannot forget the "good old days" when taxes were very low and they could do as they pleased. The nation owes these bankers, manufacturers, and merchants a tremendous lot, and should treat them with respect. Statistics show, however, that they are rapidly dying off, and their places are being taken by younger men who never knew those good old days. These younger men accept present conditions as normal and do not worry about taxes, government regulations, and other handicaps.

As I travel about the country, it is interesting to note the difference in the attitude of members of our regular chambers of commerce from the attitude of the members of the junior chambers—the "jaycees" as they are called. Most of the resolutions passed by the older groups are *against* something; they are trying to sweep back the ocean with a broom. The resolutions passed by the "jaycees" are *for* something; they are interested in

[8] E. B. Gowin: *The Executive and His Control of Men*, p. 29. 1915.

launching a ship to sail the seas! Every year more and more of these "jay-cees" are coming into positions of authority. After returning from a speaking engagement before a sedate chamber of commerce, I am a blue pessimist; but after speaking to a group of these "jaycees," I am a rip-roaring bull.[9]

Some people are especially devoted to whatever is ancient, climbing their family trees and commemorating events of times past, to bolster their self-esteem. They feel like Hardcastle in *She Stoops to Conquer:* "I love everything that is old—old friends, old manners, old customs, old wine."

C. SENTIMENT

Customs are especially enduring when they are based predominantly upon sentiment. The emotional attachment to an habitual mode of conduct may be practically indissoluble since sentimental behavior is not subject to critical judgment. In matters of sentiment cold analysis is felt to be out of place. Consider, for example, the traditional means of disposing of the dead by burial. Is it rational to pay for cemetery lots and for fancy coffins? Is it sensible to reimburse an undertaker for applying his cosmetic arts to the corpse so that it may appear more presentable to those morbid observers who want to see how the deceased "looked in death"? Think of the money spent on dead people which might better be spent on the living. Many families who cannot afford the luxury of an expensive burial become impoverished by the high cost of a funeral.[10] Some people feel that cremation is more desirable, or should we say, less undesirable. Most people, however, still feel that cremation is irreverent, prefer a "decent Christian burial." [11] Even the people who prefer cremation are so irrational as to buy expensive coffins to be destroyed within a day or two in the furnace. While all of this money is being spent on the dead, the living suffer from inadequate medical care because of insufficient funds.

D. CONSERVATISM

There are other factors contributing to the permanence of custom which we may consider under the general heading of conservatism.

[9] Tampa *Morning Tribune,* May 23, 1941.
[10] See C. M. Brown: "Reducing the High Cost of Dying." The *Christian Century* October 21, 1936. J. B. Berry: "The High Cost of Dying." *Reader's Digest,* November, 1936.
[11] P. Waxman: "The Flesh Profiteth Nothing." *Forum,* September, 1939.

The individual who is addicted to custom has a backward look; being ruled by the past, he is convinced that "what hath been, forever more shall be, world without end." People in groups are particularly prone to be conservative in so far as their behavior becomes institutionalized, or, in other words, organizations tend to become conservative as they grow older. This tendency is to be expected since the group is interested in preserving certain values which are advantageous to its members. It is natural that grown-ups should be eager to perpetuate in the younger generation the values which they themselves were trained to cherish in their own youth. When people organize for some purpose, they become more and more interested, after achieving their end, in keeping things unchanged. Once they get what they want, they are primarily concerned with conserving their gains, though the self-interest may be disguised as altruism of the noblest sort.

Ownership of property predisposes a person to conservatism. Socrates abandoned the radical views of his humble youth when he married into opulence.

He began life in a very humble stratum of society as a free artisan or even as a slave. . . . He seems to have married a woman of his own class, Xanthippe, at an early age. Later he married a lady of patrician family, one Myrto, . . . in his late forties. . . . Socrates of the Symposium moves in a very good society. He comes to the banquet from the bath, adorned like a bridegroom, and wearing sandals.[12]

Increasing material prosperity affected his philosophical view and changed Socrates from a radical to a conservative.

Even when some inventive person has discovered a new and more efficient way of doing something, many people will continue in their old ruts, muddling along in a routine they cannot abandon, so strong is the force of habit. G. Stanley Hall noticed this tendency among the farmers of his boyhood village:

They had little sympathy with new-fangled ways or even labor-saving devices which rather suggested shirking. Ends attained by hard work were more honest, and were the more desirable to secure, the harder the effort was to obtain them. My grandfather, for instance, always preferred the slow-moving oxen for all kinds of farm work to horses, and when his sons introduced the latter he was reluctant to see the improvement. These people were pretty set in the good old ways, and if they did make innova-

[12] A. D. Winspear and T. Silverberg: *Who Was Socrates?*, pp. 39, 40, 52. 1939.

tions, or progress, it was only in particular items, and it was done with a great deal of self-consciousness.[13]

A blind Negro, Hanson McCoy, pulling a plow on his small farm in Georgia as his wife guided him, exemplified reluctance to depart from an ancient practice. MyCoy quoted the Biblical precept that bread should be earned by the sweat of the brow.

1. INERTIA

This tendency to continue one's habits even though such perseveration makes the going harder is basically a matter of psychic inertia. A. H. Maslow demonstrated at Teachers College, Columbia, how easy it is for college students to get into a rut and stay in it:

The evening was hot. Fifteen girls were seated about a table copying sentences from books to the accompaniment of the monotonous beat of a metronome.

Fourteen of the girls were dressed warmly in smocks over their dresses, a living, perspiring demonstration of what a psychologist has termed "psychic inertia." For ten evenings they had sat at their warm tasks. They had been required to wear the smocks despite complaints. Now, on the tenth evening, they were told that the smock might come off. But, so strong is the tie that binds us to the familiar, only one girl removed the extra garment.

Psychic inertia is not at all the same as laziness. In fact, it might almost be thought of as the opposite. Often people will go to a great deal of trouble because of their preference for the familiar.

Used to working with pens, these girls would scorn proffered pencils even though writing on sponge-like mimeograph paper. They would laboriously copy whole sentences because they had been doing so, even though told that single words would serve the required purpose as well. . . .[14]

Cultural inertia is based on the fact that "reactions toward social institutions . . . start from an assumption of the validity of the established order." [15] The enjoyment of orderliness and routine militates against change. We like things to stay the way they are, unless existing arrangements prove too inconvenient or annoying. A sense of security usually inclines us in favor of the *status quo*. The same

[13] G. S. Hall: *Life and Confessions of a Psychologist,* pp. 56-57. D. Appleton-Century Company, 1923.

[14] See A. H. Maslow: "The Influence of Familiarization on Preference." *Journal of Experimental Psychology,* 1937, 21, 162-180. American Psychological Association, Inc.

[15] C. C. North: *Social Differentiation,* p. 243. 1926.

desire to keep everything under control by preserving what is, prompts us to exert pressure upon nonconformists to compel them to get into line.

The stability of the social order depends upon the inertia inherent in habit. People who are miserable will usually do nothing to improve their condition, since it seems easier to get adapted to evil than to try to overcome it, especially if a change is going to mean a disruption of long-established habits. The social significance of habit was described by William James:

Habit is thus the enormous fly-wheel of society, its most precious conservative agent. It alone is what keeps us all within the bounds of ordinance, and saves the children of fortune from the envious uprisings of the poor. It alone prevents the hardest and most repulsive walks of life from being deserted by those brought up to tread therein. It keeps the fisherman and the deck-hand at sea through the winter; it holds the miner in his darkness, and nails the countryman to his log-cabin and his lonely farm through all the months of snow; it protects us from invasion by the natives of the desert and the frozen zone. It dooms us all to fight out the battle of life upon the lines of our nurture or our early choice, and to make the best of a pursuit that disagrees, because there is no other for which we are fitted, and it is too late to begin again. It keeps different social strata from mixing. Already at the age of twenty-five you see the professional mannerism settling down on the young commercial traveler, on the young doctor, on the young minister, on the young counselor-at-law. You see the little lines of cleavage running through the character, the tricks of thought, the prejudices, the ways of the "shop," in a word, from which the man can by-and-by no more escape than his coat-sleeve can suddenly fall into a new set of folds. On the whole, it is best he should not escape. It is well for the world that in most of us, by the age of thirty, the character has set like plaster, and will never soften again.[16]

Once the mind gets firmly set and drives are thoroughly canalized, habits will endure. An old-time teacher wants to know why the school teachers of today are demanding so much pay and such short hours:

A good deal of money can be saved our taxpayers by the elimination of so many holidays in our schools. School conventions should be held on Saturdays, in my opinion. Forty-two years ago I taught school in Hawley for $5 a week. Today a teacher receives $25 for teaching in that same district. Why?

[16] W. James: *Principles of Psychology*, I, p. 121. 1890.

The world may change; prices and wage scales may change; economic standards and educational standards may change; but not this lady.

A missionary to Africa noticed a native woman leaning over a tub washing clothes. The missionary got the woman a chair and showed her how to wash sitting down. The next day she found the native standing on the chair, leaning over to reach the tub. When the primitives of India were given wheelbarrows by a missionary and then

"All I know is, the visiting nurse said I should use it when I take Little Eagle out for a walk!"

Schus

(Permission, Adolph Schus and *This Week*.)

shown how to use them to carry bricks, instead of carrying the bricks on the tops of their heads, it was discovered that as soon as the missionary's back was turned, the natives put the wheelbarrows full of bricks on top of their heads, since it felt more natural to bear the burden that way. People everywhere are slow to accept innovations. Such is the obstinacy of human beings when confronted with something new, something different, that calls for a shift from old habits to new ones.

2. RESISTANCE TO THE NEW

Conservatism often involves something more than mere inertia—an active resistance to change. The Lynds were impressed with this resistance in their study of Middletowners.

Everywhere in Middletown one sees these small businessmen looking out at social change with the personal resentment of one who by long defensive training asks first of every innovation, "What will it do for (or to) me?" The resulting tendency is to stress the negative aspects of new proposals and for local opinion to dwell upon and to crystallize around extremes of possible abuse which might occur.[17]

Far-fetched arguments against the Child Labor Amendment illustrate this sort of reactionary pattern which is so common among the vested interests. To the fact that people actively oppose change, any reformer can testify.

There are three devices of resistance which are particularly noteworthy: ridiculing the new, condemning it on moral grounds, or dismissing it as economically unsound.

a. *Ridicule.* The first man to adopt an innovation must be willing to withstand the taunts of those who are too cowardly to abandon the old customary way of doing things. We can see the use of ridicule to keep innovators in line in all phases of our communal life. For a sample, let us examine the field of sport.

In the early days of baseball the catcher caught with his bare hands, and so did the other players. Some daring player finally had the nerve to wear a mitt or a glove, but for his heresy he had to suffer the shame of being branded a "sissie." The modern catcher resorts to all possible means of protecting his body and no one volunteers any disparaging comments on his manhood. The man who brought about this revolution in baseball toggery was a catcher named Roger Bresnahan. He had original ideas as to the correct dress for backstops and one day a strange form came out of the dugout at the Polo Grounds. He looked as if he were dressed for the cricket-field. Very little of Bresnahan could be seen. Added to his mask and chest protector were a pair of brown leather shinguards. No foul tip could touch him in a vulnerable spot. He was sheathed like a knight of old. The crowd, we are told, set him down as a mollycoddle; his fellow players made derogatory remarks out of the corners of their tobacco-stained mouths. But Bresnahan was a sensible fellow with the courage of his convictions. He wasn't afraid of being hurt or of being called yellow. A valuable ballplayer, it seemed as wise to him to protect his legs which he needed for running, as it was to protect his face. Scorn was heaped upon him for being different; today no player suffers abuse for taking

[17] R. S. Lynd and H. M. Lynd: *Middletown in Transition,* p. 24. Harcourt, Brace and Company, 1937.

care of his hands and his shins. Though people tried to prevent the change by means of ridicule, wisdom finally prevailed.

b. *The Stigma of Immorality.* In the folkways, whatever is seems right. The folkways appear to be the right ways just because they are in operation. They seem inherently correct; they are not subject to criticism or evaluation with reference to such criteria as fairness or usefulness. If the mores seem to be moral, then any act which violates the mores, will be considered immoral. A good example of this thesis is to be found in the attitude of slave-owning Southerners, before the Civil War, toward slavery. Abolitionists in the North could see the evils resulting from the enslavement of the Negroes (as could many Southerners) but not so the slaveowners. To the white slaveowners slavery was a noble institution, ordained and blessed by the Almighty, good for the whites and especially good for the colored people, who would have starved to death if left to provide for themselves.[18] According to this credo, the Negro was naturally inferior and slavery was the best means of taking care of him. There was nothing degrading about it. Negroes did not want their freedom; only Northerners entertained the absurd idea that they did. The allegedly typical Southern slaveholder, the stereotyped Colonel sipping a mint julep, could see no wrong in slavery, because the rationalizations built up through the years to justify the practice had become so much a part of him that he could not see slavery for what it really was. The institution, as Sumner would say, had been surrounded with *pathos,* the glamor of sentiment that gives its blessing to a pet notion and protects it from criticism.[19] It is pathos that makes the mores sacred, that leads us to believe, therefore, that the folkways are beyond criticism. The slaveowner believed in slavery just as a patriotic citizen believes in his country—without reserve, without question.

How far pathos may go in the stultification of thought is exemplified in this letter to an editor, entitled "New England Gave Coolidge a Conscience."

William Allen White's biography of Calvin Coolidge is being reviewed widely, and reviews, by indirection, make it clear that the New England conscience is the key to his character.

One form of the New England conscience is a deep-seated reverence for the Creator and Master of the Universe; its sign is humility. In Coolidge's case doubtless this reverent humility was intensified by his insignificant appear-

---

[18] Study this credo in Margaret Mitchell's novel, *Gone with the Wind.* 1936.
[19] Sumner: *op. cit.,* p. 180.

ance, his lack of oratorical ability, the manners and voice of the country villager.

Such a reverence holds that the world has developed slowly through the ages, in the only way in which it could develop.   Everything is in a fine, careful balance.   There may be some features of this world which seem to us less than perfect; but who among us is omniscient?   And if we upset the delicate balance by artificially forcing a change, we cause repercussions which may have far wider and more baneful results than we can by any means foresee.

The most extreme caution must be exercised before it is ventured to throw the universe out of gear—to insult, to criticize the divine Creator who has placed here for the orderly governing of His world the twin laws of supply and demand.   Moreover, history has shown many panaceas tried to no lasting effect—the only "system" which survives is capitalism. . . .

Coolidge was not a reformer; he was not even an initiator.   He never sought change, and never went looking for trouble.   No good politician does the latter.   Whenever a big thing was thrust upon him, he did not hesitate nor temporize nor count the cost; but he never acted except under a sort of compulsion generated by circumstance.   He was always adequate for every occasion, but between occasions he seemed to some inadequate.

Between crises he was static, letting God run his world, standing by, ready, if he should be needed.   This passivity was the result of a firm belief that the best government is that which governs least.   It was an active sort of passivity.[20]

In Japan, prior to World War II, anything the government did was considered "right" because the Emperor was deemed by his subjects to be "sacred, inviolable."   The written constitution made that assertion and Prince Hirohumi Ito, who was chiefly responsible for drafting that document, wrote, in his *Commentaries on the Constitution:*

The Sacred Throne was established at the time when heaven and earth became separated.   The Emperor is heaven-descended, divine, and sacred. He is preeminent above all his subjects.   He must be reverenced as inviolable.   He has indeed to pay due respect to the law, but the law has no power to hold him accountable to it.   Not only shall there be no irreverence for the Emperor's person, but also he shall not be made a topic of derogatory comment nor one of discussion.

This traditional conception of the sacredness of the Emperor gave powerful support to the state, served to sanctify everything national, assured the apotheosis of patriotism.   Worship of the state was cen-

[20] The Boston *Herald*, November 22, 1938.

tered in the person of the Emperor, who was elevated as the supreme authority to the rank of divinity or its equivalent. Such a faith in an infallible ruler promoted a uniformity that tolerated no criticism; absolute obedience became the supreme virtue. No wonder the militarists were able to carry out their imperialistic program without running into any effective opposition. Any minority in power that could league itself with the divine, was in a position to operate without interference. Thus the national religion, Shinto,

sets up sanctions and controls by which it becomes possible for every official of the state from highest to lowest to claim for himself and his own interpretation of his authority, a participation in the inviolability of the person of the Emperor. We can understand from this why the sovereign is so hedged about with seclusion, why the army and navy claim for themselves a final responsibility to the Emperor alone, and why the sentiment of the sacredness of the imperial throne is so assiduously cultivated in the national mind as the first postulate of all education.[21]

Under these circumstances it would have been considered wrong by the Japanese for any ordinary citizen to seek to initiate a change in a political system ordained by the divine Emperor. Such an innovator would have been quickly punished for his "immorality." [22]

It is a matter of common observation that innovations are usually regarded as immoral even in such trivialities as bobbing the hair. Aimee Semple McPherson Hutton bobbed her hair and there were people who said that she was no longer fit to preach, with her shorn tresses. There were comments to the effect that a woman who would bob her hair would do other things that no respectable lady would countenance. The conviction that bobbing hair is an immoral practice is no modern whim; William Prynne, an English Puritan, was crusading against bobbed hair way back in the seventeenth century:

English gentlewomen are now growne so farre past shame, past modesty, grace and nature, as to clip their haire like men with lockes and foretops, and to make this cut the very guise and fashion of the times. . . . Even nature herself abhors to see a woman shorne or polled; a woman with cut haire is a filthy spectacle, and much like a monster . . . it being natural and comly to women to nourish their haire, which even God and nature have given them for a covering, a token of subjection, and a naturall badge to distinguish them from man.

[21] D. C. Holton: "The Sacred Emperor." *Christian Century*, February 11, 1942.
[22] Remember, on p. 169, we mentioned the charge of "immorality" leveled against a pacifist in America.

Innovations in clothing are sometimes regarded with considerable alarm, particularly if the change is toward scantier attire. Back in the 1920's the Pope warned women against immodest dress. Said he: "It is undoubtedly very painful and deplorable that clothing which by nature was intended to cover the body, has in our time, because so many women forget their dignity, served often to deaden sacrilegiously the sense of shame, and to offer to everybody, especially the young, occasion for stimulus of the senses." Note that nature intended us to conceal our bodies in clothes, and, therefore, it is unnatural to wear short skirts. This edict is reminiscent of the Mormon edict that garments shall leave only the feet, hands, and head exposed. Joseph Smith, first prophet of the Church, had also specified that undergarments should be fastened by strings, not by buttons. A meeting of 10,000 Mormons was held a few years ago to sustain an edict permitting shorter undergarments, also buttons. Among those present was a man named Paul Feil, who interrupted the meeting to take exception to the ruling of the Church authorities ordering a change in the length of underwear, for "God," he urged, "is unchanging and could not have permitted this deviation from the established custom."

A thing that is new is under suspicion; the judgment is often "guilty until proved innocent." Such was the case with the movies in their earliest days, according to Adolph Zukor, who was one of the first producers of the silent-film dramas. It took the motion picture promoters a long time to gain respectability. Zukor relates:

When movies were struggling for a foothold, stage players who ventured to pick up an occasional dollar or so working before the cameras were banned from the theater if found out, movies being such a cheap and tawdry form of expression that legitimate actors lowered their prestige by being seen in them. Minnie Maddern Fiske, one of the early pioneers in films and one of the more daring of the legitimate stage actresses, consented to make *Tess of the D'Urbervilles* on condition that her participation be kept a secret. . . . A young man who left his job as teller in a bank to join me in a production in 1912 was so degraded by such association in the eyes of his fiancée that she broke her engagement. I was in the fur business when I went into the movies and the family kept quiet about my unsavory sideline. . . .

William A. Brady, then a prize-fight promoter and yet to gain fame as a legitimate producer, was my silent partner. Ashamed of his connection with the movies he remained very much in the background. Business was poor, and Will declared that movies were just a fad. . . . I disagreed, insisting that the public was willing to accept movies if the film product would be brought to the level of the stage itself, which forbade its players to have anything to do with us. . . .

We had to walk the streets to get actors. Our "casting office" was usually in front of Hammerstein's old Victoria Theater. . . . This was a favorite hangout for actors and we would wait until a particularly hungry one would come along. . . .

Those who first went to the movies were people with a little idle time, and respectable folks did not go except to slide in occasionally and hope nobody was looking. . . .[23]

It hardly seems credible to a modern generation of movie-goers that there ever could have been a time when people were ashamed to be seen attending a motion picture theater. It is just another instance of the fact that progress can be retarded on the ground that innovations are menacing to morals.

c. *The Charge That the New Is Impractical or Unsound.* A survey of technological trends from an historical point of view shows that many inventions have been denounced and resisted with intense animosity.

The development of the railroads was opposed by turnpike companies which were profiting from tolls, by owners of stage coaches, and by tavernkeepers along the routes of the post roads. New Yorkers who had incurred a heavy debt in building the Erie Canal argued that the railroads were not as convenient as canals for travel, and they favored the practice of levying tolls upon railroads whose lines ran parallel to the canals. Objectors to the railroads pointed out that the heavy carriages could not be stopped without a great shock to the occupants; that the noise would make the cows withhold their milk; that hens would be so scared they'd stop laying eggs; that more insane asylums would be needed to house the people driven mad with terror at the sight of locomotives rushing across the country with nothing to draw them; that a speed of fifteen miles an hour would cause the blood to spurt from the passengers' noses, mouths, and ears; that such travel would encourage flightiness of intellect. Almost universally there was a stress on the hazards and imperfections of the railways, as people failed to conceive the vast potentialities inherent in the invention of the steam locomotive. Nicholas Wood, a railroad expert, declared Stephenson's claim of a possible speed of twenty miles an hour was absurd, and added, "Nobody could do more harm to the prospects

[23] A. Zukor: "From the Nickelodeon to the Picture Palace." *The New York Times Magazine,* February 28, 1937.

of building or generally improving such coaches than by spreading abroad this kind of nonsense." Later when Westinghouse tried to interest Commodore Vanderbilt in the air brakes he had invented, he was dismissed by the Commodore, who said he had no time to waste on fools.[24]

The story of the automobile is similar in many respects to that of the railroads. From the first there was widespread hostility to the horseless carriage. The editor of the Springfield *Republican,* in 1895, refused an invitation to ride in the car in which Duryea had won the first auto race, on the grounds that to do so would be incompatible with the dignity of his position. In the press automobile drivers were held up to public derision. Early tourists were regarded as fools and knaves, and had to form clubs for their own protection. Every accident on the roads was attributed to the Juggernaut. Clergymen flayed "automobilitis" as deleterious to morals and religion. Bankers refused to invest in a plaything. Chauncey Depew warned his nephew not to invest $5,000 in Ford stock because "nothing has come along to beat the horse."

Steamboats, submarines, airplanes, and subways were all considered foolish dreams and the men who proposed them were ridiculed for being so impractical. Experts testified that such ideas were unrealizable and they dismissed them with a pooh-pooh.

Even printing came in for its share of abuse. Its introduction in Paris was delayed for twenty years by the hostility of the guild of scribes. In this country, printing was denounced because it was feared that the extension of literacy to the masses would foment discontent. Governor Berkeley of Virginia expressed this alarm in 1670:

I thank God there are no free schools, nor printing, and I hope we shall not have them these hundred years; for learning has brought disobedience and heresy and sects into the world, and printing has divulged them and libels against the best government.

In a later day typewriters were opposed as impracticable. When the New York Y.W.C.A., in 1881, announced typing lessons for women, the organization was showered with vigorous protests from men who warned that the female constitution could not stand up under such a strain. The typewriter was long regarded as an affectation, a pre-

---

[24] These illustrations and some of those which follow, are largely digested from *Technological Trends and National Policy,* a report of the Subcommittee on Technology to the National Resources Committee, Part I, Section IV, "Resistances to the Adoption of Technological Innovations." 1937.

tense to authorship or professionalism on the part of a layman and therefore unbecoming an honest person. Some people looked upon the receipt of a typed letter as an aspersion upon their literacy.

By ridiculing innovators, by stigmatizing their productions as immoral, and by condemning inventions for their unsoundness, conservative people succeed in retarding progress. During the delay, however, the opposition gradually gives in, so gradually as to "save its face" by seeming not to have yielded, and finally the die-hards have to acknowledge that maybe there is something to this newfangled contraption after all.

3. EDUCATION

Cultural inertia is encouraged by education.

Education is a force which conserves culture from one generation to another, that is, education in a very broad sense as the learning that takes place outside the schoolroom as well as inside. Education is thus in very large measure the making acquainted of the young with the existing culture, and tends to strengthen the force of habit.[25]

The younger generation are trained to follow in the footsteps of their elders; harmony results when youth accept what they are told to believe.

4. CULTURAL LAG

Generally speaking, people are more inclined to accept inventions of a physical nature than they are to adopt new concepts in the field of social relations. The Lynds found that residents of Middletown were eager to have radios and electric refrigerators, but they were not so progressive in their attitudes toward birth control, divorce, and the New Deal. When the librarian of the Middletown public library was asked where people in Middletown could get information on sex, the reply was, "Not here!"[26] That people are more progressive in some respects than others is also shown in the differential gains achieved by the medical profession in the control of various diseases: smallpox, typhoid, and diphtheria have been largely eliminated, but the "social diseases" (venereal) are still rampant because the public, for moral reasons, refuses to cooperate in wiping out these menaces to

[25] W. F. Ogburn: *Social Change*, p. 179. 1922.
[26] R. S. Lynd and H. M. Lynd: *Middletown in Transition*, p. 169. Harcourt, Brace and Company, 1937.

health. This fact, that in some cultural patterns people do not progress as rapidly as in others, has been termed "cultural lag."

It is a strange thing that human beings are apparently more interested in developing the physical world than they are in improving their own lot in that world. Machines are invented and installed to speed up production; years later workmen's compensation is adopted and "safety first" campaigns are instituted. Holding companies are conceived and exploited; years later comes the Securities and Exchange Commission. Improved means are found to get more work out of employees in less time; years later come unemployment insurance and old age security. We seem to be more concerned with our physical welfare than we are with our social welfare. Another way of stating the same idea is to say that the social sciences lag behind the physical sciences. During the course of history man devoted himself to mathematics, physics, chemistry, astronomy, and biology; as an afterthought he became interested in the sciences of human relations, psychology and sociology. As a result of this lag, we know less about solving the problems of unemployment, economic depression, and war than we do about applying our knowledge of gasoline to the speeding up of transportation. Perhaps some day we shall have as clear an understanding of the principles of economics, government, and sociology as we have long since secured in the physical and biological sciences.

IV. SURVIVALS

The permanence of customs is responsible for the presence of survivals, a survival being a custom that was once useful but is no longer of value because conditions have in the meantime changed so drastically as to render it obsolete. Because of inertia and other factors conducive to conservatism a custom may be preserved long past the days of its usefulness, in which case it becomes a survival. Such survivals may be noted in ceremonials, politics, law, medicine, and economics.

A. CEREMONIALS

Ceremonials have been described as the museum of history because they tend to linger on even though out of date. Formalities are easily crystallized; once established, they endure. Formal behavior suffers from the "dead hand of the past."

Several centuries ago, when Cavaliers and Roundheads carried their swords with them into the House of Commons, there was some danger of mortal combat during the parliamentary debates. To prevent such a disaster a red line was painted across the floor and a rule was passed that no member of Parliament could speak if he set foot over that line. That red line is still there and only recently a member of the House was shouted down with hoots when he tried to speak while one of his feet had strayed across the barrier, though he had no sword to brandish at his fellow members. The unfortunate man was nonplused by the vociferous greeting showered upon him in as much as he was completely unconscious of the red line and equally unaware of its meaning. Cavaliers and Roundheads disappeared long ago but the red line lingers on.

There is an old custom in France decreeing that persons attending a funeral must walk bareheaded to the cemetery, no matter how inclement the weather. Many octogenarians, anxious to show their respect to the dead by remaining uncovered, even though it may be cold and rainy, die from exposure. Ambassador Herrick went bareheaded to Marshal Foch's funeral. Herrick caught cold and died. General Pershing went bareheaded to Herrick's funeral, caught cold, and nearly died. In spite of the folly of this custom, the taboo against riding to the cemetery and the taboo against wearing a hat still persist. Whether this practice was ever useful is dubious; certainly it is a silly custom that should be abandoned.

It is characteristic of survivals in ceremonials that the form remains, whereas the spirit which originally inspired the observance is missing. This principle is illustrated in the celebration of Thanksgiving. Originally this holiday was an occasion for giving thanks to God for the bounty of the harvests; today it is a day off for many people, a chance to see a football game and an opportunity to overeat. The religious meaning of Thanksgiving, for such persons, has been forgotten, and only the form survives.

Another survival from Puritan times is the prim Mrs. Brewster, who is the very embodiment of custom:

Mrs. Brewster, Priscilla's aunt, is the ancestor of all New England aunts. She may be seen today walking down Tremont Street, Boston, in her Educator shoes on her way to S. S. Pierce's which she pronounces to rhyme with hearses. The twentieth century Mrs. Brewster wears a high-necked black silk waist with a chatelaine watch pinned over her left breast and a spot of Gorton's codfish (no bones) over her right. When a little girl she was taken to see Longfellow, Lowell, and Ralph Waldo Emerson; she speaks familiarly of the James boys, but this has no reference to the well-known Missouri outlaws.

She was brought up on blueberry cake, Postum and the *Atlantic Monthly.*
She loves the Boston *Transcript,* God, and her relatives in Newton Center.[27]

B. Politics

The presence of survivals in politics is symbolized in the obsolete
stereotypes prevalent in political cartoons.   As David Low, the British cartoonist, has pointed out, John Bull and Uncle Sam, as symbols
of Great Britain and the United States, are no longer valid.   These
portraits may have been accurate pictures of types once upon a time.

But leaving on one side their obsolete dress, it would be difficult to find less
truthful representatives of the average present-day citizens of Britain and the
United States of America than respectively this obese, smug, side-whiskered
country squire, and this lanky, long-haired, goat-bearded farmer.   What are
these agricultural left-overs doing monopolizing the masquerade as Britain
and the United States in these industrial days?   Is this a machine age or isn't
it? [28]

The cartoon stereotypes for Russia, France, and Germany are just
as obsolete.

In defiance of the march of events these moth-eaten creations still appear, though they no longer bear any significant relationship to reality.
The modern Russian is not a bewhiskered Nihilist leading a bear and
carrying a smoking bomb of antique model, but a clean-shaven young
man, dressed in overalls, smeared with oil, running a tractor; the
modern Frenchman is not your dandy Alphonse, the modern German
not your fat Fritz, for there have been wars and revolutions, and the
present-day nationalists are men earnestly interested in shirts, salutes,
and machinery.   Adds David Low in summarizing his suggestions to
cartoonists who want to bring their art up to date:

New models are required for a world which, as it annihilates time and
space with its speed machines, its sound machines, its vision machines, is
annihilating also regional peculiarity.   Unfortunately for the cartoonists
the same kind of suits and felt hats are now worn in New York, London,
Moscow, Paris, Berlin, Tokyo, Istanbul, Peiping, Stockholm and Addis
Ababa. . . .

It is becoming both untrue and unprofitable any more to represent peoples
as being essentially different one from another. . . .

[27] From: *A Parody Outline of History,* by D. O. Stewart, copyright 1921 by
Doubleday and Company, Inc.
[28] David Low: "Streamlining the Cartoon for the Airplane Age." The New York
Times Magazine, February 7, 1937.

A bleak prospect for cartoonists. It is difficult to mature new symbols in such a world; but it becomes evident that to perpetuate the old ones is to perpetuate confusion.

"A symbol always stimulates the intellect," said Emerson in a weak moment. Well and good, if it is a symbol of living thought; but symbols which have outlived their significance, yet still persist as habits of thought, do not stimulate but only drug the intellect.[29]

The philosophy of isolationism, still embraced by some Americans, is a survival in a world which has been united by common needs and common aspirations. In the early stages of World War II there were numerous Americans who favored the policy of ignoring Europe' troubles and staying home to mind our own business. Even in the late stages of the War there were those who believed America should retire from the world scene, build up its military defenses, and tell the rest of the world to leave us alone. Tin and rubber shortages, dating from the Japanese conquests of Malaya and the Dutch East Indies in early 1942, led some of us to wonder about our self-sufficiency. Wendell Willkie reminded us that today we live in *One World*, in which we must assume the responsibilities that are in keeping with our preeminence among the great powers. The experiences we shared with other peoples, as friends and enemies, during the Second World War broadened our social consciousness. The narrow isolationism of the jingo press is certain to appear out of date as a result of our enlarged mental horizons. The modern American realizes that his well-being and his security are all tied up with the well-being and security of peoples of other nations. Even in a material sense we cannot live alone and like it, especially in an age of atomic power with all that this discovery implies in the way of social responsibility.

The average American

rises in the morning and takes a look at the thermometer filled with mercury from Spain. He cleanses his body with soap to which coconut, palm and olive trees have made their un-American contribution. He brushes his teeth with a Japanese toothbrush and pulls on a pair of socks made from silk from the same country. His shoes are as international in their composition as the League of Nations. The buttons on his coat are from the ivory palm of Colombia or Ecuador. He walks out into the dining room on a carpet or a rug whose basis is the jute yarn of India. He sits down to a table covered with Irish linen, sips a little Java coffee and proceeds to cut up a banana from Honduras on a biscuit whose constituents once

[29] *Ibid.*

ay on a Kansas wheat field in a sheaf wound with sisal fibres from Yuca-
an. He finds at his plate the morning newspaper printed on Canadian
vood pulp from ink whose gums, oils and colors came from overseas. On
eaving the house he puts on a felt hat made from the surplus Australian
abbit crop. He climbs into the seat of his automobile and finds it covered
vith mohair which once grew on the back of a goat in Asia Minor. His
rain is drawn by a locomotive to whose basic substance, steel, 40 countries
aave contributed 57 different materials. Arriving at his office he switches on
an electric light which with its connections is the product of five continents.
He then summons his secretary by the office telephone, an instrument to
which an Irishman has contributed flax, an Egyptian long cotton fibres, a
Hindoo mica, a Russian platinum, a South African gold, and a native of the
Straits Settlements rubber. While his secretary is coming he takes out a
pencil filled with graphite from Ceylon. . . .[30]

The unrealistic nature of isolationist sentiment in the world of today
is brought out likewise in this brief story entitled "Patriot":

It was a beautiful Sunday morning. Simpson, having finished reading
a paper printed with an invention made in Germany, set out with his wife
for the meeting house of a faith founded in Palestine. Contemplating the
beauty of the land, which had been discovered by an Italian in the employ of
a Spanish queen and musing on the liberty it possessed thanks to the help
of a French navy, his bosom swelled with pride. "Thank God," said Simpson fervently in a language imported from the British Isles, "I am a one-
hundred-per-cent American!"

C. Law

Survivals in the realm of law are intimately related to survivals in the
field of politics, largely because so many of our politicians are lawyers.
The situation has inspired some critics of our system to wonder whether
a government of the lawyers, by the lawyers, is for the people or not.
To determine whether a government by lawyers is good for us or not,
it will be enlightening to examine the psychology of lawyers, taking the
profession as a whole.

Lawyers adhere to the past because law is fundamentally based on
precedent. When an observer of our legal system pointed out this
fact, a lawyer offered this defense:

If there is any phase of human activity wherein adherence to, and reliance
upon precedent is absolutely vital to the welfare of society, it is, to my mind,
the administration of the law. The layman, if the truth be known, would be

[30] From a speech by Justin Nixon at the Northern Baptist Convention, June, 1931.

the first to complain and the chief loser, if the system of reliance upon precedent should be abandoned.

When a prospective litigant goes to a lawyer for advice, he presumably places before his legal adviser, in so far as he can, all of the facts in relation to his difficulties. It is the lawyer's first job to assist the client by adroit questions in obtaining these facts, and as accurately as possible. The lawyer then obtains, in so far as he is able, the facts relied upon by the other party to the controversy. Then what does he do? He either draws upon knowledge that he already possesses or he examines the law, and advises his client as to his rights and remedies, or perhaps as to his liability to his opponent.

And how does the lawyer do this? Simply by his reliance upon precedent. If the lawyer could not base his advice upon precedent, he would have to tell the prospective litigant that the outcome of the litigation might very well depend upon the whim of a judge or the caprice of a jury. The law of precedent means something secure, something steadfast, something comparatively changeless in a constantly changing world.[31]

No outsider could write a more damning indictment of the legal profession. According to this lawyer, our choice lies between either precedent or whim (caprice). There is no allowance made for the use of some intelligence by the judge or the jury because that would upset some precedents. If the law of precedent, as he asserts proudly, is "comparatively changeless in a constantly changing world," then obviously there will be a lag, with consequent maladjustment.

Roscoe Pound, former dean of the Harvard Law School, points out that our legal system was evolved to care for the problems of a pioneer America which was chiefly a rural and agricultural country. Since colonial times, with the rise of large cities, we have made the transition into an urban industrial society. But we still seek to meet the problems of the new situation with the ideas, institutions, and political machinery of our formative era. Law must be stable, Pound asserts, but it cannot stand still.

The lawyer tends to take things as they are and to keep them that way. He is aided in this task by the fact that once a law gets on the statute books, it is apt to stay there. A good example of this thesis is a Sunday blue law passed in Massachusetts in 1692, two centuries before the advent of the automobile, which lived on for 241 years, much to the detriment of certain motorists to whom it was applied by the courts.

The blue law, passed by the Colonial Legislature of Massachusetts, was known as the Lord's Day Act, and it provided among other things that "no

---

[31] Letter to the Editors, *Harper's Magazine,* December, 1931.

aveler shall travel on that day." This statement would seem to have little connection with the modern motorist, but because of it numerous Massachusetts motorists, although not in fault in any way themselves, have had to pay thousands of dollars in damages, and have been unable, themselves, to gain damages when injured. Because of it the innocent have often been adjudged the guilty.

The process whereby the Sunday blue law so evolved, through a series of judicial rulings, that it applied to motorists began on a certain Sunday in 1876. On that date a praiseworthy gentleman was walking down a Massachusetts road minding his own business, and generally behaving himself when a reckless and irresponsible fellow drove over him with a team of galloping horses. The pedestrian sued for damages and was astonished when the court informed him that he would have to pay his own doctor bills. He could collect no damages because he had been a trespasser on the highway, since he was unlawfully traveling upon it. This seemed pretty far-fetched to the Legislature which repealed the blue law the following year.

But repealing the law did not kill it. It merely slumbered until 1909. Six years before, the Legislature had passed a law which read in part: "All automobiles shall be registered, and no automobile shall be operated unless registered." It might seem that we are still a far distance from the Lord's Day Act of 1692, but this did not seem the case to the attorney of the Northampton Street Railway. A street-car of that corporation had surprised one Mr. Dudley who was in no way to blame. So, he filed suit only to find that he had been in Massachusetts more than fifteen days and should have had his car registered in this state. In other words, it was found that through a technicality he had been illegally driving. This was all the attorney for the street-car company needed. If a man was a trespasser in 1876 for breaking the 1692 law, the attorney argued, he was a trespasser in 1909 for breaking a 1903 law. If a trespasser could not collect damages in 1876, he should not be able, in all logic, to collect damages in 1909. A precedent had been made and the legal mind loves a precedent. It made slight difference that Mr. Dudley was the injured party. What's an injury to a precedent? So Mr. Dudley did not collect, and thus another precedent had been made, this one dealing with automobiles.

The rule adopted by the courts stated briefly: If an automobile was not properly registered, its driver was a trespasser, and had no legal rights as far as travel on the highway was concerned. His car could be shattered, his family killed, all through no fault of his own, and if it was shown that through some technical error his automobile was improperly registered, he could have no recourse at law.

With this decision came a host of cases which flouted every rule of logic save legal logic. For instance, a man whose correct first name was Henry and whose automobile was registered in the name of Harry (his last name was correctly stated) was the injured party in an automobile accident. The courts ruled that he was a "trespasser and could not collect damages for his injuries."

The trespasser doctrine was evolved at a time when automobiles wer frightful to most horses, and introduced a new element of danger to ordinar travelers. . . .[32]

In the state of Illinois it took from 1915 to 1934 to pass a bill requir ing the dropping of a little nitrate of silver solution into the eyes o babies right after birth. All kinds of obstacles were placed in the wa of this legislation: a governor vetoed the bill, an attorney-general de clared it unconstitutional. Babies were becoming blind while the law yers haggled over questions of legality. Finally, in 1934, the measur was passed; and in that year no babies suffered blindness in Illinois The delay in enacting this humane legislation leads one to suspect tha maybe Arnold was right when he said that legal scholars are often in terested in attaining an undesirable result if it can be achieved in a learned way.[33]

A study of the Oklahoma Ice Case reveals several significant phase concerning the operation of our legal machinery. The State of Okla homa passed a law making the manufacture of ice a public utilit and requiring that producers get a certificate of public necessity and convenience before establishing any new factories. The State thu stipulated that no man could start a new ice plant if the authorities fel there were already enough such plants to supply the demands of the consumers. The U.S. Supreme Court ruled against the law on the ground that it violated the "due process" clause of the 5th and 14th amendments to the Constitution. The "due process" clause was origi nally intended to protect individuals unjustly accused of crimes from being railroaded into prison without the opportunity of a fair trial Later the courts interpreted this clause to protect corporations against public-service regulation.[34]

Scholars in the law schools then proved that the extension of the clause to refer to corporations was not really a change in the meaning of the Constitution, after all.[35] This point is of concern to us because the Constitution is very widely regarded as a sacred instrument, un changing and steadfast, a basis for security when everything else is fal tering. In so far as the Constitution is thought of in this way it func tions as an obstacle in the path of progress. If we discard the folklore underlying this simple faith in the unalterable Constitution, we shall

[32] The Boston *Herald*, January 1, 1933.
[33] T. W. Arnold: *The Symbols of Government*, p. 5. 1935.
[34] T. W. Arnold: *The Folklore of Capitalism*, p. 22. 1937.
[35] *Ibid.*, p. 34.

iscover that the Constitution is what the judges say it is. The "due rocess" clause has in this way come to mean what the Justices of the upreme Court say it means. The interpretation arrived at by the Justices proved itself a convenient device for obstructing progressive legislation. Both the Income Tax and Minimum Wage laws were ruled nvalid by means of this device; later the Court reversed its decisions, nd the innovations, though delayed, were allowed. Thus the Court nay at times retard progress.

The Oklahoma Ice Case is of interest to us also because the dissenting opinions of Brandeis and Cardozo state so clearly the relationship f the law to the social inertia underlying survivals. The opinions nay be summarized as follows:

Brandeis: Increasingly, doubt is expressed whether it is economically wise, r morally right, that men should be permitted to add to the producing facilities of an industry which is already suffering from overcapacity. . . . The ramers of the 14th amendment did not intend to leave us helpless to correct he evils of technological unemployment and excess productive capacity which he march of invention and discovery have entailed. There must be power n the States and the Nation to remold through experimentation our economic practices and institutions to meet changing social and economic needs. . . To stay experimentation within the law in things social and economic s a grave responsibility. We should be ever on our guard lest we erect our rejudices into legal principles. If we would be guided by the light of reaon, we must be bold.

Cardozo: The needs of successive generations may make restrictions imperaive today which were vain and capricious to the vision of times past. . . . New times and new manners may call for new standards and new rules. A onstitution ought to state principles for an expanding future.

We may conclude our discussion of the conservatism prevalent in the legal profession by citing the remarks of Representative Maverick of Texas, who, speaking as one lawyer to others, accused the American Bar Association of having a "stupid, undemocratic, and behind-the-times" attitude toward child labor, business regulation, security and social legislation. In the law colleges, he added, the student is not taught the scientific necessities of the day, but is schooled "to think in terms of special interest through theories as dead as the dodo bird." [36] In protest against this conservatism of the American Bar Association, the Lawyers' Guild has been established, to promote civil rights, general welfare, and progressive legislation.

[36] The Boston *Herald*, January 10, 1937.

D. Medicine

Survivals abound in the field of medicine—obsolete practices that persist because people for one reason or another impede progress. New discoveries are often rejected until resistance is gradually worn down to the point of acquiescence. Quinine, for example, was discovered in 1638 by the Jesuits of Peru and marvelous cures were reported in connection with its administration. Since the use of quinine was a radical departure from established precedent, it was viewed with alarm. The University of Paris declared the use of quinine unconstitutional and banned the drug as dangerous.

Vesalius, in the sixteenth century, showed that Galen's description of the hip bones was wrong. This was regarded as insolent presumptuousness on the part of Vesalius, for Galen had been accepted since ancient times as the authority in anatomy. Vesalius was denounced for casting discredit upon the great Galen. When Vesalius finally proved he was correct, his denouncers backed down and admitted it, but not without excusing their error on the ground that man had changed his shape, since the days of Galen, through wearing tight trousers.

When George Boddington introduced the idea of fresh-air treatment for tuberculosis, he was reviled by the public for his inhumanity and driven out of his practice by members of his own profession. The idea was too revolutionary to be adopted without long protest.

For centuries male doctors were not allowed to practice obstetrics because it was considered indecent for a man to attend a woman during labor. During the sixteenth century the prejudice against the participation of men in midwifery was intense. A doctor named Roslin, who had probably never seen a child born, may have felt something of the humor of his position, when in 1513 he entitled his book on obstetrics: *The Garden of Roses for Pregnant Women and for Midwives*.[37] In 1522 a Dr. Wert of Hamburg, Germany, put on the dress of a woman in order to attend and study a case of labor; as a punishment for his impiety he was burned to death. In the 1840's John Stevens of London was denouncing the immorality of employing men in midwifery and dedicating his pamphlets to the Society for the Suppression of Vice. About the same time, in our country, tracts were being written declaring that "the employment of men to attend women in childbirth and other delicate circumstances is unnecessary, unnatural, and injurious." Dr. James P. White gave an obstetric demonstration

[37] H. W. Haggard: *Devils, Drugs, and Doctors*, p. 29. Harper & Brothers, 1929.

a clinic at the University of Buffalo in 1850 and immediately he was
attacked by the press for having outraged decency, members of the
medical profession joining in the clamor against him. Two years later
Dr. Charles D. Meigs of Philadelphia ingenuously argued in favor
of the propriety of male obstetricians on the ground that the first
woman must have been assisted in labor by a man since Eve could
have had no other assistance than that rendered by Adam. The doctors who were brave enough to pioneer in this field found that great
shame was attached to their calling. They were derisively referred to
as "he-grandmothers."

It is this same squeamishness about sex that accounts for our failure
to control venereal disease. Senator John McNaboe of New York
opposed a bill for the control of syphilis, in May, 1937, because "the
innocence of children might be corrupted by a widespread use of the
term. . . . This particular word creates a shudder in every decent
woman and decent man." Such an attitude is as costly as the custom
in Arabia which forbids a woman to expose any part of her body or
face to a man. She is thus deprived of surgery she may need. If a
doctor has to operate on the eyes, he is given special permission to do
so, provided he does not lift the veil. Under the circumstances the
surgeon must work through small holes cut in the veil.[38]

Dr. Victor Heiser reported in *An American Doctor's Odyssey* (1936)
many instances, encountered in various parts of the world, of the fact
that popular attitudes toward disease very seriously obstruct the practice of modern medicine. He found the inhabitants of the Philippines
resigned to their ailments, chief of which was cholera. Year after year
Heiser and his co-workers labored by every possible means to persuade
the Filipinos to boil their water. It was all in vain because the Filipinos believed boiled water was injurious. The next best thing,
Heiser realized, would be to get an appropriation from the Legislature
for the purpose of boring artesian wells as sources of pure water.
When the first well started flowing, the natives would not come near
it, for they said, "If God had intended us to drink water out of a hole
in the earth, he would have put it there." Doctors who were sent to
explain the virtues of the well water were greeted with hostility.
Rumors began to circulate. "If you drink this water," the villagers
said, "your hair will fall out. If you don't believe it, look at the
Director of Health at Manila. He drinks this water. Look at him."

Heiser encountered the same antiquated notions when he worked to
eliminate smallpox in the Philippines, in India, in the United States.

[38] J. Beatty: "Desert Doctor." *The American Magazine*, October, 1938.

Millions of people die from smallpox because they refuse to be vac cinated. Societies have been formed to promulgate the idea that al the ills of the world are due to vaccination. A chiropractor in Denve who campaigned against vaccination later contracted smallpox, fle to Arkansas where he started an epidemic, then died. According t Heiser there are very few anti-vaccinationists now in the Philippines most of them have died of smallpox.

From his wide experience, Heiser concludes:

> To change a way of existence once adopted is repugnant to our whol psychology. Life is but a tissue of habits, and we believe deeply that th old ways are the best ways. "As comfortable as an old shoe" or "like an ol glove it wears well" are favorite maxims. Age is surrounded by a shinin halo of sanctity, sometimes so blinding as to shut out the light.
>
> "Habit with him was all the test of truth; 'it must be right: I've done i from my youth.' " [39]

We cling to our old habits though it may mean disaster to do so.

E. Economics

One survival in the realm of economics is the conviction, shared b many, rich and poor alike, that "rugged individualism" is the onl system conducive to a sound social order. According to this doctrine first expounded at length by Adam Smith in his *Wealth of Nation* (1776), people prosper best when the government leaves them alone t pursue their own ends as they see fit. If the political authorities wil refrain from regulating economic activities, a system of free competi tion will be maintained under which economic laws can operate t promote the good of all the citizens. Under such an arrangement where every man is for himself, it is presumed that the individual wil render the greatest service to society by seeking his own gain.

The idea that prosperity and virtue are concomitant variables—th more virtuous you are, the more prosperous—was a contribution o seventeenth-century Puritanism. By a fortunate dispensation, it wa pointed out, the virtues enjoined upon Christians, such as diligence moderation, sobriety, and thrift, are the very qualities most conduciv to commercial success; indeed, success in business may be interpretec as a sign of spiritual grace, poverty as the evidence of moral shortcom ings. Economic greed and uncharitable covetousness, natural humar frailties, were converted into "economic enterprise" and then rational

[39] V. G. Heiser: "You Need a Change." *Collier's,* November 14, 1936.

ed as resounding virtues, for when duty is so profitable, may not
rofit-making be a duty?   The Puritan moralists stressed the moral
bligations to work hard and to avoid extravagance and luxury, thus
anonizing as an ethical principle that very efficiency that economists
vere preaching as the cure of all social ills.   The acquisition of wealth
vas converted from a temptation into a moral imperative, inspiring
nen with the zeal that changed the face of material civilization.[40]
This creed was the milk of lions, a convenient rationalization for "the
obber barons" who were busy plundering their fellow men to the
lory of God.[41]   The combination of piety and acumen reached its
enith in "Divine Right" Baer, who wrote the following letter in reply
o a request that he settle a strike in his railroad company:

PHILADELPHIA AND READING RAILWAY COMPANY
PRESIDENT'S OFFICE
READING TERMINAL, PHILADELPHIA

My dear Mr. Clark:
  I have your letter of the 15th instant.
  I do not know who you are.   I see that you are a religious man; but you
ure evidently biased in favor of the right of the working man to control
a business in which he has no other interest than to secure fair wages for the
vork he does.
  I beg of you not to be discouraged.   The rights and interests of the laboring man will be protected and cared for—not by the labor agitators, but by
he Christian men to whom God in His infinite wisdom has given the control
of the property interests of this country, and upon the successful management
of which so much depends.
  Do not be discouraged.   Pray earnestly that right may triumph, always
remembering that the Lord God Omnipotent still reigns and that His reign
s one of law and order and not of violence and crime.
Yours truly,
Geo. F. Baer, President.

Some people thought capitalism was designed by God to permit the
noblest men to rise to positions of power.
  Believers in *laissez faire* sponsored personal independence.   Self-reli-
unce was praised as the foundation of character.   Accordingly no man
could be said to have a strong character if he had to depend upon
others for sustenance.   The successful businessman fatuously assumed

[40] See R. H. Tawney: *Religion and the Rise of Capitalism.* 1926.
[41] See M. Josephson: *The Robber Barons.* 1934. Also, J. T. Flynn: *God's Gold.*
1932.

that his preeminent achievements were ascribable to his own untiring efforts and to his own ethical superiority. He was willing to take exclusive credit for his prosperity. In his self-complacency he attributed other people's failures to their moral deficiencies and he excused himself from contributing to their support on the ground that charity would complete the demoralization of their characters.

Individual freedom may have been compatible with the public welfare in the days of the pioneer, when ours was an expanding country and opportunity beckoned to every man to set out for himself into the wilderness to hew his future by the labor of his own hands. Individual initiative and ceaseless toil were of infinite value in the development of our natural resources. There were no problems of technological unemployment in those days but there are now, and in our present era man's responsibility to his fellows is being increasingly recognized as more important than the capacity a person of superior intelligence may have for taking advantage of duller wits.

In our modern world the philosophy and practice of rugged individualism, some authorities feel, are as out of place as a covered wagon would be on the Lincoln Highway. Free competition does not exist in our present social order; it is doubtful, indeed, whether competition was ever free. The phrase "free competition" is an abstraction and without specific referents it is an empty bit of gibberish, "only a noise in our heads," a verbal concept unrelated to the world of fact. Who is competing? How free is free? When we raise such semantic questions and look to the world of reality for our answers, we learn quickly that "free competition" is a propaganda device, not a description of facts, and "rugged individualism" belongs in the same category. What do we find when we examine the real world of business? Business men organized monopolies long ago to stifle competition, and strange to say, some of the people most vociferous in their praise of competition as "the motive force of progress," are the heads of those monopolies.

The person who is living in today and not in a bygone era is not interested in propagandizing for vague ideals like "freedom" and "rugged individualism." He is concerned rather with discovering some new techniques for adjusting our purchasing power to our productive capacity so that production can proceed at maximum efficiency, allowing us to raise the standards of living especially among the people of lower incomes. The time has come to cease quarreling emotionally over slogans, to start tackling our economic problems in a scientific spirit, to

k ourselves such questions as the following ones—and search for the
iswers:

Does not a lack of purchasing power among the masses perhaps serve to
revent the full employment of our productive resources?
What is the possible bearing of the distribution of income among the
ifferent groups in society upon the demand for the products of industry? [42]

An open-minded survey of our history, undertaken to learn facts that
light guide us in formulating our present policies, would reveal,
mong other things, that competition needs to be regulated in the
ublic interest, for otherwise aggressive individuals with a genius for
iking advantage of their opportunities will exploit our natural re-
ources to their private gain. Competition is not always a blessing,
nce a free-for-all may entail stupid waste. In the early days of the
ilroads, for instance, competing companies were laying duplicate
ts of tracks through the same territories, setting the rails at different
istances apart so that the cars of one company could not be used on
ie rails of another company. With nobody to stop them, competitors
uring that same period were depleting the national resources, de-
iolishing the forests for lumber, for example, without any regard for
ie consequences. Barren farm-lands, dust-ridden plains, and devas-
iting floods remain as evidence of what happens when individuals are
llowed to go their own way, unhampered by government regulation.
uch waste cannot be tolerated today: another reason why rugged in-
ividualism is an anachronism now.

The fundamental reason that rugged individualism is out of date is
iat we are living in an age of increasing interdependence.[43] How far
idividual initiative should be limited by governmental regulation is
crucial problem in our present society, as we have already observed.
he importance of this issue was recognized at the Harvard Tercen-
nary celebration in 1936, when a symposium was held on the topic,
Authority and the Individual." Speaking on the occasion of this
ieeting, Wesley C. Mitchell, Professor of Economics at Columbia, said
i part:

The growing economic prosperity of the nineteenth century pushed men
oser together while it also widened the areas from which they drew supplies

[42] H. G. Moulton: "Scientific Method in the Investigation of Economic Problems."
ientific Monthly, March, 1936.
[43] See B. Russell: *Freedom versus Organization, 1814-1914.* 1934.

and over which they marketed products. Increasing density of population makes what one man does more important in numberless ways to the health and happiness of his neighbors. Men feel the need of more common rule concerning what no one shall do and also concerning more things that every one must do for the common-weal. Government is the great agency for setting minimum standards of conduct that must be enforced upon the reca citrant, and so finds its functions multiplying as the interdependence of ind viduals becomes more intimate and intricate. So also the wider geographi scope of economic organization exposes the modern man to more and mor hazards that he cannot control, and he calls stridently upon this governmen for aid. Local regulations that served well enough in an earlier day ar replaced by national rules, supplemented by international conventions.[44]

This thesis was also advanced by the committee that made a surve of technological trends:

All inventions which make it possible for goods to travel faster and mor comfortably, or ideas to be better conveyed, in point-to-point or wholesal communication, tend, first, to build up larger, more widespread businesse These tend to outrun the powers of local regulation and taxation and to be come more and more subject to wider areas of governance.[45]

In 1932 Henry I. Harriman, then President of the U.S. Chamber c Commerce, confirmed this same point of view:

We must contemplate the adoption of devices to establish a better balanc between production and consumption. Only through such a proper co-o dination can a sane, orderly and progressive economic life be developed. freedom of action which might have been justified in the relatively simple lil of the last century cannot be tolerated today because the unwise action c one individual may adversely affect the lives of thousands. We have of nece sity left the period of extreme individualism, and are now living in a perio of national economy.[46]

That our moral concepts in the economic sphere have been modifie in recent times, is shown by the way people have revised their att tudes toward the rights of the man who does not work. It used to b a common assertion that no man had a right to eat unless he earne that right by virtue of some contribution to society in the way c

[44] W. C. Mitchell: "Intelligence and the Guidance of Economic Evolution *Scientific Monthly*, November, 1936.

[45] *Technological Trends and National Policy*, p. 36. 1937.

[46] H. I. Harriman, in a speech entitled "Sound Business Policies Essential to S curity."

labor. "No work, no eats." Conditions have changed during our own generation so that jobs, during peacetime at least, are not as plentiful as they used to be. Even in the days of high prosperity during the 1920's the number of the unemployed was steadily on the increase and when the depression of the 1930's came, many more individuals were thrown out of work. Advances in technological efficiency, making it possible for fewer men to produce more goods, have, of course, played a role in aggravating the unemployment problem. Individuals who never thought they would see the day when they'd have to "sponge" on the family or go on relief, were forced by hard times to revise their ideas about depending on the folks. Persons who were fortunate enough to have jobs during the depression of the '30's changed their attitudes toward their less fortunate fellows. Since the days when "President Hoover, echoed by most leaders of opinion in the land, was dwelling on the dreadful effects which the 'dole' would have on national morale, . . . there has been a historic revolution in American thinking" about relief and its beneficiaries' rights and duties.[47] This revolution was demonstrated in the Gallup and *Fortune* polls.

"No intelligent citizen any longer thinks that all of the unemployed are bums who won't work and should be left to starve. The majority of the American people now unquestioningly accept both the necessity and probable permanence of Relief, believe overwhelmingly that the Government should give the unemployed jobs instead of cash. But that by no means signifies that tax-paying citizens are satisfied with Relief-as-it-is." [48]

Morals change as "time marches on," and if we want to keep abreast of the times, we must take periodic inventory of our values, and make sure we are not pursuing ideals that are obsolete. As Lowell said, "New occasions teach new duties, time makes ancient good uncouth." [49] It is difficult for people to revamp their values. This task is an essential one, however, if we are going to avoid devoting our efforts to the preservation and promulgation of survivals. A new morality is in the making, in which "grim toil must be supplemented by creative labor, thrift by sharing, individualism by intelligent altruism, patriotism by internationalism, and charity by justice." [50] What we need most of all may likely be sympathy and honesty, as one observer has proposed:

---

[47] *Life*, July 24, 1939.
[48] *Ibid.*
[49] J. R. Lowell: "The Present Crisis," *Complete Poetical Works,* p. 68. 1844.
[50] C. H. Heimsath: "A Moral Code for the Future." *Harper's Magazine,* December, 1934.

Polls on Relief, 1936-39

Should the Government support the needy unemployed?

YES   NO

Jan. 1938   69%   31%

June 1939   75%   25%

Should the Government give work instead of cash relief?

YES   NO

June 1937   79%   21%

May 1939   90%   10%

Will America have to continue relief permanently?

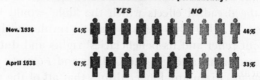

YES   NO

Nov. 1936   54%   46%

April 1938   67%   33%

Is the Government spending too much on relief?

YES   NO

Nov. 1937   49%   51%

April 1938   57%   43%

Are there any people on relief in your community who could get jobs in private industry if they tried?

YES   NO

April 1938   69%   31%

Does politics influence relief in your locality?

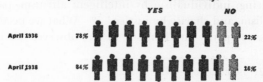

YES   NO

April 1936   78%   22%

April 1938   84%   16%

(Courtesy, American Institute of Public Opinion and *Fortune* "Survey of Public Opinion." See *Life,* July 24, 1939.)

In primeval times, the exercise of sympathy and honesty can have been of very little importance in the promotion of evolution, and so they were not as ethically important as the exercise of strength and activity. Now, however, the peaceful and helpful intercourse between nations, which is so essential for world progress, requires greater sympathy and honesty on the part of the dominant groups than ever before, and the same qualities are daily more necessary in the conduct of modern business.[51]

V. RATIONAL DISCRIMINATION

Custom as the conservator of the past is constantly an obstacle to progress, blocking the changes that are necessary if adjustments are to be made to shifting conditions. Adherence to tradition prevents experimentation unless a special effort is exerted to break away from the domination of established habits. Maladjustments result when people refuse to recognize the passage of time. We have observed that human beings suffer because they are not ready enough to change their ways in a world that never stands still. Yet there is another side to the story. Change in itself is not desirable, though there are persons who worship the Great God Change in their eagerness to try anything as long as it is something new, something different. This thought has been expressed by one of the younger generation in the following poem:

O YE OF LITTLE FLUX

They say we're atheistical,
Headstrong, and egotistical,
And cynics more sophistical
    Than young men ought to be;
Our doctrines are irrational—
Or else they are *too* rational—
    "Just younger-generational"
        Sums up our perfidy.

At sacred things we smile and boo;
We do what folks would never do—
(Although they always wanted to—)
    When father was a boy.
Nor is our girl an angel: she
Is often quite unmaidenly;
She has forgotten how to be
    Appropriately coy.

[51] P. L. Alger: "The Relation of Ethics to Human Progress." *Scientific Monthly,* August, 1942.

We are the bane, the sorrow, the
Despair of Christianity;
Our souls (excuse profanity)
    Are damned: to hell we go.
But hearken, all ye critical
Old saps so analytical,
Sincere or hypocritical,
    You need not worry so.

We get no kick from being bad;
Our heresies are just a fad;
We're, candidly, a little mad
    For anything that's strange.
Though we're not pietistical,
We are not atheistical—
There's nothing in it mystical:
    We serve the great god Change.

      . . . .

The thing that we hold dear,
    So dear:
Just anything that's queer;
    We luvvit.[52]

It is characteristic of the young to want to defy custom, to revol
against the authorities, as a symbol of arriving at maturity; it is jus
as characteristic of their elders to resist the struggle of the young for
independence, to stand by long-established customs, to point out to
the immature heretics that when they get older, they'll get wiser. In
the words of Francis Bacon: "Therefore, since Custome is the Prin
cipall Magistrate of Man's Life, Let Men by all Meanes endevour to
obtain good Customes."[53] Or as the Scotsman's prayer put it: "God
grant I may be right—for ye ken I never change."[54]

There is a happy medium between ultra-conservatism and ultra
radicalism: the practice of rational discrimination. "Be not the firs
by whom the new are tried, Nor yet the last to lay the old aside." The
intelligent person realizes that customs have grown up because they
have fulfilled definite human needs; he is also shrewd enough to per
ceive that new conditions will probably call for new ways of meeting
the situation. There is danger in discarding a custom without stop
ping to examine its original purpose. "Hold fast to that which i

---

[52] The *Dartmouth*. (Date not known.)
[53] F. Bacon: *Essays*, "Of Custome and Education." 1625.
[54] E. Brunner, quoted in *Reader's Digest*, February, 1940.

od," admonishes St. Paul, and, we might add, hold fast only to
hat's good in any particular folkway. Check it to make sure it is not
ere folklore. Double-check to determine whether the old way is no
nger useful. If it is out of date, do not allow sentiment to delude
u into abiding with the hoary practice just for old time's sake. In-
lligent adjustment involves a willingness to vary behavior to meet
anging conditions.

"Be an heir of the past, not a slave of it." "Take from the altar of
e past the fire, not the ashes." It is important that we cultivate a
ew attitude toward our institutions, an attitude that will permit us
 view our standardized modes of conduct realistically in terms of
heir fruits. Our mores are not sacred. They must not be taken for
ranted, on the ground that they lie beyond examination, beyond criti-
ism. Our institutions are merely attempts to solve problems as those
roblems arise and they are not intended to be permanent solutions
recluding any further attempts at improvement. Loyalty to our
athers does not consist in standing where their journey ended, but in
ursuing the path their vision discerned. So when you hear a person
ay, "I thought that issue was settled long, long ago," you may infer
ou are dealing with an individual whose mental arteries are harden-
ng from a stupid addiction to the past. Nothing is perfected in a
vorld of flux; nothing is settled forever.

VI. CONSERVATISM AND REVOLUTION

A revolution occurs when any social system or government, or economic system, has become so adamantine, so unyielding that new
orces cannot break through. Any set of ideas, any organization, may
become resistant to the normal process of growth, as there are sure to
arise certain persons who profit in some way from the present set-up
and who are anxious, therefore, to see the *status quo* preserved. When
conservatism reaches the degree where no agitation for change is tolerated, progressive forces, despairing of attaining their ends by orderly
means, resort to violence. It may take some time for discontent to accumulate to what we might call "the boiling point" of revolution but
sooner or later this stage will be reached in a society whose privileged
groups are stagnating in their own complacency, unwilling to see that
he old order of things is outmoded and refusing to admit that the old
must give way to something new.

The surest way to encourage the violence of revolution, then, is
o insist upon standing still. "A wise conservatism," says Harold J.
Laski, "is a strategy of adaptation, not a philosophy of resistance to

change." [55]   Individuals who want to stay in power will see the wisdom
of tolerating a little change for the sake of preventing more radical
changes.   The real inciters of revolution are the conservatives and re
actionaries who want to maintain things just as they are, defenders of
privilege who exert all their authority to discourage people who feel
"there ought to be some changes made." *Stupid* conservatives refuse
to examine rationally the appeal for concessions; they are afraid to
give way somewhere lest they be compelled to surrender everything
Intelligent conservatives recognize the wisdom of compromise; they
yield to pressure soon enough to make it appear that they conceded of
their own generous free will.   Thus revolt is given no opportunity to
get started, nobody is going to feel abused, nobody is going to nurse
any grudges against the powers that be.   Conservatives who want to
continue to enjoy their possessions, for example, will be clever if they
lend their sanction to plans for alleviating poverty.   Another course,
one that is headed for revolution, is to try to delude the poor into believing that their indigence is really good for them, in this style:

"Our Lord was born and lived all his life in abject poverty.   It's a virtue
to live a life of poverty, and millions choose that way of life, placing them
selves in the hands of God.   That is the spirit of religion."

Although he extolled poverty as a virtue, Cardinal O'Connell pointed out
that there are many fine Christians who, through native intelligence and
ability, had been able to amass fortunes which they used well while con
tinuing to live simple, healthy lives. . . .[56]

You can fool some of the people some of the time by administering
opiates of this nature but a day of reckoning will come.   If violence
be the outcome, the responsibility for the resort to force must rest
heavily upon those conservatives who stubbornly resisted orderly progress.   Social inertia is the fundamental cause of revolution.

A rigid outlook is out of place in a dynamic world.   Intransigence
may delay reforms unduly when people settle their problems by means
of formulas and slogans which they mistake for eternal verities.   Thus
many persons argued against the parcel-post system because, they alleged, it meant the government was going too far in socialistic and pa-
ternalistic legislation; reactionaries opposed the Interstate Commerce
Commission as "Anti-Christian"; die-hards stormed against the income tax, predicting ruin would result from the accelerating evils of

[55] H. J. Laski: "A Formula for Conservatives." *Harper's Magazine*, September,
1937.
[56] Boston *Herald*, May 24, 1935.

uch socialistic legislation. None of these issues was judged on the merits involved. They were resisted on behalf of inherited tags and phrases hallowed only by time. Now these reforms are all taken for granted. They might have come sooner if they had been weighed with more respect for existing needs, less respect for the past.[57] Blind reverence for tradition, as cited in the instances above, may cause a 'piling up of cultural lags." When such lags accumulate to a sufficient extent, revolution is likely to ensue.[58] The violence of political revolution when it comes is a summation of the aggressive impulses that have been thwarted time and again by people who stand unreservedly for a stubborn defense of outworn customs. "The history of revolution," Lynd observes, "is one long record of overlong resistance to recognizing the handwriting on the wall." [59] Warburg shares this view:

Trouble starts when those who have acquired power exercise it without sufficient sense of responsibility, without sufficient understanding of its ramified effects, and, above all, to protect their own position by erecting unnatural obstacles to change. When they do this they outrage the "sense of justice" of the masses and, by obstructing change, frustrate their efforts to remedy the injustice.

This is what destroys hope and leads to revolution—not the inequality of wealth and power, but their exploitation to prevent change and progress.[60]

Anne Lindbergh showed expert insight into the psychology of a society in transition when she declared: "For only in growth, reform, and change, paradoxically enough, is true security to be found." [61]

One major cause of revolution is social inertia.

[57] See F. Frankfurter: "A Rigid Outlook in a Dynamic World." *Survey Graphic*, 1938.

[58] See Ogburn: *op. cit.*, p. 280.

[59] R. S. Lynd: *Knowledge for What?*, p. 246. Princeton University Press, 1939.

[60] J. P. Warburg: "The Isolationist Illusion and World Peace." Reprint of a chapter from his book, *Our War and Our Peace*. Rinehart and Company, Inc., 1941.

[61] A. M. Lindbergh: *The Wave of the Future: a Confession of Faith*, p. 38. Harcourt, Brace and Company, 1940.

Chapter 14

FASHION

A FASHION is a uniform behavior pattern common to a large number of people. It is an innovation that "takes," something new that catches the public fancy. The people who "go in for" the novelty are vaguely referred to as *they*—"they are doing it now." There are enough of "them" to engender the feeling that "everybody's doing it now," an illusion described more technically as "the impression of universality." [1] The course of adoption normally follows a definite pattern: in the first stage there is some hesitation before most persons are ready to commit themselves; then comes a period of mad enthusiasm during which the innovation becomes "all the rage"; next a sense of satiety sets in, as people get "fed up" and bored; then "they" are ready to move on to something different that will add to the variety and spice of life. Fashions do not last long; they come and go. It is this fact that LaPiere has in mind when he describes fashions as *fugitive patterns of behavior*.[2] Fads are even more fugitive than fashions; fads affect fewer people, are shorter-lived.

I. FASHION, CUSTOM, AND CONVENTION

Customs and conventions, as we have seen, also represent uniformities of behavior. How are they distinguishable from fashions?

Customs are enduring modes of behavior, hallowed by age, whereas fashions are temporary, evanescent.

Conventions are non-competitive; fashions, competitive. A fashion is the current mode, the prevailing thing to do. If people are playing badminton, then you must go in for this sport if you want to be "in the swim." This element of competition is lacking where conventions are concerned. It is the convention, we may add, that a lady must

---

[1] Refer to Chapter 8, "The Creation and Manipulation of Crowds," where there is a discussion of the role that *number* plays in crowd psychology. See also, F. H Allport: *Social Psychology*, pp. 392-393, 1924.

[2] See R. T. LaPiere: *Collective Behavior*, p. 192ff. 1938.

wear an evening gown to a formal dinner; there is no choice in the matter, for it is a rule binding on everybody. The opportunity for variation and competition enters when fashion is considered. An evening gown it must be, but it may be the fashion to wear a long pink dress with no back one season, and it may be the fashion to wear a blue short dress with a high back another season. The girl who has to appear in last year's gown will be regarded as having satisfied the conventions but she will be considered out of the running with respect to the demands of fashion.

Another characteristic distinguishing fashion from convention is fashion's unconcern with morality. There was a time when convention decreed it immoral to use cosmetics. Later convention allowed the use of rouge, if well concealed; now the rules have been lifted so that almost anything is tolerated. In 1919 an advertisement in the *Ladies' Home Journal* announced a rouge that was "imperceptible if properly applied"; in 1929 the same magazine carried an advertisement of a lipstick which assured readers, "It's comforting to know that the alluring note of scarlet will stay with you for hours." It may be fashionable at the moment to use scarlet lipstick or maroon lipstick or no lipstick; as far as being in fashion is concerned, there is no moral issue in the matter. Fashion is simply what people for the time being are doing, regardless of ethics.

There is one more characteristic of fashion that is distinctive—it is far more irrational than custom or convention. There is usually some pretty good reason for a custom or a convention. There are reasons for fashions, too, but they are not very good ones. Fashions are adopted whether or not they are beautiful or useful. Poiret, the French designer, used to say that there was no use in a woman's trying to hold out against a silly fashion because sooner or later she would have to capitulate to social pressure.

> "I will not wear the long skirts,"
> Cried angry Kitty Blue;
> "That is, I will not wear them
> Unless the others do."

The essential irrationality of fashion lies in the desire to do as others do, whether it is becoming to the individual or not. It is reasonable to assume that any given mode of dress which is designed for women in general will not be just the thing to bring out the best points of some woman in particular. Yet the individual will don a hat resembling a flower pot, if this type of hat happens to be the rage, even though it makes of her a ridiculous spectacle. As long as the article is fashionable, the individual seems satisfied. No further recommendations are necessary. To be in the swim is enough. The irrationality of following the dictates of fashion is expressed in this advertisement:

CHRISTMAS GIVING

has become the fashion. Fashion
is like love: one does not
explain it—one submits to it.

Love is blind; so is fashion.

The person who is a slave to fashion is inclined to feel that the current mode is here to stay since it is entirely satisfactory. The present vogue is the best. It is not seen as something passing in the perspective of time.

Some years ago an authority in this field made a dogmatic prediction: "Women will wear corsets; they always have and they always will. We may as well consider this a settled fact." [3] Yet corsets disappeared, though they returned in 1939. At that time Sophie Gimbel, buyer for Saks Fifth Avenue, predicted women would wear them, no matter how uncomfortable they found them. Maybe so, but of one thing we may generally be certain, that is, no popular mode is going to prevail as *the* fashion for very long, for Dame Fashion is a capricious creature, fickle in her loyalties, and flighty in her enthusiasms.

II. MANIFESTATIONS

The term *fashion* ordinarily connotes a mode of dress. It would be a mistake, however, to limit the concept to such a narrow range. There are fashions in clothes, snuffing or smoking, literature, religion, and psychology, just to mention a few areas in which fashionable behavior plays a role.

A. CLOTHES

Fashions in clothes change rapidly, especially in women's clothes. Seldom is a dress worn until it is worn out. Often it is discarded before there are any signs of wear, in favor of something new that is more up-to-date. Thus business is accelerated. Though the waste is

[3] Marion Harland.

appalling, there is some justification—clothes are made, purchasers put money into circulation, spirits are lifted by the pleasure of donning "positively the latest creation."

B. Snuffing and Smoking

During the 1920's one of the oldest snuff factories in the world, a Scottish concern, closed in surrender to the changing moods of fashion. A snuff tray used to be regarded as an indispensable accoutrement of a gentleman. On social occasions people took a pinch of snuff and inhaled it through the nose, performing the whole operation with elegant gestures. Then just as snuff was "going strong," men, and later, women, shifted to tobacco-smoking for solace, for poise, for a lift. No longer did man sniff through his nose; now the operation was reversed as man inhaled through the mouth and, if sufficiently rugged, exhaled through the nose, though most people inhale and exhale entirely through the oral aperture. Smoking, like taking snuff in the old days, is regarded in many quarters as a valued accessory to polite conversation. Cigars, so we are informed by the advertisements, may even be considered a mark of gentility. Certainly they are a sign of masculinity, along with the pipe, as women generally restrict their puffing to cigarettes. Since the lifting of the conventional taboos against women's smoking, after World War I, tobacco has really come into its own. It is now fashionable to smoke. Chewing tobacco, however, has not yet come into style among the elite who set the fashions. Chewing gum in public is likewise taboo in the best circles.

C. Literature

There are fashions, too, in literature. Essays, dime novels, debunking biographies, realistic depictions of war, short stories, long novels, free verse, psychoanalytic explorations into the unconscious, detective mysteries, sophisticated romances, realistic fiction dealing with sociological problems, success stories, historical novels, autobiographies, popularizations of science, journalistic reports of political conditions— all enjoy their moments in the spotlight of popularity. Long descriptions, snappy conversations, tabloid illustrations, character portraits are featured according to the mood prevailing at a given time. Fashions in writing change and it is a wise author who fits his style to the predominant whim, anticipating what readers are set to like at the moment. Writing must be timely to catch the public fancy, as we have already indicated in our study of "Public Acclaim" (Chapter 9).

D. RELIGION

Fashions in religion appear from time to time. During the summer of 1939 York Village, Maine, celebrated a "Day of Our Forefathers." One part of the program was a reenactment on Sunday of a church service held originally in 1710, in the course of which the pastor delivered a famous sermon entitled "The Doleful State of the Damned," once preached by the Reverend Moody in that distant past, some 229 years previous.

"Fire! Fire! Fire!" the Rev. Millinger shouted in Moody's sternest manner.

"Where?" the congregation responded.

"In hell! For sleeping sinners," the pastor concluded. . . .

Just as did the preacher 229 years ago, the Rev. Millinger interrupted his sermon to condemn the "ungodly strut" of the notorious Mme. Ingraham, this year portrayed by Mrs. Harold Kimball.

Before the church program began, the congregation was informed that although some of the incidents that were about to take place might seem humorous, they were distinctly otherwise two centuries ago and should not be taken lightly. Two visitors who ignored the warning were pushed from their pew by the tithing man and escorted to the choir loft where they sat in disgrace for the remainder of the service.[4]

The most significant thing about this historical occasion was the mirth produced by the old-fashioned Hell-and-Damnation sermon. In the old days preachers like Jonathan Edwards used to frighten their congregations with their vivid descriptions of the goings-on in Hades. Penitent listeners used to tremble in their pews. The modern generation takes such awful predictions as a joke. Times have changed.

A parade of outstanding religious fashions would include camp meeting revivals, tabernacle evangelism with the anxious seat and the sawdust trail and the spectacular conversions, Buchmanite hobnobbing with the upper crust for Moral Rearmament, concentration on the social gospel with theological students being arrested in the picket lines. At various times it becomes the fashion to argue about free will, predestination, and other theological abstrusities, to dwell on the prospective pleasantness of the future life, to be preoccupied with personal sin, to crusade against infidels, bartenders, or purveyors of dirty pictures, to attack the money changers in the temple, to promulgate the message of the Prince of Peace, to advocate a humanistic exclusion of

---

[4] The Boston *Herald,* August 21, 1939.

God and immortality in favor of a happy life here and now—just to mention a few of the shifting interests of religious people.

E. PSYCHOLOGY

Among the fashions in psychology that may be recognized in the historical procession are psychophysics, introspectionism, functionalism, psychoanalysis, behaviorism, configurationism, and operationism. At some time or other psychologists have devoted themselves chiefly to the mind-body problem, to sensory physiology, to conditioned reflexes, to intelligence testing, to mental hygiene, to social psychology. Psychology may be elementaristic, holistic, organismic, or personalistic, depending on the current rage. People are classified into types during one period, arranged on charts of individual differences during another. Today psychology is experimental and statistical, ultra-scientific, mechanistic, mechanical, mathematical, semantical, laboratorical, anti-metaphysical, anti-philosophical, anti-religious. It is the current style to talk a lot about "the whole individual in the whole situation." *Reflex arcs* are *passé,* S-R *bonds* are obsolete, *identical elements* are no longer identical, *mental faculties* have disappeared, and the *soul* has vanished into the limbo of ancient superstitions. People who studied psychology a generation ago would be lost in trying to orient themselves to the current lingo. Terminology has changed, interests have changed, psychologists have changed, as the fashions have come and gone. We have come a long way since man first peered into his psyche.

III. FASHION AND STYLE

In the matter of dress a fashionable woman will wear what "they're all wearing this season." Whether she happens to look attractive in a pair of modish sandals and in the longer skirts, seems to be of no concern to milady when she really is determined to be abreast the latest creations. Such is the folly of fashion, the irrationality of dressing like everybody else without regard for one's own odd size and shape.

Style is something very different. The woman who is guided by style in the selection of her clothes buys those which are designed to suit her particular build, with lines that give her individuality, that enable her to make the most of her own unique "personality." Since the stylish person is interested, too, in comfort, she dresses with the idea of adapting her apparel to each situation—shorts for tennis, slacks for golf, boots for hiking, skirts that allow freedom for housework, as the case may be. Her clothes are *functional* rather than fashionable: they make sense. And since they are chosen to enhance her special attrac tiveness, she will have the "nerve" to wear her clothes for several sea sons because they are good-looking, regardless of the changing fash ions. The individual whose aim is style does what is becoming to her; the fashionable person must do what "they're all doing." This dis tinction is a significant one whether we are dealing with women's clothes, men's clothes, going to college, choosing a vocation, or any other phase of our social behavior.

Addicts of fashion believe some mode is fashionable because the ads say that everyone is adopting it. Fashion decrees that your bag must match your shoes; that you can't wear last winter's coat, even though it is in excellent condition, because it has a belt and this year "we are not showing belts"; that you can't have a bathing suit with a brassière and separate pants because "we don't carry them any more"; that you can't buy a comfortable polo shirt like the one you wore out last year because "this summer it's shirts and slacks in combination."

According to the French legend, "All beautiful clothes are designed in France and all women want them." That fallacy haunted Eliza beth Hawes and inspired her to convince American women that beau tiful clothes could be conceived by American designers and produced by American manufacturers. She has been successful in undermining the French legend, though popular delusions of that sort are not easily destroyed once they have become firmly imbedded as traditions. The chief obstacle in the way of persuading American women in general to abandon fashion in favor of style, and thus to adopt modes of dress specially designed for American wearers, is the fact that American man ufacturers of mass-production clothes stubbornly refuse to recognize that good quality, usefulness, or beauty—the functional aspects of style—are of any real importance; instead they proceed on the assump tion that unless clothes change every few months there will be no profit So fashion rather than style has been the guiding *motif* among Ameri can women. Consequently, if Lady So-and-So is wearing lace to the races at Ascot, then women must be garbed in lace to go to work in Macy's basement and then to play at Coney Island; when fashion dic tates shorter skirts, then women must wear them, no matter how un shapely their legs.

Most women are either slightly knock-kneed or bow-legged. Most women' legs are either too fat or too skinny. Most women feel awkward in skirt that barely cover the knees. Yet this spring [1939] most women will be wearing daytime skirts that are 17 or 18 inches from the ground. They really have little choice in the matter.

Short, fluttering skirts have a girlish, youthful look. When skirts are going from short to long, failure to follow the trend may make a woman look unstylish, but it will not make her look older. But, when all the Bright Young Girls are wearing girlish-looking knee-length skirts, nothing adds years to a woman's general appearance as quickly as a long droopy skirt. . . .

Dread of most stylists and fashion-conscious women is that the new short skirts will bring with them ugly longer waistlines, as was the case in 1928.[5]

However ugly a fashion may be, there is nothing to be done about it except to yield gracefully.

It takes a certain amount of courage to defy the imperious dictates of fashion. There are some individuals who have the force of character to dress as they please. If a person with this sort of independent nature wants to wear her hat on top of her head, she does so; if she wants to wear a high collar when only low necks are being worn, she goes right ahead just the same with the high collar. There is more to style than just being an independent sort of person. In addition to courage, there must be an intelligent appreciation of the kind of clothes which will minimize the individual's liabilities, maximize her assets. Such an appreciation involves an understanding of aesthetic principles. Apparently the persons are rare who have the intelligence to grasp these principles and the patience to apply them in such a way as to produce the best effect. The woman who wants to achieve style must give considerable thought to her person, resisting the temptation to take the easier path of conforming to what's fashionable.

This question of having the "nerve" to do what's sensible despite the irrational dictates of fashion may be illustrated by the failure of women at various periods to respect the functional demands in clothing. An example is, the women (p. 542) who were trying to play tennis about the year 1903 wrapped in garments which covered them like a tent. Thus, it should not be difficult to understand why most people are more fashion-conscious than style-conscious—they lack the courage to dress functionally because they might shock somebody's moral sensibilities.

There are occasions when a style would be condemned because it is in "poor taste." For example, Elizabeth Hawes, on a visit to Boston during a heavy blizzard, was prompted by the occasion to denounce "the slaves of convention [she means fashion] who struggled to work in silk stockings, swirling skirts and inadequate hats. They should have worn ski pants, jackets and ski boots, and hats which would provide

[5] *Life,* February 27, 1939. As of the present, 1947, one must read this comment in reverse. However, read either way, it proves the point.

protection, not adornment.   It would have been completely practical."
Practical, yes—but not likely, for one basic reason: people who want to
enjoy a reputation for good taste do not go to the office in ski suits.

IV. CHANGE

Periodic change is a fundamental characteristic of fashion.   A large
number of people do something for a while, thus establishing a collective behavior pattern which is temporarily fashionable, then they
get tired of it and go on to something different, thus introducing a new
fashion which will, in turn, enjoy its day and pass on.   The extent of

1903   1947
(A.P. Photo at Right, Courtesy, Pauline Betz.)

these variations is not apparent until one takes time out to retrace the
evolution of the passing show.   Test yourself on the photograph on
page 543 by guessing the year in which women were outfitting themselves in these respective garbs.

The correct dates are 1929 and 1896.   How quaint, how preposterous the old-fashioned clothes seem to us as we look back on them
from our orientation in the present scheme of things.   It seems impossible that within the lifetime of some of us, people ever looked like the
1896 and 1929 ladies depicted.   It is equally difficult to realize that
our own present-day fashions will, in a few years, appear just as out-
of-date and just as unattractive.

A. Noticeable Shifts

We may rest assured that the designers, manufacturers, and retailers
will see to it that the shifts in fashion will be noticeable enough to

keep consumers buying new clothes from season to season lest they be humiliated by being obviously and shamefully behind the times. Occasionally one observes some person who is forced by economic hardship to continue wearing clothes that are long out-of-date; the pitiableness of such a tragic character, parading his outmoded garments for all the world to see, advertises the importance to one's self-esteem of keeping abreast of the times.

Fashion changes are generally manipulated by businessmen and

(Keystone Photo.)

women who are professionally interested in exploiting the vanity of the consumer public, a public that includes all of us whether or not we can afford to keep the pace that is set for us. Organized business interests tease the money from our pockets, "egg" us on in the pursuit of fashion. They are extremely clever in this art. One September the word was passed around that every fashionable woman had to wear an Empress Eugenie hat; as soon as all the old feathers had been sold, the reign of the Eugenie was over. One season the bob came in and all the ladies rushed to have their tresses sheared; the next season it was decreed that wigs were to be worn and the girls bought their hair back at fancy prices.

High-class American designers give their customers, every four months, not just new clothes, but new *fashions*. This four-month seasonal change is the regular policy of the designers and manufacturers who charge top prices for clothes, their clientele being limited to women whose aim in life is to dress fashionably; this short-term cycle does not apply to the millions of customers who patronize the ready-to-wear business. Five-year and ten-year cycles affect women of all classes, as these longer-term cycles involve changes in silhouette, transitions from long skirt to short skirt, and other alterations of a more dramatic nature. Transformations in silhouette are engineered, not by physical culture, but by resort to undergarments. Corsets were decreed in 1929, again in 1939, exactly ten years intervening. Both edicts emanated from Paris. During this ten-year interval, a significant revolution had occurred, which explains why the 1939 ukase on corsets failed to impress American women very profoundly. 1930 was the year which marked the beginning of the break from French domination. Until that year most American clothes had been adaptations of French models; since then the American fashion industry has assumed its own leadership. New York, center for American creations, democratized fashion by ending the exclusive, expensive foreign monopoly on clothes design. Hollywood, in its eagerness to exploit feminine beauty on the screen, inadvertently supplied the models and revolutionized American tastes and values. In many cases women no longer dressed to look smart; instead they dressed to look pretty, shifting their aim from *fashion* to *style*. Cinema stars insisted upon hats which would flatter their individual faces, in each case capitalizing on special personal assets.

Hollywood has never failed to recognize that one woman's clothes are another woman's poison. And because the stars of Hollywood represent a number of different feminine types—women of every shade of coloring and shape, wide-shouldered, narrow-shouldered, long-waisted, short-waisted, wide-hipped, narrow-hipped, short-legged, and long-legged—a woman movie-goer can see with her own eyes how a first-rate clothes designer would dress *her* face, *her* figure, and *her* kind of personality.[6]

College girls, too, are now influencing the trend of fashion. Stores, like Bonwit Teller, have even taken to asking customers what they want and seeing to it that they get it. Customers and designers are beginning to pool their ideas. All of these new trends, emerging since 1930, are bound to affect the rate of seasonal change in fashions. The old five-ten-year pattern may be a thing of the past.

When fashions change abruptly, as they often do, some industries are likely to suffer financially, as business is diverted into new chan-

[6] W. Raushenbush: "Fashion Goes American." *Harper's Magazine*, December, 1941.

nels. These unexpected shifts in the public fancy are a source of constant anxiety for those persons whose livelihood depends on anticipating consumer likes and dislikes. Lloyds of London will insure against weather, or war, or twins, but they draw the line against gambling on shifts in fashion, since the element of chance (ignorance) in this field has been so large, until recently at least, as to render prediction hazardous.

During the fall of 1938 it was announced in the press that the town of Leominster, Massachusetts, was being revived by the passing of the bob. The celluloid factories in Leominster had been practically idle since the coming of bobbed hair. In the autumn of 1938 a boom was occasioned by the new "off the neck coiffure" which was forcing American women to buy side combs. The newspaper account read:

The celluloid factories, which are the economic backbone of this city of 22,000 inhabitants, are busier now than for many months, and most of the orders are marked "rush!"

It seems that American women—especially those whose hair isn't quite long enough to coil up in neat piles on top of the head—can't find enough celluloid combs and hair pins to meet their needs.

During the past two months, several factories that have been shut down for years have reopened, and there is no sign yet of a slowing down in the rush of orders for back and side combs. Leominster once was a world leader in the manufacture of hair ornaments, many of which have been brought back into style by the new coiffure.

So acute has the demand for skilled help become that Mayor Bell has found it necessary to issue an edict concerning WPA workers who have refused jobs in factories. . . .

The sudden industrial upturn called back many elderly men from retirement. These men spent most of their lives in the comb-making trade and were needed because of their skill. Some of them said they owed their retirement to bobbed hair and their emergence from retirement to the new craze. . . . Just now the people of Leominster are showing considerable enthusiasm for the new hair styles and hope they will last.[7]

Of course this trend could not last long, for there is only one thing that we can all count on in this realm of caprice—and that is flux. Always there will be flux.

Hatmakers have their headaches, too. College students are charged with at least partial responsibility for the vogue of going without hats of any sort. This is a popular practice at many colleges and boys' schools, and has spread thence to older people, as did the academic

[7] The Boston *Herald*, September 16, 1938.

vogue of wearing arctics flapping and unbuckled. Clothing advertisers have helped to popularize the vogue by picturing sturdy young men, with firm chins and resolute eyes—*hatless*. The young man standing in a lordly way by the automobile door, the young man gracefully relieving the girl of her racquet case, the young man helping the lady into a canoe—all these Apollos are without hats. So the hat manufacturers complained to the clothing advertisers. They said that the normal correspondence between the volume of men's clothes sold and the number of hats absorbed by the market was being disturbed, to the detriment of the hat industry. The hatless fad, in fact, caused a drop in the manufacture of hats of some 1,020,000 in one season, and thus constituted a threat to the workers employed in hat factories. The New England representative of the United Hatters of North America rose in meeting to deplore any fad that injures business and to urge the support of labor and its friends in frowning on the "hatless fad." [8] Milliners were worried, too, in 1941.

HATLESS TREND PUZZLES HATTERS

Do you always wear a hat on the street?

If you don't, you're part of the hatless trend, and the cause of sleepless nights for milliners. This trend has cut into millinery sales. In the New York area, where 70 per cent of the women's hats are manufactured, milliners say 750,000 fewer hats were sold from January through April than in the same period last year.

They're taking steps. The Millinery Stabilization committee, to which most of them belong, has set up a bureau to find the cause of the hatless trend and to combat it.

Why don't you wear a hat when you should, they'd like to know? Is it because a hat would spoil your front curls? Because hats are uncomfortable? Does the back elastic bind? The thing won't stay on in the wind? Or are most hats too hard to wear? Unbecoming? Too full of flowers? Too silly?

The milliners are doing something about every one of these queries. Also they've enlisted the support of movie producers and college boys. They say the movie people promise to make film stars wear hats more often. College boys are writing pro-hat editorials in campus newspapers, saying, "Men don't like hatless women. We are starting a girlcott against girls who boycott hats."

Nobody knows how the hatless trend started. But the college girl is a prime offender. When she does wear a hat, she chooses inexpensive little stuck-on-the-back-of-the-head numbers, calots or beanies, or for dress-up, Juliet caps.[9]

[8] The Boston *Herald*, July 7, 1930.
[9] The Boston *Herald*, February 10, 1941.

In the field of dress, fashions tend toward extravagance, that is, they tend to go to extremes. The psychological reason for this tendency is that the senses become negatively adapted to innovations, thus making it necessary for a person to exaggerate his differences in order to renew the impression of distinction. About the time men get so habituated to short skirts that they no longer take special notice of feminine limbs and before moral crusades can get organized to attack immodesty, skirts go long again. Hurlock points out that fashions are likely to go to ex-

The Circle of Fashion.   (Strube, in the London *Daily Express*.)

tremes of immodesty after wars, since the shortage of men compels individual women to shine if they want to attract a man. After the long foreign wars fought by Athens in ancient times, the state decreed that all women should split their tunics from the hips down.[10] Clothes, or the lack of them, are thus exploited for sexual competition.[11]

B. CYCLES

Changes in fashion follow a rhythmical pattern. Fashions come, go, and come back again.

Charting the fashions began in a professional way about 1919. Previous to this statistical recording of fashion changes, "stores were stocked thoroughly twice a year; depleted lines were replenished as

[10] See E. B. Hurlock: *The Psychology of Dress*, p. 218. The Ronald Press Company, 1929.
[11] See K. Dunlap: "The Development and Function of Clothing." *Journal of General Psychology*, 1928, 1, 64-78.

circumstances dictated, but generally at haphazard. There was no careful system of advance information to prepare a merchant for a developing new fashion or to warn him that an established one was on the wane. . . . Fashion was regarded as a whimsical jade. Sometimes one guessed right, sometimes wrong." [12]   Tables of figures and graphs, interpreted by the expert analyst, now help to guide the merchandizer in anticipating the market for a given fashion.   Investigation shows that changes in fashion, far from being whimsical as popularly supposed, follow a regular pattern, moving slowly and in cycles.

The buyer of women's apparel today goes into the market with his merchandise control sheet in one hand, telling him how many garments to buy and how much to pay for each, and in the other his chart of colors, styles, and proportion of each, provided by the fashion director.   When the manufacturer, too, has been advised by, and has cooperated with his own analyst, he offers what the buyer knows women will take.   The result is a gratifying increase of profit and decrease of loss all along the line.   Stories of expensive left-overs unsalable because the style was wrong are becoming scarcer.   Manufacturers saved from investing in thousands of yards of unneeded material because they had accurate information of skirt and coat length fill the air with their grateful praise.   The hit-or-miss storekeeper of the old type who prospered in spite of his disorderly and illogical methods . . . [is] fast surrendering to the facts-and-figures school of bright young men and women . . . who are raising merchandising to the dignity of a profession and proving that the scientific spirit is the Waterloo of waste, whether it be in manufacturing automobiles, hats, or shoes.[13]

The fashion analyst has reduced the hazard of merchandising by revolutionizing the philosophy behind the manufacturing and selling of clothes.   The old-time promoter was given the assignment of pushing the sales for a particular fashion already in production; the modern analyst looks for the answer to the people themselves, records what representative individuals are wearing and have been wearing over a period of time, then predicts what is coming.

The purpose of the fashion director is not to show the store how to sell what the manufacturer has made, but rather to show the store how to buy what the public will demand. . . .   And the public will demand, all history goes to show, what it has demanded, but with modifications, alterations, and new embellishments.   If women wear ultra-feminine things as they did in

[12] K. Casey and C. Sullivan: "Charting the Fashions." *Atlantic Monthly,* June, 1930.
[13] *Ibid.*

1921, they will go through seasons of simplified semi-masculine modes before they again demand and accept the ruffles and laces as they began to do in 1929.[14]

The spring of 1939 brought the return of the frilly lingerie blouse after a lapse of ten years. Blouse manufacturers who had been through many lean years welcomed the chance to turn out models with frills, jabots, zippers, ruffles, and lace (as much as 90 yards of ruffled lace in just one blouse).

Market analysis demonstrates that history thus repeats itself regularly, that the old may in time be old enough to be new again.

College boys, eschewing the to them slightly ridiculous tail coat, used to come to dinner in the shorter Tuxedo, and their elders and betters, dazzled by the glamour of youth, fell into line. For some years, conservative hostesses, with an appreciative eye to the formalities, deplored the fact that you couldn't get a man under ninety into anything but a dinner coat. Then the college boys, seeking change, discovered the delights of dressing up in tail coat and "topper" even as their sisters, short-skirted and bob-haired since childhood, derived a costume-party thrill from the first drooping long skirts. Last winter (1929) we saw the dignified man of middle age once more enduring the portly grace of formal attire.[15]

This same sort of revival occurs in the realm of popular music, notably in the case of *Oh Johnny, Oh Johnny, Oh!* which was a hit in 1917, a bigger hit when Bonny Baker recorded it with Orrin Tucker's band in 1939. Sales of the reincarnation exceeded those in 1917 largely because of the fad of the juke-box which in itself helped to bring the recording industry, long in a slump, back to life again.[16]

Kroeber measured evening dress illustrations in style journals from 1844 to 1919. Skirts were long until 1875 when they reached the ground, then shortened till 1887, lengthened till 1899, stayed long till about 1910, then shortened rapidly to an unprecedented degree. The complete cycle, he found, takes about 35 years.[17]

It has been observed that skirt lengths are influenced by economic conditions—they go up in times of prosperity and down in depression periods; or as Mayor McNair of Pittsburgh put it, business fluctuates with the length of women's skirts. No explanation has been offered to account for this concomitant variation. Whether the two phenomena

[14] *Ibid.*　　[15] *Ibid.*　　[16] *Time,* January 15, 1940.
[17] See A. L. Kroeber: "On the Principle of Order in Civilization as Exemplified by Changes in Fashion." *American Anthropologist,* 1919, New Series 21, 235-263.

are causally related or not, remains to be investigated. Both run in cycles, at any rate. "Short skirts run in cycles like sunspots and depressions," was the comment of Beatrice Mathieu, noted Paris style reporter. "There is a theory," she added, "that women must have a certain percentage of their bodies exposed—say 15 per cent." She would not say, and neither can we, whether prosperity brings on short skirts or short skirts presage good times. She did feel that short skirts will recur periodically, even though many women would wish it were otherwise. The cycle appears to be inevitable.

C. PRESTIGE

We have described the role of prestige in suggestion in Chapters 7 and 9. It will answer our purpose here if we consider just a few examples to show how prestige functions in the realm of fashions.

A person who has sufficient prestige can attract imitators, however eccentric he may be. When the wife of Charles VI put on a two-horned headdress, the women of the time vied with each other as to who should wear the most handsome headgear peaked like a steeple, and the tallest horns. The Paris Opera House burned down in 1760, and feminine Paris would hear of nothing in coiffures save the "burnt opera-house" variety. A firebrand thrown at Francis I during a game compelled the king to wear his hair short, and all France copied the fashion. The daughters of Louis XI wore long skirts to hide their misshapen feet and legs, and the ladies of France, no matter how shapely their feet and legs, followed suit. Madame de Montespan adopted the hoop skirt to conceal defects caused by an accident and in no time at all the hoop was the rage. Queen Elizabeth wore a high neck ruff to cover up a long, thin, ugly neck and the high neck ruff made its appearance far and wide. Henry VIII was corpulent, so his courtiers stuffed their suits to spare the king any embarrassment.[18] Edward VII was so plump he had to leave his bottom waistcoat button open in order to be comfortable. A variation of this sloppy habit was the collegiate practice of leaving the bottom button on the suit coat unfastened, a fashion that was adhered to by many undergraduates, fat or thin.

Tricks of prestige are used to exploit the public. A store is called a "Shoppe" instead of a shop. The woman who runs it is a "Mademoiselle." If her name is Helen, it appears as Hélène; if Mary, Marie. The sign in front is void of capital letters: it reads *"marie's shoppe."* The clothes come from Deauville, never from Hoboken. The clothes

[18] See Hurlock: *op. cit.,* p. 104.

are *chic* and they are shown in a *salon*. Beautiful models called manikins, or more stylishly *mannequins,* parade the clothes in graceful struts before prospective customers who are deceived into thinking they will look just as alluring in the same gowns.

Royalty is very effective in establishing a fashion. The former Prince of Wales was instrumental in popularizing colored shirts with collars to match, wide trousers, soft hats, scarfs of regimental colors, and gray-blue suits. His marriage to Wally Simpson was the talk of the world; by late June, 1937, less than three weeks after the wedding, women in America were wearing daytime versions of the Duchess of Windsor's wedding dress. It was first sold to only one shop in a city, and retailed at $25-$29. By mid-July Wally's dress had become the general fashion, retailing everywhere for $8.90.

Other sources of prestige are the smart set, the movie stars, and the collegians. Debutantes, sub-debs, post-debs, and social registerites in general lead the way.

The movies are very significant in establishing fashion trends. Clark Gable bared his undershirtless chest in *It Happened One Night* and underwear sales dropped so seriously that manufacturers went to the motion-picture producers to demand the scene be deleted. What the movie actresses wear today, a million stenographers, teachers, shopgirls and dairymaids will wear tomorrow. Not only is Hollywood the arbiter on clothes, but its dicta on hairdressing, housefurnishings, diction, and even etiquette are religiously followed by slaves of the screen. The stenographer who beautifies herself against the daily grind of the office, may be asking her roommate, "How shall I make my eyebrows today, like Betty Grable's or Greer Garson's?" Fashions there have always been, but only within the past few years have they been popularized almost simultaneously throughout the world. In the old days fashions moved sedately across the Atlantic to New York, then to the other large cities, and finally to the small towns and villages. Sometimes it took a year for the latest Paris creation to penetrate the hinterland, and there was plenty of time for manufacturers of women's clothes to keep abreast of the demand. But now Lauren Bacall displays a gown on the screens of New York and a thousand hamlets at the same moment, and overnight a new fashion is born and in a few months it is dead—everywhere. Just one more reason for gray hairs on businessmen's heads!

It was Hollywood, too, that popularized tap-dancing. A report issued in 1935 stated that dance schools were being deluged with youngsters wanting to learn tap-dancing. The economic depression had ended for dance teachers when the public took a fancy to the Ginger Rogers-Fred Astaire combination. A manufacturer of the little metal taps that go on the soles of dancing-shoes reported a 280 per cent rise in his business in 1934, a 400 per cent increase in 1935. Astaire, more than any other star, was credited with popularizing white tie and tail coat for men's evening wear, after years of dinner coats and black ties. Collegians are playing an increasing role as fashion leaders.

No one in America is more responsible for setting styles at sporty summer resorts than the Eastern college girl. . . . When college closes in the middle of June, the fashions and fads which she initiated during the year are being copied by high-school girls and vacationists all over the country. . . . Because she is an important fashion force, smart department stores have their own "College Shops." Fashion magazines make extensive surveys of her wardrobe. Manufacturers stay awake nights creating gadgets to introduce as "College Fads." But the fads which your college girl really adopts are her own innovations. Because her dress is so standardized, her fads are mostly in collars, socks, shoes, hair-dos. College-introduced fashions still worn extensively are Brooks sweaters, reversible raincoats, peasant scarfs, and saddle shoes.[19]

D. Fashion Racing

Fashion racing was mentioned in the discussion of "Suggestion and Imitation" in Chapter 7. It merits further consideration in the present context.

Fashion racing or "getting ahead of the Joneses" is especially prevalent in a democratic society where social mobility prevails. An American visitor to England made a significant comment on his return to the United States: "What I like about England is that people stay in their own class in that country." [20] Such is not the case here where the "log-cabin-to-White-House" legend is a precious tradition. In keeping with this spirit of rising from the ranks, we find maids who aspire to be nurses or school teachers, stenographers who want to be lawyers, clerks who take correspondence courses in order to become executives, dullards plowing through five-foot shelves to acquire culture. In a sense these ambitions are all laudable. Nevertheless, such lofty aspirations may keep the pluggers dissatisfied, inspire strivings often out of proportion to native endowments, make for restlessness and in-

[19] *Life*, June 26, 1939.
[20] R. Le C. Phillips: "Getting Ahead of the Joneses." *Harper's Magazine*, April, 1927.

security. With so many people bent on improving their status, the social order is bound to be unstable.

The real tragedy in all this competition, however, lies in the fact that so much of the racing is dominated by the desire to prove one's superiority by superficial signs such as expensive automobiles and "bigger and better" possessions in general. Here is a real-estate advertisement aimed to appeal to the social climber:

Georgian design with spacious rooms characterizes this fine colonial home; the generous living room is full paneled in figured walnut, fireplace of Oak Bark brick, open porch with colonial spans, library in country pine, tiled lavatory, dining room full paneled in African mahogany, glassed breakfast room, real pantry and splendid tiled kitchen with Chambers gas range; rear porch; two maids' rooms and bath entirely separate; six masters' chambers and three baths with separate dressing room and nursery, fireplace in master's bedroom, covered radiators, inlaid floors; awnings; colonial spiral staircase; three-car garage; basement finished play-room with third fireplace; gas-fired hot water heater. Buy this home and your social standing will be assured.[21]

Every suburban community is peopled with climbers who race by means of air conditioning appliances, basement playrooms, shrubs, window boxes, awnings, and bridge-club prizes.

The battle for supremacy among the plain people of the middle class is mild in comparison with the struggle that goes on in high society where a rating system helps keep the peace among the contestants. An insider explains how it works:

The seating of just ordinary society people at a dinner, easy in Washington where high sounding titles abound, is done most successfully in New York on the point possession system.

Mrs. Jones may get 10 points for a yacht while Mrs. Smith has nine points for a country home. Then, each will have points for motors, art possessions, or maybe Pekingese pillow hounds.

You add them up and maybe Mrs. Smith wins by a yacht or Mrs. Jones by a Rembrandt.[22]

Clothing is one of the most obvious marks of class distinction. In the seventeenth century the length of the train (on a dress) denoted the rank of the wearer. In the eighteenth century it was the headdress. The headgear was so bulky that ladies had to sleep upright and heads

---

[21] Boston *Sunday Herald*, September 14, 1930.
[22] Boston *Herald*, November 12, 1931.

had to be "opened" once a month to clean out the vermin nesting among the tresses. One headdress known as the "macaroni head" made it necessary to remove the top from a carriage when a lady went out for a ride.[23] An old drawing depicts a man on top of a stepladder curling the hair of a lady seated in a chair beneath him.[24] An amusing contrast to all this folderol is the custom among the Balonde Negroes of recognizing the absence of clothing as the characteristic mark of the slave.

(Courtesy, Francis Dahl and the Boston *Herald*.)

Among many of the African tribes, the subjects may approach the king, only if they are naked. When the queen of the Balonde Negroes received a call from Livingstone, she paid him the highest honor possible, by appearing in a state of complete nudity. The Australian [aborigines] require their women to remove their clothing on festival occasions as a sign of their inferiority.[25]

Status is recognized even among the aborigines, but how much simpler are the earmarks of social station!

[23] A drawing of this absurdity is reproduced in E. B. Hurlock: *The Psychology of Dress*, p. 106. Copyright, 1929, The Ronald Press Company.

[24] See G. W. Rhead: *Chats on Costume*, p. 260. 1906. Reproduced in Hurlock: *op. cit.*, p. 153.

[25] Hurlock: *op. cit.*, p. 31.

In modern America a man's social standing can be read from the clothes he wears, perhaps even more readily than in the case of his wife because fewer men than women bother to verse themselves in the fine points of correct attire.   Feeling that men should give some serious attention to their attire, Dorothy Stote wrote *Men Too Wear Clothes* (1939) to guide the poor, hapless menfolks.   Men need help.   For example, it is painfully obvious that the fellow depicted in this drawing doesn't know his way around.   The average man is apt to be

Waistcoat Showing beneath Front of Tail Coat Is Appalling. (Illustration by Nina Granada from *Men Too Wear Clothes,* by Dorothy Stote. Courtesy, J. B. Lippincott Company, Publishers.)

grossly ignorant concerning "what to wear when."   How many men (gentlemen) could tell in detail just what is expected in the way of attire at formal and semi-formal day affairs—weddings, ceremonies, etc.?   Among the specifications we note certain kinds of waistcoat and cravat—to ordinary men, vest and necktie.   Language, too, marks a difference.

It is apparent that ordinary men lack the time or energy to become informed on all these fine points.   The ordinary man goes to a sale to get a hat, sees one he takes a fancy to, says promptly, "I'll take that," and dismisses the matter from his mind.   He doesn't know whether he has acquired a Homburg or not. He wouldn't know one if he saw one. And he'll wear his one hat on all occasions, regardless of what's called for. A gentleman, by way of contrast, is that rare man who is properly attired. Of course, a gentleman must have money in order to acquire the proper wardrobe, and that's where money plays its part again in denoting social rank. Clothes tell the story because it takes money to dress correctly. Six thousand dollars a year is the budget necessary to provide the minimum wardrobe. The well-dressed man, on the authority of the Merchant Tailors Designers' Association, would have to own nineteen outfits, including: six business suits, divided among blue, gray and brown—two double-breasted, four single-breasted; one sports suit; informal walking suit; cutaway, host jacket, dinner and full dress suits; three topcoats; one overcoat; a Guard's coat, riding and yachting suits.

Fashionable people who advertise their class by their clothes are just naturally averse to nudism because nakedness would promote social anarchy. This thought is well expressed in an editorial which appeared in the *Nation:*

KEEP YOUR SHIRT ON

Fashion leaders, school principals, beach censors, and the like continue to be agitated over the question of bodily exposure. The conservatives appear to be fighting a losing battle and we confess that we take no more than an intellectual interest in their problems, but we are tired of hearing it said by liberals that the question is one of aesthetics rather than morals. We do not deny that some legs are more ornamental than others; we do not wish to maintain that beauty has nothing to do with the matter; but we do insist that both the moralists and the aestheticians take a superficial view of the subject. It belongs to the realm of political economy, and we propose, if our readers will bear with us, to give a brief outline of our Philosophy of Clothes.

Men and women are distinguished in various ways: some are rich, some are famous, some are well-born, and some are beautiful. Naturally each person prefers that form of society in which his particular excellence counts for most and naturally, therefore, the rich do all they can to promote the development of a plutocracy while the well-born look with favor upon every custom which tends to emphasize the importance of birth. But physical comeliness, the most immediately apparent of all the possible forms of human excellence, is not the necessary concomitant of any other. Let the millionaire, the philosopher, and the social leader descend to the beach, and they will discover that the social scale has been inverted in the twinkling of any eye. Here their various distinctions count for nothing. All eyes are turned toward the young Apollo who licks stamps for the millionaire and the young Venus who sold

Madam that *costume de bain* which, alas, for all its chic, does not contribute enough to the total effect to compensate for her more striking inferiorities. Let her be dressed in her official uniform, give her her pearls and an evening gown which covers as much as it can without confessing a timidity, and she is at least in a position to assert in audible terms her claims to consideration. But on the beach competition is brutally simple and the little salesgirl wins an overwhelming victory. . . .[26]

Fashion racing has been expedited by technological improvements and by installment buying. The Lynds found that a rising standard of living, accelerated by technological advances, intensified the struggle for status in Middletown. Formerly, nobody had running hot and cold water; there were no class distinctions in the matter of plumbing. When some privileged people first installed running water, others soon followed suit, and this same competition was aggravated all along the line. A small down payment, so much a month, encouraged people to live beyond their means. One resident testified, "Most of the families I know are after the same things today that they were after before the depression, and they'll get them the same way—on credit." [27] Years ago only well-to-do persons could afford silk stockings. Common people had to be content with cotton hose. Now that the new processes for producing artificial silk are making it possible for women of all classes to wear "silk" stockings, one more class distinction is being destroyed. The newest creations in the chic salons of Paris do not remain exclusive very long, for, as Elizabeth Hawes explains, professional visitors at first showings copy the patterns and relay them to America, where they are immediately reproduced on a mass scale.[28] The Paris modes are cheapened in the process, so that milady of the upper class has a difficult time keeping ahead of the working girl. Rapid transportation, efficient manufacturing processes, the larger number of young women earning money to spend on clothes, all facilitate fashion racing to an unprecedented degree. The wise lady of the upper crust takes Elizabeth Hawes' advice, abandons the hectic pursuit of fashion, and goes in for style, instead.

Two motives are responsible, among others, for fashion racing: the desire for individuation and the desire for conformity. The leaders of fashion, who are recruited from the wealthy and the social elite, are busy thinking up new ways of impressing others with their distinction.

---

[26] The *Nation*, September 25, 1929.
[27] R. S. Lynd and H. M. Lynd: *Middletown in Transition*, p. 203. Harcourt, Brace and Company, 1937.
[28] See Hawes: *op. cit.*, Chapter 4, "Copying, a Fancy Name."

Their innovations seep down to the lower classes where the common run of people are persistently eager to imitate what's being done by "the best people."　Most people have neither the money nor the time to set the pace; they are content to follow the leaders, motivated by the conviction that "one might as well be out of the world as out of fashion."　Most of us are conformers; our efforts are directed toward catching up with the brave souls who lead the way.　We see to it that the innovators do not maintain their distinctiveness any longer than we can help.　We conformists keep pushing the leaders all the time to invent new means of demonstrating their superiority.　In our democratic society the race never lets up because of the incessant urge on the part of each individual to improve his status by being fashionable and up-to-the-minute.

V. SEX DIFFERENCES

Most of our discussion of fashion has dealt with the subject from the feminine angle.　That is as it should be, especially where the psychology of clothes is concerned.　It would be a mistake, however, to assume that men are indifferent to the imperious dictates of fashion. Men, like women, want to be fashionable, in their own way, of course, and probably to a lesser degree.　Women have more time to think about clothes and they realize more than men do how important it is to dress attractively.　Indeed it is said that "a man needs a woman" to pick out his ties and to tidy him up generally.　Men have their ideas, too, as to how women should "deck themselves out" but men are inhibited when it comes right down to expressing their opinions in a verbal manner.　Masculine influence is exerted indirectly by virtue of the fact that men concentrate their attentions upon certain women who excel in garbing themselves becomingly.　Men naturally feel that the fundamental function of clothes, so far as women are concerned, is to aid in attracting a mate.　Women will deny this fatuous assumption.　Says Elizabeth Hurlock: "That modern dress has as its basis the desire to attract the opposite sex is questionable.　Few women dress for the sole purpose of attracting men.　Sensual appeal through the agency of physical appeal is too crude to be employed by any except the common harlot." [29]　Few men would endorse this "theory."

Sex display is, according to Hurlock, a minor motive in feminine psychology.　Women obviously dress for other women's eyes, she insists, vying with one another principally to see who can stand out most effectively from the group.　"The most important role that the av-

[29] Hurlock: *op. cit.,* p. 126.

erage man plays in determining the dress of women is to encourage the feminine members of the family to outdress the feminine members of another man's family." [30]   Undoubtedly this motive does operate in some cases; whether it is the most important role that man plays in the situation is certainly debatable; even more questionable is Hurlock's final dictum that "fashion is largely a battle within the sexes rather than between the sexes." [31]   Why, we may ask, are women or men engaging in such a battle? Hurlock does not probe deeply enough in her search for fundamental motivations. Why do women want to outshine each other? What are they after? What are the goals, conscious or unconscious, that spur them on? The answers to these questions await extensive research in this field. One principle should guide us in seeking light on the motives which are operating: behavior in any given situation is probably actuated by a number of motives; to look for "the one motive" or to try to reduce the explanation to a single formula, is likely to result in oversimplification. We dress for many reasons: to keep warm, to keep cool, to conceal physical defects, to enhance our beauty, to display our wealth, to attract the opposite sex, to bolster our morale, to avoid social disapproval, and to avoid getting locked up for indecent exposure.

Each sex has its own peculiar problems to worry about in trying to stay "in the swim."   Several years ago a congress of French hairdressers opened with a "pageant of the centuries" during which the caprices of fashion passed in historical review. After these opening ceremonies, a resolution was adopted to "curb the anarchy introduced by bobbed hair." It was decreed that "no woman henceforth is to have her hair bobbed. . . . Those who have been bobbed shall adopt through the intermediate period of the return to normalcy one of three approved styles—the Directoire, the Louis Philippe, or the Empress Eugenie."

Men cannot afford to laugh too hard at women's follies. Look back no more than a few centuries and you find the sterner sex curling their *chevelure,* manipulating it with crisping irons and hanging it with ribbons; sometimes it was "dressed like a crescent moon or twisted into the form of a pyramid."   In the days of the Cavalier under Charles II, a man's hair flowed out in long and luxuriant curls, to descend upon his back and shoulders in heavy masses. During the reign of George II there were wigs to mark every kind of professional and occupational activity—the "bob wig," major and minor; the "prentice minor bob," close and short; the "citizen's bob major" or "Sunday buckle";

[30] *Ibid.,* p. 42.
[31] *Ibid.,* p. 43.

the "flat top" wig of the university student; the "short-cut bob" for the country gentleman; the "tail-wig," for use in the militia; "bag-wigs" for doctors; and "tie-wigs" for lawyers. Nor have the men failed to bob their hair on occasion. It was a fad at the court of Louis XIV, and as "Dutch cut" it became the fashion among the courtiers of James I. Periwigs, curled darlings, roundheads, pompadours, provide only the barest glimpses of masculine madness.

It is proverbial that women change their minds. Through several decades of the seventeenth century the great ladies of Europe sought by artificial means to achieve gray hair. Now women will dye their locks to get rid of gray wisps on the edges. Men are apt to change their minds, too. Englishmen shaved clean for two centuries and then suddenly began to raise whiskers. Beards are rare today.

Fashions for women and fashions for men are two distinct propositions. Clothiers have to figure out how to induce women to wear more clothes, men to wear more kinds of clothes. Women, they admit, would not wear more clothes unless it were the fashion to do so. Men need to be impressed with the importance of being appropriately dressed for different occasions, the clothiers tell us. Of course this appeal could influence only those men who could afford to buy the requisite number of suits, but even among those persons, it is regretted, "informality of dress appears to have become somewhat of a fixed habit."

Women have a way, even when fashion reigns supreme, of being themselves. Arnold Bennett once remarked that "women show much wider originality and varieties in attire than men do among themselves. Half a dozen average well-dressed women will be as different from one another as half a dozen flowers of different species; you can distinguish them half a mile off." Women quoted this statement of Bennett's when Mussolini decreed a national dress as the standard garment for all the women of Italy. One fashion expert was led to exclaim: "There are as many styles and fashions as there are women. What is the use of being a woman if you cannot dress as you like. Always to wear a standard dress! Only a man would suggest it."

One reason women are more devoted to fashion is that they enjoy far more freedom than men in following their whims. During World War II the girls were wearing their fathers' and brothers' old shirts and they even had the nerve to leave the shirttails outside their dungarees. Can you imagine boys donning their mothers' old clothes, even under the pressure of war shortages?

Men, in general, are very conservative about their clothes. They have avoided colors ever since Beau Brummell established the tradition of dark clothes.[32]   He defied the fashions prevailing in his time, wore his hair short, without powder.   Avoiding bright colors, this famous dandy distinguished himself by the meticulous neatness and superb fit of his garments.   His typical costume was a dark blue or black

The White Man's Burden.   (Courtesy, Jay N. Darling
and the New York *Herald Tribune* Syndicate.)

coat, a buff-colored waistcoat, and black close-fitting trousers.   Brummell's influence is especially evident in evening clothes—tuxedos and dress suits.   Before Brummell's time men had been wearing lavender breeches, silver waistcoats, and wine-colored coats.   Man's only chance

[32] See L. Eichler: *The Customs of Mankind*, p. 524.   1924.   See also Stote: *op. cit.*, p. 69.

for color today is in neckties and lodge uniforms, and most men are very sober and solemn in their choice of neckties.

Elizabeth Hawes was puzzled by the fact that Frank Lloyd Wright, modern architect, appeared for a lecture on "Functional Design in Housing," dressed in a stiff shirt and black tuxedo. While he was talking, his shirt kept cracking and rising out of his vest. Why, Miss Hawes wondered, doesn't he apply his philosophy of functional design to his clothes? She turned to a man sitting near her who was trying to stretch his collar by wiggling his fingers inside of it, and asked if he was comfortable. "Yes," he replied churlishly, "there's nothing wrong with these clothes." Miss Hawes was not at all convinced; her curiosity was aroused. A little research revealed that men could be more comfortable in hot weather by taking their coats off. Why do they wear coats, anyhow? she pondered. Why do they wear belts when suspenders are more comfortable? Why do they wear narrow suspenders that wrinkle shirts and produce ridges in the flesh of their shoulders? Why do they have clips on the ends of their braces when they know the clips tear their trousers? Why do they choke themselves with collars and neckties? Why do they wear broadcloth shirts—90 per cent of shirts are made of broadcloth—when broadcloth is the most uncomfortable material that could be worn, being very nonporous? Why do they wear heavy shoes designed for tramping on cobblestones, instead of airy sandals? All of these questions puzzled Miss Hawes. She decided to do something about the beaten-down, overrestricted, overheated male. She drew some designs for the *American Magazine* and she persuaded a few brave souls to wear her tunics and silk trousers at a demonstration party, in 1935. No revolution resulted in men's clothes, however, though it is noteworthy that Elizabeth Hawes did continue her campaign long enough to win for men some comfort and some color, in the slack suit which was widely adopted for sportswear in 1939. Loose trousers with a shirt to match—it was a complete outfit. The shirt could be worn inside or outside the pants. It was worn open at the neck, without a necktie or vest or coat, even without underwear if so desired. The trouser crease—a piece of nonsense that costs the gentlemen of America thousands of dollars annually—was relinquished. The slack outfit was a colored suit—rust, blue, green. Men wore them without feeling too conspicuous. Hawes was hopeful: "Before long, in spite of their wives, in spite of fashion magazines, in spite of tradition, I think all the boys are coming to town in slack suits." [33] It would certainly be a new day if dignified men could sum-

[33] E. Hawes: *Men Can Take It*. 1939.

mon the courage to go to their offices in slack suits, and be comfortable.

VI. FADS AND CRAZES

A fad or craze is a fashion that flourishes intensely for a short time. People get "all excited" about some stunning novelty which has caught their fancy. Enthusiasm for the innovation becomes the rage and emotional excitement often approximates the madness suggestive of crowd behavior. A point of satiation is reached within a comparatively short time; people get bored with the novelty, and interest is focused on the next thing that's new.

The time element is an important criterion of fads. Fads do not last long. Fashions are temporary interests, too, but the life of a fashion is considerably longer than that of a fad. Since there are no exact time limits with reference to which an accurate classification can be made, the decision as to whether a given uniformity of behavior should be called a fashion or a fad is an arbitrary one.

Fads are interests which win adherents, rage for a while, die out, and may return again—like musical comedies, bicycling, knitting, and ping pong. Fads come and go because the public must have something constantly new, something different to revive waning interests.

The spirit of an age is expressed through the evanescent interests that impart to humdrum existence the spice of variety. As we survey the fad parade, we observe that dominant themes, each with variations, monopolize the public fancy.

Numerous fads of our era center about the theme of physical prowess. The endurance contest is a favorite device for demonstrating the ability to "take it." Flagpole sitting, tree sitting, rocking-chair rocking, six-day bicycle racing, and marathon dancing have tested the stamina of persevering contestants. Closely related is the competition to determine who can eat the most clams at one sitting, the most eggs, the most hot dogs, the most live goldfish. After goldfish-gulping had reached the maximum, reckless collegians, according to reports, proceeded to swallow worms, magazines, snakes, footballs, gunpowder, and phonograph records.[34] Daily the morning papers announced new champions in the several lines of competition. Coffee drinking, cigarette smoking, and going without sleep offered other marathoners satisfying outlets for their exhibitionism.

Health devotees, many of them hypochondriacs, have resorted to all manner of follies in their eagerness to gain abounding vitality. One

[34] See *Time*, April 10, 1939, and April 24, 1939.

famous dietary cultist was Dr. James H. Salisbury, who proclaimed in the middle of the nineteenth century that a rational diet should consist of one mouthful of food from the vegetable kingdom to two mouthfuls from the animal kingdom. His cure-all diet specified goodly quantities of lean meat and hot water. He made a fetish of chopped meat, a delicacy that has been named in his honor, "Salisbury steak."

Remember the Fad? (Photograph by Cory Snow.)

Another discovery was the sour-milk diet espoused by Metchnikoff, who got the idea from octogenarians and nonagenarians who attributed their long life to a bountiful consumption of sour milk, some of them consuming as much as three gallons a day.

In the early twentieth century the fad was Fletcherism, a doctrine that advocated prolonged chewing as the way to health. Since there are 32 teeth, it was ingeniously argued, every mouthful of food should be allotted 32 bites; if any teeth were missing, extra bites were stipulated. William James, one of the converts to Fletcherism, gave it up after three months of conscientious mastication, with the comment, "It nearly killed me." Fletcherites even chewed their milk. Devotees of the cult gave up the coarser foods because they found they could not reduce them to a liquid state even by exhaustive mastication.

The next development was a reaction in another direction, a concentration on the roughage found in coarse grains and raw foods. This cult was inspired by a "back to nature" motif, as enthusiasts pointed out that "nature did not create man with a cookstove by his side." Many people, otherwise rational, began consuming their quota of bran each morning. And, as a result, doctors reported an increasing number of stomach and intestinal ailments. Among the raw food faddists were the fruitarians and the nutarians who went in heavily for fruits and nuts, respectively.

Another cult was vegetarianism, whose exponents regarded their principles as dietary and moral in their implications. Vegetarians insisted that meat-eating involved an inhuman destruction of animals, that partaking of flesh would encourage the development of brute qualities in human consumers. John Harvey Kellogg predicted the extinction of the human race if people persisted in eating meat.[35] Extreme vegetarians scrupulously refused both milk and eggs, on the ground that "anyone who indulges in large quantities of milk develops the brains and mentality of a cow."

Reducing diets based on bananas or grape juice have enjoyed their turns, along with alkalizing menus and the munching of raisins for minerals. Doctrines are expounded concerning the harmful effects resulting from combining starches and proteins at the same meal, or milk and fish, or acid fruits and milk. One cult believed in eating a spoonful of sand every day, on the assumption that "the road to health was a sandy one."

Other faddists go in for strenuous exercises to build up bulging muscles, while still others devote their waking hours to sun-bathing. Sun worshipers who are unable to retire to the beaches adopt sunglasses which are worn even on cloudy days. People who had never heard of the ultraviolet rays or Vitamin D until the advertisers of sun lamps started to educate the public, were induced to believe that if exposure to the sun for a little while promotes health, then exposure for a long time will promote even better health. Sun-bathing became the vogue, the panacea for all physical ills.

Games come and go in the public fancy. Mahjong, miniature golf, Monopoly, crossword puzzles, jigsaw puzzles, 4-5-6 pick up sticks, Handies, Knock-Knock, and Matsies have enjoyed popularity at one time or another during the last few years, some of them lasting longer than others. Typical of these recreational pastimes was "Knock-Knock," a craze that kept Americans amused during the hot summer months of 1936.

> Knock! Knock!
> Who's there?
> Delia.
> Delia who?
> Delia cards off the top.

[35] Kellogg was a Seventh Day Adventist. Like the Doukhobors, the Adventists include vegetarianism among their moral commandments.

Other prize retorts were:

> *Hiawatha.* Hiawatha fool over you.
> *Tarzan.* Tarzan stripes forever.
> *Diesel.* Diesel be your last chance.
> *Astor.* Astor if she kept a diary.
> *Welcome.* Welcome up and see me some time.
> *Minerva.* Minervasa wreck from all these knock-knocks.
> *Osgood.* Osgood and tired of the whole darned game.[36]

Previous to this mania was the craze for telling Little Audrey stories. Before that time, way back in 1931, everyone was asking everyone else, "Where's Elmer?" Similarly, "Confucius Say," "Who's Yehudi," and "Kilroy Was Here," had their turns.

One of the fads popular during World War II, still continuing in 1947, is the drawing of Mr. Chad, Britain's war gremlin.

Chad has been demobilized with some of his patrons and now extends his critical activities among mere civilians. Londoners are becoming increasingly aware of the little fellow staring quizzically at them from the walls of

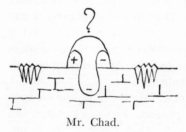

Mr. Chad.

telephone booths ("Wot, no dialing tone?"); from the shutters of fish shops closed for lack of supplies ("Wot, no bloomin' fish?"); fingered on the dusty window of an Inland Revenue income-tax office ("Wot, no rebate?"); on crates of rabbits on station platforms at Christmastime ("Wot, no turkeys?").

Mr. Chad's appearance may vary slightly in different locales, but the essentials he exposes to public view are the top of his bald head surmounted by a question mark like a solitary, curling hair, his mysterious little criss-cross eyes like addition signs and his Schnozzle Durante proboscis which droops down a section of brick wall over which he peers, hanging on by his fingers. Sometimes he is shown with jug-handle ears. With Cockney impudence or cynicism he comments monotonously, "Wot, no beer?" . . . or fags . . . or whatever it is that he misses most at the moment.[37]

Americans have depicted a similar character named Smoe, who has appeared on walls, ceilings, and everywhere a Navy man has been. Smoe also goes under the names of Kilroy, Luke the Spook, The

[36] See the *Literary Digest*, September 12, 1936.
[37] E. Reeve: "Reports." *Life*, March 18, 1946.

Womp, Finortin, Fanutin, Phenortin, The Pookie, Garvey, Alice the Goon, Oogots, Snoopie, Curley, or Joe Electron.[38]

During every economic depression schemes are evolved to gather in easy money. Bets on horse and dog races, number pools, bingo games, and treasury balances are relied upon to provide the open sesame to affluence. Townsend Plans, Ham and Egg Plans, Huey Long Plans, and other utopian schemes are invented to pull us all out of the mire by our own bootstraps. 'Twas ever so, what with the Mississippi Scheme, the Tulip Mania, and the South Sea Bubble, to mention only a few of the historical shortcuts to riches. In the spring of 1935 it was the Chain Letter craze, when the great American passion of getting something for nothing rose to a fever pitch, plunging throngs of people into giddy anticipation of sudden gold. "Have faith in your fellow-man and you will become rich and holy." Similar schemes spread like wildfire over the nation in the wake of the depressions in 1873, in the 1890's, and in the early 1900's. This sort of collective madness, diffused by suggestion, is reminiscent of the Flagellant festivals of the thirteenth century, the dancing manias of the fourteenth century, the religious revivals of the eighteenth century, and the Millerite end-of-the-world craze in the 1840's when the price of muslin skyrocketed in New York City because believers were buying white robes in which to meet the descending Redeemer.

Art is another field in which fads are common. Around 1908 it was Cubism, promoted by the Spanish artist, Pablo Picasso, who opened a campaign "against things as they are in the interest of things as they ought to be." He suggested, more specifically, that pictures be constructed out of purely abstract forms which would carry nothing but an unalloyed aesthetic content.

When the rage for Cubism had spent itself, faddists turned their attention to Futurism. "In 1911," says one historian, "the art world, scarcely recovered from the birth of Cubism, was compelled to submit to the onslaught of a new movement, originating this time from Italy. It was known as Futurism, chiefly because the impressions of the immediate past were involved in its productions." [39] Art was to be based on plastic dynamics. Devotees were exhorted to revile and repudiate old and petrified art, to allow instinct to become self-conscious, to be guided only by the "simultaneousness of states of the soul at any given moment" in portraying the innermost feelings as well as the outermost realities. Futurism was to mean a break with the inherited past.

[38] Letters to the Editor, *Life*, April 6, 1946.
[39] J. B. Manson: "Painting." *Encyclopædia Britannica*, 14th Edition, 1929.

Formerly stress had been laid on the perpendicular conception of music; futurists were to feature the horizontal conception of music. Artists for ages had been looking to the woods, fields, and streams, and especially to the human figure for inspiration; the futurists proposed that the highest motive for creative art was to be furnished henceforth by the wheels, cylinders, and pistons of the twentieth-century engine. Monuments should be made of appropriate material— one to Pirelli of rubber, one to Armstrong of steel. Ideal villages were contemplated in which the trees would give off artificial perfumes and have among their branches extraordinary birds. There were to be an aerial theater and a spiritual alphabet. People needed to be aroused to the sense of being alive. One suggestion was to exploit all possible means for making our civilization a noisier one so that fewer hours would be spent in the sheer inactivity of sleep. Signor Marinetti, the exuberant poet who launched this movement, stirred his followers to thunderous applause by bidding them reflect on the ineffable joys of a sleepless life.

During the shell-shocked years of World War I and for a short time thereafter, the rage was Dadaism, promoted avidly by a German painter named Max Ernst who was seized by a desire "to spit in the world's eye." Dadaists engaged in an organized attack on reason, expressing the post-war cynicism in a complete negation of everything. In 1920 Max Ernst and Hans Arp staged a Dada (hobby-horse) exhibition in Cologne. The entrance to the exhibition was through a public lavatory. Gallery-goers were furnished hatchets and were instructed to smash any pictures they disliked. Among the typical Dada creations were a black felt head with zipper eyes and a stuffed parrot on a hollow log, both incorrigibly senseless.

Dadaist Max Ernst did some experimenting with *collages,* the term he applied to fantastic creations made by cutting up old engravings and rearranging them in grotesque combinations, with trees growing out of horses' backs and bustled ladies with the heads of lions. A poet by the name of André Breton, who prefers a green ensemble, who smokes a green pipe, and drinks a green liqueur, a man well versed in the Freudian psychology, was inspired by the Dadaists to write "A Manifesto of Surrealism" which served to usher in a new school in 1924. Breton expressed the purpose of the new movement in these terms:

> Surrealism rests on the belief in the *superior reality* of certain forms of association neglected heretofore; in the omnipotence of the dream and in the disinterested play of thought. . . . We who have not given ourselves to processes of filtering, who through the medium of our work have been content

to be the silent receptacle of many echoes . . . are perhaps yet serving a much nobler cause.[40]

The surrealists believed in the expression of thought without the control of reason, in the exploration of the subconscious mind, and in the arousal of emotional reactions by means of objects illogically juxtaposed. Dreams and states of mind were represented, in some cases, by the assemblage of miscellaneous junk. Typical titles:

> The King and Queen Traversed by Swift Nudes
> Leaves and Navels
> The Little Tear Gland That Says Tic Tac
> Object Which Does Not Praise Times Past. [41]

One of the leading surrealists is Salvador Dali, who gave his first exhibit in America in 1934. His technique includes the depicting of watches drooping limply from the branches of a dead tree by the seaside and the representation of a nude woman with a body consisting of half-open bureau drawers. On his first arrival in the United States he explained earnestly: "I used to balance two broiled chops on my wife's shoulders, and then by observing the movement of tiny shadows produced by the accident of the meat on the flesh of the woman I love while the sun was setting, I was finally able to attain images sufficiently lucid and appetizing for exhibition in New York." At a fancy dress ball given in her husband's honor by the socialites of the East Fifties, Mme. Dali wore a dress of transparent red paper and a headdress made of boiled lobsters and a doll's head. Artist Dali was garbed with a glass case containing a brassiere on his chest. On the occasion of a lecture delivered in London, Dali wore a deep-sea diving suit with a jeweled dagger at his belt; carried a billiard cue in one hand and led a pair of Russian wolfhounds with the other. He explained that he was symbolizing the fact that he was endeavoring to plunge deeply into the human mind.

Thus artists have attained the same unreason that Gertrude Stein achieved in her literary compositions.

"How can pearls please. Pearls please me because they are accompanied by a drawing I draw merrily and I win, I win. I win I win. Pearls please me and I draw carefully and I do win. And I do wish to be that fairy. How many fairies are fair to me. One fairy is fair to me. One very fairy is fair to me." [42]

[40] A. Breton: *What Is Surrealism?* pp. 60, 61. 1936.
[41] *Time,* December 14, 1936.
[42] G. Stein: "Mildred's Thoughts," in *The American Caravan; a Yearbook of American Literature,* p. 659. Random House, Inc., 1927.

Chapter 15

SUPERSTITION

THE SOCIAL PSYCHOLOGIST is interested in superstitions because they develop and spread as persons influence one another to adopt certain beliefs traditionally accepted in their particular cultural milieu. Such beliefs serve an important use in regulating human relations within the society. Despite the fact that most of us are somewhat superstitious even in these days of scientific advancement, we are inclined to dismiss the superstitions of alien peoples as mere silly mental quirks, without pausing to ask, "Why did this or that special belief originate in that society and why did it persist for so long?" In searching for an answer, we shall find, among other things, that certain superstitions have endured because a given people has preserved them as a valuable instrument of social control, one which is effective in as much as it is highly respected by believers. Among the Kwoma of New Guinea, for example, the belief in sorcery furnishes an explanation for sickness —but further, it serves as a means of preventing criminal behavior. Theft, rape, murder, and trespass are inhibited by the fear that these crimes will bring retaliation through sorcery from the person against whom the crime is committed, or from his relatives. Similarly, the belief in ghosts and the belief in blood are not isolated, unrealistic fears, but theories which are enmeshed and intertwined with many of the important institutions of the culture. Thus it is seen that superstitions fulfill a social as well as an individual function.[1]

I. DEFINITION

A superstition is a false belief that natural events are determined by magical forces which may be influenced to operate in behalf of the believer by means of appropriate rituals, formulas, or abracadabra. The superstitious person assumes that unseen powers transcending

[1] See J. W. M. Whiting: *Becoming a Kwoma,* Chapter 8, "The Inculcation of Supernatural Beliefs." 1941.

the realm of science are the ultimate factors controlling human destinies. Natural explanations are passed over in favor of belief in spirits, demons, hoodoos, voodoos, jinxes, wishbones, amulets, witches, charms, hexes, fetishes, sorcerers, necromancers, planetary influences, and numerological vibrations. Chance is considered to be pervasive and fundamental. The turn-up of the gambler's dice is attributed to luck rather than to a combination of forces computable in terms of mathematical physics; disease is not diagnosed in terms of physico-chemical bodily processes but as evidence of the workings of evil spirits intent on punishing the victim for some alleged slight; instead of the future being predicted by surveying trends in the past, reliance is placed upon divination. It is so much easier to get a tip from some spirit than it is to arrive at a prognosis by conscientious scientific research. Mysterious skulduggery is far more intriguing than the prosaic methodology of the cautious scientist.

A. SUPERNATURAL FORCES AMENABLE TO SORCERY

A belief in supernatural forces which operate in magical ways unknown to the world of science, is basic in superstition. There is a feeling, common among college students, that it is inviting disaster to boast of "hitting an exam right on the nose for an A"; it is much safer to predict a failure and then to act surprised when the mark turns out to be an A. This attitude on the part of the student is a hangover of an ancient superstition that it is unlucky to be praised or admired because the "Evil Eye" will get peeved and will then try to get even with the proud individual by humbling him with some misfortune. Even today there are peasants in Scotland who believe that if a stranger admires a cow, the animal will waste away; to forestall this tragic ending, it is the custom to offer the stranger some of the cow's milk, thus breaking the spell.[2]

Among the uneducated Negroes of the South, faith in voodooism still persists.[3] In 1932 a Negro slayer was hounded to his death by voodoo vengeance:

Trembling lips in the Negro sections of New Orleans are whispering about the terrifying powers of the voodoo serpent god which they say drove 'Lijah Wheatley to the same watery grave that claimed his sweetheart last Sunday.

A night watchman told police he saw a Negro answering the description of Wheatley push Lucille Williams, 19, into a canal and flee.

[2] See A. A. Thomen: *Don't Believe It! Says the Doctor*, p. 258. 1935.

[3] Voodooism is the practice of invoking the aid of evil spirits by means of sorcery. Magical rites provide the liaison.

Her body was recovered and relatives buried it with the Congo voodoo rites prevalent in the old slave days of Louisiana. The ritual included a ceremony whereby the serpent god was asked to bring the murderer back to the scene of his crime.

In keeping with the voodoo creed, the young Negress was buried face downward in her coffin with a fresh egg clasped in each hand and a rope tied around each wrist.

Kinsmen of the girl told police of the ceremony and advised them to watch the canal for Wheatley's body. Meanwhile they also spread news of the rites through the Negro sections so that he would hear of it.

Early today Wheatley's body was found floating in the canal at the exact spot where the girl was drowned.

Police said they have no doubt he heard of "gris-gris" (petition to the serpent god) and went forthwith to fling himself into the water.[4]

Isn't it strange that the kinsmen of the girl were practical enough to see to it that the news of the rites were circulated in the direction of the slayer? The skeptical observer might wonder why the serpent god couldn't get the murderer single-handed, without resort to suggestion, autosuggestion, and human complicity. There is a curious mixture, in this situation, of faith in the supernatural nicely supplemented by exploitation of natural processes. The suicide of the slayer demonstrated in a concrete way his respect for the powers of the voodoo serpent god.

In the spring of 1939 there was a drought in Florida because of an excessive amount of the proverbial sunshine, and 67-year-old Lillie Stoate, who claims she can produce rain by sitting near some body of water, was hustled to Florida, on March 24, by worried citrus-growers. She assumed her post by Lake Reedy. Three days later it began raining for the first time since January.[5] Meteorologists, accustomed to accounting for the weather by reference to barometric pressures and stratospheric temperatures, remained unconvinced of the magical powers claimed by this credulous lady and dismissed the fall as "an ordinary spring disturbance." If the meteorologists were unkind enough to point out that it was three days before rain came and that it would have come irrespective of Lillie Stoate's sitting on the shore, superstitious persons, who believe that the weather can be manipulated by psychic means, would charge the scientists with closing their minds to the evidence. It had not rained for months; the lady sat down by a lake; it rained. What more proof could be desired to substantiate the

[4] New York *Times*, February 18, 1932.
[5] Miss Stoate was invited to return to Florida, expenses paid, in the fall of 1940.

lady's claims as a rain-producer? Such claims and counterclaims, were they made by the superstitious-minded and the scientific-minded, would serve to crystallize one of the difficulties involved in dealing with superstitions, namely, that there is no way of verifying the belief in the supernatural or of discrediting the belief, since empirical checks are inapplicable, immaterial, and irrelevant, from the point of view of the believer. If a person, on the one hand, believes that weather conditions are determined by the phases of the moon, he can make a statistical study of the matter and by working out his correlations arrive at a concrete answer to his hypothetical question. If a person, on the other hand, is convinced that rain can be brought about by prayers or ceremonial rigamarole, there is no scientific way of checking and double-checking the soundness of his affirmations. If such a person prays and rain comes, he is confirmed in his faith; if he prays and it doesn't rain right away, he is sure that eventually his prayer will be answered if only he has faith enough, and, in the meanwhile, is confident that the Lord or the Rain-god is delaying the answer for some perfectly good reason unknown to the believer, a reason that is for the best in the long run, a reason that is part of a great plan too big to be comprehended by limited human minds. Sooner or later it will rain; it always does.

B. Cause and Effect

It is paradoxical, but nevertheless true, that man develops superstition because he craves to be rational or, at least, to seem rational. The human being wants to feel that he understands the world about him, that he can explain, somehow, anything that happens. Anxious to find some explanation for everything he observes, man is inclined by the insecurity of his ignorance to invent some theory to account for causal relations which baffle him. He must have an explanation, a natural one if convenient, a supernatural one if necessary; in some cases, of course, man may prefer to resort to the supernatural realm for emotional reasons. As long as an effect can be attributed to some cause, no matter how far-fetched the connection, the quester after "truth" can maintain his faith in his own fundamental rationality. Let us examine the kind of logic man employs when he is in a superstitious frame of mind.

1. FALSE INFERENCES BASED ON COINCIDENCES

Many superstitions result from false inferences. If one event follows another, it is readily concluded that event No. 2 must have been caused by event No. 1: *post hoc, ergo propter hoc.* By such fallacious deductions, chance associations are interpreted in terms of cause and effect.

It may be argued that the war, the boom period, and the depression were all man-made and, therefore, that some share of responsibility for them, however little, belonged to our national leaders. But what of the drought [1934]? Is the human imagination capable of the conception that this, too, might have been averted in Washington?

Fantastic as it may seem, the answer is yes. The old primitive instinct to hold the medicine-man accountable for the acts of nature has cropped up in the corn belt. There, and perhaps elsewhere, the notion appears to be gaining ground that the drought is a direct visitation of Providence in retribution for the wholesale slaughter of little pigs and other curtailment measures decreed by the AAA. To such serious proportions has this superstition grown that Mr. Wallace, the Secretary of Agriculture, has made its refutation one of the main features of the addresses he has been delivering lately in the Middle West. It is not an easy thing to combat since minds receptive to it in the first place are not of the kind that responds readily to logic.[6]

In May, 1930, some 7000 persons were killed in an earthquake at Pegu, Burma. A gold weather-vane at Rangoon, valued at $1,250,000, crashed to the ground from the top of its golden tower. Indians regarded the earthquake and the tidal wave as punishment for the arrest of Mahatma Gandhi.[7]

Most sports figures who appear on *Time's* covers promptly lose their form:

Colonel Edward Riley Bradley (May 7, 1934). Col. Bradley had won four Derbies up to 1934. His Bazaar was one of the 1934 favorites, finished out of the money. Col. Bradley has not won a Derby since.

Cavalcade (Aug. 20, 1934). Cavalcade won the Kentucky Derby of 1934. By Aug. 1 (opening of the Saratoga season) he had won almost every important race for three-year-olds, had been defeated only once and was touted as another Man o' War. Week after Cavalcade posed for *Time's* cameraman, he tripped and bruised his foot. By the time the cover appeared on the news-stands, Cavalcade had been scratched from the Travers, didn't even run. He never won another race. . . .

Helen Hull Jacobs (Sept. 14, 1936) had won the U.S. Singles Championship four times in a row (a record). That week she was defeated by Alice Marble, 4-6, 6-3, 6-2.

Bob Feller (April 19, 1937). On April 24 Cleveland's 18-year-old ace pitcher injured his arm, pitched a few innings on May 18, was idle until the first week in July.

Baron von Cramm (Sept. 13, 1937) was defeated by Donald Budge the next week at Forest Hills. . . .

[6] The *Literary Digest,* August 11, 1934.
[7] Boston *Herald,* May 7, 1930.

Wallace Wade (Oct. 25, 1937). Undefeated but tied when Duke's Wade appeared on *Time's* cover, the Blue Devils three weeks later lost to North Carolina, 14 to 6, losing the Southern championship.

Johnny Goodman (June 6, 1938). Goodman was an 8-to-1 favorite to win the British Amateur Golf Championship in June, 1938. He never reached the quarter-finals. In the Walker Cup matches played fortnight later, Goodman lost both his matches and the U.S. lost the Walker Cup for the first time since the cup was put up in 1922.

Michigan's *Tom Harmon* (Nov. 6, 1939). Michigan then proceeded to lose to Bob Zuppke's team from Illinois, one of the major upsets of the 1939 season. To *Time,* which contributed to Michigan's overconfidence, Illinois owes thanks.[8]

No wonder athletes are superstitious about having themselves photo-graphed before a crucial contest. There are psychological reasons why publicity might undermine the human competitor, but when a horse falls down the week after being featured on a magazine cover, it looks like a jinx. One reader facetiously suggested that *Time* put Hitler on the cover again and thus assure his downfall: "It might atone for some of the innocents you have put the hex on. . . ."[9]

A person may come to believe that some garment worn during a successful deal is itself responsible for the happy ending. Eugene Foss, one-time Governor of Massachusetts, refused to part with his famous campaign coat. The coat he wore through his politcal triumphs was his favorite garment and he kept it, threadbare and dingy as it was, in his wardrobe, ready for any emergency. Jack Donahue, comedian who starred on the stage with Marilyn Miller, insisted on wearing a bathing suit when he signed a new contract with Charles Dillingham in 1926, because he was in a bathing suit at the time he signed his first contract with Dillingham in 1919, a contract that turned out to be very successful for both parties; because he was likewise so attired when he signed another contract in 1925, also eminently successful. The costume had proved its magical power to assure good fortune. Despite this faith in a charmed destiny, both Marilyn Miller and Jack Donahue died in the prime of life.[10]

A person in a superstitious frame of mind does not examine criti-cally the causal relations which he supposes to exist between two events that happen to coincide in time. If a man in his right mind

[8] *Time,* November 27, 1939.
[9] *Time,* December 11, 1939.
Joe Louis, the "Brown Bomber," finally broke the "hoodoo." See letter in *Time,* October 20, 1941.
[10] The Boston *Traveler,* January 5. 1927.

deliberately asserted that wearing a bathing suit to a business conference made him a better actor on the stage, his statement would belong
in the same category as that famous quip of Mark Twain's, to the effect
that a man who doesn't want to die shouldn't go to bed, because statistics show that most men die in bed.   Twain's suggestion is recognized as absurd, though the same
kind of reasoning often gets by un-
detected in superstition when coincidence is mistaken for causality.
One factor in a complex situation is
singled out by an uncritical person
as the one thing responsible for the
particular good fortune. Henceforth, if that one thing is kept in
mind, a happy result is assured.   It
simplifies life considerably if one
can believe that a bathing suit or a
pipe or a lucky coin will, any one of
them by itself, guarantee success,
with no need of worrying over
burdensome details.   Some people
are as misguided in their reasoning about cause and effect as Mr.
O'Toole, who was impressed by the
power house at Niagara Falls which
contained "the machinery what
pumps the water for the falls," or as
disoriented as the schoolboy who remarked, "Isn't it convenient that
rivers flow by large cities?"   The
concept of causation is slippery even
in the natural realm; how much more elusive it is when the supernatural becomes involved!

Governor Foss in His Campaign
Overcoat.   (Courtesy, the Boston
Herald.)

2. SIGNS

Assuming that certain events may be causally related, possibly in
some magical fashion that is not at all obvious at first glance, the superstitious person believes that if he does one thing, something will happen; if he does not do that one thing, something will not happen.
These contrasting rituals are known respectively as positive and negative control-signs.

a. *Positive.* On the positive side, for example, it is believed that it is necessary to get past a certain spot before a car passes or before the clock strikes, if some desirable consequence, such as a promotion with a raise in pay, is going to ensue. One individual felt that good luck would be his if he always made sure to take the same subway car (a certain number) to work. Strict adherence to this rule of procedure occasionally put him to considerable inconvenience, but he felt the extra effort involved was well worth while. At a wedding, the girl who catches the bridal bouquet is supposed to be the lucky girl next to be married. A Negro of Columbus, Mississippi, described a complicated charm guaranteed to reveal one's future wife:

> To see your future wife, pull off all your clothes at night and turn them wrongside out, hanging them on the foot of the bed. Then kneel and say your prayers backwards and get in bed backwards, entirely naked. You will see your future wife before morning.[11]

A wish may be brought true by turning over three times in bed when you hear the first whippoorwill of the year; the mourning dove will do if no whippoorwill is available. Wishes made the first night spent in a strange house always come true.[12]

b. *Negative.* On the negative side, there are certain things not to be done if ill luck is to be avoided. We are admonished to heed the following negative control-signs, among others: don't sing while eating; don't sit in the house with your hat on; don't start a journey on Friday; don't borrow salt; don't put your hat on in bed; don't whistle in the house; don't sing before breakfast if you don't want to cry before supper; don't put your left shoe or stocking on first; don't spill salt; don't open an umbrella in the house; don't turn back once you have started on a journey; don't let a black cat cross your path.

3. EMOTIONALIZED LOGIC

Superstition is based on a logic of its own, distinctly different from the logic of science. Superstitious thinking is crude, primitive, ignorant, dominated by fear and wish; it is subjective, autistic, headed for conclusions that would make life more interesting if they were true; its premises are veiled assumptions seductive in their appeal, magical in their implications. It is wishful thinking, motivated by the animistic faith that spirits govern the universe, inspired by the egocentric

---

[11] Newbell Niles Puckett: *Folk Beliefs of the Southern Negro,* pp. 329-330. Reprinted by permission of the University of North Carolina Press. Copyright, 1926 by the University of North Carolina Press.

[12] *Ibid.,* p. 354.

hypothesis that these spirits can be induced by sorcery to steer the course of nature to suit the dictates of human desire.

a. *Pseudo Science.* Error in superstitious thinking is a parody of truth. Rules are discovered that *seem* to explain, to justify what people want to believe. There is a logic, but it is pseudo logic, pseudo science. Thus a person may feel confident that lifting a ruptured child through two halves of a split tree will cure him of his ailment. The analogy underlying this bit of reasoning is strained, remote, and spurious. Nevertheless, it has about it an engaging air of plausibility. The belief that people born in February will be short of stature, since February is a short month, might be amusing as a burlesque of logic, were it not for the fact that there are people who take such analogies seriously. Crooked thinking is no jesting matter, for superstitious beliefs are practiced religiously, with results more damaging than the naïve person is likely to realize. When pseudo science parades as science, let the believer beware!

b. *Inadequate Checking.* Superstitious beliefs are not reality-tested; scientific conclusions are accepted only after they have been proved by careful verification. Superstitions do not invite tests because they thrive better on blind credulity. Because wish is the dominant theme in superstitious thinking, the evidence is selected to support a given assumption rather than to check its validity. Exceptions are discounted, ignored; successes alone are taken into account. How, for example, would the uncritical believer evaluate the following instances?

Mrs. Willimore Trotter Jones, of Madison, Ga., has found and saved thousands of four-leaf clovers. Nevertheless, she has been in five automobile wrecks, has lost three husbands, and has suffered so many misfortunes that her neighbors call her "Calamity Jane." (Denver *News*)

Mrs. Neville Coleman refused to eat at a table set for thirteen people. She waited until the rest were through, and then sat down alone. Halfway through the meal, she was stricken with a fatal heart attack. (N.Y. *Times*—A.P.)

General Emilio Mola, second in command with the Spanish Rebels, was killed in an airplane crash. When peasants picked him up, they found he was in his stocking feet. A brother officer explained that a Gypsy had once told the General he would die with his boots on, and he therefore always took his shoes off when in an airplane.[13]

By the credulous person these samples would be dismissed at once as the exceptions that prove the rule or as evidence compiled from un-

[13] "Superstitions That Soured." *Reader's Digest,* October, 1937.

reliable sources.[14]   His credence would remain unaffected by these very rare cases.

c. *Wishful Thinking*.   Error is embraced because it seems more satisfying than the truth—more interesting, more dramatic, more mysterious!   The increase in emotional satisfaction resulting from the acceptance of error prevents us rational creatures from using logic to weed out the fallacies involved in our cherished superstitions.

d. *Compulsion*.   Superstitious behavior is not only wishful—it is compulsive.   There is often a feeling of being forced against one's will to carry out some ritualistic pattern of action.   It is the same feeling that characterizes obsessions.   The obsessive person feels that he must count everything he sees: telephone poles, automobile registrations, street numbers, men with beards.   The person who superstitiously raps on wood is actuated by an inner compulsion that would make him feel uneasy if he failed to perform this rite.   The motivation involved in the compulsion is largely unconscious; there is an element of dissociation in the conflict between the believer's better judgment and the feeling that he has to do the thing, anyhow.   The individual may be vaguely aware that he ought to know better, nevertheless, the belief has an inescapable grip on him.   One person described his situation in this way: "I probably do believe . . . although I do not realize it."   The realization that the ritual is absurd does not deflect the individual from his objective because "he'd be scared stiff to do any differently."   So he raps on wood—"It isn't much bother and we'd better take no chances." [15]   Peace of mind is worth something, even at the price of inconvenience.

C. NAME-CALLING

"Superstition" is a convenient device for "name-calling."   If a person does not happen to approve of some belief, he condemns it categorically as a "superstition" and dismisses it abruptly as unworthy of serious consideration.   People who are antireligious in their sentiments may speak derisively of religion as "mere superstition" and thus seem to settle the matter by means of an epithet.   Similarly, adherents of one sect or faith may brand as "superstitious" the creeds of other churches.   Thus, the Protestant may disparage the Catholic doctrines concerning purgatory, confession, prayers for the dead, apostolic succession, holy water, transubstantiation, and the saving efficacy of

---

[14] "An exception does not prove that a general rule is true, but that it is false." R. H. Thouless: *How to Think Straight*, p. 36.   1939.

[15] A. M. Tozzer: *Social Origins and Social Continuities*, p. 228.   1925.

priestly ministrations.[16]   The Catholic, on his part, may ridicule the total immersion of the Baptists or the "second coming" of the Seventh Day Adventists.   It is very difficult to analyze such situations impartially, to discount charges and countercharges, and to arrive at an objective view of what religion would be, were its essence distilled from the unessentials that may be peculiar to the special creeds of particular sects.   In practice, though, religion is not something in general but something in particular, some definite system of beliefs that issue in concrete actions.   Each faith must be evaluated, therefore, in terms of the role it plays in producing specific kinds of behavior, patterns that may or may not fit the world of reality in a useful manner.   The question raised by some critics as to whether religious beliefs in general or some religious beliefs in particular may properly be considered "superstitious" will be discussed in a later section of this chapter.

D. Superstition and Folklore

Some false beliefs which should be more accurately designated as *folklore* are identified as superstitions.   Traditional beliefs properly belong to folklore; they are superstitions *only* in those specific cases where magical and compulsive factors are present.   There is much confusion in the literature concerning *popular fallacies,* because writers fail to distinguish between superstitious and non-superstitious false beliefs.   Faith in whiskey as a cure for snake-bite is a part of our folklore, but it is not really a superstition; the same may be said of the popular notion "that at the moment of death, especially when it occurs suddenly, the important events of a person's life are speedily recalled."

Numerous writers are guilty of ignoring this distinction between superstition in particular and folklore in general.   Thomen cites the ancient fallacy "that a good way to treat a burn is to hold the part burned before the fire to draw out the inflammation" and then adds,— "It has been aptly referred to as: 'One of those foolish superstitions.' " [17]

Popenoe also fails to make the distinction when he refers to *physiognomy* as a superstition:

It is a popular superstition that outward form gives an index to the individual's mental capacities and aptitudes.   A number of "systems" of voca-

---

[16] This comment is based on the study of a sermon delivered by W. T. Hamilton on January 23, 1848, entitled, "Superstition—Its Nature, Its Manifestations, Its Evil, and the Remedy Therefor."

[17] A. A. Thomen: *op. cit.,* p. 166.

ional selection and guidance have made money for their promoters, diagnos-
ng talent by the shape of the fingers, the contour of the jaw, and other
raits of the sort. Not one of these has any scientific basis, and all the tests
hat have been made have shown their claims to be entirely unsupported.[18]

Although character-reading by means of bodily signs is based on falla-
ious correlations, there is actually no superstition involved.

Folk cures are often based on misconceptions of a non-superstitious
nature, transmitted from generation to generation as traditional homemade forms of self-treatment. Examples:

Curing rattlesnake-bite by putting the snake's rattles in one's hatband.
Curing warts by rubbing them with meat and then feeding the meat to a
dog.
Treating chronic headache by making sure to burn the combings of hair
from the head of the sufferer, lest some bird find them and build its nest
with them; if such occurs, the person will ache until the fledglings leave the
nest.[19]

When a person carries smoothly polished pebbles as "lucky stones,"
firm in the conviction that there is magic in such a talisman, amulet,
or charm to ward off disease, or when a person assures himself of good
luck by carrying a horse chestnut or a nutmeg, he is definitely being
superstitious. Unless this trust in magic is involved, the remedy prescribed by tradition should be more broadly classified as folklore.
Sometimes it is difficult to draw the line, as in the case of the individual
who treats his warts by rubbing them with a dead cat in a cemetery.
The distinction would depend on the reason why the therapeutic
measures had to be executed in a cemetery. If the confidence of the
patient was based on a belief in good or evil spirits, then superstition
would be involved.

II. MAGIC

The essence of superstition is faith in magic, sustained by the belief
that natural events may be made to conform to the heart's desire if one
can gain the assistance of supernatural beings or can manipulate secret
forces unknown to science. Thus an enemy may be rendered ill by
using some verbal formula to cast a spell over him, a "hex" produced
by the connivance of evil spirits with whom the exhorter is mysteri-
ously in league; or rain may be ensured by the rite of sprinkling water

---

[18] P. Popenoe: *The Child's Heredity*, p. 178. 1929.
[19] See P. M. Black: *Nebraska Folk Cures*, Chapter 1, "Cures for Aches." 1935. See
also D. L. Thomas and L. B. Thomas: *Kentucky Superstitions*. 1920.

on the ground, a ceremony which will suggest to the gods that a shower is in order.   Faith in magic has given man faith in himself, since the human being feels that he can count on the cooperation of spirits when natural modes of control seem inadequate to the emergency.   Magic comes into play when chance enters the situation, when ordinary scientific techniques furnish no certain bases for prediction and control Eager to be the master of his fate, man realizes that supernatural aid may be necessary at times if such a goal is to be achieved.   When science fails him, magic provides the means for controlling his destiny so as to make his personal wishes come true.

A. Animism

Magic beliefs are usually based on animistic thinking, that is thinking which attributes natural events to the agency of spirits resident in nature.   Breaking a mirror brings bad luck because the reflection in the glass is destroyed, the reflection being the soul.   Some of the Indian natives in America were much impressed by the firearms of the early settlers because they believed that a gun released spirits and that these spirits chased the victim until they caught up with him. City walls and streets in China were laid out in a crooked line in order to frustrate the evil spirits who travel in straight lines only, according to a well-known principle of Oriental geomancy.

Primitive peoples live in constant dread of evil spirits.   An explorer who was visiting the Djukas of Dutch Guiana, tried to take a picture of a native girl.   The girl was terrified because she believed that her image on a film would give the photographer power of life and death over her.   The picture was not merely a picture, it was a spirit, a duplicate of her own soul.   Members of primitive tribes often keep their names secret because they think it would be easy for an enemy in possession of a man's name to curse him and get the evil spirits to bring him harm.

The animistic view of illness assumes that disease is produced in a person by evil spirits.   Early medicine was based on the conviction that sickness was caused by demons, that magic could be used to drive them out.   This magical concept of disease still persists among people who believe that illness is sent by God as a punishment for sin.

Calling upon demons for connivance in human schemes is accomplished by the magic arts of sorcery.   Some Southern Negroes believe that the devil himself teaches the black art of conjuring.[20]   If a person

[20] Puckett: *op. cit.*, p. 553.

wants to protect himself against the evil spirits (hoodoos) or to assure himself of some coveted good, he may resort to fetishes or charms, such as relics of the dead, bones, skulls, red flannel, red pepper, or silver dimes. Red charms are especially prized because they are sure to have spirits dwelling in them. Medicine men and priests are often consulted and requested to enlist the spirits, since these persons are supposed to be peculiarly gifted in the practice of voodooism, or black magic. If the enlisted spirits succeed in injuring the enemy, faith in the black arts is strengthened; if they fail, it is because the enemy is being guarded by spirits whom he has invoked on his own behalf. Medicine men, witch doctors, hoodoo doctors, conjure doctors, as they are variously called, are reputed to possess special powers of dealing with the supernatural because these doctors have spirits dwelling in them. If a man is rejected by the girl he loves, he concludes that she has been "tricked" or "handicapped" and so he goes to a "root-doctor" to have the spell removed, thus forcing her to change her mind in his favor. An individual who knows how to conjure on his own, may collect a debt by dusting some nails with powdered "shame-weed," thus making the debtor ashamed of his delinquency.[21]

On the morning of November 17, 1923, King Alfonso of Spain and his Queen were journeying to Italy aboard a warship to pay Spain's respects to the new Fascist state. They were met off Genoa by the Italian fleet. The moment the Spaniards came into view, a storm descended out of a clear sky. Four seamen were washed overboard from the Italian flagship and drowned. In an escorting submarine, a compressor exploded, killing a man. The Spaniards were saluted at Naples by the firing of a cannon salute. The gun exploded, killing the Italian crew. A member of the reception committee shook hands with Alfonso, collapsed, died of a cataleptic fit in a hospital later. Putting two and two together, Italians decided that King Alfonso had an evil eye, and so they called him a *jettatore*. When the King denied the imputation, as he did persistently, the people were all the more convinced that they were right, since "a *jettatore* increases his evil powers by referring to them even in depreciation."[22] Mothers spat into their babies' breasts, men grasped their iron keys whenever he approached. Nothing he could say or do would dislodge their beliefs. The destiny of Spain, certainly the fate of the House of Bourbon, was vitally affected by the implicit belief of Italians that the former Spanish King was a

---

[21] *Ibid.*, p. 283.
[22] F. Gervasi: "Evil Eye." *Collier's*, November 25, 1939.

jettatore.   Light may be shed on the strange plight of King Alfonso by quoting a passage from Sumner on this topic:

> Another direct and immediate product of primitive demonism is the notion of the evil eye.   This is a concrete dogma and a primary inference from demonism.   It is often confounded with the *jettatura* of the Italians.   The evil eye is an affliction which befalls the fortunate and prosperous in their prosperity.   It is the demons who are irritated by human luck and prosperity who inflict calamity, pain, and loss, at the height of good luck.   The *jettatura* is a spell of evil cast either voluntarily or involuntarily by persons who have the gift of the evil eye and can cast evil spells, perhaps unconsciously and involuntarily.   It follows from the notion of the evil eye that men should never admire, praise, congratulate, or encourage those who are rich, successful, prosperous, and lucky.   The right thing to do is to vituperate and scoff at them in their prosperity.   That may offset their good luck, check their pride, and humble them a little.   Then the envy of the superior powers may not be excited against them to the point of harming them.   It is the most probable explanation of the cloistering and veiling of women that it was intended to protect them, especially if they were beautiful, from the evil eye.[23]

Since an ill-advised act may provoke nasty-tempered spirits into lashing out blindly in their rage, it is a good idea to keep on the good side of the devil and his colleagues.   This is sometimes difficult to accomplish because the devil reputedly goes about on earth wearing a high silk hat and a frock coat, looking just like a gentleman.   Black cats are incarnations of the devil.   The fiddle and the banjo are instruments of Satan.   "Take your banjo to the forks of the road at midnight and Satan will teach you how to play it." [24]   If you see the devil, in the course of the day's activities, you should put your shirt on wrong-side out and look into a well.   Evil spirits in the form of witches live in stumps and hollow logs, changing their shapes from time to time, preferably prowling as buzzards or black cats.   You can tell when they're around, because "dey rides you and makes you feel down and out."   To ward off the witches, the following precautions may be used: put pepper on the witch's skin while she is out riding, so she can't get back into the skin; don't eat crickets or grasshoppers or too much grease; don't sleep on your back; keep a broom across the door, so that the witch cannot step over your threshold, a

[23] W. G. Sumner: *Folkways*, p. 515.   Ginn and Company, 1906.
[24] Reprinted from *Folk Beliefs of the Southern Negro*, by Newbell Niles Puckett, by permission of The University of North Carolina Press.   Copyright, 1926, by The University of North Carolina Press.   P. 548.

ork under your pillow, and scatter mustard seed around the house—
witches have a counting instinct which compels them to stop and
count all the seeds, thus detaining them and diverting them from their
malicious errands.

It is natural that the mystery of death should inspire a dread of what
the spirit might "be up to," once it departs from the body. The fact
that a man was well liked while he was alive does not mean at all that
the presence of his spirit is welcome after he has "gone." Primitive
peoples are disposed to take a dying person elsewhere to die; in case
they fail to get him out of the house before he dies, they burn the house
down as a precautionary measure. After the corpse has been carefully laid in a prescribed position in the grave, with food, clothes, and
pottery to care for the needs of the spirit—so he won't want to return
to haunt the living—a knife is fastened over the door of the dwelling
and an axe left on the threshold to discourage any visitations by the
spirit.[25]

Similar practices are found in parts of the South, according to
Puckett's survey.

The corpse is buried face down and deep, and the earth is pounded down
hard. These exorcising rites, called "layin' de Sperrit," include conjuration
to prevent the dead from haunting the living.

If a man calls on a widow too soon after her husband has died, the "ha'nt
will get him."

"If a ha'nt bodder you, ax him fer some money an' he'll sho' leab." One
man who was lost in the woods, surrounded by "ha'nts," recited Bible verses
and prayed to no avail, suddenly got a bright idea, took off his hat and passed
it among the spooks, and they disappeared at once.

Louisiana Negroes believe that God allows all the spirits to return to earth
on All Saints' Night, so they cook food, unsalted, especially for the dead,
to propitiate their malevolent tendencies.[26]

According to a widespread superstition, the dead are quite touchy
about being disturbed in their graves. There is an epitaph on Shakespeare's tombstone at Stratford-on-Avon which issues a warning:

> Blest be the man that spares these stones,
> And curst be he who moves my bones.

[25] See Tozzer: *op. cit.*, pp. 119-126.
[26] Reprinted from *Folk Beliefs of the Southern Negro*, by Newbell Niles Puckett,
by permission of The University of North Carolina Press. Copyright, 1926, by The
University of North Carolina Press. Chapter 2, "Burial Customs, Ghosts, and
Witches."

Shortly after Lord Carnarvon had opened up the Egyptian tomb o.
Tut-Ankh-Amen, a rumor was circulated that an ancient curse in
scribed on the walls, threatening with death anyone who disturbed the
remains, was being fulfilled.   The following mortalities were widely
attributed to this curse:

Lord Carnarvon, financier of the expedition, died from the bite of an Egyp
tian mosquito.

Colonel Audrey Herbert, his brother, died soon after visiting the tomb.

George J. Gould, American millionaire, visited the tomb and quickly passed
away.

Woolf Joel, another millionaire, yachting on the Nile, went on a sight-
seeing tour and died before he could return home.

Sir Archibald Douglas Reid began the work of X-raying the Pharoah's bones
but died before he could get under way.

Professor George Benedite of the Louvre was also taken at the height of
his enthusiasm.

Professor LaFleur of McGill University visited the tomb and died a short
while later at Luxor.

H. G. Evelyn-White, prominent Egyptologist, died, leaving a note which
read, "I knew there was a curse on me."   He killed himself.

M. Pasanova, an excavator, suddenly dropped dead.

Richard Bethell, secretary to Howard Carter, the leader, was found dead,
and his father, crying out against the *curse,* killed himself by leaping from a
window.   At his funeral the wheels of a hearse killed a boy.

Edgar Steel, working over some relics taken to the British Museum, was
found dead.[27]

Mardrus, the French Egyptologist, suggested that "the Egyptians for
7000 years have possessed the secret of surrounding their mummies
with some dynamic force of which we have only the faintest idea." [28]
Faint, indeed, is the idea, as far as scientists are concerned; for not
being mystics, scientists can see nothing in the "curse" theory but
the rankest kind of superstition.   Why not examine the records to
determine how many scores of Egyptian explorers have emerged from
their excavations with no mishap more serious than a natural fatigue?
Certainly it would be simpler to blame the fatalities on the disease
germs and mephitic vapors inevitably encountered by archaeologists
prowling around in tombs shut out for thousands of years from fresh
air and the light of day; or, in some cases, it would be simpler to

[27] See C. MacDougall: *Hoaxes,* p. 21. 1940. By permission of the Macmillan
Company, publishers.

[28] Quoted in a **Boston** *Herald* editorial, April 15, 1926.

blame the deaths on overexertion in old age. "Of the ten men present when the mummy was unwrapped, all were living ten years later.
Of the forty persons who entered the inner tomb, six have died of
natural causes in the course of years. Eventually all will die; but the
myth will live." [29]

B. Symbolism

Symbolism plays an important role in the magic of superstition.
The Easter egg, germ of life and immortality, is featured in various
rites by the Pennsylvania Dutch to assure the handing on of life from
generation to generation; it must be eaten shortly after Easter; if kept
more than a year, somebody in the family will die.[30] Among the
Southern Negroes it is believed that a baby should be taken upstairs
before he is taken down, so he'll rise in the world; seeds should be
planted at the new moon, so that the crop will grow as the moon gets
larger. Among many peoples there is the practice of planting a tree at
the birth of a child, so the child will grow, as does the tree. If the
tree happens to grow crooked, there will be a black sheep in the family.
A pregnant woman, to avoid her child's being born with red birth-
marks, should not eat mulberries. A person receiving the gift of a
knife should pay a penny for it, so that it won't cut the friendship.
The wedding ring symbolizes "love without end." Rice, the symbol
of fertility, is showered on the bridal couple, thus representing in a
roundabout way the wish that the newlyweds have a large family.
Everybody wants to get off on the right foot, and so it is important, if
one cares about his luck, to be sure to start up a stairway with the right
foot first. Thus one puts one's "best foot" forward, always a wise
procedure, if one wants to get ahead in the world. The left foot is an
evil omen, since the Latin word for left is *sinister,* a word that has
carried over into the English language to connote crafty *malice.* After
all, nobody wants a left-handed compliment, no matter how subtly
the venom is disguised.

C. Sympathetic Magic

Symbolism is the basic principle of sympathetic magic, a magic built
on the assumption that power over a thing may be achieved by getting
power over its symbol. There are two kinds of sympathetic magic:
imitative, founded on the law of association known as *Similarity;*
and contagious, founded on the law of association known as *Contigu-*

---

[29] J. Jastrow: *The Betrayal of Intelligence,* p. 37. Greenberg: Publisher, 1938.
[30] See C. Weygandt: *The Blue Hills,* pp. 358-359. 1936.

ity. The logic of these superstitions is based largely on reasoning b
analogy.

1. IMITATIVE

The person practicing imitative sympathetic magic believes that th
symbol is particularly efficacious if it resembles the object which th
believer is seeking to bring under his control. Thus the Bank I
landers stick owl feathers in a round stone—to symbolize the rays c
the sun—as a means of procuring sunshine. Among some Russian
rain is assured by having three men climb trees; one man beats a kettl
(thunder), one man makes sparks (lightning), and one man sprinkle
water (rain). The Japanese destroy the image of a god if he does no
send what is wanted, a behavior pattern similar to that of the nativ
Victorians who draw the figure of an enemy on the ground and ther
demolish the enemy by dancing around the figure and cursing it witl
incantations. A survival of this primitive practice is the spectacle o
civilized people burning an effigy as a means of venting their hatred

Imitative sympathetic magic has been widely practiced in the treat
ment of various ailments. The principle that "like cures like" wa
employed in a superstitious form long before it was adopted as a scien
tific principle by Paracelsus and later embodied in homeopathy, a
school of medical practice which is associated with the name o
Samuel Hahnemann (1755-1843). Thus, trefoil was prescribed, ir
early times, for heart disease, thistle for stitch in the side, walnut shell
for head injuries, bear's grease for baldness, lungwort for pneumonia
liverwort for liver diseases, scale of pine cones for toothache, *lacunae
filiae* (tears of a maiden in distress) for females suffering from melan
choly. Involved in this therapy was the "doctrine of signatures," the
belief that God placed distinguishing marks on various herbs to indi
cate their uses. Thus, flower of euphrasia was employed in treating
eye diseases because of its eye-like appearance. Several of the prescrip
tions mentioned above embody this same principle. "The like-cures
like principle was interpreted as in accord with the growing practice of
inoculation. Homeopathy comes into the picture as a strange projec
tion from an older ideology into modern medicine." [31]

2. CONTAGIOUS

Contagious sympathetic magic is based on the law of association by
contiguity. If a person cuts himself, he should treat the knife that has
caused the injury. A nail driven into the footprints of an enemy will

[31] J. Jastrow: *Wish and Wisdom,* p. 245. 1935.

make him lame. In ancient times the herald who brought bad tidings was executed. A hangover of this understandable reaction may be observed in the person who scolds the telephone operator for reporting that the line is busy or chides the postman for bringing no mail. Other survivals of contagious sympathetic magic are found in the beliefs that cankers on the tongue are due to lying, that "cross my heart and hope to die" is a guarantee of honesty, that swearing with a hand on the Bible will insure truthful testimony in court. This sort of logic is akin to the reasoning often employed in dream-book analogies, where verbal resemblances are interpreted as representing actual identities: to dream of a Quaker means you will meet a *friend* soon, "to dream of a dairy showeth the dreamer to be of a milksop nature," to dream of "a zebra indicates a checkered life." [32] By the same logic, eating deer meat will make a person timid, and carrying the skin of a lion will endow an individual with courage. Contiguity seems to be the vital link in tying together events otherwise unrelated, as in the case of the common superstition that if your ear burns, it means that somebody is talking about you.

III. CHANCE: THE UNKNOWN FACTOR

In spite of the fact that increasing scientific knowledge is rendering accurate prediction more likely, there still remains a large area of ignorance thwarting our desire to foretell what the future has in store for us.

People are superstitious usually because of uncertainties in their lives. The persons most likely to be superstitious are those who lead an uncertain kind of existence, such as athletes, sailors, airplane pilots, and other individuals whose occupations depend so largely upon the element of chance. The following item illustrates this thesis:

Many years ago, the reluctance of seamen to sail on a Friday reached such proportions that the British government decided to prove the fallacy of the superstition. They laid the keel of a new vessel on Friday, launched her on Friday, named her H.M.S. *Friday,* and sent her to sea on Friday.

The scheme had only one drawback—neither ship nor crew was ever heard of again.[33]

A. PREDICTION

It is natural that man, in his uncertainty and anxiety, should resort to various arts of divination: opening the Bible casually for some hint of guidance (bibliomancy), getting tips from the dead (necromancy),

[32] J. Jastrow: *Fact and Fable in Psychology*, p. 257. 1900.
[33] Quoted in *Reader's Digest*, November, 1940.

reading the lines of the hand (palmistry), analyzing vibration frequencies by counting letters in names (numerology), reading tea leaves, diagnosing planetary influences (astrology), or interpreting dreams. Omens abound, both good and bad, that are supposed to shed light on future events—prophetic signs which foreshadow destiny. Fortune is believed to depend on luck. Good luck can be assured and bad luck averted if the proper magical measures are employed in time, before it is too late to escape impending disaster.

B. LUCK

Momentous ventures are usually occasions for the ceremonious recognition of certain rites conducive to happiness. Marriage is certainly an adventure calling for the conscientious observance of every ritual that may be deemed effective in assuring harmony and joy. So the bride must wear something old and something new, something borrowed, and something blue. Certain omens may appear that should not be ignored. Happy is the bride the sun shines on. A flock of birds flying over the church during the wedding is an augury of a blessed future. If it rains on the night of the wedding, it is a bad sign. If a bride meets a hearse on her way to the church, all her babies will be born dead (contiguity). Some people would not think of getting married on a Friday.

Luck is assured by attending to (1) bad omens and (2) good omens.

1. BAD OMENS

Bad omens are known as "negative signs." Many of them are warnings of approaching death, such as:

Opening an umbrella in the house
A crack in the top of a loaf of bread
Changing a sick person from one room to another
A dish cloth hung on a door knob
Calling the doctor on Friday
A hearse drawn by two white horses
Rain in an open grave
"Building on to" a new house within a year
A window shade falling down by itself
Sneezing at the table with your mouth full
The howling of a dog at night

Thinking that these omens portend death, superstitious persons argue themselves into believing that the approaching end may be averted by resorting to counteracting charms. It is agreed among believers that if thirteen people sit at a table, the first to rise and the last to sit down are sure to die shortly; this being accepted as the certain outcome, the demises may be circumvented by having all thirteen persons, if there must be thirteen present, sit down at the same time and rise in unison. If a dog howls or an owl hoots in the *dead* of the night, various measures must be taken at once to avert death, such as turning your pockets inside out or putting your shoes upside down under the bed. The cautious person will avoid trouble by crossing his fingers. One woman was much disturbed when a picture fell from a wall in her home, because she was sure somebody was going to die. For months she lived in constant dread, wondering who it was going to be. She finally heaved a sigh of relief when she heard the news that a cousin in Australia had died.

Engine Trouble. "As soon as you were so long in dressing I knew it would be an unlucky night for us."

Some people have presentiments that things are going to go wrong, that the "breaks" will be against them. Breaking a mirror is supposed to bring seven years of bad luck. "Sing before breakfast, cry before supper." A two-dollar bill, like a black cat across the path, is a harbinger of misfortune. Passing a person on the stairs is an invitation to disaster. The author of a play should never whistle in the theater dressing room unless he is completely indifferent to success. There are times when people expect the worst. On January 25, 1938, for example, the blood-red beams of an aurora borealis were interpreted as a presage of war. Panics broke out in various parts of Europe—in Portugal, villagers rushed from their homes in fright, fearing the end of the world.

The superstition that unusual good fortune leads to misfortune, often leads to a compulsive avoidance of good fortune, or even courting of suffering.

This is of importance in puritanism, resistance to getting well, excessive worry and pessimism. . . . The idea that the powers that control fate may be moved to pity and mercy by suffering is present in the unconscious of most people. . . . It is of importance in the psychopathology of everyday life, in neuroses, and perhaps in depressions and other psychoses. . . . Essential facts are given in three cases in which a threat precipitated symptoms which seemed to be the expression of unconscious self-protection by suffering. The development of attitudes which will offset too strong a reaction of unconscious self-protection is one of the major tasks of psychotherapy.[34]

2. GOOD OMENS

Fortunately there are good omens, too, "positive signs," that, for the superstitious, point the way to better times—horseshoes, four-leaf clovers, new moons over the left shoulder, crickets in the house, picking up pins, putting on shirts inside out (providing they are left that way until 12 o'clock).

Superstitions are prevalent among the movie stars. Joe E. Brown thinks it brings him good luck if he has his photo taken the first day he starts a picture. Rita Hayworth places her faith in the number "17."

It has occurred so frequently in her life that to be without it would be like going without her eyelashes. Born Rita Carmen Cansino (which has 17 letters), on the 17th of October, she made her first professional appearance on November 17 and signed her first starring contract on April 17 when she was—of all things—17 years old. And what's still more mystical, she made her first screen test on the 17th of September in 1934, signed her first screen contract on the following January 17 and on the 17th of May signed her current stellar contract with Columbia. She should take 17 strawberries in her bowl of cream—and visit Booth Tarkington who did well with the same numerals.[35]

Director Lewis Milestone was presented with a cigarette case the day he started to direct his first successful picture, so he makes sure some character uses that case in some scene in all his productions. Alfred Hitchcock, another well-known director, insists that his brief appearance in one scene of his pictures is a guarantee of the film's success.

C. GAMES

Gamblers and athletes are particularly superstitious, relying on luck to bless their hunches and their competitive efforts. Chance is widely regarded as an important factor in games, as it seems as if fate often

---

[34] G. C. Caner: "Superstitious Self-Protection in Psychopathology." *Archives of Neurology and Psychiatry*, 1940, 44, 351-361.

[35] The Boston *Herald*, April 6, 1941.

decides who will be the winners and the losers. If the person himself wins, he is apt to attribute his victory to superior skill; if he loses, he credits the defeat to bad luck.

1. GAMBLING

A gambler at cards is inclined to feel a little uneasy if he gets off to a good start, because he has heard it said that "the winner of the first hand is loser for the night . . . good beginning, bad ending." In poker, at the roulette wheel, at the horse races, gamblers may not believe in luck, somebody has remarked, but they prefer to take no chances. Consequently, they resort to all kinds of occult guidance before committing themselves on a bet. One gambler, on hearing the number of a hymn announced in an English church, arose and departed for the gambling table, where he staked heavily on that number and won. The success attending this method of guidance led him to continue the practice. When his friends heard of the inspiration responsible for his phenomenal luck, they followed suit. The general exodus after the announcement of the hymn reached such disturbing proportions that the minister took the trouble to investigate the situation. At the next meeting he informed the congregation that in the future they would sing no hymn whose number was under 37 (the highest number on the roulette wheel).[36]

Of all the superstitious people who see omens, portents, and strange warning signs, none is quite so rationalistic in his folly as the gambler, according to Edgar Wallace, the English novelist. He was referring more particularly, he explained, to professional gamblers, not to the dilletanti who "stake their louis on the black or red." Wallace observes:

It is the amateur, the veriest dabbler in chance, who carries rabbits' feet, eschews green, and regards the passing of a funeral on his way to a racecourse as a very bad sign if he passes it coming toward him and a very good sign if he passes it from behind.

There is one superstition which persists, and that is to back the first race horse you see or the horse of the first owner you meet on your way to a racecourse. . . .

The left hand plays an important part in the superstitions of the gambler. I know men who swear they can never win at cards if the dealer is left-handed. There are players who, to change their luck, will get out and walk

[36] See F. B. Dresslar: "Suggestions on the Psychology of Superstition." *Transactions of the American Medico-Psychological Association.* 1910.

three times round the chair in which they have been sitting, but it is always right-handed—that is to say, clockwise.

Monte Carlo in the season is a welter of superstition. There is a Frenchman who goes there every year to play a system. Across his ample waistcoat is a large gold chain from every link of which depends a charm; tigers' claws, kewpies, and heaven knows what other mysterious gadgets repose in every pocket, and every finger of his hands is covered with charm rings. Nor is he unique. If you stroll round the tables you will see at every one people who have before them some potent magic to charm luck their way.

I know two or three men who bet very largely who would not dream of gambling in the accepted sense if they had started the day badly with an unpleasant letter by the morning's post or some unpleasant happening in their domestic circle. They know that they have been thrown off their balance and that reason is unseated, and since the mind is a very delicately adjusted piece of mechanism, and the mind includes such imponderable qualities as telepathy—which plays a greater part in professional gambling than most people realize—they play light.

I once saw one of the boldest betters at baccarat pass a bank when the luck was going with him. I asked him afterwards why he had taken so unusual a course.

"I knew I should lose that coup," he said. "It came to me—when I get that queer warning, I take no risks."

He told me it was the commonest experience with him to be "told," and he is not unique in this respect; scores of other men have natural powers of "reception."

And yet the non-superstitious pros have their own peculiar superstitions. I was on my way to Doncaster once with a man who bets in thousands. We were hardly out of King's Cross before he put his hand in his waistcoat pocket and took out a golden sovereign—this was after the war—and threw it through the open window.

"What's the idea?" I asked.

"My brother gave me this for luck. A new mascot always brings bad luck."

Perhaps there are no non-superstitious gamblers after all! [37]

2. ATHLETICS

Athletes, too, are inclined to be superstitious. Chimoney, the great Indian marathoner, ran a race. His baby died. He ran another race. His wife died. So Chimoney refused to run in any more marathons, though well assured of a trip to the Olympic games. The deaths in his family were a warning that the Great Spirit would not have him run in the white man's races.

Baseball players know that yellow butterflies and hunchbacked mas-

[37] *Literary Digest*, September 29, 1928.

cots are good luck. Unfortunate is the man who dreams about monkeys the night before an important game, because the omen means he won't get a hit all day. It is bad luck to walk between the umpire and the catcher on the way to the batter's box, or to step on one of the foul lines. It is good luck to touch third base between innings; the pitcher will have a good inning if the ball is thrown to him at the start by the third baseman; the batter will have a better chance of hitting if he finds a hairpin or kicks dirt on home plate. Baseball players are particularly given to faith in such hocus-pocus, since they have more time than most athletes, on and off the field, to figure things out—why they won one game or lost another. All sorts of farfetched solutions are arrived at, as illogical, most of them, as the wildest fancies of a voodoo devotee.

[Baseball] bats, for example, are loaded with superstitions. Fred Fitzsimmons, New York Giants' pitcher, once pasted a home run that clinched the National League pennant for his club. In his excitement he stepped on the bats laid out carefully in front of the dugout.

The shouts and congratulations of his teammates dwindled to a whisper as they realized the monstrous offense he had committed. He had "taken all the hits out of the bats." They had to borrow a whole new set before the World Series started.

Tris Speaker and Napoleon Lajoie had an idea they could get their bats in shape for a base hit by drawing a line in the dust just before the pitcher wound up. Ty Cobb's twenty-two spectacular seasons with the Detroit Tigers may have been the result of his ancient habit of toting three bats to the plate.

Bases, too, are important. For more than twenty years the great Babe Ruth gingerly stepped on second base every time he lumbered in from the outfield to take his turn at bat. Just a habit, but he never missed. No telling what might have happened if he had.

And gloves. Nearly every player has a pet way of throwing his on the ground between innings. "Spitball" pitchers of the old days always left theirs palms up, to prevent opponents from dropping sand in their slippery elm. Many modern non-spitballers carry on the practice, in the interests of superstition.

As in other sports, most of baseball's fetishes are individual affairs. Walter Johnson, Washington's famous pitcher, invariably warmed up in the same spot before a game. Eddie Collins, one of the greatest second-basemen of all time, liked to stick a gob of chewing gum on his cap-button to keep away the evil eye.[38]

[38] J. J. McGraw: "The Tough Days of Baseball." *Reader's Digest,* July, 1934. Condensed from four issues of *Liberty.*

Superstitions may be exploited in the interest of team morale, too. John McGraw, Giants' Manager, known to the trade as "The Master Mind," brought his team out of a slump by hiring a man to drive by the Polo Grounds every day with a wagonload of empty beer barrels, the ultimate in lucky omens. Let McGraw tell the story:

It was by playing on baseball superstitions that I gained my first pennant for the Giants, in 1902. In midseason the team went into a batting slump, losing game after game. Then one day Frank Bowerman came into the clubhouse with a smile on his face. "Saw a load of empty barrels on my way to the park today, boys," he announced. "Watch me pickle that old apple this afternoon!" And he did—four hits out of five times at bat. That gave me an idea. The next day three or four more players came in to tell about seeing a load of empty barrels. They too got out of their batting slump. Finally all the players had seen those empty barrels and opposing pitchers were being driven to the showers every day. Billy Gilbert, our second-baseman, began to get suspicious. He had seen the barrels several times but the horses were always the same. "Sure," I agreed, "I hired that teamster by the week, to meet you fellows coming in. You don't think I could afford to have him change horses every day, do you?" The players had a good laugh—but I had broken their batting slump by taking advantage of the ball players' pet superstition.[39]

Bobo Newsom, star pitcher, is reported to be the most superstitious man in baseball.

He never ties his own shoelaces—someone else does this while Bobo stands by majestically, with arms folded. He can't win unless he takes off his street socks just so, before a game, dangling them one at a time by their garters over his street shoes until they swing into his shoes without his putting a hand on them. (The left sock must go in first.) On his way to the dugout between innings he has to toss his glove over his head so that it drops on the foul line. Any deviations from this fetishist formula mean horrible bad luck.[40]

Running him a close second for confidence in hocus-pocus is Mort Cooper, another star pitcher. During the 1942 season he discarded his No. 13 shirt in disgust and from that time on he won one game after another by adhering to a certain ritual—borrowing that teammate's shirt whose number corresponded to the number of the game he wanted to win. For example, he won his twentieth game by wearing Triplett's No. 20 shirt. "That voodoo did it." [41]

[39] *Ibid.*   [40] *Time,* September 14, 1942.   [41] *Time,* September 21, 1942.

Automobile racers also rely on charms to carry them to victory. The right talisman may be more important than the correct gasoline.

Prize fighters worry a lot over certain superstitions. A boxer does not like to climb into the ring first. John L. Sullivan maintained that the first man in never could win and so he demanded that the champion be allowed to duck under the ropes after his challenger. In

Teddy-bear Mascots Bring Gar Wood (left) Luck and Victory Cups. (International News Photo.)

1892, Sullivan was tricked by William A. Brady, Jim Corbett's Manager, into entering the ring first. The champion was worried. In the twenty-first round, Corbett knocked him out—the first and only time the mighty John L. ever went down for the count.

Boxers hate to see a hat on a bed. In 1932, after Max Schmeling lost his heavyweight title to Jack Sharkey, a friend came into his dressingroom and carelessly tossed his hat on the bed. When the fighter and his handlers learned he had done this constantly at training camp, they realized why Schmeling had lost.

With the exception of Joe Louis, colored fighters are notorious for elaborate superstitions. Joe Gans, lightweight, always carried one of his pet dice; Jack Johnson thought a $10 bill worn close to his ebony skin was good luck. Joe

Walcott and Sam Langford relied on Harlem's traditional antighost medicine: rabbits' feet.

Johnny Summers, lightweight, had the odd custom of kneeling in his corner between rounds clutching his young daughter's rag doll.[42]

Athletes are commonly superstitious because many of them believe that winning or losing a contest is a matter of luck. Chance is accepted as the ruling factor in competition, as "proved" by the fact that favored teams lose, mediocre teams win. The unpredictable outcome is feared with the same dread primitive man accords the evil eye. It has been said that sailors are among the most superstitious of men, since sailors have the widest experience of disasters which no foresight can avert. If this assertion is true of sailors, then athletes cannot be far behind. In either case, magic spells the difference between success and failure.

IV. LOCAL COLOR

Residents of a particular locality develop their own peculiar superstitions to fulfill their local needs. The resulting beliefs, often borrowed from other climes, are modified, given local color, and passed along from generation to generation until they seem indigenous to the local culture. Thus certain superstitions come to be associated with the heritage of a particular place. Because of this fact, the expert in the field of superstition can often place the locale of a belief very accurately. This would be possible, for example, with many of the Negro superstitions explored by Puckett in various sections of the South, mentioned in earlier parts of this chapter.

Local color is typical, too, of the superstitions found among the Pennsylvania Dutch and the Ozark Mountain folk.

A. Pennsylvania Dutch

Popularly associated with the Pennsylvania Dutch is the belief in the *hex*. Certain individuals, such as witch doctors or powwowers, are accredited with the power of *hexing,* a power of a magical nature that can be used for good or evil. A powwower can hex a sick person by means of secret salves and potions which ward off the evil spirits responsible for the disorder. Certain people, it is believed, can bewitch live stock, causing hogs, cows, and other animals to die. The hexer may accomplish this result by boring a hole in a barn with an auger, inserting pig hair and mule hair, and plugging the hole with a wooden stopper. Some places are haunted, like the Hexenkopf, a mountain

[42] The *Literary Digest,* July 10, 1937.

where hunters find their guns so bewitched that they cannot hit the hare or woodcock or grouse, and the chestnuts are no good. There is no use cutting a cedar post from the wood on this mountain because it will rot immediately. It's all due to hexerei. Farmers prevent their animals from being "ferhexed" (bewitched) by putting symbols on the south side of the barn. The symbol that is widely trusted is a six-lobed star, patterned after the six petals of the tulip. The tulip is the sign manual of all good things in the Dutch culture. No lightning

Exotic Decorations on a Barn in Lehigh County, Pa. (From *Consider the Lilies.* Courtesy, Pennsylvania German Folklore Society.)

rods appear on the barns, since the farmers believe their symbols provide sufficient protection against the elements.

B. Ozark Mountain Folk

Hexing is a matter of grave concern, also, among the Ozark Mountain folk, according to Vance Randolph, who is an authority on the Ozark Mountain region. Sudden deaths and delirious deaths, especially, are attributed to witchcraft. When a death occurs in a family, the clocks in the house are stopped, the mirrors are covered, and black cloths are draped over the bee hives to "tell the bees" so they won't swarm—if the bees did swarm, bad luck would hit everybody. The dead person's pillow is opened to see whether the feathers have bunched themselves into a wreath called the "heavenly crown." If the feathers are found woven into such a formation, it means the deceased has gone to heaven.

Among these hill folk of Missouri and Arkansas a maiden in search of a mate advertises her readiness for marriage by hanging a chicken

Ozark Woman with Poppet Doll.   (Courtesy, Vance Randolph, David F. Fox, and *Life*.)

bone over her door, thus announcing her "debut." She takes the bone down when the right man appears. Some girls snatch down the bone when the wrong man appears. Love is the dominant theme of Ozark spells. One widely adopted charm is made of a peach stone filled with a secret lure; it is worn on the girl's leg just above the knee. Ozark children are told that babies come out of the big galls on black-oak trees. Evil spirits are kept away from the cabins by placing three-pronged cedar pegs in the pathways.

Sympathetic magic is practiced faithfully by the Ozark natives. A witchwoman may make a "poppet" (doll) of dirt and beeswax, name it after her enemy, and then drive nails into the doll's body to "hurt" corresponding parts of the enemy's body. A nail through the heart spells death. Another example of such magic is the technique used by a wife to win back her errant husband. She makes a shrine of a skull and a Bible, places before it two puppets dressed in cloth once worn by the philandering pair, and drives heavy nails into the puppet of "the other woman" in order to cause her bodily pain. She would thus break up the adulterous romance.[43]

Witchcraft gets blamed for all sorts of disasters by these backwoods people. If cows go dry, the owner goes out and shoots the witch with a silver bullet. One man found himself in a haunted house. The first thing he knew he saw a big she-cat. He shot and blew off the cat's hind feet. Just then a woman somewhere hollered "Oh my Gawd," and he swears he saw a woman's bare foot, shot up and bloody. Later he learned that a woman in the neighborhood, at just about this same time, had shot her foot off "accidental-like, died a-yowlin' an' a-spittin' like a cat." [44]

V. PSEUDO SCIENCE

It seems puzzling that so many people in this scientific era can "fall for" the superstitious chicanery of the astrologists and the numerologists who pass off their systems as legitimate branches of science. Without even a blush the gullible public accepts the wildest claims of the pseudologists that stars and numbers control human destinies. Superstition is flourishing in the guise of science.

A. ASTROLOGY

In 1933 a New York City public-school teacher, Helena A. Perota, quit her desk when she discovered she had mystic powers latent in her being, and took to fortune-telling for a livelihood. As Gypsy Lee,[45] festooned in the trappings of Romany, she pitched her tent aboard the steamers of the Hudson River Day Line and in her spare time mapped out a plan of action. She called together twenty-one leading New York seers and seeresses to form the National Association of Fortune Tellers. Then as President of the Association, Gypsy Lee summoned the nation's fortune tellers to a convention in Trenton, New Jersey. At this convention the Fortune Tellers tried to win the

---

[43] Pictures illustrating these Ozark superstitions appeared in *Life,* June 19, 1939, and in *Click,* December, 1939.

[44] See V. Randolph: *Ozark Mountain Folks,* Chapter 2, "Witches and Witch-Masters." 1932.

[45] Not to be confused with Gypsy Rose Lee.

allegiance of their time-honored rivals, the astrologers (men) and astrologists (women), but the devotees of astrology were not willing to ally themselves with the crystal-gazers, card-readers, and palmists, whom they regarded as impostors. One thing occurred at this convention which is worth mentioning—because it is so entertaining—the Association went on record against dishonesty and fraud!

Astrology enjoys in this period of garish enlightenment a vogue it has not experienced since the fourteenth and fifteenth centuries, when it was a dominating influence at the courts of Europe.[46] Jonathan Swift was supposed to have disposed once and for all of its windy pretensions in his famous "Predictions of the Year 1708 by Isaac Bickerstaff, Esq.," but only a naïve person would be optimistic enough to believe that astrology could be annihilated by one fell blow. Indeed, it was estimated in 1936 that there were some 10,000 persons practicing astrology in the United States.[47] Many of them belong to the American Academy of Astrology [*sic!*]. Popular magazines print the secrets of the Zodiac in every issue. At least 250 newspapers in the United States, including three in New York City, print daily articles on astrology. The New York *Daily News* published a daily astrological forecast, much like its weather forecast, both in its form and, perhaps, in its accuracy. Nearly a dozen magazines are devoted entirely to this humbug, with a total circulation of some half a million copies. Pamphlets on astrology are sold extensively in five-and-ten-cent stores.

The present popularity of astrology is due, in large measure, to the amazing career of Evangeline Adams, ace astrologist. Miss Adams moved from Boston to New York in 1899. Her first client was the proprietor of the Hotel Windsor, on Fifth Avenue. In his horoscope she saw disaster rushing in upon him. A few moments later the hotel burst into flames. So the proprietor told newspaper reporters. Next day Miss Adams woke up to find herself a national figure. Celebrities flocked to her door. She consulted the stars concerning the destinies of individuals and of corporations. At $50 a consultation, she advised executives as to the fitness of employees for salary increases or promotions to positions of responsibility; through her auspices the stars told hundreds of parents when to conceive and when to bring forth their young. The radio broadcasts of Evangeline Adams enjoyed a vast audience, until she was forced off the air waves by protests made to the Federal Communications Commission by the American Astro-

[46] See C. W. Ferguson: "Superstition in Cellophane." The *Christian Century,* February 17, 1932.

[47] See "Fortune-Telling's Enlarged Scope." *Digest and Review,* December, 1936.

nomical Society and the American Society of Magicians, the latter insisting that people should be told, in all fairness, when they are about to be fooled. Her work has been carried on by her husband, George Edward Jordan, Jr., whose clients number about 165,000 persons. How long the rage may last, only the stars can say. Certainly it will continue as long as there are persons who find it easier to consult a soothsayer about the future than to sit down and plan constructively some means of bringing the future under their control.

Astrology is built on the assumption that the stars are interested in what is happening to individual human beings. Just why the stars should concern themselves with our personal affairs and just how the stars go about directing our destinies are questions discreetly left unanswered by believers. In spite of such disquieting queries, devotees of the cult remain unshaken in their faith that our personal fates are in the "laps of the stars." Our word *disaster* is based on this faith in stellar determinism.

Disaster: Latin *dis-*, against, away from; and *astra,* stars. If you disregard your horoscope—play the market on Tuesday when the astrologers say Thursday, for example—you are courting *dis*aster. . . . Ill-starred has the same sense of unlucky.[48]

The belief in planetary influences is an ancient one. The tenets of the creed have been refined to make them simulate more exactly the criteria of science. The improvements, however, are evidence of a fundamental misapplication of intelligence, no matter how cleverly the schemata are devised. While the astrologer constructs a horoscope, the astronomer builds a planetarium. There is a world of difference focused in that contrast.

When we examine the presuppositions underlying astrology, it becomes increasingly difficult to understand how such a pseudology can survive in our supposedly enlightened age.

The fanciful bond between the stars and our fate rests only on the coincidence that the Greeks assigned human qualities to their gods and also named the stars after them. On the basis of mere namesake kinship, the pseudological mind decreed that a mortal born when the *planet* Jupiter is in a certain position, by that name communion, must be "jovial" in disposition because the *god* Jupiter (Jove for short) was so rated.[49]

[48] M. Ernst: *In a Word*, p. 80. Alfred A. Knopf, Inc., 1939.
[49] J. Jastrow: "Lo, the Pseudologist." *Esquire,* January, 1936.

By the same sort of farfetched analogy, it is reasoned that if Saturn happens to be in the ascendant when a child is born, the child will be gloomy (saturnine), for the time of his birth predestines him to misfortune. It sounds like a jest, a belabored one, at that—but it is no joke. There are plenty of people who take it seriously, who make no commitments until they have learned what the stars have to say.

One of the weirdest products of astrologizing is the Zodiacal man, a strange composite of anatomy and constellations.

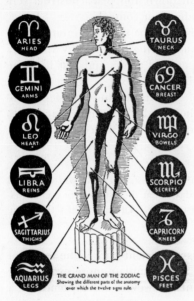

(Courtesy, *Esquire*.)

He came into imaginary existence when fancy traced in the grouping of the stars certain sketchy resemblances to animal and human forms, and by a feeble analogy of relation, assigned the *Ram* (Aries) with its prominent horns to the *head;* the big-necked *Bull* (Taurus) to the *neck;* the Fish (Pisces) at the bottom of the sea, to the *feet,* the *Twins* (Gemini), in that there are two, to the *arms,* and the *Goat* (Capricorn) because of its nimble knee-action, to the *knees.* Four hundred years ago, this construction led to no greater irrelevance than prescribing goat's grease for pain in the knees; today it gives rise to such sapience as this: "Thirty-odd years ago, the world came strongly under the influence of Uranus in Scorpio, which rules invention on the material plane. Children born during this period were sure to be interested in mechanical things like phonographs, player pianos, moving pictures, automobiles, airplanes and radios." And they were—strangely like children born at any other time.[50]

Similarly, persons born under Leo will be leonine, that is, dominant individuals fitted for positions of power, "born to the purple." It is true that Mussolini and Ford and Hoover were August-born children (*Leos*) but so are butchers and bakers and bindlestiffs. Washington and Lincoln got along all right, in spite of the fact that they were born at the wrong times, the former being a *Fish,* the latter a *Water-Bearer.* Surveys of great men show, as anybody in his lucid moments would

[50] *Ibid.*

anticipate, that no single month has a monopoly on illustrious personages.

Astrological nonsense is responsible for much anxiety among people who are inclined to give credence to such Zodiacal hocus-pocus. There are persons who believe, for example, that there is a connection between Cancer, the sign of the Zodiac, and cancer, the disease, and as a result of this superstition they are led to the conclusion that an individual born under that sign is predestined to die of cancer. This dread is so prevalent that the New York City Cancer Committee took occasion in 1932 to publish a refutation of the astrological dogma on this matter, for the benefit of ignorant people worrying themselves sick over the dread of their inevitable end.[51]

What are the benefits that astrology is supposed to confer upon those who turn to the Zodiac for guidance? An astrological consultant can answer that question for us very readily. A brochure outlining "What Astrology Means to You," is designed especially to "dispel all doubts for those who are sufficiently 'advanced' to grasp its helpful message." One benefit is health. The astrologer can tell, given the time of your birth, just what sickness you are in for in this earthly sojourn. His predictions are based on astronomical observations, though gastronomical observations might shed more light on the prognosis. The expert astrologer can predict when you are going to have a sore throat. If he is conscientious in his role of adviser, he will urge you to take preventive measures, so that you can prevent such a misfortune from happening. So the astrologer predicts a sore throat, which you don't get because you gargle in time, thus disproving the reliability of the consultant as a seer into the future. When Caruso's family consulted an astrologer, during a severe illness that had beset the great singer, they were assured that he would not die from that illness. "And all the world knows that he did not. That is a proof of the great blessing and boon of astrology."

Greek skeptics used to ask whether it was possible that all the soldiers who fell at the battle of Salamis had the same horoscope.[52] The modern skeptic might point out that the birthdays of the victims bombed in London or Berlin or Nagasaki are quite likely distributed in the same diversified manner as the birthdays of the survivors. If astrologers were sincere in their profession of scientific interest, they would make statistical studies of individual differences and of individual careers to see whether they correlate significantly with the signs

---

[51] *Cancer: Then and Now*. Published by the Chemical Foundation. 1932.
[52] See J. Jastrow: *The Betrayal of Intelligence*, p. 41. 1938.

of the Zodiac or the signs of anything else. Painstaking investigation of such relationships are not found among the publications of the astrologers. Instead, these seers continue to make vague prediction that are so indefinite that it is impossible to determine by any check whether they come true or not; unlike scientists, the astrologers see fit to ignore the negative instances when their horoscopic readings turn out to be incorrect. Mistakes in prediction may be somewhat embarrassing, as in the case of James M. Curley, who was elected Governor of Massachusetts in 1934 in spite of the fact that the stars and the Republicans were allied against him. A report from Scotland in 194 tells of a street of small shops in a much blitzed city. "Most of them were badly damaged, and practically all had their windows smashed One of them however has a little glass left, from which the proprietor has not troubled to remove the printed slogan: 'Don't worry. The stars say there will be no war.' " [53]

When events fail to conform to astrological computation, it can always be said that astrologers make mistakes but the stars never do. When events do turn out as predicted, it would be naïve to conclude from a single case or even several cases that the stars are regulating everything that happens to us. "Don't say or think 'there's something in it,' of any false system. Those who trust to false systems are setting out to sea in a sieve. A sieve is not all holes, but it will not hold water." [54] Before deciding that "there's something to it," it would be wise to ask why astrologers who can see the future so clearly don't play the stockmarket for a living instead of advising others just when to buy and when to sell. The quizzical observer may be excused for raising an eyebrow when he notes that a famous astrologer who numbered great financiers among her clients, died insolvent herself. One astrologer closed his office in 1940 because the future seemed so uncertain.

Certain signs of the Zodiac are supposed to be especially propitious for the birth of persons with marked aesthetic capacities. This claim has been checked in two ways by Farnsworth: first, by determining whether most artists were born under certain planetary influences which are supposed by astrologers to be specially conducive to art; second, by comparing the birth dates of artists with the birth dates of people in general. One important obstacle in the way of the first procedure was the ambiguity encountered in the authoritative astrological manuals. They were found to be "none too clearly written. Only

---

[53] The *Christian Century,* December 10, 1941.
[54] Jastrow: *The Betrayal of Intelligence,* p. 47. Greenberg: Publisher, 1938.

one sign, Libra, seems to be agreed upon fairly generally as an artistic sign." [55] Farnsworth's research did not reveal a preponderance of artists born under the ascendancy of Libra. An analysis of the birth dates of New York and Vienna populations failed to uncover any birth trends to confirm the claims of astrology. These results are in line with the conclusions reached by Huntington in his studies of the relationship between time of birth and noteworthy achievement, to the effect that certain seasons of the year seem to produce more than their share of great men, notably February and March (conceptions in May and June); but there is no evidence that any particular kind of greatness, such as artistic fame, is to be significantly correlated with any special season. [56]

Thousands of people are born every day at the same hour who turn out very differently, no two of them having the same kind of personality or the same profile of talents. Artists are born in all the months, scientists are born in all the months, and no one month can be said to be partial to any single professional interest or to any special sort of temperamental disposition. Why should the time of birth be so significant? Why not the time of conception? Certainly the stars could keep posted on the hour of conception and start influencing the embryo in its prenatal evolution. If a person is to believe that the time of birth is all-important, then it would seem logical to assume that the obstetrician who hastens a birth is thereby remolding indirectly the child's whole personality. Such an assumption should not prove too much of a burden for a person who can believe, as a premise, that a chunk of rock floating in space millions of miles away can influence our behavior because that chunk has the same name as some character in Greek mythology. "Would it be a greater absurdity to say that riding in a Pullman car named Venus would insure success in love?" [57]

An astrologer wrote Frank Schlesinger, director of the Yale University Astronomical Observatory, offering to give him a test prediction if he would send in the exact time, down to the minute, when somebody he knew was born. The professor gave him the time of his son's birth, and waited. Said the professor later:

I don't know whether astrologers go by standard or daylight saving time, but I gave this fellow all necessary corrections for different kinds of time at

---

[55] P. R. Farnsworth: "Aesthetic Behavior and Astrology." *Character and Personality*, 1938, 6, 335-340.

[56] See E. Huntington: *Season of Birth*, Chapter 13, "Leadership, Birth Rank, and Season of Birth." 1938.

[57] F. C. Kelly: "That Gigantic Fraud, Astrology." *Commentator*, May, 1938.

New York and elsewhere, including Peiping. Naturally at a given hour there would be a great difference in the position of the planets according to *where* you were born. . . . Not a single thing he told me about my son's life was true.[58]

The charlatanry of the astrologers is exhibited in the ease with which new functions are assigned to planets each time a new one is discovered. Uranus was discovered in 1781 and Neptune in 1846. Apparently these two planets, each of them bigger than Mercury and Mars and Venus combined, had been influencing human affairs for centuries without revealing themselves to the ken of the astrologers. Congenial jobs were found for both of them by Evangeline Adams, who passed out their assignments with majestic pomp: Uranus to rule the railroads and Neptune to govern aviation. The astronomer Herschel demonstrated exactly how he had discovered Uranus, explained why others had failed to locate it; Miss Adams, however, would have been embarrassed if she had been compelled to demonstrate the influence of Neptune on aviation.

A campaign to enlighten the public and to strengthen all state antiastrology laws was launched in 1941 by the Boston-Cambridge branch of the American Association of Scientific Workers under the leadership of Bart J. Bok and Margaret W. Mayall of the Harvard Observatory.[59] These scientists cite the following facts: the amounts of radiation from the stars and planets which are received on the earth are exceedingly small and their gravitational effects are so slight as to be negligible in comparison with radiations from near-by objects; the walls of hospitals and other buildings where babies are born are opaque to all known radiations from the planets; astrology requires an unknown mechanism for the transfer of planetary influence; astrologers assume that planets with a considerable degree of similarity affect human affairs in an entirely dissimilar fashion; the choice of the moment of birth as the one and only critical instant seems arbitrary, and one is inclined to ask why this particular moment should be favored over the time of conception; the rules by which astrologers interpret their horoscopes have not been derived from any known experiments or observations.[60]

The menace of astrology has prompted a vigorous statement on the subject from the executive council of the Society for the Psychological Study of Social Issues:

[58] *Ibid.*   [59] *Time,* January 27, 1941.
[60] See B. J. Bok and M. W. Mayall: "Scientists Look at Astrology." *Scientific Monthly,* March, 1941.

Psychologists find no evidence that astrology is of any value whatsoever as an indicator of past, present, or future trends in one's personal life or in one's destiny. Nor is there the slightest ground for believing that social events can be foretold by divinations of the stars. The Society for the Psychological Study of Social Issues therefore deplores the faith of a considerable section of the American public in a magical practice that has no shred of justification in scientific fact.

The principal reason why people turn to astrology and to kindred superstitions is that they lack in their own lives the resources necessary to solve serious personal problems confronting them. Feeling blocked and bewildered they yield to the pleasant suggestion that a golden key is at hand—a simple solution—an ever-present help in time of trouble. This belief is more readily accepted in times of disruption and crisis when the individual's normal safeguards against gullibility are broken down. When moral habits are weakened by depression or war, bewilderment increases, self-reliance is lessened, and belief in the occult increases.

Faith in astrology or in any other occult practice is harmful in so far as it encourages an unwholesome flight from the persistent problems of real life. Although it is human enough to try to escape from the effort involved in hard thinking and to evade taking responsibility for one's own acts, it does no good to turn to magic and mystery in order to escape misery. Other solutions must be found by people who suffer from the frustrations of poverty, from grief at the death of a loved one, or from fear of economic or personal insecurity.

By offering the public the horoscope as a substitute for honest and sustained thinking, astrologers have been guilty of playing upon the human tendency to take easy rather than difficult paths. Astrologers have done this in spite of the fact that science has denied their claims and in spite of laws in some states forbidding the prophecies of astrology as fraudulent. It is against public interest for astrologists to spread their counsels of flight from reality.

It is unfortunate that in the minds of many people astrology is confused with true science. The result of this confusion is to prevent these people from developing truly scientific habits of thought that would help them understand the natural, social, and psychological factors that are actually influencing their destinies. It is, of course, true that science itself is a long way from a final solution to the social and psychological problems that perplex mankind; but its accomplishments to date clearly indicate that men's destinies are shaped by their own actions in this world. The heavenly bodies may safely be left out of account. Our fates rest not in our stars but in ourselves.[61]

---

[61] Quoted by Bok and Mayall: *loc. cit.*

B. NUMEROLOGY

Numerology is another pseudo science with a wide vogue today Years ago the tenants of a fashionable apartment house in New York City began breaking their leases, tenant after tenant departing without any complaints about rental charges or lack of heat. The sudden exodus remained a puzzle until the mystery was cleared up by the police: a prominent numerologist in the city had informed the ladies that the house number at that address was bringing static to their destiny.[62]

According to the numerologists, "all names are numbers and all numbers are names." When a person or corporation is named, certain vibrations are supposed to be set in motion and "it is only by knowledge and wisdom that we can govern, direct, and adjust ourselves to these vibrations." A prominent numerologist whose classes are largely attended, announces in the daily press:

People in all walks of life are becoming interested in numerology, the science of numbers. Those who are not familiar with numerology will be interested to learn that we are all working under certain vibrations, and it is by understanding them that we are able to overcome difficulties and attain success. Numerology, correctly interpreted, shows the right way.

Many problems which disturb our peace of mind, both in the social and business world, are easily adjusted once we are set on the right path.

Many people after having their names analyzed are interested to study numerology themselves so they may be able to work in accord with the laws of vibration. It is a definite science easily applied when the underlying principles are thoroughly understood.[63]

This announcement appeared in a respectable newspaper whose editors compose wonderful editorials urging the readers to develop an intelligent outlook on the world about them.

What are the underlying principles that can be so easily applied to solve all of our perplexities? The basic idea is the determination of the number-values of a person's baptismal name. This is done by drawing up panels of traits for the nine fundamental numerological varieties of human beings and then designating each person as a "1," a "2," a "3," and so on up to a "9," with a special class of "11's" and an extra-special class of "22's." The scheme is simple:

[62] See C. W. Ferguson: "The Religion of Luck." The *Christian Century*, March 30, 1932.
[63] A Boston newspaper.

```
1 2 3 4 5 6 7 8 9
a b c d e f g h i
j k l m n o p q r
s t u v w x y z
```

The 11th letter *k* is counted as 11 and the 22nd letter *v* is counted as 22. Using the above key, John Doe's name may be analyzed as follows:

```
J o h n    D o e
1 6 8 5    4 6 5
```

That all adds up to 35. Now you divide by 9, a standard procedure, and see what you have left over as a remainder. In John's case, we are left with a remainder of "8," which means that John is an "8."

The number-values of the *vowels alone* in your name determine your *Soul-Urge;* those of the *consonants alone* shape your *Quiescent Self,* the self you dream about; the total *name* stands for your *Expression,* that is, what you actually do. After you have discovered by an analysis of this sort what kind of person you are, you are ready to grasp advice on any particular problem that happens to be facing you. You may learn, for example, that you will find yourself at *sixes* or *sevens* if you attempt to act "1" when the day says "2." Better tune yourself up a bit, so you'll vibrate in the right key.

There might have been some excuse for accepting this systematized balderdash back in the times of the Pythagoreans, who built a philosophy of numbers to explain the nature of the universe, a philosophy that was later bastardized by charlatans. The wise person will want to know today how it is possible, on numerological premises, that there can be so many different John Smiths vibrating at such different frequencies, as evidenced by their different personalities, their different professions, their different stations in life. One John Smith will vary as widely from another John Smith as any particular John Smith will differ from Algernon Higginbotham. It makes life interesting, certainly, to believe that there is mystical significance in the vibrations tied up in your house number, your telephone number, your automobile registration number, your office number, but it doesn't make sense. It would be as rational to compute your income tax return by multiplying your telephone number by the size of your hat, subtracting the number of the clubs you belong to, dividing by the number of electric lights in your house, and adding the size of your collar.

The sort of thinking that numerology is based on may fool some people because it has the earmarks of rationality. This seeming logicality is deceptive enough to convince people who really want to believe in such folderol. The superficial rationality of the numerologists was cleverly satirized by Newell Dwight Hillis in one of his famous sermons:

Nothing is easier than proving that every man in history was mythical Archbishop Whateley has shown conclusively that Napoleon never lived. By carefully scrutinizing Washington's addresses one can find cryptograms that establish the fact that Hamilton and Jefferson invented him. Why, one could prove in five minutes that Abraham Lincoln, the emancipator of slaves, and the late war are all legends, just as Renan and Straus suggest that many things in the life of Jesus are mythical. Two thousand years from now some Renan of American history will investigate the Lincoln myth. Then his argument will move along these lines:

Beyond all doubt there must have been at some early time a collision between the black race and the white race. Patriotism needs heroes. Youth feeds upon the godlike qualities in great leaders. Needing a giant, therefore the far-off American fathers created a martyr. They named him Abraham Lincoln and made him tall of body as well as mind.

But in building up the myth they were very clumsy. If they had named him John Lincoln, they might have deceived us—but Abraham—that is too much. Abraham means the freeman and the emancipator, and inasmuch as they proposed to make him free slaves, they named him Abraham. This is in itself very suspicious. Not content with casting about until they found the title Abram, they kept on until they took the name Ham, which was the name of the colored race, the children of Ham, and then they tacked the word "Ham" on to the Abram. This not only stirs suspicion, but it gives absolute certainty of the mythical origin. Having now proved beyond the possibility of a doubt that this Abraham Lincoln was a myth, we now come to other arguments though these are not needed.

In building this myth about an emancipator, they made Abraham Lincoln's Vice-President to be called Hannibal Hamlin. Inasmuch as this administration was to emancipate the slaves, who were the sons of Ham, they ventured to tack this Ham on to the Vice-President's name, calling him Hamlin. Probably they did the same thing with his given name, Hannibal. It may be that the printers of 2000 years ago changed an "m" to an "n," for without doubt the inventors named the Vice-President Hammibal Hamlin, which has been corrupted to Hannibal. But having now proved that the Vice-President also was a myth, let us now examine critically the growth of the idea that there was any rebellion on the part of the southern states.

Count the letters in the name of Abraham Lincoln and there are 14, and the letters of Hannibal Hamlin, and there are 14, giving us the exact 28

tates that they represented, showing us how the creator of the myth worked
t out mathematically.[64]

It is, of course, impossible to prove to a person who believes in as-
rology or numerology that these systems of prediction are fakes, as
pseudo as the pseudo sciences go. Respected scientists, men who be-
ong to the recognized scientific societies like the American Associa-
ion for the Advancement of Science, do not believe that the stars we're
born under govern our destinies and they do not accept the proposi-
ion that the number of letters in a person's name sets him vibrating
on the path to success in a certain year. The fact that reputable
cientists do not endorse this nonsense may be discredited, of course, as
an *argumentum ad verecundiam* (appeal to prestige). It is possible,
indeed, that a group of eminent scientists might be mistaken, but it is
much less likely than the probability that a group of uneducated persons will be disposed to accept theories unsupported by reliable evidence. If we must follow leaders, let's select good ones—astronomers
n preference to astrologists, statisticians in preference to numerologists, historians in preference to seers. We cannot be too careful in
choosing our guides.

VI. SUPERSTITION AND RELIGION

Some people feel that religion is essentially superstitious, that it is
obligatory, therefore, to emancipate ourselves from the church and
all that the church stands for, if we are to live bravely in the new
world of today. It is sometimes asserted by sophisticated persons that
only ignorant people will be gullible enough to believe in God and
immortality. Among skeptics, faith in the unseen may be regarded as
evidence of sheer naïveté. This indictment of religion merits a
thoughtful answer.

There is no doubt that some religious practices are indulged in with
the same faith in magic which characterized primitive superstition.
Tozzer reports the case of a student who made it a point to attend
chapel on the morning of an examination. The student confessed
that his attendance on these special occasions was motivated by a superstitious feeling rather than a religious feeling.[65] He meant to imply in this self-analysis that he believed his presence at the divine service in itself was an insurance of success in the day's test. He felt a
little sacrilegious in terming this act a superstition but honesty com-

[64] N. D. Hillis in the *Advance* (Chicago).
[65] See Tozzer: *op. cit.,* p. 256.

pelled him to admit that such was the case.   Probably his diagnosis was correct.   It would be overgeneralizing to conclude from this one instance that going to church is always a matter of sheer superstition

It has already been pointed out that labeling the other fellow's religion "superstition" may be the name-calling device of the propagandist.   It is easier to detect the superstitious elements in somebody else's religion than in one's own.   Let us suppose there is some element of superstition in everyone's religion.   Is it fair to jump to the conclusion that since there is some superstition in every man's religion, religion therefore, is nothing but superstition?   Some prominent scientists have unwisely pursued their own logic to that congenial interpretation Both religion and superstition involve faith in the supernatural; consequently, it is falsely asserted, religion must be superstitious.   Such a conclusion is not logically justified by the premise, since it is based on the fallacy of "the ambiguous middle term."

Freud believes that religious beliefs are the products of wishful thinking, that they have no more validity than our idlest daydreams Freud argues as follows: we want to believe in a good God; it makes us feel better to have faith in the immortality of our souls; it is a source of consolation and strength to think that God is looking out for our welfare; we have invented God in order to have somebody forgive our sins.   These beliefs are all thereupon branded by Freud as childish immature, magical, superstitious; one and all, illusions.   According to some psychoanalysts, anybody who is naïve enough to think that reality is pleasant is "kidding" himself.   Logically, the fact that I want to believe in God does not bear in any way on the question of God's existence and it is possible that I may be immortal in spite of my hope for survival.

According to Lewis Browne, religion is born solely of fear.   Early man, he recounts, was afraid of the hostile spirits that were ever threatening him with punishment for his misdeeds.   After a time he discovered that some spirits were friendly, that even the hostile spirits might be won over.   Thus a hope was raised that maybe the spirits could be exploited for the promotion of personal ends.   Sacrifices were made to the fetishes and the idols in which spirits resided.   These sacrifices were accompanied by songs of praise, for the spirits were supposed to be vain as well as hungry.   Thus prayer was born.   Animism, idolatry, priestcraft, sacrifice, prayer, the church, were all developed by man as means for gaining personal control of the universe Religion came into being as techniques were developed for persuading the deities to show some cooperation in furthering plans in which the applicant happened to be interested.   Religion never displaced primitive magic entirely and "to this day no historical religion on earth is without its adulterations of magic." [66]   The belief that the bread and wine of communion actually change into the body and blood of Christ is interpreted by Browne as a relic of an old magic rite.   "The belief that any prayer is efficacious *only* if uttered in a certain place at a certain time in a certain tongue by a certain person, or is *particularly* efficacious if concluded with the words 'We ask it in Jesus' name' or some similar formula—such a belief reveals quite obviously the degeneration of a one-time religious petition into a mere magic spell." [67]   Later the idea that God knows all and sees all and metes out punishment in the hereafter for earthly sins, haunted the believer and prompted him to take measures for getting on the right side of the God-in-the-sky. Religion began in fear, still thrives on fear.   So Browne maintains.[68]

Such is the story of religion as Browne tells it, a story far too simple to cover adequately the heterogeneous motives involved in man's spiritual needs.   Religion is the outgrowth of man's whole nature, not just one phase of it.   Certainly love and hunger and self-esteem and many other motives led primitive man to worship supernatural powers, as McDougall asserts in his *Introduction to Social Psychology,* where he calls attention to admiration (a fusion of wonder and negative self-feeling), awe (a fusion of admiration with fear), and reverence (a blending of awe with tender emotion)—all of these emotions being sentiments that enter into the religious experience.[69]   Perhaps Browne oversimplified the picture in an effort to popularize his account of the early evolution of religion.   His story gains in vividness by being so simple.   Its very simplicity, however, encourages the reader to conclude that religion is to be discredited because of its humble origin in magic and superstition.   We must remember that science, too, began in magic and superstition: astronomy grew out of astrology, chemistry out of alchemy, mathematics out of numerology.   We do not reject Kepler's laws of planetary motion because he thought that the planets were sped on their way by angels who mounted the heavenly bodies and drove them by the beating of their wings.   Both science and religion have produced their mythologies; neither should be accepted or rejected in terms of its origins (the genetic fallacy).   People who stake their salvation on science, who trust their souls to the priestcraft of

[66] L. Browne: *This Believing World,* p. 44.   1926.
[67] *Ibid.,* p. 44.
[68] *Ibid.,* Book One, "How It All Began."
[69] See W. McDougall: *An Introduction to Social Psychology,* Chapter 13, "The Instincts through Which Religious Conceptions Affect Social Life." 1908. 1921.

scientists, who believe that science is omnipotent, are perhaps just a
superstitious as those persons who justify their shiftlessness by the con
tention that "the Lord will provide." [70]   Whether religion is inher
ently superstitious must be determined by reference to the attitudes c
individual believers, not only in the past but also in the present.   Joh
Haynes Holmes has summed up the situation with profound insight
"It is not that religion is inherently superstitious but rather that mar
is superstitious, and carries over into his philosophy, and science, an
the practices of his daily life, all the irrational fads and fancies tha
make up in any one age the content of his brain." [71]

The crux of our general problem here may be formulated thus: I
religion outgrowing its superstitious past, just as science is purgin
itself of its ancient kinship with magic?   Under the critical influenc
of scientific advance, religious thinkers are getting away more and mor
from the magical forms of faith.   Religion is evolving toward a mor
intelligent view of the universe.

We see the evolution of his concept of God from an anthropomorphic con
ception of numerous deities of capricious behavior and often conflicting pur
poses, through the notion of a single God who walked and bargained witl
men, who chastised them and repented, to the conception of a great spiritua
force operating through natural laws which are understandable and depend
able and at least partly discoverable through science.[72]

Some beliefs, widely accepted a generation ago and taken very seri
ously by the pious, are a source of amusement to the present genera
tion.   Take, for example, Bellamy Partridge's story of the lawsuit tha
resulted from the efficacy of collective prayer.   Crops had been suffer
ing from a prolonged drought; Duncan McLeod, the new Presbyteria
minister, organized a town-wide prayer for rain, with everybody in th
community invited to join the intercession for five minutes starting a
noon on a hot August Saturday.   Later, at four o'clock, a thunder
storm swept the township, drenched the parched countryside with tw
inches of rain, and ignited with a bolt of lightning the large hay bar
of Phineas Dodd.   The barn burned to the ground, a total loss
Phineas Dodd had been opposed to the idea of petitioning the Al
mighty to send rain, insisting that men should not meddle in the affair
of the Lord.   When he heard how elated Mr. McLeod was over the

[70] See G. Adams: *Psychology: Science or Superstition?* 1931.
[71] J. H. Holmes: *The Sensible Man's View of Religion*, p. 6. 1932.
[72] K. T. Compton: "Religion in a Scientific Era." *Scientific Monthly*, January
1940.

rompt answer to the prayer for rain, he sued the Rev. McLeod for ne $5000 loss on the barn. Partridge's father, who was counsel for ne minister, maintained through cross-examination that the plaintiff, hineas Dodd, had failed to produce evidence that the defendants ad prayed for anything but *rain,* and he argued that the lightning as an entirely gratuitous gift from the Author of All Weather. The uit was dismissed.[73] This story would not have been considered entertaining a generation ago because people quite generally felt that iod could be influenced to fill personal orders for private benefits of ne kind or another. Partridge's account of the incident would have een thought irreverent and in bad taste. The naïveté of the belief nat God can interrupt the course of nature to suit the whims of the uithful is apparent to a generation trained to view the universe as a vorld of law and order. Science is compelling religion to abandon its rust in magic.

VII. EDUCATION AND SUPERSTITION

It is generally assumed that education is the best antidote for superstition. Certainly the ignorant person may be excused for his faith in nagic on the ground that he really "doesn't know any better." The ducated person, enlightened by an historical view of human thought, rained in the principles of laboratory science, versed in the laws of ogic, should be expected to put away childish modes of thought in avor of more mature beliefs. Investigations have shown that college tudents do grow less superstitious as they progress in knowledge, hough they still retain some of their pet superstitions even after four ears of intellectual training. The fact that college graduates may lace their trust in rabbits' feet and other charms, despite their superior intelligence and despite their superior enlightenment, shows ow emotional habits in favor of magic may override mere academic leation. Impressed by the fact that even seniors cling sometimes to he naïve ideas of childhood, Dudycha comments: "Although college nstruction is such that it does convert some few students from their aïve beliefs and superstitions, it certainly is not such as to convince ll students of the falsity of such notions as those concerning good and ll fortune, fortune-telling and other such popular beliefs."[74] The vidence suggests that college training is not as effective as it might be n eradicating wishful, unscientific modes of thinking.

[73] B. Partridge: *Country Lawyer.* 1939.
[74] G. J. Dudycha: "The Superstitious Beliefs of College Students," *Journal f Abnormal and Social Psychology,* 1932-33, 27, 457-464.

Back in the early 1900's Dresslar made an investigation of the su perstitious beliefs current at that time among students at a Souther university. The students were requested to write out all the superst tions they could think of in an hour and to indicate for each iter whether it evoked *no belief, partial belief,* or *full belief.* Tabula tions of 7176 confessions of belief or disbelief in some 300 varieties o superstitions were made and it was found that the percentage of belie was about 45. One belief mentioned was: "If you permit a baby les than a year old to look into a mirror, it will die before it is a year old. Ten out of the eleven people who listed this item, expressed an abic ing belief in the truth of it. Dresslar suggested that college student retain these superstitious beliefs because they wish to complete thei search for an answer to a particular problem, to secure relief from un certainty, to reduce experience to rules—on the assumption that an rules are better than none.[75] A later study of this same general prob lem was made by Conklin. Male and female students at the Univer sity of Oregon were asked to state any superstition which they believe or which influenced their conduct. An excellent sampling of super stitions was obtained. Forty per cent of the males and 66.6 per cent o the females indicated their acceptance of superstitions. Eighty-tw per cent of the subjects stated that they could recall having believed o having been influenced by superstitions, at some earlier time. Nine teen per cent wrote that their beliefs had been confirmed by a few ex periences that seemed to verify their assumptions; some were convince by one such experience. Most of the beliefs were attributed to socia contacts with credulous persons, especially parents.[76]

Nixon prepared a test on popular beliefs, including statements lik "Women are by nature purer and better than men." [77] (Note tha this statement, like some others in the list, does not satisfy our criteri for superstition). Gilliland used a modified form of Nixon's test a Northwestern University, where it was administered to 103 students i general psychology in the College of Liberal Arts and to 46 student taking the same subject in evening classes in the School of Commerce Liberal Arts students averaged 9.58 in acceptance before the course

[75] See F. B. Dresslar: "Suggestions on the Psychology of Superstition." *Proceed ings of the American Medico-Psychological Association.* 1910. *American Journa of Insanity,* 1910, 67, 213-226.
See also, F. B. Dresslar: *Superstition and Education.* 1907.
[76] See E. S. Conklin: "Superstitious Beliefs and Practices Among College Students. *American Journal of Psychology,* 1919, 30, 83-102.
[77] See H. K. Nixon: "Popular Answers to Some Psychological Questions." *Amer ican Journal of Psychology,* 1925, 36, 418-423.

.15 afterward; Commerce students, 11.98 before, 6.58 afterward. Despite the fact that the test included some popular beliefs non-superstitious in nature, as we have noted, the study does demonstrate the value of a course in psychology in reducing credulity. Gilliland is careful to point out that the shift toward skepticism with reference to these popular fictions should not be accredited solely to the course in psychology, as there were other influences motivating the students to reevaluate their stock of beliefs.[78]

Many of the superstitions encountered among college students concern athletic competition and examinations. Athletes may believe:

That it is good luck to wear the same uniform in a game as worn in practice.

That fortune will smile if the socks do not match.

That a hit is more likely if home plate is tapped with the bat a certain number of times.

That victory may be assured by wearing a pin on the undershirt or carrying a penny in the pants leg.

College rooters who see the team lose repeatedly may be forced to the conclusion that they are jinxing the players and that it is advisable to stay away from the games. Students facing examinations may believe that success depends on:

Using a certain pen (fetish).

Wearing no underclothes.

Putting the lecture notes under the pillow.

Wearing a special necktie.

Getting out of the right side of the bed.

Picking up a pin pointing toward the examinee.

It is a long-established superstition that shaving during the time of exams is sure to lead to flunking. Some students may take this warning to mean that one may shave part of the face but not the whole. As a result, chin whiskers, goatees, and Vandykes may bloom. Growing a beard may be effective in that it saves the time occupied in shaving and cuts down on social engagements.

It is reported that two Harvard students insisted on occupying the same seat in an examination, since both of them had enjoyed good luck in that seat in former tests. They were separated by a proctor who

[78] See A. R. Gilliland: "A Study of the Superstitions of College Students." *Journal of Abnormal and Social Psychology*, 1930, 24, 473-479.

made the suggestion that they toss a coin as an amicable way to decide the contest. To insure fair play, the proctor was required to toss the coin himself. During an examination on classical history, one student produced from his pockets three small plaster of Paris busts, which he arranged on the desk before him. One was identified as Julius Caesar, another as the poet Homer, and the third as Plutarch, the Roman historian. With these images to aid him, the student proceeded with confidence to answer the questions assigned him. It is commonly felt that the potency of any charm may be nullified if the student coming out of the exam commits the folly of saying that the exam was easy. Such optimism is merely inviting disaster.

There are a number of reasons why educated persons may be superstitious despite years of academic study. The chief reason is that faith in certain superstitions is a habit carried over from childhood and the emotional conditioning involved in beliefs makes them more or less immune to uprooting influences. Pet beliefs are protected by logic-tight compartments, dissociated from the realm of critical intelligence. Superstitions can always be excused by maintaining that chance operates when there are factors involved which remain unknown. It makes life more dramatic to suppose that mysterious forces control the universe.

There are signs that indicate progress is being made in eradicating superstition. Perhaps the most encouraging one is the sheepish look worn by the sophisticated person who gets caught by a friend in the act of performing some magic rite in order to guarantee the fulfillment of a personal desire.

Would you admit, in company, your subscription to any of the following beliefs, *without any embarrassment?*

1. Do you cross your fingers and wish on a wagonful of hay?
2. Do you say "Bread and butter" when a post or some other object comes between you and another person?
3. Do you cross your fingers when telling an untruth?
4. Do you wish on the first star of the evening?
5. Do you avoid looking at this star after you have wished upon it?
6. Do you avoid carrying two-dollar bills?
7. Do you tell a dream before breakfast?
8. If you put your clothes on wrong side out, do you leave them that way?
9. If you and another person happen to say the same thing at the same moment, do you hook fingers and wish?
10. Do you knock on wood?
11. Do you wish on a wishbone?

12. Do you avoid the number 13?

13. If you spill salt, do you throw a little of it over your shoulder?

14. Are you careful not to break a mirror for fear of 7 years' bad luck?

15. Do you believe that a shooting star means a death or birth?

16. Do you believe that if persons engaged to be married are photographed together, their marriage will never occur?

Emme reports that there is a strong negative correlation between intelligence and belief in superstition, that specific instruction reduces belief in superstitions.[79] If his findings are valid, we may still rely on education as our main hope for emancipation from the lure of magic.

---

[79] See E. E. Emme: "Modification and Origin of Certain Beliefs in Superstition among 96 College Students." *Journal of Psychology,* 1940, 10, 279-291. "Supplementary Study of Superstitious Belief among College Students." *Journal of Psychology,* 1941, 12, 183-184.

Chapter 16

PREJUDICE: DOGMATISM AND IGNORANCE

PREJUDICES are of interest to the social psychologist because they affect our interpersonal relations most vitally, setting race against race, sect against sect, nation against nation, predisposing us to like people who most resemble ourselves. We shall examine in this chapter the psychological nature of prejudice; then in the following chapter we shall investigate the origins of our prejudices and survey the possible steps we can take to minimize our biases, in the interest of conducting ourselves more intelligently in our social relations.

I. THE PSYCHOLOGICAL SIGNIFICANCE OF PREJUDICE

A prejudice is a pre-judgment, that is, a predisposition toward a particular evaluation of a person or issue, a judgment arrived at before due reflection, a commitment of a partisan nature made without respect for the relevant facts involved; in short, prejudice means "making one's mind up ahead of time." In reaching a conclusion, the prejudiced person is influenced more by his emotional inclinations than he would be were he practicing disinterested deliberation. Desire, displacing logic, exploits reason by means of cunning rationalizations, thus supporting the view that is emotionally satisfying. A prejudice is a bias which assures the conclusion before the evidence is in, a set which points thinking in a congenial direction, a determining tendency which compels reason to conform to the demands of the prevailing wish. Prejudice pervades human behavior because man is an emotional creature, not as devoted to the pursuit of logic as rationalists are wont to believe.

Judicious conduct, as an ideal, calls for the unprejudiced weighing of evidence. Emotions are set aside in the interest of justice. Personal interests are not permitted to interfere with an open-minded consideration of the facts which are being marshaled for the purpose of reaching a fair decision. The judge, who epitomizes this ideal, takes no sides, remains non-partisan while the testimony pro and con is being offered, makes his decision objectively, apart from any personal leanings one way or the other.

No one except a romanticist would believe that the average mortal ordinarily conducts himself in any such judicious manner. The realistic observer of the human scene might point out that judicious decisions are seldom exemplified in our courts of law, even in the Supreme Court of the United States. Prejudices are so basic in the legal thinking of our most esteemed Justices that it is often possible to predict the decision before a case starts. This feat was accomplished in the newsletter sent out from Washington by the Research Institute, "accurately forecasting every Supreme Court decision of major significance during the New Deal, both the decisions prior to the President's 'reform' of the Court and those following. It came close to predicting the actual division of the Court in many instances, hit the division right on the head in one instance. But this accuracy in scientific inference was itself a source of embarrassment, because it gave rise to the unjustified rumor that the Institute had a pipeline into the Court." [1] Indeed, the large number of 5-4 decisions by the Supreme Court gave rise to considerable suspicion regarding the Eternal Justice being embodied in its august judgments. The public became aware that the deliberations of the Tribunal amounted to little more than a rationalization of conservative and liberal prejudices, respectively, with legal erudition thrown in to conceal the personal predispositions which were fundamentally responsible for the decisions.

Prejudice leads a person to welcome evidence that will confirm convictions long held and treasured. It is gladdening to discover that one was right all the time. This satisfaction was enjoyed by members and their guests who attended a meeting of the W.C.T.U. Institute, as reported in a local paper:

A delightful day was spent by the members of the W.C.T.U. and friends, on Tuesday, at the Baptist church. Mrs. Holt presided. Mrs. Smith, state president, spoke on the harm done by alcohol.

Why would a group of women assemble to hear a talk designed to tell them what they already knew and believed? Why were they naïve enough to assume that the state president spoke with authority on a

[1] F. Lundberg: "News-Letters: a Revolution in Journalism." *Harper's Magazine,* April, 1940.

complicated problem requiring expert knowledge of physiology and sociology? The answer, of course, is obvious: the state president was telling them what they desired to believe. It is not surprising that they all had a wonderful time. If they had opened their meeting to a speaker disseminating propaganda for the United Brewers Foundation, they would have spent an unhappy afternoon and all would have gone home angry. Suppose, for example, the speaker of the afternoon had discussed the subject, "Beer and Brewing in America," reviewing all the good things credited to beer:

The brewing industry is one of the nation's six largest taxpayers. State beer taxes, collected by every state in the Union, have been earmarked in various states for old-age pensions, public schools, state institutions, relief, public health, blind, crippled and dependent children, aid to agriculture. . . .

The local newspaper would not have been able to report, "The members spent a delightful day."

Thinking often starts from a complex as its premise, according to Hart's thesis as developed in his *Psychology of Insanity*. The complex is a system of emotionally toned ideas, a set giving direction to a line of thought, guaranteeing a "sound" conclusion right from the beginning. The "sound" conclusion, of course, is one that fits in nicely with the individual's preconceptions. The complex thus functions as a prejudice which inspires its own justification in the form of rationalization. Reasons can easily be found for substantiating what a person really wants to believe.

Complexes may be largely responsible for making up our minds ahead of time. Blind hero worship prompted Big Bill Thompson, Mayor of Chicago, to condemn Rupert Hughes' biography debunking the idealization of George Washington. A newspaper interview on the subject was reported as follows:

"Hughes is a damned liar," Mayor Thompson said as he launched into a denunciation of the author. "He is a cheap skate trying to get some personal publicity. He lied about Washington's personal habits. In any other country they would put him where he belongs."

The mayor was asked to point out some of the specific instances of Hughes' lying. This he declined to do, but said generally, "about his personal habits."

"I was taught in school that George Washington was the greatest American patriot and that he performed great deeds for the nation. I don't care what he did between times."

Finally, after the mayor again repeated that Hughes was a liar and told a lot of untruths in his book, a reporter asked, "Mr. Mayor, have you read Hughes' book on Washington?"

"No, I haven't," he shouted, "I wouldn't read any part of it. He's just a muckraker for profit."

"I have no objections to publicity of the shortcomings of public men," he continued hurriedly, "provided these don't enter conspiracies to destroy popular heroes. All this is inspired by England to tear down our ideals."

"What's the motive behind that?" someone inquired as "Bill" stopped to take a breath.

"The motive," he said dramatically and rather confusedly, "is to sell this nation for money to whoever can get it."

The explanation wasn't very clear to the reporters who asked "Big Bill" to explain this explanation. "Just what do you mean by that, Mr. Mayor?" they asked.

"Well, just that," he replied in a hesitant and rather crestfallen manner, as if hurt because his statement wasn't accepted without comment.[2]

Obviously, Rupert Hughes was given no opportunity to make a dent on Big Bill. The Mayor's mind was made up—and closed; no disquieting evidence could penetrate the barriers of the logic-tight compartment within which his idealized heroes were protected against the taints of reality.

Prejudice is likely to play a significant role wherever evaluation is concerned. We are prone to estimate the value of a thing in terms of our own personal experiences. This fact was demonstrated in an experiment conducted by Thorndike at Harvard's Inglis Lecture in 1937, where he was discussing the topic, "The Teaching of Controversial Subjects." The audience was given the following blank to fill out.

INGLIS LECTURE EXPERIMENT

Please consider the values which you got from a hundred hours spent in the seven activities listed below at or near age sixteen. Write 1 in column I after the activity which you think did most for you. Write 2 after the activity which you think did next most. Write 3 after the activity which you think did next most; and so on. If two or more of the activities were equally beneficial give them the same number.

Then in column II rank the seven activities in the same way for the benefit which you think sixteen-year-olds in general would derive from them.

[2] The Boston *Herald*, Dec. 5, 1927.

	I For myself	II For sixteen- year-olds	d
Algebra	5	3	2
Athletic sports	3	5	2
History	1	2	1
Latin	2	4	2
Science	4	1	3
Semi-skilled labor, such as cooking, typing, or driving a car	6	6	0
Unskilled labor such as washing dishes, or low grade factory work	7	7	0
			10

The figures recorded in the above blank are those registered by the author. The last column ("d") is made up of the difference in ranks of columns I and II. Thorndike explained that if the sum of the *d's* was less than 14, the score indicated the fact that the individual was prejudiced by his own experience in school. The author offers no apology for his score since he is well aware of the tendency each person has to set himself up as the norm for others, with little or no regard for individual differences in capacity or taste. This egocentric prejudice comes naturally to each one of us.

The shrewd propagandist paves the road for his appeals by exploiting the preexisting attitudes of the people. His suggestions cannot fail if he touches off the basic prejudices of his audience. The cartoonist may find his medium particularly effective for proselytizing, even when his message is out of step with reality, if he aims his appeal accurately at some definite deep-seated bias. In early March, 1940, a "Ding" cartoon from the New York *Herald Tribune,* reproduced in the financial section of *Newsweek,* intended to portray how American business felt after seven years of Roosevelt. The long-suffering victim was battered and damaged, sat in a wheel chair and grasped crutches, with an axe sunk deep in his skull. Undoubtedly, it was easy for many a businessman to identify himself with this tragic figure, punchdrunk from the felonious assaults engineered by the New Deal. The cartoon served as a good excuse for another orgy of self-pity. Strangely enough, on the same page with the cartoon appeared a report on the financial balances of 669 of the nation's leading corporations for 1939. The statements recorded an increase of 83.1 per cent over 1938 earnings.

This sort of appeal to prejudice is usually effective because it touches off emotions of an intense nature. In this connection we need to recognize clearly the observation made by Thouless:

> Poetry, romantic prose, and emotional oratory are all of inestimable value, but their place is not where responsible decisions must be made. The common (almost universal) use of emotional words in political thinking is as much out of place as would be a chemical or statistical formula in the middle of a poem.[3]

This warning is directed against settling social issues by poetic outbursts, like, for example, the highly emotionalized article on "Fear" produced by Edna St. Vincent Millay as she brooded over the fate of Sacco and Vanzetti.

> There are two names you would not have me mention, for you are sick of the sound of them. All men must die, you say, and these men have died, and would that their names might die with them; would that their names were as names written in the sand, you say, to be dissipated by the next incoming tide! For you long to return to your gracious world of a year ago, where people had pretty manners and did not raise their voices; where people whom you knew, whom you had entertained in your houses, did not shout and weep and walk the streets vulgarly carrying banners, because two quite inconsequential people, two men who could not even speak good English, were about to be put forever out of mischief's way. *Do* let us forget, you say; after all, what *does* it matter?
>
> You are right; it does not matter very much. In a world more beautiful than this it would have mattered more. On the surface of a Christianity already so spotted and defaced by the crimes of the Church this Stain does not show very dark. In a freedom already so riddled and gashed by the crimes of the state this ugly rent is with difficulty to be distinguished at all.
>
> And you are right; it is well to forget that men die. . . .[4]

This passage is beautifully written; it is poetic in style, rhythmic, passionate, powerful, designed to sway the emotions. Nevertheless, it does not clarify the social issues involved. Getting all excited over the

[3] R. H. Thouless: *How To Think Straight*, p. 8. 1939.
[4] E. St. V. Millay: "Fear." *Outlook*, November 9, 1927.

fun of persecuting radicals is detrimental to fair dealing and clear thinking; getting all stirred up in behalf of radicals is just as inimical to intelligent deliberation.

Prejudices are apt to be especially violent where moral issues seem to be at stake. Several years ago, Maude Royden, British social worker and preacher, was scheduled to speak to a number of Methodist women's societies in the United States. At the last moment, it was learned that she smoked cigarettes. This practice being outlawed by the rules of the Methodist Church, her engagements were immediately canceled. This action was commended by a lady who was obviously prejudiced against smoking on the part of the clergy—or the laity:

It seems to me that the Methodist Women's societies that canceled her engagements to speak were not only justified in so doing, but it was to their credit.

If I remember rightly it is a rule in the Methodist discipline that ministers of that denomination shall not use tobacco. They are supposed to be representatives of Christ, and surely we cannot imagine him forming a habit that would make him obnoxious to anyone or in any way injure his influence or set a bad example to others.

D. L. Moody was once asked if a person could be a Christian and smoke. He replied, "Yes, a dirty one." We have enough "dirty" Christians in our own country without importing any and honoring them by invitations to religious gatherings. A Harvard student asked me not long ago if there was anything in the Bible against smoking. I referred him to I Cor. iii, 17. "If any man defile the temple of God, him shall God destroy, for the temple of God is holy, which temple ye are."

Prejudice inspires a person to leap to conclusions upon the slightest provocation. Sir Oliver Lodge, speaking before the British Association for the Advancement of Science in 1930, stated that scientists could not afford to limit the field of their scientific inquiry to material things, because

immense unknown powers lie beyond the range of matter. . . . We are in the midst of a spiritual world which dominates the material. It constitutes the great omnipresent reality whose powers we are only beginning to realize, whose properties and functions exhaust all our admiration. We have concentrated too much on the material. Spiritualism is one of the many fields for scientific exploration not connected with material things. *Already spiritualists have discovered that the mind can operate independently of the brain,* that a person is not necessarily limited to the performance of the organs of his body, that there exist individuals who can send messages mentally and others who can receive them. . . . *Certainly the individual continues after death and carries with him power of memory and affection. . . .*[5]

Sir Oliver Lodge would not have distinguished himself in the realm of experimental physics if he had permitted hunches of this sort to govern his laboratory procedure.   His training as a physicist was effectively dissociated from his beliefs about the Beyond because he was so anxious to believe that his dead son, killed in the First World War, was still in active touch with him, revealing his abiding affection by returning to his father in ectoplasmic form and by sending spirit messages conveying his love.   Only a person inspired by passionate longings could be driven to assert that it has been proved that the mind can function without the brain and that there is indubitable evidence for a personal life beyond the grave.   An honest person might entertain these beliefs as hopes, adopted on faith.

We often commit ourselves to conclusions when the evidence is so inadequate as to justify only a suspension of judgment.   We are inclined to take sides, as Jastrow has pointed out in this excellent description of prejudice.

Men are by nature partisans; and only the few by training and self-control approach the judicial, even the tolerant attitude.   One need not go beyond quite familiar psychology to suspect that there is some other force than logic or proof at work that sends the balance of judgment to the one conviction or the other, and usually with fervor and tenacity; and that is the measure of prejudice that is here concerned.   For prejudice is not, as commonly conceived, a crude, insensitive blindness or stubborn determination to reach, or even to jump, to conclusions that are personally, which means emotionally, acceptable.   Prejudice is formed of subtler stuff; it intrudes as a slight, subdued, often subconscious deviation of the logical eyesight that incapacitates it to see rightly.   We are all prejudiced, though some far more so than others, and differ still more significantly in the control that we exercise and are eager to exercise over our prejudicial inclinations.   The dangerously prejudiced man is he who gives in to his inclinations not only with unrestraint but with exultation.   In the attempt to buttress or protect our prejudices by reasons—with choice of fact and argument alike—and so pacify our logical conscience, we are fairly alike, differing only in the skill and frankness with which we practice this dubious art. . . .   When feeling runs high, reason runs low.[6]

[5] The Boston *Herald*, September 8, 1930.
[6] J. Jastrow: "Our Prejudices: Discussed in the Light of Psychology." *Outlook*, November 23, 1927.

Prejudice means, in essence, making one's mind up ahead of time or passing judgment without rational respect for the evidence. To insure emotional satisfaction, desire supplies the motivation toward a particular decision.

II. BIAS OR DETERMINING TENDENCY

Determining tendency is conceived by the psychologist as a set, usually unconscious, which inclines thinking or acting in certain directions. The tendency is the resultant of the ways in which the person's needs have been canalized or conditioned by experience to form characteristic habitual attitudes. Unless the individual takes the trouble to explore the origins of his sets by critical self-analysis, his personal propensities affect him without his being very much aware of their influence. These determining tendencies function as prejudices, inclining the individual to react to a particular situation in a definite manner, to reason his way to satisfying conclusions, to interpret the world about him according to patterns which are in line with his inclinations. We notice what we are set by our interests to observe and the meanings we attribute to stimuli are determined by our peculiar predispositions. The interpretation of an event is a function of the event itself and of the prejudices dominant in the observer, as in the case of the little, old, pious lady who lamented, "My nephew went to Dartmouth a Christian and came home a Democrat."

We all face the risk of unkindly misinterpretation when we rub the cynic the wrong way. The cynic is sure that all courtesy is hypocritical, that most advertising is lies, that all married men are unfaithful either in fact or intention, that all reformers practice vice in secret, that intelligent people who say they enjoy Dickens are posing, that every good deed is a blind for some nefarious purpose, that the desire for money is the real reason behind every notable achievement.[7] What chance has an honest man when the cards are so stacked against him? He stands condemned before he even gets a chance to present his case.

The influence of prejudice is fairly obvious in our personal likes and dislikes, though unconscious factors contribute to our animosities. A person may be aware that his attitude toward somebody is prejudiced without understanding fully the sources of his feeling.

> I do not like you, Dr. Fell,
> The reason why, I cannot tell,

[7] See G. Seldes: "A Super-American Credo." The *Saturday Evening Post*, July 21, 1928.

> But this I know, and know full well,
> I do not like you, Dr. Fell.

Intense likes and dislikes are very apt to be the results of prejudices, whether or not there is a clear realization of their motivation.   Some people have a knack for inspiring strong feelings, winning friends and making enemies with equal facility.   Gene Tunney belongs in this category; as "Gentleman Gene" he was known to his friends.   Professor Phelps of Yale said of him:

He is a gentleman, courteous, considerate, with irreproachable manners and with no affectations. . . .   He is a reader of good books, and has taste and intelligence. . . .   His knowledge of modern poetry and of modern fiction is good; he makes no pretenses, never tries to show off, but talks about literature in a natural, unaffected, and interesting manner.   A newspaper reporter called me up by telephone to ask if Tunney really did know something about literature, or whether that was just press-agent stuff.   I assured him that Gene Tunney's culture is genuine, that he loves books for their own sake. . . .

Tunney lectured on Shakespeare before one of Phelps' classes at Yale and did a good job of it, too, according to students' reports.   This sort of highbrow activity did not sit well with the fight fans.   Prize fighters were not supposed to read books, retire from the ring, hang on to their earnings, and marry a socialite—all of which Tunney did, in defiance of pugilistic conventions.   It is rumored that a Dempsey supporter visited Tunney's training camp before the big fight and returned to his own quarters with the comment, "The fight's a set-up; I seen Tunney reading a book."   Tunney's enemies were just as sure of his putting on airs as his friends were certain of his sincerity.   Said a Dempsey admirer:

It is not Mr. Tunney's intellectual attainments one objects to, but his intellectual pretensions.   No wonder men like Heywood Broun, Louis Bromfield, Sinclair Lewis, and H. L. Mencken have expressed a preference for Dempsey.   One has only to contrast the interviews given by these two men, Dempsey and Tunney; one simple and profound, the other a mixture of bombast and cant.

In our likes and dislikes of persons, most of us are ready to admit, under pressure, that we are prejudiced.   When it comes to evaluating public issues like political problems, we are not so likely to confess our bias, since we pride ourselves on being objective in judging social questions.   The desire to be rational in weighing political issues is apt to obscure the underlying complexes and sentiments really responsible for our opinions.   In the summer of 1932, students in a social psychology examination were asked, "Where did you get your political opinions?   Taking yourself as a sample, what do you think the prospects are for democracy?"   One girl replied:

> I have no pronounced political opinions inasmuch as I am not yet able to vote.   I think as my father, mother, sister, and all my in-laws think because we have always been Republicans, therefore I naturally would be.
>
> I'm afraid this reasoning is not in the least intelligent.   I am also against the repeal of the 18th amendment.   I'm not old enough to remember seeing men lurch from the corner saloon, but I have heard about it in our family discussions.   In college one sees drinking a lot—at least where I go.   But I know quite a few girls who don't drink now who would drink if it were no longer prohibited.   It is only their social consciousness which makes them afraid.   Our home is absolutely dry and having been brought up in such an environment I shouldn't openly become wet.
>
> Democracy's prospects don't appear very bright to me.   The Democratic party has done a lot of talking and really have said little.   Roosevelt has no definite plank except repeal.   Hoover has at least stated what he intends to do if he is re-elected.   He may not get all the things done, but his intentions are good.
>
> This is none of it intelligent, but I can't talk on what I know little about. Too many people do that as it is.

This student states that she has "no pronounced political opinions"— and then goes on to reveal a very definite pro-Republican slant and some rather decided attitudes about a number of matters.   She shows a modicum of insight in remarking that her observations are not very intelligent.

Political opinions are often determined by prejudices operating outside the awareness of the voter, as revealed by an analysis of letters written to the Boston *Herald Traveler* in October, 1928, explaining why the writers were going to cast their ballots for Hoover or Smith in the approaching presidential election.   Most of the people writing to the paper claimed that they were not influenced by the religious affiliations of the candidates.   They were, therefore, forced to find other reasons which would serve as an excuse both to themselves and to others for having decided to vote one way or the other.   Protestants were not opposed to Smith because he happened to be a Catholic, but because he wasn't "cultured," because he lacked "dignity" and "respectability."

That this was but a very thin cloak over their religious prejudices may be seen by the following quotations:

Smith's speech in Boston was the simplest and the most disgusting of anything I ever listened to. His language is more befitting to that of a parochial school education than that of a grammar school where English is taught. As for Hoover, he conducts himself like a gentleman using refined language and leaving out slanderous remarks and slang.

Mr. Hoover represents the cultured kind of people that have ruled this country the greater part of the time for sixty-eight years. The advancement of no country is comparable to that of the United States during this period. Al Smith represents something entirely different. A power seeking organization of foreign domination. He represents the worst element in America today.

Catholics, on their part, found plenty of socially acceptable reasons for believing that Hoover was unfit for office. Many of the Catholics said they were going to vote for Smith, "not because he is a Catholic, but because by voting for him we are doing away with religious bigotry."[8] There appeared to be little awareness, on the part of the Hoover or the Smith supporters, of the subtle rationalizations they had evolved for themselves to permit them to continue their faith in their own inherent rationality. This sort of self-deception comes easily to the individual who lacks insight into the prejudices underlying his explicit attitudes.

III. DOGMATISM AND IGNORANCE

It has often been said that dogmatism and ignorance tend to go hand in hand. High amount of prejudice and low amount of information often do go together. One of the most bigoted persons I have known was a man who never went beyond the grammar school. He would expound on matters he knew little about with the assurance of a person who was an expert in each of the several fields he cared to mention. He would apologize for his meager schooling and then overwhelm his audience with his aggressive positiveness. When I think of him, my thoughts turn to a statement which made an impression on me some years ago, source unknown:

The fanatic is invariably ignorant. Tolerance is the offspring of intelligence. The intelligent man knows he may be mistaken. The ignorant man

[8] W. F. Vaughan: "An Experimental Study in Political Prejudice." *Journal of Abnormal and Social Psychology,* 1930, 25, 268-274.

is certain he is right. Give me the radius of a man's intelligence and I will describe the circumference of his tolerance.

Perhaps Murphy and his collaborators stated the case more accurately when they concluded from several studies correlating belief and evidence, that "certainty of opinion is a function not of information but of desire." [9]

Extremists, whether radical or reactionary, are more emotionally convinced of the correctness of their views than are those persons who support less extreme doctrines.[10] Intensity and certainty go together where atypical opinions are involved. The correlation of certainty and extreme opinion is usually interpreted on grounds of emotional frustration, as indicative of strong prejudice and implying little knowledge, but in all fairness it should be pointed out, as Katz and Schanck do, that the greater emotionality of the non-conformist may be related to his "thinking the issue through for himself. Conclusions which a man arrives at himself are more meaningful and more intense than stereotypes he mouths without understanding." [11] In so far as this observation holds true, it would not be valid to generalize that dogmatism and ignorance are invariably concomitant.

A. IGNORANCE NO BARRIER TO OPINION

The average person is ready to offer his opinions on almost any matter, if he is asked to express his ideas, or even if he isn't asked. Trotter has given us an apt delineation of this common human frailty:

If we examine the mental furniture of the average man, we shall find it made up of a very precise kind upon subjects of very great variety, complexity, and difficulty. He will have fairly settled views upon the origin and nature of the universe, and upon what he will probably call its meaning; he will have conclusions as to what is to happen to him at death and after, as to what is and what should be the basis of conduct. He will know how the country should be governed, and why it is going to the dogs, why this piece of legislation is good and that bad. He will have strong views upon military and naval strategy, the principles of taxation, the use of alcohol and vaccination, the treatment of influenza, the prevention of hydrophobia, upon mu-

---

[9] G. Murphy, L. B. Murphy, and T. M. Newcomb: *Experimental Social Psychology*, p. 940. Harper & Brothers, 1937.

[10] See F. H. Allport and D. A. Hartman: "The Measurement and Motivation of Atypical Opinion in a Certain Group." *American Political Science Review*, 1925, 19, 735-760.

[11] D. Katz and R. L. Schanck: *Social Psychology*, p. 449. John Wiley & Sons, Inc., 1938.

nicipal trading, the teaching of Greek, upon what is permissible in art, satisfactory in literature, and hopeful in science.

The bulk of such opinions must necessarily be without rational basis, since many of them are concerned with problems admitted by the expert to be still unsolved, while as to the rest it is clear that the training and experience of no average man can qualify him to have any opinion upon them at all.[12]

Before you hasten to condemn this average man Trotter has described, test yourself as honestly as you can by observing whether you are inclined to hold rather definite opinions on the following topics. How do you feel about:

> Continuing the Japanese Emperor?
> Harsh treatment for occupied Germany?
> Universal military training?
> Maintenance of price ceilings?
> The right of unions to see the company books?
> Foreign missions?
> Spanking a child?

You probably find that you have the answers, and that you would defend them vigorously. Would your self-certainty be commensurate with your store of knowledge on these problems?

The author played a mean trick on one of his classes in social psychology. Without explaining the purpose of the questionnaire, he asked the members of the class to record their reactions by underscoring "Yes" or "No" for each of the following statements:

1. Communism is a serious menace to our civilization.	Yes	No
2. Communists should be barred from teaching in our public schools.	Yes	No
3. Even if communism should work out well in Russia, it isn't the kind of system that we want in America.	Yes	No
4. Communism is not as sound as capitalism, psychologically, because communism ignores the profit motive which is basic to human nature.	Yes	No
5. Communism comes pretty close to Christianity in its aim to promote the brotherhood of man on an international scale.	Yes	No
6. Communism believes in a fair income for everybody.	Yes	No
7. Communism asserts that a revolution by violence is inev-		

---

[12] W. Trotter: *Instincts of the Herd in Peace and War,* p. 36. Ernest Benn Limited (London), 1919.

itable as the only way by which capitalism can be over-
thrown.   Yes   No
8. Communism ignores man's spiritual nature.   Yes   No
9. Communism encourages immorality by undermining
   family life.   Yes   No
10. Communism is unequivocally opposed to Nazism.   Yes   No
11. Communists are maladjusted persons who have turned
    radical because they cannot solve their own personal
    problems.   Yes   No
12. Communism is based on fallacious economic theories.   Yes   No

This test was administered in December, 1939.   It is worth noting that
74 per cent felt that we don't want communism instituted here in
America, that 71 per cent believed that a fair income was not one of
the communists' tenets, that 62 per cent were of the opinion that man's
spiritual nature was being neglected under the communist system.

These papers were collected when completed and then each student
was given a 9 by 12 sheet of paper with the instruction at the top:
"Enumerate in brief statements the essential economic, social, and political principles of communism."   The students were allotted 15 minutes to carry out this project.   There was much head-scratching and
staring around the room during the interval, with more time devoted
to ruminating than to writing.   Thirteen students stated that communists were aiming for an equal distribution of wealth to all men;
one student said that a *laissez-faire* policy would prevail; one student
mentioned the necessity for a secret-police system; and one student,
who stated that he was a communist, expounded none of the economic,
political, or social theories, but defended communism on the ground
that "it should be the next step in the advance of man."   One is reminded of Artemus Ward's remark that "ignorance does not mean not
knowing but knowing so many things that ain't so."

After the expositions were completed and collected, it was explained
that the purpose of the experiment was to demonstrate how easy it is
to have opinions, with inadequate knowledge to support them.   Several students remarked afterward that they were ashamed when they
discovered how little they knew about such an important social problem.   The experience proved to be stimulating, as evidenced by a
number of students who asked for references so that they could inform
themselves on the subject.   None of the inquirers were familiar with
the *Communist Manifesto*.   The experiment exemplifies a pedagogical
technique that has much to recommend it.   As Socrates used to say,
the confession of ignorance is the beginning of learning.

From the semantic point of view the questionnaire leaves much to be desired. What are the referents for "fair income," or "spiritual nature," or "menace to civilization," or "communism" itself? Take the word "communism," for example. In a school gymnasium girls were required to take a shower in the presence of other girls. Parents of the pupils drew up a petition of protest. One parent stated his objection thus: "The common-shower system is a step towards communism." [13] Obviously, the term "communism" carries many shades of meaning. Stuart Chase reported these definitions:

Schoolboy: "War. . . . Something that's got to be licked."
Housewife: "A large Florida rattlesnake in summer."
Author: "I can only answer in cuss words."
Italian hairdresser: "A bunch, all together." [14]

We are all guilty of advocating or opposing causes that we know little or nothing about. We make up our minds before we learn the relevant facts.

B. FONDNESS FOR OUR CONVICTIONS

We like our prejudices and we mean to stand by them, contented as we are with our own brand of ignorance. As Lecky once said, "a false belief is rarely disproved; it merely becomes obsolete and disappears."

Cantril conducted a questionnaire to determine the effect that a radio news commentator might have on his listeners; in this case, Boake Carter. One of the findings was summarized thus: those who have standards of judgment tend to listen to a commentator whose point of view resembles their own.[15] Listeners tuned in to get Carter's slant on the news because he agreed with them, and then they could go on holding the same beliefs, undisturbed by alternative interpretations. Thus they followed in spirit the course described by Francis Bacon in his *Novum Organum:*

The human understanding, when any proposition has been once laid down . . . forces everything else to add fresh support and confirmation: and although most and abundant instances may exist to the contrary, yet [the understanding] either does not observe, or despises them, or it gets rid of and

[13] *Time,* April 1, 1940.
[14] S. Chase: *The Tyranny of Words,* p. 189 ff. 1938.
[15] H. Cantril: "The Role of the Radio Commentator." *Public Opinion Quarterly,* 1939, 3, 654-662.

rejects them by some distinction, with violent and injurious prejudice, rather than sacrifice the authority of its first conclusions.

A pet theory usually is protected by a logic-tight compartment; that is, conflicting evidence is nullified by means of the defense mechanisms of rationalization, repression, and dissociation.[16] "There are none so blind," we say, "as those who will not see." Prejudice is not simply a partial, erroneous judgment due to limited experience—it is often a willful perversion of judgment because of personal interest or passion. A biologist named Clifford once wrote to William James regarding the claims of spiritualism: "Even if such a thing as telepathy were true, scientists ought to band together to keep it suppressed and concealed. It would undo the uniformity of nature, and all sorts of other things without which scientists cannot carry on their pursuits." Here was a "scientist" denying in behalf of science the very freedom of research that is the essence of science, apparently unaware that he was getting himself involved in contradictions. Protecting science from the truth —granting that telepathy might be true, as Clifford does—is certainly a strange pursuit for a scientist. Such inconsistency is evidence of an unorganized mind, a mind that has failed to get the connections implicit in true knowledge.

The prejudiced person is apt to be suffering from a fixed idea, a mental disorder sometimes referred to as *monoideism*. Such behavior is characteristic of the paranoiac whose delusions of persecution cannot be dislodged by any amount of persuasion. If the paranoiac thinks he is being followed, then anybody walking behind him is following him and therefore must have designs on him. It will be clear, too, that those designs must be malign; otherwise the person in pursuit would speak up and explain his mission. Getting "hypped" on an idea and sticking to it regardless of reality is the basic symptom of paranoia; it is also the basic characteristic of the fanatic, the intolerant person, the bigot, the narrow-minded individual who argues around upsetting evidence, like the "psychologist" who asserted that if intelligence tests did not support Nordic supremacy, then there must be something wrong with the tests.

If a person has one idea that means very much to him, he tends, unless he guards against the temptation, to mold everything to fit his scheme of beliefs, and thus is enabled to appropriate other articles of faith as his own. For example, my father and an uncle of mine were both reared in an environment where fundamentalist theology was

[16] See B. Hart: *The Psychology of Insanity*, p. 96 ff. Fourth edition, 1937.

dominant. My father broke away from his childhood beliefs to become a liberal theologian. My uncle also cast aside the narrow theology of his youth to become a reader in the Christian Science church. When these two men discussed religion, as they were bound to do, and my father uttered an enlightened opinion, my uncle would immediately suggest, "Why, that's Christian Science." And there was no use denying it.

Behind a prejudice there is often a self-complacent ignorance. If we like a belief, we do not investigate circumstances to find out if it is true. "History is bunk," said Henry Ford. And Ford proved that his brand of history was "the bunk" at the time when he instituted a libel suit against the Chicago *Tribune*. In the course of the trial Ford described Benedict Arnold as a writer, and in reply to the question, "Have there been any revolutions in this country?" he replied, "Yes, in 1812." [17]

The American public likes to believe that rich people are indifferent to the public welfare, so they are predisposed to accept the popular tale that William H. Vanderbilt once said, "The public be damned." There is another version of the story that probably comes closer to the truth, as recounted in an advertisement sponsored by *Nation's Business:*

At 3 in the morning William H. Vanderbilt is pulled out of bed by an annoying reporter. "The public has a right to this interview," insists the reporter, as Mr. Vanderbilt grouchily refuses to talk.

"The public be damned at 3 in the morning," he roars, and "the public be damned" (without reference to the hour) has rattled down the years as typifying the attitude of that business generation toward legitimate public interest. How we do love *catch phrases!* [18]

The actual circumstances spoil the effect of the story. Consequently, they are usually omitted in its recounting. People prefer the story in its more dramatic form, influenced as they are by what Francis Bacon called the Idol of the Theater, a prejudice that inclines persons to favor news value over truth value.

Seldom does a man come out in the open to admit how fond he is of his own prejudices but that is exactly what John Grier Hibben, former president of Princeton, did in his book, *A Defense of Prejudice*. Study this passage for a classic example of rationalization:

[17] F. L. Allen: *Only Yesterday*, p. 4. 1931.
[18] The Boston *Herald*, November 19. 1929.

Strip a man of his prejudices, and only the commonplace remains. Individuality is the projection of our prejudices. Remove the prejudices and the individual is merged again with the crowd. He is only one of many. He no longer appeals to our imagination. There is no more of interest or charm or power about him. A character without a dash of prejudice in his nature always lacks intensity of conviction. There may be a glow of intellectual light, but there is a conspicuous absence of fire and driving power. There is often a certain judicial poise of mind which reveals itself in a tolerance that is an indication of weakness rather than strength. Such a man never lets himself go. He always sees two sides to every question, and can never commit himself to the one or the other. Freedom from prejudice is often indicated by a vacillation which is pitifully weak and ineffectual.[19]

The book is an able defense of prejudice. It should be examined by all those persons who are eager to improve the art of self-deception. Maybe the man was right who defined thinking as the rearrangement of one's prejudices.

C. Dependence of Learning on the Questioning Attitude

Learning presupposes curiosity. The person who "knows it all" already is not interested in searching for more enlightenment. That is why the research-department heads in Hollywood do not employ persons with extensive training in academic research, for they explain:

Those fellows know too much; if you ask them something they pop right up with the answer, and at least once out of every ten times they're wrong. A good researcher always says, "I don't know, but I'll find out." [20]

Curiosity is kept alive by encouraging the questioning attitude that goes with an open mind. Children are curious, comments Bertrand Russell, and the function of education seems to be to cure them of this habit. Unfortunately this commentary is all too true.

Looking back on his own unsatisfying education, Lincoln Steffens concluded: "It is questions that should be taught, not the answers." When somebody asked Einstein how he happened to make his great discoveries, he replied, "By challenging an axiom." [21] As long as mathematical physics accepted the authority of Aristotle and Euclid, there was no search for truth. Thinkers of the Middle Ages believed

---

[19] J. G. Hibben: *A Defense of Prejudice,* pp. 13-14. Charles Scribner's Sons, 1911.
[20] S. Colton and H. Jones: "What's Right about the Movies." *Harper's Magazine,* July, 1943.
[21] L. Steffens: *The Autobiography of Lincoln Steffens,* p. 816. Harcourt, Brace & Co., 1931.

that the truth was already known by revelation.   Hence there was no need to look further.   Science was discouraged by such complacency. The spirit of investigation was revived during the Renaissance when men again became curious about the mysteries of the universe.   It has been well said that "the wise man chooses his problems wisely and wisely keeps them problems." [22]   The quester searches and then searches some more, one problem suggesting another; that is what we mean by "*re*search."   The spirit of the quest cannot thrive in an authoritarian culture where suppression is exerted either by the prejudices of the church or by the prejudices of the state.

Questioning the eternal verities should be a vital process in a good education.   A few years ago "Five Bewildered Freshmen" at Cornell "addressed a joint letter to the Cornell *Sun* bewailing the fact that after two whole months at Ithaca they were still somewhat uncertain as to the nature and purpose of a college education and were not yet possessed of full and definite knowledge as to the mysteries of the cosmos and the destiny of man." [23]   Professor Carl Becker wrote a letter to the *Sun* congratulating the freshmen on their bewilderment and expressing the hope that they would retain the same intellectual zeal indefinitely:

I was interested in the letter of "Five Bewildered Freshmen," and in the discussion it gave rise to.   The freshmen say they have been engaged in the intellectual life for more than two months and don't know what it's all about.   This is bad, but who is to blame?   Some say the students are to blame, and some say the professors.   What is to be done about it?   You suggest a foundation or an orientation course such as is given in other universities.

For my part, I don't blame any one—not the freshmen, certainly.   It's not especially the student's fault if he doesn't know what it's all about.   If he did, he wouldn't need to come to college.   That's why, I have always supposed, young people come to college—to get some notion, even if only a glimmering, of what it's about.   They come to get "oriented."   But why expect to be oriented in two months, or a year?   The whole four years' course is a course in orientation.   It isn't a very satisfactory one indeed.   Four years isn't enough.   Life itself is scarcely long enough to enable one to find out what it's all about.

Neither do I blame the professors—not particularly.   Many people appear to think that professors possess some secret of knowledge and wisdom which

[22] W. D. Wallis: "Some Phases of the Psychology of Prejudice." *Journal of Abnormal and Social Psychology*, 1929-30, 24, 418-429.
[23] Quoted by H. E. Barnes: "Education versus Enlightenment," in *The New Generation*, V. F. Calverton and S. D. Schmalhausen (Editors), 1930.

would set the students right as to the meaning of things if they would only impart it. This, I do assure you, is an illusion. I could write you a letter on behalf of "Five Bewildered Professors" which would make the five bewildered freshmen appear cocksure by comparison. The professors are in the same boat. They don't know, either, what it's all about. They tried to find out when in college, and they have been trying ever since. Most of them, if they are wise, don't expect ever to find out, not really. But still they will, if they are wise, keep trying. That is, indeed, just what the intellectual life is—a continuous adventure of the mind in which something is being discovered possessing whatever meaning the adventurer can find in it.

This effort to find out what it's all about is, in our time, more difficult than ever before. The reason is that the old foundations of assured faith and familiar custom are crumbling under our feet. For four hundred years the world of education and knowledge rested securely on two fundamentals which were rarely questioned. These were Christian philosophy and Classical learning. For the better part of a century Christian faith has been going by the board, and Classical learning into the discard. To replace these we have as yet no foundations, no certainties. We live in a world dominated by machines, a world of incredibly rapid change, a world of naturalistic science and of physico-chemico-libido psychology. There are no longer any certainties either in life or in thought. Everywhere confusion. Everywhere questions. Where are we? Where did we come from? Where do we go from here? What is it all about? The freshmen are asking and they may well ask. Everyone is asking. No one knows; and those who profess with most confidence to know are most likely to be mistaken. Professors could reorganize the College of Arts if they knew what a College of Arts should be. They could give students a "general education" if they knew what a general education is, or would be good for if one had it. Professors are not especially to blame because the world has lost all certainty about these things.

One of the sure signs that the intellectual world is bewildered is that everywhere, in colleges and out, people are asking for "Orientation" courses which will tell the freshmen straight off what it is all about. If we were oriented we shouldn't need such courses. This does not mean that I am opposed to an orientation course for freshmen. I would like an orientation course for freshmen. I would like one for seniors. I would like one for professors and trustees. I would like one for President Farrand and President Butler. . . .

The Five Bewildered Freshmen have got more out of their course than they know. It has made them ask a question—What is it all about? That is a pertinent question. I have been asking it for thirty-five years, and I am still as bewildered as they are.[24]

Some students at Smith complained that they had become bewildered by teachers who were too much inclined to give them facts and then

---

[24] Reprinted by kind permission of Frederick D. Becker.

leave them to interpret the evidence on their own. Students, they contended, lack the background to work out their own salvation unaided. "It is highly demoralizing," they insisted, "to receive mental food in the form of two opposites of which the feeder says, 'There may be as much reason on this side as on that, and I cannot help you to decide which is right.' That sort of thing leaves us in a wavering fog." The result, they confessed, was despair.

Meiklejohn, former president of Amherst, agrees with the Smith students that a professor is not fulfilling his function when he fails to help his pupils in their judgment-making. The teacher cannot guide the student if the teacher cannot make up his own mind and come to conclusions of his own. "In a classroom in which young people are being prepared to use their minds for the doing of the world's work, the open-mindedness which refuses to commit itself to plans of action is indistinguishable in its effect from feeble-mindedness. It prepares the pupil for deciding—nothing." [25]

Lynd is also of the opinion that a good scientist has a point of view which he makes manifest in his teaching.

Without [such] a point of view he is no scientist, and as a teacher he becomes a walking equivalent of an encyclopedia or a colorless textbook. A prevalent protest by alert students in the social sciences is that the immediacies of facts and data tend to operate in the university classroom as a monopolizing concern shutting off the listener from the ripe wisdom of many a mature teacher. It is the boast of some able professors that they handle controversial subjects in the classroom in such skilful manner that the students are never able to know "what the professor himself really thinks about the problem." This amounts, in the judgment of the writer, to sabotaging the inner meaning of education. Of course, no university should have a staff all the members of which think alike on a given problem. But the blurring of explicit statement of sharp and divergent hypotheses within a faculty is almost as dangerous. [26]

Possibly there is less to fear in bewildered professors than in dogmatic professors who delight in converting their pupils to their own prejudices. There are probably fewer professors of the bewildered variety, anyway. Students, unfortunately, are inclined to assume that their teachers know all the answers. Some professors take advantage of this reverent naïveté to pose as omniscient. The wise teacher will

[25] A. Meiklejohn: "Teachers and Controversial Questions." *Harper's Magazine,* June, 1938.
[26] R. S. Lynd: *Knowledge for What?,* footnote on p. 187. Princeton University Press, 1940.

certainly take the precaution of presenting his own views as beliefs tentatively held, not as doctrines to be accepted on his authority. It is possible that "many professors are rationalizing when they answer that it is not the duty of the instructor to present his own beliefs. Many of them have no actual beliefs because they lack personal experiences or social convictions." [27]   A teacher should have *convictions;* he should not be guilty of seeking to propagate his own *prejudices* by virtue of his personal prestige.

Indecision is often a symptom of the maturing mind, for growth involves change.   A certain amount of conflict, an unsettled condition of puzzlement and wonder, must be tolerated if curiosity is to be maintained.   Hardening of the mental arteries may set in prematurely, once living ceases to raise problems.   It is not implied that a person should never make up his mind; it is suggested that he should not make it up permanently too soon.   The art of reaching decisions without sacrificing an open mind is one demanding finesse.   The problems involved call now for our consideration.

D. The Necessity for Action

Although skepticism has its value in stimulating investigation, one cannot live by skepticism alone—faith, too, is essential.   If skepticism is conducive to a reasonable faith, a faith that is repeatedly brought into line with reality, a faith that is not allowed to crystallize into absolute certainty, then doubt serves a healthy purpose.   We may well heed the counsel of Bertrand Russell who expressed his faith in terms of three propositions:

1. When experts are agreed, the opposite opinion cannot be held to be certain.

2. When they are not agreed, no opinion can be regarded as certain by a non-expert.

3. When they all hold that no sufficient ground for a positive opinion exists, the ordinary man would do well to suspend his judgment.

If these propositions were accepted, says Russell, they "would absolutely revolutionize human life." [28]

We have to make decisions, though, on the basis of what evidence we have.   We cannot postpone action indefinitely while we wait to attain certainty.   Frequently we are compelled by circumstances to act,

[27] C. L. Wood: "What Do You Believe, Professor?" *Christian Century,* December 27, 1939.
[28] B. Russell: *Skeptical Essays.* 1928.

to make up our minds one way or the other, even though the experts continue to disagree. The more we come to know, the harder it is to make decisions. Ludwig Lewisohn has said, "To know little is to dare easily; to have looked upon all sides of all mortal questions is to come near paralysis." [29] Indecision may mean that the individual is aware of puzzling complications or it may mean that he does not care deeply about the issue at stake. "The ability to rest in the negative implies either a lack of interest in the result, or a vivid sense of competing alternatives." [30] Nevertheless, there are issues we cannot ignore, situations calling for commitment, and when these crises impend, we cannot afford to be paralyzed by a sense of competing alternatives.

Suppose a person insisted on getting adequate evidence on every question before he made up his mind. He would not go to school until he had determined whether education is really worth while. He would not go to college because he had not made up his mind to go to school and because there are some things to be said for Yale and some things to be said for Harvard. He would never go to work because he would be too busy making a survey of industrial opportunities and getting tested by various vocational counselors. He certainly would never marry, for how can anybody be sure that a particular girl is meant for him and how can anybody be sure that marriage is wise, anyhow? This bewildered citizen could never vote since he would be occupied in looking up the records of all the candidates and gathering data on the issues involved in the election. The election would be over before he got around to deciding it was time to record his judgment. It is all right to be puzzled about life but one cannot be stewing in his own uncertainty incessantly. We have to act according to our best lights at the moment, confident in the belief that our faith is founded, tentatively at least, on facts that we have honestly marshaled to facilitate a wise decision. A certain amount of prejudging is inevitable. Prejudice can be minimized, not eradicated.

Some people circumvent mental paralysis by simplifying the dilemma, thus making choice an easy matter. During the depression of the 'thirties, a Methodist convention voted to remain neutral in their evaluation of our economic order, perhaps because they could not decide whether capitalism is a good or a bad system. Shortly afterward, their neutrality was deplored by members of the Methodist Federation for Social Service, who said the lack of action was an attempt to reconcile the irreconcilable, and then added:

[29] L. Lewisohn: *Up Stream*, p. 211. Liveright Publishing Corporation, 1922.
[30] W. Lippmann: *Public Opinion*, p. 356. 1922.

The time has come once again when organized society must change its way of life or go down to decay or destruction. The spirit of Jesus and the Will of God are on one side or the other. It is a joint question of economic fact and moral choice. Either the capitalist economy has broken down or it has not. Either its basic principle is right or it is wrong. Either it promotes the development of Christian values or it destroys them. How long does the church go limping between two opinions? If God is our God let us serve Him. If Mammon, then frankly serve him. But we cannot do both.[31]

Logicians would call this the fallacy of oversimplification. Capitalism has its good points and its bad ones. It would be difficult to decide whether God is for it or against it. God is against Mammon but whether Mammon is a capitalist, that is the question.

Most people were probably either for or against the League of Nations. All of us have heard vehement arguments on the subject by persons who knew very little about the international issues involved; if they had been better informed, perhaps they would not have been so sure of themselves. Cherrington conducted an experiment dealing with the international attitudes of several groups of students. One group spent most of one summer in Geneva, attending forums, lectures and seminars. They watched the League in operation. They spent considerable time in informal discussion with a wide variety of "experts." Tests administered before the summer in Geneva and afterward showed a noticeable change in the direction of increased uncertainty about the value of the League and about international problems in general. This change was attributed by Cherrington to the "sudden immersion in the intricacies of international affairs . . on the part of students whose international attitudes heretofore had been based upon altruistic feeling and purely academic instruction."[32] The question of the League was no longer oversimplified. Complications induced mild paralysis.

A similar state of indecision was induced in an editor of the *New Yorker* by a casual conversation:

Seated between two intellectual giants after dinner, we were borne lightly along on conversation's wave, from country to country, dipping into problems of empire, the rise and fall of dynasties, the loves and hates of kings, the warrings in Spain, the trends in Russia, strikes, revolutions, diplomacies, the

[31] Quoted by J. Davis: "Capitalism and the Church." *Harper's Magazine*, January, 1937.

[32] B. M. Cherrington: "Methods of Education in International Attitudes." *Teachers College Contributions to Education*, 1934, No. 5.

dissolution of peoples; and without a pause heard everything under the sun made plain. We have the deepest envy for anyone who can feel at home with great matters, and who, armed cap-a-pie with information, can see into the motives of rulers and the hearts of subjects, and can answer Yes to this, No to that. Our envy was so strong that when we returned home at midnight and our wife asked us whether, in our opinion, our dog had worms, we answered with a bold Yes, in a moment of vainglory pretending that here was a thing on which we spoke knowingly—though such was far from the case, as we both secretly knew.[33]

This inability to make up one's mind may prove quite troublesome for a person who wants to be like other people in coming to conclusions and forming sound convictions. It is exasperating to order a dessert for lunch, only to find yourself a moment later envying the superior one chosen by your companion. This sort of experience is a common one for the person who is tormented by the realization that a situation is not as simple as it looks; just as he is about to draw near a conclusion, the absolutely opposite conclusion announces itself, entirely uninvited, and being fresh to the mind, instead of stale with too much consideration, beckons to him more briskly. Such a person being preoccupied with his doubts may not appreciate how easy it is for most people to pronounce judgment on almost any topic. One man whose mind was a turmoil of perplexity testified to the shock he suffered in meeting an individual who apparently knew all the answers.

Sometimes it is possible to forget my annoying complaint when I am alone, but contact with normal people brings it on at once. For example, I sat the other day in the smoking room of a Pullman, pleasantly oblivious for the moment that I was very different from other people who travel on trains. Then a soap salesman, who, appropriately enough, was lathering his face, shattered this illusion instantly. Mistaking as a friendly overture my look of admiration at his skill in shaving on a moving train, he declared without further provocation that what we needed was a larger merchant marine. Violent twinges of my trouble set in. I felt that I would have given all I possessed if I could stand in a lurching train, with my mouth and ears full of soap, and come so readily to a conclusion about our merchant marine, or anything else. He passed without perceptible transition to the subject of prohibition, which he tersely denounced as a huge joke. Not knowing the agony he was causing me, he went on to inform me with some heat that the Soviet Government was a menace to the world, and said, with the air of a man who

[33] The *New Yorker*, January 9, 1937. Permission of the *New Yorker*, copyright, 1937, The F-R. Publishing Corporation.

knows, that Coolidge was a fine president and that Darwinism was utter rubbish. These pronouncements, bringing so mercilessly the sense of my own deficiency, left me weak and full of self-commiseration.

For these are questions—Heaven help me!—which have revolved in my wobbling mind for years without solution. I have given some of them more than casual consideration and I have had ample opportunity—if I had it in me—to reach some intelligent conclusions. But it seems hopeless.

I wish I knew what kind of president Coolidge is. To know whether a man is a strong or a weak president—certainly this would seem to the unafflicted mind a matter of the most elementary sort. Of course, I read about him in the newspapers, but he doesn't seem to crystallize into a person of clear outlines. The fact that he is a singularly silent executive who sometimes rides a mechanical horse, goes fishing in the summer, and believes in the protection of American lives and property in foreign countries, does not furnish me with a real key to his usefulness to the country. These things might all be true, might they not, of good or bad presidents? Is the nation prospering under Coolidge? Or is it prospering in spite of him? Or is it prospering? I haven't the faintest idea. He remains to me a somewhat dimly discerned figure, vague as a legend. I do not know half as much about him as I do about Achilles, Galahad, or Nero.

It seems pleasant to have in the White House such a quiet, dignified conservative, entrenched behind good old New England traditions of reserve and caution, a man who, you feel instinctively, would never be hard on the furniture. Still, wouldn't it be better to have a more dynamic, explosive sort of president? . . .[34]

It is interesting to note that this skeptic was wondering in 1927 about Coolidge prosperity when most people were taking "good times" for granted. The average person does not like to have so many questions raised, for it seems morbid to get so confused by doubts. Vacillation is usually regarded as a malady, reminiscent of the pathological Hamlet:

> . . . the native hue of resolution
> Is sicklied o'er with the pale cast of thought,
> And enterprises of great pitch and moment
> With this regard their currents turn awry
> And lose the name of action.[35]

It is easy for ignorant people to be dogmatic since they don't know enough to know that they don't know. Samuel Butler stated the case very aptly when he wrote:

[34] R. Lewis: "I Have My Doubts." *Atlantic Monthly*, December, 1927.
[35] W. Shakespeare: *Hamlet*, Act III, Scene 1.

It is only those who are ignorant and uncultivated who can know anything at all in a proper sense of the word. Cultivation will breed in any man a certainty of the uncertainty even of his most assured convictions. It is perhaps fortunate for our comfort that we can none of us be cultivated upon many subjects, so that considerable scope for assurance will remain to us; but however this may be, we certainly observe it as a fact that the greatest men are they who are most uncertain in spite of certainty, and at the same time most certain in spite of uncertainty, and who are thus but able to feel that there is nothing in such complete harmony with itself as a flat contradiction in terms.[36]

Learning depends upon the questioning attitude, upon the arousal and sustenance of curiosity. Lincoln Steffens once remarked that college teaching concentrates too much on the study of what's known and too little on the study of what's not known. It would be better for the student to organize his ignorance into a system, he suggested. Such a program would make education exciting. "If you know too surely, you cannot learn; for the purposes of research you may have theories, but never, never knowledge. . . . Ideas harden like arteries; indeed . . . convictions are identical with hardened arteries. . . . Boston was a community of fixed minds, often refined and scholarly, but . . . inhospitable to new ideas and was dying of its old convictions." [37] Steffens wanted his son to feel that there was plenty to learn, plenty to do to improve this world of ours.

So I tell him I don't know what we don't know.

One evening I took him to hear me address an audience and afterwards answer questions. On the way home he whispered a question that had evidently been in his mind all evening.

"Daddy," he said, "why do people listen to you and ask you questions? Don't they know you don't know anything?" [38]

The philosophy of keeping an open mind as an incentive for pursuing truth has been called "the cult of the questers." [39] Its basic tenet is that truth is tentative, that doubt is more important than belief. Questers preach unbelief as though it were itself a gospel. The philosophy of questing for its own sake, critics assert, may become an

---

[36] S. Butler: *Life and Habit*, p. 28. E. P. Dutton & Company, Inc., 1911.

[37] L. Steffens: *op. cit.*, pp. 375, 408, 644.

[38] From *Lincoln Steffens Speaking*, as condensed in *Reader's Digest*, January, 1937, under the title, "Unfinished Business." Reprinted by permission of Harcourt, Brace and Company, Inc.

[39] See the Editorial on "The Cult of the Questers" in the *Christian Century*, May 20, 1931.

apologetic for inaction.   As Heywood Broun put it, "It is better even to be wrong upon occasion than forever an inquiring neutral. . . . It may be true that they also serve who only stand and weigh and weigh, but into every life must come a time to step right or left, forward or back."   It is so easy to shed responsibility by losing oneself in a maze of doubt, to seek but never to find.

We are getting too problem-conscious for our own good, in the opinion of Harry Emerson Fosdick, who issues a warning against making life a tangled puzzle.   His view is worth quoting:

For multitudes of people religion has ceased being a source of confident and joyful life and has become a matter of debate.   The symbol of much modern religion is a discussion group.   Some generations are predominantly appreciative.   They enjoy their religion, live by it, make a festival of it create great music to celebrate it, build a cathedral to enshrine it.   Other generations are predominantly critical.   They ask questions, raise doubts seek for reasons, analyze their faith.

No doubt can exist as to the kind of generation we are living in.   Multitudes of people are intensely interested in religion and a midnight session on a college campus is almost sure to discuss two subjects—love and religion but it is religion as a problem to be debated, not as a privilege to be enjoyed

The tragic situation in the world at large accentuates this mood.   Everything is a problem—business, education, politics, internationalism—so that people become excessively problem-conscious, until all life appears as a tangled puzzle.   In consequence, insanity increases, suicides mount, nervous breakdowns multiply, and even more normal people lose the faith and morale to solve the very problems they worry over.

Under these circumstances it is important to see that religion is like nature or music or the family; problems do abound in all of them, but also privileges to be rejoiced in and lived by.   Granted that a man who tries to take the privileges without facing the problems is a sentimentalist! It also is true that a man who in any such realm becomes so problem-conscious that he does not rejoice in its powers and opportunities becomes dry, unhappy, and futile.

We do not need to solve all the scientific problems about nature before we enjoy the Maine coast or find health in the mountains.   No more do we need to solve all the problems about religion before we begin to live by it and draw power from it.   There are unsolved and, it may be, insoluble problems about God, Christ, prayer, and the Bible, but there are basic ideas and ideals in Christianity to be rejoiced in and lived for in the meantime.

Beware of becoming pathologically obsessed by the problematical aspect of life.   Richness of living depends on discovering the positive privileges of life under, over, and within the problems.[40]

[40] From a sermon reported in the New York *Times,* July 11, 1932.

Fosdick would find a supporter for his counsel in Carl Jung, the Swiss psychiatrist, who believes, on the basis of his wide clinical experience, that many people suffer breakdowns because they try to reason everything out instead of relying on their feelings, sacrificing their spiritual needs in the process; and another supporter in Henry Link, an American authority on personnel guidance, who states that a college education has so overintellectualized many persons that they go out into life with a morbid urge to analyze every experience as a problem to be reasoned about, instead of finding a faith they can live by.[41]

There are times when we must act, when it is folly to continue whirling in cogitation. One reason we fail to capitalize on our powers, said Francis Bacon, is the "pernicious and inveterate habit of dwelling on abstractions." Other thinkers have issued a similar warning against questing. Thomas Huxley insisted that "the great end of life is not knowledge but action." Harold Laski states that "thought has no meaning save as it is the prelude to the deed. . . . We may be more tolerant or less tolerant about ways of behavior we disapprove. We cannot be impartial about them." [42] Some people, according to Hogben, mistakenly believe that "excessive caution is the hallmark of science," erroneously assuming that knowledge should be a step to more knowledge, not to action, and when there is a need to act, such people "talk glibly, write elegantly, and argue forcibly." [43]

Probably few people need to be warned to act more, think less, since they think little enough now. Typical expression of American haste is this inspirational fight-talk from an advertising executive who is expounding the "Knack of Selling Yourself":

FASTER! FASTER!

Speed up! You have not a minute to waste. If you're enthusiastic, you demand a quick conclusion; you simply haven't the time to let nature take its course. Hurry on to your goal, stopping for nothing, deferring to nothing, racing, racing, all the time. Speed up. Dive into your subject and BEGIN THE THING. With a mighty swath you can do a life's work in an hour! For TIME even, most ruthless of all the elements, succumbs to enthusiasm.

Speed up! Work quickly, immediately, frantically. Take no time to breathe, to cool off, to rest. Your own enthusiasm is the only energy you

---

[41] See C. Jung: *Modern Man in Search of a Soul*. 1933. H. C. Link: *The Return to Religion*. 1936.

[42] H. J. Laski: "The Duty of the Intellectual Now." *Harper's Magazine*, December, 939.

[43] L. Hogben: *The Retreat from Reason*, pp. 10, 11. 1937.

need. Time and space must be given no standing whatsoever! Do it, do it now. Hurry! Hurry! Hurry! No man can loaf and be enthusiastic.[44]

The next section is appropriately entitled: "Be a Child Again."

Life is enough of a mad rush now without somebody spurring us to become more frantic. Somewhere between blind haste and meditative inaction must lie the course of wisdom, a course that gives full heed alike to the dangers of prejudice and the impracticability of mental paralysis. We cannot always wait until we are dead sure of ourselves; we do not want to "rush in where angels fear to tread." The path of compromise each man must blaze for himself.

[44] J. T. Mangan: *The Knack of Selling Yourself*, p. 54. 1938. By permission of Dartnell Corporation, Chicago.

Chapter 17

THE GENESIS AND CONTROL
OF PREJUDICE

We have observed how hard it is to get away from the pernicious habit of leaping to congenial conclusions. The prejudiced person who allows his personal biases to guide him cannot live as intelligently as the man who sees things objectively and then adjusts himself to the world of facts. What can be done to minimize the influence of prejudice in our lives? It may help us in working toward this ideal to examine some of the sources of our prejudices and some of the techniques we can use to promote the objective attitude.

I. ORIGINS

Most of our attitudes grow out of our casual personal experiences, especially the informal training we get in the home. This social derivation of prejudice is described in the lines which came to Henry Sedgwick in his sleep:

> We think so because all other people think so;
> Or because—or because—after all, we do think so;
> Or because we were told so, and think we must think so;
> Or because we once thought so, and think we still think so;
> Or because having thought so, we think we will think so.

Exposure to propaganda is also responsible for many of our attitudes, as we noted in Chapter 10.

A. Personal Experience

Our prejudices grow out of the kinds of experiences which happen to us. It makes a difference in a person's opinions on which side of the tracks he lives. In Woodworth's *Psychoneurotic Inventory* we encounter two questions designed to measure differences in adjustment, which read:

Did the teachers in school generally treat you right?

Have your employers generally treated you right?

If these questions are answered in the negative, neurotic tendencies are supposed to be indicated. It would make some difference, however, whether the testee was a white or a Negro. "A white person answering negatively may reveal a neurotic hypersensitivity; but as race prejudice is a consistent element in the social situation of the Negro, he may answer negatively, not as a neurotic but as a realist. Both may be maladjusted, yet the distinction must be made between maladjustments originating in subjective fancies and in objective fact."[1] It is easy for a white, in planning such an inventory, to ignore such distinctions because he has not suffered from such discrimination. The background of experience depends much on the race to which one belongs: one's idea of what's neurotic depends much on that background.

The forces that shape some of our most important beliefs may be more or less haphazard. Suppose you live in a factory town. A strike is going on. You pass along a certain street and you happen to see the strikers brutally beaten by the police. Your emotions are aroused. You become pro-Labor. But assume that you had taken another route home and had happened on a crowd of strikers pummeling a "scab." In this case, too, you might have been emotionally stirred, and you might have reacted to the situation by joining the Chamber of Commerce. A single experience, if it is vivid enough, may be decisive in setting one's outlook for years.

Particular experiences condition our attitudes toward certain situations or persons; then by association (conditioning) these attitudes are extended to include related objects. Thus the girl who was jilted by a medical student came to feel hostile toward all doctors. Senseless, it is true, but feelings do not always conform to the cold rules of logic. This particularistic fallacy—generalizing on the basis of a limited personal experience—plays an important role in the genesis of our prejudices. Racial animosities develop in such a manner.

The particular Jew whose bearing, mannerisms, and conduct excite a feeling of strangeness or repulsion is in part, no doubt, the cause of the ill feeling towards his race as a whole. The modern Negro, his ancestors still fresh in memory as slaves and menials, is the victim, by association and conditioning,

[1] M. Brenman: "The Relationship between Minority-Group Membership and Group Identification in a Group of Urban Middle Class Negro Girls." *Journal of Social Psychology,* 1940, 11, 171-197.

of the slave psychology. The foreigner with the name suffixed with a *ski,* regardless of rank or attainment, in the general mind is regarded with distrust, largely because his name is conditioned by the misgivings produced by some first-generation countrymen whose conduct has not conformed to the American behavior—whose reactions themselves are conditioned to an alien culture.[2]

Propagandists are quick to condition our attitudes, by name-calling and other devices, linking our old hostilities to new ones.

It is natural for us to interpret the world in general in terms of our own experiences in particular. One observer has remarked that many a prediction of a world-wide depression can be traced to a hole in the prophet's pocket. A man in Putney, Vermont, wrote to a Boston paper, in 1938, to commend an article in its financial columns on "The Red Menace." He concluded his praise by saying: "It is most timely, and I am sure that it expresses the views of business men in all sections of the country." How could a man way up in Putney, Vermont, have presumed to take himself as an index of national sentiment, especially after what happened in the presidential election of 1936? It is easy to mistake a local prejudice for a universal truth.

B. Some Agencies for Promoting Prejudice

Some of our prejudices grow out of our casual everyday experiences, as we have noted; some of them are inculcated in us by agencies bent on seeing to it that we acquire the proper biases. These are essentially the same agencies, by the way, which we considered as instruments of propaganda dissemination in Chapter 10.

1. the school

Many of our prejudices are inculcated by formal courses in the schools, though informal training in the classroom, as well as in the home, may contribute much more to the molding of attitudes. Formal training refers to the ideas expounded by textbook and teacher. Informal training refers to the personal example set by the instructor in the classroom, on the playground, and in other situations where he may exert an influence upon his pupils. It is possible for a teacher to preach tolerance, to practice intolerance. Personal example is considered to be far more influential than verbal precept.

[2] N. B. Willey and M. M. Willey: "The Conditioned Response and the Consciousness of Kind." *American Journal of Sociology,* 1924, 30, 22-28. University of Chicago Press.

Back in the 1920's an Italian made some comments on French education, which shed much light on what has happened since:

For hundreds of years, except during rare periods, the French and the Italians have disliked each other. Who is to blame? First of all, events, but also the nature of man, who is always slothful when there is a question of correcting certain defects of education. The French, who had attained their national unity four centuries before the Italians, looked upon the Italians as a people who deserved to be dominated. From the Renaissance on, the Italians were considered to be an idle race, venal and capable of the most perfidious crimes and treachery. This tradition was carefully preserved. All one has to do is to examine French literature in which the Italian appears as a base and sinister personage. The Italians, even in their saddest days, despised this contempt of them. It was hardly possible that they should respond to it by friendly expressions. This feeling of superiority, which is particularly wounding to the Italians, is rather general in the French attitude toward the greater number of foreigners.

It is the result of French education, which is so different from Italian education. In education, where we try to keep our natural spontaneity in entirety, the French, on the other hand, are formed after a fixed plan and all their movements and manner of speech must, to be correct, follow certain rules. In foreign countries a Frenchman sometimes gives the impression of posing, but the truth is that he is artificial without knowing it, because that is the way he has been brought up by his educators.

Indoctrination is inevitable in education, in the view of Ellis Freeman. As evidence for this assertion he offers his analysis of the *Thorndike Arithmetic,* published in 1917. Practically all of the problems are concerned with commerical transactions in which monetary gain is the predominant motive—selling, buying and reselling, rent, working for wages, employing others for wages, interest on loans. Thorndike was possibly unaware of the capitalistic bias determining his choice of problems. Indirectly, subtly, the examples impress the child with the idea that our commercial culture is all right. No questions are raised to suggest that perhaps our order of things might be changed for the better. Freeman, for example, proposes that problems like this should be included: "If a family needs $15 a week for food, but receives $5 on the dole, what is the percentage of undernourishment?" Such a problem would damn the book as "propagandistic and unworthy of the dignity of pure arithmetic." Thorndike's examples are just as propagandistic. They are not recognized as such, however, since they tend to perpetuate the accepted ideology. Freeman grants that Thorndike's *Arithmetic* is pragmatically justified because it is preparing the child to take his place in our particular culture, not in some abstract utopia. The point Freeman is seeking to drive home is the fact that it is practically impossible to be impartial in our teaching. His plea is that we stop deceiving ourselves about our pedagogical disinterestedness. There are social implications even in $2 + 2 = 4$, for that's a profit of 100 per cent in any arithmetic.[3]

Fanatics are not so subtle about the dissemination of their pet predilections. Parents of Philadelphia's public-school children were urged during the school year of 1940 to seek the ban of a social science textbook considered to be "very, very un-American" by Mrs. Elwood J. Turner, corresponding secretary of the Daughters of Colonial Wars. Mrs. Turner contended that the book, written by Harold Rugg, "tried to give the child an unbiased viewpoint instead of teaching him real Americanism. All the old histories taught 'My country, right or wrong.' That's the point of view we want our children to adopt." When Rugg was asked by the critics to justify himself, he queried, "What do they want—medicated history?" And the answer, of course, to that question is "Yes." The newspaper headline concerning the incident summed up the case accurately:

PHILADELPHIA SCHOOL BAN
ON "UNBIASED BOOK" SOUGHT [4]

Such candor is rather wholesome. Ordinarily a person is not so unabashed about revealing his intention to make his own prejudices prevail.

2. THE PRESS

Newspapers help to confirm us in our prejudices because we are inclined to read papers whose views coincide with our own. Allen mentions the hatred of the rich for Roosevelt during the 'thirties, an attitude of violent displeasure shared in those days by many of the wealthy in all sections of the country. Then Allen goes on to say:

It was strongest and most nearly unanimous among the very rich and in those favored suburbs and resorts where people of means were best insulated against uncomfortable facts and unorthodox opinions. To live in Locust Valley or Greenwich, let us say, to work in Wall Street, and to read only the New York *Herald Tribune* in the morning and the New York *Sun* at night, offered excellent insulation, especially if one concentrated devotedly upon the

---

[3] See E. Freeman: *Social Psychology*, pp. 263-266. 1936.
[4] The Boston *Traveler*, February 20, 1940. We mentioned Mrs. Turner's condemnation of Rugg, you remember, under "The School" in Chapter 10.

daily lamentations of Mark Sullivan and the uniformly sour interpretations of Administration policies in the financial columns of the *Sun*.[5]

The pictorial medium employed by the artist and the cartoonist is particularly effective in promoting prejudice. This *Literary Digest*

(Courtesy, Jay N. Darling.)

cover was a masterpiece in the art of building up sentiment against Prohibition. Its caricature utilizes stereotypes to gain the maximum effect, carrying its message subtly and convincingly; words could not accomplish the same end with such facility. Analyze the drawing and you will appreciate how persuasive is the argument it advances. Its appeal is direct, simple, devastating.

[5] F. L. Allen: *Since Yesterday*, p. 232. Harper & Brothers, 1940.

Many examples in literature could be cited to show how authors use their media to foster prejudice against racial groups. Shakespeare's portrayal of Shylock in *The Merchant of Venice* served to stereotype the Jew and to crystallize sentiment against him. It is significant that Shakespeare probably never saw a Jew, since Jews had been banished from England before his time.

An author may consciously, or *unconsciously,* nourish definite prejudices in the minds of his readers, as Granville Hicks points out.

One result of this deliberately uncritical attitude is that rank prejudices creep in without being challenged by the author, and often without being challenged by the reader. In Archibald MacLeish's "Frescoes for Mr. Rockefeller's City" there is a famous stanza:

> "Ain't you read in d'books you are all brudders?
> D'glassic historic objective broves you are all brudders!
> You and d'Wops and d'Chinks you are all brudders!
> Haven't you got d'same ideology? Haven't you?"

Now this not only implies that communists are dogmatic ignoramuses, which Mr. MacLeish at that time very possibly believed; it also implies that all or most communists are Jews, that these Jewish communists speak execrable English, and that they are palpably insincere since they profess that the Chinese and Italians are their brothers and yet speak derogatorily of them as "Chinks" and "Wops." Mr. MacLeish did not believe all these things, and, when Mike Gold accused him of having a "fascist unconscious," he protested. He did better than protest; he showed in words and actions that he had no sympathy with race prejudice and that he could recognize sincere revolutionary ardor. But he had allowed these assumptions, which he had not taken the trouble to examine, to enter his poem. . . .

Out of the scores of reviewers who praised Margaret Mitchell's *Gone With the Wind,* scarcely one commented on her attitude toward the Negro. If Miss Mitchell merely reproduced the prejudices of the time she is describing, we could, of course, justify it on artistic grounds; but the truth is that she makes exactly the same assumptions as were made by the slaveowners of the 'sixties. Her Negroes are preeminently happy-go-lucky, empty-headed children, and we hear much about "the excited babble of Negro voices," the "high-pitched Negro laughter," and the "grinning Negroes, excited as always at a party." They have no reasoning powers, but they have "an unerring African instinct." When a servant is stupid, it is because it is more than "the brain in her little black skull could bear." The color of the skull is carefully specified. When a servant is praiseworthy there is a "but" to mark the fact as exceptional: "Mammy was black, *but* her code of conduct and her sense of pride were as high or higher than that of her owners." Although there are some reasonably unattractive white persons in the book, it is never suggested that their vices are due to their race. Viciousness on the part of a Negro, however, is always coupled with his color. Just as Thomas Wolfe, although his Eugene Gant seems fairly preoccupied with sex, stresses the sexuality of the Jews, so Miss Mitchell, in spite of the rather active passions of Scarlett O'Hara and Rhett Butler, repeats again and again all the old phrases about Negro lust. The Ku Klux Klan is a "tragic necessity" to defend southern womanhood, and when there is talk of rape by a Negro, a lynching is regarded by the towns-people—and if Miss Mitchell disagrees, she does not say so—as "the only decent solution possible." [6]

Hitler mobilized "Mother Goose" in the form of a Nazi primer published by the Jew-baiter, Julius Streicher. Twenty-one brightly colored pages showed brute-faced Jews cheating, seducing, and poisoning handsome Nordics. The cover depicted a fox and a Jew, with this script to drive home the moral: "Trust Not the Fox by Field or Pond, Nor Any Jew upon His Bond." One jingle accompanied a picture of a fat Jewish villain accosting a noble German girl and dangling a string of pearls before her averted eyes:

> The Jew, he thinks he's pretty sly
> If he a German girl can buy.
> But see this picture of the Jew:
> For her the Yid will never do!
> For German girls, O mercy me!
> How miserable a sort is he!

In another scene, a little German girl was gazing into the display window of a toy shop. Her mother warned her: "No, that is a Jewish store. We must buy only in German stores, where we will not be cheated." On the last page there was a road with a signpost reading, "One-Way Street to Palestine," and down it were marching all the detestable Jewish characters portrayed in the book: the dirty butcher, the skinflint lawyer, the murderous doctor, the vile debaucher, and their kin. These novel nursery rhymes were composed by a young Third Reich schoolteacher named Elvira Bauer. "Her activity as kindergarten instructress," observed a Nazi comrade, "has given her a rare insight into the souls of children." [7] There can be no doubt as to what such vivid lessons would do to the impressionable minds of kindergarten children.

[6] G. Hicks: "Assumptions in Literature." The *English Journal*, 1936, 25, 709-717.
[7] See R. Thurston: "Hitler Mobilizes 'Mother Goose.'" The *Nation*, March 20, 1937.

3. THE MOVIES

The cinema contributes its share to the fomenting of prejudice. The stereotyped villain is a sneaky Oriental who would give even the hardboiled detective-story reader the creeps.   One movie goer testified: "The picture showed the Chinese with a knife, going into the man's room.   Shortly after, he came out, with a villainous, bloodthirsty, satisfied look that haunts me now, ten or more years after." [8]   Apparently this picture left its impression.   Many adults can recall just as clearly the savage Negro attacking the white girl in *The Birth of a Nation,* an effective dramatic film, from the point of view of propaganda, although the racial element was quite incidental to the main story.   In a test experiment this picture was found to exert a very decided influence on the racial feelings of children who saw it in Crystal Lake, Illinois, partly because very few of the children had known or even seen Negroes before.[9]   High-school students in Hyde Park, Illinois, filled out a paired comparison schedule registering their attitudes toward various nationalities, following the instruction to "underline the one nationality, or race of each pair that you would rather associate with."   Then they were shown *The Jazz-Singer* (a motion picture favorable to the Jews), *Michael Strogoff* (favorable to the Russians), *Four Sons* and *The Emden* (favorable to the Germans).   A subsequent retest on the paired comparison schedule revealed a slight change in the direction of favoring the nationalities depicted on the screen, though the shift was not large enough to be statistically significant. It was found, however, that *Four Sons* and *Son of the Gods* (Chinese) both produced significant attitude changes when they were shown to students in small towns.[10]

Prejudice against Americans is encouraged by some of the Hollywood films which are exhibited in other countries.   We Americans may not realize how our films affect the peoples of other nations, who may rely largely on this source for their idea of how the typical American spends his time.   An exhibitor in New Zealand reports his experience with Hollywood films:

It would be no exaggeration to say that nothing America has ever done or is ever likely to do has injured the standing of the United States as much as

---

[8] Quoted from the *Pacific Coast Race Relations Survey,* in E. S. Bogardus: *Immigration and Race Attitudes,* p. 69.   1928.

[9] See R. C. Peterson and L. L. Thurstone: *Motion Pictures and the Social Attitudes of Children,* p. 35.   1933.

[10] *Ibid.,* pp. 10-13; 17-20.

the pictures it has produced. . . . You could not persuade even a fifteen-year-old boy—

1. That every American, from the President down to the toughest gangster, is not a hard drinker;

2. That there is an honest American business man, politician, judge, or jury; and

3. That there is any such thing as a clean, honest newspaperman.

That is what the American picture producer has done with this golden opportunity.   It has gone beyond recall—the opportunity to build up throughout the civilized world the most wonderful and profitable reputation for America . . . any nation has ever had.   But what has he done?   He has taught the world that those things our mothers, our churches, our government taught us to believe in were not worth having.

He taught us to believe that clean, honest courts of justice and clean, honest home life . . . are not known in the United States . . . that marriage is a farce. . . .

America is portrayed as the land of loose women, drinking men and women, dishonest judges and juries, corrupt government, rum-runners. . . .[11]

From England, previous to World War II, a comment by the *Daily Telegraph*:

It cannot be denied that in a certain section of the community there is rapidly growing up an unpleasing feeling toward you.   These people regard an American as a lawless, immoral individual, who carries a gun in his pocket at all times, and changes his wife as easily as he changes his shirt, doping his friends, shooting his enemies, attending petting parties, and bathing "Follies" girls in champagne.   Can you blame them? [12]

From India comes a statement by Lord Irwin to the effect that "Orientals . . . ceased to respect the white race after seeing Hollywood films." [13]

4. THE RADIO

The radio bolsters prejudice in favor of the vested interests.   In order to influence the masses, the advocate who wants to evangelize in behalf of his own prejudices must have access to the instruments of propaganda, the press and the radio.   These instruments, being ex-

---

[11] Quoted by F. Eastman: "Movies and Our Neighbors' Children." *Christian Century*, June 7, 1933.

[12] Quoted, *ibid.*

[13] Quoted, *ibid.*

ensive, are available only to those who have plenty of money to foot
he bills.

Let's see how the radio is employed to prejudice the so-called mass
mind.[14]   John T. Flynn discusses the matter:

> There is no better time to catch the monster [the "mass mind"] than on
> Sunday evening.   It is relaxed.   It is in a benevolent mood.   On Sunday eve-
> ning the family is gathered in the living room when into their midst float
> the strains of music from a great symphony orchestra.   In millions of homes
> people are listening.   This goes on for half an hour.   Then as the strains
> of some well-loved old song fade from the air and the family sits around,
> thoroughly softened up, there floats into the room and into the unguarded
> chambers of their minds the voice of the propagandist.   For five or ten
> minutes the carefully planned infection flows into the monster.   It tells of
> the romantic saga of business, the great achievements, the massive wisdom,
> the matchless courage, the civilizing alchemy of the great business man as
> distinguished from the selfish and narrow ignorance and wickedness of the
> Government—the great-souled business leader compared with the small-
> minded and vicious Senator.[15]

Another program, sponsored by certain banks, features an economist
who is notorious as an apologist for big business.   There is no counter-
blast to contradict him.   The people who listen are induced to believe
that the stupid Government should leave business alone.

Another device used by big business corporations, according to
Flynn, is shirt-stuffing.   The head of a corporation is publicized as an
all-wise heroic figure under whose name the publicity department
issues articles and speeches.   Epigrams and philosophies are invented
for the stuffed shirt to proclaim as his own.   This technique for swaying the radio audience is based on the fact, states Flynn, that the American people have been led to accept

the naïve illusion that because a man knows how to make a million dollars, he knows how to run a government, how to bring back prosperity, how
to fashion and mold our culture, how to direct universities, and how, in fact,
to control our theology and govern our churches.   The result is that these
stuffed shirts become useful instruments for getting space in the papers and
time on the radio to spread the propaganda that is essential to their commercial objectives.[16]

---

[14] The "mass mind" refers to the minds of the average citizens.
[15] "Is Our Public Opinion Controlled by Propaganda?" *Bulletin of America's
Town Meeting of the Air*, April 18, 1938.
[16] *Ibid.*

Flynn suggests that measures should be taken to prevent advertisers from using the radio for political propaganda. Let them put on their orchestras and crooners; bar them from sneaking in their political nostrums. Newspapers may have a bias in favor of their advertisers but they have not reached the stage where they announce that their editorials are "coming to you through the courtesy of the Crazy Crystal Corporation." The radio even more than the newspaper serves as a propaganda instrument for the special pressure groups who can pay for the privilege of influencing the public.

II. THE SIGNIFICANCE OF INDIVIDUAL DIFFERENCES

It is felt by some observers that prejudices are traceable generally to the mere fact that individuals differ from one another. Proponents of this view insist that people who differ in appearance, interests, and cultural background just naturally take a dislike to one another. The stranger is *persona non grata* until he can prove himself *grata*. The Greeks had a word for him: they called him a *barbarian* because his foreign speech sounded like "bar-bar-bar," and that was not good Greek.

A. DIFFERENCE AND STATUS

Hostility between groups may involve the recognition of differences but the real source of strong antagonism is group competition which threatens the disruption of the individual's status, thus endangering his survival. Ordinarily, intense prejudice is not caused by mere difference; the dynamic basis of the animosity lies in the threat to status. When the dominant group fancies that the inferior group is undermining its status, those who have the upper hand feel insecure and their fears lead them to acts of aggression by which they intend to suppress the presumptuous upstarts. Thus Jews are persecuted because they presume that they are equal to or superior to Gentiles, and the Gentiles do not relish this attempt to usurp their superior position. The threat to the Gentiles' status (rating) arouses the fear of losing special privileges—economic, social, and political—which constitute their dominance. "Differences are emphasized because they offer the readiest rationalization for defence against real or fancied dangers." [17]

Bogardus takes the view that status is the basic factor in causing prejudice. Status, he says, is one's standing,

---

[17] F. Brown: "A Socio-Psychological Analysis of Race Prejudice." *Journal of Abnormal and Social Psychology*, 1933, 27, 364-374.

the personal rating given one person by his fellows. The wish for recognition is the dynamic force involved. Whatever lowers the social rating given a person or his group arouses prejudice. What boosts one or his group is likely to stimulate favoritism. . . . Where a person's status, or the status of anything he values is endangered by the members of some race, then race prejudice flares up.[18]

There is no doubt that status conflict is very significant in arousing hostility toward those ambitious persons who seek to better themselves at our expense. The fact that foreigners are segregated in the community tends to give rise to the impression that they are outsiders, possibly enemies who must be actively guarded against and suppressed. We observe this reaction occurring on a large scale in the field of economic competition. When Booker T. Washington established a program of industrial education for the Southern Negroes, with the idea that training would bring economic salvation for them, he ran into a psychological obstacle which thwarted his aim to a serious extent. The Negroes were taught how to grow better sweet potatoes. The whites retaliated by discriminating more bitterly than ever against the Negroes. A similar situation arose more recently in Memphis, Tennessee, where organized labor petitioned the school board to take the mechanical arts out of the curriculum in Negro schools.

Americans in California have for years resented the intrusion of the Japanese, whom they call "the Jews of the Orient," because the Japanese are so thrifty and industrious. It has been the practice of the Japanese to work hard, to save their money, to buy up land, to prosper at the expense of native Americans. Consequently there was a strong feeling against the immigrants from Japan, long before Pearl Harbor. This hostility was expressed by blaming the Japanese no matter what they did.

If they asked less than the going wage, they were threatening the American standard of living; if they demanded better wages, they were avaricious; if they were successful in farming and saved enough to buy their own ranches, they were driving the whites out; if they were unsuccessful, they were "wearing out the land." [19]

Persecution of the Jews, both in Germany and America, has been rationalized by embracing the belief that the Jews control every profitable enterprise. The Nazis used to explain the anti-Nazi tone

---

[18] Bogardus: *op cit.*, pp. 30, 28.
[19] E. K. Strong, Jr.: *The Second-Generation Japanese Problem*, p. 125. 1933.

of the American press by alleging that the newspapers in this country are Jewish owned.   This allegation cannot be substantiated by facts. Only 15 out of 17,000 firms publishing daily newspapers are Jewish owned.

Using the Jew as a scapegoat is a popular device; not only was this true in Germany but it is still true elsewhere.   We Americans, like others, have developed fictitious charges against the Jews to excuse our prejudice against them.   *Fortune* conducted a careful investigation in 1936 to determine whether the Jews really control our major enterprises.   The investigators discovered that the clannishness of the Jews is responsible for the Gentile prejudice against the Jews, that Gentiles invent economic grievances, such as that "the Jews monopolize American business and industry," in order to justify their animosity.   There are several reasons why it is easy for the belief to develop that the Jews are monopolizing everything.   One is the urban concentration of the Jews.   The population of New York City, for example, is about thirty per cent Jewish.   Another reason is that the Jews tend to concentrate in certain trades and professions.   The *Fortune* investigators found that the Jews were not running the banks in this country.   There were no Jews at all in the largest commercial banks.   The personnel of the Stock Exchange was only sixteen per cent Jewish.   There were very few Jews in the steel industry, although ninety per cent of the scrap-iron industry was run by Jews.   There were very few Jews in the automobile industry, very few in rubber, shipping and transportation, department-store retailing, advertising, newspapers.   There were many in the clothing business.   Jewish interests were extremely important in radio, although the vast majority of local stations outside of New York City were non-Jewish; very important in the theater, where about one-half the producers were Jews; very prominent in the production and financial control of motion pictures.   About one-third of the lawyers in New York City were Jews; but Jews constituted one-third of the population, too.   The same figures applied to medicine.   Though they excelled in both law and medicine, their power was by no means proportional to their numbers.   Jews, in 1935, made up about one-seventh of the Communist Party membership.   This is not surprising when it is recognized that both the Jews and the Communist Party center in New York City.   Certainly, when this *Fortune* report is considered as a whole, there is little or no ground for contending that the Jews are depriving American Gentiles of a chance to earn a living.[20]   The fiction of Jewish encroachment persists as a convenient

[20] "Jews in America."   *Fortune*, February, 1936.

justification for maintaining hostile attitudes and for indulging in discriminatory practices.   As long as Gentiles believe that Jews are damaging their economic status, there will be anti-Semitic prejudice.

Threat-to-status underlies most of our violent prejudices.   It is the author's conviction on this point that differences, regardless of status, promote prejudice in so far as they involve ignorance and misunderstanding.   Individual differences give rise to prejudice; endangered status aggravates the hostility.

Take, for example, the attitude of Americans toward Italians, say, around Boston.   An Italian girl living for years in Boston makes this observation: "Among most Americans there is a feeling of bias against the foreign-born in general, and sometimes it would seem as though it were directed particularly against Italians." [21]   She speaks especially of social discrimination against Italians.   This discrimination, we might point out, is not due to the fact that Italians are threatening to dislodge native Americans from their traditional prerogatives in Boston.   The Italians do not constitute a threat to the status of the natives resident in Boston.   We Yankees do discriminate against the Italians, nevertheless, largely because we feel our superior status.   Italians do menial labor, dig ditches, mow lawns, run fruit stands, work as barbers.   Consequently, we come to think of all Italians as inferior, ignoring the fact that immigrants as a rule are forced by Americans to earn their living in occupations carrying little prestige.   The social discrimination against them is felt very keenly by Italians, so much so, that the Italian may come to regard it as a high compliment for an American to say, "Why, you don't look like an Italian."

It is my belief that Americans who are prejudiced against Italians take such an unfriendly attitude primarily because Italians appear different to them.   They look different, they speak in a strange tongue, they have large families, they eat garlic and spaghetti, they reside in the slum areas.   The feeling of the American toward the Italian may be just a mild dislike involving no acts of intentional aggression, but the prejudice is there.

Now suppose the son of an Italian (race) who runs a fruit stand (occupation) takes a fancy to the daughter of an American business man; suppose the young Italian is a graduate of an American university, well mannered, cultured, handsome, intelligent, in fact, more intelligent and better educated than either the girl or her father; there you have a situation where status is endangered and the father does

[21] T. G. Talamini: *The Influence of Recreation on the Inferiority Complexes of the Italian Adolescent Girl.*   Master's Thesis, Boston University.   1932.

what you would expect him to do under the circumstances, he requests his daughter to discourage the young man's attentions.   The prejudice against Italians in general was present long before any question of status was involved; the prejudice against one Italian in particular was aggravated by his presuming—so the father felt—that he was good enough to marry into an American family.

Individual differences are the primary source of prejudice in this instance.   It is more natural for us to get to know more about people who are like ourselves, who are interested in the same things we are interested in, than it is for us to go out of our way to familiarize ourselves with people who are obviously different in their tastes and pursuits.   We tend to be prejudiced in favor of people who resemble ourselves, against those who deviate from our particular norm.

One phase of psychological warfare in World War II was that of training solders to appreciate and to respect the differences they were sure to encounter in various parts of the world; by being tolerant and friendly, to help win friends for Uncle Sam.

In the Solomons, in China, in North Africa it matters a great deal whether the native people, as well as the soldiers of Allies, like Americans or resent them.   To these people, the soldier is America's representative.   If he offends them, it will be America and Americans who seem offensive—not just the soldier himself.

An American soldier entering a Moslem church with his shoes on could counteract all the friendly councils of generals and diplomats in a palace in Algiers.[22]

Similarly, it would never do for an American to upbraid a Chinese peasant for beating "the daylights out of his tired horse," since the Chinese are brought up to feel no more sympathy for a horse than an American feels for a mosquito.[23]   The American soldier, trained from childhood to be industrious, will be inclined to look with disdain upon the custom of the siesta practiced, say, among the New Caledonians—until he has lived long enough in their climate to see the sense in their resting during the midday heat.[24]   Beliefs and habits of thought and customary ways of doing things—all of them *learned*—make up the most important national differences.   Every soldier should study the ways of his friends—and his enemies—for it will pay him to do so.

[22] A Committee of the National Research Council: *Psychology for the Fighting Man*, p. 397. 1943. See the whole chapter, 18, "Differences among Races and Peoples."

[23] *Ibid.*, p. 402.   [24] *Ibid.*, pp. 407-408.

Many American lives might have been saved earlier in this war if the soldiers had understood the Japanese way of thinking about surrender and taking prisoners. Americans, attempting to save Japs who had had to jump into the water from sinking transports, were killed in their act of mercy. They did not understand that many Japs would rather die than be rescued under such circumstances.[25]

So the soldier was advised to:

1. Try to *understand* strange customs. There are real reasons back of all of them: they are not just crazy.
2. *Respect* these customs even though you can't understand them.
3. If you cannot respect them, *suppress your disapproval*.
4. When you can respect them, *show it*.
5. When you associate with foreign people, try to *adopt their manners*. Do not expect them to adopt yours.
6. *Suppress your own peculiarities* if they conflict with the custom of the land.
7. When a foreign custom does not concern you, *mind your own business*.
8. *Be friendly*. You won't like them right away, perhaps, because no one is immediately fond of strangers. But from the start, act as though you liked them. You will find *some* things to like about people everywhere. Your friendliness, if it is genuine, will usually bring out friendliness in them. [26]
9. *Take people as they come*. Like them for what they are, not for the way they happen to measure up to your own standards. . . . Of all the billions of men and women in this world, each one is different from every other one. You are different, too. Each stranger you meet will surprise you, interest you, thrill you, or puzzle you. Each is a challenge to you to show the best that is in *you*.[27]

B. KINDS OF DIFFERENCES

Personal variations are the most prolific source of prejudice, since it is in the realm of personal relations that we give the freest rein to our feelings. We shall concentrate our attention, therefore, upon differences of a personal nature.

1. PERSONAL APPEARANCE

We tend to dislike people who look radically different from ourselves. Until we get to know them, they all look alike to us. Thus we are likely to feel hostile right from the start toward persons whose skin is of a different color, whose eyes slant, whose manner of dress seems inexcusably strange. It is easy for me to incite my neighbors

[25] *Ibid.*, p. 403.   [26] *Ibid.*, p. 412.   [27] *Ibid.*, p. 412.

to giggles of ridicule just by carrying a cane on a stroll down our street.   How much easier it is for a foreigner to arouse enmity or at least unfriendliness by appearing with a turban, or a slit kimona, or a ring through the nose (instead of through the ears), or a full-length beard.   We forget that personal worth cannot be estimated by such superficial signs.   The "stranger" gets no chance to demonstrate his admirable qualities.   Unless he happens to excite curiosity, he is rejected arbitrarily, without trial.   By straining ourselves we may extend the friendly hand and learn to tolerate his idiosyncrasies, we may even get to like him after a while, but the odds are against it.   It is much easier to like people who are images of ourselves.

2. PERSONALITY

We are inclined favorably in our relations with persons whose traits, interests, and attitudes coincide with our own and we are inclined unfavorably in our contacts with persons who vary from ourselves in these respects.   Staunch Republicans cannot understand a person with non-partisan political attitudes, a "queer" sort of person who sometimes votes for Republicans, sometimes for Democrats, sometimes even for Socialists.   They try to like him in spite of his quirk, blaming his oddity on the fact that he is aiming to be different from normal people for the sake of the distinction he can derive from being contrary. With some effort, they may tolerate this idiosyncrasy because they find in him good qualities to compensate for his political infirmity.

3. CULTURAL LEVEL

Children who go to private schools are apt to look down upon "the common herd" who go to public schools.   A prominent dean whose School of Education trained teachers for the public schools was embarrassed by a warning from a leading society matron that his daughters would not be asked to the best homes if they continued going to the public schools.

The man who dines in formal attire and the man who eats his supper in his shirtsleeves are prone to look askance at each other.   The refined person is deeply annoyed by the individual who picks his teeth in public or by the uncouth individual who sips his coffee out of a saucer in a public restaurant.   They will never meet as kindred souls.

4. RELIGION

There is much intolerance between religious believers and unbelievers, including in the latter category heathen, infidels, atheists, and agnostics; and there is likewise much enmity amongst believers who belong to differing sects.

Some religious believers, perhaps a little shaken in their faith by disturbing doubts, resent the infidel who questions their theological assumptions. Being none too sure of themselves to begin with, such believers fear for their spiritual security. Hostility is aggravated if the infidel is given to poking fun at the credulity of the believer. Enmity may be felt, however, even when the doubter is kindly and sincere in questioning the bases of faith, as in the case of Thomas Paine, for example, who was reviled as "that filthy little atheist," despite his irreproachable character.

Individual differences among religious believers are responsible for bitterly hostile prejudices. Since religious beliefs concern the values that we prize most dearly, it is natural for us to become emotionally aroused when people cross our paths who disagree with our precious version of "the eternal truth." Each sect evolves its own dogma—and then seeks to convert the benighted who dwell in sin and ignorance. Christianity is especially evangelical and Christians, it is sad to note, have too often been guilty of persecutions and inquisitions hardly consistent with professions of brotherly love. Many observers have been puzzled by this contradiction between the teachings of the Gospel and the unbrotherly way in which it has sometimes been propagated. The mystery clears when we realize how profoundly people disagree in their values. Given a number of people who have different conceptions of what is important in this life and the next, each person willing to fight for his own particular view or the creed of his group, it is not surprising that the history of religions includes many savage controversies.

As beliefs that are considered a part of religion are invested with a supernatural and divinely authorized character, it is but natural that they should be the most irrationally and fanatically held of all possible beliefs. . . . It is . . . inevitable that there will be about as many sets of values as there are individuals and that native disposition and environment acting together will cause them to form numerous religious groups. The unfortunate part of it is not that one creed limits its meat diet on Friday to fish while another abstains entirely from pork, or that one sect practices total immersion of adults while another sprinkles a little water on the heads of infants; the fact that these differences in beliefs and practices exist would not be so important if it were not for the militant advocacy of them and the attempt to convert or to exterminate dissenters. Human nature cannot be standardized in religious matters any more than in height, weight, color, disposition, or intelligence.

Tolerance is therefore needed in religion above all other things. Merely because we prefer one belief to another is by no means an adequate justification for attempting to cast all others in the same mold in which we were cast. . . . Uniformity in belief is impossible.[28]

The apocryphal story is told of an Irishman who struck a Jew he had just met on the street. The Jew, a complete stranger, was somewhat taken aback since he had done nothing to provoke the assault. He was curious to learn the reason for the sudden attack. So he inquired. The Irishman replied that the Jews had crucified Jesus. "Well, I don't believe it," responded the Jew, "but even so, that was a long time ago." "Yes," explained the Irishman, "but the first I heard of it was this morning." This amusing tale is interesting because it touches lightly on a racial animosity that is fundamentally religious in its origins and because it illustrates how fictions, invented to excuse prejudice, come to circulate as historically true. Many persons believe that the Jews crucified Jesus, though actually it was the Romans who tried him and nailed him to the cross. The fiction that the Jews were responsible persists because it is a useful rationalization to justify ill feeling.

Religious sects exist because different kinds of people require different kinds of religion to satisfy their spiritual longings. McComas points out that

the differences which appear in the religious life of different denominations have their only justification in the differences of human dispositions and not in any divine preferences. Nothing is more necessary today than the proclamation of this fact, for the heart of sectarianism is the belief that each sect is peculiarly a divine favorite. When all religious people freely acknowledge that their differences are matters of individual tastes and temperaments the real barriers to church unity will be brushed away.[29]

The ideal of church unity has been entertained as a worthy goal by a number of church leaders who see in this aim a practical means of terminating the bickerings and controversies that undermine the effectiveness of sectarian religion. There are economic reasons for unity, too, particularly in small communities which cannot afford to support several churches. Community churches have been growing in number. The chief barrier to unity is that each sect favors that unity which

[28] R. S. Ellis: *The Psychology of Individual Differences,* pp. 512-513.   D. Appleton-Century Company, 1928.
[29] H. C. McComas: *The Psychology of Religious Sects,* p. 8.   1912.

would result from its absorbing other sects. This is true of the Roman Catholic Church, whose policy in this matter was explained by the Pope in 1928 when a movement was being organized to bring about church unity. A report of progress appeared in the news on January 10, 1928.

> Protestants, Orthodox church folk, and all others dissenting from the original Roman Catholic church, must return to Rome if they really desire a union of all Christians, is the substance of a papal encyclical to the episcopacy of the world, issued today. There is no safety outside the Roman Catholic Apostolic Church, Pope Pius XI repeats once more.
>
> During the Pontificate of Benedict XV, prominent American Protestants came purposely to Rome to try to induce the Pope to send a representative to a conference for union of the churches. The Pope received them most cordially, listened to them with the greatest attention, but answered in effect: "There is nothing we desire more ardently than a union of all Christians, but this can be obtained only in one way—by the return of the wandering sheep to the fold."
>
> In this, the first encyclical of the new year, the Pope, restating the church's age-long stand on the union of Christians, emphasizes the point that while it is good to cultivate charity among Christians, it should not be done to the detriment of the faith on which that charity is founded.
>
> Recognizing the general tendency toward better international union between peoples, he deplores the fact that "some seem to wish to transfer it from the political to the religious field, thus blending the true religion with the false, holding all religions equally good and praiseworthy."
>
> "God, the creator," says the Pope, "is also the revealer to man of the way in which He wishes to be honored and served. That is the real religion for which he founded his church on earth. The duty of the human being therefore is to believe God's revelations, and consequently adhere to the church—not that which is supported by the erring, but, on the contrary, that church which in verity was willed and founded by Christ and which by the promise of Christ's assistance perseveres as one and identical throughout the centuries —namely, the Apostolic Roman Church." [30]

This pronouncement speaks for itself.

Some religious leaders have been working to promote good will among the various religious faiths by organizing conferences where Catholics, Jews, and Protestants meet to discuss their mutual problems, thus encouraging a better understanding among the several groups. The National Conference of Jews and Christians was organized in 1927

---

[30] The Boston *Herald*, January 10, 1928.

—the name has since been changed and it is now called the National Conference of Christians and Jews. Sessions are conducted regularly in which Protestants, Catholics, and Jews participate. The meetings are conducted as seminars, representatives of the several faiths contributing ideas on the sources of conflicts and offering suggestions for the improvement of their personal and institutional interrelationships. From their headquarters at 381 Fourth Avenue, New York City, the National Conference of Christians and Jews cooperates with local committees in arranging seminars to consider human relations. The Conference sponsors the observance of Brotherhood Days on the Saturday and Sunday nearest to Washington's birthday, "to encourage the three major religious groups that constitute America to cooperate without any compromise of their distinctive principles in the tasks that belong to them as citizens of a common country." Typical contributions to Conference discussions concern "Disagreement without Bigotry," "Can We Learn to Be Brotherly?" and "Joint Endeavors and the Public Good." These are efforts in the direction of promoting harmony between groups, which have, in the past, spent much of their energies in devastating conflict. There is evidence of an increasing good will in action, notably in Christian aid to Jewish refugees, in the program of the Institute of Interdenominational Studies founded at the Jewish Theological Seminary of America, in interreligious cooperation on community projects, just to mention some examples which are not considered at all exceptional.

5. RACE

Some of our most violent prejudices appear in the field of race relations. We are trained to look with favor upon members of our own race, to view with suspicion and hostility members of other races. This is the general rule. There are, of course, exceptions. One exception is the bitter enmity sometimes existing between members of the same race: between the Northern Negro and the "black trash" of the South, between orthodox and unorthodox Jews, between German and Russian Jews. More extensive, however, are the prejudices between members of different races—the Irish and the English, the Japanese and the Chinese, the French and the Italian. The term "race" is used here in its popular connotation, as will be further elucidated shortly.

Studies made of regional variations in race prejudice show that they are not very clearly defined. It is true that G. B. Watson found laborers more prejudiced against the Chinese on the Pacific Coast than elsewhere in the United States, which fact he interpreted as signifying that racial prejudice is built chiefly on self-interest.[31] University of Washington students registered more prejudice against Orientals than did a comparable group of Eastern college students but Guilford reports that such regional differences in racial prejudice, on the whole, are slight.[32] This conclusion is confirmed by Bogardus. Despite the discovery of more prejudice against the Negroes in the South than in the West, more prejudice against the Mexicans in the Southwest than in the South, he concludes that "taken by and large, and considering regional reactions to peoples of forty different racial groups, similarity rather than difference in racial attitudes prevails."[33] Reinhardt's studies showed that the ethnic preferences of West Virginia students were highly similar to those of North Dakota students.[34] In an experiment conducted by Diggins, the ranking of ten races by Columbia University and Indiana University students proved to be almost identical.[35] Regional differences are not as important as social and economic differences in determining prejudice, according to Katz and Braly.[36] This observation may be accepted as a fair interpretation of the data gathered by a number of investigators who have studied the influence of the regional factor on racial antagonisms.

Race antipathy is manifested in name-calling. Favorite names include coon, nigger, dago, wop, yid, kike, sheenee, harp, chink, greaser, gringo. These terms are, to say the least, disparaging, provoking, degrading. Their use is prompted by a desire to impress upon the persons designated a full sense of their inferiority. Calling names is a convenient means of establishing relative social status.[37] Such names help to crystallize the racial stereotypes which represent for some people what they think these races are like. These fictions enable the name-callers to flatter themselves with a sense of their own inherent superiority. "Racial animosities supplement group symbols, or fictions, and make possible concerted group activities. Group prejudices are rationalizations by which the individual maintains his self-esteem and advances his economic and other interests."[38]

[31] G. B. Watson: *Orient and Occident.* 1927.
[32] See J. P. Guilford: "Racial Preferences of a Thousand American University Students." *Journal of Social Psychology,* 1931, 2, 179-204.
[33] Bogardus: *op. cit.,* p. 161.
[34] See J. M. Reinhardt: "Students and Race Feeling." *Survey,* 1928, 61, 239-240.
[35] See E. Diggins: *A Statistical Study of National Prejudices.* Master's Thesis at Columbia. 1927.
[36] See D. Katz and K. W. Braly: "Racial Prejudice and Racial Stereotypes." *Journal of Abnormal and Social Psychology,* 1935, 30, 175-193.
[37] See F. E. Lumley: *Means of Social Control,* Chapter 12, "Calling Names." 1925.
[38] Katz and Braly: *loc cit.*

Racial stereotypes are often based, in part, upon sensory impressions which are relied upon as evidences of racial inferiority. Italians are supposed to smell of garlic, Negroes are represented as having a peculiar body odor of an unpleasant nature. Negroes, in their turn, report that white women smell like cadavers. If any Negroes or foreigners smell, it is probably because of conditions which are apt to be found among the poorer classes, to which foreigners or racial minorities are likely to belong simply by virtue of the fact that they are denied various privileges conducive to refined habits of living.[39]   There are probably group differences in body odor. Indeed, every individual has his own unique body odor. It is not surprising, psychologically, that we find members of other groups having an unpleasant body odor. We get adapted to our own odor and to the odors of our friends, observes Klineberg. Why not, he says, extend the adaptation to include those persons whom we regard as aliens?[40]

We have noted the fact that stereotypes are apt to include a good deal of fiction. Let me illustrate this point by describing the stereotype of the Negro, which is so common in the United States. A youngster was asked to give his impressions of the Negro. He replied:

Neagro. I do not like the Neagro because he fits with rasers and are verry sly.[41]

This picture accords with the one obtained by the Chicago Commission on Race Relations:

The mind of the Negro is distinctly inferior to that of the white race.

When a Negro boy grows a mustache his brain stops working. . . . The great physical development of the colored person takes away from the mental, while with the whites the reverse is true. There is proof for this in the last chapter of Ecclesiastes. [*Statement made by a teacher. If you can find the Biblical citation, you'll do better than I.*]

Negroes have a musky odor.

Every colored cook has a lover who never works and she feeds him by stealing the best part of every dish she cooks.[42]

Whenever a Negro is educated he refuses to work and becomes a criminal.

All Negroes who show any intelligence are two-thirds white and the sons of U.S. Senators.

[39] See Bogardus: *op cit.,* Chapter 4, "Origins of Race Antipathy." 1928.
[40] See O. Klineberg: *The Psychology of Race Differences,* pp. 128-131. 1935.
[41] B. Lasker: *Race Attitudes in Children,* p. 140. 1929.
[42] When the present author read this statement in class, an aristocratic Southern lady (white) involuntarily gasped, "Why, that's absolutely true."

The minute a Negro gets $8 he goes to a dentist and has one of his front teeth filled with gold.

Negroes usually carry razors. Whenever a newspaper reporter is in doubt he gives a razor as the weapon used.

Negroes habitually shoot craps.

Negroes are flashy in dress. They love brilliant colors, especially vivid red.

Negroes are fond of gin.[43]

The picture of the Negro, in the minds of white people, serves as a sanction against the colored people. The subordinate position of the Negro, accordingly, is based upon the belief that a colored person is

a lower form of organism, biologically more primitive, mentally inferior, and emotionally undeveloped. He is insensitive to pain, incapable of learning, and animal-like in his behavior. . . . To the whites, the Negro appears as an "unsocialized being." . . . He is lazy and will not work except under the compulsion of force or immediate need; he is dependent upon the whites and prefers this dependence to the struggle of existing in the present society without their protection. . . . The Negro lacks respect for property and will steal with no feeling of guilt. . . . He lacks emotional stability, is quick to laugh or to cry . . . allows his passions free rein. . . . The Negro is "childlike" and will never grow up. . . . Owing to his inherent inferiority, he can never become a mature individual.

This body of beliefs constitutes an ideological system which is used to justify the social relationships between the superordinate whites and the subordinate Negroes.[44]

One method for measuring relative degrees of prejudice toward various races is the Social Distance Scale devised by Bogardus.[45] This Scale is based on the principle that there is likely to be a steady decrease in antipathy as we proceed from intimate personal relations to more distant relations. For example, a person might object strongly to having his daughter marry a Turk, might not protest so vigorously against a Turk moving into his neighborhood, might not care particularly one way or the other about a Turk's being admitted as an American citizen. The Bogardus Scale first appeared in this form:

[43] Digested from the report of the Chicago Commission on Race Relations: *The Negro in Chicago.* 1922.

[44] A. Davis, B. B. Gardner, and M. R. Gardner: *Deep South, A Social Anthropological Study of Caste and Class,* pp. 16-20. University of Chicago Press, 1941.

[45] From "Measuring Social Distance." *Journal of Applied Psychology,* 1925, 9, 299-308.

Directions: *According to my first feeling reactions I would willingly admit members of each race (as a class, and not the best I have known, nor the worst members) to one or more of the classifications which I have circled.*

	To close kinship by marriage	To my club as personal chums	To my street as neighbors	To employment in my occupation in my country	To citizenship in my country	As visitors in my country	Would exclude from my country
English	1	2	3	4	5	6	7
French	1	2	3	4	5	6	7
Hindus	1	2	3	4	5	6	7
Mulattoes	1	2	3	4	5	6	7
Negroes	1	2	3	4	5	6	7
Turks	1	2	3	4	5	6	7

The figures 1, 2, 3, 4, 5, 6, 7, represent hypothetical steps in increasing social distance. Findings of Bogardus, confirmed by Thurstone's studies employing the method of paired comparisons, show the greatest amount of antipathy is directed against Negroes, Turks, Mulattoes, Japanese, and Hindus. A certain amount of antipathy is revealed against out-groups in general. As evidence for the validity of the tests as measures of social distance, large samples show that a group which is not accepted in a given role, will be rejected in all "nearer roles."

Racial prejudice, like other forms of prejudice, is acquired through experience. Dislike of the unlike is not present in young children. White and Negro children will play together as naturally as two children of the same race until they are warned by their elders against such "undesirable" associates. This was found to be true even in the South, as Horowitz discovered in some experiments conducted in Tennessee.[46] Photographs of white boys and Negro boys, as individuals and as groups, were presented to white pupils from kindergarten through the 8B grade. Each subject took three tests: "ranks" test, in which he indicated his order of preference among a mixed assortment of white and colored faces; "show-me," in which he selected boys he would like to take home to lunch, etc.; "social situations," in which he chose play groups he would like to join. The results indicate that white and Negro children harbor very little if any prejudice against

[46] See E. L. Horowitz and R. E. Horowitz: "Development of Social Attitudes in Children." *Sociometry*, 1938, 1, 301-338.

ach other at the kindergarten level but as they grow older they learn to avoid each other. Sanctions are imposed on white children by their parents in order to instill race consciousness, such as the promise of a "whupping" if they get caught playing with Negroes. Friendships formed between whites and Negroes in early childhood, however, persist in spite of parental opposition. In some cases repeated punishment is required before the child can be "led" to accept the mores concerning the relations of the two races. Evidence that a "consciousness of kind" is sometimes nourished at the primary-school stage was brought to light by an experiment in which the white subjects were shown pictures of a library scene containing only white persons and later they were asked, "What was the colored man doing?" According to the children's reports, the colored man was invariably dusting the books or sweeping the floor; never was he seated, reading a book. The stereotype was beginning to exert its influence.

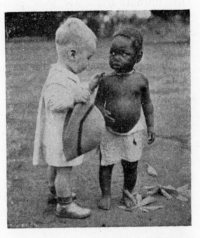

No Racial Hostility Here. (Courtesy, *Life* and Mrs. H. R. Brown.)

A study of prejudice against Italian-Americans in Boston, conducted by Kingsley and Carbone, showed a similar growth of racial antipathy through childhood and adolescence. The question was asked of Italian-Americans: "Have you ever felt that you were treated as an inferior or that you have been discriminated against by Americans because of your Italian nationality?"

The results for five age groups are shown in the following table with the percentages of males and females in each group answering this question affirmatively.

Groups	Age Range	Total Number M.	Total Number F.	Per Cent Answering "Yes" M.	Per Cent Answering "Yes" F.
I	6-10	7	8	42.8	50
II	11-19	21	26	43	50
III	20-29	17	25	71	68
IV	30-39	14	7	71	86
V	40-67	21	16	71	25

The figures indicate a tendency for the percentage who feel discrimination to increase with age. Furthermore, girls appear to feel it a little more than boys. The drop in the percentage of females in Group V is explained by the fact that these women, all foreign-born and most of them unable to understand English, had spent most of their lives in their homes, their associates for the most part having been other Italians.

By asking at what age this discrimination was first felt, it was ascertained that discrimination is practically always felt before the close of the period of adolescence.[47]

Discrimination mostly took petty forms: being called names, being snubbed after moving to a new neighborhood. Some slights amounted to insults, as in the case of the individual who reported, "Employer told me 'wops' should not use the same elevator as other employees." Reactions to the discriminatory treatment were usually anger, resentment, and hate.

Racial prejudice has varied in intensity during different periods of history. At present, racial antipathy seems to be on the increase. The Jews have been persecuted for centuries. In recent times they have served as scapegoats for the unemployment and starvation prevailing in Germany. After World War I their humiliation was engineered as a means of enabling the German citizen to take pride in the superior racial stock of the Teuton. Rauschning explained the Nazi policy frankly in his book *The Revolution of Nihilism* (1939):

> The doctrine of race, as yet developed only in regard to Jewry, offers inexhaustible opportunities of domination and of providing an ideological basis for a realist will to power. . . . The doctrine of the inequality of men and of races sweeps away all sentiment acquired during the centuries.

This arrogant assumption of racial superiority encouraged the Nazis to ignore the ethical scruples which underlie civilized man's respect for human values. The whole myth of the Aryan Teuton explodes when one is asked to visualize how a person would look "if he were as blond as Hitler, as slender as Goering, as tall as Goebbels, as long-headed as Rosenberg." [48]

It is easy for Americans to condemn the wholesale persecution which the Nazis carried on against the Jews; it is not so easy to recognize how extensively we discriminate against the Jews in our own

[47] H. L. Kingsley and M. Carbone: "Attitudes of Italian-Americans toward Race Prejudice." *Journal of Abnormal and Social Psychology*, 1938, 33, 532-537.
[48] J. S. Huxley and A. C. Haddon: *We Europeans*, p. 13. 1936.

nidst. Take the matter of employment, as a convenient example. Many employers will not hire Jews because they say Jews are character-zed by "such objectional traits as oudness, lack of good breeding, a endency toward insubordination, aggressiveness, overweening ambi-ion, clannishness, and unscrupu-ousness." [49] A study of the job ituation prompts the following omment:

Glib, sweeping criticism of all Jews s employees is generally traceable to unfortunate experiences with a single or sharply limited number of individuals. After such personal unpleasant-ness the employer tends to attribute these personality defects to the em-ployee's Jewishness and to transfer this antipathy to other and often to all Jews. Thus a superficial diagnosis becomes a ruling shibboleth.[50]

Hitler, Goering, and Goebbels.
(Courtesy, *Life* and the British Ministry of Information.)

Evidence is at hand that some employment agencies which handle Jew-sh applicants proceed on the assumption that Jews will not be accept-ible to prospective employers.

The vice-president of a great national tobacco company reported to us that the agencies with which he deals always ask his religious preference. This may be nothing more than a bit of "routine" procedure, but rarely will it fail to bring out to the fullest degree latent possibilities for discrimination. Worst of all, however, is the insidious agency manager who attempts to "flatter" his client by insinuating, "Of course, you don't want a *Jewish* stenographer." Rarely will he get the only decent response to that kind of subtle insult, such as came from a packing house superintendent who fired back: "What the hell do I care about her religion! Send me a *good* stenographer." [51]

It is difficult, in many places, for Jews to get teaching positions, or to advance in the profession.

Most racial persecution, in our country or elsewhere, is predicated on

---

[49] J. X. Cohen: "Jews, Jobs, and Discrimination; a Report on Jewish Non-Employment." This document is published by the American Jewish Congress, 1834 Broadway, New York City. 1937, reprinted 1945.
[50] *Ibid.*   [51] *Ibid.*

false assumptions: first, that clear-cut pure races exist, and second, that certain races are inherently superior to other races. The unscientifi concept of race may be contrasted with the scientific concept if the reader will take the time to compare the ideas that were held by Hitler on the subject, as expressed in *Mein Kampf,* with the treatment of the same topic by Boas, as expressed in *The Mind of Primitive Man.*[52]

Klineberg defines a *race* as a "group of human beings distinguished by unique hereditary physical characteristics which they have in com mon."[53] There is no homogeneity within a race, he says, no sharp line between one race and another. Race divisions are arbitrary classi fications. Consequently, general statements about a race will not be applicable to every member of that race; group differences do not de fine the characteristics of specific individuals. Indeed, there is a wide variability within any so-called race. Jews, for example, differ widely physically and mentally; that is, there are many kinds of Jews. There is an extensive overlapping between different groups with respect to any criteria, whether we consider the shape of the nose, skin color, eye pigmentation, hair color and texture, gross bodily dimensions, crania indices, or blood grouping. Any particular individual may have the coloring of one racial group and the cephalic index of another.

There is no racial hierarchy. The idea that one race is inherently superior to another is fallacious, and dangerous. There is no evidence to substantiate the doctrine that there are innate differences in the mental abilities of different races. Many whites believe that Negroes are just naturally endowed with inferior intelligence. The available evidence does not support such a judgment. Yerkes found by testing recruits for the U.S. Army during World War I that Northern Negroes were superior to Southern Negroes; in some Northern states, that Ne groes were superior to Southern whites.[54] Northern Negroes, it has been determined, test superior to Southern Negroes because of the better environment in the North in which to develop. Improvement is proportional to the length of time in the better environment. As the environment of the Negro approximates that of the whites, the in feriority of the colored person tends to disappear.[55] Witty and Jen-

---

[52] See A. Hitler: *Mein Kampf,* Chapter 11, "Nation and Race." 1933. F. Boas: *The Mind of Primitive Man,* Chapter 13, "The Race Problem in Modern Society." Revised edition, 1938.
[53] See Klineberg: *The Psychology of Race Differences,* p. 18. 1935.
[54] See R. M. Yerkes (Editor): "Psychological Examining in the U.S. Army." *Memoirs of the National Academy of Science,* 1921, Volume 15.
[55] See Klineberg: *op. cit.,* Chapter 8, "Intelligence Testing—the Factors Involved," and Chapter 9, "Intelligence Testing—the Problem of Selection."

ins' studies of Negro pupils, reported in 1940, reveal a level of intelligence that must astonish whites who like to believe complacently in their own native superiority. Witty and Jenkins selected the brighter children among 8,400 Negroes in the third to eighth grades of seven Chicago public schools and gave them intelligence tests. Twenty-nine proved to be "gifted" (I.Q. of 140 or above), as many as would be found in a similar group of white children; 103 were "bright" (I.Q. 120 or above), again a par score if we take whites as the standard.[56] Certainly what evidence we have does not qualify any race to gloat over its superior endowments. Without any hesitation we may agree with Klineberg that "there is nothing in the brain or blood of other races which justifies our ill-treatment of them." [57]

As a summary of this discussion no better statement could be made than the one issued in 1939 by the Executive Council of the Society for the Psychological Study of Social Issues, concerning the existence of alleged psychological differences among racial and national groups:

The [then] current emphasis upon "racial differences" in Germany and Italy, and the indications that such an emphasis may be on the increase in the United States and elsewhere, make it important to know what psychologists and other social scientists have to say in this connection.

The fascists and many others have grossly misused the term "race." According to anthropologists, the term "race" may legitimately be used only for such groups as possess in common certain physical or bodily characteristics which distinguish them from other groups. It is impossible to speak correctly of a "German race" or of an "Italian race," since both of these groups have highly diversified physical characteristics. A South German may resemble a Frenchman from Auvergne or an Italian from Piedmont more closely than he does a German from Hanover. North Italians are markedly dissimilar from those living in Sicily or Naples. More important still, the emphasis on the existence of an "Aryan race" has no scientific basis, since the word "Aryan" refers to a family of languages and not at all to race or to physical appearance. As far as the Jews are concerned, scientific investigations have shown them to be tall or short, blond or dark, round-headed or long-headed, according to the particular community studied. In the light of this wide variation in physical characteristics, almost all anthropologists outside of Germany and Italy would agree that it is scientifically impossible to speak of a "Jewish race," much less of an "Aryan race."

In the experiments which psychologists have made upon different peoples, no characteristic, inherent psychological differences which fundamentally dis-

---

[56] L. S. Hollingworth and P. Witty: "Intelligence as Related to Race." *Yearbook of the National Society for the Study of Education*, 1940, 39, 257-269.

[57] Klineberg: *op. cit.*, p. 348.

tinguish so-called "races" have been disclosed. This statement is supported by the careful surveys of these experiments in such books as *Race Psychology* by Garth, *Individual Differences* by Freeman, *Race Differences* by Klineberg and *Differential Psychology* by Anastasi. There is no evidence for the existence of an inborn Jewish or German or Italian mentality. Furthermore there is no indication that the members of any group are rendered incapable by their biological heredity of completely acquiring the culture of the community in which they live. This is true not only of the Jews in Germany but also of groups that actually are physically different from one another The Nazi theory that people must be related by blood in order to participate in the same cultural or intellectual heritage has absolutely no support from scientific findings.

Psychologists look elsewhere for the explanation of current racial hatred and persecution. It is certain that the Nazi race theories have been developed not on the basis of objective fact, but under the domination of powerful emotional attitudes. A well-known psychological tendency leads people to blame others for their own misfortunes, and the Nazis have found in the Jew a convenient psychological scapegoat for their own economic and political disabilities. In certain Czechoslovakian localities as well, Jews are now being blamed for the dismemberment of the country. There can be no doubt that economic factors are also directly involved, as the recent enormous levy on Jewish capital in Germany has amply demonstrated. Theories of Jewish plots and machinations are an excuse, a rationalization for the expropriation of badly needed property. . . .

Racial and national attitudes are psychologically complex, and cannot be understood except in terms of their economic, political, and historical backgrounds. Psychologists find no basis for the explanation of such attitudes in terms of innate mental differences between racial and national groups. The many attempts to establish such differences have so far met failure. Even if successful they would offer no justification for repressive treatment of the type now current in Germany. In the scientific investigations of human groups by psychologists, no conclusive evidence has been found for racial or national differences in native intelligence and inherited personality characteristics. Certainly no individual should be treated as an inferior merely because of his membership in one human group rather than another. Here in America, we have clear indications of the manner in which members of different racial and national groups have combined to create a common culture.[58]

Race and nationality are frequently confused in popular thought. People who speak of the German "race" are really thinking of the German nation, a state composed actually of individual citizens belonging to several races. Nationalism, indeed, is responsible for some of our racial prejudices, as we observe in the sort of person who expresses his love of country in the style of the American who put up a sign in front of his store back in 1917, which read: "One hundred per cent American—I hate Germany." The next day the proprietor of the store across the street tacked up a sign: "Two hundred per cent American—I hate everybody."

6. SEX

One of the chief problems of social adjustment in the life of a human being is getting along happily with the opposite sex. The difficulty of the problem is aggravated by the queer ideas each sex entertains about the other. These notions are largely based upon prejudice. Various groups of men and women students were asked by William Marston to list what they considered typical male and female traits. The results may be summarized as follows:

Men think women are more charming, sweeter, tender toward men and children, warm-hearted, more altruistic and "mysterious." Men also think women are less intellectual, less intelligent, "gold-diggers," morally weak and emotionally unstable, liars, treacherous, childish and petty.

Women think men are venturesome, good workers, less upset by little things, more courageous physically, steady, democratic, purposeful, loyal and persistent, but also egotistical, domineering, changeable, selfish, patronizing, ruthless, inconsiderate, less loving, arrogant, nagging, simple and easy to fool.[59]

Despite the grain of truth in some of these alleged traits, it is obvious that no satisfying social relationships can be established on such whimsical foundations. One of the important reasons men and women do not understand each other better is the fact that they allow their prejudices to distort their impressions of one another. It is easy to start on the wrong foot by assuming that it is no use trying to understand a person of the opposite sex.

The history of women, as Davies has pointed out, has been built on a series of fictions invented by men to keep women in subjection. These fictions concern the supposed differences between men and women, differences that are predicated largely on prejudice. Women are supposed to be physically weaker, mentally less active than men, more changeable in temperament. Men agree that no one can hope to understand women or please them for long. Made for maternity, women are supposedly unsuited to work save in the home and the

[59] Summarized by the *Woman's Home Companion*.

nursery. According to the male version, women have different mental processes: incapable of reasoning, they make up for this deficiency by superior intuitiveness.[60]

Man's ideas about the basic nature of woman have been evolved to serve man's purposes, though the male may not be aware that this is so. Men make sweeping claims that women are unfit for industrial work. Such claims on the part of the male "are probably based in part upon our habits of chivalry, and in part upon a rationalization of masculine economic motives. They reflect the manner in which men have wished to see women rather than the proven nature of woman herself." [61] In a similar manner man has fostered the belief that woman is a sweet creature who must be protected from evil. The motive, in this case, is primarily the jealous proprietary sex interest which the male invests in the female.

This picture of women not only gives the aggressive male the fullest opportunity for his own drives, but relieves his feeling of inferiority, palliates his moral failures, and enrolls him as the protector of home and civilization. . . . The stereotypes of sex difference are no mere idle fantasies of male thinking: they are working habits, attitudes which have become organized as an integral part of our political, economic, and social system.[62]

Despite male resistance, women have been flocking into business. Alert women are fully aware of the prejudices that belong with man's traditional prerogatives in this sphere. A woman with some experience in business offices gives a warning tip to her sex:

We women have gone into nearly every business and profession and wherever we go we are received with a surface courtesy that gives rise to the notion that sex antagonism has vanished from business. But it hasn't.

Being pent up and unexpressed vocally, the antagonism is probably bitterer now than it ever was. Nor is there any reason why it should not be worse than previously. By following the man from the schoolroom and the home into his working fields, his clubs, his bars, his barber shops, we have stolen from him his last retreats. Now he never gets away from our sex. He is surrounded by women all day in his business life just as he has always been in his domestic and his social life. Our presence may have improved his

[60] See J. L. Davies: *A Short History of Women.* 1927.

[61] Reprinted from *Institutional Behavior,* by Floyd H. Allport, by permission of The University of North Carolina Press. Copyright, 1933, by The University of North Carolina Press. P. 365.

[62] *Ibid.,* p. 370.

manners slightly, though not in all cases.   But it is questionable whether it has improved his morale.

The men have become either ashamed or afraid to say openly that they harbor resentment against women in their working life.   Some of them probably don't resent it, for in the offices especially we women have carried on the agelong custom of making our men's lives easier and smoother.   The man who says, "Wait till I ask my secretary about that," adding with a laugh, "she knows more about my business than I do," is speaking a truth wild horses couldn't drag from him unless he thought his remark were to be taken facetiously.   Men don't resent women as long as we remain underlings, but I have yet to see a man who could take orders from a woman and like it.[63]

If a suggestion for improving the business is made by a woman, a man will be inclined to reject it without realizing the motive for his opposition.   In all fairness to the idea proposed, the man should stop and ask himself, "What would I think of this idea if it were being proposed by a man?" [64]   It sometimes happens that the woman's idea is summarily rejected and then later adopted as the man's own bright idea, the source having been conveniently forgotten.

Feminists have been ardent in their insistence upon the right of women to earn their own livelihood.   Psychologists affirm that women want to find outlets for their talents, that they desire to win recognition for themselves as individuals, that they are not completely satisfied just to be glorified for "beautiful motherhood," that they crave the self-assurance resulting from economic independence.   Women also want male approval, for they are still emotionally dependent upon men.   Woman's problem is to combine the work and love interests so as to derive the most satisfaction from both.   This is difficult, according to Paul Popenoe, Director of the Institute of Family Relations in Los Angeles, who says: "Big business spoils a woman for love and marriage. The more dominant she becomes, the more she repels men.   If financially possible, a woman should never take a job, but should spend her spare time cultivating her talents. . . .   Homemaking and marriage should be her first goal." [65]   Popenoe probably arrives at this conclusion by taking into account the male prejudice that "woman's place is in the home."   Woman's problem of appeasing her man is particularly complicated for the married woman who is successful in business, since

[63] E. Cushman: "Office Women and Sex Antagonism."   *Harper's Magazine*, March, 1940.

[64] S. E. Jelliffe: "Sex Has Thrown a Bomb into Business," Chapter 3, in *Why Men Fail*, M. Fishbein and W. A. White (Editors).   1928.

[65] Quoted in the *Literary Digest*, May 15, 1937.

she must be very tactful in handling a husband who will probably resent her success, especially if she makes more money than he does.

There is not so much male prejudice against women's working as there used to be, except for the fact that it aggravates male unemployment; but there is still widespread prejudice against allowing married women to work. This feeling is accentuated if the husband is already earning enough to support the family. In November, 1937, Gallup conducted a national poll on the question: "Do you approve of a married woman earning money in industry or business if she has a husband capable of supporting her?" Eighty-two per cent of the 100,000 persons questioned answered "No." Women themselves were opposed, by seventy-nine per cent. The reason given by the majority of "no" voters was: "Why should a married woman with plenty of money take bread out of the mouths of women who need work?" Young people were twenty per cent for women working as compared with ten per cent for the nation as a whole. Some of the minority opinions were stated as follows:

> Some women have no family to raise; they might as well work as sit around the house.
> Women should have equality with men, since they are taxed as well as men.
> Many a woman earns more than her husband; let him keep house.

This issue comes to a head periodically when drives are organized to eject married women teachers from the public schools.

Women have had to fight to win the right to work. They have had to fight for the right to vote. They have had to fight for the right to get a higher education. They are fighting for emancipation from the burdens of unwanted motherhood. All along the way men have fought to keep women in subjection. Nevertheless, women are winning the battle for emancipation from the ancient taboos restricting their activities, taboos developed and enforced by the male in his effort to maintain his dominance. Prejudice plays an important role in this controversy between the two sexes. Women are determined that they are going to achieve equality; men are determined that they are not going to do so. World War I gave women an opportunity to prove their worth outside the home, in war plants and in business where they filled in capable fashion the jobs of the men called to the service. World War II provided women with another golden opportunity to show what they could accomplish in the work of production ordinarily delegated to men, with another even more significant opening to participate in the waging of war, a prerogative long monopolized by men. The Wacs, Waves, Spars, Waafs, and others succeeded, against considerable male prejudice, in demonstrating their value as an integral part of the war machine, undergoing hardships and rendering service which played an important role in achieving military victory.   Certainly the contribution of women to the war effort, both at home and abroad, will affect her socio-economic status as reflected in man's attitude toward her place in society.   Women have progressed a long way since the days of Queen Victoria.   In fact, the time may be approaching when men will have to struggle for their own emancipation.   Count Keyserling, the German philosopher, believes that moment has already arrived in America.   After a visit to the United States, he concluded that "America is governed by women. . . .   The great need of America is the emancipation of men, rather than the emancipation of women."

Our study of individual differences—personal, cultural, religious, racial, and sexual—reveals the vital relationship between these differences and the generation of prejudice.   A more extensive survey of differential psychology is recommended as a valuable means for the cultivation of tolerance and a correlative diminution of prejudice.

III. CONTROL: THE IDEAL OF OBJECTIVITY

The person who endeavors to be objective is the antithesis of the individual who resigns himself to his prejudices.   Being objective means being impartial.   It is an ideal we cannot achieve without real effort because we are so inclined to be partisans.   This fact is illustrated in an incident that occurred during World War II.   A U-boat wrecked a ship and the survivors landed in South Ireland.   Two civic guards debated as to whether they should intern the strangers.

"We ought to intern them."
"And why, I'm asking?"
"Why? Because we're neutral."
"Sure, we are. But who are we neutral against?"

It is easy for us to take sides; difficult, to suspend judgment.

A. THE DESIRE FOR ENLIGHTENMENT

Disinterestedness is essential if we want to discover the truth.   Lippmann points to this ideal as the supreme necessity for the philosopher, who, by definition, is a lover of wisdom.[66]   If we desire to see the world

[66] See W. Lippmann: *A Preface to Morals.* 1929.

in a mature fashion we must set aside our wishes; we must be willing to accept the facts whether they are pleasant or unpleasant. The truth will elude us if we are primarily interested in finding results that will confirm our prejudices. Sometimes, it is true, prejudice in favor of a certain truth facilitates its discovery, for in some cases investigation is prompted by the passionate longing of the individual to get his own faith substantiated, and, in spite of his emotional predisposition, he may arrive at the correct result. More often, however, passion will prove a hindrance rather than a help in the pursuit of knowledge, as Renan pointed out when he introduced Pasteur to the French Academy:

Truth is a great coquette; she will not be sought with too much passion, but often is amenable to indifference. She escapes when apparently caught, but gives herself up if patiently waited for; revealing herself after farewells have been said, but inexorable when loved with too much fervor.[67]

The individual with a sincere desire for enlightenment will train himself to distinguish between statements of fact and statements of opinion, even when he makes the statements himself. Most of us are not wary enough of unverifiable opinions. "If we feared the entertaining of an unverifiable opinion with the warmth with which we now fear using the wrong implement at the dinner table; if the thought of holding a prejudice disgusted us as does a foul disease, then the dangers of man's suggestibility would be turned into an advantage." [68] We like our opinions and the opinions of others who agree with us. This very human preference for believing what we want to believe must be held in check if we are to succeed in escaping our prejudices.

Acceptance of authoritarian dogma is detrimental to the search for enlightenment. A prominent religious leader was not displaying enthusiasm for open-minded inquiry when he gave the following advice to college students: "Test all things but hold fast to your faith which is the truth of God forever." There is little point in testing all things unless the premises of faith are also subjected to trial. The guarantee behind the creed should not be regarded as unconditional. It is not conducive to the spirit of research for those in authority to use their prestige for discouraging inquiry. Prejudice in favor of a religious premise is just as inimical to the pursuit of truth as any other kind of

[67] Quoted by W. D. Wallis: "Some Phases of the Psychology of Prejudice." *Journal of Abnormal and Social Psychology*, 1929-1930, 24, 418-429.

[68] W. Trotter: *Instincts of the Herd in Peace and War*, p. 45. Ernest Benn, Limited (London), 1919.

bias. The desire for enlightenment cannot operate where strong emotional sets function to inhibit cerebral activity. If thinking is to produce results, it must be unimpeded except for the restrictions imposed by the laws of logic.

Moral condemnation is often applied as a weapon against persons who dare to tell the unpleasant truth as they see it. In 1917, Charles A. Beard, the eminent historian, resigned from Columbia University because he believed a small group of the trustees were taking advantage of the War situation "to drive out or to humiliate or to terrorize every man who held progressive, liberal, or unconventional views on political matters in no way connected with the War." The New York *Times* commented on the resignation by congratulating Columbia for getting rid of Beard, a man who wrote "bad . . . books . . . grossly unscientific . . . unrelated to fact and quite unconvincing in their nature. . . . These trustees know, as every man of sound sense and unclouded vision knows, that Columbia University is better for Professor Beard's resignation." [69] Why these cheers for his exit from Columbia? Beard had enjoyed high respect as an historian, until he published his *Economic Interpretation of the Constitution* in 1913. In this book he alleged that the Founding Fathers, in drawing up the charter of our liberties, were guided less by the Holy Spirit than by the commitments they and their relatives had made in purchasing depreciated securities of the new nation. Some critics pointed out to Beard at the time that his book was one no professor should have written since it was so obviously unscientific, not based at all on a candid and competent examination of facts. "It was a book," said the *Times,* "which did Columbia much harm." Albert Bushnell Hart pronounced the book "little short of indecent." When President Taft, retired to a seat at Yale, was asked for a comment, he replied, "The facts seem right enough, but why did the damn fool print it?" [70] He did print it, nevertheless, and he took the consequences. In spite of the calumny to which he was subjected, Charles Beard—and his wife, Mary Beard—are regarded today as authorities on American history. Their book, *The Rise of American Civilization* (1927), has been a best seller. In the perspective of the years even the New York *Times* must feel that it was unfair to persecute Beard for telling the unpopular truth. Critics might have weighed the *Economic Interpretation of the Constitution* and its author more justly if they had not been blinded by a

[69] Editorial in the New York *Times,* October 10, 1917.
[70] See H. Herring: "Charles A. Beard: Free Lance among the Historians." *Harper's Magazine,* May, 1939.

naïve patriotism. The people who damned Beard were more interested in keeping their heroes untarnished than they were in learning the facts.

The desire for enlightenment is easily discouraged when the morals of youth are threatened with corruption. In 1936 the General Assembly of Virginia passed a resolution:

WHEREAS, the effects of alcohol upon the human system are required by law to be taught in the public schools of Virginia; and

WHEREAS, due to the apparent differences of opinion existing among medical authorities upon this subject, the State Board of Education does not have the necessary material for the purpose; and

WHEREAS, the General Assembly believes that the faculties of the medical school of the University of Virginia and the Medical College of Virginia are qualified and equipped to furnish accurate information upon this important subject,

Now, therefore, *Be It Resolved* . . . that they . . . make . . . the necessary investigation and study therefor, and . . . furnish within a reasonable time to the State Board of Education for use by it as a basis for material to be taught in the public schools, accurate information as to the effect of the use of alcohol upon the human system, in respect to both moderate and excessive use thereof.

The study was made, and the findings embodied in the Haag-Waddell report which was submitted to the 1938 session of the General Assembly. Despite the fact that the State Board of Education had pronounced the report "scientifically sound and very scholarly," the Assembly voted to have the report destroyed, because the investigators had come to the conclusion that the use of alcohol in moderation is not harmful. Senator Muse of Roanoke said that he accepted the authors' statements as scientific truths but he expressed the fear that the facts would be misleading if presented to minds too immature to understand them. Said he: "It might be scientifically true that the moderate use of alcohol is not harmful, but I do not want my ten-year-old son taught that." So the report was destroyed, much to the relief of one minister who wrote: "To be sure, we are grateful for any help science can give. But our supreme hope for deliverance from the corrupting influence of the liquor traffic lies in a high moral idealism and the dynamics of religion." [71] We favor scientific inquiry *but.* Enthusi-

[71] J. M. Trimmer: "Science and the Liquor Question." *Christian Century*, January 4, 1939.

asm for fact-finding is only half-hearted when it is qualified, as in the case just cited, by the reservation that the results will be accepted only if they are agreeable. It is so hard for us to deal honestly with the truth when our personal values seem to be at stake. For some people there are values superior to truth. It requires insight to appreciate how essential to our welfare is the hunger for reality, to realize that intelligent adjustment to the world in which we live is predicated on accurate knowledge of that world.

B. EDUCATION FOR TOLERANCE*

In a democracy it is especially important that the individual citizen learn to be tolerant. The democratic way of life imposes upon each person the responsibility for living peaceably with his fellows. There are all kinds of people with whom we must effect workable mutual adjustments. One way to prepare for these social adaptations is to study the nature and the extent of individual differences. When we come to realize how fundamental is the fact of individuality and when we come to accept the right of the individual to be himself, within certain bounds defined with reference to our social well-being, then we are ready to live and let live. Understanding the personality of the other fellow is a long step toward tolerating his idiosyncrasies and even forgiving his "sins." Education may promote a more charitable and humane attitude toward people who may seem strange to us because they are different in temperament, background, race.

Educating for tolerance may prove effective if it is carefully planned for that purpose and if the program is started while the individual is still young enough to learn. Youngsters should be trained from their earliest years to adapt themselves to the differences they run up against in other children. Through group activities the individual child learns that he cannot always have his own way without getting embroiled in conflict with others who have ideas and wills of their own. Gradually it dawns on the combatants that each must give in and limit his self-assertion if there is going to be any game or any other sort of cooperative activity. The leader who may succeed in imposing his will on a particular group will sooner or later find himself in situations where other dominant personalities will challenge

---

* The term *tolerance* is employed because it is popularly used in connection with programs for promoting harmony among conflicting groups. The term has the unfortunate connotation of "enduring" or "putting up with" persons who differ from us. Ideally, we seek *friendly* relations rather than mere *toleration*.

his right to dictate. Guidance by older persons wise in the ways of the world may hasten the process of socialization and carry it further along the path to completion.

There are a few suggestions for promoting tolerance that merit special mention here.

1. READING

A subscription to the *National Geographic Magazine* can be recommended, if my own personal experience is at all typical. The beautiful photographs of people in other lands and the stories of travel and adventure appeal to children and to adults as well. The colored pictures are particularly interesting to younger children who may not be mature enough to read or to listen to the descriptive articles. Looking at the strange faces, the quaint modes of dress, the "funny" houses, the odd religious ceremonies, the queer market-places, and the beautiful landscapes, the child is sure to be fascinated. In the process he is learning how differently people live in various parts of the world. Such experiences, being primarily vicarious, extend a person's mental horizon, and provide valuable training in identification. It is through this psychological process of identification that sympathy is fostered.

Madeline Brandeis has written a series of books about children of other lands, designed for young readers.[72] They include:

> *The Wee Scotch Piper.* 1929.
> *Little Philippe of Belgium.* 1930.
> *Little Anne of Canada.* 1931
> *Mitz and Fritz of Germany.* 1933.
> *Little Tony of Italy.* 1934.
> *The Little Spanish Dancer.* 1936.
> *Little Erik of Sweden.* 1938.

Older children will enjoy the *Travel and Adventure Library for Young Folks,* a series written by several authors.[73] Reading of this sort may exert a broadening influence.

Travel, of course, is the ideal way to learn about people of other lands. Reading is a fair substitute for those who cannot afford to visit foreign countries.

Biographies and autobiographies depicting the lives of foreigners may be useful in stimulating interest in folks from other lands and

---

[72] Published by Grosset and Dunlap.
See also the "Little People Everywhere" Series, published by Little, Brown and Company.

[73] Published by Doubleday, Doran and Company. 1907-1933.

thus increasing the bonds of understanding. Biography provides the "human-interest story" in its most attractive form. *Up From Slavery* (1901), the autobiography of Booker T. Washington, appealed to me when I read it as a youngster and no doubt it contributed much to my appreciation of the Negro in America. Jacob Riis' *The Making of an American* (1902), Mary Antin's *The Promised Land* (1912), Ludwig Lewisohn's *Up Stream* (1922), Michael Pupin's *From Immigrant to Inventor* (1923), and Edward Bok's *The Americanization of Edward Bok* (1923) were all helpful in expanding my racial sympathies. These are listed merely to suggest to the reader the type of book that may be valuable in encouraging the feeling that "we are all brothers under the skin." It is, of course, education on the verbal level and, as such, its effectiveness will depend upon how successfully it stimulates the reader to use his imagination in living through the experiences of the characters in the books. Biography is an excellent medium for reducing narrow-mindedness. In so far as it encourages introjection, it may foster tolerance.

2. CLASSROOM INSTRUCTION

Reports of experiments on the college level to determine the influence of a course in social science upon the prejudices of the students have not been too encouraging. Droba measured attitudes toward the Negro before and after a course on race relations. There was no reliable change as a result of the course.[74] Young found that his course on American Race Problems at the University of Pennsylvania had little effect on the students' prejudices. The course was successful from the informational standpoint but it failed to change racial prejudices. Students who passed the course made such statements as:

The Jews do all the cheating.
The Negro did well, considering.
The Italian is not a bad sort even if he did come from Italy.

In analyzing the reasons why the course failed to produce the desired changes, Young states that the time, a few hours a week, was too short for accomplishing much; the teaching method, presenting facts and theories in a logical sequence, was superficial. Factors making for race prejudices were psychologically stronger than the corrective measures. Especially significant among those factors conducive to preju-

---

[74] See D. D. Droba: "Education and Negro Attitudes." *Sociology and Social Research,* 1932, 17, 136-141.

dice was the experience of meeting someone of another race for the first time. In such fashion students had been conditioned to associate Negro with gardener or washwoman, Greek with bootblack or fruit store, Italian with laborer. Young suggests that a problem or case method might prove more effective than the pedagogical technique he employed.[75]

Schlorff tested some high-school pupils to see whether tolerance toward the Negro could be increased by a curriculum dealing with the Negro's origin, his history, his contributions, and with prejudices against the colored race. Before the course was undertaken the pupils in the control group and in the experimental group rated Negroes lowest on a social-distance scale; at the end, the control group rated them above Portuguese, Greeks, Russians, and Hungarians, from a total list of twenty nationalities. The experiment was quite successful in improving tolerance toward the Negro.[76] It is likely that the modification of racial prejudices would be easier at the high-school level than at the college level; that it would be still easier in the elementary grades. In commenting on Schlorff's investigation Murphy suggests the hypothesis that "instruction regarding a single race does not significantly change attitudes as measured on a scale involving that race only, nor does instruction regarding several races produce changes in the rank positions assigned to those races; but instruction concerning one race may significantly change the rank position of that race among others." [77]

Efforts to promote interracial good will in the schools would be more effective if more time were devoted to this important program and if the material were more intelligently organized. One organization which is doing a particularly good piece of work in this field is the Southern Regional Council, located in Atlanta, Georgia. Under the Council's auspices, curricular material has been prepared to guide the study of the race problem as it exists in the South. Among their publications is a brochure entitled "Understanding Our Neighbors: an Educational Approach to America's Major Race Problem." [78] The

[75] See D. Young: "Some Effects of a Course in American Race Problems on the Race Prejudice of 450 Undergraduates at the University of Pennsylvania." *Journal of Abnormal and Social Psychology,* 1927-1928, 22, 235-242.

[76] See P. W. Schlorff: *An Experiment in the Measurement and Modification of Racial Attitudes in School Children.* Ph.D. dissertation, New York University. 1930.

[77] G. Murphy, L. B. Murphy, and T. M. Newcomb: *Experimental Social Psychology,* p. 952. Harper & Brothers, 1937.

[78] By R. B. Eleazer. Copies of the brochure may be obtained at 10 cents per copy from the Southern Regional Council, 63 Auburn Ave., N.E., Atlanta, Ga.

pamphlet contains some valuable suggestions for public-school teachers who wish to devote time in the classroom to exploring the causes and the consequences of discrimination against the colored race.[79] Pupils begin with a study of the historical background of the Negro to discover why he has a dark skin, why he has been retarded in his cultural development, why it is silly to regard his color as a badge of inferiority, why it is a mistake to believe that the black race is by nature inferior. This survey is called "The Dark Continent." Next comes a section, "The Negro in America." The institution of slavery is considered and questions are raised as to its good effects and its bad effects:

Its best aspects: Paternal personal interest on the part of the owners, loyalty and faithful service in response. Its worst: Absentee ownership and overseer control.

The problems introduced by the Emancipation Proclamation are called to the attention of the student:

A dangerous situation: More than four million slaves suddenly set free without resources, experience, or training in self-direction; suddenly deprived of the economic security of slavery and thrust out on their own responsibility.

Then there is a review of the events of the Reconstruction period following the Civil War, during which each state established a genuine school system "providing for 'separate but equal'" opportunities for the children of the two races. Progress in reducing illiteracy since that time is traced, from 90 per cent in 1860 to 16.3 per cent in 1930. Military service rendered to the United States is recounted to show how loyal the colored race has been to the country of its adoption. Section III is on "Civic Problems." Population trends are described briefly. Related to these trends is the matter of medical care. The suggestion is made that the pupils discuss the consequences of the inadequate medical attention given to Negroes, so that they will appreciate the fact that germs do not respect the color line.

Every day more than a million Negro cooks, laundresses, and maids go into the homes of white people to prepare their food, wash their clothes, and care for their children. If these domestic helpers live in unsanitary, disease-breeding slums, what will be the inevitable effect upon the people for whom they work? What does all this suggest to the white community (1) from the stand-

[79] Similar projects have been promoted in the colleges and high schools of the South by the Southern Regional Council.

point of justice to the Negro, (2) from the standpoint of the welfare of all? What steps might be taken to improve these conditions [public health services, clinics, hospitalization, slum clearance, decent homes, sewerage, water, sanitary surroundings, etc.]?

SUGGESTIONS FOR INVESTIGATION

What are the health conditions of Negroes in this state, this county, this community? What public health facilities are available to them—medical and nursing service, clinics, hospitals, etc.? What services are available in the Negro schools? How do all these compare with those provided for white people?

Sources of information: Reports of state, county, and community departments of health. . . . Personal observation of Negro housing and community conditions, the worst and the best.

Poverty, recreation, schools, justice in the courts, and suffrage occupy the remainder of this section. Section IV lists the contributions of the Negro to "Literature and Music." At the end typical units of work in various high schools are outlined, and supplementary materials are cited.

This study has been thoroughly prepared. It is stimulating throughout, as it raises so many interesting problems, each described with an exemplary spirit of impartiality. The chief value in this project, as I see it, lies in the fact that it reveals the ramifying effects of our racial prejudices and shows how the harm done by discrimination often "comes home to roost." It may seem a long way from prejudice to illness but when you stop to trace the relation it becomes clear: because of prejudice affecting the allocation of public funds the sewer may stop where the Negro section begins, unsanitary conditions cause sickness in the cook's family, the cook passes the infection along to the point where "we-all got started," to the white man who couldn't see spending that money on a "bunch of damn ——." Students are thus impressed with the fact that their prejudices against others may ultimately affect themselves.

Another source of material for high-school courses designed to promote interracial good will may be found in a program planned under the auspices of the Council against Intolerance in America.[80] Teacher's Manual No. 1, entitled *An American Answer to Intolerance,* was published in an "Experimental Form" in 1939. The general plan of study includes a section on "Minority Groups" which embodies some suggestions prepared by the Service Bureau of Intercultural Relations.

[80] Address: Lincoln Building, 17 East 42nd Street, New York City.

For each minority group, statistics are furnished regarding the number now resident in the United States, their occupations, and the states in which they dwell. A list of leaders is provided, with a summary of their principal achievements. These names are taken largely from *Our Racial and National Minorities* (1937) by F. J. Brown and J. S. Roucek and from *We Who Build America* (1939) by C. F. Wittke. These suggestions are designed to encourage the students to gather more data on the subject as bases for class discussion. The projects are sure to prove very enlightening to those privileged to take part in them.

"The Springfield Plan" (Massachusetts) has been given much publicity, partly through the Hollywood version in a film short entitled "It Happened in Springfield." The "Plan" is simply a well-organized program of training in democratic living, the pupils being provided with opportunities to share their experiences with pupils of other races and other cultures in an atmosphere conducive to friendly feelings. School assemblies are utilized for dramatizing the values in the cultures of foreigners and curricular assignments are planned around the idea of teaching interracial cooperation as one phase of democracy. Springfield has received wide notice for its program. As a matter of fact, so I am told, similar plans in intercultural education have been operating in many other communities without so much fanfare. School programs of this sort, aiming to teach democracy by practicing it, are constructive efforts directed toward minimizing racial prejudice.

We can do no better, in concluding this discussion of what the classroom can accomplish in the way of promoting tolerance, than to cite an account of what is being done in Chicago's public schools to encourage friendliness among the races.

Unusual lessons are being taught to first-graders in Chicago's public schools. One is a story called *Billy's Ride,* which ends as follows:

"A policeman held up his hand and the cars stopped. Though Billy was usually polite, he stared and stared! He had never seen a colored policeman. 'Mother,' Billy called, 'look at the brown policeman.' 'Yes,' said Mother, 'there are many brown policemen. In our country we have many kinds of helpers.' Just then the policeman waved his hand for the cars to move on. Then Billy and Jack did have an exciting time. They were looking for more brown policemen."

While first-graders learn about Negro policemen and Pullman porters, other primary pupils (white and colored) are being told of Negro contributions to civilization, U.S. history, the war effort. Examples of Negro subject matter woven into the general class material:

2nd grade: George Washington Carver, who made many things "from funny little peanuts."

3rd grade: Life in West Africa's Dahomey as an example of the ancestors of U.S. Negroes.

4th grade: The careers of Negro notables such as Contralto Marian Anderson, Bass-Baritone Paul Robeson.

5th grade: "Chicago's first settler, Negro Jean Baptiste Point de Saible."

6th grade: Negro Captain Alonzo Pietro of Columbus' good ship *Nina.*

7th grade: U.S. slavery and its abolition.

8th grade: Negro military heroes, contemporary Chicago Negroes.

The person who originated this program and got Chicago's Board of Education to okay it is a handsome, 36-year-old Negro teacher, Madeline Robinson Morgan. She is the wife of a civilian foreman at Chicago's Army Quartermaster Depot. As a girl Mrs. Morgan knew days and nights of terror during Chicago's 1919 race riots. She got a master's degree in education at Northwestern University, taught at Chicago's Emerson School.

Mrs. Morgan got a year and a half's leave to do research, work out a curriculum, integrate it with the school program as a whole. She says she had her "fingers crossed all the time but most teachers are enthusiastic about the material and children take it as a matter of course." Mrs. Morgan hopes for a change in "quality of attitudes" but expects no miracles. She is pleased that New York City school authorities show interest, that Chicago's Catholic pedagogues are planning a similar step.[81]

3. PERSONAL CONTACTS

It would seem reasonable to assume that an individual would tend to be more prejudiced in his attitudes toward persons he knew little about, less prejudiced toward persons with whom he was familiar. This hypothesis might account for prejudices against strangers. Whether this assumption is to be accepted as sound or not will depend in part upon our definition of "prejudice." Since we have defined "prejudice" as a pre-judgment, a judgment predicated on ignorance rather than knowledge, the above hypothesis appears to make sense. This question of definition is raised at this point because *prejudice* is ordinarily used by laymen and psychologists to connote *antipathy,* ignoring the fact that likes may be just as prejudiced as dislikes.

Now it is true that dislikes are often predicated on ignorance. This proposition may be illustrated by reference to sectional prejudices. People in one part of the country, who have not traveled extensively, develop derogatory notions concerning the inhabitants of other parts of the nation.

[81] *Time,* June 21, 1943.

Pride and Prejudice

At dinner on a Florida-bound ship, a Boston lady remarked to the Captain, a South Carolinian: "I understand there are people who live in the South the whole year round."

———————

Two young girls, newcomers to New York, had stopped a policeman to ask their way about Central Park. They fell into conversation, and the policeman said he'd walk along a bit to show them the way, to be sure. He asked the girls where they came from, and one said Ohio and the other Minnesota. This caused the cop to reflect. After some meditation he observed, "Ah, well, we're all God's creatures." [82]

A reviewer of Josephus Daniels' *Tar Heel Editor* (1939), a book about North Carolina, comments: "The writer's east-Carolina prejudice against the western part of the state is plainly evident." That is sectionalism with a bang, but it cannot surpass the "ethnocentric" outlook of the schoolboy on Block Island, who concluded his essay on George Washington with these eloquent words: "All things considered, he was a great man for an off-islander."

This sort of antipathy is clearly a form of prejudice, since it is based on ignorance. Suppose the east-Carolinian still has no use for the west-Carolinian even after he gets better acquainted. The east-Carolinian may still be called "prejudiced" if he has protected his initial hostility by resort to a logic-tight compartment, which device allows the emotional elements to override the rational elements in preserving his notions about west-Carolinians. Personal likes and dislikes are prejudices if they are determined by feelings rather than by facts. Most of the experiments designed to test the correlation of knowledge and prejudice have been formulated on the assumption that *prejudice is prejudice against* somebody. Such experiments are measures of antipathy, primarily; they are studies of prejudice only in so far as the antipathy is based on ignorance or emotional predisposition. Keeping this warning in mind, let's examine some evidence on the question as to whether familiarity will facilitate tolerance.

Americans on the Pacific Coast were found to be more tolerant in their feelings toward Orientals if they knew the Chinese and Japanese intimately. The less the Americans knew about the immigrants from the Orient, the more hostile they felt toward the strangers in their midst. This was the conclusion reached by G. B. Watson in his survey

———————

[82] *Reader's Digest,* January, 1942. The first item was contributed by William E. Wilson; the second is reprinted from the *New Yorker.*

of race relations on the Pacific Coast in the 1920's.[83]   More recently Harlan has found that non-Jewish college and university students manifest more favorable attitudes toward Jews as a result of more intimate contacts with them.[84]

Graduate students in education were invited to spend two consecutive week ends in Harlem, where they listened to addresses by a prominent Negro editor, a surgeon, and a novelist.   They had tea with Negro college groups, lunch at a Negro social workers' club.   They visited churches, a hospital, and cooperative apartments.   They went to a party at the home of a distinguished Negro where they met a famous Negro poet, an artist, and a musician.   Tests and retests, with a control group for comparison, showed a reliable increment of approval toward Negroes.   In this case personal contacts produced a more friendly attitude toward the colored race.[85]

Familiarity tends to reduce prejudice toward members of other races, according to Diggins, who made a statistical survey of national prejudices among 87 foreign students and 24 American students in the International House in New York City, 25 students at Columbia, 73 at Indiana, and 78 at Occidental College, Los Angeles.   The subjects were instructed to rate each of ten national groups with respect to art, industrial progressiveness, personal preference for social contacts, and willingness to live in a neighborhood where all families were of the particular nationality.   Subjects also indicated whether they had lived in any of the countries from which these groups had come, if so how long, and whether they knew intimately at least three or more individuals belonging to a given nationality.   Results showed a definite tendency for the subjects to rate a group higher if they had lived among that group on its own soil and the longer they had resided there, the higher was the rating.   A higher rating also correlated positively with the number of intimate acquaintances the subjects had developed with members of a certain nationality.[86]

Familiarity, however, has not reduced the prejudice against the Negro in the South where the Negro is well known.   Bogardus reports that there is more feeling against the Negro among Southerners than

[83] See G. B. Watson: *Orient and Occident*.   1927.

[84] See H. H. Harlan: "Some Factors Affecting Attitude toward Jews." *American Sociological Review*, 1942, 7, 816-827.

[85] See F. T. Smith: *An Experiment in Modifying Attitudes toward the Negro.* Ph.D. thesis, Teachers College, Columbia University.   1933.

[86] See E. Diggins: *A Statistical Study of National Prejudices.*   A.M. thesis, Columbia University.   1927.   For a summary of this study, see G. Murphy and L. B. Murphy: *Experimental Social Psychology*, pp. 635-638.   1931.

among whites in other sections of the country.[87]   Reasons for this state of affairs may be gleaned from our previous discussions of the economic and cultural factors operative in the Negro's history and in his present unhappy situation.   Important among the cultural factors is the color line.   Extensive research on this matter has shown that different treatment is accorded darker skinned folk from that given those of lighter complexion; the darker the skin the less likely is the person to be allowed to participate normally in the American scene; women suffer greater disadvantages with increased pigmentation than do men of the same skin color; Negroes themselves would be "black no more," as evidenced by the sizable cosmetic industry which has developed because of the "higher social value of caucasoid features."   That skin color is so important in determining discrimination against Negroes is seen in the fact that successful Negro men, whether dark skinned or light, prefer light skinned wives.[88]

Attitudes of Northerners and Southerners toward the Negro were compared in an investigation made by Hunter.   On a good-will scale computed from answers to a questionnaire Northerners were found to be more favorably disposed toward the Negro than were Southerners.   Two questions revealed a clear-cut sectional difference in antipathy.

If you went into a cafeteria in a Northern city, sat down, and then realized that you were at a table with a Negro, what would you do?

	Percentage who would eat with a Negro
Columbia College	79
Northern adults	59
University of North Carolina	25
Southern adults	0

Does your feeling about riding in the same car with a Negro depend upon whether or not he is clean?

	Percentage answering "Yes"
Columbia College	85
Northern adults	85
University of North Carolina	31
Southern adults	21

[87] See Bogardus: *op. cit.*, p. 160.
[88] See W. L. Warner, B. H. Junker, and W. A. Adams: *Color and Human Nature,* Chapter 1, "The Negro Individual in Society."   1941.

While other questions failed to show such distinctions in sectional attitudes, the study as a whole supports the contention that familiarity in itself is not a panacea for eradicating racial antipathy.[89]

Personal contacts may influence prejudice in various ways, depending upon the nature of the contacts, and the nature of the individuals with whom one happens to be associated. "Contact of a friendly sort brings friendliness, while contact under conditions of conflict brings antagonism." [90]

What can be achieved through contacts of a friendly sort is illustrated in the "Vermont Experiment" in which 78 Negro children, nine to twelve years of age, were invited to spend two weeks during the summer of 1944 living in the homes of whites up in the hills of Vermont. The children, from the Harlem district of New York, enjoyed the rural life very much and endeared themselves to their hosts who discovered, according to the Rev. Low, the sponsor of the project, that the Negro children "were little different from their own youngsters except in color." [91] This experiment proved so successful as to lead to similar projects in New Hampshire and Connecticut during the following summer. The Vermonters are continuing their hospitality because they found the interracial associations beneficial to everyone concerned. This experiment is cited here to show how friendliness is developed when it is nourished under kindly, intelligent auspices—in this case, churches in Harlem and in Vermont.

No doubt the Rhodes Scholarships have helped to tie the United States in closer kinship with the British. Exchange fellowships for university students have contributed in many cases to better feelings between the student beneficiaries and the people with whom they come to live, for the situation as a whole in such instances is conducive to friendship. Cosmopolitan Clubs in the colleges serve a useful function in promoting friendly relations, but their value is limited by the fact that the people who need this broadening experience are the very ones who do not join the Clubs. The melting pot functions to better advantage, perhaps, on the athletic field, where foreigners mix easily with natives in group competition. Indeed, some of the football line-ups in our leading colleges look like the personnel of an immigration

---

[89] See C. W. Hunter: *A Comparative Study of the Relationships Existing between the White Race and the Negro Race in the State of North Carolina and in the City of New York.* A.M. Thesis, Columbia University. 1927. For a detailed summary of this investigation, see G. Murphy and L. B. Murphy: *Experimental Social Psychology,* pp. 639-645. 1931.

[90] Murphy, Murphy, and Newcomb: *op. cit.,* p. 995.

[91] A. R. Low: "Vermont Experiment." *Christian Century,* June 20, 1945.

quota. Contacts of this sort help to foster a happy familiarity with our new Americans.

It is difficult to predict how human beings will react to one another when their prejudices are involved. Sometimes the best intentions are frustrated, as efforts made in behalf of good will eventuate in hard feelings instead. Such was the case with the Olympic Games. Charges and countercharges of poor sportsmanship so marred these international contests that the authorities seriously considered abandoning the Games. One who·has followed the course of the Olympic Games over the years can understand how these animosities arose. More baffling is the friendly attitude of GIs occupying Germany after World War II toward their former deadly enemies, a friendliness, especially with the German girls, that had to be curbed by non-fraternization orders which imposed fines and other severe penalties for accosting and associating with inhabitants of the occupied country. It is too early, at this writing, to foretell how prejudices against foreigners have been affected by the contacts of our armed forces with the peoples of many lands, but it is apparent from the evidence at hand that the returning veteran is going to be less prejudiced against and more disposed in favor of the various peoples he got to know during his extensive travels in the course of waging war.

4. PROPAGANDA OF ENLIGHTENMENT

If education is to root out our prejudices and demolish them, our pedagogy must aim at the emotional side of our biases. The fight against fallacious convictions cannot be waged successfully on the intellectual level. Emotion must be redirected by canalizing it through different channels. Emotional appeals may offer the most effective means of changing our attitudes.

An experiment was conducted by Chen to determine whether he could employ oral propaganda to modify the prejudices of Americans with regard to the conflict of China and Japan over Manchuria. He found that "a few minutes of vigorous propaganda given orally in the classroom may, under these conditions, produce large and measurable results." [92] In another study of a similar nature, editorials were planted in a college newspaper, some derogatory and some laudatory, regarding the Hon. W. Morris Hughes, Prime Minister of Australia from 1915 to 1922. This gentleman was unknown to the subjects when

[92] W. K. C. Chen: "The Influence of Oral Propaganda Material upon Students' Attitudes." *Archives of Psychology*, 1933, 23, No. 150.

the experiment began. Students who read the favorable editorials were influenced to esteem the Hon. Mr. Hughes, while students who read the unfavorable editorials were led to think poorly of him. "Opinions," it was learned, "can be induced by means of judiciously selected selections in as short a time as seven issues of a newspaper," under the conditions described.[93]

With these experiments in mind, let us consider how the prejudice against vivisection may be undermined by cleverly designed propaganda in favor of vivisection. Being thoroughly convinced, myself, that vivisection has played an important role in the advancement of our scientific knowledge, I am naturally disposed to see the anti-vivisectionist as a person who is unduly influenced by his emotional attachments for our animal friends, so blinded, indeed, by that love, that he stubbornly refuses to open his mind to the facts. We may gain some light on the psychological bases of the controversy by examining the emotionalized appeals of the anti-vivisectionists and then analyzing an emotionalized appeal made by vivisectionists.

1. *ANTI-VIVISECTION*

Consult no physician who does not openly condemn this brutal crime. . . . Where a living being is undergoing torments, forcibly inflicted upon it, it ceases to be humane scientific research and becomes vivisection, which has rightly been called the greatest BLOT and SHAME of present-day civilization and its greatest CRIME. . . . Apart from the DEMORALIZATION caused by inflicting torture and the impossibility, in most cases, of rendering the experiment painless, the experimenting on the living body, the putting to torture of poor defenseless animals, is UNCERTAIN and MISLEADING in its results, and is often the mere aimless and CRUEL GAME played by ambitious climbers, sadistic jugglers and characters with criminal tendencies deficient in moral restraint. Forward, then, in the fight for the RIGHTS OF THE ANIMALS and against the ACCURSED PRACTICE of VIVISEC-TION. . . .

MEDICAL SCIENCE based on experimentation on living beings: VIVI-SECTION and INOCULATION are the chief factors in the decline of the race. . . . Instead of being the salvation of Humanity, present-day medical science is THE CURSE OF THE RACE.[94]

---

[93] A. D. Annis and N. V. Meier: "The Induction of Opinion through Suggestion by Means of Planned Content." *Journal of Social Psychology*, 1934, 5, 65-81.

[94] Quoted from publications distributed by an organization of German, Austrian, and Swiss medical opponents of vivisection. President: Dr. Gustav Riedlin, Karlsruhe, Germany.

TO THE HEART WE APPEAL

The universities, experimental schools and the like, under the cloak of science, practice these cruelties day in and day out throughout the year. . . .

We would like to ask some of these exponents of that theory how they would like to have their pet dog maltreated in a laboratory? And the fact that the animal cannot protest should arouse every newspaper man in the country to speak for those who cannot speak for themselves. . . . Anyone who has stood on a street corner and witnessed the appeal of a wounded dog following an automobile accident has some conception of the every-day tragedy as a result of the practice of vivisection.[95]

Through these sentimental appeals, the anti-vivisectionists have succeeded in threatening the practice of animal experimentation.

2. *VIVISECTION*

Scientists are beginning to realize that they must fight back with emotionalized propaganda methods if they are going to preserve their privilege of using animals in research. *Life* in its issue of October 24, 1938, showed how such a campaign should be waged. The first page of the article was an effective masterpiece of irony. On the next page, under the heading, "For Vivisection," appeared photographs of U.S. Surgeon General Thomas Parran, Dr. Alexis Carrel, co-inventor, with Colonel Lindbergh, of the artificial heart, Dr. Karl T. Compton, president of Massachusetts Institute of Technology, Clifford P. Morehouse, the editor of *The Living Church,* Archbishop John J. Cantwell of Los Angeles, and President Ray Lyman Wilbur of Stanford University, with a brief statement by each man extolling the values of animal experimentation. The list is well chosen to include both scientists and religious leaders and the photographs help to carry the weight of their prestige. The contrast of these gentlemen with the ladies on the page opposite is extremely dramatic. Then the *Life* investigators went to the Harvard Medical School (more prestige), where they were allowed to see and photograph all the experiments that were being carried on at the time. These pictures speak more than words ever could. We quote:

On the following pages you will see some examples of animal research which support *Life's* conclusions that:

[95] Editorial written by C. E. Broughton. Published in *The Press,* Sheboygan, Wisconsin, March 16, 1937.

(1) Medicine's tremendous progress during the past 300 years would have been impossible without animal experimentation.

(2) Millions of persons would die in pain every year were it not for discoveries resulting from vivisection.

(3) The major modern diseases can be cured only if scientists are allowed freedom in their research.

(4) A ban on animal experimentation would force surgeons to learn their art on living men and women.[96]

The first picture shows children stricken with infantile paralysis being kept alive in iron lungs, with an insert of Engineer Philip Drinker, designer of the iron lung, trying out his first experimental respirator on a cat whose breathing muscles had been paralyzed. Caption for the page is:

"Twenty-Four Cats Proved Iron Lung Could Save Children"

Another page shows medical students learning their surgery by using animal subjects and these pictures drive home the point that anesthesia and antiseptic precautions are employed to make the experimenting as humane as possible. The final demonstration shows how horse serums are prepared and tested on rabbits before being applied to a child as an inoculation against diphtheria, a precaution that saves thousands of children's lives each year. The final picture is a photograph demonstrating how the antitoxin is administered to a child. This is powerful propaganda of enlightenment prepared to combat the crusading anti-vivisectionists. While it might be unconvincing to a confirmed anti-vivisectionist, it is designed to win the approval of persons who are willing to consider the evidence pro and con. The appeal through photographs, backed by the prestige of scientists garbed in the paraphernalia of the doctor, with the emphasis on humanitarian motives throughout, is a very effective argument, linking ideas and emotions in a manner that is moving in its forcefulness.

C. Understanding the Psychology of Stereotypes

One of the most valuable ways for the individual to attain objectivity is to discover how his attitudes become stereotyped. A stereotype is a picture of what the person thinks things are like—it is an expurgated edition of reality, in which some part inaccurately represents the whole (partial identity), with the details eliminated by a process of simplification. Stereotyping depicts reality as all black or all white; there are no *ifs* or *buts*.

[96] *Life,* October 24, 1938.

A person's judgments of the different features of a situation are not so many isolated, discrete reactions to it, but rather are parts which mutually determine each other . . . [thus] an evil man begins, after a while, to look evil. . . . There also seems [to be] a tendency in judgment to arrive at a consistent, unified view, to get rid of incompatible perspectives. . . . It is rare to find settled attitudes . . . which are half-for, half-against a view. . . . The tendency toward consistency, toward unification, is frequently expressed in the phenomenon of simplification, in the trend to see the main features of a situation in the simplest possible way.[97]

A familiar example of stereotyping is the common classification of college men according to definite distinguishing traits. Students of the "big four" have been pigeonholed by their own and other college groups as follows:

Dartmouth—outdoor men, college-loyal, hard drinkers, athletic, the rah-rah type.
Harvard—blasé, indifferent, snobbish, conceited, intellectual, socialites.
Princeton—style-setting, gentlemanly, smooth, college-loyal, socialites.
Yale—college-loyal, athletic, typical college boys, hard drinkers, socialites.[98]

The fallacy of such typing becomes apparent when you come to know individual men from these various institutions of higher learning, who do not fit the types specified for their respective schools. Individual differences as established by curves of statistical distribution do not fall neatly into such categories of classification; variations shade imperceptibly into each other as a rule; discrete pigeonholing is artificial, a device more suited to convenience than reality.

Stereotypes function as prejudices in determining our evaluations. Fascism, for example, involves some very definite tenets but for many people it is a name connoting something vicious; indeed, they will reject it, even though they approve of its principles if these principles are presented without the label "Fascist." This fact was demonstrated in an experiment conducted by Raskin and Cook, in which they found that some of their subjects who liked the ideas embodied in Fascism did not like Fascism as such.

[97] S. E. Asch: "Studies in the Principles of Judgments and Attitudes: II. Determination of Judgments by Group and by Ego Standards." *Journal of Social Psychology,* S.P.S.S.I. Bulletin, 1940, 12, 433-465.
[98] See K. Fink and H. Cantril: "The Collegiate Type as Frame of Reference." *Journal of Abnormal and Social Psychology,* 1937, 32, 352-356. American Psychological Association, Inc.

There is definite evidence that the responses of numerous individuals to political party labels are at marked variance with their responses to the idea making up the corresponding party programs. The significance of this fac for an understanding of both the nature of political attitudes and the tech niques of measuring and changing them is obvious.[99]

The stereotype, "a picture in the mind" of what the verbal symbo represents, is an important determining tendency in the motivation of our social behavior.

Other studies of political judgment corroborate this finding. Indi viduals are so strongly influenced by labels that they cannot keep thei minds on the evidence they are supposed to be evaluating. Gordor Allport, in a study of Dartmouth undergraduates, reports that almos half of the students who constituted the most radical 10 per cent or his scale, favored a candidate representing a conservative party.[100] Menefee found that individuals who endorsed certain statements o political policy later rejected from 27 to 32 per cent of these same statements when they were correctly labeled fascist, radical, or com munist.[101] Hartmann discovered that people who favored socialis objectives were opposed to the Socialist Party:

The masses seem to like "socialism," but to dislike "socialists." . . . The dominant old-line major parties, "Republican" and "Democratic," occup first and second place . . . despite the fact that neither of them is officiall committed to the socialization of industry, which by implication, the greate number of those interviewed really desired. . . . Presumably the main effec of an "unpopular" name is to delay the advent of the "popular" measures tha it symbolizes. . . . The population of this study apparently would prefe to have the Republican Party be the vehicle for introducing socialism to America.[102]

Hartmann suspects that this preference for the Republican Party a the vehicle of socialism is about as unrealistic as Luther's hope tha some day the Pope would be converted to Protestantism; but only the future will tell.

[99] E. Raskin and S. W. Cook: "A Further Investigation of the Measurement of a Attitude toward Fascism." *Journal of Social Psychology*, 1938, 9, 201-206.

[100] See G. W. Allport: "The Composition of Political Attitudes." *American Jour nal of Sociology*, 1929, 35, 220-238.

[101] See S. C. Menefee: "The Effect of Stereotyped Words on Political Judgments. *American Sociological Review*, 1936, 1, 614-621.

[102] G. W. Hartmann: "The Contradiction between the Feeling-Tone of Politica Party Names and Public Response to Their Platforms." *Journal of Social Psy chology*, 1936, 7, 336-357.

Political propagandists know how to direct their appeals effectively o common stereotypes. Pinning the label of "Communism" on any-one or anything used to be (and still is, generally) a quick means of damning a person or program. Stereotyped words and catch phrases play an important role in "red-baiting." Judgment is manipulated readily by calling an opponent an "anarchist" or a "Bolshevist" or some other dreadful name. Emotionalized responses built up through years of conditioning are evoked by supplying the appropriate stimuli. The inclinations are loaded, ready for some demagogue to release them.

Bogardus cites an interesting case to illustrate how stereotypes affect us in our human relations. During World War I a French woman hated "Germans" (institutionalized symbol). In spite of this hostility, she was prompted by pity to help a German prisoner of war, whom she regarded not as a "German" but as a human being.[103] In this example we discover how an understanding of stereotypy can help us to get rid of our prejudices. The secret lies in the art of learning to regard a person as a human being rather than as a member of a certain race. A prominent Negro athlete stated that his college career had turned out to be a curse to him, because in college he was admired as an athlete and as a person, but when he graduated into the non-academic world, he learned to his sorrow that he was still just another Negro. Some people have come to the point where they can think of Roland Hayes or Paul Robeson or Marian Anderson as marvelous singers, artists deserving glorification for their skill, and the matter of race has become irrelevant. Approximately 75,000 people assembled to hear Marian Anderson sing on the steps of the Lincoln Memorial in Washington at Easter-time, 1939, after she had been denied the privilege of singing in the D.A.R.'s Constitution Hall, and many more people listened to her thrilling performance over the radio. When Philadelphia bestowed its highest honor for the year 1940 upon this great Negro contralto, many Americans hailed the award with satisfaction. Such experiences contribute their bit to encourage admiration for great human beings regardless of race, though we are not justified in leaping to the conclusion that we are ushering in a new era of universal good will. The fact that Roland Hayes can sing to appreciative audiences in the South and the fact that Paul Robeson can play the leading role in *All God's Chillun* opposite a white woman are indications that anti-racial feeling is subsiding in some places and among some people, at least. One more evidence of this trend is the report

[103] See E. S. Bogardus: "Mutations of Social Distance." *Journal of Applied Sociology*, 1926, 11, 77-84.

that the Fellowship of Southern Churchmen convened in April
1943, for a four-day series of meetings at Raleigh, North Carolina
There was no segregation of whites and Negroes. "For many it wa
the first experience of Christian fellowship unmarred by the violatioi
of brotherhood generally imposed by custom and by law." [104]

We must be ever on our guard against the intrusion of stereotypee
reactions in our social relations if we are going to get away from preju
diced attitudes. If we analyze ourselves to discover the nature of ou
stereotypes and then if we discount them in determining our judg
ments, we are more likely to be objective in our behavior. This un
qualified respect for personal merit we find embodied in great scien
tists like Thomas Edison, who invited George Washington Carver, th
Negro genius, to join his laboratory.[105] Edison did not care at al
what the color of the man's skin was. His invitation was promptee
by his regard for the man's ability. It was one man calling to anothe
man for help, not a white self-consciously beckoning a Negro to forge
the color line. That line was ignored because both men were awar
that more important issues were involved. And we find the same in
difference to a man's color in orchestra leader Artie Shaw, who hac
scheduled a tour through the South to raise $25,000 which he needec
to start "his dream band," a big band with which he could play con
cert jazz. One of his feature players was a Negro trumpeter, "Ho
Lips" Paige. Despite the prospect of $2,500 per engagement, fiv
nights a week,

leader Shaw last week canceled 32 such golden dates in the South an
Southwest, where he has never played. Reason: he was asked to shelve Negr
Paige during that part of his tour. The South can take all-Negro bands lik
Cab Calloway's, and it doesn't mind small mixed combinations; against
Negro in a large white band it tends to draw the color line. But Artie Shaw
like most musicians, is color-blind.[106]

D. MEASURING PROGRESS TOWARD FAIR-MINDEDNESS

If fair-mindedness is truly one of the main goals of education, as s
many leaders tell us it is, then we should certainly develop some tech

[104] Correspondence in the *Christian Century*, May 5, 1943. The author is awar
that there are instances of rising tension between whites and Negroes in some lo
calities. One Negro leader asserts that the increased tension is due to the Negro
insistence that he be recognized as a first-class citizen, in other words, as a persor
[105] *Reader's Digest*, June 12, 1937.
[106] *Time*, September 22, 1941.

ique for determining whether we are making any progress toward
hat objective.

The need for a measuring instrument to check the effectiveness of
ur educational program in this respect prompted Goodwin Watson
o develop a test for measuring fair-mindedness. "Fair-mindedness,"
e discovered, was variously identified with open-mindedness, scien-
ific-mindedness, and freedom from prejudice. Turning to Dewey, he
ound an educational philosophy centered about the ideal of open-
indedness. Dewey noted that prejudices arrest development, that
closed mind represents a premature old age. "Open-mindedness is
ot the same as empty-mindedness. To hang out a sign, 'Come right
1; there is no one at home' is not the equivalent of hospitality. . . .
The well-educated person will exhibit an] open-minded preference
or conclusions that are properly grounded." [107]

Obviously Watson could not label his questionnaire "A Test of Fair-
indedness" since that would expose its purpose, invalidate the results.
his pitfall was avoided by entitling the test "A Survey of Public
pinion on Some Religious and Economic Issues." Watson assumed
hat the examinee would furnish evidence of his fair-mindedness by
ecording his attitudes on certain issues. Prejudice, or a lack of fair-
indedness would be revealed if the subject:

(1) Crossed out controversial words as disagreeable or annoying (Cross-
ut Test).

(2) Accused sincere, competent persons of being insincere or incompetent
they differed in opinion (Degree of Truth Test).

(3) Drew conclusions in accord with his bias, conclusions unjustified by the
vidence (Inference Test).

(4) Condemned actions in one group, which he condoned in another
Moral Judgment Test).

(5) Gave blanket approval to one set of arguments as all of them strong, or
he opposite, as all of them weak (Arguments Test).

(6) Attributed to all persons in a group characteristics belonging only to
ome of the members of the group (Generalization Test).[108]

A Gross Score may be obtained which expresses the strength of a
erson's prejudices. The tests also provide the data for computing,

[107] J. Dewey: *Democracy and Education,* pp. 204-206. The Macmillan Company,
930.
[108] The "Watson-Glaser Tests of Critical Thinking" (1943) have supplanted Wat-
n's "Survey of Public Opinion on Some Religious and Economic Issues." The
lder test has been cited because it fits the present context more exactly.

according to a standardized key, the Analytical Score. This score indicates the direction of the prejudices, as to whether they agree with a typical capitalist, a typical Roman Catholic, and the like. There are 18 typical lines of bias in all. The Analytical Score may be represented graphically in a Prejudice Profile.

Watson raised several questions concerning the validity of his test. Does it measure fair-mindedness? He answered this question in the affirmative. Critics, however, leveled objections against its validity. Some of them suggested that the test was a measure of empty-mindedness, that it was unfair to call enlightened opinions "prejudices," that a person who made a low score on the test was called "fair-minded" when he might really be a wishy-washy person handicapped by ignorance and minus convictions. Watson nullified these objections by pointing out that the nature of the test items was such as to provide a *fair* measure of prejudice, that the subject was given an opportunity to express his opinions with no necessity for going so far as to call names or to draw unwarranted conclusions, that results showed high correlations with judgments passed by the subjects' colleagues. To illustrate this last point, he called attention to the fact that students at the Yale Divinity School and at Union Theological Seminary proved on the test to be more open-minded on religious issues than the ordinary college student. It would be unreasonable, he said, to assume that the divinity students were poorly informed on these matters or that they were empty-headed. Judgments by colleagues indicated that the test scores in this instance were valid.

One observation that Watson makes, on the basis of data obtained through his test, should be cited. There is good evidence, he says, that well-informed persons can be very prejudiced.[109] Note that he does not say well-informed persons are prejudiced; he merely states they can be.

One individual who took the Watson Test objected that the test did not differentiate between prejudice and conviction.[110] This was possibly a neat rationalization on the part of a person who preferred to think of his strong opinions as convictions, not as prejudices. Another subject did not think it correct to attribute "fair-mindedness" to individuals "lacking in virile moral convictions." [111] High com

---

[109] See G. B. Watson: *The Measurement of Fair-Mindedness*, p. 33. 1925.
[110] *Ibid.*, p. 58. Profile No. 31.
[111] *Ibid.*, p. 60. Profile No. 46. Available since 1942 are the "Watson-Glaser Test of Critical Thinking," published by the World Book Company, Yonkers-on-Hudson, New York. There are two Batteries: "Discrimination in Reasoning," and "Logical Reasoning."

endation for such weak persons, he thought, was most unfortunate. 'his commentary was probably another rationalization, one that is ommon in the moral sphere where prejudices are not likely to be 'cognized as such, where open-mindedness is liable to be misinter- reted as empty-mindedness.

Watson believed that this test could be used to measure how effec- ve are lectures, sermons, and discussion groups as means of influ- acing opinion in the direction of fair-mindedness. Any instrument : this kind that will make it possible for us to check our progress •ward the realization of objectivity is sure to be valuable. By testing .ir attitudes from time to time, we can learn how to revise and im- ·ove our educational techniques. Most of us have not as yet made iy serious attempt to root out our prejudices. Once we have come • appreciate how much harm is done by our biases, we can see the nportance of discovering the best ways for getting rid of them, or : least minimizing their influence upon our thinking and our con- .ict. The task can be accomplished if we care enough to make the ecessary effort. It is an ideal that cannot be realized by the mere :t of willing oneself to become a broad-minded person. One must nderstand the psychological principles involved in the genesis of prej- dice and in the rooting out of prejudice and then put those prin- ples into effect through a persistent process of reeducation in order • achieve satisfactory fair-mindedness.

Part V

INSTITUTIONAL PATTERNS OF
SOCIAL BEHAVIOR

MAN, as a social being, living with others in various kinds of groups, learns early and learns well that it is the part of wisdom to conform to regulations, standards, codes, and sanctions, which are imposed and enforced by organized opinion. We have explained that social psychology studies the individual in social situations. In order to understand the patterns of behavior that characterize the human being in his social relations, we must examine the nature of the institutions which come to control his every thought, his every deed.[1]

An institution, from the point of view of behavior, is an organized system of group habits. It refers to ways of doing things according to a standardized routine. "People always will find ways of meeting existing needs group-wise, and these collective ways are their social institutions at the time."[2] So people have developed recognized ways of doing business, establishing a home, worshiping God, conducting a government. These customary patterns of organized behavior we call institutions: business, family, church, state, as the case may be.

"All social institutions may be thought of as founded upon the mores. Institutions represent formal trends in the mores."[3] The mores are the customs, the prevalent habits of thought, which define the functions of the individual in a particular community. These norms of conduct are compelling because they are supported by the prestige of a long past. Things institutional, like all things built on custom, are enduring. This lasting quality may be attributed, in part, to the fact that every institution seeks to prolong its existence, to con-

---

[1] See our section on this topic in Chapter 1.
[2] J. P. Lichtenberger: *Divorce: a Social Interpretation*, p. 421. Whittlesey House, copyright, 1931, by the McGraw-Hill Book Company, Inc.
[3] W. Waller: "War and Social Institutions," in *War in the Twentieth Century*, p. 485, W. Waller, Editor. 1940.

serve its role in the communal life. Institutions last a long time, resisting change in a changing world, remaining static because people hesitate to make a break in the routine of their familiar habits. Living "for God, for Country, and for Yale," as we all do, literally or figuratively, means being loyal to the old traditions, the ancient founders, the old-timers who have gone before.

This dominance of the past may entail serious maladjustments, for, as Veblen says, "institutions are products of the past process, are adapted to past circumstances, and are therefore never in full accord with the requirements of the present." It is respectable to be a conservative, vulgar to be an innovator. Under such circumstances we are inclined to give allegiance to our institutions, strong in the faith that our way of doing things is divinely ordained and obviously the best. Thus as we stand by our habits, we commend ourselves for our good judgment.

An institution may be described in terms of its concept and its structure. Its concept includes its functions and purposes; its structure refers to the instruments by means of which the purposes are realized and to the ways in which the instruments are used. The concept is represented in the essential characteristics of an institution.[4] Some of these are:

First, a social institution arises out of and is a result of repeated groupings of interacting human individuals in response to elemental needs or drives (sex, hunger, fear, etc.).

Second, common reciprocating attitudes and conventionalized behavior patterns develop out of the process of interaction (affection, loyalty, cooperation, domination, subordination, etc.).

Third, cultural objects . . . embody symbolic values . . . become the cue stimuli to behavior conditioned to them (the idol, cross, ring, flag, etc. . . . charged with emotional and sentimental meaning).

Fourth, cultural objects . . . embody utilitarian values . . . become the means of satisfying creature wants for warmth, shelter, etc. (buildings, furniture, etc.).

Fifth, preserved in oral or written language, externally stored and handed down from one generation to the next, there are description and specification of the patterns of interrelationship among these elemental drives, attitudes, symbolic culture traits, and utilitarian culture traits. . . .[5]

[4] Adapted from F. S. Chapin: "A New Definition of Social Institutions." *Social Forces*, 1928, 6, 375-377.
[5] See M. F. Nimkoff: *The Family*, pp. 8-12. Houghton Mifflin Company, 1934.

Thus we may see the family in terms of the following characteristics:

Attitudes and behavior patterns	Love
	Affection
	Devotion
	Loyalty
	Parental respect
Symbolic culture	Marriage ring
	Crest
	Coat of arms
	Heirloom
Utilitarian culture	Home equipment
	Personal property
Oral or written specifications	Will
	Marriage license
	Genealogy
	Mores[6]

The structure may be defined in terms of the personnel constituting the group, its equipment, and its organization.

Institutional behavior represents the influence of a fairly permanent, well-organized group upon individuals who come within its jurisdiction. Membership in such traditional groups as the family, the school, or a business firm involves subscribing to certain regulations. Members must fall in line, to remain welcome. Thus individualities are sacrificed, as persons merge into the likenesses of other members of the herd.

Prominent among our institutions are business, family, church, and state. Each of these deserves our attention; each is covered rather comprehensively, in the order just mentioned, in Chapters 18, 19, 20, and 21, respectively.

[6] *Ibid.*

Chapter 18

INDUSTRY

SOCIAL PSYCHOLOGY is just beginning to explore the complex problems of human relations in the field of industry. Interest in the human factor in business is developing rapidly because of the discovery that a happy worker is a more productive worker. The machine is important but more important still is the mental condition of the man who operates the machine. His state of mind is going to be affected very much by the people with whom he is associated on the job. If he does not like his immediate superior or if he fails to get recognition for his efforts, he is going to suffer some decrement in his productive efficiency and his frustrations are going to be communicated to his fellow workers. Mental hygiene being fundamentally a matter of satisfying human relations, it is obvious that a congenial group to work with is a psychological necessity for sound morale. An understanding boss and a loyal employee make an ideal combination. This is a fact of profound concern to the social psychologist who is interested in learning how individuals can get along together happily as they labor to earn a living.

I. HUMAN RELATIONS

The study of human relations in industry is so new that the psychologist at this stage must limit himself to a few fundamental principles and to suggesting further lines of research that are sure to be followed through in the near future by investigators who are concentrating their attention upon this field of psychological interest. It is a pioneer field offering large opportunities to psychologists with initiative and insight into human motivation.

We may assume, at the start, that a business concern is established as an organized group effort to achieve a definite goal—in our capitalistic economy, the objective of making money. This end will be attained by offering the public a product or service which will satisfy some need. It is axiomatic, likewise, that any concern must operate at a profit since no businessman is in business "just for his health." Profits will depend upon the productive efficiency of the group. Thus arises one problem calling for study, that of determining what kind of group structure will be most conducive to effective operation. What are the patterns of interrelationships that will enable the participants in an enterprise to attain their objectives pleasantly and efficiently? One type of organization is the one man organization, that is, one man is the leader and he alone makes all the decisions. In another type of organization the head delegates much of his authority to other executives who in turn delegate authority to their subordinates and so on down the line. Which of these two kinds of structures is the more desirable will depend upon the size of the company, the nature of its product, the personalities of the people involved. In the old days the head of a small business knew all his employees intimately and consequently he was in a position to evoke loyalty of a very personal nature to the company, with which the worker easily identified himself. Today, when many organizations are so big that the boss cannot possibly know many of his subordinates, the company tends to become an impersonal abstraction for which the employee only "goes through the motions." We have oversimplified the situation, of course, merely to formulate the problem in a general way.

Another phase of group structure is the contrast between the organization of management and the organization of a labor union. The head of the company may make decisions on his own which are regarded as binding; the union leader can only express the will of the members by whom he is elected and by whom he is employed. These contrasting structures affect the dealings which management and union have with each other. Little is known at present as to just what the psychological effects are of these dissimilar arrangements, particularly as they affect collective bargaining.

Many of the significant relationships in industry are of the superior-to-subordinate sort. The nature of this kind of relationship can best be understood by comparing it to the relationship of parent and child.[1] This analogy suggests two avenues of exploration. First is the prototype of the stern father who maintains discipline by relying largely upon punishment. He is comparable to the business executive who

[1] I am indebted to Douglas McGregor of the Massachusetts Institute of Technology for first calling this analogy to my attention. Rosenstein also recognizes the similarity: "We must bear in mind that the executive-subordinate relationship is the same as the parent-child relationship." J. L. Rosenstein: *Psychology of Human Relations for Executives*, p. 9. McGraw-Hill Book Company, Inc., 1936.

uses threats to force his employees to obey his decrees. The employee is likely to react as does the child, by resenting his humiliating position and looking about for some convenient means of "getting even" through sabotage, idling on the job, or striking for more pay. A second basis of comparison is the father who believes that he has discharged his full responsibility as a parent when he "brings home the bacon," thereby providing for the material needs of his family. We know now the terrible tragedy of the child who feels unloved, starving for affection. There is a similarity here between the unloving father and the superior who thinks that adequate pay is all that is needed to keep his employees happy. Little does such an employer realize how much zest for the job is lost because he does not manifest a personal interest in each employee, asking after their families, calling them by name, praising them for work well done—in other words, to put it boldly, by showing his subordinates some affection. We must note, in both of these analogous situations that we have described, the significance of the psychoanalytic teaching that the employee re-enacts toward his boss the very patterns of emotional love and hate which he originally felt toward the parent in childhood. The wise boss, therefore, will strive to be "a good father" if he expects to merit respect and loyalty on the part of his subordinates.

The aim in setting up a business enterprise and maintaining it successfully will be to nourish a healthy organization. Such an organization will be characterized by the absence of serious friction, but more than that it will endeavor to see to it that the workers enjoy their work, enjoy it because they have been trained to understand the meaning of what they are doing and because they get an emotional "kick" out of cooperating with friendly persons in a common task. Superiors and subordinates alike will need psychological help in order to improve their relations. It is a cardinal principle of social psychology in this context that people must first be shown they need help before such aid can be given to good advantage. Executives, in particular, are apt to indulge in much wishful thinking with respect to the psychological conditions prevailing in their organizations, complacently convincing themselves that all is well.[2] Experimental studies of worker morale may be required to reveal the need for modifying existing arrangements and the desirability of revamping management policies.

The psychologist who has some worth-while suggestions to offer man-

[2] See W. D. Scott, R. C. Clothier, S. B. Mathewson, W. R. Spriegel: *Personnel Management*, Third Edition, p. 507. 1941.

agement for improving the human satisfactions among the members of the organization, must first of all sell the idea to management. The best appeal is a demonstration that a change in policy will result in higher production and lower costs. For example, management will be kindly disposed toward delegating more authority to labor if such action will mean less absenteeism and less turnover. It is likely that "the top management in a factory fails to use democratic methods not primarily because of opposition to democracy, but rather because of unfamiliarity with democratic methods appropriate to the problems of factory management." [3] Here, then, is a major assignment for the social psychologist: to discover appropriate democratic techniques and to show by actual results that these democratic methods of handling problems in human relations really pay dividends in terms of greater production and greater emotional satisfaction. Rosenstein may have had these possibilities in mind when he wrote:

The most important single factor in industry today is the human being at work, yet comparatively few executives have learned . . . the "proper techniques" of dealing with the worker . . . few . . . have made any attempt to gain an understanding of the goals, the purposes, the drives and emotions of the worker on the job. . . . Any move made by an executive, which might in the slightest degree destroy the belief in his absolute sincerity of purpose and wholehearted interest in the employees' welfare, will wreak more havoc than any number of errors made by employees. The executive must spend more time trying to devise plans for getting the employee to talk, and devote less to figuring out ways of "getting him told." [4]

We might add that it would be even more democratic for the executive to invite his employees to join with him in devising plans for sharing ideas, a practice that is gaining acceptance.

Training in psychology is an asset to an executive because it gives him a mode of approach to human problems which is based upon understanding and upon an objective attitude. With a background in clinical and genetic psychology, the executive will confront a situation like that of a disloyal employee by asking himself how the person "got that way." What is his background? What sort of a personality did he bring to the job? Did his immediate superior precipitate some emotional maladjustment by clumsy handling of a personal difference?

[3] J. R. P. French in *Human Nature and Enduring Peace*, p. 329, G. Murphy (Editor). 1945.
[4] Reprinted by permission from *Psychology of Human Relations for Executives*, by J. L. Rosenstein. Copyrighted, 1936, by the McGraw-Hill Book Company, Inc.

What is the meaning of the employee's behavior? Disloyalty is thus regarded merely as a symptom of some underlying difficulty needing further investigation. How does such a sympathetic point of view work out in practice?

If we should find a workman deliberately refusing to carry out the orders of a foreman, we should *not* have sufficient cause for discharge. We should consider the actions of the worker only symptoms or signs that the past relationship between the two has been such that there gradually developed a pent-up emotional pressure which ultimately resulted in this "blowoff." We should not consider this "blowoff" as ground for discharge but as a demand for investigation of causes and for a complete knowledge of the history of events leading up to the act of insubordination. Study of causes may show that the foreman himself is the influence instigating insubordination and that he needs to learn some newer techniques of dealing with men.[5]

The executive who is objective will recognize that management may be "wrong," and he will wisely admit it when he knows a mistake has been made; he will even go so far as to set up the machinery for correcting the error and preventing the occurrence of similar ones in the future. A reputation for fair dealing, thus acquired, will contribute to an important degree toward establishing confidence of employees in their management.

A list of some typical problems in human relations in industry will indicate how social psychology must inevitably become more and more concerned with this field of social behavior:

Is the worker really dissatisfied with his wage or is his real grievance an upset over a superior who irritates him?

Is the important thing the level of pay or the fact that the worker feels he is entitled to as much as some other employees are getting?

How will the workers react if time studies are made to determine the rate of pay?

How can suggestions from the men at the bottom be secured without embarrassing their superiors who may feel their subordinates are trying to "show them up" as incompetent?

How far should management concern itself with the worker's activities outside the plant that may be affecting his efficiency adversely?

[5] Reprinted by permission from *Psychology of Human Relations for Executives*, by J. L. Rosenstein. Copyrighted, 1936, by the McGraw-Hill Book Company, Inc.

Is it wise for boss and subordinate to address each other by first names Will the practice encourage undue familiarity?

What can be done about the executive who bullies his employees to compen sate for his own sense of insecurity?

How can impractical suggestions be rejected without hurting the suggester' feelings?

How can promotions be engineered so as to place men at their highes level of ability, without saddling them with responsibilities beyond thei capacity to bear?

How can a leader handle such problems as the man who thinks he is being exploited, the one who resents criticism of any kind, the worker who belittle the other fellow's ideas, the person who feels imposed upon, the individua who feels he is not really accepted by the group, the man who is constantl looking for an argument, the employee who is guilty of insubordination, th "yes-man," the girl who "overdresses," the person who prefers conversatio to working, the experienced man who is reluctant to teach the newcomer th technical skills of his craft, the employee who seems to be a privileged perso because he is a relative of the owner, the worker who spends more time thar he needs to in the lavatory, the girl who is primarily interested in attractin the men, the employee who devotes working time to selling tickets for a clul benefit show?

These are just a few of the problems in social relations that must be contended with and solved if a company is going to function smoothly It is clear that the selection of supervisory personnel must be directe by consideration of a person's ability to handle others, an ability tha is all too rare, unfortunately.

As we have just remarked, supervisory personnel is frequently re cruited from workers who have demonstrated superior skill at the bench, without sufficient regard for their leadership skill. Thus the typical foreman lays aside his tools, and becomes a leader, a role fo which he may not be duly qualified by personality or by training One old-timer explained how he handled a new employee.

"I just stand there . . . and stare him down, to kinda show how dumb h is."

"And then?"

"Then I spit." [6]

[6] Quoted by S. Chase: *Men at Work*, p. 44.   1945.

We have stated that it is important for management to understand what the job means to the employee. There are four *job values* which must be taken into account:

1. The *reality value,* which is represented in wages and salaries as they offer individuals economic security and a satisfactory standard of living.
2. The *social-saturation value*—that is, the value that the job has in helping the individual to experience the saturation of his emotional needs for interpersonal relationship. . . .
3. The *integration value,* contained in the opportunites offered to the individual in his job to express his specific abilities in productive work. . . .
4. The *role value* . . . which permits the individual to [achieve a satisfying status in the community].[7]

Basic to all these values is the principle that a person's job adjustment is a major factor in the assurance of sound mental health. In our culture it is essential to one's self-respect, for most people, to have a job; further, it is a blessing to be engaged in the kind of work which satisfies one's emotional needs.

One more problem in human relations to challenge the social psychologist is the perennial conflict between management and labor. The violence of this conflict was somewhat lessened by the National Labor Relations Act, backed by decisions of the Supreme Court and strengthened by the growth of labor's political power. The signing of a labor-management charter by Eric Johnston, Philip Murray, and William Green, representing the United States Chamber of Commerce, the Congress of Industrial Organizations, and the American Federation of Labor, respectively, was a manifestation of good will and, therefore, a move in the right direction. It is too early, at this writing, to forecast the effect of the Taft-Hartley Act of 1947 on the labor-management conflict. Industrial peace, however, cannot be secured by any of these measures as long as there remain areas of dispute which leaders of labor and leaders of management refuse to tackle. There are three major areas of dispute demanding intelligent and courageous attention:

First, and most disturbing, is the question, What is a fair wage? . . . Can wages be said to be fair when they equal the highest paid in the industry or trade? . . . Or do fairness and justice lie in giving to labor some share of the profits of industry? If so, what proportion? . . .

[7] B. Solby: "A Theory of Mental Hygiene in Industry." *Mental Hygiene,* 1945, 29, 353-371.

It all depends, of course, on the point of view.

Historically, business looked on labor as a commodity necessary for the operation of a factory, to be purchased in much the same way as coal or raw materials are purchased. Enlightened industrialists no longer try to keep wages at the lowest possible level, for they have learned that in the last analysis it is the working people who have to buy what their plants produce. Accordingly, wages have been raised, sometimes generously. But so long as the profit motive dominates industry, management will reach a far different conclusion from that which labor will reach as to what constitutes a fair wage.

WHERE THE TROUBLE LIES

As labor sees it, wages represent an opportunity to live. No worker will ever be satisfied with subsistence wages. He wants a larger share of the good things of life which can be purchased only by a larger income. When he contemplates the fact that no goods could be produced without his toil, he wants to know why his share of the total income is not larger.

It is from this divergence as to what constitutes a fair wage that most labor disputes spring. Industry and labor are not agreed on a basic standard of values in the light of which the wage issue can be solved. Until they can approximate such a common standard, controversy will continue. Much harm can be done at this point by imputing insincerity to either side. We have here an owning class point of view and a working class point of view which have never been brought to judgment before some firm moral standard in the light of which their claims and assumptions can be evaluated. Until that is done the only peace we are likely to get in the field of industrial relations will be a peace dictated by fear or power.

WHO IS TO CONTROL?

A second issue prolific of industrial conflict centers in the question of control. Mr. Johnston succeeded in including in the labor-management charter a statement of the rights of management to direct the operation of its own enterprises. Perhaps he had in mind the fact that a large proportion of disputes before the War Labor Board center in the issue of joint management. As a matter of unvarnished fact, industry today does not have the kind of unlimited control of its enterprises which this charter claims for it. Under some contracts management can employ only those whom the union selects. It can discharge an undesirable employee only for certain causes but must discharge a good employee who breaks union rules and is expelled from the union. It may not choose whom it pleases for new jobs nor promote whom it pleases to openings in old jobs. In a score of ways it is limited by some union contracts. . . .

Here again is a basic clash. The right of ownership to do what it pleases with its property goes back to the earliest days of the industrial revolution. So deeply rooted is this conviction that one who challenges that right can almost

e accused of subversive tendencies. Yet labor is doing that very thing.
Every union contract aims to place in labor's hands the authority either to
determine its rights and duties or to check on the authority which does so
determine. It seeks a share in control because such control spells protection
against what it regards as arbitrary power wielded by a ruling class.

DIFFERENT POINTS OF VIEW

The trouble is that management and labor come to this problem with
different points of view and what seems fair to one does not seem fair to the
other. There is today no generally accepted standard by which this issue can
be judged. Until such a standard is discovered and accepted, conflict is
likely to continue.

A third area of controversy is found in the issue of security. . . . What
obligation does industry have to labor beyond the payment of wages? Historically the answer is *none*. British mill-owners at the dawn of the nineteenth
century could discard a broken-down worker as easily as a broken-down mule,
and probably with less regret. But those days have passed.

The seniority provisions of labor contracts are based on the assumption
that an employee acquires through long service certain rights which are over
and above the right of adequate wages. . . . Next to adequate wages the most
precious thing that an employee has is security in his job.

The present drive for an annual wage has back of it the conviction that
labor has a right to the security of a steady income. But how much security?
Where will the line be drawn in industries, many of which are none too secure
themselves? In a system of private competitive capitalism . . . there can be
no guaranteed security for any business. But in such security as there is, labor
asks to share. It is because there has been no meeting of minds in this area
that controversy continues.

This analysis of the fundamental sources of management-labor conflict
is based upon extensive experience on the War Labor Board during
World War II. The author, Edwin A. Brown, asserts that these issues
which "divide industry and labor are not merely economic. They are
fundamentally moral issues. In every one of these three basic problems, human values are paramount. If solutions are to be found they
will be found by agreement upon what is basically just and fair. If
we are to have industrial peace which goes beyond a mere armistice
we shall have to discover an ethical code for industrial relations which
will commend itself to the consciences of both labor and management." [8] Brown feels that neither management nor labor is likely

[8] E. A. Brown: "The Church and Industrial Conflict." *Christian Century*, August 8, 1945.
The reader will relate this discussion to what we learned about values in Chapter

to arrive at valid standards of economic justice because of their his
torical biases; that, consequently, some agency like the Church should
provide the ethical insights necessary to the attainment of satisfactory
harmony.

The contrasting value systems of management and labor became
more and more manifest in the strikes following World War II. Sev
eral new concepts of its rights, on the part of labor, have been
emerging. Walter Reuther, head of the United Automobile Workers
advanced the claim that labor has a right to examine the company's
books and then to help decide in what percentages profits are to be
distributed to employees in the form of wage increases. This revolu
tionary principle is not supported by the American Federation of
Labor or by the United Mine Workers, for these organizations insis
that labor should concern itself solely with wages and working con
ditions and leave such matters as prices and profits to management
Management, of course, is strongly opposed to the idea of opening it
books to union scrutiny, convinced that such a step would amount to
according labor the privilege of taking over an essential function of
management, namely, the decision of how much of the profits will be
assigned to wages.

A different approach to the solution of these management-labor con
troversies is that sponsored by Julius Hochman, head of the New York
Joint Board of Dress and Waistmakers Unions, largest componen
of the International Ladies' Garment Workers Union. Hochman is
hailed as the man "responsible for the most important innovation in
collective bargaining in a generation." His policy is based on the
conviction that "good times for the bosses mean good times for the
workers." In a pamphlet entitled "Industry Planning through Col
lective Bargaining," published in 1941, he recommended that in the
renewal of its contract the union ask neither more pay nor a cut in
hours, but, instead, ask for a program of efficiency in production and
in sales promotion. The contract, therefore, embodied an "efficiency
clause" obligating management to insure effective supervision, time
saving procedures, rational routing of work; and a "promotion clause"
in which labor agreed to finance plans to stimulate demand for dresses
This suggestion, startling to both management and labor, has produced
excellent results 'which vindicate, in the garment industry at least

4 and to what we said about bringing our ethical codes up to date in the section on
"Collective Immorality" at the close of Chapter 5. The reader should also keep
this statement of Brown's in mind when we deal in Chapter 20 with the oppor
tunities for leadership beckoning to the Church.

Hochman's philosophy that "only management can assure organized labor that security of status which makes cooperation possible." [9]

II. THE "FOLKLORE OF CAPITALISM"

Many of the problems concerning human relations in the industrial sphere can be understood more clearly by studying industry against the background of our economic culture. Business in the United States is organized and conducted according to the tenets of capitalism. Property rights are highly respected, sometimes even more than human rights, as we noted in Jones' study of Akron cited in Chapter 4. In such cases it seems we revere our economic institutions so much that we lose sight of the human values which are really of supreme importance to us.

In our culture, the conventional business man will believe in the beneficence of free competition, the partnership of capital and labor, the profit motive as a spur to creative endeavor, the sacredness of private property. "We believe in the capitalistic system, as we used to believe in democracy, not as a tool, but as a set of abstract principles to be followed." [10] Many of these formulas which we endorse are fictions, not at all descriptive of actual conditions today. They belong to our economic mythology, persisting because they provide effective weapons for opposing dangerous innovations. Trust in the desirability of free competition, for example, is a naïve faith in a theory that has not worked out too well in practice, a fact that would have been recognized long ago, were we not so infatuated with the shibboleth of "private enterprise." This emotional stake in this slogan has blinded us to serious abuses for which remedial measures have been unduly postponed. Isadore Lubin, Federal Commissioner of Labor Statistics, has described the situation accurately:

For more than 150 years we and other nations have relied on the competitive system to furnish us with the essentials of life. We have assumed that if we were all free to act on our own initiative those who can most effectively meet our needs will come out on top. In the race for economic supremacy we have assumed that the victory would go to the most efficient producer.

We know only too well that it is not necessarily those who produce most efficiently or those who render the greatest service to society who secure the lead in the race for economic returns. All too frequently the honors—profits— go to those who can take the greatest advantage of their fellow men. By

[9] See E. Lyons: "A Remarkable Union—and Union Leader." *Reader's Digest,* April, 1946, condensed from *The New Leader,* April, 1946.
[10] T. W. Arnold: *The Folklore of Capitalism,* p. 45. 1937.

cutting wages, compelling labor to work inhumanly long hours, many a producer has not only weathered economic storms, but has actually profited from them.

And he has usually done so at the expense of his competitor who has refused to stoop to similar tactics. In too many instances the ability to sweat one's labor has supplanted efficiency as the determinant of business success.

Competition, in short, has failed to work in the way we have assumed it to work. Instead of a well-ordered race with well-defined rules which enabled the best man to win, we have had a chaotic system in which the employer with high standards has been forced by unscrupulous competitors to adopt policies detrimental to his workers, his industry, and society as a whole. The plane of business morals has too often been forced far below that of the majority of business and industry. Many an employer has been obliged to yield to rules of business conduct he despises. He has been forced to live a dual existence. Despite indignation at the employment of children, long hours of labor and low wages, he has been compelled to pursue such practices because of the pressure of competition from employers who lack a sense of social responsibility.

Employers with a social conscience are now assured by the Wages-and-Hours Law that they will no longer be compelled to conform to the standards of competitors with blunted social sensibilities. The law does not curtail competitive action. It only determines the manner in which competition shall take place. It seeks to create a situation in which the ideals of the better rather than those of the worst employers shall prevail. It incorporates into law standards which, even though acceptable to the majority, could not be put into effect without governmental authority as long as a handful of men in any given industry refused to conform to them. It aims to establish by law a plane of competition far above that which could be maintained in the absence of government edict.[11]

This enlightening commentary on our economic system calls our attention to a vital principle of institutional behavior, one that is stressed by Allport, namely, that respect for an institution in the abstract may serve to divert attention from behavior in the concrete which does not measure up to professed principles.[12] Some of the staunchest defenders of "free competition" are corporation heads who have used the weapon of monopoly to put their competitors out of business.

III. INDUSTRIAL ORGANIZATION AS A SOCIAL SYSTEM

An industrial organization is a social system. This was the conclusion drawn by the investigators who studied personnel problems in

---

[11] Boston *Herald*, July 19, 1938.
[12] See the discussion of the "Group Mind Fallacy" in Chapter 1.

the Hawthorne Works of the Western Electric Company in Chicago. This research project was originally intended as an experiment to determine "the relation between conditions of work and the incidence of fatigue and monotony among employees." [13] Unexpectedly, the attempt to control the human element in the experimental conditions revealed the necessity of taking into account the personal interrelations among the employees under observation. By steps that we shall trace in more detail, the study of fatigue led to an exploration of the social factors operating in the work situation. The findings could not be understood as long as these social influences were ignored.

When a company is described as a "social system," the term "system" connotes a whole in which each part bears a relation of interdependence to every other part. This concept is a useful one for interpreting the activities of individuals who work as members of a large industrial concern.

An industrial organization performs two functions: creating a product; providing employees with a medium for personal satisfaction. The first is the economic function, evaluated in terms of cost, profit, technical efficiency; the second is a psychological function, evaluated in terms of employee relations, cooperation, and good will between management and worker. These two functions—turning out an article at a profit and promoting happy employee relations—are often treated as if they were separate functions, even antithetical. The Hawthorne study showed that these two industrial problems are intimately related to each other.

Industrial leaders have devoted more attention to improving methods of efficient production than to developing techniques for securing cooperation, apparently oblivious to the fact that "getting people to work together effectively and with satisfaction to themselves" affects the economic operations of the company. The intelligent employer, appreciating the interdependence of technological progress and human relations, will plan his policies with due consideration for both the technical organization and the human organization of the plant.

A. Prestige and Social Equilibrium

The human organization of a plant is a social organization in which individuals, with different backgrounds, combine to achieve a collective purpose. Executives, technical specialists, supervisors, factory workers,

[13] Reprinted by permission of the publishers from F. J. Roethlisberger and W. J. Dickson: *Management and the Worker.* Cambridge, Mass.: Harvard University Press, 1939. P. 3.

and office workers interact with one another in carrying out their respective assignments.   From these associations definite patterns of personal interaction evolve, prescribed by various differences in status.

Some relationships fall into routine patterns, such as the relationship between superior and subordinate or between office worker and shop worker. Individuals conscious of their membership in certain groups are reacting in certain accepted ways to other individuals representing other groups.   Behavior varies according to the stereotyped conceptions of relationship.   The worker, for example, behaves toward his foreman in one way, toward his first-line supervisor in another way, and toward his fellow worker in still another.   People holding the rank of inspector expect a certain kind of behavior from the operators—the operators from the inspectors.   Now these relationships, as is well known from everyday experiences, are finely shaded and sometimes become complicated.   When a person is in the presence of his supervisor alone he usually acts differently from the way he acts when his supervisor's supervisor is also present.   Likewise, his supervisor acts toward him alone quite differently from the way he behaves when his own supervisor is also there.[14]

These subtle distinctions are based on social evaluations through which definite values become attached to individuals and to groups performing certain functions.   The nature of their respective tasks is a criterion for ranking individuals in a scale of social prestige.   Thus, each person has a definite status in the organization.   This hierarchy is maintained by a state of social equilibrium.   Any move on the part of the management which affects an individual's place in this equilibrium, by altering the status of the worker, will be resented by the worker as unjust and unfair.

It is very important to comprehend the significance of this process of social evaluation among the employees, for the desire to maintain rank explains many reactions encountered among the workers.   This observation describes the essential discovery made in the Hawthorne study.

Every item and event in the industrial environment becomes an object of a system of sentiments.   According to this way of looking at things, material goods, physical events, wages, hours of work, etc., cannot be treated as things in themselves.   Instead they have to be interpreted as carriers of social value. The meanings which any person in an industrial organization assigns to the events and objects in his environment are often determined by the social situation in which the events and objects occur.   The significance to an em-

[14] Roethlisberger and Dickson, *op. cit.*, p. 555.

ployee of a double-pedestal desk, of a particular kind of pencil, of a handset telephone is determined by the social setting in which these objects appear. If people with double-pedestal desks supervise people with single-pedestal desks, then double-pedestal desks become symbols of status or prestige in the organization. As patterns of behavior become crystallized, every object in the environment tends to take on a particular social significance. It becomes easy to tell a person's social place in the organization by the objects which he wears and carries and which surround him. In these terms it can be seen how the introduction of a technical change may also involve for an individual or a group of individuals the loss of certain prestige symbols and, as a result, have a demoralizing effect.[15]

B. SENTIMENTS

The "logic of sentiments" expresses the values of the informal organization; the logic of cost and efficiency, the values of the formal organization. Business has been conducted too much on the basis of the latter logic, as if the worker were actuated solely by economic motives. The Hawthorne research demonstrated the error of assuming that the worker is interested primarily in making money. The influence of sentiments pertaining to social relations, instead, proves to be the paramount consideration in determining employee reactions. Whether a given policy is going to cause satisfaction or dissatisfaction among the workers will depend largely upon how that policy affects each individual's position in the social organization of the company, his sentiments about his status as related to the status of his fellow employees, and his opportunities for getting the emotional returns which he has come, by temperament and past social conditioning, to expect from his job, as a member of the company and as a member of the community outside the plant. The worker has his own ideas about the function of his occupation, ideas that he shares with the men who labor with him in his own particular group. Some of these sentiments are:

(1) You should not turn out too much work. If you do, you are a "rate-buster."

(2) You should not turn out too little work. If you do, you are a "chiseler."

(3) You should not tell a supervisor anything that will react to the detriment of an associate. If you do, you are a "squealer."

(4) You should not attempt to maintain social distance or act officious. If you are an inspector, for example, you should not act like one.[16]

[15] *Ibid.*, p. 557.
[16] *Ibid.*, p. 522.

Thus each group exercises social control over the output of its members. Sarcasm, "binging" (striking a person on the upper arm), and ridicule are used to discipline nonconformists who dare to transgress the code.

Each employee possesses a system of sentiments that reflect the social organization of the company. This organization involves a class stratification in which each employee's rank is defined. Status depends on various factors, such as sex, length of service, office or shop duties. Office workers are differentiated from shopworkers by method of payment, conditions and hours of work. Supervisors are distinguished from workers by method of payment, privileges, and duties. Old-timers get the preference in hourly rates and chances for promotion (seniority rights). These distinctions in status are recognized all down the line. Inspectors are known to be superior to operators by means of various outward signs. When wiremen and soldermen, during the experiment, left their jobs to be interviewed, they appeared, without exception, in shirt sleeves or sweaters, whereas inspectors came dressed in coats and vests. This matter of dress is very significant. Foremen wore business suits with coats and vests, the vest being optional. Section chiefs wore vests but not coats, white shirts, neckties. Operators wore neither coats nor vests, with the choice open for a white shirt unbuttoned at the throat, perhaps with a tie dangling loosely at an angle. These differences which appear so trivial are fraught with meaning because they reflect the social status of the individual in the company. And this matter of status becomes even more significant when we learn that there is a close correlation between occupational status in the company and social status in the community. Hours of work and wages are clearly more than economic matters; to the worker they are tied up with his whole system of values. Thus the working environment is permeated with social significance.

C. Job Satisfaction

Job satisfaction, Hoppock found in his survey of the workers residing in New Hope, Pennsylvania, is connected with family relationships, relative status in the community, pleasant relations with superiors and associates. A person is satisfied with his work if his labors bring him a sense of success, self-respect, admiration from others. "Self-esteem means more to most individuals than money . . . when they seek riches they do so principally because of the effect that wealth has upon the respect in which they are held by others, and consequently upon the respect with which they feel justified in regarding themselves." [17]   A successful attorney answered in the negative when asked, "Are you satisfied with the effect of your job on your social position?" and a Negro deliveryman replied in the affirmative to the same question.   Obviously the subjective factor was more decisive than external circumstances in determining their respective attitudes.   The deliveryman had been employed for fourteen years and during that period there was "nothing he ever disliked about his job."   At one time his pay had been $25 a week.   During the Depression it was reduced to $21.   This cut did not disturb him seriously because he was still getting higher pay than his father and not less than his half-brothers and sisters.   He enjoyed his work because he liked the people around town he delivered to.   He preferred his job to his recreations, " 'Cause," he explained, "I meet different people, learn lots of things." In commenting on this case, Hoppock says: "The significant fact, of course, is not that [he] earns $21 a week but that he is satisfied with $21 a week.   Apparently neither high earnings nor exalted social status is essential to contentment, in this case at least, although the man's relative status in his own circle of friends may really be superior." [18]

Many factors enter into the derivation of satisfaction from a job: earnings, hours of work, variety, freedom from too much supervision, tangible results, opportunities for advancement, competition, pleasure in skillful performance, security, adaptation to unpleasant aspects of the work, means of remedying or expressing annoyances, appreciation, social status.   This last factor is certainly one of the most important, according to authorities on industrial morale.   Whiting Williams concurs in this judgment, as a result of his intimate associations with the workingman.   He says:

Everywhere among the workers a man determines the social standing of himself and his family, not so much by the earning power as by the *nature* of his job. . . .

It is impossible, therefore, to judge the effect of either wage or other conditions of work apart from the relationships the work permits with other persons. What every worker knows is this: that sooner or later the final joy of his work is settled, not by him, nor by his employer, but by the social standing awarded him by his fellow citizens.[19]

Young people, in choosing a vocation, are considerably influenced by the social status attached to a given line of work.   Indisposed to

[17] R. Hoppock: *Job Satisfaction*, p. 34.   Harper & Brothers, 1935.
[18] *Ibid.*, pp. 72-73.
[19] W. Williams: *Mainsprings of Men*, pp. 58, 62.   Charles Scribner's Sons, 1925.

soil their hands in manual toil, many youths prepare themselves for white-collar jobs, only to be disillusioned when they discover later that there are not enough of these "clean" jobs to go around.   "Clearly the majority of American youth are showing conventional vocational interests and plans which are so out of proportion to economic reality that the work life begins with disappointment. . . .   Dissatisfaction is a major phenomenon throughout adult work life." [20]   In view of such conditions, it is encouraging to note that many high schools are beginning to recognize their responsibility for educating more realistically the large majority of youngsters who are not going on to college but directly into factory or office.   Pupils are being advised to survey the seasonal and long-term trends in the labor market so that they may fit themselves for lines of work in which there are good chances of steady employment.

Job dissatisfaction is more prevalent than it should be.   Hoppock found among the inhabitants of New Hope, Pennsylvania, that 15 per cent did not like their jobs; 66 per cent got more satisfaction from their jobs than from their spare-time activities.   Reviewing 32 investigations of job satisfaction, he reported that two-thirds of the studies showed less than one-third of employees dissatisfied, and concluded that "most people really like their jobs." [21]   (One-third discontented seems tragic to me.)   New Hopers are not typical, however, if we are to accept the authority of *Fortune's* "Survey on Occupational Contentment." To the question: "If you could go back to the age of eighteen and start life over again, would you choose a different career or occupation?" the following trends were noted:

Of the total group studied, 41 per cent would have chosen a different career, 39.2 per cent were satisfied with their jobs; and the remaining group were uncertain.

The figures are about the same for the 20-40 age group, though the number expressing dissatisfaction is slightly smaller.   Among those over 40, a slightly greater number express regret over their present status as compared with the younger group.

Even among the prosperous, only 55.4 per cent are satisfied with their careers.   The figure for professional people is 53.3 per cent.   Among the poor, half would have preferred different jobs; 30.2 per cent seemed satisfied. Factory laborers show the most pronounced dissatisfaction, 61.3 per cent expressing discontent.

[20] See H. Bell: *Youth Tell Their Story*, pp. 134, 436.   American Council on Education, 1938.

[21] Hoppock: *op. cit.*, pp. 6, 8, 18.

Pacific Coast residents express more satisfaction than those in the Mountain States, and as expected, discontentment is greatest in large cities, least in rural areas.[22]

One of the chief problems in social science is to discover political and industrial techniques for providing every citizen with the opportunity to work and the privilege of contributing to the national economy, without resort to Nazi-type tyranny or Fascist regimentation. Unemployment weakens a nation and brings untold suffering to the man without a job; its psychological consequences are devastating. Hard times impress upon us the psychological values found in work. Overstreet has called attention to the human need for a job:

> Only the sheer inability to find work seems to have brought us to the realization of the profound satisfactions that we normally find in work. Curiously enough, when we are busily on the job, we usually fail to be conscious of the deep sub-current of satisfaction that runs through our life. For the most part we give no credit for our happiness to work itself. But when work goes, we know that the tragedy is more than economic. It is psychological. It strikes at the center of our personality. It takes from us something that rightly belongs to every self-respecting human being.[23]

Here is a need that must be provided for in a healthy industrial civilization. When an able-bodied man wants to work, organized efforts should be made to help him find some way to satisfy this desire, for the man who wants to work deserves every encouragement. This is a primary obligation in the reconversion period as we shift from war to peace.

IV. CRITIQUE OF OUR ECONOMIC CULTURE

We are inclined to believe in "the permanence and normality of the prevailing business system." [24] Even before World War I there were many,

> not themselves suffering conspicuously from the system, who challenged its beneficence and permanence, in the name of justice, economy, and the best and highest interests of mankind as a whole. Since the war many more have come to the conclusion that business as now conducted is not merely unfair, exceedingly wasteful, and often highly inexpedient from a social standpoint,

[22] *Fortune* Survey, January, 1938.
[23] H. A. Overstreet: "When Work Is Like Play." *Occupations*, 1935, 13, 389-394.
[24] J. H. Robinson: *The Human Comedy*, p. 223. Harper & Brothers, 1937.

but that from an historical standpoint it is intensely unusual, unstable, complicated, unreliable, and temporary. It may prove to be the chief eccentricity of our age.[25]

Robinson was thinking of the chronic distress inflicted upon us by periodic depressions, of starvation in the midst of plenty, of poverty in the midst of abundance. The remarkable thing is the tolerance for needless suffering that so many people develop. The have-nots, during economic crises particularly, are often praised for their patience and courage in enduring their lot without complaint. Maybe it would be more conducive to their well-being if they were not so easily habituated to coming out of the short end of the horn. Thoughtful people question whether a system makes sense which permits the few to corner more wealth than they need while the many who create that wealth, live on, poorly fed, poorly housed, poorly clothed, poorly educated. More people would evaluate our economic order in terms of its assets and its shortcomings were it not for the fact that our industrial behavior is institutionalized and because it is institutionalized we are inclined to accept it as the only fair way of conducting business. Negative adaptation (habituation) renders us blind to the defects that might be remedied to make our system more fit to survive.

A. Motivation for Work

As a psychologist the author's principal interest is in describing how people react to present conditions. It is not his function to advocate any particular system: capitalism, state socialism, or communism. Nor is it his function to solve our economic or industrial problems. It *is* his function to investigate the psychological aspects of our business institutions, to find out whether our setup might be improved as an instrument for promoting human satisfaction.

What are the motives that make us want to work?

1. DESIRE FOR ESTEEM

We work in order to acquire property, the conventional basis of esteem. The purpose of ownership is really to win emulation, not to achieve mere subsistence. The psychological need for owning property is insatiable, particularly so in people whose self-esteem is insecure. Since the accumulation of property is a means of acquiring honorable status in our social hierarchy, aggressiveness, greed, "predatory efficiency" are highly valued, though euphemistically labeled as

[25] *Ibid.*, p. 224.

shrewdness and cleverness. The typical American can never get enough money to satisfy him, mainly because wealth is a value for him in that it permits him to indulge in display, conspicuous consumption, and conspicuous leisure. One example of the way money fulfills psychological needs is the collecting of rare objects, such as paintings or stamps—a conventional means of demonstrating superiority. Twenty-five thousand dollars spent for a rare stamp ought to impress almost anybody.

People expect to gain from their work a satisfying status, knowing that this prestige will spread from the job to relations in the larger community.

Most of us want the satisfaction that comes from being accepted and recognized as people of worth by our friends and work associates. Money is only a small part of this social recognition. The way we are greeted by our boss, being asked to help a newcomer, being asked to keep an eye on a difficult operation, being given a job requiring special skill—all of these are acts of social recognition. They tell us how we stand in our work group. We all want tangible evidence of our social importance.[26]

2. THE "PROFIT MOTIVE"

Much has been said about the profit motive as the fundamental incentive for working in a capitalistic society. Some people have even gone so far as to claim that the desire for profit is inherent in human nature, that it is responsible for America's preeminent prosperity, that it is the inspiration for invention and the spur to industrial enterprise. Before we comment upon these claims, we should clarify in our own minds just what is meant by "profit," for the term is employed loosely to cover all sorts of income: wages, salaries, bonuses, commissions, fees, honorariums, gifts, royalties, wagers, prizes, graft, barter, sales, rent, interest, dividends. Some of these sources of revenue may be properly designated as "profit," some of them hardly belong in that category. Salary and rent are not "profit" in the same sense. There should be a differentiation between income derived from personal effort and income derived from the ownership of property, for surely "this is a distinction of incalculable social significance." [27] The word "profit" should be used only when reference is being made to dividends accruing to owners and investors as the surplus available after costs of

[26] Reprinted by permission of the publishers from F. J. Roethlisberger: *Management and Morale*. Cambridge, Mass.: Harvard University Press, 1941. P. 24.

[27] K. Page: "What Is the Profit Motive?" *Christian Century*, March 20, 1935.

operation have been deducted from the gross income. "Profit" and "income" are not at all synonymous. Most of us work in the expectation of earning some income by our efforts, very few of us expect to derive profits. Maybe the large majority of workers labor in the vague hope that some day they may become owners and live on the profits of their investments, but more immediately the source of their daily inspiration is the pay envelope with enough cash in it to pay the grocer and the landlord. The "profit motive" is a misnomer, a slogan that is more useful for rallying resistance against change than accurate for describing human motivation. The "profit motive" is becoming a myth, according to some authorities, because the government is levying heavier taxes, fixing wage levels, and in general taking the profits out of the "profit motive."

Money is not so important as personal status anyhow in the eyes of the worker. Employees of the Hawthorne Works restricted their output when a new system of group piecework was imposed, even though their "slow-down" meant lowering their individual earnings. The workers slowed down because they resented the interference of management with their established interpersonal relationships. The men had been functioning in four different social groups. The new wage-payment system which was introduced no longer recognized the important distinctions involved in these "four different ways of life" and the men cut down production—and their *pay*—to force management to alter its policy.[28] "Social motives, far more than expectations of economic gain, determine individual action."[29]

Money affects our personalities in manifold ways, especially if we think we are not getting our share of it, or at least not as much as we need to maintain ourselves on a standard of living to which we feel our personal worth entitles us. Pressey and his collaborators sum up a few significant observations concerning the relation of economics and psychology under the heading of "Wealth, Income—and Psychology":

In conclusion, three points must here be noted. In the first place, the data on wealth and income exhibit in striking fashion the fact of individual differences. From the subnormal shiftless hobo to the keen, acquisitive driving, hard business leader, there is an enormous range *and* variety of abilities, attitudes, motives, potentialities. Knowledge of a person's economic status is a very important datum about him. In the second place, there are exhibited the facts on which are based most discontents, jealousies, strivings

[28] See Roethlisberger: *op. cit.*, pp. 57-58.
[29] *Ibid.*, p. 52.

nd also most class antagonisms and solidarities and snobberies. Study of
notivation and social psychology might take a beginning from such facts.
inally, these data show an extraordinary range as regards opportunities for
uman development; and they show large numbers of the total population to
e seriously handicapped and restricted in opportunities for realization of
heir total potentialities of ability and personality.[30]

3. OTHER MOTIVES

Why do people work, then, if the profit motive is not the dominant
nspiration? Most people work because they prefer to do something
ather than nothing (provided working does not involve excessive
train or frustration); because they fear the social censure which is
directed against the idler and the loafer; because they want money as
n instrument for getting things they desire: food, clothes, shelter,
ducation, entertainment, power, self-approval, and the approbation
of others. Some people enjoy their work because it gives them a "psy-
hic income," satisfaction in doing something useful, as in the case
of George Washington Carver, Tuskeegee scientist, who did so much to
rehabilitate the South with no thought for his own financial gain, or
George Herbert Palmer, Harvard philosopher, who said he would
gladly pay for the privilege of teaching, were he in a position to do so.
Men devote their lives to research, spurred in the main by curiosity,
as was Ehrlich, the discoverer of "magic bullets." In medical school,
his professor inquired as to what he was doing in the "lab" when he
was obviously not carrying out a class assignment, and Ehrlich replied,
"*Ich probiere*," which freely translated, meant, "Oh, just fooling
around, trying to find out something." He "probed" most of his life;
the discovery of "606" was his reward. Many are the motives that
impel people to work. The economic motive is only one of them;
the "profit motive" is of minor importance, if we are using our terms
accurately.

B. Effects of Our Culture

Among the psychological effects of our economic culture there are
three that are of particular social significance.

1. PREEMINENCE OF BUSINESSMEN

The first is the preeminence of businessmen in our society, men who
distinguish themselves in manufacture, trade, or finance. They dom-

---

[30] S. L. Pressey, J. E. Janney, R. G. Kuhlen: *Life: a Psychological Survey*, p. 64.
Harper & Brothers, 1939.

inate our politics, our education, and our religion, just as in earlie
times leadership belonged to the religious or to the military castes.

Most religious institutions make easy terms with business, and, far fro
interfering with it or its teachings, on the whole cordially support it.   Bus
ness has its philosophy, which it holds to be based upon the immutable trai
of human nature and as identical with morality and patriotism.[31]

2. PREOCCUPATION WITH EARNING A LIVING

A second effect of our business culture is to make work predominan
among our interests.   The gospel of diligence keeps us plugging an
the devil finds no mischief for our busy hands.   Recently a tow
official forbade the erection of benches in a park on the ground tha
they would only serve to encourage idleness.   We Americans do no
know how to loaf without feeling guilty, as Lin Yutang reminde
us in his *Importance of Living* (1937).   We toil on, devoting th
better part of our lives to material things, designing things, manufac
turing them, selling them, owning them, using them, discarding them
destroying them, repairing them, until we find there is little lef
over for anything else.

Industry itself has come to hold a position of exclusive predominanc
among human interests, which no single interest, and least of all the provisio
of the material means of existence, is fit to occupy.   Like a hypochondria
who is so absorbed in the processes of his own digestion that he goes to th
grave before he has begun to live, industrialized communities neglect the ver
objects for which it is worth while to acquire riches in their feverish preoccu
pation with the means by which riches can be acquired.[32]

When grown-ups get together in the evening, the women talk abou
diseases and the men discuss their work.   We do not know when to
quit our labors, or how to leave ourselves time for enriching our lives
with broader, non-commercial interests.   In other words, we spend
so much of ourselves in earning a living that we have little time or
energy left over to enjoy reading, hobbies, music, travel.

3. CONCENTRATION OF POWER

A third consequence of our economic system is the concentration of
power in the hands of a few persons of superior intelligence who excel, among other things, in aggressiveness, greed, and cunning, by vir-

[31] Robinson: *op. cit.,* p. 222.
[32] R. H. Tawney: *The Acquisitive Society,* pp. 183-184.   1920.

ie of which qualities they are able to amass more worldly goods than
ieir competitors. Business, like the game of "Monopoly," is a contest
i which the participants see who can get hold of the most property;
ie person who can corner most of the available wealth is declared the
inner with all the honors appertaining thereto. When one per cent of
ie population come to own sixty per cent of the nation's wealth and
ome thirteen per cent corner ninety per cent of it, a situation is created
hich is not conducive to the greatest happiness of the greatest num-
er of people. Lundberg called attention to some of the social conse-
uences that follow from this concentration of control in some "sixty
imilies." [33] A more accurate study made by the Securities and Ex-
iange Commission found:

Of an estimated 8,500,000 U.S. stockholders, less than 75,000 (.06% of the
opulation) own fully one-half of all corporate stock held by individuals.
More than 80% of individual stockholders had a dividend income of less
ian $500, probably received not much over 10% of the total dividend income
f individuals.
The 13 most potent family groups' holdings were worth $2,700,000,000;
omprised over 8% of the stock of the 200 corporations surveyed.[34]

'his concentration of power is not an ideal arrangement for anybody
oncerned, for as Lumley says: "Ideally, social control would be in
ie hands and the interests of the inclusive group whatever it is; prac-
ically, however, it is in the hands of, and often in the interests of,
ome few members who have usurped power and know how to use
t." [35] The government's inquiry into the salaries of the executives of
0,000 corporations revealed conditions that carry many implications
or social psychology. It is more than a matter of economic concern
hat a steel corporation paid an executive $5,497,000 in five years—
ven though Thorndike maintains that such high pay is deserved.[36]
The fact that a bank president could receive as much as $1,700,000 in
year," states Odum, "had some social bearing upon the thousands of
american citizens who had lost their savings and investments." [37] It is
f interest, in this connection, to note that rich people give away large
ortions of their wealth to endow universities, hospitals, and charity

[33] F. Lundberg: *America's 60 Families.* 1937.
[34] "The Distribution of Ownership in the 200 Largest Non-Financial Corpora-
ions." 1940.
[35] F. E. Lumley: *Means of Social Control,* pp. 13-14. 1925.
[36] See E. L. Thorndike: *Human Nature and the Social Order,* p. 95. 1940.
[37] H. W. Odum: *American Social Problems,* p. 328. 1939. See especially Chapter
0, "Industry and Work."

organizations, thus getting satisfaction from a sense of benevolence–
and perhaps a sense of superiority. The question naturally arises
Would it be more satisfying to more people if the rules of the gam
were modified in such a way as to steer funds into worth-while ente
prises without routing them through the detour of a few plutocra
who may or may not know how—who may or may not want—to di
burse their capital for the highest benefits of the general public? S
much depends upon the wisdom of the benefactor's judgment or hi
sense of social responsibility. Certainly a man's ability to make a fo
tune is no guarantee of his ability to use that money intelligently.

V. HUMAN VALUES IN OUR INDUSTRIAL
CIVILIZATION

Industry has been developed more in the interest of efficiency tha
in the interest of emotional satisfaction. Technological improv
ments in machinery and speed-up plans have been geared to a deman
for increased profits rather than to desire to promote human happ
ness. Industrial management has generally exploited the worker
efforts and ignored his personal interests.

A new concept of management is emerging, one in which the em
ployer sees production in relation to the personal satisfaction his em
ployees may be deriving from their work. "The true business leade
is not merely a clever manipulator of men. He is an interpreter a
well as an organizer and a supervisor; that is, he helps subordinate
understand the meaning of their labors by explaining company policie
to them, by sharing common problems with them." [38] If new mach
inery is to be installed, the intelligent manager, aware of his respons
bilities to his men, reeducates the workers, endeavors to find jobs fo
persons who have to be let out, and changes equipment gradually be
cause he realizes that sudden changes precipitate unrest. Throug
the whole process of installing new machines and readjusting relation
ships, he knows that direct personal contact between management an
labor will serve to secure cooperation. Smith and Nyman express
growing conviction when they state that there has been too much em
phasis on technological changes as such and far too little on the ne
and more exacting task of management. What we need, they say, i
rapport established by fairness, frankness, and friendliness on the pa
of management. [39]

---

[38] H. W. Hepner: *Human Relations in Changing Industry*, p. 32. 1938.
[39] See E. D. Smith and R. C. Nyman: *Technology and Labor: a Study of the Hu
man Problems of Labor Savings*. 1939.

Smith Johnson exemplifies this sort of friendly management in his ubber factory in Middlefield, Ohio. His talk-it-over policy has achieved

he happy kind of labor relations that efficiency experts never even dream of. . . . He tries to get every workman to understand the product he's turning)ut, what it is used for, the cost, the relation of good workmanship and labor osts to more orders and steady work. . . Several [workers reported] . . . hat they had been offered more money elsewhere but they'd rather have their)lant's friendly atmosphere and steady work. . . . [Smith Johnson] believes hat labor relations are bound to be harmonious as long as both workman and)oss can continue to regard each other as human beings.[40]

Industrial psychology is devoting more attention to the human relationships involved in business. There is a real need for more stress)n the human side of work, as shown by the Hawthorne study. (See)p. 732-36.) In that study the investigators ran into problems of motivation which they had not anticipated. They started out to explore the effects of working conditions, especially the influence of fatigue and monotony on production. Much to their surprise, they found sentiments more important than amount of pay or hours of work. By merely asking the employees to help in the investigation, the persons in charge of the study made the workers feel important. The opportunity to cooperate in an enterprise whose purpose was made clear to them, gave their jobs a new meaning. Under the experimental conditions which were set up by the investigators, the workers were given more freedom than they were accustomed to and they responded with a keener sense of their own responsibility for self-discipline and teamwork. Morale improved. Each worker began to see that he belonged to a group in which he had a vital part to play, a function to discharge that gave him a sense of importance and a feeling of security. He realized his performance counted for something and this realization enabled him to gain more satisfaction from his labors.

Interviewers at the Hawthorne plant asked the employees to tell them what they felt they had a right to kick about, what they thought of their jobs, their working conditions, their bosses, and their company. The interviewers had prepared a questionnaire with great care but they found the workers were often inclined to wander off the subject on to grievances that seemed rather trivial to the interviewers. After a while the interviewers woke up to the fact that these digres-

[40] D. Wharton: "They Call Him Smith." *This Week Magazine,* April 20, 1941. Copyright, 1941, by United Newspapers Magazine Corp.

sions were the most important data they were gathering. So they laid aside their questionnaires. The workers confessed that they felt a lot better for getting their complaints off their chests and the management discovered that the employees had made valuable suggestions for improving plant operation. The chance to have a say about the way things were being run made the workers feel that it was *their* company, that they were working *with,* not merely for, the management.

In general practice, the main objective of employers has been efficiency. Consequently, relatively little heed has been given to the maintenance of cooperation.[41] The Hawthorne study uncovered the great need for the development of collaboration. It became clear that working together may be a subject for research as well as a topic for exhortation. The value of securing such cooperation among the workers was discovered more or less by accident. The investigators, aiming to study the physical conditions governing output, had to consult the operators concerning the changes to be introduced. In the very act of taking the workers into their confidence, the researchers altered the entire experimental situation and uncovered by chance a principle far more important than anything they had originally been looking for, namely, that production can be improved by the impetus of friendlier cooperation between management and the worker.

"Our technological development in the past hundred years has been tremendous. Our methods of handling people are still archaic." [42] Industrial leaders have been blind apparently to the elementary fact that workers are human beings, governed more by sentiment than by logic. Because they crave understanding more than economic gain, their feelings should always be taken into consideration in determining company policies. This means that management must inform itself constantly as to how the workers feel about their boss, their jobs, their company. This end can only be achieved by keeping the avenues of communication wide open from top to bottom, from bottom to top in the organization.

The enlightened management will see clearly that efficiency is an inadequate ideal in itself, and that technology, even when it is designed to help the worker, may do much harm indirectly. An example of this principle may be cited from the Hawthorne study:

Carefully thought out wage plans are intended to reimburse the worker with a wage proportional to his efforts. The simplification of his job, whether

[41] See Roethlisberger: *op. cit.,* p. xix.
[42] *Ibid.,* p. 26.

hrough a change in process, division of labor, or elimination of random
novements, is supposed to make his work easier and less fatiguing. If fatigue
s eliminated, the worker, theoretically, can produce more and can thereby
arn more money.

Now it happens frequently that these logical plans to promote efficiency and
ollaboration do not work out as intended. From the point of view of senti-
nents, they involve consequences which sometimes defeat the logical purposes
f the plan as conceived. Let me point out some of these possible non-logical
onsequences. When skill is divorced from the job at the work level and
ut in the hands of a group of technologists, a situation is created whereby the
vorker is put in a position of having to accommodate himself continually to
hanges which he does not initiate . . . many of these changes deprive him
f those very things which give meaning and significance to his work. In
he language of the sentiments, it is as if the worker were told that his own
ndividual skills, his acquired routines of work, his cultural traditions of
raftsmanship, his personal interrelations, had absolutely no value. Now,
uch non-logical consequences have devastating effects on the individual.
They make him feel insecure, frustrated, or exasperated.[43]

For a long time management has assumed that if technological effi-
iency is taken care of, the human factor will take care of itself. This
onviction still prevails. It is made evident in the common attitude
hat

rom the economic viewpoint most personnel people are considered super-
umeraries. Most of their duties are concerned with the routine carrying
ut of policies that have been settled by other groups or with settling as best
hey can human problems that have already been created. There is a tend-
ncy in modern industrial organization to separate the economic function
rom all the social interrelations and to believe that in the settlement of eco-
omic ·problems it is not necessary to consider any other aspect of human
rganization.[44]

What we need is a management that combines a view of the economic
vith a view of the social functions of the workers. Such a management
vill have found the answer to this question: "How can a plant be or-
anized so as to fulfill its technical objective of manufacturing a
roduct at a minimum cost and at the same time fulfill a social func-
ion of providing for its employees a socially significant way of life?" [45]

Employers in general are not aware of the need for improving hu-
nan relations in industry.

[43] *Ibid.*, pp. 36-37.   [44] *Ibid.*, pp. 53-54.   [45] *Ibid.*, p. 112.

No automobile manufacturer would be insulted or hurt if it were suggested that this year's model of his product could be improved; yet he resents an implication that all is not what it might be in the area of human relations. He would lead us to believe that either everything is perfect or there is a strike. Just because the employees of a plant are not striking, everything in the human relations area is entirely satisfactory.[46]

Roethlisberger deplores this stupid oversight of the human problem in industry, for the truth is that in any business organization there are numerous tensions. These strains produce an unbalance which is bound to interfere with efficiency and personal satisfaction. A constant adjustment is required "between what is being asked of the individual and what he is asking of the situation. . . ."[47] Such a dynamic concept of employer-employee relations provides a frame of reference for clarifying the role of the human factor in business.

"The executive may *believe* that morale is high, and that his plant has no sore spots in it, but without some quantitative measure of morale, he cannot be sure."[48] In order to obtain definite information on the mental condition of the workers, industrial leaders should institute a definite system of measuring morale, with these minimum requirements in mind:

1. Information about attitudes of employees and their working conditions
   a. Opportunity for the employee to express his feelings on a large number of specific points (i.e., his relations to other employees, supervisors, hours, pay, etc.).
   b. Determination of the relation of these specific feelings to morale
   c. Calling of attention to specific "sore spots," both in the plant and in specific situations.
2. The opening of a wealth of material for the use of scientists, training of supervisors, etc.
3. Production of a healthy, cathartic effect upon the individuals studied [giving them an opportunity to get their troubles off their chests].[49]

Indirect methods of measuring morale include such indices as labor disorders, labor turnover, absences, grievances, employee representation

---

[46] *Ibid.*, p. 131.   [47] *Ibid.*, p. 120.

[48] A. B. Blankenship: "Methods of Measuring Industrial Morale," Chapter 15 in *Industrial Conflict: a Psychological Interpretation*, G. W. Hartmann and T. Newcomb, Editors. The Dryden Press, 1939.

[49] *Ibid.*

nd output at work. Direct methods involve observation, clinical in-
erviews, and questionnaires. Exit interviews, to find out why workers
.re leaving a company, have proved especially fruitful in uncovering
ources of poor morale—and in preventing men from quitting. The
py system is not recommended as a technique of observation. Heed
nust be given to details, as little things may make a great difference
n morale. Workers' attitudes have been found to be specific rather
han general. Their attitudes, according to Schultz, are not so much
:oncerned with management policies as with personalized simple things
.bout the job, specific factors in the work situation affecting their
norale, more emotional than factual in nature.[50]

The technique of ascertaining occupational morale may be illustrated
)y describing the approach used by the Houser Associates of New York
3ity. Under their auspices all employees of a given company answer
elf-administering, objective questionnaires consisting of sixty to eighty
eparate questions, dealing with general attitude toward the company
)r employer, with attitudes toward pay, hours, working conditions,
.upervision, the kind of work done, and a variety of other specific as-
)ects of the job situation. As an independent research organization,
he Associates promise anonymity to the employees by assuring them
hat the answered questionnaires will remain in the possession of the
'outside" organization, that no one connected with their company will
:ver see them, and that the report to their company will show only
'counts of the answers" and no individual replies. Sample questions:

Are there other companies in which you would rather work at the same
:arnings if you could get a job for which you feel equally qualified?
( ) I would rather work in *any* of the others.
( ) I would rather work in *almost any* of the others.
( ) *Some* of the others.
( ) *Very few* of the others.
( ) *None* of the others.

When there is a better job vacant, how often do you feel that the best-
qualified person gets promoted to the vacancy?
( ) Rarely.
( ) Sometimes.
( ) Usually.
( ) Almost always.
( ) Always.

[50] See R. S. Schultz: "Psychology in Industry." *Personnel Journal*, 1937, 16, 1-4.

If you had any cause for dissatisfaction, what would your chances be of getting a fair hearing and a square deal?

( ) Very little chance, if any.
( ) Poor.
( ) Fair.
( ) Reasonably good.
( ) Very good.

The large majority of workers who have filled out these questionnaires have attained morale scores above 50, the theoretical midpoint on the scale. This favorable showing is due, in part, to the fact that the sample has been representative largely of the "better" companies where considerable attention is devoted to personnel and industrial relations. It is likely, too, that the average worker develops a bias in favor of his own company. Noteworthy is the fact that larger variations in morale score occur between departments in the same company than between companies. This variation holds true even when the comparable departments are performing essentially the same operation for the same pay, with identical hours. The difference in morale from department to department depends principally upon the sort of person who is the supervisor, for the personality of the immediate boss constitutes a "tremendously important factor in the determination of employee morale." [51] Other findings include these pertinent observations:

> The quality of immediate supervision . . . appears to create a mental set which carries over to and influences attitudes on factors of the job situation which are not controlled by the supervisor. . . . In the selection of its supervisors business has paid far too little attention to qualifications for personnel administration. . . . The results fail to show any high relationship between morale scores and type of work done, nor does there seem to be any significant correlation between morale and general wage level. . . . The average morale score increases with the amount of responsibility involved. . . . In the majority of situations, indeed, factors such as fair treatment of grievances, credit for suggestions, and consideration on the part of the immediate supervisor have proved to be more highly associated with morale than are pay and hours.[52]

One important reason why management has overlooked the emotional aspects of industrial life is the conventional attitude that it is unbecoming for a manager to indulge in sentiment.

[51] R. L. Hull and Arthur Kolstad: "Morale on the Job," Chapter 17 in *Civilian Morale*, G. Watson (Editor). Houghton Mifflin Company, 1942.
[52] *Ibid.*

It is interesting to note that in business today, particularly in manufacturing organizations, it is not considered quite appropriate for the executive to indulge in statements of sentiment when talking to his employees and fellow-associates. This form of behavior is the province of his salesforce when appealing to a particular customer, or when talking to the public on the air, or through other mediums of advertising. With regard to employer-employee relations, however, the executive code dictates that employers should interact with their employees merely on the basis of fact. This code has led to a curious state of affairs. It has blinded some executives to what is going on around them. It has forced some into a position of trying to handle matters of sentiment as if they were matters of fact. And when matters of sentiment so blatantly arise that even the most obtuse cannot fail to label them for what they are, they have no techniques for dealing with them.[53]

Temple Burling, in a discussion of "Mental Hygiene in Business and Industry," also notes that American businessmen are a little ashamed of their humanitarian impulses. Speaking for himself, he confesses that his function as a physician in an industrial organization is to promote efficiency—and to help individuals.

I am very glad that this is so. If it were not, I should be able to get no real satisfaction from my job. The point of this is that I believe that most business executives really feel much the same way, but it is not good form at the present time to admit it. H. L. Mencken and Sinclair Lewis and the rest of that tribe did such a thorough job of debunking business idealism a decade and a half ago that businessmen of the present day are afraid to admit that interest in the welfare of their employees can have any motive *in addition* to that of pure profit-seeking, lest they be thought hypocritical.

I think it is hypocritical to pretend that the profit motive is not reinforced by simple human interest in other people. I think this is important, because unwillingness on the part of a business leader to admit that he is interested in making his plant a pleasant place in which to work—not only because it will increase profits, but also because he himself, like his employees, gets satisfaction out of being connected with a pleasant place in which to work—interferes with realistically thinking through methods of achieving that purpose.

I am not for a moment decrying economic motives. People study medicine for economic motives. But if only economic motives were acknowledged by physicians, the discussions at medical conventions would not have advanced the art to its present state. Can you imagine a surgeon saying to his colleagues: "Boys, I've got a new operation and it is a whiz! It cuts down overhead by 15 per cent and at the same time enables me to jack up the fees by 25 per cent." No—they discuss their new achievements in terms of benefit to the patient. Not that they don't expect to get a living out of their work.

[53] Roethlisberger: *op. cit.*, p. 103.

Occasionally they will say about some new procedure: "And, incidentally, this is a help to the physician as well, because by reducing the patient's other expenses, it enables him to pay his doctor more promptly." More often, however, in their scientific discussions, all take it for granted that they have an economic interest in their work. I am willing to grant that the primary object of the businessman is to make a profit, provided it is understood in discussions that we both take for granted that he is also interested in the human satisfaction of the people who work with him.

But at the present time businessmen won't admit the truth of that assumption. Often I have seen a businessman discuss personnel plans to make his employees happier, literally with his eyes sparkling, and then suddenly catch himself, remember that he is a businessman with a role to act, and say: "Well, of course, I am interested in this *only* because it will increase profits."

This is hypocrisy and, like all hypocrisy, it stands in the way of sound planning and action.[54]

Instead of the negative objective of minimizing trouble, a positive industrial policy will aim to increase production by improving the satisfaction workers find in their jobs. "Now is the time," says William Hard, "to go beyond 'rights' of labor and management into the field of their opportunities and duties."[55] Minimum wage and maximum hour regulations help to distribute the national income but they do not increase it; collective bargaining laws protect labor but they do not increase labor's contribution to our economic welfare; strikelessness is desirable, though unprogressive, *per se*. Workers may work against a company unless constructive harmony is established between management and worker. Happier conditions would exist for all concerned if unions were democratically organized and if a desire prevailed among the union members to *supplement* rather than to *supplant* the efforts of management. The democratic and cooperative idea is to secure "more and better pay through more and better production." A constructive program should "aim at producing American union members who control their own dues and their own strikes and their own officers, and who on top of that are conscious participants, along with management, in the basic American economic duty of making an America that is really efficient and really prosperous."[56] Such a charter of cooperation implies a new system of values for both manage-

[54] T. Burling: "Mental Hygiene in Business and Industry." *Mental Hygiene,* April, 1941.

[55] W. Hard: "Needed Now!—A *Positive* Labor Policy for *Production*." *Reader's Digest,* April, 1942.

[56] W. Hard: "Regulating Unions for the Common Good." *Reader's Digest,* September, 1942.

ment and the worker, a charter embodying the thesis: more output by all, more income for all.

Incentive pay, rightly conceived, can achieve such a goal, as Charles E. Wilson, President of the General Electric Company has demonstrated in his policy of paying workers more if they produce more. Unfortunately, because of unfair dealing in the past, "incentive" has come to have an unhappy meaning for a vast multitude of American workers, to wit:

Management sends a time-study man to observe a worker at a machine. This lofty character has a watch which divides a minute not merely into 60 parts but into a hundred. With its help he decides the exact length of time required for a certain operation.

So the worker gets to work. He "speeds up." He beats the time-study man's time. He climbs, let us say, to $1.50 an hour. *Then management cuts the number of cents per operation till the worker is earning no more going fast than he used to earn going slow.*

This has happened to a million workers in American industry. To my knowledge it has happened repeatedly even since the war began. It makes workers wary. It makes them hold back. It causes great masses of them habitually to work way below their productive power. *Here is the greatest single loss of human energy in American life.*[57]

Wilson's idea is to pay all the workers in a plant ten per cent more if production rises ten per cent, and accordingly for further rises. The base or standard is set by time-study experts representing *both* the management and the union. The Murray Corporation in Detroit has shown what can be done on such a basis. An incentive was offered:

The standards will stick right where they are. But for every one per cent more of production we get, we will hand out one per cent more pay.

The basic production rose to 25 per cent above normal and stayed there for weeks, with pay increases calculated by reference to the combined performance of *all the individuals on a given group job.* This is a sound principle of social psychology: "every man in the group has a money interest in the performance of every other man in the group." [58] As a result of this cohesion and inter-stimulation, production is stepped up. This whole program is predicated on a new system of values, as

[57] W. Hard: "Incentive Pay: For More War Production, For More Peace Prosperity." *Reader's Digest*, August, 1943.
[58] *Ibid.*

we remarked, a system of values suggested by two questions and the answer:

> Ought not management to try to get rid of the idea that a worker can earn "too much"? Ought not labor to try to get rid of the idea that it is a bad thing if management makes "more"? Here is a case in which both sides can make "more." [59]

Some managements are so addicted to old habits of thinking in this connection that they can't see but that Mr. Wilson's "incentive pay" plan gives everything to labor. What is the truth of the matter?

> What happens when you pay 25 per cent more money to labor for 25 per cent more work? The cost of the investment in the plant, of interest on borrowed money, and of all management remains the same. Hence, 25 per cent greater output means that your net cost goes down and your net income goes up.[60]

The idea of consulting the workers about company policies is coming to be recognized as sound psychological wisdom. Indeed the workers are demanding a say. Collective agreements increasingly "include provisions giving to the workers a voice in workshop planning and in other functions which the employers have long considered exclusively their own prerogative." [61] The International Ladies' Garment Workers, as we noted earlier in this chapter, in preparing their 1941 contract insisted upon their right to demand efficient management of the shops in which they were working, on the ground that the worker stands to prosper if the business is well run and to suffer if it is poorly run. This demand was a recognition—long delayed by the attitude of employers who felt that they could run their business as they pleased—of the fact that a manufacturing concern, whatever its financial setup, is really a cooperative enterprise in which management and workers share a common interest; each "side" is entitled to do something about it if the other "side" falls down on its job. There was some opposition to this proposal but it went through just the same.

The manufacturers admitted that something had to be done to extricate the industry from its depressed state, but some of them were piqued that

---

[59] *Ibid.*   [60] *Ibid.*

[61] L. Huberman: "Historical and Economic Backgrounds of the Current Conflict Situation," in *Industrial Conflict: a Psychological Interpretation*, p. 35, G. W Hartmann and T. M. Newcomb (Editors). The Dryden Press, 1939.

he union had taken the initiative. They considered it an infringement of
heir managerial prerogatives.[62]

The Steel Workers Organizing Committee has undertaken a similar
cooperative program in numerous plants, with resulting increases of
efficiency. One of the obstacles the steel union had to overcome was
reported to be "the hostility of foremen and plant managers, who fear
hat their inefficiency will be shown up." [63] Evidence of cooperation
has been exhibited, too, in the accomplishments of the Amalgamated
Clothing Workers.

These plans of collaboration between worker and management "do
not yet represent the dominant tendency in industrial relations. But
hey are straws in the wind, harbingers of a new sort of economic
ife." [64] The objective behind these policies of cooperation is to get
everybody in a plant to thinking about the means of improving plant
operation, instead of leaving the headaches of problem solving to "a
ittle group of thinkers in a room by themselves." [65] The advantage
of pooling ideas is becoming obvious. Constructive suggestions emanate frequently from the most unexpected quarters. This trend toward
collaboration—from the master-servant relationship to one of colleague-
ship—is very significant because it brings our business economy more
into accord with the democratic tradition. It is a trend that is likely
o continue because it has already been demonstrated that union-
management cooperation can increase production.

In this connection it is enlightening to study what has been accomplished for the cause of industrial harmony by the Steel Workers Organizing Committee. Under capable, far-seeing leadership, this Committee has succeeded notably in winning for labor a voice in management. This objective has been attained, according to Golden and
Ruttenberg, through the instrumentation of the union (closed) shop,
which serves as a means of providing the workers with the security
requisite for making their collective bargaining effective. Such an instrument was needed because management, as a rule, has used its
power to dominate the individual employee and to keep him duly submissive to authority. Labor, once it gets properly organized, can stand
up for its rights. The union shop has compelled management to
concede to union demands for a say in determining company policies.
Individual employees are no longer at the mercy of dictatorial bosses

---

[62] I. Ross: "Labor, Capital and Co.: Unions and Management Get Together."
Harper's Magazine, September, 1941.
[63] *Ibid.*   [64] *Ibid.*
[65] W. Hard: "Adventures in Industrial Citizenship." *Reader's Digest*, March, 1940.

who can hire and fire in an arbitrary fashion, commanding dumb acquiescence "or else." Working through his union the modern worker has gained satisfaction for some of his imperative needs:

1. Economic—an adequate plane of living and the necessary amount of job and wage protection.
2. Psychological—the personality needs of freedom of action, self-expression, and creative outlets.
3. Social—the ties and bonds of group relations and community life.[66]

When organized labor discovered that it could tell the boss "where to get off" and get away with it, there was a temptation to manifest an attitude of hostility. This immature policy of retaliation is being replaced by a desire for cooperation, a metamorphosis that is being effected by leaders with a constructive outlook, who assume the responsibility for reeducating union members. Workers are trained to appreciate the benefits that may be theirs if labor and management stop dissipating their energies fighting each other, and get together. Thus the way is pointed toward improving production, with the promise that an equitable share in the increments can be secured through collective bargaining.

The idea of granting labor a share in running the business used to be regarded as a rank heresy by industrial leaders. Workers were given orders; they were not consulted. The men who ran the machines could figure out better ways of operating the machinery but they could not get anybody to listen to them, since suggestions implied a reflection upon the intelligence of persons higher up who had failed to effect such improvements themselves. Hard times and World War II necessitated the adoption of union-management cooperation in order to step up efficiency and cut costs. When Donald Nelson assumed the chairmanship of the War Production Board, he asked management and labor to form joint committees to speed up production. More than 800 plants soon formed such committees, collected valuable ideas from the workers, and boosted efficiency—in some cases as much as 50 per cent. Despite management's fears that it would be unwise to take labor into its confidence, the plan proved its effectiveness. Union-management collaboration has demonstrated its value by promoting efficiency and by enlarging the opportunities for work satisfaction for both worker and manager. The speed-up becomes a source of pride, rather than

[66] C. S. Golden and H. J. Ruttenberg: *The Dynamics of Industrial Democracy*, p. 7. Harper & Brothers, 1942.

ground for grievance, when labor shares the responsibility for increasing productive efficiency.

Developments in union-management cooperation since 1937 have shown conclusively that working together on common problems is mutually advantageous. A policy which encourages every employee to exercise his intelligence, each one contributing what he has learned about his particular job, is good psychology—and good business. Men take more interest in their work when they see that they are respected and esteemed by their managers and fellow workers. Sharing in a common enterprise is democracy in action; it is good for the morale of all concerned. In order to achieve this *esprit de corps,* management has had to forego the privilege of dictating; labor has had to forget its grievances of days gone by. Leaders, both in management and labor, are needed, men who can think in terms of teamwork rather than conflict.[67] The pattern of union-management relations has been revised to meet more adequately our modern needs. Intelligent planning on a large scale is necessitated by war, and just as truly by the needs of peacetime, in order to secure the stabilization of employment, the equitable distribution of necessities, and the improvement of work satisfaction. The promise of abundance and security in an economic democracy spurs the workers to give their best efforts. This is the thesis of Golden and Ruttenberg in *The Dynamics of Industrial Democracy* (Harper and Brothers), a book in which they report their experiences in union-management cooperation from the point of view of the Steel Workers Organizing Committee. We quote some of their more significant observations:

Joint union-management cooperation on such elementary matters as wage rates, job evaluations, and setting work standards develops a pattern of cooperation that can be used later for more fundamental matters and on a broader scale. When collective bargaining in a local industrial establishment reaches maturity it is then possible for the union and management to cooperate to increase efficiency, reduce wastes, and otherwise cut costs of production. . . .

Industrial peace is a means toward achieving the goal of optimum efficiency and full employment and production, and not an end in itself. . . .

The extent to which creative participation in production raises a worker's social prestige and gives him personal satisfaction and a vital sense of belonging and being important, is one of the underlying motives for union-management cooperation. . . .

[67] Labor leaders are being trained in collective bargaining and other relevant matters, on "labor fellowships" at Harvard and Yale. See *Time,* August 31, 1942.

Unfortunately there is no magic formula to produce this singleness o. purpose. It is the product of group reactions. . . . Neither union leader and members alone nor management alone can achieve it, because, by its very nature, a singleness of purpose by two traditionally contending groups is a cooperative human endeavor. . . .

Workers are not a miscellaneous assortment of individuals moved primarily by personal economic incentives, but social beings guided by a combination of social, psychological, and economic motives; as a consequence, their technical knowledge can find expression only through group participation in management.[68]

The wisdom of listening to what the other person has to say, was demonstrated by Hortense Odlum's success as president of Bonwit Teller Company in New York City. She instituted the policy of consulting her employees and asking for their advice. She invited disgruntled purchasers to tea, insisted on seeing them herself. She set up a consumers' advisory committee to counsel her on the operation of the store. Bonwit Teller prospered. In 1940 Mrs. Odlum retired with the explanation that she was not interested in making money, that she had promised herself to stay long enough to prove whether the principles she believed in would or would not work when applied to business.

Kindliness, consideration for customers and employees alike, courtesy, appreciation, are human qualities which I believed, with good merchandise, would create a store that women would like to shop in. . . . Those qualities have proved themselves. . . . A store does not have to be hardboiled or high-hat or high-pressure to be successful. The thing that has given me an abiding sense of accomplishment is that we have been able to get results through good human methods.[69]

This personal testimony is in line with a trend toward the policy of having producers and consumers get together to determine production plans, as reported by Wulfeck: "The willingness to reshape industrial policies in terms of public attitudes is based upon the recognition that the whole democratic economic structure is jeopardized by industrial policies which run contrary to the public interest." [70]

"Labor doesn't want favors or concessions; labor wants what is its right," says Henry L. Nunn, president of the Nunn-Bush Shoe Com-

[68] Pp. 188, 227, 249-250, 265, 277.
[69] Quoted in an editorial in the *Christian Century,* October 23, 1940.
[70] W. H. Wulfeck: "Social Changes in Relation to Industrial Management." *Journal of Social Psychology,* 1942, 15, 145-151.

pany of Milwaukee, Wisconsin. Its right, he feels, is a proportionate share in production. Consequently, the wage scale must be flexible, subject to downward as well as to upward revision. Demands for higher wage rates and fewer working hours are not based on any realistic concept of justice, for labor ought to accept its share in the risks of production. Collective action on the part of labor is a necessity, though the recognition of this fact has taken a long time, as an historical study of labor unions will show. Continuity of pay at a fairly stable level, based on a proportionate share in the value of production, gives the worker security and a sense of partnership with the management.[71] Security is also provided by a policy of "no arbitrariness in management," dating back to 1915 when the management called the workers together and voluntarily relinquished the right to fire an employee; since that time no man has been discharged until his case has been reviewed and sanctioned by his fellow workers. Says Mr. Nunn: "It is really so simple that I don't see why employers can't see it. As soon as you remove arbitrariness from industry, as soon as you make arbitration the ultimate appeal, then you have removed fear from the employee's mind, and there is no occasion for violence from either side." [72] This policy is certainly better psychology than the one advocated by Judge Gary, former head of the U.S. Steel Corporation, who recommended that the worker be kept in constant fear of losing his job because this anxiety kept him "on his toes." Professor Carlson described this type of situation more accurately in a faculty meeting at the University of Chicago. Several faculty members had charged that that University was not giving certain of its teachers secure tenure of their jobs. President Hutchins admitted the truth of the complaint, but claimed that this practice kept the professors on their toes. "Vot you mean," Carlson burst out, "is dot it keeps dem on deir knees." [73] You can judge for yourself whether that is the best posture for effective work.

The importance of studying personal problems as a program of industrial research has been stressed by Elton Mayo of the Harvard School of Business Administration, who speaks as an expert in this field. He points out that company policy cannot be administered with a take-it-or-leave-it attitude, as a doctor gives medicine to a recalcitrant patient. The worker wants to understand his work situation,

[71] This policy of the Nunn-Bush Shoe Company is portrayed in a motion picture entitled, "Fifty-Two Pay Checks a Year," obtainable from Burton-Holmes Company, Armitage St., Chicago, Illinois.

[72] See J. W. Cyrus: "No Strikes on Him." *Christian Century*, September 18, 1940.

[73] *Time*, February 10, 1941.

for otherwise he labors against opposition from himself, harassed by a sense of futility and a feeling of exasperation. The rationale of management policies should be communicated all "down the line." These policies should be based upon an appreciation of the fact that human social factors are more fundamental than economic considerations. Wise management is predicated on a comprehension of the worker's needs: the desire to live in social relations, the desire to be conscious of his value to the group, the desire to be aware of his economic function. Consequently, time spent by the management in promoting a spirit of teamwork and understanding throughout the personnel of the organization is time well spent, as the Hawthorne study has demonstrated. Mayo was one of the counselors in the planning of that investigation. What he says about this need for cooperation is applicable in areas far more extensive than the industrial field: "Misunderstanding between employers and workers . . . has persisted for a century without any sign of amelioration. . . . At no time since the industrial revolution has there been, except sporadically here and there, anything of the nature of effective and whole-hearted collaboration between the administrative and the working groups in industry." [74]

Scientists are becoming increasingly aware of the problems that we human beings are facing as we try to adjust ourselves to our industrial civilization. Business affects people in various ways and it is important to learn just how individual persons react to different kinds of environmental conditions, whether they can work effectively, whether they find in living the satisfactions that they deem essential to their happiness. Social psychology is calling attention to the importance of understanding human relations in business and in all other realms of social activity. There is a special need for research in the field of Industrial Relations in these troublous times. The Massachusetts Institute of Technology, in 1941, initiated a new graduate course providing

opportunities for integrated research that will cut across the traditional barriers that have separated economics, business and engineering administration, sociology and psychology. . . . We think it important for an institution of this sort to start training men who not only understand the actual processes and procedures of industry but also have a broad enough background to contribute in universities, industrial concerns, labor unions, and government agencies to a solution of the very difficult economic and social problems of

[74] E. Mayo: *The Human Problems of an Industrial Civilization*, pp. 177-178, 179. 1933.

readjustment and reconstruction in industry with which we are bound to be faced at the end of the war.[75]

The program "major" gives a general idea of the scope of study. The candidate will be expected to take a general examination covering economic theory, socio-psychological theory, industrial relations and industrial economics, industrial technology, statistical method and theory, economic history, and the State in relation to industry.[76] Here is a program that recognizes the breadth of experience a person should have who intends to deal adequately with Industrial Relations. A training just as broad in scope should be planned for all students preparing themselves for personnel work, a field that is attracting many young persons today. Knowledge, and more particularly wisdom, are necessary for solving the manifold problems involved in human relations. As our culture grows in the complexity of its personal demands, individuals find it increasingly difficult to cope with the conflicts and frustrations they encounter. They need all the help that the social sciences can offer them.

[75] Quoted from a letter sent by W. Rupert Maclaurin.
[76] Quoted from the announcement of the "Graduate Work in Industrial Economics."

Chapter 19

THE FAMILY

We have defined an institution as a system of behavior patterns to which individuals must conform as members of an organized group. Institutional behavior is characteristic of family life, as we shall now observe.

Marriage and the *Family* are interrelated institutions in our culture, for it is expected that people get married before having children. Marriage is a civil or sacramental contract which formally sanctions wedlock and procreation. Occasional couples live together without this sanction and sometimes children are born out of wedlock; both of these heresies are generally frowned upon, even severely condemned. It is possible to have a family without the blessing of the church or state; in our culture it is not the accepted arrangement. There are couples, too, who share the marriage relationship, duly celebrated by public or private ceremony, without any offspring. In such cases, there is a marriage but no family, since it is "improper to speak of the family where no children are involved." [1] There are childless marriages, no childless families. These various instances have been mentioned to show that *marriage* and *family* are not synonymous, even though they are usually or normally interrelated.

I. AN EVOLVING INSTITUTION

The traditional pattern of sexual maturation is courtship, engagement, wedding, honeymoon, children, in that order. Some persons either by divorce or bereavement may go through the sequence again; some persons even run the gauntlet repeatedly, hope triumphing over experience, as divorce and marriage alternate in the sort of "tandem polygamy" we associate with Hollywood.

In the case of the family, as in the industrial field, we are dealing with an institution that is designed to regulate human relations so that

[1] M. F. Nimkoff: *The Family*, p. 8. Houghton Mifflin Company, 1934.

people may get along together with a minimum amount of friction and with a maximum amount of stability, with some insurance that all persons involved will find in the home enduring satisfactions. Social interactions within the family are informal, spontaneous, intimate, face to face. Through these relations human beings learn the give and take that is so necessary to the art of living together in the larger society outside the home. Around the symbolic hearth are kindled loyalties that grip us as the strongest emotional ties we know. Devotion to kin should not exclude interest in friends outside the home, as it did in the case of the family circle that operated as a closed system:

> God bless me and my wife
> My son John and his wife
> Us four and no more.

The socialization of the individual in the home should aim to cultivate family loyalty as the prototype of more extensive loyalties. Though the family has been declining in influence, it is still true that personalities are shaped largely by the experiences which children get through interacting with their parents. It makes a lot of difference to a child whether his parents love each other, whether they are dominating, whether they are kind, considerate, intelligent, happy. "Like father, like son" embodies a fundamental psychological truth.

Our interactions inside the family circle are determined by the ideas we have of one another. If we expect the father to be "the head of the house," then we are inclined to see him in that role. If Father thinks of himself as the supreme authority, he will assume that role, counting on the rest of the group to show by their deference that they feel, too, that it is proper for children to obey their parents, particularly Father. Perhaps Mother, on the other hand, is submissive, as becomes "a woman who knows her place," having promised at the altar to "love, honor, and obey." If the home functions on such a basis, we recognize at once that Dad and Mom are old-fashioned, for things have changed now. The father used to be the breadwinner, the mother the homemaker, but in these days Mother may have a job that brings in a better income than Father can earn. And in the modern home a wife does not kowtow to her mate, because she knows she is just as good as he is, and knowing this, she intends to deal with him as an equal. She is no longer gullible enough to believe that "a woman's place is in the home." She suspects that some man invented that slogan and called it Nature's decree, in order to keep women in subjection.

A. Traditional Norms and Functions

Our traditional norms of family life specified "properly legalized sex relations, unrestricted procreation, female domesticity, male domination, economic self-sufficiency, and permanency." [2] Some of these norms are rather passé now.

Our marriage institution, despite numerous modifications, remains essentially monogamous, one man joined to one woman till death parts them. According to Hornell Hart and Ella Hart, those persons who live within the framework of the mores in this respect are usually happier than those who follow unconventional patterns in their sexual adjustments. [3] Waller concurs in this judgment, upon the basis of his observations, and adds his own comment to the effect that most of us, with the old moral codes enshrined in our consciences, cannot assimilate non-conformity in the face of opposition from the rest of society. It is not that people are happy because they adhere to conventional morality, he points out;

perhaps the true statement is that they are conventional because they are happy—or merely that they are conventional because they are capable of being conventional. Certainly nothing is gained by exhorting persons who are dissatisfied with the present order to begin leading conventional lives in order that they may be happier. It seems just enough to make clear to the young the costs of unconventionality, as the leaders have been doing for countless centuries. But when the world is as upset as it now is, when our conventions are as conflicting and on the whole as little productive of human happiness as they are, is it not fair to add a word or two on the costs of conformity? [4]

All things considered, people are to be counted fortunate who find adequate satisfaction within the bounds of matrimony. Since their style of life fits easily into the conventional mode, they do not become involved in secret rendezvous, they do not expose themselves to censorious gossip, and they do not complicate their emotional lives by dividing their loyalties. One of the chief things to be said in favor of monogamy—prosaic, dull, or bourgeois as it may seem to radicals— is that it limits sexual rivalry, thus saving for other purposes much time and effort which would otherwise be consumed in courtship.

[2] J. P. Lichtenberger: *Divorce: a Social Interpretation,* p. 339. Whittlesey House, copyright, 1931, by the McGraw-Hill Book Company, Inc.

[3] See H. Hart and E. Hart: *Personality and the Family,* p. 210. 1934.

[4] Willard Waller: *The Family: a Dynamic Interpretation,* pp. 451-452. 1938. Reprinted by permission of The Dryden Press, Inc., the publishers.

The institution of the family came into existence as an instrument for satisfying definite human needs: sexual desire, economic cooperation, and the rearing of children. Marriage provides an answer to the craving for a more intense and trustworthy comradeship, the longing for intimate response. The family also involves responsibility for children as one of its primary functions. "All other things being equal, sex expression in marriage proves to be more satisfying than sex expression apart from marriage," says Nimkoff, who goes on to point out that the love interest is more adequately satisfied in family life because it is integrated with other needs, particularly emotional security for both parents and children. The functions of the family are thus both marital and filial. The stability of the family as an institution is based on the community of interests shared by all who are included in the family circle. Assumption of responsibility contributes to the maturity of the parents; children gain in orientation and socialization under parental tutelage.

The ideal marriage aims at (1) the gratification, under favorable conditions, of the craving for complete sexual love; (2) perpetuation of kind as the fulfillment of biological destiny for both man and woman; (3) the enhancement of personal growth through the enriching experiences of family relationships; (4) transmission of the cultural heritage to the younger generation; (5) provision of the opportunities by means of which children can attain physical, intellectual, and emotional maturity.[5] Marriage, ideally, issues in the family, and the functions of these two institutions are closely intertwined. The family is needed to give the sex relation its greatest emotional value, to rear children in an atmosphere of intelligent affection, to socialize the individual, and to prepare the child, consciously or unconsciously, for satisfactory mating in the future.

B. Its Basis in Custom

To the student of anthropology or comparative sociology, there is nothing sacred about the institution of marriage or the institution of the family. The patterns of institutional behavior represent relationships sanctioned by the mores of the time, the customary mode of mating and living together. Sexual relations between man and wife are "right" in that custom makes them proper. Customs change. Today, for example, we are coming to recognize that mutual affection is more essential than legal bonds for sanctifying sexual intimacy. Neverthe-

[5] See B. Glueck: "Psychoanalysis and Child Guidance." *Mental Hygiene*, 1930, 14, 813-827.

less, the Catholic Church teaches that sex relations are justified only if they are practiced solely for procreation, though it has compromised to the extent of allowing pleasurable contacts during the "safe period," according to the doctrine of "the rhythm." This conviction that birth control is wrong because it violates the divine law, does not carry authority except for Catholics who want to believe it. Contraception would be immoral if the majority of the people believed it was "wrong." The mores determine morals; whatever the majority of people do is "right." [6]

The comparative method of studying customs is very enlightening. The Bible forbids us to commit adultery. The Biblical ruling on this matter is the view which prevailed among the Jews. Adultery, however, is not considered a sin by all peoples everywhere, even though the Bible does tell them that it is. The Eskimos, for example, do not accept the prohibition of adultery, for it is customary among the Eskimos for the host to invite his guest to share the wife's bed. Says one observer:

The exchange and loaning of wives is a custom which is practiced not only by the western Eskimos, but it is found among many of the earth's primitive peoples. It may take place as an amusement, as a matter of deference and hospitality shown to distinguished visitors, or the reason may be a practical one. Among the western Eskimos all three of these factors are responsible for the practice. In the region of the Yukon and the Kuskokwim Delta the author frequently found himself honored by a village chief offering his wife as a bedfellow during the duration of the visit. This was his customary way of showing his respect and hospitality to visitors prominent among his people. Refusal of this offer is a base insult, which can be assuaged only by presenting the host with a very fine gift. Murdock speaks in the following manner concerning this practice among the Point Barrow Eskimos, "A curious custom, not peculiar to these people, is the habit of exchanging wives temporarily. For instance, one man of our acquaintance planned to go to the rivers deer-hunting in the summer of 1882, and borrowed his cousin's wife for the expedition, as she was a good shot and a good hand at deer-hunting, while his own wife went with his cousin on a trading expedition to the eastward. On their return the wives went back to their respective husbands. The couples sometimes find themselves better pleased with their new mates than with the former association in which case the exchange is made permanent." [7]

[6] See W. G. Sumner: *Folkways*, Chapter X, "The Marriage Institution." 1906.

[7] C. M. Garber: "Marriage and Sex Customs of the Western Eskimos." *Scientific Monthly*, September, 1935. The Murdock quotation cited by Garber is from the Ninth Annual Report, Bureau of American Ethnology, p. 413.

There may be better ways for the Eskimos—or, indeed, for all of us—but they will be considered immoral until custom gives them sanction.

C. CHANGING MORES

As attitudes toward love and marriage and family change with the passing years, the alert observer can detect the small variations that contribute to the evolution of our moral values. For example, the social climate in the late 1930's was not the climate we knew in the early 1920's. The decade following World War I saw a revolution in manners and morals, with

a younger generation addicted to knee-length skirts, hip flasks, mixed drinking in the speakeasy, petting in the parked car, uninhibited language, a second-hand knowledge of Freudian complexes, and a disposition to defy their more puritanical parents and ridicule the whole Puritan tradition. Already by the end of the nineteen-twenties the revolution was playing itself out. . . . The older generation were gradually becoming accustomed to the outlandish ways of their progeny and relaxing somewhat their own codes of conduct, and the younger generation were getting older and learning the practical advantages of moderation.[8]

An analysis of magazine articles during this period, by Hornell Hart, showed that the accent on sex freedom reached its highest point in the years 1923-1927; by 1930 sex was being discussed in a conservative tone; in 1930 there was more emphasis on the values of marriage and family life, than there had been in 1920.[9] By the time of the middle 1930's sex had taken a back seat—it was no longer news, as the editors of *Fortune* pointed out in a survey of college youth.[10]

In 1938—after several years of economic depression had exerted an effect—Bromley and Britten's study of 1364 juniors and seniors in 46 colleges and universities from coast to coast reported that half the young men and a quarter of the girls had engaged in pre-marital sexual intercourse.[11] Pre-marital sex experience has been increasing.[12] Terman predicts that if the present trend continues, virginity at marriage "will be close to the vanishing point for males born after 1930 and females born after 1940. . . . It will be of no small interest to see how

---

[8] F. L. Allen: *Since Yesterday*, pp. 129-130. Harper & Brothers, 1940.

[9] H. Hart: "Changing Social Attitudes and Interests," in *Recent Social Trends.* 1933.

[10] "Youth in College." *Fortune,* June, 1936.

[11] See D. D. Bromley and F. H. Britten: *Youth and Sex.* 1938.

[12] See E. S. Wile: *The Sexual Life of the Unmarried Adult.* 1934.

long the cultural ideal of virgin marriage will survive as a moral code after its observance has passed into history." [13]   Whether Terman is correct or not in his prophecy, it is clear to anyone who can see, that we have come a long way since the Victorian era when a woman was branded with perpetual shame if she lost her virginity before marriage, since her purity was more precious than life itself.   The development of contraceptives, disease prophylaxis, and rapid transportation, have all contributed to a disregard for the ban on pre-marital experience, on the part of many persons.   That this shift in moral values has taken place on a fairly wide scale is evidenced in Terman's finding that "pre-marital chastity has lost most of its significance so far as relation to marital happiness is concerned." [14]

Getting back to the transition from the 1920's to the 1930's, we find the change summarized by Frederick Lewis Allen, in these words:

In short, although there was considerable public acceptance of pre-marital sex relations as inevitable and not sinful, and a tendency to approve of what one observer has called "a single standard, and that a low one," nevertheless marriage seemed to have become more highly prized as an institution than in the nineteen-twenties.   The family seemed to have become more highly prized as an institution.   "Sixty per cent of the college girls and fifty per cent of the men would like to get married within a year or two of graduation, and fifty per cent of each sex would like to have children soon after marriage," reported the editors of *Fortune* in their 1936 survey.   The fact that the college girls of the nineteen-thirties were more eager for early marriages than those of the nineteen-twenties was noted by many college administrators.   These same undergraduates and their contemporaries were on the whole less scornful of their parents and of parental ideas, less likely to feel that family life was a mockery, than the young people of ten years before.[15]

Marriage and family mores do change—slowly.   Most of us hesitate to experiment with sexual innovations.

"Much of the present trend towards the disruption of family life, which the purists assign to the vicious teachings of free-lovers, sociologists, and psychoanalysts, is due to the coming of the Industrial Revolution and the entry of women and children into industry." [16]   Many

[13] L. M. Terman et al.: *Psychological Factors in Marital Happiness*, p. 323.   Mc-Graw-Hill Book Company, 1938.

[14] *Ibid.*, p. 320.

[15] Allen: *op. cit.*, p. 135.   See also his discussion of the nineteen-twenties in *Only Yesterday*. 1933.

[16] H. E. Barnes: "Sex in Education," in *Sex in Civilization*, p. 328, V. F. Calverton and S. D. Schmalhausen (Editors). 1929.

influences have affected marriage and the family. The economic independence of women has enabled women to bargain on an equal
footing with men when marriage is under consideration; they can
marry or not, for they are free to choose on their own terms, with
no compulsion to marry a man as a "meal-ticket." For the same reason, a woman can divorce her husband if she finds that he falls short of
what she wants in a man. She doesn't have to stay married if she
doesn't want to. (It is significant to note here that in 1900 the married constituted 15 per cent of all working women; in 1940, about 30
per cent.) [17] Woman's status has also been improved by the development of birth control, for she is no longer subjected to the oppression
of involuntary motherhood; again she can make her own choice. She
can postpone parenthood, thus she is free to marry sooner if she wants
to; she can even remain intentionally childless without incurring
serious criticism.

There is less family solidarity today because many people do not
live long enough in one house to make it a "home." Many modern
couples live in apartments or small houses that are easy to take care of,
and easy to move out of. What memories can cluster about his "childhood home" for a child who was born in a hospital and who has been
uprooted periodically by his parents who are in search of cheaper rents
or better janitor service? People who do not own their homes do not
"stay put" long enough to become neighbors—they live merely as
"neigh-dwellers." Fewer cooperative tasks are performed in the home
than in the days before the Industrial Revolution, as people do not
make their own furniture, grow their own food (except under the
stress of war), or make their own clothes. The modern home is a
center of consumption, not a center of production. Recreation is
found largely outside the home. With no chance for privacy in the
living room on nights when the family does stay in, the daughter and
her caller head for the darkness of a movie or a deserted spot on a
country road.[18] The close quarters of the modern apartment afford
plenty of opportunity for rubbing tempers the wrong way and there
is no room up in the attic where a bruised soul can retire for a few
moments' peace.

The family has undergone two fundamental changes in its functions,
according to Ogburn, who reported these conclusions in the survey
he made for *Recent Social Trends* (McGraw-Hill Book Company):

[17] For the 1900 figures, see *Recent Social Trends*, p. 715. 1933.
[18] See R. S. Lynd and H. M. Lynd: *Middletown*, p. 99. 1929.

One is the decline of the institutional functions. Thus the family produces less food and clothing than it did formerly. The teaching functions of the family also have been largely shifted to another institution, the school. Industry and the state have both grown at the family's expense. The significance of this diminution in the activities of the family as a group is far-reaching.

The other outstanding conclusion is the resulting predominant importance of the personality functions of the family—that is, those which provide for the mutual adjustments among husbands, wives, parents and children, and for the adaptation of each member of the family to the outside world. The family has always been responsible to a large degree for the formation of character. It has furnished social contacts and group life. With the decline of its institutional functions these personality functions have come to be its most important contribution to society. The chief concern over the family nowadays is not how strong it may be as an economic organization but how well it performs services for the personalities of its members.[19]

Changes in the mores have been far-reaching, as we discover when we take time to survey our recent history. The Puritan ban on sex has been lifted, partly under the leadership of Freud, and young people are demanding enlightenment concerning the "facts of life." The Methodist Episcopal Church has abandoned its taboo against dancing. Y.W.C.A.'s conduct charm classes. Cosmetics have come into general use. Birth control has been sanctioned by the Federal Council of Churches and by the American Medical Association (both in 1937). Public-health campaigns are educating people concerning venereal diseases and calling them by name.[20] All along the line we notice a greater tolerance for many actions that used to be condemned.

Looking at the history of marriage, we can discern a trend toward the secularization of this institution. The Christian concept of marriage as a sacrament prevailed in Western culture until the time of the Protestant Reformation. In accordance with the teachings of the Apostle Paul, marriage was preferable to burning, wedlock was of value as a preventive against sin (fornication), sex was not to be enjoyed except for procreation, virginity and celibacy were more conducive to spiritual growth.[21] For ages Church doctrine declared marriage indissoluble; outright divorce, admitting of the remarriage of either party, was utterly forbidden, as it is still forbidden in the Roman Catholic Church; but marriages were annulled for a price by resort to

[19] See the complete discussion, pp. 664-700.
[20] See E. W. Burgess and L. S. Cottrell: *Predicting Success or Failure in Marriage*, pp. 7-10. Prentice-Hall, Inc., 1939.
[21] See I Corinthians, the seventh chapter.

all kinds of ingenious casuistry—indeed, "it might be said that, for a sufficient consideration, a canonical flaw could be found in almost any marriage." [22]

It was Luther who repudiated the sacramental concept of marriage as a priestly invention, and who denounced its exclusive control by the Church as an unwarranted usurpation. He rejected the ascetic attitude toward sex relations in favor of an interpretation of marriage as a normal relationship, pure and noble because it gave expression to natural impulses divinely implanted for the perpetuation of the race. The legitimate satisfaction of these natural desires he commended as a social duty. "Matrimony," Luther declared, "is a temporal, worldly thing" which "does not concern the church." [23]

This view of Luther's represents the *civil-contract* concept of marriage, a theory that gained its first official recognition in England's Civil-Marriage Act of 1653, which transferred matrimonial jurisdiction from spiritual to civil tribunals and pronounced marriage an unequivocally secular affair. In the United States this civil-contract concept of marriage has been in force ever since Colonial times. Accordingly, the intervention of a priest was declared "unnecessary and out of place." [24] Gradually the Puritan prejudice against ecclesiastical rites subsided and laws were enacted allowing ministers of all denominations to perform the ceremony; that is, clergymen were constituted civil officers for this purpose.

This historical background will clarify the conflicting attitudes toward marriage that are still confusing many of us and obscuring the issues involved. Though the theory of the sacrament no longer prevails legalistically, the feeling still persists that there is an inherent sanctity about marriage that makes it a religious as well as a secular union. This feeling explains the long resistance to legislation permitting easier divorce, a resistance that has persisted despite the fact that public sentiment has grown more tolerant toward the dissolution of a marriage tie where mutual affection no longer blesses the union. Secular control of our domestic institutions is slowly but surely increasing, as people are more and more coming to feel that marriage exists for human happiness and that its continuance, therefore, is only justified, in particular cases, by the successful fulfillment of that end. "If the increasing divorce rate does not represent increasing

---

[22] C. F. Thwing: *The Family*, pp. 112-113. Revised edition, 1913.
[23] G. E. Howard: *History of Matrimonial Institutions*, Volume I, pp. 387-388. 1904.
[24] See *Ibid.*, Volume II, pp. 127-138.

marital unhappiness, it does indicate a profound change in mores as to the inviolability of marriage. Fifty years ago the sanction of American mores was still enforced against divorce as inimical to social welfare. Today our mores condone, if they do not approve, divorce as one solution of the problem of marital unhappiness." [25] It was, in fact, the increasing divorce rate that called attention to the importance of studying the personal adjustments involved in marriage.

The State has appropriated the right to legislate concerning "these subjects which have as their end the promotion of human happiness and well-being." The Church still retains as its proper function the "fostering of ethical ideals in respect to marriage and divorce, as in all other important human relations," and the privilege of advocating civil legislation which will conform to its standards.[26] The traditional attitude that marriage is a sacrament still survives, nevertheless, exerting its influence on our conduct. As a consequence, many of us intellectually accept modern ideas on love and marriage while we emotionally reject them. When we try to be more tolerant, our expanding broadmindedness shocks us and makes us feel uneasy. It would be difficult for anybody to regard marriage as a natural relationship between two human beings deeply in love with each other, if he took seriously such views as were represented in these resolutions passed secretly by the Anglican Bishops in their Lambeth Conference of 1931, to wit: "The sexual relationship even in marriage must be regarded as a regrettable necessity. . . . Except where children are desired, married persons should remain celibate after marriage, as before." But why? If human happiness in this life is important, it is clear that such a policy of deliberate frustration is contrary to our own best interests. The ascetic view of life is waning in its appeal; changing attitudes toward marriage exemplify one aspect of that decline. People get married today, not to suffer together, but to share those human experiences that enrich life and give it meaning. Marriage is an instrument, not an end in itself. It is not a sentence to be served. It is not intended to be an endurance contest with a prize for the one who can suffer longer. Self-discipline and forbearance are necessary, but they are not the primary aims of marriage.

The institution of marriage has been changing without our realizing just what has been going on. Judge Lindsey brought this ob-

[25] Burgess and Cottrell: *op. cit.*, p. 1.
[26] J. P. Lichtenberger: *Divorce: a Social Interpretation*, p. 99. Whittlesey House, copyright, 1931, by the McGraw-Hill Book Company, Inc.

servation dramatically to public attention in his advocacy of "companionate marriage." He insisted that "companionate marriage" was nothing new but simply a frank recognition of the kind of marriage that most people were already practicing. Bishop Manning did not agree with Lindsey on this point and said so in a sermon delivered on Golden Rule Sunday, December 7, 1930, in the Cathedral of St. John the Divine. Lindsey, present in the congregation, heard himself scorned as the author of a book, "the most filthy, insidious, and cleverly written piece of propaganda ever published in behalf of lewdness, promiscuity, adultery, and unrestrained sexual gratification." The Bishop's discourse was dotted with:

break down the moral defenses of the young . . . sexual passions . . . Bertrand Russell . . . efforts being made to destroy the moral foundations of our life . . . foul and wicked thing . . . a man who stands openly and publicly for legalized free love under a cover of the term "companionate marriage."

Lindsey arose and strode forward to protest against the misrepresentation of his views. Somebody shouted, "Lynch him." In a moment, pandemonium broke loose. Order was restored by the police.[27] The incident is related here to show how violent people are inclined to be when they think their traditional institutions are being threatened by an innovator. Reactions are apt to be particularly emotional when proposals are made for revising our sex mores.

Let's examine Lindsey's suggestions to see whether the Bishop was justified in denouncing companionate marriage as a cloak for free love. Lindsey contended that the majority of marriages today are companionate, and that he was merely advocating an honest recognition of the fact. He said that customs, not ceremonies, make marriage what it is—the habits of the people, not the bell, book, and candle of the Church, not the laws in the statute books. There are four main points in his plan:

1. Birth control.
   Most married people practice birth control now.
   Lindsey proposed that we legalize it and place dissemination of information about it in the hands of specialists accessible to the poor as well as to the rich. He deplored the present situation where information is "bootlegged" in unscientific and inaccurate forms. Most people want to limit the size of their families and they do not intend to do so by means of continence. Birth

[27] Boston *Herald,* December 8, 1930.

control is an important phase of the plan because it means that a couple can get married sooner, reasonably confident that they will not be saddled with children until they can afford them; because it means that a couple can postpone the arrival of children until they are fairly sure that they are suited to each other and that their marriage gives promise of permanence.

One aim of earlier marriage is to reduce the amount of sexual promiscuity that now prevails. There would not be so much provocation to illicit love if young folks were encouraged to get married sooner.

2. Divorce.

Childless couples should be privileged to get a divorce by mutual consent.

People get divorced by mutual consent now but because of our antiquated divorce laws they have to resort to subterfuge, lies, and collusion. Lindsey proposed to put divorce on an open, honest basis.

A board of reconciliation would interview the couple in an endeavor to iron out their difficulties. If the board failed to settle the differences, the couple should have free access to divorce, for it would be better for them to part company than to live together under compulsion.

3. Sex education at the expense of the state.

4. No alimony except in rare cases.

5. Companionate marriage is legal marriage, in the nature of a contract. This contract is to have the same status as conventional marriage if there are children. In case there are no children, the partners may void the contract by mutual consent at the end of the first year.[28]

Stated Lindsey: "I am not suggesting that society should establish companionate marriage, but merely that it recognize it—since we already practice it. We already have it; and we ought to recognize the childless marriage as a separate thing from procreative marriage, instead of stupidly treating them as if they were one and the same thing. We ought to recognize that regulations which are perfectly reasonable in the one are absurd and irrational in the other."[29]

Critics of Lindsey's plan feared that the opportunity for marrying and unmarrying so easily would promote legalized promiscuity. The Judge answered this objection by explaining that most young people who fall in love with each other propose to stay together. They are disposed to believe that their union will be permanent.

Emotional ties grow up between people when they are in close daily association, especially in the intimacy of married life. Such a relationship sends out roots, like a growing tree; and it resists being torn up and transplanted.

[28] See B. B. Lindsey and W. Evans: _The Companionate Marriage._ Liveright Publishing Corp., 1927.

[29] B. B. Lindsey: "The Moral Revolt." _Redbook_, June, 1927.

Nearly everybody genuinely prefers to find a stable relationship in marriage. In nearly all cases people seek divorce only if they find anything else unendurable. It is the least of the evils confronting them; it is a last resort. The presence in society of a few polygamous freaks does not alter this essential fact that *human beings are normally monogamous;* and that this passion for monogamy is predominant even in men and women who are physically "unfaithful" to their mates.[30]

Add to these emotional ties the sense of personal decency, the sense of social responsibility, and the pressure of public opinion, and you can see that the evidence favors a stable relationship. So said the Judge.

Our changing mores with respect to pre-marital sex experience and with respect to birth control have been mentioned. These two phenomena are interrelated, of course, and they are important enough to merit further consideration.

Terman and others have evidence that seems to indicate that young folks in general are indulging more and more in pre-marital sex relations.[31] Some authorities, like Popenoe, feel that this trend is bound to have an unhappy effect on marriage, since promiscuity overemphasizes the role of passion, undermines self-control, and cultivates a taste for variety that is incompatible with the constancy demanded of husband or wife.[32] It is possible, of course, that the mores may take a turn toward a stricter code of sex morality, as a reaction against the present emphasis on uninhibited self-expression.

While early marriage has been proposed as a means of canalizing the sexual interest within the bounds of matrimony, thus minimizing the temptation of promiscuity, it must be noted that there are some disadvantages in assuming marital responsibilities prematurely. Early marriage, as Groves says, is apt to be dominated by physical attraction.[33] An older person is presumably more mature and his choice of a mate will be determined by personal qualities that are more essential to a stable marriage. Early marriage may interfere with professional advancement, especially if children come along before the young folks are prepared financially and emotionally to assume family responsibilities.

Marriage seems to present serious problems, whether it is entered

---

[30] *Ibid.*   [31] See Terman: *op. cit.,* pp. 324-335.

[32] See P. Popenoe: *The Conservation of the Family,* Part II, Chapter 3, "Delayed Marriage." 1926.

[33] See E. R. Groves: *Marriage,* Chapter 8, "Early Marriage, Its Advantages and Disadvantages." 1933.

into earlier or later. The release of sex tension is not the only factor to be considered in weighing the advantages or disadvantages of marrying young. Younger people, on the one hand, are likely to be more flexible in their social adaptation, their habits have not yet become settled in the individualistic ways of the bachelor, they can adjust themselves more readily to the petty annoyances and the personal idiosyncrasies that contribute to marital friction. On the other hand, younger persons are apt to be lacking in emotional maturity. The relation between flexibility and maturity was investigated by Burgess and Cottrell. They were much impressed with the "unfortunate effects of very early marriages," where the wife was younger than nineteen and the husband under twenty-two. The optimum age for marriage success proved to be twenty-eight to thirty. At this age there is the most favorable balance, apparently, between flexibility and maturity.[34] Men over thirty-one were found to be poor marriage risks, possibly because they were losing in flexibility without gaining in maturity. The best age for getting married, of course, will differ for individuals. The problem is mentioned here to indicate that early marriage is not to be commended simply because it may reduce promiscuity, for it may introduce difficulties even more damaging to the success of family life.

Changes in the mores are also observable with respect to the practice of birth control. "No marriage norm of the past has become so completely obsolete within recent years as that of unrestricted procreation."[35] The idea that fecundity should be controlled has been almost universally accepted among the more favored social and economic groups, as attested by the small families on the higher social levels, and by the testimony of persons who have been interviewed concerning the use of contraceptives. According to a 1940 Gallup Poll, 77 per cent of U.S. citizens favor dissemination of birth control information through Government health clinics. Davis and Hamilton have both found that birth control is practiced by most married people.[36]

In 1939, South Carolina made birth control one of its official public health services. Adopted by the State Medical Association, which functions as the State Board of Health, this new service is one phase

---

[34] Burgess and Cottrell: *op. cit.*, pp. 115-117.
[35] Lichtenberger: *op. cit.*, p. 350.
[36] See K. B. Davis: *Factors in the Sex Life of Twenty-two Hundred Women*, p. 13. 1929. Also, G. V. Hamilton and K. MacGowan: *What's Wrong with Marriage*, p. 98. 1929.

of a campaign to reduce maternal and infant mortality, both of which had grown to an appalling total. Birth control is now prescribed for mothers, when it is indicated, by physicians in charge of maternal and child-health clinics operating in every county of the State. This program has lowered the mortality rate of women who, for various reasons, are unfit for child-bearing. There are more live births now, more infants surviving the first year. With public funds to finance the enlightenment of thousands of indigent mothers, medical care has been extended to many who had never received regular attention before. This care has cut down the toll of toxemias, which are due in part to poor nutrition and too frequent pregnancies. Spacing of children has helped, too, by relieving the economic burdens which affect the health of the poorer families.

This birth-control program met no public opposition in South Carolina. Indeed, "it is now, and has been since 1936, legal throughout the United States, except in Massachusetts and Connecticut, for a physician to give pregnancy-spacing advice to his patient when her health requires it." [37] In these two states the use of contraceptives is forbidden by law, even though the patient's condition may require medical prescription of measures to prevent pregnancy. With the exception of these two New England bulwarks of conservatism, "the public hue and cry which attended the first years of birth-control promotion in this country has died." [38] Margaret Sanger, who languished in jail for "obscenity" a number of times years ago, must be delighted to see such a revolutionary change in sentiment during her own lifetime. The National Committee for Planned Parenthood working in conjunction with the Birth Control Federation of America is making progress. There is still much to be done, however, in bringing contraceptive knowledge to the poorer classes who need it most.

With the legal and moral status of birth control clarified, the growing concern of medicine is to make birth control serve the broadest social purposes. Prescribed by doctors to their private patients or in the 560 birth-control clinics in various parts of the country, it can be brought only to a limited section of the population. To reach those who need it most, birth control must become, as in North and South Carolina, an official public-health measure.[39]

[37] Quoted from "Planned Parenthood, Its Contribution to Family, Community, and Nation." Published by the Planned Parenthood Federation of America.
[38] *Life*, May 6, 1940.   [39] *Ibid.*

That there is a need for enlightenment among the poorer classes is demonstrated by the fact that nearly a quarter of a million children were born in 1934 to American parents who were already dependent upon public relief.[40]   A study of 504 families who had been dependent for years on public relief in Los Angeles County showed that they had been producing children steadily at public expense. Popenoe was led to conclude that "the longer a family is dependent on charity, the more children it produces." [41] This phenomenon is not peculiar to Los Angeles County. Mr. and Mrs. S—— were on relief when they welcomed their sixteenth child in seventeen years. Mr. and Mrs C—— of East St. Louis, Illinois, on relief in 1935, were blessed with triplets, increasing their roster to nine. Said Mrs. C——: "If the Lord sees fit to give them to us, we'll see fit to provide for them." Whom does Mrs. C—— mean by "we"?

Bromley reports that in 1932 there were 48 per cent more births in families without any employed workers than in families with one or more full-time workers. Families that were actually receiving relief had a birth rate 54 per cent higher than those not on relief. The fecundity of the family on relief is not due to idleness—to the fact that the man of the house is home so much of the time—for the same persons who were prolific in 1932 were also prolific in 1929.

The man who shows no judgment about the number of children he sires is likely to be the man who loses his job in a crisis, perhaps because he lacks judgment all along the line. . . . The depression has made realists of many well-meaning workers who formerly believed that the same Providence which sent little children into the world would see that they were taken care of.[42]

Birth control is tied up with many of our social problems: malnutrition, high mortality rates, poverty, unemployment, and war. It is no coincidence that the most war-prone nations have been the most prolific, too. Overpopulation calls for territorial expansion to insure the supplies necessary to sustain more people, and expansion means war at somebody's expense. It is true, of course, that nations bent on aggression encourage fertility in order to amass the man power and woman power requisite to the successful prosecution of war. It is a vicious circle, ending in a cry for *Lebensraum*. If population is

[40] Information supplied by the Birth Control League of Massachusetts.

[41] P. Popenoe: "Fecundity of Families Dependent on Public Charity." *American Journal of Sociology*, 1934, 40, 214-221.

[42] D. D. Bromley: "Birth Control and the Depression." *Harper's Magazine*, October, 1934.

outrunning subsistence, a lower birth rate would seem to be a sensible solution. Restriction of the birth rate, however, may be suicidal for any one nation in a world where military strength is so important. At this stage in human progress we still depend upon the ravages of war to keep our population within bounds. It is clear that birth control, as a social policy, cannot be considered apart from its social implications.

The practice of contraception must also be related to its effects upon personality. The fear of pregnancy, prevalent among people who do not have access to scientific knowledge on birth control, is a significant factor in causing neurotic disorders, as many clinics can testify.[43] This fear robs the sexual relationship of complete psychic satisfaction, and the resulting sense of frustration is attended by unhappy effects upon family harmony. Sexual happiness cannot be attained when anxiety permeates the marital relations. Birth control is a great boon to ease of mind and emotional security. Its value to family life can be further recognized in many spheres, notably in the spacing of children so that health and financial welfare can be assured. Tired mothers and worried fathers are apt to breed misery as well as neurotic children. The couple who are without the means for contraception, through ignorance or through religious scruples, must either resign themselves, if they are normally endowed with the sexual drive, to having ten to fifteen children, or "they must so limit their physical relations as to cause serious frustrations and harmful emotional tensions, which are bound to lead to unhappiness and perhaps to the destruction of their love and their marriage. . . . Birth-control—the most revolutionary invention of any century—is an inescapable necessity. It is, indeed, an inescapable fact."[44]

Despite all of these benefits, both personal and social, that are procurable by the practice of birth control, the Roman Catholic Church still denounces contraception as immoral, shameful, and intrinsically vicious. Artificial family limitation is declared sinful because it violates the will of God, because it interferes with nature, because it frustrates the primary purpose of marriage which is procreation, because it encourages the pursuit of personal pleasure, because it degrades the moral nature by elevating passion above spiritual values. The Church recommends self-control as the most honorable method of birth control, on the ground that the self-denial involved in

[43] D. E. Hall and G. J. Mohr: "Prenatal Attitudes of Primiparae: a Contribution to the Mental Hygiene of Pregnancy." *Mental Hygiene*, April, 1933.

[44] Hamilton and MacGowan: *op. cit.*, pp. 93-94.

the practice of continence is good for the soul. Pope Pius XI, in one of his encyclicals, spoke of "the great excellence of chaste wedlock" which he endorsed as the path of virtue. Contraception has been referred to by priests as the "murder of the unborn," and in this connection it has been argued that men like Benjamin Franklin, who was fifteenth in a line of seventeen, would never have been born if his parents had interfered with nature.

The ascetic life espoused by the Church is a hard one. It is well known that many Catholics do not obey the injunction of the Church against the use of contraceptives. Communicants are apt to lose respect for the Church if rules are imposed that are sure to be violated by a proportion of the members. People are discovering that voluntary parenthood is a means of achieving numerous ends which are important to their welfare.

The general trend of the mores is toward the secularization of marriage; the widespread adoption of birth control is just one phase of that evolution. Marriage and the family are both headed for a larger emphasis on the personal satisfactions afforded by the home.

II. HUMAN RELATIONS IN THE HOME

Interest in the psychology of family relations was stimulated to an important degree by the studies of the psychoanalysts, notably the explorations of Freud into the complicated emotional attachments involved in the development of the Oedipus and Electra complexes.[45] Alfred Adler, at one time a pupil of Freud, also devoted much attention to the influences of family relationships, especially as they affect the social aspects of the individual's personality. According to Adler, the basic function of the home is the development of social interest, a social-mindedness which will find expression in the recognition of obligations to the larger community beyond the confines of the family. Behaviorist Watson's *Psychological Care of Infant and Child* (1928) was a pioneer contribution to this field of human relations within the family. His warnings against the demonstration of parental affection proved so disconcerting to fond parents as to excite widespread notice. Incidentally, Watson's counsel is no longer regarded as sound.

We shall explore some of the problems of social adjustment which are common in family life, concentrating our attention first upon the husband-wife relationships involved in married life and then follow-

[45] Incestuous attachment of son to mother and of daughter to father, respectively

ing this discussion with a description of parent-child relationships, and last of all, relationships among siblings.

A. Marriage: Husband and Wife Relationship

The art of living together is exemplified on its highest plane in a happy marriage. A husband and wife must first understand each other, then practice all the skills of social adjustment at their command. A successful marriage is a manifestation of emotional maturity on the part of both partners.

1. mutual adjustment

The idea has been advanced by various students of the psychology of sex that the love relationship is inherently a union of incompatible persons, that conflict is inevitable, that mutual adjustment is attainable only by self-sacrifice, forbearance, and social insight. Psychologists do not believe that "marriages are made in heaven," that people marry and automatically "live happily ever after." The high incidence of divorce suggests that marriage leads rather easily to friction and discord. A realistic view of married life recognizes that personal dissension is inherent in the very intimacy of such a union; also that rich emotional rewards are to be won when passion is transmuted into love and differences are translated into harmony. Living together is a difficult art, under any circumstances; when it is complicated by love, all the insight that psychology can afford will be necessary.

a. *Courtship.* The basis for a happy or unhappy marriage is established, to an important degree, during the courtship period. In our culture the natural configuration—the rise of tension and the release of tension—is blocked by taboos against pre-marital sex experience. Many young persons, we have already noted, are not following the ideal of chastity recommended by their parents and their religious teachers.[46] This widespread defection from the moral standards of the elder generation must not be interpreted to mean the taboos are no longer operative. There is far more frustration than satisfaction in the love-life of the average couple who have started "going around together." Their relations cramped by conventional restrictions, young lovers are forced to endure much thwarting of desire, especially after the announcement of the engagement gives the go-ahead signal for "heavy petting." The mutual frustration is liable to result in mutual hostilities that are kept repressed until the honeymoon is

[46] See M. C. Banning: *The Case for Chastity.* 1937.

over. As long as concupiscence is thwarted, the sex-object is over-valued, the individual finding solace for his restless yearnings in day-dreaming and in idealizing the beloved. With the fulfillment of desire in the intimacy of marriage, the stimulus for idealization is removed, fancy gives way to reality. Disillusion follows the disappointment of fondest dreams, and pent-up animosities break out, much to the surprise and confusion of the lovers. When the husband or wife comes to realize how far individuality has to be sacrificed to the demands of love, the hostility of rebellion is added to the antipathies attending disillusionment. Love and hatred are experienced as marriage gives vent to ambivalent feelings, a conflict that has been so vividly described by the psychoanalysts. It is the critical nature of these emotional problems that leads Waller to say that "intelligent adjustments or counseling during the courtship period is perhaps the best possibility for the improvement of family life." [47]

The mores of courtship are expounded by writers of books of etiquette, by advisers to the lovelorn, by deans of women. "Whether all these counselors mean all that they say would be a difficult question, but it is significant that they seem to agree." [48] It is a general rule that a young man and a young woman do not address each other until they are formally introduced. The privilege of making advances is reserved to the man, who may ask for a date if he is so inclined; if she accepts, he foots the bills. The girl plays the role of the "pursued," acting nonchalant in order to give point to the chase, but not so indifferent as to discourage interest. It is the man who does the wooing, though the woman may "egg him on" if she is subtle enough about it. After the engagement is announced, the engaged couple are not supposed to go out individually with another person of the opposite sex, for love is to be exclusive and "property rights" are jealously guarded.

Previous to the one great love, nearly every person goes through a series of puppy loves, or calf loves, each of which may be mistaken for a providential leading. These early loves are taken very seriously by the boy and girl, though their parents may "josh" them in an attempt to keep them from getting in "too deep." Usually puppy loves do not last very long. Each time they collapse, the young person leaves behind a little of his capacity to love. Jilted, "given the air," with

---

[47] Reprinted by permission of The Dryden Press, publishers of *The Family: A Dynamic Interpretation,* by Willard Waller, 1938. P. 176.

[48] *Ibid.,* p. 177.

his ego hurt and his dreams shattered, the lover avenges himself by setting out to exploit the opposite sex. Emotional traumas and heartless brutality may issue from this malicious resolve. Affair follows affair, with contacts transitory, as each person looks for thrills. Relations are unstable on such a basis. There is a "high contact mobility," which is the sociologist's way of describing the flitting hither and yon in search of excitement. The boy spends the money and expects fun in return. The girl uses coquetry to lead him on. They dally, they flirt, each one handing the other a "line," endeavoring to ensnare the other without getting "roped in." It's a jungle law: exploit or get exploited. The process is one of bargaining, the man trying to get sexual gratification through "necking" or going the limit, while the girl seeks to go as far as she can without sacrificing her chastity. "The ultimate bargain of the courtship process is marriage, a bargain to end all bargaining." [49] This last step is a "scary" one for it means committing oneself, burning the bridge behind. There is an impulse to go ahead and fall in love all over; there is also an urge to be prudent, to think of what it is going to cost in terms of money and personal restrictions. The tendency to love is released only when certain conditions are satisfied—family background, education, social class, financial status, age, beauty, sexual attractiveness.[50]

The experiences of courtship are supposedly a preparation for the more lasting emotional reciprocity of the marital relationship but in actual practice "courtship educates for courtship more than for marriage." [51] The psychological situation before marriage differs from the psychological situation after marriage. The norms of desirability are different. It is important at the adolescent stage to have a partner who is a good dancer, one with "a smooth line," one with a few whims which keep interest at a high pitch. Such a person might prove rather boring in marriage unless possessed of other qualities of more permanent value. It may be fun to go with a girl who is unpredictable but it is not easy to live with her. The novelty soon wears off. When a person is immature, he is attracted to one of the opposite sex primarily as one he can fall in love with. This means the sort of person whom he can idealize easily. This kind of person, however, may not elicit the same worship in the close routine of marital existence. Choosing a partner because you fall in love with her, not because you believe she will make a good wife, is as irrational as it would be to choose a surgeon because he had wavy, blonde hair.

[49] *Ibid.*, p. 241. [50] *Ibid.*, p. 242. [51] *Ibid.*, p. 227.

The atmosphere of courtship is fictitious, dreamy, delusional. Perhaps that explains why "many neurotics appear quite normal during the courtship period." [52]

Romantic infatuation may become a mania, a consuming passion, an obsession that monopolizes all thought and action. At its best, romance is a flimsy basis for marriage. Romance there should be, but more, too, in the way of cooperative effort and the sharing of responsibilities. A happy marriage, prosaic as this may sound, depends fundamentally upon habits of coordination, organized routine, mutual adaptation. Even the art of quarreling successfully is an important part of the technique of marriage: the disagreement must be limited in range, some decision must emerge from the conflict, reconciliation must be effected.[53] Gradually accusations and denunciations will give way to deliberation and discussion. Thus love will be strengthened as "crises . . . lead to successive re-definitions of the relationship in increasingly meaningful terms." [54]

b. *Conflict and Incompatibility.* Some of the difficulties which complicate marital adjustment are traceable to the differences between the courtship situation and the marriage situation, as we have remarked. "Most of the habits of the courtship period are manifestly unsuitable for marriage." [55] The idealizing relation is not likely to continue in the close contacts under one roof; trouble results from the newlyweds' expecting the rosy haze to persist. After getting accustomed to mutual flattery, it is quite a come-down to discover each other's faults. Once marriage is established, the couple, so to speak, get back to normal and return to their natural egocentricity. Prides and envies and unintended slights and disgusting mannerisms rub the wrong way. In some cases the husband and wife set out to remedy the bad bargains of courtship and to redress the wrongs that have been nursed in secret. There may be a delusive solidarity which conceals unexpressed grievances. These repressed animosities may erupt in feuds during which past wrongs are rehearsed and relatives are insulted. Release for these tensions is occasionally found in jokes about marriage, such as "married people don't live longer, it just seems longer," or George Bernard Shaw's jest that "no man dare write the truth of marriage while his wife still lives, unless he hates her."

[52] *Ibid.*, p. 298.
[53] See R. C. Binkley and F. E. Binkley: *What's Right with Marriage: an Outline of Domestic Theory*, Chapter 17, "Marriage and Art." 1929.
[54] Waller: *op. cit.*, p. 270.
[55] *Ibid.*, pp. 305-306.

A ranking of domestic complaints by husbands and wives has been drawn up by Terman to illustrate the "sex differences in the seriousness of thirty-five grievances:"

Rank Order for Husbands			Rank Order for Wives
Not affectionate	1.	1.	Selfish and inconsiderate
Selfish and inconsiderate	2.	2.	Untruthful
Complains too much	3.	3.	Argumentative
Quick tempered	4.	4.	Complains too much
Conceited	5.	5.	Not affectionate
Insincere	6.	6.	Nervous or impatient
Criticizes me	7.	7.	Insincere
Narrow minded	8.	8.	Management of income
Argumentative	9.	9.	Criticizes me
Untruthful	10.	10.	Not faithful
Spoils children	11.	11.	Lazy
Management of income	12.	12.	In-laws
In-laws	13.	13.	Influenced by others
Insufficient income	14.	14.	Narrow minded
Nervous and emotional	15.	15.	Insufficient income
Influenced by others	16.	16.	Interested in other women
Jealous	17.	17.	Amusement and recreation
Lazy	18.	18.	Quick tempered
Amusement and recreation	19.	19.	Attitude toward drinking
Too talkative	20.	20.	Intellectual interests
Choice of friends	21.	21.	Respect for conventions
Interested in other men	22.	22.	Conceited
Lack of freedom	23.	23.	Choice of friends
Respect for conventions	24.	24.	Spoils children
Intellectual interests	25.	25.	Lack of freedom
Attitude toward drinking	26.	26.	Too talkative
Not faithful	27.	27.	Religious beliefs
Religious beliefs	28.	28.	Jealous
Education	29.	29.	Swears
Swears	30.	30.	Drinks
Tastes in food	31.	31.	Education
Wife older	32.	32.	Husband older
Smokes	33.	33.	Tastes in food
Drinks	34.	34.	Smokes
Younger	35.	35.	Younger[56]

[56] L. M. Terman, *et al.: Psychological Factors in Marital Happiness*, p. 105. McGraw-Hill Book Company, 1938.

In love there ought to be *at least* as much respect for individuality and freedom as in friendship. Threats to individuality through the loss of privacy may become a serious source of dissatisfaction.

The impact of one person upon the other is often incalculably heavy. And the marriage situation, aggravated by the extreme intimacies of early marriage, is a crushing weight upon the idealized pictures of marriage. As the area of privacy diminishes, the opportunity for idealization diminishes at an equal pace. As intimacies increase, opportunities for disgusts are multiplied. As personalities become known, imagined accords and agreements are destroyed. As the revelations of the past of the other person proceed, something ordinary replaces the imagined clouds of glory. As we have seen, it is of the nature of early marriage interaction to tend toward an unusual intimacy. It is not surprising, therefore, that the honeymoon so often ends in conflict.[57]

Resentment against encroachments upon one's individuality may accumulate because the resentment is not easily expressed; indeed, the individual may not be aware of the basis for his alienation and even if he does recognize the origin of his hostile feelings, he may not wish to reveal them. It is usually very embarrassing to speak to one's partner about personal matters that are displeasing. The individual learns from experience that it is difficult to talk over such touchy subjects without becoming involved in a heated quarrel, and so he develops the habit of keeping his grievances to himself, brooding over them perhaps, leaving his darksome thoughts unsaid.

"You should never marry a man to reform him" is a popular saying which emphasizes the need for practicing tolerance in marriage. Each partner must accept the other's personality. Subtle campaigns looking toward substantial reform of the other one's nature are inadvisable. Trouble is likely to result from efforts to make the mate over in one's own image.

Mr. Brown is a highly intelligent man with a deliberate, reflective, critical type of mind. He is a bit rigid and conventional in his thinking and he shows only a moderate amount of originality. In disposition he is inclined to be suspicious and secretive at all times and occasionally acutely jealous. His general emotional tone is serious rather than merry, although he is not actually gloomy. His wife has an alert uncritical mind that is certainly far from profound, but she is both facile and ingenious. Her reaction-time is fast, and the kind of thinking she does at all she does on the dead run. She is the type of person who thinks up a new way to hang curtains while she is scrubbing

[57] Reprinted by permission of The Dryden Press, publishers of *The Family: A Dynamic Interpretation,* by Willard Waller, 1938. P. 313.

a bathtub, or evolves the perfect discipline for Junior while the dentist is pulling one of her teeth. In disposition she is generous, affectionate, and naïve; she gives away time, love, ideas, money, or work to anyone who seems to need them. Her emotional tone is cheerful, but she has a tendency to become excited and she loses her temper easily. Mr. Brown's deliberate carefulness looked to Mrs. Brown like security, and her vivacity seemed to him charming and thrilling. All would be well if each were willing to leave the other alone, but the one trait they share is a conviction that his or her way is the only way. Mr. Brown constantly urges his wife to stop and think, the way he does; she gets annoyed because he is unable to think on his feet as she does. He is sure her quickness is nothing but carelessness, and she regards his deliberation as sheer stupidity. She scoffs at his fear that someone will steal his inspirations, and he froths at the mouth when she lightheartedly gives away a good idea. He regards her casual way of picking up acquaintances as in bad taste, and she thinks his caution and suspicion to be cowardly and undemocratic. He warns her that people will criticize her, and she replies blithely "O.K., let 'em," and goes on her way. She tries to reform his seriousness, and he tries to dampen her gaiety. Each of them has precisely the qualities the other needs, but instead of valuing their individual differences they criticize, deride, abuse, and quarrel—each trying to re-create the other in his own likeness.[58]

Some of the collisions in family life are due to the fact that duties and privileges are obscurely defined in our culture. If the wife thinks that a husband should help with the baby, wash the dishes, turn the wringer, wax the floors, and if he has different ideas about what he should be doing in his spare time, it is obvious that a clash is in the offing. If the husband thinks his wife should do all the shopping, press his trousers, clean the windows, do her own housework, and she thinks her list of responsibilities does not include all of these particular assignments, then again it's a case of an irresistible force up against an immovable object. There is considerable confusion in our time concerning the role of the married woman. There are at least three common roles, each implying certain privileges and obligations:

(1) The *wife-and-mother* role is the traditional role of the married woman. It implies as privileges security, the right to support, alimony in the case of divorce, respect as a wife and mother, a certain amount of domestic authority, loyalty of the husband to one who has borne him children, and a more or less sentimental gratitude from husband and children. Corresponding obligations include bearing and rearing children, making a home, rendering domestic

---

[58] From *Attaining Maturity*, by Luella Cole, copyright, 1944, by Luella Cole Lowie, and reprinted by permission of Rinehart and Co., Inc.

service, loyal subordination of self to the economic interests of the husband, an
acceptance of a dependent social and economic status, and the acceptance of a
limited range of interests and activity.

(2) The *companion* role is essentially a leisure-class phenomenon. The

Up Window—Down Window. (Courtesy, Ted Key. Reproduced
by special permission from the *Saturday Evening Post,* copyright
1941, 1943, 1948, by the Curtis Publishing Company.)

privileges pertaining to this role include sharing pleasures with the husband,
receiving a more romantic emotional response, being the object of admiration,
receiving funds adequate for dress and recreation, having leisure for social
and educational activity, and the receiving of a certain amount of chivalrous
attention. On the other hand, it implies as obligations the preservation of
beauty under the penalty of marital insecurity, the rendering of ego and
libido satisfaction to the husband, and the cultivation of social contacts ad
vantageous to him, the maintenance of intellectual alertness, and the responsibility for exorcising the demon of boredom.

(3) Finally, there is the *partner* role, corresponding to a new definition of
the cultural situation which is gradually emerging. This entails the privileges
of economic independence, equal authority in regard to family finances, ac-

:eptance as an equal, exemption from one-sided personal or domestic service :o the husband, equal voice in determining locale of residence, and equality in :egard to social and moral liberty. The obligation side of the balance sheet .vould include renouncing alimony save in the case of dependent children, :omplete sharing of the legal responsibilities of the family, willingness to dispense with any appeal to chivalry, and equal responsibility to maintain the family status by success in a career.[59]

There is much overlapping of these various roles and consequent confusion. Personality conflicts are generated because a woman cannot decide which role she wants to fill, because she may play one role and wish it were another, because she may be performing one role while her husband is expecting her to adopt another, because she may assume the obligations without enjoying the correlative privileges.

Another source of conflict is the possibility that two persons who are well mated at the start may grow in disparate directions with the passing of the years. The bride who was gay may turn into a household drudge; the groom who was intellectually alert may deteriorate mentally as his business comes to consume all of his waking hours. One partner may mature as life unfolds, the other may regress to childish dependence and refuse to grow up. "Since personalities are not static but are in the process of development, a combination favorable to the functioning of the personality at one time may not be so for a later period in that personality's development; and hence a period, or recurring periods, of unadjustment may provide conditions of 'growth' until a relatively mature and stable level of personality organization is achieved." [60] Mutual adaptation may not be effected if the differences are so radical as to overtax the capacities for adjustment. The relationship is reciprocal; if mates do not grow together, they are going to grow apart. Joined at the beginning by sex appeal, perhaps, they may part in time as one continues on this basis and the other lapses into a mere desire for companionship. Children complicate the marriage situation. Mates who have been happy in each other may lose their *rapport* when affection is spread to sons and daughters.

The problem of the in-laws and other obvious vexations in marriage and family life have not been discussed. Our attention has been directed to some of the psychological adjustments which are not so

[59] Reprinted by permission of The Dryden Press, publishers of *The Family: A Dynamic Interpretation*, by Willard Waller, 1938. Pp. 323-324.
[60] E. W. Burgess and L. S. Cottrell: *Predicting Success or Failure in Marriage*, p. 11. Prentice-Hall, Inc., 1939.

generally taken into account by young folks contemplating marriage. Such concentration upon the frustrations and disappointments may create the false impression that we are endorsing Keyserling's view that married life is basically a tragic state of tension. "Marriage," he says, "apart from all its advantages, demands daily and hourly self-sacrifice, renunciation, and the shouldering of responsibility." [61]   True enough, but let's not forget that there are "advantages," as he suggests. The darker side is not the only side. Our thesis is that happiness is not a gift from the gods but something to be created by facing the facts and surmounting the difficulties. We agree with Nimkoff that happy family life is achieved "not by the absence of trials and tribulations, but by the conquest of them." [62]   It is with this possibility in mind that we have stressed the "trials and tribulations."

Incompatibility is considered as ground for divorce in some states. Somehow the impression is created that incompatibility is something unusual in marriage. It is important to correct this fallacy, as the late Felix Adler often pointed out in his lectures and writings on the subject. In one interview he expounded his views as follows:

It behooves us to face the fact that incompatibility in personal relations is the rule, and natural, and that harmony and complete compatibility are the ideal—something to be created, not the gift of the gods. We do not naturally come into tune with each other. No two faces are alike, no two characters are alike.

The more developed a person is the more he has discrepancies, peculiarities, not shared by others. You often find one with a strong and dominating will, another yielding, devoted, self-effacing. But that is not harmony, it is obliteration, whether on the side of the man or the woman. A man may do everything within his ability to give a delightful home to his partner, but that is not harmony—it is submergence of the personality. Wherever there is growing character and mind, there you inevitably get differences, and the art of composing these differences in such a way that they shall dove-tail with one another, shall be compensatory, is the subject of the new ethics I am trying to teach. . . .

In all human relationships, parenthood and childhood, friendship, marriage, business, citizenship and international relations, we are dealing with natural incompatibilities. . . .

It is clear that mutual adjustment is constantly required in family life, where individual differences are too patent to be ignored and too

---

[61] Count H. Keyserling: *The Book of Marriage,* p. 47.   Harcourt, Brace and Company, 1926.

[62] Nimkoff: *op. cit.,* p. 506.

persistent to be glossed over by superficial assurances that "all is well."

The high incidence of divorce among persons involved in hasty marriages during World War II is evidence of the fact that it takes a long time and plenty of continuous association for two people in love to learn how to get along happily with each other. Short acquaintance, a hurried honeymoon, and a long separation do not furnish a satisfactory basis for a stable marriage. Inspired by feelings of patriotic devotion and a sense of "now or never," unions were consummated without adequate emotional preparation and commitments made with little thought for the long-range future. Many of these war marriages are going "on the rocks," leaving the young lovers disillusioned and perhaps wiser.

Mixed marriages, that is, marriages contracted by persons of divergent religious faiths, do not turn out well, either. There are so many sources of incompatibility in the marriage relationship under normal conditions; the addition of one more area of friction often proves the "last straw." Statistics show that marriage between two persons of the same religious faith is more likely to be successful. It is clear from the evidence that religion is an important matter to consider in selecting a mate, important because religious training touches marital adjustments at so many vital points. The records of mixed marriages demonstrate that among Catholics and Protestants who marry, one-third are successful, one-third survive despite their unhappiness, and one-third end in divorce. There is more likelihood of success when the wife is a Catholic and the husband a Protestant, than when the situation is reversed. A Catholic and a Jew stand a better chance of success than a Catholic and a Protestant. A liberal Christian and a liberal Jew will find their prospects better than those of a liberal Christian married to an orthodox Jew.[63]

Warnings against mixed marriages have been issued by Catholic, Jewish, and Protestant authorities. We shall quote a representative of each of these faiths, in turn.

CATHOLIC

Don't ever permit yourself, dear non-Catholic friend, to fall in love with a Catholic, for love is unreasoning and lures its victims into thinking that there are exceptions to all rules and experiences.

Should you determine to marry a Catholic, you would first have to make an agreement, binding in conscience, never to interfere with the full performance of your wife's religious beliefs and practices—to have all your children

[63] See G. S. Overton: *Marriage in War and Peace*, pp. 166-167. 1945.

baptized in the Catholic faith, raised in it, educated in it. And this you would have to continue to do even should your wife die when the children are still babies.

If you were to wed a Catholic, a priest—and only a priest—could marry you; nor would a second ceremony by the minister of your own church be permitted.

Should you marry a Catholic, your family would always be divided, religiously speaking, and you would be the lone outsider left at home when the rest went to mass or benediction, or going alone to your own church of a Sunday or trailing along with your wife and children, a spectator, but not a participant in their worship. And some day you would wonder just what to answer when the children who belonged to you would ask why you, too, didn't go to confession or Holy Communion along with them.

In the Catholic Church marriage is a sacrament which calls for spiritual advancement as well as physical love. It calls for children without unnatural hindrance—Catholic children, all of them. Marriage, too, is a contract made before God and man which is totally binding on both "till death us do part."

The Catholic Church does all in its power to discourage mixed marriages and permits them only with the greatest of reluctance. Its marriage laws were enacted not to antagonize those of other creeds, nor to work a hardship on anyone, but to safeguard the faith of the Catholic.

Of course, dear neighbor, you may not concur with all this, but perhaps what we have said will, from the non-Catholic viewpoint, make you agree that our advice is good when we say it: Don't marry a Catholic! [64]

JEWISH

"What about the marriage of Jews and Gentiles?" I asked Rabbi James G. Heller, distinguished President of the Central Conference of American Rabbis. "From the non-Jewish viewpoint we are advising against these interfaith unions. Is that the position of Judaism?"

"Yes, very decidedly so," was the quick answer. "The traditional Jewish religious attitude is that such a marriage is forbidden either by Scripture or rabbinical law or both and is therefore a sin.

"In the reform group, on the other hand, opposition is not on the grounds of sin, but of expediency. The final determination is left to the couple themselves, but about two-thirds of the rabbis in this group will not officiate at the wedding because among the Jews a wedding is considered a religious ceremony in which the non-Jew cannot truly participate.

"Jews today view the future with grave concern. They feel strongly a need for community of interests. As a social group their continued existence de-

---

[64] This statement, entitled "Don't Marry a Catholic," was prepared by the Narberth Movement. It appeared first in a symposium in *Classmate*, October, 1943; later was reprinted by the National Conference of Christians and Jews. For other authoritative statements by the several faiths, see Overton: *op. cit.*, pp. 167-179.

pends upon the maintenance separately of Jewish tradition, custom, and religion. To step outside their group for mates is to endanger their solidarity.

"Intermarriages are also inexpedient because of the difficulties in adjustment of Jewish and non-Jewish religion and customs. The husband and wife are better able as adults to make necessary readjustments. But the cultural gap between them may be so great that it is very difficult for the wife to feel at ease in the husband's family circle or the husband in his wife's. One cannot completely ignore relatives and friends with their divergent and sometimes quite antagonistic viewpoints.

"Any attempt to escape religious conflicts by giving up church attendance and activities is nothing short of a spiritual disaster. Both mates and their children need to cultivate religious ideals and practices. Failure to do so robs them of the highest satisfactions and fullest attainments known to human beings.

"I urge a couple to consider perhaps above everything the possible plight of their children. It is folly not to be realistic. Anti-Semitic prejudices are widespread and often unbelievably vindictive. The non-Jew who marries a Jew may be able as an adult to withstand the attacks of bigotry when they are directed at him. But how will he feel about having exposed his child to them? And what will they mean to the sensitive child himself?

"The Jewish-Gentile marriage should be discouraged. You can say that for me as a rabbi and for all thoughtful Jewish people." [65]

PROTESTANT

She was a beautiful girl—more beautiful, in fact, than she had been the evening I conducted her wedding ceremony. There was something about her maturity that made her even more attractive than she had been as a girl. But it was plain that she was in very great trouble. Every line of her lovely face betokened anxiety.

"Ted's a wonderful fellow," she said, "and he's kind and considerate. But it's his religion. I don't know what to do."

Some of us had been greatly concerned when this fine Protestant girl had fallen so deeply in love with that splendid Catholic boy. Both were excellent young people, and they deserved the best that life could give. However, knowing the genuine devotion of each, we greatly feared the outcome of the marriage.

"It's not that we quarrel," she went on. "But you see, the deepest and most precious thing in life is something we cannot share with one another. Ted believes his way, and I believe mine, and I think we'll never get together. He's as honest as I am, and I know I'm as honest as he is. My church and my religion have been the most precious things I have had in life, and it's the

[65] Interview with Rabbi James G. Heller, originally appearing under the title, "Consider the Children," in *Classmate*, October, 1943; it was later reprinted by the National Conference of Christians and Jews.

same with Ted. But now we've discovered it's something we just can't talk about."

She was making the discovery that thousands of other young people have made, when it is too late: the thing that should be drawing and holding them together was actually separating them.

"Not long ago our baby was sick, and very sick, too. Ted and I were almost frantic. And in that awful hour we discovered we couldn't pray together for her. Ted had been trained to pray one way, and I had been trained to pray another. When we tried to pray together it just didn't work. It was terrible."

She really wasn't an unreasonable girl. I remembered how, before her marriage, she tried to "be broad-minded about it all." And Ted was not narrow or bigoted either—the empty place in their marriage was as painful to him as to her. But the difference in the religion and religious training was something too deep and broad to be overcome by broad-mindedness and "tolerance."

It was not that they had quarreled over the matter. They had not. It was just that the most sacred and fundamental thing in life was something that had to be shut away and never discussed. When she was in a tight place she asked Ted to pray for her, and in his way he did. When she knew Ted was going out to meet a bad situation in his work, she never failed to send up her prayers. But this difference in their church life and religious experience made it impossible for them to pray for each other, together!

"And now that the baby has come it's tragic. I agreed that any child should be reared a Catholic, but I made that agreement when I didn't know what it would mean to a mother. If that baby is to be a Catholic it means that I will not even have my own child! Ted says to let the thing ride, that it will come out somehow, but the longer we let it ride the worse it gets. And it seems we can't even talk about that. It's not that Ted gets angry or that I lose my head. It's all so deep and desperate."

And in spite of the fact that she loves Ted, and in spite of the fact that he takes good care of her, providing her with all the clothes and other things necessary, she begged me to say to other girls, "Make sure you know what you're doing before you marry a Catholic." [66]

c. *The Art of Love.* The success of marriage, in so far as sex is concerned, depends essentially on the knack of converting a fugitive desire into a lasting emotion. Making love last is an art. "It is easier," said Byron, "to die for a woman one loves than to live with her." Keeping

---

[66] R. L. Smith: "Know What You Are Doing." *Classmate*, October, 1943. Later reprinted by the National Conference of Christians and Jews. See also: "If I Marry a Roman Catholic." Prepared by The Commission on Marriage and the Home of the Federal Council of the Churches of Christ in America. 1945. Procurable for five cents at 297 Fourth Avenue, New York City.

the spirit of romance alive requires thought and intelligence. It is important that the partners have some insight into each other's attitudes regarding the place of sex in their union, the number and timing of children, their management and discipline, the role of the wife as a homemaker, extramarital friendships, and the responsibility of the family in the community. Mutual understanding is promoted by frank discussion of personal preferences with respect to perfume, twin beds, gum chewing, smoking, open windows, menus, convertible coupés, and a host of other trivia that add up to the difference between contentment and dissatisfaction. This point is stressed because so many people feel that romance is just something that happens to one, that it is just a matter of chance whether love is going to last or not. Such a naïve faith in luck needs to be corrected by the recognition that there is no harm in knowing whither in general you expect to be going on the sea of matrimony and how in particular you expect to get there. Something more definite than a vague yearning is necessary to make a success of marriage. It is true that no exact formulas can be laid down for sure guidance. The deftness of the skilled artist is called for. Even the artist must have a pretty good idea of what he's doing.

There is one principle fundamental in the art of marriage, according to Keyserling, and that is the precept of keeping an appropriate "distance," just the opposite of what most lovers dream of as the ideal.

> The validity of this principle is indisputable; a relation that is essentially contingent upon tension, if it is not self-sustaining, can be maintained only by means of a consciously practiced reserve. And this applies more especially, the more intimate the relation on which the state of tension is based. . . . Man and woman should never endeavor to be completely merged in one another; on the contrary, the more intimate they are, the more strictly should they cherish their own individuality, and it should be the unwritten law that neither must encroach on the rights of the other. In the case of highly differentiated people, conjugal happiness wholly depends on this sound principle of keeping one's distance; and in this respect, a by no means unimportant art is to sense the right time for separating for a short while. But in reality this principle is equally valid everywhere. It's application is obvious as regards the maintenance and preservation of passion; in this case, if no restrictions are imposed, allurements soon fade.[67]

Woe is the man whose wife is convinced that neither one should have a secret from the other, or vice versa. There is no justification for a

[67] Keyserling: *op. cit.,* p. 36.

policy of insisting that each should be accountable to the other for every action or speech, that questions such as "Who's the letter from?" should be asked and should be answered, that each should feel it a right to inquire into all the doings of the other, that there should be no reticences, no reserves. Life would be pleasanter if each person disciplined himself to "mind his own business" without being reminded to do so. There can be no peace in a home where there is ever present the menace of an unannounced intrusion.[68] "The only time I am alone," complained one man, "is when I am in my bath." It is unfortunate that so many persons today fail to respect the wisdom of preserving some mystery, for it is easy for marriage to degenerate into a prosaic routine under conditions of uninhibited familiarity. Monogamy may become monotony if each party is an open book to the other with no surprises ahead to hold the reader's interest.

The art of love usually connotes "the art of making love." The art of love, of course, is really a broader term that includes not only the sexual side of marriage but all the other fine points of living together which contribute to the deepening of love and the achievement of lasting happiness. Most students of marriage agree that sexual adjustment is an important aspect of family solidarity. Popenoe asserts that sexual maladjustment is the most important factor in most divorces, though the parting couple may not be aware of the reason underlying their separation.[69] De Pomerai asserts: "The sex relationship is a comparatively small thing in marriage if it is satisfactory . . . but a very big thing if it is not all right. . . . The real underlying cause of most marital unhappiness and divorce is invariably sexual discontent."[70] These observations are made with the full knowledge that sex is not a thing apart—it is a relation that is intertwined with all the other relationships of married life. The husband who has been inconsiderate during the day is more than likely to find his wife incapable of affectionate response at night; and the husband who is constantly belittled or nagged at by his wife will discover he has little appetite for her when they come into physical contact. Mowrer calls attention to the "importance of sexual adjustment in promoting harmonious adjustment in other relations";[71] it is just as essential to point

---

[68] See V. T. Van de Water: "Does Your Family Cramp Your Style?" *This Week Magazine,* April 30, 1939.

[69] See Popenoe: *op. cit.,* pp. 79-80.

[70] R. de Pomerai: *Marriage,* p. 226. 1930.

[71] E. R. Mowrer: *The Family; Its Organization and Disorganization,* p. 197. 1932.

out that sexual adjustment is affected by the showing of courtesy and consideration in all the interactions of domestic coexistence.

There are two occasions when a husband's tact, sympathy, and self-control are urgently needed, if he is to be an expert in love and life: in the first days of married life, and in the first days of the monthly ebb, when feminine tinder is highly inflammable and an angry retort to an overwrought wife may be the powder train leading to an explosion. If a husband can extinguish the smoldering brand and not fling it back, there will be fewer quarrels and a closer bond between them. The situation offers the man a real chance to generate a peculiarly masculine type of sympathy and affection. This solicitude will not go unnoticed. For although women may approach the irrational at such times, they are keenly aware of the little overtures made by the one closest to them in an all too lonely world. It is a husband's greatest opportunity to instill a deep-rooted and abiding devotion.[72]

Authorities on marriage and divorce can cite many cases where ignorance concerning the art of love has proved costly in terms of human frustration and human sorrow. The blame for this unnecessary suffering should be laid where it belongs, on the puritanical attitude still poisoning the minds of well-meaning folks who see in sex something nasty and unclean. The enlightened person binds sex with inexorable standards, not because it is ugly and therefore to be feared, but because it is beautiful and therefore to be revered. All the loveliness in sex, man has made; its romance, its sanctity, its beauty, are all his. It is man's genius which has spiritualized the physical union and converted marriage into a work of art.

To a person with insight, the art of love is only one phase of the larger art of living together. Domestic adjustment is more than sex adjustment. Marriage, as Keyserling sees it, and he sees it clearly, is a struggle for adaptation, an experiment in unselfishness, an adventure in mutual and self-sacrificing love, a discipline in patience, kindness, sympathy, renunciation, and utter devotion not to oneself but to another. Wedlock is not an open sesame to untrammeled joy; it is a test of personal resources, bringing out the best and the worst in human nature. Succeeding in love means more to human happiness than any other venture in life. Emotional creatures that we are, there is nothing so important as happy family life. The achievement of this end is worth every effort, as Dorothy Dix says so well:

[72] From "Marital Pitfall No. 1," by Gretta Palmer, *Reader's Digest,* February, 1938. Copyright, 1938, by The Reader's Digest Association, Inc. This statement is based on an observation made by T. H. van de Velde in his book, *Ideal Marriage.* 1936.

A prominent college announces that it is going to establish a course for the study of Family Relationships.

This should fill a long-felt want, for there is no other subject under the sun about which the great majority of people are so abysmally ignorant as they are about how to get along harmoniously with their own blood and kin and in-laws, nor is there any other one thing about which they are in such sore need of enlightenment as about how to make themselves really popular with those of their own households.

Strangely enough, this branch of the humanities has never been thought worthy of serious study. Our colleges have taught their eager-eyed young pupils the dead languages, but not how to speak the diplomatic word that averts strife in the home circle. They have been taught how to read the stars and calculate the eclipse of the moon, but not how to interpret the signs and portents on father's brow, or in mother's air that presage a storm and that make it unsafe to ask for an advance in an allowance or the use of the car. They have been taught how to handle the most intricate chemical formulas, but not how to blend the antagonistic dispositions of a bride and bridegroom so that when brought together they will not make an explosion that will wreck a home.

Why the higher culture has not included a good working knowledge of how to deal with those with whom Fate has cast our lot, it is hard to say. Certainly no education could be more valuable to us than that which would teach us how to manage our husbands and wives and parents and children and make them like it; how to gumshoe around the angles in their temperaments and how to pour oil on the troubled domestic waters. Those of us who could do that would have a right to consider ourselves really accomplished and be qualified for our M.A. degrees, for we would be truly masters of arts.

The most important thing in the world to every one of us, from the highest to the lowest, is our family relationship. The plaudits of the multitude are as empty as sounding brass and tinkling cymbals to the man who must go home from a cheering mob to a fault-finding and nagging wife. Bushels of pearls and strings of limousines do not compensate a wife for a husband who gives her everything but love and companionship.

No other sorrow can tear men's and women's hearts to tatters and bend their heads so deep in shame as can the children who bring disgrace upon them. The poorest child that is rocked to sleep in its mother's arms and that grows up in a home where there is love and tenderness is happier and more fortunate and has a better chance in life for success than have the children of millionaires who are turned over to hirelings to rear, whose only homes are boarding schools and camps, and who have a succession of stepfathers and stepmothers.

Of course, heretofore we have believed that a knowledge of how to deal with family relationships came by nature, just as Dogberry thought that a knowledge of reading and writing did. We have had the artless idea that every man and woman knew by instinct how to be good husbands and wives and parents and that all children honored their parents and that it was no trick at all to establish a happy home.

Perhaps that is why we have never thought it worth while to devote any time and study to the domestic group who through neglect threaten to become as extinct as any of the prehistoric animals. So it is encouraging to learn that our higher institutions of learning are about to take this subject up in a large way and try to prepare their students for marriage as they would for any other profession that they elected to follow.

Just what the curriculum is to be has not been stated, but the most important thing that can be taught in the course of Family Relationships is just ordinary politeness. If all the members of a family would treat each other with the courtesy and consideration that they show to every outsider on whom they wish to make a pleasant impression, there would be no domestic problem. It would solve itself, and the dove of peace would take up its perpetual roosting place on every rooftree.

It is a strange and unaccountable thing that we show our worst sides to those we love the most, and that we do everything possible to alienate from us those whose affections we desire above all others. It is only to our nearest and dearest that we say the things that stab like knives and that leave wounds that never heal.

Our whole happiness depends on our keeping our husbands and wives in love with us, admiring us, interested and entertained, and yet it is for strangers that we save our good clothes, our witty stories, our listening expression, our efforts at being charming. We agonize over our children leaving us and yet we drive them from us by our criticisms, our restrictions and our petty tyrannies.

If every husband made as much effort to be as fascinating and agreeable to his wife as he does to the woman he takes to dinner; if every wife jollied her husband as she does the men she meets at a party; if parents tried as hard to "sell" themselves to their children as they do to other nice young people, and if children were as well behaved at home as they are abroad, there would be no divorces and no unhappy homes.

So I trust that whatever else they teach in the course of Family Relationships they will teach good manners and to treat those of your own household as well as you do strangers.[73]

[73] Dorothy Dix, syndicated column printed on September 25, 1932.

d. *Inner Cohesion.* Modern marriage is based on love, not on legal compulsion. People today feel "that a willing loyalty in marriage is the only loyalty worth having." [74] Solidarity is founded on free choice rather than outer coercion. This insistence that the association of husband and wife be continued only on the condition that they wish to stay together because of mutual affection is now embodied in our marriage mores as a consciously recognized ideal, that marital security is hardly worth the struggle unless it is sought in a spirit of mutual love.

It is not a sense of duty that draws Darby and Joan ever closer to each other as the years pass: to the pleasures they originally shared, there has been added the fact that they feel *at home* together, and "strange" when they happen to be separated. These are the real "ties that bind" in marriage, yet they do not gall the husband and wife because they have grown up from within, instead of having been imposed from without.[75]

In expecting too much of marriage, husband and wife may not be as tolerant as they should be of each other's faults. The modern attitude that a couple should stick together only as long as they are united by love may incline the mates to part company on slight provocation, their incompatibilities being mistaken for irreconcilable differences. There is some point in the facetious remark, "True love endures—it has to." There are times when it seems to one or both partners that they "just can't go on this way any longer"; on such occasions a kindly patience may give love a chance to come back, for moods change from hostility to affection, as moods will with a little encouragement. It is significant that divorces fall off when business declines.

There are fewer divorces sought during depression years than there are during good times. Women seem to be more tolerant of the faults of their husbands during depressed periods. Perhaps it is not as easy to get another husband in such times.[76]

Be that as it may, married people are more apt to stay married during hard times. Whether they do so because they are overlooking the defects in each other, we cannot say. It may be true of some homes that the preservation of marriage "in name alone" only adds its incre-

[74] J. M. Murry and J. C. Young: "Modern Marriage." *Forum*, January, 1929.
[75] L. Gould: "How 'Normal' Is Jealousy?" *Esquire*, October, 1938.
[76] Statement made by Arthur W. Sullivan, reported in the Boston *Herald*, January 30, 1939.

ment to the sum total of human misery; it may be true of other homes that the force of economic necessity keeps the husband and wife together long enough to discover that they really love each other after all. These comments are offered with the idea of impressing on the reader the importance of examining our newer ideals carefully in order to assess them with respect to both their advantages and their limitations. Most of us will agree, I think, that inner cohesion, as a modern ideal, is an improvement on the old-fashioned ideal of "sticking it out regardless"; but we should be fair enough to see the virtues, whatever they were, in the old-fashioned readiness "to put up with a lot for the sake of keeping the family together." It may be that we moderns are in too much of a hurry to sever the bonds of matrimony.

2. DIVORCE

"A low divorce rate," says Lichtenberger, "is no absolute ground of assurance that marriage conditions are ideal." [77] Another way of putting this same observation is to note that it is an error to judge the success of a marriage by the length of time that it endures. The general trend of the divorce rate has been upward ever since the Civil War, a development that is shocking and alarming to some people. We must analyze this situation carefully before deciding that "we are going to the dogs." What are the facts? What do they mean?

Desertion and adultery have been declining as grounds for divorce; cruelty has come into increasing favor as the best available charge. This does not mean that people are growing more cruel than they used to be. It simply signifies that it is less defaming to the spouse's character to charge him with cruelty than it is to pin adultery on him, and that wives who are out to get a decree are decent enough to want to do it in a refined manner. It is the women, mostly, who sue for divorce; it is to them the decree is usually granted. Husbands ordinarily agree to be the ones sued; they agree to admit they've been cruel or at least they agree not to speak out of turn if a witness makes up a good tale about harsh words and severe beatings; they are cooperative when collusion is proposed. Men are never so chivalrous as when their wives request them to be good sports and "get into the spirit of the thing" when a suit is being filed. It is this sort of conspiracy amongst husbands and wives and lawyers that Judge Lindsey sought to abolish by proposing "honest divorce" as one feature of the companionate-marriage program.

[77] Lichtenberger: *op. cit.*, p. 111.

Divorces are occurring earlier in marriage than formerly. More of them take place in urban areas than in rural areas. Possibly the higher incidence of divorce in the cities is due to the smaller influence of religious orthodoxy, the absence of community restraints, and the weakness of the home ties. College graduates are less involved, maybe on account of their superior intelligence and their marrying later in life.[78]   Divorces are more apt to occur in childless families. This fact does not imply necessarily that it is the absence of children *per se* which contributes to the frequency of divorce, for such a conclusion, popular as it may be among advocates of large families, is supported "neither by the statistics nor by logical inference." [79]   Mowrer warns against interpreting too simply the relation between childlessness and divorce:

Just because there were no children, however, does not necessarily mean that had there been offspring there would have been no divorce. . . .   It may be that to a large degree the persons who get divorces are those who do not want children, and for much the same reason, i.e., because they wish to retain their personal freedom.[80]

Divorce and childlessness may both be attributable to the same cause: highly individualized life patterns in husband and wife who do not want children and who do not want each other after the bond begins to bind.[81]

The higher divorce rate may be interpreted as indicative of a rise rather than a decline in our standards of morality.   Moral values have changed.   More is demanded of marriage; living together in mutual hostility and hatred is no longer condoned.   Some observers contend that people are freer, more intelligent, more moral today than people used to be, and they cite as evidence of higher moral standards, the insistence on mutual affection as the only decent basis for marriage.

The increase of divorce is symptomatic of wide social changes in the institution of the family—changes that we have already outlined as significant in the declining importance of the home as the center of social life.   Frequent divorce seems to be the norm toward which we are moving.   The non-divorce of people involved in unsatisfactory

---

[78] Co-ed wife: "Co-education Makes Good Marriages." *Scribner's Magazine*, November, 1931.

[79] Lichtenberger: *op. cit.*, p. 137.

[80] E. R. Mowrer: *The Family; Its Organization and Disorganization*, p. 73.   1928. A second edition of this book appeared in 1939.

[81] See Waller: *op. cit.*, pp. 528-529.

narriages may be viewed as a matter of "culture lag," that is, conervative adherence to old-fashioned attitudes. We must recognize hat the stability of the family, as people used to know it, is a thing of the past, gone because the conditions that made for such stability no longer prevail. An institution cannot remain changeless in a social framework that is subject to such constant flux.

The idea of the rightness of divorce is now accepted by a large majority of the women in America, according to a poll conducted by the *Ladies' Home Journal* in 1938. The investigators report that

A majority of the women of America believe:

In divorce; 69 per cent said "yes."

That there should be a uniform divorce law in all states; 94 per cent said 'yes."

That money is the chief source of friction in marriage.

That "in-laws" cause relatively little trouble between husband and wife.

That grounds for divorce should be—in the order named—adultery, desertion, cruelty, habitual drunkenness, failure to provide, venereal disease contracted before marriage, drug or dope habit.

That young people should be taught more about sex before they get married.

That sex instruction should be given by their parents.

That girls should not marry with a mental reservation that divorce can free them.[82]

The interviewers found the women of America eager to speak their minds on these questions. There can be no doubt of the trend of public opinion on the subject of divorce.

Despite this trend toward an overwhelming approval of divorce, there are still some die-hards who refuse to give their blessing, who protest that "there ought to be a law against it." There are already plenty of laws against it, and the funny thing is that the more stringent the laws become, the higher goes the divorce rate. Legal obstacles are of no avail. More effective would be constructive measures: adequate preparation for marriage; education in the psychology of family relationships; inculcation of wholesome attitudes toward sex; enlarging the range of choice by improving the opportunities for young people to meet each other; and provision of good low-cost houses to

[82] H. F. Pringle: "What Do the Women of America Think about Marriage and Divorce?" *Ladies' Home Journal*, February, 1938. Reprinted, by special permission, from the *Ladies' Home Journal*. Copyright, 1938, The Curtis Publishing Company.

encourage settling down in one spot for a while—in other words, doing everything possible to stabilize life in the home and to give the family a position of central importance.

Alienation is implicit in every marriage, a fact that we are prone to overlook. "Marriages which end in divorce are not greatly different from other marriages. . . . There is conflict in all marriages." [83] The line between success and failure is a fine one. Favorable conditions might conceivably tip the scales toward the preservation of the marital status. A constructive attack on the problem of divorce could prove fruitful.

It is important for us to give serious thought to the means available for reducing divorce because family disintegration is so expensive in terms of mental cost. Divorce is a tragedy because it involves wounds to pride, because it is an advertisement of personal failure, and because it is difficult for the divorced person to find a new role in the community where social occasions are planned for the married, the divorcés, together with the widows, being left out.[84] Divorce is evidence of misfortune, too, the sad plight of unhappy parents who are apt to have unhappy children. The children suffer from the unhappy marriage rather than from the divorce; in most cases the children are better off after the granting of the decree, for it is mentally unwholesome for children to live with squabbling parents.[85]

Opinion on grounds for divorce has not yet been crystallized. The legal grounds include adultery, cruelty, desertion, drunkenness, nonsupport, neglect to provide, insanity, and incompatibility. In New York adultery is the only ground; in South Carolina there are no grounds.

Although adultery is cited as the formal ground in less than ten per cent of U. S. divorces and so rates far down the list after cruelty and desertion, some divorce lawyers insist that adultery is the real cause about ninety per cent of the time. Such are American morals, however, that even where known adultery exists, most people prefer to be branded—or to brand their spouses—as tyrants, deserters, anything but adulterers. Hence the airing, under the label of "cruelty," of types of marital meanness which vary from forcing a wife to make pancakes for use as poker chips to putting itching powder in her corsets; from refusing to take baths to refusing to have a child because it would cost too much and then buying a horse; from holding a wife's false

[83] Waller: *op. cit.*, pp. 540, 525.
[84] See W. Waller: *The Old Love and the New: Divorce and Readjustment.* 1930
[85] See Lichtenberger: *op. cit.*, p. 140.

eeth for two dollars' ransom to "allus shootin' his mouth off about other
ames." [86]

The Roman Catholic Church still prohibits divorce on any ground;
most of the Protestant churches have given their sanction to di-
orce. The laws on divorce are not uniform, ecclesiastical opinion
s not unified. The contradictory attitudes expressed through our
ivil and religious institutions help to aggravate the mental conflict
ormenting individuals who have to face the possibility of divorce and
add to the confusion of friends who want to adopt an intelligent
policy in their personal contacts with the alienated couple.

Contrary to the popular impression on the matter, the great ma-
ority of divorced persons do not remarry.[87] The number who get
divorced to remarry immediately is small, despite the prevailing opin-
on to the contrary. The few who do remarry at once lay themselves
open to censure for their apparent indifference to the sanctity of the
marriage bond.

Several kinds of agencies have been set up to deal with domestic discord and to obviate divorce by effecting reconciliation. Courts of
Domestic Relations have not been very successful in this task of fore-
stalling family collapse, partly because the case has become hopeless
by the time it reaches the court, partly because the court situation itself is not conducive to a peaceful settlement of differences.[88] Family
Guidance Clinics have proved more effective in heading off divorce.
These clinics, which date back only to 1929 in this country, are growing in number. They are privately supported, some of them functioning under church auspices as a division of social-service work, some of
them operating under university direction. The best-known clinic, the
one doing the most extensive work in this field, is the Institute of
Family Relations at Los Angeles. The program of such a clinic
includes the clarification of family troubles, the provision of information on household management and other related matters, and the
remotivation of the alienated couple so that a "change of heart" may
be brought about.[89]

Harriet Mowrer, Domestic Discord Consultant of the Jewish Social Service Bureau in Chicago, reports a high degree of success in
settling marital difficulties. She finds that her clients are usually

[86] *Life*, September 3, 1945. [87] See Nimkoff: *op. cit.*, p. 447.
[88] See E. R. Mowrer and H. R. Mowrer: *Domestic Discord*, p. 149. 1928.
[89] See Nimkoff: *op. cit.*, pp. 490-503.

ready with explanations as to the basis for their troubles and invari
ably it is the other person who is to blame. The individual know
that he has been wronged and goes to the consultant to get suppor
for his conviction that he is not the one responsible for the impasse
The therapist, of course, is not interested in fixing blame; his func
tion is to help the client see his situation objectively. This end i
achieved by showing the husband and wife that their difficulties ar
possibly traceable to early training, to differing cultural backgrounds
or to fundamental personality traits of long standing. Since people
meet the marriage situation by resorting to the same patterns they
have followed in adjusting to other problems, a genetic study of the
personality is made which furnishes an historical perspective throug
which the individual gains insight into the sources of his domestic dis
cord. The interviewer probes the past for light on the present con
flict:

Was the person the oldest, youngest . . . child in the family? Was he
pampered or ignored? Did he feel misunderstood? Who was considered the
head of the family?

What economic class did the individual's family belong to?

How much knowledge of sex was there at the time of marriage?

What did they expect of marriage? How has that hope been modified or
abandoned? [90]

The consultant learns all he can about the early family organization,
the cultural patterns prior to marriage, the social interactions between the family and the community, the conflicts within the family
group, and the rationalizations advanced to explain the difficulties.
Then he enlightens the partners and their relatives, so that all persons
concerned may cooperate in "ironing out" the differences which are
preventing reasonable harmony between husband and wife. Time
and patience are required; a happy solution is well worth the effort.

The range of services that are rendered by a well-staffed clinic is
exemplified in the work being done at the Alto Psychologic Center in
San Francisco, where counsel is offered to men and women contemplating marriage, to the unhappily married, to the divorced, to the
unmarried adult, and to parents who want guidance in the sex education of their children. From their experience in counseling, the staff
makes a plea for reliance upon all that scientific psychology can provide in the way of insight:

[90] See H. Mowrer: *Personality Adjustment and Domestic Discord,* Chapter 2,
"The Interview." American Book Company, 1935.

The sex or marriage problems of any individual must be regarded as problems of his particular personality. Problems that are similar in appearance may have to be approached and solved in widely differing ways because they have developed in different personalities.

More than this, there are very frequently complex and subtle inter-relationships between the problems of sex and marriage and the problems of vocational dissatisfaction, of social ineffectiveness, of parent-child difficulties, of alcoholic indulgence, and of personality frustrations of various kinds.

Every resource of the scientific psychology of the emotions, of motivation, and of learning must be used to study each personality, and to devise the most appropriate means for the prevention or solution of its problems. For all these reasons the best sex and marriage counseling requires the expertness of professional psychologists.[91]

Something more is needed than the simple rules for marital happiness formulated by Judge Sabath, who based his advice upon the domestic grievances aired in his court for years and years. Advises the Judge:

1. Have patience with each other.
2. Work together, play together, grow together.
3. In all disputes avoid excited talk.
4. Do not conceal little differences until they accumulate to the breaking point; discuss them calmly.
5. Be frank with each other.
6. Sympathy and mutual understanding are the pillars of the home.
7. Good humor in parting in the morning and a cheerful greeting at night are important.
8. Share responsibilities.
9. Establish a home of your own.
10. Make your bedtime prayers a review of the day and never go to sleep without a clean slate.[92]

Good, Judge, but how do you "work together, play together, grow together" if you don't feel like it or if your partner doesn't feel like it? It's all very well to say, "Discuss calmly," but how do you proceed to reason with a spouse who insists on being irrational and on raising his (or her) voice the minute you mention a point you'd like clarified? The real problem is how to carry out the Judge's maxims. That's where psychology comes in.

---

[91] Quoted from a brochure by H. de Fremery distributed by The Alto Psychologic Center, 210 Post Street, San Francisco, California.
[92] *Literary Digest,* December 23, 1931.

One reason for the prevalence of divorce is the prevalence of faitl in romance as an infallible basis for marriage. De Rougemont main tains that we are predisposing ourselves to disaster by overemphasiz ing passionate love. He cites the ancient Greeks and Romans whc regarded love as a mental aberration and the Orientals who fee that way about erotic courtship even now. Only in our Wester culture do we apotheosize romantic love as the number-one value il life.[93] We have glorified Romeo and Juliet, Tristan and Iseult, for sc long that we are blind to the risks involved in gambling on the se> thrill. The investment of the emotions should certainly merit a much study and care as the investment of money. Speculativ hunches are dangerous in either field. The lover, like the get-rich quick optimist, is easily misguided by superficial signs. Affection ma> be "counterfeited by mere sex attraction without genuine sym pathy." [94] Lovers don't want to look before they leap because they feel that deliberation is out of place in Cupid's realm. This is ; grave error, as Groves warns: "The purpose of intelligence in th mating experience is not to act as a check upon passion, a conception far too often held, but to clarify the experiences that influence choic and to interpret the needs that require fulfillment for matrimonia success." [95]

Fantastic as it may seem to one who has been through the mill, there are still many people at large who are naïve enough to believe that folks get married and then just naturally live happily ever after. I would be just as sensible to say, "They both found jobs and so they lived happily ever after." Our love stories—in novels, or songs, ou movies—nourish the absurd assumption that when the time comes for the lovers to embrace in the purple dawn, happiness has been found

We live in a world where it is well to remember that dreams do not always come true. Dreaming of his future, a man fancies his wife wil be a clever housewife, a good mother, and a sparkling comrade; if it turns out that she embodies one of these ideals, and one alone, he should thank his lucky stars. Girls, too, dream of the ideal existence ahead, of life with a man who is going to be the answer to a maiden's prayer, a successful business man, a handy man about the house, a thrilling lover, three in one, all combined in one person. That's

[93] See D. de Rougemont: *Love in the Western World.* 1940.

[94] E. R. Groves and W. F. Ogburn: *American Marriage and Family Relationships,* p. 29. 1928.

[95] E. R. Groves: *Marriage,* p. 67. 1933.

oo much to ask of any man.[96] Woe is the man or the woman who is
upposed to be the answer to these dreams. The specifications are
mpossible of fulfillment. The chances of a happy marriage would
e improved if our hopes and aspirations were more realistic.[97] If the
ounger generation were enlightened concerning the real values at-
ainable in marriage and family life, there would be fewer persons
vedding in haste and repenting at leisure. The best insurance against
divorce is a program of education that meets the realities of marital
oexistence with an honest appreciation of the problems that must be
olved if happiness is to be achieved.[98]

3. REDUCING THE GAMBLE

We have just observed that there would be less risk in getting married if prospective brides and prospective grooms were better prepared to face the problems ahead of them. There are means available for taking the guesswork out of choosing a mate. Any person
contemplating matrimony will naturally be interested in finding out
before it is too late whether his selection is a wise one. Kepler, the
famous astronomer, determined, after one unhappy marriage, to proceed more cautiously and more scientifically in embarking on a second
matrimonial venture. He listed all the available women, then weeded
them out until he had reduced the number of candidates to eleven.
Each of these women was then rated carefully, her assets on one side
of the ledger, her liabilities on the other. A score was computed and
the winner was the one he married. The marriage turned out worse
than his first venture. He gave up, disappointed, swearing that the
problem did not fall within the scope of mathematical precision. He
lived too soon, for we now have statistical analyses to guide us in
choosing a mate.

Predicting Success or Failure in Marriage, by Burgess and Cottrell,
is a report of an investigation into the various factors that predispose
men and women to happy or unhappy marriages.[99] The questionnaire method was used, supplemented by some intensive case studies.
A list of items relevant to marriage adjustment was assembled, garnered from published researches, from preliminary soundings by the

[96] See A. Black: *American Husbands.* 1925. Condensed in *Reader's Digest,* November, 1934.
[97] See J. K. Folsom (Editor): *Plan for Marriage,* Chapter 1, "Romance and Real-
ism in Love and Marriage." 1938.
[98] See Nimkoff: *op. cit.,* pp. 503-512.
[99] Published in 1939.

authors, from suggestions made by technical observers and by every
day married people. Two lists were compiled from these items, on
dealing with impersonal matters upon which subjects would be read
to give information without any inhibitions, the other dealing wit
the more intimate sex and family relationships upon which subject
would be less inclined to speak their minds freely. The first grou
of items was used in constructing the questionnaire; the secon
group was arranged in an outline to guide the interviewer and t
help persons writing autobiographical accounts of their marrie
lives. This plan was followed in order to circumvent resistance agains
filling out the questionnaire and to obtain by case studies reliabl
data on personal matters.

The questionnaire items were arranged in the following categories

1. Items on the husband's premarital background.
2. Items on the wife's premarital background.
3. Items on the postmarital attitudes and experiences of the couple.
4. An abbreviated personality inventory which might give some indication
for the presence or absence of neurotic tendencies in the person filling ou
the questionnaire.[100]

The questionnaires were filled out by 526 young married couples in
Illinois, mostly city folk, college or high school graduates, Protestants
more than half with an income of $1800 or more, all married from
one to six years, a majority having no children.

Happiness was taken as the criterion of successful marriage. The
subjects themselves furnished the marital-happiness ratings. 55.4 per
cent of the husbands rated their marriages very happy, 24.7 per cent
happy, 11.9 per cent average, 5.6 per cent unhappy, and 2.4 per cent
very unhappy; 51.8 per cent of the wives, very happy, 27.5 per cent
happy, 12.3 per cent average, 6 per cent unhappy, and 2.4 per cent very
unhappy. In 71.4 per cent of the cases, husbands and wives agreed in
their ratings; 24.6 per cent differed by only one step on the scale
Friends' ratings agreed with the couples' ratings in 48.5 per cent of the
cases, differed by only one degree in 42.7 per cent.

These happiness ratings were correlated with measures of marital
adjustment, secured through the administration of the questionnaire,
for the purpose of ascertaining what factors are conducive to a happy
marriage. Happy couples are those who agree on the handling of
family finances, who kiss each other frequently, who are in accord with

---

[100] Burgess and Cottrell: *op. cit.*, p. 18.

respect to intimate relations, who agree on friends and relatives—all indicative of "an intimate and affectionate companionship." [101]

How can a person tell ahead of time that his marriage with a certain person will turn out happily? What indices can he use for predicting success or failure? Significant facts in the backgrounds of successful couples were explored to serve as a guide to good matrimonial risks. Good risks are those whose parents have been happily married, who are strongly attached to their parents [*sic!*], who are the oldest children, who possess a similar family background, who attend Sunday School, who belong to three or more organizations. A man is desirable if he has a regular income no matter what its size, and if he has the kind of job that permits him to come home from work every day. The girl who has worked before marriage is a better risk than one who hasn't; she is especially desirable if she has been a teacher or a skilled office worker. Marriage is more likely to be a success if the couple have known each other for a long time, at least five or more years, with a courtship of three to five years' duration, and an engagement lasting two years. Affection and companionship are better signs of happiness ahead than infatuation and romance, since infatuation does not necessarily mean that sexual adjustment will be satisfactory when the marriage is consummated. Wanting to own a home is a good sign; so is the desire for children. Married persons are less happy after the children have come.

The findings of this pioneer study are recapitulated as follows:

1. Contrary to prevailing opinion, American wives make the major adjustment in marriage.

2. Affectional relationships in childhood, typically of the son for the mother and the daughter for the father, condition the love-object choice of the adult.

3. The socialization of the person, as indicated by his participation in social life and social institutions, is significant for adjustment in marriage.

4. The economic factor in itself is not significant for adjustment in marriage, since it is apparently fully accounted for by the other factors (impress of cultural background, psychogenetic characteristics, social type, and response patterns).

5. With the majority of couples, problems of sexual adjustment in marriage appear to be a resultant not so much of biological factors as of psychological characteristics and of cultural conditioning of attitudes toward sex.

6. Prediction before marriage of marital adjustment is feasible, and should and can be further developed through statistical and case-study methods.[102]

---

[101] *Ibid.*, p. 52.
[102] *Ibid.*, p. 349.

Terman and a group of collaborators conducted a similar investigation of marriage and happiness, using a marital-adjustment index much like that employed by Burgess and Cottrell. Terman and his staff applied their scale to 792 middle-class couples (average income: $2,450) in California, and the predictive value of the examination, in the experience of the investigators, led them to conclude: "Our data suggest that marital happiness can be predicted by our scale almost as accurately as the college success of a high school graduate can be predicted from an intelligence test." [103] This investigation leads to the conclusion that if an individual scores in the top quarter on the test, the chances are four out of five that his marriage will be average or above average in happiness.

According to Terman, happily married subjects differ from the unhappily married with respect to the following background variables:

Their parents were on the average decidedly more happy in marriage (this factor more differential for husbands than for wives). They had a much happier childhood. They much less frequently report conflict with the mother. Their home discipline was more often "firm, not harsh," less often very strict or lax, and much less often irregular (discipline more differential for wives than husbands). They were punished less severely and less frequently. They were more attached to both parents (more differential for husbands). They had less conflict with father (more differential for wives). Their early questions about sex were more frankly answered by their parents (more differential for husbands). Their premarital attitude toward sex was less often one of disgust and also less often one of eager and passionate longing (more differential for husbands). Happy husbands are less often markedly superior to their wives in mental ability, and happy wives are less often superior to their husbands.[104]

There is no evidence that a couple's income, religious training, differences in age or education have any distinguishing effect upon marital happiness. To a surprising degree the happiness of one spouse is independent of the other's. Satisfactory sexual mating is not the prime requisite for a happy marriage; personality and background factors are more important. Virginal couples have slightly higher chances for a happy marriage than others. Among the sex factors, the most significant are the relative strength of the sex drive in husband and wife, and the wife's ability to reach complete sexual satisfaction.

[103] L. M. Terman *et al.*: *Psychological Factors in Marital Happiness*, p. 6. McGraw-Hill Book Company, 1938.
[104] *Ibid.*, pp. 265-266.

Terman's study concentrated more than did the research of Burgess and Cottrell upon the temperamental factors differentiating happily and unhappily married persons. The thoroughness of his analysis in this respect is demonstrated in the description of happy and unhappy wives:

Happily married women, as a group, are characterized by kindly attitudes toward others and by the expectation of kindly attitudes in return. They do not easily take offense and are not unduly concerned about the impressions they make upon others. They do not look upon social relationships as rivalry situations. They are cooperative, do not object to subordinate roles, and are not annoyed by advice from others. Missionary and ministering attitudes are frequently evidenced in their responses. They enjoy activities that bring educational or pleasurable opportunities to others and like to do things for the dependent or underprivileged. They are methodical and painstaking in their work, attentive to detail, and careful in regard to money. In religion, morals, and politics they tend to be conventional. Their expressed attitudes imply a quiet self-assurance and a decidedly optimistic outlook upon life.

Unhappily married women, on the other hand, are characterized by emotional tenseness and by ups and downs of moods. They give evidence of deep-seated inferiority feelings to which they react by aggressive attitudes rather than by timidity. They are inclined to be irritable and dictatorial. Compensatory mechanisms resulting in restive striving are common. These are seen in the tendency of unhappy wives to be active "joiners," aggressive in business, and overanxious in social life. They strive for wide circles of acquaintances but are more concerned with being important than with being liked. They are egocentric and little interested in benevolent and welfare activities except in so far as these offer opportunities for personal recognition. They also like activities that are fraught with opportunities for romance. They are more inclined to be conciliatory in their attitudes toward men than toward women and show little of the sex antagonism that unhappily married men exhibit. They are impatient and fitful workers, dislike types of work that require methodical and painstaking effort. In politics, religion, and social ethics they are more often radical than happily married women.[105]

These are broad generalizations, Terman explains, perhaps too broad, but they are derived from a solid ground of concrete evidence.

Various criticisms have been leveled at these attempts to predict marital happiness. It is obvious that "happiness" is subjective, elusive, and indefinite, and, therefore, it is naïve to believe that ratings are an accurate index of the true state of affairs. How does a person

[105] *Ibid.*, p. 146.

know whether he is happily married, or unhappily married? Perhaps he would give one estimate this week and another very different one a month later. Weighting of the items in the scale, some being given a position of more importance than others, was determined by an arbitrary allocation of values. All the objections to the questionnaire technique may be raised against the investigations, as Hollingworth points out in citing a passage from Terman that damns the whole procedure, to wit: "Unhappy spouses display an irresistible [*sic!*] inclination to account for their unhappiness in terms of almost anything that is suggested." [106] This halo effect vitiates the entire technique of exploration. It is true, too, that people may say one thing and believe another. When husbands offer the opinion that infidelity in the wife is less serious than "not having meals on time," one begins to wonder if they really mean it or whether they are "spoofing." Certainly there would be grounds for suspecting that husbands might not be so nonchalant about an unfaithful wife if they really found out that she was untrue to the marriage vow. Hollingworth is not favorably impressed by Terman's study, as the following comments suggest:

> If this volume ever gets into the hands of the newspaper boys they will get a lot of fun out of the solemn discovery that it is unfavorable for happiness for spouses to disagree on their liking for Pershing, that it is ominous for both mates to feel the same way about crossing the street to avoid meeting someone and that among the best differentiating items of happy from unhappy spouses are mutual interest in dental work and joint fondness for men who use perfume. Thus low have the personality traits fallen. . . .

> If "the approach which relies upon direct questioning of the subject about his grievances can be and perhaps usually is grossly misleading" (p. 109), then it is doubly distressing that the personality indicators and case history data utilized in the five chapters to follow in the search for "causal factors" were secured in the same way. Not only are they mere "correlates," but they also may be expected to be "colored" correlates, perhaps just as "colored" as the domestic grievances. Even the combined "estimates of three psychologists" (p. 119) can do nothing to mitigate this misfortune. After all, it might have been safer and cheaper to rest with the main "theory," advanced in this chapter and later reaffirmed, that happy marriages are those made by happy people

> The ratios of specific complaints as between happier and less happy individuals are taken not as measures of any causal influences but merely as "rationalization indices," and it is declared that "viewed as factual testimony, the responses to the grievance items are next to worthless" (p. 95). In the light

[106] *Ibid.,* p. 314.

PROFILE PROPHETIC OF MARITAL HAPPINESS

David D. Vaughan

Grade the individual from 0 to 100% by putting a dot on the line at the right of trait, quality or history item rated. Connect these dots by a line. If this broken line is far to the left of the 75% vertical line, be careful in considering the person graded as a favorable prospect.

	TRAIT, QUALITY, HISTORY.	0 / 25%	50%	75% / 100%
1	MARITAL HAPPINESS OF PARENTS.	VERY UNHAPPY.		PERFECT HAPPINESS.
2	CHILDHOOD HAPPINESS.	VERY UNHAPPY.		PERFECT HAPPINESS.
3	CONFLICT WITH PARENTS.	FREQUENT VIOLENT CONFLICT.		PERFECT HARMONY.
4	BALANCED HOME DISCIPLINE.	DISCIPLINE ABSENT OR VERY HARSH.		FIRM. KIND. FAIR.
5	STRONG NORMAL LOVE FOR PARENTS.	HATRED FOR PARENTS.		STRONG NORMAL LOVE.
6	SEX FRANKNESS BY PARENTS.	SHAME, EMOTIONAL ANTIPATHY.		SCIENTIFIC, WHOLESOME.
7	CAPACITY FOR CONJUGAL AFFECTION.	COLD, NO AFFECTION.		AFFECTIONATE.
8	DOMESTIC INTEREST, LOVE OF CHILDREN.	NONE.		KEEN.
9	APPEARANCE, STYLE SENSE, CLEANLINESS.	SLOVENLY, REPELLENT.		GOOD TASTE, CLEAN.
10	DISPOSITION.	QUARRELSOME, MOODY, JEALOUS.		CHEERFUL, MAGNANIMOUS.
11	CHARACTER, PERSONAL INTEGRITY.	UNRELIABLE, DISHONEST, INSINCERE.		ABSOLUTELY DEPENDABLE.
12	EMOTIONAL BALANCE, PATIENCE.	VIOLENT TEMPER, UNBALANCED.		PATIENT, BALANCED.
13	SOCIAL MINDEDNESS, UNSELFISHNESS.	SELF-CENTERED, TYRANNICAL, INCONSIDERATE.		ALTRUISTIC, CONSIDERATE.
14	SENSE OF RESPONSIBILITY, SELF-RELIANCE, AMBITION.	IRRESPONSIBLE, COWARDLY, LAZY.		MEETS OBLIGATIONS, AMBITIOUS.
15	SKILL IN ORGANIZING LIFE.	PLANLESS LIFE.		FORESIGHT, ORGANIZING SKILL.
16	HABITS, ALCOHOL, ETC.	REPULSIVE, INTEMPERATE.		WHOLESOME, SELF-DISCIPLINED.
17	COMMON INTERESTS, COMRADESHIP.	DISSIMILAR TASTES, NON-COÖPERATIVE.		PERFECT HARMONY.
18	HEALTH.	VERY POOR.		PERFECT.
19	AGE DISPARITY.	WIDE DIVERGENCE.		COMPATIBLE.
20	INTELLIGENCE, EDUCATION.	WIDE DIVERGENCE, INADEQUATE.		COMPATIBLE, ADEQUATE.
21	SOCIAL INHERITANCE.	CRUDE, DEPENDENT, DELINQUENT.		FAMILY CULTURED, RESPECTED.
22	FAMILY EUGENIC RECORD.	DISEASED, MENTALLY DEFICIENT.		ALL SOUND IN MIND AND BODY.
23	RELIGIOUS COMPATIBILITY.	WIDE DIVERGENCE.		HARMONIOUS.
24	SENSE OF HUMOR.	NONE, DULL.		KEEN.
25	INCOME.	INADEQUATE, INSECURE.		ADEQUATE, SECURE.

PERCENTAGE RATING.

of this declaration the value of any other item reported in the questionnaire becomes infected with grave suspicion. . . .

The prestige of the authorship and sponsorship will give this volume a halo of authenticity that will put its tentative intimations into the fireside journals as the final conclusions of science, and the science will be psychology, which already has a hard enough job defending its precarious status. . . .[107]

In all fairness to Terman it is worth while to reiterate Hollingworth's general contention that the limitations of the study for predicting marital happiness were appreciated by Terman. The danger lies in the likelihood that amateur digesters of the research will give the conclusions more weight than they are entitled to and jump to interpretations the authors never intended. This is a new field. The pioneers have merely blazed the trail of exploration.

If Kepler were alive today—and still contemplating marriage—he might welcome opportunity to use the *marriage score card* to reduce the marriage hazard; or better still, the improved variation of this card, a *Profile Prophetic of Marital Happiness*.[108] This Profile may be used either for personal self-appraisal or for an estimate of a marriage prospect. This systematic evaluation is "helpful in adding reason to romance . . . it is useful in reducing to figures what would otherwise be left in the realm of hazy opinion." [109] Such a listing of desirable qualities in a prospective mate may serve a valuable purpose as a guide to a wise selection of a life-partner. Any scheme that will encourage the lovers to use some deliberation in weighing their mutual suitability is all to the good, for impulse is liable to prove an unreliable beacon. Choosing a mate is one of life's most important decisions; the choice should be determined by insight rather than by hunches.

B. PARENT-CHILD RELATIONSHIPS

Home may be viewed as a place for training people in the fine art of living together. The right kind of person will welcome the opportunity, provided by the family circle, for practicing considerateness and courtesy. Unfortunately, some people look upon home as a place where you know the other persons so well that you can afford to cast

[107] Review by H. L. Hollingworth, in the *Psychological Bulletin*, 1939, 36, 191-197.
[108] Devised by David D. Vaughan, formerly Professor of Social Ethics, School of Theology, Boston University. (See page 817.)
[109] *Boston University Radio Institute Journal*, January 8, 1940. For other self-tests and rating scales applicable to fiancé or mate, see P. Popenoe: *Marriage, Before and After*. 1943.

aside your manners, be unkind, talk back, slam doors, and relax into an uncivilized mood of uninhibited aggressiveness. Family life under such circumstances may become a battleground where the contestants are trained for combativeness instead of peaceful cooperation.

It is the parents who establish the basic patterns which prevail in the home. Of fundamental importance is the matter of marital harmony, for happy husband-wife relations tend to create happy family relations, and vice versa. In one study of these interrelationships,

forty-two boys and thirty-four girls in preschool, ages one year six months to five years seven months, were observed, and data were collected concerning their adjustment. Data were also collected from their parents by psychiatric social-work type interviews concerning interparental tensions. Child adjustment was significantly related to interparental tensions over sex, lack of consideration, inability to talk over differences, lack of expressed affection . . . while tensions over items, such as work and friends, showed little relation to child adjustment. Significant tensions seemed to be closely related to fundamental affectional and ego values. While there was no statistically significant difference between the effects of interparental tensions on boys and their effects on girls, it appeared that the girls were somewhat more affected.[110]

In view of such evidence it is an unwise policy for a husband and wife who cannot get along together successfully, to resort to procreation as a means of straightening out their personal difficulties. " 'Having a baby,' " Levy and Monroe warn, "is in itself no solution for the sufferings of mismated couples." [111] It is well to remember, too, that parents who exemplify in their own lives that marriage is worth while may expect their children to wish to follow their good example when they grow up. Education for parenthood begins in childhood as parents themselves set the style of life for their youngsters.

Harmony in the family does not mean that complete agreement is necessary on every issue which comes up for discussion. Parents can afford to disagree, Travis and Baruch insist, if they really love each other. It is even permissible, under such conditions, for Father to criticize Mother for the way in which she is endeavoring to impose discipline. For example:

[110] D. W. Baruch and J. A. Wilcox: "A Study of Sex Differences in Preschool Children's Adjustment Coexistent with Interparental Tensions." *Journal of Genetic Psychology*, 1944, 64, 281-303.
[111] J. Levy and R. Monroe: *The Happy Family*, p. 241. 1938.

It does no harm for father to say, "I don't think Sarah should be allowed to dabble in the water." It does no harm for father and mother to argue the point out in front of Sarah.

After all, what does Sarah get? She gets the fact that grownups, even though they love each other, are nonetheless entitled to their individual opinions. She gets also a concept of the democratic mode of life. She sees that where different people and differing opinions enter, each has a right to freedom of speech. From the sally, Sarah gets constructive value.

Parents can disagree if their disagreements are actually aimed at the question on which they are disagreeing. Their differences may, however, be aimed as missiles at each other. If they disagree because of fundamental, deep-seated differences, it is not the argument that creates harm. The devastating part of the matter is that the basic tension exists. Smiling in sweet, hypocritical accord will be readily unmasked.[112]

The family is fulfilling its main psychological function when it encourages a wholesome interplay of personalities, an interplay that inculcates habits of mutual respect and patterns of interpersonal compromise. "We measure the success of the family, not in terms of its size or its income or its dwelling place, but rather in terms of the quality of its human relations." [113] A good home, like Thorndike's good city, will be characterized by good people who are learning how to live with each other in an atmosphere of sympathy and affection.

The achievement of family harmony depends principally on how wisely the parents deal with their children's problems.

Where the relations between children in the same family are commendable, it will be found as a rule that the parents have observed three considerations: (1) they have emotionally prepared each child for the coming of the next, (2) they have been equally considerate of each child, and (3) they have inculcated in each child a sense of responsibility for the others.[114]

It is especially important to instill in the minds of the children that the new baby is "our baby," for this idea facilitates identification (family pride) and prevents the impression from materializing that the recent arrival is an unwelcome intruder upon the family scene. Pleasant family relations are more likely to develop in a home that is skillfully managed, a home in which each person is assigned specific responsibilities, work is routinized according to an established sched-

---

[112] L. E. Travis and D. W. Baruch: *Personal Problems of Everyday Life*, pp. 290-291. D. Appleton-Century Company, 1941.

[113] Nimkoff: *op. cit.*, p. 340.

[114] *Ibid.*, p. 347.

le, obligations are clearly defined. In such a home everybody gets
he sense of participating in a common enterprise and each contributor
njoys the feeling of being an essential member of the group. Chil-
ren need to appreciate their duties as well as their privileges. It is
ell for them to respect their parents, still better if the parents are
eople who merit the loyal devotion they expect from their offspring.
Certainly it is of no avail for a mother, through her sobs, to remind an
nappreciative child of all the sacrifices she has made in his behalf,
ecause this kind of plaintive appeal does not strike a responsive
hord.

In answer to the question, "Why Have Children?" Ernest R. Groves
nd Gladys Hoagland Groves tell us:

Marriage may begin with romantic love; but children give it abiding
rength. . . .

Most people, when they marry, assume that they will have children. . . .

Parenthood, however, is so fundamental a part of marriage that it too often
taken for granted. There are important facts about it which should be dis-
ussed beforehand. If you are to be good parents of healthy, happy children,
ou must know that your mate feels as you do about having them; and that
ou agree in general on the kind of home and education you hope to give
hem.

How do children benefit marriage?

In many important regards. First, in a deep and mystical way, children
nk us with the future. It is not only that they carry on the name, traditions
nd possessions of a family; in a very real sense they represent immortality.
or, as long as children are born to us with something of our features, facial
xpressions, voice or mannerisms, then we too are projected into the years
head. . . .

But children have other values, practical ones, for marriage. They keep
arents young in mind, alert in interests. . . . We adults can ward off the
ear that age so often brings if, like them, we welcome new experiences and
nake them teach us—but never defeat us.

If we are close to our children we cannot close our minds to progress and
ew ideas. . . .

Parenthood is emotionally maturing, just as marriage is. We must be truly
dult if we are to meet even the physical needs of children. For instance,
t requires patience and unselfishness for a woman to follow the unremitting
outine of feeding and care that are necessary to give her infant a good,
ealthy start in life.

Our children make us grow up mentally, for as soon as they can talk they
egin to ask questions. Children's questions are much harder to answer than
hose of adults because they are direct and simple and require answers equally
irect. . . .

But just as important as physical care is the understanding we owe them for although their feelings for us during childhood may range from adoration to hatred they can never be indifferent to us. To nobody else are we so important as to our children, especially during their early years. To them, until we prove otherwise, we are the handsomest, the strongest, the wisest people in the world. . . .

Homes are less likely to break up when men and women are striving for common objective—to give their children "better than we had." There incentive to work hard when there are children to reap the benefits.

The emotional warmth, the gaiety, even the hazards that every family encounters, the building up of family customs like birthdays and Christmas—all these are active factors in making marriage and home secure.

The healthy functioning of the community itself depends upon children for married couples who are also parents have more reason to be interested in school and community affairs than have childless couples. . . .

In a long-range look at marriage, it is children that give meaning to the relationship. A never-ending development comes from sharing the joy sorrows, dangers and accomplishments of your children. You can touch life at more points through your sons and daughters than you can alone.[115]

Parents have become increasingly aware of the need for psychological insight in rearing their children. The open sesame to wisdom may be sought by reading a book on child psychology. Such a procedure may be a case of a little knowledge being dangerous, particularly if the baffled parent learns the words but not the music. As general principle, it is true that "the best parents are not necessarily those who know the most about the physical, mental, and emotional growth of children, but those who are themselves well-adjusted and well-integrated persons." [116]

Authorities on child-rearing—contrary to Watson's prohibition against demonstrating affection—insist that, above all else, the child must be made to feel he is loved and wanted. Kisses and hugs afford the youngster convincing testimony that his parents are fond of him Loving a child does not mean spoiling him. Spoiling does not issue from real love, love that is ever thoughtful of the child's well-being and mindful of his need to grow toward mature independence. Spoiling occurs when motives of a different sort are operating, when parents are seeking to make up for their own unhappy childhood or indulging themselves by proxy. Fear and punishment are to be avoided as much as possible on the ground that it is better to have an aggressive

---

[115] *Look*—"America's Family Magazine," January 22, 1945.
[116] F. K. Berrien: *Practical Psychology*, p. 88. 1944.

hild who is difficult to handle than one who has been intimidated.
t is unwise to make a child feel inferior. Parents will avoid such a
mistake if they respect the young one's feelings. Love is manifest in
many ways besides cuddling, in interest shown in what the child is
doing, in expecting of him growth and improvement rather than per-
ection. Discipline, of course, there must be; a healthy discipline will
•e one motivated by affectionate firmness.[117]

Another principle endorsed by several authorities on family life is
he value of frankness and directness in parent-child relationships.
This directive is offered with one thought uppermost in mind: "It is
ust as human for parents to hate children as to love them." [118] Am-
•ivalent attitudes of this kind are normal in all close personal contacts.
3lood relationships, indeed, make our loves and hates even more in-
ense. Parents are apt to feel guilty when they experience resentment
gainst their children; compensating for guilt, they are induced to be
•verattentive in an impulsive manner which is characterized more by
n unintelligent emotional release than by honest solicitude for the
hild. Children are apt to get emotionally confused when parents
•old in their feelings. It is recommended, therefore, that parents
how their love and also their annoyance, thus enabling the child to
liscover exactly where he stands in each situation. Such a straight-
orward expression of normal affection and normal resentment is
much better than any set of rules for parental guidance.[119]

A good home will produce balanced personalities, according to
Klein.[120] Mutual trust and considerateness will prevail in such a
iome. Very young children, accordingly, will be treated as *persons,*
iot as troublesome creatures with merely a nuisance value. Poise is
a manifestation of a sense of security which is derived from assurance
hat the parents genuinely care for their offspring. Alert parents will
•ppreciate the bearing of happy relations in the home upon the child's
uture.

His eventual thoughts on the meaning of marriage, on how one ought to
•ring up children, on the place of a father in the home, on the role of the
mother may be given shape and substance by what he notices in this early

---

[117] See M. Levine: *Psychotherapy in Medical Practice,* Chapter 10, "Basic Attitudes
oward Children." 1942.

[118] Levy and Munroe: *op. cit.,* p. 259.

[119] See Levy and Munroe: *op. cit.,* pp. 259-280. Travis and Baruch: *op. cit.,*
p. 278-279.

[120] See D. B. Klein: *Mental Hygiene,* Chapter 10, "Home and the Balanced Per-
onality." 1944.

domestic psychological laboratory. This is an "obvious" truth tragicall overlooked by tyrannical fathers, shrewish wives, overindulgent parents, jea ous husbands, and selfish mothers.[121]

Respect for children will prompt parents to be tactful in their har dling of problems in the home. An effort will be made to adjust th children to differences in treatment, as in the case of a younger chil who is compelled to go to bed earlier than his older siblings. Th tactful parent will not discourage initiative by anticipating ever want or by imposing a system of repressive regimentation involvin needless frustration and a disregard of personal needs. The chil will be taught to appreciate the delicate balance between individua rights and group rights. Parents should ask themselves, What shal I do *for* this child? instead of the question, What shall I do *to* thi child? The chief business of parents is to guide the young ones i their care, to help them grow up into persons capable of intelligen self-direction. If this goal is to be achieved, there is a *continued* nee for more and more emancipation from parental management.

The three major mistakes perpetrated by parents are overprotec tion, rejection, and inconsistency, in the opinion of Berrien.[122] Over protective mothers, particularly, show little insight into the harm they are doing. In fact, it is quite common for parents to fail to rec ognize their own deficiencies in the misbehavior of their children Good intentions are certainly not enough to guarantee wholesom child rearing. Levy has found that overprotective mothers repeatedl assure the psychiatrist that the child is badly behaved in spite of al they have done for it, thus defending themselves against the possibl accusation that the fault may be theirs.[123] Strange as it may seem overprotective mothers whose lives are run by their tyrannical chil dren, usually play the dominating role in their relationships witl their husbands and friends. It is only in the peculiar *rapport* of par ent and child that such mothers submit to tyranny. Unfortunately the child who has been protected gets so used to such treatment tha he finds it hard to grow up. During adolescence he will revolt. Th revolt will be directed against the parents, provoking a release of an tagonisms on both sides, but really the rebellion is actuated by th adolescent's protest against his own sense of dependency.[124]

Rejection is another serious problem. The unwanted child—un

[121] *Ibid.*, p. 255.
[122] Berrien: *op. cit.*, Chapter 4, "Mental Hygiene and Guidance."
[123] See D. M. Levy: *Maternal Overprotection*, p. 105. 1943.
[124] See Levy and Munroe: *op. cit.*, p. 17.

wanted because his parents may have been economically or emotionally unprepared for his arrival, or because they may have prized their own freedom so much as to resent being tied down—this unwanted child senses his unhappy position and retaliates by adopting a hostile attitude of his own toward his parents and society. The results are often observable in delinquency and neuroticism.

Inconsistency is the third error specified by Berrien. Inconsistent treatment breeds confusion and a sense of injustice. Nevertheless, there is much to be said on the other side. Travis and Baruch, for example, assert that "acting appropriately is much more important than acting consistently." [125] Discrimination between situations is more likely to be the intelligent mode of behavior, than rigid adherence to absolute rules, for, as we remarked in Chapter 4 on the Art of Living, there are times to be stern and times to be gentle, times to help and times to insist on the child's helping himself. It is not sensible to treat the same person always in the same way regardless of circumstances nor is it sensible to try to treat all the children in a family exactly alike. Each child should be handled according to his individual needs. One may be qualified for music lessons, another for summer camp, another for a new suit. It is naïve to provide music lessons for everybody regardless of talent or interest or to buy new suits for everybody just because one is momentarily enjoying that special privilege. Of course, there must be no playing of favorites; indeed parents must try to avoid even conveying the impression of favoring one child over another, even though inwardly they may prefer one to another.

It is clear to any student of family relations that no two children in a home are brought up in the same environment.

Take the Smith family. When Sarah, their eldest, is born, the Smiths are young and eager. They have been married only a year. They are thrilled over the baby's advent. Sarah comes into an environment consisting of father and mother, thrilled, very young, very eager. Then Bob is born. He comes two years later. Mother is a little tired. Father has been working hard. The first bloom is off their romance. They are acceptant of the fact that another baby is coming, but they are not thrilled by it. Bob, then, comes into an environment consisting of father, mother, and Sarah—father and mother not so young, not so eager, not so thrilled. And Sarah with a good chance of being jealous. Obviously the environment for these two children is not the same. Never in their lives is it exactly the same. Even around the breakfast

---

[125] Travis and Baruch: *op. cit.*, p. 283.

table on any morning, the environment is different. The mere bare fact that for Sarah it contains Bob, and that for Bob it contains Sarah, makes it different For one, it contains a boy sibling; for the other one, a girl. Other facts, not so bare, enter aplenty. Father's feelings toward Bob are different from his feelings toward Sarah. Mother's likewise. The ramifications are many.

Here, then, are two children. They are different individuals. They have different biological equipment. They have different environments. They have different emphases in their needs. The moral? Treat each according to his own fashion. Never treat two children alike.[126]

Another way of looking at this variation in environment:

Parents have used up all their energy in training the older children and regard the younger ones with more the attitude of grandparents, enjoying them and letting them grow up as best they can.[127]

Children do not instinctively love their parents—they learn to love them or to hate them as conditioning proceeds. Children feel so helpless in a world of adults. They are awed by the overwhelming size of their parents, even when the elders are merely normal in stature and weight. Young children fear the parental might, they tend to regard their guardians as omniscient and infallible, and they are very sensitive to slights as expressed in neglect or overattention to another sibling.

Children often seem ungrateful to their parents. Youngsters do not like it when mother or father keeps reminding them of all the sacrifices they are making for their children. Young children take everything that is done for them as a matter of course. No one really enjoys feeling indebted to another person, anyhow. Those parents who look upon their children in terms of expense, who complain constantly about being tied down, who grumble about having to wear last year's coat because Johnny has to have his teeth straightened, reap the ingratitude they deserve.

Children complain that their parents interfere with their friendships and their loves. They charge that parents are unfair when they lay down rules which are not followed in other homes. They resent it when they are scolded for staying out too late. They object to chores that are suddenly thrust upon them, which upset their schedules and their plans without any regard for their legitimate fun.

[126] *Ibid.*, pp. 289-290.
[127] Blanche C. Weill: *Through Children's Eyes*, p. 31. The Island Press, Inc., 1940

"Why don't they talk over the things they want done with you?" [one boy] asks indignantly. "Why do they think a boy's not worth consulting and his plans aren't important?"

"Sometimes they say they don't need you and then just as you start doing something important they tell you to go to the store and say it won't take a minute, but when you get home they send you right back again for something they forgot the first time. A thing like that uses up a whole afternoon." This complaint has been made by a number of boys.

"It's not the amount of work we object to," a thoughtful lad hastens to explain. "We just don't like jobs sprung on us, regardless of what else we have to do."

As all the boys see it, the biggest possible improvement in life at home would be the streamlining of these chores.

In their opinion, the present slapdash assignments cause more bad family feeling than almost anything else. When the boys rebel, parents conclude that their sons are selfish. The boys think parents are inconsiderate.

"But there is a solution," says a spokesman for all of them. "Here's what we suggest: Let parents give us, early in the week, a list of chores they want us to do. Then leave it to us to work out a schedule. That will put the responsibility on us and will be a genuine sign of respect."

"I already got my mother to give me a list like that," another boy says. "It used to be so awful in our house I couldn't stand it any more. But the new plan works fine." [128]

Parents would learn a great deal if they could see the world through children's eyes. It is easy for the child, with his literal mind, to conclude he is not loved enough. He is forced to this conclusion by the evidence: he is asked to do things, his little brothers are never imposed upon in the same way; when things go wrong, it is always his fault; his mother never picks him up and hugs him as she does the baby and father never rocks him on his knee. The psychologist can relieve this suffering by explaining to the youngster that he is older, therefore his parents count more on him for help; that he is not taken on father's lap because that sort of thing is just for babies. The child is advised:

Act as if you were perfectly sure that your parents loved you as much as the other boys, and that you are proud that they treat you like a responsible, almost grown-up person.[129]

Parents can give such a child more assurance of their love by thanking him and praising him, instead of just scolding him for all his mistakes;

[128] G. Turner: "Parents Aren't Fair." *This Week*, March 4, 1945. Copyright, 1945, by United Newspapers Magazine Corp.

[129] Weill: *op. cit.*, p. 7.

by compelling the younger child to respect the property and othe rights of the older child, instead of jumping into the conflict to pro tect the younger one against the older one's threats of aggression; b understanding that a naughty child is always an unhappy child; b avoiding remarks before a daughter about wanting a son or exultin over the arrival of "a son at last," and avoiding comments before a so that "it's too bad the boy got the curls." Inconsiderate remarks an actions may hurt a child deeply, though no meanness is intended.

We have discussed at some length parent-child relationship There are other relationships of an elder-youngster alignment whicl involve psychological problems, such as the presence of stepparent parents-in-law, grandparents, and other relatives in the home. On stepmother reports her experience as follows:

Your stepchildren either have a real mother some place, whom they prob ably visit for definite periods each year, or they have the memory of a mothe who has died. In either case "Mother" is a very real person whose specia rights and functions they are not inclined to honor in another. No one els can be so good to them as Mother. And no one else is ever allowed to be a hard on them.

Every time the stepmother does something "motherly" she is subject to th child's unrelenting and analytical eye. The first time she checks to see if he stepchild really brushed his teeth or just dampened the toothbrush, she stepped into the part. Yet a stepmother's job is to take a mother's place.

A second unbeatable factor is that the children, no matter how warm you sympathy for them or how responsive they are, just aren't *your* children They don't *look* like you; they don't feel or act like you.

And third, there is the children's mother. A stepmother is foolish if she expects to win her over. The best she can hope for is an armed truce.[130]

Grandparents can complicate family life by being overindulgent, b interfering with parental discipline, by being "old fogies" and crit icizing the ways of the new generation. The presence of two genera tions in a home is a challenge to strive for teamwork; a third gen eration adds another set of problems to be solved if harmony is to be achieved. Attention to an infirm grandparent may impose a heav burden upon a tired mother and the old folks may overtax the famil budget so much as to introduce additional anxieties into the situa tion, because parents may feel they should be devoting their money to their youngsters' health and education.

[130] Anonymous: "My Life as a Stepmother." *Coronet*, January, 1945. Copyrigh by Esquire, Inc.

C. SIBLING RELATIONSHIPS

"Getting Along with One's Family" was the subject of a Group Guidance Unit recently compiled by a college professor and his class. One of the objectives was defined as the aim of enabling "the individual student to appreciate that problems in family relationships are not accidents or necessarily results of personal deficiencies but are natural and to be expected in family life." Then under the heading, "Problems of Brother-Sister Relationships," the following were listed as "possible battle lines":

1. Using the other's property without permission.
2. Dividing and completing chores.
3. Securing privacy.
4. Jealousy and envy over family attention, possessions.
5. Accompanying the other—an enforced measure.
6. Tattling.
7. Teasing.
8. Being object of unfavorable comparison with brother or sister.[131]

Sibling relationships, of course, include brother-brother and sister-sister as well as brother-sister contacts. Each of these several situations involves its own peculiar tasks of mutual adjustment. Common are such difficulties as the following: the older bosses the younger sibling, belongings are appropriated, rights and privileges are envied and guarded and debated, concessions to a delicate child are demanded, older children feel their parents are less strict with the younger, the younger insist upon going with the older everywhere the older goes; there is quarreling over the selection of radio programs, over boys being given more freedom than girls, over relative amounts of money given as allowances, over comparative times of going to bed; in addition, the model older brother or sister may be setting a pace that is hard to match, parents may be taking sides in quarrels and intervening to protect the younger from physical harm at the hands of the older; and there are numberless other interpersonal differences.

It is up to the parents to guide the natural rivalry between children into constructive channels, which is a big assignment. The task

---

[131] J. W. Yeo and class: "Getting Along with One's Family." *Education*, October, 1944.

When I informed my wife that I was spending the day writing on brother-sister relations, she suggested, "Instead of writing about them, why don't you do something about them?"

is rendered somewhat easier if the sibling conflicts can be viewed in a large perspective as requiring a basic program of educating the participants in the art of getting along with other people. A child's life is complicated by the presence of siblings; at the same time, his experience is incalculably enriched by the variety of interpersonal problems which have to be solved. Quarreling, tedious and annoying as it may be, may be providing the means of sharpening wits, inculcating respect for one's opponent, teaching the domineering child that he cannot always have his own way. Excessive bickering would indicate the need for investigating whether the antagonists were getting enough sleep, enough fun out of life, adequate sense of achievement. Unfortunately, weary parents are apt to deal with squabbling children in terms of their own need for quiet; if the needs of the children were respected, it might be discovered that occasional "spats" served a valuable function in releasing hostilities better brought out in the open, discharged, and then possibly forgotten.[132] Psychologists quite generally are advocating that parents allow the children to settle their own differences in their own way, interceding only to see that rules of "fair play" are respected and that no excessive violence is perpetrated by either party.[133]

The family constellation, which is the structure of interpersonal relationships based on birth order, is of great psychological significance. The situation is different for each child, depending on whether he is the first born, the middle child, the youngest, a boy among girls, a girl among boys, and so on. Generally parents have dreamed ahead of time of their ideal family, first a son, then a daughter, and no more, if they fit the picture of the typical home depicted in the advertisements where father, mother, older son, younger sister complete the circle. Frequently, children do not arrive in the order planned. In such a case, a girl as the first-born child may not be so welcome as a son would have been. This situation may have serious psychological repercussions.

The oldest child is an only child for a while and he may feel dispossessed when a sibling arrives, especially because baby is likely to monopolize attention, needing extra care as babies inevitably do. The parent can prevent undue jealousy by devoting exclusive attention to the older child at least for a short time each day. Investiga-

[132] See R. Brickner: "When Brothers and Sisters Disagree." *Parents' Magazine,* October, 1933.

[133] See, for example, Travis and Baruch: *op. cit.,* pp. 190-191.

tions have shown that jealousy is common among oldest children.[134] The wise parent will warn the child that a baby brother or sister is expected and then go even further by soliciting his cooperative interest. It is important to take these psychological problems into account, for, as Adler maintains, "Almost every discouragement in childhood springs from the feeling that someone else is preferred." [135] Feeling deprived of mother's love, the oldest child often turns to father and becomes devoted to him.[136]

The oldest child is in a favorable position in some respects. He is privileged to wear new clothes; siblings who follow wear his "hand-me-downs." The oldest is fortunate, though he may not think so, in being entrusted with responsibilities which aid him to mature. He is likely to regard himself as the guardian of law and order, is more inclined, consequently, to become a conservative, the sort of person who exaggerates the value of preserving the *status quo,* who is sure no rule should be changed or exceptions allowed. He is in a position to use force, and therefore may learn to be a bully or to be protective. Adler found that most problem children were oldest children.[137]

The second-born child is in a unique psychological position, according to Adler, who cites the Biblical story of Jacob and Esau as a typical account of the relationship between the first child and the second child. Adler feels that the second-born develops a "race-course attitude," being constantly under steam to overtake the older child who is ahead as a pacemaker.

The youngest child is "the baby," gets more attention than any of the older siblings. The story of Joseph in the Bible is a good study of the psychology of the youngest child. Being the smallest, he is considered most in need of help. In some cases, he is stimulated to prove he is somebody, to excel, to gain power; in other cases, lacking self-confidence because he feels so young and so inferior, he becomes the chronic plaintiff who is chiefly concerned with evading his obligations. He enjoys one advantage in that he knows he cannot be dethroned, which is some consolation. He also is in a position to bene-

---

[134] See S. Foster: "A Study of the Personality Makeup and Social Setting of Fifty Jealous Children." *Mental Hygiene,* 1927, 2, 53-77. B. M. Ross: "Some Traits Associated with Sibling Jealousy in Problem Children." *Smith College Studies in Social Work,* 1931, 1, 364-376.

[135] A. Adler: *What Life Should Mean to You,* p. 142. 1931.

[136] *Ibid.,* p. 146.

[137] *Ibid.,* pp. 147-148.

fit from the teachings of the older siblings, a good fortune if he takes advantage of his opportunities. He may get a good perspective on himself, too, because there are plenty of older persons to pass along their criticisms. Siblings are frank in their criticisms, a policy that may be socializing or demoralizing, depending on how well the youngest can tolerate candid "public" opinion.

The only child is given undivided attention by his parents. He has also been given much attention by psychologists. It was G. Stanley Hall who put so much stress on the misfortune of being an only child and psychoanalysts generally supported his view.[138] There are other students of family relationships who are more optimistic about the chances for happiness which are open to the only child. Among the findings are the following observations. Vetter discovered more only children in the atypical, reactionary, and radical groups. "It somehow seems peculiarly fit," he says, "that the more extreme positions should contain more only children; they have a reputation for more unusual emotional development." [139] According to Guilford and Worcester, the only child is superior in personal orderliness, cleanliness, initiative, self-control, industry, truthfulness, dependability, and courtesy; less superior in cooperativeness and fairness.[140] Goodwin Watson reports that only children are not unhappy when they grow into adults.[141] Lester and Barnette concluded from their study that there is no marked tendency for the only child to be adjusted or unadjusted.[142] Only children, states Maller, are above average in intelligence, moral knowledge, cultural background, and honesty; average in cooperativeness; below average in inhibition.[143] These experimental findings are cited to show that research does not bear out the theorist who thinks the only child is likely to become a social misfit for lack of companionship with playmates. Campbell concludes his survey of numerous investigations concerning the only child by

[138] See especially A. A. Brill: *Psychoanalysis: Its Theory and Practical Application*, Chapter 14, "The Only or Favorite Child in Adult Life." 1922.

[139] G. B. Vetter: "Measurement of Social and Political Attitudes." *Journal of Abnormal and Social Psychology*, 1930, 25, 149-189.

[140] See R. B. Guilford and D. A. Worcester: "A Comparative Study of the Only and Non-Only Child." *Journal of Genetic Psychology*, 1930, 38, 411-426.

[141] See G. Watson: "Happiness Among Adult Students of Education." *Journal of Educational Psychology*, 1930, 21, 79-109.

[142] See O. P. Lester and W. L. Barnette: "Some Factors Relative to Adjusted and Maladjusted Personalities." *Journal of Juvenile Research*, 1932, 16, 319-325.

[143] See J. B. Maller: "Size of Family and Personality." *Journal of Social Psychology*, 1931, 2, 3-27.

asserting: "Whatever role the mere presence or absence of siblings may play in the development of personality, its importance is certainly not crucial." [144]

Only children, in the light of such evidence, can adjust to life successfully, despite the lack of sibling relations and despite the monopoly of parental attention. In the case of an only child, parents must take special precautions against being overprotective, against being overanxious about matters of health, against pampering and spoiling, and they must make special efforts to provide associations with other children outside the home. Of decisive psychological importance in the situation is the reason why there is only one child: it would make a difference whether the parents limited themselves to one offspring in order to have more money to spend on themselves, or whether they disliked their child so much they did not want any more like him, or whether for physiological reasons pregnancy was impossible or inadvisable. All of these possibilities should be explored by the person who wants to understand the psychology of the only child.

D. The Trend toward Democracy in the Home

We have already mentioned the changes in the mores which have established equality as a basic principle governing the relationships between husband and wife. Some men are behind the times in thinking of themselves as the supreme potentate in the home; in such homes conflict is inevitable if the wife takes seriously her rights to the role of partner. Despite the competitive struggle for status which vitiates the husband-wife relationships in occasional homes, I believe it is accurate to state that equality is being increasingly accepted as the prevailing norm.

The same trend toward democracy is observable in parent-child relationships, too, here in America. In Puritan America the father laid down the law and his wife and children were expected to submit with unquestioning obedience. A sense of duty was paramount and people were relentlessly moralistic and intolerant in their attitudes toward themselves and toward others. Parental attitudes were revealed in a combination of rigid discipline and insecurity in the handling of children. This combination is very unfavorable to the development of healthy personalities. The American Puritan home accordingly produced maladjusted personalities characterized by excessive shyness,

[144] A. A. Campbell: "The Personality Adjustments of Only Children." *Psychological Bulletin*, 1934, 31, 193-203.

withdrawing tendencies, inferiority feelings, sex repression, and concealed resentments.[145]

American children are not favorably disposed to autocratic parents, as a rule, in our day. Consequently, the imposition of discipline in dictatorial style is apt to breed open rebellion. Parents who adhere to the older autocratic modes of child rearing, in our present social climate, are inviting trouble. The inevitable difficulties come

out into the open when the biologically helpless, and therefore, submissive, "baby" becomes a willing person and his will begins to assert itself by refusing to remain a passive tool of parental domination. It is perhaps for this reason that, in so many complaint statements, the word willfullness is used as a synonym for stubbornness and obstinacy. There are parents who find the emergence of the will inconvenient and upsetting. They cannot accept it for what it is—a natural and desirable acquisition in the evolution of personality. "Will," which finds expression in the presence of alternatives, is deprived from the start of the guided opportunity to choose between alternatives. Nothing except compliance with the parent's will is tolerated. Any show of initiative and spontaneity which does not strictly conform to parental demands is bewailed as "disobedience" and raises the issue of "discipline." And discipline, to such people, means a lesson in unquestioning, uncritical, unconditional surrender.

Disciplinarianism as a basis for child rearing is made respectable by traditional convention. The rod has, since Biblical days, functioned as a symbol of prophylaxis against spoiling. Children who are seen and not heard are still extolled by some as the ideal products of child rearing. Bending of the twig is still often recommended in a way which takes little precaution against over-bending or even breaking. Habit training is often interpreted as agitated habit enforcement.

The conventional concept of discipline comes as a godsend to rejecting parents. It sanctions and, in fact, prescribes parental autocracy. If the child does not capitulate—and no healthy child does—his remonstrance, in spite of all the seeming inconveniences which it entails, serves as a welcome justification for an attitude of nonacceptance: "How can I be satisfied with a child who does not obey, refuses his cereal, does not empty his bowel at the exact time when I want it emptied, and throws a temper tantrum when I insist? Such a child is 'bad,' and I am entitled to a 'good' child. His badness must be inherited or the result of some physical illness." This is how the resort to pseudo-genetics and pseudo-medicine fits into the picture.

Psychologists have recognized children's early remonstrance as a normal phenomenon of growth. Some have spoken of a "period of resistance" in the second and third years of life as a natural stage of psychological develop-

[145] C. Bühler in *Human Nature and Enduring Peace* (p. 99), G. Murphy (Editor). 1945.

ment. There was a tendency to ascribe this resistance to attributes contained in the *Anlage;* a predisposition to transitory negativism was supposed to be dormant in the newborn, as the milk teeth are hidden in the jaws, to appear in the course of infancy, and to give way to conformity, as the milk teeth give way to permanent teeth. Clinical studies, however, show clearly that the pointing to chromosomal origins disregards something much more real and more readily demonstrable. It shows that so-called resistance is nothing more nor less than a first exercise in choosing between available alternatives, a first attempt at self-assertion. Since the choice cannot, and does not, always coincide with parental expectations, the instances of divergence tend to impress impatient parents as evidences of resistance.

The degree of resistance depends largely on the extent to which force is used in trying to obtain compliance. Force creates an atmosphere of hostility. A child, finding himself surrounded by disapproving autocrats, has the choice between allowing himself to be crushed and fighting back. Most children have enough stamina to fight back. They discover that their refusals are powerful, and the only, weapons at their disposal. "Discipline" acts as a boomerang. The parents, frustrated and offended, meet resistance with counter-resistance, and a vicious circle is established. The child and the parents are contestants in constant warfare. They get "on each other's nerves." The less genuine affection there is for the child, the lower is the threshold of parental annoyance.

Not long ago at a social gathering, the mother of two boys who are now serving overseas in the Armed Forces reported how delighted she used to be when in years past her sons came down on Sunday mornings, sprawled out on the living room carpet and read the funny papers. A short time afterwards, another mother brought her 7-year-old boy to our clinic. She insisted that Tommy was very bad. One of the examples of his badness was his habit of coming down on Sunday morning, sprawling out on the living room carpet, and reading the funny papers. It was the same behavior in both instances. To the fond parent, it gave pleasure and a pleasant memory. The rejecting mother, whose threshold of annoyance was very low indeed, was irked by it and saw in it one more "reason" for her accusing attitude. The two soldier sons had a secure, happy childhood. They had no need for behavioral backfiring. Tommy was a crushed child, in danger of giving up and withdrawing, but still, luckily, possessed enough vitality to continue his struggle, which would have been hopeless without intensive psychiatric assistance.[146]

The modern school has been described as child-centered; the same thing might be said of some modern homes. The child-centered home is not a democracy but an autocracy in which the child is the dictator rather than the parent. Parents have their rights, too, and a demo-

[146] L. Kanner: "Convenience and Convention in Rearing Children." *Scientific Monthly,* October, 1944.

cratic regime will preserve those rights by curbing untrammeled self-expression on the part of the children. Democracy and anarchy are not synonymous. There must be some semblance of order if any social group is to operate successfully, whether it is the state or the family. Leadership, therefore, is as necessary in the home as it is elsewhere, a leadership that exerts an organizing influence based upon the respect of the governed. In the democratic home, accordingly, children will be given an opportunity to express their ideas in group discussion as a preliminary to group decisions. Policies are apt to be more acceptable to persons who have been privileged to participate in their formulation.

Democracy in the home is advocated by Reilly in his book, *How to Improve Your Human Relations by Straight Thinking,* in which he describes how it functions in his own home. A conscious effort is made by the whole family to set up the necessary conditions for living peacefully with one another. Common agreements on what is right and on what is wrong are reached at weekly conferences in which all the members of the family have a say. Rules are established at these "business meetings" by joint discussion. A person who violates a rule is all the more willing to pay the penalty because he has had a part in setting up the regulation and specifying the fair punishment for breaking the "law." The Reilly family report that children feel more secure when they know the rules and appreciate that the rules "make sense." [147]

In a democratic home children will be consulted about their wishes and their preferences will be taken into consideration even though they are not regarded as "the last word." Weill tells about a little girl who was making a great fuss about eating. Here is the way the psychologist handled the situation. It was explained to this child, after she had engaged in a few games with other children, how big children acted in contrast to what babies did. Then she was asked why she thought people ate food.

" 'Cause things taste good," was all she knew about it. She was interested in finding that food helped children grow. She was anxious to be considered "big."

"Let's make two lists, one of things you like to eat, and one of things you don't like. Then we can tell your mother and plan some meals." [148]

[147] See W. J. Reilly: *How to Improve Your Human Relations by Straight Thinking,* pp. 150-154. 1942.

[148] Weill: *op. cit.,* p. 319.

The child's eating habits were straightened out gradually, partly because she had her say in the selection of menus.

In another case described by Weill, illness of the parents forced them to extend a great deal of freedom and responsibility to their children. The youngsters "had the run of the house and the say about what clothes they should wear and even what clothes they should buy." The principle adopted by the parents was this:

As much responsibility as they can bear at each age. As much freedom to make mistakes as is consistent with physical safety. On our part as little nagging as possible.[149]

The very mothers who criticized this arrangement because they were sure the children would lose all respect for their parents, were amazed to notice how these children, in contrast to their own, ran to their father and mother with all their joys and sorrows, sharing their experiences with the easiest confidence. These parents did not seek to run their children's lives, to choose their friends, to impose their own values. The children profited by their freedom, grew up into mature persons.

One more family described by Weill, is worthy of mention here. Their mode of family government is similar to that of the Reilly family referred to above.

"It's really much easier to get along well in a large family than in a small one," said a mother who knew what she was talking about, for she had not only been one of nine herself, but could point proudly to seven sons and five daughters, each planned for, welcomed and trained into cooperative and loving responsibility.

"You can have such good times, with teams ready to hand, and it's so sociable," she went on. "Oh, yes, there are quarrels, plenty of them, but if tension gets too high, their father has trained them to select a referee, put on the gloves, go into the back yard and have a go at each other. There is always an audience too, and that adds to the interest. The older ones are mostly away now and things are not so exciting. But for my part, I found the house even easier to run when it was full of children.

"It wasn't that I was naturally a good manager. I take very little credit myself. My husband made the original suggestion and laid most of the plans to run the house on a cooperative scheme, as much like a business concern as we could. He said if we were going to have the large family we wanted, we would have to grease the household machinery as much as possible

---

[149] *Ibid.*, p. 333.

and that the more grease the children could supply of themselves, the better equipped they would be for living outside the home later on.   So we sat down and worked out a scheme that had three main facets.

"The first was the general skeleton of the routine of the house, just as a business has its general routine.   We were all to be bound by this, so as to save time arguing, pleading, trying to decide.   At the same time we realized we must never let ourselves become slaves to routine.   So we made allowance for very special occasions, such as staying up later for birthday parties, and the like.   Then within the limits of the schedule we all had great freedom. For instance, if it were a fine evening, the group in charge of supper might announce that we would eat out-of-doors.   Or if it were a howling, dreary night, they'd decide that we'd have a floor picnic around the big fireplace in the living room.

"The second phase of the scheme was that the work of the household should be organized into jobs, and these jobs carefully studied and graded according to their difficulty, their wearisomeness and their responsibility.   Then they were to be handed around according to age, ability and reliability. As often as possible, the jobs were given to groups, instead of to individuals, in order to avoid lonesomeness and monotony.   When the oldest children were tiny, only the simplest jobs were given them, but as they grew older, they advanced to more and more difficult and responsible ones, while breaking in their next younger brothers and sisters to take over their work.   They always seemed to get a great deal of satisfaction out of playing teacher in this way. They could trade jobs if they liked.   But both sides had to be satisfied, and the job equally well done."

"How did you get them to be willing to accept such responsibility?" I asked.

"Well, that is where the third part of the scheme came in. Every Sunday and oftener if necessary, we had a family conference.   Dad was the head, but each member had not only the right, but was expected to take part.   That was the time to offer suggestions or to consider the suggestions of the others as to better methods, eliminations or new projects.   Dad sat at the head of the table and listened respectfully while each child learned to present and defend his own case.

"It was excellent training for them all and one of the by-products was the growth of a belief in the wisdom and fairness of the pooled opinion of the group.   It led, too, to a surprising amount of cooperation and confidence in each other. . . .

"As for routine, that has been, of course, the backbone of our living, but like a backbone, it combines strength with flexibility.   We all like a fair amount of certainty.   And of course a schedule we really live by eliminates, as I said before, quantities of waste time, effort and emotion by eliminating arguments and fussing.   The children all understand *why* we use schedules. They all have learned to feel that they are cooperators and producers as well ns mere receivers of protection and consumers; and the schedule helps. They really like it. It makes them feel important and worthwhile. The flexibility comes in whenever necessary. Our schedule isn't dead and as each child knows that he can make suggestions in regard to it, none of us is irritated by feeling that we live according to rule.

"Enough of the children have grown up now so that we can begin to judge results. As they go away from home and have to depend more and more on themselves, they seem to carry with them a fund of knowledge of situations and of people that stands them in good stead. They welcome responsibility, or at least they accept it instead of resenting it or trying to avoid it, as we have seen so many young people do. And they also go at a job in constructive fashion. They differ widely in their interests. That pleases us too. They have been used to earning and spending money since babyhood, making budgets and keeping accounts, so they do not become overwhelmed by manipulating an allowance when they start off for college, or by living within their salary as they start on their first jobs." [150]

This family exhibits very clearly what we mean by democracy in the home.

The trend is definitely in the direction of democratic family life, as exemplified in the cases we have cited. The evidences of such a trend can be observed in various present-day practices.

Wives, husbands and children have attained more privacy, more freedom, more personal dignity. The "heavy" father, the self-appointed Jehovah of the home, now is a piece of early Americana currently inciting uproarious laughter in the theater. Wives have advanced from being clinging vines and recipients of financial doles from their lords and masters to handlers of home finance and to enjoying the attendant personal self-expression. Children have a voice in their own destinies, are not arbitrarily told what they must do or become.[151]

[150] Weill: *op. cit.*, pp. 346-351.
[151] M. Lindsay: "Yes, We've Acquired More Sense." *Reader's Digest,* June, 1944. Condensed from the Washington *Post* of April 12, 1944. The play referred to in the above passage is undoubtedly Clarence Day's *Life with Father.*

Chapter 20

THE CHURCH

THE CHURCH is a third institution which exerts considerable influence upon our social conduct. It is under the care of organized religion that most of us acquire the ideals which constitute the basis of character, the values which inspire our endeavors. It is in the church that we get most of our formal moral training. This phase of our preparation for socialized living is extremely important. Psychologists, unfortunately, have neglected this field of investigation too long partly because of a notion that morals are not a proper subject for scientific research, partly because of a disinclination to probe the sacred precincts of the spiritual life. While religionists have been raking scientists over the coals for plunging civilization into destruction, the scientists on the whole have been adhering to a "hands-off" policy as far as religion is concerned. Ministers have been making forays into the field of psychology; psychologists, on the whole, have been nervously steering clear of religious problems. The time is ripe for an evaluation of the church in the light of modern psychology. How does it function as a social institution? Does it promote our happiness or hinder our attainment of a satisfying life? How can it be improved as an instrument for human welfare? The psychological approach to these problems will afford us a new insight into the assets and liabilities of our traditional religious practices. Persons sincerely interested in the church will welcome any constructive suggestions we can offer in the light of our investigation, for religion is definitely on trial in many parts of the world today. If the influence of the church is to be preserved and extended, loyal believers must re-examine their religious training, weed out the superstitions and the follies, and then concentrate on a gospel of social reconstruction that will satisfy the demands of critical intelligence.

I. RELIGION AND RELIGIONS

Students of semantics tell us that we should have definite referents in mind when we use words. Many discussions of religion and the hurch proceed on the implicit assumption that there is one religion r one church that is being referred to. Actually, there are many eligions, many churches, many communicants; statements made about ne religion may be entirely inapplicable to another. This warning vill be kept in mind by the author as he tries to be careful in his hoice of terms. He will try to be definite, to be concrete, to limit iis observations to the exact situations of which they are really de-criptive. References will not be made to religions in general but to pecific practices engaged in by people who are following the teach-ngs of their minister or priest. Unless otherwise specified, religion vill connote "Christianity," as the author does not feel qualified to reat Judaism, Confucianism, Mohammedanism, Buddhism or other aiths, with authority. The author is aware that "Christianity" is an ndefinite term, that there are Christians and Christians, some of whom lo not see eye to eye with others passing by the same name, as Prot-:stants and Catholics who marry each other can bear witness.[1] The :laim that not all Christians share the same outlook simply because hey are called "Christians" may be substantiated by citing the atti-.udes of Protestants toward Catholics in a small Connecticut town vhere a survey was conducted by *Commonweal,* a Catholic publica-ion. It was found that:

An overwhelming proportion of the Protestants would refuse to marry a Catholic, vote for a Catholic for President, or approve the selection of one for he Supreme Court. A majority said they would hesitate to employ a Catholic as nurse for their children, as a guardian, as private secretary, or as a mem-er of the school board. They expressed willingness, however, to pray with a Catholic, approve one as a schoolteacher or librarian, select one as Fourth of July orator, and to have one as an intimate friend. Practically all were willing to recognize Catholics as Christians.[2]

T. P. O'Connor was thinking of the differences that set Christian over against Christian when he remarked: "Ireland is in a devil of a way. Down here we have the Catholics, and up there we have the Protes-tants, and they're at each other's throats all the time. I often wish they were all of them heathen, so they could live together like Chris-tians." [3]

---

[1] Anonymous: "What It Means to Marry a Catholic." *Forum,* June, 1929. Refer to the discussion of mixed marriages on pp. 793-96.

[2] Quoted by P. Odegard: *The American Public Mind,* p. 68. Columbia Uni-versity Press. 1930.

[3] Quoted, *Ibid.,* p. 76.

Nevertheless, despite the countless variations in creed and practice some observations may be made about religion that apply to religiou people in general.

When Reinach defines religion as "a sum of scruples which imped the free exercise of our faculties," he is speaking of one phase of re ligion that is common to all behavior dominated by reverence for the Divine Will.[4] It is natural for the believer, no matter what his spe cial creed, to be dogmatic about his faith, since his convictions mean so much to him. Religious experience depends upon believing; skep ticism is discouraged. There is a finality about religious certaintie that shuts out the attitude of suspending judgment. The very fac that the emotions are so intensely involved in religious experienc suggests the likelihood that calm deliberation will not occur unde such "moving" conditions. The danger of yielding to the lead o such stirring emotions makes it all the more important for us to ex amine the nature of religious behavior.

Speaking, again, of human experience in general, one discerns the opposite danger of trying to live by reason alone, without any regard for spiritual longings. Good mental hygiene demands a wholesome respect for the deep-seated convictions which nourish confidence and courage when discouragement, misfortune, suffering, and sorrow threaten to overwhelm us. At such times there is strength and hope in believing unreservedly that there is an Intelligence immanent ir the universe giving life a purpose and a meaning, that there is for giveness for our mistakes and our transgressions, that bodily pain and personal bereavement may be blessings in disguise, that justice will ultimately prevail, that immortality awaits us. Beliefs of this nature perhaps unproved before the bar of reason, contribute to mental poise, and there are times when skeptics probably wish they could believe these heartening articles of faith for the consolation they pro vide. Jung concludes from his long experience as an analytic psy chologist that many nervous breakdowns are due to the spiritual bankruptcy that results when religious faith is discarded, and there is nothing to replace it.[5] Morale suffers when a person rejects his re ligion ideationally, though still clinging emotionally and uncon sciously to the faith instilled in childhood. Link supports Jung in asserting that persons with scientific training are apt to place too much

[4] Quoted by H. E. Fosdick: *As I See Religion*, p. 3. 1932.
[5] See C. G. Jung: *Modern Man in Search of a Soul*, Chapter 10, "The Spiritual Problem of Modern Man." 1939.

tress on the intellect, not enough on the feelings.[6] Unbelief is common among scientists, as Leuba discovered, with no regrets reported.[7] More ordinary people, with a mere touch of the scientific "I'm from Missouri, you'll have to prove it" skepticism, gained from a couple of courses in college, may not have the personal resources with which to face the cold, impersonal universe when bereft of their religious faith.[8] These are the unfortunate souls who are upset and demoralized by our modern education. It is a rare person who can reconcile his spiritual yearnings and his rational judgment, or better still, integrate them into an effective philosophy of life.

We have made two general statements about religion: that it may impede deliberation and that it may minister to our emotional needs. These affirmations apply to any kind of religion.

Criticisms of religion are sometimes issued in such sweeping form as to imply that they are applicable inclusively to any and all religions, when, in fact, they are properly relevant only to certain specific kinds of religion. In some cases, for instance, the critic of religion may be reacting against the narrow, outmoded teachings he encountered in his own childhood, having failed to bring his theology up to date along with the advances on other sectors of his intellectual front. Sometimes this hostility to religion is tied up with rebellion, perhaps unconscious, against parental authority, or with the effort to eradicate puritanical inhibitions associated with early moral instruction. James Harvey Robinson fits the former description, if I read correctly between the lines of his *Mind in the Making* and his *Human Comedy*. In the latter book, he makes this sweeping indictment: "To the candid historical student the evil workings of religion are, to say the least, far more conspicuous and far more readily demonstrated than its good results." [9] In this same book, Chapter 11, "The Twilight of the Gods," there is abundant evidence to justify the suspicion that he is predicting the end for religion largely because he had become acutely conscious of the fact that the naïve conceptions of his childhood could not stand the test of his mature judgment. It is not fair, of course, to present religion in its worst or weakest form in order to facilitate a demolishing attack on its foundations. Apparently

[6] See H. C. Link: *The Return to Religion*, Chapter 4, "Fools of Reason." 1937.
[7] J. H. Leuba: "Religious Beliefs of American Scientists." *Harper's Magazine*, August, 1934.
[8] Freud feels that religion is a refuge for weak persons who cannot meet life on their own power. See his book, *The Future of an Illusion*. 1928.
[9] Page 263.

Robinson the historian, owing to an emotional bias, was not awar
that religion, too, may have a history in the life of the individual a
he grows older and puts away childish notions. It is unfair of him t
ridicule his own childhood beliefs as if they were representative o
religion in general. Many persons have started in childhood witl
a naïve creed which they have replaced with a more intelligent set o
beliefs as they have grown up and gained in understanding. Robir
son's theological development seems to have been arrested in hi
youth. His attacks on religion were really a rejection of the outwor
creeds that had dominated his childhood days. This sort of reactio
against an outmoded theology is evident also in the writings o
Mencken, Barnes, Asbury, and others.[10] If some of these critics woul
put themselves out to visit a number of churches, they might be su
prised to learn how things have changed since they were childrer
Even the traditionally anti-religious *American Mercury* is fair enougl
to publish an article taking the critics to task, in which the author
Roger Riis, says:

> And I state with assurance that the critics of the churches today don't knov
> what they are talking about. True, a minority of churches still offer a dul
> repellent form of salvation, some in ugly buildings, some with painful musi
> some with humdrum ministers. But you don't have to go to those churche
> nor need you condemn all churches because some fail.
> It is obvious that the assailants of churches do not go to church. The
> don't know what the churches are doing these days.[11]

When Harry Emerson Fosdick says that "much of our contempo
rary Christianity is not making people better, but worse," he is carefu
to specify that he is not making a wholesale indictment against th
churches.[12] Religion, he elaborates, makes some people generou
sympathetic, understanding, kind—but it also makes some peopl
lazy, useless, soft, unduly optimistic, socially apathetic. Some of thes
psychological effects of religion we are going to enlarge upon late
They are mentioned at this point to emphasize the necessity for lir
iting and qualifying our comments if we aim to be accurate and fai
There are all kinds of religions and all kinds of people who are a

[10] See H. L. Mencken: *Treatise on the Gods*. 1930. H. E. Barnes: *The Twiligh
of Christianity*. 1929. H. Asbury: *Up from Methodism*. 1926.
[11] R. W. Riis: "Why I Go to Church." *American Mercury*, January, 1941. Cor
densed under the title, "Now I am for the Churches" in the *Reader's Digest*, Jar
uary, 1941.
[12] The quotation is from his book, *Adventurous Religion*, p. 276. 1926.

fected in all sorts of ways by their "religion," some good, some bad, some indifferent.

II. FUNCTIONS OF THE CHURCH

Worship, evangelism, education, and community welfare are four primary functions of the church.[13]   These services are personalized in the role of the minister—or parson as he used to be called—who cares for his parishioners, acting as "adviser in daily affairs, officiator at birth, marriage, and death, consoler in time of grief, at moments of stress physician to their souls.   He must also manage a large institution, pick his way through conflicting opinions, act as model to his neighbors, meet the world with unimpeachable good humor and compassion." [14]

There are two responsibilities of the church that are of special concern to the social psychologist: one is the provision of opportunities for fellowship; the other, the direction of motivation.

First of all, human beings, gregarious as they are, enjoy the privilege of sharing their joys and sorrows.   Confession is social as an exchange of experiences, satisfying to both confessee and confessor. The Oxford Group Movement has featured the value of sharing as one of its cardinal principles, and a Buchman house party where devotees recount their personal transgressions is reminiscent of the old-fashioned prayer meeting with its call for personal testimony.   Christ promised to be present wherever two or three gathered together in his name.   This social appeal has been one of the strongest assets of Christianity, from its earliest days when converts were urged by Paul to regard themselves as members of the body of Christ, a mystical symbol for the need of expressing the common faith by the sharing of mutual hopes and enthusiasms.   "The right hand of fellowship" is a ritual of welcome into the recognized communion of kindred souls.

This impulse for sharing the blessings of religious experience is encouraged by the evangelistic nature of Christianity.   The Christian, imbued with the missionary spirit, is eager to tell others "the old, old story of Jesus and His love," the good news of salvation promised those who give themselves to the service of Him who died upon the Cross to save us from our sins.   In former days this zeal to win converts was inspired by the belief that heretics would be damned eternally unless they surrendered themselves to Christ.

[13] According to Luther A. Weigle, President (1940-1941) of the Federal Council of Churches of Christ in America.
[14] *Life,* February 3, 1941.

The social function of the church is fulfilled, in part, by the cultivation of worship. The liturgy, celebrated in the High Mass, or the Low Mass, or the Protestant communion, is an occasion for the experiencing of group consciousness. No one can get the full value from a service of public worship by listening to a radio broadcast in the privacy of his home.

Protestant churches are beginning to see the values in ritualizing the worship service as a means of inducing a reverent mood in the congregation. The Catholic Church has always appreciated the importance of pomp and ceremony and atmosphere in the evocation of a worshipful state of mind.

The second function of the church that is of special interest to the social psychologist is found in its program for instilling good motives. It is not the job of the pastor to solve all our economic, political, or social problems. "Let the minister tend to his knitting," suggest the critics when a preacher wanders from religion into the fields of business or medicine—realms in which his opinion may be worth no more than the guess of the average parishioner. Perhaps such out-of-bounds pronouncements are actuated by confusion in the minister's mind as to just what his function is. There are some people who feel that the pastor's task should be the kindling of impulses toward good will, unselfishness, and kindness in the bankers, educators, doctors, and politicians in his congregation so that each of them will be inspired to use his special knowledge in his own field for noble ends. Here is a real challenge, for the mess the world is in today is attributable, in Sorokin's opinion, to religion's failure to promote good will among men, to spiritualize mentality, to socialize conduct, to ennoble social relations.[15] Of course this responsibility does not belong to the church alone but certainly it is a responsibility falling peculiarly within the sphere of religion.

Here, then, is a big assignment for the church: to inspire people so that they will want to be good and—to enlighten them with respect to their concepts of right and wrong so that their moral endeavors will be intelligently directed. Conscience needs to be educated to a proper sense of values. People who think that God cares whether they wear short skirts or play cards may become so preoccupied with their peccadillos as to overlook their more serious transgressions. A complete ethical code will not concern itself solely with sexual temptations. It will be inclusive enough to embrace the "sins" of dishonesty, hypocrisy, self-complacency, avarice, envy, callousness, incon-

[15] See P. A. Sorokin: *The Crisis of Our Age.* 1941.

siderateness, meanness, and the like, big sins and little sins that make it difficult for us to live together harmoniously and happily.

The responsibilities of the minister and the functions belonging to the church, change with the times. The midweek prayer meeting and the Sunday evening service have been abandoned in many communities, owing to competitive attractions offered by the movies and the radio. Some ministers are taking to the radio themselves as a medium for spreading their message to larger audiences, and it is noteworthy that their sermons are delivered with less of an air of authority, more in the vein of discussion and inquiry. The church building is open more of the time now, particularly in some of the big cities where people come to consult the pastor—just the reverse of the custom of former times when the parson went the rounds, making his pastoral calls in the parlors of his parishioners. The minister who has to deal with a large congregation is less of a personal pastor; indeed, his only contacts with some of his spiritual charges are made at weddings, christenings, and funerals, times when even the most indifferent feel the proprieties call for the presence of the pastor in his official capacity. In the large churches the minister is now an executive with assistants who carry out their respective assignments under his direction. Individuals who need help of one kind or another, vocational guidance or psychiatric counsel perhaps, may be referred, under such a regime, to the proper social agencies, if it is the policy of the church not to undertake functions performed just as well by nonsectarian agencies. In the smaller parishes the minister may still attempt to be preacher, confessor, vocational counselor, psychiatric aide, spiritual guide, educational adviser, clinical psychologist, and marital conciliator—a large job for any one man.[16]

III. TRENDS

We have surveyed some of the functions of the church. Now we shall analyze the program undertaken by the typical modern church and then proceed to examine some of the factors responsible for the declining influence of the church as a social institution.

A. The Modern Program

There are certain features that deserve special mention in a review of what the churches are doing today to serve the community: re-

---

[16] Some of these comments have been culled from C. L. Fry: "Changes in Religious Organization," Chapter 20 in *Recent Social Trends*. McGraw-Hill Book Company, 1933.

ligious education, mental hygiene, unity through fusion, and the propagation of the social gospel.

1. RELIGIOUS EDUCATION

Modern religious leaders are fully aware that the continuing prosperity of the church will depend in large measure upon training the young in habits of attending services of divine worship and participating in the various activities sponsored by the organization. The time to win loyal support is right from the start when the child is still impressionable. Religious instruction used to be handled by anybody who was willing to teach a Sunday-school class. Volunteers were enlisted in the Lord's work whether or not they were qualified to explain the Biblical parables and whether or not they were fit persons to influence the child in the forming of his ideals. This haphazard selection of teachers has been replaced in many churches by a well organized program under the leadership of a paid Director of Religious Education specifically trained for his job by university courses in this field. In some instances there is a professional staff trained in the techniques of religious instruction, who are paid for doing this important work of preparing the young to walk in the paths of righteousness. Sunday-school programs have been standardized by an International Council of Religious Education, in operation since 1922, whose job it is to direct the preparation of graded lessons for the Protestant churches. The Catholic Church has been expanding the parochial schools to make sure that its young people are given the proper ideas on religion and morals. Pope Leo XIII stated the policy of the Church: "It is necessary not only that religious instruction be given to the young at certain fixed times but also that every other subject taught be permeated with Christian piety." [17]

Since Church and State in the United States have remained distinctly separate as a matter of policy, religious instruction, other than the reading of the Bible, has been forbidden in the public schools. Catholics feel that their children are being reared as pagans under public school teachers, and therefore they are doing everything possible to foster parochial school education. Protestants are aware, too, that one hour a week in Sunday school is hardly enough time for religious training, and consequently they are promoting weekday and vacation Bible schools.[18] Anyone familiar with genetic psychology will agree

---

[17] Quoted in an encyclical issued by Pope Pius XI.

[18] In some states laws have been passed to permit the local school boards to excuse pupils from public school at certain times for religious education, to be pro-

that it is important to give children an enlightened education in religion and morals, for many an atheist has been produced by an outmoded theology inculcated in him during his defenseless tender years.

All education, one may urge, should be religious, in the sense that
the student should develop an appreciation for things worth while.
Certainly the enlightened person should have a good sense of values
with due reverence for whatever ideals there are that merit his respect.
The great scientists like Millikan, the believer, and Einstein, the agnostic, revere the mysteries of this remarkable universe. There is no
place in our schools for the teacher who has a mania for tearing down
everything his pupils believe in, who is an iconoclast with an irresistible urge to upset his protégés, who believes in nothing himself except
the goal of undermining other people's faith. Teachers of this sort,
who employ ridicule and mockery to confuse immature minds, are
just as much a menace as religious fanatics who oppose the teaching of
evolution. Some of these iconoclasts feel that they have a mission to
perform, like the atheist who enrolled in a school of theology because,
he explained, he wanted to undermine the church from the inside.
"Runner-downers" feel no responsibility for offering something constructive and their continued blasting of youthful hopes is apt to defeat
one of the main purposes of education: finding something worth while
to believe in. This search for values is the chief aim of Religious Educators. It is a very important task. The responsibility for helping
students in this search is one that all educators must assume. It is
not an obligation resting solely on the Sunday school.

One of the disadvantages in Religious Education, as we have already
hinted, is its tendency to impose a particular creed sponsored by the
particular church which is giving the children instruction, instead of
allowing the pupils to work out their own philosophy of life. Some
church schools are consciously guarding against this inclination by encouraging the use of project and discussion methods in true progressive style. Under this modernized system children are no longer given
dogma, doctrinal precepts, maxims, and proverbs to memorize, on the
assumption that the verbal repetition of these sayings will implant
sound moral principles which will subconsciously influence conduct in
the right directions in later life. Today children are given problems
to discuss and they are left to find the solutions for themselves with
some guidance from their instructors. Projects give the pupils an opportunity to pick up useful information on the way, information that

---

vided under the auspices of the religious group with which the particular child's
family is affiliated.

will facilitate the achievement of an intelligent orientation to the moral and spiritual problems of man.

2. MENTAL HYGIENE

The modern theological student, preparing himself for the ministry, is trained in clinical psychology and mental hygiene on the theory that a good part of his pastoral work will consist in advising people about their emotional problems, their frustrations, their ambitions, their disappointments, their sorrows, their personal difficulties, their maladjustments in general. In the course of his preparation the embryonic parson may spend some time in residence at a psychiatric hospital where he gets acquainted with the various neuroses and psychoses by witnessing their respective symptoms in the raw.[19] This experience— an internship dealing with personal maladjustments of an extreme sort—is intended to give him a background for understanding the personal problems of normal people and a foundation for detecting incipient mental disorders in his parishioners. There is some chance, after such training, that the parson in his ministry may become overanxious about the trivial eccentricities of his charges. A little knowledge of psychopathology may prove very dangerous, especially so if the minister is foolish enough to prescribe for conditions needing the professional attention of a psychiatrist.

On the other hand, it is a real advantage for a church to have a pastor who can give personal counsel based on training in psychology. There are many people who would be embarrassed about going to the office of a psychiatrist for an interview, many who could not afford to pay the fees charged for such a visit. Such persons would feel more inclined to have a heart-to-heart talk with their pastor. If the pastor is versed in mental hygiene, he may be able to help the individual to find a satisfactory solution for his difficulties; if he suspects symptoms indicative of serious psychopathic conditions, he may send the individual to a psychiatrist for consultation; or he may have a psychiatrist on the church staff, if he has a large church with adequate funds at his disposal. Granting Jung's theory that most neuroses are brought on by moral or spiritual disintegration, it is reasonable to assume that

---

[19] Clinical training of clergymen may include residence in general hospitals, too, where the student gains an intimate knowledge of human beings and their personal problems. See P. Morell: "Ministers in White." *Saturday Evening Post*, July 25, 1942. See also, "What Clinical Training Does for Clergymen." *Information Service*, May 21, 1938. Published by the Department of Research and Education, Federal Council of the Churches of Christ in America, 297 Fourth Avenue, New York, N.Y.

the clergyman is in a unique position to render help in time of trouble. Mental healing has been associated with the church since the time of Christ, who was himself a master of the art, and there is no doubt that Christian Science gives many people just the faith they need for overcoming sickness and adversity. The belief that religion has curative powers is an old one and a sound one: it was the cardinal principle of the Emmanuel Movement initiated by Elwood Worcester at the Emmanuel Episcopal Church in Boston, where the mental hygiene approach was incorporated as an integral part of the pastoral service.[20]

One difficulty in the psychotherapeutic situation as it exists today may be expressed in the form of a dilemma: should the person in distress turn to a clergyman who probably knows very little psychiatry or should he unburden his troubles in the consultation room of a psychiatrist who may have very little religious faith? This statement, of course, oversimplifies the actual state of affairs. Nevertheless, it is near enough to reality to approximate the alternatives which aggravate the confusion of the distraught individual. Some maladjusted people find the answer in the helpful ministrations of their pastor; some, in the services of a psychoanalyst or a psychiatrist. The clergy and the medical profession compete sometimes for the privilege of lending a helping hand. In this competition doctors are encouraged by the fact that people are coming increasingly to realize that science with its insistence upon the knowledge of laws and the fulfilling of conditions provides the surest means of achieving health and prosperity. Some observers feel that science is displacing religion as a way of gaining what human beings want to get out of life.[21] In so far as this is true, doctors of medicine will profit at the expense of doctors of divinity. One man who had found the psychologist more helpful than the clergyman testified:

> I'm fed up on lectures. . . . A fellow would like to talk to his clergyman now and again . . . about little troubles . . . but they won't let you get anything off your chest. . . . They shake hands with their gloves on. . . . A bunch of theology. . . . But I have a friend who is a psychologist. . . .[22]

Some people complain that when they have confided their troubles and worries to the minister, the clergyman will then assure them that

[20] For a description of this work, see E. Worcester, S. McComb, and I. H. Coriat: *Religion and Medicine.* 1908.
[21] See H. E. Fosdick: "The Real Point of Conflict between Science and Religion." A sermon delivered on the National Vespers program. March 10, 1940.
[22] Quoted by J. H. Preston: "D.D. versus M.D." *Reader's Digest,* July, 1936. Condensed from *Scribner's Magazine.*

true penitence will bring absolution from a benevolent Creator, that God will forgive those who have faith. Mystical reassurances of this sort may repel the modern person who wants a concrete answer to the question, "How can I clear the way for success in living?" Disappointed in his pastor, the troubled individual may then go to a psychologist and tell him the whole story.

The psychologist tells him the reasons for these difficulties; ferrets into his past, holds to light some ancient fear, some ancient illness, misunderstanding or maladjustment, and shows how they bear upon his present state of mind. Here, at last, is something the modern man can understand. . . . Here is a man who grasps at once all the ailments that have seemed so mysterious and unconquerable, and reduces them to utter simplicity. . . . The clergyman urges blind faith in cosmic benevolence, and seems unable to help him face the realities of living. The psychologist gives him causes, effects, reasons.[23]

The psychologist or psychiatrist will lend an attentive ear without any tinge of moral censure, thus providing the best kind of attitude for facilitating a catharsis. In this respect the scientist has an important advantage over the clergyman who is apt to react with shock and moral condemnation when the confession gets too sordid for him. There is another point of superiority in favor of the scientist: the patient pays him for his advice. The minister gives his counsel for nothing and subconsciously the patient may be inclined to conclude that that is about all the advice is worth.

The wise minister who is eager to build up his church as an influence in the community will be alert enough to feature mental hygiene as one of the pastoral services for his communicants; he will keep in touch with medical men who can be called upon to handle cases requiring special care; he will not become so obsessed with the clinical spirit as to lose sight of other functions that are equally important in the total program of the church. The parson, because of his position in the community, comes to know intimately the trials and tribulations of his flock and he should sense his obligation, as a confessor and a confidante, to equip himself with every instrument available for helping his charges to solve their personal problems. People will turn to him for help; if he fails them in their hour of need, their loyalty to the church is bound to suffer. The clergy has a wonderful opportunity in this field of counseling. The minister can be a guide, a sort of personnel counselor, if he prepares himself to meet the need that he is sure to face as a pastor.

[23] *Ibid.*

3. FUSION AND COOPERATION

Many different sects have grown up within Christianity because individuals want various kinds of religious experience to satisfy their particular needs. The Catholic Church and the High Episcopal Church use the aesthetic appeal in creating the spirit of worship, with incense, robes, chants, and beautiful cathedrals to stir reverence for the Divine. One lady expressed her preference for the Episcopal service, with its incense, by explaining that she liked to smell her religion. There is something to that—for sense experience is vivid and real. The Protestant churches are beginning to realize the value of sensory cues in the stimulation of worshipful attitudes. Their emphasis in the past has been more on the intellectual side, as in the Unitarian Church, or on the emotional side, as in the Methodist Church. Protestants discuss, debate, and argue about the bases of faith; Catholics speak with authority. Different sects, different denominations, suit different temperaments. Sectarianism is definitely in line with the needs revealed by differential psychology.

Unfortunately religious sects encourage strong prejudices and violent animosities among the several groups, each of which is partial to its own creed and its own way of doing things.[24] These partisan loyalties are so intense that it is virtually impossible for a Protestant and a Catholic to marry without becoming involved in a disrupting conflict. They must be married by a priest or they are not married at all; the children must be reared in the Catholic faith. The Protestant may protest—in vain. These obstacles to harmony are by no means limited to the conflicts of family life. When Al Smith ran for the Presidency in 1928, the rift between the faiths gave rise to many bitter arguments and hostile accusations of narrow-mindedness on both sides. Some Protestants saw the menace of the Pope moving into the White House. Living together would be much easier if we were not separated by creedal barriers and divisive loyalties.

There are some indications that the barriers are breaking down as the churches move toward unity. Leaders are calling attention to the fact that the churches cannot promote universal brotherhood very effectively when there is so much squabbling in the ranks. Various developments are pointing to the advantages of fusion, besides that of better fellowship.

[24] The influence of sectarianism on religious prejudices has been discussed in Chapter 17.

There are plenty of other arguments in support of church unity. There is the taxpayer's argument that it is a burden to the community to exempt from taxation more church buildings and building sites than are needed. There is the businessman's argument that it is a waste of money and of men to support a dozen churches and ministers in a community that could be served by two. There is the missionary's argument that in foreign lands denominational differences are often worse than meaningless.

Some of the denominational names cannot be translated into Chinese without provoking smiles among that delightfully humorous and intelligent people. It is not easy to present a religion of universal brotherhood against the background of a home base where brotherhood is not realized. But strongest of all the arguments for unity is this new one, this terrible pressure from without of alien and anti-Christian ideologies which seek to dominate the world.[25]

Economic necessity has been an important factor in promoting church unity. In numerous small towns the various churches have fused into a community church espousing the fundamentals of faith accepted by most religious believers.

Some authorities feel that we shall merge our denominational and sectarian differences ultimately into one religion for all. Hocking is strongly of this opinion. As chairman of the Appraisal Commission for the Laymen's Foreign Missions Inquiry he was impressed with the need for cooperation and mutual understanding. In *Re-Thinking Missions* (1932), the Commission shocked conservatives by proposing that Christians should cease attacking non-Christian religions and try to work with them in a spirit of common sympathy. After pondering over this idea for several years, Hocking gave expression to his convictions in *Living Religions and a World Faith* (1940), in which he maintains that the world's religions must be replaced by one religion. He deplores the "scandal of plurality," the fact that religion, by its very nature universal and one, is everywhere local, partisan, sectarian. A world faith will not be brought about by the kind of missionary who goes out into the foreign field with a zealous purpose for making his own particular religion universal. If we are going to achieve a world religion, we must proceed with a different set: the desire to find the elements that people of all faiths can agree upon. This fusion of beliefs will culminate in a religion that is God-centered rather than Christ-centered: "God is in His world, but Buddha, Jesus, Mohammed

[25] H. C. Robbins: "Present-Day Progress toward Church Unity." *Christian Century Pulpit,* July, 1940.

are in their little private closets, and we shall thank them but never return to them." [26]   The urgency behind a search for a universal religion is not a desire for propagating a particular creed as the one true faith but a desire for world citizenship.   "There is a universal science; there should be universal law; why may we not expect a world faith?" [27]   Hocking looks forward to the achievement of such a faith as one aspect of a new world culture that is coming into being.   In his aspiration for a universal faith, Hocking is speaking as a philosopher, not as a Congregationalist, for ardent denominationalists are not enthusiastic over the prospect of fusing with anybody and sacrificing perfectly sound doctrines for a sickly eclectic faith.   As long as believers remain champions of sectarian religion, the prospect of a world faith is a distant one.   There are more denominationalists than there are Hockings and it is likely that his proposals will not strike a responsive chord among his fellow members in the local church—even in Cambridge.

Though sectarianism still thrives, there are definite trends toward cooperation among the various churches.   The Northern and Southern Methodists, split since the division over the slavery issue back in the 1840's, voted in 1939 to unite into one church.   The Baptist World Alliance has been seeking to coordinate the work of this denomination on a world-wide scale.   A merger of Presbyterians and Episcopalians has been under consideration.   Cooperation among the several Protestant churches is fostered by the Federal Council of the Churches of Christ in America, founded in 1908.   This council publishes a monthly *Federal Council Bulletin,* subtitled "A Journal of Inter-Church Cooperation."   The National Catholic Welfare Conference has been coordinating the efforts of the Catholic churches since 1919.   In 1940 the North American Council of Churches was established to correlate the religious interests of the United States and Canada, and to promote friendly contacts around the world.   There is a World Council of Churches which is very active in promoting the ecumenical movement.   This list of cooperative agencies is not intended to be exhaustive.   The cases cited exemplify two trends characteristic of the church as an institution today: the merging of separate divisions, sects, denominations into a community church or a united church, and the wider cooperation among the churches within interdenominational organizations.   These institutional changes are repre-

[26] W. E. Hocking: *Living Religions and a World Faith,* p. 22.   1940.
[27] *Ibid.,* p. 21.

sentative of changing attitudes toward religion, common among present-day church members, and seconded by many people who are not included within the official folds.

There are numerous instances of this trend toward cooperation. One is a report of a Conference on Religion in the World, held at Harvard University in July, 1941. Participants agreed that religion is, or should be, a unitive force in society. Professor Auer, an exile from The Netherlands, affirmed that "religion is the power that endeavors to bring men together," and that it can bring men together in mutually helpful cooperation in spite of the widest differences of opinion. President Bixler of Colby College stated that if religion is to have a unifying influence, "it must be a religion of a liberal type . . . a rational, ethical religion, purged of superstitious fear, of all obscurantism and reliance on authority, and dedicated to the moral ideal which men share because they are men, not because they are Christians or Jews, Aryans or Semites."

Further evidence of the movement toward unity is a report (1941) concerning missionary activities in Mexico. The story speaks for itself:

PROTESTANT CONGRESS
BRINGS COOPERATION

The holding of the International Congress on Christian Education in Mexico City (July 16-20) will be a big help toward interdenominational cooperation in this country. All the denominations working in Mexico are participating. It is very significant that the missionaries and the mission boards are joining in the congress with a beautiful spirit. Denominational divisions were brought to the Mexicans by the missionaries of the pioneering days. One must not indulge in too harsh criticisms of them. They were ardent evangelists. They were up against tremendous difficulties and suffered with patience and fortitude hardships and persecutions.

EARLY MISSIONARIES OFTEN
STRESSED PECULIARITIES

But, men and women of their times that they were, their denominational zeal was for them one and the same thing with their evangelical faith. So they held bravely not only to the simple gospel of Christ but to the peculiarities of their particular denomination as well. They thought it was their duty as good soldiers of Jesus Christ to stress as much as possible the differences rather than the likenesses of the denominations, to hold out the characteristics of their own denomination as the last word in the pure interpretation of the Gospel and to warn and guard their little flocks against contamination with the "errors" of other denominations.

OPEN WARFARE
ENSUED

The result was a picture of isolated evangelical groups, spying with jealousy and hostility at each other through the wall-holes of denominational exclusiveness. Naturally, in this sort of climate, clashes were frequent. God only knows how many tons of paper in the church periodicals were miserably wasted, to the joy of hostile outsiders, in bitter attacks on other denominations.

NEW GENERATION
COOPERATIVE

Fortunately, a new generation of missionaries is in the field now. They have become convinced that the policy of their predecessors was wrong at that point. They belong now with the more devoted advocates of cooperation. It is as if they wished to atone for the sins of the past. All the future of missionary work and of individual missionaries in Mexico lies in their will and effectiveness for cooperation. There is no place nor hope for a missionary who would revert to oldtime policies of disruption and non-cooperation. Missionary participation in the International Congress indicates that times have changed and that the missions are one with the national churches in the promotion of Christian brotherhood.[28]

Fourteen major Protestant denominations agreed, by V-J Day, that they would join in a united Christian program when they resumed missionary work in Japan. These various denominations plan to pool personnel, resources, and administration in a thoroughgoing effort to rise above sectarian differences. This integration of missionary enterprises was undertaken by the fourteen churches as members of the Committee on Cooperation in Japan of the Foreign Missions Conference. Eight other denominational boards are associating themselves with the Committee on Cooperation in a consultative relationship. For the first time in history, Protestant missionary work in Japan will be conducted on a unified basis.

World War II has exerted an influence toward fusion. Men in the service came into intimate contact with chaplains of various faiths and were privileged to witness these men of the cloth ministering to the needs of our fighting men regardless of differences in religious connections. When men are sharing the dangers and hardships of the battlefield, creedal distinctions seem inconsequential. Some of these returning veterans are going to be deeply interested in breaking down denominational barriers in favor of a cooperative merging of religious interests.

[28] Correspondence from G. B. Camargo in the *Christian Century*, August 6, 1941.

4. THE SOCIAL GOSPEL

From time to time ministers shift their emphases from theological dogma to the implications of Christianity for the social order. Leaders in the social-gospel movement have sought to determine what should be done to carry out God's will in human society. Sheldon wrote *In His Steps,* first published in 1898, to answer the question, "What would Jesus do if he were living here today?" The influence of this book can be estimated roughly by the fact that it has sold more copies than any other book except the Bible.

There has been a revival of interest in the social applications of Christianity since the advent of the economic depression in 1929. The crisis brought religious persons to a realization that they were personally responsible, individually and collectively, for the failure to usher in the reign of justice and love implicit in the teachings of Jesus. Many thoughtful persons studied the tenets of socialism to ascertain whether a socialistic system would come nearer than a capitalistic system to embodying the principles advocated by the Master. Religious conferences examined our society with a critical eye, found it wanting in many respects, and passed resolutions in favor of radical alterations in our scheme of living. Under the slogan of *social action,* church members considered and lamented the irresponsibility prevailing in our "unchristian" economic system, the unequal distribution of wealth, unemployment, class privilege, poverty, social injustice, disregard of personal rights, the profit motive, child labor, low living standards, insecurity; and on the positive side they proclaimed themselves in favor of the service motive, social planning, social engineering, orderly change, political action, and education stressing the need for correcting the evils of our present industrial order.[29]

Some critics of Christianity have raised the objection that religious people are too much concerned with the next life and not enough with this one here on earth. No one could justly make such criticism with respect to a religion that becomes involved in the social issues facing modern society. The social gospel is practical Christianity. There are plenty of theories, to be sure, but they are not left to perish in the realm of abstraction. Advocates of social reform, following the example of the Master himself, go out and practice what they preach.

---

[29] For a summary of these indictments and proposals, see H. F. Ward and W. L. Chappell (Editors): *The Social Service Bulletin.* Published by the Methodist Federation for Social Service, 150 Fifth Avenue, New York, N.Y.

They join the picket lines; they preach against racial discrimination; they go to jail for their convictions. They suffer for a righteous cause as did the martyrs of old. These sponsors of the social gospel furnish the best answer to the Communist charge that religion is just an opiate to lull people into a lethargic acceptance of things as they are.[30]

B. The Decline in Influence

Disinterested observers agree that the influence of the church has been declining. There is nothing today to compare with "the astonishing movement [in the thirteenth century] by which the church remodeled all the ideas and institutions of the age, and integrated all social interests into a system of which it made itself the center, and controlling authority";[31] and there is nothing today to compare with the position of the church in colonial America when the New England clergy were preaching a political philosophy, based on the Bible, that espoused the natural rights of man, freedom of conscience in civil affairs, freedom of the press and of speech, and the sanctity of contracts.[32] During the nineteenth century the clergy were leaders in their communities; men like Henry Ward Beecher and Phillips Brooks were national figures. The churches were a dominant influence in establishing schools, colleges, and universities, in fostering prohibition, in abolishing slavery, in rationalizing capitalism, in stimulating and directing charitable enterprises. No one would dispute Latourette's assertion that "Christianity, and notably Protestant Christianity, was a major factor in shaping the ideals of the United States," [33] for it was the church, more than any other social institution, that functioned as the primary agency in guiding the mores. Social scientists, however, would be very skeptical of Latourette's judgment when he says in reference to the influence of the church in 1914, "in spite of some tendencies in the opposite direction, on the whole Christianity was a growing force in the nation's life." [34] They would be more apt to ratify and to feature an observation that Latourette relegates to a position of secondary importance:

[30] An analysis of some sermons published between 1929 and 1940 indicates an increase in social pessimism and a movement away from the "social gospel" in Protestant pulpits. See T. Hamilton: "Social Optimism and Pessimism in American Protestantism." *Public Opinion Quarterly,* 1942, 6, 280-283.

[31] W. G. Sumner: *Folkways,* p. 411. Ginn and Company, 1906.

[32] See A. M. Baldwin: *The New England Clergy and the American Revolution.* 1928.

[33] K. S. Latourette: *The Great Century,* p. 388. Harper & Brothers, 1941.

[34] *Ibid.,* p. 423.

Was that influence growing or declining? Was Christianity a waxing or a waning force? Exact measurements are impossible.

To some, especially in intellectual circles, on the eve of 1914 Christianity seemed to be losing its hold. The complexity and drive of industrialized life, particularly in the larger cities, was appearing to wean men's attention from the churches. The scientific approach and the knowledge accumulated by it were held by many to render Christianity obsolete.[35]

Evidence of the decline in the churches' prestige is to be found in *Recent Social Trends* (1933). Hornell Hart recorded the data and interpreted the signs of the times. While "traditional Christianity has been sinking to a new low point in public interest and esteem as expressed in magazines," deeper interest is manifested in what Hart terms "the rise of 'open-minded religion,'" in which the avowed goals are "fulfillment of personality, the attainment of rich experience, and the achievement of basic values here on earth." These conclusions are "based almost entirely upon statistical analyses of interests and opinions expressed in leading general magazines, supplemented by analyses of certain books and newspaper indexes." Most of the data were collected by William B. Mills, a Protestant, and Francis L. McGarraghy, a Roman Catholic.

The reliability of the results is indicated by the fact that the same general trends in discussion and opinion appear in a number of independent sources at the same time. The weakened grip of traditional Christianity upon educated opinion in the United States has been found reflected in general "intellectual" periodicals, in scholarly journals, in the number of religious books published, in declining relative circulations of religious journals, and in the attitudes reflected in mass circulation magazines. Evidence of the recent rebellion against authoritative monogamistic mores, has been found not only in magazine articles, but in short stories, moving pictures, and stage plays. . . .

Toleration of extramarital sex relations by the general public, as reflected in short stories, moving pictures and plays, has lately been several times as great as it was in 1900.

The women's periodicals gave far more attention and toleration to breaches of the sexual morality code in 1931-32 than the magazines of 1900-1905. More attention and more toleration were given by the mass circulation magazines of 1931-32. Much more attention and still more toleration or approval were given by the "intellectual" magazines of 1931-32. More interested still, but avowedly most opposed to extramarital relations, were the sensational periodicals.

[35] *Ibid.*, pp. 421-422.

Moving pictures were more apt than any class of magazines studied to resent divorce and sexual irregularities in an approving light.

The waning power of religious sanctions is closely related with the recent se of antagonism against monogamistic sex mores. . . .

Changes in sex attitudes have probably been connected to some extent ith technological developments, such as the introduction of the automobile nd the dissemination of birth-control devices; with the results of industrial evelopment such as the growth of cities; with the transfer of functions from ne home to the factory; and with the disintegration of patriarchal family onceptions. The evidence, however, suggests to the investigator that a major ictor in recent shifts of attitudes toward sex behavior has been the breakdown f traditional religious control and partially worked-out attempts to substitute :ientific criteria.

Among the other trends observed by Hart:

Antagonistic criticism of the Church, of ministers, and of traditional creeds eached a maximum in 1925-1928 in general magazines, and still exceeds the olume of favorable comment. The leading part in antagonistic criticism has een taken by the periodicals circulating among the more highly educated part f the population; periodicals read by the great masses of the people reflect a rowing lack of interest in, rather than aggressive criticism of religion. Favorble discussions of God, or religion in relation to science and of the spiritual ife, reached a new high peak in 1925-1928. Analysis of short stories suggests hat even this type of religion has definitely less grip on the public in 1932 than t had in 1900-1905.[36]

During the period 1930-1942, according to Hart, magazine discussion f religious topics decreased still further. The general public still elieved in a personal God and in life after death, but such beliefs ubsided rapidly among scientists.[37]

Some observers expected that the Depression of the 1930's would re- ive the sagging interest in the church, but this prediction proved to be allacious. "The long slow retreat of the churches into less and less ignificance in the life of the country, and even in the lives of the ma- ority of their members, continued almost unabated. . . . The shock f the Depression did not find the churches, by and large, able to give vhat people thought they needed," was the report of Frederick Lewis Allen in his volume of contemporary history, *Since Yesterday*.[38]

[36] H. Hart: Chap. 8, in *Recent Social Trends*. McGraw-Hill Book Company, 1933.
[37] See H. Hart: "Religion." *American Journal of Sociology*, 1942, 47, 888-897.
[38] Pp. 155, 157. Harper & Brothers, 1940.

The Lynds concurred in this observation as a result of their secon
visit to "Middletown" in 1935. They had paid their first visit in 192-
1925 when from a year and a half of attendance at religious servic
and from talking with individual citizens, they got the dominant in
pression of "unalert acceptance, punctuated periodically in the le-
socially sophisticated churches by bursts of religious energy during
revival." [39] Would this element of lethargy be less apparent in 193
as the churches endeavored to meet the spiritual needs of a people i
the throes of an economic depression? Several new church building
had been erected during the 1925-1935 interval, but there was no spiri
of vitality to correspond to the physical expansion. Any hope for
new interest in religion

evaporated as one began again to attend church services and to read the se:
mons reprinted in the Monday-morning newspaper. Here, scattered throug
the pews, is the same serious and numerically sparse Gideon's band—two-third
or more of them women, and few of them under thirty—with the same star
ring of empty pews "down front." The audiences seem older than former
and, especially in the business-class churches, persons between fifteen an
twenty-five years of age seem fewer, although this is only an impression.[40]

The same preponderance of gray-haired persons was noted in th
working-class churches. A rally of Sunday-school superintendents i
1932 considered what they were going to do about it when the religiou
awakening followed the hard times. The very raising of the questio
indicated "that there had been no marked upsurge up to that time." [4
The minister of one of the smaller and more primitive sects compose
entirely of working-class people testified: "There has been only a ver
small turning to religion during the depression." [42] A revival in 193
almost "died on the hands" of the sponsors and toward the end of th
four weeks it became very difficult to get attendance. One ministe
involved said: "I don't think these churches have much stomach fo
trying it again." [43] Speaking of the younger generation, a schoo
teacher close to the high-school students made this comment: "Chil
dren are growing farther and farther from religion." [44] The minister
in town seemed to be suffering from a "troubled morale." All o
these observations offer further confirmation for our statement that th
influence of the churches has been declining.

[39] R. S. Lynd and H. M. Lynd: *Middletown in Transition*, p. 259. Harcour
Brace and Company, 1937. See the full report of this first survey in their book
Middletown, Chapter 23, "Religious Observances." 1929.
[40] R. S. Lynd and H. M. Lynd: *Middletown in Transition*, p. 297.
[41] *Ibid.*, p. 301.   [42] *Ibid.*, p. 301.   [43] *Ibid.*, p. 302.   [44] *Ibid.*, p. 304.

The Church

863

Some people expected World War II to inspire a new interest in the church. This expectation was manifest in the observation, "There are no atheists in foxholes." Persons who saw the fighting men in action do not corroborate this assertion. Bishop Henry Knox Sherrill, then Episcopal Bishop of Massachusetts, was one authority who seriously questioned the existence of "fox-hole religion" and the likelihood of a big spiritual revival after the war. On the basis of numerous conferences, on various fronts, Bishop Sherrill asserts that the chaplains of all the churches were agreed that men and women who came into the service with religion and from religious homes had kept and in many cases deepened their faith; those who had little religion had not been changed as a result of the war. There were no great evidences of changed hearts and minds on the home front, either. Praying to God for help in an emergency is one thing, living a Christian life on a high moral plane and practicing religion regularly in private or public worship is quite another.

All of the Chaplains united in feeling that our young men and women in the service revealed, again in general, the lack of religious training in the home. The ignorance of American young manhood and womanhood in matters of religious faith is colossal. This is not their fault but is the reflection of failure in the home, the Church and the school. . . .

However, it should be added that in countless cases the war experience has deepened the faith of many. The best evidence of this is the very large number of men in the service who have signified their interest in studying for the ministry of their Church upon their discharge.

In other words, if we may expect no great spiritual revival there is at least no ground for greater discouragement than the Churches face in normal times. I do not see why we should expect war to generate spirituality. However necessary we may feel it to be as a second choice, it is a denial of the very principles upon which religion is based.[45]

Social scientists seem to agree that the church is losing ground. This trend has been documented with considerable evidence. We shall note further aspects of this decline. While we are doing so, we shall pause occasionally to analyze the psychological reasons for the diminution of interest in the church. Our discussion will be predicated on the assumption that religion would naturally appeal to people, being concerned as it is with man's vital interests, if it were the kind of religion that answered present human needs. Perhaps Christianity—which is the religion we are considering—will have to be mod-

[45] Boston *Sunday Herald*, August 12, 1945.

ified, revised, brought up to date if it is to experience an upswing
Such revision seems to be needed if the church is to hold the younge
generation who are not so enthusiastic about the church as their par
ents are, for the children are moving away from parental attitudes i
this regard. This is shown in one set of replies to the *Thurstone
Chave Scale of Attitude toward the Church* in which it appeared tha
"between the ages of 17 and 30 there is a steady decrease in favorabl
attitude toward the Church." [46]

1. CHURCH ATTENDANCE

Only about one-half the inhabitants of the United States—52 pe
cent—belong to any church or actively practice any religion.[47] I
is true that church membership has been steadily increasing in recen
years, 25.5 per cent in the United States between 1926 and 1942, whil
estimated population increased 14.3 per cent during that period.[48]
Statistics of this nature, however, do not tell the whole story. Ther
is no uniform criterion, for example, by which to determine wha
persons should be counted as church members. Still more serious i
the difficulty concerning inactive members. How inactive must the
become to be counted out? The indifference of church members, a
manifested in their non-attendance, is so widespread that a Nationa
Christian Mission toured the country in 1940 to "reach the unreached"
and to inspire them to return to "active duty." A more accurat
estimate of the strength of religious interest in the United States coul
be obtained if church members could be "weighed as well as counted,"
that is, if their loyalty could be evaluated in terms of financial suppor
and personal participation.

2. PRESTIGE OF THE CLERGY

The local minister used to be the only educated man in town. Th
universities, many of them, were founded to train men for the Chris
tian ministry and the majority of the graduating class, in the old days
headed for the ministry. Today the situation is different. Colleg
students preparing to become clergymen are, today, a small minority
Consequently, the present-day parson finds himself in a communit

[46] See G. Murphy, L. B. Murphy, and T. M. Newcomb: *Experimental Social Psy
chology*, pp. 921-922. Harper and Brothers, 1937.
[47] *Yearbook of American Churches.* 1945.
[48] *Information Service*, January 1, 1944. Department of Research and Educatior
Federal Council of the Churches of Christ in America.

where there are many persons as well or better educated than he is, and he is no longer looked up to as the authority on all matters. Free tuition at theological seminaries sometimes attracts students who are looking for the easy path to some kind of livelihood, often men of inferior economic and social background. The clergyman who is lacking the social graces and handicapped, besides, by a low income, cannot hope to compete with other professions in the matter of prestige, for in our culture prosperity is widely considered as a mark of intelligence and worth. The minister, therefore, like the teacher, often suffers in the race for social prestige.

Poteat notes the vanishing influence of the clergyman under the impact of the rising spirit of secularism which characterizes our modern age. As evidence for the waning prestige of the minister, he cites a personal experience. He was appearing at a public hearing before a judiciary committee to oppose a bill which carried grave implications for the state. Poteat spoke "with great earnestness and small effect." He was then called aside by a prominent newspaper editor who whispered to him, "The trouble with your opposition is that this crowd is tired of having the preachers tell them what they shall do. They won't pay any attention to you, no matter what you say." The remark was made in all friendliness. Poteat, thinking it over later, made the following comment upon the declining status of the clergy:

This was a dramatic illustration of the puzzling condition to which I have alluded—namely, the loss of conspicuous and effective leadership which the modern minister has suffered in the so-called secular world. It was not ever thus.

For centuries the Christian minister spoke the authentic and clarifying word in nearly every area of dispute and confusion. From the beginning of the Christian era, his ascent led him to a pinnacle in 326, when Constantine subjected Rome to a corporate induction into the religion he preached. Beginning with the Reformation and the age of scientific rationalism, his place began to yield to new and combative ideas and forms of thinking, and his dominance in affairs was gradually withdrawn. So definite has been his decline in influence that today we observe in the fields of thought and morals —where the ministers' interests are largely focused—changes which he seems impotent to withstand and to which he does not find it altogether easy to adjust himself. He seems to be spinning about in eddies off the main current of modern life—or already cast up on barren sand bars, to dry out in the sun. Our intellectual leaders are not churchmen. Those who dominate thought are not of the cloister. We are under the influence of secularists in science, philosophy, politics, and education. The preacher is faced with at least the possibility of being progressively eliminated until his touch will become light as air on our social complex.[49]

In seeking to find the reasons for the loss of prestige suffered by the clergy, Poteat arrived at the conclusion that the minister has not kept up-to-date mentally with the changes in ideas, emotions, and moral standards which have generally been accepted as an integral part of our secular culture. Two changes in ideas are particularly significant: the Copernican discovery that the earth is not the center of the universe and Darwin's discovery that man has evolved from the lower animals. The Rev. John Doe does not take kindly to either of these ideas, so revolutionary are their effects upon man's concept of his own importance and upon his convictions concerning his special relationship to the Deity. Similarly, the Reverend Doe has failed to comprehend the meaning of new developments in man's emotional orientation to life and changes in his moral standards, and the Reverend Doe has likewise failed to approach these altered conditions constructively. In an endeavor to ascertain how "The World Looks at Dr. Doe," Poteat circulated a questionnaire. Respondents remarked that the minister's "religion is out-of-date, mostly," that he is preserving institutions which are "venerable but vulnerable," that the "divisions and machinery" of religious institutions strike "the lay mind as outmoded, inefficient, wasteful, and unnecessary."[50]

Some promising young people are hesitant to elect the ministry as a career because they have observed that so much is expected of a man in such a position, in fact, more than any human being can live up to. Critics wait for a false step as an excuse for deriding the errant clergyman and the clergy in general. The pastor's conduct is supposed to be exemplary at all times. Living under the spotlight of public inspection is a strain for any man who is human—and for his wife, too, for she is at the mercy of other women who are capable of making her life miserable if they feel so inclined.[51] The minister may find his social relations handicapped by the fact that laymen feel constrained in the presence of a clergyman. This social obstacle may be an important factor in deterring a young man from entering the

[49] E. McN. Poteat: *Reverend John Doe, D.D.*, pp. 29, 30-31. Harper & Brothers 1935. Poteat is a Baptist minister, formerly President of Colgate-Rochester Theological Seminary.

[50] *Ibid.*, Chapter 2, "The World Looks at Dr. Doe."

[51] See H. Spence: *One Foot in Heaven*. 1940.

ministry, especially if he is the sort of person who enjoys social life and likes to feel free to be himself.[52]

3. SOCIAL CENTER

The church is no longer the principal social center in the community. Up to the end of the last century people in the small towns used to concentrate practically all of their social life in the various activities of the church. There were the all-day-sewing-meetings, the sociables or socials, the bazaars, the suppers, the annual picnic, the receptions, and even the midweek prayer meeting was an occasion for fellowship. The women were particularly loyal in supporting all these activities. The church was a natural place to get together with friends for a social evening. There were few competitors in the field.

How different the modern situation! The automobile, the radio, the motion-picture theater, golfing, or dancing at the country club, ski trains or camera trains for week-end outings—with all these the church finds it very difficult to compete. So many diversions attract the young people that the pastor is seriously handicapped when he attempts to win support for the church through a social program—the chief inducement for getting the younger set into the habit of churchgoing. Social committees are hard put to it to think up ways of providing entertainment, limited as they are to stunts, charades, and "Guess Who," frolics that seem pretty tame to young folks who have become accustomed to jitterbugging to the blatant music of a juke box or staying out late at a country-club dance. Habituated to excitement, the young folks are apt to find the Christian Endeavor Get-Acquainted Meeting or the Epworth League Valentine Social rather dull going.

Many churches have met the competition by offering movies and dancing in the parish house, with the hope that young persons might be enticed by these attractions into exposing themselves to religious influences. "Piety," wrote Mencken, "was cunningly disguised as basketball, billiards, and squash; the 'sinner' was lured to grace with Turkish baths, lectures on foreign travel, and free instruction in stenography, rhetoric, and double-entry bookkeeping." [53] One parson resigned from the ministry with this message of despair: "Church suppers, ballyhoo, bowling alleys, sugar-coating the pill of salvation, and uproarious evenings in the church basement—I'm tired of them

---

[52] The author is a son of a Baptist clergyman.
[53] H. L. Mencken: *A Book of Prefaces.* Alfred A. Knopf, Inc., 1918.

all." He went on to say that gathering a flock and keeping it to
gether is a much more difficult job than it might seem to the layman
and it was becoming too much for his weary soul. He was giving up
the struggle—and we should not be too hard on him, for the modern
minister must be extremely resourceful if he is going to compete suc
cessfully with all the counterattractions that divert interest away from
religion. The social program, nevertheless, represents one of the im
portant functions of the church. It is up to the church to provid
wholesome entertainment for young and old, to offer opportunitie
for marriageable "lonely hearts" to meet each other, and to foster
spirit of neighborliness and fellowship that will promote kindlie
relations throughout the community at large.[54]

4. FOREIGN MISSIONS

Christianity has been an evangelistic religion ever since Jesus and
his disciples first spread the gospel. The vitality of the Christian church
has been founded on this urge to win new followers for the Kingdom
The Foreign Missionary Movement was one phase of this campaign
to add more persons to the list of those who were publicly committed
to taking Christ as their Saviour. Evangelists at home and abroad
carried the message that Christ had died upon the Cross to redeen
us from our sins, that converts could be saved by confessing their faith
in the Lord and pledging their loyalty to the church, that it was well
to be enlisted among the hosts of the Redeemer on the Judgment Day
This belief in the urgency of knowing about Jesus had tremendous
driving power in it. Christians set out for foreign lands inspired
with a zeal for telling the heathen the gospel and gathering in "de
cisions" for Christ. The enthusiasm over foreign missions was ex
pressed in the slogan of the Student Volunteer Movement for Foreign
Missions: "The evangelization of the world in this generation."[55]
This sanguine outlook for the immediate universalization of Chris
tianity was inspired by an unparalleled missionary zeal. The ide
that "all should go and go to all" seemed very convincing to people
who were being stirred a generation ago to heed the challenge, "G
ye into all the world and preach the Gospel to every creature." Lead
ers who were recruiting missionaries even went so far in their plea
as to assert that "because of the greater need in other lands and th

[54] The reference to "lonely hearts" is not intended to be facetious. It is very dif
ficult for people in large cities to meet others and to make friends. The cit
churches are rendering a great service by welcoming strangers and helping then
to establish personal contacts.
[55] See J. R. Mott: *The Evangelization of the World in This Generation.* 1900

maller number of Christians there to tell of the Christian Gospel, very true Christian should ask himself not why he should go . . . ut why he should not go." [56]

Missionary activity has been affected by the increasing enlightenment hat makes many older beliefs untenable. The newer generation is ot so sure the heathen need to be saved. Some of the older generation ave been wondering, too, whether the dynamics behind the old-fashoned drive for evangelizing the pagans was not founded on fallacious ssumptions. Pearl Buck, a Presbyterian missionary to China, who on the Nobel Prize for her novel *The Good Earth,* was brought efore the Presbyterian Board of Foreign Missions for questioning oncerning certain heresies that seemed to call for her removal from he field. An article she had written in *Harper's Magazine,* January, 933, renounced the theory of pagan damnation. She referred to the octrine that the heathen races are damned unless they hear the ;ospel, as a belief belonging to a magic religion, and she added: "I gree with the Chinese, who feel that their people should be protected rom such superstition." Mrs. Buck was also brought to task by the 'resbytery for stating that she did not consider a belief in the Deity f Christ essential, that she did not believe in the miracles described n the New Testament, and that she did not believe in original sin. 'earl Buck's services were terminated because it was felt that she had ost the faith that gave the spark to the whole missionary enterprise.

Re-Thinking Missions, the report of the Laymen's Commission vhich Hocking headed, expressed the view, now widely held, that nissionaries should concentrate less on dogma and more on medicine, .griculture, and education; that they should cooperate with the forigner to promote social justice, racial equity, and world friendship. `he study of comparative religions is sure to awaken in the thoughtful erson an appreciation of the contributions made by other religions esides Christianity. It is an obligation incumbent on the intelligent nissionary to learn sympathetically the lessons that the "heathen Chiee" and others can impart to him. The missionary conference in Jerualem in 1928 had given voice to this modern approach: the chief bjective is not giving, but sharing spiritual values. This shift in emhasis marks a desertion, practically speaking, of the old goal of evangelizing the world for Christ. It is a program of tolerance far removed rom the bigoted assumption that only one religion is right, all others vrong.

[56] Latourette: *op. cit.,* p. 97. This plea was embodied in Robert E. Speer's pamhlet, reprinted again and again, "What Constitutes a Missionary Call."

When *Re-Thinking Missions* was published in 1932, it fell like
bombshell among many circles already disheartened over the drop i
evangelistic interest. Presbyterians rallied in Philadelphia to d
nounce the report. Robert E. Speer cheered the gathering by voicin
their belief in Jesus Christ as *the* Saviour of the world. They agree
that Christ is not *a* Saviour but *the* Saviour, that Christianity is not on
of many religions, possibly only a little better than the rest, but
supernatural religion with a unique Saviour and a unique atonemen
The discussion at this meeting resulted in a conviction, shared by man
persons devoted to the missionary cause, that *Re-Thinking Missior*
"instead of being a platform on which Christians might rally to a con
mon standard, might prove to be the most divisive statement in this ge
eration." [57]   These loyal souls were right in fearing that evangelisti
passion could never be kept at white heat by the broadminded view th;
other religions might do almost as well as Christianity. It is this ve
attitude of objective neutrality, the readiness to see the good in th
other man's faith and the willingness to forsake any monopoly o
religious insight, that has taken some of the zeal out of the missionar
enterprise.

Another setback to missions has come from the growth of nationa
ism, especially in China. Foreign peoples like the Chinese have bee
stimulated by their rising patriotism to look upon missionaries as th
forerunners of Western capitalism, parties to imperialistic design
underminers of national loyalties. Many of the Chinese believe th;
Christian missionaries are responsible for dividing the people of Chin
at a time when they need to be united. The natives in China hav
learned to resent the large amount of property accumulated by Amer
can mission boards in their country. Chinese patriots object to ha
ing foreigners teach their children in the schools, and there is now
regulation that every foreign school must have a Chinese principa
They do not want their young people thinking in foreign terms, a
sorbing outside propaganda. Nationalistic feeling has helped to brir
about "devolution," a process by which the American missionary trai
a native Chinese to help him, later to replace him. "At first th
missionary was the leader, the native an assistant, but of late th
tendency has been toward equalization of responsibility, and in som
places, notably Japan, to make native leadership dominant." [58]   Ame
ican missionaries were withdrawn from Japan with the advent of w;

[57] *Christian Century* correspondence from Philadelphia.
[58] C. L. Fry, "Changes in Religious Organization," Chapter 20 in *Recent Soci*
Trends. McGraw-Hill Book Company, 1933.

n 1941. Christian missionaries from America were *persona non grata*
n Japan even before the war. Nationalism, whatever the country,
s not friendly toward the cosmopolitanism of Christianity. The
rotherhood of all mankind is not a watchword among super-national-
sts.

There is a possibility that Christianity will find a heartier welcome
n China as a consequence of American-Chinese cooperation in World
Var II. *Time,* in 1941, predicted:

CHRISTIANITY IN CHINA

Christianity is staging a comeback in China this year—a comeback almost
nbelievable to those who remember its plight there in 1927. The change
s due entirely to the war with Japan and the part missionaries have played in
he struggle. . . .

In 1927 the Chinese revolutionaries hounded churchmen from one end of
he Yangtze to the other as "running dogs of imperialism"—and the imperial-
sm they hated was largely Anglo-American. Today England and America,
10 longer hated, are two Christian friends on whose support Christian Chiang
Kai-shek is counting to free China from the non-Christian Japanese invad-
rs. . . . In Chungking, the Christian leader of China rules with his
Christian wife, aided by a Christian Finance Minister and a host of other
Christian officials. . . .

Government money subsidizes Christian colleges, Christian hospitals, Chris-
ian service councils. Government appropriations are made for Christian
vangelists who go to the tribal districts of China's far western frontier. Mis-
ion universities are now backed in every possible way so that they may train
rains for the new China. Their 1940-41 enrollment is a record 7,734, up 20
er cent from peacetime 1937. Once forbidden by law to require religious
tudy, they can now make the weekly compulsory Sun Yat-sen memorial meet-
ngs a forum for religious education.

In 1940 the National Christian Council alone treated almost 300,000
rounded Chinese soldiers. The Y.M.C.A. has put 120 stations into operation
1 war zones. Here soldiers find people who will write their letters for them,
aagazines and newspapers to read, hot baths, tea, occasionally one of the Y's
nree mobile sound-movie units. Impressed by such omnipresent faithfulness,
ven China's Communists have become friendly towards Christianity. . . .

For a century, the U.S. has supplied two-thirds of the Protestant mission-
ries, and it now provides over half the overseas financial support for Catholic
nd Protestant missions alike. These Americans have been the spearhead of
hinese social change. They were the first to penetrate the interior, taking
Vestern ideas, clothes, techniques, medicines, preparing desires and attitudes
nat opened the way for Western commerce. In every Chinese change of the
ast generation—with the exception of the 1926-27 revolution—the share of

the missionaries has been large. They led the movements for famine relief and Western agricultural methods, led in the attacks on opium, foot-binding daughter slaughter, concubinage.

In China, Christian institutional and educational work looms as large as evangelism. The 271 Protestant hospitals and the 267 Catholic hospitals and asylums have in the past generation worked themselves into the consciousness of Chinese of every class. The humblest rickshaw coolie knows where to go to have his mucus-draining eyes treated, or who will help when his wife has childbed fever. The 13 Protestant colleges, 255 Protestant middle schools six Protestant medical schools and three Catholic colleges today are some of the chief sources of Government leadership. The best engineers, doctors, and scientists come from mission universities. . . .

Converting one per cent of the Chinese in 100 years is not in itself a cheering statistic for the missionaries, but the time may be riper than they realize for a far broader acceptance of their faith. . . .[59]

The heroism of the Christian missionaries in the Orient during World War II may do much to restore interest in the missionary enterprise. Joy Homer was skeptical about the missionaries when she first visited war-torn China, but she changed her mind after she had lived with them and seen how their work endured. The story of her adventures, *Dawn Watch in China* (1941), constituted a tribute to these brave Americans. In 1942 President Roosevelt cited Dr. Crydon M. Wassell, a missionary "well known for his good works in China," for his valiant achievement in evacuating twelve wounded men from Java to Australia, a feat of loyalty and courage which merited the award of the Navy Cross. Public recognition of such sacrificial devotion on the part of individual missionaries may create new support for the missionary effort. Whatever the future may hold, we may feel sure that the philosophy behind foreign missions will have to be enlightened if the movement is to enjoy any sustained success.

5. SABBATH OBSERVANCE

The declining influence of the church may be attributed in part to the secularization of Sunday—which means that people don't go to church because they are going other places, to the golf course, to the flower gardens in the yard, to the ski trails, to the movies, almost anywhere except to church. The automobile must accept some of the responsibility for taking people in ungodly directions. The Sabbath Day was supposed to be kept holy; now it has become, for many, a day of recreation. Sunday is just one day in a gay week end. Churches

[59] *Time,* April 28, 1941.

nd ministers are naturally upset.   Now and then they issue a protest
ke the one reported in this news item:

LORD'S DAY LEAGUE HEARS WARNING
OF SUNDAY GAMES, LIQUOR, BETTING

Commercial sports, amusements, liquor traffic and gambling are seeking to
apture the Christian Sabbath, guaranteed as a national day of rest by the
Inited States Constitution, declared the Rev. Dr. Harry L. Bowlby of New
ork in an address last night at the annual meeting of the Lord's Day League
f New England in the Cathedral Church of St. Paul.

"Every attack on the Sabbath is an assault on the sanctuary, and every in-
asion of Sunday is an infringement of some people's rights," he said.   He
sked for the combined influence of good citizenship and church membership
ɔ halt commercialization of the Lord's Day.

He particularly deplored the tendency of business enterprises which, be-
ause of sharp competition, were turning to Sunday operation.   "Especially
ɔ this true," he said, "of the great railroads of the country, bidding for the
unday excursionist with their attractive and discriminatory low fare induce-
nents." [60]

[he Lord's Day League will find it increasingly difficult to stem the
ide.   People have ideas about spending Sunday that do not fit into
he program the parson would design if he were planning their week
nds for them.   Many persons still observe the Sabbath, but not in
. pew.

Some critics of the church, notable by their absence on Sunday
nornings, are unaware of the numerous changes which this religious
nstitution has undergone during the last generation.   A visit to a
:hurch service may provide a surprising experience for such an absen-
ee.   Roger Riis, "happening into a church" for the first time in
wenty-two years, testified that he found "the churches today are dis-
ɔensing something I need, and that church and religion go together."
[he service was simple, reverent.   The sermon was on the perma-
ɪence and beauty of the church.   "It fell on my spirit like water on
ι desert, and I went out stirred and grateful," he tells us.   Curiosity
ɔrompted him to attend another church, on one of his journeys, and
ιgain he discovered the service was "helpful."   There are run-down
:hurches featuring a stupid form of salvation, but "you don't have to
ʲo to those churches."   Riis convinced himself by going to church that
ʲou can find something uplifting and satisfying if you go with a "sym-
ɔathetic, hopeful attitude," like the attitude you take with you to the

[60] The Boston *Herald,* January 25, 1939.

movies—"that's the least you should bring to church." Most sermon
are surprisingly good. "The most successful churches are those whos
clergymen set forth uncompromising Christianity." Explore a littl
and you will surely find in every community some church that wi
give you what you want. In evaluating the church, take note of th
fact that "the nations where the churches flourish are the democra
cies." Riis is for the church because it is one institution that en
courages a high opinion of man, one institution that transcends race
nation, and class, one institution that is loyally undertaking to re
lieve human suffering and to carry on a ministry of reconciliatio
among men.[61] Riis found something helpful in the church. Peopl
who go to find fault or who stay at home and criticize what they didn
go to hear, cannot expect to share Mr. Riis' enthusiasm for the churcl

Link discovered in his counseling experience that he was relyin
heavily on religious principles in recommending measures which h
clients should adopt in order to regain their mental and physica
health. His observations convinced him that self-discipline, interes
in others, participation in group activities, Sunday-school attendanc
active support of the church, are all important factors in building an
maintaining a healthy personality. It dawned on the counselor tha
he should take some of his own advice and go to church himself—
and he did. He tells us in his *Return to Religion* how it all hap
pened:

My reason for attending church again is that I have recommended it to s
many others. I go because I would rather lie in bed late on Sunday morning
the only chance for a good sleep I have during the week. I go because
would rather read the Sunday papers. I go because I know it will please m
old father, when he learns of it, and my parents-in-law whom I shall un
doubtedly see there. I go because I shall meet and have to shake hands wit
people, many of whom do not interest me in the least; because, if I don't g
my children consider that they have a good reason for not going to Sunda
School; because I might be asked to do something I don't want to do; becaus
I may disagree with what the minister has to say. I go because some of m
best friends, who know the details of my life, consider me a hypocrite. I g
because I do not believe all the doctrines of this church, or any other church
I go, in short, because I hate to go and because I know that it will do m
good.[62]

[61] See R. W. Riis: "Why I Go to Church." *The American Mercury*, January, 194
Condensed under the title, "Now I Am for the Churches," in the *Reader's Diges*
January, 1941.
[62] From H. C. Link: *The Return to Religion*, p. 19. 1936. By permission of Th
Macmillan Company.

6. FAILURE IN LEADERSHIP

The editors of *Fortune* attribute the declining prestige of the church to the failure of this institution to provide people with the religious leadership they expect and demand. When people, in their confusion, turn to the clergy for guidance, they want to hear a voice of authority telling them which way to go; instead, says the editorial, they get an echo for an answer. The indictment by the editors, charges:

The Christian leadership has passed from the hands of the church to the hands of the active and practical laity—the statesmen and educators, the columnists and pundits, the scientists and great men of action. And this is another way of saying that there is no true Christian leadership at all. Hence the future of Christianity, and of its derivative political and social doctrines, has become imperiled. . . .

As laymen dedicated to the practice of Christianity we can merely record our certainty that in order for humanity to progress it must *believe;* it must have faith in certain absolute spiritual values, or at least have faith that absolute spiritual values exist. The church, as teacher and interpreter of those values, is the guardian of our faith in them. And as laymen we do not feel that that faith is being guarded. . . . [63]

For decades prior to the Civil War the churches in the North and in the South did not insist that all men, black or white, are free, as they should have insisted in keeping with the Christian view of man; instead, they rationalized slavery. In 1917 and again in 1941 the churches reversed their position regarding war, opposing war in peacetime and promoting it in wartime. "It used to be said among the troops, with a kind of clairvoyant bitterness, that if the Y.M.C.A. didn't win the war, then the preachers back home surely would." The editorial continues:

Their [the preachers'] position today [January, 1940] is almost exactly what it was in 1914 [versus war], and their arguments are almost the same. How much will it take to get them over on the other side of the fence? The answer would seem to be clear: the pastors will go over to the other side when, as, and if the people go over to the other side. . . . Thus the flock is leading the shepherd. . . . The voice of the church today, we find, is the echo of our own voices. And the result of this experience, already manifest, is disillusionment. . . . This is a profound and absolute spiritual disillusion-

[63] The Editors: "War and Peace." *Fortune,* January, 1940.

ment, arising from the fact that when we consult the church we hear onl
what we ourselves have said.[64]

Fortune's editors express the layman's disappointment in the churc
Apart from the rightness or wrongness of the church's shifts durin
crises, people look for leadership, and feel cheated when they find th
clergy are mere reflectors of public opinion.

. The churches have a habit of being pacifist in times of peace, mil
tant in times of war. "Organized religion seems to have a way o
getting on the band wagon and going along with the parade."
Rational thought is inhibited when religious and patriotic emotior
combine. Symbols of nationalism and symbols of Christianity wor
together handily because they are so similar in many respects. Thei
parallelism becomes immediately apparent when they are arrange
side by side:

The flag	The Cross
The Constitution and the Declaration of Independence	The Bible
Tradition of the Founding Fathers	Sacred tradition and theolog
Patriotic slogans	Holy words and phrases
Patriotic songs	Hymns
Uniforms	Gowns, surplices, etc.
Patriotic parades	Religious processions
Hero worship	Worship of saints
The sword	The sword of the Spirit

Preachers Present Arms (1933), by Abrams, is an excellent study o
the way ministers gave their blessing to World War I. Some quota
tions:

Joseph Fort Newton: "Think it all through, and at bottom, the war is r
ligious." [66]
James A. Francis: "I look upon the enlistment of an American soldier as
do on the departure of a missionary for Burma." [67]
George Parken Atwater, speaking of the Church militant: "The arm
today is the Church in action . . . its choir is the crash of cannon and th
thrilling ripple of machine guns." [68]

[64] *Ibid.*
[65] "Soldiers of the Lord." *Propaganda Analysis,* April 1, 1940. See also, "R
ligious Propaganda against the War." *Propaganda Analysis,* January 25, 1941.
[66] R. H. Abrams: *Preachers Present Arms,* p. 57. 1933.
[67] *Ibid.,* p. 57.   [68] *Ibid.,* p. 123.

Daniel A. Poling spoke of the "moment when the American army was baptized by fire into the sacrificial comradeship of democracy's international Calvary." [69]

Thoughts on the holiness of war as fought by our side were epitomized by the little girl *évacuée* from London who, saying her prayers for her hostess at a country house, repeated the familiar "Now I lay me down to sleep" and then improvised her own postscript: "And God, please protect Daddy and Mummy from those German bombs. And, do, dear God, take good care of yourself—because if anything happens to you, we're sunk." [70]

It is one function of the church as a social institution to transform the world according to the pattern of Christian ideals. Too often it has failed in this task by capitulating to the existing order. The church, flattered by its prestige as the bulwark of things-as-they-are, has in many instances sacrificed its opportunities for leadership in order to become polite, genteel, and respectable. That is what the editors of *Fortune* meant when they wrote that the church had failed as a source of guidance and authority.

IV. ORGANIZED RELIGION AS A SOCIAL FORCE

The communists, as we have pointed out before, have charged that religion is an opiate, used by the capitalist class to quiet discontent among the working people. Religion, according to Lenin, is the worst implement of class exploitation. Evidence can easily be found to support this indictment that Christianity is sometimes misused for exploitative purposes.

People who denounce communism as the sworn enemy of Christianity might spend their time to better advantage in studying the criticisms leveled against the Christian church to find out whether there is any truth in the charges. The most effective way to defend Christianity would be to evaluate religion by weighing its effects upon human behavior and then to modify the practice of religion where it fails to fit human needs. What does religion do to people? Does it promote human happiness or does it impede its attainment? What kind of religion is desirable? These are important questions that deserve thoughtful answers. Religion can be very stupid at times, as Mrs. Hepburn observed when she clashed in debate with Father Coughlin at a congressional birth-control hearing. "Human beings have always done so many stupid things under the most righteous

[69] *Ibid.*, p. 175.   [70] The *Reader's Digest,* December, 1940.

terms that it is very difficult for us really to use our intelligence about anything." [71]   Let us examine institutionalized religion impartially Perhaps we can uncover defects that need remedying—and then do something about them.

It is true that religion functions as a conservative force, tending to perpetuate the *status quo* with its injustices and its deficiences.   But that is not the whole story of religion as a social institution, for it is equally true that the church has been the advocate and the sponsor of radical social reforms.   We cannot get a fair picture of the church's influence in society unless we include both its conservatism and its radicalism.

A. Conservatism

Social change is often retarded by the obstructionist influences of the church.

Conservatism is not peculiar to the church, however, for most institutions tend toward the preservation of things-as-they-are.   As soon as people get organized into a successful, recognized institution, they devote themselves largely to preventing change, unless, of course, it be in some group brought together for the specific purpose of revolution (Even revolutionists become conservatives after they are successful in attaining their objective.)   Interest in maintaining the *status quo* is characteristic of such organizations as the American Bar Association the American Medical Association, the American Legion, the Daughters of the American Revolution, and the local Chambers of Commerce.   Members of these organizations may favor new ways of doing little things but they are not disposed to countenance any proposal for radical alterations in the fundamental bases of the present social order.   Now the church is like these other institutions in its conservatism—but even more conservative, because the church deals with what is sacred.   In bestowing its blessing upon any particular custom, the church can lift the practice above criticism, whether the custom be mother love or respect for other people's property.   Religious sentiment often inhibits critical thinking and thus discourages the idea of changing existent conditions.[72]

The reactionary tendency of the church may be illustrated in the field of ethics.   For centuries Christians have taken the Ten Commandments as the authoritative word in moral principles.   Muzzey

[71] The Boston *Herald,* January 19, 1933.

[72] Institutional opposition to change was discussed at length in Chapter 13, or "Custom."

the eminent historian, questioned whether it was intelligent to follow Moses uncritically and suggested that we should test the Ten Commandments in the light of our own judgment. Should we be good because we are told we must, or should we be good because human experience shows it to be desirable? Muzzey proposed that we should stress the beauty of a good life, that we should replace the old method of saying, "thou shalt not," with the new pedagogy of showing what it is desirable to do. The editor of the *Reformed Church Messenger* was provoked to refute Muzzey, stating that it is fatuous to believe the aesthetic appeal is universal or has in it the mighty power of "the categorical imperative." Recalling that Kant had said he was filled with ever-increasing wonder and delight not only by the starry heavens above him but by the moral law within, the *Messenger* maintained:

> If it be true, as Dr. Muzzey admits, and as we believe, that the precepts of the Ten Commandments have not been invalidated, and that truth is truth, whether some of the younger (or older) generation believe it or not, what right have we to abandon the proclamation of God's will, revealed at Sinai, or to emasculate the Commandments of the Most High into mere recommendations or polite requests, which folks may "take or leave"?
>
> No, if we are not weary of well-doing, we must reiterate and reemphasize the ancient formula, "Thus saith the Lord," no matter how many moderns may sneer at it. Surrender to the will of God remains the essence of all true wisdom.[73]

Psychological studies attest to the conservatism of church members. Harris, Remmers, and Ellison found church members relatively reactionary as compared with non-church members.[74] Among college students Christians are more conservative than Jews, and reactionaries are inclined to be very pious, according to Vetter.[75] Religious affiliation correlates highly with conservatism, especially so in the case of Catholics—this was the finding of Carlson, in a study of college students.[76] An investigation by Zimmerman revealed that 29 per cent more religious than non-religious students favored prohibition, according to the questionnaire used; twice as many non-religious as

---

[73] *Literary Digest*, February 20, 1932.

[74] See A. J. Harris, H. H. Remmers, and C. E. Ellison: "The Relation between Liberal and Conservative Attitudes in College Students, and Other Factors." *Journal of Social Psychology*, 1932, 3, 320-335.

[75] See G. B. Vetter: "The Measurement of Social and Political Attitudes and the Related Personality Factors." *Journal of Abnormal and Social Psychology*, 1930, 25, 149-189.

[76] See H. B. Carlson: "Attitudes of Undergraduate Students." *Journal of Social Psychology*, 1934, 5, 202-212.

religious students believed that the existing moral code is too rigid; 23 per cent more non-religious than religious students favored birth control; socialism was approved by more than twice as many non-religious students; and religious students were overwhelmingly in favor of making divorces harder to obtain.[77] Bird comments on the influence of religion by stating that "the primacy of religious training and its persistence throughout childhood and adolescence probably erect barriers against which contrary doctrines and scientifically established facts, as taught in college, make few inroads." [78]

The communists, we have said, charge that religion is an opiate, a drug for relieving discontent and for inducing inaction. Just how can religion function as an opiate? Particularly Christianity?

First of all, otherworldliness has been uppermost in the minds of many Christians. We refer to those persons who believe that this life is unimportant in itself—a period of testing character, a preparation for the eternal life hereafter. For persons who adopt this premise it makes no real difference whether we are happy or not in the here-and-now because suffering will be compensated in the life-beyond-death. Deny ourselves now and we will be all the happier in the future life. The communists do not accept this idea of ignoring the present situation and they sing their rejection, "I don't want my pie in the sky, bye and bye, I want it now." Critics of the Christian view would endorse the sentiment of Sir Arthur Keith, who said, "For if men believe, as I do, that this present earth is the only heaven, they will strive all the more to make a heaven of it."

Otherworldliness has been a very effective weapon of exploitation. People have been induced to tolerate their misfortunes by being persuaded that suffering helps to build character. Thus religion serves as an escape mechanism, providing an excuse for doing nothing to eradicate sources of trouble. A devout church member in Cleveland protested in a letter to the Cleveland *Press* that he was going to church to forget his troubles but that the minister wouldn't let him:

> I write as a respectable member of one of our foremost churches where have attended for many years.
> I think it is a disgrace and insult to our wonderful Christian edifices for some of their members, and some ministers, too, I am sorry to say, to carry the economic ills into their church. When I go to church I want to forget the physical and all earthly things.

[77] See F. K. Zimmerman: "Religion a Conservative Social Force." *Journal of Abnormal and Social Psychology*, 1934, 28, 473-474.

[78] C. Bird: *Social Psychology*, pp. 179, 180. D. Appleton-Century Company, 1940.

Instead, I am reminded, even from the pulpit, of the injustices in the world and even urged to assist in bettering conditions on earth.

I'm brought into contact with common people who are advocating a one-class society, in which everyone would have the same opportunities and advantages.

Most of these people would not have sense enough to take advantage of an opportunity if one was offered. They have no aspirations or they would not be where they are.

We have always had poor people in this world and always will have; the Bible says so, so why try to make a leveled society? I am surprised that some of my own acquaintances indorse these ridiculous ideas.

I think it is high time for the church to put aside all thoughts and preachings of the physical needs and confine itself to the spiritual.

This man writes as a *respectable* church member. He evidently wishes to stay respectable; and he wants his religion to stay that way, too.

A second reason why religion may function as an opiate is found in its sacred character. Being holy, it must not be profaned by criticism. It is considered impious to analyze the effects of religion upon personality; it is like pulling one's mother apart to see whether she is guilty of instilling an Oedipus complex. Sean O'Casey's play *Within the Gates* was banned in Boston because, in the opinion of the censors, it portrayed the futility of Christianity. The censors did not pause to consider whether some forms of Christianity might be futile for some people. The theme was religion; the objective, criticism; the censors ruled a determined "No," prodded by a leading divine who urged that "this insidious attack on religion be kept from the stage of Boston." [79] This attitude is similar to the sentiment expressed by a university student who was interviewed concerning a professor's dismissal. According to report, "he thought that Dr. Blank was a menace to the Christian faith, and should not be allowed to teach in a Christian school. He said that he thought the church should never be criticized." [80]

Customs enjoy the sanctions of the gods. Traditions become holy with the sanctification of time. The mores, blessed by religion, are considered immune to criticism. This protection of whatever is customary is an obstacle in the way of clear thinking and intelligent behavior, as Burtt observes when he says:

[79] The Boston *Herald*, January 16, 1935.
[80] *Bulletin of the American Association of University Professors*, March, 1935.

Nothing, assuredly, will so affront the deceased ancestors of the tribe as laxity in preserving the beliefs which they wholeheartedly embraced when alive. Nothing, accordingly, will be surer to draw immediate and devastating punishment on the tribe than toleration of any individual who takes lightly the sacred traditions. Unquestioning belief in the creed of the ages, and readiness to act implicitly upon it, thus become primary religious virtues. . . Religion becomes the mightiest force of all for intellectual conservatism.[8]

Thus the church and the priesthood become sacrosanct and any policies or ideas they sponsor carry an authority brooking no criticism.

There is a naïve trust that religion is *ipso facto* good, that religious people are indubitably doing the right thing just because their hearts are in the right place. Surprising as it may seem, "good" people may do wrong, no matter how honorable their intentions may be, if they are lacking in intelligence or insight. This observation is clearly applicable to crowd situations where people engage in lynching parties or other brutal pastimes, rationalizing their sadism as "the protection of womanhood" to excuse their cruelty. Virtuous intentions, unverbalized or professed, should not throw us off our guard. Scoundrels often disguise their nefarious purposes under a cloak of righteousness.

Institutional inertia is another factor contributing to the opiate effect of religion. There is an evolution from vitality to rigidity as religion becomes formalized, organized, institutionalized, creedalized, ritualized. There is the religion of Jesus and there are religions about Jesus, as Fosdick puts it. Religion may grow cold as it hardens into second-hand Christianity. If Christ could return to earth and witness some of the things that are done in His name, He would be moved to announce, "If this is Christianity, then I am no Christian."

Committed to an authoritarian outlook, with the Bible as an infallible guide and a creed as an absolute faith, it is natural that some religious people should regard anything new with suspicion, just as Pope Pius IX once damned a long list of discoveries in his famous Syllabus of Errors. Some irreligious soul, commenting on the Syllabus, described it as "an admirable summary of the intellectual and scientific progress of the three previous centuries." The devout are often inclined to view new ideas as sacrilegious just because nobody has thought of them before and because they are not mentioned in the Bible. A theological bias may close the mind to experimental evidence, as the Florentine doctor, Redi, found when he sought to dem-

---

[8] E. A. Burtt: *Principles and Problems of Right Thinking*, p. 44. Harper Brothers, revised edition, 1931.

onstrate that dead meat could not turn into live maggots by itself. "He placed a piece of gauze over the meat, thus preventing flies from laying eggs to produce maggots. The holy men were enraged, and charged Redi with having limited the 'power of the Omnipotent.' " [82] Luther Burbank ran into the same kind of stubborn resistance from pious people when he started improving on nature. He reported some of the reactions to his experiments evolving "new creations":

> A perfect storm arose, in the heat and wind of which I was called a good many names stronger than blasphemer; I was preached about, talked at, written, telegraphed, scolded, abused, and vilified; the more extreme of my critics said that I was setting myself up as a competitor of Omnipotence, and the mildest of them called me a falsifier. Of course I had neither thought nor said anything either impious or blasphemous, unless it is impious and blasphemous to work with Nature, utilize her laws, direct her work, apply intelligence to plastic forms, and then claim a victory in getting useful and beautiful results. [83]

It would be only fair to add that Burbank's innovations were so radical a departure from tradition that "even the nurserymen were skeptical."

The clergy, immersed in their own particular dogmas, have done much in the past to hinder medical progress, and some of them are still doing their bit to retard advancement in this field, notably in battling against birth control and the eradication of venereal disease. Ministers used to oppose anaesthesia on the ground that pain was the ordained lot of mankind and, therefore, the act of preventing it was a sacrilege. Men of the cloth were especially vehement in denouncing the use of anaesthetics in childbirth, as Dr. Channing found out when he tried to introduce ether for cases of childbirth in Boston. The preachers protested on the ground that "the very suffering which a woman undergoes in labor is one of the strongest elements in the love she bears her offspring." One clergyman stated the case against the relief of pain: "Chloroform is a decoy of Satan, apparently offering itself to bless women; but in the end it will harden society and rob God of the deep, earnest cries which arise in time of trouble for help." Vaccination for smallpox was resisted on theological grounds, too. "Smallpox," the ministers said, "is a visitation from God, and originates in man: but the cowpox is produced by presumptuous, impious

[82] S. Chase: *The Tyranny of Words*, p. 215.   1938.
[83] L. Burbank: *The Harvest of the Years*, p. 70.   Houghton Mifflin Company.

man.   The former Heaven ordained; the latter is a daring and profane
violation of our holy religion."   Haggard concludes from his survey
of medical history that the church has done much to impede progress:

> So long as medicine was subordinate to religion, it could not advance. . .
> Before civilization can apply the knowledge to prevent pestilence it must ad-
> vance beyond the belief that disease is of supernatural origin.   Pestilences
> have occurred in those times when theology was at its greatest heights of faith.
> In each year of the Civil War, 1,000 out of every 100,000 died of typhoid.
> In the World War, five out of every 100,000.   This decrease in the prevalence
> of typhoid was due to preventive medicine and not to theology.   The care
> of drinking water took the place of incantations. . . .   Prophylactic inocula-
> tion against the disease replaced the wearing of charms and holy relics. . .
> In the twentieth century the screening out of flies was found more effective in
> preventing the spread of typhoid than all the prayers of the pious.   Nothing
> has retarded the growth of scientific medicine during the past 2,000 years so
> much as the iron grip of theology in maintaining practices based on belief
> in the supernatural origin of disease.[84]

Changes have been resisted by church people in fields outside
medicine.   The winnowing machine was opposed because it was considered irreligious of man to raise his own winds—it reflected discredit
on God who alone was supposed to take care of the wind.   The Panama Canal was denounced, when it was first proposed, as a blasphemous attempt to improve on God's creation.   If God had wanted the
oceans joined, he would not have interposed the "mountains and
iron rocks which can stand the fury of the seas."   When the Tennessee Valley Authority told the homesteaders about the flooding of
certain property, a native objected: "I wouldn't have no lake.   If the
Lord had wanted a lake He would have created it in His own way.'
Any alteration of the existent state of things is to be regarded as
a sacrilege.   This ultraconservatism, scandalized by new discoveries
constitutes "a lamentable blunder which always reacts disastrously
upon the fortunes of religion." [85]
Another way in which Christianity may serve as an opiate is evidenced in an attitude of passive resignation, a philosophical acceptance of whatever comes, an outlook that was borrowed by some early
Christians from the Stoics.   Whatever happens thus becomes God'
will, to which the stoical Christian submits without protest, praying

---

[84] H. W. Haggard: *Devils, Drugs, and Doctors,* p. 297.   Harper & Brothers, 1929
The quotations cited in the preceding paragraph are also taken from this book.
[85] H. E. Fosdick: *Adventurous Religion,* p. 103.   1926.

"Thy will, not mine, be done." A student summarized this philosophy of life in a nutshell: "Religion makes poor women believe that large families, dissolute husbands, and badly reared children are the will of God."

A Brooklyn mother, in 1930, watched her son who was near death while five physicians testified that his life could be saved by a simple operation. She refused to permit the operation on the ground that God had given her son to her and if it was His will to reclaim him, then she would not complain. While she prayed, city officials forced action through the courts, the boy was operated on and recovered, though the mother fought the doctors to the bitter end.[86] A similar situation arose in Philadelphia where a boy was suffering from a tubercular leg infection. An operation was imperative to save his life, but the parents protested. The father said, "It isn't right to take matters like this out of God's hands. Somebody will have to answer for it on the Judgment Day." The mother said, "The Lord giveth and the Lord taketh away." The doctors operated and saved the boy's life. The case was headlined by the *Literary Digest* as another clash between faith and medical science.

An examination made by Kimball Young of 3,000 Protestant hymns, showed that more than one-third of them featured an "infantile" leaning on God as their dominant theme.[87] Some individuals, relying on the theory that "the Lord will provide," do nothing to insure their economic security. It is an easy way to shift the responsibility of caring for one's own needs—just leave it up to God.

No better example could be found to substantiate the charge that religion is an opiate than the philosophy of passive resignation recommended by Cardinal O'Connell in a speech delivered in 1935 with the professed aim of quieting the hysteria of those malcontents who were busy advocating a change in our society. The Cardinal said, in part:

There are a million ways in which any citizen of America can voice his views, but they ought to be done with self-respecting honesty and, above all, the proper respect due to superiors. That is the underlying principle of Christian conduct. . . .

Our Blessed Lord walked among the poor all his life. He was poor himself. He loved the poor. Look to his life and you will never find one word, the

[86] W. B. Pitkin: *A Short Introduction to the History of Human Stupidity*, p. 36. 1932.

[87] See K. Young: "The Psychology of Hymns." *Journal of Abnormal and Social Psychology*, 1926, 20, 391-406.

utterance of a single phrase, that would do anything to upset the beautiful harmony of life which ought to exist in every orderly community. . . .

The office of the priest and bishop of the Catholic church is to continue to love poverty, to love the poor, to respect the poor, and to teach them, to help them and to guide them, not to ill-gotten wealth or anarchy or discontent in their lives, but to bring them, through the grace of God, the word of God and the sacraments, peace and happiness in whatever condition of life they may happen to be. . . .

And the good Catholic who is in straightened circumstances shows a cheery faith and a loyal heart and is not ashamed of his position, but is happy in the love of God and the strength of his faith and goes about in the fullest confidence that somehow God will make it all right.

Isn't that the most beautiful thing that one can aspire to in the life o. humanity? [88]

If the Cardinal is asking for an honest answer, it must be definitely "No."

The final way in which Christianity may act as an opiate is found in its encouragement of a reliance upon magic. Some Christians believe in miracles effected by God, who uses His omnipotence to set aside momentarily the laws of nature. Pitkin reports the case of a Russian farmer who tried to get rid of grasshoppers by having a priest sprinkle holy water on his fields.[89] During a flu epidemic in Denver in 1937 Christians resorted to prayer as a means of checking the spread of the disease. Some religious people do not seem to realize that there are natural laws which cannot be abrogated just to suit somebody's earnest desire. Prayers can only be answered when the supplicant prays according to the rules: not asking for the impossible, not depending on divine intervention, not delegating the solution entirely to the Almighty. Thus it is in keeping with the laws of nature to pray—*if* the individual follows his prayer with some practical measures for alleviating his situation. Praying for the end of an epidemic is more likely to be effective if the schools are closed, if public meetings are canceled, if dish-washing regulations in restaurants are enforced more strictly, if the doctors organize their services. The trouble with praying lies in the temptation of the supplicant to pray and then to let it go at that, substituting prayer for action. John Dewey once asserted: "Men have never used the powers they possess to advance the good in life, because they have waited upon some power external to themselves and to nature to do the work they are responsible for

---

[88] The *Boston Herald*, May 24, 1935.
[89] See Pitkin: *op. cit.*, p. 121.

doing. Dependence upon an external power is the counterpart of surrender of human endeavor." [90] There is nothing new about this kind of heroic thinking, comments a clergyman who knows his Bible, for long ago the Almighty said to Moses: "Why callest thou upon me? Speak to the children of Israel that they go forward."

B. RADICALISM

While religion may be an opiate, as we have observed, it is equally true that it may be a stimulant, providing an invigorating urge to transform the world. Religion is what we make it. If the emphasis has been concentrated on a religion of escape, it is because people have felt the need for "getting away from it all." Christianity is not inevitably an invitation to retreat from reality, for the church has inspired, and is inspiring today, many humanitarian enterprises and campaigns for social reform.

The modern Marxian indictment of religion as the source of conservatism and political reaction is so familiar and so generally accepted even among non-Marxians that Spengler's thesis of the religious basis of radicalism will be regarded as strange and bizarre. Yet it is probably true. It is at least as true as the counter-indictment. The real fact is that religion is the source of both radicalism and conservatism; for the light of its sanctities can be used with equal success to obscure the imperfections of society and to bring them into bold relief.[91]

The monk who flees the world is not the prototype of the Christian. There are the prophets, too, who have led people in crusades that have revolutionized society.

Progressive achievements accredited to the church include its leadership in behalf of the abolition of slavery, and for temperance, woman suffrage, peace, public schools and universities, political freedom, and democracy. In this connection it is *à propos* to mention the brave fight for freedom that the Christians of Germany waged against totalitarian oppression, a stand that landed many of them in concentration camps where 80 per cent of the prisoners were not Jews but Christians. Their courage evoked a tribute from Albert Einstein, Jew and agnostic, who paid his respects in these words:

Being a lover of freedom, when the revolution came in Germany, I looked to the universities to defend it, knowing that they had always boasted of their

[90] J. Dewey: "The Liberation of Modern Religion." *Yale Review*, June, 1934.
[91] R. Niebuhr: "Religion as a Source of Radicalism." *Christian Century*, April 11, 1934.

devotion to the cause of truth; but, no, the universities immediately were silenced. Then I looked to the great editors of the newspapers whose flaming editorials in days gone by had proclaimed their love of freedom; but they, like the universities, were silenced in a few short weeks. . . .

Only the Church stood squarely across the path of Hitler's campaign for suppressing truth. I never had any special interest in the Church before, but now I feel a great affection and admiration because the Church alone has had the courage and persistence to stand for intellectual truth and moral freedom. I am forced thus to confess that what I once despised I now praise unreservedly.[92]

The church has been progressive in championing changes in society destined to bring in the reign of justice, equality, and fraternity, sometimes referred to as "the Kingdom of God on earth." The central theme in Christianity is the worth of the human person. The embodiment of this conviction in business, in politics, in international relations would cause such a revolution in our habits as to suggest that "radical" is a mild word for the dynamics inherent in the social gospel. If the church has often been reactionary and lethargic, indifferent to its social responsibilities, its lack of vigor must be interpreted as a symptom of the failure to take Christ's teachings seriously. Moral rearmament, whether it is sponsored by Frank Buchman or by some other religious leader, is an objective that should inspire action rather than spiritual slumber. Religion can furnish us with ideals challenging us to exert ourselves to the utmost in doing our bit to make this world a better place to live in. The progress of invention and the accumulation of wealth cannot bring us happiness if freedom is lost. In "A Message for Easter Day," 1941, entitled "What You and I Need Most," Arthur H. Compton, famous scientist, spoke of freedom and the need of preserving it:

And no achievements of science alone, no matter how wonderful, will be enough to save it. The test tube and the scales, the microscope and mathematics cannot reach those intangible, yet real, qualities of life in which is rooted human freedom.

I speak of the virtues by which man lives and progresses, on which civilization is built and by which alone it can endure. I speak of the spiritual elements of love and sacrifice, justice and honor, integrity, equality and good will. Call them intangibles if you will—yet they are real and they are indispensable. They are the qualities on which democracy and freedom are built. They are the qualities which must be strengthened if we would safeguard our liberty and our civilization.

[92] *Time*, December 23, 1940.

These qualities in turn are rooted deep in religion. To strengthen them we must strengthen our faith, for faith is the cornerstone of religion. . . .

The realization that a Supreme Intelligence brought the universe into being . . . and created Man . . . is the first step in the growth of Faith. The second is the understanding that God, who created life, has given it a meaning and a destiny. There is a purpose for our being and doing, and faith in that purpose spurs man to struggle and to progress.

Here is no room for cynicism, for defeatism, for frustration. True, there is chaos in parts of the world, but in the midst of that chaos we see human progress. Hospitals and colleges, asylums and orphanages gird the world, founded on the impulse given by the cardinal element of religious faith: the Fatherhood of God and the Brotherhood of Man. Science and religion join hands in the battle against ignorance, superstition, disease, poverty and under-privilege.

Religious faith exalts man and gives him freedom. It spurs progress because it teaches an unfolding destiny for every man, woman and child, with opportunity for all. These concepts are the heart and soul of democracy, in which governments become the servants of men.[93]

Religion can be a "spur to progress." That's the kind of religion that the church should feature if it wants to assume leadership in the modern world.

[93] From "What You and I Need Most," by Arthur H. Compton. Reprinted from *This Week* by permission. Copyright, 1941, by United Newspapers Magazine Corporation.

Chapter 21

THE NATION

IN POPULAR USAGE, the terms *nation* and *state* are employed interchangeably. We shall follow the same practice, though aware that the *nation* is a cultural configuration, the *state* a political organization. Actually, the state and the nation would coincide only when all the persons sharing the same culture were organized into one political unit.

I. NATIONALISM AND THE STATE

A nation is not to be thought of merely as a physical territory or as a single government, but more essentially as a group of people unified in sentiment. Nationality may be described as a configuration of citizens each of whom regards himself as belonging to the whole. "The nation's 'mind,'" as Stratton says, "is the minds of its citizens organized for national purposes."[1] There is no "group mind" belonging to a nation. The nation is a psychological entity merely in the sense that members think of themselves as belonging together that way. In pre-Revolutionary days the people in the colonies were really not "Americans" because they had not yet come to think of their country as a nation. They were still thinking of themselves in local terms. Even at the time of the Constitutional Convention many individuals were still thinking in terms of separate states rather than in terms of a *United* States. We did not become a nation until we had achieved a common attitude which could be accurately described as *"E Pluribus Unum."*

The concept of the nation should not be confused with the concept of race. Nationality is a matter of psychological attitude; race, a matter of physical constitution. Identification of the two is due to a confusion of concepts, a confusion which is sometimes deliberately perpetrated for purposes of political exploitation.

[1] G. M. Stratton: *International Delusions*, p. 227. 1936.

A nation comes about as a product of conditioning. The attachments of a man to his countryside and to very personal experiences around which the memories of youth have cast a halo of sanctity, constitute the basis of patriotism. The universal beneficences of nature come to be interpreted as blessings showered upon our particular group by virtue of divine favoritism. Symbolism plays a large role in nourishing the love of country.

THIS LAND AND FLAG

What is the love of country for which our flag stands? Maybe it begins with love of the land itself. It is the fog rolling in with the tide at Eastport, or through the Golden Gate and among the towers of San Francisco. It is the sun coming up behind the White Mountains, over the Green, through a shining glory on Lake Champlain and above the Adirondacks. . . .

It is men at work. . . . It is the farmer riding his great machine in the dust of harvest, the dairyman going to the barn before sunrise, the lineman mending the broken wire, the miner drilling for the blast. It is the servants of fire in the murky splendor of Pittsburgh, between the Allegheny and the Monongahela, the trucks rumbling through the night, the locomotive engineer bringing the train in on time, the pilot in the clouds. . . .

It is small things remembered, the little corners of the land, the houses, the people that each one loves. We love our country because there was a little tree on a hill, and grass thereon, and a sweet valley below; because the hurdy-gurdy man came along on a sunny morning in a city street; because a beach or a farm or a lane or a house that might not seem much to others was once, for each of us, made magic. It is voices that are remembered only, no longer heard. It is parents, friends, the lazy chat of street and store and office, and the ease of mind that makes life tranquil. It is summer and winter, rain and sun and storm. These are flesh of our flesh, bone of our bone, blood of our blood, a lasting part of what we are, each of us and all of us together.

It is stories told. It is the Pilgrims dying in their first dreadful winter. It is the Minute Man standing his ground at Concord Bridge, and dying there. It is the army in rags, sick, freezing, starving at Valley Forge. . . .

The land and the people and the flag—the land a continent, the people of every race, the flag a symbol of what humanity may aspire to when the wars are over and the barriers are down. . . .[2]

We cherish our common traditions and our common hopes for the future. In so far as we share these experiences we are a nation.

To the casual observer a person's concept of the state might seem to be an insignificant triviality, a distant abstraction, hardly worth men-

---

[2] Editorial in the New York *Times*, June 14, 1940.

tioning; but to the social psychologist a person's ideas regarding the nature of the state are seen to result in far reaching consequences. The Hegelian philosophy of the state, for example, provided the intellectual justification for Germany's *"Deutschland über alles"* nationalistic ambitions. Hegel believed that the state should be the supreme object of devotion, that the state is a super-individual organism, with a consciousness of its own, actually transcending the mind of the individual. All virtue accordingly is embodied in service to the state. Hegel's philosophy was appropriated to rationalize Prussian militarism; later it culminated in the Nazi philosophy which saw a personification of the nation in the *Führer,* a Superman Leader of a Superstate. Hitler, like Hegel, held that great men and ordinary persons are significant only in so far as each is useful, in his own sphere, to the organic whole, for as Herr Hitler said, *"Du bist nichts; dein Volk ist alles."* (You are nothing; your people are everything.)

From Hegelism through Nazism the notion of a super-individual consciousness was extremely profitable. . . . Its corollary was the consistent repudiation of all opposing ideas and institutions. . . .

If, following generations of preparatory indoctrination through philosophy, literature, and interpretation of history, a people comes to accept its own unique group mind as a settled condition for achieving its Grand Mission, certain consequences are inevitable. To begin with, all other groups must be viewed exclusively in terms of their supposed serviceability or hindrance to that mission.[3]

It is no accident that Hegel's philosophy enjoyed a revival in Fascist Italy where Croce and Gentile, good Hegelians, devoted their intellectual gifts to sustaining Mussolini.[4]

The state may be regarded as a cooperative organization established and maintained for the purpose of solving the problems involved in living together. Authority is delegated to representative officials who enforce regulations set up to protect the citizens from criminals, to guard the public health, and to provide other services necessary to satisfying communal relations. The state is sometimes exploited by special-interest groups who use the political instruments available to gain special privileges. "Historically we always find that any system of government is dominated by those who at the time wield economic

[3] E. Freeman: *Conquering the Man in the Street; A Psychological Analysis of Propaganda in War, Fascism, and Politics,* pp. 135-136. The Vanguard Press, 1940.
[4] Refer to the section on "The Group-Mind Fallacy" in Chapter 1.

power; and what they mean by 'good' is for the most part the preservation of their own interests." [5]

"Patrioteering" is a term applied to the activity of citizens who exploit patriotism by identifying loyalty to country with loyalty to a special set of beliefs which they happen to cherish as the only sound principles. Thus "the prevailing social mode is sanctified, and given a stronger hold on the loyalty of the people by being represented as necessary to the life of the community." [6] In this way patriotism is used as a means for blocking orderly change and adjustment, in the interest of keeping things as they are.

The confusion of patriotism with devotion to some particular set of political or economic arrangements is an ancient and common fallacy. A militaristic system of "national defense," a laissez-faire system of competitive industry, a financial system which makes private profit the motive for every enterprise and distributes rewards without reference to the value of services rendered—all those are among the articles of political faith most dearly cherished by those who [believe] that adherence to the constitution is equivalent to a defense of the status quo.[7]

Anything new may be discredited simply by labeling it "un-American." This sort of patrioteering encourages mere loyalty to institutions as they are, without any thought as to whether the established practices promote the welfare of all the people. Hunter has proposed the term "communalism" to designate loyalty to the general interest of the whole community.[8]

II. FORMS OF GOVERNMENT AND "HUMAN NATURE"

If we accept the view that the state exists for persons, it is important for psychologists to determine how individuals are affected by various forms of political organization. A pioneer experiment in this field was reported in 1939 by Lewin, Lippitt, and White, who worked with clubs of boys. The subjects were equated and placed in three distinct groups:

(1) *Authoritarian,* in which the leader determined all the policies and maintained an aloof attitude, while the followers were kept in the dark as to what was going to happen next.

[5] H. Laski: *Foundations of Sovereignty,* p. 238. 1931.
[6] C. L. Hunter: *A Sociological Analysis of Certain Types of Patriotism,* p. 79. 1932.
[7] G. Boas: "Technic of Mob Rule." *Harper's Magazine,* May, 1935.
[8] Hunter: *op. cit.,* p. 250.

(2) *Democratic,* in which the group engaged in discussion and decision, with active encouragement and assistance from the leader, who suggested alternatives for making choices, gave information upon request, and stimulated self-guidance.

(3) *Laissez faire,* in which there was complete freedom for the group or for individuals to make the decisions; the leader in this section gave information but did not participate in the group discussion.

Each of the leaders, during the course of the experiment, headed each of these three types of organization in turn. The democratic setup was evaluated as the best because it produced a friendlier *rapport* between members and leaders; there was much less aggressiveness directed toward fellow members; scapegoating was rare; there was more toleration for individual differences; and better techniques were developed in the way of cooperative planning.[9] Americans would be inclined to endorse this conclusion heartily without demanding any more substantial evidence for the decision in favor of democracy.

Any system of government depends for its success, as an instrument of human welfare, upon the habits of its citizens. A socialist order cannot endure unless the participants are psychologically prepared for it. Neither can democracy succeed where people are accustomed to regimentation. Accordingly, it would be psychologically unwise for any nation to attempt to impose its own form of government upon other nations—a natural temptation that may stir up trouble in programs of post-war planning, however generous intentions may be. "We must make up our minds to deal with governments and their social systems as they are and not as we should like them to be. . . . Personal liberty cannot be imposed by machine guns. . . . It must grow in the minds and spirits of men." [10]

What sort of government is best suited to human needs? Whose particular needs, when, where? You and I may want freedom but do all kinds of people want freedom? There are persons who prefer regimentation, according to Eric Fromm, persons who enjoy living in a society where somebody else takes the initiative, makes the decisions,

---

[9] See K. Lewin, R. Lippitt, and R. K. White: "Patterns of Aggressive Behavior in Experimentally Created 'Social Climates.'" *Journal of Social Psychology*, 1939, 10, 271-299. See the excellent report of these data prepared especially for *Readings in Social Psychology* (1947) by R. Lippitt and R. K. White, entitled "An Experimental Study of Leadership and Group Life."

Refer to the section on "Political Science" in Chapter 2 and to the section entitled "Organizing Society to Meet Human Needs: Democracy" in Chapter 4.

[10] H. Hoover and H. Gibson: "New Approaches to Lasting Peace." *Collier's,* June 5, 1943.

shoulders the responsibilities.[11] We must confess that there are people even in America who would rather have security than freedom, who are perfectly willing to turn over their cares and worries to a benevolent Government. We must know more about what people want before we can determine what the ideal form of government would be under the existent conditions. It may be that communism suits the Russians just as well as or better than our system satisfies us.

III. NATIONALISM AND PATRIOTISM

Nationalism and patriotism may be conveniently discussed together because they are different phases of the "love of country." One might become patriotic in his devotion to his neighborhood or his town, but patriotism ordinarily connotes loyalty to the nation. Hayes, the historian, defines nationalism as "an emotional fusion of nationality and patriotism," and, as such, it is a modern phenomenon. He points out that nationalism involves a belief in the independent sovereignty of each nation, the heartening conviction that one's own nation is the greatest in the world, and the acceptance of this devotion to country as the supreme loyalty.[12]

Patriotism, popularly conceived, connotes particularly the willingness to bear arms for one's country in case of war. The flag is looked upon as a symbol for the nation in its martial capacity. Thus to the Briton the British flag means Nelson and Trafalgar, not Shakespeare, not Darwin, not Newton. War, conquest, heroism in battle are the thoughts that come to our minds when we are in the patriotic mood. We have not come to realize, in the naïveté of our patriotism, that the best deeds of Englishmen have been performed by them not as Englishmen, but as individuals. A Jewish student who was preparing a book on famous Jewish scientists wrote to Albert Einstein requesting him to provide the data for a résumé of Einstein's scientific career. In his reply, Dr. Einstein suggested that this young man also write a book on redheaded scientists. The German version read: *"Warum nicht die Rothaarigen?"* This was Einstein's way of insinuating that a scientist should be considered as a scientist and not as a Jew, for in such matters race is an irrevelant factor.

Patriotism will not come of age until we are mature enough to become as enthusiastic over the illustrious achievements of our artists and scientists as we now become over our military heroes. The verdict of history will probably rule that Harry Emerson Fosdick was

---

[11] See E. Fromm: *Escape from Freedom.* 1941.
[12] See C. J. H. Hayes: *Essays on Nationalism.* The Macmillan Company, 1926.

overoptimistic when he declared, in 1929, in his joyful celebration of the Kellogg Peace Pact: "The militarists have long had a monopoly on Patriotism. They can hold it no longer. The Peacemakers are now the Patriots, and that change is one of the most crucial in history."

A. BENEFITS

As an instrument for waging war the state has proved useful in gaining for its citizens material benefits which they otherwise could not enjoy. Nationalistic territorial expansion has resulted in the acquisition of valuable natural resources which make possible a high standard of living.

We shall concern ourselves primarily with the psychological benefits that are derived from nationalistic patriotism.

Patriotism gives the individual the opportunity to bolster up his pride without feeling any sense of boastfulness. By praising the superiority of the group, the individual can vicariously pat himself on the back, and thus engage in a subtle form of self-approbation. This sort of tribal arrogance may foster group cohesion. It was easy for us to detect the conceit and the vainglory of the German who insisted that he belonged to a super-race. It is not so easy for us to recognize our own chauvinistic arrogance. It is important to realize that the members of every nation are given to this sort of patriotic self-glorification. Nationalistic pride encourages members of each nation to draw apart from people of other nationalities and to distrust all outsiders. Each nation has its own sense of destiny, a conviction that it has been chosen to lead the backward peoples of the world toward a higher civilization.

Patriotism develops the "We" feeling, thus satisfying our need for belonging to some important group. In moments of patriotic ardor, we can expand agreeably and enjoy the exaltation of ourselves as individuals. Singing the praises of our own particular nation, we are given to an exaggerated esteem of our own achievements and to a lack of appreciation for the contributions that other nationalities have made to our common culture. An objective recognition of the cooperative nature of civilization would help to chasten our national conceit. Patriotism, a territorial emotion, by sanctifying our prejudices and narrowing our loyalties, frequently obscures the common interests of humanity. We glorify loyalty to our own group, then exult in hostility toward all "outsiders."

Patriotism affords us a vicarious compensation for frustration, enabling us to transcend our own limitations by "ganging up" on some other "party." Nationalism permits a release of aggression by directing hatred toward the "out-group." Blaming the foreigner is an easy way of evading personal responsibility for hard times. A convenient scapegoat serves as an object upon whom pugnacious tendencies can be vented. Patriotism provides an excellent outlet for our pent-up aggressive feeling, thus relieving our sense of frustration.

B. MANIFESTATIONS

We may gain some insight into the psychological significance of patriotism by examining its expressions in ethnocentrism, economic self-sufficiency, and national sovereignty.

1. ETHNOCENTRISM

The feeling that one's own racial or ethnic group is superior to all other groups is referred to as *ethnocentrism*. The term is now used to refer also to nationalistic self-complacency. Patriotism may take the form of "national egocentrism," a jingoistic preoccupation with one's own merits.[13] This feeling of superiority is one of the chief characteristics of nationalism, according to Hayes, who has made an exhaustive study of this phenomenon. Hayes says:

Nationalism is partly love of country, but chiefly something else. Nationalism is a proud and boastful habit of mind about one's own nation, accompanied by a supercilious or hostile attitude toward other nations; . . . and it has easily recognisable symptoms of selfishness, intolerance, and jingoism, indicative of the delusions of grandeur from which it suffers. Nationalism is artificial and it is far from ennobling; in a word, it is patriotic snobbery.[14]

It was Herbert Spencer who pointed out that an excess of egoism is regarded everywhere as a fault but that an excess amount of patriotism generally meets with approval among one's fellow citizens.[15] One reason for the acceptance of patriotism is the fact that it is a disguised form of self-love. We do not tolerate bragging in individuals who boast of their own personal attainments. If the same self-satisfaction, however, is expressed in the form of nationalistic self-satisfaction, we respect and honor the person for being proud of our group. When we encounter the ethnocentric type of attitude on a small scale,

---

[13] See Hunter: *op. cit.*, Chapter 5, "Type III: National Egocentrism."
[14] C. J. H. Hayes: *Essays on Nationalism*, p. 275. The Macmillan Company, 1926.
[15] See H. Spencer: *The Study of Sociology*, pp. 206-207. 1873.

localized in its scope, we see how absurd is group snobbery. For example:

When R. E. Lee Marshall was at school in Virginia, it was the custom of the headmaster to call on one of the boys each morning to read a passage from the Scriptures. One day a boy began the 25th chapter of St. Matthew:

"Then shall the kingdom of Heaven be likened unto ten Virginians, which took their lamps and went forth to meet the bridegroom. And five of them were wise and five were foolish."

The headmaster stopped the boy and told him to repeat the passage. The boy read it exactly as before. Again the headmaster stopped him, and remained a few moments in deep thought. At last he said sadly: "Well, if the Bible says so it must be true. But I would never have believed that there were five foolish Virginians." [16]

A similar incident amused the author, who is not a native of Massachusetts. Dyed-in-the-wool Bay Staters probably read, without even batting an eyelash, this front page editorial published on the eve of a Massachusetts state election in 1934, which read, in part: "Let no voter underestimate the importance of this election. We live in a state which may have its shortcomings, but it is clearly the superior of any other in the Union." [17]

The psychology underlying the evolution of ethnocentrism is well described by Smertenko, who writes:

When the immigrant wrote back to his people in Ireland that in America every man is just as good as his neighbor, if not better, he expressed in a typical Irishism a universal sentiment, which is undoubtedly as old as it is widespread. Every man feels in some way superior to his neighbor, whether because he is rich or poor, modest or proud, giant or pigmy, carnal or pious, quick-witted or plodding, for it is in every man's power and it is every man's custom to make a virtue of his special condition and characteristics. Moreover, in this task of marking "Superior Brand" on distinctive traits and qualities, the individual does not stop with himself; he exalts similarly his family, his clan, and his tribe, thus unconsciously creating a vicious circle by admiring what he has because he has it.

What is true of individuals is equally true of nations. From the earliest times a given nation's feeling of superiority to its neighbors has been one of the most powerful forces influencing and molding the life of peoples. There is hardly a nation which has not suffered because at some time in its history it acted in the belief that this feeling was a fact. Furthermore, both the records

---

[16] C. B. in the Baltimore *Sun*, quoted under the heading "Of Pride and Prejudice," in *Reader's Digest*, February, 1939.

[17] Boston *Herald*, November 5, 1934.

of ancient civilization and the history of our more immediate past show us that the nations have followed an identical formula to justify this national arrogance.[18]

Ethnocentrism is a serious obstacle to international harmony. National conceit makes for bad feeling, just as personal vanity proves annoying in interpersonal relations. It is easier, of course, to detect the attitudes of superiority in members of other nations than it is to recognize the same assumption of arrogance among ourselves. It might take the edge off the conceit on all sides if each group could see itself as others see it.

The ethnocentric outlook, based as it is upon self-complacency, tends to encourage the disparagement of other races and nationalities, and thus interferes with international understanding. If, for example, we take a look at ourselves through the eyes of the European press, we observe the United States as a grotesque image in a distorting mirror. When the American Legion had a noisy but good-natured convention in New York City, the London *Daily Mirror* featured it in a headline which read: "Four Hundred Thousand Troops Terrorized Broadway in Wild Orgy." According to the London *Daily Express* the South is "lawless and half savage." The correspondent of the *Daily Express* used to be fascinated by the feuds and lynchings which were supposedly part of the routine of life in Kentucky. Lynchings, he reported, were "regarded as good evening's entertainment after a boring day of drinking moonshine on the hot back porch."

Both in England and on the Continent trivial and freakish items tend to drown out other American news. The editors play up the serious news from Berlin and Rome. Then, to balance their papers, they print the story about the mule in Kansas that had its face lifted. It is like the news stories in American papers which hastily pass over a crisis in the French government to print a half-column on a brawl in a Parisian night-life cafe.

It's hard to realize how much the foreign conception of us is based on such silly, fly-by-night little items that are tucked away in the corners of our newspapers. We have our own brand of humor; we can take these items for what they are worth. But they get copied abroad, go ricocheting around the Continental press and leave a deposit of enduring beliefs and opinions as solid as they are perverse. . . .[19]

[18] J. J. Smertenko: "The Claim of 'Nordic' Race Superiority." *Current History Magazine,* April, 1924.
[19] E. Muller: "America through the Looking Glass." *Christian Century,* June 22, 1938. World War II has helped to reduce some of this international misunderstanding.

An Englishwoman, in 1939, told Americans confidentially about the Briton's genius for not understanding the United States. The English, she said, have not tried to understand us. The English were in the habit of mentioning America at times but they did not investigate us. Consequently their impressions of American life were sketchy and erroneous. This Englishwoman, Helen Bryant, informed us how we looked to the average Englishman:

Americans are still considered a hustling, pushing race with no manners. They die of heart-failure in early middle age. They have perverted the English language and speak it with an atrocious accent. . . . They have two chief cities, New York, where everybody "goes on" in an extraordinary way, and Chicago, devoted to gangsters. Americans have no home life; divorce is a habit with them, like afternoon tea with the British. . . . America also strays into English literature lessons . . . there is an American writer to whom English educational authorities are partial: Washington Irving. But they prepare the ground so badly that the small Briton emerges from contact with him with conclusions somewhat as follows:

Washington Irving wrote some rather dull ghost stories of an inferior brand, and this Washington man also founded the United States and the Americans thought a lot of him, but it is hard to see why. Alfred was a hero because he burned the cakes, and Canute because he told the sea to retreat and it didn't, and Henry VIII because he had wives, and Elizabeth because she was a Virgin Queen. But what did Washington do? Nothing but write these tepid stories. . . .

The United States, when it got free of England, had a civil war about slavery, and after Lincoln had won it for them, they shot him. That's the wild way they go on over there.[20]

The discovery that others do not see us in as happy a light as we see ourselves should prove helpful in tempering our national conceit. Ethnocentrism, however, is probably incurable. When a Scotsman met an American for the first time he asked him where he came from. "God's country," replied the American. Responded the Scotsman, "You've lost your accent." The misunderstanding between ourselves and foreigners, fostered by nationalistic exclusiveness, is represented in this simple poem:

> I always thought that foreign boys
> Were those across the sea
> Until I got a letter
> From a boy in Italy.

[20] Helen Bryant: "1776 and All That." New York *Times Magazine,* April 23, 1939.

"Dear little foreign friend,"
It said, as clearly as could be,
And now I wonder who is foreign,
The other boy or me?

2. ECONOMIC SELF-SUFFICIENCY

The spirit of nationalism inspires the aim for economic self-sufficiency, since each nation wants to feel independent, both physically and emotionally.[21] "Buy British," exhort a thousand advertisements in British newspapers girdling the globe. India, meanwhile, launches a "Buy Native" campaign. These movements, developing in various nations all over the world, instead of solving our financial problems, are apt to make them worse. Nationalistic isolationism, an anachronism in a world united by airplane and radio, still manifests itself in tariffs and embargoes which restrict the very entrance of goods into a country and decrease their availability by raising prices once they are in. The rejection of economic internationalism in favor of even partial nationalistic insulation must mean, inevitably, a decline in the standard of living. The mass production which is rendered possible by a world-wide market means lower prices, bringing within the reach of everyone things which would otherwise be luxuries available only to the rich.

There are three ways in which each nation can secure the raw materials and the manufactured materials its people need: (1) become self-sufficient by imperialistic expansion through conquest; (2) become self-sufficient by development of *Ersatz* products (substitutes, like nylon for silk); (3) learn to trade satisfactorily with other nations. The United States will probably follow policies (2) and (3).

America in its present state is very much dependent upon foreign trade. Some economists feel that much is to be gained by specialization of effort on the part of each individual nation, since this has been found to result in increased productive efficiency, making possible much higher standards of living. In the opinion of Francis B. Sayre, formerly Assistant Secretary of State, we may assume that as a corollary to increased wealth for each nation will come increased dependence on the product or markets supplied by other nations. Trade agreements, by promoting international trade, are an aid to peace. Sayre explains his position on this point thus:

No nation is so abundantly endowed with natural resources and technical skill that each can be economically sufficient unto itself and remain prosperous. Trade constitutes the very life blood of nations.

[21] See the section on "Survivals—in Politics" in Chapter 13, "Custom."

If orderly processes of trade break down as means for securing the ready exchange of goods and the distribution of the necessary raw materials of the world, conquest and the march to imperialism become well-nigh irresistible. Economic nationalism and its corollary, imperialistic expansion, alike lead to perpetual conflict.[22]

A "Buy American" movement is sure to become identified by some persons with patriotism. Thus William Randolph Hearst instructed his editors to campaign for "patriotic policies," beginning with: "Buy American and Spend American. See America first. Keep American money in America, and provide employment for American citizens." And for three days in succession, in compliance with Hearst's request, the New York *American* proclaimed the "Buy American" crusade in huge editorials spread over a third of a page, with a typical sentence running like this: "Americans Must Buy American Goods—the products of American labor and American capital—to the exclusion of any other goods, or any other products, of any other services, of any other labor—whatever part of the world they proceed from and at whatever price they are offered." [23] Patriots of this type are apt to lose sight of the fact that if we "Think American and Buy American," we cannot expect, at the same time to "Sell Foreign."

Scientific discoveries of new ways for manufacturing essential products may alter the whole international situation. Science is learning how to make automobile steering wheels from soy beans, piano keys from cottage cheese, metal and rubber substitutes from corn cobs, synthetic gas from coal. Inventions of this sort may be ushering in a new day in which each nation will come closer to approximating self-sufficiency. It is possible that this evolution will minimize the causes of international conflict, since the pressure for political control of ore deposits, coal fields, oil pools, and other natural resources will be diminished. Thus the physical basis of international jealousy may be liquidated and "at last the intelligence of science may make it truly practical to beat our swords into ploughshares, our spears into pruning hooks." [24]

3. NATIONAL SOVEREIGNTY

Another expression of nationalism is the faith in national sovereignty. According to this philosophy each nation is the sole judge of

[22] F. B. Sayre: "World Trade and American Recovery." Speech on America's Town Meeting of the Air Program, December 3, 1936.

[23] Reported in the *Literary Digest*, January 7, 1933.

[24] Kirtley Mather, Harvard professor.

its own practices, and the result of the doctrine is international anarchy. Someone has compared the international situation to a community where sixty different sovereigns were trying to live together with no plain citizens upon whom they could exercise their powers; in such a community each man would be king and each would insist on having his rights regardless of any protests registered by the fifty-nine other sovereigns. No community could exist for long on such a basis. If we look upon nations as citizens of a world community instead of as ends in themselves, we see how backward we have been in developing any ideology or any instruments for settling international disputes in a rational, law-respecting, civilized manner.

Nations, standing apart, independent, viewing each other with mutual distrust, cannot help living in a state of jealous disunion. Stratton insists that "their jealous love of separation in a world today all knit together in its interests is a childish refusal to deal with reality." [25] Under such conditions, where basic rights and duties are so ill-defined, international anarchy will continue to exist. Just as individuals need to function under certain restraints, so people organized as nations need the help of others in limiting their powers for the common good, for otherwise the international situation will be a free-for-all.

During World War II, the German propaganda office delighted in quoting from Britons who, at some time in the past, had made statements which belied the British claim of fighting in defense of freedom. The following excerpt will serve as an apt illustration of this technique. It is included here because it shows the sort of thing that happens when nations feel that they are in the right in satisfying their ambitions irrespective of the rights of others.

WHEN BRITONS STILL SPOKE HONESTLY

Today Great Britain never misses an opportunity to pose as the defender of all nations and all liberties. Her own record, however, certainly bears the strongest testimony against her hypocritical claims, and plenty of Englishmen have acknowledged this last sad fact. Here is a typical example:

Major Stewart L. Murray had this to say in his book, *The Future Peace of the Anglo-Saxons:* "There is no such thing as International Law. What is wrongly called by that name is nothing but international usage. If a nation is sufficiently strong, it can add a new usage at any moment. *We Britishers have made ourselves guilty of more breaches of international agreements than any other nation.* We have often used our sea power in order to make surprise

---

[25] Stratton: *op. cit.,* p. 95.

attacks on other countries. . . . It cannot be stressed too much that international law merely protects the strong and that the only laws recognized by the Great Powers as binding are those of might and military preparedness."

It matters little that an Englishman made this statement and it matters little that he said it way back in 1905, since it describes the common procedure pursued by nations that are strong enough to get away with such a policy. It was another English author, Norman Angell, who asserted in his book *The Unseen Assassins* (1933) that nationalism or, specifically, nations insisting on sovereignty and independence, is the basic cause of modern warfare. In effect, he pointed out, such a doctrine means that every nation insists on the right of being prosecutor, judge, and jury in all cases which involve its interest. Thus every nation insists that it should enjoy rights the exercise of which involves the denial of the same rights to every other nation. In civil life this mood produces crime and racketeering; in international life it produces anarchy and war. Yet the people have been taught to cling blindly to nationalism and in doing so they are themselves responsible for the miseries which they deplore.

Two newspaper headlines in 1935 may be cited to illustrate the doctrine of national sovereignty in practice. The first one appeared on April 30, 1935:

HITLER SAYS NATIONS MUST NOT SIT AS JUDGES OF GERMANY

It is interesting to note that an accompanying headline in the same newspaper referred to a pending local trial in these words: "Hultman Evidence May Go to Court." The significance of the contrast between these two simultaneous headlines lies in the fact that members of the same nation settle their disputes by resort to a court, while a nation, if it wants something badly enough, refuses to submit its disputable claims to extra-national adjudication.

The second headline illustrating national sovereignty, which appeared on June 21, 1935, was the following:

ITALY PREPARED TO QUIT LEAGUE

Will Do So if It Intervenes In Her Dispute with Ethiopia

No wonder that Warburg makes this prediction:

> Just as within the nation we shall have to curtail the sovereignty of economic man and distribute economic power, as we have distributed political power—so we shall have to change and limit an outworn concept of national sovereignty. The government of a nation must have the power to do *within its nation* whatever the people of that nation desire it to do; *it must not have the power to do things which affect the people of other nations without their, too, having a voice in the matter.*[26]

It is a paradox that patriotism transmutes individual unselfishness into national egoism. Unqualified devotion to country is the very basis of the nation's power and of the license to use that power without moral restraint. Thus the unselfishness of individuals makes for the selfishness of nations. What lies beyond the nation—the community of mankind—seems too vague to inspire devotion.

IV. INTERNATIONAL RELATIONS

We shall now deal with some of the psychological factors involved in war, peace, and internationalism.

A. WAR

We have already observed how ethnocentrism, the desire for economic self-sufficiency, and the doctrine of national sovereignty contribute to the conditions that facilitate war. We do not need to resort to any hypothetical instinct of pugnacity, accordingly, to account for our periodic international combats. The source of war is traceable to the institutions we have developed rather than to native aggressiveness. We are all capable of anger—the ways in which we express our rage are *conditioned* by habit. Watson in his experiments with Albert demonstrated this thesis; comparative anthopologists have uncovered corroborative evidence that behavior is *culturally determined.*[27] In Chapter 1, under the heading of "Institutional Behavior," we stated that men resort to arms because war has been established as the *habitual* mode for settling international differences; under the heading "Group-Mind Fallacy," we observed how the concept of national

---

[26] J. P. Warburg: *The Isolationist Illusion and World Peace.* Pamphlet No. 11 in a series entitled "America in a World at War." This pamphlet is a chapter in Warburg's book, *Our War and Our Peace.* Rinehart and Company, Inc., 1941. See also *Nationalism*, a report by a study-group of members of the British Royal Institute of International Affairs. 1940.

[27] Refer to section on Anthropology in Chapter 2.

honor contributes to the causation of war.   These are institutional influences.   Let us examine now other factors in the situation.

Many people express the view that men do not want wars but that they are forced to fight them.   This sentiment was expressed by Lincoln Steffens in his *Autobiography* (1931): "Wilson did not mean peace, not literally; nor do we Americans, nor do the British, mean peace.   We do not want war; nobody in the world wants war; but some of us want the things we can't have without war." [28]   Some observers feel very strongly that this idea of people not wanting to fight, is erroneous.   H. L. Mencken, for example, writing in *Liberty,* says:

War, to the typical young fellow, is a colossal release.   The problem of making a living in a stupid and unappreciative world departs from his shoulders.   He ceases to be a nonentity and becomes a public figure, cheered by his relatives, his friends, and the populace in general.   There is someone to clothe him, and someone to tell him what to do.   He has a gun in his hands and feels like a man.   His country needs him and tells him so with many a slap on the back, though in a little while it may forget him.   No more lordly life is imaginable.   It combines all of the advantages of a sure income, good and racy company, and a job full of thrills.   The soldier stands proudly above all the ordinary laws.   Even the laws of economics are repealed for him. . . .

All the rules are suddenly suspended . . . every girl has two beaus, and every boy has three girls.   The old fellows make speeches, hunt spies, try to get their share of the easy money. . . .[29]

Discounting the fact that Mencken is exaggerating for the sake of literary effect, we must give heed to the truth that there are satisfactions gained in wartime from group loyalty, freedom from ordinary taboos, release of aggressive tensions, and the like.   These appeals are overlooked by persons who are inclined to think that man would be peaceful if the warmongers would only leave him alone.   Any adequate investigation of the psychological factors involved in war must give due consideration to the psychological possibility that human beings, in some respects, like war.

We must remember that man is not entirely a rational being and that his war-making may be the consequence of motives of which he is unaware.   The psychiatrists tell us that there is much evidence to indicate that our animal nature still persists underneath the civilized veneer, that there are aggressive tendencies which develop and

[28] P. 783.   Harcourt, Brace and Company.
[29] H. L. Mencken: "Peace—When Human Nature Changes."   *Liberty,* December 26, 1936.   Condensed in *Reader's Digest,* June, 1937.

reappear as a result of frustration, whether the frustration concerns "id-desires" for food, shelter, love, and security, or highly elaborated idealistic superimposed "super-ego desires." Paraphrasing this description one might say that aggressiveness follows the frustration of the simple animal desires or the frustration of our moral ideals. In any case, psychologists would agree that there is a great deal of aggressiveness in human beings, which finds a satisfying release in war.

Psychiatrists generally are of the opinion that war satisfies certain human cravings which are likely to emanate from the Unconscious. Freud insisted that wars result from man's innate destructiveness. Human aggression, however, frequently finds sublimated outlets, according to Alexander, who suggests that, instead of wasting our time seeking the causes of war, we might spend our time more profitably by considering under what conditions peace is possible. There are two important conditions for peace as he sees the situation: first, human beings must be united in one large, well integrated social organization; second, there must be a technique

"See, Men Are Superior Because They Have the Power to Reason." (Courtesy, Carl Rose and the Boston *Herald*.)

for settling conflicting interests. In the meantime, there will be a need for coercion until the peoples of the various nations have come to realize that cooperation is their common concern.[30]

Psychiatrists meeting at The Hague in 1935 considered as one of their chief topics for discussion the question as to why there is a seeming contradiction between the conscious individual aversion to war and the collective preparedness to wage war. They agreed that there are unconscious factors impelling people to war, factors that operate without any effective inhibitions because they are ordinarily ignored when individuals think about war. The behavior, the feelings, and the thoughts of an individual as an individual are quite different from

[30] See F. Alexander: "The Psychiatric Aspects of War and Peace." *American Journal of Sociology*, 1941, 46, 504-520.

those of the same person as a part of a collective whole. The psychiatrists endorsed the view that civilized twentieth-century man still possesses strong, fierce, and destructive drives which have not been sublimated, or only partly so, and which break loose as soon as the community to which he belongs feels itself threatened by danger; the unconscious desire to give rein to the primitive impulses, not only without punishment but even with reward, furthers, in a great measure, the preparedness for war.

We psychiatrists declare that our science is sufficiently advanced for us to distinguish between real, pretended, and unconscious motives, even in statesmen. The desire to disguise national militarism by continual talk about peace will not protect political leaders from the judgment of history. . . . International organization is now sufficiently advanced to enable statesmen to prevent war by concerted action. Protestation of peace and the desire for peace, however sincere, do not guarantee the self-denying spirit necessary for the maintenance of peace, even at the cost of national sacrifice. . . .[31]

The main point for our consideration is the hypothesis that man is more warlike than he is inclined to admit even to himself. Certainly it is true that human beings have devoted themselves far more to developing institutions for the prosecution of war than they have to establishing institutions for the insurance of peace.

Psychiatrists have learned by experience that violence provokes counter-violence, as shown by the fact that whereas patients treated gently react with self-restraint, patients subjected to brutal handling react with unrestrained anger. Chains and armaments are symbols of violence and as such they stir up animosity and rebellion. Strecker points out that the history of psychiatry has demonstrated the futility of violent treatment, even when it is politely camouflaged as "restraint." This, he says, is an "extremely important lesson which psychiatry has learned—a lesson with social and cultural implications."[32] Strecker's contention is confirmed by other observers who are convinced by the evidence that we cannot get peace by unpeaceful means, that we cannot get democracy by undemocratic means. Students of the international situation note that we all share the ideals of peace and justice. If we ask ourselves why we don't attain these desirable ends, we may find the answer in our choice of the wrong methods. Most wars—from the time of the Romans—have been fought in the interests of peace. If psychiatric experience is a valid criterion, we

---

[31] Statement quoted by the New York *Times*, October 20, 1935.
[32] E. A. Strecker: *Beyond the Clinical Frontiers*, p. 154. 1940.

can be fairly certain that peace will not be attained by resort to methods of violence. Even while people are engaged in fighting they turn their thoughts to the peace they are fighting for, unconvinced by history's abundant evidence that war is almost invariably, if not inevitably, followed by frustration, insecurity, aggression, and persecution, culminating eventually in another war for peace. It is sad but true that nations are always not yet convinced of the futility of fighting wars to end wars.

We shall achieve peace only when we have learned enough about ourselves to understand the causes of war and the ways of circumventing war. Ignorance on these problems is expensive. The popular explanation for war is to attribute it to an instinct of pugnacity or a "war instinct." In 1932, Fletcher asked members of the American Psychological Association to answer the following question: "Do you, as a psychologist, hold that there are present in human nature ineradicable instinctive factors that make war between nations inevitable?" Of the 378 members who replied, 91.6 per cent answered "No," 2.6 per cent answered "Yes," and 5.8 per cent recorded answers which could not be classified.[33] Obviously, psychologists no longer resort to a war instinct to explain why we keep on having wars. The trend among psychologists who deal with the problem of war is toward the explanation of conflict in terms of habits and institutions which are man-made rather than in terms of hereditary endowment.

The primary cause of war, according to this modern view, lies, as we have already observed, in the type of nationalism which is fostered by education. Nationalistic bias is often instilled in history courses. Writers of history textbooks frequently distort the facts because of their nationalistic bias, as Walworth shows in his book, *School Histories at War* (1938). He mentions the advertisement of a widely used school history which sets up five tests of merit in a textbook, without naming accuracy as one of them. He also cites the prospectus of an American Legion history text published just after World War I, which promised to speak the truth but assured the reader that it would "tell the truth optimistically." [34] English history books, treating the American Revolution, stated that George III might have been inept but that his policies were just; Americans were pictured as law-breaking tax dodgers who were so uncooperative as to refuse to pay part of the cost of maintaining army protection against the Indians. One-half of

[33] See J. M. Fletcher: "The Verdict of Psychologists on War Instincts." *Scientific Monthly*, August, 1932.
[34] Quoted by A. Walworth: *School Histories at War*, p. xix. 1938.

the English texts do not mention the rout of the Hessians at Trenton, an event that is featured in American texts. One striking statement in an American version of the Revolution is Muzzey's comment that the defeat at Bunker Hill was "a moral victory" for the Americans.[35] Walworth's study is concerned with the present influence of secondary school histories on public opinion. In this connection it is important to note that history courses play a significant role in attitude-formation, for such courses are taught from the first grade to the last; more pupils take history in the elementary school than in high school, and more pupils in high school than in college.

Bessie L. Pierce published the results of an extensive investigation of history books in *Public Opinion and the Teaching of History* (F. S. Crofts and Co., 1926). In this book she stated:

Since the World War [I], an ardent patriotism has swept the country, resulting in a widespread investigation of the teaching and writing of history. Sponsored by various groups, the movement has gained considerable momentum, until history teaching and history textbooks are in danger of being an expression of certain religious, racial, or other partisan opinions. These groups hold, in common, that American histories, as now written, neglect heroic characters in American history, especially in the Revolutionary War, and that they are distorted by a pro-British bias. Propaganda, indeed, makes strange bed-fellows. In this new praetorian guard of the temple of American patriotism are found the Hearst newspapers, an element of the Knights of Columbus and of the Irish-Americans, the German-Americans and finally patriotic societies of this country.[36]

There is a close psychological connection between nationalism and war. It is safe to assume, therefore, that we shall have wars as long as any considerable number of educators continue to encourage a jingoistic nationalism. Montagu sums up the case very well:

Man has reached his present supremacy of reason through the inhibitive and integrative powers of his mind, the ability to reject and suppress what he considers to be undesirable, the ability to *control*. Human society depends upon the maintenance of the ability of the mind to control, not so much the brute in man—for there is really little that is brutal in him that is not forced upon him—but those elements which under miseducation are capable of making a brute of him. All that is fine, noble, beautiful, and desirable in our civilization has been achieved by the supercession of mind over Nature, and much of this has been achieved through the resolute determination of indi-

[35] *Ibid.*, p. 13.   [36] P. 206.

vidual minds not so much to conquer and to vanquish what is customarily called "Nature," red in tooth and claw, but to enlist the aid of "Nature" in the service of man, and to control it effectively. All that is so ugly and inhuman and so destructive in our civilization is due to the activities of those who are anxious to exploit their fellow men to their own advantage and who use measures of control only towards this end. To them war is a profitable activity, for it increases their fortunes and thus their power. It is individuals of this order, in all countries, and from the earliest historical times, who make wars, not Nature: "The fault, dear Brutus, lies not in our stars, but in ourselves." . . .

Men, it seems, only fight when and if they want to; there is nothing within their native structure, no *primum mobile*, no innate prejudice, save for such prejudices as have been cultivated in them by education, that originally forces them to fight. . . .

The tradition of thought which renders possible such glib talk of war and its supposed natural causes . . . represents the bequest to us from the remote past of obsolete modes of thought which are conspicuous for their profound irrationality. . . . At present this tradition of thought constitutes the sole constrictive force operating upon the mind of man as well as the main impediment in the way of its rational functioning, coercing the good in him towards evil and, in short, representing a tyranny of the strongest and subtlest power. If man is to be saved from himself before it is too late this tyranny must be broken, and this can only be achieved by the unequivocal action that must follow upon the reasoned dissolution of such errors of belief and thought as form so great a part of our traditional social heritage today.[37]

B. Peace

It is foolish for people to say dogmatically, "There is no use trying to promote peace because history proves wars are inevitable." The fact of the matter is we have never tried seriously, on any extensive scale, to educate for peace. "If we are to have peace on earth, men must prepare for peace and must think peace, have peace in their hearts. Today those who shout for bigger armaments are called practical men; those who work for peace are called visionaries."

With things as they are one is forced to admit that it is easier to prepare men for war than it is to prepare them for peace. We all say that we want peace but we must confess that war is far more exciting. Peace is not so easily dramatized. Zinsser, speaking in the third person of his own experiences in World War I, made this significant observation:

[37] M. F. Ashley Montagu: "The Nature of War and the Myth of Nature." *Scientific Monthly*, April, 1942.

He did bring back a profound faith in these infantrymen, and often wondered why some peacetime formula could not be found to bring out the magnificent latent traits of courage, patience, and cooperative enthusiasm which the circumstances of war and danger appear to call forth in individuals who, in times of peace, are second-rate, or worse. What a nation they would make. What a triumphant democracy, if this secret could be discovered.[38]

Children are particularly susceptible to militaristic influences, perhaps as a result of the training to which most adults have been subjected and which they pass along to their own young ones. Children get a thrill out of playing with guns, they love bands and parades, they enjoy holidays commemorating war heroes. A survey of war and peace ideas among children was made by Case and Limbert of Teachers College, Columbia, in 1932. Nearly four hundred students ranging in age from ten to fifteen years, were tested. In the light of our traditional culture it is not surprising to learn that 71 per cent declared every park should have a cannon or some other military symbol to remind people of the heroes of the past. The ignorance of some of these youngsters concerning peace was astounding: a third of them thought that the Kellogg Peace Pact was "a company that makes breakfast food"; over two-thirds thought that the United States was a member of the League of Nations.[39] Someone commenting on the results said sadly: "The replies to the questions put by the investigators are most disheartening to the lovers of peace, for it appears that the militarists and superpatriots still have the admiration and confidence of the children and adolescents."

An education for peace would mean revolutionizing our current practices in school and in society. The extent of the change required for such a transition can be appreciated by studying the type of textbook that Rugg prepared for the secondary schools. His conception of history is radically different from that which dominated the school textbook of the past generation. We have already mentioned Rugg's books and the "warm reception" they received in many quarters from people who found his type of history distasteful in its unmilitaristic treatment of our national past. Rugg's aim was to banish overemphasis on war from the school books by placing the emphasis on "an eco-

[38] H. Zinsser: *As I Remember Him,* p. 242. Little, Brown and Company and the Atlantic Monthly Press, 1940.
[39] Data from a test, "Around the World," by A. T. Case and P. M. Limbert. Series of Character and Personality Tests, published by the Association Press, 347 Madison Ave., New York City.

nomic and industrial interpretation of the world in place of the age-
old story of strife and bloodshed."

When this program first got under way, Wayne Parrish described the
experiment in these words for his New York *Herald Tribune* readers:

Scrapping the separate subjects of history, civics, geography, economics, and
sociology, Dr. Rugg has combined them all into a new course, which he calls
"Social Science," in which all the elementary grades and high-school children
will be provided with an economic, rather than political, interpretation of the
world's history.   He has been encouraged and aided financially by Teachers
College, which supplied him with a laboratory and research facilities with
which to work.

Newspaper headlines, newspaper style, cartoons, and graphs have been
used freely and frequently.   The texts have been so "jazzed" up by Dr. Rugg
that no old schoolmaster would recognize them.   Mechanical and industrial
conquests are told as "fairy-tales," with emphasis on a literary style found
mostly in fiction books.

The rise and fall of kings and empires are often told in lines and sentences.
The World War receives 1,700 words.   The assassination of President Abraham Lincoln is told in thirty-eight words.   The Civil War, given chapters in
every text today, is presented in 2,000 words in these revised texts.   Mechanical and industrial conquests are told in chapters, with whole books being devoted to social and ethical problems which Dr. Rugg says have never before
appeared in schoolbooks. . . .

An example of how this educational experiment works is found in the
treatment of the Civil War, which Dr. Rugg has mentioned in the abstract in a
small section of the first volume of his "America's March Toward Democracy."
. . .   A paragraph of what the children will read about the Civil War is typical
of the whole treatment:

"In the excitement of the moment much of the horror that civil war must
mean was not realized.   The first few battles, however, shocked people into
the knowledge that it was not a war to be quickly or easily won.   Indeed, it
was to last four long years.   Seven hundred thousand men lost their lives in
its battles.   In order to pay the expenses of war, the Government had to
borrow enormous sums of money, which it could not repay for many years.
When the war was ended the South was a ruined land; her plantations deserted, many of her cities burned; her commerce completely destroyed.   The
Civil War was one of the most terrible wars that the world had yet known."

Perhaps the most pertinent and the most dramatic example of Dr. Rugg's
wholesale revision is told in America's part in the World War, which is given
in the second volume of "America's March Toward Democracy."   On page
105 is the statement: "On April 6 war with Germany was declared."   On page
110, five pages later, is the sentence: "On November 11, 1918, peace between
the warring countries finally came."

The whole story of the World War is told in about 1,700 words, again with scarcely any mention of a battle, and then only in a perfunctory manner. War is mentioned in the abstract. A few paragraphs concerning the World War are:

"A war in the modern world is no comic-opera affair. A war engaged in by industrial nations is vast and complicated. It involves industry of all kinds, it depends upon fleets of ships and thousands of miles of railroad.

"Now in order to transport millions of men to the front, in order to feed and clothe them and supply them with ammunition, in order to feed and clothe the home population, in order to keep industries going and railroads running, in order to raise money to do all the other things, some one must control all these people, all these armies, all these industries, all these means of transportation. Who or what is big enough to do this job? Only the Government. Therefore, when the United States Government found itself in the greatest war in history, it had to take on itself greater powers than it had ever before assumed.

"The Government had to persuade 100,000,000 people to enter the war, it had to build ships, it had to run railways, it had to manage industry, it had to feed armies, it had to send goods to the Allies and keep some at home for the home population, and it had to raise huge sums of money." . . .

This is what Dr. Rugg gives the school children in place of descriptions of the battles of the Marne, Château-Thierry, the Hindenburg Line, and the like. The story of the World War is essentially one of how the Government was forced to enter all branches of activity, the tremendous costs, and loss of life.

Dr. Rugg considers his move to be the first attempt ever made to "condition" the minds of school children of a whole nation to tolerance, peace, and understanding of the world's peoples and problems. . . .

Another effort in this direction which should be mentioned is a book entitled *Educating for Peace* (1940) which was edited by Jacobs and De Boer. This volume, consisting of materials on the relation of education to peace, is a report of a committee on international relations of the National Council of Teachers of English. The committee, in preparing this report, aimed to avoid the romantic, rhapsodic laudation of peace, and to challenge the assumption, too common in the interpretation of both history and literature, that war is a normal instrument of human progress and the finest expression of heroic qualities.

Popular opinion in favor of peace can be created effectively through the medium of carefully planned propaganda—preferably in the form of pictures which any ordinary person can understand. Posters were used very effectively in arousing the American citizens to an enthusiasm for a war against the Kaiser's Germany. Some of these posters were extremely stirring in their appeal. Similar pictorial propa-

The Orange Memorial.   (Courtesy, Jack Frost.)

ganda was used by World Peaceways, portraying in a graphic form the horrors and the futility of war.

Public statues in the past have been designed to commemorate war. An innovation is the idea of symbolizing peace, as expressed in a thoughtful memorial erected in Orange, Mass.[40]

[40] "In 1934 the town of Orange unveiled this memorial to its citizens who served in World War I. The statue attracted national attention as it was a new way of representing a community's appreciation to its veterans.

Preparation for peace, as we have said, must begin with the education of the child.

It is comparatively easy to make young people realize the horrors of war . . . it is much harder to make them see that the best and only sure way . . . of keeping American boys out of war . . . is to lend our efforts to keeping the French, German, English and Italian boys out of war as well. . . . To underrate the difficulty of that task, to make our education the vehicle of superficial propaganda, to preach nostrums even with the best of intentions in the sacred name of peace, is not merely to fail of our object, but also to do harm to the cause. . . .

The most popular short cut in this country (as in almost every other) is to teach our school children that we are the most peace-loving nation on earth, that all our wars have been uniformly righteous and successful, that all the nations opposing us were wicked or mad, that, if the rest of the world would follow our example, the millennium would dawn. . . .

We must end anarchy if we are to have peace. Disputes between nations will continue to arise and will continue to be settled by war until the law-abiding nations of the world are ready to stand together not merely to resist aggression, but also to administer justice. . . .

The problem of peace . . . is the problem of importing into the relations between the nations the same concepts of law and order and reasonableness which are necessary to ensure domestic peace.

Life in the world today is a continual lesson in the value of peace, and the desire for peace is well nigh universal. What is needed is a clearer realization of the means we must use to obtain it. . . .[41]

The Psychologists' Manifesto, endorsed by numerous psychologists in 1944, is an excellent formulation of the principles which must be put into practice if peace is to be won. I quote the document in full:

"It has been aptly called a war memorial dedicated to peace. The Rev. Wallace G. Fiske, pastor of the Orange Universalist Church, was chairman of the committee for the memorial, and he made sketches himself to convey the idea the committee wished displayed.

"The committee demanded that the work in no way glorify the idea of arms and military equipment for the younger generation, feeling that these almost stereotyped supplements to war memorials only served as advertisements for munitions makers.

"The sculptor, Joseph P. Pollia of New York, considered it one of the best of his creations. The soldier is describing the futility of war to the listening child whose clenched fist signifies a vow that he will never permit another—that 'It Shall Not Be Again.'" Boston *Herald*, May 28, 1937.

[41] Speech delivered by Frank Aydelotte before the Public Education Association in 1937.

HUMAN NATURE AND THE PEACE

A STATEMENT BY PSYCHOLOGISTS

Humanity's demand for lasting peace leads us as students of human nature to assert ten pertinent and basic principles which should be considered in planning the peace. Neglect of them may breed new wars, no matter how well-intentioned our political leaders may be.

1. *War can be avoided: War is not born in men; it is built into men.* No race, nation, or social group is inevitably warlike. The frustrations and conflicting interests which lie at the root of aggressive wars can be reduced and re-directed by social engineering. Men can realize their ambitions within the framework of human cooperation and can direct their aggressions against those natural obstacles that thwart them in the attainment of their goals.

2. *In planning for permanent peace, the coming generation should be the primary focus of attention.* Children are plastic; they will readily accept symbols of unity and an international way of thinking in which imperialism, prejudice, insecurity, and ignorance are minimized. In appealing to older people, chief stress should be laid upon economic, political, and educational plans that are appropriate to a new generation, for older people, as a rule, desire above all else, better conditions and opportunities for their children.

3. *Racial, national, and group hatreds can, to a considerable degree, be controlled.* Through education and experience people can learn that their prejudiced ideas about the English, the Russians, the Japanese, Catholics, Jews, Negroes, are misleading or altogether false. They can learn that members of one racial, national, or cultural group are basically similar to those of other groups, and have similar problems, hopes, aspirations, and needs. Prejudice is a matter of attitudes, and attitudes are to a considerable extent a matter of training and information.

4. *Condescension toward "inferior" groups destroys our chance for a lasting peace.* The white man must be freed of his concept of the "white man's burden." The English-speaking peoples are only a tenth of the world's population; those of white skin only a third. The great dark-skinned populations of Asia and Africa, which are already moving toward a greater independence in their own affairs, hold the ultimate key to a stable peace. The time has come for a more equal participation of all branches of the human family in a plan for collective security.

5. *Liberated and enemy peoples must participate in planning their own destiny.* Complete outside authority imposed on liberated and enemy peoples without any participation by them will not be accepted and will lead only to further disruptions of the peace. The common people of all countries must not only feel that their political and economic future holds genuine hope for themselves and for their children, but must also feel that they themselves have the responsibility for its achievement.

6. *The confusion of defeated people will call for clarity and consistency in*

the application of rewards and punishments.   Reconstruction will not be possible so long as the German and Japanese people are confused as to their status. A clear-cut and easily understood definition of war-guilt is essential.   Consistent severity toward those who are judged guilty, and consistent official friendliness toward democratic elements, is a necessary policy.

7. *If properly administered, relief and rehabilitation can lead to self-reliance and cooperation; if improperly, to resentment and hatred.*   Unless liberated people (and enemy people) are given an opportunity to work in a self-respecting manner for the food and relief they receive, they are likely to harbor bitterness and resentment, since our bounty will be regarded by them as unearned charity, dollar imperialism, or bribery.   No people can long tolerate such injuries to self-respect.

8. *The root-desires of the common people of all lands are the safest guide to framing a peace.*   Disrespect for the common man is characteristic of fascism and of all forms of tyranny.   The man in the street does not claim to understand the complexities of economics and politics, but he is clear as to the general directions in which he wishes to progress.   His will can be studied (by adaptations of the public opinion poll).   His expressed aspirations should even now be a major guide to policy.

9. *The trend of human relationships is toward ever wider units of collective security.*   From the caveman to the twentieth century, human beings have formed larger and larger working and living groups.   Families merged into clans, clans into states, and states into nations.   The United States are not 48 threats to each other's safety; they work together.   At the present moment the majority of our people regard the time as ripe for regional and world organization, and believe that the initiative should be taken by the United States of America.

10. *Commitments now may prevent postwar apathy and reaction.*   Unless binding commitments are made and initial steps taken now, people may have a tendency after the war to turn away from international problems and to become preoccupied once again with narrower interests.   This regression to a new postwar provincialism would breed the conditions for a new world war. Now is the time to prevent this backward step, and to assert through binding action that increased unity among the people of the world is the goal we intend to attain.

C. INTERNATIONALISM

The most important social problem of our time is the problem of preserving what is worth while in nationalism and at the same time transcending patriotism to achieve a loyalty that embraces other nationalities.   Patriotism in the past has too often involved the rejection of the ideal of an inclusive humanitarianism.   The patriot characteristically feels impelled to glorify his own people at the expense of others.   In our more rational moments we may recognize the illogical basis of our chauvinism. That we are wholly good and others wholly bad, is never true.

One of our favorite myths is the belief in our own inventive supremacy. It is pleasant for us to believe that most of the great inventions have been made by clever Yankees. For example, we accept the myth that Robert Fulton invented the steamboat. Actually, about thirty steamers, more or less successful, had been built before his *Clermont* plowed the Hudson in 1807. William Symington had been churning the water with a paddle-wheel boat in England in 1787, and his *Charlotte Dundas* had been a notable success in 1802. Similarly, if you trace the automobile to its origin, you will probably be surprised to learn that very little of it turns out to be American. The streamlining of the airplane was done largely in Europe. If you tell a German that Alexander Graham Bell invented the telephone, he will inform you that Philip Reis had sent music over a wire in 1861—fifteen years before Bell. We think of Edison as the inventor of the electric incandescent lamp; an Englishman named Joseph Swan came out simultaneously with a lamp whose filament was considered by some authorities to be even better than Edison's.

Self-glorification is not an American monopoly. Every country cherishes the illusion of greatness. Try to tell a European that Samuel F. Morse invented the telegraph about 1837 and you will make astonishing discoveries in patriotism as well as in technological history. The Germans will say with reason that Von Sömmering was telegraphing electrically in 1809 and that Steinheil was applying the induction principle simultaneously with Morse. In England, schoolteachers inform the young that Cooke and Wheatstone invented in 1837 a needle telegraph which is so good that it has not yet been abandoned. . . .

As we review the procession of inventors who have made this the machine age, we forget nationalities, forget the childish patriotism that ascribes this or that achievement to our unique genius. These great mechanics who spring from a dozen soils seem like fellow craftsmen working successfully through centuries at the same problem. . . .[42]

Progress toward international understanding is blocked by a number of delusions which characterize nationalistic thinking among our own countrymen and among the citizens of other nations. Among these delusions we may list the following:

Our own nation is the most ardent lover of peace.
We are arming for defense only.

[42] W. Kaempffert: "Who Invented It?" *Reader's Digest*, December, 1936.

Our war is a righteous one.

What we want we cannot live without.

Others are responsible for our harsh treatment of them.

Our nation is an upright nation among knaves.

Such beliefs make nations bad neighbors. Enlarging the mind's span so that we can all live in a large world, working together in loyalty to a common cause, will take time, just as it took time for the German states to become a union, with each citizen fully conscious of the union's importance. We must learn to pay a price for world order just as individuals must forego certain things if the state commands them to make the sacrifice. Though we are becoming aware of a larger community, we are not yet eager to do the things required to bring about international amity: to keep promises, to respect territory, to refrain from war; to recognize that "nations, as personifications, have moral duties to one another." [43] The spirit of internationalism will be closer to realization when we apply the truth of the sentiment expressed on the statue of Alexander Hamilton in Chicago: "The established rules of morality and justice are applicable to nations as well as to individuals." We are a long way from embodying that ideal in our international behavior.

International understanding would be greatly facilitated if language barriers could be transcended by the adoption of a universal language. It is significant that the populations of the earth speak about 350 languages and sub-languages, to say nothing of the bewildering variety of scripts in which they are written. How can the peoples of the world reach a common sympathy when they can communicate with each other for the most part only through interpreters and translations? There are two serious impediments in the way of a universal language. First, there is no organization which would seriously venture to propose English, or any other tongue as "*the* world language." Second, in view of international rivalries there is little likelihood of all the nations agreeing to any such attempt at ending the present confusion of tongues. Each of the peoples has a literary inheritance bound up with its own language, and anything like consent to a separation of the two is psychologically inconceivable. It has been predicted that some day by the process of borrowing and interchange, at least several of the great languages will come to resemble each other so much as to suggest a merger of them as being desirable. Growing contacts may hasten such an amalgamation. Perhaps the

[43] Refer to the section on "Collective Immorality" in Chapter 5.

time may come when Esperanto or Basic English will find favor. In the meantime, our language barriers impede international understanding.

A common language, in itself, though, is not enough to ensure mutual understanding and harmonious relations, as we can witness in the prejudices and antagonisms that sometimes vitiate the contacts between Americans and Englishmen, despite the fact that we have fought side by side as allies in two World Wars. Anglo-American misunderstanding is attributed by Nicolson, British writer and diplomat, to certain *general* faults and to certain *particular* faults.

> It is a general, and wholly natural, fault for the individuals composing any community to identify themselves with that community and to regard other communities as "different" and therefore as in some sense opposed to themselves. It is a general, and again natural, fault for the ordinary man or woman to be distrustful of the unfamiliar, to note differences rather than similarities and to approach these differences in a mood of suspicion.[44]

In addition to these general barriers there exist certain particular barriers between the ordinary American citizen and the ordinary British subject, barriers one does not find, to the same degree at any rate, between the Englishman and the Norwegian or the American and the Frenchman. Why is there so much distrust in the relations between Americans and Englishmen? One explanation stems from what children learn in their study of history. "The average British boy or girl," Nicolson explains, "looks upon the American War of Independence as an unfortunate episode caused by Lord North's bungling; he has no idea that there was a second war in 1812." The average American's idea of our break from the Mother country is that it was analogous to the departure of a smart son who decides that he has endured enough abuse from his tyrannical parents and feels that it's time to leave home with no intention of keeping the old ties alive. Americans, Nicolson continues,

> are exposed, however, not merely to an anti-British bias but also to an anti-European bias, for a large number of Americans feel that their forbears left Europe because they did not like it. I have often been surprised on visits to the United States to realize how frequently the ordinary American looks upon "Europe" as some maleficent extension of "England." The more simple-minded American, loving his own great country passionately and desiring to

[44] H. Nicolson: "Anglo-American Misunderstanding." *American Scholar*, Vol. 12, No. 1, Winter, 1942-1943.

be left in undisturbed enjoyment of his own opportunities and standard of living, inclines to regard Europe as a distasteful arena of imperialist squabbles into which America is drawn against her will. He tends to suspect England of being some connecting membrane through which the poisons of Europe infect the great white soul of America. . . .

To these historical and political barriers a social barrier must be added. To the Britisher the average American seems likely at moments to identify, if only subconsciously, the Great Britain of today with the somewhat distorted picture of eighteenth-century England received at school. Americans do not realize that within the last two centuries we have changed from an aristocratic and agricultural community into a community that is mainly socialist and industrial in character. Their misunderstanding is increased by their occasional contacts with the visiting Englishmen—only the rich or highly cultivated Englishmen can afford to cross the Atlantic. Nor does the ordinary American always remember that the vast majority of our population is composed of working people who are as conscious of their political and social rights as he is. The misconceptions thereby occasioned are increased by the marked difference between the British and the American manner. Americans are likely to interpret our British reserve as being due to arrogance, whereas in almost every case it is due to our deplorable shyness. Conversely the English are likely to accuse the Americans of boastfulness when in fact they are merely ill at ease and desirous of making a good impression. If only our respective peoples could be convinced that each is acutely shy of the other (that the Englishman cowers in shyness as a tortoise in his shell and that the American seeks to reassure himself by talking a little louder than he would at home) much of this particular barrier would disappear. . . .

Americans tend sometimes to adopt toward us a "holier than thou" attitude that we find wounding and misplaced. We do not see that intrinsically there is very much difference between your "manifest destiny" and our "imperialism" nor are we convinced that the extension of your frontier, the incorporation of Texas, or the acquisition of the Panama Canal were achieved by methods wholly different from those giving us our colonial Empire. Since the record of both nations is murky in spots we rather resent the assumption that your questionable deeds should be forgotten while ours should be held against us all of the time. Each of us has his good moments and if we are to like each other better it is best to concentrate on them.

Popular good will must be created if Americans and Englishmen— or any other peoples—are to get along without undue friction. Nicolson believes there is much good will in Great Britain toward America, a lesser proportion of good will in the United States toward Great Britain. Many prejudices, misconceptions, and assumptions will have to be removed by a process of education. The adoption of a socialist regime, with the nationalization of coal mines, banks, railroads and many other enterprises, will probably make it more difficult for Americans, with their capitalistic bias, to understand their British Allies. The appeal of His Majesty's Government for American capital to finance an experiment in socialism in England is evidence that the English still have much to learn about the psychological attitudes and reactions of Uncle Sam.

Steps can be taken to build up a better understanding between Englishmen and Americans. Personal contacts of Americans and English people during World War II have increased mutual understanding, on the whole. English children evacuated to America returned to their native country with a new appreciation for the people who took care of them in a time of need, and no doubt their parents will learn through their children more about American ways. American servicemen quartered in England got acquainted with many of the local inhabitants. Some friction was bound to occur, since Americans had more money to spend and more aggressiveness in dating the girls. The English voiced their complaint in the statement that "the Yanks were overpaid, overdressed, oversexed, and over here." Despite the hardships resulting from the American "occupation," mutual understanding between the Allies was undoubtedly facilitated. Some observers have asserted that the English vote for the Socialist program in 1945 was due, in part, to the conviction that something should be done to bring to the English people the abundant life so obviously manifest in the affluence of their American visitors.

It is encouraging to observe the growth of organizations devoted to the promotion of international amity. This trend holds some promise for the future. Among the organizations promoting internationalism we may mention the World Council of Churches, the Carnegie Endowment for International Peace, the American Friends Service Committee, the World Peace Foundation, the World-Wide Broadcasting Foundation, the Foreign Policy Association, the Williamstown Institutes, American Youth for a Free World, the International Bureau of Education, the Institute of Intellectual Relations, the Geneva School of International Studies, the Inter-American Educational Foundation, the United Nations Educational, Scientific and Cultural Organization, the World Federation of Trade Unions, and various Foreign Missions societies.

The Rockefeller Foundation must certainly be accorded front rank among the organizations fostering internationalism. The scope of its benevolences has been world-wide, providing financial support for medical programs, educational programs, scientific research, in all parts of the globe, irrespective of race, creed, or color. A study of the Foundation's annual reports will afford abundant evidence that its funds are so dispersed as to assure dividends in well-being the world over. President Vincent, former head of the Foundation, stated the aim in these words: "The search for truth and its application to hu-

(Courtesy, George White and the Tampa *Morning Tribune*.)

man need is a vast, world-wide cooperative task which demands constant interchange of ideas and more intelligent teamwork among workers. Every country should seek entangling alliances in a league for scientific progress."

Throughout the first twenty-five years of its activities, the Foundation was guided by the objective written into its charter: "The well-being of mankind *throughout the world*." In reviewing the activities of the Foundation for 1937, President Fosdick stated some basic principles which were guiding the trustees in formulating their policies:

In accordance with this purpose the aim of the trustees has been to maintain the work of the Foundation on an international plane without consideration of flags or political doctrines or creeds or sects. Particularly in a program based on the advancement of knowledge it is imperative to disregard the geographical boundaries which arbitrarily and often unhappily divide the earth into a patchwork of senseless antagonisms. For in the last analysis knowledge cannot be nationalized. No successful embargoes can be maintained against the export or import of ideas. Whether new conceptions of atomic physics come from Copenhagen or from Cambridge, England; whether the cure for cancer is developed in New Haven or in Berlin; whether it is a Russian or an Italian or an American who takes the next step forward in mankind's struggle with virus diseases—we are all of us, under whatever flag, the joint beneficiaries of the intellectual property of the race. In all the clash of competing nationalisms there is here an underlying principle of unity: the single aim and language of science in the discovery of truth. It is this principle which challenges the twentieth century with the conception of civilization as a cooperative achievement and with the ideal of intellectual capital as an international possession. . . . Disease knows no frontiers and has never been a respecter of flags. In this field of public health, more clearly perhaps than any other phase of human effort, one sees the complete inadequacy and meaninglessness of the conception of the absolute sovereignty of the state.[45]

In reporting the Foundation activities for 1939, Fosdick cited an excellent example of what international cooperation can mean in the field of medicine:

The amazing development and application of sulfanilamide—that beneficial gift to mankind—has been the result of a collaboration in which flags and boundary lines have been non-existent. The first hint of it was discovered in Germany, oddly enough in connection with the commercial dye industry, and the drug was given the name prontosil. With this hint as a basis, in 1935 a German scientist—Dr. Gerhard Domagk—published the results of his experiments with mice under carefully controlled laboratory conditions, showing the extraordinary effect of prontosil on streptococcus. The Pasteur Institute in Paris then picked the matter up, and subjecting prontosil to organic analysis discovered that its activity was localized in one distinctive part of its molecular structure. This potent factor in prontosil, separated from the

[45] R. B. Fosdick: *The Rockefeller Foundation: A Review for 1937.*

rest of the molecule, is what we now know as sulfanilamide. At this point Queen Charlotte's Hospital in London, with a grant from the Rockefeller Foundation, tried the drug on women suffering from streptococcal infection associated with puerperal or childbirth fever, immediately reducing the death-rate from such infections by 25 per cent. The Johns Hopkins School of Medicine was the next institution to carry forward the experiments, and in the last three years research on this drug has been developed, with brilliant results, in laboratories and hospitals on both sides of the Atlantic.

Achievement in science, more often than not, is the result of the sustained thinking of many minds in many countries driving toward a common goal. The creative spirit of man cannot successfully be localized or nationalized. Ideas are starved when they are fenced in behind frontiers. The fundamental unity of modern civilization is the unity of its intellectual life. . . .[46]

One sequel to this story should be related. Professor Domagk was awarded the Nobel prize for physiology and medicine in November, 1939, in recognition of his discovery of prontosil, but as a citizen of the Reich, he could not accept it. "Simultaneously came the announcement that sulfanilamide compounds would be administered to all wounded British soldiers to reduce the death rate from infection. Thus the wonder-drugs cut across the barriers between nations, to work their 'sulfa-miracles' in war as in peace." [47]

Under the significant title, "The Search for Unity," Fosdick discussed the internationalism of science, particularly medical science, in his report for 1941:

If we are to have a durable peace after the war, if out of the wreckage of the present a new kind of cooperative life is to be built on a global scale, the part that science and advancing knowledge will play must not be overlooked. For although wars and economic rivalries may for longer or shorter periods isolate nations and split them up into separate units, the process is never complete because the intellectual life of the world, as far as science and learning are concerned, is definitely internationalized, and whether we wish it or not an indelible pattern of unity has been woven into the society of mankind.

There is not an area of activity in which this cannot be illustrated. An American soldier wounded on a battlefield in the Far East owes his life to the Japanese scientist, Kitasato, who isolated the bacillus of tetanus. A Russian soldier saved by a blood transfusion is indebted to Landsteiner, an Austrian. A German soldier is shielded from typhoid fever with the help of a Russian, Metchnikoff. A Dutch marine in the East Indies is protected from malaria

[46] R. B. Fosdick: *The Rockefeller Foundation: A Review for 1939.*
[47] L. M. Miller: "Sulfa-Miracles." *Hygeia,* September, 1940.

because of the experiments of an Italian, Grassi; while a British aviator in North Africa escapes death from surgical infection because a Frenchman, Pasteur, and a German, Koch, elaborated a new technique.

In peace as in war we are all of us the beneficiaries of contributions to knowledge made by every nation in the world. Our children are guarded from diphtheria by what a Japanese and a German did; they are protected from smallpox by an Englishman's work; they are saved from rabies because of a Frenchman; they are cured of pellagra through the researches of an Austrian. From birth to death they are surrounded by an invisible host—the spirits of men who never thought in terms of flags or boundary lines and who never served a lesser loyalty than the welfare of mankind. The best that every individual or group has produced anywhere in the world has always been available to serve the race of men, regardless of nation or color.[48]

If everybody could acquire the attitude common to the research scientist in medicine and the practitioner of medicine, namely that nationality is a matter of small importance, the problems of internationalism would be more readily solved.

Cooperation of scientists the world over is going to be an important means of cementing friendly relations among the various peoples. The American Association for the Advancement of Science expressed this hope in a resolution passed in 1943, which included these statements:

In devotion to the search for knowledge and wisdom scientists are not separated from one another by national boundaries. What they seek may be discovered in any land; their findings are placed in the service of all.[49]

The meeting of the International Scientific Congress in Russia in 1945 was a dramatic demonstration of the interdependence and the international solidarity of scientific workers. Harlow Shapley, chairman of the American delegation, described the Congress in these words:

It was a conclave for good will, closer collaboration among the world men of science, and greater cultural intercourse in international relations.[50]

When we stop to think of it—and we seldom do—the blessings of science, of art and of music are shared by peoples everywhere, regardless of nationalistic boundaries. Wagnerian operas belong to the

[48] R. B. Fosdick: *The Rockefeller Foundation: A Review for 1941.*
[49] *A. A. A. S. Bulletin,* June, 1943.
[50] Boston *Sunday Herald,* July 15, 1945.

world and to the ages, not to Germany alone. "Everything is internationalized but nations," says Anne O'Hare McCormick, eminent observer of the state of the world. As she remarks, "It is necessary to travel far to get away from the movies, the music, the cocktails, the fashions, even the wisecracks of Broadway," for improved means of communication have bound the whole world together.

Yet, despite all the influences conducive to internationalism, there are still some very definite psychological obstacles to a happy understanding between the nations. Nationalism may be either conscious or unconscious; the latter type sets our attitudes without our being aware of their source. The unconscious nationalist is a dangerous person: "Seeing everything through his national spectacles, but not knowing that he carries them on his nose—or even denying that such is the case—he lives in the naïve belief that he sees things objectively 'as they are' and as they should be seen by 'every reasonable person.' To him the 'others,' those who see things in a fundamentally different way, are not, as for the conscious nationalist, un-English, un-German, un-American, but simply 'unhuman'; or at least, if he is very 'tolerant,' unreasonable." [51] The following obstacles are listed by Ichheiser:

1. *Ethnocentrism.*

Every nation has a tendency to regard its own habits, its own ways of thought and of living, its own values and its institutions, and its own points of view, not only as its own but also as a kind of norm which unconsciously underlies the judgment of everything "foreign." The "other," the "foreign," is perhaps not necessarily "evil," but it is always considered at least as a kind of "deviation," a kind of "distortion" of the "right." . . .

The average Frenchman, Englishman, German, American, is ignorant of the fact that he holds certain opinions only because he is a Frenchman, Englishman, German, American, only because he has grown up in a certain social environment. He lives in the belief that he holds these opinions because they are "good" and "right." . . .

2. *Rationalization.*

We are unwilling to admit to ourselves our bad qualities. We try to hide them not only from the others but also from ourselves. . . . Instead of the real motives which actually underlie our behavior, we invent fictitious motives to justify our action. It is not because we are all sometimes dishonest with ourselves but because we pretend that we are always quite honest, that realistic discussion and settlement of human relationships become so complicated.

[51] G. Ichheiser: "Some Psychological Obstacles to an Understanding between the Nations." *Journal of Abnormal and Social Psychology,* 1941, 36, 428-432.

Even among devils some kind of social order would be possible on the basis of mutual self-interest; the formation of a social order in a society of devils who are pretending to be angels, on the other hand, is almost completely impossible. . . .

Yet the fact that the real basis of the conflicts is not admitted, but rather kept hidden, makes the complications . . . more difficult . . . and their solution no easier. . . .

It is much easier to see through the illusions and the prejudices of others than our own . . . every nation sees through the rationalizations of other nations without difficulty and indeed with a sense of superiority; but every nation is completely blind as far as its own collective illusions and prejudices are concerned. . . .

3. Stereotypy.

Members of every nation have in their consciousness a more or less vague image of the other nations. Subject to various changes, this image is always stereotyped, simplified, and distorted. For such a conception is only partly . . . the product of factual, rational experience. . . . To the larger extent it is the product of irrational forces . . . short term propaganda, history taught from the nationalistic point of view, the illusion caused by distance . . . all . . . help to produce a distortion of the conceptions which nations have of one another. Members of most nations would be amazed if they knew how other nations regard them.[52]

The chief obstacle is still the enthronement of patriotism as an absolute ideal. Under the statue of Edith Cavell were carved these words:

Edith Cavell—Brussels—Dawn, October 12, 1915

Patriotism is not enough. I must have no hatred or bitterness for anyone.

This sentiment is even more applicable to the international situation today than it was in 1915. There is still a greater need to rise above patriotism to a larger loyalty, just as in the past people have risen above family loyalty to a love of nation. Parochialism and provincialism are anachronistic in a world where big maps are called for. Having transcended warfare between towns, we can look back with amusement on the situation that developed many years ago when war was about to break out between the towns of Norwalk and Stamford, Connecticut. It seems ridiculous to us that two communities should engage in battle, but it did not seem ridiculous to those two towns. Their young men were quite ready to lay down their lives for their

[52] Ibid.

respective localities. Eventually, the day may come when warfare between nations will seem just as ridiculous. Before that day arrives we must evolve from local partisanship to some form of federalism.

Light on this development may be gathered by citing an incident from our own history here in America. It was only after a prolonged struggle that the thirteen colonies agreed to give up some of their sovereignty in the interests of a federal union. Each colony hesitated to sacrifice its own rights. When the convention gathered for the ratification of the Constitution, Alexander Hamilton had to overcome plenty of opposition before he could convince the stubborn colonists that federation would be a blessing to all parties. Our subsequent history has vindicated Hamilton's judgment.

In the larger sphere of international relations we must ultimately pass through a similar evolution, sacrificing some of the sovereign prerogatives of nationhood. We cannot have peace as long as each nation feels that it has a right to do as it pleases. Peace can only be assured when the nations surrender their freedom of action in some respects to international control. The idea of submitting international disputes to arbitration was embodied in Article XIX of the League of Nations Covenant. War as an instrument of national policy was renounced in the Pact of Paris.[53]

Hamilton Fish, a contender for nomination for the Presidency in 1940, announced as his platform: "Americanism versus Internationalism." This belief that internationalism means a complete renunciation of nationalism is a false limitation of alternatives. As we have said before, we can preserve the *values* of nationalism even while we move forward to a *practice* of internationalism.

Some new ideal must be born, if any of us are going to enjoy security in the future. America can assume a position of leadership in international affairs by developing a realistic foreign policy, something we have never had in the past, according to the editors of *Fortune:*

We have always been able to dodge behind what went by the name of international peace. That kind of peace was negative, based upon a balance of economic and military power; it was merely not-war. Nevertheless, in combination with the oceans, it served well enough to enable the United States to participate in trade without incurring any real political responsibility. . . .
There remains, finally, the possibility of leadership. If the United States should take this . . . course, it would have to participate in formulating and

[53] See J. T. Shotwell: *War as an Instrument of National Policy and Its Renunciation in the Pact of Paris.* 1929.

implementing an entirely new order of peace to replace the old one that has broken down. Moreover, the participation would involve something much more than a mere suggestion or peace plan. It would involve commitments toward peace, a definite implementation of the new order. To provide such leadership, the United States would have to take its place among the nations as a *force* for peace.

Now this is something that the American people have never been willing to do. . . .

Most peace has been negative—that is, not-war. But every so often a group of separate political units, discovering a community of interests, integrate themselves into a new area, called a nation; an area in which peace becomes the rule rather than the exception; an area of positive peace, in that, by the consolidation of resources, man power, traditions, and laws, the whole becomes greater than the sum of its parts. Most modern nations are compositions of this kind. . . .

Now the striking fact is that, with obvious setbacks and temporary reversals of trend, the size of these integrations has persistently increased. The task of integrating the little island of England once seemed insuperable; today, the U.S.S.R. is integrating one-seventh of the land area of the globe. The reason for this lies in the development of transportation, communication, and other technologies, which bear upon the problem in two ways. First, they make the integration possible by linking the political or financial or industrial centers together; and second, they make integration *desirable* by creating a community of interests where there was none before. In the days of the horse a community of interests was defined largely by natural barriers. If these happened to be mountains, as in Switzerland, the community might be very small. If they happened to be oceans, as in the United States, it might be very large. But however small or however large, the community of interests tended to expand under the pressure of technology. When New York was six weeks removed from London, no true community of interests existed between them, even though "relationships" might be friendly (i.e., negative peace). But today, when New York is closer to London than it used to be to Philadelphia, a community of interests, while it may not exist, is certainly not inconceivable.

As a means of integration for a modern community of interests, federal union has no equal. In federal union the autonomy of the constituent states is retained; only a limited portion of their powers is forfeited to a central government for the purposes of integration. . . .[54]

The Bretton Woods Conference, the Dumbarton Oaks Conference, and the San Francisco Conference were all indications that the United States intends to live up to its international responsibilities. The

[54] Editorial entitled "America's Choice for Peace," in *Fortune*, December, 1939. Condensed in the *Reader's Digest*, February, 1940.

signing of the United Nations Charter in 1945, ushering in the establishment of a World Security Organization, marked, it is to be hoped, the beginning of a new era in international relations. Various organizations were busy, meanwhile, arousing interest in a Federal Union of the World or some form of Federal World Government.

The task of building support for a world organization of some kind is essentially a matter of changing people's attitudes. Such a project is more apt to succeed if we understand the existent attitudes which are going to be modified. What is the nature of the evidence so far uncovered?

International attitudes, as Neumann has noted, tend to be specific. His study of the international attitudes of a large number of high-school students showed a pronounced *nationalism* concerning the superiority of the United States among other nations, but a strong *internationalism* concerning the obligations of the United States to the rest of the world.[55] This observation is confirmed by Goodwin Watson who found that good will is not a cause of world-mindedness, but is rather the result of thinking in certain ways about specific problems. Good will is not a general trait, for the same individual may look upon one people with favor, another people with hatred. Citing Symonds' study of attitudes among Honolulu children, which showed that as children progressed in school and information increased, attitudes remained constant, Watson suggests that education seems to reinforce attitudes already held. The amount of information seems to be less significant than the "proportionate emphasis within that information and the condition under which it was given." Watson reports that he discovered no significant relation between world-mindedness and intelligence; bright people may be more, or less, prejudiced than dull people.[56] These studies suggest that more effective techniques must be developed if we are going to educate the new generation to adopt attitudes favorable to a federated world. Much progress has been made in this general direction, for the polls show that the American people have largely abandoned isolationism in favor of participation in international security plans.[57] The advent of the atomic age will probably facilitate this trend still further.

[55] See G. Murphy and L. B. Murphy: *Experimental Social Psychology*, pp. 646-647. 1931.

[56] See G. B. Watson: "Does World-Mindedness Depend upon Good Will or Information? Upon Character or Intelligence?" *Religious Education*, 1926, 21, 188-194.

[57] See W. A. Lydgate: *What Our People Think*, Chapter 4, "Is Isolation Dead?" 1944.

Educating people to appreciate the desirability of federation will include the development of a new state of mind. Involved in this task are the following factors:

1. There must be assurance of the federation's power and willingness to protect the interests of the participating units.
2. There must be some assurance that the federation will be able to supply economic needs.
3. A sentiment of loyalty to the federation must be created.
4. This sentiment must be linked to existing loyalties.
5. Some form of psychological compensation must be worked out to make up for the loss of national military power and the abrogation of complete national autonomy.
6. People must be aroused to feel ashamed of the present low standard of morality governing international conduct.
7. Cohesion within a federation can be produced more readily in the face of a real or imaginary external threat.
8. Means should be provided for deflecting aggressiveness from human enemies to other ends.
9. These other ends may be framed in such a way as to serve as "moral equivalents" of war.[58]

Collective security and peace will be achieved only by a reorientation of our combative attitudes and the establishment of a sense of unity among the nations. Political, juridical, and military negotiations cannot succeed in bringing about unification unless they are accompanied by a thoroughgoing modification of our traditional system of values. Emotional reconstruction must precede any permanent social reconstruction.[59] Such a radical change in our habits and institutions will require time and sound psychological insight.

[58] See J. C. Flügel: "The Psychological Appeal of Federalism." *New Commonwealth Quarterly*, 1940, 6, 102-115. By permission of the London Institute of World Affairs.

[59] In his final report as Chief of Staff of the Army (February 15, 1948) General Dwight D. Eisenhower wrote:

"Were as much study and research devoted to the causes and prevention of war as have been to the causes and prevention of disease we should in time attain the same control over its eruption and spread as we have over the physical plagues.

"And were the study of war, its causes and prevention given the place in our education curricula that its importance to the individual citizen merits, we would have better hope of finding a practical basis for enduring peace."

INDEX

Abrams, R. H., 876
Academic degrees, prestige and, 240
Acclaim, public, 318-327
  books and, 318-321
  errors in predicting, 318-324
  fickleness of, 326-327
  plays and, 321-323
  sampling, 324-326
  songs and, 323
  speeches and, 323-324
Ackermann, A. S. E., 293
Action, leadership and, 272-273
  uniformity of, 254-257, 268
Actors, social consciousness and, 395
Adams, Evangeline, 602
Adams, G., 616fn.
Adams, W. A., 703fn.
Adler, Alfred, 782, 831
Adler, Felix, 792
Adler, Mortimer J., 135
Advertisers, exploitation of suggestion
  by, 245-247
Advertising, 166
  civilian morale and, 446-449
  relative effectiveness of visual and
    auditory appeals, 227-228
Age, suggestion and, 229-230
Aggression, 27
  frustration and, 4, 420, 907
Akron, Ohio, corporate property study,
  113-116
Aladdins of Industry, 366
Albert, 905
Alexander, F., 118fn., 907
Alexander, J., 175fn.
Alfonso, King, 583-584
Alger, G. W., 157fn.
Alger, P. L., 529fn.
Alimony, 776
Allen, F. L., 153fn., 657, 639fn., 769fn.,
  770, 861
Allport, F. H., 15, 25, 35, 36, 68, 69, 70fn.,
  227fn., 269, 534fn., 634fn., 686fn.
Allport, Gordon W., 37fn., 39fn., 100,
  309-310, 432, 443fn., 710
Alto Psychologic Center, 808

Amalgamated Clothing Workers, 757
American Academy of Astrology, 602
American Anthropological Association,
  60
American Association for the Advance-
  ment of Science, 212-213, 613, 927
American Association of Scientific
  Workers, 608
American Astronomical Society, 602-603
American Bar Association, 519, 878
American Board of Psychiatry and Neu-
  rology, 193
American Civil Liberties Union, 479
American Committee for Democracy and
  Intellectual Freedom, 370, 479
American Committee on Maternal Wel-
  fare, 477
American Council on Education, 94
American Economic Association, 60
American Federation of Labor, 414, 727,
  730
American Friends Service Committee,
  923
American Historical Association, 60
American Institute of Public Opinion,
  78, 79, 81, 84, 207, 528
American Legion, 367-368, 878, 899, 909
American Medical Association, 148, 150,
  151, 152, 772, 878
American Political Science Association,
  60
American Psychiatric Association, 188
American Psychological Association, 38,
  39, 60, 108, 909
American Society of Magicians, 603
American Sociological Society, 60
American Statistical Association, 60
American Youth Commission, 94, 121,
  125
American Youth for a Free World, 923
Ames, R. S. 362fn.
Amory, C., 410fn.
Anastasi, A., 684
Ancestor worship, 490
Anderson, Marian, 700, 711
Angell, Norman, 337, 904